BARTLETT'S
BOOK OF ANECDOTES

BARTLETT'S®
BOOK OF ANECDOTES

Clifton Fadiman and André Bernard
General Editors

— ✺ —

Little, Brown and Company
Boston   New York   London

FIRST REVISED EDITION

This book is an updated and revised edition of *The Little, Brown Book of Anecdotes,* edited by Clifton Fadiman.

Designed by Interrobang Design Studio

Library of Congress Cataloging-in-Publication Data

Bartlett's book of anecdotes/Clifton Fadiman and André Bernard, general editors. — 1st rev. ed.
    p. cm.
  Rev. ed. of: Little, Brown book of anecdotes, 1985.
  Includes bibliographical references and indexes.
  ISBN 0-316-08267-8 (hc)
  1. Biography — Anecdotes. 2. Biography — Dictionaries. 3. Anecdotes I. Fadiman, Clifton, 1904–1999. II. Bernard, André. III. Little, Brown book of anecdotes.
CT109.B37 2000
920'.003 — dc 21   00-020356

10 9 8 7 6 5 4 3 2 1

Copyright acknowledgments may be found at the back of the book, following the indexes.

Printed in the United States of America

And once when saying his prayers, which he [Sydney Smith] always did out loud, he was overheard to say: "Now Lord, I'll tell you an anecdote."

— Patrick Mahony,
Introduction to *Barbed Wit and Malicious Humor*

CONTENTS

PUBLISHER'S NOTE

———◆———

THIS BOOK IS FOR THE MOST PART A COLLECTION OF ANECDOTES ABOUT READILY IDENTI-
FIABLE PEOPLE AND IS ORGANIZED ALPHABETICALLY BY PERSON. Where doubt exists as to
whom an anecdote should be ascribed, we have usually chosen the more familiar name. In
as many cases as possible, we have placed the anecdote with that person whose character
is most revealed. Some anecdotes included here are connected with obscure or unfamiliar
names or places. They were so interesting in their own right that we included them in no
particular order. To distinguish them from the regular text, they are boxed.

We hope *Bartlett's Book of Anecdotes* has value as a work of reference as well as one
of entertainment. It does not, however, claim to be a work of exact scholarship, and should
not be used as an infallible encyclopedia. Anecdotes are by nature often well worn; while
in circulation (and after decades or even centuries) attributions can be mixed up, dates can
be changed, and the very point of the stories can be lost. But we have done our best to verify the historical accuracy of those anecdotes we have included in this volume. We hope
it presents a lively mix of the hoary and the fresh, to give a full tour of the world of the
anecdote.

The editors are especially grateful to a few exceptionally fine collections of anecdotes
that are available to the general reader and that have provided us with source material. All
collections like ours are in part the product of pilferage; we have tried to stop short of pil-
lage. Foremost among our sources are the volumes prepared by Paul F. Boller, Jr., which include *Presidential Anecdotes, Presidential Wives, Hollywood Anecdotes,* and *Presidential
Campaigns,* all published by Oxford University Press. While stories about presidents, their
wives, and their campaigns can be found readily, Mr. Boller has collected, selected, and
written the best, and his extensive listing of sources attests to his thorough and original re-

search. The reader is urged to turn to his books for a more complete and definitive collection on his chosen subjects. The same recommendation can be made for the great poet Donald Hall's work on *The Oxford Book of American Literary Anecdotes*.

A complete bibliography lists all of our sources. In addition, the source for each anecdote is given, when known, in a Source List at the back of this book, preceding the bibliography. Every effort has been made to credit sources; where information is missing or incorrect (and with material as diverse as is included in this long volume, some gaps may be inevitable), the publisher regrets the omission and will print the correct information with full credit in subsequent printings.

ACKNOWLEDGMENTS

———— ✺ ————

Bartlett's Book of Anecdotes is a revised, edited version of *The Little, Brown Book of Anecdotes,* the last edition of which was published in 1985. For that version, Clifton Fadiman, as General Editor, contributed and wrote anecdotes, made the final selection, and edited the volume. He also was responsible for the translations from French and German sources. Among the contributors were Joe Bryan III, Annalee and Kim Fadiman, Albert Friendly, Leo Counce Hopkins, George Lang, Henry D. Smith II, and Don and Siu Zimmerman; Ann Sleeper and Betsy Pitha; Colleen Mohyde, Margaret Freudenthal, and Virginia Creeden; and Susanne McNatt and Mary George. For the 2000 edition the editors are grateful to our editor at Little, Brown, Chip Rossetti, and especially to our copy-editor, Pamela Marshall, who made valuable suggestions and heroic corrections; both were patient and good-natured beyond any reasonable expectation.

INTRODUCTION

---◌◦◌---

ANCESTRY

*H*OW FAR BACK DO ANECDOTES GO?

As with so many other good things, what we now call anecdotes may have started in classical Greece. Joseph Epstein quotes the Italian scholar Arnaldo Momigliano, who, in his *Development of Greek Biography*, conjectures that the anecdote's founding father may have been the musical theorist Aristoxenus of Tarentum (born c. 370 BC): "Perhaps [Aristoxenus] was . . . the first to make anecdotes an essential part of biography. . . . I suspect that we owe to Aristoxenus the notion that a good biography is full of good anecdotes."

Though we borrowed the term from the French, *anecdote* ultimately derives from an almost identical Greek word meaning "things not given out," or, as we would say, unpublished. It is in this sense that Cicero uses it to describe some of his own manuscripts, a usage followed later by Renaissance scholars to denote manuscripts discovered in libraries and afterward published.

From the outset there seems also to have been attached to the word a connotation of secrecy or perhaps merely gossip. As a biographical device it was and remains anti-official, anti-panegyrical. It surprises the human being in question *en pantoufles*.

The anecdote's shady reputation probably derives from the sixth-century Byzantine historian Procopius, who called his posthumously published, scandalous account of the Emperor Justinian *Anecdota* or *Historia Arcana* (Secret History).

It is during the Renaissance, with the rise of cities, royal courts, a true leisure class, and the cult of the individual that the anecdote, a form of condensed gossip, begins clearly to show its face. It begins to shake off its association with the merely scandalous.

In his *Dissertation on Anecdotes* Isaac D'Israeli (1766–1848) tells us that the French broadened the term to make it apply to "any interesting circumstance." In the eighteenth century Samuel Johnson defined it as "a *biographical incident;* a minute passage of *private life.*" The suggestion of amusing triviality now begins to emerge, so that two centuries later Winston Churchill could call anecdotes "the gleaming toys of history." In the transactions of biographers they function as petty cash.

The eighteenth century also marked the beginning of the association of anecdotes with the wit of old men. You can trace it in the French aphorist Rivarol (1753–1801). The frayed pejorative pun "anecdotage" may have been invented by John Wilkes (1727–1797) or perhaps by Thomas De Quincey (1785–1859). It was made fashionable by Benjamin Disraeli in *Lothair* (1870): "When a man fell into his anecdotage it was a sign for him to retire from the world." But in 1835, thirty-five years earlier, an anonymous scribbler in *Blackwood's Magazine* had already made fierce play with the word: "The disgusting perversions of their anile anecdotage." It would seem that in youth we sow our wild oats, in old age our tame anecdotes.

We may conjecture that by the beginning of the eighteenth century the form had come of age in Western Europe. Continuing to develop, it becomes more and more luxuriant as we approach our own time. Hence this anthology's decided slant toward the modern.

ANATOMY OF THE ANECDOTE

An anecdote, so *Merriam-Webster's Tenth Collegiate Dictionary* informs us, is "a usually short narrative of an interesting, amusing, or biographical incident." This collection confines itself to "biographical incidents." We admit, however, that on occasion we have stretched the notion of incident so as to accommodate a reasonable number of origin stories, traditional tales, or wisecracks of the Groucho Marx–Dorothy Parker stripe.

Such witticisms gain in interest when placed in a setting, but it has not always been possible to provide one. We are, for example, ignorant of the circumstances in which the composer Mascagni stated that the Italian language has three degrees of comparison: *stupido, stupidissimo,* and *tenore.* Ditto for a learned mathematics professor, Badke by name, who once defined a point as an angle from which the two sides have been removed. These noncontextual examples failing to qualify as anecdotes, I have dishonestly smuggled them into this paragraph so that they may not be forever lost. But they really belong in *Bartlett's Familiar Quotations,* with which this book is not in competition.

Webster's says: "a usually short narrative." We have in general obeyed this requirement but in a few instances violated it in order to illustrate what entertained men and women of generations long past. Our predecessors, at least to the mid-ninetenth century, valued prolixy as we do terseness. They had more time. And it was worth less money.

Furthermore, Webster's adjectives "interesting" and "amusing" may not seem to us to apply to many anecdotes that apparently gave them pleasure. A dusty collection called *The Percy Anecdotes* offers items like this: When the late Marquis of Cornwallis was leaving a nobleman's house and stepping into his carriage, a servant offered to hold an umbrella over him. "Take that thing away," said his lordship. "I am neither sugar nor salt, to suffer by a shower of rain." To us this seems flat. It is too *reasonable.* The metaphor is one you and I might have thought of without any notion that it might pass for wit. Still, our forefathers prized such conversational junk jewelry, giving it the name of anecdote.

We must keep in mind that the author of the foregoing was a marquis. That helped. The undeservedly forgotton essayist Frank Moore Colby once remarked, "Never destroy an uninteresting letter is the first rule of the British aristocracy." Second rule: Always remember to record an uninteresting action or remark. This rule has generated a revered tradition, featuring the peerage at its dullest. Horace Walpole felt the need to record for posterity that the contemporary dowager Duchess of Devonshire stayed up "every evening, till it was dark, in the skittle-ground keeping the score. . . ." Though we have salvaged a few of these antiquities — see Thomas Herbert Pembroke 1 — we must for the most part think of them as *ana* rather than anecdotes.

Our dictionary defines *ana:* "collected items of information, esp. anecdotal or bibliographical <Americ*ana*> <Johnsoni*ana*>." We would call it *miscellany.* The Percy miscellany is a kind of free-form substitute for a magazine. It is a potpourri of historical episodes, potted biographies, oddities of literature and history, excerpts from trial proceedings, classical legends, records of sensational events, believe-it-or-nots, travel memoirs, snippets from Plutarch, Herodotus, Macrobius; ghost and horror stories; oddities of natural history; records of the lives of eccentrics, geniuses, and other abnormals; edifying examples of virtuous speech and action; excerpts from letters; essaylets on the arts, sciences, and vocations. Indeed in many respects it is an unsystematic mini-encyclopedia of manners, persons, arts, sciences, and professions.

A representative collection such as *The Lounger's Commonplace Book; or, Alphabetical Anecdotes,* the work of Jeremiah Whitaker Newman (1759–1839), tends to conceive the anecdote as an extended short biography, often of an obscure person whose life is in some respect striking or unusual. Moralizing is a feature of the genre. The notion of point or humor hardly enters. It was not until almost the twentieth century that the anecdote became sparser, more isolated from a larger narrative context, achieving an economical effect with corresponding economy of means (see HENRY JAMES 2).

It is not always easy to distinguish between anecdote and episode. The seventh-century BC Greek poet Archilochus composed satires against his prospective father-in-law, Lycamber, so powerful that the poor man and his daughter both hanged themselves. This is beyond a doubt brief (I have told you all I know), it needs no larger context, it is far from prosy. Yet one thinks of it as an episode rather than an anecdote. If we are to admit all the striking episodes to be discovered in any eventful life (say Napoleon's), we would come up with a book quite different from the one you are now reading. Thus the story of van Gogh's ear composes a fascinating chapter in his biography, but is too complex, in a sense too *important,* to qualify as an anecdote. Many unforgettable episodes of history fall into this nonanecdotal category. In 1347 Edward III, having starved Calais into submission, required six men to deliver the keys of the town and castle dressed "in their shirts and with halters about their necks." They sacrificed themselves for their town. Though a moving story, is this an anecdote? I think not.

What makes rules interesting, however, are the exceptions. Therefore in this repository we have included a number of such anecdote-episodes whenever they seemed to us effective in brief form and diverting or striking or, as with EDITH CAVELL 1, a treasured item of our folk memory.

A career may be crowded, it may be a model of high achievement and yet in our sense produce few real anecdotes. Goethe, a titan, did not generate titanecdotes. His countrymen preserve as anecdotes his *sayings,* which range from the magnificent to the magnificently banal. Within this range you may place according to your taste this typical example: To a friend who regretted that he had never seen Italy, Goethe said, "Good, for if you had, our own sky would never seem blue enough."

However, so that certain supremely great names may be at least represented, we have on occasion smuggled in an anecdote or two that may be only moderately striking (see J. S. BACH 1). But not all greats are linked to trivia; the reader will note the absence of many famous figures.

Just as a first-rate anecdote should be more than merely a good saying, so it should be more than an odd biographical fact. It is well known, for instance, that Schiller worked better when inhaling the odor of overripe apples kept in his desk drawer. And we learn from Gordon Rattray Taylor's *The Great Evolution Mystery* that the world's leading authority on giant clams, Professor Sir Maurice Yonge, is the only man who has read *The Decline and Fall of the Roman Empire* from cover to cover while sitting on the Great Barrier Reef. Such eccentric particulars make for delightful reading but in the strict sense they are not anecdotal and few will be found in these pages.

Oddity alone, then, will not quite do. King Frederick Augustus of Saxony was in the course of his career elected king of Poland and became known as Augustus the Strong. He would astonish his dinner guests by picking up two of his state trumpeters, one in each hand. For five minutes he would keep them dangling while they played a fanfare. It is not clear just what earned Augustus his epithet — this kind of thing or his fathering of 354 bastards. The latter achievement recommends him to Guinness, but he doesn't quite fit into this book.

Similarly, we have generally ignored practical jokes, except when they are not only amusing but have some kind of narrative form and are connected with a famous personage (JOHN PARTRIDGE 1).

Finally, a book of biographical anecdotes must be just that, whether the individual created or provoked the anecdote. We have pinned each item to a single person (on occasion we were compelled to use a straight rather than a safety pin). But in the past less restrictive views obtained. Isaac D'Israeli thought "there are *anecdotes* of the art as well as the Artist; of the war as well as the General; of the nation as well as the Monarch." Such anecdotes we prefer to leave to the history books. It is true, however, that a biographical anecdote can throw light on an important *aspect* of an entire nation (see PABLO PICASSO 5).

The preceding comments underline the obvious: that the definition of anecdote shifts with the centuries. For our purposes anecdotes remain what D'Israeli called them — "minute notices of human nature and of human learning," even if today we are less interested in the latter than in the former. The witty, the humorous, those crackling with the whiplash of a tagline, tend to circulate most widely, to conform more closely to the modern sensibility. But there is plenty of room for the quieter anecdote whose value lies in the illumination of character or the inculcation of a moral lesson.

We prefer our anecdotes to be short, free-standing, with a nub or point or center. This book, nevertheless, contains many of which this cannot be said. EDWARD GIBBON 1 has no identifiable "point." But it continues to interest us as a famous statement made by a famous person about a critical event in his life. Some anecdotes are really mini-dramas appealing to our tenderest emotions (BRONSON ALCOTT 1; CHARLES DE GAULLE 4). Others — indeed, many — strip us of our dignity. Some depend on mere word-play and do not rate a second reading, while others (ALBERT EINSTEIN 13) set the mind pondering. Some may not even depend on words at all (GEORGE ANTHEIL 1).

WHERE DO ANECDOTES COME FROM?

With many exceptions, anecdotes seem to be dominantly urban. Our Mountain Men, our pioneers, produce yarns, not anecdotes; desert and peasant cultures are rarely anecdotal seminaries. The atmosphere of the court, the great house, the capital, favors the anecdote as do many institutions and vocations associated with the city: the club, the dinner party, the university, the theater, the studio and gallery, the law court, parliaments and senates. The anecdote is a social product; it does not flourish in isolation. One qualifies immediately: certain personalities, irrespective of their environment or calling, may be anecdotal naturals.

Still, in these pages highly social beings are generally prominent. They tend to be associated in fair part with the arts and in consequence exhibit relatively unconventional temperaments: Tristan Bernard, Whistler, Sarah Bernhardt, George Kaufman. On the other hand, statesmen too may be loci of anecdote: Churchill (but he was also a painter); Lincoln (but he was also a great writer); Talleyrand. Money men are far less in evidence — though there is J. P. Morgan, of course, and one of our most profound and prescient anecdotes is about a banker (JAMES STILLMAN 1). Show business is replete with lively minds. It is fairly well represented in these pages. Children, as you must know from your own childhood, are naturally brighter than adults, and in theory should provide a mine of anecdotes. However, the rules of our game require that notable names be attached to them, which limits the field.

The case of politicians is interesting, Many politicians, of course, have been vivid or witty personalities; but the general run are either by nature unamusing or are afraid to be thought amusing. That Adlai Stevenson was an interesting man with a quicksilver mind proved a political handicap. This is not true, of course, for the genuine greats, a Lincoln, a Disraeli, a Churchill. But the need to provide an image (or, as with Richard Nixon, a selection of images) tends to inhibit the kind of conduct that generates anecdotes. Still, look at Coolidge, who in some odd manner contrived to be both witty and dull.

This collection is sadly deficient in anecdotes about women. The reason is apparent: the chronicle of humankind has been written by the winners — at least up to our own day. One would wager that the index of a compilation like this, but published a century hence, will contain the names of a vast number of women. Yet even our sparse representation suggests that when women are amusing or trenchant or intellectually provocative they are often far more so than are men. The four samples from Sophie Arnould reveal a subtler spirit than the twelve items associated with so renowned a wit as Sir Thomas Beecham.

Finally, in trying to identify the loci of anecdotes, we must keep in mind that the collector can work only with what has been recorded. Because he was a great monarch much of what Louis XIV said and did in public, whether dull or interesting, was bound to show up in memoirs of the period. It is, however, quite possible that thousands of remarkable or funny stories by or about obscure figures have been recounted in forgotten conversations. Such oral anecdote is lost forever. In the space-time continuum, one imagines, there exists a whole library of such anecdotes. But it is unwritten.

ANECDOTES AND NATIONALITY

A woman once asked Dr. Johnson why his dictionary defined "pastern" as "the knee of a horse." "Ignorance, madam, pure ignorance," he replied. This book's editors are equipped with plenty of pure ignorance. Worse still, they are not linguists. They handle adequately only three languages. Hence the anecdotes are mainly of British, American, French, and German origin.

Nevertheless, admitting our ignorance and language limitations, we consider these pages not unduly parochial. A genius for or interest in anecdote is not universal. The national traits that give birth to these airy trifles seem less marked in other countries than in those mentioned above. Perhaps Scandinavians and Swiss and Poles are not so receptive to eccentricity. Or it may be that they have not chanced to evolve certain social or class institutions that tend to generate anecdotes.

Even when the language is open to us our selections may be insufficiently representative. We are conditioned by an Anglo-American culture. Consequently what pleases us may not please those differently conditioned, and vice versa. For example, we include from the German many anecdotes we think entertaining or instructive. But we have also omitted many that make a special appeal to the Germanic temperament. Here is one:

> A lady suffering from headache consulted the famous Berlin physician Heim and, in some embarrassment, asked whether she could try a remedy that had been recommended to her as infallible: covering her head with sauerkraut. Heim replied: "Excellent — but don't forget to mix a bratwurst with it!"

As one moves eastward, the divergence of taste becomes more radical. We would have liked to find some anecdotic reflection of the magnificent cultures of India, China, and Japan. This book presents a faint reflection of that reflection. But after admittedly superficial research, one is led to conclude that anecdotically East is East, and West is West, and never the twain shall meet. Oriental "anecdotes" tend either to be moral parables — bits and pieces of wisdom literature — or longish historical episodes. Rarely do they seem to be the bubbles that form and break on the surface of social intercourse. The East, whether Near, Middle, or Far, is not attuned to our kind of anecdote, just as it does not appear to produce our kind of light verse. (Search these pages carefully enough, however, and you may find one or two Ottomanecdotes.)

With respect to our subject, it is not true to say that Americans and British are separated by a common language. The American anecdotal *tone* differs slightly and interestingly from the British, but no vast gulf separates our mutual appreciation. However, again we must qualify. We have included a few cricket stories that will baffle many Americans. To be fair, we have included enough baseball stories to infuriate our British cousins.

AUTHENTICITY

Leslie Stephen in his life of Milton remarks that no good story is quite true. A sobering thought.

Anecdotes are the thistledown of biography. To establish authenticity in all cases is impossible. We have done our best. Where we strongly suspect an anecdote to be apocryphal, we have so stated. We do not, however, claim to have identified every possible case and we welcome corrections from our readers.

We have tried to keep in mind the words of the venerable president of Magdalen, Oxford, Martin Joseph Routh (1755–1854). Approaching the century mark, he was once asked by a disciple what single wisdom-crammed axiom or precept he could abstract from his long life's experience. The president reflected, then, after a long pause, said, "I think, sir, since you come for the advice of an old man, sir, you will find it a very good practice *always to verify your references!*"

Well said. But difficulties abound. There is, for example, the self-effacing anecdotalist (more often simply a jokesmith) who, in the interest of wider circulation, prefers to hide his own light under another's bushel. Samuel Johnson once described the process: "Pointed axioms and acute replies fly loose about the world, and are assigned successively to those whom it may be the fashion to celebrate." Thus in the nineteenth century a *bon mot* turning on the contrast between wealth and poverty might naturally be credited to a Rothschild.

The philosopher Immanuel Kant, listening to a string of anecdotes about a famous personality of the time, remarked, "It seems to me I recall similar anecdotes about other great figures. But that is to be expected. Great men are like high church towers: around both there is apt to be a great deal of wind." In this century Churchill, Dorothy Parker, and Samuel Goldwyn became high church towers.

Long before them came Talleyrand. He worked overtime; it was said that he never fashioned so many brilliant *mots* during his life as he did after his death. It requires great wit to utter post-mordancies. On the other hand (the authority is his brother, who may have suffered from sibling jealousy), Talleyrand is said to have abstracted many of his good things from *L'Improvisateur français,* a compilation of anecdotes in twenty-one duodecimo volumes.

We know of one interesting case in which Talleyrand created an anecdote by fiat. It has to do with the Bourbon Restoration. On the evening of the day on which the Comte d'Artois, later to become King Charles X, entered Paris, Talleyrand asked a group assembled in his drawing room what the Bourbon prince had said. "Nothing at all" was the answer. Talleyrand, not satisfied, ordered a well-known political writer to leave the room and compose an appropriately memorable remark. The writer made three tries, all inadequate. Finally he returned with the words: "Nothing is changed in France; there is only one Frenchman more." Talleyrand applauded; the Duke of Artois had been assigned his *mot;* and another famous anecdote was added to "history."

It is probable that at least five percent of the items in this book consisted originally of confected or current jokes that were then fathered on notables.

The question of authenticity arises perhaps most particularly in the case of Lincoln stories. Here the source-hunters have been busy and conscientious. Yet questions remain. We may never be able to say of certain Lincoln anecdotes, "Yes, this is authentic," but we have tried to avoid the inclusion of too many doubtful items. Those die-hards who prefer a scholarly tracking down of Lincoln stories are referred to *Abe Lincoln Laughing: Humorous Anecdotes from Original Sources by and about Abraham Lincoln,* edited by P. M. Zall (University of California Press, 1982). This is a first-rate job of scholarship.

Sometimes an anecdote may be credited to two or more different persons, though it is obvious only one can be responsible. The famous quip "And if you were my wife, I'd drink it" (WINSTON CHURCHILL 7) is (almost) surely the great man's. Yet it has also been ascribed to Senator Robert Taft, who could not have said it had the presidency come with it. The dress designer Edith Head, who knew Grace Kelly in Hollywood, was, at the time of Miss Kelly's marriage, asked for anecdotes about the princess. Said Miss Head, "Grace doesn't allow anecdotes to happen to her." Neither did Taft.

The retort "That will depend on whether I embrace your lordship's mistress or your lordship's principles" is assigned to various personages, of whom we have chosen John Wilkes as the most credible. Many such putdown retorts, in our time often attributed to Dorothy Parker or Groucho Marx, or others, were probably never actually said to anyone at all.

There are legacy-anecdotes, whose birth lies in the obscure past, but are rediscovered, refurbished, and with each passing generation assigned new paternities. It was Donatus who uttered the classical curse: *Pereant qui ante nos nostra dixerunt!* (A plague on those who said our good things before we did!) Doubtless some of these good things, truly of ancient lineage, have turned up in this book dressed in modern clothes.

WHAT DO ANECDOTES DO?

Chiefly, they entertain. They form a minor genre, even a trivial one; they are not history and biography but the decoration on history and biography. Yet, when more than just good jokes, they may on occasion perform nontrivial functions.

We moderns look for the *ping* of the unexpected, the glint of heterodoxy. True enough, the Old and New Testaments contain some of the greatest *stories* ever told. Yet in one sense they are not anecdotes, and in this collection the Bible is represented only by SOLOMON 1.

The ancient Hebraic temper and the anecdotal temper do not have much in common. The same appears to be more or less true with respect to early religious leaders of other faiths.

Classical figures prized their anecdotes as narrative condensations of generally acknowledged truths. That the paths of glory lead but to the grave was pointed out by Thomas Gray in 1751. But the sobering truism was more vividly expressed by Diogenes in explaining to Alexander the Great why he was examining a heap of human bones: "I am searching for the bones of your father, but I cannot distinguish them from those of his slaves." No great wit here, certainly no shock of surprise, yet a telling early statement of a universal insight.

It is by such light that we must consider the anecdotes of the ancients, some of whose bearded quips are herein collected. Besides, it is instructive to discover what amused or titillated our forefathers. You may even find some of the hoary items diverting. One man's chestnut is another man's *marron glacé*.

From its beginnings the anecdote has acted as a leveling device. It humanizes, democratizes, acts as a counterweight to encomium. Perhaps that is why it flourishes best in countries that, like Britain and the United States, enjoy a strong democratic tradition. It may bring home to our hearts social and political ideals that, expressed by politicians, elicit yawns. It may do this through phrasing of great elegance (EDWARD EVERETT 1) or of casual, bitter irony (JACKIE ROBINSON 1).

Men of high philosophic mind have valued the anecdote less for its capacity to divert, more for its power to reveal character. This value was first classically formulated by Plutarch, quoted by Boswell: "Nor is it always in the most distinguished achievements that men's virtues or vices may be best discerned; but very often an action of small note, a short saying, or a jest, shall distinguish a person's real character more than the greatest sieges, or the most important battles."

From anecdotes, thought Prosper Mérimée, one "can distinguish a true picture of the customs and characters of any given period." Nietzsche was confident that "three anecdotes may suffice to paint a picture of a man." Isaac D'Israeli, whose *Dissertation on Anecdotes* affords a perfect reflection of his time's anecdotal preferences, thought anecdotes accurate indices to character: "Opinions are fallible, but not examples." Says Ralph Waldo Emerson: "Ballads, bons mots, and anecdotes give us better insights into the depths of past centuries than grave and voluminous chronicles." His contemporary William Ellery Channing agreed: "One anecdote of a man is worth a volume of biography."

Perhaps such claims are excessive. Like statistics, an anecdote, unless measured against the whole record of a life, may be a damned lie. But a reasonable number of them, drawn from different phases of a given career, may give us an imperfect yet authentic sense of character. Try reading the sections on, let us say, Henry James, Max Beerbohm, Pablo Picasso, Johannes Brahms, Pope John XXIII. You don't get the whole man, but you do learn something valuable and generally easy to fix in the memory. The intimidating, downright character of the Iron Duke flashes out at once in WELLINGTON 16.

Beyond these functions anecdotes may perform at least three others.

The first is illustrated by such traditional stories as KING ALFRED 1. We include no more than a scattering of these quasi-legendary items, for we do not propose to compete with such massive compilations as Brewer's *Dictionary of Phrase and Fable*. But there are enough here to suggest one of the book's minor purposes. Our present educational system sees to it that Macaulay's schoolboy should not exist in our country. The editors cannot create him, either, but at least we can dig a few hundred historical and biographical postholes of traditional reference, familiar in other days to every, or at least Macaulay's, schoolboy.

An assiduous reading of anecdotes can, then, light up odd corners of the past that we should all recognize. But it can, far more valuably, shake us out of our quotidian rut, administer a slight and salutary shock of surprise or delight. At its finest, an anecdote signalizes the intervention of the unexpected. It mounts a small-scale assault on the banality of normal intercourse.

Finally, if one were asked to name the *kind* of book that within one set of covers most adequately reflects the sheer multifariousness of human personality, it might well be a book of anecdotes. *Ana* would not do, for much *ana* is mere information not revelatory of character. A biographical dictionary would not do either, for its editors do not have the space or the desire to set down the quirks and oddities of their subjects. But a reasonably ample gathering of anecdotes, drawn from many times and climes, may reconcile us to our human nature by showing us that, for all its faults and stupidities, it can boast a diversity to which no other animal species can lay claim.

Clifton Fadiman

NOTE TO THE REVISED EDITION

————— ❧ —————

"Perhaps few authors are wholly original as far as their plots are concerned; indeed Shakespeare seems to have invented nothing, while Chaucer borrowed from both the living and the dead. And to come down to a somewhat different plane, the present writer is even more derivative, since for these books he has in general kept most doggedly to recorded actions, nourishing his fancy with logbooks, dispatches, letters, memoirs, and contemporary reports." So writes Patrick O'Brian in the introduction to *The Far Side of the World,* the tenth volume in his incomparable Aubrey/Maturin series. His words might be applied to this volume, which collects the best, and occasionally the best-known, anecdotes about a wide range of people — scholars, politicians, crowned heads, sports figures, movie stars, scientists, and the occasional unknown — throughout human history. We have scoured many sources for the anecdotes included here, finding them in biographies, in newspaper accounts, in histories, and in general reference works, among other places. Some have surfaced in conversation, others in collections, and have been chosen as touchstones of the genre. Familiar or unfamiliar — and inevitably many of these anecdotes will be known to readers, *as they should be* — they aim to amuse and enlighten.

This new edition is a revised version of *The Little, Brown Book of Anecdotes,* published in 1985. Some entries which proved of ephemeral interest, or those whose *mots* did not continue to sparkle in the intervening years, have been dropped from this volume. We have added many new people whose quips, situations, or dilemmas we feel are of sufficient interest to warrant inclusion, and we have also added anecdotes about well-known people of the past that have come to light more recently; Queen Victoria, for instance, or Mozart, or Yogi Berra.

As this manuscript was being delivered to its publisher, its General Editor, Clifton Fadiman, died at the age of ninety-five. Kip, as he was widely known, collected and wrote many of the entries contained herein and was very much involved in its revision. Perhaps because he had a long and most distinguished career as an anthologist, essayist, and editor — at Simon & Schuster, at *The New Yorker,* and especially at the Book-of-the-Month Club, where for over fifty years he served on its editorial board, and thus helped shape, in a very real way, the reading tastes and interests of the general public — one of his chief interests was good talk and the sharing of fine, often droll, stories. In conversation he was witty and learned, sharing bits of history and discovery with an excitement and a confidence in the interests of others that made the dissemination of his tales a complete delight. The anecdotes we have selected reflect his wide familiarity with men and women of distinction and accomplishment, his fascination with relationships and historical events, and above all his delight in elegant or amusing turns of phrase. His accumulated store of such tales was unsurpassed, and is offered here in the hopes that the reader will enjoy the reading as thoroughly as Kip did the relating.

André Bernard

BARTLETT'S
BOOK OF ANECDOTES

A

AARON, Henry Louis ["Hank"] (1934–), *US baseball player. He broke Babe Ruth's home-run record, hitting 755 in all.*

1 During the 1957 World Series, Yankee catcher Yogi Berra noticed that Aaron grasped the bat the wrong way. "Turn it around," he said, "so you can see the trademark." But Hank kept his eye on the pitcher's mound: "Didn't come up here to read. Came up here to hit."

2 Aaron, who surpassed Babe Ruth's "unsurpassable" home-run record of 714 home runs in 1974, never saw any of his famous hits flying through the air. While running to first base he always looked down until he touched the bag, feeling that "looking at the ball going over the fence isn't going to help."

3 Asked how he felt about breaking Ruth's record — an achievement that was both admired and somewhat controversial given the great reverence and affection Ruth inspired even years after his death — Aaron said, "I don't want them to forget Ruth. I just want them to remember me!"

4 Aaron was known as a hitter who rarely failed, the bane of pitchers. As a pitcher on a rival team once said of him, "Trying to sneak a pitch past Hank Aaron is like trying to sneak a sunrise past a rooster."

ABERNETHY, John (1764–1831), *British physician.*

1 A titled gentleman who consulted Abernethy was received by the great doctor with the rudeness for which he was notorious. The patient lost his temper and told Abernethy that he would make him "eat his words." "It will be of no use," responded Abernethy, "for they will be sure to come up again."

2 When Abernethy was canvassing for the post of surgeon to St. Bartholomew's Hospital, London, he called upon one of the governors, a wealthy grocer, in the man's shop. The grocer loftily remarked that he presumed Abernethy was wanting his vote at this important point in his life. Nettled by the man's tone and attitude, Abernethy retorted, "No, I don't; I want a pennyworth of figs. Look sharp and wrap them up. I want to be off."

3 "Mrs. J—— consulted him respecting a nervous disorder, the minutiae of which appeared to be so fantastic that Mr. A. interrupted their frivolous detail by holding out his hand for the fee. A £1 note and a shilling were placed into it; upon which he returned the latter to his fair patient, with the

angry exclamation, 'There, Ma'am! go and buy a skipping rope; that is all you want.'"

4 Despite his brusqueness with his private patients, Abernethy was conscientious and kindly toward the poor under his care in the charity hospital. Once as he was about to leave for the hospital, a private patient tried to detain him. Abernethy observed, "Private patients, if they do not like me, can go elsewhere; but the poor devils in the hospital I am bound to take care of."

5 A patient complaining of melancholy consulted Dr. Abernethy. After an examination the doctor pronounced, "You need amusement. Go and hear the comedian Grimaldi; he will make you laugh and that will be better for you than any drugs." Said the patient, "I am Grimaldi."

6 Abernethy was renowned for his dislike of idle chatter. With this in mind, a young lady once entered his surgery and, without a word, held out an injured finger for examination. The doctor dressed the wound in silence. The woman returned a few days later. "Better?" asked Abernethy. "Better," replied the patient. Subsequent calls passed in much the same manner. On her final visit, the woman held out her finger, now free of bandages. "Well?" inquired the doctor. "Well," she replied. "Upon my word, madam," exclaimed Abernethy, "you are the most rational woman I have ever met."

ACHESON, Dean [Gooderham] (1893–1971), US statesman and lawyer; secretary of state (1949–53).

1 On leaving his post as secretary of state, Acheson was asked about his plans for the future. He replied, "I will undoubtedly have to seek what is happily known as gainful employment, which I am glad to say does not describe holding public office."

2 In April 1963 Winston Churchill was made an honorary citizen of the United States. At the ceremony in the White House, his letter of acceptance was read by his son Randolph, as he himself was too frail to attend. It contained a passage rejecting the idea that Britain had only a "tame and minor" role to play on the international scene. Dean Acheson recognized this as an oblique allusion to his own famous and greatly resented remark that Britain had lost an empire and failed to find a new role. "Well, it hasn't taken Winston long to get used to American ways," commented Acheson. "He hadn't been an American citizen for three minutes before he began attacking an ex-secretary of state."

3 A rather flustered elderly lady once accosted Acheson in a Washington hotel. "Pardon me," she said, "I am somewhat embarrassed. My zipper has stuck and I am due at a meeting. Could you please help me out?" As the zipper was firmly stuck halfway down her back, Acheson was obliged to undo it completely, averting his eyes as best he could, before pulling it back up to the top. The lady thanked him profusely. "I think that I should tell you," she added, "that I am vice president of the Daughters of the American Revolution."

"My dear lady," replied Acheson, "what a moment ago was a rare privilege now appears to have been a really great honor."

ACTON, Harold (1904–97), *British author whose works include poetry, histories, memoirs, and novels.*

1 "One summer afternoon Acton, then a celebrated undergraduate poet at Oxford, was asked to perform at a Conservative Garden Fete. He decided he could do no better than recite [T. S. Eliot's] *The Waste Land* from beginning to end. His audience's good manners were severely tested, as this dirge for a god-

less civilization, delivered in Harold Acton's rich, resounding voice, swept irresistibly above their heads; and one or two old ladies, who were alarmed and horrified but thought that the reciter had such a 'nice, kind face,' rather than hurt the young man's feelings by getting up and leaving openly, were obliged to sink to their knees and creep away on all fours."

ADAMS, Alexander Annan (1908–), *British air commander.*

1 At the end of the Battle of Britain, Adams was driving to a meeting at Fighter Command Headquarters when he came upon a sign: ROAD CLOSED — UNEXPLODED BOMB. Adams called over the policeman on duty, hoping he might be able to suggest an alternative route. "Sorry, you can't go through," said the policeman as he approached the car. "The bomb is likely to go off at any minute now." Then he caught sight of Adams's uniform. "I'm very sorry, sir," he said, "I didn't know you were a wing commander. It is quite all right for you to go through."

ADAMS, Ansel (1902–84), *US landscape photographer (particularly of the mountainous West) and conservationist.*

1 During his early years Adams studied the piano and showed marked talent. At one party (he recalls it as *"very* liquid") he played Chopin's F Major Nocturne. "In some strange way my right hand started off in F-sharp major while my left hand behaved well in F major. I could not bring them together. I went through the entire nocturne with the hands separated by a half-step." The next day a fellow guest complimented him on his performance. "You never missed a wrong note!"

ADAMS, Franklin Pierce (1881–1960), *US journalist, writer of light verse, and wit.*

1 Adams belonged to a poker club that included among its members an actor called Herbert Ransom. Whenever Ransom held a good hand, his facial expression was so transparent that Adams proposed a new rule for the club: "Anyone who looks at Ransom's face is cheating."

2 Adams accompanied Beatrice Kaufman (wife of the playwright George S. Kaufman) to a cocktail party where, feeling a little out of things, she sat down on a cane-seated chair. The seat suddenly broke, leaving Beatrice immobilized inside the frame, legs in the air. As a shocked silence gripped the party, Adams said severely, "I've told you a hundred times, Beatrice, that's not funny."

3 "Whose birthday is it today?" Adams once asked Beatrice Kaufman. "Yours?" she guessed. "No, but you're getting warm," replied Adams. "It's Shakespeare's."

4 Alexander Woollcott had been asked to sign a first-edition copy of his book *Shouts and Murmurs.* "Ah, what is so rare as a Woollcott first edition?" he sighed as he wrote. "A Woollcott second edition," replied Adams.

5 A friend was recounting to Adams an apparently interminable tale. He finally said: "Well, to cut a long story short —"
"Too late," interrupted Adams.

ADAMS, Henry (1838-1918), *US diplomat and writer known particularly for his autobiography,* **The Education of Henry Adams.**

1 Adams was very fond of his teenage niece Gabrielle. During one visit, they sat together in the library after dinner as Uncle Henry be-

gan to speak. His monologue was extraordinary, and ranged over the cosmos, the nature of God and man, and his own hopes and disappointments. For a long time he talked, then broke off and sat quietly for a moment. "Do you know why I have told you all this?" he asked her. "It is because you would not understand a word of it and you will never quote me."

———— ✃ ————

ADAMS, John (1735–1826), *US statesman, 2d President of the United States (1797–1801).*

1 Adams loathed being vice president; even in those early days of the Republic, the job was ill defined and not much respected. Of his role as Washington's secondary partner, he wrote, "My country has in its wisdom contrived for me the most insignificant office that ever the invention of man contrived or his imagination conceived."

2 During his presidency Adams's grand style, which contrasted unfavorably with the simpler dignity of the Washington regime, made him many enemies. A scandalous story circulated that he had sent General Charles C. Pinckney to Britain to select four pretty girls as mistresses, two for the general and two for himself. When this slander came to Adams's ears, he wrote complainingly to a friend, "I do declare, if this be true, General Pinckney has kept them all for himself and cheated me out of my two."

3 Adams received a letter from his wife, Abigail, that was highly critical of the impending marriage of a young lady she knew to a much older man. She called it the union of "the Torrid and the Frigid Zones." Adams immediately wrote back, saying, "How dare you hint or list a word about Fifty Years of Age? If I were near, I would soon convince you that I am not above Forty."

4 Although failing fast, Adams was determined to survive until the fiftieth anniversary of the signing of the Declaration of Independence — July 4, 1826. At dawn on that day he was awakened by his servant, who asked if he knew what day it was. He replied, "Oh, yes, it is the glorious fourth of July. God bless it. God bless you all." He then slipped into a coma. In the afternoon he recovered consciousness briefly to murmur, "Thomas Jefferson lives." These were his last words. Unknown to him, Thomas Jefferson had died that same day.

———— ✃ ————

ADAMS, John Quincy (1767–1848), *US statesman, 6th President of the United States (1825–29). From 1831 to his death he served in the House of Representatives.*

1 John Quincy Adams, an enthusiastic swimmer, used to bathe naked in the Potomac before starting the day's work. The newspaperwoman Anne Royall had been trying for weeks to get an interview with the President and had always been turned away. One morning she tracked him to the riverbank and after he had got into the water stationed herself on his clothes. When Adams returned from his swim, he found a very determined lady awaiting him. She introduced herself and stated her errand. "Let me get out and dress," pleaded the President, "and I swear you shall have your interview." Anne Royall was adamant; she wasn't moving until she had the President's comment on the questions she wished to put to him. If he attempted to get out, she would scream loud enough to reach the ears of some fishermen on the next bend. She got her interview while Adams remained decently submerged in the water.

2 In 1846 John Quincy Adams suffered a stroke and, although he returned to Congress the following year, his health was clearly fail-

ing. Daniel Webster described his last meeting with Adams: "Someone, a friend of his, came in and made particular inquiry of his health. Adams answered, 'I inhabit a weak, frail, decayed tenement; battered by the winds and broken in upon by the storms, and, from all I can learn, the landlord does not intend to repair.'"

3 One wintry day in 1848 Adams was busy writing at his desk when the Speaker of the House rose to ask a question. Adams rose to answer, then fell into the arms of his neighboring member. He was carried into the Speaker's chamber, where he spent the next two days in a semiconscious state. His final words were, "This is the last of Earth. I am content."

———∘⁄∘———

ADDAMS, Jane (1860–1935), *US social reformer. A supporter of racial equality, female suffrage, and pacifism, she shared the 1931 Nobel Peace Prize with the educator Nicholas Murray Butler.*

1 In 1900 the Daughters of the American Revolution elected Jane Addams to honorary membership. However, her antiwar stance during World War I and her insistence that even subversives had a right to trial by due process of law caused them to expel her. She commented that she had thought her election was for life, but now knew it was for good behavior.

———∘⁄∘———

ADDISON, Joseph (1672–1719), *British writer and politician.*

1 Addison's natural diffidence made him an ineffective parliamentary debater. On one occasion he began, "Mr. Speaker, I conceive — I conceive, sir — sir, I conceive —" At this point he was interrupted by a voice saying, "The right honorable secretary of state has conceived thrice and brought forth nothing."

2 The Duke of Wharton, hoping to animate Addison into wit, plied him so generously with wine that the writer was taken ill. The duke observed with disgust that he could "get wine but not wit out of him."

3 A friend of Addison's with whom he was accustomed to have long discussions on topics of mutual interest borrowed some money from the author. Soon afterward Addison noticed a change in his behavior; before the loan the two friends had disagreed on a number of subjects, but now the borrower fell in with every line that Addison himself adopted. One day when they were talking on a point on which Addison knew his friend had previously held an opposite view to his own, he exclaimed, "Either contradict me, sir, or pay me my money!"

———∘⁄∘———

ADE, George (1866–1944), *US humorist and playwright.*

1 Following a well-received after-dinner speech by George Ade, a noted lawyer rose to speak. His hands buried deep in the pockets of his trousers, he began: "Doesn't it strike the company as a little unusual that a professional humorist should be funny?" Ade waited for the laughter to die down before replying: "Doesn't it strike the company as a little unusual that a lawyer should have his hands in his own pockets?"

———∘⁄∘———

ADEE, Alvey Augustus (1842–1924), *US diplomat.*

1 When Adee was asked by President McKinley the best way to say no to six European ambassadors who were coming to see him to try to prevent war against Spain, he wrote on

the back of an envelope: "The Government of the United States appreciates the humanitarian and disinterested character of the communication now made on behalf of the powers named, and for its part is confident that equal appreciation will be shown for its own earnest and unselfish endeavors to fulfill a duty to humanity by ending a situation the indefinite prolongation of which has become insufferable."

The President read this message verbatim to the ambassadors.

———— ∽ ————

ADENAUER, Konrad (1876–1967), *German statesman and first chancellor of the Federal Republic (1949–63).*

1 Essentially a Rhinelander, Adenauer never liked or trusted the Prussians and his compatriots in eastern Germany. In the interwar period he used frequently to have to go by train to Berlin. It is said that every time he crossed the River Elbe on this journey he would frown and mutter to himself, "Now we enter Asia."

2 Adenauer received many marriage proposals in his mail when he was chancellor, even after he became an octogenarian. When they were brought to his notice he used to tell his secretary patiently: "Put them in the nonaggression pact file."

3 When Adenauer, still chancellor, was approaching the age of ninety, he succumbed to a heavy cold. His personal physician, unable to be of very much help, had to put up with Adenauer's impatience. "I'm not a magician," protested the harassed doctor. "I can't make you young again."

"I haven't asked you to," retorted the chancellor. "All I want is to go on getting older."

———— ∽ ————

ADLER, Hermann (1839–1911), *British rabbi (chief rabbi of London).*

1 Adler found himself sitting beside Herbert Cardinal Vaughan at an official luncheon. "Now, Dr. Adler," said the cardinal mischievously, "when may I have the pleasure of helping you to some ham?"

"At Your Eminence's wedding," came the prompt reply.

———— ∽ ————

AESCHYLUS (525–456 BC), *Greek poet. Some of his tragedies are the earliest complete plays surviving from ancient Greece.*

1 Aeschylus died and was buried at Gela in Sicily. Ancient biographies record the tradition that his death came about when an eagle, which had seized a tortoise and was looking to smash the reptile's shell, mistook the poet's bald head for a stone and dropped the tortoise upon him.

———— ∽ ————

AGASSIZ, Jean Louis Rodolphe (1807–73), *Swiss naturalist and paleontologist.*

1 An emissary from a learned society came to invite Agassiz to address its members. Agassiz refused on the grounds that lectures of this sort took up too much time that should be devoted to research and writing. The man persisted, saying that they were prepared to pay handsomely for the talk. "That's no inducement to me," Agassiz replied. "I can't afford to waste my time making money."

———— ∽ ————

AGRIPPINA (AD 15–59), *mother of Emperor Nero by her first husband. Her third marriage was to her uncle, Emperor Claudius, whom she later poisoned.*

1 Agrippina was consumed by her ambition to place her son Nero on the imperial throne.

She consulted the soothsayers, who told her, "Nero will reign, but he will kill his mother."

"Let him kill me, then," said Agrippina.

2 Agrippina proved less easy to eliminate than Nero expected. According to Suetonius, he tried poison three times (she had taken the antidote beforehand), a collapsible ceiling in her bedchamber (someone warned her), and an unseaworthy boat (she swam to safety). Finally he sent a centurion with orders to kill her. The centurion struck her first on the head, as he had been ordered, but she bared her breasts, crying out, "Strike rather these, which have nurtured so great a monster as Nero."

AIDAN, Saint (d. 651), *Irish monk who became bishop of Northumbria (635) and founded the monastery at Lindisfarne.*

1 King Oswin, ruler of the former British province of Deira and a friend of Aidan's, gave the bishop a fine horse. Soon afterward Bishop Aidan met a beggar who asked him for alms; he at once dismounted and gave the horse, with all its costly trappings, to the poor man. When this charitable deed came to the king's ears, he taxed Aidan: "Why did you give away the horse that we specially chose for your personal use when we knew that you had need of one for your journeys? We have many less valuable horses that would have been suitable for beggars." Replied Aidan, "Is this foal of a mare more valuable to you than a child of God?" The king pondered, then, suddenly casting his sword aside, knelt at Aidan's feet and begged his forgiveness. Aidan, greatly moved, begged the king to go to his dinner and be merry.

As Aidan watched the king go, he became very melancholy. When the bishop's chaplain asked why, Aidan replied, "I know that the king will not live long, for I have never seen a king so humble as he is. He will be taken from us as the country is not worthy to have such a king."

The foreboding was proved correct: King Oswin was treacherously killed by his northern neighbor, King Oswy.

ALBEMARLE, William Anne Keppel, 2d Earl of (1702–54), *British soldier and ambassador.*

1 Sent as plenipotentiary to Paris in 1748, Albemarle took with him his mistress Lolotte Gaucher, an actress described by contemporaries as cunning and rapacious. One evening, seeing her gazing pensively at a star, the earl remarked, "It's no good, my dear, I can't buy it for you."

ALBERT, Prince (1819–61), *prince consort of Great Britain; husband of Queen Victoria.*

1 Prince Albert had a chronic inability to stay awake late at night. At a concert given at Buckingham Palace and attended by various distinguished guests, Queen Victoria noticed that her husband was asleep. Half-smiling, half-vexed, she prodded him with her elbow. He woke up, nodded approval of the piece being performed, and fell asleep again, still nodding. The queen had to wake him up all over again. A guest at the concert reported, "The queen was charmed, and cousin Albert looked beautiful, and slept quietly as usual."

2 A picture at Balmoral portrayed all the royal children and various birds and animals. Someone asked which was Princess Helena. "There, with the kingfisher," said Albert, adding, "a very proper bird for a princess."

ALBERT, Eugène d' (1864–1932), *German pianist and composer.*

1 D'Albert was married six times. At an evening reception which he attended with his fifth wife shortly after their wedding, he presented the lady to a friend who said politely, "Congratulations, Herr d'Albert; you have rarely introduced me to so charming a wife."

——— ❧ ———

ALCIBIADES (c. 450–404 BC), *Greek general and politician.*

1 Alcibiades was telling Pericles, forty years his senior, how best to govern Athens. This did not amuse Pericles. "Alcibiades," he said, "when I was your age, I talked just as you do now."

"How I should like to have known you, Pericles," replied Alcibiades, "when you were at your best."

——— ❧ ———

ALCOTT, [Amos] Bronson (1799–1888), *US educator and writer, father of the writer Louisa May Alcott.*

1 The Alcott family finances were very low, but they placed great hopes on Bronson Alcott's latest lecture tour. When he arrived home one night in February, the family gathered around to welcome him, offer him food and drink, and rejoice in his homecoming. Then a little silence fell, and it was daughter May who asked the question in all their minds: "Did they pay you?" Slowly Bronson Alcott drew out his pocketbook and displayed its contents — a single dollar. "Another year I shall do better," he said. There was a stunned hush in the group around him. Then Mrs. Alcott flung her arms around his neck and said stoutly, "I call that doing very well."

——— ❧ ———

ALCOTT, Louisa May (1832–88), *US novelist, author of* Little Women *(1869).*

1 When Louisa Alcott became a celebrity, she often found her fame tiresome. A supporter of the fight for women's suffrage, she attended the Women's Congress in Syracuse, where she was accosted by an effusive admirer. "If you ever come to Oshkosh," said the lady, "your feet will not be allowed to touch the ground: you will be borne in the arms of the people. Will you come?"

"Never," replied Miss Alcott.

——— ❧ ———

ALEMBERT, Jean le Rond d' (1717–83), *French mathematician.*

1 The illegitimate son of an aristocrat, d'Alembert was abandoned by his mother soon after his birth and was brought up by a glazier named Rousseau and his wife. When d'Alembert's extraordinary talents became known, his mother attempted to claim him. D'Alembert rejected her, saying, "My mother is the wife of the glazier."

——— ❧ ———

ALENÇON, Sophie-Charlotte, Duchesse d' (d. 1897), *Bavarian-born duchess who married the Duc d'Alençon in 1868.*

1 On May 4, 1897, the duchess was presiding over a charity bazaar in Paris when the hall accidentally caught fire. Flames spread to the paper decorations and flimsy walls of the booths and in seconds the place was an inferno. In the hideous panic that followed, many women and children were trampled as they rushed for the exits, while workmen from a nearby site performed incredible acts of heroism, rushing into the blaze to carry out the trapped women. Some rescuers reached the duchess, who had remained calmly seated behind her booth. "Because of my title, I was the first to enter here. I shall be

the last to go out," she said, rejecting their offer of help. She stayed and was burned to death, along with more than 120 others, mainly women and children.

ALEXANDER, Sir George (1858–1919), *British actor.*

1 "On the first night of that unfortunate play [Henry James's] *Guy Domville,* produced by George Alexander, it was soon evident from the attitude of the gallery that the play was not going to be a success, but the seal of failure was set on it when Sir George uttered the line, 'I am the last of the Domvilles.' Scarcely were the words out of his mouth than a voice came from the gallery, 'Well at any rate, that's a comfort to know.'"

ALEXANDER, Grover Cleveland (1887–1950), *US baseball pitcher.*

1 Although he became an alcoholic during his twenty-year career, Alexander remained one of the best pitchers until the end. At thirty-five he pitched superbly in the World Series of 1926 between his St. Louis Cardinals and the New York Yankees. After winning the full sixth game of the best-of-seven set and tying the series at three games each, Alexander spent that night celebrating. Since pitchers usually rested three days between starts, he went out to the bull pen next day, with the relief pitchers, and snoozed away the final game until he was, surprisingly, summoned to pitch the seventh of the nine innings. There were three men on base, one out needed to end the inning, and a one-run lead. Alexander faced the feared Tony Lazzeri and struck him out, ending the inning to the cheers of the crowd. He then stopped the Yankees in their last two innings to win the game and give his team the title.

Afterward Alexander was asked how he felt. "I feel fine," he said. "It's Lazzeri you should ask how he feels," and added, "I owe it all to clean living." And he went out and got drunk.

ALEXANDER, Harold, 1st Earl [Alexander of Tunis] (1891–1969), *British field marshal.*

1 Alexander's assistant once commented on his habit of tipping into his Out tray any letters remaining in his In tray at the end of the working day. "Excuse me, sir," he asked. "Why do you do that?"

"It saves time," explained Alexander. "You'd be surprised how little of it comes back."

ALEXANDER, Samuel (1859–1938), *Australian-born philosopher and university professor who lived most of his life in England.*

1 The professor of philosophy on his beloved bicycle was a familiar sight around Manchester. On one occasion he rode over to Liverpool to dine and spend the night at the house of a wealthy shipowner. The host's valet noticed that the professor had arrived without luggage and reported the fact to his employer, who courteously said that he would not dress for dinner that evening. He also instructed the valet to put out a spare pair of pajamas in the professor's room. A short time later, however, the valet rushed into his master's dressing room with the message: "I have just seen Professor Alexander going downstairs and he's wearing a dinner jacket." The host made a rapid change. The following morning the valet returned the spare pajamas, unused, to his master, remarking: "The professor had his own, after all." Curiosity finally overcame the shipowner. As he was seeing his guest off on his

bicycle, he asked, "Do you not have any luggage?"

"I'm wearing it," replied the professor.

———— ❧ ————

ALEXANDER I (1777–1825), *czar of Russia (1801–25).*

1 The way for Alexander's accession to the throne was cleared through the murder of his savage, megalomaniac father, Czar Paul I, by a group of aristocratic conspirators. Thus in two generations history repeated itself, for Alexander's grandmother, Catherine the Great, had connived at the murder of her husband, Peter III, in order to seize power herself less than forty years before. The youthful archduke had had prior warning of the plot against Czar Paul, but had preferred to think that the conspirators' intention was merely to depose and imprison his father. When news of the murder was brought to him, he almost collapsed with horror. This incident haunted him for the remainder of his life, but the strongest proof of his complicity was in his treatment of the conspirators; they all continued in his favor and some became his closest counselors. A French spy, the Countess de Bonneuil, reported to her master Fouché on the situation in St. Petersburg: "The young emperor goes about preceded by the murderers of his grandfather, followed by the murderers of his father, quite surrounded by his friends."

2 When Alexander was in Paris, following the defeat of Napoleon, he attended anniversary celebrations at one of the hospitals. The ladies who had organized the affair passed plates around for contributions. An extremely pretty girl was delegated to take a plate to the czar. Alexander dropped in a handful of gold and whispered, "That's for your beautiful bright eyes." The young lady curtsied and immediately presented the plate

again. "What? More?" said the czar. "Yes, sire," she replied, "now I want something for the poor."

3 The czar heard of a new invention, a calculating machine, that could apparently work faster than any person. He summoned the inventor, Abraham Stern, to his court to demonstrate the device. After inspecting it, Alexander challenged Stern to an arithmetic contest. A prearranged list of calculations was read out, and both Stern and the czar, who worked the numbers with a quill pen, set to. As Alexander was completing the first calculation, Stern announced that his machine had finished. The czar read over the results, looked at Stern and his machine, then said to his attendant, "The machine is good, but the Jew is bad."

———— ❧ ————

ALEXANDER III [Alexander the Great] (356–323 BC), *king of Macedon (336–323).*

1 Gossip surrounded the birth of Alexander. Doubt as to whether Philip was really his father later allowed Alexander to declare that he was a god and the son of Jupiter. Alexander's mother, Olympias, preferred to leave the matter obscure. When news was brought to her of Alexander's claim to divine paternity, she said, "Please — I don't want to get into any trouble with Juno."

2 A Thessalian brought an exceptionally beautiful horse, named Bucephalus, to the Macedonian court, offering to sell it to King Philip. However, when the royal grooms tried to test its paces, it proved wild and unmanageable. The young Alexander asked his father for permission to try his skill. Philip reluctantly agreed, saying that if the prince failed to ride Bucephalus he was to pay his father a forfeit equal to its price. Alexander walked quickly to the horse's head and

turned it to face into the sun, for he had noticed that the horse's own shadow was upsetting it. He calmed it, then mounted it, and Bucephalus obediently showed off his paces.

The court, which had feared for the prince's safety, broke into loud applause. Philip was overjoyed. He kissed his son, saying, "Seek another kingdom that may be worthy of your abilities, for Macedonia is too small for you."

3 Alexander, setting out on his conquest of Asia, inquired into the finances of his followers. To ensure that they should not be troubled over the welfare of their dependents during their absence, he distributed crown estates and revenues among them. When he had thus disposed of nearly all the royal resources, his friend General Perdiccas asked Alexander what he had reserved for himself. "Hope," answered the king. "In that case," said Perdiccas, "we who share in your labors will also take part in your hopes." Thereupon he refused the estate allocated to him, and several other of the king's friends did the same.

4 At Gordium in Phrygia (Asia Minor) a chariot was fastened with cords made from the bark of a cornel tree. The knot was so cunningly tied that no ends were visible, and the tradition was that the empire of the world should fall to the man who could untie it. When Alexander conquered Gordium, he confronted the famous puzzle. Unable to untie the knot, he drew his sword and with one slash severed it.

{Hence the phrase "cut the Gordian knot" for finding a quick and drastic solution to an intricate problem.}

5 On his march through Asia Minor, Alexander fell dangerously ill. His physicians were afraid to treat him because if they did not succeed, the Macedonian army would suspect them of malpractice. Only one, Philip the Acarnanian, was willing to take the risk, as he had confidence in both the king's friendship and his own drugs.

While the medicine was being prepared, Alexander received a letter from an enemy of Philip's that accused the physician of having been bribed by the Persian king to poison his master. Alexander read the letter and slipped it under his pillow without showing it to anyone. When Philip entered the tent with the medicine, Alexander took the cup from him, at the same time handing Philip the letter. While the physician was reading it, Alexander calmly drank the contents of the cup. Horrified and indignant at the calumny, Philip threw himself down at the king's bedside, but Alexander assured him that he had complete confidence in his honor. After three days the king was well enough to appear again before his army.

6 After Alexander had conquered Egypt, the Persian king, Darius, sent a letter offering generous terms for peace and future friendship with the Macedonian king: 10,000 talents to be paid in ransom for Persian prisoners, all the countries west of the Euphrates to be ceded to Alexander, and Darius's daughter to be given to him in marriage. Alexander consulted his friends about how he should respond. His general Parmenion said, "If I were Alexander, I would accept these offers."

"So would I," retorted Alexander, "if I were Parmenion."

7 The captured Indian king Porus was brought before Alexander, who asked how he wished to be treated. "Like a king," was the reply. Alexander asked if he had anything else to request. "Nothing," said Porus, "for everything is comprehended in the word 'king.'" Alexander restored Porus's lands to him.

8 Alexander's final command before a certain battle was that the beards of his soldiers

should be shaved off. "There is nothing like a beard to get hold of in a fight," he explained.

9 Alexander the Great was marching across the desert with a thirsty army. A soldier came up to him, knelt down, and offered him a helmet full of water. "Is there enough for ten thousand men?" asked Alexander. When the soldier shook his head, Alexander poured the water out on the ground.

———— ✧ ————

ALEXANDER VI (c. 1431–1503), *pope (1492–1503) who used his office to advance the prospects of his illegitimate children, especially his son Cesare Borgia.*

1 Alexander VI's illegitimate daughter Lucrezia was married in 1502 to her third husband, Alfonso d'Este, son and heir of the Duke of Ferrara. Not long after the marriage the Ferrarese envoy to the papal court reassured Pope Alexander that all was well with the newlyweds; Alfonso, he reported, made love to Lucrezia nightly. Alfonso, the envoy added, also made love with equal regularity to other women during the day, but that was unimportant. "Well, he is young," said the pope, "and that is how it should be."

———— ✧ ————

ALEXANDRA (1844–1925), *Danish princess who in 1863 married the Prince of Wales (later King Edward VII of Great Britain).*

1 On May 10, 1910, King Edward VII died. At first, as he lay on his deathbed, his long-suffering queen, who had turned a blind eye to his infidelities and his pursuit of his pleasures in every fashionable resort on the Continent, was stricken with grief. But it was not long before her sense of humor reasserted itself. She remarked to Lord Esher, "Now at least I know where he is."

———— ✧ ————

ALFONSO X (c. 1221–84), *king of Castile and León (1252–84), known as Alfonso the Wise.*

1 The most celebrated of the works undertaken under Alfonso's sponsorship was the compilation of the "Alfonsine Tables," which were published on the day of his accession to the throne and remained the most authoritative planetary tables in existence for the following three centuries. The preparation of the tables was very laborious and was based, of course, upon the Ptolemaic scheme of the universe. Alfonso remarked that if God had consulted him during the six days of creation, he would have recommended a less complicated design.

———— ✧ ————

ALFONSO XIII (1886–1941), *king of Spain (1886–1931).*

1 One would-be assassin leaped suddenly in front of the king's horse as he was riding back from a parade and pointed a revolver at him from barely a yard away. "Polo comes in very handy on these occasions," said Alfonso afterward. "I set my horse's head straight at him and rode into him as he fired."

———— ✧ ————

ALFRED [Alfred the Great] (849–899), *king of Wessex.*

1 At one time during his wars with the Danes, Alfred was forced to seek refuge incognito in a hut belonging to a poor Anglo-Saxon family. The woman of the house, who had to leave for a short time, asked the fugitive to keep an eye on some cakes she was baking. Alfred, deep in thought, did not notice that the cakes were burning. When his hostess returned, she gave the unrecognized king a hearty scolding for being an idle good-for-nothing.

2 As a young boy Alfred received little formal schooling. He did possess a highly retentive

memory and particularly enjoyed listening to the court bards reciting poetry. One day his mother, holding a fine manuscript book in her hand, said to Alfred and his elder brothers, "I will give this book to whichever one of you can learn it most quickly." Although he could not read, Alfred was greatly attracted to the book and was determined to own it. Forestalling his brothers, he took it to someone who read it through to him. Then he went back to his mother and repeated the whole thing to her. This talent was the foundation of Alfred's later reputation as scholar, translator, and patron of learning.

—◌◌—

ALGREN, Nelson (1909-81), *US writer known especially for his National Book Award–winning novel,* **The Man with the Golden Arm.**

1 Algren's career in Hollywood was short-lived. As he described it, "I went out there for a thousand a week, and I worked Monday and I got fired Wednesday. The man who hired me was out of town Tuesday."

—◌◌—

ALI, Muhammad (1942–), *US boxer, Olympic gold medalist, and world heavyweight champion (1964–71, 1974–78, 1978–80). Born Cassius Clay, he converted to Islam.*

1 In the fight film *Rocky II*, a character apparently based on Muhammad Ali taunts the hero with the words "I'll destroy you. I am the master of disaster." After seeing a private screening of the film, Ali wistfully remarked, "'Master of disaster': I wish I'd thought of that!"

2 Just before takeoff on an airplane flight, the stewardess reminded Ali to fasten his seat belt. "Superman don't need no seat belt," replied Ali. "Superman don't need no airplane, either," retorted the stewardess. Ali fastened his belt.

3 Irritated by Ali's perpetual boasts of "I am the greatest," a colleague asked the boxer what he was like at golf. "I'm the best," replied Ali. "I just haven't played yet."

4 At a New York party, violinist Isaac Stern was introduced to Ali. "You might say we're in the same business," remarked Stern. "We both earn a living with our hands."

"You must be pretty good," said Ali. "There isn't a mark on you."

5 Ali went into his now-legendary fight with Sonny Liston in 1964, the fight that secured his title as heavyweight champion, as a seven-to-one underdog. He was seen as more of a clown in the ring than a true fighter. Sportswriters all agreed that he couldn't fight as well as he could talk. But fight he did, and he repeated his victory in 1965 in their second title bout. As Liston lay on the mat, Ali stood over him with his fist clenched, yelling, "Get up and fight, sucker!"

6 A young person once asked Ali what he should do with his life. He could not decide whether to continue his education or go out into the world to seek his fortune. "Stay in college, get the knowledge," advised Ali. "If they can make penicillin out of moldy bread, they can make something out of you!"

—◌◌—

ALLAIS, Alphonse (1854–1905), *French humorist, writer, and dramatist.*

1 In Alphonse Allais's library was a volume of Voltaire in which he had inscribed: "To Alphonse Allais, with regrets for not having known him. Voltaire."

2 Asked to deliver a lecture on the subject of the theater, Allais began: "I have been asked to talk to you on the subject of the theater, but I fear that it will make you melancholy. Shakespeare is dead, Molière is dead, Racine

is dead, Marivaux is dead — and I am not feeling too well myself."

— ✧ —

ALLEN, Dick (1942–), *US baseball player.*

1 Allen, who played for numerous teams, including the Cardinals, the Dodgers, the Cubs, and the A's, liked to write words in the dirt around first base. This distracted the other players, and finally baseball commissioner Bowie Kuhn told the Philadelphia Phillies to put a stop to this practice. Allen's immediate response was to write three words in the dirt: *No, why,* and *Mom.* Why Mom? "To say she tells me what to do," Allen said, "not the man up there."

— ✧ —

ALLEN, Ethan (1738–89), *US patriot, leader of the "Green Mountain Boys" during the Revolutionary War.*

1 Ethan Allen with a group of associates attended a Sunday service led by a stern Calvinist preacher. He took as his text "Many shall strive to enter in, but shall not be able." God's grace was sufficient, observed the preacher, to include one person in ten, but not one in twenty would endeavor to avail himself of the offered salvation. Furthermore, not one man in fifty was really the object of God's solicitude, and not one in eighty — here Allen seized his hat and left the pew, saying, "I'm off, boys. Any one of you can take my chance."

2 In the early morning of May 10, 1775, Ethan Allen led a small force in a surprise attack on the British garrison at Ticonderoga. Having overpowered the sentries, Allen demanded to be taken to the commanding officer's quarters. He shouted at him to come out immediately or he would kill the entire garrison. The commander appeared, his breeches still in his hand. Allen ordered the instant surrender of the fortress. "By what authority?" asked the British officer. "In the name of the great Jehovah, and the Continental Congress," said Ethan Allen. The garrison surrendered.

3 When Allen's first wife, notorious for her sourness and bad temper, died, a local man offered to help transport the coffin to the church. "You could call on any of the neighbors," he said to the widower. "There's not a man in town wouldn't be glad to help out."

4 Allen lay ill. The doctor examined him and said, "General, I fear the angels are waiting for you."

"Waiting, are they?" said the bluff frontiersman. "Waiting, are they? Well — let 'em wait."

— ✧ —

ALLEN, Fred (1894–1956), *US comedian, writer, and radio star.*

1 "If somebody caught him in an act of kindness, he ducked behind a screen of cynicism. A friend was walking with him when a truck bore down on a newsboy in front of them. Allen dashed out and snatched the boy to safety, then snarled at him, 'What's the matter, kid? Don't you want to grow up and have troubles?'"

2 Spying a haggard, long-haired cellist in the orchestra pit of a vaudeville house in Toledo, Ohio, Allen called out to him, "How much would you charge to haunt a house?"

3 The radio and TV comic Jack Parr, of the *Tonight* show fame, idolized Allen. On their first meeting he stammered, "You are my God!" Allen replied: "There are five thousand churches in New York and you have to be an atheist."

4 The script for one of Allen's radio shows was returned to him with extensive alterations scrawled across the pages in blue pencil. Allen flipped through it impatiently. "Where

were you fellows when the paper was blank?" he asked.

———— ✺ ————

ALLEN, Woody (1935–), *US film actor, director, and writer.*

1 A fan rushed up to Allen on the street calling, "You're a star!" Allen replied, "This year I'm a star, but what will I be next year — a black hole?"

2 Allen was revered by the French, who saw in him a true genius of the medium. And American critics were adulatory as well, dubbing him one of the great directors of modern times. Allen himself was more sanguine: "I don't want to achieve immortality through my work. I want to achieve it through not dying!"

———— ✺ ————

ALLINGHAM, Margery (1904–), *British mystery writer.*

1 Allingham was born into a family of bookworms, and from her earliest days was surrounded by editors and journalists. One day, as the seven-year-old Margery was sitting on the floor writing a story in her notebook, the housemaid saw her and said, "Master, missus, and three strangers all sitting in different rooms writing down lies and now YOU starting!"

———— ✺ ————

ALMA-TADEMA, Sir Lawrence (1836–1912), *Dutch painter who adopted British nationality in 1873.*

1 A friend of Alma-Tadema had just become the proud father of twins. The painter made his congratulatory visit immediately after concluding a rather excessive drinking bout. Though still a bit muzzy, he was prudent

enough to exclaim, "What an enchanting baby!"

———— ✺ ————

ALTENBERG, Peter (?1862–1919), *Austrian poet.*

1 Though in fact he maintained a very solid bank balance, Altenberg had a mania for begging. The poet and critic Karl Kraus tells how Altenberg besought him again and again to give him a hundred kronen, and on every occasion Kraus refused him. Finally, his patience at an end, Kraus burst out, "Look, Peter, I'd gladly give it to you, but I *really, really,* don't have the money."

"Very well, I'll lend it to you," said Altenberg.

———— ✺ ————

ALTMAN, Robert (1925–), *US film director.*

1 Hollywood had always found Robert Altman difficult to work with; and Altman returned the feeling, loathing the pretentiousness and excess of the big studios. A maverick filmmaker, he had made his way with his own rules. His movie *The Player* was an irreverent, sometimes savage look at modern moviemaking, an in-joke on the whole industry. At a special screening Altman was delighted to observe that, during a scene showing a snake, studio mogul Barry Diller "jumped a foot out of his chair." Chuckled Altman, "I guess he didn't expect to see a relative."

———— ✺ ————

ALVANLEY, William Arden, 2d Baron (1789–1849), *British aristocrat and society leader.*

1 After emerging unscathed from a duel fought in a discreetly secluded corner of London, Lord Alvanley handed a guinea to the hack-

ney coachman who had conveyed him to the spot and home again. Surprised at the size of the largesse, the man protested, "But, my lord, I only took you a mile." Alvanley waved aside the objection: "The guinea's not for taking me, my man, it's for bringing me back."

2 Owing to the careless driving of their coachmen, Lord Alvanley and another nobleman were involved in a collision. The other peer jumped out of his coach, rolling up his sleeves and making ready to thrash his negligent servant, but on seeing that he was elderly and abjectly apologetic, contented himself with saying significantly, "Your age protects you." Alvanley likewise hopped out of his coach, ready to thrash his postilion, but, finding himself confronting a very large, tough-looking lad, he thought better of it. "Your youth protects you," he said, and climbed back into his coach.

⸻ ✿ ⸻

AMBROSE, Saint (?340–397), *Italian cleric, born at Trier in Germany.*

1 The emperor appointed Ambrose provincial governor of northern Italy, residing at Milan. In this capacity he was called out in 374 to the cathedral, where a riot was threatening between two rival factions of Christians, each intent on winning its own candidate's nomination to the bishopric. Ambrose quelled the riot but was unable to persuade the warring parties to agree on a bishop. Finally someone suggested Ambrose himself, and the nomination was enthusiastically greeted on all sides. In vain Ambrose protested that he was not even christened. He was hurriedly baptized, then ordained, and finally consecrated bishop — all within the space of a single week.

⸻ ✿ ⸻

AMMONIUS, *early Christian monk.*

1 In the year AD 420 the monk Ammonius, who wished to be left alone in contemplation and prayer, was approached by a group of villagers who wanted him to become their bishop. In front of them he cut off his own left ear, saying "From now on be assured that it is impossible for me, as the law forbids a man with his ear cut off to be an ordained priest. And if you compel me, I will cut out my tongue as well."

⸻ ✿ ⸻

ANAXAGORAS (500–428 BC), *Greek philosopher.*

1 Anaxagoras took refuge at Lampsacus on the Hellespont, and the Athenians condemned him to death in absentia. When he heard the news of the sentence he observed, "Nature has long since condemned both them and me."

⸻ ✿ ⸻

ANAXIMENES (4th century BC), *Greek philosopher born at Lampsacus in Asia Minor.*

1 Anaximenes accompanied Alexander the Great on his expedition against the Persians, in the course of which the Macedonian forces captured Lampsacus. Anxious to save his native city from destruction, Anaximenes sought an audience with the king. Alexander anticipated his plea: "I swear by the Styx I will not grant your request," he said. "My lord," calmly replied Anaximenes, "I merely wanted to ask you to destroy Lampsacus." And so he saved his native city.

⸻ ✿ ⸻

ANDERS, William A[lison] (1933–), *US astronaut. A member of the crew of* Apollo 8, *he circumnavigated the moon in December 1968.*

1 Anders received his fair share of publicity after the *Apollo 8* moon trip. Tired of being ac-

costed by pressmen, photographers, and the admiring public, he "escaped" with his wife for a brief vacation in Acapulco. A few days after their arrival, however, as they relaxed on the patio of their holiday villa, a young man called and asked if he could take some photographs. Groaning, Anders replied, "Okay, come on in."

"Thanks," said the young man enthusiastically as he marched across the patio. "You've got the best view of the bay in the whole place."

2 Anders's son asked his father who would actually be driving the *Apollo 8* craft as it hurtled into space. Anders told him, "I think Isaac Newton is doing most of the driving now."

———— ✺ ————

ANDERSEN, Hans Christian (1805–75), *Danish writer famed for his fairy tales.*

1 As a young man Hans Christian Andersen read one of his plays to the wife of another Danish writer. She soon stopped him: "But you have copied whole paragraphs word for word from Oehlenschläger and Ingemann!" Andersen was unabashed: "Yes, I know, but aren't they splendid!"

2 Visiting with Charles Dickens's family in England, Andersen rather overstayed his welcome. One of Dickens's daughters summed up the guest as "a bony bore, and [he] stayed on and on." Dickens himself wrote on a card that he stuck up over the mirror in the guest room: "Hans Andersen slept in this room for five weeks — which seemed to the family AGES."

3 Hans Christian Andersen was discussing the march for his funeral with the musician who was to compose it: "Most of the people who will walk after me will be children, so make the beat keep time with little steps."

4 Despite his evident love of children, Andersen never married. Late in life his health declined rapidly; first he developed chronic bronchitis, then the more serious, and ultimately fatal, liver cancer. Unable to care for himself, he moved into the house of some friends near Copenhagen, where he could see the ocean from his room. One morning he quietly finished his tea, and was found a few minutes later in his bed, dead. In his hands was a farewell letter written forty-five years earlier by the only woman he had ever loved.

———— ✺ ————

ANDERSON, Sherwood (1876–1941), *US author best known for his collection* Winesburg, Ohio.

1 (Anderson describes a chance meeting in New Orleans with Horace Liveright, the publisher, who was a well-known womanizer.)

"He was with a beautiful woman and I had seen him with many beautiful women. 'Meet my wife,' he said and 'Oh yeah?' I answered. There was an uncomfortable moment. It *was* Mrs. Liveright. I was sunk and so was Horace."

2 Anderson's first publishers, recognizing his potential, arranged to send him a weekly check in the hope that, relieved of financial pressure, he would write more freely. After a few weeks, however, Anderson took his latest check back to the office. "It's no use," he explained. "I find it impossible to work with security staring me in the face."

———— ✺ ————

ANDRE, Major John (1751–80), *British army officer during the American Revolution.*

1 The British army major who plotted with Benedict Arnold to overthrow West Point was finally captured in 1780 by the shores of the Hudson River and was condemned to

death. When Andre appealed to General Washington to be shot instead of hanged, Washington declined to help, saying that if Andre was a traitor, he should die a spy's death; if he was to be considered a prisoner-of-war, he should not be executed at all. As Andre was led to his death, he nearly fainted to see the hangman's noose awaiting him. But he swiftly recovered his composure, helped the hangman adjust the noose around his own neck, and offered his handkerchief to be used to bind his hands. "All that I request of you gentlemen," he told his captors, "is that you will bear witness to the world that I die like a brave man."

ANDREW, Father Agnellus (1908–), *British Franciscan.*

1 Father Andrew was the BBC's adviser on Roman Catholic affairs. A producer who was planning programs on the subject wrote him asking how he could ascertain the official Roman Catholic view of heaven and hell. The answering memorandum contained just one word: "Die."

ANNE, Princess (1950–), *daughter of Queen Elizabeth II of the United Kingdom.*

1 Watching the annual show-jumping event at Hickstead in Sussex one afternoon, Princess Anne was accosted by a fellow spectator. "Has anyone ever told you that you look like Princess Anne?" he inquired. Anne replied: "I think I'm a bit better-looking than she is."

2 In 1974 a deranged man tried to kidnap Princess Anne in the very public site of the Mall. In his attempt he fired six shots, wounding her bodyguard and several other people. Her father, Prince Philip, later said, "If the man had succeeded in abducting Anne, she would have given him a hell of a time in captivity."

3 At a dinner party Anne spent the entire meal talking about horses with one of her dinner companions. Her neighbor on the other side was ignored throughout the meal as Anne talked, until at last she turned to him to ask for the sugar. The slighted man put two lumps of sugar on his open palm and held them out to her.

ANTHEIL, George (1900–59), *US composer, especially of film music.*

1 Among Antheil's early avant-garde pieces, none caused a greater sensation than his *Ballet mécanique,* scored for automobile horns, airplane propeller, fire siren, ten grand pianos, and other instruments. When it was performed at Carnegie Hall in 1924, a concertgoer near the orchestra could stand no more than a few minutes of the racket. Tying his handkerchief to his cane, he raised the white flag.

ANTHONY, Marc (d. 30 BC), *Roman soldier, lover of Egypt's Cleopatra.*

1 Octavius's invasion of Egypt spelled doom for Marc Anthony. So Cleopatra's lover summoned his servant Eros and asked him to fulfill a promise made earlier: to kill Marc Anthony when the chips were down. Eros drew his sword, but at the last moment plunged it into his own heart. "Well done, Eros," said Marc Anthony, "you could not do it yourself, but you teach me to do what I must." So saying, he drew his own sword and killed himself.

ANTHONY, Susan B. (1820–1906), *US suffragette and social reformer.*

1 "You are not married," the well-known abolitionist Samuel May once said to Susan Anthony. "You have no business to be discussing marriage."

"You, Mr. May, are not a slave," she retorted. "Suppose you quit lecturing on slavery."

2 At a reception given to honor her many decades' struggle for equal rights for women, Anthony was showered with bouquets of flowers. Commenting on her initial forays into politics and marveling that her status had certainly changed over the years, she noted, "They threw things at me then — but they were not roses."

3 On her deathbed Anthony was asked if she was happy about the course her life had taken. "Oh, yes, I'd do it all again," she said. "The spirit is willing yet; I feel the same desire to do the work, but the flesh is weak. It's too bad that our bodies wear out while our interests are just as strong as ever."

———— ᴄᴧᴑ ————

ANTISTHENES (c. 440–c. 360 BC), *Greek philosopher.*

1 Antisthenes dressed with ostentatious poverty. Socrates once mocked him, saying, "I can see your vanity, Antisthenes, through the holes in your cloak."

2 Overcome by a distaste for life, Antisthenes was offered a dagger by Diogenes with the words: "Perhaps you have need of this friend?" Antisthenes replied, "I thank you, but unfortunately the will to live is also part of the world's evil, as it is part of our nature."

———— ᴄᴧᴑ ————

APELLES (4th century BC), *Greek painter.*

1 While Apelles was being acclaimed at the court of Alexander the Great, Protogenes, the only man worthy to be considered his rival, was living poor and obscure on Rhodes. Apelles went to visit him, but when he arrived, Protogenes was away from home. The old woman servant asked Apelles who she should tell her master had called on him in his absence. In reply Apelles took a brush and traced upon a panel, with a single continuous line, a shape of extreme delicacy. When Protogenes returned and saw the panel he remarked, "Only Apelles could have drawn that line." He then drew an even finer line inside that of Apelles, telling the old woman to show it to his visitor if he returned. In due course Apelles came back and added a third line of even greater fineness between the first two. When Protogenes saw it, he admitted that Apelles was his master and he hurried out to find him so that they could celebrate together.

2 A certain cobbler had found fault with the shoes of a figure in one of Apelles' paintings. Not wishing to disregard the advice of an expert, Apelles corrected the mistake. The cobbler, flattered, went on to criticize the shape of the figure's legs. This was too much for Apelles. "Cobbler, stick to your last!" he cried, dismissing the would-be critic from his workshop and contributing a phrase that has endured for more than two millennia.

———— ᴄᴧᴑ ————

AQUINAS, Saint Thomas (c. 1225–74), *Italian Dominican theologian and scholastic philosopher who was canonized.*

1 As the pupil of the scholastic teacher Albertus Magnus in Paris, Aquinas made a poor impression on his fellow students, who nicknamed him "the dumb ox." Albertus summoned him to a private interview at which

they discussed all the subjects in the university curriculum. At the next lecture the master announced, "You call your brother Thomas a dumb ox; let me tell you that one day the whole world will listen to his bellowings."

———— ✿ ————

ARCHELAUS (5th century BC), *king of Macedon (413–399 BC).*

1 A barber, talkative like the rest of his profession, asked King Archelaus how he would like his hair cut. "In silence," replied the king.

———— ✿ ————

ARCHER, George (1939–), *US golfer.*

1 Archer won nineteen Masters tournaments during his career, playing hard. But as he approached retirement he was at a loss as to how to occupy himself. When asked what he would do when the time came, he shook his head, saying, "Baseball players quit playing and take up golf. Basketball players quit and take up golf. Football players quit and take up golf. What are we supposed to do when we quit?"

———— ✿ ————

ARCHER, William (1856–1924), *British drama critic and playwright.*

1 (Max Beerbohm relates an anecdote about Archer to his biographer, S. N. Behrman.)
"'Did you know that Archer, who always wished to demonstrate that, though a drama critic, he could write a play, had one night of triumph when he felt that he had achieved a beautiful play? He told me this himself. One night, between sleeping and waking, it seemed to him that he had evolved a perfect plot, saw the whole thing from beginning to end. He saw that it only remained to write it — like that!' [Max snapped his fingers.] 'Then he fell into a blissful sleep. When he wakened he went over the whole plot again in his mind. He had a disillusioning, a frightful revelation. What he had dreamt was *Hedda Gabler.*'"

———— ✿ ————

ARCHIMEDES (287–212 BC), *Greek mathematician and scientist.*

1 Hiero believed that an artisan to whom he had given a quantity of gold to shape into a crown had adulterated the metal with silver. He asked Archimedes if there was any way that his suspicions could be proved or disproved. According to the traditional story, the answer occurred to Archimedes while he was taking a bath. He noticed that the deeper he went into the water, the more water overflowed, and that his body seemed to weigh less the more it was submerged. Leaping from the bath, he is said to have run naked through the streets of Syracuse crying, *"Eureka!"* (I have found it!) The concept he had grasped, now known as Archimedes' Principle, is that the apparent loss of weight of a floating body is equal to the weight of water it displaces, and that the weight per volume (density) of a body determines the displacement. Archimedes realized that by immersing first the crown, then the same weights of silver (less dense) and gold (more dense), different volumes would be displaced, and so he was able to demonstrate that the crown was indeed adulterated.

2 His vision of the possibilities opened up by his inventions of the lever and the pulley led Archimedes to make his famous utterance: "Give me a place on which to stand, and I will move the earth." Hiero challenged him

to put his words into action and help the sailors to beach a large ship in the Syracusan fleet. Archimedes arranged a series of pulleys and cogs to such effect that by his own un-aided strength he was able to pull the great vessel out of the water and onto the beach.

3 The lack of a suitable surface could not deter Archimedes from drawing mathematical diagrams. After leaving his bath he would anoint himself thoroughly with olive oil, as was the custom at the time, and then trace his calculations with a fingernail on his own oily skin.

4 When the Roman general Marcellus eventually captured Syracuse, he gave special orders that the life of Archimedes should be protected. A Roman soldier, sent to fetch the scientist, found him drawing mathematical symbols in the sand. Engrossed in his work, Archimedes gestured impatiently, indicating that the soldier must wait until he had solved his problem, and murmured, "Don't disturb my circles." The soldier, enraged, drew his sword and killed him.

—— ⚬⅃⚬ ——

ARDITI, Luigi (1822–1903), *Italian composer and opera conductor.*

1 While staying in Birmingham, England, Arditi was advised by a friend to spend a day at Stratford-upon-Avon. "It would be a pity to leave the area without visiting the birthplace of Shakespeare," said his friend. "But who is this Shakespeare?" asked the conductor. His friend looked at him in amazement. "Haven't you heard of the man who wrote *Othello* and *Romeo and Juliet* and *The Merry Wives of Windsor*?" he asked. "Ah," replied Arditi after a moment's thought, "you mean ze librettist."

—— ⚬⅃⚬ ——

ARISTIDES (?530–468 BC), *Athenian statesman and military commander known as "Aristides the Just."*

1 Under the Athenian system of ostracism every free adult male could specify the man he wished to see ostracized by scratching the name on a potsherd and dropping it into an urn. An illiterate Athenian, not recognizing Aristides, asked him to write on his potsherd on his behalf. Asked what name the man wanted written, he replied, "Aristides." Surprised, the statesman inquired whether Aristides had ever injured him that he should wish to see him banished. "No," replied the man, "I don't even know him, but I am sick and tired of hearing him called 'the Just.'" Aristides in silence wrote his own name on the potsherd and handed it back to the man.

—— ⚬⅃⚬ ——

ARISTIPPUS (?435–?356 BC), *Greek philosopher.*

1 Aristippus, asked by a rich Athenian to teach his son philosophy, demanded 500 drachmas. The Athenian protested, "What! I could buy a slave for that much."

"Do so," replied Aristippus. "Then you will have two slaves."

2 During his sojourn at the court of Dionysius, tyrant of Syracuse, Aristippus requested a favor for a friend. Dionysius refused. Aristippus pleaded with the tyrant, abasing himself at his feet, until the favor was granted. Criticized for this conduct as being unworthy of a philosopher, Aristippus retorted, "But that is where the tyrant's ears are."

3 Dionysius asked Aristippus why it was that philosophers paid court to princes, but not vice versa. Aristippus answered, "It is because philosophers know what they need, and princes do not."

—— ⚬⅃⚬ ——

ARLEN, Michael [Dikran Kouyoumdjian] (1895–1956), *British writer born in Bulgaria of Armenian parents.*

1 Down on his luck, Arlen went to New York in 1944. To drown his sorrows he paid a visit to the famous restaurant "21". In the lobby, he ran into Sam Goldwyn, who offered the somewhat impractical advice that he should buy racehorses. At the bar Arlen met Louis B. Mayer, an old acquaintance, who asked him what were his plans for the future. "I was just talking to Sam Goldwyn —" began Arlen. "How much did he offer you?" interrupted Mayer. Arlen hesitated. "Not enough," he replied evasively. "Would you take fifteen thousand for thirty weeks?" asked Mayer. No hesitation this time. "Yes," said Arlen.

2 Arlen had had lunch with William Saroyan, the American author of Armenian origin, and gave his wife a glowing account of the encounter. "What are you so excited about?" she asked him. "After all, the day before you lunched with the king of Greece!" Arlen replied, "For an Armenian to lunch with a king — that's natural, but for an Armenian to lunch with another Armenian — that's something to be proud of!"

———— ◆ ————

ARMOUR, Philip Danforth (1832–1901), *US industrialist, founder of the meat-packing company Armour and Co.*

1 Noting that the employees in a certain department of Armour and Co. had greatly increased their efficiency, Armour decided to present each of them with a new suit of clothes. Every man was asked to order the suit of his choice and send the bill to Armour. One particularly greedy young man decided on a suit of evening clothes costing eighty dollars. Armour agreed to pay the bill, commenting to the clerk as he did so, "I've packed a great many hogs in my time, but I never dressed one before."

———— ◆ ————

ARMSTRONG, Louis ["Satchmo"] (1900–71), *US jazz trumpeter and singer, band leader, and composer.*

1 (Satchmo recalls this incident from his earlier years.)
"One night this big, bad-ass hood crashes my dressing room in Chicago and instructs me that I will open in such-and-such a club in New York the next night. I tell him I got this Chicago engagement and don't plan no traveling. And I turn my back on him to show I'm so cool. Then I hear this sound: SNAP! CLICK! I turn around and he has pulled this vast revolver on me and cocked it. Jesus, it look like a cannon and sound like death! So I look down at that steel and say, 'Weelllll, maybe I do open in New York tomorrow.'"

2 When Armstrong's band played a command performance for the king of England, Satchmo was not too overawed by the sense of occasion. "This one's for you, Rex," he called out to George VI as the band took up their instruments.

3 Armstrong was once asked whether he objected to the impressions of him frequently given by other singers and comedians. "Not really," he replied, shrugging his shoulders. "A lotta cats copy the *Mona Lisa*, but people still line up to see the original."

4 Armstrong disliked all efforts to define his music. When someone asked him if jazz was synonymous with folk music, he said, "Man, all music is folk music. You ain't never heard no horse sing a song, have you?"

5 A new musician joined Armstrong's band the night of a concert. When his turn came for a piano solo, the man played well but hammed it up as well, mugging and smiling through-

out his musical effort. When he was finished, Armstrong came over to the piano and, leaning over the keyboard, said, "Look here, Pops, I do all the eye-rolling in this band."

6 Upon the death of his faithful assistant Doc Pugh, Armstrong was asked by friends what had ailed the man. "What was wrong with Doc?" asked Armstrong with a sad look. "When you die, *everything* is wrong with you."

ARMSTRONG, Neil (1930–), *US astronaut who was the first man on the moon.*

1 On July 20, 1969, Neil Armstrong became the first human being to set foot on the moon. President Nixon authoritatively acclaimed the event as the greatest since the Creation. Armstrong himself, as he took the last step from the ladder of his lunar module onto the moon's surface, said, "That's one small step for a man, one giant leap for mankind."

2 Photographer Yousuf Karsh and his wife were having lunch with Neil Armstrong after a photographic session. Armstrong politely questioned the couple about the many different countries they had visited. "But Mr. Armstrong," protested Mrs. Karsh, "you've walked on the moon. We want to hear about *your* travels."

"But that's the only place I've ever been," replied Armstrong apologetically.

3 Armstrong, a devout Christian, visited the Old City of Jerusalem. At the Hulda Gate, which leads to the Temple Mount, Armstrong wanted to know if Jesus had walked on those very steps. Assured that he did, Armstrong said, "I have to tell you, I am more excited stepping on these stones than I was stepping on the moon."

ARNE, Thomas Augustine (1710–78), *British composer of operas and incidental music, most notably "Rule, Britannia!"*

1 Arne's father, who was both an upholsterer and an undertaker, wanted his son to become a lawyer. Thomas Arne, therefore, had to acquire his early musical training by stealth. His violin teacher, the eminent violinist Michael Festing, found Arne on one occasion practicing with his music propped up on the lid of a coffin. Not a little disturbed, Festing said he himself would be unable to play under such conditions for fear there might be a body in the coffin. "So there is," replied Arne coolly, raising the lid to provide proof.

ARNIM, Harry Karl Kurt Eduard, Count von (1824–81), *German diplomat.*

1 At the close of the Franco-Prussian War Bismarck had an interview with Arnim at Versailles. Lord John Russell, the British prime minister, happened to be waiting in the anteroom. As Arnim emerged from his meeting, he said to Russell, "I don't know how Bismarck can stand it! He never stops smoking those strong Havanas of his. I had to request him to open the window." When it was Russell's turn, he walked in to find Bismarck standing at the open window, laughing. "Russell, Arnim was just in here, and he had so much scent on him that I simply couldn't stand it. I had to open the window."

ARNO, Peter [Curtis Arnoux Peters] (1904–68), *US cartoonist whose work appeared regularly in* **The New Yorker.**

1 Peter Arno imported a racing car from Europe for his own personal use. Among its unique features were fenders made of platinum. Once the car was safely through customs at New York, Arno had the fenders

taken off and replaced by ordinary steel fenders. He then sold off the platinum at a large profit.

———— ✧ ————

ARNOLD, Matthew (1822–88), *British poet and critic who was professor of poetry at Oxford (1857–67).*

1 Arnold's cold reserve and critical eye did not endear him to the Americans on his American tour in 1883. There is a story that when his hostess offered him pancakes, Arnold passed the plate on to his wife with the comment: "Do try one, my dear. They're not nearly as nasty as they look."

2 As critic and moralist, Arnold attacked the philistinism of the British middle class of his time, upholding rather severe, even dismaying standards of intellectual rigor and moral seriousness. Shortly after his death Robert Louis Stevenson remarked, "Poor Matt. He's gone to Heaven, no doubt — but he won't like God."

———— ✧ ————

ARNOULD, [Madeleine] Sophie (1740–1802), *French actress and opera singer.*

1 The dancer Marie Guimard was a star of the Paris Opéra; her art consisted mainly in rhythmical arm movements and graceful poses, and her fame resided principally in her celebrated liaisons with members of the aristocracy. When Mlle Guimard's arm was broken by some falling scenery, Sophie Arnould remarked, "What a pity it wasn't her leg; then it wouldn't have interfered with her dancing."

2 After a supper she had given for several distinguished personages, Sophie Arnould was visited by the lieutenant of police, demanding their names. She replied that she could

not remember one. Said the lieutenant, "But a woman like you ought to remember things like that."

"Of course, lieutenant, but with a man like you I am not a woman like me."

3 A rival actress had been presented by her lover with a magnificent diamond *rivière*. The necklace was rather too long and as worn by the actress it seemed to be about to disappear down her cleavage. Sophie Arnould commented, *"C'est qu'elle retourne vers sa source"* (It's just returning to its source).

4 Another actress consistently produced a child every year, with predictable consequences to her figure. The result was that she regularly lost both theatrical engagements and lovers. "She reminds me of those nations that are always extending their boundaries but cannot retain their conquests," remarked Sophie Arnould.

———— ✧ ————

ARRIA (d. AD 42), *wife of the Roman senator Caecina Paetus.*

1 Accused of involvement in a plot against the emperor, Paetus was ordered to commit suicide. When he hesitated, Arria took the dagger from him, stabbed herself, and handed the dagger back with the words: *"Paete, non dolet"* (Paetus, it does not hurt).

———— ✧ ————

ASCHE, [John Stanger Heiss] Oscar (1872–1936), *Australian actor, playwright, and theatrical manager.*

1 Asche was once playing a particularly bad game of golf on a Scottish course. After an uncharacteristically good stroke, he risked a casual remark to his caddie: "You'll have

seen worse players than I am." When the caddie, an elderly Scot, did not reply, Asche assumed that he had not heard and repeated the remark. "I heard ye afore," said the caddie. "I was just considerin'."

ASOKA (d. c. 232 BC), *emperor of India (c. 273– c. 232 BC), the greatest of the kings of the Mauryan dynasty.*

1 At the outset of his reign Asoka ruled with the savagery that had characterized the previous rulers of the kingdom of Magadha in northern India. At his capital (modern Patna), there was a fearful prison called "Asoka's Hell," from which, it was decreed, none could emerge alive. One of its victims was a Buddhist saint who had been wrongfully accused. When the torturers threw him into a cauldron of boiling water, he remained unscathed. The jailer informed the king that he should come and see this miracle. Asoka came and wondered. He was about to depart when the jailer reminded him of the edict that no one was to leave the prison alive. Asoka thereupon gave orders that the jailer was to be thrown into the boiling cauldron.

His experience in the prison deeply affected Asoka's outlook. Shortly afterward, he gave orders that the prison was to be demolished and he himself became a convert to Buddhism. The pillars containing his edicts bear witness to the humanity and justice of his rule after his conversion.

ASQUITH, Herbert Henry, 1st Earl of Oxford and Asquith (1852–1928), *British statesman and Liberal prime minister (1908–16).*

1 "The nineteenth-century Rothschild family kept great state in, among other places, their home in Waddesdon, where Alfred Rothschild lived. One day Prime Minister Asquith, who was staying from Friday till Monday, was waited on at teatime by the butler. The following conversation ensued: 'Tea, coffee or a peach from off the wall, sir?' 'Tea, please.' 'China, Indian or Ceylon, sir?' 'China, please.' 'Lemon, milk or cream, sir?' 'Milk, please.' 'Jersey, Hereford or Shorthorn, sir? . . .'"

ASQUITH, Margot (1864–1945), *second wife of Lord Herbert Henry Asquith.*

1 When Jean Harlow, the platinum-blonde American movie star of the 1930s, met Lady Asquith for the first time, she addressed Lady Asquith by her Christian name. She made the further mistake of pronouncing the word as if it rhymed with *rot*. Lady Asquith corrected her: "My dear, the *t* is silent, as in *Harlow*."

2 Margot Asquith did not like the famous British sportsman Lord Lonsdale, renowned for his fine horses and his courage in the hunting field. Someone in Lady Asquith's hearing once praised his prowess as a rider to hounds. "Jump?" she interrupted. "Anyone can jump. Look at fleas."

3 Her stepdaughter, Violet Bonham-Carter, once asked if she planned to wear a certain hat trimmed with ostrich feathers to Lord Kitchener's memorial service. Margot replied, "How can you ask me? Dear Kitchener saw me in that hat twice!"

4 Lady Asquith had a poor opinion of several of George V's advisers. After his death the king's doctor, Lord Dawson, was one of those who fell victim to her sharp tongue. She once remarked to Lord David Cecil, "Lord Dawson was not a good doctor. King

George himself told me that he would never have died had he had another doctor."

———— ᴄʌ◦ ————

ASTAIRE, Fred [Frederick Austerlitz] (1899–1987), *US stage and film dancer.*

1 Attracted by Hollywood as a young dancer, Astaire submitted himself for the usual screen test. The verdict has become part of film history: "Can't act. Slightly bald. Can dance a little."

2 (David Niven tells a story about his good friend Astaire, who had become the owner of a winning string of racehorses.)

"The most balanced of men in every sense of the word, he only once to my knowledge went mad. At dawn one day Fred called me and announced his mental aberration. 'I'll never know what made me do it,' he moaned, 'but I had this overpowering urge . . . so I got up in the middle of the night and drove all over Beverly Hills painting the mailboxes with my racing colors.'"

3 Fred's wife Phyllis Astaire and David Niven came to RKO to watch the filming of his "Cheek to Cheek" number in the musical *Top Hat,* with his partner, Ginger Rogers. Ginger came in for the first take in a dress composed entirely of red feathers. "She looks like a wooster," giggled Phyllis.

It turned out the dress was ready only just in time. The dance began. "Slowly, one at a time at first, the feathers parted company with the parent garment. Then, as Fred whirled Ginger faster and faster about the gleaming set, more and more flew off. It became reminiscent of a pillow fight at school, but they pressed bravely on with the number, and by the end Ginger looked ready to spit. . . . Phyllis pulled my sleeve. 'Let's get out of here,' she said, 'Fwed will be so embawassed.'"

———— ᴄʌ◦ ————

ASTOR, John Jacob (1763–1848), *US financier who was reputed to be the richest man in the United States.*

1 Astor once observed to Julia Ward Howe, "A man who has a million dollars is as well off as if he were rich."

2 Astor sold a lot near Wall Street for $8,000. The buyer, confident that he had outsmarted Astor, could not resist a little self-congratulation after the signing of the papers. "Why, in a few years this lot will be worth twelve thousand dollars," he gloated. "True," said Astor, "but with your eight thousand I will buy eighty lots above Canal Street, and by the time your lot is worth twelve thousand, my eighty lots will be worth eighty thousand dollars."

———— ᴄʌ◦ ————

ASTOR, Mary Dahlgren (c. 1850–94), *wife of financier William Waldorf Astor.*

1 When her friends Elizabeth Marbury and Elsie de Wolfe (Lady Mendl) began to throw large and rather daring parties at Irving House (their Manhattan home), with colorful personalities as the attraction, Mrs. Astor was determined not to be left out. "I am having a bohemian party, too," she announced. Asked who would be there to provide the necessary spice, she said, "J. P. Morgan and Edith Wharton."

———— ᴄʌ◦ ————

ASTOR, Nancy Witcher Langhorne, Viscountess (1879–1964), *US-born politician who became the first woman to take a seat in the British House of Commons.*

1 Male antagonism toward Nancy Astor as the first woman to gain a seat in the House of Commons showed itself on several occasions, Winston Churchill in particular being guilty of discourtesy. When she challenged

———— ᴄʌ◦ ————

him about his behavior, he told her that it was because he found her intrusion into the all-male preserve embarrassing — as embarrassing as if she had burst into his bathroom when he had nothing to defend himself with. "Winston," she retorted, "you are not handsome enough to have worries of that kind."

2 Particularly irksome to the antifeminists in the House of Commons was Lady Astor's opinion that it was unnecessary for her to prove herself the equal of her male colleagues since women are the superior sex. "I married beneath me — all women do," said she.

3 Since Lady Astor believed in making her presence felt in the House of Commons, she rather too frequently interrupted other speakers. Castigated for this on one occasion, she protested that she had been listening for hours before interrupting. "Yes, we've *heard* you listening," said an exasperated colleague.

4 During a formal dinner, Lady Astor remarked to her neighbor that she considered men to be more conceited than women. Noticing that her comment had been heard around the table, she continued in a loud voice: "It's a pity that the most intelligent and learned men attach least importance to the way they dress. Why, right at this table the most cultivated man is wearing the most clumsily knotted tie!" The words had no sooner left her lips than every man in the room surreptitiously reached up to adjust his tie.

5 At a dinner given by Theodore Roosevelt, Nancy Astor was given precedence over Grace Vanderbilt. By way of excuse and consolation she remarked to Mrs. Vanderbilt, "The Astors skinned skunks a hundred years before the Vanderbilts worked ferries."

6 "[During the early thirties Winston] Churchill's critics called him rash, impetu-

ous, tactless, contentious, inconsistent, unsound, an amusing parliamentary celebrity who was forever out of step. 'We just don't know what to make of him,' a troubled Tory MP told Lady Astor. She asked brightly: 'How about a nice rug?'"

ATKINSON, Christopher Thomas (1874–1964), *British academic at Oxford.*

1 During one course of lectures Atkinson found himself confronted with a group of girl students. He began by saying that his talk that morning would be on the sexual prowess of the natives of the Polynesian islands. The shocked ladies made a concerted rush for the door. Atkinson called after them, "It's all right, ladies, you needn't hurry. There's not another boat for a month."

ATLAS, Charles (1894–1972), *US circus strongman, born Angelo Siciliano.*

1 In his early days Atlas performed with the Coney Island Circus Side Show. His demonstrations of strength included lifting two men off the floor, tearing telephone books in half with his bare hands, and lying on a bed of nails with three members of the audience standing on his chest. Of this last feat he once remarked: "Women used to faint when I did that. They couldn't stand watching a beautiful body like mine being abused."

AUBER, Daniel François Esprit (1782–1871), *French composer.*

1 An infant prodigy had written a score that caused a sensation on account of the "originality" displayed by one so young. Said Auber, "This lad will go far when he has less experience."

2 A friend of Auber's engaged him in conversation as they descended the grand stairway at the Opéra. "My friend, we're all getting older, aren't we?" he observed. Auber sighed. "Well, there's no help for it. Aging seems to be the only available way to live a long time."

3 Auber refused to think about death and whenever reminded of the approach of his last hour would say, "I'll pay no attention to it." But in his late old age he began to accommodate himself to his own mortality. At a funeral service that he was compelled to attend, he remarked to one of his fellow mourners, "I believe this is the last time I'll take part as an amateur."

———— ✧ ————

AUBERNON, Euphrasie (1825–99), *French salonnière and woman of letters.*

1 Mme Aubernon presided as an absolute autocrat over her salon: she decided the topics to be discussed, dictated who should speak and for how long, prohibited any asides or tête-à-têtes, and enforced her guests' attention by ringing a little hand bell. A surprising number of the Parisian intelligentsia meekly submitted to this conversational tyranny, but there were occasional rebellions. On one occasion the witty and charming Mme Baignières arrived rather late. Before she had time to catch her breath, Mme Aubernon rang her bell and said, "We are discussing adultery, Mme Baignières. Will you give us your opinions?" Mme Baignières replied, "I'm so sorry. I've only come prepared with incest."

2 A young matron keen to set herself up as a salonnière came to Mme Aubernon for counsel. Mme Aubernon's advice: "Don't try. You have far too luscious a bosom to keep the conversation general."

3 One of Mme Aubernon's guests was relating a conversation with his young son.

"Papa," the child had asked, "when you and Maman went on your honeymoon in Italy, where was I?"

"What did you tell him?" asked Mme Aubernon eagerly.

"I thought for a moment," replied the guest, "then I said, 'You went there with me and came back with your mother.'"

———— ✧ ————

AUBIGNÉ, Jean Henri Merle d' (1794–1872), *Swiss Protestant divine.*

1 When Dr. d'Aubigné was staying with the Scottish divine and preacher Thomas Chalmers, he was served a kippered herring for breakfast. He asked his host the meaning of the word "kippered" and was told "kept" or "preserved." This item of information had a sequel at morning prayer, when the guest, leading the household in their devotions, prayed that Dr. Chalmers might be "kept, preserved, and kippered."

———— ✧ ————

AUDEN, Wystan Hugh (1907–73), *British poet who became an American citizen.*

1 The Nazis, opposed to the anti-Nazi material in her routines, deprived the cabaret artiste Erika Mann, daughter of novelist Thomas Mann, of her passport. She appealed to the homosexual Isherwood as an available Englishman to marry her so that she could obtain an English passport. Isherwood dodged, but Auden generously agreed to marry her and she duly obtained her English passport. Soon afterward a former stage associate of Erika's, who had also lost her passport on account of her anti-Nazi stand, appealed to the Audens for help. Searching around among his acquaintances, Auden found another member of their homosexual circle who gal-

lantly agreed to marry the second lady. "What else are buggers for?" observed Auden.

2 Auden was surprised to learn from a third party that Mike De Lisio, his sculptor friend, wrote poetry in his spare time and had had some of his verses published in *The New Yorker.* "How nice of him never to have told me," said Auden.

3 Auden, about to begin a course of lectures on Shakespeare at the New School for Social Research in New York City, noted that every seat was filled. Surveying the sea of faces extending right to the back of the large auditorium, Auden announced: "If there are any of you who do not hear me, please don't raise your hands because I am also nearsighted."

4 As a young, little-known writer, Auden was once asked what effect fame might have upon him. "I believe," he said after a moment's reflection, "that I would always wear my carpet slippers." When fame did eventually come, Auden was always to be seen in carpet slippers, even when wearing evening dress.

5 Just before a lecture Auden was to give at Harvard on *Don Quixote*, he was seen to have a few too many martinis. When he began speaking, he first apologized for his new set of dentures, then admitted he'd never actually read through the entire book and doubted whether anyone in the crowd had either.

6 Just after acquiring his first set of dentures, Auden attended a tea party given by some ladies in Boston. When his hostess asked him to blow out the flame under the teapot, Auden did so with gusto. "My dear," he later said, "the *din!* My uppers went crashing into my neighbor's empty teacup!"

7 Dorothy Day, founder of the Catholic Worker Movement, was fined $250 because her hostel for indigents was not up to code. As she headed to work the next morning, she walked through a group of homeless men, one of whom stepped out and, saying he had heard she was in trouble, handed her a check. "Here's two-fifty," said the man. Day looked at the check later, but instead of the $2.50 she thought she had received, it was for the entire sum, and it was signed "W. H. Auden." "Poets do look a bit unpressed, don't they?" Day later said.

8 Three of Auden's great admirers happened to be together when the news of his death was reported on the radio: the poet Richard Wilbur, the critic Alfred Kazin, and Kazin's wife, Ann Birstein. In one voice they immediately said, "Earth, receive an honoured guest"— a line from Auden's elegy for W. B. Yeats.

AUERBACH, Arnold Jacob ["Red"] (1917–), *US basketball executive, manager of the Boston Celtics.*

1 On tour with the Boston Celtics, Auerbach met three of his players, each with an attractive young woman on his arm, in the hotel lobby at five o'clock in the morning. One of the players covered his embarrassment by introducing the young woman as his "cousin." Auerbach nodded politely. The player, desperately trying to make the unlikely tale sound more convincing, continued, "We were just on our way to church." Auerbach, relating this story on a later occasion, remarked, "I couldn't take that. I fined him twenty-five dollars for insulting my intelligence."

2 Auerbach often said that basketball was a simple game, a thought that confounded sports fans. When asked why, he said, "The ball is round and the floor is flat."

———— ❧ ————

AUGUSTINE OF HIPPO, Saint (354–430), *North African theologian; one of the fathers and doctors of the Church. His* City of God *and* Confessions *are among the greatest Christian documents.*

1 In his *Confessions* Augustine recounts the sins of his youth and how even his prayers for repentance were tainted with insincerity: *"Da mihi castitatem et continentiam, sed noli modo"* (Give me chastity and continence, but not yet).

———— ❧ ————

AUGUSTUS [Gaius Julius Caesar Octavianus] (63 BC–AD 14), *first Roman emperor (31 BC–AD 14), heir of Julius Caesar.*

1 The evening before the crucial battle of Actium, Octavian (the young Augustus) set up his camp on a hill overlooking the bay and the two fleets — his own and Anthony's — near what is now the town of Preveza in northwestern Greece. In the morning as he emerged from his tent he met a peasant driving a donkey. He asked the man his name. "Eutyches" (Good Fortune) was the answer. And the donkey's name? "Nikon" (Victor).

2 An old soldier was involved in a lawsuit that seemed likely to go against him. He therefore accosted his former commander, Augustus, in a public place, asking him to appear in court on his behalf. The emperor at once selected one of his suite to appear for the man and introduce him to the litigant. But the soldier, rolling back his sleeve to reveal his scars, shouted, "When you were in danger at Actium, I didn't choose a substitute but fought for you in person." Chagrined, Augustus appeared in court on the veteran's behalf.

3 Several people trained birds to make complimentary greetings to the emperor. Augustus would often buy the birds for generous sums of money. A poor cobbler acquired a raven, intending to train it to make such a remark. The bird turned out to be such a slow learner that the exasperated cobbler often used to say to it, "Nothing to show for all the trouble and expense." One day the raven began to repeat its lesson as Augustus was passing. This time the emperor declined to buy, saying, "I get enough of such compliments at home." The bird, however, also remembering the words of his trainer's usual complaint, went on, "Nothing to show for all the trouble and expense." Amused, Augustus bought the raven.

4 Augustus had ordered a young man of bad character to be dismissed from his service. The man came to him and begged for pardon, saying, "How am I to go home? What shall I tell my father?"

"Tell your father that you didn't find me to your liking," the emperor replied.

5 A certain Roman nobleman died, leaving enormous debts that he had successfully concealed during his lifetime. When the estate was put up for auction, Augustus instructed his agent to buy the man's pillow. To those who expressed surprise at the order he explained, "That pillow must be particularly conducive to sleep, if its late owner, in spite of all his debts, could sleep on it."

6 The conduct of Augustus's daughter Julia was so blatant that a group of influential Romans threatened to denounce her as an adulteress in front of the whole court. Augustus anticipated them by banishing his daughter to a barren island. Her lovers were variously punished. One of Julia's attendants, the freedwoman Phoebe, hanged herself rather than give evidence against her mistress. "Oh, that I had been Phoebe's father, not Julia's,"

exclaimed Augustus when he heard of the suicide.

AUMALE, Henri, Duc d' (1822–97), *French aristocrat, son of King Louis Philippe.*

1 The Duc d'Aumale was one of the most aristocratic of the lovers of Léonide Leblanc, a fashionable courtesan. Léonide eventually hit on a subtle way to discourage unwanted lovers. She had a lifelike wax model of the duke set up at a table in a room of her house. When pestered by a suitor, she would half-open the door to that room, then close it quickly, and say, "Ssh! The duke is here."

2 The Duc d'Aumale's residence at Chantilly was at a distance from Paris convenient for the visits of Léonide Leblanc. One day she traveled out to Chantilly by train, sharing the compartment with a group of society ladies who began vying with each other to prove on what friendly terms they were with the duke. "We dined with His Highness last night," said one. "We shall be lunching there tomorrow," said another. "Of course, we went to the ball there last week," said a third. Léonide Leblanc held her peace until the train drew into Chantilly station. Then she stood up, said, "And I, ladies, am sleeping with His Highness tonight," and stepped lightly from the train.

3 During the Franco-Prussian War Marshal Achille Bazaine commanded the French troops in the fortress of Metz. It was his hesitations, misjudgments, and ultimate surrender that deprived France of the last forces capable of withstanding the German advance. In 1873 the marshal was arraigned before a French military court presided over by the Duc d'Aumale; he was charged with neglecting to do everything required by duty and honor before capitulating to the enemy. At one stage in the proceedings the marshal

sought to exonerate himself by reminding the court of the state of affairs at the time of his surrender: "There was no government, there was no order, there was nothing." "There was still France," said the Duc d'Aumale.

4 Aumale, a great patriot, yearned for military glory in the cause of his beloved France. Commissioned as a sublieutenant in the infantry at the age of fifteen, he announced, "My only ambition is to be the forty-third Bourbon to be killed on the field of battle."

5 The Duc d'Aumale was renowned for his youthful love affairs, but in his old age he felt his powers failing. "As a young man I used to have four supple members and one stiff one," he observed. "Now I have four stiff and one supple."

AUSTIN, Alfred (1835–1913), *British poet and dramatist.*

1 Someone once chided the poet laureate for grammatical errors in his verses. Austin excused himself by saying, "I dare not alter these things; they come to me from above."

AUSTIN, Warren Robinson (1877–1962), *US politician and diplomat.*

1 In a debate on the Middle East question, Austin exhorted the warring Jews and Arabs to sit down and settle their differences "like good Christians."

2 Someone once asked Austin whether he did not become tired during the apparently interminable debates at the U.N. "Yes, I do," he replied, "but it is better for aged diplomats to be bored than for young men to die."

AVEMPACE [Abu Bekr Ibn Bajja] (c. 1095–1138), *Spanish Muslim scholar.*

1 The Muslim governor of Saragossa was so delighted by the excellence of Avempace's verses that he swore the young scholar should walk on gold whenever he entered his presence. Avempace feared that the governor would soon regret his exuberant vow and that his own welcome at court would suffer as a result. He therefore sewed a gold piece into the sole of each of his shoes, so that the governor's oath could be kept at no expense to himself.

———∾———

AVERY, Oswald [Theodore] (1877–1955), *Canadian-born bacteriologist and the discoverer of DNA as the basic genetic material of the cell.*

1 Professor Avery worked for many years in a small laboratory at the hospital of the Rockefeller Institute in New York City. Many of his experimental predictions turned out to be wrong, but that never discouraged him. He capitalized on error. His colleagues remember him saying, "Whenever you fall, pick up something."

———∾———

AYMÉ, Marcel (1902–67), *French novelist, essayist, and playwright.*

1 A journalist was complaining to Aymé that the modern world hinders the free development of the human being. "I don't agree," said Aymé mildly. "I consider myself perfectly free."

"But surely you feel some limits to your freedom."

"Oh, yes," replied Aymé, "from time to time I find myself terribly limited by the dictionary."

———∾———

AZEGLIO, Massimo Taparelli, Marchese d' (1798–1866), *Italian statesman and writer of historical novels.*

1 Azeglio's second marriage, to Luisa Blondel, was not very successful and the couple separated. In 1866, however, hearing that Azeglio was dying, Luisa rushed to his deathbed. "Ah, Luisa," sighed the marchese, "you always arrive just as I'm leaving."

B

BABBAGE, Charles (1792–1871), *British inventor and mathematician.*

1 Babbage objected to Tennyson's lines from *The Vision of Sin,* "Every moment dies a man, / Every moment one is born," saying that if that were true "the population of the world would be at a standstill." In the interests of accuracy, he wrote to Tennyson, the lines should be emended to read, "Every moment dies a man, / Every moment one and one-sixteenth is born."

2 Babbage liked to talk. At a dinner he was completely outtalked by Thomas Carlyle, who spent the whole meal haranguing the company on the merits of silence. After dinner Babbage went up to Carlyle and thanked him grimly for his interesting lecture on silence.

BACALL, Lauren (1924–), *US movie actress who married Humphrey Bogart.*

1 Lauren Bacall attended a New Year's Eve party at which the Shah of Iran was one of the distinguished guests. He complimented her on her dancing: "You dance beautifully, Miss Bacall."

"You bet your ass, Shah," she replied.

2 When Humphrey Bogart died, Lauren Bacall placed in the urn with his ashes a small gold whistle inscribed, "If you want anything, just whistle." She had spoken this line to him in their first film together, *To Have and Have Not.*

3 When Bacall took a break from making movies to have children with her husband, Humphrey Bogart, she had mixed feelings. "I'll miss Hollywood," she said. "Of the twenty friends I thought I had, I'll miss the six I really had."

BACH, Carl Philipp Emanuel (1714–88), *German composer; third son of Johann Sebastian Bach.*

1 As court musician to Frederick the Great in Berlin, one of C. P. E. Bach's duties was to accompany the king when the latter played the flute. Since Frederick prided himself on his ability, Bach's services as accompanist were frequently requested. At the end of one such royal performance a sycophantic courtier burst out with "What rhythm!"

"What rhythms!" grumbled Bach sotto voce at the piano.

BACH, Johann Sebastian (1685–1750), *German composer and instrumentalist.*

1 While at school at Lüneburg, Bach more than once walked to Hamburg, fifty kilometers away, primarily to hear J. A. Reincken, organist of the Katharinen-Kirche there. One day, returning almost penniless to Lüneburg, he rested outside an inn. Someone threw two herring heads onto the rubbish heap. Picking up this unsavory offering to see if any part was edible, Bach found a coin in each head. Not only did he have his meal, he was able "to undertake another and more comfortable pilgrimage to Herr Reincken."

BACON, Francis, 1st Baron Verulam and Viscount St. Albans (1561–1626), *British lawyer and experimental philosopher.*

1 While lord chancellor, Bacon presided over a criminal appeal in which the plaintiff was a man called Hogg. Hogg facetiously pleaded that he should be let off on the grounds of his kinship with the judge. "For," he claimed, "Hogg must be kin to Bacon."

"Not until it has been hung," was the chancellor's reply.

2 Sir John Hayward's *History of Henry IV,* published in 1599, immediately landed its author in serious trouble with Queen Elizabeth, who believed that under the pretense of writing history he was criticizing her own policies. Summoning her legal officers, she consulted them as to whether it might not be possible to prosecute Hayward for treason. Bacon demurred: "I cannot answer for there being treason in it, but certainly it contains much felony."

"How?" asked the queen. "And wherein?"

"In many passages," Bacon replied, "which he has stolen from Tacitus."

3 Queen Elizabeth I visited her lord chancellor at his house at Gorhambury in Hertford-shire. "What a little house you have gotten," she remarked, being used to the lavish establishments of the great lords who vied to entertain her. Bacon replied with consummate tact, "The house is well, but it is you, Your Majesty, who have made me too great for my house."

4 In the court of James I there was present a rather unremarkable envoy from France. After giving audience to this lanky, overgrown nobleman, the king asked Bacon his opinion of the marquis. "Your Majesty," replied Bacon, "people of such dimensions are like four- or five-story houses — the upper rooms are the most poorly furnished."

5 Bacon's experimental method was directly responsible for his death. In March 1626, as he was being driven in a coach past snowy fields near Highgate, north of London, the idea occurred to him that snow might be used as a means of preserving food. He stopped the coach at the foot of Highgate Hill and entered a poor woman's house where he bought a chicken, killed and drew it, and then packed the interior of the carcass with snow. This endeavor brought on such a chill that he was unable to return home. He went instead to the Earl of Arundel's house in Highgate, where he was installed in a somewhat damp bed. An attack of pneumonia followed, from which he died within three days.

BADER, Sir Douglas Robert Stuart (1910–82), *British aviator.*

1 Warring countries usually communicate with bombs, bullets, and propaganda. In World War II this rule was briefly broken when an RAF plane flew over a German airfield and dropped a package by parachute. It was addressed "To the German flight commander of the Luftwaffe at St. Omer," where Bader was held prisoner in the hospital. The package

contained an artificial leg, bandages, socks, and straps. The Germans, after capturing Bader, had radioed England that he was well but missing one of his tin limbs. The parachute drop followed shortly.

Once back on both tin legs, Bader made four attempts to escape before the Germans deprived him of his artificial limbs at night. After three years and eight months in a maximum-security prisoner-of-war camp, he was freed by the American Third Army.

BAEYER, Johann Friedrich Wilhelm Adolf von (1835–1917), *German chemist who was awarded the Nobel Prize for Chemistry in 1905.*

1 Entering his laboratory one morning, Baeyer found his assistants using mechanical stirrers operated by water turbines. Such complex machines would not normally have received the professor's approval, but he was soon fascinated by them. Anxious to communicate this new discovery to his wife, he summoned her from their neighboring apartment. Frau Baeyer watched the apparatus at work in silent admiration for a while, then exclaimed, "What a lovely idea for making mayonnaise!"

BAHR, Hermann (1863–1934), *Austrian playwright, author, and theater director.*

1 Bahr once received from a young poet a historical tragedy together with a request for his opinion: "If you find any faults, please tell me the truth. Words of criticism from a source so judicious would make me feel ennobled." Bahr returned the manuscript with a brief comment: "I'd like to make you at least an archduke."

BAILLY, Jean Sylvain (1736–93), *French astronomer.*

1 Bailly remarked to his nephew the day before his appointment with the guillotine, "It's time for me to enjoy another pinch of snuff. Tomorrow it will be impossible. My hands will be bound."

BAKER, Josephine (1906–75), *US dancer and singer who lived a large part of her life in France.*

1 In 1929 Crown Prince Adolf of Sweden visited her in her dressing room. Late that night she boarded his private railway carriage and was installed in an enormous swan-shaped bed to await his return. When the prince arrived, she complained of being cold — a condition he attempted to remedy by attaching a three-stranded diamond bracelet to her arm. He was greatly amused when she complained that the other arm was still cold. She got the matching bracelet.

2 In World War II Josephine Baker joined the French Resistance. Her marriage to a Jewish businessman, Jean Léon, brought her to the notice of Goering and the Gestapo, who decided to murder her. Goering invited her to dinner, having arranged to put cyanide in her fish course. Forewarned, Josephine excused herself as the fish was served, planning to drop down the laundry chute in the bathroom to a rendezvous with Resistance workers below. Goering produced his gun and ordered her to eat the fish before allowing her to retire to the bathroom. She managed to reach the chute, slid down, and her colleagues rushed her to a doctor, who pumped out her stomach. After a month of sickness she recovered, but lost all her hair (she always wore a wig thereafter).

BAKST, Léon (1866–1924), *Russian artist and designer, court painter to the Romanovs.*

1 Diaghilev was sitting with Bakst watching a rehearsal when he suddenly turned to the designer and asked, "What are the three most beautiful things in this theater today?"

"Olga Spessiva [the great ballerina], the little boy with the big brown eyes [dancer Anton Dolin], and me," replied Bakst without hesitation.

———— ✂ ————

BALANCHINE, George (1904–83), *choreographer, born in Russia.*

1 (Bernard Taper, in his biography of Balanchine, tells the following story.)

"I was complaining to Balanchine one day about the scarcity of documentary materials pertaining to his life, particularly his inner life. I had been reading some biographies of literary figures — abounding in quotations from the subjects' diaries, letters, journals, and memoirs — and, as a biographer, I was feeling deprived. Balanchine had never journalized, had written perhaps fewer letters than the number of ballets he had choreographed, and had kept no scrapbooks to preserve what others had said about him. Balanchine listened to my complaint and then replied, 'You should think of your task as if you were writing the biography of a racehorse. A racehorse doesn't keep a diary.'"

———— ✂ ————

BALDWIN, Stanley, 1st Earl (1867–1947), *British politician, three times Conservative prime minister (1923–24, 1924–29, 1935–37).*

1 As financial secretary to the treasury, Baldwin was appalled at the extent of the British war debt after the 1914–18 war. In 1919 he wrote an anonymous letter to *The Times* urging the wealthy to impose a voluntary tax upon themselves to help relieve the national burden. Estimating his own personal estate at £580,000, Baldwin realized 20 percent of its value and invested £150,000 in government war-loan stock. He then destroyed the stock certificates, thus making his £150,000 a gift to the treasury. The rich, however, did not stampede to follow Baldwin's example.

2 (Stanley Baldwin's daughter, Lady Lorna Howard, tells a story that illustrates the relationship between her father and the workers at the family plant.)

"An embarrassed newlywed employee came to Baldwin and told him he had broken the bridal bed. Baldwin said it could be repaired free at the family ironworks, but the man feared it would make him the laughing stock of all his mates. So the broken bed was brought to the back door of Baldwin's house at night, wheeled through the hall the following morning, and taken across the road for repair as if it were Baldwin's own."

———— ✂ ————

BALFOUR, Arthur James, 1st Earl of (1848–1930), *British statesman; prime minister (1902–05).*

1 Balfour was once asked if the rumor that he intended to marry Margot Tennant (later Asquith) had any foundation. He replied, "No, I rather think of having a career of my own."

———— ✂ ————

BALMAIN, Pierre (1914–82), *French couturier.*

1 "During the years of cold and shortages Gertrude [Stein] and Alice [B. Toklas] became friends with a neighbour at Aix, a simple young man named Pierre Balmain, with a taste for antiques and a natural bent for de-

signing women's clothes. In fact he made with his own hands heavy tweeds and warm garments for Gertrude and Alice to wear during the hard winters. Now he has opened a shop in Paris. At his first showing to the Press Gertrude and Alice arrived with their huge dog, Basket. Gertrude, in a tweed skirt, an old cinnamon-coloured sack, and Panama hat, looked like Corot's self-portrait. Alice, in a long Chinese garment of bright colours with a funny flowered toque, had overtones of the Widow Twankey. Gertrude, seeing the world of fashion assembled, whispered, 'Little do they know that we are the only people here dressed by Balmain, and it's just as well for him that they don't!'"

BALSAN, Consuelo (1878–1964), *US society leader.*

1 (Cass Canfield, who was connected with Harper and Row, the publishers of her book, *The Glitter and the Gold,* entertained Mme Balsan, whose ideas were still colored by the grandeur of her first marriage to an English nobleman.)

"At Fishers Island, New York, where we have a tiny two-room house on a beach, she came to tea; we chatted on the terrace adjoining our cottage, and after a pleasant hour she rose to leave. 'I've had such a nice time,' she said, 'and your place is lovely. But *where* is the house?'"

BALZAC, Honoré de (1799–1850), *prolific French novelist.*

1 When he was thirty-three, Balzac received an interesting letter from the Ukraine signed "The Stranger." Following it up, he found that the writer, Evelina Hanska, was the wife

of a baron. Their affair lasted for seventeen years, and although the baron died in 1841 the couple did not marry until five months before Balzac's death. "It is easier," wrote Balzac, "to be a lover than a husband, for the same reason that it is more difficult to show a ready wit all day long than to produce an occasional *bon mot.*"

2 During his years of poverty Balzac lived in an unheated and almost unfurnished garret. On one of the bare walls the writer inscribed the words: "Rosewood paneling with commode"; on another: "Gobelin tapestry with Venetian mirror"; and in the place of honor over the empty fireplace: "Picture by Raphael."

3 A Parisian bookseller, hearing of Balzac as a young writer of outstanding promise, decided to offer him 3,000 francs for his next novel. He found Balzac's address, situated in an obscure quarter of the city. Realizing that he was not dealing with a gentleman of fashion, he dropped his price to 2,000 francs. He went to the house, saw that the writer was living on the top floor, and dropped the price another 500 francs. When he entered Balzac's garret, he found him dipping a bread roll in a glass of water. He thereupon dropped the price to 300 francs. The manuscript sold this way was *La Dernière fée.*

4 Balzac, who enjoyed his own celebrity, was discoursing one evening on fame. "I should like one of these days to be so well known, so popular, so celebrated, so famous, that it would permit me . . . to break wind in society, and society would think it a most natural thing."

5 One night a thief broke into Balzac's single-room apartment and tried to pick the lock on the writer's desk. He was startled by a sardonic laugh from the bed, where Balzac, who he had supposed was asleep, lay watching him. "Why do you laugh?" said the thief. "I

am laughing to think what risks you take to try to find money in a desk by night where the legal owner can never find any by day."

6 (Edmond de Goncourt writes in his journal:)
"I have had happily confirmed the confidences of Gavarni on the economical manner in which Balzac dispensed his sperm. Lovey-dovey and amorous play, up to ejaculation, would be all right, but only up to ejaculation. Sperm to him meant emission of purest cerebral substance, and therefore a filtering, a loss through the member, of a potential act of artistic creation. I don't know what occasion, what unfortunate circumstance caused him to ignore his pet theory, but he arrived at Latouche's once, exclaiming, 'This morning I lost a novel.'"

7 On his deathbed Balzac is reported to have said to the doctor attending him, "Send for Bianchon." (Doctor Bianchon was a character in *La Comédie humaine*.)

8 The geographer von Humboldt once asked a doctor friend, while on a trip to Paris, if a dinner could be arranged during which he could meet a lunatic. The doctor put together a guest list, which included one man dressed in black who sat through dinner in silence and another tousled and extremely unkempt man who could not stop talking. Over dessert von Humboldt leaned over to the doctor and said that he had much enjoyed the company of the lunatic, indicating the disheveled man. "But it's the other one who's crazy," exclaimed the doctor. "Your dinner partner was Monsieur Honoré de Balzac!"

9 Balzac always dressed in a particular costume when he wrote: he wore Moroccan slippers and a white robe, secured by a belt from which hung scissors, a paperknife, and a penknife. But he was ever anxious about his need to produce more books. "To be forever creating!" he would exclaim. "Even God only created for six days!"

BANCROFT, Sir Squire (1841–1926), *British theater manager.*

1 Sir Squire Bancroft was notoriously tight-fisted, his style of management being in complete contrast to that of another contemporary theatrical impresario, Sir Herbert Beerbohm Tree. Tree once took Bancroft to view His Majesty's Theatre, which Tree had recently had built and lavishly equipped. Gazing at the building from the opposite side of the street, Bancroft remarked, "There'll be an awful lot of windows to clean."

BANKHEAD, Tallulah (1903–68), *US actress famous for her flamboyant life-style —"more of an act than an actress," as an anonymous wit said.*

1 At the opening-night party for Lillian Hellman's *The Little Foxes,* in which she starred, Tallulah got into an argument with the writer Dashiell Hammett. Hammett, commenting on her addiction to cocaine, told her that he did not much like people who took drugs. Tallulah retorted, "You don't know what you're talking about. I tell you cocaine isn't habit-forming and I know because I've been taking it for years."

2 At a party given by Dorothy Parker, Tallulah Bankhead became rather drunk and behaved indecorously. As she was being escorted out, Dorothy Parker called out, "Has Whistler's mother left yet?"
The following day the actress, observing herself in a small mirror, said, with a glance at Mrs. Parker, "The less I behave like Whistler's mother the night before, the more I look like her the morning after."

3 Alexander Woollcott took Tallulah Bankhead to see a rather bad revival of a Maeterlinck

tragedy. They decided to leave, and as they rose to go, Tallulah murmured, "There's less here than meets the eye."

4 Tallulah's volubility was notorious. The magician Fred Keating came away from an interview with her saying, "I've just spent an hour talking to Tallulah for a few minutes."

5 When Tallulah Bankhead first became successful in London, she bought herself a Bentley, which she greatly enjoyed driving. The London streets bewildered her, however, and she tended to get lost. After a while she took to hiring a taxi to lead the way while she drove behind in the Bentley.

6 Dropping a $50 bill into the tambourine held out to her by a Salvation Army player, Tallulah waved aside the man's thanks. "Don't bother to thank me. I know what a perfectly ghastly season it's been for you Spanish dancers."

7 (Former *Tonight* show host Jack Paar related the following Tallulah story. Miss Bankhead was in a stall in a ladies' room.)

"She could not find any toilet paper in her stall, and asked the lady in the next booth, 'Darling, is there any tissue in there?'

" 'Sorry, no.'

" 'Then have you any Kleenex?'

" 'Afraid not.'

"Then Tallulah said, 'My dear, have you two fives for a ten?' "

8 Miss Bankhead's father, William Brockman Bankhead, was Speaker of the US House of Representatives. Checking in at a New York hotel one evening, he was pleasantly surprised by the receptionist's exclamation: "Not *the* Mr. Bankhead?" He replied, "Why, yes — Congressman Bankhead." The receptionist's face fell. "Oh," she said. "I thought, maybe, you were Tallulah's father."

9 A fellow actress once said of Miss Bankhead: "She's not so great. I can upstage her any time." "Darling," retorted Tallulah, "I can upstage you without even being onstage." At the next performance, she set out to prove her point. In one scene, while the other actress was engaged in a long telephone conversation, Tallulah had to put down the champagne glass from which she had been drinking and make her exit upstage. That evening, she carefully placed the half-full glass in a precarious position at the edge of the table, half on and half off. The audience gasped, their attention riveted to the glass, and the other actress was totally ignored. She later discovered that Miss Bankhead had surreptitiously stuck a piece of adhesive tape on the bottom of the glass to ensure the success of her moment of triumph.

10 Miss Bankhead had been to see a screen adaptation of Tennessee Williams's play *Orpheus Descending,* and was unimpressed. She later told the playwright: "Darling, they've absolutely ruined your perfectly dreadful play."

11 Actor Donald Sutherland had a memorable first encounter with Tallulah Bankhead. He was making up in his dressing room when he heard a noise behind him. Turning around, he was astonished to see Tallulah standing there, stark naked. "What's the matter, darling?" she asked. "Haven't you ever seen a blonde before?"

BANKS, Sarah Sophia (1744–1818), *sister of Sir Joseph Banks, the British naturalist and explorer.*

1 A visitor once idly remarked to the eccentric Sophia, "It is a fine day, ma'am," to which she retorted, "I know nothing at all about it. You must speak to my brother upon that subject when you are at dinner."

BARBIROLLI, Sir John (1899–1970), *British conductor of French-Italian descent.*

1 One of the players in the Hallé Orchestra had an affair with a singer and after a time his wife heard of it. Intending to enlist Sir John Barbirolli's help, she went to his room in Manchester's Free Trade Hall and sobbed out her story. Sir John listened sympathetically and when she had finished tried to find words of comfort for her. He concluded, "You know, there's nothing to worry about. He's playing better than ever."

———◈———

BARHAM, Richard Harris (1788–1845), *British clergyman and humorist.*

1 At Oxford Barham regularly failed to attend morning chapel. His tutor demanded an explanation. Barham excused himself. "The fact is, sir, it's too late for me," he said. "Too late!" said the astonished tutor. "Yes, sir," Barham continued. "I'm a man of regular habits and I can't sit up until seven o'clock in the morning. Unless I get to bed by four, or five at the latest, I'm good for nothing next day."

2 Richard Bentley, the publisher of *Bentley's Miscellany,* in which many of the *Ingoldsby Legends* first appeared, mentioned to Barham that he had had trouble in selecting the name for his magazine, and had first intended to call it *The Wits' Miscellany.* "Well, you needn't have gone to the other extreme," remarked Barham.

———◈———

BARNES, Djuna (1892–1982), *US novelist; author of* Nightwood *and other experimental works.*

1 Eccentric and reclusive, Djuna Barnes lived for many years in a tiny Greenwich Village apartment. Her neighbor E. E. Cummings would occasionally shout across to her from his windows: "Are ya still alive, Djuna?"

2 Guy Davenport, learning that poet Louis Zukofsky frequently saw Djuna Barnes when he went for his morning paper, inquired whether they ever exchanged pleasantries. "No," replied Zukofsky. "What do you say to the Minister's Black Veil?"

3 Barnes once wrote a play that she showed to T. S. Eliot. He told her that, while it was obviously a magnificent work, he couldn't understand it. Later she showed the play to her friend Janet Flanner, who admired the vocabulary but was unclear about its meaning. Scornfully, Barnes told her, "I never expected to find that you were as stupid as Tom Eliot."

———◈———

BARNUM, Phineas Taylor (1810–91), *US showman. He founded his famous circus — "The Greatest Show on Earth"— in 1871.*

1 In 1841 Barnum purchased Scudder's American Museum in New York, soon turning it into a prize attraction. So many people flocked to see the exhibits that it was a problem to keep them moving, and long lines built up outside the entrance. Barnum solved the problem by posting up inside the museum a sign reading "TO THE EGRESS."

2 For a time Barnum employed an elephant to do the plowing on his farm. A neighboring farmer, a friend of Barnum's, noticed the beast at work. He then got into an argument with its owner, who insisted the elephant was just another working animal about the farm. After wrangling for a time about the economics of feeding it and the amount of work it could do, the farmer said to Barnum, "I would just like to know what it can draw." Barnum smiled. "It can draw the attention of twenty million American citizens to Barnum's Museum," he said.

3 Barnum's business instincts did not desert him on his deathbed. His last reported words were: "How were the receipts today in Madison Square Garden?"

4 In April 1891, the great showman realized his end was near. Hearing that his last wish was to read his own obituary, the New York *Evening Sun* obliged, running a four-column death notice the day before he actually died. Barnum was said to have greatly enjoyed reading it.

———— ✦ ————

BARR, Stringfellow (1896–1981), *US educator, co-founder of the Great Books program at St. John's College, Annapolis, Maryland.*

1 The four-year Great Books program was based on the works of great writers and thinkers from Homer to such twentieth-century giants as Freud. Someone once asked Barr, why a Great Books program? "Don't you feel sorry for all the students in all the other colleges who have no one to teach them but oafs like me?" Barr asked.

———— ✦ ————

BARRIE, Sir J[ames] M[atthew] (1860–1937), *British journalist and playwright known especially for* Peter Pan.

1 Barrie had for a long time looked forward to meeting A. E. Housman. When this was eventually arranged and the two placed next to each other at a dinner in Cambridge, neither found much to say to the other. Barrie, returning to London with this unprofitable encounter weighing on his mind, penned the following note to Housman: "Dear Professor Houseman, I am sorry about last night, when I sat next to you and did not say a word. You must have thought I was a very rude man: I am really a very shy man. Sincerely yours, J. M. Barrie." Back from Cambridge came

Housman's reply: "Dear Sir James Barrie, I am sorry about last night, when I sat next to you and did not say a word. You must have thought I was a very rude man: I am really a very shy man. Sincerely yours, A. E. Housman. P.S. And now you've made it worse for you have spelt my name wrong."

2 The pallbearers at Thomas Hardy's funeral included distinguished writers (Rudyard Kipling, G. B. Shaw, A. E. Housman) and politicians (Stanley Baldwin, Ramsay MacDonald). Shaw, the tallest and most obviously impressive, later remarked that he himself had looked well at the ceremony, but "Barrie, blast him! looked far the most effective. He made himself look specially small."

3 *Peter Pan* premiered in London in 1904. In it Peter told the Darling children that if they believed strongly enough that they could fly, they *would* fly. Barrie soon began to hear from parents with children who had taken Peter's word literally, and hurt themselves in consequence. Barrie at once included in the play a cautionary statement that the children could fly, but only if they had first been sprinkled with "fairy dust." From then on, fairy dust being in short supply, all has gone well.

4 The success of Barrie's play owed a great deal to the author's close attention to production details and his presence at rehearsals. Late one night after an exhausting and unsatisfying rehearsal of *Peter Pan,* when the director had just told the cast that they could go, Barrie suddenly demanded that they all be brought back onto the stage. "Impossible," shouted the weary director. "Why?" asked Barrie. "Crocodile under fourteen — gone home," was the response.

5 One of the reactions to *Peter Pan* that Barrie most enjoyed was that of a small boy who had been given a seat in the author's box to watch the play. At the end he was asked which bit he had liked best. The child

replied, "What I think I liked best was tearing up the program and dropping the bits on people's heads."

6 (Peter, one of the sons of the Davies family of whom Sir James Barrie was very fond, recalled an incident that throws a curious light on Barrie's sense of humor.)

"One evening at dusk I was summoned to J. M. B.'s room, to find him sitting in a somehow dejected attitude, at the far end of the room in the half light. As I entered he looked up, and in a flat lugubrious voice said: 'Peter, something has happened to my feet,' and glancing down I saw to my horror that his feet were bare and swollen to four or five times their natural size. For several seconds I was deceived, and have never since forgotten the terror that filled me, until I realized that the feet were artificial (bought at Henley's), made of the waxed linen masks are made of, and that I had been most successfully hoaxed."

7 Barrie, valuing the privacy of his home, tended to react violently when it was invaded. A reporter turned up on his doorstep and when Barrie came to the door said brightly, "Sir James Barrie, I presume?"

"You do," said Barrie, and slammed the door.

8 Barrie was sitting next to George Bernard Shaw at a dinner party. The vegetarian Shaw had been provided with a special dish of salad greens and dressing. Eyeing the unpleasant-looking concoction, Barrie whispered to Shaw, "Tell me, have you eaten that or are you going to?"

9 "You'll be sick tomorrow, Jack, if you eat any more chocolates," said Sylvia Llewelyn-Davies to her young son. "I shall be sick tonight," said the child calmly, as he helped himself to yet another. Barrie, who overheard this exchange, was so delighted with it that he incorporated it in *Peter Pan* and paid the young Llewelyn-Davies a copyright fee of a halfpenny a performance.

10 While producing one of his own plays, Barrie was approached by an inexperienced member of the cast. Although his part was a very minor one, the young actor, anxious to give it the right interpretation, sought Barrie's advice. Sir James gave the matter some thought. "I am glad you have asked me," he finally replied. "I should like you to convey when you are acting it that the man you portray has a brother in Shropshire who drinks port."

―――― ⚬⁄ₒ ――――

BARROW, Isaac (1630–77), *British clergyman and mathematician.*

1 There was no love lost between Barrow and King Charles II's favorite, the Earl of Rochester, who had called the clergyman "a musty old piece of divinity." One day at court, where Barrow was serving as the king's chaplain, he encountered the earl, who bowed low and said sarcastically, "Doctor, I am yours to my shoe-tie."

"My lord," returned Barrow, "I am yours to the ground."

"Doctor, I am yours to the center."

"Doctor, I am yours to the antipodes."

"Doctor, I am yours to the lowest pit of hell."

"And there, my lord, I leave you," said Barrow, turning smartly on his heel.

―――― ⚬⁄ₒ ――――

BARROWS, Sidney Biddle (1952–), *famed for running a discreet prostitution business.*

1 Called "The Mayflower Madam" due to her Waspy family background, Barrows ran a highly successful prostitution ring in New York City. During the trial of another Madam, Heidi Fleiss, whose business encompassed the movie-studio world of Holly-

wood, Barrows was hired as a television commentator to describe for viewers the inside world of prostitution. Barrows was once asked to explain how — and why — she was offered this role. "If you want an expert on war, you get a retired general. I'm not exactly a general, but I am retired."

———— ⌀ ————

BARRYMORE, Ethel (1879–1959), *US actress, member of a remarkable acting family (Lionel and John were her brothers).*

1 Miss Barrymore was in her Hollywood dressing room one day when a studio usher knocked on the door and called: "A couple of gals in the reception room, Miss Barrymore, who say they went to school with you. What shall I do?"

"Wheel them in," came the reply.

2 Ethel Barrymore was exact in manners and expected from others the same courtesy. When she invited a young actress to dinner, her guest not only failed to appear but did not even bother to account for her absence. Several days later, the two women met unexpectedly at New York's Gallery of Modern Art. Lamely, the young woman began, "I think I was invited to your house to dinner last Thursday night."

"Oh, yes," replied Ethel. "Did you come?"

3 In her old age Barrymore was confined to her bed with heart disease and arthritis. Her room was kept full of fresh flowers and at a near-freezing temperature. On her last evening she awoke from a nap, clasped her nurse's hand, and said, "Is everybody happy? I want everybody to be happy. I know *I'm* happy." She then fell asleep for the last time.

———— ⌀ ————

BARRYMORE, John (1882–1942), *US actor. Throughout his successful career on stage and screen he always thought of himself primarily as a great classical actor.*

1 In his youth Barrymore was extremely lazy and had already acquired an unhealthy taste for alcohol. In 1906 a heavy night of drinking enabled him to sleep through the great San Francisco earthquake. The next morning he was pressed by the army into helping clear the rubble — an event that caused his uncle to remark, "It took a calamity of nature to get him out of bed and the US army to make him go to work."

2 Although Hamlet was to become one of Barrymore's most famous roles, the actor was not at all happy with his first performance. He was sitting despondently in his dressing room after the show, when a distinguished-looking gentleman came in. Throwing himself at the actor's feet, the stranger kissed Barrymore's hand and gushed, "O Master! I enjoyed your performance so much!"

"Not half so much as I am enjoying yours," replied Barrymore.

3 During rehearsals for a play the leading lady and Barrymore had a furious row. Barrymore told her pungently what he thought of her parentage and her offstage pursuits. "Kindly remember I am a lady!" snapped the actress. "I will respect your secret, madam," retorted Barrymore.

4 In accord with his frequently professed contempt for the film medium, Barrymore refused to learn his lines for any of his movie roles. This necessitated having a small army of stagehands hold up boards with the star's lines written on them so that Barrymore could see and read them during filming. When directors or his fellow actors remonstrated with him about his inconvenient habit, he always produced the same answer: "My memory is full of beauty — Hamlet's soliloquies, the Queen Mab speech, King Magnus' monologues from *The Apple Cart,*

most of the Sonnets. Do you expect me to clutter up all that with this horseshit?"

5 When the filming of *A Bill of Divorcement* was complete, Katharine Hepburn turned to co-star John Barrymore, saying, "Thank God I don't have to act with you anymore!"

"I didn't know you ever had, darling," he replied.

6 The assistant to a movie mogul telephoned Barrymore, explained that she was speaking for her boss, and invited Barrymore to a party the following day. Barrymore replied, "And I am speaking for John Barrymore, who has a previous engagement which he will make as soon as you have hung up."

7 In 1938 Orson Welles broadcast throughout the United States a radio production of H. G. Wells's story *War of the Worlds,* which tells of a Martian invasion. The broadcast was so realistic that it almost caused a coast-to-coast panic. John Barrymore was among those convinced that the Martians had landed. He managed to contain his fear until it came to the point at which the invaders are marching down Madison Avenue. Rushing out to the kennel in which he kept his twenty St. Bernards, he flung open the gate and released the dogs, crying, "Fend for yourselves!"

8 While appearing in the play *Redemption,* Barrymore was irritated by the audience's constant coughing. In the next act, as soon as the coughing began again, he pulled from his clothes a large fish and flung it into the seats. "Chew on that, you walruses, while the rest of us get on with the libretto!"

9 Barrymore faced his end with a last gesture of gallantry. In the hospital and aware that he was dying, he called for a priest, who came to his bedside accompanied by an old and extremely ugly nurse. Asked if he had anything to confess, Barrymore replied,

"Yes, Father, I confess to having carnal thoughts."

"About whom?" asked the nervous priest.

"About her," said Barrymore, pointing to the nurse.

———— ∞ ————

BARRYMORE, Maurice (1847–1905), *Britlish-born actor, father of John, Lionel, and Ethel Barrymore.*

1 When Maurice Barrymore was being laid to rest, the straps supporting the coffin became twisted. The coffin, already lowered into the grave, had to be raised again so an adjustment could be made. As it reappeared, Lionel impulsively nudged John and whispered, "How like Father — a curtain call!"

———— ∞ ————

BARTÓK, Béla (1881–1945), *Hungarian composer and pianist. In 1940 he moved to the United States, where he died in poverty.*

1 (Isidore Philipp, a great teacher of piano, was visited by Bartók in Paris.)

"[Philipp] offered to introduce the young Hungarian composer to Camille Saint-Saëns, at that time a terrific celebrity. Bartók declined. Philipp then offered him Charles-Marie Widor. Bartók again declined. 'Well, if you won't meet Saint-Saëns and Widor, who is there that you would like to know?' 'Debussy,' said Bartók. 'But he is a horrid man,' said Philipp. 'He hates everybody and will certainly be rude to you. Do you want to be insulted by Debussy?' 'Yes,' said Bartók."

———— ∞ ————

BARTON, Clara (1821–1912), *founder and president of the US Red Cross.*

1 Miss Barton, who never bore grudges, was once reminded by a friend of a wrong done to her some years earlier. "Don't you remem-

ber?" asked her friend. "No," replied Clara firmly, "I distinctly remember forgetting that."

2 At a meeting of the National Woman Suffrage Association, Barton was told, "Every woman should stand with bared head before Susan B. Anthony." "Yes," was her reply, "and every man as well."

———— ✧ ————

BARUCH, Bernard Mannes (1870–1965), *US financier and presidential adviser.*

1 Baruch was telephoned one night when giving a dinner party. His side of the conversation was clearly audible to his guests. "Consolidated Gas — good," they heard him say, then, "Yes — good — fine." A lady who was present rushed out the following morning and bought a substantial holding of Consolidated Gas. Over the next few months the stock fell disastrously. When the lady next met Baruch, she reproached, him saying she had bought Consolidated Gas on his recommendation.

Baruch was puzzled, but when she reminded him of the telephone conversation, light dawned. The call had been from a consultant whom he had briefed to investigate Consolidated Gas and who had said that Baruch's suspicions were well founded. Baruch's words had been his expression of satisfaction that his hunch had proved correct.

2 A man who had often spoken to Baruch about his love for hunting was eventually invited to the financier's South Carolina estate for a turkey shoot. For two days the hapless guest toiled around the plantation, firing at every gobbler he saw, but without hitting a single one. Baruch said nothing. On the third morning, however, the guest noticed a particularly fine turkey sitting motionless in a tree right by the path. He crept up silently to the

turkey and fired point-blank. The bird dropped at his feet. With great joy he hastened to stuff his trophy into his bag and it was only then that he noticed the card tied around the bird's neck. It read: "With the compliments of Bernard Baruch."

———— ✧ ————

BASIE, "Count" [William] (1904–84), *US jazz pianist.*

1 On tour in London in 1957, Basie went shopping for gifts for his family. He had decided on fur gloves for his daughter, but in several shops he was advised that mittens were more practical for children. "Yeah?" said Basie. "How're they going to count in the wintertime?"

———— ✧ ————

BAUM, L[yman] Frank (1856–1919), *US writer and journalist, author of* The Wonderful Wizard of Oz *(1900).*

1 Baum had a weak heart and was not allowed to smoke, but he often held an unlit cigar in his mouth. Once, when standing on a lakeshore, he was asked whether he ever actually lit the cigar. "I only light up when I go swimming," replied Baum. "I can't swim, so when the cigar goes out I know I'm getting out of my depth." To illustrate this bizarre explanation, he lit the cigar, walked into the lake until the water reached the level of his mouth, then returned to the dry land, the cigar extinguished. "There, now," he said triumphantly, "if it hadn't been for the cigar I would have drowned."

2 Baum's first book began when a group of children, including his own four sons, asked him to tell them a story one evening at his house in Chicago. He launched directly into a tale about a Kansas farm girl, Dorothy, and spun out her adventures. When one of the

children asked him what country Dorothy had landed in, Baum looked about for inspiration. The first thing he saw was a filing cabinet, labeled O–Z. "The land of Oz!" he cried.

BAYLIS, Lilian (1874–1937), *British theater manager.*

1 Miss Baylis was notoriously discouraging of romances between members of her company. A young actor and actress went hand in hand to her office. For a time she affected not to notice them, then, scarcely looking up from her desk, said, "Well, what is it?"

"We're in love, Miss Baylis," stammered the actor, "and we — er — want to get married."

"Go away," said Miss Baylis. "I haven't got time to listen to gossip."

2 Chronic financial problems beset Lilian Baylis's theatrical ventures. For these, as for other matters, she was unabashed about seeking divine aid. Members of her company were frequently embarrassed by her habit of going down on her knees in her office. It was said that at one particularly stressful moment she was overheard to pray, "O Lord, send me a good tenor — cheap."

3 Elated by her recent acquisition of Sadler's Wells as an opera and ballet house, Miss Baylis stepped off the sidewalk outside London's Old Vic theater without looking and was knocked down by a passing cab. An elderly gentleman rushed to her aid. "Blimey," he exclaimed, "if it ain't Miss Lilian Baylis of the Old Vic." Raising her head with some difficulty, Miss Baylis announced proudly, "And Sadler's Wells, too!" And lapsed unconscious.

BAYLOR, Elgin (1934–), *US basketball player.*

1 When Baylor was the leader of the Los Angeles Lakers, he agreed to take a vote among the players as to whether to buy blue or gold blazers. The vote went for gold, but Baylor ordered blue. When his rival, Bill Russell, heard about it, he asked Baylor to explain. "I told 'em I'd give 'em the vote, I didn't say I'd count it," Baylor replied.

BEAN, Roy (?1825–1903), *US frontier judge and saloon keeper.*

1 Bean was the proprietor of the Jersey Lily tavern in Langtry, Texas, close to the railroad. One day when a train stopped to take on water, a passenger rushed into Bean's bar for a bottle of beer. Bean lazily told him to help himself, which the man did, rushing out again without paying. Incensed, Bean grabbed his gun and ran up to the train, telling the conductor to hold it. He found his customer in the smoking bar and, cocking his gun, demanded the money for the beer. Alarmed, the man handed over a $10 bill. Bean took it and said, "Fifty cents for the beer, nine dollars and fifty for collecting. This squares your account. You can keep the bottle." Then stepping down from the train, he told the conductor, "You can go ahead now as soon as you damn well please."

BEATON, Sir Cecil (1904–80), *British photographer, designer, and society portraitist.*

1 In 1926 the young Beaton, uncertain about his future plans, begged the advice of a friend, Kyrle Leng. "What on earth can I become in life?" he asked in a letter, and received the reply, "I wouldn't bother too much about *being* anything in particular, just become a friend of the Sitwells, and wait and see what happens."

2 (At an informal dinner party soon after the engagement of Princess Margaret and Anthony Armstrong-Jones was announced, Cecil Beaton was shown one of the first wedding presents, painted by one of the guests.)

"One of the painters present had given them a large picture of a great number of hysterical-looking naked figures milling together in what appeared to be a blue haze or an earthquake or a trench scene of the 1914–18 war. Princess Margaret said, 'They're all dancing.' I took a gulp of champagne and said, 'Oh, I'm so glad it isn't a disaster.' Princess Margaret laughed so much that she had to lie flat in an armchair."

———— ✧ ————

BEATTY, David Beatty, 1st Earl (1871–1936), *British admiral.*

1 Beatty commanded one arm of the British fleet at the battle of Jutland in 1916. He was not wholly prepared with all ships in position when he encountered the German fleet, and a brisk battle soon developed. The *Lion* was hit first and then the *Indefatigable* was blown up; soon afterward the *Queen Mary*, with her crew of 1,200, was sunk. Admiral Beatty observed to his flag captain, "There seems to be something wrong with our bloody ships today, Chatfield."

———— ✧ ————

Ernie Byfield, who used to run Chicago's legendary Pump Room, was once asked why real caviar was so expensive. His reply: "After all, it's a year's work for the sturgeon."

———— ✧ ————

BEAUMONT, Francis (1584–1616), *British dramatist, collaborator of John Fletcher.*

1 At one stage in their collaboration Beaumont and Fletcher were arrested on suspicion of treason. As they were sitting in a tavern working out the plot of a tragedy, one had been heard to remark to the other, "I'll kill the king."

———— ✧ ————

BEAVERBROOK, William Maxwell Aitkin, 1st Baron (1879–1964), *British newspaper publisher and politician, born in Canada.*

1 In the washroom of his London club, Beaverbrook happened to meet Edward Heath, then a young MP, about whom he had printed a rather insulting editorial a few days earlier. "My dear chap," said Beaverbrook, embarrassed by the encounter, "I've been thinking it over, and I was wrong. Here and now, I wish to apologize."

"Very well," grunted Heath. "But next time, I wish you'd insult me in the washroom and apologize in your newspaper."

———— ✧ ————

BECKETT, Samuel (1906–89), *Irish novelist, playwright, and poet who was awarded the Nobel Prize for Literature in 1969.*

1 Beckett was listening while his friend Walter Lowenfels expounded at length his views on the relationship of art and the desolate condition of society. Beckett nodded but said nothing, until his friend burst out, "You sit there saying nothing while the world is going to pieces. What do you want? What do you want to do?" Beckett crossed his long legs and drawled, "Walter, all I want to do is sit on my ass and fart and think of Dante."

2 In 1962 Beckett married his longtime companion, Suzanne. Soon afterward their relationship became soured by her jealousy of his growing fame and success as a writer. One day in 1969 the telephone rang. Suzanne answered it. She listened for a moment, spoke briefly to the caller, and hung up. Then she turned to face Beckett, looking stricken, and whispered, *"Quel catastrophe!"* (What a catastrophe!) She had just been told that the

Swedish Academy had awarded him the Nobel Prize for Literature.

———— ✧ ————

BECKFORD, William (1760–1844), *British eccentric and collector.*

1 Beckford built a high wall around his estate at Fonthill to discourage visitors. One determined young man managed to slip unobserved through the main gate during a tradesman's call. Heading across the park, he came to a walled vegetable garden. A man who had been digging potatoes came over and asked the intruder to identify himself. The young man explained that he had heard a great deal about the beauties of Fonthill and finding the gate open had taken the opportunity of having a look. The gardener seemed sympathetic, showed him around the greenhouses, and then said, "Would you like to see the house and its contents?"

After a comprehensive tour of the house, the young man's guide pressed him to stay and have some dinner, then revealed his true identity; he was, of course, William Beckford. The young man readily agreed to stay, and he and Beckford had a magnificent meal and thoroughly enjoyable conversation. On the stroke of eleven Beckford withdrew to bed. A footman showed the guest to the door. "Mr. Beckford ordered me to present his compliments to you, sir," he told the young man, "and I am to say that as you found your way into Fonthill Abbey without assistance, you may find your way out again as best you can, and he hopes that you will take care to avoid the bloodhounds that are let loose in the gardens every night. I wish you good evening, sir."

With the door resolutely shut behind him, the young man ran as fast as he could to the nearest tree and climbed up out of reach of the hounds. There he spent a night of acute terror and discomfort until the day dawned

and he was able to make his way in safety to the main gate and escape.

2 Beckford's vast and assorted collection did not win universal admiration. After financial constraints forced its owner to disperse it, the essayist William Hazlitt remarked, "The only proof of taste he has shown in this collection is his getting rid of it."

———— ✧ ————

BEECHAM, Thomas (1820–1907), *British industrialist; grandfather of the conductor Sir Thomas Beecham.*

1 Beecham's fortunes were founded on his pills, which became a popular panacea and were sold with the slogan "Worth a guinea a box." It is said that this phrase was suggested to Beecham by a satisfied customer who came up to him while he was peddling the pills in the marketplace at St. Helens, Lancashire. When Beecham became wealthy, he used to send samples of the pills to the old people of the Oxfordshire village in which he had once been a shepherd. In the bottom of each box he would put a guinea.

———— ✧ ————

BEECHAM, Sir Thomas (1879–1961), *British conductor and impresario.*

1 As a young man Beecham was the subject of many stories relating to his dashing style. One tells how he was walking in London's Piccadilly on a balmy summer evening when he began to feel that he was too warmly dressed. He hailed a cab, tossed his redundant topcoat into it, and ordered the driver, "Follow me." He then completed his stroll unencumbered.

2 Beecham was not a great admirer of the music of the British composer Ralph Vaughan Williams. During a rehearsal of a Vaughan Williams symphony he seemed to be doing

no more than listlessly beating time — indeed, he was still beating time after the orchestra had stopped. "Why aren't you playing?" Beecham mildly asked the first violinist. "It's finished, Sir Thomas," came the reply. Beecham looked down at his score, turned the page, and found it empty. "So it is, thank God!" he said.

3 Sir Thomas Beecham was traveling in a no-smoking compartment on a train belonging to the Great Western Railway. A lady entered the compartment and lit a cigarette, saying, "I'm sure you won't object if I smoke."

"Not at all," replied Beecham, "provided that you don't object if I'm sick."

"I don't think you know who I am," the lady haughtily pointed out. "I am one of the directors' wives."

"Madam," said Beecham, "if you were the director's *only* wife, I should still be sick."

4 When rehearsing Handel's *Messiah* Beecham said to the choir, "When we sing 'All we, like sheep, have gone astray,' might we please have a little more regret and a little less satisfaction?"

5 Riding in a New York cab, Beecham irritated his companion by repeatedly whistling a passage from Mozart. Eventually the man exclaimed, "Must you do that?" Beecham replied, "You may be able to hear only my whistling; I can hear the full orchestra."

6 In the foyer of a Manchester hotel Beecham saw a distinguished-looking woman whom he believed he knew, though he could not remember her name. He paused to talk to her and as he did so vaguely recollected that she had a brother. Hoping for a clue, he asked how her brother was and whether he was still working at the same job. "Oh, he's very well," she answered, "and still king."

7 The rehearsal had not been going well, with some players apparently unable to keep time.

Beecham addressed one of the main offenders: "We cannot expect you to be with us the whole time, but maybe you would be kind enough to keep in touch now and again?"

8 In the first half of a concert Beecham was conducting a Mozart concerto. He and the pianist did not get on together; his conducting lacked luster and the pianist's playing was mediocre. During the intermission some adjustments to the stage became necessary. The person in charge asked Beecham, "Should we take the piano off or leave it on?" Beecham mentally ran over the second half of the program, for which a piano was not required. "You might as well leave it on," he said. "It will probably slink off by itself."

9 Beecham and violinist Jean Pougnet were appearing with an orchestra that seemed overawed at rehearsal. The start of the main piece was disastrous. Sir Thomas kept going, and after a while the players began to settle down. He leaned forward to Pougnet and said: "Don't look now, Mr. Pougnet, but I believe we're being followed."

10 A lady asked Sir Thomas's advice on an instrument for her son, concerned about the misery his first efforts on the violin or trombone might inflict upon the household. What instrument would Sir Thomas recommend? Beecham replied, "The bagpipes; they sound exactly the same when you have mastered them as when you first begin learning them."

11 When Beecham conducted the opening night of Richard Strauss's *Elektra* at Covent Garden in 1910, he judged the singing not up to standard. He urged the orchestra to play louder and louder: "The singers think they are going to be heard, and I'm going to make jolly well certain that they aren't."

12 Beecham was once asked why he always chose such generously built ladies for the

leading soprano roles in his productions, rejecting the more shapely and attractive candidates. "Unfortunately," replied the conductor with a wistful sigh, "those sopranos who sing like birds eat like horses — and vice versa."

---◌◐◌---

BEECHER, Henry Ward (1813–87), *US Congregational minister and author.*

1 In the middle of one of Henry Ward Beecher's most eloquent political speeches, a member of the crowd gave a perfect imitation of a cock crow. The audience roared with laughter, but the speaker gave no sign of annoyance, simply pulling out his watch and studying it until the noise had died down. Then he said, "That's odd. My watch says it's ten o'clock. But there can't be any mistake. It must be morning, for the instincts of the lower animals are absolutely infallible."

2 Arriving at Plymouth church one Sunday, Beecher found in his mail a letter containing just one word: "Fool." During the service that morning, he related the incident to his congregation, adding the remark: "I have known many an instance of a man writing a letter and forgetting to sign his name, but this is the only instance I have ever known of a man signing his name and forgetting to write the letter."

3 During the Civil War, Beecher traveled to England with the aim of arousing British support for the Northern cause. Addressing a turbulent crowd of rebel sympathizers in Manchester, he was asked: "Why didn't you whip the Confederates in sixty days, as you said you would?"

"Because," retorted Beecher, "we found we had Americans to fight instead of Englishmen."

4 Beecher possessed a beautiful globe depicting the various constellations and stars of the heavens. Robert Ingersoll, visiting Beecher one day, admired the globe and asked who had made it. "Who made it?" said Beecher, seizing the opportunity to attack his guest's well-known agnosticism. "Why, nobody made it; it just happened."

---◌◐◌---

BEERBOHM, Sir Max (1872–1956), *British writer, caricaturist, and wit.*

1 (Sir James Barrie, although a Scot, was frequently to be seen as a pallbearer at the funerals of major figures of the English literary establishment. Beerbohm recounted an incident at the funeral in 1909 of George Meredith.)

"As I left . . . a young woman rushed up to me, crying, 'Mr. Barrie, Mr. Barrie — you are Mr. Barrie, aren't you? — will you write something for me in my autograph book. Here it is!' . . . I know it was in poor taste; I said nothing, but when I took the volume my pen ran away with me, and I wrote, 'Ay, Lassie! It's a sad day the noo. J. M. Barrie.'"

2 Max had no time for the new psychological theories that pervaded literature in his latter years. Reflecting on his own happy family life, he wondered aloud to a friend what the psychologists would make of him. "I adored my father and mother and I adored my brothers and sisters. What kind of complex would they find me a victim of? Oedipus and what else?" He paused for a moment and then went on, "They were a tense and peculiar family, the Oedipuses, weren't they?"

3 Max's eccentricities may in part have been inherited from his father, Julius Beerbohm. On one occasion, at a party he was not enjoying, one of Julius's daughters-in-law came across him groping his way around the room. She asked if he was looking for something. "The door," exclaimed Mr. Beerbohm.

4 Elisabeth Jungmann, reading about Newton, observed to Max that she would have liked to have met the great scientist. Max, to whom scientific matters were a closed book, said that he would not have understood him. "He would have liked you," persevered Elisabeth. Max was amused: "I would have taught him the law of levity," he said.

———⌾———

BEETHOVEN, Ludwig van (1770–1827), *German composer.*

1 At a reception, Beethoven, who was then still known only as a pianist, mentioned his desire to have an arrangement with a publisher similar to that enjoyed by Goethe and Handel. That is, anything he wrote would belong to the publisher in perpetuity in return for a guaranteed lifetime income. "My dear young man, you must not complain," sneered his interlocutor, "for you are neither a Goethe nor a Handel, and it is not to be expected that you will ever be, for such masters will not be born again."

2 On one occasion when Beethoven was walking with Goethe, Goethe expressed his annoyance at the incessant greetings from passersby. Beethoven replied, "Do not let that trouble Your Excellency; perhaps the greetings are intended for me."

3 When Beethoven composed, he considered himself at one with the Creator and took endless pains to perfect his compositions. On one occasion a violinist complained to him that a passage was so awkwardly written as to be virtually unplayable. Beethoven replied, "When I composed that, I was conscious of being inspired by God Almighty. Do you think I can consider your puny little fiddle when He speaks to me?"

4 Beethoven's Third Symphony, *Eroica,* composed in 1803, was originally entitled "Bonaparte." This was intended as a tribute to the hero of revolutionary France, then First Consul and almost exactly the same age as Beethoven. But Beethoven's admiration soon gave way to disillusionment when Napoleon proclaimed himself emperor in May 1804. Beethoven was in Vienna when he heard of this; in a rage he went to the table where the score lay and tore the title page in two. On publication the symphony was given its present title, *Eroica* (Heroic), and it was described as having been composed "to celebrate the memory of a great man."

5 Performing a new piano concerto at the Theater An der Wien, Beethoven forgot that he was the soloist and began to conduct. At the first *sforzando,* he threw out his arms with such force that he knocked down the lights on the piano. He began the concerto again, this time with two choir boys holding the lights. On reaching the same *sforzando,* Beethoven repeated his dramatic gesture. He hit one of the boys, who was so frightened that he dropped his light. The other boy anticipated what would happen and dodged the blow. Enraged by the audience's laughter, Beethoven struck the piano with such force that at the first chord six strings broke.

6 His Ninth Symphony (the *Choral*) completed, Beethoven was urged to conduct his latest work at a Vienna concert. After a particular passage, unaware of the thunderous ovation, the composer stood still turning the leaves of his score. Finally one of the singers pulled at his sleeve and pointed to the audience. Beethoven turned, and bowed.

7 Beethoven fired his housekeeper, who had taken excellent care of him, because she once shielded him from an unpleasantness by fibbing about it. "Anyone who tells a lie has not a pure heart," he said, "and cannot make pure soup."

8 Beethoven once happened to hear someone playing his Variations in C minor. After a

short time he asked who had written the piece. When told he was its author, he exclaimed, "Such nonsense by me! Oh, Beethoven, what an ass you were!"

9 Beethoven failed quickly at the end of his life, suffering from rheumatism, kidney disease, and the general effects of a lifetime of bad health. In the winter of 1826–27 jaundice and a severe cold finally felled him. At 6:00 on the evening of March 26, as he lay in a stupor in his bed, a loud thunderclap roused him. He sat up, shook his fist at the sky, and fell back dead on his pillow.

———cɯɔ———

BEGIN, Menachem (1913–92), *Israeli statesman and prime minister* (1977–83) *who together with President Anwar Sadat of Egypt was awarded the 1979 Nobel Peace Prize.*

1 In September 1940 Begin was playing chess with his wife when Russian soldiers burst into his home to arrest him. As they dragged him away, he shouted to Mrs. Begin that he conceded the game.

———cɯɔ———

BEHAN, Brendan (1923–64), *Irish playwright.*

1 (During one of his alcoholic periods, Behan arrived at his publisher's office en route for Euston station, wearing his pajamas under his suit. The publicity director, a friend of the family, was to accompany Behan to the station to meet his parents. She had the task of making him a little more presentable.)

"On our way to the station we stopped at an outfitter's in a side street off the Euston Road, and although the clothes in the window had little in common with Brendan, we went in. As I busied myself informing the immaculately dressed assistant that we wanted an overcoat, shirt, and a tie, I did not notice that Brendan was preparing himself enthusiastically for the fitting until, too late, he

stood in front of us with not a stitch between himself and his Maker, his suit and his pajamas bunched in a pile by his tiny bare feet. With a dignity that is essentially the mark of a perfect English gentleman, the assistant did not raise an eyebrow as he helped Brendan into his new shirt and back into his trousers as though the sight of a naked customer in his shop was an everyday occurrence."

2 Behan was originally a housepainter by trade, and while in Paris was asked to paint a sign on the window of a café to attract English tourists. He painted, "Come in, you Anglo-Saxon swine / And drink of my Algerian wine. / 'Twill turn your eyeballs black and blue, / And damn well good enough for you." After receiving payment for the job, Behan fled before the café proprietor had time to have the rhyme translated.

3 Behan was asked what he thought of drama critics. "Critics are like eunuchs in a harem," he replied. "They're there every night, they see it done every night, they see how it should be done every night, but they can't do it themselves."

4 Just before he died, Behan looked up at the nursing nun who was taking his pulse. "Bless you, Sister," he said with a weak smile. "May all your sons be bishops!"

———cɯɔ———

BELL, Alexander Graham (1847–1922), *Scottish inventor most noted for his invention of the telephone.*

1 On March 10, 1876, Bell made the first telephone communication over a line set up between two rooms in a building in Boston. The epoch-making words recorded by Mr. Watson, Bell's assistant, were simply: "Mr. Watson, come here; I want you."

2 As professor of vocal physiology at Boston University, Bell had many deaf pupils, includ-

ing Mabel Hubbard, who later became his wife. They lived happily together for forty-five years. As Bell lay dying after a long illness, Mabel whispered to him, "Don't leave me." Unable to speak, Bell traced with his fingers the sign "No." With this last silent message, the inventor of the telephone took his final leave of his wife.

BELL, Joseph (1837–1911), *Scottish surgeon, the model for Sir Arthur Conan Doyle's Sherlock Holmes.*

1 Bell used a standard experiment to test the powers of perception of each new class of medical students. He held up a tumbler of liquid, explaining that it contained a potent drug with a very bitter taste. "We might easily analyze this chemically," he said, "but I want you to test it by smell and taste and, as I don't ask anything of my students which I wouldn't be willing to do myself, I will taste it before passing it around." The students watched uncomfortably as Dr. Bell dipped a finger into the liquid, put his finger to his lips, and sucked it. Grimacing, he then passed the tumbler around the class and each student in turn dipped a finger into the unknown substance, sucked it, and shuddered at the bitter taste. The experiment over, Dr. Bell announced: "Gentlemen, I am deeply grieved to find that not one of you has developed this power of perception, which I so often speak about. For, if you had watched me closely, you would have found that, while I placed my forefinger in the bitter medicine, it was the middle finger which found its way into my mouth!"

2 Dr. Bell once attempted to demonstrate the deductive method of diagnosis to a group of students gathered around the bed of one of his patients. "Aren't you a bandsman?" he asked the sick man. His patient nodded. "You see, gentlemen, I am right," said Dr.

Bell triumphantly. "It is quite simple. This man has a paralysis of the cheek muscles, the result of too much blowing at wind instruments. We need only inquire to confirm. What instrument do you play, my man?"

"The big drum, doctor."

BELLOC, [Joseph] Hilaire [Pierre] (1870–1953), *British biographer, novelist, and critic.*

1 Belloc's passionate convictions prompted him in 1906 to seek election as an MP, although he knew that, as a Roman Catholic, he would have a struggle to overcome the voters' religious prejudices. On the occasion of his first campaign speech at Salford he appeared on the rostrum with a rosary in his hand and made the following declaration: "I am a Catholic. As far as possible I go to Mass every day. As far as possible I kneel down and tell these beads every day. If you reject me on account of my religion, I shall thank God that he has spared me the indignity of being your representative." He was elected.

2 Belloc was a master of insult. The novelist and critic Wilfrid Sheed recalls that an unidentified man came up to Belloc, saying, "You don't know me."

"Yes, I do," replied Belloc, turned on his heel, and walked off.

3 (A. N. Wilson, in his biography of Belloc, states that he heard the following story from several sources but has never been able to substantiate it. It illustrates the strain under which Belloc often worked, turning out book after book, not always up to his highest standard, merely in order to make a difficult livelihood.)

During the 1930s in a railway carriage Belloc noticed a man in front of him reading a volume of his *History of England*. He leaned forward, asked him how much he had paid for it, was informed of the price, took a corresponding sum out of his pocket, gave it to the man, snatched the book from his hand, and tossed it out the window.

———— ↔ ————

BELLOWS, George Wesley (1882–1925), *US painter known for his prizefight series.*

1 Joseph Pennell once accused Bellows of nonauthenticity for having painted the execution of nurse Edith Cavell by the Germans in 1915 without having been an eyewitness of the event. Bellows retorted that although he had not been present at the execution, "neither had Leonardo da Vinci been present at the Last Supper."

———— ↔ ————

BEMBO, Pietro (1470–1547), *Italian scholar who was later created a cardinal.*

1 In Rome Cardinal Bembo gave a splendid dinner. Among the distinguished guests was the Count Montebello, famous for his perfect breeding. During the banquet the count rose from his seat and looked around. He observed the priceless carpets, the mirrors, the bronzes — and shook his head. He let his gaze wander over the wall tapestries, the gold and crystal table service, and shrugged his shoulders. Then his eyes roved over the servants, dressed in silk and satin, ranged against the walls. Finally he walked up to one of the lackeys and spat straight into his mouth. The cardinal, shocked, looked in astonishment at his guest. Montebello explained, "My lord, it was the only place I could find in the whole room where I could spit."

———— ↔ ————

BENCHLEY, Robert (1889–1945), *American humorist.*

1 When Benchley visited Venice for the first time, he sent a cable to Harold Ross, the editor of *The New Yorker,* reading, "Streets full of water. Please advise."

2 At a Hollywood party the guests were playing a game in which each one had to compose his or her own epitaph. An actress, whose marriages and love affairs were notorious, sat next to Benchley. She complained that she could not think what to write about herself. The humorist suggested: "At last she sleeps alone."

3 (Benchley had himself admitted to the hospital to escape an engagement.)

"The doctor who examined him was the kind that interprets a hangnail as the early symptom of something obscure and hideous. 'Lucky for you this case fell into my hands,' he told Benchley. 'I don't want to alarm you, but all we can do is prescribe in a general way and watch the effects of the treatment, although we don't know precisely what they'll be. Now, these pills —'

"Next day the patient was moaning feebly. 'Those pills!' he managed to gasp. 'Doctor, they must have been — you don't suppose —' The frightened doctor whipped back the sheets. Benchley had glued pillow feathers from his shoulder blades to his knees."

4 Leaving the Algonquin after a particularly alcoholic session, Benchley found himself face to face with a uniformed man whom he took to be the doorman. "Would you get me a taxi, my good man?" he requested. The other drew himself up proudly. "See here, I happen to be a rear admiral in the United States Navy," he snapped. "Perfectly all right," said Benchley, "just get me a battleship then."

5 Caught in a rain shower one afternoon, Benchley arrived home soaking wet. "George," he called to his servant, "get me out of this wet suit and into a dry martini."

6 Benchley was attending the Broadway premiere of a play during which a telephone

rang on an otherwise deserted stage. "I think that's for me," remarked Benchley, and he rose and left the theater.

7 Benchley and Dorothy Parker were visiting a speakeasy when a man showed them what he said was an indestructible watch. They tested this by hitting it against the table top, then throwing it on the floor and stamping on it. The owner picked it up, put it to his ear, and said in incredulous dismay, "It's stopped."

"Maybe you wound it too tight," said Benchley and Mrs. Parker in chorus.

8 Attending the premiere of *The Squall* in 1926, Benchley was exasperated by the play's use of pidgin English. He whispered to his wife that if he heard one more word of it he was going to leave. At that moment a gypsy girl on stage prostrated herself at the feet of another character and announced, "Me Nubi. Nubi good girl. Me stay." Benchley rose to his feet and said, "Me Bobby. Bobby bad boy. Me go." And he went.

9 The office Benchley shared with Dorothy Parker in the Metropolitan Opera House building was so tiny that Benchley observed of it, "One cubic foot less of space and it would have constituted adultery."

10 Someone asked whether Benchley knew the playwright Robert Sherwood, distinguished for his great height — he was six feet seven inches tall. Benchley hopped onto a chair and raised his hand to a level just below the ceiling. "Sure," he said, "I've known Bob Sherwood since he was *this* high."

11 Benchley was stuck on a piece one day, unable even to get started. To clear his head he took a walk, then returned to his room and typed out the word "The." Back out he went, joining a friendly poker game and having a few drinks. He returned to his work in better humor but still could make no headway. Sitting at his typewriter, he stared at the page for a moment, then typed out, "hell with it" to complete the sentence, and left for the day.

12 Benchley died of a cerebral hemorrhage in New York City on November 21, 1945. His widow and son Nathaniel took the urn in which his ashes were kept to Nantucket for burial, but when they opened it, the urn was, oddly, completely empty. Mrs. Benchley was quiet for a moment, then began to smile. "You know," she told her son, "I can hear him laughing now."

BEN-GURION, David (1886–1973), *Israeli socialist statesman, born in Poland. When the new Jewish state of Israel was established in 1948, Ben-Gurion became its first prime minister (1948–53) and was prime minister again from 1955 to 1963.*

1 Members of the Israeli cabinet did not hesitate to register their disapproval when Ben-Gurion addressed Parliament wearing neither jacket nor tie. Parrying their protests, the prime minister claimed to have Winston Churchill's permission for his unconventional state of dress. "On my last visit to London," he explained, "I wanted to take off my jacket and tie. Churchill stopped me. 'Mr. Prime Minister,' he said, 'you can only do that in Jerusalem.'"

BENNETT, [Enoch] Arnold (1867–1931), *British writer and theater critic.*

1 In his review of Arnold Bennett's *The Old Wives' Tale,* the critic Frank Harris complained that the famous public execution scene was obviously written by someone who had never witnessed such an event. He accused Bennett of having a warped imagination and proceeded to write his own version of the scene. This was so appalling and so ex-

plicit that Bennett wrote to Harris saying that if Harris's description had been published before *The Old Wives' Tale* had been written, he would have gladly utilized it in the book. He wound up by admitting that he had never actually seen an execution.

"Neither have I," wrote back Harris.

2 Bennett usually took great pleasure in getting detail perfect in his fiction. He used to boast that Darius Clayhanger's death in the Clayhanger series could not be bettered: "I took infinite pains over it. All the time my father was dying I was at the bedside making copious notes."

3 Bennett had a serious speech impediment. Once while being presented at court, he saw the Duke of York, later George VI, moving in his direction. The duke also had a speech impediment.

"Great Scott," Bennett confided to a neighbor, "if he s-s-speaks to me I'll p-p-probably spend my last days in the Tower of London."

4 Irascible and nervous, Bennett was intensely wary of approaches by strangers. One day in London a luckless passerby asked Bennett to tell him the quickest way to Putney Bridge. "There are e-e-eight million people in London," erupted Bennett. "Why the devil can't you ask somebody else?"

5 At a literary luncheon one day, Bennett was autographing copies of his latest book. One young man had arrived clutching three copies of the first edition, but was too embarrassed to ask the author to sign all three at once. Having received his first autograph, he returned to the end of the line, hoping that Bennett would not recognize him when his turn came again. The author signed the second book without comment, and the young man patiently repeated the procedure. Presented with the third copy, however, Bennett paused for a moment. Then he penned on the flyleaf: "To ———, who is fast becoming an old friend."

⁓

BENNETT, James Gordon (1841–1918), *US newspaper owner and eccentric who launched the Paris edition of the* New York Herald.

1 During World War I, whenever news was lacking, Bennett filled in the empty space with "Deleted by French censor."

2 Since Bennett and William Randolph Hearst were never on the best of terms, it did not come as welcome news to the former that Hearst was trying to buy Bennett's paper, the ailing *Herald*. When Hearst tried to find out what it would cost, Bennett cabled him: "Price of Herald three cents daily. Five cents Sunday. Bennett."

3 Bennett's primary goal was to spend all his money. On one occasion he gave a tip of $14,000 to the guard on the Train Bleu between Paris and Monte Carlo. The guard stepped off the train, resigned his job, and opened a restaurant.

4 Night after night Bennett would return to the same restaurant in Monte Carlo because of the perfect way it prepared a mutton chop. One evening someone else was occupying his favorite table. He ordered the owner to sell him the restaurant and purchased it for $40,000. Bennett then asked the diners at his table to leave, even though they were only halfway through their meal. When Bennett had finished his meal of mutton chops, he left a very large tip: he gave the restaurant back to the owner.

⁓

BENTON, Thomas Hart (1782–1858), *US senator from Missouri for thirty years* (1821–51).

1 When Benton's house in Washington was destroyed by fire, he was summoned from Con-

gress to view the ruin. He gazed at it for a while, then said, "It makes dying easier. There's so much less to leave."

2 Benton had never been on good terms with Senator Henry S. Foote of Mississippi. Foote once threatened to write "a little book in which Mr. Benton would figure very largely." Benton was unperturbed. "Tell Foote," he replied, "that I will write a very large book in which he shall not figure at all."

BERG, Moe (1902–72), *US baseball player.*

1 Unusual in a player, Berg had an extensive higher education, including a doctorate and degrees from Princeton and the Sorbonne. A linguist, he also served as a spy during World War II. But once a White Sox teammate who saw him strike out twice with the bases loaded approached him and said, "Moe, I don't care how many of them college degrees you got. They ain't learned you to hit that curveball any better than me."

BERIA, Lavrenti Pavlovich (1899–1953), *feared head of the Russian secret police.*

1 Stalin's death is reputed to have been caused by a seizure suffered during a fit of rage brought on by an argument with Kliment Voroshilov during a Presidium meeting. Livid with fury, Stalin leaped from his seat, only to crash to the floor unconscious. While other members of the Presidium stared at the apparently dead figure, Beria jumped up and danced around the body shouting, "We're free at last! Free at last!" Stalin's daughter forced her way into the room and fell on her knees by her father. At this point Stalin stirred and opened one eye. Beria at once dropped down beside him, seized his hand, and covered it with kisses.

BERNADOTTE, Jean Baptiste Jules (c. 1763–1844), *French general who became King Charles XIV John of Sweden (1818–44).*

1 During the days of the Terror, Bernadotte fought in the French revolutionary army. Later, when king of Sweden, he fell ill and to the consternation of the attending physician, steadfastly refused to be bled. As his condition grew worse, the doctor begged the king to allow him to bleed him. At last the king capitulated. "You must swear," he said, "that you will never reveal to anyone what you have seen." The doctor swore, picked up his lancet, and rolled back the patient's sleeve. On the king's upper arm was a tattoo: the red Phrygian cap and under it the words: "Death to all kings."

BERNARD, Tristan (1866–1947), *French dramatist and novelist.*

1 A young playwright sent Bernard a play of his to read and sometime later asked Bernard for suggestions for a title. Bernard, who had not read the manuscript, thought for a few seconds, then asked: "Are there any trumpets in your play?"

"No," said the young dramatist, rather puzzled.

"Or any drums?"

"No."

"Well, then, why not call it *Without Drums or Trumpets?*"

2 One afternoon, during a rather unsettled phase in his first marriage, Bernard was found by a friend gazing despondently into a shop window in the pouring rain. Having ascertained that Bernard had no specific reason for being there, his friend offered to take him for a meal, or at least a drink. The dejected writer declined both invitations. "Surely

you're not going to stand out here in the rain!" exclaimed his friend. "Why don't you go home?"

"I don't dare," replied Bernard. "My wife's lover is there." His friend was about to voice some expression of sympathy when Bernard continued, ". . . and he's a goddam bore!"

3 A friend saw Tristan Bernard on the promenade at Deauville wearing a jaunty new yachting cap. When he remarked on it, Bernard replied that he had just bought it with his winnings from the previous night's play at the casino. The friend congratulated him. "Ah," said Bernard, "but what I lost would have bought me the yacht."

4 Tristan Bernard strongly disliked female journalists. One was seated next to him at a press luncheon and said, "Forget that I am a woman; treat me as you would a male colleague." Bernard steadily ignored her existence throughout the meal. At the end, he tapped her on the shoulder and said, *"Allons pisser."*

5 Bernard's frankness often went to extremes. One evening, he had been invited to a dinner party at a house renowned for its excellent cuisine. An hour after the appointed time, Bernard still had not arrived, and his hostess, anxious that the meal should not be ruined, telephoned him to ask what had happened. "I'm so sorry," said Bernard, "but I'm not coming."

"Not coming?"

"No," replied Bernard. "I'm not hungry."

6 Bernard was about to start off in a fiacre one day when the horse either took fright or had some sort of insane seizure. It reared, kicked, pawed the air with its front hoofs, then fell onto its knees and eventually flopped over, supine, on the ground. Climbing down from the fiacre, Bernard quietly asked the coachman, "Is that all the tricks he knows?"

7 Bernard hated the effort of writing. His apparently spontaneous output was, in fact, a grim, plodding labor, which he would postpone whenever he could. If anyone suggested coming to see him, he would say, "Please do. And preferably in the morning. That's when I work."

"A notorious tiepin was once flaunted by Barney Barnato, the cockney 'card' who sold the Kimberley tip to Cecil Rhodes for a bucket of the sparklers. After he had retired to Park Lane, this man with a heart of pure diamond became a famous giver of gifts and a well-known wag. Once, when he was bidden out on the town by some friends, the invitation arrived too late for him to go home and dress, so on his way to dinner Mr. Barnato popped into an outfitter on the Charing Cross Road and bought a pair of paste studs and a paste tiepin of splendiferous vulgarity. Over dinner, as the champagne flowed and the Whitstable oysters slipped smoothly down the throats of one and all, the Diamond King's fellow roisterers were unable to take their eyes off the beacon of light glittering on his shirt front.

" 'By Jove, that's a cracker — good old Kimberley!' one of them finally exclaimed.

"Barnato waved his Romeo y Julieta expansively. 'Anyone who wants it — all he has to do is pay for the wine tonight,' he said.

"They almost knocked the wine steward over in their rush to pick up the tab; and only when copious Krug for six had been duly paid for did Barnato reveal that the tiepin, together with the studs, had cost him ninepence."

— David Frost and Michael Deakin,
David Frost's Book of Millionaires, Multimillionaires, and Really Rich People

---

BERNERS, Gerald Tyrwhitt-Wilson, 14th Baron (1883–1950), *British musician and artist.*

1 "One of his acquaintances was in the impertinent habit of saying to him, 'I have been sticking up for you.' He repeated this once

too often, and Lord Berners replied, 'Yes, and I have been sticking up for you. Someone said you aren't fit to live with pigs, and I said that you are.'"

2 "A pompous woman of his acquaintance, complaining that the head waiter of a restaurant had not shown her and her husband immediately to a table, said, 'We had to tell him who we were.' Gerald, interested, inquired, 'And who were you?'"

3 Lord Berners was lunching with guests one day when his butler came in with a large placard. "The gentleman outside says would you be good enough to sign this, my lord," he said. Lord Berners read the message on the placard, "An appeal to God that we may have Peace in our Time," and shook his head. "It wouldn't be any use," he replied. "He won't know who I am — probably has never heard of me."

4 (Ballet dancer Robert Helpmann had been invited to take tea with the eccentric Lord Berners.)

"Helpmann was shown into the drawing room of the peer's mansion near Oxford and found him with an elegant silver tea service and a horse. Lord Berners greeted Helpmann, asked whether he took cream and sugar, and fed buttered scones to the horse. No explanation was offered, and after the animal had been told it had eaten enough, it was led out through the french window. Much later, Helpmann asked about the horse's presence.

"'I'm very nervous,' Lord Berners explained. 'When people see the horse, they become as nervous as I am, so that after a while I get over it. Then we can have a normal conversation.'"

5 At his estate in England, where he kept white doves dyed many colors, Lord Berners built them a tower and posted the following sign on its door: "Members of the Public Committing Suicide From This Tower Do So At Their Own Risk."

BERNHARDT, Sarah (1844–1923), *French actress, famous for her interpretation of great tragic roles, her beautiful voice, and her striking personality.*

1 Bernhardt's debut in the title role of Racine's *Iphigénie* was unimpressive. The scrawny figure of the seventeen-year-old girl was not flattered by the classical Greek dress that she wore, and at the beginning she was plainly suffering from stagefright. At one point in the drama Iphigénie stretches out her arms imploringly to Achilles. As she did this a voice from the balcony called out, "Careful, monsieur, or you'll impale yourself on her toothpicks!"

2 When Bernhardt was twenty-two, she persuaded Félix Duquesnel, the owner of the Odéon, to give her a contract. His partner, Charles-Marie de Chilly, demurred, as he had no wish to gamble on the continuing success of a young actress who already had a reputation for a difficult temperament. "If I were alone in this, I wouldn't give you a contract," he told Sarah. "If you were alone in this, monsieur, I wouldn't sign," was the retort.

3 Sarah Bernhardt was playing Cleopatra in Shakespeare's *Antony and Cleopatra* (one of her most celebrated emotional roles) to a packed theater in Victorian London. She stabbed the messenger who brought her the news of Antony's marriage to Octavia, stormed hysterically, smashed some of the props, and finally, as the curtain fell, flung herself to the floor in a fury of despair. As the rapturous applause died away, a lady's voice was heard to remark, "How different, how very different, from the home life of our own dear queen!"

4 A friend, watching Bernhardt making up for the part of Cleopatra, was intrigued to see her painting the palms of her hands a terracotta red. "No one in the audience will possibly see that," objected the friend. "Maybe not," replied the actress, "but if I catch sight of my hands, then they will be the hands of Cleopatra."

5 The actress Madge Kendal, though an admirer, once complained that Bernhardt always acted in roles requiring such displays of passion that Mrs. Kendal felt she could not take her daughter to see her. Bernhardt replied, "But, madame, you should remember that were it not for passion, you would have no daughter to bring."

6 Clergymen across the United States, in fact, denounced Sarah Bernhardt from their pulpits as the "whore of Babylon," thereby ensuring massive attendance at her performances. The Episcopalian bishop of Chicago having delivered a particularly effective piece of publicity, Bernhardt arranged for her agent to send him a note and a bank draft. "Your Excellency," the note read, "I am accustomed, when I bring an attraction to your town, to spend $400 on advertising. As you have done half the advertising for me, I herewith enclose $200 for your parish."

7 It was such common knowledge that Sarah Bernhardt, celebrated for her almost skeletal thinness, was given to wild exaggeration that Dumas *fils* was driven to comment, "You know, she's such a liar, she may even be fat!"

8 In 1915, as the result of an accident while Sarah Bernhardt was playing the title role in Victorien Sardou's drama *La Tosca*, one of her legs had to be amputated. While she was convalescing, the manager of the Pan-American Exposition at San Francisco asked permission to exhibit her leg, offering a fee of $100,000. Sarah cabled two words in reply: "Which leg?"

9 An admirer of a certain young English performer was discussing her acting with Sarah Bernhardt, who was not at all convinced of the young woman's talent. "But surely," said the man, "you will at least admit that she has some wonderful moments."

"Maybe, but also some terrible half-hours," countered Sarah.

10 Sarah Bernhardt was so idolized by her colleagues in the Paris theater that the callboy would notify her of the first-act curtain with the words: "Madame, it will be eight o'clock when it suits you."

11 Shortly after World War I, Lucien Guitry was asked to play opposite Bernhardt in a charity performance. The great actress was by now in her seventies, her former beauty had vanished, and she walked on a wooden leg. The magical quality of her voice, however, and her ability to deliver even the most ordinary lines with emotion still shone through. At the first rehearsal of the scene, Bernhardt read to the end of her first long speech and waited for Guitry's reply. Hearing no response, she looked up from her script to find him overcome, tears running down his cheeks.

12 In her later years, Sarah Bernhardt lived high up in a Paris apartment block. An old admirer arrived at her door one day, gasping for breath after the long climb. When he had recovered his strength a little, he inquired, "Madame, why do you live so high up?" "My dear friend," replied the actress, "it is the only way I can still make the hearts of men beat faster."

BERNOULLI, Jacques (1654–1705), *Swiss mathematician.*

1 "[Bernoulli] had a mystical strain which . . . cropped out once in an interesting way toward the end of his life. There is a certain spiral (the logarithmic or equiangular) which

is reproduced in a similar spiral after each of many geometrical transformations. [Bernoulli] was fascinated by this recurrence of the spiral, several of whose properties he discovered, and directed that a spiral be engraved on his tombstone with the inscription *Eadem mutata resurgo* (Though changed I shall arise the same)."

BERNSTEIN, Henri (1876–1953), *French dramatist.*

1 Shortly before his death Bernstein visited Hollywood. He was unimpressed. "Genius and geniuses every way I turn!" he lamented. "If only there were some talent!"

BERNSTEIN, Leonard (1918–1990), *US conductor, composer, and pianist.*

1 Bernstein's father was criticized for not having given his talented son more encouragement when he was a child. "How was I to know he would grow up to be Leonard Bernstein?" he protested.

2 Arriving at an airport one day, Bernstein was asked by a photographer if he would mind posing for a picture astride a motorcycle. Bernstein objected. "I don't ride a motorcycle," he said. "It would be phony." The photographer tried to persuade him. He showed him the controls, explaining briefly how to operate them. "I'm sure you could ride it if you tried," he said encouragingly. Bernstein climbed onto the machine and, to the horror of his colleagues, shot off at top speed across the airfield. After a few other maneuvers he returned, grinning broadly. "Now you can take your picture," he announced. "I'm a motorcycle rider."

3 At an opera rehearsal that featured an especially difficult singer, Bernstein finally lost his temper. "I know it's the historical prerogative of the tenor to be stupid," he shouted, "but you, sir, have abused the privilege."

4 Talking with his fellow composer Ned Rorem one day, Bernstein said, "The trouble with you and me is that we want everyone in the world to personally love us, and of course that's impossible. You just don't *meet* everyone in the world."

"The perils of irony were never better illustrated than in the following example: Lord Justice Bowen, when acting as a Puisne Judge, had before him a burglar who, having entered a house by the top story, was captured below stairs in act of sampling the silver. The defence was more ingenuous than ingenious. The accused was alleged to be a person of eccentric habits, much addicted to perambulating on the roofs of adjacent houses, and occasionally dropping in 'permiscuous' through an open skylight. This naturally stirred the judge to caustic comment. Summing up, he is reported to have said:

"'If, gentlemen, you think it likely that the prisoner was merely indulging in an amiable fancy for midnight exercise on his neighbour's roof; if you think it was kindly consideration for that neighbour that led him to take off his boots and leave them behind him before descending into the house; and if you believe that it was the innocent curiosity of the connoisseur which brought him to the silver pantry and caused him to borrow the teapot, then, gentlemen, you will acquit the prisoner!'

"To Lord Bowen's dismay, the jury *did* instantly acquit the prisoner."

— DANIEL GEORGE,
A Book of Anecdotes

BERNSTEIN, Robert (1923–), *US book publisher.*

1 As a quite young man, Robert Bernstein had a job at New York's radio station WNEW. Albert Leventhal, head of sales of the publishing house of Simon and Schuster, liked

the looks of the tall, red-headed, engaging Bernstein and enticed him into publishing. Bernstein turned out to be a phenomenon of energy. Once Leventhal, happening to enter the office at the early hour of 7:30 AM, found his protégé already busy at work. Bernstein looked up at his boss and said: "I'm ambitious. What's your excuse for being here at this unearthly hour?"

BERRA, Lawrence ["Yogi"] (1925–), *US baseball player who is most famous for his verbal confusions.*

1 His minor-league batting coach once told Berra to concentrate better on the pitches he was facing. But doing so led to more strikeouts for Berra, who, after one disastrous inning during which he struck out in three swings, said, "You can't think and hit at the same time."

2 Taken to a famous restaurant of which he had never heard, Yogi looked around the packed place and observed, "No wonder nobody comes here — it's too crowded."

3 Yogi Berra read only the sports pages, so he was clearly at a loss when introduced to novelist Ernest Hemingway in a restaurant. Someone asked Berra if he had ever heard of the famous author. "I don't think so," Berra admitted. "What paper does he write for?"

4 On "Yogi Berra Day" in St. Louis, his home town, Berra opened his acceptance speech by saying, "I want to thank all the people who made this night necessary."

5 Berra once received a $25 check for a radio interview with sportscaster Jack Buck. Berra glanced at the check, which was made out to "Bearer," and promptly complained: "How the hell long have you known me, Jack? How could you spell my name like that?"

6 Having ordered a pizza, Berra was asked whether he would like it cut into four or eight pieces. "Better make it four," said Yogi. "I don't think I can eat eight."

7 Said to have gotten his nickname because he sat cross-legged like a yogi from India — or so said his boyhood chums, after seeing a movie set in that country — Berra was once told by New York mayor John Lindsay that he looked cool in his new summer suit. "Thanks," replied Berra, "you don't look so hot yourself."

8 It is said that when he emerged from the movie theater after seeing *Dr. Zhivago* and was asked his opinion of the film, he replied, "It sure was cold in Russia in those days."

9 Another *Dr. Zhivago* story has Berra coming home early after a game had been rained out and asking his wife where she had been that afternoon. Told she had taken their son to see *Dr. Zhivago,* Berra reportedly asked, "What the hell's wrong with him now?"

10 One day Berra participated in an interview with Bryant Gumbel, during which he was asked to do some free association: Gumbel would mention some names, and Berra would say the first thing that he thought of in response. After going over the format a few times, they were ready to begin. Gumbel said, "Mickey Mantle." "What about him?' responded Berra.

11 He loved to read comic books in the dugout, a habit that made him the target of much teasing. But Berra had a good rejoinder to his teammates: "If that's so silly, how come every time I put one down, somebody else picks it up?"

12 When Phil Rizzuto complimented him on his beautiful new house in Montclair, New Jersey, Berra demurred: "It's nothing but rooms."

13 In the early 1980s Berra was a coach with the Houston Astros. When he got into a hot tub after a game, he yelped. A trainer asked if the water was too hot. "I don't know," said Berra. "How hot is it supposed to be?"

14 When he was first named manager of the New York Yankees in 1964, someone asked him if he really felt qualified to do the job. "You observe a lot by watching" was his response.

15 Berra once arrived ten minutes late for a meeting with Joe Garagiola, a lapse that left Garagiola unhappy. After being rebuked, Berra pleaded, "But this is the earliest I've ever been late!"

16 Driving with his wife to the Baseball Hall of Fame in Cooperstown, New York, Berra realized that they were not only very late but hopelessly lost. When his wife complained, Yogi told her, "That's all right. We're making good time, though."

17 Commenting on a season when baseball teams were not drawing the attendance they hoped for, Berra said to baseball commissioner Bud Selig, "If the people don't want to come out to the park, how are you gonna stop them?"

18 Berra's malapropisms and verbal stumblings have become legend, of course. He is now more famous for his stumbles in interviews than for his prowess on the baseball diamond. In response to those who made fun of his gaffes, he once said, "I really didn't say everything I said."

———— ◇ ————

BETTY, William Henry West (1791–1874), *British actor.*

1 After Betty's triumph, the English stage was beset by a multitude of juvenile imitators. Dorothea Jordan, the actress who was mistress of the Duke of Clarence (later William IV), surveying the throng of would-be Bettys, exclaimed, "Oh, for the days of King Herod!"

———— ◇ ————

BEUNO, Saint (d. c. 640), *abbot of Clynnog (North Wales).*

1 When the chapel in which the saint's bones were believed to be interred was being renovated, it was necessary to open the tomb itself. This offered an opportunity to discover more about the relics. An anthropologist was called in to inspect the skeleton. He pointed out that its pelvis contained the bones of a fetus. The man in charge of the renovation was unsurprised. "Saint Beuno was a very remarkable man," he observed.

———— ◇ ————

BIALIK, Chaim Nachman (1873–1934), *Jewish poet, born in the Ukraine.*

1 (A few days before Bialik's death, the newspapers were full of speculation that he would be awarded the Nobel Prize for Literature.)

"When the prize was awarded to another writer, Bialik was asked for his reaction. 'I'm very glad I didn't win the prize,' he said. 'Now everybody's my friend and feels sorry for me. My, my how angry they are on my behalf! "Now isn't that a scandal," they say. "Imagine such a thing — Bialik, the great poet Bialik, doesn't get the Nobel Prize! And — tsk! tsk! — just look who they gave it to! To X, that so-and-so! Why, he can't even hold a candle to Bialik!"

"'On the other hand, what if I had been awarded the Nobel Prize? Then, I'm sure, some of the very same people who are now so indignant on my account would have said, "Nu, nu, what's so wonderful about getting the Nobel Prize? Why, even that poet Bialik got one!" ' "

---◦ᴖ◦---

BING, Sir Rudolf (1902–97), *Austrian-born opera administrator best known for his years as general manager of New York's Metropolitan Opera.*

1 At one of the early Glyndebourne seasons, Bing engaged the Italian singer Salvatore Baccaloni. Artistically the engagement was a success, but Baccaloni could be very temperamental. The problems were exacerbated by the fact that he could speak only Italian while Bing spoke none at all. Baccaloni would storm into Bing's office and deliver a flood of Italian, to which Bing would listen uncomprehendingly. When he seemed to have finished what he had to say, Bing would solemnly hand him a £5 note. This always seemed to appease Baccaloni.

2 When Bing arrived in the United States in November 1949 to take up his appointment at the Metropolitan Opera, he was interviewed on board ship before it docked. The reporter began, "I am supposed to ask tactless questions." Bing replied, "And I am supposed to give evasive answers."

3 (Birgit Nilsson had a magnificent success in *Tristan und Isolde* in New York. A few days later, Tristan, sung by Ramon Vinay, fell ill, and each of the two possible substitutes was similarly sick. It was too late by then to change the program.)
   "I consulted with Miss Nilsson and then spoke with my three tenors again. None of them felt up to an entire *Tristan;* could each of them take an act? They agreed. When the house lights went down, before the music began, I came onto the stage, and was greeted by a great moan from all corners of the house — the general manager appears only to make the most important announcements,

and everyone thought he knew that this announcement had to be: Miss Nilsson has canceled.

"So I began by saying, 'Ladies and gentlemen, Miss Nilsson is very well,' which brought a sigh of relief from almost four thousand people. Then I went on: 'However, we are less fortunate with our Tristan. The Metropolitan has three distinguished Tristans available, but all three are sick. In order not to disappoint you, these gallant gentlemen, against their doctors' orders, have agreed to do one act each.' There was laughter in the house. I added, 'Fortunately, the work has only three acts.' "

4 Bing disliked the negotiations with the trade unions at the Metropolitan Opera because of the hysteria and sense of confrontation they generated. At one session with representatives of the stagehands, he leaned across the table toward the trade union's lawyer and said, "I'm awfully sorry, I didn't get that. Would you mind screaming it again?"

5 Bing was mugged one day while walking his dog in Central Park, losing his money and his watch. Although the watch was worth only about $25, its loss particularly grieved Bing since it was a British Army watch, a souvenir of his time as a fire warden in Britain during World War II. This incident found its way into the newspapers. Next day at the opera house he was severely rebuked by soprano Zinka Milanov. "The general manager of the Metropolitan Opera does not carry a watch worth only twenty-five dollars," she said sternly.

6 In Sir Rudolf Bing's *5000 Nights at the Opera* there is a photograph of the author sitting all alone in the old Metropolitan Opera House, a solitary figure in a sea of empty seats. On seeing this picture his brother commented, "No wonder you have a deficit."

7 When Bing engaged Maria Callas to sing the Queen of the Night in *The Magic Flute,* the star expressed mild surprise at the fee he offered her: "It doesn't make sense for you to pay me such a big fee for such a small part."

"I have a solution," said Bing, "reduce your fee."

8 When Bing canceled Maria Callas's contract with the Metropolitan Opera, in 1958, he engaged Leonie Rysanek to sing Lady Macbeth in Verdi's opera. He was fearful, however, that the audience, resenting the absence of Callas, would give Rysanek a hostile reception. He therefore hired a claqueur to shout "*Brava,* Callas," as Rysanek made her first entrance. As he had guessed, the Met audience rallied to the stand-in, and the performance was a great success.

9 A flu epidemic hit the cast of the New York Met, so Bing pinned up a list of precautions to prevent further spread of the infection. The last item on the list read: "Confine your kissing to the irresistible."

———cₙ⊃———

BION (2d century BC), *Greek philosopher.*

1 Bion undertook a sea voyage on a vessel manned by a particularly dissolute and wicked crew. A storm blew up and the sailors began to pray loudly to the gods for deliverance. Bion advised them to keep quiet: "Rather let them *not* know where you are."

———cₙ⊃———

BISMARCK, Otto Eduard Leopold, Prince von (1815–98), *German statesman; first chancellor of the German Empire (1871–90).*

1 Bismarck's career in the Prussian civil service was unsuccessful and brief. He fell in love, overstayed his leave, got into debt, and eventually tendered his resignation. He was then twenty-four years old. Five years later he tried to make a fresh start in the civil service, but resigned in less than a month, saying, "I have never been able to put up with superiors."

2 The Seven Weeks' War between Prussia and Austria in 1866 was almost entirely engineered by Bismarck, who wished to establish Prussia's position as leader of the German states instead of Austria. Sanctioning the advance of the divisions under General Manteuffel's command across the River Elbe into Austrian territory, Bismarck telegraphed the general: "Treat them as fellow countrymen, homicidally if necessary."

3 During the Franco-Prussian War of 1870 a German prince complained to Bismarck that the Iron Cross was being too freely awarded to the undeserving. Bismarck replied that unfortunately this was unavoidable; a certain number of persons would have to be decorated for reasons of protocol or out of mere politeness. He added, "After all, Your Highness, you and I have it too."

4 At a ball in St. Petersburg Bismarck entertained his attractive partner with the usual pleasant flatteries. But she would have none of it, exclaiming, "One can't believe a word you diplomats say."

"What do you mean?" said Bismarck.

"Well, when a diplomat says, 'Yes,' he means 'perhaps.' When he says 'perhaps,' he means 'no.' And if he should say 'no' — well, he's no diplomat."

To which Bismarck replied, "Madam, you are quite right, it's part of our profession, I fear. But with you ladies the exact opposite is the case."

"How so?"

"When she says 'no,' she means 'perhaps.' When she says 'perhaps,' she means 'yes.' And if she says 'yes' — well, she's no lady."

5 Bismarck, a stickler for formality, was once seated at dinner next to a young, ebullient

American lady. At first she addressed him as "Your Highness." With the next course he became "Mr. Chancellor" and with the third course "My dear Mr. Bismarck." As the plates were changed once more, he smiled and said amiably, "My first name is Otto."

6 He had been conversing for rather a long time with the English ambassador when the latter posed the question: "How do you handle insistent visitors who take up so much of your valuable time?" Bismarck answered, "Oh, I have an infallible method. My servant appears and informs me that my wife has something urgent to tell me." At that moment there was a knock at the door and the servant entered with a message from his wife.

7 In 1878 Disraeli and Bismarck were among those representing their countries at the Berlin Conference. As part of the Berlin settlement Britain managed to win Cyprus from Turkey. Bismarck seemed very pleased on Disraeli's behalf and told him, "You have done a wise thing. That is progress. It will be popular. A nation likes progress." Describing this encounter later to Queen Victoria, Disraeli observed of Bismarck, "His idea of progress was evidently seizing something."

8 Bismarck developed cancer, and his wife, Johanna, brought in a new, young doctor to attend him. At their first meeting the chancellor told him brusquely, "I don't like questions." "Then get a veterinarian," replied the doctor. "They don't question their patients."

—— ✿ ——

BLACKWELL, Alexander (d. 1747), *British adventurer.*

1 Sentenced to be decapitated, Blackwell came to the block and laid his head on the wrong side. The executioner pointed out his mistake. Blackwell moved around to the correct side, observing that he was sorry for the mis-

take, but this was the first time that he had been beheaded.

—— ✿ ——

BLAKE, Eubie [James Hubert Blake] (1883–1983), *US jazz pianist and composer.*

1 Asked why he played so many of his compositions in complicated sharp or flat keys, Eubie replied, "Down South where I come from, you don't go round hittin' too many white keys."

2 On Sunday, February 13, 1983, the London *Observer* carried in its feature "Sayings of the Week" a quotation from centenarian Eubie, who had smoked since he was six and refused to drink water. "If I'd known I was going to live this long, I'd have taken better care of myself," he was reported as saying.

—— ✿ ——

BLAKE, William (1757–1827), *British artist, poet, and mystic.*

1 Blake and his wife, Catherine, were once sitting naked in their garden, reciting to each other passages from *Paradise Lost*. Blake was not at all embarrassed when a visitor called on them. "Come in!" he cried. "It's only Adam and Eve, you know."

2 When Blake was fourteen years old, his father planned to apprentice him to the engraver William Ryland. He took the boy to visit Ryland's studio and the arrangement seemed acceptable to both parties, when young Blake suddenly took a violent dislike to his future master. The only justification he could make to his father was: "I do not like the man's face. He looks as if he will live to be hanged." Ryland was then a famous and respected figure, so the boy's objection seemed totally irrational, but his father was

obliged to forgo his original intention and apprentice William to the comparatively unknown engraver James Basire.

Many years later Ryland became bankrupt after the failure of his business and in his desperation committed a forgery. His crime was discovered and he was hanged.

3 From childhood Blake had seen visions. One of the earliest stories recounted of him was that he told his parents he had seen a tree full of angels. This angered his father, who thought the boy was willfully telling lies. In later years Blake habitually talked about the supernatural subjects of his pictures as being actually present in his studio when he was drawing them. A visitor once surprised him hard at work on a picture of an invisible sitter. He looked and drew, drew and looked, apparently intent on capturing a likeness. "Do not disturb me, I have one sitting to me," he said. "But there's no one here," exclaimed the visitor. "But I see him, sir," replied Blake haughtily. "There he is — his name is Lot — you may read of him in the Scriptures. He is sitting for his portrait."

BLECH, Leo (1871–1958), *German composer and conductor.*

1 At a rehearsal of the orchestra of the Berlin State Opera Company, one of the players could not follow Blech's beat. "You're new here?" asked Blech. "Yes, I started only yesterday," replied the player. "Well, your difficulty is understandable," said Blech. "Let's work at it till we get it right." He spent two hours working with the performer, then said, "Now it sounds right and tomorrow at the premiere you'll be perfect." The player replied, "But I won't be here tomorrow. I'm only here to help out with the rehearsals."

BLESSINGTON, Marguerite, Countess of (1789–1849), *British author and society leader.*

1 In the late 1830s, between his first and second abortive attempts to regain the French throne, the future Emperor Napoleon III frequented Lady Blessington's salon. But when she arrived in Paris, pursued by scandal and debts, Napoleon, then returned from exile and president of the Republic, felt it would be an embarrassment to recognize her. After waiting in vain for an invitation from her former protégé, Lady Blessington managed to accost him at a reception. *"Ah, Miladi Blessington!"* said Napoleon distantly. *"Restez-vous longtemps à France?"* (Are you staying in France for some time?) Lady Blessington curtsied. *"Et vous?"* (And you?) she inquired sweetly.

BLOMBERG, Ron (1948–), *US baseball player.*

1 Blomberg, who played for the Yankees, was the first designated hitter in major-league baseball, a position that has remained controversial to this day. Blomberg himself said of his role, "I've been a DH all my life — Designated Hebrew."

BLUME, Judy (1938–), *US writer of realistic stories for and about young teenagers.*

1 Judy Blume was once accosted by a woman who had been so upset by two pages about wet dreams in Ms. Blume's novel *Then Again Maybe I Won't* that she had torn them out of her son's copy. "What if they had been about a girl's menstruation?" inquired the author. "Would you still have torn the pages out?"

"Oh, no, that's normal," said the mother.

BLUMENTHAL, Oskar (1852–1917), *German playwright, journalist, and critic.*

1 Blumenthal and his friend critic Ludwig Sternaux were discussing a play that had opened the previous night. "I'm amazed the audience didn't hiss it," observed Sternaux. "Well, you can't yawn and hiss at the same time," said Blumenthal.

——— ✧ ———

BOGART, Humphrey (1899–1959), *US film star.*

1 Taking Verita Peterson, his hairdresser and mistress, to Romanoff's restaurant for the first time, Bogart introduced her to Mike Romanoff as Petée Gonzales, a Mexican actress who spoke very little English. Somewhat surprised, Verita played along with the joke, talking in mock Spanish to Bogart and in very broken English to Romanoff. As they left, she complained to Bogart that she would now have to take on this persona every time she went to Romanoff's. Bogart said he had a solution. When they returned to Romanoff's a few days later, "Good evening, Señorita Gonzales!" cried the proprietor. A look of horror passed across Bogart's face. "What the hell's the matter with you, Mike?" he growled. "You getting senile or something? This is my executive secretary, Verita Peterson. Christ! Can't you tell one broad from another? This is really *embarrassing!*"

——— ✧ ———

BOGDANOVICH, Peter (1939–), *US film director.*

1 For his film version of Larry McMurtry's novel *The Last Picture Show* director Bogdanovich cast Cloris Leachman as a lead and predicted that she would win an Academy Award. When Leachman asked him how he could be sure, Bogdanovich answered that any actress who played that role would get an Award. For the rest of the filming, after every shot, Leachman would turn to him, saying, "Okay? An Oscar?"

——— ✧ ———

BOHR, Niels Henrik David (1885–1962), *Danish physicist who was awarded the Nobel Prize in 1922.*

1 A visitor to Niels Bohr's country cottage, noticing a horseshoe hanging on the wall, teased the eminent scientist about this ancient superstition. "Can it be that you, of all people, believe it will bring you luck?"

"Of course not," replied Bohr, "but I understand it brings you luck whether you believe or not."

——— ✧ ———

BOILEAU (-Despréaux], Nicolas (1636–1711), *French satirist and critic.*

1 Boileau once introduced an impoverished poet to a prospective patron with the words: "I present to you a person who will give you immortality; but you must give him something to live on in the meantime."

2 Louis XIV showed Boileau some poems he had written, and asked his opinion of them. The great poet was also an accomplished courtier: "Sire, nothing is impossible for Your Majesty. Your Majesty has set out to write bad verses and has succeeded."

——— ✧ ———

BOLEYN, Anne (1507–36), *second queen consort of Henry VIII, mother of Elizabeth I.*

1 Henry, desperate for a male heir, decided that Anne was no better as a "broodmare" than Catherine of Aragon had been. He therefore had Anne accused of infidelity with five men, one of them her own brother. She and all her supposed lovers were convicted of treason and condemned to death. For Anne's execu-

tion the services of the executioner of Calais were engaged. He used a sword for the beheading, according to French practice, instead of the ax used by English executioners. Anne refused to be blindfolded and the executioner found her so disarming that he persuaded someone to attract her attention so that he could steal up silently behind her to carry out the death penalty.

2 Anne did not repine at her fate and cheerfully acknowledged the boon that Henry granted her in allowing her to be decapitated by a sword instead of an ax. "The king has been very good to me," she said. "He promoted me from a simple maid to be a marchioness. Then he raised me to be a queen. Now he will raise me to be a martyr."

BOLINGBROKE, Henry St. John, Viscount (1678–1751), *British orator and statesman.*

1 Bolingbroke's marital infidelities were a source of considerable scandal. Voltaire reports that when Bolingbroke took office, a courtesan remarked to her friends, "Seven thousand guineas a year, my girls, and all for us!"

BOLT, Tommy (1919–), *US golfer known for his graceful swing and terrible temper.*

1 Anecdotes of Tommy Bolt's quirky temperament still light up darkened clubhouses. Once, after lipping out six straight putts, he shook his fist at the heavens and shouted, "Why don't You come on down and fight like a man!"

2 Another time, trying to enliven a clinic, he asked his fourteen-year-old son to "show the nice folks what I taught you." The son obediently hurled a nine-iron into the blue sky.

BONNER, John (1920–), *US biologist.*

1 Bonner's specialty is the slime-mold *Distyostelium,* discovered in 1935 by Kenneth Raper. It may contain as many as 40,000 amoebae which under certain circumstances form themselves into a sausage-shaped slug, crawl about, and exhibit other remarkable talents. Bonner was once explaining his work to two Russian university rectors. They betrayed no sign of interest until he wrote on the blackboard the words "social amoebae." At this they at once perked up, delighted with the idea that even one-celled animals could form collectives. Apparently a slime-mold too may be used to justify Karl Marx.

BOONE, Daniel (1734–1820), *US pioneer.*

1 The American artist Chester Harding, painting Daniel Boone's portrait, asked the old frontiersman, then in his eighties, if he had ever been lost. Boone replied, "No, I can't say I was ever lost, but I was bewildered once for three days."

BOOTH, Junius Brutus (1796–1852), *US Shakespearean actor, father of John Wilkes Booth.*

1 A young actor playing a minor role with Booth in *Richard III* inadvertently made his entry from the wrong side of the stage. After the scene he apologized abjectly to the great actor, expecting to be given a royal dressing down. "Young man, it makes no difference to me," said Booth kindly. "Only come on; I'll find you."

2 (Booth's profile was marred by a broken nose.)
   "You're such a wonderful actor, Mr. Booth," gushed a female admirer one day, "but to be perfectly frank with you, I can't get over your nose."

"There's no wonder, madam," replied Booth. "The bridge is gone."

3 Booth was famous for his eccentricities, many of them doubtless a consequence of his wholehearted addiction to the bottle. Once, it is said, when playing Othello, he prolonged his death scene for quite some time. Finally terminating it, he got up and asked the audience, "How did you like *that?*"

4 In later life Booth's addiction to rum made him a problem to theater managers, though his vast experience often enabled him to perform when a lesser man would have been incapacitated. One story tells how the aged actor, putting the last touches to his makeup, staggered from his dressing room at curtain time, inquiring, "Where's the stage, and what's the play?"

———— ∾ ————

BORGES, Jorge Luis (1899–1986), *Argentinian poet and short-story writer.*

1 During the Perón era, Borges's refusal to hang a portrait of the dictator in his office led to his expulsion from the presidency of the Society of Writers. One night an ardent Peronista called on his mother and threatened to kill her and her son. "Well," she replied, "if you want to kill my son, it's very easy. He leaves home for his office every morning at eight; all you have to do is wait for him. As for myself, señor, I have turned eighty, and I advise you to hurry up if you want to kill me, because I might very well die on you beforehand."

———— ∾ ————

BORGHESE, Princess Marie Pauline (1780–1825), *sister of Napoleon I.*

1 A lady expressed surprise that the princess should have posed naked while Antonio Canova modeled his famous statue of her as Venus Victrix. "But," said Princess Pauline demurely, "there was a fire in the room."

———— ∾ ————

BORROMEO, Saint Charles (1538–84), *Italian archbishop who was later canonized.*

1 Cardinal Borromeo was once rebuked for the great pleasure he took in exercising his skill at chess. "What would you do if you were busy playing and the world came to an end?"
   "Continue playing," replied Borromeo.

———— ∾ ————

BOSQUET, Pierre François Joseph (1810–61), *French soldier.*

1 The British cavalry attack on the Russian guns at Balaclava, the charge of the Light Brigade, was carried out with parade-ground steadiness of pace and discipline, despite the murderous fire from all sides. Watching the doomed advance of his allies, General Bosquet was moved to the memorable utterance, *"C'est magnifique, mais ce n'est pas la guerre"* (It's magnificent, but it's not war).

———— ∾ ————

BOSSUET, Jacques Bénigne (1627–1704), *French Roman Catholic bishop and preacher.*

1 Bossuet was a precocious child, already preaching with skill and grace at the age of eight. Vincent Voiture was present at one of the boy's sermons, which on this occasion went on until midnight. The poet was heard to remark on leaving, "I have never heard a sermon so early — or so late."

2 Shortly after Louis XIV had collated Bossuet to the bishopric of Meaux, the king asked some of the citizens whether they were pleased with their new bishop. They replied, rather uncertainly, that they liked him pretty well. "'Pretty well!' Why, what's wrong with him?" asked the monarch. "To tell Your

Majesty the truth, we should have preferred a bishop who had completed his education. Whenever we call to see him we are told that he is at his studies."

BOSWELL, James (1740–95), *Scottish lawyer, author of the famous biography of Dr. Samuel Johnson.*

1 After their first meeting in the back of Tom Davies's bookshop, Boswell assiduously cultivated the acquaintance of Johnson. Johnson enjoyed his company and conversation, and decided to grant him friendship. "Give me your hand," he said. "I have taken a liking to you." Some of Johnson's other friends were less impressed by the new arrival in their circle. "Who is this Scotch cur at Johnson's heels?" asked someone. "He is not a cur," replied Oliver Goldsmith, "he is a burr. Tom Davies flung him at Johnson in sport, and he has the faculty of sticking."

2 During their Scottish tour, Boswell took Johnson to his home in Edinburgh, and Johnson there met Boswell's wife. Mrs. Boswell did not much care for Johnson, although she received him civilly enough. She was scornful of her husband's devotion to this ungainly, lumbering, ill-complexioned man whose manners displeased her. "I have seen many a bear led by a man, but I never before saw a man led by a bear."

BOTTICELLI, Sandro [Alessandro di Mariano Filipepi] (c. 1445–1510), *Italian painter.*

1 A weaver set up his eight-loom workshop next to Botticelli's house. The noise drove the painter nearly mad, but his protests remained unheeded. Botticelli hoisted a vast rock onto the roof of his own house, balancing it in such a way that it overhung the neighbor's roof and threatened to come crashing down upon it at the slightest disturbance. The weaver, eyeing this novel sword of Damocles, came to terms.

BOTTOMLEY, Horatio William (1860–1933), *British journalist and financier.*

1 Horatio Bottomley called to see Lord Cholmondley. "I wish to speak to Lord Cholmondley," he said to the butler. "Lord *Chum*-ley, sir," said the butler, correcting his pronunciation. "Oh, all right," said Bottomley. "Tell him that Mr. Bumley would like to see him."

2 An acquaintance found Bottomley in prison stitching mail bags. "Ah, Bottomley," he said, "sewing?"
"No," Bottomley replied, "reaping."

BOUHOURS, Dominique (1628–1702), *French Jesuit grammarian.*

1 On his deathbed Bouhours announced, "I am about to — or I am going to — die; either expression is used."

BOULANGER, Georges Ernest Jean Marie (1837–91), *French general.*

1 When Boulanger's mistress, Marguerite de Bonnemain, died of tuberculosis in 1891, the heartbroken general had her tombstone inscribed with the simple message: "Marguerite. See you soon." He returned to the grave two and a half months later to fulfill his promise. Drawing his pistol, he held it to his head and pulled the trigger. (Another version of the story says he stabbed himself.)
Boulanger's tombstone, erected beside that of his beloved Marguerite, was inscribed as requested: "Georges. Could I really live two and a half months without you?"

———— ❧ ————

BOULANGER, Nadia [Juliette] (1887–1979), *French composer, conductor, and teacher of composition.*

1 (US composer Roy Harris once described how Nadia Boulanger selected her pupils.)

"Nadia Boulanger told me this way she has of deciding who to accept for students. Those who have no talent, and those who have no money; these are not acceptable. There are those who have talent but no money. These she accepts. Those who have little talent but much money she also accepts. But those who have much talent and much money she says she never gets."

———— ❧ ————

BOULT, Sir Adrian (1889–1983), *British conductor.*

1 At the BBC Boult frequently found himself in conflict with the administrators over their parsimony and their ignorance of music. On one occasion, when Boult was planning to perform a piece scored for two piccolo players, he was told that the budget allowed for only one. He protested, but the administrators were adamant. He took his complaint to the head of the department, Charles Carpendale. Carpendale was torn between his wish to oblige Boult and his dislike of overruling his subordinates. Having pondered for a minute, he proposed a compromise: "How about using one piccolo, and placing it closer to the microphone?"

———— ❧ ————

BOWEN, Elizabeth (1899–1973), *British writer, born in Ireland.*

1 (Howard Moss described a dinner party given by Elizabeth Bowen one hot summer evening.)

"She had been detained and had to shop at the last minute. When I arrived, the drinks were impeccable, everything went swimmingly. After drinks, you went into another room for a stand-up dinner. And that was rather unbelievable. Elizabeth was notoriously nearsighted and she must have gone into some delicatessen and ordered a buffet. There was a salad that looked as if it had been briefly shampooed. The lettuce leaves had suspicious ruffles. I was standing next to her, and she tasted the salad first. She turned to me and said, 'You know, this just doesn't have that *je ne sais quoi.*'"

———— ❧ ————

BOWEN, Louise de Koven (1859–1953), *US suffragist.*

1 Mrs. Bowen, originally from Chicago, spent her summers from 1882 to the 1940s in fashionable Bar Harbor. Though very rich and well connected, she met with some difficulty in establishing friendly relations with the tonier eastern seaboard families. Once, driving her pony cart down a country road, she was dumped out of it when the pony shied and upset the cart. Two Philadelphia ladies came along in their carriages, noticed the dazed figure lying on the road, stopped, got out, and examined Mrs. Bowen briefly. Said one to the other, "Who *is* she?" Her companion shook her head. They took no further action. Finally a native islander happened to come along and sent for help.

———— ❧ ————

BOWLES, Paul (1910–99), *US expatriate novelist, short-story writer, and composer.*

1 A German journalist came to Tangier, where Bowles had long made his home, to conduct a television interview. During the course of the session Bowles became more and more irritated, observing that each of her questions

began with the word "Why?" When he told her that, in his opinion, questions beginning with "why" couldn't be answered intelligently or truthfully, her next question was, "Why not?"

———— ◈ ————

BOWLES, William Lisle (1762–1850), *British clergyman.*

1 When Bowles gave a Bible to Bessie Moore, wife of the poet Tom Moore, she asked him to inscribe it. She was startled to see that the absentminded divine had written: "from the Author."

2 Bowles's usual daily ride took him along a road through a turnpike gate at which he had to pay twopence to the tollkeeper to allow his horse through. One day he passed that way on foot and tendered the twopence as usual. The gatekeeper, puzzled, asked:
"What's this for, sir?"
"For my horse, of course!"
"But, sir, you have no horse!"
"Oh, am I walking?" exclaimed Bowles.

———— ◈ ————

BOWRA, C. Maurice (1898–1971), *British classical scholar.*

1 Parsons' Pleasure, the stretch of river at Oxford set aside for men's bathing, is out of bounds for women. One day Bowra and a group of other dons were bathing there *au naturel* when a boatload of women, disregarding the "Men Only" signs, rowed into their midst. The dons on the bank hurriedly grabbed towels and fashioned impromptu loincloths — with the exception of Bowra, who threw his towel over his face. When the intruders had gone, Bowra explained, "I believe, gentlemen, that I am recognized by my face."

———— ◈ ————

BRADFORD, John (?1510–55), *British Protestant martyr.*

1 Bradford was in the habit of saying, when he saw criminals going to their execution, "But for the grace of God, there goes John Bradford."

———— ◈ ————

BRADLEY, Henry (1845–1923), *British philologist.*

1 Bradley was very helpful to other scholars, supplying them with advice and material to such an extent that he once remarked that some of his best work was in other men's books. When another scholar attacked the competence of a certain philologist, Bradley put up some defense for the victim. "Well," said the detractor, "I suppose the man can't be an absolute fool as he did supply that brilliant reading in ———" naming a particular work. Bradley shifted uneasily in his chair: "To tell you the truth, I sent him that."

———— ◈ ————

BRADY, William A. (1863–1950), *US theatrical producer.*

1 "To keep up morale in my staff," Brady once recalled, "and to fool rival producers and theatrical reporters, I always instructed managers of my road companies to add three hundred dollars to their nightly reports of box-office receipts. The system worked fine until one of them wired, 'Only theatre in town burned to the ground this afternoon. No performance. Receipts $300.'"

———— ◈ ————

BRAHE, Tycho (1546–1601), *Danish astronomer.*

1 Brahe died in Prague of, well, politeness. The astronomer had neglected to relieve himself before a long banquet given by the Baron of

Rosenberg, and his good manners prevented him from excusing himself from the table during the endless meal. His bladder burst, and the resulting infection killed him not two weeks later.

———— ✺ ————

BRAHMS, Johannes (1833–97), *German composer.*

1 Brahms came from a humble background, and the financial welfare of his parents was an anxiety to him. As he made his way in music, he contributed to the upkeep of their home out of his increasing but still slender resources. Knowing that his father was rash in money matters, he provided against an unforeseen economic crisis in his own way, before leaving home. "If things go badly with you the best consolation is always in music," he advised his father. "Read carefully in my old *Saul* and you'll find what you want." His father found this advice rather puzzling. Nonetheless when difficulties arose he took down the score of *Saul* and opened it; there between the pages was a substantial supply of banknotes.

2 During the period in which Brahms was still considered advanced, the Boston Symphony Orchestra ventured to play one of his compositions. Some wag changed the exit sign to read: EXIT IN CASE OF BRAHMS.

3 As a celebrated composer, Brahms conducted his two piano concertos in Berlin and attended a dinner given for him. His host proposed a toast to "the most famous composer." Brahms, seeing what was coming, interposed hastily, "Quite right: here's to Mozart!" and clinked glasses all round.

4 Although Brahms could be agreeable and interesting, he could also be difficult, sarcastic, and rude. Even his friends were not immune to unprovoked verbal attacks. On one occasion he upset a gathering of friends with a se-

ries of offensive remarks, then rose to his feet and left the room, stopping briefly at the door to say, "If there is anyone here whom I have not insulted, I beg his pardon."

5 A great wine connoisseur invited Brahms to dinner and in his honor brought out some of his choicest bottles. "This is the Brahms of my cellar," he announced to the company as wine from a venerable bottle was poured into the composer's glass. Brahms scrutinized the wine closely, inhaled its bouquet, took a sip, and then put down his glass without comment. "How do you like it?" anxiously asked the host. "Better bring out your Beethoven," murmured Brahms.

6 A young musician complained bitterly to Brahms about delays in the publication of his first opus. Brahms counseled him to be patient. "You can afford not to be immortal for a few more weeks," he said.

7 Brahms and Johann Strauss the Younger, each of whom had great admiration for the other's work, once met in Vienna. Strauss handed Brahms his autograph book and asked if he would do him the honor of signing it. Opening the book at a blank page, Brahms transcribed the first few bars of *The Blue Danube* and wrote underneath, "Unfortunately not by Johannes Brahms."

8 Brahms, who enjoyed his food, was distressed when he became ill and his doctor prescribed a strict diet. "But this evening I am dining with Strauss and we shall have chicken paprika," he protested. "Out of the question," said the doctor. "Very well, then," said Brahms. "Please consider that I did not come to consult you until tomorrow."

9 Finding himself cornered by a group of rather talkative ladies, Brahms made several vain attempts to escape. Finally, in desperation he took out a large cigar and lit it. Engulfed in smoke, the ladies reproached the

composer for this lack of courtesy. "A gentleman doesn't smoke in the presence of ladies," they reminded him. Continuing to puff at his cigar, Brahms replied: "Ladies, where there are angels there must also be clouds."

10 In his old age Brahms announced to his friends that he was going to stop composing music and enjoy the time left to him. Several months went by without Brahms's writing a note. But there came the day when a new Brahms composition made its debut. "I thought you weren't going to write any more," a friend reminded him. "I wasn't," said the composer, "but after a few days away from it, I was so happy at the thought of no more writing that the music came to me without effort."

BRAITHWAITE, Dame [Florence] Lilian (1873–1948), *British actress who made her name in Noël Coward's play* **The Vortex.**

1 It was the opening night of *The Vortex* in Washington, D.C. At one of the most dramatic moments of the play, Miss Braithwaite had to snatch a box of drugs from Coward's hands and hurl them out of an open window. One of the stagehands, unfamiliar with the script, helpfully threw the box back into Miss Braithwaite's hands. The bewildered actress had no option but to throw the box again, this time with such force that it broke the edge off the window as it sailed through.

2 Drama critic James Agate, finding himself alone with Miss Braithwaite, made the controversial remark: "My dear lady, may I tell you something I have wanted to tell you for years: that you are the second most beautiful woman in the United Kingdom." Expecting the actress to ask the obvious question, Agate had prepared a suitable reply. Miss Braithwaite, however, did not take the bait.

"Thank you," she said. "I shall always cherish that, as coming from the second-best dramatic critic."

BRANCUSI, Constantin (1876–1957), *Rumanian sculptor.*

1 Brancusi moved to Paris in 1904. In 1906 Auguste Rodin invited him to work in his studio. Brancusi refused, remarking: "Nothing grows well in the shade of a big tree."

BRANDEIS, Louis Dembitz (1856–1941), *US Supreme Court justice.*

1 Brandeis was once criticized for taking a short vacation just before the start of an important trial. "I need the rest," explained Brandeis. "I find that I can do a year's work in eleven months, but I can't do it in twelve."

"Victor Biaka-Boda, who represented the Ivory Coast in the French Senate, set off on a tour of the hinterlands in January 1950 to let the people know where he stood on the issues, and to understand their concerns — one of which was apparently the food supply. His constituents ate him."

— JOHN TRAIN, *True Remarkable Occurrences*

BRANDT, Willy (1913–92), *German socialist chancellor (1969–74) who was awarded the Nobel Peace Prize in 1971.*

1 On a visit to Israel as mayor of West Berlin, Brandt was invited to view the great new Mann auditorium in Tel Aviv. Having expressed his appreciation of Israel's naming the concert hall for Thomas Mann, the German writer, Brandt was politely corrected by his host. The hall was actually named for a

certain Frederic Mann of Philadelphia. "What did he ever write?" exclaimed Brandt. "A check," came the reply.

⁓

BRAQUE, Georges (1882–1963), *French painter.*

1 The painter Roland Penrose, calling on Picasso, found that Braque and his wife were also visiting. "You know Penrose?" Picasso said to Braque as greetings were being exchanged. "Oh, yes," said Braque, "but I haven't seen him for about twenty years and at first sight I didn't recognize him; he's changed so little."

⁓

BRENDEL, Alfred (1931–), *Austrian pianist.*

1 Brendel gave a concert in Copenhagen in November 1981, a cold, damp time of year in that city. The audience coughed and sneezed a good deal, enough to make the pianist stop in the middle of a piece. Glaring from the stage, he said very quietly, "Ladies and gentlemen, I can hear you, but I doubt if you can hear me."

⁓

BRIAND, Aristide (1862–1932), *French socialist politician and prime minister.*

1 In September 1926 Briand arranged to meet the German statesman Gustav Stresemann, with whom he shared that year's Nobel Peace Prize. They met at a small village in the Jura where they could discuss postwar problems in privacy. After lunch the two statesmen wrangled amicably about the bill. "No, I'll pay for the lunch," said Briand. "You take care of the reparations."

2 Briand tended to be somewhat lazy. He once rebuked a Latin American diplomat who brought him a massive armful of documents

to study, "You don't suppose I've lost my incapacity to work, do you?"

⁓

BRIDGER, Jim (1804–81), *US frontiersman and fur trapper.*

1 A man dressing a serious wound that Bridger had received in the course of one of his numerous skirmishes with hostile Indians or wild animals expressed the fear that the wound would suppurate. Bridger told him not to worry: "In the mountains meat never spoils."

2 Bridger sold a yoke of cattle worth $125 to obtain a copy of the complete works of Shakespeare and then engaged a wagon boy at $40 a month to read the plays to him. In the middle of *Richard III,* Bridger gave up the business in disgust. "I won't listen anymore to the talk of a man who was mean enough to kill his mother."

⁓

BRILLAT-SAVARIN, Anthelme (1755–1826), *French writer and gastronome.*

1 A lady inquired whether he preferred Burgundy or claret. Brillat-Savarin replied, "That, madame, is a question that I take so much pleasure in investigating that I postpone from week to week the pronouncement of a verdict."

⁓

BRITTEN, Benjamin (1913–76), *British composer.*

1 In his early thirties Britten was once found walking unsteadily along a hotel corridor in Edinburgh. Asked what he was doing, Britten replied that he was trying to avoid the red in the hall carpet. "If I can get up and down the corridor without touching the lines, it will mean that I am a composer."

2 On a visit to Russia, Britten began discussing music with the great composer Dmitri Shostakovitch. When Shostakovitch asked Britten's opinion of Puccini, Britten said, "His operas are dreadful." "No," replied Shostakovitch, "he wrote marvelous operas but dreadful music."

———— ❧ ————

BRODIE, Sir Benjamin Collins (1783–1862), *British surgeon.*

1 Brodie, deeply immersed in the preparation of a paper, was dragged away from his work to attend a fashionable evening party. After drinking with the gentlemen there for a while, he went to the men's room. Intending then to make his escape, he tucked his hat under his arm, emerged, and walked past a number of arriving guests. The men all sniggered and the women tittered and turned their heads away. In the hall he was accosted by his host: "Good Lord, Brodie, is that a usual part of your attire?" Brodie looked, too. Instead of his hat, he had absentmindedly picked up the toilet-seat cover.

———— ❧ ————

BRODIE, Steve (fl. 1880s), *US saloonkeeper.*

1 In 1886 Steve Brodie jumped off the Brooklyn Bridge into the East River, a fall of some 135 feet, to win a $200 wager. The police arrested him for this suicidal leap, though at the time many people doubted whether Brodie had actually jumped; some people believed that he had just thrown a dummy off the bridge. Sometime later the father of the heavyweight boxer Jim Corbett met Brodie. "So you're the fellow who jumped over Brooklyn Bridge," he said. "I jumped *off* it," corrected Brodie. Old Mr. Corbett was disgusted: "I thought you jumped over it. Any damn fool could jump off it."

———— ❧ ————

BRODIE, William (d. 1788), *Scottish head of the Incorporation of Edinburgh Wrights and Masons.*

1 A respected figure in Edinburgh, Brodie was also a highly successful burglar. No suspicion fell upon him until an accomplice turned king's evidence. Brodie fled to Amsterdam but was apprehended, brought back to Edinburgh for trial, and condemned to death. He is credited with an invention that was first tested at his own execution — the drop. Before that time, the person to be hanged was simply pushed off a height; Brodie thought up the system of a trapdoor and lever that became standard wherever hanging was the means of legal execution. On the gallows the hapless inventor inspected the arrangements, pronounced them satisfactory, and was efficiently launched into eternity.

———— ❧ ————

BRONTË, Charlotte (1816–55), *British novelist and poet, author of* Jane Eyre.

1 During one of Charlotte Brontë's spells as a governess, a child whom she had scolded burst into penitent tears and ran to her crying, "I love you, I love you, Miss Brontë."

"Love the *governess,* my dear?" icily queried the mother, who was in the room.

2 In her first desperate rebellion against her role as a teacher Charlotte wrote in 1836 to the poet laureate Robert Southey, asking whether he thought she could earn her living as a writer. Southey wrote back: "Literature cannot be the business of a woman's life, and it ought not to be. The more she is engaged in her proper duties, the less leisure will she have for it, even as an accomplishment and recreation. To those duties you have not yet been called, and when you are you will be less eager for celebrity."

———— ❧ ————

BROOKFIELD, Charles Hallam Elton (1857–1913), *British actor.*

1 Chatting to Brookfield one day, a theatrical colleague sensed that the actor was looking at him rather oddly. "What's up?" he asked. "Is my tie wrong?"

"No," replied Brookfield, "but you have a little dried soap in your right ear."

"How filthy!" exclaimed his colleague.

"Oh, no," said Brookfield, "not filthy at all; a little ostentatious perhaps."

———— ∾ ————

BROOKS, Phillips (1835–93), *US Episcopal bishop, author of the hymn "O Little Town of Bethlehem."*

1 Recovering from a serious illness, Brooks refused to receive any visitors, even his closest friends. When the agnostic Robert Ingersoll called, however, the bishop did not turn him away. Ingersoll, conscious of the privilege, was curious to know the reason behind it. Said the bishop, "I feel confident of seeing my friends in the next world, but this may be my last chance of seeing you."

———— ∾ ————

BROUGHAM, Henry Peter, Baron Brougham and Vaux (1778–1868), *British lawyer and statesman; Lord Chancellor (1830–34).*

1 When Lord Brougham arrived at the theater for a performance of Handel's *Messiah*, Sydney Smith remarked, "Here comes counsel for the other side."

2 When Sydney Smith was living in London he saw Lord Brougham's one-horse carriage pass him in the street and noticed the splendid B surrounded by a coronet on the panel of the coach. "There goes a carriage with a B outside and a wasp within," he commented to a friend.

3 It distressed Lord Brougham to learn that his eldest son was having an affair with a young French actress. To bring the erring youth to his senses, his father wrote to him tersely: "If you do not quit her, I will stop your allowance." His son wrote back: "If you do not double it, I will marry her."

———— ∾ ————

BROUN, [Matthew] Heywood Campbell (1888–1939), *US journalist.*

1 Reviewing a play in 1917, Broun described the performance of actor Geoffrey Steyne as "the worst to be seen in the contemporary theater." Steyne immediately sued. While the case was pending Broun had occasion to review the actor's performance in another play. This time he wrote: "Mr. Steyne's performance was not up to his usual standard."

2 A large, shambling, awkward man, Broun was noted for the disarray of his dress. During World War I, serving as a correspondent, he resisted wearing an officer's cap with his uniform, preferring a fedora. His son recalls: "The dishevelment of that uniform, bought at the Galeries Lafayette department store, led one exasperated major at an inspection of correspondents to ask fretfully, 'Mr. Broun, have you fallen down?'"

———— ∾ ————

BROWN, Charles Brockden (1771–1810), *US author of Gothic novels.*

1 An English visitor found America's first professional author huddled in his dark and dingy room, writing at a cramped desk, and asked if he could not write better if he looked out over a view of Lake Geneva or some other bucolic setting. "Good pens, thick paper, and ink well diluted," replied Brown, "would facilitate my composition more than the broadest expanse of water, or mountains rising above the clouds."

BROWN, Gates (1939–), *US baseball player.*

1 Brown's talents as a ballplayer were discovered while he was at the Mansfield State Reformatory, in Ohio, where he had been sent for breaking and entering. The team coach wrote to various baseball teams alerting them to Brown's skills, and he soon found himself playing for the Detroit Tigers, helping them get to the 1968 World Series. Much later he returned to his high school to talk to the students. When the principal, in introducing him, said, "I'm sure some of our students would be interested to know — what did you take when you were in school?" Brown replied, "Overcoats, mostly."

2 Not long after Brown joined the team, the Tigers were considering another prospect, Ron LeFlore, who had been incarcerated for robbery. While trying out for them, LeFlore did well, but one player was quite upset at the idea of a convict joining the group. Asked the manager, "Where do you think you got Gates Brown from — kindergarten?"

BROWN, John Mason (1900–69), *US critic and lecturer.*

1 One of Brown's first important appearances as a lecturer was at the Metropolitan Museum of Art. He was pleased, but also rather nervous, and his nerves were not helped when he noticed by the light of the slide projector that someone in the room was mimicking his every gesture. At length he broke off, announcing with dignity that if anyone was not enjoying the lecture he was free to leave. Nobody did, and the mimicking continued. It was only after another ten minutes that Brown realized that the mimic was his own shadow.

2 At a party given by a collector of modern art, Brown paused to study a large sculpture by Jean Arp that was supposed to depict the female form. Peering through a large hole in the middle of the sculpture, he exclaimed, "Ah, a womb with a view!"

BROWNING, Elizabeth Barrett (1806–61), *British poet, wife of Robert Browning.*

1 During the early months of 1846, encouraged by Browning and in preparation for their elopement, Elizabeth Barrett began to rid herself of the habits acquired as an invalid, practicing standing without assistance and then walking where she had previously been carried. In January she reported to Browning a notable advance: "I put on a cloak and walked downstairs into the drawing room — walked, mind!" Her brother, who was in the room, was so startled by the unexpected sight that he exclaimed, "So glad to see you!" as if she were a stranger.

2 The love poems in *Sonnets from the Portuguese* were written for her husband, poet Robert Browning. Never intended to be more than a private declaration of love, they were published because, as he said, "I dared not keep to myself the finest Sonnets written in any language since Shakespeare's." They have nothing to do with Portugal; Browning's pet name for his dark-complectioned wife was "my little Portuguese."

BROWNING, Robert (1812–89), *British poet.*

1 Browning's *Sordello* was published in 1840. On the face of it the story is simple enough, the tale of an unknown heir to a dukedom in thirteenth-century Italy. But it is considerably complicated by Browning's interest in the development of the human soul and the motives that sway it toward a practical or

disinterested course of action. Tennyson is reported to have said that there were only two lines in it that he could understand, and both of them were lies: "Who will may hear Sordello's story told" and "Who would has heard Sordello's story told." Baffled readers resorted to the poet for an explanation. Members of the London Poetry Society asked Browning for an interpretation of a particularly obscure passage. Browning read it through twice, frowned, and then shrugged his shoulders. "When I wrote that, God and I knew what it meant, but now God alone knows."

2 Cornered by a bore at a party, Browning had to listen to a volley of questions concerning his work. Eventually the poet managed to escape. "But my dear fellow, this is too bad. I am monopolizing you," he exclaimed, and fled.

3 (During the months of suspense before his marriage to Elizabeth Barrett, Browning was one day seized with a whimsical notion of attempting divination while he was at work in his library.)

"'What will be the event of my love for Her?' he questioned the book that fell under his hand, opening it at a random passage. The volume, of all inauspicious ones, turned out to be Cerutti's Italian grammar. He hoped he might come upon a word like *conjunction* or at least a possessive pronoun. To his amazement his eyes lighted upon the sentence in an exercise for translation: 'If we love in the other world as we do in this, I shall love thee to eternity.'"

———cł๑———

BRUCE, James (1730–94), *British explorer.*

1 Someone once asked Bruce what musical instruments were used in Abyssinia. Bruce, unprepared for the question, hesitated before saying, "I think I only saw one lyre there."

George Selwyn whispered to his neighbor, "Yes, and there is one less since he left the country."

———cł๑———

BRUMMELL, George Bryan (1778–1840), *British society figure known as Beau Brummell, arbiter of fashion during the Regency period.*

1 A friend, seeing Beau Brummell limping, inquired the reason. He recounted the story of the injury, concluding, "And the worst of it is that it is my favorite leg."

2 Beau Brummell found the fashionable romantic raptures about scenery rather boring. An acquaintance, knowing he had recently visited the English Lake District, asked which of the lakes he had most admired. Beau Brummell summoned his valet. "Which of the lakes did I most admire?" he asked. "Windermere, sir," replied the valet. "Ah, yes, Windermere," said Beau Brummell to the inquirer.

3 Beau Brummell's quarrel with his former friend the prince regent shook fashionable society. Various versions of the row were current. Brummell himself said that the prince delivered the first cut; he was riding with a friend in the park in London when they met the regent, who spoke to the friend but ignored Brummell. When the regent moved on but was not yet quite out of earshot, Brummell asked loudly, "Who's your fat friend?"

4 After his quarrel with the prince regent, Beau Brummell found that many London hostesses who had previously been eager for his presence now excluded him from their guest lists. Among these was a certain Mrs. Thompson. Beau Brummell managed to discover that she had invited the regent to a party. Near the time that he might be expected to arrive, Beau Brummell sauntered into her house. In terror lest the regent encounter his enemy, the hostess bustled up to

eject the unwanted guest, telling him to leave at once as he had not been invited. "Not invited, ma'am? But surely there must be some mistake. I have a card." Brummell began to feel in all his pockets, very leisurely, while Mrs. Thompson was on tenterhooks in case the regent arrived. At length Beau Brummell found a card and handed it to her. "But this is from Mrs. Johnson," she exclaimed. Beau Brummell appeared deeply surprised and contrite. "From Mrs. Johnson? How very unfortunate, Mrs. John—er, Thompson, I mean. Johnson and Thompson, Thompson and Johnson, so very much the same kind of thing." He bowed low and made a dignified exit.

5 Someone commiserated with Beau Brummell for having a cold. He explained that he had caught it at an inn on the Brighton road: "My infidel valet put me in a room with a damp stranger."

6 Beau Brummell at one period had a whim to eat no vegetables. A lady asked him if he had ever in his life eaten any. "Yes, madam," replied the dandy, "I once ate a pea."

7 At Ascot a fashionable man-about-town complimented Brummell on his exquisite turnout. Brummell replied, "I cannot be elegant, since you have noticed me."

8 (An acquaintance asked Beau Brummell where he had dined the previous night.)

"Why, with a person of the name of R——. I believe he wishes me to notice him, hence the dinner; but to give him his due, he desired that I would make up the party myself, so I asked Alvanley, Mills, Pierrepoint, and a few others, and I assure you the affair turned out quite unique; there was every delicacy in and out of season; the Sillery was perfect, and not a wish remained ungratified; but, my dear fellow, conceive my astonishment when I tell you that Mr. R—— had the assurance to sit down and dine with us."

———— ✧ ————

BRUNET, George (1935–91), *US baseball player.*

1 The left-handed pitcher played for thirty different teams over his career, much of which was spent in the minor leagues. Eventually an American League team member, Brunet ended his career as a much older player in the Mexican League. Overweight and sloppy, he never wore a protective cup under his uniform. He admitted, "Getting out of the way of ground balls up the middle has cost me a few singles over the years."

———— ✧ ————

BRUNO, Giordano (1548–1600), *Italian philosopher, theologian, and astronomer.*

1 Denounced to the Venetian Inquisition in 1592, Bruno put up a plausible defense. However, the much more relentless Roman Inquisition demanded that he be handed over to them. Over the next seven years Bruno's trial progressed to its inevitable conclusion. On February 8, 1600, eight cardinals excommunicated him (yet again) and with customary hollow recommendation to mercy turned him over to the secular law. "Perhaps your fear in passing judgment is greater than mine in receiving it," commented the unrepentant ex-monk. On February 17 Bruno was led barefoot to the stake and burned alive — gagged to restrain him from uttering further heresies in his final agony.

———— ✧ ————

BRYAN, William Jennings (1860–1925), *US politician and perennial presidential candidate.*

1 Admiral Togo, whose brilliant tactics had destroyed the Russian fleet at the battle of the Sea of Japan, visited the United States shortly after the Russo-Japanese War. At a state din-

ner arranged in his honor Bryan was asked to propose the toast. A strict Prohibitionist, he absolutely refused to drink champagne, and it was feared that an embarrassing breakdown of protocol was about to occur. When Bryan rose to propose the toast he held up his glass, saying, "Admiral Togo has won a great victory on the water, and I will therefore toast him in water. When Admiral Togo wins a victory on champagne, I will toast him in champagne."

2 On a campaign Bryan was asked to speak to a crowd of people assembled in a field. As he climbed up onto the manure spreader that served as an impromptu dais, he remarked, "This is the first time I have ever spoken from a Republican platform."

3 In a burst of patriotism, J. P. Morgan announced, "America is good enough for me!"
"Whenever he doesn't like it, he can give it back to us," was William Jennings Bryan's comment.

BUCHANAN, James (1791–1868), *US politician, 15th President of the United States (1857–61).*

1 In 1845 President Polk appointed Buchanan secretary of state. Ex-President Andrew Jackson made a strong protest. "But you yourself appointed him minister to Russia in your first term," said Polk defensively. "Yes, I did," said Jackson. "It was as far as I could send him out of my sight, and where he could do the least harm. I would have sent him to the North Pole if we had kept a minister there."

2 On leaving the White House in March 1861, Buchanan said to the incoming President, Abraham Lincoln, "If you are as happy, my dear sir, on entering this house as I am in leaving it and returning home, you are the happiest man in this country."

BUCKINGHAM, George Villiers, 2d Duke of (1628–87), *British statesman.*

1 On a royal ceremonial occasion Charles II was being addressed by the full battery of his titles. When the master of ceremonies got to the epithet "Father of his people," Buckingham added, in an undertone, "or quite a lot of them." Even Charles could not overlook this *lèse-majesté,* and Buckingham was told to withdraw from the court for a while.

BUCKLAND, William (1784–1856), *British geologist and paleontologist.*

1 Professor Buckland had great gastronomic curiosity. John Ruskin, once his student, tells us (in *Praeterita*) that he "always regretted a day of unlucky engagement on which I missed a delicate toast of mice."
The professor, who disdained virtually nothing organic, once decided that a mole was the nastiest thing he had ever tasted. Later on he awarded the palm to blue-bottles. He was once shown the heart of a king of France, preserved in a snuff box. Said the professor, "I have eaten some strange things, but never the heart of a king." And swallowed it.

2 Buckland once gave a dinner party at which a delicious but unusual soup was served. He challenged his guests to name the chief ingredient, but none guessed correctly. They were subsequently horrified to learn that they were eating the remains of an alligator Buckland had dissected earlier in the day. Two or three were obliged to make a hasty exit from the room. "See what imagination is," said Buckland. "If I told them it was turtle, or terrapin, or bird's-nest soup, they would have pronounced it excellent, and their digestion would have been none the worse." One of the remaining guests ventured to ask if the

soup had really been made from the dissected alligator. "As good a calf's head as ever wore a coronet," answered Buckland with a smile.

BUCKLEY, William F[rank] (1925–), *US author, conservative Republican figure, and word lover.*

1 In 1965, Buckley stood as Conservative candidate for the office of mayor of New York City. The likelihood of victory being almost nonexistent, the campaign was not taken very seriously, even by Buckley himself. A reporter asked him what his first action would be if elected. "I'd demand a recount," replied Buckley.

2 Buckley once sent fellow author Norman Mailer a copy of his latest book. Mailer, disappointed to find that Buckley had not written any message on the flyleaf, promptly turned to the index to see if he had been mentioned. Alongside Mailer's name in the index was the handwritten greeting "Hi!"

BUDDHA, Gautama (563–483 BC), *Indian prince whose teachings formed the basis of Buddhism.*

1 After his enlightenment the Buddha decreed, as an act of personal humility, that no one was to make an image of him or to paint him. However, one nameless artist, seeing him sitting deep in contemplation on the banks of the Ganges at Benares, was so moved by his saintly demeanor that he could not resist attempting to portray the Buddha in some way. He reasoned that if he used as his model, not the Buddha himself, but his reflection in the rippling waters of the Ganges, he would be able to secure for posterity a portrait of the great man without defying the injunction. For this reason many representations of the youthful Buddha have

folds in their garments known as the water-ripple effect.

2 A man interrupted Buddha's preaching with a flood of abuse. Buddha waited until he had finished and then asked him, "If a man offered a gift to another but the gift was declined, to whom would the gift belong?"

"To the one who offered it," said the man.

"Then," said Buddha, "I decline to accept your abuse and request you to keep it for yourself."

The old Duc de Broglie, reminiscing in company about memorable letters he had received, recalled, "The one that gave me the greatest satisfaction was one I got from a very lovely lady. It consisted of only one word."

"And that was?" said one of the guests.

"Friday."

— W. SCHOLZ,
Das Buch das Lachens

BUDÉ, Guillaume (1467–1540), *French humanist scholar.*

1 Budé's servant came running to him one day to tell him that the house was on fire. "Tell your mistress," Budé replied, waving him away. "You know I leave all household matters in her hands."

BUDGE, J. Donald (1915–2000), *US tennis player.*

1 In 1937 Budge met Baron Gottfried von Cramm of Germany in the deciding match of the Davis Cup final at Wimbledon. Just as the game was due to begin, watched by Queen Mary, von Cramm was called to the telephone. "You can't keep Queen Mary waiting," said an official severely. "I can't keep der Fuehrer waiting," responded von Cramm. The caller was Adolf Hitler, order-

ing the baron to win for the honor of Germany.

---cłs---

BUFFALMACCO, Buonamico (?1262–?1340), *Italian painter.*

1 Buffalmacco once lived next door to a rich woolworker, whose wife worked throughout the night at her spinning wheel. The noise of the wheel frequently kept the painter awake. In desperation he devised a plan to remedy the nuisance. Having noticed a small hole in the communicating wall, directly above the neighbors' cooking pot, Buffalmacco hollowed out a cane, pushed it through the wall, and was thus able to add a large amount of salt to the woolworker's dinner every evening. After two or three inedible meals, the woolworker began to beat his wife for her carelessness, and her screams brought a number of their neighbors, including Buffalmacco, to their door. "This calls for a little reason," said the painter when he had heard his neighbor's case. "You complain that the pot is too much salted, but I marvel that this good woman can do anything well, considering that the whole night she sits up over that wheel of hers and has not an hour's sleep. Let her give up this all-night work and sleep her fill, so she will have her wits about her by day and will not fall into such blunders." The woolworker accepted Buffalmacco's advice, and from that time on the painter enjoyed an undisturbed night's rest.

---cłs---

BULL, John (?1563–1628), *British composer.*

1 "The queen's will being to know the music, her Grace was at that time at the virginals: whereupon, he, being in attendance, Master Bull did come by stealth to hear without, and by mischance did sprawl into the queen's majesty's presence, to the queen's great disturbance. She demanding incontient the wherefore of such presumption, Master Bull with great skill said that wheresoever majesty and music so well combined, no man might abase himself too deeply; whereupon the queen's majesty was mollified."

2 Hearing of a famous musician at St. Omer's, Dr. Bull, pretending to be a novice, visited him. The man showed Bull a song with forty parts, boasting that it was so complete and full that no one could add to it or improve it. Bull requested pen, ink, and ruled paper and then asked to be locked up in the cathedral music school for two or three hours. The musician locked Bull in as he desired. Before his return Bull had added another forty parts to the original song. The musician tried the music, examined it, then exclaimed that the hand that had added the extra forty parts must be either that of the devil or of Dr. Bull. Bull thereupon disclosed his identity and the St. Omer man fell at his feet in homage.

---cłs---

BULLER, Sir Redvers Henry (1839–1908), *British general.*

1 On one of the numerous occasions when Buller was forced to retreat by the Boers, he put the best face possible on the setback by saying that he had retreated without losing a man, a flag, or a cannon. "Or," added Whistler, when the story was told to him, "a minute."

---cłs---

BÜLOW, Hans Guido, Baron von (1830–94), *German conductor and pianist.*

1 The kaiser wearied of von Bülow's eccentricities and let fall a heavy hint: "If anyone doesn't care for the way things are in Germany, let him shake the dust from his shoes." At the end of von Bülow's last concert in Berlin, he laid down his baton, took out a

handkerchief, and elaborately dusted his shoes. And left next day for Egypt.

2 Invited to play for Napoleon III, von Bülow was annoyed to find that the emperor soon ceased to attend to the music and began talking animatedly to one of his guests. Von Bülow stopped playing. "When his majesty speaks," he said, "all must be silent."

3 A young composer asked von Bülow to listen to his latest composition, a piece that turned out to be notable mainly for the extent of its borrowings from other composers. "How do you like it?" asked the man when he had played it through. "I have always liked it," replied von Bülow.

4 Musicians could assure themselves of the approval of a certain music critic only by taking moderately priced lessons from him. "That's not too bad," observed von Bülow. "His fees are so low one might almost call him incorruptible."

BUNSEN, Robert Wilhelm (1811–99), *German chemist; the Bunsen burner is named for him.*

1 At the end of one of Bunsen's courses, a student of completely unfamiliar appearance presented his certificate to the professor for endorsement. "But, Herr Dingskirch," said Bunsen, glancing at the name on the card, "I've never seen you at any of my lectures."

"Quite so," replied the student. "You see, I always sit behind the pillar."

"What a lot of you sit there," remarked Bunsen, endorsing the certificate with a sigh of resignation.

BUÑUEL, Luis (1900–83), *Spanish film director.*

1 Buñuel was brought up as a Catholic by the Jesuits. When asked, in later life, if he had been deeply affected by his Jesuit education, he replied, "I am an atheist, thanks be to God."

BURKE, Edmund (1729–97), *British statesman, political philosopher, and writer.*

1 The barrister Arthur Murphy opposed Burke in the discussion during the early 1770s on the question of whether perpetual copyright could exist in literary property. Murphy argued the case of those who contested the booksellers' endeavor to establish such a principle. Discussing the question with Murphy, Burke observed, "But you must remember the booksellers deal in commodities they are not supposed to understand."

"True," said Murphy, "some of 'em do deal in morality."

2 David Hartley, son of the famous philosopher of the same name, was an exceptionally dull speaker. As member of Parliament for Hull, he regularly emptied the House of Commons when he rose to speak. On one occasion in 1783 his audience had dwindled from about three hundred to eighty, most of these half asleep. He seemed about to wind up his oration when he demanded that the clerk of the House read the text of the 1715 Riot Act to illustrate some point he had made. At this Burke leaped to his feet, shouting, "The Riot Act? The Riot Act? To what purpose? Don't you see that the mob is already quietly dispersed?"

3 Someone observed to Burke that the democratic faction in Parliament never seemed to hold together for any length of time. Burke replied, "Birds of prey are not gregarious."

4 Burke's celebrated nine-day speech made in 1794 at the trial of Warren Hastings, the former colonial administrator in India, on charges of corruption, was widely acclaimed as a masterpiece of eloquence. The greatest

tribute, however, came from Hastings himself. "For half an hour," he confessed, "I looked up at the orator in a reverie of wonder, and during that space I actually felt myself the most culpable man on earth."

5 Edward Thurlow was moved to the patriotic exclamation: "When I forget my king, may my God forget me!"

"And the best thing God can do for him," muttered Burke.

———— ∽ ————

BURNETT, Carol (1934–), *US actress.*

1 Climbing out of a cab one day, Miss Burnett inadvertently caught her coat in the door. As the driver continued on his way, unaware of the accident, the comedienne was obliged to run alongside the moving vehicle to avoid being pulled off her feet. A quick-thinking passerby, noticing her plight, hailed the cab and alerted the driver. Having released Miss Burnett's coat, the driver asked her anxiously, "Are you all right?" "Yes," she replied, still gasping for breath, "but how much more do I owe you?"

———— ∽ ————

BURNS, George (1896–1996), *US actor and radio comedian.*

1 Burns worked in radio for many years with his wife, Gracie Allen. After her death he visited her grave regularly. An interviewer jokingly asked him if he told her what had been going on. "Sure, why not?" was the reply. "I don't know whether she hears me, but I've nothing to lose and it gives me a chance to break in new material."

2 George Burns was lunching one day at a restaurant with his friend Jack Benny. Benny could not make up his mind about whether he should put butter on his bread. "I hate bread without butter," he sighed. On the other hand, his wife, Mary, had put him on a diet specifying no butter. What should he do? Perhaps he should ring up Mary? At this point George Burns cut across his deliberations with, "Please, Jack, just make this one decision yourself!" So Benny had the butter.

At the end of the meal when the bill was brought, Burns told the waiter to give it to Benny. "Why should I pay?" asked Benny. "If you don't, I'll tell Mary about the butter," said Burns.

3 On reaching the age of eighty-five, George Burns observed that this was a very comfortable stage of life: "I was always taught to respect my elders and I've now reached the age when I don't have anybody to respect."

4 Ed Sullivan happened to mention in his newspaper column one day that George Burns wore a toupee. Burns later reproached Sullivan for publicizing this embarrassing piece of information. "But, George," said Sullivan, "I didn't think you'd mind."

"If I didn't mind," retorted Burns, "why would I wear a toupee?"

———— ∽ ————

BURR, Aaron (1756–1836), *US politician and lawyer.*

1 Burr was inordinately proud of his reputation as a lady-killer. A friend asked him, shortly before his death, why he allowed a woman to saddle him with the paternity of a child when he knew he was not its father. Burr replied, "Sir, when a lady does me the honor to name me the father of her child, I trust I shall always be too gallant to show myself ungrateful for the favor."

2 Burr had had a tumultuous personal life. At the age of seventy-seven he married a wealthy ex-courtesan, Mrs. Jumel, whose fortune he quickly squandered before leaving her. At the age of eighty, still squabbling with his soon-to-be-ex-wife, he fell gravely ill. His

friend Dr. P. J. Van Pelt, who was at his bedside, asked him if he was prepared to accept salvation. Burr replied, "On that subject I am coy." A few minutes later, and two hours after his divorce was finalized, he died.

———— ✑ ————

BURTON, Richard (1925–84), *British stage and screen actor, married twice to actress Elizabeth Taylor.*

1 During the filming of *The Assassination of Trotsky,* Burton was playing a scene with French actor Alain Delon. Delon, as the nervous killer, was swinging an ice ax around; at one point the ax came dangerously close to Burton's head. "You'd better be careful how you handle that ax," cried Burton. "There are plenty of French actors around, but if you kill me, there goes one-sixth of all the Welsh actors in the world."

2 As a young actor Burton was famed for his Hamlet. At a theater in London, on the opening night of a run, he heard someone mumbling the lines along with him from the very first scene. The next time he was backstage he screamed, "Will someone throw that old codger who's doing my lines with me — OUT!" Burton couldn't see over the footlights, but a stagehand went to look and returned, saying, "Sorry, Mr. Burton, but it's the prime minister, Mr. Churchill."

———— ✑ ————

BURTON, Sir Richard (1821–90), *British scholar and explorer, translator of* **The Arabian Nights.**

1 In Boulogne after his return from Sind, Burton was attracted by a young woman called Louisa, cousin of his future wife, Isabel Arundell. Unsavory rumors about Burton's adventures in Sind had spread through the fashionable English colony in Boulogne, and Louisa's mother summoned the young man

to her presence, "because," she said, "I think it my duty to ask what your intentions are with regard to my daughter." Burton, who regarded his relationship with the lively young Louisa as little more than a pleasant flirtation, was amused and somewhat taken aback by the formality of the interview.

"Your duty, madam?"

"Yes, sir."

"Alas," sighed Burton. "Strictly dishonorable."

2 Isabel Arundell always wanted to marry Richard Burton, and her joy was boundless when at last he proposed to her. Their engagement somewhat prolonged by Burton's continued traveling, Isabel spent the time actively preparing for the marriage she so ardently desired. She learned to milk cows, groom horses, ride astride. She sought out a celebrated fencer and demanded he take her on as a pupil. "What for?" he asked. "So that I can defend Richard when he is attacked," said she.

———— ✑ ————

Anthony Burgess was taking a bath in a Leningrad hotel when the floor concierge yelled that she had a cable for him. "Put it under the door," he cried. "I can't!" she shouted. "It's on a tray."

— ANTHONY BURGESS, Preface, in
Modern Irish Short Stories,
ed. Ben Forkner

———— ✑ ————

BUSBY, Richard (1606–95), *British teacher.*

1 As Dr. Busby was showing King Charles II around his school, it was noticed that, contrary to etiquette, the headmaster kept his hat on in the royal presence. Busby excused himself in these words: "It would not do for my boys to suppose that there existed in the world any greater man than Dr. Busby."

2 Dr. Busby was very short. One day in a crowded London coffeehouse he was addressed by an Irish baronet of huge stature: "May I pass to my seat, O giant?"

"Certainly, O pygmy!" said the doctor, making way.

The bulky baronet started a clumsy apology: "My expression alluded to the size of your intellect."

"And my expression to the size of yours," retorted Busby.

———— ✧ ————

BUSCH, Fritz (1890–1951), *German-born Swiss orchestra conductor.*

1 One of the favorite stories at the Glyndebourne Festival Opera concerned Busch's very first orchestral rehearsal. He raised his baton and then quickly dropped his arms to his sides before anyone had played a note. Addressing the orchestra, he said in his thickly accented English, "Already is too loud."

———— ✧ ————

BUSH, Barbara (1925–), *wife of President George Bush (1989–93).*

1 Enormously popular with the public, Barbara Bush was known for her down-to-earth sense of humor and style. She often made fun of her appearance — her prematurely white hair, weight, and unfashionable clothing — which only helped her popularity. She once told a reporter, "There is a myth around I don't dress well. I dress very well — I just don't look so good."

2 On a foreign tour with her husband, then vice president, Mrs. Bush sat next to Japan's Emperor Hirohito at a luncheon in Tokyo. Commenting on her surroundings, she praised the architecture and decor of the Imperial Palace but wondered at its seeming newness. Was the former palace so old it crumbled? "No," replied the emperor stiffly, "I'm afraid that you bombed it."

3 During her commencement address at Wellesley College in 1990, she made headlines when she said, "Somewhere out in this audience may even be someone who will one day follow in my footsteps and preside over the White House as the President's spouse. I wish him well."

———— ✧ ————

BUSH, George (1924–), *US politician; 41st President of the United States (1989–93).*

1 Bush was often teased for his stiff, correct manner, when he served as a fairly bland vice president under the most personable of modern presidents, Ronald Reagan. He noted that it was very important for a vice president not to upstage his boss, and then said, "You don't know how hard it has been to keep my charisma in check these last few years."

2 The Bushes' pet springer spaniel, Millie, gave birth in the White House to a fine litter of puppies. The President was delighted to tell reporters, "They're sleeping on the *Washington Post* and the *New York Times.* It's the first time in history these papers have been used to prevent leaks."

3 Bush scandalized the world when, overly fatigued by travel and suffering from a flu, he threw up in the lap of his host, Prime Minister Kiichi Miyazawa, at a state dinner in Japan. Sometime later Bush invited the prime minister to attend the opening of the Bush Presidential Library, quipping, "This time the dinner's on me."

4 Bush loved to play golf, though his game was not much better than that of his predecessor, Gerald Ford. After having returned to private life for a year or so, he noted, "It's amaz-

ing how many people beat you in golf once you're no longer President."

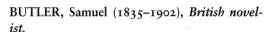

BUTLER, Benjamin Franklin (1818–93), *US general and politician.*

1 As commander of the Union forces occupying New Orleans in 1862, Butler made himself thoroughly unpopular. After some women had abused Northern soldiers he issued the notorious proclamation that if any woman insulted or showed contempt for "any officer or soldier of the United States, she shall be regarded and shall be held liable to be treated as a woman of the town plying her avocation." This provoked furious outcry; Butler was dubbed "Beast" Butler, and the enraged ladies all turned their backs on him whenever they met him. He remarked, "These women know which end of them looks best."

2 A Confederate soldier, brought before Butler to take the oath of allegiance at the end of the Civil War, impudently remarked, "We gave you hell at Chickamauga, General!" The furious Butler warned him that if he did not take the oath immediately he would be shot. With some reluctance, the rebel duly took the oath. Then he looked Butler in the eye and said, "General, I suppose I am a good Yankee and citizen of the United States now?" The general replied benignly, "I hope so." "Well, General, the rebels did give *us* hell at Chickamauga, didn't they?"

BUTLER, Henry Montagu (1833–1918), *British academic.*

1 Dr. Butler used to invite freshmen at Trinity to have breakfast with him. Finding a nervous group awaiting him one wintry day in the breakfast room, he glanced toward the window and remarked, "Well, we have a little sun this morning." At this the shyest of the young men responded with "I hope Mrs. Butler is all right."

BUTLER, Samuel (1835–1902), *British novelist.*

1 (Butler and his companion Henry Festing Jones visited the Palazzo Reale in Palermo. They were cheated by the custode at the entrance to the Capella Palatina, who gave Butler a bad lira in his change and refused to exchange it despite their remonstrances.)

"When we came out we had recovered a little, and the custode . . . returned our umbrellas to us with an obsequiousness capable of but one interpretation. 'I shall not give him anything,' said Butler severely to me. 'Oh yes, I will though,' he added, and his eyes twinkled as he fumbled in his pocket. Then, with a very fair approach to Sicilian politeness, he handed the bad lira back to the old gentleman. The custode's face changed and changed again like a field of corn on a breezy morning. In spite of his archiepiscopal appearance he would have been contented with a few soldi; seeing a whole lira he beamed with delight; then, detecting its badness, his countenance fell and he began to object; almost immediately he identified it as his own coin and was on the point of bursting with rage, but suddenly realizing that he could have nothing to say, he laughed heartily, shook hands with both of us, and apologized for not being able to leave his post as he would so much have liked to drink a glass of wine with us.

"'There, now we have made another friend for life,' said Butler as he drove away."

2 As a result of his studies in Homer, Butler became convinced that the *Odyssey* was writ-

ten by a woman. In 1897 he published *The Authoress of the Odyssey*. Shortly after this work appeared, Anne Thackeray Ritchie, Thackeray's intelligent and witty daughter, asked him what he was working on now, and was told a book of Shakespeare's sonnets. "Oh, Mr. Butler," she said playfully, "do you know my theory about the sonnets? They were written by Anne Hathaway." Butler never understood that she was mocking him and told the story everywhere against her: "Poor lady, that was a silly thing to say!"

3 (An admirer asked Samuel Butler to write her "a rule of life." Butler thought that her own common sense ought to be a better guide than any precepts he might deliver, and wrote back in a lighthearted tone.)

"'Get as many nice people about you as you can, more particularly Jones and myself. Snub snobs. Stick to the Ten Commandments — they never forbid swearing — and really I do not know what else there is!' She said she did not find my letter as comforting as she hoped it would be."

4 "The first time that Dr. Creighton asked me to come down to Peterborough before he became Bishop of London, I was a little doubtful whether or not to go. As usual I consulted Alfred [his servant and confidant], who said: 'Let me have a look at his letter, sir.'"

"I gave him the letter, and he said: 'I see, sir, there is a crumb of tobacco in it; I think you may go.' I went and enjoyed myself very much."

5 (Samuel Butler's notebooks reveal him as not the most comforting of deathbed companions.)

"'Promise me solemnly,' I said to her as she lay on what I believed to be her deathbed, 'if you find in the world beyond the grave that you can communicate with me — that there is some way in which you can make me aware of your continued exis-

tence — promise me solemnly that you will never, never avail yourself of it.' She recovered and never, never forgave me."

———⌘———

BYNG, John (1704–57), *British admiral, court-martialed and shot for failing to relieve the island of Minorca, then under French attack (1756). He was the subject of Voltaire's witticism that in England "il est bon de tuer de temps en temps un amiral pour encourager les autres" (it is thought desirable to kill an admiral from time to time to encourage the others).*

1 When Byng came to stand before the firing squad, some officers suggested that his face be concealed with a handkerchief lest the sight of him breed reluctance in his execution. Byng replied, "If it will frighten *them*, let it be done; *they* will not frighten me."

———⌘———

BYRD, William (1674–1744), *US tobacco planter, diarist, and colonial official.*

1 (The entry for July 30, 1710, in *The Secret Diary of William Byrd of Westover 1709–1712*, reads:)

"In the afternoon my wife and I had a little quarrel which I reconciled with a flourish. Then she read a sermon in Dr. Tillotson to me. It is to be observed that the flourish was performed on the billiard table."

———⌘———

BYRON, George Gordon, Lord (1788–1824), *British Romantic poet.*

1 While he and Robert Peel were schoolmates at Harrow, one day Byron saw Peel being beaten unmercifully by a senior boy. Having no hope of fighting because of his clubfoot, Byron nevertheless approached the bully and bravely asked how many stripes he was intending to inflict upon his poor friend.

"What's that to you?" thundered the bully. "Because, if you please," replied Byron, trembling with rage and fear, "I would take half."

2 (Byron was to meet Thomas Moore at the house of Samuel Rogers, although he did not know his host. Rogers describes the evening.)

"When we sat down to dinner I asked Byron if he would take soup? 'No, he never took soup.' — 'Would he take some fish?' 'No, he never took fish.' Presently I asked if he would eat some mutton? 'No, he never ate mutton.' — I then asked if he would take a glass of wine? 'No, he never tasted wine.' It was now necessary to inquire what he *did* eat and drink; and the answer was, 'Nothing but hard biscuits and soda water.' Unfortunately neither hard biscuits nor soda water were at hand; and he dined upon potatoes bruised down on his plate and drenched with vinegar. — My guests stayed till very late discussing the merits of Walter Scott and Joanna Baillie. — Some days after, meeting [Byron's friend John Cam] Hobhouse, I said to him, 'How long will Lord Byron persevere in his present diet?' He replied, 'Just as long as you continue to notice it.' I did not then know what I now know to be a fact — that Byron, after leaving my house, had gone to a club in St. James's Street, and eaten a hearty meat supper."

3 After the well-publicized breakup of his marriage, Byron was cut by London society. At one social gathering, he was standing near a doorway through which a group of aristocratic ladies were passing, all of whom ostentatiously ignored him. The procession ended with a pert brunette who nodded to him and whispered, "You see, you should have married me, and then this wouldn't have happened to you."

4 Byron gave his publisher, John Murray, a handsomely bound Bible with a flattering inscription. Murray was rather proud of this gift and used to leave it on a table where his guests might see it. One day a visitor who was admiring the book remarked that at John 18:40, in the sentence "Now Barabbas was a robber," Byron had deleted the word "robber" and substituted "publisher." After this discovery Byron's present no longer appeared on Murray's table.

C

CABELL, James Branch (1879–1958), *US novelist.*

1 None of Cabell's other works quite lived up to the success of *Jurgen*. In later years he was amused to receive a letter from a fan: "Dear Mr. Cabell, I have chosen you as my favorite author. Please write to me immediately and tell me why."

CADBURY, George (1839–1922), *British Quaker and cocoa manufacturer.*

1 When King George V and Queen Mary visited the Cadbury works, George Cadbury led the way with the queen while his wife walked behind with the king. Cadbury had removed his hat as a mark of respect for royalty. It was, however, very cold, and Queen Mary was concerned lest the old man should get a chill. "Mr. Cadbury, please put on your hat," she said. George Cadbury demurred. "Please, Mr. Cadbury — or I'll ask the king to command you to do so!" Her host still hesitated. Then from behind them came the ringing tones of Elizabeth Cadbury: "George, put your hat on." He did.

CAEN, Herbert Eugene (1916–98), *US journalist.*

1 (Herb Caen followed hard on the heels of the troops at the D day landings in Normandy. The writer Barnaby Conrad records the contents of a postcard that Caen sent describing an incident just after the landing.)

"When we landed at Carentan it was so great — I was elated and excited and scared and I had to go to the bathroom desperately. I saw an old guy there who was too old-world-French to be true, with the smock and the white mustache and the beret, and I rushed up to him and said, *'Monsieur, pardon, où est le lavabo?'* (Excuse me, sir, but where is the bathroom?) And he answered, tears of happiness streaming down his cheeks and gesturing around him expansively, *'Mais, toute la belle France, mon ami, toute la belle France!'* " (All of beautiful France, my friend, all of beautiful France!)

CAESAR, Gaius Julius (100–44 BC), *Roman general and statesman.*

1 A tall, fair man, Caesar was conservative in all matters except his clothing. To his purple senatorial tunic he added wrist-length sleeves with long fringes, and he never fastened his belt. This nonconformity caused Sulla to

warn members of the aristocratic party, "Beware of that boy with the loose clothes!"

2 At one stage in Caesar's early career political feelings were running so high against him that he thought it expedient to leave Rome for a while and go to Rhodes to take a course in rhetoric. En route the ship was attacked by pirates. Caesar was captured and held for a ransom of 12,000 gold pieces. His staff were sent away to arrange the ransom, and Caesar spent nearly forty days with his captors. During this time he would often jokingly say to the pirates that he would capture and crucify them, a threat they found greatly amusing. When the ransom was paid and Caesar was set at liberty, the first thing he did was to gather a fleet and go after the pirates. He caught them and crucified them to a man.

3 In 61 BC Caesar's second wife, Pompeia, was involved in a scandal concerning the religious rites known as the Feast of the Great Goddess. Only women were admitted to the rites, but on this occasion it was rumored that the notorious profligate Publius Clodius had attended them in female dress and had there committed adultery with Pompeia. Caesar divorced Pompeia. At the subsequent inquiry into the desecration various members of Caesar's family gave evidence. Caesar himself declined to offer any testimony against Pompeia. The court therefore asked him why he had divorced her. "Caesar's wife must be above suspicion," was the reply.

4 Caesar's confrontation with the senatorial party came to a head in 49 BC, when he was ordered to relinquish control of the armies he had commanded as governor in Gaul. Realizing that his opponents would not rest until they had destroyed him, Caesar decided to invade Italy. However, when he reached the Rubicon River, which formed the boundary between Gaul and Italy itself, he could scarcely bring himself to issue the fatal order

to cross. As he hesitated, a figure of superhuman size was seen on the bank. It snatched a trumpet from a soldier, blew a mighty blast on it, and then ran into the river and crossed over. Caesar accepted this as a sign from the gods and led his troops over with the words: *"Iacta alea est"* (The die is cast).

5 When Caesar sailed from Italy at the end of 49 BC to attack Pompey in northwestern Greece, he was hampered by lack of transport for his troops and by the midwinter storms that made crossing the Adriatic a hazardous enterprise. When the transports he had sent back to Brindisi to fetch reinforcements failed to return (some had been lost to enemy action and the remainder were afraid to sail), Caesar resolved to return to Brindisi himself and reorganize them. Disguised as a slave, Caesar set out in a small boat against the wind. The sea became so stormy that the pilot gave orders to turn back, but Caesar stood up and encouraged him to persevere. "Go on and fear nothing," he cried. "You carry Caesar and his fortune."

6 In the Alps Caesar came upon a poor and miserable village. One of his company idly wondered whether there was competition for civic honors in such a place, whether the village's men struggled and schemed to be head of their wretched community. With great earnestness, Caesar said, "For my part, I would rather be the chief man in this village than the second man in Rome."

7 While he was dining with friends on the evening of March 14, the question arose: "What is the best kind of death?"

"A sudden one," exclaimed Caesar before the others could answer. The next day he was assassinated.

8 Early in March of 44 BC the augur Spurinna warned Caesar that a great danger would befall him on the Ides of that month. On the Ides Caesar set off as usual for the Senate

house; he encountered Spurinna and said to him with a smile, "The Ides of March have come."

"True, they have come," answered Spurinna, "but not yet gone."

9 Among the conspirators who attacked Caesar on the fatal Ides of March in the Roman Senate house was Marcus Junius Brutus, whom Caesar had trusted and favored as a son. In the accounts of the assassination by Roman historians, Caesar is said at first to have resisted the onslaught of the assassins. But when he saw Brutus among them with his dagger drawn to deliver a blow, he ceased to struggle, and pulling the top part of his robe over his face, said, "You too, Brutus?"

CAGLIOSTRO, Alessandro (1743–95), *Italian alchemist and adventurer.*

1 Among the stories attaching to this famous charlatan was a rumor that he was three hundred years old. One of his servants, asked to confirm this, replied, "I can't. I've only been in his service a hundred years myself!"

CAGNEY, James (1899–1986), *US film actor.*

1 (His wife was proud of Cagney's incredible memory. She recalled one instance of it.)

"One day not long ago, we were getting into the car in New York, and he saw a man across the street. 'You see that fellow over there?' Jimmy said to me. 'He sat next to me in school. His name is Nathan Skidelsky.' 'Prove it,' I told him. 'Go say hello.' So he did. And you know what? It *was* Nathan Skidelsky. The only problem was, he didn't remember who Jimmy Cagney was."

2 Cagney was presented with a Life Achievement Award by the American Film Institute for his great contributions to film. After thanking those in his profession who had advanced his career as a movie star, he paused, then said, "And the names, the names of my youth — Lagerhead Quinlivan, Artie Klein, Pete Leyden, Jake Brodking, Specs Toporcer, Brother O'Mara, Picky Houlihan . . . the unmistakable touch of the gutter without which this evening might never have happened at all."

3 Near the end of his life Cagney agreed to see an old friend. He had not socialized for years, and no one knew what to expect. But the luncheon was a great success. Cagney told stories and cried as he remembered companions long past. When he was kidded about his tears, Cagney dabbed at his eyes and said, "Ah, you know the Irish, we cry at card tricks."

CAINE, Hall (1853–1931), *British novelist.*

1 Fame, it seems, can vanish as quickly as it comes. Few people now know the name of Hall Caine, for instance, who was internationally admired in the first half of the twentieth century. His books were translated into every known language, and his appearance (not unlike Shakespeare's) was familiar to everyone. When Maksim Gorki visited London and was introduced at a party to such literary greats as Hardy, Conrad, Shaw, Wells, and Bennett, he inspected the guests for the famous face and, not finding it, demanded, "Where is Hall Caine?"

CALHERN, Louis (1895–1956), *US actor.*

1 Calhern was starring in an obviously doomed play that was having its first — and as it turned out, its last — night in Boston. Halfway through the first act the actors realized that the audience consisted of three people. Advancing to the proscenium, Cal-

hern courteously invited them to join the cast so they wouldn't feel so lonely.

---⚭---

CALIGULA [Gaius Caesar] (AD 12–41), *Roman emperor. His nickname means "Little Boots," a reference to the small military boots he wore as a boy.*

1 Caligula was much addicted to gladiatorial games and other gory sports. On one occasion when the assembled Romans cheered on a team that the emperor did not support, he leaped to his feet in a rage, shouting, "I wish all you Romans had only one neck!"

2 At full moon, in accordance with his claim to be on an equal footing with the gods, Caligula used to invite the moon goddess to his bed. "Did you not see her?" he demanded of Aulus Vitellius (himself later to become emperor). "No," said Vitellius tactfully, "only you gods can see one another."

3 At a banquet Caligula was suddenly seized with a fit of helpless laughter. The consuls reclining next to him asked if they might share in the imperial merriment. Caligula, wiping the tears from his eyes, managed to gasp, "You'll never guess! It suddenly occurred to me that I had only to give a single nod, and both your throats would be cut on the spot."

4 Caligula was so hairy, and his legs so spindly, that he proclaimed it a capital offense to mention goats in his presence.

5 Caligula had a bridge built across the Gulf of Baiae, near Rome. Three and a half Roman miles long, it was made of boats lashed together with planking for a surface. He liked to ride back and forth over the bridge, and did so over and over. Years earlier, when his grandfather Tiberius was trying to select a successor, an astrologer had proclaimed, "Caligula has no more chance of becoming Emperor than of riding a horse dryshod over the Gulf of Baiae."

---⚭---

CALLAS, Maria (1923–77), *operatic soprano born in the United States of Greek parentage.*

1 When Maria Callas was singing at the Metropolitan Opera in New York, she was interviewed by a reporter who said, "You were born in the United States, you were brought up in Greece, you are now practically an Italian. What language do you think in?" Miss Callas replied, "I count in English."

2 Signing a contract to perform at the 1958 Festival of Two Worlds at Spoleto, Italy, Callas explained to Gian Carlo Menotti that he was actually saving money by employing her. He would not need to spend vast amounts on elaborate decor, which might distract the audience's attention from her voice. An expensive tenor would also be unnecessary, as the crowds would flock to hear the great Callas regardless of the quality of the other performers. "I've signed up Luchino Visconti as director," said Menotti. "Wonderful!" cried Callas. Then, after a moment's thought, she added, "But he lacks just one thing. He lacks humility."

3 Hearing a recording of her rival Renata Tebaldi, Callas said, "What a lovely voice — but who cares?"

---⚭---

CAMBRIDGE, George William Frederick Charles, 2d Duke of (1819–1904), *British field marshal.*

1 Making the rounds of a hospital with Florence Nightingale during the Crimean War, the duke recognized a sergeant of the guard who had had a third of his body shot away. The duke addressed him by name, and asked jovially, "Aren't you dead yet?" Later the

wounded man said to Miss Nightingale with tears in his eyes, "So feelin' of 'is Royal 'ighness, wasn't it, ma'am? Bless 'is 'eart, 'e wondered why I ain't dead yet!"

———— ⌘ ————

CAMBRONNE, Pierre-Jacques, Baron de (1770–1842), *French general.*

1 Cambronne commanded the French imperial guard at Waterloo. The circumstances of his capture by Colonel Hugh Halkett, a Hanoverian officer serving in the British army, are confused. The traditional account is that when Halkett called upon Cambronne to surrender, the Frenchman replied, *"La garde meurt, mais ne se rend pas"* (The guard dies but does not surrender).

"Damned humbug," Halkett later remarked of this famous utterance, leaving it unclear whether he was referring to its authenticity or its sentiment.

———— ⌘ ————

CAMBYSES II (d. 522 BC), *king of Persia (529–522 BC), son of Cyrus the Great.*

1 Cambyses was a drunken despot, yet one of his actions shows that he was not without a sense of poetic fitness. When a judge was found guilty of corruption, Cambyses ordered him to be flayed alive. After the sentence had been carried out, the skin was used to cover the seat from which judgments were handed down. Cambyses then appointed the dead judge's son to his father's position.

———— ⌘ ————

CAMERON, Julia Margaret (1815–79), *British photographer.*

1 Julia Cameron used to present her friends with inappropriate and rather eccentric gifts that had caught her eye — a pair of yew trees for the poet Alfred Tennyson to plant, old

catalogues for his children to read, rolls of wallpaper, legs of mutton from her sister's estate, a violet poncho for Mrs. Tennyson's father. Her gifts were not always graciously received. Thomas Carlyle once unwrapped a Christmas parcel and found a prayer book. "Either the Devil or Julia Cameron must have sent me this!" he exclaimed.

———— ⌘ ————

CAMERON OF LOCHIEL, Sir Ewan (1629–1719), *Scottish highland chieftain, reputed to have killed the last wolf in Scotland.*

1 Sir Ewan was out camping in the highlands with his young grandson, Donald Cameron (1695–1748), later known as "the Gentle Lochiel." There had been a heavy fall of snow and the Cameron of Lochiel noticed that his grandson had rolled up a snowball to make a pillow. Sir Ewan kicked the snowball away. "I'll have no effeminacy here, boy," he snarled.

———— ⌘ ————

CAMPBELL, Mrs. Patrick [Beatrice Stella Campbell, *née* Tanner] (1865–1940), *British actress, famous for her wit as well as her dramatic tantrums.*

1 Mrs. Patrick Campbell was rehearsing William Butler Yeats's *Deirdre* at the Abbey Theatre, Dublin. After a particularly wild display of her famous temperament, she walked downstage and peered out at the author, who was pacing up and down the stalls. "I'd give anything to know what you're thinking," she shouted. "I'm thinking," replied Yeats, "of the master of a wayside Indian railway station who sent a message to his company's headquarters saying: 'Tigress on the line: wire instructions.'"

2 When Mrs. Campbell went to Hollywood in the early 1930s to be considered for film

roles, she was handed the customary mimeographed publicity form. As requested, she gave details of her name, the color of her hair and eyes, her height, her hobbies, and so forth. When she came to the sheet headed "Experience," she wrote, "Edward VII."

3 At dinner Mrs. Patrick Campbell was sitting next to a biologist who could talk of nothing but the marvelous social organization of ant colonies. "Do you know," he said enthusiastically, "they have their army and their own police force?"

"What, no navy?" said Mrs. Campbell.

4 Mrs. Campbell once attempted to smuggle her pet Pekingese through customs by tucking him inside the upper part of her cape. "Everything was going splendidly," she later remarked, "until my bosoms barked."

5 During the course of an American tour, Mrs. Pat once lost her usual control of the situation. A rather shy, unobtrusive little man was taking her in to dinner. She turned her magnetic eyes on him and, in her most effective histrionic tones, said, "*Tell* me which would you sooner do — love passionately or be loved passionately?" The little man took a deep breath, considered, then ventured, "I'd rather be a canary."

6 Sara and Gerald Murphy, talented in their own right, were wealthy, well-connected friends of the novelist F. Scott Fitzgerald. Sara was also a favorite of Mrs. Pat Campbell, so much so that Mrs. Pat, whenever out shopping for clothes for her theater appearances, would insist on Sara's accompanying her. "Sara, darling," she would say, "does the dress walk? Or does it make me look just like a cigar?"

7 Mrs. Campbell was once asked by a rather pompous gentleman why it was that women were so devoid of any sense of humor. "God did it on purpose," replied the actress, "so that we may love you men instead of laughing at you."

8 Her genius did not always include tact. In her latter years, during an American tour, she was introduced to a distinguished gentleman who happened to be virtually bald. They had met many times before, but each time she had failed to recognize him. So it was in this latest encounter. The gentleman finally muttered something expressing irritation. Mrs. Pat's lovely voice filled with tears as she murmured brokenly, "I'm so sorry — I think it's because you do your hair differently!"

Chertkov, a disciple of Tolstoy, was a wealthy aristocrat. Tolstoy once reprimanded him for traveling first class, suggesting that, to demonstrate his humility, he should go second. On his next journey the obedient Chertkov hired an entire second-class coach for himself.

— FROM MICHAEL SCAMMEL,
Alexander Solzhenitsyn: A Biography

CAMPBELL, Thomas (1777–1844), *British poet, known especially for his war songs and narrative poems.*

1 At the height of the Napoleonic wars Campbell attended a literary dinner at which he proposed a toast to "Napoleon Bonaparte." An angry clamor broke out among the patriotic guests. Campbell raised his voice and continued: "Gentlemen, you must not mistake me. I admit that the French emperor is a tyrant. I admit that he is a monster. I admit that he is the sworn foe of our nation, and, if you will, of the whole human race. But, gentlemen, we must be just to our enemy. We must not forget that he once shot a bookseller."

The audience, nearly every one of them an author, broke into applause.

2 Attending Paisley races with John Wilson, Campbell bet his companion £50 that a certain horse, Yellow Cap, would win the first race. When the race was over, Campbell, thinking his horse had lost, turned to Wilson and said, "I owe you fifty pounds; but really, when I reflect that you are a professor of moral philosophy, and that betting is a sort of gambling only fit for blacklegs, I cannot bring my conscience to pay the bet."

"I very much approve of your principles," replied Wilson, "and I mean to act upon them. In point of fact, Yellow Cap has won the race, and, but for conscience, I ought to pay you the fifty pounds. But you will excuse me."

CANE, Facino (1360–1412), *Italian condottiere.*

1 Facino Cane's marauding bands of soldiers were greatly feared. One day a rich man, dressed in a fine doublet, came to complain that one of Cane's soldiers had held him up and robbed him of his coat. "Were you wearing that doublet on the day of the robbery?" inquired Facino Cane. The complainant said that he was. "Get out," said the condottiere. "It wasn't one of my soldiers who robbed you. None of *them* would have left you that doublet."

CANNING, George (1770–1827), *British Tory prime minister (1827).*

1 Sydney Smith said that Canning in office was like a fly in amber: "Nobody cares about the fly. The only question is — how the devil did it get there?"

2 Canning was a master of the putdown. He once attended a church service, following which the clergyman asked his opinion of the sermon. Canning replied, "You were brief."

"Yes," said the clergyman, "you know I avoid being tedious."

"But you *were* tedious," said Canning.

CANNON, Cornelia James (1876–1969), *US novelist.*

1 (The Cannons' daughter Marian Cannon Schlesinger, ex-wife of historian Arthur Schlesinger, Jr., tells this story about her mother.)

"A year or two later [she was about ninety], when sitting in the car waiting for my sister, who was buying apples in an orchard farm near Franklin [New Hampshire], my mother suddenly called out to her, 'I'm dying, Linda. We must go home. This is such an undignified place to die!' When my sister exclaimed, 'Mother, how do you know you're dying?' she said, 'How *can* I know, I've never died before.'"

When Vera Czermak learned that her husband had betrayed her, she decided she would end it all by jumping out of her third-story window. Some time later she awoke in the hospital to discover that she was still alive, having landed upon her husband. Mr. Czermak, however, was dead.

— JOHN TRAIN,
True Remarkable Occurrences

CANUTE [Cnut] (?994–1035), *Danish king of England (1014–35).*

1 The story of how Canute rebuked the flattery of his retainers is told in a twelfth-century chronicle. Tiring of their extravagant praises of his greatness, power, and invincibility, Canute ordered his chair to be set down on the seashore, where he commanded the waves not to come in and wet him. The incoming tide soon proved the futility of hu-

man commands, and the chronicler adds that from this time on Canute never wore his crown again, but hung it upon a statue of the crucified Christ.

CAPA, Robert (1913–54), *US photojournalist, born Andrei Freidmann in Hungary.*

1 Capa was in the Basque town of Bilbao in 1937 during the German bombing. He was out photographing when a German plane swooped low overhead. With two other men he jumped for shelter into a ditch. Thinking that he needed somehow to introduce himself, Capa turned to his companions. "I am a photographer," he said. "I am a Basque Catholic," said the second man. The last man snarled, "Those are two professions that are of no use at this moment."

CAPONE, Al (1899–1947), *US gangster of Italian birth. He dominated the Chicago underworld in the 1920s.*

1 The US Bureau of Internal Revenue astounded Capone by demanding millions of dollars in back taxes. "They can't collect legal taxes from illegal money," he objected.
{They could; in 1931 Capone was imprisoned for tax evasion.}

CAPUS, Alfred (1858–1922), *French playwright and novelist.*

1 Capus attended a rehearsal of a play in which an incredibly bad performance was given by the ingenue in the main female role. "How could such an important part be given to such an inexperienced ninny?" Capus demanded of the director. The director explained that the show's producer was "interested" in the girl. "Ah, *bon,*" said Capus, "but that's not brought out enough in the first act."

CARAY, Harry (1920–98), *US ballpark announcer.*

1 Born Harry Carabina, Caray became legendary for his work as a stadium announcer, first for the Cardinals and then for the Cubs. A hard drinker, he loved to rouse the fans to sing "Take Me out to the Ball Game" and kept up a steady patter of witty remarks throughout the games. At one point he was said to have gotten romantically involved with a woman who had married into the Busch family — the owners of the Cardinals. He resigned his job, saying, "I'd rather have people believing the rumor and have my middle-aged ego inflated than deny it and keep my job."

2 In 1968 Caray was hit by a car as he crossed the street, breaking his shoulder, nose, and both legs. The next season, on Opening Day, he stumbled out of the dugout as he was announced to the crowd. Crossing the foul line he threw away one cane; heading into the field he threw away the other. The crowd roared as he walked unaided to the field microphone. "Well, it's all show business," he said. "I hadn't needed those canes in weeks."

CARDANO, Girolamo (1501–76), *Italian mathematician and astrologer.*

1 Cardano was renowned throughout Europe as an astrologer, even visiting England to cast the horoscope of the young king, Edward VI. A steadfast believer in the accuracy of his so-called science, Cardano constructed a horoscope predicting the hour of his own death. When the day dawned, it found him in good health and safe from harm. Rather than have

his prediction falsified, Cardano killed himself.

Caesarius of Heisterbach (c. 1170–c. 1240), Cistercian monk and medieval chronicler, tells of a Cistercian lay brother who was heard to pray to Christ: "Lord, if Thou free me not from this temptation, I will complain of Thee to Thy mother."

— WILL DURANT,
The Story of Civilization, IV

CARDOZO, Benjamin (1870–1938), *US Supreme Court Justice.*

1 A group of Supreme Court justices once took an outing by boat as a break from the pressures of the law. Justice Cardozo, well known for his courtroom dispassionateness, began to feel seasick. A colleague, noticing his discomfort, hurried over to him and asked whether there was anything he could do. "Yes," replied the judge, "overrule the motion."

CARÊME, Marie-Antoine (1783–1833), *gastronome and the first famed French chef.*

1 One of fifteen children born to an impoverished family, Carême was eleven when his father led him by the hand into a strange neighborhood of Paris and, leaving him there, bid him find his fortune. As night fell he went to the first lighted window he saw, which was that of a bakery. Over the next thirty-eight years Carême perfected his craft to become the greatest chef in Europe, cooking for Talleyrand and Napoleon, among others. Near the end of his relatively short life he commented on his years in the great kitchens of the world. "The charcoal is killing us, but what does it matter? The fewer the years, the greater the glory."

CARILLO, Mary (1957–), *US tennis player.*

1 On being called, in a frenzy of adulation, "the best woman tennis player or anything else with the word woman in it," Carillo snapped, "I don't want to be graded on a curve."

CARLETON, Henry Guy (1856–1910), *US playwright and wit.*

1 Carleton suffered from a stutter, but he did not let that worry him unduly. Greeting his friend Nat Goodwin, the comedian, he said, "G-G-Goodwin, c-c-can you sp-p-pare m-m-me f-f-fifteen m-m-minutes?"

"Certainly, what is it?"

"I w-w-want f-f-five m-m-minutes' c-c-conversation w-w-with you."

CARLOS I (1863–1908), *king of Portugal (1889–1908).*

1 At the end of a visit to England King Carlos was asked by his host, King Edward VII, which aspects of the country had impressed him most. "The roast beef," replied the Portuguese monarch. "Is that all?" pursued his host, mildly disappointed. King Carlos pondered, then said, "Well, the boiled beef is quite good too."

CARLTON, Steve (1944–), *US baseball player.*

1 Known as "Lefty," the four-time Cy Young Award–winning pitcher Carlton was unusually reserved, keeping his life very private and rarely giving interviews to the press. So silent and distant was he that when the *St. Paul Pioneer-Press* published a photo of the 1987 World Champion Twins meeting with

the President at the White House, he — wearing sunglasses — was identified as "unnamed Secret Service agent."

2 Carlton was so angry with Philadelphia's sports reporters that he stopped talking with them entirely. Even during the postgame party celebrating the Phillies' victory in the 1980 World Series, he was silent, preferring to celebrate alone, away from journalists' questions. Later in his career, as his game faltered and he bounced from team to team, Carlton began opening up to reporters, boasting about highlights of games he had played and predicting great things for the future. Said one scribe, "Carlton finally learned to say hello when it was time to say good-bye."

CARLYLE, Thomas (1795–1881), *British historian, born in Scotland.*

1 (When Carlyle had completed the first part of *The French Revolution,* he lent the whole manuscript to John Stuart Mill, who had aided him with advice and loans of books. Carlyle's *Journal* for March 7, 1835, takes up the story:)

"Last night at tea, Mill's rap was heard at the door: he entered pale, unable to speak; gasped out to my wife to go down and speak with Mrs. Taylor [whom Mill later married]; and came forward (led by my hand, and astonished looks) the very picture of desperation. After various inarticulate utterances to merely the same effect, he informs me that my First Volume (left out by him in too careless a manner, after or while reading it) was except four or five bits of leaves irrevocably ANNIHILATED! I remember and can still remember less of it than of anything I ever wrote with such toil. It is gone, the whole world and myself backed by it could not bring that back: nay the old spirit too is fled. I find it took five months of steadfast, occa-

sionally excessive, and always sickly and painful toil. — Mill very injudiciously stayed with us till late; and I had to make an effort and speak, as if indifferent, about other common matters: he left us however in a relapsed state. . . ."

2 Carlyle found that the American Civil War confirmed his somber views on the human condition. "There they are cutting each other's throats, because one half of them prefer hiring their servants for life, and the other by the hour."

3 Commenting on the marriage of Thomas and Jane Welsh Carlyle, a mutual acquaintance suggested to Tennyson that it was a pity because with anybody else each might have been quite happy. Tennyson disagreed: "By any other arrangement *four* people would have been unhappy instead of two."

4 Carlyle was among those who used to provide financial aid to Leigh Hunt, who was notoriously careless about money. (He suggested the character of Harold Skimpole to Charles Dickens when the latter was writing *Bleak House.*) A friend calling on Carlyle, who was not rich himself at that time, noticed two gold sovereigns lying on the mantel and inquired what they were for. Carlyle tried to fob him off with an evasive answer, but his visitor persisted. "Well," said Carlyle reluctantly, "the fact is, Leigh Hunt likes better to find them there than that I should give them to him."

5 Carlyle was walking with Ralph Waldo Emerson in his native Scotland. Emerson found the landscape quite rough and asked his companion what crops could possibly grow there. Carlyle responded, "We grow *men.*"

CARNEGIE, Andrew (1835–1919), *Scottish-born US businessman and philanthropist. He* *considered that the rich had a responsibility toward society.*

1 Andrew Carnegie was a generous supporter of the New York Philharmonic Society, meeting its annual deficits in its early years. One year the society's secretary came as usual to Carnegie's mansion, this time requesting a subvention of $60,000. Carnegie was just about to sign the check when he paused and said, "No, I've changed my mind. Surely there are other people who like music enough to help with their own money." He then told the secretary to go out and raise half the necessary amount, promising to match it with the other half when this had been done.

The following day the secretary was back at the Carnegie mansion, announcing that he had raised the requisite money. Carnegie commended the man's enterprise and wrote out and signed his check for $30,000. As he handed it over he said, "Would you mind telling me who gave you the other half?"

"Not at all. Mrs. Carnegie."

2 Carnegie did not marry until he was fifty-one, although in earlier years he had sought the company of various eligible girls. When one of these married a rival, he said complacently, "If anybody else in the world can win her, I don't want her."

3 A fervent socialist visiting Carnegie spoke at some length about the evils of capitalism and the need for the fair distribution of wealth. Carnegie called his secretary and asked for two figures: the total value of his assets and possessions, and the latest estimate of the world population. After a simple calculation he instructed his secretary: "Give this gentleman sixteen cents. That's his share of my wealth."

4 Questioning Frank Doubleday about the publishing business, Carnegie asked bluntly, "How much did you make last month?"

Doubleday tried to dodge the question, explaining that publishing profits could not be calculated on a month-to-month basis. Carnegie was unimpressed. "Frank," he said, "I'd get out of it."

5 Once Carnegie was going over his accounts with his secretary and asked how much money he had given away over the course of his life. $324,657,399, he was told. "Good Heavens!" exclaimed Carnegie. "Where did I ever get all that money?"

CAROL II (1893–1953), *king of Rumania (1930–40).*

1 While in exile King Carol told his friend, the British diplomat Sir Robert Bruce Lockhart, that during his reign he had selected fourteen of the brightest Rumanians for special training in the government service. He sent seven to England and seven to the United States, to study their political and economic systems. "The seven who went to England were very smart — they all achieved great success in the government in Bucharest," said Carol.

"What about the seven you sent to the States?" asked Lockhart.

"They were even smarter," said the king. "They stayed there."

CAROLINE, Duchesse de Berri (1798–1870), *Italian wife of Charles Ferdinand, Duc de Berri (1778–1820), son of Charles X of France.*

1 The Duc de Berri was a notorious libertine, a fact to which his wife was quite resigned. In 1820 she was visited by about a score of women from Nantes, all of them claiming to be with child by the duke. The duchess asked one of her household how long the duke had been at Nantes. "A week, madame."

"Ah, then in that case, it's quite possible," sighed the duchess.

CAROLINE of Ansbach (1683–1737), *wife of George II, king of Great Britain and Ireland (1727–60).*

1 Queen Caroline went to see an exhibition of portraits of English royalty by the painter Jonathan Richardson. She observed the picture of the plain-looking Cromwell hung between Charles I and Charles II. To the artist she said, "Surely that personage is not a king."

"No, madam," replied Richardson. "He is no king, but it's good for kings to have him among them as a memento."

2 Though George II was notoriously unfaithful to Queen Caroline and kept a series of mistresses, when she lay on her deathbed he was sincerely grieved and sat weeping. The dying queen begged him to marry again, but George replied through his tears, "No, I shall have mistresses."

"Ah, that need not hinder you," said Queen Caroline.

CAROLINE of Brunswick (1768–1821), *wife of King George IV of Britain.*

1 When the then Prince of Wales first set eyes on his future wife at St. James's Palace in April 1795, he was appalled at her graceless appearance. As etiquette demanded, he kissed her and then, stepping back, called out to his aide, "I am unwell; bring me a glass of brandy."

2 At her trial in 1820 before the House of Lords, various salacious details of Caroline's behavior on her foreign travels were produced in evidence against her. One line of inquiry concerned her conduct with the dey (governor) of Algiers. The chief justice, Lord Norbury, remarked, "She was happy as the dey was long."

3 When Caroline returned to England in 1820, popular enthusiasm for her was intense. George IV and his ministers, determined to prevent her establishing her position as queen, were threatened by mobs on the London streets. The Duke of Wellington was accosted by a group of men armed with pickaxes, who demanded that he express his loyalty to Caroline. The duke replied, "Well, gentlemen, since you will have it so, 'God save the Queen' — and may all your wives be like her!"

4 George IV's groom of the bedchamber announced to him the portentous news of Napoleon's death: "Sir, your bitterest enemy is dead."

"Is she, by God!" exclaimed Caroline's husband.

CAROTO, Giovanni Francesco (c. 1480–1555), *Italian painter of the Veronese school.*

1 A priest objected to Caroto's figures on the grounds that he made them too lascivious. "If painted figures move you so," retorted the artist, "how are you to be trusted with living flesh and blood?"

2 Caroto had executed a painting for the Chapel of the Cross at San Bernadino. The picture, portraying Christ kneeling before his mother, was criticized by the guardian of the monastery, who thought that Christ should have been kneeling on both knees to show true reverence to her. By way of reply Caroto asked the guardian to kneel down and stand up again. This he did, grudgingly, lowering his right knee to the ground first as he knelt and raising his left leg first as he rose. When he was standing again, Caroto said to him, "Did you observe, Father Guardian, that you neither knelt down nor stood up with both

knees together? This Christ of mine is correct, because one might say he is either coming to his knees before his mother or, having knelt a while, is in the process of rising."

———— ∞ ————

CARROLL, James (1943–), *US novelist.*

1 (Carroll once told the following story:)

"On the occasion of the publication of my novel *Mortal Friends* in 1978, I was honored with a special tour of the Little, Brown warehouse in a suburb of Boston. My host and tour guide, a Little, Brown executive, showed me the assembly line along which workers wrapped, boxed, and mailed off books to wholesalers and bookstores. At one point he introduced me to one of the workers who said, 'Mr. Carroll, we all just love your book.'

"I took that as the greatest compliment an author could receive. To think that these workers had actually troubled to read my book.

"But then she went on. 'We just love it. It's the perfect size for packing.'"

———— ∞ ————

CARROLL, Lewis [Charles Lutwidge Dodgson] (1832–98), *British mathematician and author of* Alice in Wonderland *and* Through the Looking-Glass.

1 Queen Victoria was so delighted with *Alice in Wonderland* that she had a letter sent to the author stating that Her Majesty would be graciously pleased to accept any other works by the same pen. She was somewhat disconcerted to receive in due course a copy of Dodgson's *Syllabus of Plane Algebraical Geometry.*

2 (The amusement Lewis Carroll derived from logical problems is illustrated in an anecdote related by his younger cousin, Alice Raikes.)

"The room they had entered had a tall mirror standing in one corner. Dodgson gave his cousin an orange and asked her which hand she held it in. When she replied, 'The right,' he asked her to stand before the glass and tell him in which hand the little girl in the mirror was holding it. 'The left hand,' came the puzzled reply. 'Exactly,' said Dodgson, 'and how do you explain that?' Alice Raikes did her best: 'If I was on the *other* side of the glass,' she said, 'wouldn't the orange still be in my right hand?' Years later she remembered his laugh. 'Well done, little Alice,' he said. 'The best answer I've had yet.'"

3 Carroll caught a cold on a walk near his room at Christ Church College, Oxford, and died shortly thereafter. At his funeral, one of the floral wreaths placed near his bier stated simply, "Alice."

———— ∞ ————

CARSON, Johnny (1925–), *US television entertainer, longtime host of the* Tonight *show.*

1 When Carson signed for the *Tonight* show, he was so beset by reporters that he compiled a list of ten answers to which the journalists could furnish the questions to suit. They were: "1. Yes, I did. 2. Not a bit of truth in that rumor. 3. Only twice in my life, both times on Saturday. 4. I can do either, but I prefer the first. 5. No. Kumquats. 6. I can't answer that question. 7. Toads and tarantulas. 8. Turkestan, Denmark, Chile, and the Komandorskie Islands. 9. As soon as possible, but I'm not very good at it yet. I need much more practice. 10. It happened to some old friends of mine, and it's a story I'll never forget."

2 Actress Angie Dickinson was a frequent guest on Carson's show. One night she appeared wearing a peculiar-looking flowing red outfit. Carson jokingly asked why she was wearing pyjamas, then pursued the sub-

ject, asking, "Do you dress for men or for women?" "Well," said Dickinson, "I dress for women, and I undress for men."

3 Once when Carson announced a station break for a Sara Lee commercial, he paused to joke that actually no one had ever seen Sara Lee, and that she was probably "some little alcoholic old lady in the Midwest" who was drunk much of the time. The show's sponsor could not have been more displeased — the owner of Sara Lee had named the product for his beloved young daughter.

4 Carson was struck during the 1976 presidential campaign by the bland, uninspiring nature of both Jimmy Carter's and Gerald Ford's campaigns. He noted that making a choice between the two candidates would be very difficult, saying, "It boils down to fear of the unknown versus fear of the known."

———— ❧ ————

CARTER, Jimmy (1924–), *US politician, 39th President of the United States (1977–81)*.

1 During the 1976 presidential election Jimmy Carter's wife, Rosalynn, was asked what her husband had that his opponent Gerald Ford didn't. "He has me," she said simply.

2 As he campaigned by bus in the summer of 1976, Carter told reporters that they had in fact treated him pretty well. "Compared to what?" they asked. "To the way you treated Nixon," he said.

3 In 1976 Carter attended a party in Los Angeles thrown in his honor by Warren Beatty. The crowd was largely Hollywood people, a group that had not previously met the Georgia governor. Just before leaving the scene of the festivities Carter, a straight-laced Southern Baptist, noted, "It is a real thrill to meet the famous people here tonight. I hope I don't get to know too much about you!"

4 For all his religious fervor, Carter was still a competitive politician. He once noted, "Show me a good loser, and I'll show you a loser."

5 Carter's devout Southern Baptist background frequently led reporters to question him on his stance on moral issues. "How would you feel if you were told that your daughter was having an affair?" a reporter asked him. "Shocked and overwhelmed," replied Carter, adding, "but then, she's only seven years old."

6 Before moving into the White House Mrs. Carter was anxious to discover whether the chef there could cook the kind of meals the Carters enjoyed at home in the South. "Yes, ma'am," was the reply. "We've been fixing that kind of food for the servants for a long time."

7 Carter was asked, in the spring of 1979, whether his young daughter, Amy, ever boasted about her father's presidential status. Mindful of the heavy criticism that his administration was attracting, Carter replied, "No, she probably apologizes."

8 With candor rare among celebrities, the President's daughter, Amy Carter, when asked by a reporter if she had any message for the children of America, answered: "No."

9 While visiting Egypt on a state visit he was told that the Great Pyramid of Giza had taken twenty years to build. "I'm surprised that a government organization could do it that quickly," Carter said.

10 During the 1980 presidential campaign Carter, as the incumbent, increasingly referred to his experience in the job and warned that Ronald Reagan, the Republican nominee, was too much of a novice to become President. Replied Reagan, "I haven't had Jimmy Carter's experience. I wouldn't be caught dead with it."

"Splendid," exclaimed the future diva. "We do it tomorrow."

CARTLAND, Barbara (1902–2000), *British novelist specializing in popular romances.*

1 Barbara Cartland came into remote contact with royal circles when her daughter Raine's stepdaughter became the Princess of Wales in 1981. When Miss Cartland was interviewed for the BBC radio program *Today,* the woman interviewer asked her whether she thought that class barriers had broken down in Britain. "Of course they have," replied Cartland, "or I wouldn't be sitting here talking to someone like you."

CARUSO, Enrico (1873–1921), *Italian tenor renowned for his roles in the operas of Verdi and Puccini.*

1 Caruso was caught in the great 1906 San Francisco earthquake and fire. He swore he would never again go back to such a city, "where disorders like that are permitted."

2 A group of reporters once asked him what he thought of Babe Ruth. Caruso, who was unfailingly polite and amiable, replied that he didn't know because unfortunately he had never heard her sing.

3 Caruso once reported an extraordinary conversation with a lady who was anxious to learn to sing, believing it possible that within a month she would be a recognized artist. "I'm leaving the country next month," she said, "and need twenty-five lessons before my departure."
    "Impossible, madam."
    "Why? Couldn't I take two lessons each day?"
    "True enough," said Caruso. "I hadn't thought of that. But in that case why not take all twenty-five lessons in one day?"

CARVER, George Washington (1864–1943), *US agricultural researcher, the son of black slaves.*

1 Carver lost his entire life savings, some $70,000, in the crash of the Alabama bank in which the money was deposited. Carver, however, was apparently unperturbed. "I guess somebody found a use for it," he remarked. "I was not using it myself."

CASALS, Pablo (1876–1973), *Spanish cellist and conductor.*

1 Casals found his greatest fulfillment in conducting, which he always wanted to do even when, at the height of his career as a cellist, he had little time for anything outside his cello performances. On his first American tour in 1901 a falling rock injured the fingers of his left hand. His first reaction was: "Thank God I won't have to play the cello anymore."

2 At his Viennese debut Casals suffered from nerves. When he came to pick up his bow to play the first note, he found that his hand was too tense. To loosen it he tried a little twirl, but the bow flew from his fingers and landed in the middle of the orchestra. As it was carefully passed back to him along the rows of musicians, he remembered his mother's maxim about calmness and steadiness in the pursuit of one's purpose. By the time the bow was returned to him his hand was steady. The concert was one of his greatest triumphs.

3 While playing a piece that she knew well and had played many times, a pupil suffered a lapse of memory. Casals said, "Fine — everything should be new every time you play it."

4 (The famous photographer Yousuf Karsh remembers photographing Casals with his back to the camera. Karsh recalls:)

"I was so moved on listening to him play Bach that I could not for some moments attend to photography. I have never posed anyone else facing away from the camera, but it seemed just right.

"Years later when the photograph was on exhibition at the Museum of Fine Arts in Boston, I was told that every day an elderly gentleman would come and stand for many minutes in front of it. Full of curiosity, a curator finally inquired gingerly, 'Sir, why do you come here and stand in front of this picture?'

"He was met with a withering glance and the admonition, 'Hush, young man. Can't you see I am listening to the music!'"

———— ⁊ ————

CASSATT, Mary (1845–1926), *expatriate US artist and promoter of the Impressionists.*

1 Mary Cassatt was always generous in her praise of her fellow Impressionists, but never of her own work. At an exhibition one day she was talking with some people who did not know her. "But you are forgetting a foreign painter that Degas ranks very high," said one of the strangers in the course of the conversation. "Who is that?" Mary Cassatt inquired with interest. "Mary Cassatt," came the reply. "Oh, nonsense!" exclaimed the artist with conviction. "She's jealous," murmured the stranger as he turned away.

———— ⁊ ————

Frank Case was manager of the Algonquin Hotel in New York City. He would never charge the Algonquin Round Table celebrities for their lunches, but this did not stop them from saying what they thought of the food he served. On one occasion they declared it inedible and arranged to have their food sent over from the Colony the following week. The

week after that the group, doubtless feeling that they had made their point, assembled at the Algonquin as usual and were greeted by small cards that Case had put on their table, saying, "Basket parties welcome." No one was embarrassed.

— CASKIE STINNETT, *Travels with Marc*

———— ⁊ ————

CASTIGLIONE, Nicchia, Countess di (1837–99), *aristocratic beauty at the court of Empress Eugénie, wife of Napoleon III.*

1 The countess's public appearances in a state of virtual undress caused considerable scandal. At a diplomatic ball she appeared dressed as the Queen of Hearts, her breasts covered only by a strip of gauze onto which two hearts had been sewn to conceal the nipples, and another heart sewn onto her transparent skirt concealing her vaginal mound, but leaving her pubic hair clearly visible. Empress Eugénie looked at her and said, "Countess, your heart seems a little low."

———— ⁊ ————

CASTLEROSSE, Valentine Browne, Lord (1891–1943), *Irish nobleman.*

1 "Gross in appetite and appearance, with nimble wit concealed beneath buffoon's exterior, Lord Castlerosse was Beaverbrook's court jester. 'What is your handicap?' Nancy Cunard asked him on the golf-course. 'Drink and debauchery,' he answered sadly but correctly."

———— ⁊ ————

CASTRACANI, Castruccio (1281–1328), *Italian condottiere, later nobleman.*

1 The Quatigiani family of Lucca had been Castracani's friends and supporters. They quarreled, and after Castracani defeated them, he treated them with the utmost severity. One of his advisers warned him that

people were censuring him for dealing so harshly with his old friends. "I am not dealing with old friends," was the reply, "but with new enemies."

———— ❧ ————

CASTRO, Fidel (1927–), *Cuban revolutionist and political leader.*

1 A meeting in 1959 between then Vice President Richard Nixon and Fidel Castro turned out, as might have been expected, to be a disaster. Just before the meeting, as the Cuban delegation waited, a functionary entered, announced as "Mister So-and-So, in charge of Cuban Affairs." To which Castro replied, "And I thought I was in charge of Cuban affairs."

2 On a flight to New York in 1960, Fidel turned to Ramiro Valdes and asked if there would be an escort plane accompanying them. Valdes stuttered out a no. "We're in danger. If I were running the CIA, I'd shoot down the plane at sea and report the whole thing as an accident." Silence. Fidel went on, "At least we should have had an escort. What a mistake." Everybody started to look around. Suddenly there was a huge roar: a squadron of planes was heading toward them. Yankee fighters. Everybody panicked. The fighters came closer, but US territory was just ahead. Fidel was calm, probably having said all those things just to see the reaction. There were too many planes for an attack. They were an honorary escort. The plane entered US territory literally under the CIA's wing.

———— ❧ ————

CATHER, Willa (1873–1947), *US novelist and short-story writer.*

1 Friends begged her to withdraw from publication her story "The Birthmark," which was based on the life of another friend, say-

ing that it would ruin the friend's reputation, at a minimum, and might ruin her life. Cather refused, saying, "My art is more important than my friend."

———— ❧ ————

CATHERINE of Aragon (1485–1536), *first queen of Henry VIII of England, whom she married in 1509. She bore him a daughter, Mary (later Mary I).*

1 Catherine was imprisoned, deprived of her titles and the company of her daughter, and died in suspicious circumstances. One of her last acts before her death was to dictate an affectionate letter to Henry VIII, beseeching him to be kind to their daughter, Mary. The last words were: *"Oculi mei te solum desiderant. Vale"* (Mine eyes desire thee only. Farewell).

———— ❧ ————

CATHERINE II [Catherine the Great] (1729–96), *empress of Russia (1762–96).*

1 As part of her plans for reform in Russia, Catherine dreamed of founding great cities that would be centers of industry and progress in her backward country. During a state visit from the Austrian emperor Joseph II, the two rulers proceeded to lay the foundation stones of one of these proposed metropolises. Catherine laid the first stone, the emperor laid the second. Joseph commented, "I have finished in a single day a most important business with the empress of Russia; she has laid the first stone of a city and I have laid the last."

———— ❧ ————

CATO [the Censor] (234–149 BC), *Roman statesman.*

1 Cato was the chief instigator of the third Punic War, convinced that Rome could never

be secure while the great city of Carthage on the North African coast remained its rival. Whenever called upon to speak in the Senate, whatever the subject under debate, he always concluded his speech with the words: *"Carthago delenda est"* (Carthage must be destroyed).

2 The eighty-year-old Cato surprised his friends by setting himself the task of studying Greek. Asked how he could contemplate such a lengthy course of study at his advanced age, he replied that it was the youngest age he had left.

3 As Cato had deserved well of the Republic, someone once asked him why no statue had been erected to him. Cato replied, "Better that question than the question: 'Why have they erected a statue?'"

CAVELL, Edith Louisa (1865–1915), *British nurse.*

1 As a Red Cross nurse in Belgium during World War I, Edith Cavell helped Allied soldiers to escape from behind the enemy lines. The Germans captured her, and in a court-martial sentenced her to death. As she was led before the firing squad, she is reputed to have said, "I realize that patriotism is not enough; I must have no hatred or bitterness towards anyone."

CECIL, William (1863–1936), *bishop of Exeter.*

1 Traveling by rail to a confirmation ceremony, the absentminded bishop mislaid his ticket and was unable to produce it for the ticket collector. "It's all right, my Lord," said the collector, "we know who you are."

"That's all very well," replied the bishop, "but without the ticket how am I to know where I'm going?"

CERF, Bennett (1898–1971), *US book publisher and radio wit.*

1 During World War II Random House, where Cerf was the longtime president, wanted to publish a book for servicemen called *The Ten Commandments* — but the page count was too long to be economical. It was suggested that only five of the commandments be printed and the book retitled *A Treasury of the World's Best Commandments.*

CERVANTES SAAVEDRA, Miguel de (1547–1616), *Spanish writer, best known for* **Don Quixote.**

1 When King Philip III of Spain noticed a man reading beside the road and laughing so much that the tears were rolling down his cheeks, he commented: "That man is either crazy or he is reading *Don Quixote.*"

CETEWAYO (1826–84), *king of the Zulus.*

1 Cetewayo, like the Zulu kings before him, would not allow the young men in his regiments to marry until they had "washed their spears," that is, killed enemy warriors in battle. When one of his regiments had passed this test, he ordered the men to find wives. One of the women chosen did not want to marry the man allotted to her. To avoid marriage she put on the *isidwaba,* the long full skirt worn by married women. Her deception discovered, she was taken to a high waterfall and thrown over. The *isidwaba* billowed out as she fell, breaking her fall and saving her from being drowned or smashed on the rocks. When night came she crept away and found refuge with some European settlers. The waterfall, in the Mangeni Gorge in Zululand, is still called the Isidwaba Falls.

CÉZANNE, Paul (1839–1906), *French Post-impressionist painter.*

1 Cézanne worked very slowly. His friend, the famous art dealer Ambroise Vollard, underwent no fewer than 115 sittings for a single portrait. Cézanne commented, "I am not entirely displeased with the shirt front."

CHALIAPIN, Feodor Ivanovich (1873–1938), *Russian bass singer.*

1 Once when Chaliapin was on tour, he spent a night with a young woman of the town. In parting he offered her two tickets for the opera in which he was singing that evening. The girl said she was poor and hungry, and opera tickets did not buy bread. "If it was bread you wanted," retorted Chaliapin, "why didn't you spend last night with a baker?"

2 During a seemingly interminable delay in a rehearsal, the singers began to show signs of impatience. A stagehand offered to fetch a chair so that Chaliapin could sit down until the difficulty was worked out. Chaliapin said, "It is not my body that is tired, it is my soul. But my soul has no ass. So forget the chair."

3 Chaliapin was afflicted with lifelong stagefright, which he eased with vodka. On one occasion, he was dozing comfortably after a particularly strong dose of vodka when Eddie ("Papa") Senz, the makeup man at the Metropolitan Opera in New York, made him up. Suddenly, he opened his eyes and inspected his reflection in the mirror. "Vot is dis face you giff me?" he exclaimed.
   "Mefistofele," replied Senz.
   "Not Boris?" asked the great bass, apparently expecting to appear in the name part of Mussorgsky's *Boris Godunov.* "Holy mother! Send for de *Faust* score! I must see de score."

CHALONER, John Armstrong (1862–19?), *US financier.*

1 In 1897 Chaloner was certified as insane and incarcerated in a New York lunatic asylum. There was a tremendous family and public scandal over the episode; speculation was revived when he escaped, fled across the state border, and was pronounced sane by two other doctors. Sometime later Chaloner's brother, known as Sheriff Bob, announced that he was intending to marry the tempestuous singer Lina Cavalieri. Chaloner sent his brother a telegram: "Who's loony now?"

CHAMBERLAIN, Joseph (1836–1914), *British politician.*

1 Chamberlain was once guest of honor at an important civic dinner. The main part of the meal over, the mayor whispered to Chamberlain as the coffee was being served, "Shall we let the people enjoy themselves a little longer, or had we better have our speech now?"

CHAMBERLAIN, Sir [Joseph] Austen (1863–1937), *British statesman.*

1 Offered the post of chancellor of the exchequer in 1919, Austen complained that the prime minister, David Lloyd George, had not sent for him with the customary formality, but had simply thrown the office at him — like a bone to a dog. "Stop a minute, Austen," said Lloyd George to him, "there is a good deal of meat on that bone."

2 Chamberlain and his wife were dining one evening with the well-known London hostess Mrs. Ronnie Greville. The excellent food and wine were marred only by the fact that the butler had obviously been drinking.

Rather than make a scene in front of her guests, Mrs. Greville surreptitiously scribbled a note and handed it to him. The message read: "You are drunk — leave the room at once." The butler dutifully laid the slip of paper on a silver salver, tottered around to the other side of the table, and presented it to Austen Chamberlain.

CHAMBERLAIN, Wilt (1936–99), *US basket-ball star.*

1 Despite his personal successes, Chamberlain was criticized for not taking his team to titles. Then in 1967, when his Philadelphia team finally won a championship, someone asked Chamberlain if he thought that everybody would get behind him now. "No way," he said.

"Why not?"

"Nobody roots for Goliath," was the answer.

CHANDLER, Raymond (1888–1959), *US crime-story writer, creator of the immortal Philip Marlowe, private investigator.*

1 Chandler wrote the screenplay for his novel *The Big Sleep*, which was being made into a movie by Howard Hawks. During the filming Hawks wrote to Chandler, asking him to clarify who in the movie killed the chauffeur Owen Taylor, who ended up in the Sternwood family limousine under ten feet of water at the movie's end. Chandler reread his novel, reread his script, then wired back, "I don't know."

CHANEL, Coco [Gabrielle Chanel] (1883–1971), *French fashion designer.*

1 When Cocteau's *Antigone* was produced in Paris in 1924 the playwright specified that Mlle Chanel was to make the gowns worn by the princesses in the play. "She is our leading couturière," he said, "and I cannot imagine Oedipus's daughters promoting a 'little dressmaker.'"

2 When the mini-skirt came into fashion in the mid-1960s, Chanel was asked whether she approved of girls' exposing their knees and thighs in this way. "Thighs — of course," she replied. "But knees — never!"

3 Chanel never married, although many men fell desperately in love with her. Upon a proposal of marriage by the Duke of Westminster, Chanel replied, "There have been several Duchesses of Westminster — but there is only *one* Chanel!"

CHANNING, Carol (1921–), *US actress and singer.*

1 As part of a nightclub act, Carol Channing sometimes encouraged the members of the audience to ask her personal questions. "Do you remember the most embarrassing moment you ever had?" asked one man. "Yes, I do," replied Miss Channing. "Next question?"

CHAPLIN, Charlie (1889–1977), *British-born film actor.*

1 In 1931 Chaplin invited Albert Einstein, who was visiting Hollywood, to a private screen-

ing of his new film *City Lights*. As the two men drove into town together, passersby waved and cheered. Chaplin turned to his guest and explained: "The people are applauding you because none of them understands you and applauding me because everybody understands me."

2 Charlie Chaplin entered a Charlie Chaplin look-alike competition in Monte Carlo. He came in third.

3 (The playwright Charles MacArthur had been brought to Hollywood to do a screenplay, but was finding it difficult to write visual jokes.)

" 'What's the problem?' asked Chaplin.

" 'How, for example, could I make a fat lady, walking down Fifth Avenue, slip on a banana peel and still get a laugh. It's been done a million times,' said MacArthur. 'What's the best way to *get* the laugh? Do I show first the banana peel, then the fat lady approaching: then she slips? Or do I show the fat lady first, then the banana peel, and *then* she slips?'

" 'Neither,' said Chaplin without a moment's hesitation. 'You show the fat lady approaching; then you show the banana peel; then you show the fat lady and the banana peel together; then she steps *over* the banana peel and disappears down a manhole.' "

4 Chaplin was entertaining guests at a Hollywood dinner party with his impressions of famous figures. He concluded his performance with an excellent rendering of an operatic aria. "Why, I never knew you could sing so beautifully!" exclaimed one of his guests. "I can't sing at all," replied Chaplin. "I was only imitating Caruso."

5 A child named Jackie Vernon sent a steady stream of letters to his idol, Charlie Chaplin. But he never received a response. Many years later Vernon had the opportunity to meet his great hero. When he heard his name, Chaplin immediately said, "Tell me, why did you stop writing?"

---⊶---

CHAPMAN, John (1774–1845), *US frontiersman who earned the nickname "Johnny Appleseed" for his work seeding and pruning apple trees across the Ohio River countryside.*

1 Johnny Appleseed once entered a house in Washington Territory, Ohio, barefoot, and introduced himself to the occupants. The man of the house asked why he was wearing no shoes. Johnny Appleseed, who had recently trodden on a snake, held out one of his feet and said, "Sir, this foot had been guilty of offense in treading unmercifully upon one of God's creatures, and as a corresponding punishment I am now exposing it to the inclemency of the weather."

2 Johnny Appleseed carried his reverence for other forms of life to what other people would consider extremes. It is said that once when he had been bitten by a rattlesnake, someone asked him what had become of it. "The poor thing!" replied Johnny Appleseed, his eyes filling with tears. "Hardly had it touched me than I, overcome by godless passion, cut off its head with my sickle. The poor, poor innocent thing!"

---⊶---

CHAPMAN, John Jay (1862–1933), *US dramatist, critic, and political reformer.*

1 After a high-spirited dinner at Harvard's Porcellian Club in 1887, Chapman horsewhipped a classmate who he thought had made insulting remarks about his fiancée. Sobering up, Chapman was so ashamed of his behavior that he went to the open fireplace and held his left hand in the flames. It was so badly burned that it had to be amputated.

—⚬—

CHARLEMAGNE (?742–814), *king of the Franks (768–814) and Holy Roman Emperor (800–814).*

1 The great French white wine Corton-Charlemagne owes its existence, according to local legend, not to the emperor but to his wife. The red wines of Corton stained his white beard so messily that she persuaded him to plant vines that would produce white wines. Charlemagne ordered white grapes to be planted. Thus Corton-Charlemagne.

—⚬—

CHARLES, Prince of Wales (1948–), *eldest son of Queen Elizabeth II and heir apparent to the throne of the United Kingdom.*

1 Actress Susan Hampshire, wearing an extremely low-cut dress, was presented to Prince Charles at a show-business function. Without a trace of embarrassment, the prince greeted Miss Hampshire with the words: "Father told me that if I ever met a lady in a dress like yours, I must look her straight in the eyes."

2 Charles briefly attended a school in Australia. One Sunday, the rector of the local parish church was surprised to see the prince at his morning service. There was only a scanty congregation that day, for which the rector apologized as his royal visitor left the church. "Being bank holiday weekend," he explained, "most of the parishioners are away."

"Not another bank holiday!" said the prince. "What's this one in aid of?"

"Well," replied the rector, a little embarrassed, "over here we call it the queen's birthday."

—⚬—

CHARLES II (1630–85), *king of England, Scotland, and Ireland (1660–85).*

1 Charles's attempt to recover the throne by force ended in his defeat at Worcester in 1651. Despite the reward offered for his capture and the extreme penalties threatened to any who concealed or aided him, Charles eventually made his escape to the continent. An early part of his journey was accomplished with the aid of some brothers, one of whom lent him the horse from his mill. Charles, accustomed to more sprightly steeds, complained after a while of the heavy, lumbering pace of his mount. The miller at once defended his horse with the words: "No wonder, sire, that the horse goes so heavily, as it bears the weight of three kingdoms on its back."

2 (John Aubrey tells a charming story:)

"Arise Evans had a fungous nose, and said, it was revealed to him, that the king's hand would cure him, and at the first coming of King Charles II into St. James's Park, he kissed the king's hand, and rubbed his nose with it; which disturbed the king, but cured him."

3 Charles II enjoyed talking and in particular telling anecdotes of his own life. His courtiers, who had all heard the stories many times, found them very tedious, and used to withdraw from the king's presence if they could, leaving him with a much diminished audience. The Earl of Rochester said of this trait that he wondered that a man could so well remember every detail of a story yet not remember that he had told it to the same people only the day before.

4 In contemporary satires Charles sometimes features under the name of "Old Rowley," a stallion with a reputation for breeding fine foals. One of the king's young ladies was sitting in her apartment singing the satirical ballad "Old Rowley the King," when

Charles II knocked at her door. She asked who was there. "Old Rowley himself, madam," the king replied with his customary good humor.

5 There are several versions of Charles's encounter with the Quaker William Penn, whose creed enjoined him to refuse to remove his hat as a mark of respect to his social superiors. Seeing Penn's hat remaining on his head, the king with a flourish removed his own. "Friend Charles, why dost thou uncover thyself?" asked the Quaker. "Friend Penn," replied the king, "in this place it is the custom for only one man at a time to keep his hat on."

6 On his morning walk one day in London, Charles dismissed most of his attendants and strolled into Hyde Park with just two lords attending him. As he crossed the road, his brother, James, Duke of York, drove up in his carriage, attended by an armed guard. The duke stopped his coach, expressed surprise at seeing the king almost alone, and hinted that it was unwise to expose himself to danger in this way. "No danger," said King Charles, "for no man in England would take away my life to make *you* king."

7 The king asked Edward Stillingfleet, bishop of Worcester and a popular preacher, why when Stillingfleet preached at court he always read his sermons. He had heard that when he preached elsewhere he always delivered his sermons extempore. Stillingfleet explained that awe of the king made him afraid of forgetting what he had to say, so he preferred to read when he had royalty in the audience. Emboldened by the king's favorable reaction to this diplomatic reply, the bishop then asked if he might put a question of his own. Why, he asked Charles, did he always read his speeches to the House of Commons, when it could not be that he was in awe of his audience? Charles replied good-naturedly,

"I have asked them so often, and for so much money, that I am ashamed to look them in the face."

8 The Earl of Rochester once wrote on the door of the king's bedchamber: "Here lies our sovereign lord the king, / Whose promise none relies on; / He never said a foolish thing, / Nor ever did a wise one." Charles skillfully replied to the insult with the observation: "This is very true, for my words are my own, and my actions are those of my ministers."

9 Seventeenth-century monarchs died as they lived, very much in the public eye. To the attendants and notables gathered around his deathbed Charles II said, "I have been a most unconscionable time a-dying; but I beg you to excuse it."

———— ✧ ————

CHARLES V (1500–58), *Holy Roman Emperor (1519–56) and king of Spain (1516–56).*

1 In 1521, when Charles renewed his struggle with the French king, Francis I, over the empire's Italian lands, the emperor remarked, "My cousin Francis and I are in perfect accord — he wants Milan, and so do I."

2 When Hernando Cortéz, the celebrated explorer of the New World, returned to Spain and made a report of his findings to the king, one of his chief recommendations was that a passage to India be effected by digging a canal across the Isthmus of Panama. Charles considered this suggestion with his advisers and finally rejected it: "What God hath joined together let no man put asunder."

———— ✧ ————

CHARLES X (1757–1836), *king of France (1824–30).*

1 When Louis XVIII became king, the Comte d'Artois continued to treat his brother with

easy familiarity, bordering on disrespect. Eventually this became so marked that M. de Maurepas was entrusted with the delicate task of dropping a hint to Charles that now that Louis was king, he should observe a more formal approach. Maurepas put his case to the count, concluding by saying that if he continued in his informal ways, the king might be offended. "Offended, eh?" said Charles. "Well, and what if he is? What can he do to me?"

"He can pardon you, sir," replied Maurepas suavely.

2 Charles X, oblivious of his brother's flight on March 20, 1815, justified his absolutist policies to Talleyrand by saying that for the Bourbons "there is no middle course between the throne and the scaffold."

"Your Majesty is forgetting the postchaise," Talleyrand reminded him.

CHARLES FRANCIS JOSEPH [Charles I of Austria] (1887–1992), *Austrian emperor.*

1 Informed of the death of Francis Joseph, Charles, now elevated to the throne, was deeply moved. He seized his adjutant's hand and in his emotion stammered, "What should I do? I think the best thing is to order a new stamp to be made with my face on it."

CHARLOTTE of Mecklenburg-Strelitz (1744–1818), *wife of George III, king of Great Britain and Ireland (1760–1820).*

1 Queen Charlotte was never a beauty, being short, pale, and very thin at the time of her marriage. As she grew older, her appearance improved, inspiring her chamberlain to remark, "I really do think that the bloom of her ugliness is going off."

CHARONDAS (6th century BC), *Greek legislator.*

1 One of Charondas's laws forbade citizens to carry weapons into the public assembly. Forgetting this, he wore his sword into the public meeting one day. A fellow citizen reproached him for violating his own law. "By Zeus, I will confirm it," said Charondas instantly, and, drawing his sword, killed himself.

CHASE, Ilka (1903–78), *US actress and playwright.*

1 A short while after her just-divorced husband, Louis Calhern, married Julia Hoyt, Miss Chase was going through some boxes and found a packet of visiting cards on which was engraved the name "Mrs. Louis Calhern." Thinking it a pity to let them go to waste, she wrapped them up and mailed them to her successor with a note: "Dear Julia, I hope these reach you in time."

CHASE, Salmon Portland (1808–73), *US statesman, Chief Justice of the Supreme Court (1864–73).*

1 Shortly after the Civil War, Chief Justice Chase was introduced to a striking beauty from Alabama. "I must warn you that I'm an unreconstructed rebel," she archly informed him. "In your case, madam," responded Chase gallantly, "reconstruction — even in the slightest degree — would be nothing short of sacrilege."

CHATEAUBRIAND, François René, Viscomte de (1768–1848), *French author and statesman.*

1 Chateaubriand's exalted opinion of himself drew some acerbic comments from his con-

temporaries, among them Napoleon, who gave him a post in the French legation in Rome in 1803. Chateaubriand soon became disaffected. Napoleon observed, "The difficulty lies not so much in buying Monsieur Chateaubriand, but in paying him the price he thinks he's worth."

2 In his later years Chateaubriand suffered from deafness, an affliction that evoked a biting comment from his old enemy Talleyrand: "He thinks he's deaf now that he no longer hears himself talked about."

CHATTERTON, Thomas (1752–70), *British poet.*

1 Walking with a friend in a London churchyard one day, engrossed in the melancholy pastime of reading the inscriptions on the gravestones, Chatterton stumbled and fell into a newly dug grave. His friend immediately came to his rescue, and in an attempt to make light of the matter, said he was glad to have been present at the resurrection of a genius. Chatterton took a more gloomy view of the accident: "I have been at war with the grave for some time, and I find it not so easy to vanquish it as I imagined. We can find an asylum to hide from every creditor but that." Three days later he killed himself.

CHEKHOV, Anton Pavlovich (1860–1904), *Russian short-story writer and dramatist.*

1 In Chekhov's story "The Malefactor," a peasant removes the nuts from railroad ties to use as weights for his fishing lines, unaware that this comparatively trivial theft could endanger the lives of hundreds of railroad travelers. A lawyer asked Chekhov how he would have punished the peasant had he been judge at his trial. "I would have acquitted him," said Chekhov. "I would have said

to him: 'You have not yet ripened into a deliberate criminal. Go — and ripen!'"

2 Chekhov was walking with Tolstoy at Gaspra, in the Crimea, discussing the art of drama, when Tolstoy put his arm around Chekhov's shoulders and said, "Shakespeare's plays are bad enough, but yours are even worse."

3 One night a writer came to see Chekhov and questioned him about his work. Chekhov told him that he considered his writing merely a diversion from his medical studies. "You want to know how I write my stories?" he asked the young writer. "Here!" And he picked up the first thing he looked at, which was an ashtray. "If you like, it will be a story tomorrow. 'The Ashtray.'"

CHERUBINI, Maria Luigi (1760–1842), *Italian composer known mainly for his choral works.*

1 An acquaintance of Cherubini's handed him a score, saying that it was by Étienne Méhul. Cherubini studied it. "This isn't by Méhul, it's too bad!" he said. "Then will you believe me if I tell you that it is mine?" asked the other man. "No," Cherubini replied, "it's too good."

2 Cherubini once granted an audition to a man possessed of a very powerful voice. Asked for a demonstration of his talents, he sang so forcefully that the windowpanes rattled. "Do you think anything can be made of me?" he asked Cherubini at the conclusion. "Certainly," was the reply. "An auctioneer."

3 During Cherubini's directorship of the Paris Conservatoire, a student who had written an opera that was being considered for production begged him to be present at the tryout. Cherubini consented. He listened to the first act, then the second, but uttered not a word

of comment. The young composer, nervously haunting the box in which Cherubini sat, could no longer conceal his impatience. "Master, haven't you anything to say to me?" Cherubini grasped the young man's hands, replying kindly, "My poor chap, what can I say to you? I've been listening to you for two hours and you haven't said anything to me either."

4 "What is worse than a flute?" mused Cherubini, and immediately supplied his own answer: "Two flutes."

———∽———

CHESTERFIELD, Philip Dormer Stanhope, 4th Earl of (1694–1773), *British politician and writer.*

1 The popularity of the preacher George Whitefield was such that the Privy Council debated whether steps should be taken to prevent his vast evangelical rallies. Chesterfield listened, then struck in with a practical suggestion: "Make him a bishop, and you will silence him at once."

2 Lord Chesterfield's sister, Lady Gertrude Hotham, was an active Methodist. When her brother fell ill, she tried to coax him into going to a Methodist seminary in Wales to recuperate, partly because she genuinely believed that the environment would improve his health, but also because she hoped to convert him to Methodism. She extolled the virtues of the place, in particular its views and its mountains. Lord Chesterfield, guessing her intentions, broke in, "I do not love mountains. When your ladyship's faith has removed them, I will go thither with all my heart."

3 Increasing deafness, political disappointment, and the unsatisfactoriness and eventual death of his son and namesake Philip clouded Lord Chesterfield's last years. His friend and contemporary Lord Tyrawley also suffered setbacks, being ignominiously dismissed from his post in Portugal in 1763 on the grounds that he was too old. Near the end of his life Chesterfield was asked by a mutual acquaintance how Lord Tyrawley was. He replied, "Tyrawley and I have been dead these two years, but we do not choose to have it known."

4 In the last few months of his life Lord Chesterfield was so infirm that when he rode in his carriage the horses were usually led at a slow walking pace. An acquaintance, meeting him on such an expedition, congratulated him on being able to take the air. His lordship thanked the man, adding, "I do not come out so much for the air, as for the benefit of rehearsing my funeral."

———∽———

CHESTERTON, G[ilbert] K[eith] (1874–1936), *British essayist and novelist who wrote a series of detective stories centered on the character of Father Brown, a Roman Catholic priest.*

1 Chesterton's prosperous middle-class parents, wedded to respectability, attached great importance to "proper" speech and the right accent. At the age of three GKC must have known this. He once screamed for his hat: "If you don't give it to me, I'll say *'AT'*!"

2 Chesterton was an imposing figure, very tall and burly. "Oh, Mr. Chesterton," gushed an admirer, "how wonderful it must be to be so famous that everyone knows who you are."
"If they don't, they soon ask," he replied.

3 Despite his large bulk, Chesterton had a mild falsetto voice, which he sometimes used to surprising effect. Before giving his first lecture on a tour of the United States, he was introduced in embarrassingly florid terms by a pompous and long-winded chairman. Sens-

ing the audience's restlessness, Chesterton got to his feet and murmured, "After the whirlwind, the still, small voice."

4 George Bernard Shaw, tall and thin, stood in vivid contrast to the corpulent Chesterton. They differed about other matters too. Once Shaw is reported to have said to Chesterton, "If I were as fat as you, I'd hang myself." Chesterton replied amiably, "And if I had it in mind to hang myself, I'd use you as the rope."

5 Once when G. K. Chesterton's economic views were abused in print by George Bernard Shaw, his friends waited in vain for him to reply. Historian Hilaire Belloc reproached him.

"My dear Belloc," Chesterton said, "I have answered him. To a man of Shaw's wit, silence is the one unbearable repartee."

6 Chesterton's vast bulk afforded him certain consolations. He once remarked that it gave him opportunity for gallantry. "Just the other day in the Underground I enjoyed the pleasure of offering my seat to three ladies."

7 During World War I, a young lady handing out white feathers in Fleet Street accosted Chesterton with the question: "Why are you not out at the front?"

"My dear madam," replied the portly novelist, "if you will step round this way a little, you will see that I *am*."

8 G. K. Chesterton was not embarrassed by his girth. In Pittsburgh he told a delighted audience: "I want to reassure you I am not this size, really — dear me, no. I'm being amplified by the mike."

9 Chesterton's mind was so preoccupied that he frequently forgot to keep appointments and was obliged to write apologetic notes explaining his absence. He once astonished his publisher by arriving punctually at the agreed hour. He then handed the man a letter containing an elaborate explanation of why he was unable to keep the appointment.

10 The absentminded Chesterton was devoted to his mother. When he became engaged to be married, he was so eager to share the happy event with her that he went straight home and wrote her a long letter. Mrs. Chesterton was delighted with her son's news, although she was not at all surprised to receive his letter. She was in the room with him when he wrote it.

11 "Chesterton relied on his wife in all practical matters. Once on a lecture tour he sent her the following telegram: 'Am in Birmingham. Where ought I to be?' She wired back: 'Home.'"

12 Alexander Woollcott met Chesterton for lunch at a London restaurant. Chesterton expounded on various philosophical topics, including the relationship between power and authority. "If a rhinoceros were to enter this restaurant now, there is no denying he would have great power here. But I should be the first to rise and assure him that he had no authority whatsoever."

13 Chesterton was once asked what books he would most like to have with him if he were stranded on a desert island. "Thomas's *Guide to Practical Shipbuilding*," he replied.

14 On his American travels, Chesterton was taken one night to view the brilliant lights of Broadway blazing the names of brand products and shows through the blackness. After staring at the spectacle for a few minutes Chesterton remarked, "How beautiful it would be for someone who could not read."

15 Chesterton was once chided by a magazine editor about his increasing size: "Ah, Gilbert, pregnant, I see." Chesterton replied, "Well, at least I don't suffer from your monthly periodicals."

CHEVALIER, Maurice (1888–1972), *French singer and actor.*

1 Chevalier was once asked why he had chosen to remain a bachelor. "You're not going to believe this," he replied, "but it's for a very good reason. When I get up in the morning, I like to have the choice of getting out of bed from either side."

2 Chatting to comedian Phil Silvers backstage, the seventy-three-year-old Chevalier heaved a deep sigh as a group of pretty showgirls trooped past them. "Ah, if only I were twenty years older," he said. "Don't you mean twenty years younger?" asked Silvers. "No," replied Chevalier. "If I were twenty years *older,* then these girls would not bother me the way they do."

CHIGI, Agostino (1465?–1520), *wealthy Italian banker, who lived at the Villa Farnese in Rome.*

1 When Agostino Chigi held dinner parties *al fresco* at the Villa Farnese, overlooking the Tiber, he would impress his guests by instructing them to jettison their dishes and cutlery into the river at the end of each course. The gesture was less extravagant than it seemed, however, for the banker had had the servants rig up nets just below the surface of the water before each party, so that none of his valuable tableware was lost forever in the mud of the Tiber.

CHOATE, Joseph Hodges (1832–1917), *US lawyer and diplomat.*

1 Choate was asked at a private dinner who he would like to be if he were not himself. He thought rapidly through a list of world celebrities, and then, catching his wife's eye, said, "If I could not be myself, I would like to be Mrs. Choate's second husband."

2 Once during a Supreme Court hearing it was pointed out to Choate that he was arguing directly contrary to what was stated in his brief. Choate was not at all abashed. "Oh well, I have learned a great deal about the case since the brief was prepared."

3 Fellow-lawyer Chauncey M. Depew was a rival wit with whom Choate had many skirmishes. At one dinner Depew introduced Choate with the words, "If you open Mr. Choate's mouth and drop in a dinner, up will come a speech." When Choate rose to speak he began, "Mr. Depew says that if you open my mouth and drop in a dinner, up will come a speech. But I warn you that if you open your mouths and drop in one of Mr. Depew's speeches, up will come your dinners."

4 Visiting at a certain ducal residence, Choate happened to be standing near the front door when an English nobleman came into the hall and, mistaking him for the butler, said to him, "Call me a cab."

"You are a cab," Choate obligingly replied.

The nobleman complained to his host and was gently told that Choate was the American ambassador. At this the nobleman returned to Choate to apologize. Choate said, "Pray don't apologize. If I had known who *you* were, I would have called you a hansom cab."

5 In a case at the New York courts Choate was opposed by an attorney from Westchester County, a residential area lying north of New York City. The attorney, having a poor case, fell back upon an attempt to belittle Choate, ending with a warning to the jury not to be taken in by Choate's "Chesterfieldian urbanity." Choate waited until his summing up,

then urged the jury not to be unduly influenced by "my opponent's Westchesterfieldian suburbanity."

———— ✑ ————

CHOPIN, Frédéric (1810–49), *Polish composer and pianist.*

1 Chopin was lionized by Parisian hostesses who imposed upon him by inviting him to dinner and then asking him to play something by way of free entertainment. One lady was particularly unsubtle in her approach, so much so that Chopin murmured in response to the inevitable request, "But, madame, I have eaten so little!"

2 Chopin was extremely fastidious; one point on which he was particularly sensitive was the physical appearance of his manuscripts. Knowing this, a friend to whom Chopin lent the manuscript score of his Concerto in E Minor donned white gloves to turn the pages and returned the manuscript to the composer without a spot or mark upon it. On opening it Chopin grimaced with displeasure. "My dear fellow, you were smoking when you read it!" he exclaimed.

———— ✑ ————

CHRISTIAN X (1870–1947), *king of Denmark (1912–47).*

1 During the occupation, but before his imprisonment, the king noticed a Nazi flag flying over a Danish public building. He immediately called the German commandant, demanding that the flag be taken down at once. The commandant refused to comply with the king's request. "Then a soldier will go and take it down," said the king. "He will be shot," returned the commandant. "I think not," replied the king, "for I shall be the soldier."

The flag was taken down.

———— ✑ ————

CHRISTIE, Dame Agatha (1891–1976), *British writer of detective fiction, creator of the Belgian detective Hercule Poirot.*

1 Agatha Christie's second husband, Max Mallowan, was a distinguished archaeologist who made his name excavating in Mesopotamia. On her return with her husband from the Middle East Miss Christie was asked how she felt about being married to a man whose interest lay in antiquities. "An archaeologist is the best husband any woman can have," she said. "The older she gets, the more interested he is in her."

2 In 1977, a young Arab girl was flown to England in a semiconscious state and admitted to a London hospital. The doctors were baffled by her condition, which continued to deteriorate over the next five days. On the sixth day, the child began to lose her hair. The nurse watching over her was suddenly struck by the similarity of her symptoms to those of a series of murder victims in Agatha Christie's *The Pale Horse,* which she was reading at the time. The fictional characters had been killed by thallium poisoning; subsequent tests on the Arab girl revealed that she had high levels of thallium in her urine. Three weeks later, the child was fit enough to return home, and the case was written up in the *British Journal of Hospital Medicine,* with a note of thanks to the observant nurse and the late Dame Agatha Christie.

———— ✑ ————

CHRISTINA (1626–89), *queen of Sweden (1644–54).*

1 Having abdicated, Christina journeyed south through Europe and in Innsbruck was received into the Roman Catholic Church, no doubt to the huge satisfaction of the local priests, who made a grand ceremony out of

her abjuration. After the solemn ritual in the cathedral, the next item on Christina's agenda in Innsbruck was a visit to the theater. "It is only fair," she remarked, "that you should treat me to a comedy, after I have treated you to a farce."

———— ✄ ————

CHURCHILL, Randolph Frederick Edward Spencer (1911–68), *British journalist, son of Sir Winston Churchill.*

1 Randolph Churchill never won a contested election, though he was a member of Parliament for Preston during the wartime coalition in the 1940s. People naturally speculated that this failure to emulate his father was an embittering factor in his life. Someone, possibly Noël Coward, unkindly remarked, "I'm so fond of Randolph. He's quite unspoiled by his many failures."

2 Churchill was known for his temperamental character, and for his rudeness to complete strangers. Once, during a dinner party, he shouted at an executive of British petroleum, "You have nothing to contribute to this. You are only a clerk in an oil store." When a tumor was discovered in his lung (he was a chain smoker), many people openly hoped for the worst. But it was discovered to be benign. When Lord Stanley of Alderberry learned Churchill would make a complete recovery, he remarked, "What a pity to remove the one part of Randolph that is not malignant."

———— ✄ ————

CHURCHILL, Lord Randolph Henry Spencer (1849–95), *British politician, father of Winston Churchill.*

1 Lord Randolph Churchill was buttonholed on the stairs of his club by the resident bore,

who embarked on a long-winded tale. In desperation Lord Randolph summoned a footman. "Listen until his lordship finishes," he instructed the man and made his escape.

———— ✄ ————

CHURCHILL, Sir Winston (1874–1965), *British statesman, prime minister during and after World War II.*

1 In the early 1900s, Churchill gave a lecture on his escape from prison during the Boer War. He had been provided with a large map of the relevant part of South Africa, which he used from time to time during the talk. Describing his movements immediately after the escape, he suddenly broke off, looked closely at the map, and carefully placed the tip of his pointer on a tiny dot. "That's me!" he announced.

2 As a young subaltern Churchill sported a mustache. At a smart dinner he fell into argument with a grand dowager who, thinking to quell him, snapped, "Young man, I care for neither your politics nor your mustache."

"Madam," responded Churchill, "you are unlikely to come into contact with either."

3 Soon after Edward Marsh became Churchill's private secretary in 1905, he accompanied Churchill on an election campaign in his Manchester constituency. Their canvassing took them into the slums. Churchill looked at the rows and rows of squalid little houses with horror. "Fancy living in one of these streets," he observed to Marsh, "never seeing anything beautiful, never eating anything savory — never saying anything clever!"

4 Edward Marsh was waiting at a railroad station with Mrs. Churchill for Churchill to join them to catch a train. It was getting late and Mrs. Churchill began to worry that her husband would miss the train. Marsh soothed her by observing, "Winston is such a sports-

man that he always gives the train a chance to get away."

5 (Violet Asquith describes a conversation with Churchill at the dinner-table.)

"For a long time he remained sunk in abstraction. Then he appeared to become suddenly aware of my existence. He turned on me a lowering gaze and asked me how old I was. I replied that I was nineteen.

"'And I,' he said almost despairingly, 'am thirty-two already.'

"On reflection he added thoughtfully, 'Younger than anyone else who counts, though.' Then, savagely, 'Curse ruthless time! Curse our mortality. How cruelly short is the allotted span for all we must cram into it!' He burst into a diatribe about the brevity of life and ended: 'We are all worms. But I do believe that I am a glowworm.'"

6 A group of political friends who had achieved high office comparatively early in life were discussing their careers. Someone asked whether they had ever expected to be where they were then. They all said, "No," with the exception of Churchill, who was then home secretary at the age of thirty-five. "Yes," he said. "Napoleon won Austerlitz at my age."

7 Shortly before World War I Nancy Astor, the American-born wife of Waldorf, Viscount Astor, visited Blenheim Palace, the ancestral home of the Churchill family. In conversation with Churchill, she expounded on the subject of women's rights, an issue that was to take her into the House of Commons as the first woman member of Parliament. Churchill opposed her on this and other causes that she held dear. In some exasperation Lady Astor said, "Winston, if I were married to you, I'd put poison in your coffee." Churchill responded, "And if you were my wife, I'd drink it."

8 Despite holding important posts in the Liberal administration just before World War I, Churchill found that his salary from the government did not cover the expenses of his growing family. He was obliged to supplement his income by lecturing and journalism. "I live from mouth to hand," he remarked.

9 At one stage of World War I Churchill went across to France as a volunteer to observe the fighting at first hand. In his sandbagged shelter at the front line, he was brought a message from a visiting general, a former acquaintance, who wanted to see him. He was to walk to a crossroads about three miles away, where a car would pick him up and take him to the general. After waiting at the crossroads for nearly an hour, Churchill was joined by one of the general's officers. The car had been sent to the wrong crossroads and now it was too late for the meeting to take place.

Churchill began the long trudge back to the trenches in the dark and the rain, in a very bad humor, cursing the thoughtless general. When he got back to his shelter, however, he found that it no longer existed. Five minutes after he had left a shell had come through the roof, killing the man left inside. As Churchill records, "Suddenly I felt my irritation against General X pass completely from my mind. All sense of grievance departed in a flash. As I walked to my new abode, I reflected how thoughtful it had been of him to wish to see me again, and to show courtesy to a subordinate when he had so much responsibility on his shoulders."

10 Winston Churchill's powers of oratory became a legend; his broadcasts to the nation and his speeches in the House of Commons during World War II are world famous. Not all his friends, however, were complimentary. In the 1920s, for example, F. E. Smith complained, "Winston has devoted the best

years of his life to preparing his impromptu speeches."

11 In the House of Commons one afternoon, Churchill was attacking a certain aspect of government policy. Referring to Stanley Baldwin, then prime minister, Churchill declared: "History will say that the right honorable gentleman was wrong in this matter." After a brief pause, he added, "I know it will, because I shall write the history."

12 In 1938 Churchill published a collection of his speeches under the titles *Arms and the Covenant.* There was to be an American edition of the work, but the publishers felt that the title would not mean much to US readers, who were not very interested in the League of Nations. Churchill was asked to suggest an alternative. In due course he sent a cable suggesting "The Years of the Locust." Somehow the phrase got garbled in transmission and arrived in the publishers' offices as "The Years of the Lotus." The editors puzzled over what was intended and eventually, following through the association of lotuses and slumber, came up with the title *While England Slept.* The book duly appeared under this title and was a great success.

13 When Winston Churchill became First Lord of the Admiralty at the outbreak of World War II, he visited a naval base to see the Asdic antisubmarine defense system in operation. He was taken on board a warship, which sailed to an area in which there were known to be submerged wrecks. In due course the Asdic located one. Churchill asked what happened next. The naval officer in charge explained that they would then depth-bomb the target. Churchill asked to see this part of the operation as well, so a depth-charge was dropped overboard. A few seconds later there was a tremendous underwater explosion and quantities of water and wreckage erupted. Amid the wreckage was

an apparently intact door bearing upon it the letters W. C. Churchill afterward observed, "The navy always knew how to pay proper compliments, bless them."

14 Churchill made his first address to the US Congress on Boxing Day 1941. He remarked on this occasion, "If my father had been American and my mother British, instead of the other way round, I might have got here on my own."

15 In the summer of 1941 Sergeant James Allen Ward was awarded the Victoria Cross for climbing out onto the wing of his Wellington bomber, 13,000 feet above the Zuider Zee, to extinguish a fire in the starboard engine. Secured only by a rope around his waist, he managed not only to smother the fire but also to return along the wing to the aircraft's cabin. Churchill, an admirer as well as a performer of swashbuckling exploits, summoned the shy New Zealander to 10 Downing Street. Ward, struck dumb with awe in Churchill's presence, was unable to answer the prime minister's questions. Churchill surveyed the unhappy hero with some compassion. "You must feel very humble and awkward in my presence," he said.

"Yes, sir," managed Ward.

"Then you can imagine how humble and awkward I feel in yours," said Churchill.

16 "Before the Battle of El Alamein, he summoned General Montgomery and suggested that he study logistics. Montgomery doubted that he should become involved in such technical matters. 'After all, you know,' he said, 'they say that familiarity breeds contempt.' Churchill replied: 'I would like to remind you that without a degree of familiarity we could not breed anything.'"

17 Churchill was accosted at a wartime reception by a rather overbearing American lady. "What are you going to do about those wretched Indians?" she demanded.

"Madam," replied Churchill, "to which Indians do you refer? Do you refer to the second greatest nation on earth, which under benign and munificent British rule has multiplied and prospered exceedingly? Or to the unfortunate North American Indians, which under your present administration are almost extinct?"

18 Once when Churchill was visiting the White House, President Roosevelt wheeled himself along to the British premier's bedroom and opened the door unexpectedly. Churchill was standing in the middle of the room stark naked and unembarrassed. "You see, Mr. President," he said, "we British have nothing to hide."

19 F. D. Roosevelt had expressed hopes that the Yalta conference would not last more than five or six days. Remarked Churchill: "I do not see any way of realizing our hopes about world organization in five or six days. Even the Almighty took seven."

20 President Charles de Gaulle, a six-foot-four-inch humorless Frenchman with "a head like a banana and hips like a woman" (as Hugh Dalton remarked), did not hit it off with the much more compact and sparkling Churchill. Each had his own ego problem; each saw himself as the embodiment of his nation. On one occasion, during dinner at Chequers, Churchill was informed by his butler that de Gaulle wished to speak to him on the phone. Churchill, in the middle of drinking his soup, refused to take the call. De Gaulle, vehemently persisting through the intermediary of the butler, eventually persuaded the British leader to abandon his soup. When Churchill returned to the table ten minutes later, he was still crimson with rage. "Bloody de Gaulle! He had the impertinence to tell me that the French regard him as the reincarnation of John of Arc." Pause.

"I found it necessary to remind him that we had to burn the first one."

21 Churchill's actress daughter Sarah was married for a time to the music-hall entertainer Vic Oliver. Churchill did not particularly like him. Out walking one day, Oliver asked his father-in-law whom he had admired in the war. "Mussolini," growled Churchill surprisingly, adding, "He had the courage to have his son-in-law shot."

22 During a visit to America, Churchill was invited to a buffet luncheon at which cold fried chicken was served. Returning for a second helping, he asked politely, "May I have some breast?"

"Mr. Churchill," replied his hostess, "in this country we ask for white meat or dark meat."

Churchill apologized profusely.

The following morning, the lady received a magnificent orchid from her guest of honor. The accompanying card read: "I would be most obliged if you would pin this on your white meat."

23 George Bernard Shaw sent Churchill a note inviting him to the first-night performance of *Saint Joan*. He enclosed two tickets, "One for yourself and one for a friend — if you have one." Expressing his regret at being unable to attend, Churchill replied, asking if it would be possible to have tickets for the second night — "if there is one."

24 A critic (or editor) once had the temerity to correct a Churchillian sentence on the grounds that he should not have ended the sentence with a preposition. Churchill scribbled a note of his own: "This is the sort of English up with which I will not put."

25 A proud mother remarked that her baby looked exactly like Churchill. "Madam, all babies look like me," said Churchill.

26 He had few illusions about his oratorical effectiveness. When one of his friends asked, "Aren't you impressed to see ten thousand people gather to hear you speak?" he replied, "No — because ten times as many would come to see me hanged."

27 At a dinner for Commonwealth dignitaries, a chief of protocol approached Churchill, who was presiding, and whispered in his ear that one of the distinguished guests had been seen to slip a silver salt shaker into his pocket. Churchill promptly pocketed the matching pepper shaker. At the end of the meal he slid up to the offending guest, murmuring, "Oh, dear, we were seen. Perhaps we had both better put them back."

28 During an after-dinner conversation Churchill's son Randolph was trying to make a point when his father interrupted him to express his own opinion. Randolph listened for a moment, then attempted to bring the conversation back to his own line of reasoning. "Don't interrupt me when I am interrupting!" snapped his father.

29 Entering the men's room in the House of Commons one day, Churchill found Clement Attlee already standing at the urinal. Churchill took up his stance at the opposite end of the urinal. "Feeling standoffish today, are we, Winston?" asked Attlee. "That's right," replied Churchill. "Every time you see something big, you want to nationalize it."

30 At a dinner party one evening, there was a heated exchange between Churchill and a female MP. At the end of the exchange the lady scornfully remarked, "Mr. Churchill, you are drunk."

"And you, madam," replied Churchill, "are ugly. But I shall be sober tomorrow."

31 Returning home exhausted one evening, Churchill felt he could not face his last appointment of the day — a visit from a rather tiresome colleague who always outstayed his welcome. "When Sir —— arrives," he told his valet, "tell him I'm out." Then, after a moment's thought, he added, "And to convince him, smoke one of my cigars when you open the door."

32 While in New York, Churchill visited publisher Henry Luce, who had one of the former prime minister's landscapes hanging in his private office. "It's a good picture," remarked Luce, "but I think it needs something in the foreground — a sheep, perhaps." The following morning, Luce was horrified to receive a call from Churchill's secretary, requesting him to send the painting back. Luce complied, distressed to think that his criticism had caused such offense. A few days later, however, the canvas was returned — with a single sheep grazing placidly in the foreground.

33 One of Churchill's bodyguards also enjoyed painting in his spare time. He showed a few of his canvases to the former prime minister, who was quite impressed. "They're much better than mine," he remarked. "But yours will have to be judged on merit."

34 Asked why he chose to paint landscapes rather than portraits, Churchill replied: "Because no tree has ever complained about its likeness."

35 The photographer who had been photographing Churchill on his eightieth birthday said courteously that he hoped he would photograph him on his hundredth. "I don't see why not, young man," said Churchill. "You look reasonably fit to me."

36 In his eighties, Churchill paid a visit to the House of Commons. His appearance distracted attention from the debate then in progress. An MP said irritably, "After all, they say he's potty."

"They say he can't hear either," said the aged former prime minister.

———— ✣ ————

CHWOLSON, Daniel Abramovich (1819–1911), *Russian archaeologist.*

1 Asked whether his decision to join the Orthodox Church had been made through conviction or for expediency, Chwolson replied: "I accepted baptism entirely out of conviction — the conviction that it is better to be a professor in the Academy in St. Petersburg than a teacher in a *cheder* in Vilna."

———— ✣ ————

CIBBER, Colley (1671–1757), *British actor and dramatist who became poet laureate.*

1 Colley Cibber worked his way up in the theater from the humblest of beginnings. His very first role was a brief appearance to hand a message to a character played by the great Thomas Betterton. Paralyzed with stage fright, he made a mess of it and upset the other actors. Afterward, Betterton angrily asked the prompter for the name of the youth who had caused the disturbance. "Master Colley," replied the prompter.

"Master Colley. Then fine him!"

"But, sir, he has no salary."

"No?" said Betterton. "Then put him down for ten shillings a week and fine him five shillings."

———— ✣ ————

CICERO, Marcus Tullius (106–43 BC), *Roman orator and statesman.*

1 Caesar greatly increased the number of Roman senators, a practice that caused much resentment among those who were already entitled to senatorial rank. One day at the games a newly created senator walked along the rows, looking for a seat. As he passed Cicero, the latter said to him, "I should have been happy for you to sit beside me were I not already short of room," intending both to snub the interloper and to make plain his contempt for the enlarged senate. Mindful of Cicero's reputation for political fickleness, the man replied, "I am surprised that you of all people should be short of room, since you make a habit of sitting on two seats at once."

2 Caninius Rebilus was consul for only one day. Cicero, who deplored the disintegration of the ancient and dignified offices of the Roman Republic, made several observations on this event, including, "We have a consul of such vigilance that during his entire term he never slept a wink." And, on being reproached for not practicing the usual courtesy of calling on the consul during his consulship, Cicero explained, "I was on my way, but night overtook me."

———— ✣ ————

CIMON (d. 499 BC), *Athenian admiral and statesman.*

1 A barbarian prince who had formerly supported the Persian cause abandoned his ally and came to Athens, seeking to place himself under Cimon's protection. To ensure his welcome he brought two vessels, one filled with gold pieces and the other with silver, and placed them before Cimon's door. Cimon looked at them and smiled. "Would you prefer to have me as your mercenary or as your friend?" he asked.

"As my friend," replied the man.

"Go," said Cimon, "and take these things away with you. For if I am your friend, your money will be mine whenever I have need of it."

———— ✣ ————

CINQUE, Joseph (?1813–80), *African slave who led the mutiny aboard the Spanish ship* Amistad *in 1839.*

1 In his later years Cinque became an interpreter at a Christian mission in Sierra Leone. He was asked whether, if he were faced with the situation aboard the *Amistad* again, he would not now pray for the captain and cook instead of killing them. "I would pray for them," he replied, "and kill them too."

—◌◌—

CLAIRE, Ina (1895–1985), *US actress.*

1 Between 1929 and 1931 Ina Claire was married to John Gilbert, the romantic hero of the silent screen. A reporter asked her how it felt being married to a celebrity. "Why don't you ask my husband?" replied Mrs. Gilbert.

—◌◌—

CLARK, George Rogers (1752–1818), *US soldier.*

1 Impoverished and crippled, Clark applied to the Virginia legislature for a military pension. He was sent a ceremonial sword in token of his many heroic exploits. "When Virginia needed a sword, I gave her one. Now she sends me a toy," the old hero said. "I want bread." So saying, he broke the sword in two with his crutch.

—◌◌—

CLARK, Mark Wayne (1896–1984), *US general.*

1 Clark was once asked what was the best advice he had ever been given. "To marry the girl I did," he replied.

"And who gave you that advice?" was the next question.

"She did," said the general.

—◌◌—

CLAY, Cassius Marcellus, Sr. (1810–1903), *US abolitionist and diplomat.*

1 A cousin of the great Henry Clay, he remained loyal to the Union during the Civil War and fought numerous duels with fellow Kentuckians who disagreed with him. Though he was an expert duelist (he never lost an encounter), his first confrontation was a failure. As both he and his opponent missed their allowed three shots, the encounter was called off. It was well known that Clay could normally hit a suspended string at ten paces three times out of five. Asked to explain his inaccurate fire, he replied, "That damned string never had no pistol in his hand."

—◌◌—

CLAY, Henry (1777–1852), *US statesman and orator, nicknamed "the Great Compromiser" on account of his compromises to preserve the Union over the issue of slavery.*

1 Henry Clay's forceful and brilliant style of oratory won him the acclaim of the House but also the jealousy of certain older and more ponderous speakers whose long-windedness showed up badly in comparison. One such speaker approached Clay and tried to deflate him by pointing out that Clay's speeches, aimed at immediate impact, were for the present generation while most senior orators were speaking for posterity. "And it seems, sir, that you are resolved to speak until the arrival of your audience," retorted Clay.

2 John Randolph of Roanoke and Henry Clay were deadly rivals. On one occasion the two politicians found themselves walking toward each other on a footpath so narrow that they

could not pass. "I never give way to scoundrels," said Randolph, standing stock-still. "I *always* do," said Clay, stepping off the curb.

3 Jefferson's vision of the westward expansion of America fired the imagination of the young Henry Clay. On his way home from Washington to Kentucky he stepped from the stagecoach, bent down, and put his ear to the ground. "What are you listening for?" inquired the driver. "I'm listening for the tread of unnumbered thousands of feet that will pass this way westward," said Clay.

4 "You don't remember my name," said a lady to Henry Clay. "Madam, I do not," said Clay, bowing, "for when we last met, I was certain that your beauty and accomplishments would soon cause you to change it."

5 In about 1850 Clay observed in a speech, "I would rather be right than be President," a sentiment not borne out in his own unsuccessful struggle to achieve the supreme political office. John C. Calhoun, who had been vice president in 1824, commented, "I guess it's all right to be half right, and vice president."

6 Speaking at a meeting one day, Clay found himself struggling against a number of slave-owners who were trying to drown out his voice by hissing. "Gentlemen," he cried, "that is the sound you hear when the waters of truth drop upon the fires of hell."

7 Clay was sitting outside the old National Hotel in Washington with Daniel Webster, then US senator from Massachusetts. Watching a man walk by with a pack of mules, Webster remarked, "Clay, there goes a number of your Kentucky constituents."

"They must be going up to Massachusetts to teach school," commented Clay.

CLEMENCEAU, Georges (1841–1929), *French statesman, prime minister (1906–09, 1917–20), known as "the Tiger."*

1 Clemenceau told the following story of himself, and it perhaps illuminates his diplomatic methods. On a tour in the East he took a liking to a statuette offered for sale by a dealer. The man said he could have it for only 75 rupees, "because it's you." Clemenceau offered 45 rupees. The bargaining went on, with Clemenceau firmly sticking to his 45-rupee offer. Eventually the dealer flung up his hands indignantly. "Impossible! I'd rather give it to you!" he exclaimed. "Done!" said Clemenceau, pocketing the statuette. "You are exceptionally kind and I thank you, but such a gift could only come from a friend. I hope you will not be insulted if I offer you a gift in return." The bemused dealer said that he would not. "Here," said Clemenceau, "are forty-five rupees for you to use in charitable works." The dealer accepted the rupees and they parted on excellent terms.

2 Clemenceau once awarded the Legion of Honor to a business magnate whose only claim was his large contribution to the Tiger's political funds. Pinning on the decoration, Clemenceau said, "Sir, you wanted the Legion of Honor. Here it is. Now all you have to do is deserve it."

3 At a Paris railroad station on the way to one of his numerous duels, Clemenceau surprised his second by asking for a one-way ticket. "Isn't that a little pessimistic?" asked the second. "Not at all," replied Clemenceau. "I always use my opponent's return ticket for the trip back."

4 Clemenceau fought a duel with his longtime political rival Paul Deschanel. Every time Clemenceau lunged, Deschanel retreated a little farther. Eventually Clemenceau shrugged, tucked his sword under his arm, and said, "Monsieur is leaving us."

5 When Clemenceau was appointed home secretary, he arrived punctually at the department to inspect his new offices and staff. As he and his aide walked around the building, flinging open door after door, they found every office empty. At last they entered a room to discover a staff member slumped over his desk, fast asleep. As the aide darted forward to rouse him, Clemenceau put out a restraining hand. "Don't wake him," he said. "He might leave."

6 A supporter rushed into Clemenceau's office in great excitement, crying out, "Your son has just joined the Communist party." Clemenceau looked up calmly. "Monsieur, my son is twenty-two years old. If he had not become a Communist at twenty-two I would have disowned him. If he is still a Communist at thirty I will do it then."

7 Clemenceau's contrariness was invaluable in shaking France out of its torpor during World War I, but it was altogether less of an asset during the subsequent peace. This trait emerged even in trivial matters. Going into a grand garden party at Versailles, the bowler-hatted Clemenceau met the British foreign secretary, Lord Balfour, wearing a top hat. "They told me top hats would be worn," said the British diplomat. "They told me too," said Clemenceau.

8 After Wilson's departure from the Versailles conference following World War I, Clemenceau, on his way to a meeting with Colonel House, Wilson's adviser, was fired on by a young anarchist, Emile Cottin. As Clemenceau's car sped away, Cottin fired seven (some say eight) more shots. One hit Clemenceau near his heart. Cottin was apprehended and the death penalty demanded. Clemenceau intervened: "We have just won the most terrible war in history, yet here is a Frenchman who misses his target six times out of seven. . . . Of course the fellow must

be punished for the careless use of a dangerous weapon and for poor marksmanship." He recommended eight years in prison "with intensive training in a shooting gallery."

10 Clemenceau loathed flying and always avoided it whenever possible. Before one flight he was heard to admonish the pilot, "Fly very cautiously, very slowly, and very low."

CLEOPATRA (69–30 BC), *queen of Egypt renowned for her beauty.*

1 The lover of Julius Caesar and Marc Anthony among others knew the end — not only of her reign as queen of Egypt but of her life — was near when Octavian's invasion of her country produced Marc Anthony's corpse. Octavian sent his emissary, P. Cornelius Dolabella, to tell Cleopatra that instead of being killed, she would be taken to Rome and exhibited to the people. Cleopatra bathed and, with several of her court ladies, enjoyed a final meal. When Cornelius and his soldiers arrived, they found the queen dead along with a lady-in-waiting; the other courtier lay dying on the floor. "Was this well done by your lady?" Cornelius asked angrily. In her final throes Cleopatra's servant replied, "Exceedingly well, as became a descendant of a long line of kings."

CLEVELAND, Frances Folsom (1864–1947), *wife of Grover Cleveland, 22d and 24th President of the United States.*

1 At a White House dinner given during one of the Cleveland terms of office a young European attaché was served a salad that included a worm. He was on the point of raising a

protest when he caught Mrs. Cleveland's eye, fixed on him in a challenging stare. The attaché then proceeded to devour the salad, worm and all. Mrs. Cleveland smiled approvingly. "You will go far, young man," she told him. Fifteen years later that same attaché returned as a full ambassador.

CLEVELAND, [Stephen] Grover (1837–1908), US politician; 22d and 24th President of the United States (1885–89, 1893–97).

1 Cleveland, though constantly at loggerheads with the Senate, got on better with the House of Representatives. A popular story circulating during his presidency concerned the night he was roused by his wife crying, "Wake up! I think there are burglars in the house."

"No, no, my dear," said the President sleepily, "in the Senate maybe, but not in the House."

2 A reporter was pestering President Cleveland to make a statement on a major issue of foreign policy. "That, sir, is a matter of too great importance to discuss in a five-minute interview — now rapidly drawing to its close," said Cleveland firmly.

CLINTON, William Jefferson (1946–), US politician, 42d President of the United States (1993–2001).

1 When hecklers interrupted a speech Clinton was giving in Denver one evening, he responded with a quote from Mark Twain: "Every dog needs a few fleas because they keep him from worrying so much about being a dog."

2 Ours is an inquisitive age, with little privacy afforded public figures. Clinton's eating habits became a favorite focus of the media, which frequently published photos showing his weight gains and losses. Clinton had a sense of humor about his love of food, saying, "People say to me, 'Like Harry Truman, if you can't stand the heat, get out of the kitchen.' That's the only room in the house I don't want to leave."

3 A favorite story of Clinton's was about a man who saw a sign on a highway: "George Jones, Veterinarian-Taxidermist. Either way, you get your dog back."

4 After his election Clinton lunched with the publisher of the *New York Times*, Arthur Sulzberger, Jr., who told the new President, "The best way of describing our relationship with you is 'tough love.'" "Well, just don't forget the 'love' part," laughed Clinton.

5 About his relationship with reporters, Clinton once said, "Never pick a fight with people who buy ink by the barrel."

CLIVE, Robert, Baron Clive of Plassey (1725–74), British administrator in India.

1 In polite eighteenth-century society, diners were called upon for "sentiments," that is, epigrammatical observations or wishes expressed in the manner of roasts at the end of the meal. Clive's used to be: "Alas and alackaday!" (a lass and a lac — 100,000 rupees — a day).

2 The opportunities for corruption on the part of British officials in India were astounding. When Clive was being cross-examined on this score during the parliamentary proceedings against him in 1773, he burst out, "By God, Mr. Chairman, at this moment I stand astonished at my own moderation."

CLURMAN, Harold (1901–80), US *theatrical director and drama critic.*

1 With Lee Strasberg and Cheryl Crawford, Clurman was one of the directors of the Group Theatre, an influential theatrical force in the thirties. Out of it came the playwright Clifford Odets as well as a host of actors who later achieved fame on stage and screen. One of these, Stella Adler, married Clurman. Her affection was not alloyed by sentimentality. Robert Lewis, one of the youngest members of the Group, once asked her why Clurman continually studied his face, turning it from side to side, in the mirror. Stella Adler replied, "He's trying to imagine how he's going to look on that horse when he's a statue in Central Park."

2 Robert Lewis, visiting Clurman in Hollywood, shared a bedroom with him. He noted with some alarm that throughout the night in his sleep Clurman would emit a variety of dramatic sounds, including those of clicking teeth, affection, and rage. Stella Adler reported that she once awakened him and suggested, "Harold, don't sleep like a great man. Just sleep."

COBB, Irvin S[hrewsbury] (1876–1944), US *humorist and writer.*

1 As a young reporter in New York, Cobb suffered from the ill humor of his boss at the *World*, Charles E. Chapin. Arriving for work one day, Cobb found that Chapin was home ill. "Nothing trivial, I trust," commented Cobb.

2 As a correspondent during World War I, Cobb was sent to Belgium to cover the German invasion. Traveling to the Belgian army headquarters by taxi, he and his three colleagues were captured by the Germans and questioned. The interrogation lasted throughout the night and well into the next day, and Cobb's nervousness grew increasingly apparent. Finally he called out to the interrogating officer: "Sir, whether or not you intend to shoot us, will you at least grant us one request?" The German, a little surprised, asked, "What is that?" Replied Cobb: "Will you please tell the driver of our taxicab to stop the meter?"

COCTEAU, Jean (1889–1963), *French writer, artist, and occasional film director.*

1 Someone asked Cocteau what he would take if his house were on fire and he could remove only one thing. "I would take the fire," replied Cocteau.

2 Dissatisfied with one of his productions, Cocteau confided his disappointment to a group of his film students: "It's my worst work." One of his loyal disciples said, "Among us it's generally understood that you aren't its author."

3 Cocteau was once asked if he believed in luck. "Of course," he replied. "How else do you explain the success of those you don't like?"

4 Cocteau's publisher, Bernard Grasset, had put forward the view that publishers are more important than authors. "In that case," retorted Cocteau, "perhaps you ought to imitate the film producers. Announce a BOOK BY GRASSET in big characters, and then, in tiny letters, 'Words by Cocteau.'"

5 When the subject of heaven and hell was broached in conversation one day, Cocteau politely declined to offer any opinion. "Excuse me for not answering," he said. "I have friends in both places."

COHAN, George M. (1878–1942), *US actor, songwriter, and theatrical producer.*

1 Cohan auditioned an actor for a role and finally dismissed him. As the door closed, Cohan said to one of his staff, "I hate that rat. Remind me never to hire him again unless we need him."

2 When the Actors' Equity Association was officially organized in 1913, one of its foremost opponents was George M. Cohan. He ran a signed advertisement in the New York newspapers reading: "Before I ever do business with the Actors' Equity, I will lose every dollar I have even if I have to run an elevator to make a living." The next day a sign appeared hanging out of the office window of the Equity headquarters: "WANTED — ELEVATOR OPERATOR. GEORGE M. COHAN PREFERRED."

3 At the height of his success as a theatrical producer, Cohan was dining with his father at an expensive hotel. Listening to the violinist playing skillfully in the background during their meal, Cohan was reminded of the unsuccessful violin lessons of his childhood. "Say, Dad," he remarked, "perhaps if I had given more attention to my violin lessons I might be playing here."

"Yes, you might," replied his father. "But you wouldn't be eating here."

4 Jim Moore, founder of a famous New York restaurant, had many friends in the theatrical world. As he grew older several of them died and were sorely missed by Moore. One Friday afternoon he made a pilgrimage to the graves of those departed friends, remonstrating with them for their thoughtlessness in dying. When he got to George M. Cohan's grave he took out a parcel of fish and thumped it against the headstone. "In case you don't know," he shouted, "today's Friday, and I just want you to see what you're missing."

COHEN, Morris Raphael (1880–1947), *US educator, born in Russia.*

1 At the end of an introductory course in philosophy, one of Cohen's students complained, "Professor Cohen, you have knocked a hole in everything I've ever believed in, and you have given me nothing to take its place!"

"Young lady," replied the professor sternly, "you will recall that among the labors of Hercules he was required to clean out the Augean stables. He was not, let me point out, required to fill them."

COHN, Harry (1891–1958), *US movie producer, head of Columbia studios.*

1 Though Harry Cohn was greatly disliked in Hollywood, there was a large turnout for his funeral. An observer remarked: "It only proves what they always say — give the public something they want to see and they'll show up to see it."

2 Cohn's brother Jack once suggested to Harry that they produce a biblical epic. "What do you know about the Bible?" cried Harry. "I'll lay you fifty dollars you don't even know the Lord's Prayer." After a moment's thought, Jack began, "Now I lay me down to sleep . . ." Harry pulled $50 out of his pocket. "Well, I'll be damned," he said, handing the money to his brother. "I didn't think you knew it."

3 Cohn announced to his staff one day that he was planning a trip to New York. "Take me with you, Mr. Cohn?" asked the screenwriter Norman Krasna. "You? What the hell do I need *you* for?" stormed Cohn. "You'll need me, Mr. Cohn, because on trains you have to write out your order for your meals," replied

Krasna. "So what?" demanded Cohn. "So what?" replied the screenwriter. "*You* can't write. You'll starve to death!"

———cNo———

COKE, Sir Edward (1552–1634), *British lawyer and Chief Justice.*

1 In 1598 Coke (pronounced "cook") married as his second wife, Lady Elizabeth Hatton, the widow of Sir William Hatton and grand-daughter of Lord Burghley. There was much speculation at the time as to why a lady with such grand connections should ally herself with a man of Coke's plebeian origins. An anecdote preserved by John Aubrey suggests a reason. In bed with his new wife, Coke put his hand on her belly and felt a child stir. "What? Flesh in the pot?" he exclaimed. "Yes," said the lady, "or else I would not have married a cook."

———cNo———

COLAVITO, Rocky (1933–), *US baseball player.*

1 During a game with the Cleveland Indians, batter Moose Skowron hit a pitch into right field, where Colavito missed the catch, falling onto the ball instead. Looking wildly around him as he sat on the field, Colavito was unable to locate the ball — but the fans knew he was sitting right on it. Out from the dugout rushed manager Joe Gordon, who yelled, "Somebody tell him to get off the ball before he hatches it!"

COLE, Dr. Harry (?1500–1580), *British clergyman, Dean of St. Paul's Cathedral.*

1 In 1558 Cole was given a commission to suppress the Protestants of Ireland. En route to Dublin, he stopped for the night at Chester, where he lodged with the mayor, to whom he showed his commission, boasting, "Here is what shall lash the heretics of Ireland." The mayor's wife, overhearing these words,

feared for her brother, a Protestant living in Dublin. Seizing an opportunity when Cole's back was turned, she opened the box, removed the commission, substituted a pack of playing cards, and resealed the box. The following day Cole went on his way unsuspecting.

As soon as he landed in Ireland he went to a meeting of the Privy Council, where he announced his errand to the lord deputy. When the lord deputy opened the box, all he found was the pack of cards, with the knave lying uppermost. "Let us have another commission," said he, "and in the meantime we will shuffle the cards." So Cole was obliged to return to England, but before he could reach Ireland again with a fresh commission Queen Mary died and Elizabeth ascended the throne. It is said that Elizabeth gave the resourceful wife of the Chester mayor an annual pension for her part in preserving the Irish Protestants from persecution.

———cNo———

COLERIDGE, Samuel Taylor (1772–1834), *British poet, critic, and philosopher.*

1 In 1796 Coleridge launched a periodical called *The Watchman,* a collection of prose and verse with the motto: "That all might know the truth, and that the truth might make us free." The enterprise was a total failure; it was discontinued after the ninth issue and a large number of unsold copies lay around Coleridge's house. One morning the poet saw his servant-girl laying a fire and it seemed to him that she was being unnecessarily prodigal with the amount of paper she was using. "Don't worry, sir," she reassured him, "it's only *Watchmen.*"

2 (Coleridge tells the story of the genesis of "Kubla Khan.")

"In the summer of 1797, the author, then in ill health, had retired to a lonely farm-house between Porlock and Linton, on the

Exmoor confines of Somerset and Devonshire. In consequence of a slight indisposition, an anodyne had been prescribed, from the effects of which he fell asleep in his chair at the moment of reading the following sentence, or words of the same substance, in Purchas' *Pilgrimage:* 'Here the Khan Kubla commanded a palace to be built, and a stately garden thereunto. And thus ten miles of fertile ground were inclosed with a wall.' The author continued for about three hours in a profound sleep, at least of the external senses, during which time he has the most vivid confidence that he could not have composed less than from two to three hundred lines; if that indeed can be called composition in which all the images rose up before him as *things,* with a parallel production of the correspondent expressions, without any sensation or consciousness of effort. On awaking he appeared to himself to have a distinct recollection of the whole, and taking his pen, ink, and paper, instantly and eagerly wrote down the lines that are here preserved. At this moment he was unfortunately called out by a person on business from Porlock, and detained by him above an hour, and on his return to his room, found, to his no small surprise and mortification, that though he still retained some vague and dim recollection of the general purport of the vision, yet, with the exception of some eight or ten scattered lines and images, all the rest had passed away like the images on the surface of a stream into which a stone has been cast, but, alas! without the restoration of the latter."

3 (Charles Lamb recalls an encounter with Coleridge in London.)

"Brimful of some new idea, and in spite of my assuring him that time was precious, he drew me within the door of an unoccupied garden by the road-side, and there, sheltered from observation by a hedge of evergreens, he took me by the button of my coat, and closing his eyes commenced an eloquent discourse, waving his right hand gently, as the musical words flowed in an unbroken stream from his lips. I listened entranced; but the striking of a church clock recalled me to a sense of duty. I saw it was of no use to attempt to break away, so taking advantage of his absorption in his subject, I, with my penknife, quietly severed the button from my coat, and decamped. Five hours afterwards, in passing the same garden on my way home, I heard Coleridge's voice, and on looking in, there he was, with closed eyes — the button in his fingers — and his right hand gracefully waving, just as when I left him. He had never missed me!"

4 Coleridge was once involved in discussion with a man who firmly believed that children should not be given formal religious instruction of any kind. They would then be free to choose their own religious faith, he reasoned, when they reached the age of discretion. Coleridge did not disagree, but later invited the man into his somewhat neglected garden.

"Do you call this a garden?" exclaimed the visitor. "There are nothing but weeds here!"

"Well, you see," explained Coleridge, "I did not wish to infringe upon the liberty of the garden in any way. I was just giving the garden a chance to express itself and to choose its own production."

5 Shortly after Coleridge's tragedy *Remorse* appeared, he was sitting in a public room of a hotel when he heard his name being read out by a gentleman who was studying a newspaper report of a coroner's inquest. Coleridge asked if he might see the paper, and the stranger handed it over to him. "Extraordinary that Coleridge should have hanged himself just after the success of his play, but he always was a strange mad fellow," he remarked. "Indeed, it is the most extraordinary thing," said Coleridge, "that he should

have hanged himself, be the subject of an inquest, and yet should be here at this moment speaking to you." Greatly disconcerted, the other man began to apologize, but Coleridge had taken no offense and was scanning the coroner's report. It seemed that the body of a man had been cut down from a tree in Hyde Park, and no papers had been found in his pockets to identify him, but inside his shirt was a label reading "S. T. COLERIDGE." Coleridge could readily explain that; in his travels he very frequently mislaid or otherwise lost shirts.

6 Coleridge was out riding with a friend near his home in the Lake District, wearing his customary shabby clothes. Seeing some people approaching, Coleridge suggested that he pass himself off as his friend's servant. "No," said his companion. "I am proud of you as a friend, but would be ashamed of you as a servant."

7 "Did you ever hear me preach?" Coleridge asked Lamb. Replied Lamb, "I have never heard you do anything else."

———— ⌘ ————

COLETTE [Sidonie Gabrielle Claudine Colette] (1873–1954), *French writer.*

1 In a memoir written in her forties, Colette said that she owed all her success as a writer to the appeal that her mother made to her constantly in her childhood, as she did her farm chores, to "Look, look!" Colette died in Paris in 1954, during the worst thunderstorm to visit Paris in sixty-seven years. She was eighty-one then, but her passion for observation was undiminished. Her last conscious act was to gesture toward the flashing lightning and exclaim, "Look, look!"

———— ⌘ ————

Samuel Butler told this story about the poet Herbert Clarke's little boy aged ten: "His mother had put him to bed and, as he was

supposed to have a cold, he was to say his prayers in bed. He said them, yawned and said, 'The real question is whether there is a God or no,' on which he instantly fell into a sweet and profound sleep which forbade all further discussion."

— *Samuel Butler's Notebooks: Selections,*
ed. Geoffrey Keynes and Brian Hill

———— ⌘ ————

COLLINS, Joan (1933–), *British-born actress and popular novelist known especially for her television appearances.*

1 Miss Collins had been friendly with the director George Englund. When his wife, Cloris Leachman, revealed symptoms of pregnancy, Miss Collins understandably lost her temper. "That's *my* baby she's having!" she screamed at Englund.

———— ⌘ ————

COLLINS, Michael (1890–1922), *Irish nationalist leader.*

1 One of the leading figures on the British side during the 1921 negotiations over the Irish treaty was F. E. Smith, who supported a compromise on the basis of a division that allowed Ulster to remain under British control. This encountered opposition in Britain, and after signing the treaty Smith observed as he laid down his pen, "I may have signed my political death warrant tonight."

"I may have signed my actual death warrant," said Collins.

Eight months later Collins was gunned down by republican extremists opposed to the compromise with Britain.

———— ⌘ ————

COLUMBUS, Christopher (1451–1506), *Italian-born navigator who was a discoverer of America (1492).*

1 On Columbus's first voyage west, in 1492, his crew was understandably uneasy about

the trip through unknown waters, to an unknown destination, and for an unknown period of time. To reassure the sailors and disguise the true length of the journey, Columbus kept two logs: one the real distances traveled as he reckoned them, and the other giving shorter ones so that the crew would think they were closer to home than they actually were. The irony is that it turned out the falsified figures were more accurate than the ones Columbus kept in the "true" log.

2 At a banquet given by the grand cardinal of Spain, Columbus was seated at the most honored place at table and served with great deference and ceremony. A courtier, jealous of the foreigner's success, asked him rudely whether he thought that if he had not discovered the New World somebody else would have done so. Columbus did not reply at once, but, taking an egg in his hand, invited the guest to make it stand on one end. All tried and failed, whereupon Columbus cracked the egg against the table in such a way as to flatten one end. Then he set it standing on the crushed part. The moral was plain to the company: once he had shown the way, anyone could follow it.

3 At his anchorage off Jamaica in 1504 Columbus faced a dangerous situation with supplies of food running low and the Jamaican Indians refusing to sell him any more. Consulting his almanac, he noticed that a lunar eclipse was due a few days later. On the day predicted he summoned the leaders of the Jamaicans, telling them that that night he would blot out the moon unless they resumed food trading. The Jamaicans laughed at him, but that night, when the lunar eclipse began, they came hurrying back in a state of great terror. Columbus said he would restore the moon if they would bring him food, an offer that they gladly accepted. The moon was duly restored and the Ja-

maicans hurried to bring food supplies they had withheld.

COMTE, Auguste (1798–1857), *French philosopher.*

1 Knowing that he was about to die, Comte murmured, "What an irreparable loss!"

CONDORCET, Marie Jean Antoine Nicolas de Caritat, Marquis de (1743–94), *French writer, mathematician, and philosopher.*

1 After the Jacobins came to power, Condorcet was sheltered by a widow who bravely insisted that the outlaw remain with her despite the knowledge that she would certainly be killed if he were discovered. Concerned for her safety, Condorcet slipped away and went into hiding for three days in a stone quarry until hunger forced him out to a tavern in the village of Clamart. Here he ordered an omelet. The cook asked how many eggs he wanted. With an aristocrat's ignorance of the usual number of eggs for such a dish, Condorcet ordered a dozen. Suspicions aroused, the taverner demanded his trade. "Carpenter," lied Condorcet. The man snatched the fugitive's hands and studied them. "You're no carpenter," he declared, and Condorcet was dragged off to prison. The next day he was found dead on the floor of his cell.

CONFUCIUS (c. 551–479 BC), *Chinese philosopher and political administrator.*

1 Ejected from yet another state, Confucius and his disciples were passing through a remote and deserted region when they came upon an old woman weeping beside a grave. The master asked her why. A tiger had killed

her husband, she explained, and her husband's father; now it had recently slain her only son. "Why then do you live in this savage place?" asked Confucius. "Because there is no oppressive government here," was the reply. "My children," said Confucius to his followers, "remember that oppressive government is worse than a tiger."

2 Confucius and his disciples, traveling through dry country, were all suffering from thirst. One disciple, however, managed to discover a hidden rain puddle, filled his rice bowl, and offered it to the Master. Confucius was about to raise it to his lips when he observed the faces of his disciples. At once he emptied the bowl on the ground, saying, "It would be too much for one, too little for all of us. Let us continue our walk."

—⊶—

CONGREVE, William (1670–1729), *British dramatist.*

1 After 1700 Congreve wrote little, preferring to lead the life of a gentleman supported by various pensions and sinecures obtained for him by his friends. Voltaire had the highest admiration for Congreve's comedies and on his visit to England sought out the elderly ex-dramatist. Much to Voltaire's disgust, Congreve spoke slightingly of the profession of author, although he owed to it his lasting fame and worldly fortunes, telling Voltaire that he wished to be thought of merely as an ordinary gentleman. Voltaire told Congreve sharply that if he had been so unfortunate as to have been only "a mere gentleman," he would never have come to visit him.

—⊶—

CONNELLY, Marc (1890–1980), *US dramatist.*

1 Connelly was almost totally bald. One afternoon at the Round Table in the Algonquin dining room a man ran his hand over the dramatist's bare head and observed, "That feels just like my wife's behind." Connelly stroked his head thoughtfully. "So it does," he replied.

2 Connelly was traveling in Portugal with a group of US pressmen, although his own credentials for joining the party were nonexistent. At a formal dinner all the members were invited by their Portuguese hosts to say a few words about the publications they represented. Some of the touring Americans wondered how Connelly would get out of what was potentially an embarrassing situation. When his turn came, Connelly got to his feet with perfect dignity, announced his name, and said, "I am editor of *Popular Wading,* the magazine of shallow water sports." He then went on to deliver a fifteen-minute oration on the imaginary publication, praising its editorial policy and excoriating the rival magazine *True Wading,* which catered only to "those sports reaching the ankle." When he sat down, the touring press group gave him an enthusiastic ovation. The Portuguese maintained a bemused silence.

—⊶—

"Primo Carnera was the hulking giant who captured the boxing world's imagination during the 1930's. Not much on defensive skills, he seemed willing to absorb a hundred punches if he could get off one good one himself. It was during his fight with Max Baer, with Baer giving Primo a thorough boxing lesson, that Grantland Rice remarked, 'The big fellow sure can take it.' 'Yes,' said another writer, Heywood Broun, 'but he doesn't seem to know what to do with it.'"

— R. L. Crouser, *It's Unlucky to Be Behind at the End of the Game*

—⊶—

CONNOLLY, Cyril (1903–74), *British writer and critic.*

1 (Connolly was easily moved to tears, sometimes for the most trivial reasons. Stephen Spender recalls such an occasion.)

"At a restaurant dinner given on some fairly grim PEN Club Conference occasion, he [Connolly] was sitting opposite me and I noticed the tears start in his eyes and then trickle down each cheek. Suddenly he got up from the table, came over to me, and insisted on changing places. Intense boredom with the conversation of the lady journalist on his left had driven him to this extreme course of action."

————— ✎ —————

CONSTABLE, John (1776–1837), *British artist.*

1 Before the opening of the Royal Academy's annual exhibition, Constable and the other artists were there doing the final touching-up to their work. Constable paused to look at a landscape by Clarkson Stanfield and particularly singled out the sky for praise. A little while later he met his friend Ramsay Reinagle and told him to look at Stanfield's work. "Take particular note of the sky; it looks just like putty," he added. Reinagle went to look. "But I like the sky!" he exclaimed, half to himself, after studying the picture. Stanfield overheard him and demanded to know what he meant. "Well, Constable told me the sky was like putty," Reinagle said. Incensed, Stanfield sought out Constable and accused him of being a humbug. "You singled out the sky for particular praise, and then you tell Reinagle it looks like putty!"

"So what?" said Constable. "I happen to like putty."

2 It is said that Constable and William Blake met on only one occasion. Constable showed the older artist some of his drawings, and Blake exclaimed enthusiastically, "Why, this is not drawing, but inspiration!"

"I never knew it before," replied the prosaic Constable. "I meant it for drawing."

3 While Constable was painting *The Cenotaph,* he was asked whether he would have trouble deciding on how to represent a certain brown tree. "Not in the least," replied Constable, "for I never put such a thing into a picture."

————— ✎ —————

CONSTANTINE [Constantine the Great] (c. 285–337), *Roman emperor in the West (312–24) and sole emperor at Byzantium (312–37). He was the first emperor to be converted to Christianity.*

1 In the first decade of the fourth century AD six men claimed the leadership of Rome. Chief among them were Maxentius, proclaimed emperor by the Roman Praetorian Guard, and Constantine. In 312 Constantine advanced across the Alps toward the forces of Maxentius and challenged him at the Mulvian bridge over the Tiber. On the afternoon before the battle Constantine saw a flaming cross outlined against the sun; on it were the Greek words *"En toutoi nika"* (In this sign you shall conquer). The next morning Constantine heard a voice in a dream commanding him to have his soldiers mark upon their shields the chi rho — the monogram for Christ. Constantine obeyed, fought Maxentius, and won.

————— ✎ —————

CONTI, Prince Louis-Armand II de (1695–1727), *a member of one of the most influential French families, who was often called a monster of vice.*

1 The prince was as ugly as his wife was witty. One day, about to depart on a journey, he said to her in jest, "Madame, I would advise

you above all things not to make me a cuckold during my absence." Her reply: "Monsieur, you may leave without any anxiety, for it is only when I look at you that I have any wish to deceive you."

———— ⋈ ————

COOK, Thomas (1808–92), *British tour operator*.

1 Cook himself was a zealous supporter of temperance, but his non-teetotal clients on continental tours took a different view. At an Italian railroad station his flock surged toward the buffet in search of cheap local wine. He tried to halt them with the cry: "Gentlemen, don't invest your money in diarrhea!"

———— ⋈ ————

COOLIDGE, [John] Calvin (1872–1933), *30th President of the United States (1923–29)*.

1 On returning from church one day, Coolidge was asked on what topic the minister had preached. After a moment's thought he replied, "Sin."
  "And what did he say about sin?"
  "He was against it."

2 A lady sitting next to Coolidge at dinner tried to coax him into talking to her. "I have made a bet, Mr. Coolidge, that I could get more than two words out of you."
  "You lose," said Coolidge.

3 While Coolidge was governor of Massachusetts, two of the state senators had an argument, which ended in one telling the other that he could "go to hell." The insulted politician went to see Coolidge to ask him to do something about it. Coolidge said calmly, "I have looked up the law, senator, and you don't have to go."

4 When Coolidge became vice president, he was succeeded as governor of Massachusetts by Channing H. Cox, who came to Washington to call on his predecessor. Cox was impressed by the fact that Coolidge was able to see a long list of callers every day and yet finish his work at five PM, while Cox found that he was often detained at his desk up to nine o'clock. "How come the difference?" he asked Coolidge. "You talk back," said Coolidge.

5 During the first days of his presidency, Coolidge and his family had not yet left their third-floor suite at the Willard Hotel in Washington. In the early morning hours the President awoke to see a cat burglar going through his clothes, removing a wallet and a watch chain. Coolidge spoke: "I wish you wouldn't take that. . . . I don't mean the watch and chain, only the charm. Read what is engraved on the back of it." The burglar read: "Presented to Calvin Coolidge, Speaker of the House, by the Massachusetts General Court." Coolidge then identified himself as the President, persuaded the burglar to relinquish the watch charm, led him into a quiet conversation, found out that the young man and his college roommate were unable to pay their hotel bill and buy train tickets back to their campus, counted out $32 from the wallet (which the dazed young man had also relinquished), declared it to be a loan, and advised the student to leave (in order to avoid the Secret Service) as unconventionally as he had entered.

6 During his presidency Coolidge was taken around the horticultural conservatories of Pierre S. Du Pont's estate at Longwood, Pennsylvania. The party passed through greenhouses containing magnificent orchids, extraordinary and grotesque cacti, and exquisite tropical ferns, none of which brought a word of comment from the President. At last they came to the conservatory devoted to

tropical trees. The President gazed about him for a few seconds and observed with interest, "Bananas."

7 Visiting the Amherst home of the poet Emily Dickinson, Coolidge was given a special guided tour of the house and allowed to see and handle many relics normally kept under lock and key. In the small room upstairs where Emily Dickinson had done most of her writing he was shown the greatest treasures of all: the holograph manuscripts of some of her most famous poems. He studied the handwritten sheets with some interest and then made the only observation of his entire visit: "Wrote with a pen, eh? I dictate."

8 A lady admirer burst into Coolidge's office to congratulate him on a speech he had made the previous day. She reported that the hall had been so crowded she had been unable to get a seat, so "I stood up all through your speech."

"So did I, madam," said the President.

9 President and Mrs. Coolidge, visiting a government farm, were taken around on separate tours. At the chicken pens Mrs. Coolidge paused to inquire of the overseer whether the rooster copulated more than once a day. "Dozens of times," said the man. "Tell that to the President," requested Mrs. Coolidge. The President came past the pens and was told about the rooster. "Same hen every time?" he asked. "Oh, no, a different one each time." Coolidge nodded. "Tell that to Mrs. Coolidge," he said.

10 "The ambassador of a great nation called at the White House one day for an important and private conversation with the President. Mrs. Coolidge came in as the ambassador was preparing to leave. 'Why don't you offer the ambassador a drink?' she suggested. 'He's already had one,' said the President testily. The next day, correspondents asked if he had anything to say about the conference.

'No,' said Coolidge. 'I have nothing to say about anything else either.' As they were leaving, he called after them, 'And don't quote me!' "

11 An overnight guest at the White House was mystified when he saw the President at breakfast pouring some milk from his cup into a saucer. Fearful of committing some breach of etiquette, the guest imitated him. Coolidge said nothing but smiled slightly. Bending down, he placed the saucer on the floor for the cat, which had been waiting quietly under the table.

12 Senator Selden P. Spencer of Missouri, walking around the White House grounds with Coolidge, pointed to the Executive Mansion. "I wonder who lives there," he said facetiously. "Nobody," replied Coolidge glumly. "They just come and go."

13 When Will Rogers was to be presented to President Coolidge, a friend bet him that he would not be able to make Coolidge laugh inside two minutes. "I'll make him laugh in twenty seconds," retorted Rogers. The introduction was performed: "Mr. President, this is Mr. Will Rogers; Mr. Rogers, President Coolidge." Rogers held out his hand, then a look of embarrassment and confusion stole over his face. "Er, excuse me, I didn't quite get the name." Coolidge grinned.

14 Coolidge became an enthusiastic angler, but his skill did not match his keenness. Asked how many trout there were in one of his favorite fishing places, Coolidge replied that there were estimated to be about forty-five thousand. Then he added, "I haven't caught them all yet, but I've intimidated them."

15 Coolidge was once invited to break ground for the cornerstone of a public building. Having performed this ceremonial duty, he was expected to make a speech. Pointing to the broken earth, he observed solemnly,

"That's a mighty fine fishworm," and then departed.

16 A biography of George Washington containing libelous observations having recently been published, a group of reporters visited Coolidge to get his reaction. The President merely moved to the window, pulled back one of the curtains, revealing the Washington Monument, and murmured, "I see it's still there."

17 "President Coolidge had a group of guests on the presidential yacht cruising the Potomac. As he stood alone at the rail, looking out at the expanse of water, someone exclaimed, 'Look at that slight and slender figure! Look at that head, bowed over the rail! What thoughts are in the mind of this man, burdened by the problems of the nation?' "Finally, Coolidge turned around, and joined the others, saying, 'See that sea gull over there? Been watching it for twenty minutes. Hasn't moved. I think he's dead!'"

18 A talkative young lady had failed to get any response from Coolidge throughout the course of a dinner party. "You go to so many dinners," she finally remarked. "They must bore you a great deal." Without lifting his eyes from the table, Coolidge replied, "Well, a man has to eat somewhere."

19 Asked at a press conference whether he would be attending a certain trade fair the following day, Coolidge replied, "I think the press already knows that I am expecting to attend."

"It isn't likely you will say anything tomorrow at the fair?"

"No," replied the President. "I am just going as an exhibit."

20 One day Coolidge was waiting to get his hair cut when the local doctor came in, sat beside him, and asked, "Did you take the pills I gave you?" Coolidge was characteristically silent for a few minutes, then said, "Nope."

The doctor then asked if he was feeling better. Another long pause, then Coolidge replied, "No." After his haircut Coolidge started to leave the barbershop when the barber suggested that he had forgotten to pay for his haircut. "Oh, I'm sorry," said Coolidge. "I was so busy gossiping with the doctor, it slipped my mind."

21 A visitor to the White House approached Coolidge in a receiving line and introduced himself, saying, "Mr. President, I'm from Boston." "You'll never get over it," replied the President.

22 At the end of his elected term of office, President Coolidge issued his famous "I do not choose to run" statement. Anxious reporters pressed persistently for a more detailed statement. One managed to bar his way: "Exactly why don't you want to be President again, Mr. Coolidge?"

"Because," answered the President, brushing him aside, "there's no chance for advancement."

23 Soon after he had left the White House, Coolidge had to fill out a form confirming his membership in the National Press Club. After writing his name and address, he moved on to the space marked "Occupation," in which he wrote "Retired." Next came "Remarks." Coolidge paused for a moment and then wrote, "Glad of it."

24 A newspaper reporter visited Coolidge in his retirement and noted the number of sightseers driving past the house. "It must make you proud to know that even as an ex-President you are not forgotten. Just look at the number of those cars."

"Not as many as yesterday," replied Coolidge, "there were sixty-three then."

25 Someone came up to Dorothy Parker and blurted out the news that Coolidge was dead. "How can they tell?" she inquired.

COOPER, Lady Diana (1892–1986), *British social leader renowned for her beauty and wit.*

1 As part of a publicity stunt for a play due to open in New York with Diana Cooper as leading lady, the rumor was put about that another actress had been engaged for the role. Alarmed, Lady Diana cabled the impresario Morris Gest to know if she was still wanted. He replied, "Come to America and I'll treat you like a queen."

"Which queen?" Lady Diana cabled back. "Mary Queen of Scots?"

2 Lady Diana was known for the notes she would leave on her car's windshield as excuses for parking illegally. One note read, "Dear Warden — taken sad child to cinema — please forgive." One day she left a note that read, "Old cripple's car. Gone for lunch." When she returned, she found a parking ticket together with a message from the police officer: "Hope you had a good lunch, dear."

COOPER, Gary (1901–61), *US actor and film star.*

1 Originally named Frank, Cooper was renamed by a movie agent who felt his name was not evocative enough. She hesitated over several choices, then dubbed him Gary, after her hometown, Gary, Indiana. Cooper later noted, "It's a good thing she didn't come from Poughkeepsie!"

2 When Gary Cooper first came to Hollywood from Montana, he was taken under the wing of a glamorous member of the international set, the Countess di Frasso. She wanted her handsome but gauche young lover to acquire the proper poise and sophistication. To this end she took him with her to Europe. Gene

Fowler remarked one day that he had not seen the countess and her young man recently, and was told where they had gone. "Oh, well," he said, "everyone knows the best way to go to Europe is on the Countess di Frasso."

3 While he was writing the script for *Along Came Jones,* Nunnally Johnson lent Cooper, who was to produce and act in the film, a copy of the novel on which it was based. A couple of weeks later, Johnson asked Cooper: "How did you like the book?"

"Oh, fine, I'm about halfway through," came the reply. "I'm reading it word by word."

COOPER, Dame Gladys (1888–1971), *British actress.*

1 As Dame Gladys, weakened by illness, brushed her hair on the last evening of her life, she peered into the mirror and remarked to her nurse, "If this is what virus pneumonia does to one, I really don't think I shall bother to have it again." She then tottered back to her bed and died peacefully in her sleep.

COOPER, James Fenimore (1789–1851), *US novelist best known for his works of frontier life.*

1 One evening Cooper was reading aloud to his wife, who lay ill in bed. After a few chapters, though, he threw aside the book, saying, "I could write you a better book than that myself." His wife, knowing that Cooper hated even writing letters, challenged him on the spot to try, which he did with gusto. And so began his writing career.

COOPER, Sir William (d. 1664), *British merchant.*

1 Sir William Cooper was a guest at a banquet held by the London Clothworkers' Company. Having partaken liberally of his hosts' brandy, he made his way home, where he dropped dead on arrival. Lady Cooper accused the Clothworkers of killing her husband with their noxious brandy, and when she died left a sum of money to the company with which to buy gin as a wholesome alternative.

The choice of brandy or gin is still offered at the Clothworkers' feasts with the words, "Do you dine with Alderman or Lady Cooper?"

⁂

COOTE, Robert (1909–), *British character actor.*

1 The British arrived in Hollywood as an invading army of expert settlers who formed themselves rapidly into polo clubs and cricket teams and gave tea parties for each other on Sunday afternoons. During one of these weekly gatherings, Robert Coote called across to Gladys Cooper in tones of disapproval: "Darling, there seems to be an American on your lawn."

⁂

COPE, Edward Drinker (1840–97), *US paleontologist.*

1 A Quaker, Cope refused to take a gun with him on his fossil-hunting forays, despite the fact that these led him into territories populated with hostile Indians. On one occasion, finding himself surrounded by a distinctly unfriendly band, Cope distracted his captors from their murderous intentions by removing and putting back his false teeth. Enthralled by this performance, they made him do it over and over again and eventually released him unharmed.

⁂

Sebastien Roch Chamfort was a French aphorist and playwright, an ardent supporter of the Revolution and an enemy of high society. One of his favorite stories was that of the marquis at the court of Louis XIV who, on returning to his wife, found her in the arms of a bishop. The nobleman walked calmly to the window and began blessing the people in the street below. When the startled wife asked what he was doing, the marquis replied: "Monseigneur is performing my function, so I am performing his."

— SIGMUND FREUD, *Wit and Its Relation to the Unconscious*

⁂

COPLAND, Aaron (1900–90), *US composer.*

1 Browsing in a bookshop one day, Copland noticed a woman buying a copy of his book *What to Listen For in Music,* together with a paperback edition of a Shakespeare play. As the customer left the shop, Copland stopped her and asked, "Would you like me to autograph your book?" Looking blankly into the composer's beaming face, the woman asked, "Which one?"

⁂

COPPÉE, François Edouard Joachim (1842–1908), *French poet.*

1 The wife of a not too distinguished writer once asked Coppée to support her husband's candidacy for a place in the French Academy. "I beg you, vote for my husband," she pleaded. "He'll die if he's not elected." Coppée agreed, but his vote failed to ensure the writer's success.

A few months later, another seat became vacant and the lady returned to Coppée to ask him to vote for her husband again. "Ah, no," replied the academician. "I kept my promise but he did not keep his. I consider myself free of any obligation."

———— ∽ ————

CORDAY, Charlotte (1768–93), *French noblewoman who assassinated the Jacobin leader Marat in his bath and was guillotined.*

1 Corday and Samson, the executioner, sat side by side in the tumbril on the way to the guillotine. To make conversation he said politely, "Perhaps you find the trip too long?"

"Bah, we're sure to get there," was the reply.

———— ∽ ————

CORNELIA (2d century BC), *Roman aristocrat, daughter of Scipio Africanus, wife of Tiberius Sempronius Gracchus.*

1 Most of Cornelia's children died young, but two, Tiberius and Gaius, grew up to become the famous reformers of Rome's agrarian laws. When the two Gracchi were still boys, Cornelia once received at her house a wealthy Roman lady who proudly showed off her jewelry to her hostess. She then challenged Cornelia to show off her own jewels. Cornelia gestured toward her sons, who had just entered the room. "These are my jewels," she said.

———— ∽ ————

CORNETT, Leanza (1973–), *Miss America, 1993.*

1 A serious activist who worked to support victims of AIDS among other causes, Cornett disliked wearing the rhinestone crown that was the symbol of her role as Miss America. "Who's going to take me seriously with this thing on my head?" she asked.

———— ∽ ————

COROT, Jean-Baptiste Camille (1796–1875), *French landscape painter of the Barbizon school.*

1 The caricaturist Honoré Daumier was very poor in his old age. On his sixty-fifth birthday, nearly blind, he was threatened with eviction from his little cottage at Valmondois because he could not pay the rent. Then he received a letter from Corot: "I have a little house at Valmondois which I could not, for the life of me, think what to do with. Suddenly I thought to give it to you, and liking the idea, I have had your ownership legally confirmed. I had no idea of doing you a good turn. The whole scheme was carried out to annoy the landlord. Ever yours, Corot." In his reply, Daumier wrote, "You are the only man from whom I could accept such a gift and not feel humiliated."

2 Even when very short of money, Corot found so much pleasure in having his pictures around him he could not rejoice unreservedly when he at last made a sale. "Alas, my collection has been so long complete, and now it is broken!" he exclaimed.

3 To a lady admirer who persisted in searching for hidden meanings in Corot's pictures, he replied: *"Non, madame, la peinture est plus bête que cela"* (No, madame, painting is too stupid for that).

———— ∽ ————

CORRIGAN, Douglas (1907–95), *US aviator.*

1 In 1937 Corrigan applied to the Bureau of Air Commerce for permission to make a solo flight across the Atlantic in his 1929 Curtiss-Robin monoplane (nicknamed *Lizzy*). After inspecting the aircraft the bureau refused permission on the grounds that it could not condone suicide: *Lizzy* lacked any safety de-

vices, radio, or beam finders, and the extra fuel tanks that Corrigan had put on completely obscured the pilot's forward view, so he had to look out of the side windows to see where he was going. Undaunted, Corrigan flew from Los Angeles to New York in twenty-seven hours in mid-July 1938. The following morning he told the airfield manager at New York that he was returning home. *Lizzy* was so weighed down with fuel that she traveled 3,200 feet along the runway before achieving takeoff. Just twenty-three hours and thirteen minutes later, Corrigan landed at Baldonnel Airport, Dublin. "I've just flown from New York," Corrigan announced to the airport official. "Not in that thing!" said someone, and told Corrigan where he was. "I flew the wrong way!" exclaimed the man who shortly (and forever after) would be known as Wrong-way Corrigan.

COTTEN, Elizabeth (1892–1987), *US musical performer.*

1 Cotten didn't begin her career as a singer, composer, and performer until she was sixty-seven; until then she had worked as a housekeeper. Her performance on the album *Elizabeth Cotten Live!* won her a Grammy Award in 1984, an experience she later described by saying, "I was just glad to get the Grammy. I didn't know what the thing was. It was the honor I loved."

COURTELINE, Georges [Georges Moineaux] (?1858–1929), *French playwright.*

1 A pretentious young writer, hoping to gain publicity, wrote to Courteline demanding satisfaction for some minor insult. The hand-writing of the letter was barely legible and the spelling atrocious. Courteline picked up his pen and replied: "My dear young sir. As I am the offended party, the choice of weapons is mine. We shall fight with orthography. You are already dead."

Gay Talese tells this story about Frank Costello, US racketeer:

"Even in jail Costello baffled the law. He continued to smoke English Ovals, although nobody knew how he smuggled them in. He ate steak — ebony on the outside, claret on the inside, just as he'd ordered at '21' — and yet it was impossible to uncover the source of the steaks. The unbelievable power that Costello was able to wield despite his imprisonment was demonstrated some years later when he performed a behind-bars miracle for his attorney, Edward Bennett Williams.

"Williams, during a visit to Costello's jail, seemed concerned about something, and Costello, detecting it, asked, 'What's bothering you, Mr. Williams?'

"Williams explained that he and his wife were taking her parents out that night to celebrate their thirty-fifth wedding anniversary and that he had promised them tickets to *My Fair Lady*; but the particular agent who had promised Williams the tickets — a person who'd always been reliable in the past — had suddenly failed on this occasion.

"'Mr. Williams,' Costello said, 'you shoulda told me; maybe I coulda helped.'

"Williams admitted it had never occurred to him that a man in jail could help get four tickets at the last minute to a hit Broadway show.

"Costello shrugged.

"It was then 5 PM.

"When Williams returned to his hotel room, he heard a soft rap on the door. Upon opening it, a broad-shouldered man under a slouch hat grunted something, handed over an envelope containing four tickets to that evening's performance of *My Fair Lady*, then quickly disappeared down the hall."

— GAY TALESE, *Fame and Obscurity*

COWARD, Sir Noël (1899–1973), *British playwright, actor, and wit.*

1 During rehearsal a young actor kept interrupting Coward with questions about the motivation behind the character he was playing. Finally Coward snapped, "Your motivation is your pay packet on Friday. Now get on with it."

2 The author Edna Ferber was fond of wearing tailored suits. Noël Coward, meeting her on an occasion when she was wearing a suit very similar to the one he himself was wearing, greeted her with the words: "You look almost like a man."

"So do you," said Miss Ferber.

3 Lady Diana Cooper, the society beauty who played a starring role in Max Reinhardt's famous production of *The Miracle,* observed to Coward that she had seen him in *The Vortex* (his domestic drama of the 1920s) and did not think that he had been very funny. Coward replied, "I saw you as the Madonna in *The Miracle,* and I thought you were a scream."

4 (The press unanimously damned Coward's *Home Chat* and *Sirocco,* but when he starred in S. N. Behrman's *The Second Man,* the critics praised his performance in extravagant terms. Raymond Massey describes an incident in Coward's dressing room after the second night.)

"Hannen Swaffer, a critic and theatre writer on the *Daily Express,* entered unannounced. He had been insufferable in his abuse of Noël (and of me, too). 'Nowley,' he sneered in his assumed cockney accent, 'I've always said you could act better than you write.' 'And I've always said the same about you,' was Noël's instant reply."

5 Coward was walking along the seafront at Brighton with Laurence Olivier and Olivier's young son. Observing two dogs copulating, the boy innocently asked what they were doing. "It's like this, dear boy," explained Coward. "The one in front is blind, and the kind one behind is pushing him."

6 During a rather stormy rehearsal of *Blithe Spirit,* actress Claudette Colbert screamed at Coward, "If you're not very careful, I may throw something at you!" "You might start with my cues," replied Coward.

7 Coward was strolling around an art exhibition at the Victoria and Albert Museum in London when a friend rushed up to him with an invitation to dinner. Noël politely declined, explaining that he was about to leave for Jamaica. "When will you be back?" asked his friend. "In the spring," replied Coward. "With the swallows. You'll recognize me easily among them."

8 Actor Clifton Webb was devoted to his mother, who had campaigned on his behalf with producers and directors throughout his career. A tireless exhibitionist, she was still dancing the cancan at Hollywood parties in her ninetieth year. When she finally died, Webb's health rapidly declined. "Poor dear," remarked Coward. "The late sixties is rather late to be orphaned."

9 The American writer Barnaby Conrad was badly gored in a bullfight in Spain in 1958. The columnist Leonard Lyons recorded a subsequent conversation between Eva Gabor and Noël Coward at a New York restaurant. "Noël dahling," said Eva, "have you heard the news about poor Bahnaby? He vass terribly gored in Spain."

"He was *what?*" asked Coward in alarm.

"He vass gored!"

"Thank heavens. I thought you said he was bored."

10 Coward once spent a rather uncomfortable night at a bug-ridden hotel in the Seychelles. "May I put up a sign reading 'Noël Coward

Slept Here'?" asked the manager as his distinguished guest checked out. "Certainly," replied Coward, "if you'll add one word — fitfully."

———— ✧ ————

COWL, Jane (1884–1950), *US actress.*

1 When John Barrymore was starring in *Hamlet* on Broadway, Jane Cowl attended one of the matinee performances. Her arrival caused a considerable stir in the theater and her audible comments throughout the play further distracted the audience. Barrymore himself gave no sign of noticing her presence until he took his curtain call. After thanking the audience, he bowed deeply in the direction of Miss Cowl's box and said, "Finally, I would like to take this opportunity to thank Miss Cowl for the privilege of co-starring with her this afternoon."

———— ✧ ————

CRANE, Stephen (1871–1900), *US journalist and writer.*

1 Crane participated in the invasion of Puerto Rico during the Spanish-American War. Once he was met outside a town by an American colonel, who, recognizing Crane and eager to be immortalized by the great war reporter, offered to include him in the next day's planned capture of the town. "This town!" cried Crane. "I'm really very sorry, Colonel, but *I* took this town myself before breakfast yesterday morning!"

———— ✧ ————

CRANMER, Thomas (1489–1556), *archbishop of Canterbury (1532–56).*

1 Mary I loathed Cranmer for his role in her mother's divorce from Henry VIII. In time, and accusing him of heresy, she forced him to sign a recantation, but when brought to St.

Mary's Church, Oxford, to make a public declaration of his former errors, he said that his conscience would not let him save his life by recanting. He bitterly regretted having signed the recantation, promising that when he was brought to the stake, the hand that had done the signing would be the first to burn. This promise he kept, holding his right hand steadfastly in the flames.

———— ✧ ————

CRAWFORD, Joan (1904–77), *US film actress and Academy Award winner.*

1 Leaving New York's "21" one day, Miss Crawford decided to take advantage of the sunny weather and walk home. "But, madam," protested her chauffeur, "you'll be mobbed."
  "I should certainly hope so," she replied.

2 During World War II Crawford, like other stars of the time, spent evenings helping to entertain soldiers on leave in the Hollywood Canteen. One night she was dancing with a sailor who looked hard at her and said, "You look just like Joan Crawford. Whatever happened to her?" When Crawford told him she *was* Joan Crawford, the sailor said, "Yeah? Whatever happened to you?"

3 After decades in the spotlight as one of the great screen stars, Crawford served on the board of directors of Pepsi-Cola. On a national tour promoting the soft drink, Crawford was asked what she really wanted to be — actress or spokesperson. Her reply: "What people want me to be."

———— ✧ ————

CRENSHAW, Ben (1952–), *US golf champion.*

1 Often compared to Sam Snead for his mastery of the game, the Masters champion Crenshaw has been self-deprecating nevertheless. Once early in his playing career a journalist asked him how far he felt he was

from being a great player. "About five inches," he said, "the distance between my right ear and my left ear."

2 Crenshaw tried to compete in the British Open of 1992 but failed to qualify. After his loss he entered a pub near the course, where the barkeep asked what he could bring him. "Arsenic," replied the dejected golfer.

———— ✑ ————

CROCKETT, Davy (1786–1836), *US frontiersman, member of Congress, and folk hero.*

1 When he first returned from Washington, Crockett remarked on the curiosity of the people in his home town about how people in the capital lived. Crockett told them, "They have breakfast when the sun is one or two hours high, and when you fellows have done practically half a day's work. About one or two o'clock in the day they have what they call lunch, and 'way in the night, they have their dinner."

"Then when do these people have their supper?" asked a constituent. "They don't get that until the next day," Crockett replied.

2 At a menagerie exhibition in Washington, Crockett amused his friends by pointing out a similarity between the features of one of the monkeys on display and those of a certain member of Congress. Turning around, Crockett found the member in question standing right behind him. "I suppose I ought to apologize," he said, "but I don't know whether to apologize to you or to the monkey."

———— ✑ ————

CROCKFORD, William (1775–1844), *British gambler, founder of the famous gambling club that still bears his name.*

1 Crockford's horse Ratan was favorite for the 1844 Derby. A few days before the race the horse was poisoned. Crockford's rage and disappointment brought on a fit of apoplexy that proved fatal. This put his gambling friends in a quandary as Crockford also had a heavily backed filly entered for the Oaks, which is run at the same Epsom meeting as the Derby itself. If the owner's death became known, the filly would be disqualified. They therefore propped Crockford's body up at a window in his house at Epsom, overlooking the racecourse, where it would be clearly visible to the crowd, who would thus discount any rumor of Crockford's demise. The filly won the race and the punters duly collected their winnings before their ruse was discovered.

———— ✑ ————

CROESUS (6th century BC), *king of Lydia in Asia Minor (560–546 BC). From his great wealth comes the phrase "rich as Croesus."*

1 Deliberating whether to attack the Persians, Croesus asked the oracle at Delphi if the undertaking would prosper. The oracle replied that if he went to war, he would destroy a great empire. Encouraged, Croesus invaded the Persian realms. He was decisively beaten and the Persians then invaded Lydia, captured its capital, and threw Croesus himself into chains. Croesus again sent an embassy to Delphi, this time with the question, "Why did you deceive me?" The priestess of the oracle replied that she had not deceived him — Croesus had indeed destroyed a great empire.

———— ✑ ————

CROLL, James (1821–90), *Scottish geologist and meteorologist.*

1 As he lay dying he was offered a glass of whiskey, although he had been a strict teetotaler all his life. "I'll take a wee drop o' *that,*" he said. "I don't think there's much fear o' me learning to drink now."

CROMWELL, Oliver (1599–1658), *lord protector of England (1653–58).*

1 Cromwell sat for Peter Lely, the portraitist. The painter already had a reputation for his portraits of the handsome noblemen and beautiful ladies of Charles I's court. Cromwell said, "Mr. Lely, I desire you would use all your skill to paint my picture truly like me, and not flatter me at all; but remark all these roughnesses, pimples, warts, and everything as you see me, otherwise I will never pay a farthing for it."

2 In April 1653 the Long Parliament had sat for more than twelve years, presiding over Britain's decline into civil war and constitutional chaos. It looked ready to entrench itself and its incompetence forever. Cromwell, with the army behind him, intervened and dissolved the Parliament by force, with a band of musketeers. The musketeers led away the Speaker and ejected the MPs. In front of the Speaker's chair lay the mace, emblem of parliamentary authority. "What shall we do with this bauble? Take it away," Cromwell commanded, and it was removed.

3 Cromwell addressed his troops as they were about to cross a river to attack the enemy. He concluded with the famous exhortation: "Put your trust in God, but mind you keep your powder dry."

4 There is an old but probably unreliable tradition that toward two AM on the night after the execution of Charles I, when the body was lying in the banqueting hall at Whitehall, a dark figure, closely muffled, entered the room and gazed upon the face of the dead king. The Earl of Southampton and the other man keeping vigil by the body could not see his face, but they heard him sigh the words: "Cruel necessity!" before he glided out of the room. The earl swore that the mysterious visitor had the figure and gait of Cromwell.

5 One of the changes that came with the rise to power of Oliver Cromwell was the nation's coinage. New coins were struck on the obverse of which was engraved "God with Us" and on the reverse, "The Republic of England." One old nobleman, a Royalist and anti-Puritan to the core, saw the coins and commented: "Quite proper that God and the Republic should be on different sides."

CROSBY, Bing [Harry Lillis] (1904–77), *US singer and actor.*

1 Crosby was asked once by the interviewer on a television show why he had such a calm and unruffled air. He reached into his pocket and pulled out an enormous wad of dollar bills. "That helps!" he said.

CUKOR, George Dewey (1899–1983), *US film director.*

1 In 1953 Jack Lemmon came to Hollywood to make his first film, *It Should Happen to You,* co-starring with Judy Holliday. The director was George Cukor. During the first rehearsals Cukor, after each of Lemmon's tries, would cry, "Less, less, less!" Lemmon, frustrated and bewildered, finally broke out with "Don't you want me to act at *all?*"

"Dear boy," said Cukor, "you're beginning to understand."

CUMMINGS, E[dward] E[stlin] (1894–1962), *US poet and painter.*

1 Departing with Marion, his wife, from a fashionable New Year's Eve party, Cummings realized that he did not have enough

money for the subway fare. They stepped into the elevator, which was already occupied by a portly gentleman. "Excuse me," said Cummings politely, placing his hat with a flourish at the man's feet, "would you care to step on my hat?" The man, somewhat taken aback but nevertheless impressed by Cummings's aristocratic demeanor, nodded assent. "I'm afraid it will cost you five dollars," added Cummings. The portly fellow stepped on the hat and paid his fee, enabling Cummings and his wife to travel home by taxi.

CUNARD, Emerald, Lady (1872–1948), *British society hostess.*

1 Lady Cunard was a guest at one of the first balls to be given in London after World War II had ended. Encouraged by limitless champagne, patricians of English high society danced away the night in elegant surroundings. A fellow guest, the diarist Henry ("Chips") Channon, gestured toward the glittering assembly and said, "*This* is what we fought the war for."

"Oh, do you mean they are all Poles?" inquired Lady Cunard.

2 (Edward Marsh tells the following story:)

"Later in life I had a beautiful object-lesson in behaviour to the unpunctual. The scene was a luncheon-party at the Broughams': the appointed time, one-thirty. Till one-forty-five we waited for Lady Cunard; and at two o'clock she arrived, full of apologies — she had been buying a chandelier. Old Lord Brougham, a handsome patriarch with magnificent silver hair, looked straight in front of himself and said in a pensive tone: 'I once knew a man who bought a chandelier *after* luncheon.'"

CUNNINGHAME GRAHAM, Robert Bontine (1852–1936), *Scottish writer and nobleman.*

1 A dinner partner, impressed by tales of Cunninghame Graham's aristocratic ancestry, asked him: "Is it true that there is royal blood in your family?"

"Madam," replied Cunninghame Graham, "if I had my rights I should be king of England — and what a two weeks *that* would be!"

CURIE, Marie (1867–1934), *Polish chemist who shared the 1903 Nobel Prize for physics with the discoverer of radioactivity, Henri Becquerel, and who won the 1911 Nobel Prize for chemistry.*

1 An American newspaperman tracked the Curies down to the remote cottage in Brittany where they were vacationing. He found a rather dowdy woman sitting outside the door. "Are you the housekeeper?" he began.

"Yes."

"Is your mistress inside?"

"No."

"Will she be back soon?"

"I don't think so."

The reporter sat down. "Can you tell me something confidential about your mistress?" he went on.

"Madame Curie has only one message that she likes to be given to reporters," said Marie Curie. "That is: be less curious about people and more curious about ideas."

CURLEY, James Michael (1874–1958), *Boston politician.*

1 In 1946 "the Purple Shamrock," as Curley was often called, managed to get reelected as mayor of Boston, only to find himself facing fraud charges and appearing in the dock.

Convicted, the new mayor was obliged to fulfill his duties from a prison cell. This was clearly inconvenient, so he sent a demand to the court for his release on the grounds that he was suffering from twelve potentially fatal illnesses. Summoned before the court (wearing a shirt three times too large for him), the former governor of Massachusetts was asked to name one of his twelve illnesses. "An imminent cerebral hemorrhage," the mayor declared. He was not released.

CURRAN, John Philpot (1750–1817), *Irish lawyer and judge.*

1 Curran detested all those who had voted for the union of Ireland with the rest of Britain. One day as he was in the part of Dublin near the disused Parliament Building, he was accosted by one of the pro-union peers who happened to remark on the building's present uselessness and how he disliked the sight of it. "No wonder, my lord," said Curran. "I never heard of a murderer who was not afraid of a ghost."

2 One of the high court judges had a dog he occasionally brought into the courtroom. During a trial in which Curran was expounding a particularly involved argument, the judge, perhaps intending to indicate disregard of Curran's case, bent down and began ostentatiously to pet the dog. Curran stopped. The judge looked up inquiringly. "I beg pardon, my lord," said Curran. "I thought your lordships were in consultation."

3 During Curran's last illness, his doctor, paying an early morning call, observed that he was coughing with difficulty. "That is surprising," retorted Curran, "for I have been practicing all night."

CURTIZ, Michael (1888–1962), *Hungarian-born US film director.*

1 During the filming of *The Charge of the Light Brigade,* Curtiz directed the release of a hundred riderless chargers by ordering, "Bring on the empty horses." David Niven and Errol Flynn, the stars of the film, doubled up with laughter. Curtiz saw them and yelled, "You and your stinking language! You think I know fuck nothing. Well, let me tell you, I know fuck all!"

2 Curtiz, always keen on realism, had extras throw authentic spears at Errol Flynn during a characteristic scene of derring-do. The star, dodging the hail of lethal weapons, felt the stress of real peril and started across the set after Curtiz. "Lunch!" yelled Curtiz, beating a hasty retreat.

CUSHMAN, Charlotte (1816–76), *US stage actress.*

1 Charlotte Cushman's final appearance on the New York stage was an emotional occasion with presentations, speeches, a torchlit parade, and finally a huge display of fireworks organized by the theater's business representative, Joseph H. Tooker, who was also one of the Tammany Hall stalwarts. The finale of the fireworks display was a huge portrait bust. "Who's that?" asked Miss Cushman. "Shakespeare," replied Mr. Tooker, and Miss Cushman's delight knew no bounds. Actually it was a gigantic head of Boss Tweed, left over from a Tammany Hall festivity.

CUVIER, Georges Léopold, Baron (1769–1832), *French zoologist.*

1 Cuvier's outstanding achievement resulted from his ability to reconstruct whole skeletons from fragmentary remains through his understanding of the way in which any par-

ticular feature entailed the presence or absence of other characteristics. This logical approach brought no little discomfiture to a group of students bent upon a practical joke. They broke into Cuvier's rooms in the middle of the night, and one, dressed in a devil's outfit with horns, tail, and hoofed feet, approached his bed, intoning, "Cuvier, I have come to eat you!" Cuvier woke up, gave him a single glance, and announced, "All animals with horns and hooves are herbivorous. You won't eat me." Then he promptly went back to sleep.

CYRUS II [Cyrus the Great] (d. 529 BC), *king of Persia and founder of the Achaemenian Empire.*

1 On one occasion, Cyrus reprimanded his son, Cambyses, for his arrogant behavior and rudeness. Like many fathers before and since, Cyrus told his son that he would never have spoken to his own father in the way that Cambyses spoke to him. "But you were the son of a nobody," replied Cambyses, "whereas I am the son of Cyrus the Great."

D

DAHN, Felix (1834–1912), *German jurist and historian*.

1 After a lecture in Hamburg, Dahn was invited to be the guest of honor at a dinner. He declined, giving as his reason that he had once spent six weeks in Hamburg doing nothing but sleeping and drinking; he did not want to repeat this time-wasting experience. His host, troubled, asked him when this had happened. "During the first six weeks of my life," was the answer.

DALE, Valentine (d. 1589), *British diplomat*.

1 When his employment in Flanders was first proposed, Dale was told by Queen Elizabeth that he would receive 20 shillings a day expenses. "Then, madam, I shall spend nineteen shillings a day," he said. "What will you do with the odd shilling?" inquired the queen. "I will reserve that for my wife and children," replied Dale. Elizabeth took the hint and increased the allowance.

DALI, Salvador (1904–89), *Spanish surrealist painter*.

1 (Luis Buñuel told this story:)

"As a young man [Dali] was totally asexual. . . . Of course he's seduced many. . . .

But these seductions usually entailed stripping [American heiresses] in his apartment, frying up a couple of eggs, putting them on the women's shoulders and without a word showing them to the door."

2 (Dali was staying in the same New York hotel as the Igor Stravinskys. One day as they were walking down a corridor Dali suddenly appeared before them carrying a small silver bell. Stravinsky recounted the episode to a friend.)

" 'It was the little silver bell carried before the priest when he goes through the street to bring the viaticum to a dying person,' said Stravinsky.

"He paused and greeted Dali, who replied, 'Bonjour, Igor, bonjour, Madame,' and then stood waiting. . . . It was in the period when Dali wore waxed spikes of mustache which reached to the corners of his eyes. 'But I said nothing, and Vera said nothing, we smiled très doucement, and started to go by.'

"At that Dali rang his little silver bell.

" 'What is your little silver bell doing there?' asked Stravinsky.

" 'I carry it and I ring it,' replied Dali, and Stravinsky imitated him, 'so people will see my mustaches.' "

3 Dali went into a New York bookstore one day and asked for a copy of his *Secret Life of*

Salvador Dali. The young clerk, instantly recognizing his distinguished customer, fetched the book and began to wrap it up.

"Have you read it?" asked the artist.

"No, I'm afraid not," replied the young man, handing over the package.

"Take it," said Dali magnanimously, pushing the book back across the counter. "It is my gift to you. Would you like me to autograph it for you?" The clerk eagerly tore open the package and handed the artist a pen.

Only after Dali had left the store did the young man, gazing at the treasured autograph, realize that the artist had omitted one important detail. He had neglected to pay for the book.

4 Dali had bought a castle in Spain for his wife, Gala. In one of the rooms there was a rather obtrusive radiator, and Gala asked her husband if he would paint a screen for it. Dali obliged with what he later called "Le more realistic of my paintings" — a picture of the radiator itself.

5 A female admirer asked Dali, "Is it hard to paint a picture?"

"No," replied the artist. "It's either easy or impossible."

6 Dali once took his pet ocelot with him to a New York restaurant and tethered it to a leg of the table while he ordered coffee. A middle-aged lady walked past and looked at the animal in horror. "What's that?" she cried. "It's only a cat," said Dali scathingly. "I've painted it over with an op-art design." The woman, embarrassed by her initial reaction, took a closer look and sighed with relief. "I can see now that's what it is," she said. "At first I thought it was a real ocelot."

7 When Dali was given his first raw oyster to try, he grimaced and refused to touch it, saying, "I'd as soon eat a piece of Mae West!"

DALTON, John (1766–1844), *British chemist and the originator of modern atomic theory.*

1 Dalton shunned the honors that the scientific world attempted to bestow upon him and refused to be presented to the king on the grounds that as a Quaker he could not wear the elaborate court dress etiquette then demanded. In 1832, however, he was presented with a doctor's degree at Oxford, and since the scarlet doctoral robes were considered sufficiently formal dress it was arranged that Dalton should also be presented to King William IV on the same occasion. A hitch arose when it was pointed out that Quakers could not wear scarlet any more than they could wear court dress. Dalton's color-blindness saved the day. The scarlet robes appeared to him as gray and he consented to wear them and meet the king.

DANA, Richard Henry (1815–82), *US lawyer and author of the maritime classic* Two Years Before the Mast.

1 In 1876 Dana was nominated for the post of minister to England. His campaigns on behalf of sailors and slaves and his attitude with respect to the legal aspects of the Civil War had made him objectionable to many senators. Senator Simon Cameron helped to quash the nomination with the remark, "One of those damn literary fellers."

D'ANNUNZIO, Gabriele (1863–1938), *Italian poet, dramatist, flying ace, and fascist politician.*

1 Isadora Duncan told the story of D'Annunzio's adoption of a goldfish belonging to a hotel where he stayed. The poet would feed

the goldfish, which he christened Adolphus, talk to it, and watch it swimming around its bowl. After his return to Italy, he telegraphed the hotel at frequent intervals asking: "How is my beloved Adolphus?" Eventually the goldfish sickened and died and the maître d'hôtel threw the corpse out. Almost immediately there arrived a telegram from D'Annunzio: "Feel Adolphus is not well." The maître d'hôtel cabled back: "Adolphus dead. Died last night." D'Annunzio telegraphed: "Bury him in the garden; arrange his grave." The maître d'hôtel took a sardine, wrapped it in silver paper, and buried it in the garden under a little cross inscribed: "Here lies Adolphus." When D'Annunzio returned he asked to see the grave, laid flowers upon it, and stood over it, weeping.

2 At the end of one of his love affairs D'Annunzio sought refuge in a decaying castle in the Italian hills. The flutter that this arrival caused among the local peasantry and neighbors died down, winter set in, and the prospect seemed bleak and tedious. Suddenly the neighborhood was electrified by news of a lady in a flowing white cloak seen riding a white horse into the castle courtyard at midnight. She appeared again on subsequent nights, and speculation was rife about the poet's new mistress and her secret visits to him. The explanation? It was D'Annunzio himself in disguise seeking to recreate the atmosphere of romantic mystery in which he loved to live.

DANTE ALIGHIERI (1265–1321), *Italian poet, author of* La divina commedia [The Divine Comedy], *his vision of hell, purgatory, and paradise that is generally held to be the greatest medieval work of literature.*

1 Dante had an uneasy relationship with his patron and protector, Can Grande della Scala, at whose court he lived for some time.

Another member of Can Grande's court was a conceited ignoramus who nonetheless delighted his master with jests and fooleries and was lavishly rewarded with gifts of money. One day this man said to Dante, "How is it that I, who am so ignorant and foolish, should be so rich and favored, while you, who are so learned and wise, should be a beggar?" Dante replied, "The reason is that you have found a lord who resembles you, and when I find one who resembles me, I shall no doubt be as rich as you are."

2 Deeply immersed in meditation during a church service, Dante failed to kneel when the holy sacrament was elevated. His enemies at once hurried to the bishop and demanded that Dante be punished for his sacrilege. When Dante was brought before the bishop, he excused himself by saying, "If those who accuse me had had their eyes and minds on God, as I had, they too would have failed to notice events around them, and they most certainly would not have noticed what I was doing."

DANTON, Georges Jacques (1759–94), *French revolutionary leader.*

1 At his trial before the revolutionary tribunal on the charge of having betrayed the people, Danton treated the accusations with haughty contempt. Condemned to death, he maintained on the guillotine his unflinching calm. "Show my head to the people," he instructed the executioner. "It is worth it."

DARIUS I (550–486 BC), *king of Persia (521–486).*

1 In about 512 BC, as Darius led his armies north of the Black Sea, the Scythians sent the Persian king a message comprising a mouse, a frog, a bird, and five arrows. Darius sum-

moned his captains. "Our victory is assured," he announced. "These arrows signify that the Scythians will lay down their arms; the mouse means the land of Scythia will be surrendered to us; the frog means that their rivers and lakes will also be ours; and the Scythian army will fly like a bird from our forces." But a cunning adviser to the king put a different interpretation on the message. "The Scythians mean by these things that unless you turn into birds and fly away, or into frogs and hide in the waters, or into mice and burrow for safety in the ground, you will all be slain by the Scythian archers."

Darius took counsel and decided that the second was the more likely interpretation. By beating a prudent retreat, he managed to extricate his army from the Scythian territory.

2 The tomb of Nitrocris, queen of Babylon, bore the following inscription: "If any king of Babylon after me should be short of money, he may open this tomb and take as much as he wants, but only if he really is in need of it." Darius, although he had no genuine need for the money, thought it a shame that such riches should go to waste. He had the tomb opened, only to find no money there at all. Beside the body of the queen, however, was a second message: "If you had not been greedy of gold and fond of base gain, you would not have thought of ransacking graves of the departed."

DARROW, Clarence Seward (1857–1938), *US lawyer renowned for his conduct of labor litigation and murder cases.*

1 Reporters would on occasion tease the energetic and hard-working Darrow about his disheveled appearance. Darrow retorted, "I go to a better tailor than any of you and pay more for my clothes. The only difference is that you probably don't sleep in yours."

2 A female client whose legal problems Darrow had solved burbled, "How can I ever show my appreciation, Mr. Darrow?"

"Ever since the Phoenicians invented money," replied Darrow, "there has been only one answer to that question."

3 In 1925 Darrow defended John T. Scopes of Tennessee, tried for teaching the theory of evolution. The prosecution attempted to discredit Darrow by labeling him an agnostic. He replied, "I do not consider it an insult but rather a compliment to be called an agnostic. I do not pretend to know where many ignorant men are sure."

4 After a speaking engagement at a Women's Club meeting, Darrow was cornered by a couple of ladies who wanted to discuss birth control. One asked him what he thought of birth control for the masses. "My dear lady," replied Darrow, "whenever I hear people advocating birth control, I always remember that I was the fifth child."

5 Darrow was being interviewed for a magazine article on the reasons given by prominent men for their success. "Most of the men I've spoken to so far attribute their success to hard work," said the interviewer.

"I guess that applies to me, too," said Darrow. "I was brought up on a farm. One very hot day I was distributing and packing down the hay which a stacker was constantly dumping on top of me. By noon I was completely exhausted. That afternoon I left the farm, never to return, and I haven't done a day of hard work since."

DARWIN, Charles Robert (1809–82), *British naturalist, author of books including* On the Origin of Species *and* The Descent of Man.

1 Darwin spent the eight years from 1846 to 1854 in a detailed study of barnacles. At one time there were no fewer than ten thousand

barnacles in the house. His children accepted their presence as a part of normal life. One of Darwin's sons, on a visit to a friend's house, once inquired of the other boy where his father "did his barnacles."

2 Emma Darwin, though a loving wife, did not share Darwin's enthusiasm for his work, nor did she pretend to find his experiments interesting. One day she accompanied him to a scientific lecture, during the course of which he turned to her and said, "I am afraid this must be very wearisome for you."

"Not more than all the rest," she replied politely.

3 Charles Darwin was standing near the hippopotamus cage at the zoo one day when he overheard a little boy and girl talking. The hippopotamus had closed its eyes for a minute. "That bird's dead," said the little girl. "Come along."

———— ◁ɤ ————

DARWIN, Erasmus (1731–1802), *British poet and physician, grandfather of Charles Darwin.*

1 Darwin was once offended by a young man's asking him whether he did not find his stammer very inconvenient. "No, sir," he replied. "It gives me time for reflection, and saves me from asking impertinent questions."

———— ◁ɤ ————

DAUDET, Alphonse (1840–97), *French writer.*

1 Alphonse Daudet's *L'Arlésienne,* for which Bizet composed the incidental music, was far from a success when it opened at the Odéon theater. This was in 1872, at a time when the politician and polemical journalist Victor-Henri Rochefort was beginning to regain some of the popularity he had enjoyed a few years before. At a social gathering Rochefort boasted, "I have only to raise my little finger and one hundred thousand Parisians will leave their homes and follow me wherever I wish." Daudet, also present as a guest, was heard to murmur, "Oh, if you could only lead them to the Odéon."

———— ◁ɤ ————

DAVENANT, Sir William (1606–68), *British dramatist.*

1 As the result of an illness Davenant lost his nose — a misfortune that evoked much merriment and ribaldry among his literary friends. A simple old countrywoman once blessed Davenant's eyesight. Rather surprised, the poet inquired why. She explained that if his eyesight should fail he would be in serious difficulty, as he lacked the means to support a pair of spectacles.

2 Apologizing because he could not finish a poem on which he was working, Davenant said, "I shall ask leave to desist, when I am interrupted by so great an experiment as dying."

———— ◁ɤ ————

DAVID, Sir Edgeworth (1858–1934), *Australian geologist and explorer.*

1 During the South Polar expedition, Sir Edgeworth's assistant, Douglas Mawson, was working in his tent one day when he heard a muffled cry from outside. "Are you very busy?" called the voice, which Mawson recognized as that of Sir Edgeworth.

"Yes I am," he replied. "What's the matter?"

"Are you really *very* busy?"

"Yes," snapped Mawson, losing his patience. "What is it you want."

After a moment's silence, David replied apologetically, "Well, I'm down a crevasse, and I don't think I can hang on much longer."

———— ◁ɤ ————

DAVIES, Lady Eleanor (d. 1652), *English religious fanatic; wife of the poet Sir John Davies.*

1 As a result of her prophecies, considered potentially dangerous in the troubled religious climate of Charles I's reign, Lady Eleanor found herself before the Court of High Commission. She had discovered that the letters of her name, with an *l* substituted for the final *s,* could be rearranged to form the words: "Reveal, O Daniel!" On the strength of this anagram, she attempted to persuade the court that she was possessed by the spirit of the prophet Daniel. The bishops, convinced that she was quite mad, tried to reason with her, but she had a ready reply for all their arguments. At last, one of the deans of the Arches, who had been scribbling furiously for some time, announced that he had irrefutable "proof" of Lady Eleanor's insanity, and read out the anagram: "Dame Eleanor Davies — never so mad a ladie!" The prophetess's pretensions were dismissed in a wave of ridicule.

———∽———

DAVIES, Marion (1897–1961), *US film actress.*

1 Marion Davies was among the first of the silent screen stars to realize the impact that talking pictures would have on their careers. She asked the MGM publicity manager to accompany her to see *The Jazz Singer,* the first film of the sound era, and sat quiet and totally absorbed throughout the performance. At the end she turned and said in a small voice, "M-m-mister Voight, I-I-I have a p-p-problem."

———∽———

DAVIS, Adele (1904–74), *US nutritionist and food writer.*

1 The famed nutritionist, whose movement promoting good health by eating healthy foods influenced millions, was to her horror diagnosed with terminal bone cancer. "I thought this was for people who drink soft drinks, who eat white bread, who eat refined sugar," she said when she got the news. "I have been a failure."

———∽———

DAVIS, Bette (1908–1989), *US movie actress and Academy Award winner.*

1 Bette Davis's attorney told her a rumor was spreading throughout New York that she had died. Miss Davis was unworried: "With the newspaper strike on I wouldn't consider it."

———∽———

DAVIS, Miles (1926–91), *US trumpeter and jazz musician.*

1 Davis loved to drive fast. One night he was driving his car up a highway in New York so fast that his wife became frightened and pleaded with him to slow down. Davis only smiled. "I'm in here too," he told her.

2 Davis often invited John Coltrane to join in playing with his band. And Coltrane often did; but it was well known that once Coltrane started, he couldn't stop. Someone asked him why his solos were so extended, and Coltrane said, "I get involved in this thing and I don't know how to stop."

"Try taking the saxophone out of your mouth," responded Davis.

———∽———

DAVY, Sir Humphry (1778–1829), *British chemist.*

1 Davy's fame was international. A letter reached him safely from Italy although it bore only the direction:

"SIROMFREDEVI/LONDRA."

2 One clear night Davy was passing through the London streets when he saw a man show-

ing the moon through a telescope. He stopped to look and offered the showman the penny fee. The man, recognizing his customer as the great Sir Humphry Davy, refused the money, saying, "I could not think of taking money from a brother philosopher."

3 On his return from a visit to Paris Davy was asked how he had liked the picture galleries there. "The finest collection of frames I ever saw," was his reply.

DAYAN, Moshe (1915–81), *Israeli statesman.*

1 Stopped for speeding by a military policeman, Dayan argued: "I have only one eye. What do you want me to watch — the speedometer or the road?"

DEAN, Jay Hanna ["Dizzy"] (1911–74), *US baseball player.*

1 After Dizzy Dean had pitched a one-hitter in the first game of a double-header, Paul Dean pitched a no-hitter in the nightcap. Dizzy commented, "Shucks, if I'd known Paul was gonna pitch a no-hitter, I'd a pitched one too."

2 Accused of corrupting English language students with his unruly diction and grammar, Dean retorted, "A lot of people who don't say ain't ain't eatin'."

3 An English interviewer, frustrated by Dizzy Dean's idiosyncratic relationship with language, exclaimed, "Mr. Dean, don't you know the king's English?" Dizzy reflected for a moment. Then, "Sure I do, and so's the queen."

DEBS, Eugene Victor (1855–1926), *US socialist, trade unionist, and frequent presidential nominee of the Socialist party.*

1 In 1918 the pacifist Debs made a speech condemning World War I and criticizing the persecution of persons charged with sedition in violation of the 1917 Espionage Act. This brought him a ten-year prison sentence. He ran his 1920 presidential campaign as Convict 2273 in the federal penitentiary in Atlanta, receiving nearly a million votes. On Christmas Day 1921 Debs was released on the orders of President Harding. Surprised but unrepentant, he remarked, "It is the government that should ask me for a pardon."

DEGAS, [Hilaire Germain] Edgar (1834–1917), *French painter and sculptor.*

1 By nature Degas was conservative. His friend the etcher Jean-Louis Forain believed in progress. Forain had recently installed that newfangled invention, the telephone. Arranging to have a friend phone him during the meal, he invited Degas to dinner. The phone rang; Forain rushed to answer it, then returned, beaming with pride. Degas merely said, "So that's the telephone. It rings and you run."

2 Degas attended an auction at which one of his pictures was sold for an enormous sum. Asked what it felt like to witness such a transaction, Degas replied, "I feel as a horse must feel when the beautiful cup is given to the jockey."

3 Degas took great care to appear misogynistic. Explaining to someone that he disliked the idea of marriage, he said, "I was quite terrified that I'd finish a painting and then hear my wife say, 'Oh it's really very pretty, what you've done this time.'"

4 When Degas knew he was dying, he called his friend Forain to him, instructing him that there was to be no formal oration. Then he added, "But if there has to be one, Forain, you get up and say, 'He greatly loved drawing. So do I.' Then go home."

———— ❧ ————

DE GAULLE, Charles André Joseph Marie (1890–1970), *French statesman and general; president (1958–69).*

1 Clementine Churchill was sitting next to General de Gaulle at luncheon, and during one of the many silences found herself thinking how difficult Mme de Gaulle's life must be. Her reverie was interrupted by the general's observation to her, "*Vous savez, madame, it must be very difficult, being the wife of Mr. Churchill.*"

2 De Gaulle's touchiness about the honor of France and his own position during World War II made him a difficult ally, and personal antagonism frequently flared between him and Churchill. After one such incident Churchill remarked, "Of all the crosses I have to bear, the cross of Lorraine is the heaviest."

3 De Gaulle was once likened by a speaker to Robespierre. The general's reaction was, "I always thought I was Jeanne d'Arc and Bonaparte. How little one knows oneself!"

4 The de Gaulles' daughter Anne, born in 1928, was retarded from birth and needed constant care and attention, for she could not feed or clothe herself and was unable to speak properly. Mme de Gaulle devoted herself to caring for the child and so did her husband. The pains that the aloof soldier took to entertain the little girl astonished those who knew him only in his dealings with adults; he would spend hours playing simple games with her and at night would hold her hand until she fell asleep. In 1948 Anne contracted

a lung ailment and died. After her body had been placed in the family vault at Colombey-les-Deux-Eglises, de Gaulle turned to his wife and said, "Now at last our child is just like all children."

5 When Jacques Soustelle was governor-general of Algeria (1955–56), he complained to de Gaulle that all his friends were attacking him for supporting the general's Algerian policies. De Gaulle's reply was brief: "*Changez vos amis*" (Change your friends).

6 A French diplomat, about to take up a new ambassadorship, visited President de Gaulle before leaving the country. "I am filled with joy at my appointment," he said enthusiastically. The president frowned. "You are a career diplomat," he said. "Joy is an inappropriate emotion in your profession."

7 At the height of one of the many crises that beset de Gaulle's political career, he exclaimed in frustration, "How can one govern a country that has three hundred and fifty kinds of cheese?"

8 Mrs. Sargent Shriver, the wife of the US ambassador to France, was seated beside de Gaulle at a state banquet. Charmed by his conversation, she found herself saying, as the meal drew to a close, "Mr. President, my only regret is that you're not twenty years younger and that I'm not twenty years younger." Without thinking, she repeated the remark to Mme de Gaulle later that evening. "Ah, yes, Mrs. Shriver," said the president's wife. "But just remember, I would then be twenty years younger, too."

9 Lunching with English friends at the time of her husband's retirement, Madame de Gaulle was asked what she was looking forward to in the years ahead. "A penis," she replied without hesitation. The embarrassed silence that followed was finally broken by the former president. "My dear," he murmured, "I

think the English don't pronounce the word quite like that. It's ''appiness.'"

10 An assassination attempt on de Gaulle was made in August 1962 when he and Mme de Gaulle were being driven through the outskirts of Paris. Bullets punctured the car tires, it swerved violently, and the bodyguard in the front seat yelled at the de Gaulles to get down. Neither moved. When the car came to a stop they got out, brushing the glass from a shattered rear window out of their clothing. "They really are bad shots," observed the general calmly.

Mme de Gaulle, asked later if she had been frightened, retorted, "Frightened of what? We'd have died together, and no old age."

———— ❧ ————

DE LA MARE, Walter (1873–1956), *British poet, novelist, and anthologist.*

1 De la Mare suffered a severe illness and for some time his life lay in the balance. During his convalescence, his daughter came to see him and asked if there was anything she could get him — fruit or flowers. "No, no," said the poet weakly, "too late for fruit, too soon for flowers."

———— ❧ ————

DE MILLE, Cecil [Blount] (1881–1959), *US film director and producer.*

1 One afternoon, while De Mille was directing *The King of Kings,* his epic about the life of Jesus, he spotted one of his actresses — who played a slave to Mary Magdalene — sneaking into the set late with another of the actors. Both were obviously disheveled. De Mille picked up his megaphone and, from his perch high above the set and in front of all his large cast, called, "Leave my Jesus Christ alone! If you must screw someone, screw Pontius Pilate!"

———— ❧ ————

DE MOIVRE, Abraham (1667–1754), *British mathematician of French Huguenot descent.*

1 (In his old age, twenty hours' sleep a day became habitual with De Moivre.)

"Shortly before [his death] he declared that it was necessary for him to sleep some ten minutes or a quarter of an hour longer each day than the preceding one. The day after he had reached a total of over twenty-three hours he slept up to the limit of twenty-four hours and then died in his sleep."

———— ❧ ————

DEMOSTHENES (c. 384–322 BC), *Greek orator.*

1 Demosthenes is generally considered the greatest orator of classical antiquity, but in his day he had a strong rival in the Athenian general Phocion. "One of these days the Athenians will kill you when they are in a rage," observed Demosthenes. "And you too," retorted Phocion, "when they are in their right minds."

2 Demosthenes' first success as a speaker came when he made a claim against his guardian, who had defrauded him. The fortunate outcome prompted him to embark on the career of an orator. When he first took part in the public debates, his speech was so torturous and feebly delivered that the audience could not understand him and laughed him out of the assembly. The actor Satyrus caught up with him as he was going disconsolately homeward and then and there gave him a lesson in how to deliver a speech. Demosthenes thereupon made himself an underground study where he stayed for weeks at a time, practicing his oratory. To protect himself against the temptation of going out into society, he shaved one side of his head so that he

would be too embarrassed to show himself in public. He cured his stammer by speaking with pebbles in his mouth and his shortness of breath by declaiming poetry while running uphill. Thus he eventually acquired the skill to hold an Athenian audience spellbound.

———— ✥ ————

DEMPSEY, Jack [William Harrison] (1895–1983), *US boxer, world heavyweight champion.*

1 On September 23, 1926, Dempsey lost his title to Gene Tunney. To his wife he explained, "Honey, I just forgot to duck."

{This remark was quoted by President Ronald Reagan after he was wounded in an assassination attempt in 1981.}

2 J. Paul Getty was one of the wealthy men who frequently came to watch Dempsey train. Himself a keen amateur boxer, he asked to be allowed to spar for a round with the champion. Getty put up quite a creditable performance until he made the mistake of saying, "Hit me a little harder, Jack." Dempsey knocked him out.

3 Dempsey was staying overnight in a California hotel. Just after midnight, he received a call from the reception clerk. "There's a man down here who says he can lick you," said the clerk, "and he won't go away." Tired of being challenged by drunks wherever he went, Dempsey replied wearily, "Tell you what you do — tell him he can have my title, but I want it back in the morning."

———— ✥ ————

DENHAM, Sir John (1615–69), *British poet.*

1 The Puritan poet George Wither was imprisoned in the Marshalsea and sentenced to death for his rather innocuous anti-Royalist satires. Sir John Denham, though on the king's side, nevertheless successfully interceded with Charles I for his fellow poet's life

on the ground that "If Your Majesty kills Wither, I will then be the worst poet in England."

———— ✥ ————

DENIS, Marie-Louise (c. 1710–90), *French femme du monde.*

1 Mme Denis was once complimented on the skill with which she had played the role of Zaïre at one of her uncle's private theatricals at Ferney. She replied, "Alas, to handle the role properly one must be young and pretty."

"Ah, madame, you are a complete proof of the contrary."

———— ✥ ————

DENNIS, John (1657–1734), *British playwright and critic.*

1 In one of Dennis's plays, *Appius and Virginia* (1709), a clap of thunder is called for. This Dennis provided by a machine he had invented. However, in a later performance of *Macbeth* at the same theater he heard an identical clap of thunder, which he correctly assumed emanated from his own machine. "Damn them," he is reported to have cried. "See how the rascals use me! They will not let my play run, and yet they steal my thunder!"

2 On one occasion Dennis visited a tavern with the composer Henry Purcell. Purcell rang the bell to summon the drawer (waiter) to provide them with two glasses of ale. The summons was not answered. Purcell with some annoyance tapped the table. "Why does the table remind you of this tavern?" he asked his companion. Dennis looked blank. "Because it has no drawer," said Purcell.

———— ✥ ————

DEPEW, Chauncey Mitchell (1834–1928), *US lawyer, politician, and wit.*

1 Chauncey Depew and Mark Twain were both billed to speak at a banquet. Twain spoke first for about twenty minutes and was loudly applauded. When Depew was called upon, he rose and said: "Before this dinner Mark Twain and I agreed to trade speeches. He has just delivered mine and I am grateful for the reception that you have given it. Unfortunately I have lost his speech and I cannot remember a word of what he had to say." And he sat down.

2 When Chauncey Depew was quite old, he was sitting at dinner next to a young woman wearing a very low-cut, off-the-shoulder dress. The old lawyer peered at her décolletage, leaned toward her, and asked, "My dear, what is keeping that dress on you?" "Only your age, Mr. Depew."

DESCARTES, René (1596–1650), *French philosopher and mathematician.*

1 To Queen Christina Descartes tried to explain his mechanistic philosophy: the view that all animals are mechanisms. The queen countered this by remarking that she had never seen a watch give birth to baby watches.

2 Descartes's coordinate system was one of his main contributions to the development of mathematics. It is said that the idea came to him during a period of illness in his military service as he lay on his bed watching a fly hovering in the air. He realized that the fly's position at every moment could be described by locating its distance from three intersecting lines (axes). This insight was the basis of Cartesian coordinates.

3 Descartes once constructed a robot in the form of a girl, which he later had occasion to transport by sea. The ship's captain, out of curiosity, looked into the chest in which the robot was packed and was horrified by the lifelike form, which moved like an animated being. Thinking that this could only be the devil in disguise, he threw the chest and its contents into the sea.

DE SERVERSKY, Alexander Procofieff (1894–1974), *US aviator and aeronautical engineer, born in Russia.*

1 De Seversky was visiting a fellow aviator in the hospital. The young man had just had his leg amputated; de Seversky, who had been walking on an artificial limb for some time, tried to cheer him up. "The loss of a leg is not so great a calamity," he said. "Look at me. I dance, I fly, I drive a car, I go everywhere. And another thing: if you get hit on a wooden leg, it doesn't hurt a bit! Try it!" The patient raised his walking-stick and brought it down on de Seversky's leg with considerable force. "You see," said de Seversky cheerfully. "If you hit an ordinary man like that, he'd be in bed for five days!" With these words he took his leave of the young man and limped out into the corridor, where he collapsed in excruciating pain. The aviator had struck him on his good leg.

DETOURBEY, Jeanne (d. 1908), *Comtesse de Loynes, salonnière of the Second Empire.*

1 "Once while discussing the wave of anticlericalism which was sweeping the country, an ardently Romanist guest declared that when it came to his loyalties, he was a Catholic before he was a Frenchman. "Catholic before being French?" the comtesse exclaimed. "Oh, happy the man who has been baptized before being born!"

———⟨∽⟩———

DE VALERA, Eamon (1882–1975), *three times prime minister of Ireland (1932–48, 1951–54, 1957–59) and subsequently president (1959–73).*

1 As a young man De Valera visited France. On his return he announced, "All I can say is that sex in Ireland is as yet in its infancy."

2 In the middle of a fiery political speech at Ennis, De Valera was arrested. After a year's imprisonment, he was released. At once he hastened back to Ennis, summoned a meeting, and began to speak: "As I was saying when I was interrupted —"

3 After the Easter rebellion of 1916 De Valera was sentenced to penal servitude. En route to his prison he took out his pipe and was about to light it when he stopped suddenly and said, "I will not let them deprive me of this pleasure in jail!" He immediately threw away the pipe and from that day never smoked again.

———⟨∽⟩———

DE VALOIS, Dame Ninette (1898–), *British ballet dancer and choreographer.*

1 Ninette de Valois always disliked publicity and the cult of the star performer; she herself resolutely shunned the limelight. After one of the Royal Ballet's triumphant tours, the audience at Covent Garden clamored for the company's director after their first performance back in their home theater. Ninette de Valois came reluctantly to the front of the stage and made one of the briefest curtain speeches on record: "Ladies and gentlemen, it takes more than one to make a ballet." And then she withdrew.

———⟨∽⟩———

DEVONSHIRE, Spencer Compton Cavendish, 8th Duke of (1833–1908), *British statesman.*

1 The Duke of Devonshire was renowned for his passion for sleep — a passion he often indulged in the House of Lords. One afternoon he fell asleep in the chamber. When he awoke he was heard by Lord Portland, who was sitting nearby, to complain: "Good heavens, what a bore, I shan't be in bed for another seven hours." Earlier on in his career he impressed Disraeli when he yawned in the middle of his maiden speech in the House of Commons. "He'll do," said Disraeli. "To anyone who can betray such languor in such circumstances the highest posts should be open."

2 In 1894 the Liberal chancellor of the exchequer, Sir William Harcourt, introduced death duties that gravely threatened the privileged position of the upper classes, as they saw it. The budget incorporating this tax was of course vigorously opposed by the enormously wealthy Duke of Devonshire.

One evening at dinner the duke was seated next to Lady Harcourt. She remarked, "Your Grace, I feel you would like to hang my husband."

"No, madam," he replied, "merely suspend him for a period."

———⟨∽⟩———

DEWEY, Mrs. Thomas E. [Frances E. Hutt] (1903–70), *wife of US politician Tom Dewey, governor of New York (1942–1954), who twice ran unsuccessfully for US President.*

1 In the 1948 presidential contest between Truman and Dewey, the latter looked like a winner. On election night, Dewey asked his wife, "How will it be to sleep with the President of the United States?" She replied, "A high honor, and quite frankly, darling, I'm looking forward to it."

Next morning, at breakfast, after Dewey's defeat, Mrs. Dewey said, "Tell me, Tom, am I going to Washington or is Harry coming here?"

———— ❧ ————

DE WOLFE, Elsie (1865–1950), *US fashion designer.*

1 In 1933 Elsie traveled to Greece with some friends. Like most visitors, Elsie found her first sight of the Acropolis a stirring experience. "It's beige! My color!" she cried.

———— ❧ ————

DIAGHILEV, Sergei [Pavlovich] (1872–1929), *Russian impresario.*

1 Diaghilev produced Stravinsky's *The Rite of Spring* in 1913, a ballet celebrating the primitive nature of Russian folk rituals. When the opening-night audience heard the strange, pulsing rhythms and saw the nature of Nijinsky's dancing, they began to shout and whistle in protest. Diaghilev leapt to his feet. "Listen first! Whistle afterwards!" he cried.

2 In the twenties in Paris, when Diaghilev was triumphing with his Ballets Russes, his problem was to continue to surprise a sophisticated public. Jean Cocteau, who had undertaken to provide a scenario for a new ballet, asked the great impresario for some direction. Diaghilev replied only, *"Etonnemoi!"* (Astonish me!)

3 Henri Matisse once visited a rehearsal of *Parade,* by Erik Satie and Jean Cocteau, with sets by Picasso, which Diaghilev was choreographing. At a break in proceedings, Matisse asked the great choreographer what was meant "when that little ballerina skips and then falls down and kicks her legs in the

air?" Diaghilev adopted a tone of amazement that Matisse had not understood. "Why," he cried, "it's quite simple. That's the *Titanic* disaster."

———— ❧ ————

DIANA, Princess of Wales [*née* Lady Diana Spencer] (1961–1997), *wife of Prince Charles.*

1 In 1983, the Prince and Princess of Wales visited Australia and New Zealand on a royal tour. Walking freely among the crowds in South Australia, the princess made for a group of young children, the nearest of whom she patted affectionately on his tousled head. "Why aren't you at school today?" she inquired.

"I was sent home," the lad replied, "because I've got head lice."

———— ❧ ————

As Count Jean Dauger lay dying, he spoke these last words to his son: "You'd better not wait . . . better be off to bed . . ." Then: "On the other hand, maybe you're right. You'd better stay. Nobody can watch a father die twice."

———— ❧ ————

DiCAPRIO, Leonardo (1974–), *US film actor.*

1 At a party at New York's Russian Tea Room given for Academy Award nominees, the young DiCaprio was introduced to veteran actress Celeste Holm, who had won a Best Supporting Actress Award in 1947 for her role in *All About Eve.* Holm had never heard of the young star, and when told of his latest movie, *What's Eating Gilbert Grape,* she said, "Lord, I wouldn't see that. Sounds like a pie-eating contest." For his part DiCaprio had never heard of Holm, nor of *All About Eve* or *Gentleman's Agreement.* "Rent them and learn the history of your industry,"

Holm said sternly. "And take my advice, prepare a speech. I didn't."

———⌁———

DICKENS, Charles (1812–70), *popular and prolific English novelist.*

1 Dickens's childhood was overshadowed by his father's inability to keep out of debt and subsequent imprisonment. Hardship and frequent changes of address were visited upon John Dickens's family, and the future novelist at the age of ten was forced to work at a factory pasting labels on pots of shoe blacking. When old John Dickens was later asked where his famous son had been educated, he replied, "Well, he may be said to have — ah — educated himself."

2 Like most of Dickens's works, *The Old Curiosity Shop* (1841) was first published in serial form. The novel won a vast readership in both Britain and the United States, and interest in the fate of the heroine, Little Nell, was intense. In New York, six thousand people crowded the wharf at which the ship carrying the magazine with the final installment was due to dock. As it approached, the crowd's impatience grew to such a pitch that they cried out to the sailors, "Does Little Nell die?"

3 The monthly installments of *The Pickwick Papers* were also eagerly awaited by all. A clergyman spent some time administering spiritual comfort to a sick parishioner. When he got up to leave, he felt satisfied that he had done some good. As the door closed behind him, he heard the invalid say, "Well, thank God, *Pickwick* will be out in ten days anyway."

4 While Dickens was acting as editor of the weekly periodical *Household Words,* a young poet called Laman Blanchard sent him a contribution entitled "Orient Pearls at Random Strung." Dickens's rejection slip read, "Dear Blanchard, too much string — Yours, C. D."

5 When Charles Dickens moved into Tavistock House, he made sure that every detail of it was to his taste. One of the features he installed was a hidden door to his study, made to look like part of an unbroken wall of books, complete with dummy shelves and fictitious titles. Dickens clearly derived much amusement from the invention of titles for these volumes. They ranged from the purely facetious — *Five Minutes in China,* with three volumes, and *Heaviside's Conversations with Nobody* — to straight puns such as *A Carpenter's Bench of Bishops* and *The Gunpowder Magazine.* These stood alongside more satirical titles such as *The Quarrelly Review* and *Hansard's Guide to Refreshing Sleep* in "as many volumes as possible." Further additions in later years included *Strutt's Walk, Noah's Arkitecture, Shelley's Oysters, Cat's Lives* (nine volumes), *History of a Short Chancery Suit* (twenty-one volumes), and *The Wisdom of Our Ancestors,* which consisted of volumes on ignorance, superstition, the block, the stake, the rack, dirt, and disease. The companion *The Virtues of Our Ancestors* was so narrow the title had to be printed sideways.

———⌁———

DIDEROT, Denis (1713–84), *French philosopher.*

1 In 1773 Diderot spent some months at the court of St. Petersburg at the invitation of the Russian empress, Catherine the Great. He passed much of his time spreading his gospel of atheism and materialism among the courtiers, until it was suggested to the empress that it would be desirable to muzzle her guest. Reluctant to take direct action, Catherine requested the aid of another savant, the Swiss mathematician Leonhard Euler, a devout Christian. As Diderot was al-

most entirely ignorant of mathematics, a plot was hatched to exploit this weakness. He was informed that a learned mathematician had developed an algebraical demonstration of the existence of God, and was prepared to deliver it before the entire court if Diderot would like to hear it. Diderot could not very well refuse. Euler approached Diderot, bowed, and said very solemnly, "Sir, *(a + b^n)/n = x,* hence God exists. Reply!" Diderot was totally disconcerted, and delighted laughter broke out on all sides at his discomfiture. He asked permission to return to France, and the empress graciously consented.

———— ✃ ————

DIETRICH, Marlene [Maria Magdalene von Losch] (1901–92), *German actress and singer.*

1 Asked whether she objected to being imitated by other performers, Dietrich replied, "Only if they do it badly."

———— ✃ ————

DIETZ, Howard (1896–1983), *US lyricist and publicist.*

1 During the course of an argument, critic Alexander Woollcott asked Dietz, "Are you trying to cross me?" Surveying Woollcott's ample girth, Dietz replied, "Not without an alpenstock."

———— ✃ ————

DiMAGGIO, Joseph (1914–1999), *US baseball player, one of the greatest heroes of the game.*

1 Joe DiMaggio married movie actress Marilyn Monroe. She knew nothing about baseball, but was attracted to the tall, elegant, reserved baseball player. With his blessing, she interrupted their honeymoon to make a tour of American troop installations abroad. Returning in triumph, she told him, "Oh, Joe, it was so exciting. The boys were thrilled. You never heard such cheers." Quietly DiMaggio observed, "Yes, I have."

———— ✃ ————

DIOGENES (?412–323 BC), *Greek philosopher, principal exponent of the Cynic school of philosophy.*

1 When Alexander the Great visited Corinth, Diogenes was living in a large earthenware tub in one of the city suburbs. Alexander went to see the philosopher and found him sunning himself. The king politely asked if there was any way in which he could serve him. "Stand out of my sun," replied the surly Cynic. Alexander's courtiers began ridiculing Diogenes as a monster, but the king said, "If I were not Alexander, I should wish to be Diogenes."

2 On being asked of what country he was a citizen, Diogenes replied, "I am a citizen of the world."

3 Someone was speaking enthusiastically of Callisthenes, Alexander the Great's historian. "What a fortunate man, a part of Alexander's household, privileged to be present at his feasts!"

"Say rather, how unfortunate a man," said Diogenes, "who can neither dine nor sup except at Alexander's pleasure."

4 By assiduous flattery the hedonistic philosopher Aristippus had won himself a comfortable sinecure at the court of Dionysius, tyrant of Syracuse. One day, observing Diogenes preparing some lentils for a meager meal, Aristippus offered some worldly wisdom to his fellow sage: "If you would only learn to compliment Dionysius, you wouldn't have to live on lentils."

"And if you would only learn to live on lentils, you wouldn't have to flatter Dionysius," retorted Diogenes.

5 One day a woman, accompanied by her small son, came to Diogenes, complaining that the boy was rude and ill behaved and asking what she should do to improve his conduct. Diogenes' answer was to strike the mother in the face.

6 Alexander the Great was puzzled to find Diogenes examining a heap of human bones. "What are you looking for?" he inquired.

"I am searching for the bones of your father," replied the philosopher, "but I cannot distinguish them from those of his slaves."

7 Diogenes was once noticed begging from a statue. Asked the reason for this pointless conduct, he replied, "I am exercising the art of being rejected."

———— ⚭ ————

DIONYSIUS II (c. *395–343* BC), *tyrant of Syracuse (367–356, 346–343).*

1 Dining one day with Dionysius, Philip II of Macedon spoke scornfully of the tyrant's father, who had spent his leisure time writing poetry and plays. "How could the king find leisure to write such trifles?" he asked. "In those hours that you and I spent in drunkenness and debauchery," replied Dionysius.

———— ⚭ ————

DIRICHLET, Peter Gustav Lejeune (*1805–59*), *German mathematician.*

1 Dirichlet was opposed to writing letters; many of his friends had in the course of their entire lives received no communications from him. However, when his first child was born he broke his silence; he wired his father-in-law: "2 + 1 = 3."

———— ⚭ ————

DISNEY, Walt[er Elias] (*1901–66*), *US film producer.*

1 "How does it feel to be a celebrity?" Disney was once asked. "It feels fine," he replied, "when it helps to get a good seat for a football game. But it never helped me to make a good film or a good shot in a polo game, or command the obedience of my daughter. It doesn't even seem to keep fleas off our dogs — and if being a celebrity won't give one an advantage over a couple of fleas, then I guess there can't be much in being a celebrity after all."

———— ⚭ ————

DISRAELI, Benjamin, 1st Earl of Beaconsfield (*1804–81*), *British Conservative statesman and prime minister (1868, 1874–80).*

1 In 1835 Daniel O'Connell, the Irish Roman Catholic leader, attacked Disraeli in the House of Commons. In the course of his unrestrained invective he referred to Disraeli's Jewish ancestry. Disraeli replied, "Yes, I am a Jew, and when the ancestors of the right honorable gentleman were brutal savages in an unknown island, mine were priests in the temple of Solomon."

2 Gladstone and Disraeli frequently clashed in parliamentary debates. "Mr. Disraeli cannot possibly be sure of his facts," roared Gladstone in one debate. "I wish," responded Disraeli, "that I could be as sure of anything as my opponent is of everything."

3 Disraeli was once asked to define the difference between a calamity and a misfortune. Taking the name of his great rival, Gladstone, as his example, Disraeli said, "If, for instance, Mr. Gladstone were to fall into the river, that would be a misfortune. But if anyone were to pull him out, that would be a calamity."

4 Disraeli had a standard acknowledgment for people who sent him unsolicited manuscripts for his opinion: "Thank you for the manuscript; I shall lose no time in reading it."

5 Disraeli, plagued by an applicant for a baronetcy, found various reasons why it was impossible to confer the desired honor. "You know I cannot give you a baronetcy," said Disraeli, "but you can tell your friends that I offered you one and you refused it. That's much better."

6 Disraeli had a standard method of covering up if he forgot the name of the person to whom he was talking. "When I meet a man whose name I can't remember, I give myself two minutes; then, if it is a hopeless case, I always say, 'And how is the old complaint?'"

7 When asked about his motives for writing novels, Disraeli explained the every so often he was overcome by the urge to read a novel, and in order to have one at hand he would write it himself.

8 Disraeli had been criticized for his harsh verbal attacks on John Bright, who was, after all, a self-made man. "I know he is," retorted Disraeli, "and he adores his maker."

9 Disraeli was the guest of honor at a public dinner. As the kitchen was some way from the banqueting hall, most of the food was stone-cold by the time it reached the table. Sipping his champagne after the meal, Disraeli murmured, "Thank God! I have at last got something warm."

10 A young lady was taken to dinner one evening by Gladstone and the following evening by Disraeli. Asked what impressions these two celebrated men had made upon her, she replied, "When I left the dining room after sitting next to Mr. Gladstone I thought he was the cleverest man in England. But after sitting next to Mr. Disraeli I thought I was the cleverest woman in England."

11 Disraeli was especially skilled in dealing with his sovereign, Victoria — in marked contrast to his predecessor, Gladstone. When asked how he managed to maintain such cordial relations with the queen while Gladstone's relationship with her was so frosty, he said, "Gladstone treats the queen like a public department; I treat her like a woman."

12 Queen Victoria once paid Disraeli the honor of visiting him at his country house near Beaconsfield. On his deathbed he declined another royal visit. "No, it is better not. She will only ask me to take a message to Albert."

———— ✑ ————

DIVINE, Father (1877–1965), *US revivalist preacher, born George Baker.*

1 Father Divine taught that heaven was on earth and established "heavens" for his followers in which spiritual life was centered on the worship of himself. The segregation by sexes, even of married couples, in these "heavens" caused considerable scandal. One of his confidential lady "secretaries" revealed Father Divine's favorite seduction technique. "Mary wasn't a virgin," he would murmur.

2 The goings-on at Father Divine's house of worship in Saybrook drove his neighbors to bring a court case against him as causing a public nuisance. On November 16, 1931, Justice Lewis J. Smith fined the preacher $500 and sentenced him to a six-month jail term. Four days later, on November 20, the judge, without warning, pain, or premonition, dropped dead. This extraordinary coincidence unleashed a storm of publicity. Father Divine kept his head and told the reporters clamoring for his comments on the affair, "I hated to do it."

———— ✑ ————

DIX, Dorothea Lynde (1802–87), *US philanthropist, noted for her work on behalf of the insane and for her organization of the nursing corps during the Civil War.*

1 The diarist and philanthropist George Templeton Strong described Miss Dix as a "philanthropic lunatic." Her impulsive ways led her into conflict with the Sanitary Commission, "because we do not leave everything else and rush off the instant she tells us of something that needs attention." Miss Dix once burst into a meeting of the commission in great excitement to report that a cow was dying of sunstroke in the Smithsonian grounds. She was very peeved when the commission did not immediately adjourn to investigate.

―◌◦◦―

DOHERTY, John (1783–1850), *Irish politician, Lord Chief Justice of Ireland.*

1 Attending a ball at Dublin Castle, Doherty and another gentleman were scandalized by the décolletage of a certain young lady. "Did you ever see anything like it since you were born, Doherty?" exclaimed the friend. "I can't say since I was *born*," Doherty answered, "but certainly since I was weaned."

―◌◦◦―

DOLE, Robert (1923–), *US politician, Senate Majority leader and Republican presidential nominee (1996).*

1 At a White House event, Dole observed three former Presidents standing together: Jimmy Carter, Gerald Ford, and Richard Nixon. "There they are," he said, "See no evil, hear no evil, and speak no evil."

2 When Elizabeth Dole was appointed secretary of transportation by President Reagan in 1985, magazines covered the Dole marriage — she as cabinet member, he as powerful senator. After a photo ran that showed them making up the bed in their apartment, a man wrote a complaining letter to Bob Dole, praising Elizabeth's skills but adding, "You've got to stop doing the work around the house. You're causing problems for men across the country." "You don't know the half of it," Dole wrote back. "The only reason she was helping was because they were taking pictures."

3 It was said that one of the challenges the notoriously cranky Dole faced in preparing to accept his party's nomination for President was to stand in front of the mirror and work on his acceptance scowl.

4 Dole's greatest ambition in life was to be elected President, a prize he was fated never to capture. He often joked about it, though. When he was awarded the Presidential Medal of Freedom by President Clinton in 1997, three days before Clinton's second inaugural and two months after his loss at the ballot box, he began his remarks by saying, "I, Robert J. Dole, do solemnly swear . . . Sorry, wrong speech."

5 On an appearance on the television show *Larry King Live* Dole revealed he was a test subject for the new drug Viagra, saying that it was so effective he wished he had bought stock in the company. Of his revelation, comedian Jay Leno noted that "only a Republican would think the best part of Viagra is the fact that you could make money off of it."

6 Shortly after his wife decided to campaign for the presidency herself, Dole let slip to a reporter that he would most likely contribute money to one of her opponents, his old friend Senator John McCain. When asked about this, Elizabeth Dole said that her husband had been "sent to the woodshed" for his gaffe. And McCain noted that he had

tried to call Bob Dole to accept his contribution, but the woodshed had no phone in it.

DONATELLO (c. 1386–1466), *Italian Renaissance sculptor.*

1 The Signori of Venice commissioned Donatello to make the equestrian statue of the condottiere Erasmo da Narni ("Gattamelata") and plagued the artist with their demands that he hurry up and finish it. Exasperated by their importunities, Donatello smashed with a hammer the nearly completed head of the statue. The Signori threatened him with similar treatment, to which Donatello retorted, "Quite agreeable, as long as you feel you will be able to reshape my head as I will do Gattamelata's."

DONNE, John (1572–1631), *British poet, who entered the Church (1615) and became dean of St. Paul's, London (1621–31).*

1 Donne secured the post of secretary to Sir Thomas Egerton, Keeper of the Great Seal, in 1598. He outraged his employer's family by a clandestine marriage to Anne More, the niece of Sir Thomas's wife, and lost his job. The young couple took refuge in a house at Pyrford in Surrey. There Donne scratched on a pane of glass the words: "John Donne / An Donne / Undone."

2 Donne was persuaded, after he took holy orders and repudiated his former ambitious and worldly life, to have his portrait painted. He posed for the painter in a winding sheet with his body and hands arranged like those of a corpse. When the picture was completed, he had it placed beside his bed as a constant reminder of mortality.

DOUGLASS, Frederick (c. 1817–95), *US orator and journalist.*

1 Douglass was traveling by boat from New York to Boston on a stormy night. As his Negro blood disqualified him from occupying a cabin or any of the public rooms, he was obliged to curl up in a corner of the deck to sleep. An officer came across him there and took pity on him. Knowing that he could find Douglass a stateroom if he could pass him off as an American Indian, the officer approached him with the words, "You're an Indian, aren't you?" Douglass at once grasped the significance of the question. Looking the officer straight in the eyes, he replied, "No, sir, I'm a nigger," and curled up in his corner again.

DOYLE, Sir Arthur Conan (1859–1930), *British writer, creator of the detective Sherlock Holmes and his colleague, Dr. Watson.*

1 Joking with Doyle during a rehearsal for one of his plays, a young three-pound-a-week actor called Charlie suggested that he and Sir Arthur should pool their incomes and take half each for the rest of their lives. Though amused by the proposal, Doyle declined for obvious reasons. "I don't think so, Mr. Chaplin," he replied.

2 In later life, Doyle became a fervent spiritualist and gave many public lectures on the subject. At one of these meetings, gesticulating enthusiastically as he spoke, he accidentally spilled a glass of water over some of the reporters in the front row. "So sorry," said Doyle. "I seem to have baptized you, even if I don't succeed in converting you!"

3 When Doyle did not arrive for a scheduled lecture on spiritualism, Cambridge students mounted a placard bearing the announcement: "Sir Arthur Conan Doyle has failed to materialize."

4 As part of his belief in the spiritual world, Doyle thought communication with the dead was possible. A friend once asked him to visit a fellow author who was seriously ill.

"I'll call in tomorrow," promised Doyle.

"Tomorrow could be too late — he may not last the night," said his friend.

"In that case," replied Doyle breezily, "I'll speak to him next week."

DRAKE, Sir Francis (?1540–1596), *English admiral and explorer.*

1 Drake's most famous exploit, the "singeing of the king of Spain's beard," by which he destroyed thirty ships in Cadiz harbor where they were fitting out for the invasion of England, was carried out in the face of Queen Elizabeth's reluctance to provoke the Spaniards. She hoped, despite the evidence of Spain's warlike preparations, to reach a negotiated settlement. It was only with the utmost unwillingness that she gave the order allowing Drake, who had been hanging around in Plymouth harbor for some time, to set off on his hostile errand. No sooner had she given the order than she had second thoughts, and another dispatch rider was sent racing off toward Plymouth to countermand it. Drake however had guessed that such a second order might be forthcoming and as soon as he received the first he put to sea. A speedy boat was sent after him, but curiously enough it failed to locate his fleet. The queen was very angry, but there was nothing she could do to stop him.

2 With the English fleet in harbor, Drake and the other commanders were playing bowls on Plymouth Hoe when the news was brought on July 19, 1588, that the Spanish Armada was sailing up the English Channel. Lord Howard of Effingham, lord admiral, wanted to put to sea at once, but Drake insisted on finishing his bowls. "There is plenty of time to win this game and beat the Spaniards after." Only when the game was over did the English captains go to their ships.

DREISER, Theodore (1871–1945), *US novelist.*

1 During World War I Dreiser became friendly with H. L. Mencken, made him his literary executor, and confided to him that he had chosen his own last words. They were to be "Shakespeare, I come!"

2 When Horace Liveright sold film rights for *An American Tragedy* for the unprecedented sum of $85,000, he couldn't wait to tell Dreiser, and arranged to have lunch with him and Bennett Cerf. Dreiser was ecstatic at the news, but when Liveright reminded him that, by contract, Liveright would get a percentage, Dreiser exploded. "Do you mean to tell me you're going to take $17,500 of my money?" he shouted. Throwing a steaming cup of coffee in Liveright's face, he stalked off. Liveright mopped himself dry, and said wryly, "Bennett, let this be a lesson to you. Every author is a son of a bitch."

DREW, John (1853–1927), *US actor.*

1 To play in *Rosemary* Drew shaved off his mustache, which greatly altered his appearance. Soon afterward he met Max Beerbohm but failed to recall who the latter was. Beerbohm, however, recognized Drew and said, "Mr. Drew, I'm afraid you don't recognize me without your mustache."

DREYSCHOCK, Alexander (1818–69), *Czech pianist.*

1 "At Dreyschock's first court appearance [in Vienna] he played before the emperor [Francis Joseph] in a very hot room, with closed

windows. Dreyschock began to perspire. The emperor listened intently and watched him even more closely. When the pianist got up and faced the emperor, he was afraid to wipe his face. The emperor approached. 'My dear Dreyschock, I have heard Moscheles play.' Dreyschock bowed. 'I have heard Thalberg.' Dreyschock bowed lower. 'I have heard Liszt.' Dreyschock bowed very low indeed. 'I have heard all the great players. But I never, never, never saw anybody perspire as you do.'"

———— ∽ ————

DRYDEN, John (1631–1700), *English critic and poet laureate.*

1 Dryden often played hooky from classes at Westminster School in London and rarely spent much time preparing his lessons. Once when the class had been told to compose a poem on the gospel story of the conversion of water into wine, Dryden hastily scribbled: "The modest water, awed by power divine, / Beheld its God, and blushed itself to wine." By comparison with the turgid effusions of his classmates, this couplet brought Dryden an accolade from the master, who saw in it a portent of future poetic greatness.

2 Dryden described himself as a man of grave demeanor without much of a sense of humor. However:

On one occasion his wife, Lady Elizabeth Howard, bustled into his study, feeling herself to be somewhat neglected. "Lord, Mr. Dryden," she exclaimed, "how can you always be poring over those musty books? I wish I were a book, and then I should have more of your company." Dryden replied, "Pray, my dear, if you do become a book let it be an almanac, for then I shall change you every year."

3 Dryden was enjoying a convivial meeting with a group of fashionable wits, including the earls of Buckingham and Dorset. Someone proposed a poetic competition, each man present to write an impromptu composition, and Dryden to judge which was the best. The Earl of Dorset was the first to hand in his piece of paper. Dryden waited until all the contributions had been completed before he began to read them. His face showed his pleasure as he studied the succession of witty or beautiful verses, but the broadest smile spread over his countenance as he opened the Earl of Dorset's paper. "I will have to award the prize to my Lord Dorset," he said and then read out the earl's contribution: "I promise to pay John Dryden, or order, on demand the sum of £500. Dorset."

———— ∽ ————

DU BARRY, Marie Jeanne Bécu, Comtesse (?1743–93), *French aristocrat, mistress of Louis XV.*

1 Louis XV always maintained that women could never attain to the highest excellence as cooks. Mme du Barry took the opposite view and invited the king to a supper that had been prepared by the best cuisinière in France. At the end of the meal Louis said, "Who is your cook? I must have him in the royal household." Mme du Barry replied, "It is not a cuisinier, but a cuisinière. I demand a recompense worthy both of Your Majesty and of her. I cannot accept anything less than a cordon bleu." The king agreed, and it was in this way that the cordon bleu — the blue ribbon of the grand cross of the Order of the Holy Spirit, the highest chivalric order under the Bourbon kings — became the accolade of an outstanding cook.

———— ∽ ————

DUCLOS, Charles Pinot (1704–72), *French writer and historian.*

1 Jean-Pierre Bougainville, eminent man of letters and elder brother of the famous explorer,

suffered from ill health. While electioneering for admission to the French Academy, he never failed to stress this fact. As he had not long to live, he would plead, he would soon give place to another. Duclos was unmoved by this argument: "Apparently, sir, you imagine that among the Academy's other prerogatives is that of giving extreme unction."

DU DEFFAND, Marie Anne, Marquise (1697–1780), *French noblewoman and salonnière.*

1 Cardinal de Polignac told Mme du Deffand, at great length and in inordinate detail, the story of how Saint Denis was decapitated at Montmartre and then walked a whole league to the village named after him, carrying his head in his hands. Seeing his narrative was evoking no response, the cardinal explained, "Do you deny that he carried his head in his hands for a whole league?"

"It's only the first step that counts," said Mme du Deffand.

2 Asked whether she believed in ghosts, Mme du Deffand replied, "No — but I'm afraid of them."

DUDLEY, John William Ward, 1st Earl of (1781–1833), *British politician.*

1 Lord Dudley was notoriously absentminded. One of his eccentricities was his habit of rehearsing audibly, using two voices, one gruff and one shrill, what he was going to say to others. On one occasion, when he had been asked to present a country gentleman at court, everything went smoothly until their carriage became stuck in a fearful traffic jam as they were leaving the palace. Dudley's protégé was startled to hear his companion say, "Now this tiresome country squire will be expecting me to ask him to dine. Shall I? Or shall I not? On the whole I think not; I think

he might be a bore." The country squire was momentarily confounded, then he too soliloquized, "Now this tiresome old peer will of course be asking me to dine with him today. Shall I or not? No; I am pretty sure it would be a bore." It was the earl's turn to be startled, but he quickly recollected himself, laughed, and with genuine pleasure asked the squire to dine with him.

DUKE, Vernon [Vladimir Dukelsy] (1903–69), *US composer, born in Russia.*

1 Inspired by Duke's famous song, a friend of the composer's decided to spend a few weeks in Paris one April. The weather was appalling. On his return, the traveler complained at some length about his disappointing trip. "Whatever made you go to Paris in April?" asked Duke. "The weather is always terrible then." His friend looked at him in astonishment. "I went because of your song," he replied. "Ah, well," explained the composer apologetically, "we really meant May, but the rhythm required two syllables."

DULLES, John Foster (1888–1959), *US statesman.*

1 Asked whether he had ever been wrong, Dulles considered the question for some time before replying. "Yes," he finally admitted, "once — many, many years ago. I thought I had made a wrong decision. Of course, it turned out that I had been right all along. But I was wrong to have *thought* that I was wrong."

DUMAS, Alexandre [*père*] (1802–70), *French novelist and playwright, often called Dumas* *père to distinguish him from his illegitimate son and namesake, Dumas* fils.

1 Dumas's prodigious output was greatly assisted by his corps of ghost writers. Meeting his son and namesake, Dumas inquired, "Have you read my new novel yet?" Alexandre *fils* replied, "No. Have you?"

2 A reporter was questioning Dumas about his ancestry. "Is it true that you are a quadroon?" he asked. Dumas replied that it was.

"So your father was a mulatto?"

"Yes."

"And your grandfather was a negro?"

"Yes."

Incautiously the reporter persisted: "And your great-grandfather was — ?"

"A baboon, sir," roared Dumas, his patience exhausted. "A baboon! Which means that my family begins where yours ends."

3 A well-known theater manager visited Dumas and, without removing his hat, rather unceremoniously asked if it was true that the famous playwright had sold his latest play to another, smaller theater company. Dumas confirmed this. The manager then made an enormous rival bid, but was unable to change Dumas's mind. "Your competitor," said Dumas, "got the play much more cheaply by a very simple procedure."

"And that was — ?"

"While enjoying the honor of conversing with me, he took off his hat."

4 A committee asked Dumas to contribute toward the funeral of a man who had died in poor circumstances. Dumas asked whether the deceased had been a member of the artistic circle of Paris. "Not exactly," was the reply, "but he sort of moved in and out among us. He was the district bailiff."

"How much will it cost to bury him?" inquired Dumas.

"Twenty-five francs."

"Here are fifty francs," said Dumas. "Go bury two bailiffs."

5 Dumas's quarrel with a rising young politician became so intense that a duel was inevitable. As both were superb shots, they decided to draw lots, the loser agreeing to shoot himself. Dumas lost. Pistol in hand, he withdrew in silent dignity to another room, closing the door behind him. The rest of the company waited in gloomy suspense for the sound of the shot that would end Dumas's career. It rang out at last. They ran to the door, opened it, and there was Dumas, smoking revolver in hand. "Gentlemen, a most regrettable thing has happened. I missed."

6 During the premiere of one of his plays at the Théâtre Français, Dumas mentioned to a friend that on the previous night at the same theater he had witnessed Fournet's *Gladiator*.

"How was it?"

"Tedious," answered Dumas. "People simply fell asleep."

At this moment the friend noticed a member of the audience sunk in deep slumber and remarked with a smirk, "Well, apparently your own play doesn't seem especially gripping either."

"My dear friend, you are mistaken. He's left over from last night."

7 "How do you grow old so gracefully?" exclaimed an admirer of the elderly Dumas. "Madame, I give all my time to it," was the reply.

———ᴄʌᴏ———

DUMAS, Alexandre [*fils*] (1824–95), *French novelist and playwright, often known as Dumas* fils *to distinguish him from his father.*

1 At a Paris salon Dumas overheard a woman describe him as a "boor with whom one could never spend more than an hour." Some months later Dumas found himself staying in

the same seaside hotel as the woman. Her husband was away in Paris for most of the week; she was thoroughly bored and ready for a little intrigue. Dumas exerted all his charm to seduce her, and in the end gained his objective of an assignation. At the end of exactly one hour he got up and marched to the door. "Madame, the time is up. Good day." He bowed and left the room.

2 Before the first night of a Dumas play a pretty young actress rushed up to Dumas all aflutter with stage fright. "Oh, Monsieur Dumas," she gasped, "just feel how my heart is beating." Dumas, of course, was only too happy to oblige. "How does it feel?" pursued the soubrette after a pause. "Round," said Dumas.

3 One night Dumas *fils* set out to go to the theater, but, deterred by pouring rain, returned home. His wife, Ida, had already gone to bed, so Dumas settled down to read by the fire in their bedroom. Suddenly the closet door burst open, Dumas's friend Roger de Beauvoir, clad only in a shirt, emerged, shaking with cold. "I don't see why I should die of pneumonia while you sit there warming yourself by the fire," he exclaimed. A heated altercation ensued, at the end of which Dumas started to hustle de Beauvoir outside. Seeing the pelting rain, however, he paused to reflect; after all, de Beauvoir was an old friend. "You can explain tomorrow," he said, "in the meantime I am going to bed and you can sleep in the armchair."

At first all was peaceful, but as the fire died down de Beauvoir's teeth began to chatter again. Dumas awoke. "Come to bed," he called magnanimously to de Beauvoir, who hopped in at once beside Ida. The three of them slept cosily till morning, when Dumas woke up the guilty pair. "As old friends, Roger, we shouldn't quarrel, even about a wife," he said. "Let us be reconciled as the ancient Romans were — on the public thoroughfare." So the two of them shook hands across the still sleeping Ida.

4 Dumas listened in silence as his friends discussed the physical attributes of two courtesans. One of the ladies had a magnificent figure, the other a beautiful face. "Which would you prefer?" they asked. "I would prefer to go out with the second," replied the writer, "and come home with the first."

DUNCAN, Isadora (1878–1927), *US dancer.*

1 Duncan was dancing with a young man when Paris Singer, a millionaire industrialist with whom she was having an affair, entered the room and threw him out. Duncan, visibly angry, tore off her diamond necklace, scattering the jewels. "If you treat my friends like that," she cried, "I won't wear your jewelry." As she left the room she whispered to another man present, "Pick them up."

2 At her home in Nice in September 1927, Isadora Duncan stepped into her brand-new, low-slung Bugatti racing car, driven over from the dealer's by a mechanic. She wrapped her beloved long red scarf around her neck, flung back the end of it, waved gaily to her friends, crying, *Adieu, mes amis! Je vais à la gloire!* The driver started up and the car moved off with a roar. The long red scarf became entangled in the spokes of the oversized rear wheel, twisted, and snapped Isadora's neck, killing her instantly.

DUNSANY, Edward John Moreton Drax Plunkett, 18th Baron (1878–1957), *Irish poet, short-story writer, and playwright.*

1 Dunsany Castle, the home of Lord Dunsany in County Meath, Ireland, was sacked by the Black and Tans (a British armed force sent to

Ireland to combat the republican movement, Sinn Fein). As the soldiers departed, leaving a trail of destruction in their wake, Lord Dunsany's butler politely inquired, "Who shall I say called?"

———— ✧ ————

Mme du Martel, one of Mme du Deffand's circle in eighteenth-century France, shared her gentle, smiling philosophy. Very ill and facing death, she said to a friend at her bedside, "My consolation is that I am confident that somewhere at this very moment people are making love."

———— ✧ ————

DU PONT, Thomas Coleman (1863–1930), *US entrepreneur and politician.*

1 On arrival at a Chicago hotel, Du Pont found that a lady who had previously occupied his room had left behind a frilly nightgown. He summoned the manager, handed him the garment, and instructed, "Fill it, and bring it back."

———— ✧ ————

DUROCHER, Leo (1906–91), *US baseball player and manager.*

1 Asked if he didn't feel sorry to have beaten such a "nice bunch of guys" as the New York Giants when he was manager of the Brooklyn Dodgers in the 1940s, Durocher coined the classic "Nice guys finish last."

———— ✧ ————

DUSE, Eleonora (1859–1924), *Italian actress.*

1 On her California tour Eleonora had as her personal press representative a charming journalist named Sam Davis. He was the editor of the *Carson Appeal* and also wrote for the *San Francisco Examiner.* Duse grew very fond of him and when it came time for her to return to New York, just before the "All

aboard!", she kissed him first on one cheek, then on the other, and finally on the mouth. "The right cheek is for the *Carson Appeal,* the left for the *Examiner,* and the mouth, my dear friend, for yourself." Davis thanked her, then added, "I also represent the Associated Press, which serves three hundred and eighty newspapers west of Kansas."

2 Eleonora Duse offered to look after the year-old baby of some friends while they went out. The parents wondered about the famous actress's competence with babies, but she assured them that she was full of dodges for entertaining infants. When the parents returned, they found their child sitting up gazing transfixed at the baby-sitter, who was lying on the sofa, snoring sonorously. Duse opened one eye. "Ssh," she said. "If I stop snoring for an instant she yells." She had, she reported, run through her whole gamut of singing, dancing, face-pulling, and other tricks and the baby had wailed throughout. The moment she had begun pretending to snore the baby had sat quite silent, mesmerized.

———— ✧ ————

DUVAL, Claude (1643–70), *British highwayman, born in Normandy.*

1 Duval's exploits were the subject of many ballads and pamphlets around the time of his trial and execution. The most famous of these concerns his reputation for gallantry toward ladies and his appreciation of the finer arts of life, which he had no doubt learned when he was page to the Duke of Richmond. It was said that one day on Hounslow Heath Duval and his gang stopped a coach in which sat a knight and his young wife. The lady, to show her unconcern, took a flageolet from her pocket and proceeded to play upon it. Thereupon, Duval also took out a flageolet and the highwayman and his victim played very prettily to-

gether. "Sir," said Duval, "your lady plays excellently and I doubt not she dances quite as well. Will you please to get out and let me have the honor of a dance with her upon the Heath?" The knight did not think it prudent to oppose the highwayman's wishes, so the lady got out and she and the highwayman danced upon the Heath. When the dance was over, Duval turned to the husband. "You have forgotten to pay for the music," he said. "No, I have not," replied the knight, and handed Duval a bag containing £100. Now Duval knew well that the couple had another £300 concealed in their coach, but he accepted the £100 with a good grace, bade the lady a courteous farewell, and rode off.

DUVEEN, Joseph, Baron Duveen of Millbank (1869–1939), *British art dealer.*

1 In 1920 Duveen and some of the other major art dealers decided on a determined attempt to divert some of Henry Ford's millions into the art market. They clubbed together to produce exquisite full-color reproductions of the "hundred greatest paintings in the world" and had these plates bound into three magnificent volumes, which they took along to the Ford residence. Ford was delighted, admired the pictures extravagantly, and thanked the delegation of dealers for showing him their splendid books. The dealers thought the time ripe to broach the real busi-

ness. By a curious coincidence, they explained, every one of the pictures represented in the books was for sale and they would be happy to assist Mr. Ford in any way they could to acquire these art treasures for his own. A look of puzzlement spread over Ford's face. He explained courteously that he was not really in the market for buying such big expensive books. Duveen hastened to reassure him: the books were a gift. Ford protested that he could not possibly accept such a valuable present from strangers. At this impasse Duveen was obliged to come clean and explain that the books had been specially made up to interest him in buying the originals of the pictures. At last Ford understood. "But gentlemen," he protested, "why would I want to buy originals when the pictures here in these books are so beautiful?"

DYSON, Sir Cyril (1895–?), *British jeweler.*

1 Presenting the graduation prizes at a girls' school, Dyson found it difficult to think of something different to say to each girl. As an attractive seventeen-year-old approached him across the platform, he could come up with nothing more original than "And what are you going to do when you leave school?" With a coy flutter of her eyelids, the girl replied, "Well, I *had* thought of going straight home."

E

EAKINS, Thomas (1844–1916), *US realist portrait painter.*

1 Once Eakins's wife entered his studio and, looking at his work, said, "Oh, that hand is beautifully painted. I've never seen you do one better." Upon which Eakins took a knife and scraped it right off his canvas. "That's not what I wanted," he said. "I wanted you to *feel* the hand."

EASTWOOD, Clint (1930–), *US film actor and director.*

1 Once Eastwood was asked how he defined the essence of a Clint Eastwood movie. His reply was, "To me, what a Clint Eastwood picture is, is one that I'm in."

2 Eastwood was walking across the Warner lot one day when he was suddenly accosted by a hostile young woman, who shouted, "You're a no-good sonafabitch, always making Mexicans the bad guys in your films and killing them." "Don't be angry," responded the actor. "I kill lots of other people too."

3 When he heard that Eastwood had been elected mayor of the California town of Carmel-by-the-Sea, Ronald Reagan was delighted. "What makes him think a middle-aged movie actor who's played with a chimp could have a future in politics?" crowed the President.

EDDY, Mary Baker (1821–1910), *US religious leader, founder of the Church of Christ, Scientist, in Boston.*

1 Bronson Alcott, the philosopher and father of Louisa May Alcott, came one day to visit the Massachusetts Metaphysical College, which Mrs. Eddy had established to train practitioners of Christian Science. He encountered by chance a young man named George Barry and fell into conversation with him. Much impressed by Barry's mental ability, he asked him his age. "Five years old," was the response. Then, noting Alcott's puzzlement, Barry continued: "It's five years since I first met Mrs. Eddy."

EDEN, [Robert] Anthony, 1st Earl of Avon (1897–1977), *British statesman; prime minister (1955–57).*

1 Shortly before Eden became prime minister, the journalist Alistair Cooke asked the aging Bertrand Russell his opinion of Eden. "Not a gentleman; dresses too well," was the verdict.

———∾———

EDEN, Sir William (1849–1915), *British baronet, father of Anthony Eden (later Lord Avon).*

1 As the father of a future prime minister, Sir William Eden could be surprisingly undignified at times. Although he usually restricted himself to dry comments, such as "the progress of civilization is the decay of taste," he could be stirred to more violent action. On one occasion, when the weather had looked promising but then turned to rain, Sir William shook his fist at the clouds beyond the window and yelled, "Just *like* you, God!" He then tore the barometer, which still indicated "Fair," off the wall and threw it through the same window with the cry, "There, you damned fool, see for yourself!"

———∾———

EDISON, Charles (1890–1969), *US politician, son of Thomas Alva Edison*

1 Campaigning for the governorship in 1940, Edison was anxious to dissociate himself from his father's renown. "I would not have anyone believe I am trading on the name Edison," he would explain as he introduced himself. "I would rather have you know me merely as the result of one of my father's earlier experiments."

———∾———

EDISON, Thomas Alva (1847–1931), *US inventor responsible for about thirteen hundred inventions, the most famous of which are the electric light bulb, the gramophone, and motion pictures.*

1 Edison was asked to sign a guest book that had the usual columns for name and address, as well as one for "Interested in." In this last column Edison entered the word: "Everything."

2 Edison was concerned about the way in which acquaintances visiting his office helped themselves to his Havana cigars. As he could not be bothered to lock them up, his secretary suggested that a friend of his in the cigar trade should roll some cigars made from cabbage leaves in brown paper and that these should be substituted for the Havanas. Edison agreed, then forgot about it, and only remembered some time later when the Havanas started vanishing again. He called his secretary and inquired why the bogus cigars had not arrived. The secretary said they had and that he had handed them over to Edison's manager. The manager explained that, not knowing what they were, he had packed them in Edison's bag when he had gone away on a visit. "And do you know," Edison concluded, "I smoked every one of those damned cigars myself!"

3 Someone remarked on the huge number of failures Edison had encountered in his search for a new storage battery — fifty thousand experiments before he achieved results. "Results?" said the inventor. "Why, I have gotten a lot of results. I know fifty thousand things that won't work."

4 Edison had a summer residence of which he was very proud. He enjoyed showing visitors around his property, pointing out the various labor-saving devices. At one point it was necessary to pass through a turnstile in order to take the main path back to the house. Considerable effort was needed to move the turnstile. A guest asked Edison why it was that, with all the other clever gadgets around, he had such a heavy turnstile. Edison replied, "Well, you see, everyone who pushes the turnstile around pumps eight gallons of water into a tank on my roof."

5 After a series of electrical storms at Orange, New Jersey, the vestrymen of a certain church there discussed the desirability of

placing lightning rods on the structure. Then they sought Edison's advice, who asked them what sort of building it was. "A church," was the reply. "By all means put lightning rods on," said Edison. "You know Providence is absentminded at times."

6 Henry Ford had Edison's electrical laboratory moved from Menlo Park to Dearborn. The reassembled building was opened on October 29, 1929. After the ceremony Henry Ford asked Edison what he thought of it. "It's ninety-nine-and-a-half percent perfect," replied Edison. "Why, what's wrong?" asked Ford, who prided himself on the accuracy of the reconstruction. "Well, we never used to keep the place so clean," said Edison.

7 Edison found formal dinners extremely tedious. On one occasion, the company was so dull that the inventor made up his mind to escape to his laboratory at the earliest opportunity. Unfortunately, his host accosted him as he hovered near the door. "It certainly is a delight to see you, Mr. Edison," he said. "What are you working on now?"

"My exit," replied Edison.

8 Edison was plagued with deafness all of his adult life. When asked if he knew what had caused his infirmity, he recounted an episode from his youth: as a twelve-year-old boy, he had raced to catch a train. As his arms were full of newspapers, he could not hold on to the train, which was already moving, and the conductor reached down and, grasping his ears, pulled him bodily up. "I felt something snap inside my head," he said, "and the deafness has progressed ever since."

EDMAN, Irwin (1896–1954), *US philosopher and educator.*

1 By a private arrangement Professor Edman had access to the swimming pool of his friend, the book publisher Bob Haas. On one occasion Edman bathed alone and, still in his wet bathing suit, wandered into Haas's living room. There he spotted a volume of Thucydides and sat down to read a few pages. Later on, after Edman had left, Mrs. Haas returned to find a pool of water in the middle of her living room. "It's that dog again!" she cried angrily. The French maid quickly put her right: "No, madame, not the dog. The professor!"

2 Professor Edman's absentmindedness, in fact, was his trademark and the source of much humor at Columbia University. One day he stopped a student on Riverside Drive and asked, "Pardon me, but am I walking north or south?" The student answered, "North, Professor." "Ah," replied Edman, "then I've had my lunch."

EDWARD I (1239–1307), *king of England (1272–1307).*

1 After the death in 1282 of Prince Llewelyn ab Gruffydd, leader of the Welsh resistance to English encroachment, Edward I promised the Welsh a new Prince of Wales "who would not speak a word of English." In fulfillment of this promise he presented the assembled Welsh chieftains with his infant son (later Edward II) a few days after his birth in Caernarvon Castle. According to some reports he held the royal baby aloft in his arms and proclaimed in Welsh, *"Eich dyn"* (literally, "This is your man").

EDWARD III (1312–77), *king of England (1327–77).*

1 Edward's military adventures made him eager to attract Europe's best soldiers into his service. He therefore decided to found an order of knighthood based on King Arthur's legendary Round Table. On St. George's Day,

1344, he arranged a grand jousting tournament and banquet at Windsor Castle. By some accounts, it was at this banquet that the order of the Knights of the Garter was founded. The Countess of Salisbury, accidentally or otherwise, dropped her garter while dancing with the king. He instantly retrieved it. Observing the knowing nudges and looks of the bystanders, Edward fastened the garter around his own leg, saying (in Old French), *"Honi soit qui mal y pense"* (Shame on him who thinks ill of it).

2 Edward the Black Prince, Edward's eldest son, sixteen years old at the battle of Crécy, was in the forefront of the fighting. A messenger hurried up to the English king, reporting that the Black Prince was in some danger. Edward refused to send reinforcements or to recall his son. "Let the boy win his spurs," was all he said.

EDWARD VII (1841–1910), *king of the United Kingdom (1901–10).*

1 While Edward VII was Prince of Wales, one of his closest associates was Lord Charles Beresford. Once when the prince invited him to dinner, Beresford cabled back: "VERY SORRY CAN'T COME LIE FOLLOWS BY POST."

2 In turn-of-the-century Paris one of the most dedicated social climbers was Mrs. Kate Moore, an American millionairess. After energetically pursuing him for some time she captured her prize trophy: the Prince of Wales accepted an invitation to dine at her Biarritz palace. The future Edward VII, far from being irritated by her assiduousness, was amused at her good-natured vulgarity: "Madam, you should have lived in the days of Louis the Fourteenth," he remarked. "In those days there were kings everywhere."

3 Edward's self-permissive conduct, as Prince of Wales and king, was partly a reaction to his mother's impossibly virtuous standards of conduct. When Lady Beaconsfield once suggested that her son must be a great comfort to her, Queen Victoria replied, "Comfort! Why, I caught him smoking a fortnight after his dear father died!"

4 During the 1897 Diamond Jubilee, Edward often had to represent his mother at public events. One of the hymns frequently sung and played on these occasions was "Eternal Father, Strong to Save." He once murmured, "It's all very well about the Eternal Father. But what about my eternal mother?"

5 As Queen Victoria lay dying, a member of the royal household discussed the imminent event with Edward, the Prince of Wales. "I wonder if she will be happy in heaven?" he mused.

"I don't know," said the prince. "She will have to walk *behind* the angels — and she won't like that!"

6 As king, Edward would alternate social charm with an irritable demandingness that often made things hard for his friends and courtiers. One of his hostesses, Lady Brougham, noticing his black mood, sought to cheer him up. "Did you notice, sir, the soap in Your Majesty's bathroom?"

"No!"

"I thought you might, sir. . . . It has such an *amorous* lather!"

It is reported that the king's cheerfulness was restored.

7 When the opera *The Wreckers* was first staged in 1909, influential friends of the composer, Dame Ethel Smyth, persuaded Edward VII to grace the opening night. Later, conductor Sir Thomas Beecham asked the king's private secretary, who had accompanied him to the opera, what the king had thought of it. "I don't know," said the pri-

vate secretary. "Didn't he say anything?" persisted Beecham. "Well, yes," admitted the private secretary. "He did say something. He suddenly woke up three-quarters of the way through and said, 'Fritz, that's the fourth time that infernal noise has roused me.'"

8 A pompous young minister once used the royal pronoun "We," referring only to himself, in the presence of Edward VII. The king picked him up at once: "Only two people are permitted to refer to themselves as 'We' — a king, and a man with a tapeworm inside him."

9 Edward was not remarkable for his wit, but there is something endearing in his mild rebuke to a footman who accidentally emptied a jug of cream over him: "My good man, I'm not a strawberry."

EDWARD VIII (1894–1972), *king of the United Kingdom (1936).*

1 On a visit to the United States in the twenties, while Prince of Wales, Edward was nearly caught in a raid on a nightclub run by the celebrated hostess Texas Guinan. The police, however, never realized his identity, thanks to the quick thinking of Texas, who hurried him out to the kitchen, put a chef's hat on his head and a skillet in his hand, and told him to keep cooking eggs until the raid was over.

2 Addressing a group of friends on the subject of remaining on friendly terms with one's wife, the Duke of Windsor remarked, "Of course, I do have a slight advantage over the rest of you. It helps in a pinch to be able to remind your bride that you gave up a throne for her."

3 The Homestead is a luxurious resort hotel in Hot Springs, Virginia, the haunt of many distinguished visitors, among whom have been counted the Duke and Duchess of Windsor. In 1943 they spent an entire happy month there. As they prepared to leave, the bill was presented. The duke looked at it blankly and muttered, "Now what do I do with *this?*"

The bill has not yet been paid.

EINSTEIN, Albert (1879–1955), *German-born physicist of Jewish descent who won the Nobel Prize for Physics in 1921.*

1 (Otto Neugebauer, the historian of ancient mathematics, told a story about the boy Einstein that he characterizes as a "legend" but that seems fairly authentic.) As he was a late talker, his parents were worried. At last, at the supper table one night, he broke his silence to say, "The soup is too hot." Greatly relieved, his parents asked why he had never said a word before. Albert replied, "Because up to now everything was in order."

2 An expedition to observe the 1919 solar eclipse verified Einstein's prediction, based on his general theory of relativity, concerning the curvature of space. A pupil asked him, "What would you have said if there had been no confirmation of this kind?"

"I would have been obliged to pity our dear God," replied Einstein. "The theory is correct."

3 Einstein praised the father of quantum physics, Max Planck, but noted that he didn't really understand physics. When asked what he meant, Einstein said, "During the eclipse of 1919, Planck stayed up all night to see if it would confirm the bending of light by the gravitational field of the sun. If he had really understood the way the general theory of relativity explains the equivalence of inertial and gravitational mass, he would have gone to bed the way I did."

4 When Einstein and his friend and colleague Philipp Frank were to visit the Berlin Astrophysical Observatory, they agreed to rendezvous on a certain bridge at Potsdam. Frank, who did not know the town well, was worried that he might be late, but Einstein told him not to worry, that he would wait on the bridge. Frank said he was concerned that that might waste Einstein's time. Einstein dismissed the objection. "The kind of work I do can be done anywhere. Why should I be less capable of reflecting about my problems on the Potsdam bridge than at home?"

5 "On a visit to Palestine in 1921 Einstein went to look at a kibbutz. . . . He asked a great many questions of the twenty-two-year-old girl who was head of the young community. One of his questions was, 'What is the relationship here of men to women?' Thinking that he was one of the many visitors who were of the opinion that women were common property in the kibbutz, she stammered with embarrassment, 'But, Herr Professor, each man here has one woman.' Einstein's eyes twinkled. He took the girl's hand and said, 'Don't be ashamed at my question. We physicists understand by the word "relationship" something rather simple, namely, how many men are there and how many women.'"

6 In 1927 the physicist Werner Heisenberg enunciated his principle of uncertainty, or indeterminacy. This states (roughly) that the position and velocity of an object cannot both be measured exactly at the same time.

Einstein never accepted the principle, for it would play havoc with the strict determinism in which he believed. As he often said and wrote, "God does not play dice with the universe." He and Niels Bohr carried on a controversy for many years. In 1930 at the Solvay conference in Brussels they had a celebrated discussion of the matter. Einstein had invented an imaginary device involving clocks and scales, which, he affirmed, appeared to violate the uncertainty principle. But, following a sleepless night, Bohr found that Einstein in the course of his argument had forgotten to take into account the consequences of one of his own discoveries — in a gravitational field clocks run slower. The uncertainty principle still stood firm.

7 (When L. L. Whyte was a young theoretical physicist studying in Berlin in the late 1920s, an acquaintance arranged for him to meet Einstein. Whyte, diffident about intruding upon the great man, was delighted to receive a friendly letter from Einstein, inviting him to call. The letter concluded, "Don't be put off by Frau Einstein. She's there to protect me." Whyte recounts what happened during his visit to Einstein's home.)

"After we had been talking for about twenty minutes the maid came in with a huge bowl of soup. I wondered what was happening and I thought that this was probably a signal for me to leave. But when the girl left the room Einstein said to me in a conspiratorial whisper, 'That's a trick. If I am bored talking to somebody, when the maid comes in I don't push the bowl of soup away and the girl takes whomever I am with away and I am free.' Einstein pushed the bowl away, and so I was quite happy and much flattered and more at my ease for the rest of the talk."

8 Speaking at the Sorbonne during the 1930s, Einstein said, "If my relativity theory is verified, Germany will proclaim me a German and France will call me a citizen of the world. But if my theory is proved false, France will emphasize that I am a German and Germany will say that I am a Jew."

9 After Einstein had gone into exile, a hundred Nazi professors published a book condemning his theory of relativity. Einstein was unconcerned. "If I were wrong," he said, "one professor would have been enough."

10 The classical scholar Gilbert Murray one day encountered Einstein sitting in the quadrangle of Christ Church, Oxford. The exiled scientist was deep in thought, with a serene and cheerful expression on his face. Murray asked him what he was thinking about. "I am thinking that, after all, this is a very small star," Einstein answered.

11 Einstein's wife was once asked if she understood her husband's theory of relativity. "No," she replied loyally, "but I know my husband and I know he can be trusted."

12 It is alleged that when Einstein and his wife visited the Mount Wilson Observatory in California, Mrs. Einstein pointed to a particularly complex piece of equipment and asked its purpose. Their guide said that it was used to determine the shape of the universe. "Oh," she said, not at all impressed, "my husband uses the back of an old envelope to work that out."

13 Einstein and an assistant, having finished a paper, searched the office for a paper clip. They finally found one, too badly bent for use. They looked for an implement to straighten it, and after opening many more drawers came upon a whole box of clips. Einstein at once shaped one into a tool to straighten the bent clip. His assistant, puzzled, asked why he was doing this when there was a whole boxful of usable clips. "Once I am set on a goal it becomes difficult to deflect me," said Einstein.

14 A certain distinguished astronomer once declared at a scientific meeting: "To an astronomer, man is nothing more than an insignificant dot in an infinite universe."

"I have often felt that," said Einstein. "But then I realize that the insignificant dot who is man is also the astronomer."

15 "The laws of physics should be simple," said Einstein, lecturing at Princeton. "But what if they are not simple?" came a voice from the audience. Replied Einstein: "Then I would not be interested in them."

16 During his stay in Princeton, New Jersey, Einstein used to play his violin in a string quartet. He enjoyed these sessions, but the other musicians were less enthusiastic about his skills. Complained one of the other players after a private performance, "He can't count."

17 Einstein's scientific theories and investigations were an impenetrable mystery to his second wife, Elsa. "Couldn't you tell me a little about your work?" she complained one day. "People talk a lot about it, and I appear so stupid when I say I know nothing." Einstein thought for a minute or two, frowning deeply as he searched for a way to begin his explanation. Suddenly, his face cleared. "If people ask," he said, "tell them you know all about it, but can't tell them, as it is a great secret!"

18 In the course of conversation at an American dinner party Einstein's neighbor, a young girl, asked the white-haired professor: "What are you actually by profession?" Einstein replied: "I devote myself to the study of physics." The girl looked at him in astonishment. "You mean to say you study physics at your age?" she exclaimed. "I finished mine a year ago."

19 A young friend of Einstein's proudly presented his eighteen-month-old son to the great scientist. The child looked up into the old man's smiling face and promptly began to howl. Einstein patted him on the head and said fondly, "You're the first person for years who has told me what you really think of me."

20 As the hydrogen bomb was being developed, Einstein was asked how the Third World War would be fought. Einstein answered that

he had no idea what kind of weapons would be developed for the next war, but he could assure his questioner that the war after that would be fought with stones.

21 Einstein was asked why he always sought a single principle to explain a given natural phenomenon. Why not have five or six? "It is all a matter of *good taste*," said Einstein.

22 Einstein was alone in his house when the local fuel dealer called to get the quantity of heating oil Einstein needed for the coming winter. Einstein calculated the cubic capacity of the house, estimated the heat loss from the walls and roof, determined the temperature range he liked, and, having arrived at a figure, called back to place his order. When his wife returned home he told her about the call. "For goodness sake," she told the dealer. "What made you ask the professor? He knows nothing about things like that. I think this winter will be colder than last, so add a hundred gallons to last year's order — and pay no attention to him!"

23 A friend of Einstein's was asked if it was true that only ten people in the world understood the man. After thinking for a moment, the friend said, "Oh, no. There are at least twenty, but Einstein is not one of them."

———— ✧ ————

EISENHOWER, Dwight David (1890–1969),
US general and statesman, 34th President of the United States (1953–61).

1 After the successful landings in France, Eisenhower was inspecting a British section of the Allied lines when German planes came over and strafed them. The party dived for cover. As soon as it was safe to emerge a senior British officer hurried across to see if Eisenhower was all right. Finding him unharmed, he expressed his relief in fervent terms. Ike thanked him for his solicitude. "Oh," said the officer, "my concern was just that nothing should happen to you in *my* sector."

2 Marlene Dietrich, who had been on the furthest line of the front entertaining GI's, was once asked if the rumor about her affair with General Eisenhower was true. "How could I?" she replied. "He was never that close to the front line!"

3 During the Allied advance into Europe in 1943, Eisenhower's mother, Ida, was asked if she was proud of her son. "Which one?" she asked. She had six.

4 Shortly after the Second World War had ended, Eisenhower and General MacArthur had dinner together, during the course of which MacArthur speculated that one of the two of them would become President. Eisenhower demurred, claiming that he believed strongly in the separation of politics from the military and asserting that he had no interest in high office. MacArthur leaned over as Eisenhower concluded his comments, and said, "That's all right, Ike. You go on like that and you'll get it for sure."

5 Eisenhower loved to play golf, and did so as often as his schedule permitted. On the course he was known for one eccentricity: in trying to identify his ball, he would use his club to roll the ball over until the trademark was visible, instead of bending over to look more closely at the ball. Once, at the Burning Tree Golf Club, when he rolled a settled ball over, it lodged against a rock. Eisenhower's caddie, seeing the President upset, said, "Mr. President, I'm afraid you've overidentified your ball."

6 Some months after the end of his term as President, Eisenhower was asked if leaving the White House had affected his golf game. "Yes," he replied, "a lot more people beat me now."

———— ✧ ————

ELEANOR of Aquitaine (c. 1122–1204), *French queen consort. She was first the wife of Louis VII of France, then divorced him in 1152 and married Henry II of England in 1154.*

1 Eleanor's petition for divorce from Louis VII was based on the pretext that they were too closely related for their marriage to be legal in the eyes of the church. The divorce was granted. Two years later, when Eleanor married Henry II, she remarked with satisfaction, "I am queen of England by the wrath of God."

———⌒ↄ———

ELIOT, Charles William (1834–1926), *US educator, president of Harvard for forty years (1869–1909).*

1 During his many years as president of Harvard, Charles W. Eliot expressed frequent misgivings about sports. At one point Eliot announced at the end of a successful baseball season that he was thinking of dropping the sport. Pressed for an explanation, he said, "Well, this year I'm told the team did well because one pitcher had a fine curve ball. I understand that a curve ball is thrown with a deliberate attempt to deceive. Surely that is not an ability we should want to foster at Harvard."

———⌒ↄ———

ELIOT, John (1604–90), *British missionary who devoted his life to proselytizing the American Indians.*

1 While translating the Bible into a language of the American Indians, Eliot found himself unable to translate the word "lattice" in the sentence: "The mother of Sisera looked out at a window, and cried through the lattice." He described the object in question to a number of Indian friends, one of whom offered what he thought to be an appropriate translation. Years later Eliot discovered, to

his great amusement, that his rendering of the passage in the Indian Bible read: "The mother of Sisera looked out at a window, and cried through the eel-pot."

———⌒ↄ———

ELIOT, T[homas] S[tearns] (1888–1965), *American-born poet who won the 1948 Nobel Prize for literature.*

1 I. A. Richards, the eminent literary critic and scholar, knew T. S. Eliot when he was a junior member of the staff of Lloyd's Bank in Queen Henrietta Street, London, at the end of World War I. By chance he met one of Eliot's superiors on holiday in Switzerland and the two men discovered that the poet was a mutual acquaintance. The senior banker was a pleasant man who seemed unable to frame a question that he obviously wanted to put to Richards. Eventually it came out: did Richards think that Eliot was a *good* poet? Richards replied that in his opinion, which would not be shared by everyone, Eliot was a good poet. The other man was pleased to hear it. Some of his colleagues considered that banking and poetry did not go together, but in his view if a man had a hobby and did it well it helped him in his work. He ended by telling Richards that he could tell Eliot that if he continued to do as well as he was doing at the bank, "I don't see why — in time, of course, in time — he mightn't even become a branch manager." Richards found great delight in relating this conversation to Eliot.

2 On his way to Stockholm for the Nobel prize ceremony, Eliot was interviewed by a reporter who asked him for which of his works the prize had been awarded. Eliot replied that he believed it was for the entire corpus. "And when did you publish that?" asked the reporter. Eliot observed afterward that *The Entire Corpus* might make rather a good title for a mystery story.

3 At a meeting of the Oxford Poetry Club Eliot was the guest of honor and agreed to answer questions about his work. An undergraduate asked him what he meant by the line from *Ash-Wednesday:* "Lady, three white leopards sat under a juniper-tree." Eliot answered, "I mean, 'Lady, three white leopards sat under a juniper-tree.'"

4 An American arriving in England in 1961 for postgraduate study went to visit Eliot. As he was leaving, he noticed that the poet was apparently searching for the right remark with which to bid him farewell. "Forty years ago I went from Harvard to Oxford," Eliot began. "Now, what advice can I give you?" There was a prolonged pause while the younger man waited breathlessly for the poet's words of wisdom. Finally Eliot said, "Have you any long underwear?"

5 W. H. Auden, finding Eliot engrossed in a game of patience, expressed surprise at his apparent enjoyment of this trivial occupation. "Well," said Eliot thoughtfully, "I suppose it's the nearest thing to being dead."

6 Publisher Robert Giroux once asked Eliot whether he agreed with the widely held belief that most editors are failed writers. Eliot pondered for a moment, then said, "Yes, I suppose some editors are failed writers — but so are most writers."

7 A charming American woman was seated next to Eliot at a dinner. The company drank good wine, the conversation was excellent, and after a while Eliot asked his companion to call him "Tom." "Oh, I couldn't," she said. "You were required reading!"

ELIZABETH I (1533–1603), *queen of England and Ireland (1558–1603).*

1 Many doubted the abilities of Elizabeth, who assumed her throne at a young age. In particular, the memory of her father, Henry VIII, and his outsized personality and force of opinions was strong. To one who compared father and daughter unfavorably, she replied, "Although I may not be a lioness, I am a lion's cub, and inherit many of his qualities."

2 Shortly after Elizabeth came to the throne, a knight who had behaved insolently toward her when she was living in disgrace and obscurity during the reign of her half-sister Mary threw himself at her feet to beseech her pardon. Elizabeth gestured to him to rise, dismissing him with the words, "Do you not know that we are descended of the lion, whose nature is not to prey upon the mouse or any other such small vermin?"

3 On one occasion, as he was bowing low to Queen Elizabeth, Edward de Vere, the Earl of Oxford, audibly broke wind. Deeply embarrassed, the earl withdrew from court and traveled abroad for several years. Upon his return he went to court to pay his respects, and was greeted by the queen. Her first words were: "My lord, I had forgot the fart."

4 The diplomat Valentine Dale, on a mission to Flanders, found himself running short of money. The queen's notorious parsimony was such that he feared he would be unlikely to receive a draft before he became seriously embarrassed for cash. Nonetheless, he wrote to the queen about the affairs of state and his financial position; by the same packet he also sent an affectionate letter to his wife, giving an intimate account of his stage of health and mentioning his monetary difficulty. However, the letter intended for the queen was addressed to his wife and vice versa, so that Elizabeth was startled and amused to find herself reading a familiar letter interspersed with such endearments as "sweetheart" and "dear love." The mix-up appealed to her sense of humor, and Dale's financial problem to her sense of diplomatic honor. She

promptly sent off a further supply of money, never suspecting that the "mistake" of course had been deliberately contrived by the artful diplomat.

5 Elizabeth was on her barge on the Thames River when an assassin shot at her; the bullet hit her boatman instead. The queen immediately removed her scarf to bind up his wounds, saying, "Be of good cheer, for you will never want, for the bullet was meant for me, not for you."

6 Upon hearing rumors of her death, the queen smiled and said, "Dead — but not buried." She reigned for another four years.

7 The Archbishop of Canterbury knelt at her deathbed and prayed with her, then began extolling the virtues and glories of her long reign. But Elizabeth interrupted him, saying, "My lord, the crown which I have borne so long had given enough of vanity in my time. I beseech you not to augment it in this hour when I am so near my death." Those were her last words.

"The nineteenth century produced great preachers in Wales, some of whom are remembered to this day. John Elias was one such. It is said that the power of his oratory was so great that people would come from miles around to hear him preach. But then, 'preach' is hardly the right word. It was not a sermon, it was a performance with a sense of theatre and enough dread to give it spice. The story is told of his preaching in a small village in mid-Wales on the way the finger of God touched every man. At the height of his peroration he flung out his arm, having carefully arranged the candles before hand so that the huge shadow of his finger fell upon the wall. Seeing this monstrous arm, the congregation fled."

— IVOR RICHARD, *We, the British*

ELIZABETH II (1926–), *queen of the United Kingdom (1952–).*

1 Princess Elizabeth rushed to announce the birth of her younger sister, and came first upon Lady Cynthia Asquith. "I've got a baby sister, Margaret Rose," she crowed, "and I'm going to call her Bud." "Why Bud?" asked Lady Asquith. "Well," came the reply, "she's not a real Rose yet, is she? She's only a bud."

2 On the morning of Edward VII's abdication in 1937, Princess Elizabeth wondered why there was such a commotion outside her family's front door. A footman told her the news — that her Uncle David had stepped down from the throne, and her father was to be king. When her sister, Margaret, learned that Elizabeth would then be in line to become queen, she tried to consoler her older sister, saying, "Poor you!"

3 At their wedding Elizabeth and her husband Philip displayed their gifts on a series of large tables. One gift came from Gandhi: he had woven them a tray cloth. As Elizabeth's grandmother, Queen Mary, surveyed the gifts, she spotted the cloth and shuddered. "What a horrible thing!" she exclaimed, mistaking it for a loincloth. Gandhi's gift was discreetly hidden before her next visit to the tables.

4 The regulations of some of the older London clubs are sacrosanct. One has the rule that no visitors are allowed in the lounge. The queen, arriving at the club for a private dinner party, quickly looked into the room to admire the pictures. "Not in there, Bet," said Prince Philip, and the queen retreated. An elderly member of the club, dozing by the fire, caught sight of her as she left. "Who was that woman? What's she doing here?" he rumbled. "That was the queen, my lord," said a waiter. "Well, dammit, she shouldn't be here," snapped the old man. "Members only, you know."

5 During a visit to the Bahamas the queen's host was seen to take a silver pencil from his pocket and use it to swizzle the bubbles out of a drink. "That's all right in our company," said Queen Elizabeth, "but what happens in high society?"

6 The queen and Prince Philip paid a visit to the White House during Gerald Ford's presidency. Dressing for dinner that evening, the Fords' son Jack mislaid the studs for his dress shirt and rushed to his father's room to see if he could borrow some. He stepped into the elevator, his shirt unfastened and his hair in disarray, only to find it already occupied by his parents and their royal guests. Mrs. Ford, visibly embarrassed, introduced her son. Taking in at a glance the young man's unkempt appearance, the queen remarked sympathetically: "I have one just like that!"

7 "During an interview with the queen, a British ambassador returning from the Middle East was struggling to explain the character of the head of government with whom he had to deal. He approached it from this angle, and that angle, and roundabout, using increasingly long words with a psychological tinge, until his sovereign extricated him from his misery. 'Are you trying to tell me,' Her Majesty inquired, 'that the man is just bonkers?'"

8 Two women in tweedy suits were leaving a Norfolk tea shop with a basket of cakes when a customer stopped one of them and remarked on her resemblance to the queen. "How very reassuring," said Queen Elizabeth, as she got into her car to take her back to Windsor Castle.

9 During a drive near the royal residence at Sandringham a woman walking along the road was splashed with mud by the Queen's car. "I quite agree with you, madam," said Elizabeth. Philip asked what the woman had said, "Bastards!" replied the queen.

10 A new Master of the Household found that he had much trouble keeping food warm on plates, given the constant crush of guests and the long distances food had to travel. One day the food he served the queen was stone cold. "Don't worry," she said. "People come here not for the food but to eat off the gold plate."

11 The painter Norman Hepple was painting a full-length portrait of Elizabeth in full ceremonial robes. After an hour or so he asked if she would like to sit and rest. "No," came her reply. "I am used to standing. I have been standing all my life."

12 On one state occasion Prime Minister Margaret Thatcher was embarrassed to find that her gown matched that of the queen. Calling Buckingham Palace to ask if there was a way to avoid such sartorial conflict, she was informed, "Do not worry. The queen does not notice what other people are wearing."

———— ⚬ ————

ELIZABETH the Queen Mother (1900–), *wife of George VI of the United Kingdom, whom she married in 1923.*

1 During the Blitz of London in 1940 the king and queen set an example of steadfastness and devotion to duty. Queen Elizabeth was particularly affected by the sufferings and gallantry of the poor people of London's East End, many of whom lost their homes and all they possessed. One day Buckingham Palace received a direct hit from a bomb. The queen, surveying the damage, remarked that she was not entirely sorry: "Now we can look the East End in the face."

2 When asked whether the little princesses (Elizabeth and Margaret Rose) would leave England after the Blitz, the queen replied: "The children will not leave unless I do. I shall not leave unless their father does, and

the king will not leave the country in any circumstances whatever."

3 On a royal tour of South Africa in 1947, King George VI and Queen Elizabeth did much of their traveling by train. A warm welcome was not always assured at some of the stops where the Nationalist sentiments of Afrikaners ran high.

One of the first stops was at Swellendam, well known for Nationalist leanings. At the station, where the queen greeted the crowd, an old Afrikaner farmer said bluntly that, much as he was delighted to meet the Royal Family, he did not like the overseeing from Westminster. The queen, daughter of a Scottish earl, sweetly replied, "I understand perfectly. We feel the same in Scotland."

4 King George and Queen Elizabeth went to see a Noël Coward–Gertrude Lawrence production at a London theater. As they entered the royal box, the whole audience rose to its feet to honor them. Gertrude Lawrence, standing in the wings, said, "What an entrance!"

"What a part!" said Coward.

5 During a state visit to Australia, the Queen Mother found herself surrounded by a group of inquisitive Australians at a garden party. Still nodding and smiling graciously as the circle pressed closer, she remarked in an undertone: "Please don't touch the exhibits."

6 Cecil Beaton was showing the Queen Mother a selection of photographs of herself from a sitting she had recently given him. After she had chosen one, Beaton suggested that he could have the picture discreetly retouched to conceal a few wrinkles. The Queen Mother rejected the proposal. "I would not want it to be thought that I had lived for all these years without having anything to show for it," she explained.

ELLENBOROUGH, Edward Law, 1st Baron (1750–1818), *British lawyer, lord chief justice (1802–18).*

1 Ellenborough had a redoubtable reputation for sarcasm and severity. A young lawyer, making his first appearance in court, was petrified and, rising to speak, could only stammer, "My lord, my unfortunate client — my lord — my unfortunate client — my lord —"

"Go on, sir, go on," said Ellenborough. "As far as you have proceeded hitherto, the court is entirely with you."

2 Asked to identify himself, a witness in a case began pompously, "I employ myself as a surgeon."

"But does anyone else employ you as a surgeon?" interrupted Ellenborough.

———— ⌘ ————

ELLIOT, Hugh (1752–1830), *British diplomat.*

1 In 1777 Elliot was sent as envoy to the court of Frederick the Great at Berlin. His opposite number in London was a notoriously disreputable individual whom Frederick had sent thither to annoy and indicate his contempt for the British government. Frederick mockingly asked Elliot what he thought of the Prussian envoy. "Worthy to represent Your Majesty," replied Elliot suavely.

———— ⌘ ————

ELLISTON, Robert William (1774–1831), *British actor.*

1 Elliston sat down to play at cards with Charles Lamb. His hands were excessively grimy. Lamb looked at them with distaste for some time and then observed, "If dirt were trumps, what a hand you'd have!"

———— ⌘ ————

ELMAN, Mischa (1891–1967), *US violinist.*

1 As a child of seven, Elman was asked to give a violin recital for friends of the family. He embarked on Beethoven's *Kreutzer* sonata, which he played with ease and great virtuosity. During one of the many long rests in the piece, one of his listeners, a kindly old lady, tapped him on the shoulder and whispered confidentially, "Play something you know, dear."

"Henry Erskine, Lord Advocate of Scotland toward the close of the eighteenth century, had a tutor who was very absent-minded. So much so that Erskine, who thought a great deal of the old man, was one day flabbergasted to hear him say: 'I was very sorry, my dear boy, you have had the fever in your family; was it you or your brother who died of it?' 'It was I,' Erksine replied. 'Ah, dear me, I thought so — very sorry for it — very sorry for it.' And the old man walked away."

— HERBERT V. PROCHNOW,
The Public Speaker's Treasure Chest

EMERSON, Ralph Waldo (1803–82), *US writer, Transcendentalist philosopher, and exponent of individualism, known as "the Sage of Concord."*

1 When he moved to his house in Concord, Emerson was particularly delighted with the orchard. He spent an hour each morning tending the trees; he did his writing in the orchard when possible, and received his friends there. He sent some of his pears to the local cattle show, and was pleased when he received a visit from the committee of the horticultural society who asked whether they might examine his pear trees. Emerson received them with modest pride, and then discovered that they had not come to congratulate him — they had come to look at the soil that had produced such poor specimens of such a fine species.

2 Among the sages whom Emerson sought out on his visit to Europe was the notoriously reticent and difficult Thomas Carlyle. He called on Carlyle one evening and was given a pipe, while his host took one himself. They sat together smoking in perfect silence until bedtime, and on parting shook hands most cordially, congratulating each other on the fruitful time they had enjoyed together.

3 Emerson was asked to speak on the occasion of the two-hundredth anniversary of the founding of Concord, which was also the sixtieth anniversary of the famous battle. He considered this a great honor and, determined to do his very best, decided to produce a fresh literary version of the encounter. He began by questioning the surviving veterans, and in the course of his researches came across a barefooted farmer who was driving his oxen in Concord. Emerson asked him whether all the people thereabouts went without shoes and stockings, and the farmer replied, "Wal, some on 'em doos, and the rest on 'em minds their own business."

4 While at Harvard, Oliver Wendell Holmes, Jr., wrote a fifteen-page critical essay on Plato and showed it to Emerson for his comments. Emerson returned it with the observation: "When you shoot at a king, you must kill him." Holmes destroyed his essay.

5 John Greenleaf Whittier once asked Emerson what he prayed for. "When I first open my eyes upon the morning meadows and look out upon the beautiful world," replied Emerson, "I thank God I am alive and that I live so near Boston."

6 A lady once asked a scrubwoman who regularly attended Emerson's lectures at Concord if she understood Mr. Emerson. "Not a word," was the reply, "but I like to go and

see him stand up there and look as though he thought everyone was as good as he."

7 Warned by a member of a religious cult that the world was going to end in ten days' time, Emerson calmly replied, "Well, no doubt we will get on very well without it."

8 On the publication of Walt Whitman's *Leaves of Grass,* Emerson sent Whitman the now-famous letter that included the line, "I greet you at the beginning of a great career." When the next edition was ready, Whitman sent a copy to Emerson, who saw to his dismay that his name and comment — which he had considered part of a private communication — were emblazoned in gold across the front cover. Emerson gave the copy to a friend, saying that the inside of the book was worthy of attention even though it came from a person capable of so misusing the cover.

9 In Emerson's later years his memory began increasingly to fail. He used to refer to it as his "naughty memory" when it let him down. He would forget the names of things, and have to refer to them in a circumlocutory way, saying, for instance, "the implement that cultivates the soil" for plow. Worse, he could not remember people's names. At Longfellow's funeral, he remarked to a friend, "That gentleman has a sweet, beautiful soul, but I have entirely forgotten his name." Perhaps most touching was his term for umbrella — "the thing that strangers take away."

———— ❧ ————

EMPEDOCLES (5th century BC), *Greek philosopher and scientist.*

1 Various accounts of Empedocles' death are given in ancient sources. His enemies said that his desire to be thought a god led him to throw himself into the crater of Mount Etna so that he might vanish from the world com-

pletely and thus lead men to believe he had achieved apotheosis. Unfortunately the volcano defeated his design by throwing out one of the philosopher's sandals.

———— ❧ ————

ENESCO, Georges (1881–1955), *Rumanian violinist and conductor.*

1 Enesco, wishing to help a young friend making his debut at Carnegie Hall, offered to accompany him on the piano. The idea diverted the pianist Walter Gieseking, who said he would turn the pages. A review next morning read: "The man who should have been playing the piano was turning the pages, and the man who should have been turning the pages was playing the violin."

———— ❧ ————

ENGELS, Friedrich (1820–95), *German socialist leader and political philosopher.*

1 Friedrich Engels was the son of a prosperous manufacturer of textiles. The father, to familiarize the six-year-old Friedrich with his eventual inheritance, once showed him through the factory. The little boy was profoundly shocked by the miserable working conditions under which children hardly older than himself had to labor. Before his stern father he disguised his feeling, but on his return home in great agitation he asked his beloved mother, "Must I too go to work soon in the factory?"

"No, my dear, thank God you won't have to. You can be glad that the factory belongs to us."

"And how about the children? Are they glad?"

"No, Friedrich, not like you. But it's better for you not to trouble your little head about it. No one can change things, even you."

The boy slept little that night. In the morning his mother awakened him. He looked at her. "Mother, suppose I *want* to change things — then what . . . ?"

EPSTEIN, Sir Jacob (1880–1959), *British sculptor, born in New York of Russo-Polish descent.*

1 On a visit to Epstein's studio, George Bernard Shaw noticed a huge block of stone standing in one corner and asked what it was for. "I don't know yet," said the sculptor. "I'm still making plans." Shaw was astounded. "You mean you plan your work? Why, I change my mind several times a day!" he exclaimed. "That's all very well with a four-ounce manuscript," replied Epstein, "but not with a four-ton block."

ERASMUS, Desiderius (1466–1536), *Dutch humanist scholar and writer.*

1 Reproached for not observing the Lenten fast, Erasmus replied, "I have a Catholic soul, but a Lutheran stomach."

ERIC the Red (late 10th century AD), *Norwegian navigator.*

1 The terrain of Greenland is covered mainly with glaciers and barren rock, with only a few patches of tundra and habitable land. Eric named it Greenland on the principle that colonists would be keen to go there if the country bore an attractive name.

ERSKINE, Thomas, 1st Baron (1750–1823), *British politician who became lord chancellor (1806–07).*

1 Lord Erskine had a standard practice for dealing with letters soliciting his subscription to various causes. "Sir, I feel much honored by your application to me, and I beg to subscribe" — here the reader had to turn over the notepaper — "myself your very obedient servant."

2 Erskine, who was fond of puns, was told that such word-play was the lowest form of wit. "That's very true," he replied, "and therefore it is the foundation of all wit."

ERVING, Julius (1950–), *US basketball player.*

1 The University of Massachusetts wonder, Nets star and future Hall-of-Famer, "DR. J," as he was known, was born Julius Winfield Erving II on Washington Irving's birthday in 1950. His mother was urged to call him Washington as well — Washington Erving — but reason prevailed.

ESTE, Borso d' (1413–71), *Duke of Modena and Reggio and Duke of Ferrara.*

1 Duke Borso sent a letter in Latin to the mayor of an outlying village asking him to catch a sparrowhawk (*accipitrem*) and send it to Ferrara trussed up in a sack to prevent its escape. When the letter was delivered, it caused great consternation; the villagers read it as a demand for the surrender of their archpriest (*arciprete*). Although they knew of no reason for the duke's apparent displeasure with the popular priest, they thought they had better obey his command. The luckless cleric, protesting his innocence, was duly popped into a sack and taken to Ferrara. At the ducal palace, the official to whom the package was delivered was totally perplexed. "Have you a letter?" he asked. The letter, of course, made all things clear. Duke Borso, to save the villagers' face, solemnly sent back a message saying that he had changed his mind and they could set their victim free. After

that he took care to write to his rustic subjects in the vernacular.

———— ✼ ————

EUCLID (fl. 300 BC), *Greek mathematician who lived and worked in Alexandria, Egypt.*

1 Euclid was employed as tutor of mathematics in the royal household. King Ptolemy I complained about the difficulty of the theorems that Euclid expected him to grasp, wondering whether there was not an easier way to approach the subject. Euclid gently rebuked him: "Sire, there is no royal road to geometry."

2 A student who had just begun his studies asked Euclid, after he had learned the first theorem, what would be his reward. Euclid called his slave and said to him, "Give him three obols, since he must make gain out of what he learns."

———— ✼ ————

EUGÉNIE (1826–1920), *empress of France (1853–70), wife of Napoleon III.*

1 The empress and her lady-in-waiting, Mme de Pourtalès, were playing patience in a remote corner of the palace garden at Saint-Cloud when a masked man appeared brandishing a gun. He demanded their jewels, which they duly handed over. He then told them to undress. They had begun to do so when Mme de Pourtalès suddenly recognized the intruder. "It's Poché!" she exclaimed, naming a young courtier who was known for his pranks. As they scolded him, the sound of running feet was heard — the imperial security guards alerted by the women's raised voices. Realizing that even Poché might find it difficult to explain his mask and gun, Eugénie said, "Quick, hide

under my crinoline!" So, until the guards had withdrawn, there he remained.

2 The day after an attempt by Felice Orsini and two accomplices to assassinate the imperial couple, Napoleon was implacably resolved to seek the death penalty for the conspirators, a step Eugénie implored him not to take. The argument grew heated. Eugénie, seeking an ally, burst from their private apartments, wearing nothing but a transparent peignoir, and ran into the adjacent library where her private secretary, a plain, rather stolid man, was working. She begged him to help her make her case to the emperor. He was deeply embarrassed by the virtually naked empress and scarcely knew where to look. "Your Majesty seems to forget that there is a man under the secretary," he mumbled in painful confusion. Eugénie, her nerves on edge, glanced at the solid secretaire in the corner. "What? A man hidden in here under the furniture?" she shrieked.

———— ✼ ————

EULER, Leonhard (1707–83), *Swiss mathematician.*

1 (Says E. T. Bell:)
  "After having amused himself one afternoon calculating the laws of ascent of balloons — on his slate, as usual — [Euler] dined with Lexell [a mathematical colleague] and his family. 'Herschel's Planet' (Uranus) was a recent discovery. Euler outlined the calculation of its orbit. A little later he asked that his grandson be brought in. While playing with the child and drinking tea he suffered a stroke. The pipe dropped from his hand, and with the words, 'I die,' Euler ceased to live and calculate."

———— ✼ ————

EURIPIDES (c. 480–406 BC), *Greek tragic playwright. He wrote some ninety plays, of which* *fewer than twenty survive, among them* Medea *and* The Trojan Women.

1 Euripides once confessed that it had taken him three days to write three verses. His astonished interlocutor, a poet of inferior abilities, exclaimed, "I could have written a hundred in that time!"

"I believe it," replied Euripides, "but they would have lived only three days."

EVANS, Sir Arthur [John] (1851–1941), *British archaeologist.*

1 "[Evans] kept his powers into extreme old age and on his ninetieth birthday on 8 July 1941 welcomed a party of friends who went to pay honour to him. He seemed remarkably spry and talked about a new Roman road which he had discovered. Very soon afterwards a man in the Intelligence Corps, with Greece as his special province, who liked to be a bit of a 'know-all,' told him that the Germans had destroyed Knossos. Evans was stricken to the heart, believing that his life's work had been ruined. He died three days later, and the tragic irony was that, so far from destroying Knossos, the Germans had taken pains to see that nothing was damaged."

EVANS, Dame Edith (1888–1976), *British actress, celebrated for her Shakespearean performances.*

1 When Edith Evans was playing the role of Miss Betsey Trotwood in a film adaptation of Dickens's *David Copperfield,* she had to carry a cat in a basket on her arm during one scene. The cat was sedated but in the middle of a long speech it began making efforts to climb out of its prison. Scarcely pausing in her speech, Edith Evans shoved it back into the basket. "Don't be such an ambitious pussy. You're not in *Dick Whittington,*" she hissed in an aside.

2 (In 1966 Bryan Forbes directed Edith Evans, then seventy-eight, in the role of Mrs. Ross in the film *The Whisperers.*)

"We only had one meeting prior to shooting when we discussed the script. Edith asked if I would insert one additional line of dialogue for her. Although she greatly admired Eric Portman [her co-star] as an actor she was not . . . enamoured of his private personality. 'Do you think,' she said, 'you could add a line to indicate that she married slightly beneath her?' I promised to consider it. A few days later I met with Eric to discuss his reactions to the script. He admired Edith as an actress without qualification, but confessed, with more bluntness than Edith, that there were aspects of her offstage personality that grated on him. 'Do you think, dear boy,' he said, 'you could somehow insert an extra line which would indicate she married a much younger man?' I kept both confidences to myself, duly made the amendments and neither of them ever referred to it again."

EVERETT, Edward (1794–1865), *US statesman and orator.*

1 While Everett was president of Harvard, a storm arose over the proposed admission of a Negro to the college. Everett replied, "If this boy passes the examination he will be admitted; and if the white students choose to withdraw, all the income of the college will be devoted to his education."

F

FAGIUOLI, Giovanni Battista (1660–1742), *Italian poet.*

1 As court poet to Archduke Cosimo III of Tuscany, Fagiuoli was also a kind of court clown. One day he presented his master with a list of names. "What do these names stand for?" asked the archduke.

"They're a list of all the fools of my acquaintance."

"But," exploded the archduke, "my name heads the list!"

"Your Highness, that's because yesterday you commissioned that botanist in England to collect and bring you a collection of rare plants. But — you paid him in advance!"

"I see nothing foolish in that. Suppose he delivers them in accord with my instructions?"

"In that case I'll erase your name and substitute his."

FAIRBANKS, Douglas (1883–1939), *US film actor.*

1 As he was driving back to his mansion, Pickfair, Fairbanks saw an Englishman of aristocratic mien and familiar face trudging along the road in the heat. He stopped to offer him a ride, which the stranger accepted. Still unable to remember the man's name, Fairbanks invited him for a drink, and in the course of conversation attempted to elicit some clues as to his visitor's identity. The Englishman seemed to know many of Fairbanks's friends and was evidently well acquainted with the estate, for he made approving comments on some recent changes. Eventually Fairbanks managed a whispered aside to his secretary, who had just entered the room. "Who's this Englishman? I know he's Lord Somebody, but I just can't remember his name."

"That," replied the secretary, "is the English butler you fired last month for getting drunk."

FALLIÈRES, [Clement] Armand (1841–1931), *French statesman; eighth president of the Third Republic (1906–13).*

1 Fallières, visiting sculptor Auguste Rodin's studio, looked around him at the assemblage of unfinished work — hands, feet, heads, torsos. Then he remarked, "Well, I can see that the movers haven't been particularly careful."

FARADAY, Michael (1791–1867), *British chemist and physicist.*

1 Faraday's interest in knowledge for its own sake sometimes baffled people with a more practical turn of mind. William Gladstone, watching Faraday at an experiment from which he could discern no practical result, asked, "Of what use is such a discovery?" Faraday retorted, "Why, you will soon be able to tax it."

———— ❧ ————

FAROUK I (1920–65), *king of Egypt (1936–52).*

1 After being driven from his throne in 1952, Farouk remarked bitterly, "One day there will be only five kings left: hearts, spades, diamonds, clubs, and England."

———— ❧ ————

FARQUHAR, Sir Walter (1738–1819), *British physician.*

1 One of Sir Walter's patients, an elderly lady with an ill-defined complaint, took it into her head that it would do her the world of good to take the waters at Bath for a few weeks. Sir Walter encouraged her in this scheme, and to allay her worries at the prospect of being separated from her usual physician, he promised to recommend her to a very clever doctor in Bath, a friend of his, and to write a letter for her to take with her, detailing her case. The old lady set out happily for Bath, but on the way fell to thinking that although Sir Walter had been her physician for years, he had never told her precisely what was wrong with her. Her curiosity about the contents of the letter grew. At the first overnight stop she announced to her traveling companion that she was going to open it. Her companion protested about the breach of trust, but to no avail. The letter was opened. It read: "Dear Davis, Keep the old lady three weeks and send her back again."

———— ❧ ————

FARR, Heather (1965–93), *US golfer.*

1 Farr died of cancer at the age of twenty-eight, a fight she had waged for several years. Asked how she had dealt with her health problems, she said, "You play through it. That's what you do. You just play through it."

———— ❧ ————

FARRAGUT, David Glasgow (1801–70), *US Union admiral during the Civil War.*

1 In August 1864 Admiral Farragut led the attack on Mobile Bay, to give the Union forces control over a large slice of Confederate territory. The bay was well defended by mines, forcing any approaching ships to sail close to Fort Morgan, the Confederate fortress that dominated the channel. The Confederate ironclad, the *Tennessee*, also covered the approaches. Farragut's first ship, the *Tecumseh*, eager to attack the *Tennessee*, incautiously crossed the minefield and was blown up. Then the *Brooklyn* faltered, and in an instant the lines of ships were in disarray, with the tide sweeping them closer to the guns of Fort Morgan. "Damn the torpedoes, go ahead!" shouted Farragut, swinging his own ship, the *Hartford*, clear of the *Brooklyn* and heading straight across the minefield. They heard the mine cases clatter against the hull of the *Hartford*, but none exploded, and the rest of the attacking force sailed into Mobile Bay after Farragut. In a very short time the *Tennessee* and the shore forts had surrendered.

———— ❧ ————

FAULKNER, William (1897–1962), *US novelist. He was awarded the Nobel Prize for Literature in 1949.*

1 One of the many jobs Faulkner took before he established himself as a writer was as postmaster at the University of Mississippi post office. When he found that his official duties interfered with his writing, he wrote the following letter to the postmaster general: "As long as I live under the capitalist system I expect to have my life influenced by the demands of moneyed people. But I will be damned if I propose to be at the beck and call of every itinerant scoundrel who has two cents to invest in a postage stamp. This, sir, is my resignation."

2 "I [Leland Hayward, literary and dramatic agent] got a call one day from Metro. They were completely confused over there and they wanted to know where in hell was my client, [William] Faulkner! They were pretty sore — nobody was supposed to walk out of Metro without letting the front office know where he'd gone. I didn't know where Bill was. He hadn't told me he was going anywhere. I got the office to start making calls all over the damned place, and finally we thought of trying him at his home in Mississippi, and sure enough, there he was. 'What the hell are you doing down there?' I yelled on the phone, and he said, 'Well, ah asked my producer if ah could work at home, and he said fine, so heah ah am.'"

3 Frank Case, the manager of the Algonquin Hotel in New York, met Faulkner one morning in the hotel lobby looking decidedly sorry for himself. Case asked him what was the matter. "I feel like the devil. My stomach's upset," Faulkner grumbled. "Too bad," sympathized Case. "Something you wrote, no doubt."

4 Faulkner was on a shooting expedition with director Howard Hawks and actor Clark Gable. In the course of conversation, Gable asked Faulkner to name the five best authors of the day. Replied Faulkner: "Ernest Hemingway, Willa Cather, Thomas Mann, John Dos Passos, and myself."

"Oh," said Gable maliciously, "do you write for a living?"

"Yes," retorted Faulkner, "and what do *you* do?"

5 When Faulkner's office at the Hollywood Warner Brothers studio was cleaned out after his departure, the only items found were an empty bottle and a sheet of yellow paper on which he had written, five hundred times, "Boy meets girl."

6 On a vacation trip to New York, Faulkner had agreed to meet a reporter for an interview. He did not appear at the appointed time, nor could he be found for several days. Finally, Bennett Cerf, his publisher, learned that he had slipped in the bathroom and had badly burned himself on the radiator, spending several days in the hospital. When Cerf remonstrated with him about having spent his first vacation in years in the hospital, Faulkner replied quietly, "Bennett, it was *my* vacation."

7 Faulkner was once asked why he had agreed to serve as writer-in-residence at the University of Virginia. "Because I like your country, Virginia, and Virginians," said Faulkner. "Virginians are snobs. I like snobs. A snob spends so much time being a snob, he has none left to bother other people."

———— ⚬⌀ ————

FAURÉ, Gabriel Urbain (1845–1924), *French composer known especially for his songs.*

1 Fauré was once asked what the ideal tempo for a song should be. He replied, "If the singer is bad — very fast."

FAVRAS, Thomas de Mahay, Marquis de (1744–90), *French aristocrat.*

1 Favras's trial lasted nearly two months; the evidence against him was inconclusive and the witnesses disagreed, but in the end he was found guilty. Before being led to the scaffold he was handed his death sentence, written down by the clerk of the court. He read it through, then said, "I see, monsieur, that you have made three spelling mistakes."

FAWKES, Guy (1570–1606), *British Roman Catholic conspirator.*

1 Guy Fawkes was disenchanted with the lot of the Roman Catholics in England under James I. Serving with the Spanish army in the Netherlands, he was invited by one Robert Catesby to join a conspiracy to blow up the king and Parliament. Fawkes agreed. Having rented a cellar under the House of Parliament, the conspirators managed to secrete thirty-six barrels of gunpowder there behind a stack of wood and coal. The day that King James was due to open Parliament (November 5, 1605) was the date set for the explosion. However, one of the conspirators wrote an anonymous note to a friend who was a member of Parliament, warning him not to attend the opening. The MP alerted the authorities, the cellar was searched, and the conspirators arrested. Catesby was killed resisting arrest and Fawkes was captured and tortured. He betrayed the names of the other conspirators and all were tried and executed. This is the origin of the celebrations in Britain on November 5 with fireworks and bonfires, during which an effigy, called a guy, is burned.

FELLER, Bob (1918–), *US baseball player.*

1 In the mid-1930s Feller's parents traveled to Chicago to see their son pitch in a game played on Mother's Day. The first three innings went well; then, in the fourth, Feller pitched to Marv Owen, who fouled the ball into the stands. The ball hit Feller's mother, breaking her glasses and requiring numerous stitches around her eyes. After he determined that she was taken care of medically, Feller returned to the mound and immediately struck Owen out.

FERDINAND I (1793–1875), *emperor of Austria (1835–48).*

1 Ferdinand's one recorded notable saying was: "I am the emperor, and I want dumplings."

FERDINAND I (1861–1948), *king of Bulgaria (1908–18).*

1 Led by Russia, the European powers withheld recognition of Ferdinand's status in Bulgaria. When Ferdinand entered a room at Chantilly on a visit to his elderly uncle, the Duc d'Aumale, who did not like him, the old man seemed not to recognize him. An aide whispered in the duke's ear. "Ah, Ferdinand," said Aumale, "I am behaving like the rest of Europe; I did not recognize you."

FERDINAND IV (?1286–1312), *king of Castile (1295–1312).*

1 Ferdinand had rejected an appeal by two prisoners, Peter and John de Carvajal, condemned to death on circumstantial evidence. The two men, still proclaiming their inno-

cence, summoned Ferdinand to appear before God within thirty days. On the thirtieth day the king, still fit and well, appeared to have defied the "summons." The following morning, he was found dead in his bed.

FERGUSON, Sarah (1959–), *Duchess of York, formerly married to Queen Elizabeth II's third child, Prince Andrew.*

1 Sarah Ferguson loved the active social life she led before her marriage into the House of Windsor, which thrust her into a role she found difficult and constraining. Commenting on her years behind the walls of the English royal family, she said, "It was dreadful. They tried to put the little redhead in a cage."

FERGUSSON, George, Lord Hermand (d. 1827), *Scottish judge.*

1 Lord Hermand was convivial to the point of believing that drinking could improve one's behavior. He was a member of a panel of judges trying a young man who had accidentally killed a drinking companion. A verdict of culpable homicide was brought in and the majority of the panel thought a lenient sentence would be appropriate; a short term of imprisonment was imposed. Lord Hermand dissented: "We are told that there was no malice, and that the prisoner must have been in liquor. In liquor! Why, he was drunk! And yet he murdered the very man who had been drinking with him! They had been carousing the whole night; and yet he stabbed him! After drinking a whole bottle of rum with him! Good God, my laards, if he will do this when he's drunk, what will he not do when he's sober?"

FERMAT, Pierre de (1601–65), *French mathematician renowned for his contribution to the theory of numbers.*

1 As Fermat engaged in mathematics for his own amusement, many of his most important contributions were recorded in margins of books or in notes to his friends. In about 1637 he scribbled on his copy of Diophantus's *Arithmetic*, "The equation $x^n + y^n = z^n$, where x, y, and z are positive integers, has no solution if n is greater than 2," and added, "I have discovered a most remarkable proof, but this margin is too narrow to contain it." The problem went down in mathematical lore as "Fermat's Last Theorem," and generations of mathematical adepts taxed their ingenuity to reconstitute the proof. In 1994 Andrew Wiles was the first person to prove Fermat's Last Theorem.

FERMI, Enrico (1901–54), *Italian-born physicist, winner of the 1938 Nobel Prize for Physics.*

1 In 1942 in his laboratory at the University of Chicago stadium, Fermi built the first atomic pile, using specially produced graphite blocks into which several tons of uranium were inserted. The first controlled nuclear chain reaction began on December 2 at 2:20 PM and lasted twenty-eight minutes. Afterward Arthur Compton, the American physicist who collaborated with Fermi, put through a call to James Bryant Conant at Harvard's Office of Scientific Research and Development. "The Italian navigator has reached the New World," he announced. "And how did he find the natives?" asked Conant. "Very friendly," came the reply. Thus was the atomic age announced.

FEYDEAU, Georges (1862–1921), *French play-wright.*

1 There was some question hanging over Feydeau's parentage, as his mother had a reputation as a flirt and Emperor Napoleon III had been seen to pay her marked attention. Mme Feydeau was indignant at the suggestion: "How could anybody imagine that a child as intelligent as Georges could be the son of such an idiotic monarch?"

2 At a restaurant Feydeau was served a lobster with only one claw. When he protested, the waiter explained that sometimes the lobsters fought in their tank, and such mutilations resulted. "Take this one away," ordered Feydeau, "and bring me the victor."

3 A tiresome acquaintance, whose wife was notorious for her infidelities, was boring Feydeau with a recital of the virtues of his small son. "He's so devoted to his mother and so loving," said the proud father. "He's always under her skirts."

"Where he must meet a lot of others," murmured Feydeau.

4 In Feydeau's early days as a playwright, his comedies were not always well received. At one such disastrous opening night he stationed himself in the aisle and joined in the hissing and booing. "Have you taken leave of your senses!" exclaimed a friend who had run down the aisle after him. Feydeau shook his head. "That way I can't hear them," he explained, "so it doesn't hurt so much."

———o∿o———

FEYNMAN, Richard (1918–88), *US physicist and co-winner of the 1965 Nobel Prize for Physics for his research into quantum electrodynamics.*

1 After his many books and eccentric public persona won him the acclaim of a popular audience, *Omni* magazine called him the world's smartest man. To this his mother, Lu-

cille, retorted, "If that's the world's smartest man, God help us."

2 Feynman was once asked by a physicist to explain in simple terms a standard item, why certain particles obey Fermi-Dirac statistics. He was unable to do so. "I couldn't reduce it to the freshman level," Feynman said. "That means we really don't understand it."

———o∿o———

FIELD, John (1782–1837), *British pianist and composer.*

1 Field's friends, attending him during his last hours, felt the need of a clergyman to administer the last rites. But they were not sure of Field's religious affiliation. "Are you a Papist or a Calvinist?" they asked him. "I am . . . a pianist," replied the dying artist.

———o∿o———

FIELD, Marshall, III (1893–1956), *US founder of the* **Chicago Sun** *(afterward the* **Chicago Sun-Times***).*

1 "When Marshall Field III was a small child, he displayed some of the cautious shrewdness which made his grandfather the greatest merchant prince in America.

"Being left alone in a hotel lobby for half an hour, young Marshall approached an old lady and asked if she could crack nuts.

" 'No, dear,' replied the old lady. 'I lost all my teeth years ago.'

" 'Then,' said master Field, extending both hands full of pecans, 'please hold these while I go and get some more pecans.' "

———o∿o———

"I had a very elderly and esteemed relative who once told me that while walking along the Strand he met a lion that had escaped from Exeter Change menagerie. I said, 'What did you do?', and he looked at me with contempt as if the question were imbecile. 'Do?' he said. 'Why, I took a cab.'"

— FORD MADOX FORD,
Ancient Lights

FIELDING, Henry (1707–54), *British novelist, playwright, and lawyer.*

1 Andrew Millar, the publisher, bought Fielding's novel *Amelia* in 1751 for the then enormous sum of £800, relying upon the previous success of *Tom Jones* and the great reputation Fielding currently enjoyed. He ordered a large number of copies printed, but then became nervous and showed the manuscript to a friend whose judgment he trusted. The friend said that *Amelia* was by no means up to the standard of *Tom Jones*. Millar decided to dispose as quickly as possible of the whole edition. When next he was auctioning some of his stock to other members of the trade, he began by saying, "Gentlemen, I have several works to put up for which I shall be glad if you will bid. But as to *Amelia,* every copy is bespoke." The ploy worked, as rival booksellers rushed to get their names put down for the next edition. In this way Millar disposed of the whole stock of *Amelia.*

2 When he was once in the company of the Earl of Denbigh, whose family name was Feilding, the conversation turned to Fielding's membership in the same family. The earl inquired why the names were spelled differently. Fielding replied that he could give no reason, "except maybe that my branch of the family was the first to know how to spell."

FIELDS, W. C. [William Claude Dukenfield] (1879–1946), *US film actor and comedian.*

1 A reporter interviewing Fields asked him, off the record, for his views on sex. "On or off the record," replied Fields, "there may be some things better than sex, and there may be some things worse. But there's nothing exactly like it."

2 During Prohibition, Fields and a friend heard that an acquaintance on Long Island had just received two cases of contraband Irish whiskey. They drove over to his place and helped him put part of the liquor beyond reach of the law. About dawn they left for home, taking along several bottles from which they refreshed themselves from time to time. After several hours they remarked upon the surprising length of Long Island — but kept going. When they asked filling-station attendants how far it was to the Queensboro Bridge, they got only blank stares of laughter in response. Eventually they found themselves in a hotel room. Fields fell asleep. His friend noticed a palm tree outside the window, went out to buy a paper, and learned that they were in Ocala, Florida. "We're in Ocala, Florida!" he said, shaking Fields awake. "I always said those Long Island roads were poorly marked," observed Fields.

3 Fields always kept a thermos of martinis at hand when he was filming, maintaining that it contained nothing but pineapple juice. One day someone tampered with the flask and Fields's anguished cry rang out across the set: "Somebody put pineapple juice in my pineapple juice!"

4 "Can I fix you a Bromo-Seltzer, sir?" asked a waiter of Fields, who was groaning in the grip of a fearful hangover. "No," moaned Fields, "I can't stand the noise."

5 A lifelong agnostic, Fields was discovered reading a Bible on his deathbed. "I'm looking for a loophole," he explained.

FIENNES, Ralph (1962–), *British film actor.*

1 The movie *Quiz Show* told the story of the notorious television game-show scandals of the late 1950s, during which the handsome and gifted Charles Van Doren was revealed to have cheated in order to get higher ratings for the sponsoring television station. Fiennes played the young Charles, and director Robert Redford hoped to cast his old friend Paul Newman as Charles's patrician father, the poet Mark Van Doren. Newman wasn't interested, but Redford kept delaying the actual scenes in which the father was present, shooting every other scene possible. Fiennes was driven to distraction, and eventually was seen to wander the set, saying softly, "Who's my father?"

———— ✧ ————

FILLMORE, Millard (1800–74), *US politician; 13th President of the United States (1850–53).*

1 Fillmore's presidency is regrettably encapsulated in a story (possibly of malicious invention) that circulated in Washington soon after he was sworn in. He decided that he needed a new carriage, and a White House attendant, Edward Moran, was detailed to find a suitable one. He discovered a handsome equipage that was being sold off quite cheaply since its owner was leaving the town. Fillmore inspected it, approved it, but was troubled. "How would it do, Edward, for the President of the United States to ride around in a secondhand carriage?" Moran replied reassuring, "But sure, Your Excellency is only a secondhand President!"

———— ✧ ————

FINLEY, Charles (1918–97), *US baseball executive.*

1 The owner of two teams, the Royals and the A's, Finley found it impossible to stop interfering with his managers. But he was espe-

cially combative with baseball commissioner Bowie Kuhn. Once, in public, he called him a "village idiot." Later he changed his opinion to say, "I apologize to all the village idiots of America. He's the nation's idiot."

———— ✧ ————

FISHER, M. F. K. (1908–92), *US culinary writer and gastronomic muse.*

1 When asked why she had devoted herself to writing about food and drink instead of weightier subjects, such as serious world issues or even love, Fisher replied, "The easiest answer is to say that, like most other humans, I am hungry."

———— ✧ ————

FISKE, Minne Maddern (1865–1932), *US stage actress.*

1 The actress Margaret Anglin once left a message attached to the mirror in Minnie Fiske's dressing room. It read: "Margaret Anglin says Mrs. Fiske is the best actress in America." Mrs. Fiske read it, added two commas, and returned it to Miss Anglin. The revised note read: "Margaret Anglin, says Mrs. Fiske, is the best actress in America."

2 Fiske, who was revered by the stage actors and actresses of her generation, often gave the same advice to thespians eager to achieve her greatness. "Above all, ignore the audience."

———— ✧ ————

FITZGERALD, Ella (1918–96), *US jazz singer, especially famous for her "scat" singing.*

1 Ella once performed at Columbia, South Carolina, before an audience of children. The show seemed to go well, the children all joining in such songs as "Old MacDonald

Had a Farm." A television interviewer went around the audience afterward. "What did you think of Ella Fitzgerald?" one little boy was asked. "Well, I liked her singing all right," he replied, "but she didn't break no glass."

———⌘———

FITZGERALD, F[rancis] Scott [Key] (1896–1940), *US writer, notably of* **The Great Gatsby.**

1 Producer Joseph L. Mankiewicz, stubbornly convinced that the film *Three Comrades* would make more money if the leading female character did not die, asked Fitzgerald to change the script. "*Camille* would have made twice as much if Garbo had lived," he argued. "How about *Romeo and Juliet* — you wouldn't have wanted Juliet to live, would you?" asked Fitzgerald. Mankiewicz, whose cultural experience did not extend beyond the film world, cast his mind back to the unsuccessful 1936 film version of the play. "That's just it," he retorted triumphantly. "*Romeo and Juliet* didn't make a cent."

2 When Thomas Wolfe dedicated his first, very lengthy, novel to his editor, Maxwell Perkins, a proof copy was sent to F. Scott Fitzgerald for his views. "Dear Max," ran Fitzgerald's reply, "I liked the dedication, but after that I thought it fell off a bit."

3 The Fitzgeralds were famed for the parties they gave, great riotous affairs full of drunkenness and high jinks. After a particularly vigorous period of entertaining, they hung a framed set of house rules on their living room wall, which read: "Visitors are requested not to break down doors in search of liquor, even when authorized to do so by the host and hostess. Weekend guests are respectfully notified that invitations to stay over Monday, issued by the host and hostess

during the small hours of Sunday morning, must not be taken seriously."

———⌘———

FITZSIMMONS, Robert (1862–1917), *British heavyweight boxer.*

1 Due to meet James J. Jeffries, a considerably bigger man, in San Francisco in July 1902, Fitzsimmons was asked if he was worried about the disparity in size. "The bigger they are, the harder they fall," he is supposed to have said.

———⌘———

FLAHERTY, Robert (1884–1951), *US film director.*

1 As a young man Robert Flaherty spent many months making arduous journeys in the far north in a search for iron ore and cod. He found neither, but in the course of his travels he shot over seventy-thousand feet of film. To salvage something from the wasted enterprise, Canadian financier Sir William Mackenzie encouraged him to edit the film and make a documentary. Flaherty toiled for weeks in a garret room and at last had an edited motion picture. Lighting a celebratory cigarette, he dropped the match on the floor. There was a tiny spurt of flame and in an instant the room was an inferno; every scrap of the highly inflammable celluloid was destroyed and Flaherty himself was badly burned, surviving only because he managed to jump out through a window onto the fire escape. His reaction to this disaster was a determination to return to the far north and make a film of Eskimo life "that people will never forget."

He did just that, and the result was the classic documentary *Nanook of the North* (1922).

———⌘———

FLANNER, Janet (1892–1978), *US foreign reporter, for many years the Paris correspondent for* The New Yorker *magazine.*

1 Jill Krementz, noted New York photographer, specializes in literary portraits. One of her subjects was Janet Flanner. Ms. Krementz asked if she had ever been married. Ms. Flanner replied, "I'm sure I have, but the precise details of the union escape me."

———— ❧ ————

FLAUBERT, Gustave (1821–80), *French writer best known for his novel* Madame Bovary.

1 Flaubert was once asked outright who the real-life Emma Bovary was. With a wistful smile the author replied, "*I* am Madame Bovary."

2 Some friends came to visit on a Friday and invited him to join their weekend outing. Flaubert declined, as he had far too much work to do. When his friends returned on Sunday night, they asked how his work had gone. Exceedingly well, they were told. But they noticed that he was at exactly the same place he had been before they left — in the middle of a sentence, marked by a comma. How was that possible? Flaubert noted complacently that, on Saturday, he had changed the comma to a semicolon, and on Sunday he had changed it back, thus making wonderful progress.

———— ❧ ————

FLEETWOOD, Sir William (?1535–94), *British lawyer.*

1 Fleetwood was famous for his rigorous prosecution of highwaymen. Determined to get their own back, a gang of them, halter at the ready, waylaid him near the gallows at Tyburn, bound his servants, tied his hands behind his back, and led him on his horse under the gallows. They then fixed the rope around his neck and left him to the mercy of his horse. Obedient to his master's desperate "Whoa, whoa," the horse stood quite still for a quarter of an hour or more until someone passed by and released Fleetwood from his predicament.

———— ❧ ————

FLEMING, Sir Alexander (1881–1955), *British microbiologist who shared the Nobel Prize for Medicine in 1945 with two other scientists for their discovery of penicillin.*

1 Fleming's discovery of penicillin was made by accident when a speck of dust happened to land on an uncovered culture plate. Touring a modern research laboratory some years later, he observed with interest the sterile, dust-free, air-conditioned environment in which the scientists worked. "What a pity you did not have a place like this to work in," said his guide. "Who can tell what you might have discovered in such surroundings!"

"Not penicillin," remarked Fleming with a smile.

———— ❧ ————

FLEMING, Ian (1908–64), *British suspense-story writer famous for his creation of Secret Service agent James Bond.*

1 The English literary critic Peter Quennell was a guest at the Flemings' country house. Queried on the point by Mrs. Fleming, Quennell stated that he was an early riser. Mrs. Fleming then gently requested, in case he should care to walk about outside in the early morning, that he not disturb the dew on the spider webs on the lawn. Ian, it seemed, liked to look at them first thing in the morning when he awoke.

depths. The colonel waited for his pronouncement. At length Foch stepped back from the brink and spoke: "What a marvelous place to drop one's mother-in-law!"

5 An American once complained to Marshal Foch about the insincere politeness of the French. "There is nothing in it but wind," he said.

"There is nothing but wind in a tire," replied Foch, "but it makes riding in a car very smooth and pleasant."

FOCH, Ferdinand (1851–1929), *French military commander.*

1 Marshal Foch's driver was often bothered by newspapermen anxious to get inside information on his master and his thinking about the war. "When does the marshal think the war will end?" they would ask, and the driver would promise to tell them if Foch divulged anything to him. One day he said, "This morning the marshal spoke." The reporters clustered around eagerly. "He said, 'Pierre, what do you think? When is this war going to end?'"

2 A young officer had been disciplined by his colonel for showing fear in battle. When Foch learned of the incident, however, he chose to reprimand the colonel rather than the officer. "None but a coward," he said, "dares to boast that he has never known fear."

3 (Sir Basil Thomson tells the following:)
"When the German delegation came to Marshal Foch at the end of the war to ask for armistice terms, the Frenchman picked up a paper from his desk and read a set of conditions.

"'But — there must be some mistake,' the leader of the German officers stammered in dismay. 'These are terms which no civilized nation could impose on another!'

"'I am very glad to hear you say so,' replied Foch gravely. 'No, gentlemen, these are not our terms. These are the terms imposed on Lille by the German commander when that city surrendered.'"

4 On a visit to the United States, Marshal Foch was escorted on a sight-seeing tour by a colonel who spoke French fluently. The distinguished visitor was taken to see the Grand Canyon. He gazed thoughtfully down into its

---

FONDA, Henry (1905–82), *US movie actor and Academy Award winner.*

1 Henry Fonda was asked to say in one phrase the one most important thing that any young actor has to know. Fonda answered, "How to become an old actor."

2 During the filming of *War and Peace* Fonda rebelled against some dialogue he found impossible. "I can't say that; it doesn't feel real," he told King Vidor, the director. Replied Vidor, "Of course it isn't real — it's a movie!"

FONDA, Jane (1937–), *US movie actress, daughter of Henry Fonda.*

1 When Henry Fonda's daughter, Jane, was nominated for an Academy Award for her role as a prostitute in *Klute,* he worried that she would use the ceremony as a platform to air her very public opposition to the Vietnam War, and begged her not to. Jane won, and as she accepted the statuette she said, "There is a great deal to say, and — I'm not going to say it tonight."

2 In *The Electric Horseman* Fonda had a scene in which she passionately kissed co-star Robert Redford, who was playing an ex-rodeo star. Director Sydney Pollack shot and

reshot the scene, eventually shooting forty-eight takes and running from early one morning to the evening of the next day. A studio accountant blanched at the costs the shooting had incurred — $280,000 — and growled, "It would have been cheaper if Redford had kissed the horse."

———— ✑ ————

FONTANNE, Lynn (1887–1983), *US actress, who with her husband, Alfred Lunt, made a highly successful team.*

1 The fees paid by the film studios to actors sometime amazed those accustomed to the comparatively slender Broadway salaries. When the Lunts made *The Guardsman* for MGM, they were asked by a reporter if it was true that they were getting $60,000 for their part in the film. Lynn Fontanne dumbfounded the MGM executives sitting in on the interview by replying, "Alfred and I would have worked for less, but nobody asked us."

———— ✑ ————

FONTENELLE, Bernard de (1657–1757), *French writer and philosopher.*

1 Fontenelle was conversing one day with Louis XIV when the king remarked that he had little faith in the existence of honorable men. "Plenty of honorable men exist, sire," said Fontenelle, "but they do not seek the company of kings."

2 In his great old age Fontenelle feebly but gallantly tried to pick up a fan a young lady had dropped. As she moved to help him, he exclaimed, "Ah, if I were only eighty again!"

3 At a reception in his ninety-eighth year, Fontenelle spent the first part of the evening saying gallant things to an attractive young lady. When the guests were summoned to dinner, however, he passed ahead of her to secure his place at table. "So that's what your gallantries are worth!" said the lady. "You walk straight past me without even looking at me."

"Madame, if I had looked at you I could not have passed you," replied the old man.

4 "Death has forgotten us," said an aged friend to the equally aged Fontenelle. "Sh-sh!" said Fontenelle, bringing his finger to his lips.

5 Fontenelle died just a few weeks short of his hundredth birthday. When asked how he was feeling, he replied, "I feel nothing, apart from a certain difficulty of being."

———— ✑ ————

FOOTE, Samuel (1720–77), *British actor and playwright.*

1 In 1755 Charles Macklin, the famous actor, boasted in Foote's presence that he could repeat any speech after hearing it only once. Foote challenged Macklin to repeat the following: "So she went into the garden to cut a cabbage leaf to make an apple pie; and at the same time a great she-bear, coming up the street, pops its head into the shop — What! no soap? So he died and she very imprudently married the barber; and there were present the Picninnies, and the Joblillies, and the Garyalies, and the grand Panjandrum himself, with the little round button at top. . . ."

2 The Duke of Cumberland once applauded Foote's wit with the words: "Mr. Foote, I swallow all the good things you say."

"Indeed, sir," said Foote, "then Your Royal Highness has an excellent digestion, for you never bring any of it up again."

3 Foote once asked a man why he was continually singing one particular tune. "Because it haunts me," the man replied. "No wonder,"

retorted Foote, "since you are forever murdering it."

4 A group of people were discussing the long and happy marriage of a lady who had led a wild life before her wedding. They ascribed the successful outcome of the match to the fact that she had confessed all her previous affairs to her husband before they married. They were loud in her praise: "What candor! What courage!"

"Yes, and what a memory!" added Foote.

5 Foote went into White's Club in London with a friend, who wished to write a note. While his friend was busy at the desk, Foote stood around uneasily; since he was not a member of White's, which had a very different political complexion from his own, many of the men in the room were strangers to him. The compassionate Lord Carmarthen thought of a pretext for approaching him with a few friendly words. "Mr. Foote, your handkerchief is hanging out of your pocket," he began. "Thank you, my lord, thank you," said Foote, misunderstanding the casual remark as a warning against pickpockets and quickly pushing the handkerchief back into the pocket. "You know the company here better than I do."

6 A member of the royal court complained to Foote that he had been thrown out of a second-floor window for cheating at cards, and asked his advice. "Do not play so high," replied Foote.

7 Samuel Foote was equaled in tightfistedness by his friend and fellow-actor David Garrick. On one occasion when they were out together Foote, reluctantly pulling out his purse to pay for the entertainment, dropped a guinea. Both men fell to their knees and started groping about on the floor. "Where on earth is it?" exclaimed Foote in exasperation after they had hunted vainly for some time. "Gone to the devil, I suppose," muttered Garrick. "Well, you always were one for making a guinea go further than anyone else," Foote remarked.

⎯⎯⎯ ∞ ⎯⎯⎯

FORD, Betty (1918–), *Wife of President Gerald Ford (1974–77)*.

1 Betty Ford loved her domestic life, a situation that became difficult to maintain once her husband became President upon the resignation of Richard Nixon. "I wish I'd married a plumber," she once said. "At least he'd be home by five o'clock."

2 A minor scandal was caused when newspapers revealed that Betty and Gerald Ford would share the same bed once ensconced in the White House (this was the 1970s). Betty was amused by the brouhaha, noting to her press secretary, "Something no one seems to expect is for a First Lady to sleep with the President!" Later on she commented that she was asked everything under the sun except how often she slept with her husband. She was happier to answer that than some of the other prying questions reporters insisted on asking: "As often as possible!"

3 Addressing a group of journalists on a visit to Washington many years after leaving the White House, she told them, "You've heard me say many times that what makes Jerry happy makes me happy. And if you all believe that, you're indeed unsuited for your profession."

⎯⎯⎯ ∞ ⎯⎯⎯

FORD, Gerald R. (1913–), *US politician; 38th President of the United States (1974–77)*.

1 Ford was not a scintillating speechifier, and knew it. He told of a trip he took to Omaha, where an old woman approached him after a speech he gave. "I hear you spoke here tonight," she said. "Oh," said Ford, "it was nothing." "So I heard," she responded.

2 About his strongest rival for the 1976 Republican presidential nomination, Ford quipped, "Ronald Reagan doesn't dye his hair — he's just prematurely orange."

3 During the 1976 campaign primary season Ford found unexpectedly fierce competition for the Republican nomination from Ronald Reagan. From the beginning Reagan seemed the stronger candidate, and Ford was advised to change his style — in clothing as well as in speaking — to better compete. On hearing that he was perceived as less dynamic, Ford protested. "Governor Reagan and I do have one thing in common," he reminded his advisers. "We both played football. I played for Michigan. He played for Warner Brothers."

4 After losing the presidency to Georgia governor Jimmy Carter, Ford attended a dinner honoring the memory of Vince Lombardi. He worried that the other guests might resent his presence; after all, they had paid to attend while he was still President, and now they might feel let down. "Don't worry," said his wife, Betty, "it's me they're coming to see."

———— ✻ ————

FORD, Henry (1863–1947), *US businessman who pioneered the mass production of automobiles.*

1 In the early stages of World War I, Henry Ford launched his chartered Peace Ship, which sailed to Europe with a passenger list of eminent pacifists. The intention was to appeal to heads of state to "get the boys out of the trenches by Christmas." Three weeks later Henry Ford was back in the United States. "I didn't get much peace," he said, "but I learned that Russia is going to be a great market for tractors."

2 Henry Ford once called in an efficiency expert to examine the running of his company. The expert made a favorable report, but had reservations about one employee. "It's that man down the corridor," he said. "Every time I go by his office he's just sitting there with his feet on his desk. He's wasting your money."

"That man," replied Ford, "once had an idea that saved us millions of dollars. At the time, I believe his feet were planted right where they are now."

3 A visitor to the factory of the Ford Motor Company happened to meet Henry Ford himself. Pointing to a finished car, Ford proudly declared, "There are exactly four thousand, seven hundred and nineteen parts in that model." Impressed that the president should have such details at his fingertips, the visitor subsequently asked a company engineer if the statement were true. The engineer shrugged his shoulders. "I'm sure I don't know," he replied. "I can't think of a more useless piece of information."

4 While on vacation in Dublin, Ireland, Ford was asked if he would contribute to a collection for a new orphanage. Judging the cause worthy, Ford promptly wrote out a check for £2,000. His generosity made headline news in the local paper the following day. The amount of the check, however, was wrongly quoted as £20,000. The director of the orphanage called on Ford at his hotel to apologize. "I'll phone the editor straight away and tell him to correct the mistake," he said.

"There's no need for that," replied Ford, taking out his checkbook and pen. "I'll give you a check for the remaining eighteen thousand pounds, but only on one condition. When the new building opens, I want this inscription on it: I WAS A STRANGER, AND YOU TOOK ME IN."

5 Ford was once asked why he made a habit of visiting his executives when problems arose rather than calling them to his own office. "I go to them to save time," explained Ford.

"I've found that I can leave the other fellow's office a lot quicker than I can get him to leave mine."

6 Ford was discussing education with a young man who found himself frustrated by what he felt to be Ford's narrow view of schooling. The fellow begged to differ. "These are different times — this is the modern age —" Ford interrupted to snap, "Young man, I invented the modern age."

FORD, John (1895–1973), *US film director, notable for his westerns.*

1 Asked why in his movie *Stagecoach* the Indians didn't just shoot the horses in order to stop the stagecoach, Ford said, "If they had, it would have been the end of the picture, wouldn't it?"

2 As the filming of *Stagecoach* progressed, Ford became more and more convinced of its possibilities with the public, and predicted success for its actors. He said to John Wayne, "If this picture is half as good as I think it is, you're actually going to have to buy some clothes."

3 Seeing John Wayne's performance in *Red River,* Ford said to director Howard Hawks, "I never knew the big son of a bitch could act."

4 While Ford was directing a film for Sam Goldwyn, the shooting schedule fell one day behind. Goldwyn visited the set, pointed out this fact, and inquired what the director was going to do about it. "Sam, about how many script pages do you think I should shoot a day?" asked Ford. "About five," was the rather uncertain response. Ford picked up the script and ripped out five pages. "Okay," he said, "now we're on schedule."

FORDYCE, George (1736–1802), *British physician.*

1 Dr. Fordyce sometimes drank a great deal at dinner. It was after one of these heavy sessions that he received an urgent summons to a lady patient taken ill with an unspecified complaint. Dr. Fordyce hurried to her house, aware that he was far from sober. He had considerable difficulty locating her pulse, and was then unable to count its beats. Muttering under his breath, "Drunk, by God!" he wrote out a prescription and hurriedly left the room. The following morning a letter came for the doctor from his patient. He opened it in expectation of a severe rebuke. Instead, the gist of the letter was as follows: she well knew the unfortunate condition in which he had found her the previous day and she begged him to keep the business confidential in consideration of the enclosed — a bank note for £100.

FORGY, Howell Maurice (1908–83), *US naval chaplain.*

1 Forgy was a chaplain aboard the cruiser *New Orleans* when the Japanese attacked Pearl Harbor on December 7, 1941. As the Japanese planes roared overhead, it was discovered that the man with the keys to the ammunition locker had gone ashore. A group of crewmen managed to break into the locker, only to face a second obstacle — the power ammunition hoist was out of action. So the men, Forgy among them, formed a human chain, passing the shells from hand to hand up to the gun deck. Noticing that some of the men were weakening under the weight of the shells, Forgy slapped his neighbor on the back and cried, "Praise the Lord and pass the ammunition!"

FORREST, Nathan Bedford (1821–77), *US general, Confederate cavalry commander.*

1 Forrest was reminiscing with General John Hunt Morgan about their respective exploits in Tennessee and Kentucky in the summer of 1862. Morgan was keen to know how Forrest had achieved his remarkable success at Murfreesboro, where he had captured the garrison and stores in defiance of the federal forces that filled the surrounding countryside. Forrest's terse reply was "I just took the short cut and got there first with the most men."

FOSDICK, Harry Emerson (1878–1969), *US Protestant minister and teacher.*

1 One winter night Fosdick was awakened by a tipsy young student banging on his door. After Dr. Fosdick had admitted him, the young man asked him to explain to him the difference between modernism and fundamentalism. "Go home and sober up," advised Fosdick, "and come back when you have slept it off and I will gladly give you the answer." The young man began to sob: "The trouble is, doctor, when I'm sober, I won't give a damn!"

FOSTER, Stephen Collins (1826–64), *US song composer.*

1 Though an accomplished flutist, Stephen Foster composed his melodies without needing to work them out on any instrument. At the height of his popularity he was invited to a party at which he suspected it was not his company that was sought but his flute-playing ability. He stayed home and sent his flute to the party.

FOUCHÉ, Joseph, Duc d'Otrante (1763–1820), *French politician and police functionary.*

1 Napoleon found Fouché an able minister, but resented his freedom of speech and independent attitude. Seeking to disconcert him, the emperor once reminded Fouché that he had been one of those who had voted in favor of executing Louis XVI. "True," said Fouché, unabashed. "That was the very first service that I had occasion to perform for Your Majesty."

2 On Napoleon's escape from Elba, Fouché, who had been making overtures to the victorious allies, turned coat with his customary promptitude. During the Hundred Days he was employed in compiling a list of those whom Napoleon intended to punish once he had reestablished his ascendancy. After the battle of Waterloo, this list was something of an embarrassment to its compiler, particularly when it fell into the hands of Talleyrand, whose name of course was on it. Running his eyes over the list, Talleyrand remarked, "One must at least do him the justice of acknowledging that he has omitted none of his friends."

FOWLER, Gene (1890–1960), *US journalist, biographer, and novelist.*

1 Fowler was a master of creative expense-account writing. In 1921, while on Hearst's *New York American,* he traveled to northern Canada to interview three US navy balloonists who had turned up, after being missing for a month, at a remote spot called Moose Factory. While most of their fellow journalists waited at Toronto, Fowler and five colleagues loaded a private railroad car with choice food and drink and set out for Moose Factory.

The cost of the expedition worked out at $7,200 — $1,200 for each of them. Fowler got back to the *American* offices and began drawing up his expense account. He listed all manner of items that might be thought necessary for an expedition to the far north — mittens, parkas, snowshoes — but was still short of the necessary total. He added on the purchase of a secondhand dogsled and a team of huskies to draw it. The *American*'s auditor returned the account; it still did not balance. Fowler added a mention of the death of the lead dog and compensation of $80 paid to its owner, plus a commemorative headstone for the same dog — $20. Again the account was returned, this time just a trifle short. Fowler added the final item: "Flowers for the bereft bitch — $1.50."

FOX, Charles James (1749–1806), *British statesman.*

1 Fox's father severely reprimanded him for his immense debts, concluding his rebuke by saying that he wondered that he could sleep or take any pleasure in life with these hanging over him. "Your lordship need not be surprised," his son coolly replied. "You should rather be astonished that my creditors can sleep."

2 In November 1779 William Adam, a politician who had lately become one of Lord North's supporters, challenged Fox to a duel over a speech he had made attacking the government. When the pistols had been loaded and handed to the combatants, Fox took his position facing Adam squarely. He was told to stand sideways, to lessen the chance of his opponent's shot hitting him. Fox, who had done his best to find an honorable way to avert the duel, merely said, "I am as thick one way as the other." The signal to fire was given. Adam fired; Fox did not. The seconds called to Fox that he must fire. "I'll be damned if I do; I have no quarrel," he said. The combatants then advanced to shake hands. Fox said, "Adam, your shot would have killed me if you had not been using *government* powder."

3 On September 15, 1784, Fox went with his brother to Moorfields in London to watch the Italian Lunardi make an ascent in a balloon. As they were standing in the dense crowd, Fox felt a hand at his pocket. He quickly turned and grabbed the would-be pickpocket's wrist. "You have chosen an occupation that will bring you to utter ruin, my friend," he observed. The thief begged for mercy, saying that he had been driven by desperation to turn to crime, his wife was starving, his children were ill, and he was penniless. Moved by this tragic tale, Fox gave the man a guinea and warned him to mend his ways.

At the conclusion of the show Fox felt for his watch and found it gone. His brother said that he had seen his "friend" take it. "You saw him take it, and yet you made no move to stop him?" said Fox, astounded. "Well," replied his brother, "you and he appeared to be on such good terms with each other that I did not choose to interfere."

4 When Fox went to see the play *The Gamester,* the newspapers sensed the opportunity for an edifying paragraph on how the notorious gambler had been moved to tears at this theatrical depiction of a gambler's career. In fact, Fox just watched attentively and in silence until the point at which the hero announces that he will borrow money upon the reversion of his uncle's estate. Fox turned to his friend Richard Brinsley Sheridan and whispered, "Rather odd, eh, that he had not thought of that before?"

5 While canvassing, Fox asked a respectable tradesman for his vote. "I admire your abilities," the man replied, "but damn your principles." Fox replied, "And I applaud your sincerity, but damn your manners."

—◁▷—

FOX, George (1624–91), *British religious leader, founder of the Quakers.*

1 Among the people influenced by Fox's teachings was William Penn. The son of a distinguished admiral, Penn used to wear a sword as a reminder of his own and his family's martial tradition. As he came further under the spell of the Quaker doctrine of nonviolence, he began to doubt whether it was appropriate for him to wear such an ornament. He sought Fox's counsel. "Wear the sword as long as thou canst," was the Quaker leader's advice. A few weeks later when Fox met Penn, he asked him with a smile, "Where is thy sword?" Replied Penn, "I wore it as long as I could."

—◁▷—

FRAGUIER, Claude François (1666–1728), *French scholar.*

1 Over a twenty-year period the Abbé Fraguier persisted in prosecuting a case at law that he could not, as his friends continued to tell him, possibly win. Finally it was decided against him. His friends all reminded him that had he never engaged in the case he could have spared himself much sorrow and heartbreak. The abbé replied, "Every night before falling asleep I've managed to win this case. Do you call that nothing?"

—◁▷—

FRANCIS I (1494–1547), *king of France (1515–47).*

1 Francis, a great lover of strenuous exercise, was a proficient tennis player. Once when he was playing tennis with a monk as a partner, the monk hit a fine stroke that decided the set in Francis's favor. The king applauded his partner: "That is the stroke of a monk!"

"Sire," said the man of God, "whenever it shall please you, it shall be the stroke of an abbot." Francis took the hint and the monk received his preferment.

—◁▷—

FRANCIS II (1768–1835), *Holy Roman Emperor (1792–1806) and, as Francis I, emperor of Austria (1804–35).*

1 Even the Austrian army's fearful defeat by Napoleon at Austerlitz in 1805 failed to impress the Austrians with the seriousness of war. Francis II, arriving back at Vienna at the head of his vanquished troops, announced quite cheerfully to his courtiers, "Well, here we are! Well beaten!"

2 A certain distinguished person was recommended to the emperor as a fine patriot, intensely loyal to the empire. "But is he a patriot for *me*?" inquired the great autocrat.

—◁▷—

FRANCIS FERDINAND (1863–1914), *archduke of Austria.*

1 On the fatal day at Sarajevo, the conspirators had placed a number of assassins in the crowd. The first one to act was a young man who threw a bomb at the archduke and his wife. The bomb bounced off the vehicle in which they were traveling and failed to explode. The would-be assassin ran off into the crowd and the day's ceremonial duties continued. In the course of the mayoral reception Francis Ferdinand was told the bomb thrower had been captured. He commented wryly, "Wait and see: instead of locking that fellow up, they'll be proper Austrians and award him the medal of merit."

FRANCIS JOSEPH (1830–1916), *emperor of Austria (1848–1916).*

1 The emperor, having heard the conversational abilities of the famous comedian Girardi much praised, asked the actor to tea, in expectation of a flood of brilliant talk. But Girardi said almost nothing, speaking only when spoken to, and then replying in tones of the greatest respect. The disappointed emperor finally remarked, "But my dear Girardi, I've been told so much about your extraordinary conversational gifts." Girardi wiped his forehead and replied, "Majesty, sometime you just try chatting with an emperor."

2 The emperor was basically a simple man. On one occasion he and two companions were out hunting near Bad Ischl in Austria, dressed in hunting clothes. A passing peasant stopped his cart to offer them a lift. As they were some way from their lodge, they accepted and soon fell into conversation with their benefactor. The peasant asked one of his passengers who he was. "The king of Saxony," was the supercilious reply. The peasant nodded and asked the next man the same question. "The king of Bavaria," said the second passenger. "And you?" said the peasant, indicating Francis Joseph, "I suppose you are the emperor of Austria?"

FRANCIS of Assisi, Saint (c. 1182–1226), *Italian friar; founder of the Franciscan order, later canonized.*

1 Saint Francis, who traveled quite extensively on missionary work, in 1219 visited Egypt, where he hoped to convert the sultan, al-Malik al-Kamil. The sultan laid a trap for the saint, spreading a carpet decorated with crosses in front of his divan. "If he treads on the crosses, I will accuse him of insulting his God, and if he refuses to tread on the carpet, I will accuse him of insulting me." Saint Francis walked straight onto the carpet, to the jeers of the sultan. "Our Lord was crucified between two thieves," said the saint, undisturbed. "We Christians have the True Cross. The crosses of the thieves we have left to you, and I am not ashamed to tread on those."

FRANCO, Francisco (1829–1975), *Spanish general and fascist dictator.*

1 Franco had remarkable powers of endurance and persisted in surviving long after the time that even many of his supporters considered appropriate. On his deathbed his aide announced that a General Garcia wanted to be admitted to say good-bye to him. Franco asked, "Why, is Garcia going on a trip?"

FRANKLIN, Benjamin (1706–90), *US statesman, diplomat, scientist, and inventor.*

1 In Paris in the early 1770s after the death of his wife, Franklin thought seriously of marrying Madame Helvétius, the attractive widow of the famous philosopher. Meeting him after a few days during which the pressure of his other commitments had prevented him from seeing her, she chided him for not paying her a visit. "Madam, I am waiting until the nights are longer," was the reply.

2 When a committee sat to examine the wording of Jefferson's draft of the Declaration of Independence, the proud author was somewhat discomfited by their editorial revisions.

Franklin noticed his colleague's distress and told him a little story. When he was a young man, Franklin said, he had a friend who had completed his apprenticeship as a hatter and was about to open up in business for himself. He was anxious to have a fine signboard and composed one with the inscription "John Thompson, hatter, makes and sells hats for ready money," over the depiction of a hat. He then showed it to his friends and asked them what they thought. The first one remarked that "hatter" was superfluous, as "makes and sells hats" showed the nature of the business. The second pointed out that "makes" could be left off the sign, as customers were unlikely to be interested in who had made the hats. The third friend said that as it was not the custom locally to sell on credit, the words "for ready money" were superfluous, and they too were struck out, leaving just: "John Thompson sells hats." "No one would expect you to give them away," said the fourth friend, "so what is the point of 'sells'?" Finally someone said that it seemed unnecessary to have the word "hats" on the board since there was the painted picture of a hat. So the board eventually read "John Thompson" with a picture of a hat underneath the name. Jefferson was much mollified by this story, and it was generally agreed that the committee's editorial work had improved the wording of the Declaration of Independence.

3 At the signing of the first draft of the Declaration of Independence John Hancock, one of the signatories, observed, "We must be unanimous, we must all hang together." Franklin replied, "We must indeed all hang together — or, most assuredly, we shall all hang separately."

4 After the Declaration of Independence each state assembly busied itself with drafting new constitutions and laws to take the place of the old. The Pennsylvania Assembly passed

two or three months in such business, but at the end of the time the delegates were no closer to agreeing on a new form of government than they had been when they started. The citizens of Pennsylvania, on the other hand, had gone quietly about their daily lives, and affairs in the state had run pretty smoothly without the benefit of a new constitution. Franklin pointed out to his fellow delegates the dangers of this situation: "Gentlemen, you see we have been living under anarchy, yet the business of living has gone on as usual. Be careful; if our debates go on too much longer, people may come to see that they can get along very well without us."

5 A French well-wisher remarked enthusiastically to Franklin in 1776 that the revolutionary states of America offered a great spectacle. "Yes," Franklin agreed, "but the spectators don't pay."

6 Shortly after Washington's victory at Yorktown, Benjamin Franklin, as America's minister in Europe, attended a dinner in Paris at which the French foreign minister and the British ambassador were also present. The Frenchman proposed a toast to his king: "Louix XVI, who like the moon fills the earth with a soft benevolent glow." The British ambassador followed with: "George III, who like the noonday sun spreads his light and illumines the world." Franklin rose and said, "I give you George Washington, general of the armies of the United States, who, like Joshua of old, commanded both the sun and the moon to stand still and both obeyed."

7 When Franklin was dining out in Paris, one of the other diners posed the question: "What condition of man most deserves pity?" Each guest proposed an example of such a pitiable condition. When Franklin's turn came, he offered: "A lonesome man on

a rainy day who does not know how to read."

8 Franklin was walking with friends along the banks of a small stream. The wind that day was strong enough to form waves on the surface of the water. Announcing that he had the power to calm the waves, Franklin walked a little way upstream and solemnly waved his walking stick three times over the water. His companions watched in amazement as the surface of the stream became as smooth as glass. Franklin later enlightened them: he had shaken a few drops of oil from the hollow joint of his bamboo cane.

9 When Franklin was in France, he frequently used to play chess with the elderly Duchess of Bourbon. On one occasion Franklin put her king in check and then took it. "We do not take kings so," remonstrated the duchess. "We do in America," replied Franklin.

10 Franklin was taken to a meeting of the French Academy at which Voltaire was also present. The members of the Academy all wished to see the two famous men introduced to each other, and there was a buzz of expectation as the introduction was made. The two bowed and spoke, as politeness demanded, but the onlookers, who felt they were witnessing a historic moment, thought there ought to be something more. The great men, slightly embarrassed and puzzled, took each other by the hand. Still the onlookers felt cheated and the noise increased. *"Il faut s'embrasser, à la française* [You need to embrace like the French do]," someone explained. So Franklin and Voltaire threw their arms around each other and kissed each other on the cheeks, to the tumultuous applause of the Academy members. One witness exclaimed, *"Qu'il était charmant de voir embrasser Solon et Sophocle!"* (How delightful to see Solon and Sophocles embrac-

ing!) and these words spread throughout Europe as epitomizing this momentous encounter.

11 At a meeting of a Parisian literary society Franklin found himself a bit at sea as flowery compliments in French were exchanged. He decided that it would be safest to clap only when he saw a lady of his acquaintance applauding. After the gathering was over, Franklin's little grandson said, "But, Grandpapa, you always applauded, and louder than anyone else, when they praised you."

12 At the conclusion of the Constitutional Convention, a lady asked Franklin, "Well, doctor, do we have a republic or a monarchy?"

"A republic — if we can keep it," Franklin replied.

13 An English peer invited Franklin, during his stay in London, to admire a house the peer had recently had built for himself. Behind the handsome colonnaded facade, the house was oddly and inconveniently laid out on account of the narrow and irregular plot on which it had been constructed. "All you need to do to enjoy your house, my lord," Franklin observed, "is to rent a spacious apartment directly across the street."

14 Seeing Franklin lying in an awkward position during his last hours, his daughter tried to raise him into a more comfortable attitude, hoping, as she said, to enable him to lie easier. "A dying man can do nothing easy," said Franklin.

15 Franklin composed his own epitaph, which reflected his belief in life after death:

"The body of B. Franklin, printer,
Like the cover of an old book,
Its contents torn out,
And stript of its lettering and gilding
Lies here, food for worms.
But the work itself shall not be lost;
For it will, as he believed, appear once more
In a new and more elegant edition,

Corrected and amended
By its author."

———— ◦◊◦ ————

FRANKS, Sir Oliver Shewell (1905–92), *British diplomat.*

1 In December 1948, a Washington radio station telephoned various ambassadors in the capital, asking what they would like for Christmas. The unedited replies were recorded and broadcast in a special program the following week. "Peace throughout the world," proclaimed the French ambassador. "Freedom for all people enslaved by imperialism," demanded the Russian ambassador. "Well, it's very kind of you to ask," came the polite voice of Sir Oliver. "I'd quite like a box of crystallized fruit."

———— ◦◊◦ ————

FREDERICK II [Frederick the Great] (1712–86), *king of Prussia (1740–86).*

1 On a campaign in Silesia, Frederick gave orders that all fires and lights were to be extinguished in his camp by a certain hour. To make certain that his order was obeyed he himself went the rounds. Passing by the tent of a certain Captain Zietern, he saw the glimmer of a candle, and upon entering found the officer sealing a letter to his wife. Frederick demanded to know what he thought he was doing; did he not know the orders? The captain threw himself at the king's feet, unable to deny or excuse his disobedience. Frederick told him to sit down and add a postscript to the letter, which he dictated: "Tomorrow I shall perish on the scaffold." Zietern wrote what he was told and was duly executed the following day.

2 Frederick arranged a tour of inspection of the prison in Berlin. The prisoners fell on their knees before him, all vigorously protesting their innocence. One man alone remained silent and aloof. Frederick called to him, "You there. Why are you here?"

"Armed robbery, Your Majesty."

"And are you guilty?"

"Yes, indeed, Your Majesty. I entirely deserve my punishment."

Frederick summoned the warder. "Guard, release this guilty wretch at once. I will not have him kept in this prison where he will corrupt all the fine innocent people who occupy it."

3 One of Frederick's worst setbacks during the Seven Years' War was in 1757 at the battle of Kolin, when he was forced to abandon the siege of Prague. As his cavalry streamed past him in full retreat, Frederick tried to rally them with shouts of "Rogues! Cowards! Would you live forever?"

4 Rossbach (1757) was one of Frederick's greatest victories, when, with very little damage to itself, the Prussian army inflicted heavy losses on the opposing French and German forces. Many French officers were captured. Frederick, who had justifiable hopes of weaning the French away from the alliance against him, invited them to share his table. He apologized for the scanty provisions, saying, "But, gentlemen, I did not expect you so soon, and in such large numbers."

5 After the disastrous defeat suffered by Frederick's forces at Kunersdorf, many men deserted from the Prussian army. One was caught and taken before the king, who asked him why he had deserted. "Because things were going badly for Your Majesty." Frederick reflected for a moment, then said mildly, "I suggest that you wait a week. Then, if things are still going badly, we'll desert together."

6 His cook Noël one day served some marvelous pastry to which the king paid due honor. After complimenting Noël, he added,

"But don't serve this too often. Gluttony is a sin, and we may both in consequence have to burn in hell." The cook replied, "That shouldn't frighten us — everyone knows that neither of us is afraid of fire."

7 The worthy General von Winterfeldt had long been in disfavor with the king. Happening to encounter the monarch in Potsdam, he saluted him with the greatest respect, but Frederick simply turned his back on him. "I am happy to see that Your Majesty is no longer angry with me," murmured Winterfeldt. "How so?" demanded Frederick. "Because Your Majesty has never in his life turned his back on an enemy," replied the general.

8 A soldier in one of the Prussian regiments had a watch chain of which he was very proud. Because he could not afford a watch he used to wear a bullet attached to the chain's free end. One day Frederick noticed this curious ornament and, deciding to have some fun with the man, took out his own diamond-studded watch. "My watch tells me that it is five o'clock," he said. "What time does yours tell?" Replied the soldier: "My watch does not tell me the hour, but tells me every minute that it is my duty to die for Your Majesty." Frederick was so pleased with this response that he handed his own watch over to the man, saying, "Take this so you may be able to tell the hour also."

9 In 1770 Frederick's court was visited by General Gideon von Laudon. Before his retirement in 1763 Laudon had been one of Austria's most successful military commanders and had inflicted heavy defeats on Frederick himself at Kunersdorf and Landshut during his country's Seven Years' War with Prussia. At a formal dinner the general was placed across the table from Frederick. When the king, never slow to acknowledge military skill even in an adversary, saw where Laudon had been seated, he called out for all his court to hear, "Pray, sir, take place here at my right. I do not feel at ease to have you opposite me, even at table."

10 When the time came to sign the treaty for the first partition of Poland in 1772, Maria Theresa, Archduchess of Austria, wept. "I sign because so many great and wise men want me to," she said. "But a long time after my death, the world will witness the results of an act that has gone against all precedent of what is accepted as sacred and just." Frederick the Great was unmoved by her tears. "She is always weeping," he observed, "but always annexing."

11 The great physician Georg von Zimmermann was summoned to attend Frederick the Great on his deathbed. The king remarked ironically, "You have, I presume, sir, helped many a man into the next world."

"Not as many as Your Majesty," replied the doctor, "nor did so much glory accrue to me."

FREDERICK AUGUSTUS I (1750–1827), *elector (1763–1806) and king (1806–27) of Saxony.*

1 The king had a barber who, like himself, had no prejudice against wine. Once the barber happened to nick the monarch badly. The latter broke out, "That comes from all that damned alcohol!"

"Unfortunately true, Your Majesty," said the barber humbly. "Alcohol does tend to dry the skin."

FREDERICK WILLIAM I (1688–1740), *king of Prussia (1713–40).*

1 Frederick William was deeply disappointed by his son, the future Frederick the Great, who in his youth seemed more interested in

French culture, music, and literature than in the military virtues. The father's disaffection turned to actual hatred, and his treatment became so harsh that the young prince decided to run away, with the aid of two accomplices, Lieutenants Katte and Keith. Their plan was discovered; Keith escaped, but the prince and Katte were captured and court-martialed. Katte was sentenced to life imprisonment, Frederick to solitary confinement. Frederick William, deciding that Katte's sentence was too lenient, had him beheaded in the presence of Prince Frederick. This drastic measure had the desired effect; Frederick asked the king's pardon and began to apply himself to acquiring the Prussian military philosophy.

2 The pastor attending Frederick William on his deathbed warned him that if he wished to go to heaven he must forgive all his enemies. The king's thoughts immediately turned to his hated brother-in-law, George II of England. "In that case," he told his wife reluctantly, "write to your brother and tell him I forgive him, but be sure not to do it until after my death."

3 The priest sent to console the dying Frederick William read to him out of the Book of Job: "Naked came I out of my mother's womb and naked shall I return thither." The king replied, "No, not quite naked. I shall have my uniform on." And died.

———⚬⚬———

FREDERICK WILLIAM IV (1795–1861), *king of Prussia (1840–61).*

1 The citizens of the town of Gumbinnen petitioned the king for leave to change the name of their local river, the Pissa. Frederick William endorsed the petition: "Granted. Recommend Urinoco."

2 The king attended the performance of a lengthy, tedious, and now justifiably forgot-

ten play. As he left the royal loge, he noticed the loge attendant slumped in his chair, fast asleep. "An eavesdropper," whispered the king to his aide.

———⚬⚬———

FREUD, Sigmund (1856–1939), *Austrian psychiatrist, founder of modern psychoanalysis.*

1 On a visit to the United States Freud admitted to Carl Jung that he found American women disturbing and that they gave him erotic dreams. "I continue to dream of prostitutes," he complained. "Why don't you do something about it then?" asked Jung. Freud was shocked. "But I'm a married man," exclaimed the crusader against repression.

2 Cigar smoking is often thought of as a symbolic activity, the cigar itself frequently interpreted as a phallic symbol or emblem of masculinity. Freud himself was an inveterate cigar smoker. A curious student once asked him if his cigar smoking carried any particular symbolic weight for him. He puffed reflectively, then replied, "Sometimes a cigar is just a cigar."

3 In a raid on Vienna in 1938, the Germans ransacked Freud's office and emptied his safe. On his return, Freud simply shrugged his shoulders and remarked, "I would never have taken so much for a single visit."

———⚬⚬———

FRITH, William Powell (1819–1909), *British artist.*

1 The superstition that if thirteen people sit down to a meal together the first one to rise from the table will die within the year is supported by an anecdote told of Frith's wife, Isabelle. The Friths were dining with eleven others and at the end of the meal Mrs. Frith

got up saying, "I will be the first because I can best be spared." Her friend, the widowed Mrs. Brooks, immediately leaped up too. "Well, I'll be the second, for if you died, I shouldn't want to live."

Within a month Mrs. Frith was dead, and Mrs. Brooks died five months later.

FROHMAN, Charles (1860–1915), *US theatrical manager.*

1 When the unarmed British passenger ship *Lusitania* was sunk by a German submarine in the Atlantic, Charles Frohman was among the nearly twelve hundred people who perished. Trying to encourage a group of passengers as the ship was sinking, he shouted, "Why fear death? Death is only a beautiful adventure," thus paraphrasing a line from Barrie's *Peter Pan* ("To die will be an awfully big adventure").

FROST, Robert Lee (1874–1963), *US poet.*

1 After a dinner party Robert Frost and the other guests went out onto the veranda to watch the sunset. "Oh, Mr. Frost, isn't it a lovely sunset?" exclaimed a young woman. "I never discuss business after dinner," Frost replied.

2 A journalist once called at Frost's house for an interview. "Do you have one of those machines — those tape recorders?" asked the poet suspiciously as he opened the door. "No, sir," replied the journalist. Frost's manner changed instantly. "Well, come on in!" he cried. "Those people who take down every word never get anything right."

3 Frost had just recited one of his poems, and was asked to explain it. "What do you want me to do?" he replied. "Say it over again in worser English?"

FUGGER, Johann (late 11th century), *German bishop.*

1 In the year 1110 Bishop Fugger set out from his German diocese for Rome to attend the coronation of Emperor Henry V. He sent his majordomo ahead to sample the fare provided by the taverns along the proposed route and to write *"Est"* (it is) over the doors of all those that served good wine. When the man reached the little hill town of Montefiascone in Lazio, just north of Rome, he was so enthusiastic about the local wine that he wrote, *"Est! Est! Est!"* over the inn door. His master agreed with the recommendation; during the remainder of his life he drank the Montefiascone vintage and was buried in the town. Under the terms of the bishop's will, a barrel of wine was to be poured over his grave once a year, but this wasteful stipulation was later altered and the barrel of Est! Est! Est!, as the wine is still called, was diverted to the local seminary where it could be enjoyed by trainee priests.

FULLER, Margaret, Marchioness d'Ossoli (1810–50), *US writer and philosopher.*

1 Margaret Fuller cried out enthusiastically, "I accept the universe." Hearing of this, Thomas Carlyle, the Scottish historian, snarled, "By God, she'd better!"

2 Meeting her by chance in the street one day, Mrs. Horace Greeley noticed that Miss Fuller was wearing kid gloves. "Skin of a beast!" she said, shuddering with distaste.

"Why, what do you wear?" asked Margaret.

"Silk," replied Mrs. Greeley.

Miss Fuller wrinkled her nose with equal distaste. "Entrails of a worm!" she said.

FULLER, Melville Weston (1833–1910), *US lawyer; Chief Justice of the US Supreme Court (1888–1910).*

1 Chief Justice Fuller was chairing a church conference at which one of the speakers launched into a tirade against the pernicious influence of higher education, thanking God that his own mind had never been polluted by contact with a university. "Are we to understand that the speaker is thanking God for ignorance?" broke in Fuller. "Well, yes, I suppose you could put it like that," was the reply. "In that case," said Fuller, "the speaker has a very great deal to thank God for."

FULLER, Richard Buckminster (1895–1983), *US architect and engineer.*

1 A student at the Massachusetts Institute of Technology once asked Fuller whether he took aesthetic factors into account when tackling a technical problem. "No," replied Fuller. "When I am working on a problem, I never think about beauty. I think only of how to solve the problem. But when I have finished, if the solution is not beautiful, I know it is wrong."

FULTON, Robert (1765–1815), *US inventor.*

1 Fulton constructed a submarine for the French to use against the British. In 1801 it was tested in Brest harbor. After the trial the inventor was withered by a French admiral who snorted, "Thank God, sir, France still fights her battles above the waves, not beneath them."

FURTWÄNGLER, Wilhelm (1886–1954), *German conductor.*

1 Gregor Piatigorsky was present at a rehearsal in which Furtwängler pulled the orchestra up over a certain phrase. "Gentlemen, this phrase must be — it must be — it must — you know what I mean — please try it again." Afterward, Furtwängler remarked to Piatigorsky complacently, "You see how important it is for a conductor to convey his wishes clearly?"

FUSELI, Henry [Johann Heinrich Füssli] (1741–1825), *British painter.*

1 Following the death of Reynolds, the Royal Academy in London met in 1794 to elect a new president. There was one vote for the American John Singleton Copley, one for the royal coach-painter Catton, and one for the Swiss painter Mary Moser. But most of the votes went to the previously nominated Benjamin West, the renowned historical painter. The vote for Mary Moser came from Fuseli — not because he had any particular esteem for her, but out of sheer animosity toward West. Asked why he had cast his vote for one whose sex obviously (in those days) made her unelectable, he replied, "Because I thought one old woman might be as good as another."

2 At the Royal Academy Fuseli showed the great portrait painter George Romney a sketch he had made, which he called *The First Kiss*. It was notable for the distorted, almost acrobatic pose of the two figures. Romney examined the sketch attentively, then said "Looks to me more like *The Kiss of the Laocoön Family*."

G

GABIN, Jean (1904–76), *French film actor*.

1 Arriving in New York during World War II, Gabin was asked by a reporter about the French attitude toward the British. "We are both pro-British and anti-British," Gabin replied. "Those who are pro-British say every night in their prayers, 'Dear God, let the gallant British win quickly,' and those who are anti-British pray, 'Dear God, let the filthy British win very soon.'"

GABOR, Zsa Zsa (1919–), *Hungarian-born US film and television actress*.

1 Zsa Zsa was asked if she was not embarrassed to have had so many marriages — seven at the last count. She replied, "Why should I be, dah-link? Other women have many more affairs. They are the ones who should be embarrassed. At least I marry my affairs."

2 Asked how many husbands she had had, Miss Gabor looked puzzled. "You mean apart from my own?" she inquired.

3 A women's magazine once printed the replies of a number of famous women to the question: "What is the first thing you notice about a woman?"

"Her way of speaking," was Agatha Christie's answer.

"Her hands," said Maria Callas.

"Her husband," replied Zsa Zsa.

GAINSBOROUGH, Thomas (1727–88), *British portraitist and landscape painter*.

1 Gainsborough, who found actors difficult subjects, experienced some problems with his portrait of Sarah Siddons. At one sitting he finally burst out in exasperation, "Damn your nose, madame; there's no end to it!"

2 Having discovered a malignant tumor on his neck, Gainsborough began with courage and composure to prepare himself for death. He had not been on good terms with Sir Joshua Reynolds, his rival for royal favor, but he sent for him and the two artists were reconciled. Turning to Sir Joshua with a contented smile, Gainsborough said, "We are all going to heaven and Van Dyck is of the company."

"Jack Good, after a period of top secret work for the British Navy and a Fellowship at Oxford, zoomed off to the USA and is now a Distinguished Professor of Statistics at the Virginia Polytechnic Institute. His impeccable scientific credentials — he has a list of about a *thousand* published scientific papers, reports and notes in his curriculum vitae — do not prevent his enjoying an idiosyncratic approach to life. His keen interest in palindromes (phrases like ABLE WAS I ERE I SAW ELBA) led him on one occasion to write to Her Majesty the Queen suggesting that she appoint him a peer of the realm. His reason for making his request was that when people saw him approaching they would certainly remark, "Good Lord, here comes Lord Good.'"

— CHRISTOPHER EVANS,
The Micro Millennium

⎯⎯⎯ ⌘ ⎯⎯⎯

GAISFORD, Thomas (1779–1855), *British classical scholar, dean of Oxford's Christ Church (1831–55).*

1 Gaisford once ended a sermon with the following advice: "Nor can I do better, in conclusion, than impress upon you the study of Greek literature, which not only elevates above the vulgar herd, but leads not infrequently to positions of considerable emolument."

⎯⎯⎯ ⌘ ⎯⎯⎯

GALBRAITH, John Kenneth (1908–), *Canadian-born US economist and diplomat.*

1 On the morning that *The New York Times* published a profile of Galbraith, he was having breakfast with President Kennedy. When Kennedy asked him what he thought of the article, Galbraith said it was all right but he could not understand why they had to call him arrogant. "I don't see why not," said the President, "everybody else does."

⎯⎯⎯ ⌘ ⎯⎯⎯

GALEN (c. AD 129–199), *Greek physician who practiced in Rome.*

1 Galen was called to attend the wife of a Roman aristocrat. Her doctor had been treating her for an organic complaint, but she had not improved. Galen, while taking her pulse,

mentioned the name of an actor with whom her name was linked in the gossip of the town. Her pulse immediately bounded. Then Galen leaned down and whispered something in her ear that made her laugh. That laugh began her cure and is one of the earliest instances of a psychiatric treatment for psychosomatic illness.

⎯⎯⎯ ⌘ ⎯⎯⎯

GALIANI, Ferdinando (1728–87), *Italian writer, economist, wit, and friend of the Encyclopédistes.*

1 Even after Sophie Arnould, the famous eighteenth-century opera singer, was no longer in full control of her voice, she continued to charm audiences with the appeal of her stage presence and the allure of her figure. After one concert, the Abbé Galiani, noted as a connoisseur of music, was asked his opinion of her performance. He replied: "It's the most beautiful asthma I have heard in my whole lifetime."

⎯⎯⎯ ⌘ ⎯⎯⎯

GALILEO [Galileo Galilei] (1564–1642), *Italian astronomer and physicist.*

1 In 1632, after years of silence on the Copernican issue, Galileo published his *Dialogo dei due massimi sistemi del mondo* (Dialogue on Two Chief World Systems). The Inquisition summoned the aged author to Rome, where he was examined and threatened with torture. Galileo recanted and was sentenced to house arrest for the remainder of his life. As he rose from his knees after making a solemn renunciation of the Copernican doctrine, he was heard to mutter, *"Eppur si muove"* (But still it moves).

⎯⎯⎯ ⌘ ⎯⎯⎯

GALLI-CURCI, Amelita (1889–1963), *Italian opera soprano.*

1 Relaxing in her dressing room after a concert one evening, Galli-Curci heard a knock at the door. Quite accustomed to receiving visits from aspiring young singers seeking free advice and encouragement, she sighed wearily and opened the door. There stood a rather timid young girl clutching a small bunch of roses. Galli-Curci invited her in, taking the flowers from her admirer's trembling hand. "Do you sing?" she asked. "Oh, no!" exclaimed the girl, a little taken aback by the question. "Well then, do you play?" asked the soprano, gesturing toward the piano. "No," replied her visitor, adding somewhat apologetically, "I just listen." Galli-Curci smiled and impulsively embraced the girl. "I had quite forgotten," she said, "that there were people left who *only* listen."

GALLUP, George Horace (1901–84), *US statistician, founder of the American Institute of Public Opinion.*

1 The Gallup poll conducted before the presidential election of 1948 wrongly predicted a win for Thomas E. Dewey. Shortly after the announcement of Harry Truman's victory, Gallup was stopped by a policeman for driving down a one-way street in the wrong direction. On reading the name on Gallup's driving license, the policeman grinned broadly and exclaimed, "Wrong again!"

GALOIS, Évariste (1811–32), *French mathematician.*

1 At the hospital to which Galois, fatally wounded, was taken, his younger brother sat weeping at his bedside. Galois tried to comfort him. "Don't cry," he told him, "I need all my courage to die at twenty."

GALVANI, Luigi (1737–98), *Italian anatomist and physiologist, for whom the galvanometer is named.*

1 (Wilder Penfield tells this story:)
"One evening in the late eighteenth century an Italian woman stood in her kitchen watching the frogs' legs which she was preparing for the evening meal. 'Look at those muscles moving. . . . They always seem to come alive when I hang them on the copper wire.'

"Her husband [Luigi Galvani] looked. . . . The cut end of the frog's nerve was in contact with the copper wire, and electric current produced by the contact was passing along the nerve to the muscle. As a result, the muscle was twitching and contracting. . . .

"He had discovered the key to electricity, and to nerve conduction, and to muscle action. Here was the basis of all animal movement, reflex and voluntary, in frog and man."

GANDHI, Mohandas Karamchand [Mahatma] (1869–1948), *Indian statesman and spiritual leader.*

1 Even after becoming an internationally recognized statesman, Gandhi persisted in following an extremely spartan lifestyle. He wore the simple clothes of the poor, traveled on foot whenever possible, preferred staying in the slum areas of cities, and always used the cheapest class of railway travel. In view of the danger to which such behavior exposed Gandhi, Lord Louis Mountbatten, the British viceroy, expressed surprise to an eminent member of Gandhi's party on one occasion at a railroad station. He was told that all the Untouchables in the carriage had been carefully selected and checked by the security

services: "You have no idea what it costs to keep that old man in poverty!"

2 Gandhi gave a lecture to a select gathering of maharajahs, exhorting them to give up their money and possessions and embrace a life of poverty and simplicity. One by one his distinguished audience slid out until there was nobody left except (as Gandhi afterward said) "God, the chairman, and myself." After another few minutes the chairman himself melted away. "Poor fellow," observed Gandhi, "he must have been very uncomfortable in that strange company."

3 In 1931 Gandhi went to call on Mussolini, complete with the goat that he took around with him at the time. Mussolini's children laughed at the incongruous figure, but *Il Duce* reproved them: "That man and his goat are shaking the British Empire."

4 As Gandhi stepped aboard a train one day, one of his shoes slipped off and landed on the track. He was unable to retrieve it as the train was moving. To the amazement of his companions, Gandhi calmly took off his other shoe and threw it back along the track to land close to the first. Asked by a fellow passenger why he did so, Gandhi smiled. "The poor man who finds the shoe lying on the track," he replied, "will now have a pair he can use."

5 Mahatma Gandhi was once asked what he thought about Western civilization. "I think," he replied, "that it would be a very good idea."

———— ◑◐ ————

GARBO, Greta [Greta Louisa Gustafsson] (1905–90), *Swedish film actress.*

1 After such films as *The Torrent* and *Flesh and the Devil,* Garbo decided to exploit her box-office power and asked Louis B. Mayer for a raise — from $350 to $5,000 a week. Mayer

offered her $2,500. "I tank I go home," said Garbo. She went back to her hotel and stayed there for a full seven months until Mayer finally gave way.

2 David Niven remembered a conversation with Greta Garbo one day in a rainstorm: "I often wondered if something of [vertigo] had overtaken Garbo at the pinnacle of her career, so seeing her before me, carefree and happy, munching away contentedly with the rain cascading off the table, I decided it might be a propitious moment to try and find out.

"'Why *did* you give up the movies?' I asked.

"She considered her answer so carefully that I wondered if she had decided to ignore my personal question. At last, almost to herself, she said, 'I had made enough faces.'"

3 Long after she retired from moviemaking — which she did at the age of thirty-six — she was flattered about her genius. Gently she corrected her interviewer: "My talents fall within definite limitations. I am not as versatile an actress as some think."

4 Some years after her retirement (at a very young age) from acting, Garbo visited Hollywood in the company of her good friend, designer and photographer Cecil Beaton. As they approached the city Garbo turned to her friend and said, "This is where I have wasted the best years of my life."

———— ◑◐ ————

GARDNER, Erle Stanley (1889–1970), *US lawyer and writer of detective stories. His best-known character is lawyer-detective Perry Mason.*

1 In the early days of his career, Gardner churned out stories for pulp magazines at the rate of two hundred thousand words a month. As he was paid by the word, the

length of the story was more important to him than its quality, and he tended to draw the maximum potential from every incident. His villains, for example, were always killed by the last bullet in the gun. Gardner's editor once asked him why his heroes were always so careless with their first five shots. "At three cents a word," replied Gardner, "every time I say *bang* in the story I get three cents. If you think I'm going to finish the gun battle while my hero has got fifteen cents' worth of unexploded ammunition in his gun, you're nuts."

GARDNER, Isabella Stewart ["Mrs. Jack"] (1840–1942), *US social leader and art collector.*

1 New York–born Mrs. Jack Gardner, who once out of boredom walked a lion cub down Tremont Street, Boston, on a leash, never felt secure in Boston society. Once when she was visited by a grande dame who told her, "I am here to accept your donation to Boston's Charitable Eye and Ear Association," she replied: "Really? I didn't know there was a charitable eye or ear in Boston."

2 "Isabella Stewart of New York never thought much about ancestry until she married into the Gardner family of Boston. In Boston, she endured a good deal of fairly dull conversation on the subject, so, eventually, she had her Stewart descent traced directly back — all the way to King Fergus I of Scotland, a contemporary of Alexander the Great! ... After having the Stewart lineage engrossed and illuminated in colors on a long scroll, Isabella Stewart Gardner was in a position to make one of her famous, much-quoted remarks. She had listened to a monologue by a Boston dowager concerning that lady's American Revolutionary ancestry. 'Ah yes,' said Isabella. 'They were much less careful about immigration in those days, I believe.'"

3 Mrs. Jack, received by Chicago's "queen of the White City," Berthe Honore (Mrs. Potter) Palmer, in her battlemented castle, summed up her feelings about Midwest splendor and contemporary social art when shown the pantry. Mrs. Palmer's eighteen-year-old son exhibited gold and silver plates and endless towers of porcelain dishes. "Mother has fifty of everything," said he. "What does she do," asked Mrs. Gardner, "when she has a really *big* party?"

GARFIELD, James Abram (1831–81), *20th President of the United States (1881).*

1 When President Lincoln was assassinated in 1865, Garfield was staying in New York. There was an excited crowd in the street and Garfield was implored to address them. When he had won their attention, he said simply, "My fellow citizens, the President is dead, but the Government lives and God Omnipotent reigns."

GARLAND, Judy [Frances Gumm] (1922–69), *US singer and film actress.*

1 Comedian Alan King once took Judy Garland to Chinatown in New York for dinner. King ordered as a first course stir-fried chicken, lobster, and Chinese vegetables. The magnificent dish arrived. On top was a big, black, round thing. Judy asked what it was. "That's a very rare and exotic Chinese mushroom," King told her. "It's such a delicacy they only use one to a portion, just as a French chef uses a slice of truffle." As he spoke, the exotic mushroom began to move, off the plate, across the table, and up the wall. Judy began to scream, tears rolling down her cheeks. The alarmed King was sure she was hysterical and slapped her. She stopped, then slapped him back. "What the

hell's the matter with you, you idiot? I'm not hysterical. I'm laughing."

———— ✧ ————

GARRICK, David (1717–79), *British actor and theater manager.*

1 The actor and wit Samuel Foote kept a small bust of Garrick on his bureau. "You may wonder," he said, "that I allow him so near my gold, but see — he has no hands."

2 A nobleman tried to persuade Garrick to put himself forward as a candidate for election to Parliament. Garrick declined, saying, "I had rather play the part of a great man on stage than the part of a fool in Parliament."

———— ✧ ————

GARRISON, William Lloyd (1805–79), *US abolitionist.*

1 At antislavery meetings Garrison was well used to handling insults and dodging missiles from the crowd. The British Anti-Slavery Society gave a banquet in his honor and presented him with a gold watch. "Well, gentlemen," said Garrison, "if this had been a rotten egg I should have known what to do with it, but as it is a gold watch, I am at a loss for words."

———— ✧ ————

GARROD, Heathcote William (1878–1960), *British classical scholar.*

1 During World War I, Garrod, already a distinguished scholar, worked at the Ministry of Munitions in London. The practice of handing white feathers to able-bodied men who were not in uniform was in full swing. Garrod was handed one by a woman in a London street with the withering comment, "I am surprised that you are not fighting to defend civilization." Garrod replied, "Madam,

I am the civilization they are fighting to defend."

———— ✧ ————

GARTH, Sir Samuel (1672–1719), *British physician and poet.*

1 At a convivial meeting of the Kit-Kat Club Garth announced early on in the proceedings that he would have to leave shortly to attend to his practice. However, under the influence of absorbing conversation and excellent wine, he stayed on until Sir Richard Steele thought to remind him of his waiting patients. At that, Garth pulled from his pocket a list containing fifteen names. Said he, "It is no great matter whether I see them tonight or not, for nine of them have such bad conditions that all the physicians in the world can't save them, and the other six have such good constitutions that all the physicians in the world can't kill them."

———— ✧ ————

GARVEY, Steve (1948–), *US baseball player.*

1 The first baseman for the Dodgers and the Padres, Garvey was handsome and extremely popular with fans and the media. After winning the National League championship over the Padres in 1984, Garvey was flying from San Diego to Detroit for the upcoming World Series. The movie shown on the flight was *The Natural,* and during the scene when Robert Redford hit his crucial home run, fans on the flight stood, chanting, "Gar-vey! Gar-vey!"

———— ✧ ————

GATES, John Warne (1855–1911), *US industrialist, speculator, and gambler.*

1 He once bet the wealthy John Drake, whose family founded Drake University, $11,000. The wager turned on whose bread, dunked

in coffee, would attract the most flies. Gates won. He had not bothered to let young Drake know that he had put six spoonfuls of sugar in his own cup.

———cvo———

GAUSS, Karl Friedrich (1777–1855), *German mathematician.*

1 At school, Gauss showed little of his precocious talent until the age of nine, when he was admitted to the arithmetic class. The master had set what appeared to be a complicated problem involving the addition of a series of numbers in arithmetical progression. Although he had never been taught the simple formula for solving such problems, Gauss handed in his slate within seconds. For the next hour the boy sat idly while his classmates labored. At the end of the lesson there was a pile of slates on top of Gauss's, all with incorrect answers. The master was stunned to find at the bottom the slate from the youngest member of the class bearing the single correct number. He was so impressed that he bought the best available arithmetic textbook for Gauss and thereafter did what he could to advance his progress.

2 Someone hurrying to tell Gauss that his wife was dying found the great mathematician deep in an abstruse problem. The messenger blurted out the sad news. "Tell her to wait a minute until I've finished," replied Gauss absently.

———cvo———

GEHRIG, [Henry] Lou[is] (1903–41), *US baseball player.*

1 Gehrig had been playing poorly when he asked his manager not to use him on a certain day in early May 1939. He said that he did not know why he was not playing well, but it would not be fair to his team or himself to go on. It was then discovered that he was suffering from a fatal illness; he was to die within twenty-five months. Before that he was given a "day" in his honor before a full house in New York's Yankee Stadium. Hearing the cheers, Gehrig said, "Today I consider myself the luckiest man on the face of the earth."

———cvo———

GELON (d. 478 BC), *tyrant of Syracuse (485–478).*

1 Gelon suffered from bad breath, but was unaware of it for a long time until one of his foreign mistresses mentioned the fact to him. Gelon went to Bilia, his wife, and scolded her for never telling him, when she was the person with the best opportunities for doing so. She replied that as she had never been at close quarters with any other man, she had assumed that all men had disagreeable breath.

———cvo———

GEOFFRIN, Marie-Thérèse (1699–1777), *French* salonnière.

1 Mme Geoffrin one day was overheard quarreling vigorously with one of her intimates, a man of letters who responded with equal warmth and vivacity. Baron d'Holbach, who had been listening for a while in silence, approached them, smiling, and inquired, "By any chance are you two secretly married?"

———cvo———

GEORGE I (1660–1727), *king of Great Britain and Ireland (1714–27).*

1 The collapse in 1720 of the South Sea Company, of which George I was governor, was a financial disaster that affected many people in Britain. The king was overheard to say, "We had very good luck, for we sold out last week."

GEORGE II (1683–1760), *king of Great Britain and Ireland (1727–60).*

1 George II was invited to attend the first performance of Handel's *Messiah* in London in 1743. The audience was extremely moved by the music, as was the king. When the words "And he shall reign for ever and ever" were sung in the "Hallelujah Chorus," he leaped to his feet, believing, because of his poor command of English, that this was a personal tribute to him from his protégé. The audience, seeing the king on his feet but perhaps not understanding his motive, also rose to their feet. It is still the custom for the audience to stand during this part of the performance, although not everyone knows why.

2 The keeper of a village inn at which King George stopped for a brief meal served him an egg, for which he charged a guinea. His Majesty smiled and commented, "Eggs must be very scarce around here."

   "Oh, no, sire," said the innkeeper, "it is kings that are scarce."

GEORGE III (1738–1820), *king of Great Britain and Ireland (1760–1820).*

1 Greatly impressed by astronomer William Herschel's forty-foot telescope, George invited the archbishop of Canterbury to view the magnificent new instrument. "Come, my lord bishop," he urged. "I will show *you* the way to Heaven."

2 In the stables at Windsor George III met a boy and asked him what he did and what he was paid. "I help in the stable," replied the lad, "but they give me only my food and clothes."

   "Be content," said the king, "I have no more."

3 When Lord Eldon received the Great Seal of the office of lord chancellor from George III in 1801, the king was very affable. At the conclusion of the interview, he said, "Give my remembrance to Lady Eldon." Lord Eldon thanked the king for his kindness and condescension. "Yes," said the king, "I know how much I owe to Lady Eldon. You would have made yourself a country curate; she has made you my lord chancellor."

4 The acclaimed musician Johann Peter Salomon gave violin lessons to George III, but found the king neither an apt nor a diligent pupil. Torn between exasperation and the wish to encourage the royal fiddler, Salomon delivered the following pronouncement: "Your Majesty, fiddlers may be divided into three classes: the first, those who cannot play at all; the second, those who play badly; the third, those who play well. You, sire, have already attained the second class."

5 During a fit of madness George insisted on ending every sentence with the word "peacock." This was a grave embarrassment to his ministers whenever he spoke in public until one of them thought of telling him that "peacock" was a particularly royal word and should therefore only be whispered when the king addressed his subjects. The suggestion helped.

6 George's equerry, Colonel Manners, brought him dinner one day only to find the king hidden under the sofa. Imperturbably Manners laid a place for the king on the carpet and left the food there. As he was quietly leaving, from under the sofa came the words, "That was very good . . . Manners."

7 The King hated his doctor, the Reverend Francis Willis. During one consultation he noticed Willis was wearing a black costume, and, referring to the doctor's previous life in the clergy, asked if he preferred medicine to preaching. When Willis answered that he

did, adding, "Sir, our Saviour Himself went about healing the sick," George retorted, "Yes, yes, but He had not seven hundred pounds a year for it."

———— ✣ ————

GEORGE IV (1762–1830), *king of Great Britain and Ireland (1820–30)*.

1 In the closing months of his life George IV kept almost entirely to his overheated apartments, where he consumed vast draughts of cherry brandy. He was troubled by delusions of riding a winning horse in a race and of commanding a battalion at the battle of Waterloo. His physician and confidant, the levelheaded Sir William Knighton, observed, "His Majesty has only to leave off cherry brandy, and, rest assured, he will gain no more victories."

2 Frequent repetition of his supposed feats at the battle of Waterloo reinforced the king's belief that he had actually been there. After one such recital he turned to the Duke of Wellington and said, "Was it not so, duke?"

"I have often heard Your Majesty say so," replied Wellington.

3 At a convivial dinner Wilkes, George III's courtier, offered a toast to the aging monarch, "God save the King!" When the Prince of Wales sarcastically asked him how long he had been loyally offering such a toast, Wilkes replied, "Ever since I became acquainted with your Royal Highness."

———— ✣ ————

GEORGE V (1865–1936), *king of the United Kingdom (1910–36)*.

1 George V was an enthusiastic stamp collector. A private secretary once remarked to him, "I see in *The Times* today that some damn fool has given fourteen hundred pounds for a single stamp at a private sale."

"I am that damn fool," said the king.

2 During a dinner-table conversation with the US ambassador to Britain during World War I, George V asked, "How long a term is it that your American President serves?"

"Four years."

"My God!" said the king. "If I could get through in four years, I'd never run again."

3 When Charles Lindbergh, first aviator to fly across the Atlantic Ocean alone, was presented to the king, George asked the usual questions including one that must have put the young aviator immediately at ease. "Now tell me," said the king, "there is one thing I long to know. How did you *manage?*"

4 The young Prince of Wales never got along with his father, a no-nonsense type, abrupt and cold with his children. Lord Derby once mildly suggested that the king might be a little more relaxed with Prince Edward. George replied, "My father was frightened of his mother; I was frightened of my father; and I am damned well going to see to it that my children are frightened of me."

5 In 1917 George V proclaimed that he was changing the surname of the royal family from the German Saxe-Coburg-Gotha to the solidly British Windsor. When his cousin and enemy, Kaiser Wilhelm of Germany, heard the news, he observed that he would look forward to the next performance of *The Merry Wives of Saxe-Coburg-Gotha.*

6 The great between-the-wars Cunard liner *Queen Mary* was originally to have been christened *Queen Victoria.* George V was told by a Cunard executive that the company wanted to name it after "the greatest of all English queens." The delighted king exclaimed, "Oh, my wife *will* be pleased."

7 Pedestrian crossings marked by black-and-white poles surmounted by an orange globe (called "Belisha beacons" for the minister of

transport, Leslie Hore-Belisha) were introduced toward the end of George's reign. Driving through London with Queen Mary one day, the king, eager to test one of the new crossings, ordered the chauffeur to stop the car and let him out. He returned a few minutes later, chuckling with delight. "One of my devoted subjects," he declared, "has just called me a doddering old idiot."

8 A courtier once approached the king wearing pants with cuffs, as was the new fashion. George looked at them and said, "I was not aware that my palace is damp."

9 His doctor assured the dying George V that he would soon be convalescent and able to go to his favorite seaside resort of Bognor Regis on the south coast of England. "Bugger Bognor," said the monarch and expired.

"Two gangsters, James Gallo and Joe Conigliaro, set about to murder a stool pigeon, Vinny Ensulo, alias Vinnie Ba Ba, alias Vincent Ennisie.

"On November 1, 1973, they jumped him on Columbia Street, Brooklyn, and took him for a ride. Gallo pointed a gun at his head from the right, and Conigliaro covered him from the left. The car swerved violently. The two gangsters shot each other.

"The *New York Daily News* described the sequel: 'Conigliaro, hit in the spine, was paralyzed. Every year after that Vinny Ensulo sent wheelchair batteries to Conigliaro. A small card with the batteries always said, "Keep rolling, from your best pal, Vinny Ba Ba."'"

— JOHN TRAIN,
True Remarkable Occurrences

GEORGE VI (1895–1952), *king of Great Britain and Northern Ireland (1936–52).*

1 Although George VI was distinguished in several fields, he could not claim to be well versed in modern art. Looking at the paintings of the modernist John Piper, who specialized in storm scenes, all the monarch could think of to say was, "Pity you had such bloody awful weather."

2 In 1939 King George VI and Queen Elizabeth, on a tour of the United States, were entertained at cocktails, mixed by their host, President Franklin D. Roosevelt. The President's mother looked on with disapproval. "My mother," Roosevelt explained, "thinks you should have a cup of tea. She doesn't approve of cocktails." The king accepted the drink gratefully. "Neither does my mother," he said.

GEORGE-BROWN, Baron (b. 1914), *British statesman, born George Alfred Brown.*

1 Lord George-Brown, at one stage of his career, was known to be a heavy drinker. At a certain diplomatic function when the orchestra struck up, he felt that as the senior British minister present he should start the dancing. Spying a gorgeously robed figure, he said, "Beautiful lady in scarlet, will you do me the honor of waltzing with me?" "Certainly not," was the sharp response. "In the first place you are drunk; in the second this is not actually a waltz but the Venezuelan national anthem; and, thirdly, I am not a beautiful lady in scarlet, I am, in fact, the papal nuncio."

GERARD, James Watson (1867–1951), *US lawyer and diplomat.*

1 In 1916 Arthur Zimmerman became German foreign minister. Gerard once described him as "just and friendly toward America." But relations between the two countries deteriorated. Zimmerman, whose intelligence service was unreliable, once remarked to the ambassador that if the United States entered the war, "there are half a million trained

Germans in America who will join the Irish and start a revolution." Gerard replied, "In that case there are half a million lampposts to hang them on."

GERSHWIN, George (1898–1937), *US composer and songwriter.*

1 The pianist and wit Oscar Levant, Gershwin's close friend, once asked the composer confidentially, "Tell me, George, if you had to do it all over, would you fall in love with yourself again?"

2 When Gershwin started psychoanalysis, Oscar Levant, who used to scoff at it, asked him, "Does it help your constipation, George?" Gershwin replied, "No, but now I understand why I have it."

3 Oscar Levant complained to Gershwin that when they traveled together on trains he always had to take the upper berth while Gershwin had the lower. "That's the difference between talent and genius," said Gershwin.

4 At one time Gershwin thought of taking some lessons from Ravel in Paris, but nothing came of it. Later a story went the rounds explaining what happened. Gershwin had asked the French composer for lessons, and was answered with the question: "How much do you earn a year from your compositions?"

"Between one hundred and two hundred thousand dollars," replied Gershwin.

"Then it is I who must ask you to teach me to compose."

5 At the end of a magnificent piano recital by a Spanish virtuoso, Gershwin's companion turned to him and said enthusiastically, "Isn't he great, George?"

"Yes, he's a genius," agreed the composer. "A Spanish Gershwin."

GERSHWIN, Ira (1896–1983), *US lyric writer. He collaborated with his brother, George Gershwin, on a number of the latter's songs and musical comedies.*

1 Gershwin was a keen poker player, but very unlucky. After a particularly disastrous evening, he announced to his friends: "I take an oath. I'll never pick up a card again." After a moment's pause, he added, "Unless, of course, I have guests who want to play. . . . Or unless I am a guest in another man's house." He paused again. "Or whatever circumstances arise."

GESVRES, Bernard François Potier, Marquis de (1655–1739), *French aristocrat and courtier.*

1 (The diarist Saint-Simon records a blunder made by the marquis.)

"In the king's apartments one day, he was holding forth in praise and criticism of the fine pictures there. Pointing to several Crucifixions by great masters, he maintained that they had all been painted by the same artist. People began to mock him, pointing out the various painters and how they might be recognized by their personal styles. 'Nonsense,' exclaimed the marquis, 'The painter of all of them was called "INRI," cannot you read his signature?' You may imagine the silence that followed this gross blunder, and what became of the ignoramus."

GETTY, J[ean] Paul (1892–1976), *US oil executive and art collector.*

1 Getty once received a request from a magazine for a short article explaining his success. A check for two hundred pounds was enclosed. The multimillionaire obligingly wrote: "Some people find oil. Others don't."

2 A newspaper reporter once asked Getty if it were true that the value of his holdings, at that time, amounted to a billion dollars. Getty was silent for a minute or two. "I suppose so," he replied thoughtfully. "But remember, a billion dollars doesn't go as far as it used to."

GHIBERTI, Lorenzo (c. 1378–1455), *Italian Renaissance sculptor and goldsmith.*

1 Awarded the commission for the baptistry doors of the Duomo in Florence in 1402, Ghiberti spent most of the rest of his life working on them. When he saw them, Michelangelo exclaimed, "These designs are worthy to adorn the gates of paradise."

GIAMATTI, A. Bartlett (1938–89), *US academic and baseball executive.*

1 The baseball commissioner's most controversial action was to ban legend Pete Rose from baseball for life for betting on the game. Said Giamatti about his decision, "People will say I'm an idealist. I hope so."

GIAMPETRO, Joseph (1866–1913), *German actor, born in Vienna.*

1 Elegant and accomplished, Giampetro was an indefatigable Don Juan. A friend, encountering him in a coffeehouse looking somewhat worried and holding a letter in his hands, asked sympathetically if he had received bad news. "No," was the reply, "but the sender of this letter says that he will strangle me if I keep on paying attention to his wife." "Well," advised the friend, "I'd lay off the lady, if I were you."

"But *which* lady?" cried Giampetro. "The damn letter is anonymous."

GIBBON, Edward (1737–94), *British historian. He is remembered for his epic and ironic treatment of Christianity in* The History of the Decline and Fall of the Roman Empire.

1 When Gibbon was staying in Lausanne in 1757, he met and fell in love with an accomplished and beautiful French girl, Suzanne Curchod. He was invited to her home, and had some hopes that she would agree to marry him. However, when he raised the subject with his father, Gibbon senior emphatically refused to agree to allow his son to marry a foreigner. Destitute without his father's consent to the match, Gibbon gave up his love, later writing, "After a painful struggle I yielded to my fate: I sighed as a lover, I obeyed as a son."

2 Gibbon's ventures in the direction of matrimony were ill-fated. In middle age he wooed Lady Elizabeth Foster, who at the time was governess in the Duke of Devonshire's family. On an occasion when Gibbon was engaging the lady in close conversation, one of his rivals, a French doctor, could not contain his irritation: *"Quand mi lady Elizabeth Foster sera malade de vos fadaises, je la guérirai"* (When my lady Elizabeth Foster becomes sick of your nonsense, I shall cure her). Gibbon's riposte was: *"Quand mi lady Elizabeth Foster sera morte de vos recettes, je l'immortaliserai"* (When my lady Elizabeth Foster dies from your prescriptions, I shall immortalize her).

3 William, Duke of Gloucester, brother of King George III, permitted Gibbon to present him with the first volume of *The Decline and Fall.* When the second volume appeared in 1781, Gibbon not unnaturally sought an audience with the prince to present him with a copy. He was received affably. "Another damned, thick, square book!" said the prince. "Al-

ways scribble, scribble, scribble! Eh! Mr. Gibbon?"

"*Clientelismo* [patronage] offers the only safety, and the one sin Naples inevitably punishes is ambition. Some years ago, a *mille-mestieri* nicknamed Giovanni the Immortal made a good economic thing out of stepping in front of moving automobiles. He survived twenty-six accidents and was regarded as something of a local hero in his *vicolo* because he not only supported his family by sticking the insurance companies but also provided an income for the neighborhood cronies who inevitably testified in court on his behalf. The day inevitably came when he misjudged a car's speed and was fatally run over on the Via del Duomo. At his funeral, a reporter for a local television program asked one of the mourners, an old man who had been a frequent witness at Giovanni's court appearances, how he felt about his benefactor's demise. The old man shrugged and said, 'This time he exaggerated.'"

— WILLIAM MURRAY,
Italy: The Fatal Gift

GIBBONS, Euell (1911–75), *US botanist and writer.*

1 The authority on wild foods came by his interest the hard way. As a boy his father, looking for work, left his broke and starving family to fend for themselves in New Mexico. When they had only a few pinto beans left, Gibbons walked up into the mountains and returned with his knapsack full of mushrooms and prickly-pear fruit. The foraged food lasted the family a month. After he found success writing books about the nutritional value of wild foods, he was asked how one might put together a good wild meal quickly. "Start with raccoon pie and cattail salad," he said. "They never hurt anyone."

GIBSON, Bob (1935–), *US baseball player.*

1 During the 1967 pennant race, Cardinals pitcher Gibson broke his leg. He was so hounded by reporters asking after his health and pitching prospects that he taped a piece of paper to his shirt front that read, "1. Yes, it's off. 2. No, it doesn't hurt. 3. I don't know how much longer."

GIDE, André (1869–1951), *French novelist.*

1 Paul Claudel, the Catholic mystic poet, once tried to convert the free-thinking Gide. He was unsuccessful. On February 19, 1951, Gide died. A few days later, on a bulletin board in a hall of the Sorbonne, a telegram appeared bearing Gide's signature. It read: "Hell doesn't exist. Better notify Claudel."

GIELGUD, Sir John (1904–2000), *British actor.*

1 Gielgud's first production was the Oxford University Dramatic Society's *Romeo and Juliet* in 1932. The youthful cast was a glittering one and the production launched several people on their theatrical careers, notably Peggy Ashcroft in the role of Juliet. For the role of the Nurse, Gielgud had the inspired idea of asking Edith Evans, already a considerable star, and she agreed to play the part. There were various hitches at the first performance and by the time of the final curtain Gielgud was in a state of acute nervous tension. All the flowery compliments that he had intended to pay Edith Evans and Peggy Ashcroft flew out of his head as he stepped to the front of the stage. What he actually ended up doing was thanking "two leading ladies, the like of whom I hope I shall never meet again."

2 After the evening performance, a man came to Gielgud's dressing room to offer his congratulations. "How pleased I am to meet you," said Sir John, recognizing the man's face. "I used to know your son, we were at school together."

"I don't have a son," replied the man coldly. "*I* was at school with you."

3 Comedienne Carol Channing once invited Gielgud to a sports event at which she was to award the prizes. Sir John, suffering from a virus infection at the time, scribbled the following note in reply: "Sorry, love, cannot attend. Gielgud doesn't fielgud."

4 Discussing the character of Othello, Gielgud once remarked, "I don't really know what jealousy is." A moment of reflection. Then: "Oh, yes, I do! I remember! When Larry [Olivier] had a success as Hamlet, I wept."

GILBERT, Sir Humphrey (?1539–83), *English solider and navigator, half-brother of Sir Walter Raleigh.*

1 Despite the advice of his lieutenants, Gilbert refused to abandon his little ten-ton frigate, the *Squirrel,* which was overloaded and unseaworthy. Having paid a visit to his men on board the other remaining ship in his fleet, the *Golden Hind,* he insisted on returning to the *Squirrel.* On the afternoon of September 9, 1583, the frigate was almost overwhelmed by the waves, but finally was recovered. Gilbert, sitting near the stern with a book in his hand, shouted out to the *Golden Hind* as it came within earshot, "We are as near to heaven by sea as by land." That night the watch on the *Golden Hind* saw the lights of the *Squirrel* suddenly vanish, and he cried out, "The general is cast away." This was indeed true, and of the five ships that set out on the expedition, only the *Golden Hind* re-

turned to England to tell the tale, together with Gilbert's noble last words.

GILBERT, John (1895–1936), *US film actor. A great screen lover of the silent film days, Gilbert found his career ruined by the advent of sound.*

1 Gilbert was once called upon at short notice to play the role of the heroine's father in a Chicago production. He learned his lines in record time, but was still struggling to remember the name of the character he was playing, Numitorius, when the play opened. A colleague having helpfully suggested the book of Numbers as a mnemonic, Gilbert rushed on stage with renewed confidence that evening and delivered his opening line: "Hold, 'tis I, her father — Deuteronomy."

GILBERT, Sir W[illiam] S[chwenck] (1836–1911), *British writer famous mainly for his collaboration with Sir Arthur Sullivan in the Savoy operas.*

1 Soon after the death of a well-known composer, someone who did not keep up with the news asked Gilbert what the maestro in question was doing. "He is doing nothing," was the answer.

"Surely he is composing," persisted the questioner.

"On the contrary," said Gilbert. "He is decomposing."

2 At the Garrick Club in London, Gilbert was once baiting a group of Shakespeare admirers. "Take this passage, for example," he said. "I would as lief be thrust into a quickset hedge, As cry 'Plosh' to a callow throstle." One of the group at once sprang to Shakespeare's defense: "That's perfectly clear. It just means that the speaker would prefer to

be scratched all over in a thorny bush rather than disturb the bird's song. Er — what play is that from?" Gilbert smiled triumphantly. "No play," he said. "I made it up — and jolly good Shakespeare it is, too!"

3 The Gilbert and Sullivan partnership was frequently stormy, with Gilbert particularly irritated by Sullivan's oft-repeated intention of pulling out so that he could write "better music." Gilbert observed, "He is like a man who sits on a stove and then complains that his backside is burning."

4 An actor whom Gilbert was attempting to browbeat turned on his tormentor and said, "See here, sir, I will not be bullied. I know my lines."

"Possibly," retorted Gilbert, "but you don't know mine."

5 The actress Henrietta Hodson had a long-running feud with Gilbert, whose dictatorial methods in the theater she strongly resented. At a rehearsal for a Gilbert comedy she missed the chair and sat down heavily on the stage. Gilbert applauded from the stalls. "I always thought you would make an impression on the stage someday," he said.

6 When Gilbert lived in his mansion, Grims Dyke, in Stanmore just outside London, his neighbors on the adjoining estate were the Blackwells, a family of solid tradespeople who had built up a thriving business in jams and pickles, which sold under the trade name "Cross and Blackwell." They were totally unaware that their attempts to pass themselves off as landed gentry caused a considerable amount of local amusement. On several occasions Gilbert's dogs wandered onto the Blackwells' land, an intrusion not permitted to pass unnoticed. Gilbert received a stiff note of complaint. His reply was brief: "Dear Sir, I will take care that in future my dogs do not trespass on your preserves. Kindly pardon the expression."

7 At rehearsals one day, Gilbert was anxious to speak to a particular actress and asked a stagehand where she might be found. "She's round behind," replied the stagehand.

"Yes, I know that," said Gilbert, "but where is she?"

8 Gilbert watched one of his actors give an appalling performance. Bursting into the man's dressing room after the show, he cried, "My dear chap! Good isn't the word!"

9 Gilbert once visited an actress who was lying ill in a darkened room. Her mother, who was tending her, said, "I won't ask what you think of her appearance, for you can hardly see her." Gilbert replied, "Her appearance matters nothing. It is her disappearance we could not stand."

GILLESPIE, [John] "Dizzy" (1917–93), *US trumpeter, composer, and jazz musician.*

1 One night Dizzy was playing in a small club where he liked to try out simple, sometimes old-fashioned tunes. One such number, "Hey Pete, Let's Eat Mo' Meat," was received scornfully by a group of musical sophisticates sitting right in front of the stage. Dizzy noticed their mockery, positioned himself directly in their vision, and played an extended burst of astoundingly difficult and beautiful jazz improvisations. Leaning over them, he said, "See?," then quietly resumed his playing of "Hey Pete."

GIOLITTI, Giovanni (1842–1928), *Italian statesman.*

1 Someone mindful of Giolitti's tumultuous political career once asked him if it was difficult to govern Italy. "Not at all," replied the old statesman, "but it's useless."

—✤—

GIORGIONE [Giorgione da Castelfranco] (c. 1477–1510), *Italian painter of the Venetian school.*

1 On one occasion a group of sculptors were maintaining the superiority of their art to that of the painter. Giorgione was not impressed, claiming that a painting could show at once all that was necessary, without obliging the viewer to walk around the object. He offered to show in a single view the front, back, and both sides of a figure in one painting. The sculptors were skeptical, but Giorgione fulfilled his promise by painting a nude with her back turned to the viewer, a pool of water at her feet to reflect the front, a burnished corselet reflecting one side, and a mirror the other.

—✤—

GIOTTO [Giotto di Bondone] (c. 1266–1337), *Italian painter and architect.*

1 Pope Boniface VIII, thinking to employ Giotto, sent a messenger to the painter to ask for a sample of his work. With one continuous stroke of his hand, Giotto drew a perfect circle. When this was shown to the pope, he realized that Giotto was preeminent among painters of the time.

2 While studying with Giovanni Cimabue, Giotto painted a fly on the nose of a figure in one of his master's paintings. So realistic was the insect that when Cimabue returned to work on the picture, he tried repeatedly to brush the fly away. It was some time before he realized that he had fallen victim to one of Giotto's practical jokes.

3 When he first encountered Giotto's children, Dante was struck by their ugliness. "My friend," he exclaimed, "you make such handsome figures for others — why do you make such plain ones for yourself?" The unruffled Giotto replied, "I paint for others by day."

GIPP, George (1895–1920), *US football player.*

1 In December 1920 a throat infection turned to pneumonia and Gipp died at the height of his career. On his deathbed he told Notre Dame's coach, Knute Rockne, "Someday, when things look real tough for Notre Dame, ask the boys to go out there and win one for the Gipper." In 1928 Notre Dame had had a catastrophic season. They were in New York to play Army, burdened with the memory of an 18–0 defeat in the previous year's Army game. In the locker room Rockne gathered the team around him and repeated to them Gipp's deathbed request. "I've never used Gipp's request until now," he concluded. "This is that game. It's up to you." The Notre Dame team went out and played like men inspired. The final score was Army 6, Notre Dame 12. The following day the *New York Daily News* headline read: "Gipp's Ghost Beats Army." The game was known thereafter as "the Gipp Game" and "Win one for the Gipper" entered the American language.

—✤—

GLADSTONE, William Ewart (1809–98), *British statesman, four times Liberal prime minister (1868–74, 1880–85, 1886, 1892–94).*

1 Mrs. Gladstone was presiding over a gathering in her drawing room when some of her visitors launched into a spirited controversy over the interpretation of a biblical passage. Presently one of the party, feeling that the discussion was becoming too heated, tried to put a stop to it by remarking piously, "Well, there is One above who knows all things." Mrs. Gladstone's face brightened. "Yes," she said, "and Mr. Gladstone will be coming down in a few minutes."

2 Gladstone, visiting an antique dealer's shop, admired an early seventeenth-century oil painting depicting an aristocrat dressed in old Spanish costume with a ruff, plumed hat, and lace cuffs. He wanted it badly but thought the price too high.

Sometime later, at the house of a rich London merchant, he came upon the portrait he had so admired. His host, noticing Gladstone's absorption, approached him. "You like it? It's a portrait of one of my ancestors, a minister at the Court of Queen Elizabeth." Said Gladstone: "Three pounds less and he would have been *my* ancestor."

GLEASON, Jackie (1916–87), *US comedian.*

1 While performing at a nightclub in a seaside town, early in his career, Gleason stayed at a local boardinghouse. Finding himself unable to pay the rent, he devised a way of escaping from his lodgings without raising suspicion. He packed up his belongings, lowered the suitcase out of his bedroom window into the arms of a waiting friend, then strolled nonchalantly out of the house in his swimming trunks, heading for the beach. Some three years later, anxious to pay off his debt, he returned to the boardinghouse. The landlady, recognizing him at once, stepped back in horror as if she had seen a ghost. "Oh, my Lord!" she exclaimed. "I thought you were drowned!"

GLUCK, Christoph Willibald (1714–87), *German opera composer.*

1 Walking along the rue St. Honoré one day, Gluck accidentally broke a shopkeeper's glass pane. The value being put at thirty sous, Gluck offered him a coin worth about double that. The shopkeeper was about to run next door to get change when Gluck stopped him. "Why bother? I'll make it even." And he broke another pane.

GLYN, Elinor (1864–1943), *British writer of feverish romances, who popularized the term "it" for sex appeal.*

1 Mrs. Glyn's first manuscript was rejected by a number of publishing houses. Trying a bolder approach, she sent it to another publisher with the following note attached: "Would you please publish the enclosed manuscript or return it without delay, as I have other irons in the fire." The manuscript was returned a few days later, together with a rejection slip on which the editor had scribbled: "Put this with your other irons."

GODARD, Jean-Luc (1930–), *French movie director.*

1 Filmmaker Georges Franju, laying down the law at a symposium, said, "Movies should have a beginning, a middle, and an end."

"Certainly," agreed Godard, "but not necessarily in that order."

GODIVA, Lady (c. 1040–80), *English noblewoman.*

1 A story first mentioned in 1236 by the chronicler Roger of Wendover relates how Lady Godiva, in the year 1057, exasperated her husband by persistently pleading with him to reduce the taxes on the people of Coventry. To silence her, Leofric declared he would do so only if she rode naked through the town's marketplace. The seventeen-year-old Godiva called his bluff and set out for the town next day on horseback completely naked. However, by concealing most of her body with her long and copious tresses of hair, she pre-

served both her own modesty and her husband's pride, enabling Leofric to reduce the taxes without loss of face.

GODOWSKY, Leopold (1870–1938), *Russian-born piano virtuoso and composer.*

1 When the child prodigy Jascha Heifetz made his American debut at Carnegie Hall in 1917, the audience included Mischa Elman, the violinist, and Leopold Godowsky. As the sixteen-year-old Heifetz played, Elman grew restless, fidgeting and wiping his brow. "It's awfully hot in here," he whispered to Godowsky, who shared his box. "Not for pianists," replied Godowsky.

GOERING, Hermann Wilhelm (1893–1946), *German military commander, founder of the Nazi secret police force, the Gestapo.*

1 Making his way along a crowded railroad platform in Rome, Goering happened to collide with an Italian aristocrat. The nobleman demanded an apology. "I am Hermann Goering," snapped the marshal.

"As an excuse that is not enough," replied the Italian coldly, "but as an explanation it is ample."

2 Goering's many titles included that of Master of the German Forces. He was particularly concerned with the Bialowieza National Park, which had lost much of its wildlife during World War I. Goering had the forest restocked with game and put a restriction on the number of hunting permits issued. So it was that one of the most powerful members of the Nazi party had on the wall of his office the notice: "He who tortures animals wounds the feelings of the German people."

GOETHE, Johann Wolfgang von (1749–1832), *German poet, novelist, playwright, and scholar.*

1 As Goethe's mother lay on her deathbed, a servant girl brought her an invitation to a party. The old lady directed her thus: "Say that Frau Goethe is unable to come; she is busy dying at the moment."

2 In 1830 Goethe's dissipated son August, who had caused his father much disappointment and care, died in Rome. When the news was brought to Goethe, he said, "I was not unaware that I had begotten a mortal."

3 During Goethe's last years a disciple, Johann Peter Eckermann, recorded his conversations and also took down his last words: "Open the second shutter so that more light may come in."

4 When a new edition of Goethe's autobiography was produced by the greatest of the German annotators, a curious footnote crept in. After Goethe's confession, "With her, for the first time in my life, I really fell in love!" the scholarly editor added an asterisk and the information: "Here Goethe was in error."

GOGARTY, Oliver [Joseph] St. John (1878–1957), *Irish poet.*

1 Entering a tavern one day, Gogarty caught sight of a friend wearing a patch over one eye. He greeted him: "Drink to me with thine only eye."

2 (In January 1923 during the Irish civil war Gogarty, who had played a prominent role in the founding of the Free State, was seized by Republican extremists. William Butler Yeats continues:)

"[He was] imprisoned in a deserted house on the edge of the Liffey with every prospect of death. Pleading a natural necessity, he got into the garden, plunged under a shower of revolver bullets and as he swam the ice-cold December stream promised it, should it land him in safety, two swans. I was present when he fulfilled that vow."

———— ✧ ————

GOLDSMITH, Oliver (1728–74), *British poet, playwright, and novelist, born in Ireland.*

1 Goldsmith was talking about the writing of fables, and how necessary it was to make the animals talk in character so that little fishes spoke like little fishes. Samuel Johnson was overcome by laughter. "Why, Dr. Johnson," said Goldsmith smartly, "this is not so easy as you seem to think, for if you were to make little fishes talk they would talk like WHALES."

———— ✧ ————

GOLDWATER, Barry [Morris], (1909–98), *US politician.*

1 Goldwater's family owned a department store in Phoenix, Arizona. At a party Goldwater was seen in a garish, flowery tuxedo. "One thing about owning a store," he told the amused guests. "You've got to wear the things that don't sell."

2 About his fateful run for the presidency, when he was defeated in a landslide of historic proportions, he noted, "It's a great country, where anybody can grow up to be President — except me."

———— ✧ ————

GOLDWYN, Samuel (1882–1974), *US film producer.*

1 In place of his original surname, which was Polish and unpronounceable, Goldwyn adopted the name Goldfish on arrival in the United States. Goldwyn, the company name, was an amalgam of Goldfish and the name of an early partner, Edgar Selwyn. A lawsuit was brought challenging his right to use the invented name. In the course of the hearing, the judge, who eventually ruled in Goldwyn's favor, observed, "A self-made man may prefer a self-made name."

2 In Goldwyn's office the rows with his top director, William Wyler, were so noisy that Merritt Hulbert, head of Goldwyn's story department, asked to have his office moved to another floor. "Quiet story conferences make quiet pictures," retorted Goldwyn firmly. Eventually, however, he and Wyler arranged a truce. "Look, Willie," he said, "from now on when we meet, we each put a hundred-dollar bill on my desk and the first one to shout loses his money."

"Okay," said Wyler.

As a result Hulbert stayed on in his office while, next door, appalling insults were traded in whispers.

3 Edward G. Robinson told Goldwyn that his studio was going to make Shakespeare's *Merchant of Venice* and that they wanted him to play Shylock. Did Goldwyn think he ought to accept the part? Goldwyn's response: "Screw 'em — tell 'em you'll only play the Merchant."

4 Goldwyn is said to have been eager to buy the film rights to Radclyffe Hall's *The Well of Loneliness,* a controversial novel dealing with lesbianism. "You can't film that," a studio adviser said. "It's about lesbians."

"All right," said Goldwyn, "where they got lesbians, we'll use Austrians."

5 A ghostwriter was employed to write a series of articles purporting to be by Samuel Goldwyn. Halfway through the assignment the ghostwriter fell ill and a substitute had to be found. Goldwyn, reading a piece by the

stand-in writer, expressed dismay: "That's not at all up to my usual standard."

6 Goldwyn, coaxed to change his mind about a particular script, stood firm: "I am willing to admit that I may not always be right," he conceded, "but I am never wrong."

7 As Goldwyn and another studio chief both wanted a certain big star at the same time, there was a wrangle about the contract. In the end someone suggested that the dispute be settled by arbitration. Goldwyn agreed reluctantly: "Okay, as long as it's understood that I get him."

8 Goldwyn boasted that the greatest living writers were on his team of authors and he would spare no expense to get them, even if his ideas about their output were rather vague. One of the literary celebrities he lured to Hollywood was the Belgian writer Maurice Maeterlinck, winner of the 1911 Nobel Prize for Literature and author of the enormously successful *La Vie des abeilles* (The Life of the Bee). When Maeterlinck arrived, fearful of his ignorance of motion-picture technique, Goldwyn reassured him: "I know you don't understand picture technique. That doesn't matter. All I want you to do is just go away and write your greatest book in the form of a scenario."

A few weeks later Maeterlinck returned with a manuscript. Goldwyn was delighted and retired beaming into his office, taking the manuscript with him to read. A couple of minutes later he rushed out again screaming. "My God," he yelled, "the hero is a bee!"

9 Goldwyn's secretary came to him to ask if she could destroy the files that were more than ten years old. "Yes," said Goldwyn, "but keep copies."

10 David Selznick was once greatly alarmed when Goldwyn telephoned him at midnight and said in ominous tones, "David, you and I are in terrible trouble." His mind racing over possible disasters, Selznick asked what was the matter. "You've got Gable, and I want him," replied Goldwyn.

11 When *The Best Years of Our Lives,* probably Goldwyn's greatest film, was due for release, the producer called a mammoth press conference. "I don't care if it doesn't make a nickel," he told the assembled reporters. "I just want every man, woman, and child in America to see it!"

12 Goldwyn found on his office desk one morning a copy of *The Making of Yesterday: The Diaries of Raoul de Roussy de Sales, 1938–1942,* which someone had submitted as possible movie material. Goldwyn looked at the book in amazement. "How do you like that?" he said. "Four years old and the kid keeps a diary!"

13 Goldwyn had invited writer Louis Bromfield to Hollywood. After two months, however, Bromfield had still been given nothing to do. Exasperated, he finally complained to Goldwyn. "Be patient," said Sam, "take your time."

"But why did you hire me?" asked Bromfield.

"For your name, Mr. Bronstein, for your name."

14 His inability to get names straight was part of the Goldwyn legend. One of his stars, Joel McCrea, was always Joe MacRail. Once, in a meeting, Mr. McCrea gently corrected him: "It's Joel McCrea, Mr. Goldwyn." At which Goldwyn burst out, "Look! He's telling me how to pronounce his name, and I've got him under contract!"

15 Director William Wyler had been trying in vain to explain a particular scene to Goldwyn. Exasperated, he finally turned to Goldwyn's fifteen-year-old son and asked, "Do *you* understand it, Sammy?"

"Sure," replied the boy. "It's perfectly clear to me."

"Since when are we making pictures for kids?" growled Goldwyn.

16 During the making of a film, Goldwyn had a habit of phoning his associates whenever an idea came to him, regardless of the hour. N. Richard Nash, who was writing the screenplay for *Porgy and Bess,* was the unfortunate recipient of such a call, at three o'clock in the morning. "Do you know what time it is?" he snapped. Goldwyn paused for a moment, then turned to his wife. "Frances," he said, "Mr. Nash wants to know what time it is."

17 Goldwyn was not given to flights of (uncalculated) sentiment. He and some colleagues, visiting him at his home, were once engaged in a bitter dispute over a script. One of them walked over to the window looking out on Goldwyn's luxurious lawn. He stood there for a moment, then called out to the other, "Come look. Here we are fighting, and this marvelous, peaceful event is taking place in nature right under our noses. We should be ashamed of ourselves." The others, Goldwyn last, trooped over. Parading across the lawn were a mother quail and her five little chicks. They stood there for a short time; then the silence was broken by the unappeasable Goldwyn: "They don't belong here."

18 Goldwyn and Louis B. Mayer did not love each other. In the locker room at the Hillcrest Country Club in Los Angeles, Mayer backed Goldwyn into a corner and then pushed him into a laundry hamper. Later, chided by a friend about the noisy altercation, Goldwyn said, apparently honestly astonished, "*What?* We're like friends, we're like brothers. We love each other. We'd do anything for each other. We'd even cut each other's throats for each other!"

19 Once Goldwyn spotted an advertisement for his new movie *We Live Again,* which

boasted, "The directorial skill of Mamoulian, the radiance of Anna Sten and the genius of Goldwyn have united to make the world's greatest entertainment." Nodding, Goldwyn agreed. "That is the kind of ad I like. Facts. No exaggeration."

———— ⌘ ————

GORDON, Lord George (1751–93), *British political agitator responsible for fomenting the anti–Roman Catholic Gordon Riots in London in 1780.*

1 After his release from the Tower of London, Gordon was accosted by a beggar. "God bless you, my lord," he said. "You and I have been in all the prisons in London."

"What do you mean?" said Gordon. "I was never in any prison but the Tower."

"That is true, my lord, and I have been in all the rest."

———— ⌘ ————

GORKI, Maksim [Aleksei Maksimovich Peshkov] (1868–1936), *Russian novelist and short-story writer.*

1 On a visit to the United States Gorki was taken by his hosts to spend a day at Coney Island. The huge amusement park was thronged with tourists in holiday mood, and Gorki and his hosts joined in, spending the whole day sampling the sights. As they were leaving the park, they asked Gorki what he had thought of it all. After a moment's pause he said simply, "What a sad people you must be!"

———— ⌘ ————

GOSSAGE, [Rich] "Goose" (1951–), *US baseball player.*

1 In the 1978 playoff games between the Yankees and the Red Sox, Gossage found himself pitching to Carl Yastrzemski at the bottom of

the ninth inning with the tying run on third base and the winning run on first. Yaz had hit a home run earlier in the game, and Gossage felt he couldn't pitch. But suddenly he found the ability, and he forced an easy pop-out from the famed Red Sox hitter. Later Gossage described what went through his mind. "The worst thing that could happen if we lose is that at this time tomorrow I'll be skiing in the Rockies."

GOSSE, Sir Edmund (1849–1928), *British biographer and translator.*

1 After Swinburne's death Gosse worked on an edition of the poet's works in collaboration with the bibliographer and forger T. J. Wise. One afternoon when Gosse was entertaining at his house, a maid took a message from Wise on the telephone that she, not knowing of Swinburne's death, misunderstood. She announced loudly to Gosse, "Mr. Swinburne to speak to you on the telephone, sir." There was a startled hush in the room. Gosse said, "Mr. Swinburne to speak to me on the telephone? I shall certainly not speak to Mr. Swinburne. I don't know *where* he may be speaking from."

GOULD, Jay (1836–92), *US financier and railroad magnate.*

1 Gould built up a vast railroad empire, the Gould system, in the southwestern states. Just before an impending strike he is said to have observed, "I can hire one half of the working class to kill the other half."

2 The rector of Gould's church sought the magnate's advice concerning the investment of his life's savings, amounting to about $30,000. Gould suggested, in the strictest confidence, that he should buy Missouri Pacific. The preacher followed this advice and

the stock began to rise steadily, only to fall disastrously some months later. The preacher complained to Gould that he had lost all his savings. He was somewhat taken aback when Gould promptly presented him with a cheque for $40,000 to cover his losses. Guiltily he confessed that he had also told several members of his congregation about Gould's tip. "Oh, I know that," said Gould. "They were the ones I was after."

GRABLE, Betty (1916–73), *US actress, singer, and dancer.*

1 Betty Grable's five-year-old niece, who was staying with her, asked her aunt if she could join her in the bathtub. "Sure," was the reply. "Climb right on in." The little girl did as she was invited. Betty noticed the child staring at her very intently. She asked what was the matter. "I'm just wondering," said the child, "why it is that I'm so plain and you're so fancy."

GRAFTON, Sue (1940–), *US mystery writer.*

1 Grafton has often been questioned about the life and habits of her fictional detective Kinsey Millhone, protagonist of her many highly popular mystery novels. One reader wondered why Millhone seemed not to be a cat lover. "Because she'll end up talking baby talk to the cat," said Grafton. "That's the way it is, and how can a P.I. do that?"

GRANT, Cary (1904–86), *US actor born in England as Archie Leach.*

1 A journalist was writing a story about Grant and needed some background information. Wiring to Grant's publicist, he asked, "How old Cary Grant?" Grant wired back, "Old Cary Grant fine. How you?"

—⚬—

GRANT, Ulysses Simpson (1822–85), *US military commander, 18th President of the United States (1869–77).*

1 Out driving in a buggy with Julia Dent, whom he was courting, Grant found that their route took them across a flooded creek spanned by a flimsy bridge. Grant assured the apprehensive Julia that it was safe. "Don't be frightened, I'll look after you," he said. "Well," said the girl, "I shall cling to you whatever happens," and she held tightly onto his arm with both hands as they drove across. Safely on the other side Grant drove on in thoughtful silence for some minutes, then cleared his throat, and spoke: "Julia, you said back there that you would cling to me whatever happened. Would you like to cling to me for the rest of our lives?" They were married in August 1848.

2 At Cairo, Illinois, in 1861 Grant had cause to reprimand a young recruit for deserting his post while on guard duty. Rather than punish the lad, he gave him a lesson in handling a gun and warned him, "Orders must be strictly and promptly obeyed always." Some days later the same recruit was put on guard of a steamboat laden with ammunition. His orders were to prevent anyone with a lighted pipe or cigar from approaching the boat. In due course General Grant appeared and made to board the vessel, one of his beloved cigars between the teeth. "Halt!" cried the recruit, and raised his gun. The general, surprised and annoyed at this apparent impertinence, demanded an explanation. "I have been taught to obey orders strictly and promptly," replied the solider, "and my orders are to allow no one to approach this boat with a lighted cigar. You will please throw yours away." Grant was forced to smile on hearing his own words quoted back

at him, and obediently tossed his cigar into the river.

3 In February 1862 the Confederate commander of Fort Donelson, Tennessee, sent a message to Grant, commander of the besieging Northern forces, suggesting an armistice. Grant replied, "No terms except an unconditional and immediate surrender can be accepted. I propose to move immediately upon your works." This message became famous and won Grant the nickname of "Unconditional Surrender Grant."

4 Shortly before the attack on Fort Donelson in 1862, a deserter from the fort turned up in Grant's camp. At this point Grant had not decided whether to attack the fort immediately or give his tired men a day's rest. However, on learning that the deserter, along with the other troops in the fort, had been given six days' rations, Grant made up his mind. He addressed his men: "Gentlemen, troops do not have six days' rations served out to them in a fort if they mean to stay there. These men mean to retreat, not to fight. We will attack at once."

5 Grant had major successes in 1862 with his capture of the Confederate stronghold of Fort Donelson and at the battle of Shiloh, where he averted a disaster for the Union side, turning likely defeat into a narrow victory. Nevertheless, his heavy drinking caused many of President Lincoln's advisers to urge the general's dismissal. This step Lincoln could scarcely afford to take, in view of the incompetence of the other Union generals. "I can't spare this man; he fights."

The complaints continued, but so did Grant's successes. Lincoln is said to have exclaimed, "If I knew what brand of whiskey he drinks, I would send a barrel or so to my other generals!"

6 Undistinguished and often shabby in appearance, Ulysses S. Grant did not recommend

himself to strangers by his looks. He once entered an inn at Galena, Illinois, on a stormy winter's night. A number of lawyers, in town for a court session, were clustered around the fire. One looked up as Grant appeared and said, "Here's a stranger, gentlemen, and by the looks of him he's traveled through hell itself to get here."

"That's right," said Grant cheerfully.

"And how did you find things down there?"

"Just like here," replied Grant, "lawyers all closest to the fire."

7 On his way to a reception held in his honor, Grant, caught in a rain shower, offered the shelter of his umbrella to a stranger walking in the same direction as himself. The stranger was also bound for the reception, but confided that he was going only to satisfy a personal curiosity, having never seen Grant. "Between us, I have always thought that Grant was a very much overrated man," he explained. "That's my view also," Grant said.

8 For a great general, Grant took surprisingly little interest in military affairs, an attitude that he seemed to reveal especially when meeting other military notables. Introduced to the second Duke of Wellington, he said with bland innocence, "They tell me that your father was also a military man."

9 Someone remarked in Grant's hearing that Charles Sumner did not believe in the Bible. "Why should he?" inquired Grant. "He didn't write it."

10 Grant, having no appreciation of music, found it hard when he was obliged, as President, to attend concerts. After one such occasion someone asked him if he had enjoyed the evening. "How could I?" was the response. "I know only two tunes; one of them is 'Yankee Doodle' and the other one isn't."

11 A friend of Grant's once took the President to a golf course in the hope of encouraging him to take up the game. After watching a beginner hack the grass around the tee for several minutes without touching the ball, Grant remarked: "That does look like very good exercise. But what is the little white ball for?"

12 After the close of Grant's presidency, in the spring of 1877, the Grants embarked on a world tour, in the course of which they were entertained at dinner by Queen Victoria at Windsor Castle. The queen retired early, pleading "fatiguing duties." Mrs. Grant is said to have assured the queen that she quite understood: "I too have been the wife of a great ruler."

13 When Grant lay dying of cancer of the throat, he was attended by a popular Methodist minister who sprinkled water over the unconscious patient and then announced to the press that he had been converted and baptized. A little while later the doctor who was also in attendance succeeded in temporarily reviving him. When the minister was informed of this rally, he cried, "It is Providence. It is Providence."

"Not at all," said the doctor, "it was the brandy."

——— oஃo———

GRASSINI, Giuseppina (1773–1850), *Italian contralto.*

1 Following his second victorious Italian campaign, Napoleon brought back with him to Paris an Italian opera company. The Parisians, starved for pleasure and entertainment after the terrible years of the Revolution, enthusiastically stormed the opera house.

Napoleon, proud of his grasp of mass psychology, bestowed upon Girolamo Crescendi, the company's great bel canto star, the Cross of the Legion of Honor. While this pleased the opera lovers, the same was not true of the army. One staunch old warrior complained to the beautiful singer Giuseppina Grassini (with whom Napoleon was wont to console himself for Josephine's infidelities): "It's unheard of! To think that this decoration, intended for the bravest of the brave who have suffered wounds on the battlefield, should be given to a castrato!"

Replied Grassini: "And how about the wound Crescendi endured for art's sake? Doesn't that count?"

———— ◌◊◌ ————

GRAVES, Robert Ranke (1895–1985), *British poet and novelist.*

1 Graves's mother tried not to appear shocked when four-year-old Robert, after saying his evening prayers, casually asked her if she would leave him any money when she died. "If you left me as much as five pounds, I could buy a bicycle," he said. "Surely you'd rather have me, Robby," protested Mrs. Graves. "But I could ride to your grave on it," reasoned the child.

———— ◌◊◌ ————

GRAY, Thomas (1716–71), *English lyric poet. His fame rests on a single poem, "Elegy Written in a Country Churchyard" (1751).*

1 Gray once attended a sale of books with a friend. One lot particularly appealed to him: an elegant bookcase containing a collection of finely bound volumes of French classics. The hundred guineas demanded, however, was far beyond Gray's means, and his disappointment on learning the price was obvious. The Duchess of Northumberland, who had witnessed the incident and was acquainted with Gray's companion, asked the identity of the disconsolate bibliophile. Later the same day, Gray was overwhelmed with delight to find that the coveted bookcase had been de-

livered to his lodgings. The gift was accompanied by a note from the duchess, in which she apologized for making so small an acknowledgment of the intense pleasure she had derived from reading Gray's "Elegy Written in a Country Churchyard."

———— ◌◊◌ ————

GRAZIANO, Rocky [Thomas Rocco Barbella] (1922–90), *US boxer, world middleweight champion.*

1 (R. L. Crouser tells this anecdote:)
"Rocky Graziano was making the perilous leap from the sweet science of boxing to the precarious world of showbiz. So someone asked him if he planned to polish up his syntax with some training at a place like the famous Actors Studio. 'Why should I go to a place like that?' said the Rock. 'All they do is learn guys like Brando and Newman to talk like me.'"

———— ◌◊◌ ————

GREELEY, Horace (1811–72), *US journalist and politician, founder and editor of the* New York Tribune *(1841).*

1 Traveling on a train in New York, Greeley observed a fellow passenger reading the *Sun.* Always interested to discover what made people buy the rival newspaper, Greeley opened a conversation, at first on general topics and then leading up to the question, "Why don't you read the *Tribune?* It's a much more informative paper than the *Sun.*"

"I take the *Tribune* too," replied the other man. "I use it to wipe my arse with."

"Keep it up," said Greeley, "and eventually you'll have more brains in your arse than you have in your head."

2 Greeley served in Congress for three months. In the course of conversation one day, an-

other congressman boasted that he was a self-made man. "That, sir," replied Greeley, "relieves the Almighty of a great responsibility."

3 Under the will of Stephen Girard endowing Girard College in Philadelphia, no clergymen were to be admitted to the campus. Greeley, who affected a rather clerical style of dress, one day approached the portals and was challenged by the guard. "You can't come in here," he said. "The hell I can't," retorted Greeley angrily. "I beg your pardon, sir," said the guard. "Go right in."

4 Greeley had one linguistic quirk: he insisted that the word "news" was plural. Accordingly, he once sent a cable to a member of the *Tribune* staff that read: "ARE THERE ANY NEWS?" Back came the reply: "NOT A NEW."

5 Greeley, renowned for his illegible handwriting, once wrote a note to a member of his staff on the *New York Tribune,* dismissing him for gross neglect of duty. Meeting Greeley several years later, the journalist told his former chief how useful his note of dismissal had proved. "I took it with me," he said. "Nobody could read it, so I declared it a letter of recommendation, gave it my own interpretation, and obtained several first-class situations by it. I am really very much obliged to you."

6 Greeley's notorious handwriting was, in fact, unreadable by all but one of the *Trinbune*'s compositors. One day, while this expert was at lunch, two of his colleagues caught a couple of pigeons, inked their claws, and allowed them to scamper back and forth across a sheet of paper. This page was then substituted for Greeley's copy.

That afternoon, the compositor struggled through most of the inky scrawl, but there was one "paragraph" that he was totally unable to decipher. In desperation, he consulted

Greeley. Casting his eye over the inky claw-marks, Greeley snapped impatiently: "What's the matter with you? Do you expect me to print it myself? Here, I'll rewrite the whole page."

7 A collector for a certain charitable organization once asked Greeley for a donation. "Your money will save millions of your fellow men from going to hell," was the encouraging promise. "Then I'll not give a damned cent," retorted Greeley. "Not half enough of them go there now."

8 On his deathbed Greeley beckoned the acting editor of Greeley's *Herald Tribune* to his side and whispered, "You stole my paper, you son of a bitch!" Others in the room wondered what Greeley had said. "Know that my Redeemer liveth,'" said Reid calmly.

GREEN, Hetty [Henrietta Howland] (1834–1916), *US multimillionairess, known as "the Witch of Wall Street."*

1 Like J. P. Morgan, Jr., and many other exceedingly wealthy people, Hetty Green was wary of giving financial tips. Asked to suggest a good investment, she replied, "The other world."

2 Mrs. Green's most faithful friend was a mongrel dog, which had the unfortunate habit of biting her visitors. Most of the dog's victims, anxious not to offend the millionairess, tolerated the animal, but one friend had had enough. "Hetty," she said reproachfully, "that dog just bit me again. You've got to get rid of him."

Hetty refused. "He loves me," she explained, "and he doesn't know how rich I am."

GREEN, Joseph Henry (1791–1863), *British surgeon.*

1 On his deathbed Green behaved very coolly. "Congestion," he observed, and then took his own pulse. "Stopped," he said, and died.

———cdo———

GREENE, [Henry] Graham (1904–91), *British novelist and short-story writer.*

1 An English magazine had run a competition for the best parody of Graham Greene's work. A week after the prizewinning entry was published, a letter appeared from Greene himself. He was delighted that Mr. John Smith had won the contest, although he felt that two of the other competitors, Mr. Joe Doakes and Mr. William Jones, also deserved prizes. Greene had sent in all three entries himself — they were not parodies, but passages from some of his earlier novels, which he had not considered fit for publication.

2 Greene had sent the manuscript of *Travels with My Aunt* to his publisher, but the response was less than happy. The publisher hoped he would consider changing the title, which was not perceived as exciting enough. Greene replied with a simple telegram: EASIER TO CHANGE PUBLISHER THAN TITLE. GRAHAM GREENE.

3 Graham Greene was never awarded the Nobel Prize, despite widespread opinion that he ought to have been. Asked if he was disappointed, Greene replied that he was awaiting a much better prize than the Nobel. "What prize?" he was asked. "Death."

———cdo———

GREENWOOD, Frederick (1830–1909), *British journalist.*

1 In the early 1900s Lord Riddell acquired the sensational London newspaper *The News of the World.* Meeting Greenwood at his club one day, Riddell mentioned that he owned a newspaper, told Greenwood its name, and offered to send him a copy. The next time they met Riddell asked Greenwood what he had thought of *The News of the World.* "I looked at it and then I put it in the wastepaper basket," said Greenwood, "and then I thought, 'If I leave it there the cook may read it,' so I burned it."

———cdo———

GREGORY I, Saint (?540–604), *pope (590–604).*

1 In 586 Gregory was appointed abbott of the monastery of St. Andrew's in Rome. The traditional story is that he happened to see some beautiful Angle children put up for sale as slaves in Rome's market. Struck by their appearance, he asked what nation they came from, and was told that they were Angles. *"Non Angli, sed angeli* [not Angles, but angels]," said Gregory, and he decided then and there to convert this pagan nation to Christianity.

2 Inspired by his sight of the Angle children, Gregory received permission to lead a mission to England. The party had not gone far when Gregory was halted by a sign: a locust dropped onto the Bible that he was reading. *"Locusta!"* he exclaimed, "That means *loca sta* [remain in your place]." He returned to Rome and was soon elected pope.

———cdo———

GREY, Edward, 1st Viscount Grey of Fallodon (1862–1933), *British statesman.*

1 (On August 3, 1914, Grey made his appeal to the British Parliament to support France and Belgium against Germany; a few hours later Germany declared war on France, making the violation of Belgium's territory certain.)

"In Whitehall that evening, Sir Edward Grey, standing with a friend at the window as the street lamps below were being lit, made the remark that has since epitomized the hour: 'The lamps are going out all over Europe; we shall not see them lit again in our lifetime.'"

2 Grey was deeply attached to his country estate at Fallodon in Northumberland. Once when Lloyd George was inveighing against Grey's policies during World War I, Churchill came to the foreign secretary's defense. If the Germans held a gun to Grey's head, stated Churchill, and threatened to shoot him if he did not sign a treaty, Grey would absolutely refuse to be intimidated and would simply tell them that a British minister would not bow to such pressure. "Ah, but the Germans wouldn't threaten to shoot him if he didn't sign," said Lloyd George. "They'd threaten to scrag all the squirrels at Fallodon. That would break him."

⌗

GRIMM, Charlie (1898–1983), *US baseball executive.*

1 Win or lose (and when he was manager it was mostly lose), Charlie Grimm always kept his sense of humor. One time, when the Cubs were digging deep in the barrel for new talent, one of Grimm's scouts excitedly phoned him from somewhere in the sticks.

"Charlie," he shouted, "I've landed the greatest young pitcher in the land. He struck out every man who came to bat — twenty-seven in a row. Nobody even got a foul until two were out in the ninth. The pitcher is right here with me. What shall I do?"

Back came Grimm's voice. "Sign up the guy who got the foul. We're looking for hitters."

⌗

GROTE, Harriet (1792–1878), *British writer.*

1 Mrs. Grote was noted for her eccentricity, which extended to her dress. Sydney Smith, after a few seconds' contemplation of her turban, remarked, "Now I know the meaning of the word 'grotesque.'"

⌗

GUGGENHEIM, Peggy (1898–1979), *US art collector and patron of modern artists.*

1 Among the pieces Peggy Guggenheim displayed in her garden in Venice was a horse and rider that had been cast for her by Marino Marini (1901–80). To express the rider's ecstasy the artist had cast him with an erect penis. The fact that the penis was detachable saved the collector much embarrassment on holy days, when a group of nuns habitually passed the garden.

⌗

GUIMOND, Esther (fl. 19th c.), *French courtesan.*

1 Traveling in Italy, Esther Guimond was detained at a customhouse by an officious bureaucrat because her passport did not list her occupation. "I am a courtesan," she told him clearly. "Now please repeat that to the Englishman over there, who appears to be rich."

⌗

GUINES, Adrien-Louis de Bonnières, Duke of (1735–1806), *French diplomat.*

1 Guines was enormously fat, but nonetheless a great dandy. His wardrobe contained two pairs of breeches for each outfit — one for days when he would have to sit down and the other, much tighter, for days when he would only have to stand. In the morning his valet's first question would be: "Will monsieur be sitting down today?"

GUITRY, Sacha (1885–1957), *French actor and playwright.*

1 Guitry was married five times. When his fifth wife exhibited signs of jealousy of her four predecessors, Guitry consoled her with the words: "The others were only my wives. But you, my dear, will be my widow."

GUNTHER, John (1901–70), *US journalist and writer.*

1 "John and Frances Gunther's son, Johnny, died in his eighteenth year, and was buried on July 2nd [1947]. He was a handsome, tall, fair-haired boy. He went to Deerfield Academy, where he majored in mathematics and chemistry. For fourteen months he had suffered from a brain tumor for which he had had two operations. But even after the second, and about two weeks before he died, he passed his examinations for Columbia. He was one of the finest, bravest boys we've ever known. After his first operation, the doctors asked John and Frances about the advisability of telling Johnny what was the matter with him. He was so intelligently interested that the doctors thought it wiser to explain, and the older Gunthers agreed. The surgeon went to Johnny alone and told him the full gravity of a brain tumor. The boy listened carefully, then looked the doctor in the eye and asked, 'How shall we break it to my parents?'"

GUTHRIE, Tyrone (1900–71), *British stage director and producer.*

1 Alec Guinness recalled working with Guthrie on Shakespearean drama. Guthrie would re-

fer to the different plays by one word: Spite, for instance, for *The Merchant of Venice,* or Ambition *(Macbeth),* Spiritual Pride *(Measure for Measure),* or Adolescence *(Romeo and Juliet).* Guthrie once asked Guinness to say in one word what *Hamlet* was about, but before he could answer, Guthrie said, with an appalling smile, "Mummy."

GWENN, Edmund (1875–1959), *Welsh-born actor, Academy Award winner.*

1 On his deathbed Gwenn was visited by the American actor Jack Lemmon, who asked him frankly how hard it was to be facing death. "Oh, it's hard," Gwenn said in the whispery voice that was left to him, "very hard indeed. But not as hard as doing comedy."

GWYN, Nell [Eleanor] (1650–87), *English actress and mistress of Charles II.*

1 In 1675 Nell Gwyn paid a visit to Oxford with Charles II. The crowd, believing that the king was accompanied by Louise de Kérouaille, his unpopular Roman Catholic mistress, angrily shook the coach in which Nell was riding. With an instant appraisal of the situation, she leaned out of the window, calling, "Pray, good people, be civil; I am the Protestant whore."

2 One day in the king's presence Nell Gwyn shouted at her son by Charles, "Come here, you little bastard." The king rebuked her for her language. "But, sire, I have no better name to call him by," Nell protested. King Charles took the hint and soon afterward created the boy Baron of Headington and Earl of Burford.

H

HADRIAN (76–138), *Roman emperor (117–138).*

1 A woman came to Hadrian with a petition, but the harassed emperor brushed her aside, saying that he had no time to listen to her. "Cease then to be emperor," she retorted. Hadrian accepted the rebuke and heard her petition.

HAESELER, Count Gottlieb von (1836–1919), *German general.*

1 Count Haeseler was sitting in a railway waiting room, enjoying a cigar. The room's other occupant, a young lieutenant, was not quite so comfortable. "You shouldn't be smoking that cabbage-leaf of yours in good company," he said, offering Haeseler one of his own cigars. The count accepted it, slipped it into his pocket, and continued to smoke his own. "Sir, why are you not smoking my cigar?" demanded the lieutenant angrily. "I think I'll wait, as you suggest, until I'm in good company," Haeseler replied.

HAGAN, Walter (1892–1969), *US golfer. The first great golfing professional in the United States.*

1 Hagan won and spent more than $1 million during his career. After winning one of his major titles, he was asked the secret of his success. Said Hagen, "You're only here for a short visit, so don't hurry, don't worry, and be sure to smell the flowers along the way."

2 On his first visit to England to play, he found that, by tradition, only members dined in the clubhouses, while visitors had to sit outside and make do. Accordingly, at his next match, he hired a Rolls, a chauffeur, and a butler, and, drawing up next to the clubhouse, had a magnificent picnic lunch of salmon and champagne while the members inside seethed over their beer and sausages. Never again was a professional player refused entrance to a clubhouse during a tournament in England.

HALBE, Max (1865–1945), *German naturalistic playwright.*

1 As a young man Halbe had difficulty making ends meet and was continually behind with his rent. Eventually his usually amiable landlady lost patience: "Herr Halbe, if you don't pay up now, I'm afraid I shall have to sue you."

"My dear lady, please don't," cried Halbe. "Let me make another suggestion — raise my rent."

———— ᴄⱳᴏ ————

HALDANE, J[ohn] B[urdon] S[anderson] (1892–1964), *British biochemist.*

1 Haldane was engaged in discussion with an eminent theologian. "What inference," asked the latter, "might one draw about the nature of God from a study of his works?" Haldane replied: "An inordinate fondness for beetles."

2 A discussion between Haldane and a friend began to take a predictable turn. The friend said with a sigh, "It's no use going on. I know what you will say next, and I know what you will do next." The distinguished scientist promptly sat down on the floor, turned two back somersaults, and returned to his seat. "There," he said with a smile. "That's to prove that you're not always right."

———— ᴄⱳᴏ ————

"In one of his autobiographical works, the English author Augustus John Cuthbert Hare described the experience of a certain lady who awoke in the middle of the night with the sense that someone else was in her room. The sound of footsteps going to and fro across the room and the impression of hands moving over the bed terrified the poor lady so much that she fainted. Only when morning came was it discovered that the butler had walked in his sleep and set the table for fourteen places upon her bed."

— Daniel George, *A Book of Anecdotes*

———— ᴄⱳᴏ ————

HALDANE, Richard Burdon, Viscount Haldane (1856–1928), *British statesman.*

1 At a dinner in London, Lord Haldane was teased by some of his peers on account of his considerable bulk. He countered by maintaining that fatness did not necessarily mean unfitness. To prove it he offered to set off then and there to walk the sixty miles to Brighton in his evening clothes, resting no more than two minutes in every hour, and to send his dining companions a telegram when he got there. And that is precisely what he did.

———— ᴄⱳᴏ ————

HALE, Nathan (1756–76), *US revolutionary patriot.*

1 In September 1776 Hale volunteered for a spying mission behind the British lines in New York. He was disguised as a Dutch schoolteacher, but was betrayed, arrested, and hanged on the following day. On the scaffold he is reported to have said, "I only regret that I have but one life to lose for my country."

———— ᴄⱳᴏ ————

HALIFAX, Charles Montague, 1st Earl of (1661–1715), *British statesman.*

1 In the Glorious Revolution of 1688 Lord Halifax was one of the first to take up arms on behalf of the prince of Orange. Once the prince was established on the English throne as William III, office-seekers swarmed to court claiming rewards for assisting the revolution. Referring to the sacred geese whose cackling alerted the Roman garrison in time to repulse a night attack by Celts in 390 BC, Halifax remarked, "Rome was saved by geese, but I do not remember that these geese were made consuls."

———— ᴄⱳᴏ ————

HALIFAX, Edward Frederick Lindley Wood, Earl of (1881–1959), *British Conservative statesman and diplomat.*

1 On a train journey to Bath, Halifax shared a compartment with two rather prim-looking

middle-aged ladies. All three were strangers to one another, and the journey passed in silence until the train went through a tunnel. In the total darkness of the compartment, Halifax placed a number of noisy kisses on the back of his hand. As the train emerged from the tunnel, the former ambassador turned to his companions and asked, "To which of you charming ladies am I indebted for the delightful incident in the tunnel?"

———— ✧ ————

HALL, Sir Benjamin (1802–67), *British politician.*

1 The tall and portly "Big Ben" Hall was involved with the building of the Houses of Parliament after a fire in 1834. In September 1856 Parliament was much concerned with the pressing question of a name for the new fourteen-ton bell being installed in the clock tower. "How about Big Ben?" someone offered. To a man, Parliament rang with delighted applause, and Sir Benjamin's nickname was immortalized.

———— ✧ ————

HAMILTON, Alexander (1755–1804), *US statesman.*

1 Talleyrand had met Hamilton while visiting the United States, and was much impressed by him. He observed to George Ticknor, in a conversation recorded in the latter's journal, that although he had met many distinguished men in his time, none had been Hamilton's equal. Ticknor felt that as a fellow American he ought to demur; surely, he said, the statesmen and generals of Europe had been involved with wider issues and larger numbers of people than Hamilton had ever encountered. "*Mais, monsieur, Hamilton avait deviné l'Europe* [But, sir, Hamilton had foretold Europe]," replied Talleyrand.

———— ✧ ————

HAMMERSTEIN II, Oscar (1895–1960), *US lyricist.*

1 For years Hammerstein had failed to receive his proper due from the critics. With *Oklahoma!* and *Carmen Jones* he made the breakthrough; praise was lavished on him for his part in the shows' successes, and offers of work suddenly flooded in. That year Hammerstein took space in the traditional annual issue of *Variety* in which show-business people sent season's greetings to one another and also announced the work that they had done in the past twelve months. The advertisement ran: "Holiday Greetings from Oscar Hammerstein II, author of *Sunny River* (6 weeks at the St. James), *Very Warm for May* (7 weeks at the Alvia), *Three Sisters* (7 weeks at the Drury Lane), *Ball at the Savoy* (5 weeks at the Drury Lane), *Free for All* (3 weeks at the Manhattan). I've Done It Before and I Can Do It Again!" The advertisement caused a sensation.

Hammerstein himself offered two explanations, not necessarily contradictory. The first was that on Broadway a person is either very, very good or terrible and "I'm the same guy I used to be, except now I've got hits instead of flops. The ad was just a gentle reminder that times change and keep changing." The second, less subtle motive was to "thumb my nose and say: 'Well, you hyenas, so you thought I was all washed up?'"

2 Hammerstein's wife, Dorothy, was always ready to speak out for her husband when she felt that he was being pushed out of the limelight by one of his collaborators. Whenever somebody referred to Jerome Kern's "Ol' Man River," Dorothy would immediately retort, "Oscar Hammerstein wrote 'Ol' Man River.' Jerome Kern wrote 'Ta-ta dumdum, ta ta-ta dumdum.'"

3 Hammerstein, suffering from cancer, was surrounded in his room by his five children.

When his son Jimmy burst into tears contemplating his father, Hammerstein snapped, "Goddamn it, I'm the one who's dying, not you!"

HAMMETT, Dashiell (1894–1961), *US novelist.*

1 During the eight years that Hammett worked as a detective for the Pinkerton agency, he found out how resourceful a sleuth must be. A man he had been assigned to tail wandered out into the country and managed to lose himself completely. Hammett had to direct him back to the city.

2 The chief of police of a southern city once sent Hammett a detailed description of a wanted criminal, which included even the mole on the man's neck. The description omitted, however, the fact that the wanted man had only one arm.

3 Hammett lived for many years with playwright Lillian Hellman. During a quarrel when they had both been drinking heavily, she was raging at him and pacing about the room when she noticed that he was grinding a burning cigarette into his cheek. "What are you doing?" she demanded. "Keeping myself from doing it to you," was his reply.

HAMSUN, Knut (1859–1952), *Norwegian author, winner of the 1920 Nobel Prize for Literature.*

1 During the winter of 1894–95 Hamsun visited Paris for the first time. On his return home someone asked him, "At the beginning, didn't you have trouble with your French?"

"No," replied Hamsun, "but the French did."

Greek orator and satirist Lucian described an ill-fated debut: "Harmonides, a young flute-player and scholar of Timotheus, at his first public performance began his solo with so violent a blast that he breathed his last breath into his flute, and died upon the spot."

— FROM CHARLES BURNEY,
A General History of Music

HANCOCK, John (1737–93), *US statesman.*

1 As president of the Continental Congress, Hancock was the first signatory of the Declaration of Independence. Having written his name in a fine, bold hand, the paradigm for signatures thereafter, he commented, "There, I guess King George will be able to read that."

HANDEL, George Frideric (1685–1759), *German composer who lived in England.*

1 Handel once sent word to a local tavern ordering dinner for two. When he arrived, he asked for the dinner to be brought. The landlord came up, begged his pardon, and said he had understood that his honor had been expecting company. "I am the company," said Handel, and duly ate his way through the dinner for two.

2 (Charles Burney tells a story about the preparation at Chester Cathedral for the first performance of *Messiah* in Dublin.)

"During this time, [Handel] applied to know whether there were any choirmen in the cathedral who could sing *at sight;* as he wished to prove some books that had been hastily transcribed, by trying the choruses which he intended to perform in Ireland. . . . Among them [was] a printer of the name of Janson, who had a good bass voice. . . . A time was fixed for this private rehearsal . . .

but alas! on trial of the chorus in the Messiah, 'And with his stripes we are healed,' poor Janson, after repeated attempts failed so egregiously, that Handel, . . . after swearing in four or five languages, cried out in broken English, 'You shcauntrell, tit you not dell me dat you could sing at soit?' 'Yes, sir,' says the printer, 'and so I can, but not at *first sight.*'"

3 The famous soprano Francesca Cuzzoni, who came to England in 1722, treated Handel to a display of prima-donna temperament by refusing to sing the song that he had written for her London debut. Handel picked her up bodily and threatened to drop her out of the nearby window unless she did as she was told.

She sang the song.

4 While rehearsing his opera *Flavio*, Handel, accompanying the singers upon a harpsichord, fell afoul of the tenor, who objected to the composer's playing. "If you don't follow me better than that," he grumbled, "I'll jump on your harpsichord and smash it up."

"Go right ahead," retorted Handel, "only please let me know when and I will advertise it, for more people will come to see you jump than to hear you sing."

HANNIBAL (247–?183 BC), *Carthaginian military commander.*

1 After the final defeat of King Antiochus III's forces by the Romans at Magnesia in 189 BC, the victors insisted that the aged Hannibal be surrendered to them. Hannibal fled to Crete and then to Bithynia in Asia Minor, where a detachment of Roman soldiers caught up with him and surrounded his hiding place. Hannibal took out the phial of poison that he always carried with him and drank it. "Let us relieve the Romans of the fear which has so long afflicted them," he said, "since it

seems to tax their patience too hard to wait for an old man's death."

HARDY, Thomas (1840–1928), *British novelist and poet.*

1 During the furor that followed the publication of *Jude the Obscure*, the novel was burned by a bishop. Hardy took this phlegmatically, ascribing the action to the ecclesiastic's chagrin, "presumably, at not being able to burn me."

HARLOW, Jean (1911–37), *US film actress.*

1 Once Harlow cabled the great playwright Eugene O'Neill, asking him to write a play specifically for her. Would he cable back his reply, collect, but limiting his telegram to the standard twenty words. Back came O'Neill's telegram: "No no no no no no no no no no no no no no no no no no no Eugene O'Neill."

HARRIMAN, W[illiam] Averell (1891–1986), *US diplomat.*

1 Averell Harriman, a phenomenally hard worker, expected his staff to be the same. One afternoon he left his office at the unprecedented time of 5:30. "I'm not coming back tonight," he called to his staff, "so you can declare a half-holiday."

2 During his ambassadorial stint in Moscow, Harriman was shadowed everywhere by the Soviet secret police. One weekend he was invited to visit a British diplomat at his country retreat. The house was accessible only by means of a four-wheel-drive vehicle, a fact of which Harriman considerately warned his shadows. Nonetheless, the police followed Harriman's jeep in their customary heated sedan, which soon became hopelessly bogged

down. A resolute operative set off doggedly on foot, and the jeep slowed down to allow him to keep up. Harriman, concerned that the policeman would freeze to death before they reached their destination, offered him a ride, promising that he would tell no one about the incident. The man accepted, and ambassador and policeman rode together for the rest of the journey.

———❦———

HARRIS, Frank [James Thomas] (1856–1931), *British writer and critic.*

1 Frank Harris was an unashamed plagiarist in his conversation, on one occasion relating as his own an anecdote everyone in his audience recognized as the property of Anatole France. There was a slightly embarrassed silence, broken by Oscar Wilde's saying, "You know, Frank, Anatole France would have spoiled that story."

2 Rushing to catch a train, the well-known pornographer went into Sylvia Beach's Parisian bookstore Shakespeare & Co. to find some reading material. Asked if she could suggest something, Beach mentioned *Little Women*. Harris's eyes gleamed, and, no doubt mistaking the nature of the book, bought it on the spot and hurried off.

3 In later years someone asked Max Beerbohm, an acquaintance of Harris's during the 1890s, whether Harris had ever been known to speak the truth. "Sometimes," replied Max, "when his invention flagged."

———❦———

HARRISON, Benjamin (?1726–91), *US statesman.*

1 The English government offered a large reward for the names of those who had signed the Declaration of Independence, which it declared an act of high treason, punishable by death. Benjamin Harrison, who had played an active role in drafting the declaration, was amused at the threat. He was a large, heavy man, while his fellow signatory, Elbridge Gerry, was a small, frail one. "When the hanging comes," he said to Gerry, "it will be all over with me in a minute, but you will be kicking the air for an hour after I'm gone."

———❦———

HARRISON, Benjamin (1833–1901), *US politician; 23d President of the United States (1889–93). Grandson of President William Henry Harrison.*

1 Harrison took the 1888 election results very calmly. His chief interest seemed to be in his own state of Indiana. When the results from Indiana were safely announced, around 11:00 PM, he went to bed. The following morning a friend, having called to congratulate him at midnight, asked why he had retired so early. The President-elect explained, "I knew that my staying up would not alter the result if I were defeated, while if I was elected I had a hard day in front of me. So a night's rest seemed the best in either event."

———❦———

HART, Moss (1904–61), *US playwright and theatrical producer.*

1 Hart, though later a happily married man, for many years prized his independent bachelor life. Oscar Levant was a guest at a dinner party when Hart entered, the beautiful actress Edith Atwater on his arm. "Ah," said Levant, "here comes Moss Hart and the future Miss Atwater."

———❦———

HARTE, [Francis] Bret (1836–1902), *US writer.*

1 Bret Harte once attended a lecture in Richmond, Virginia, suffering from a miserable headache. Afterward, to clear his head, he took a walk with a Richmond friend, who expatiated on the city's wholesome air and location, adding proudly that its mortality statistics reflected only one death per day. Harte, still in agony with his headache, exclaimed, "Heavens, let's hope today's candidate is already dead."

HARTLEBEN, Otto Erich (1864–1905), *German poet.*

1 The poet, feeling quite ill, consulted a doctor who after a thorough examination prescribed complete abstention from both smoking and drinking. Hartleben picked up his hat and coat and started for the door. The doctor called after him, "My advice, Herr Hartleben, will cost you three marks."

"But I'm not taking it," retorted Hartleben, and vanished.

HATTO (?850–913), *archbishop of Mainz (891–913).*

1 The story of the mice is the best known of many apocryphal tales about Hatto's cruelty and treachery. At a time of famine, Bishop Hatto was besieged by poor people who wanted him to release some of the grain stored in the archiepiscopal granaries. Hatto assembled his petitioners in a large barn to which he set fire, burning them all to death. He then retired to a fortified tower in the middle of the Rhine, thinking himself safe from retribution. But a great army of mice swam across the river, gnawed their way into the tower, and ate Bishop Hatto alive.

HAVEMEYER, Louisine Waldron Elder (1855–1929), *US art collector and philanthropist.*

1 "Mrs. Havemeyer, whose collection of paintings is today the pride of New York's Metropolitan Museum, was once confronted by a wealthy, bejewelled dowager who asked, rather scornfully, why she spent so much money on dabs of paint on paper and canvas. Mrs. Havemeyer examined the dowager's pearl necklace for a long and studious moment before answering: 'I prefer to have something made by a man than to have something made by an oyster.'"

HAWTHORNE, Nathaniel (1804–64), *US novelist best known for* The Scarlet Letter *(1850) and* The House of the Seven Gables *(1851).*

1 As Hawthorne's son, Julian, was also a writer, father and son were frequently mistaken for each other. "Oh, Mr. Hawthorne, I've just read *The Scarlet Letter,* and I think it's a real masterpiece," gushed a lady to whom Julian Hawthorne had just been introduced. "Oh, that," said Julian, shrugging modestly, "that was written when I was only four years old."

2 In March 1864, an ill Hawthorne was traveling with his old friend and publisher James Ticknor. Driving through Philadelphia, the bad weather turned even colder and rainier. Ticknor took off his coat and put it around Hawthorne's shoulders to protect him. It helped Hawthorne — but Ticknor caught a severe case of pneumonia and died a few days later.

3 By mutual agreement, Hawthorne's wife never disturbed him during the course of his writing. On the night he finished *The Scarlet Letter,* he read the last chapter to her. "It broke her heart," he said later, "and sent her up to bed with a grievous headache, which I look upon as a triumphant success."

———∞———

HAWTHORNE, Nigel (1929–), *British actor.*

1 Hawthorne had played many roles before rocketing to fame in the United States in the movie *The Madness of King George III,* in which he played the title role. Hawthorne's opinion of his American audience can be guessed by his comment to producer Samuel Goldwyn, Jr., to whom he said, "That title is no good for America. They'll stay away thinking they've missed parts one and two."

———∞———

HAWTREY, Sir Charles Henry (1858–1923), *English actor, producer, and theater manager.*

1 Hawtrey directed the first production of Ben Travers's farce *The Dippers* in 1922. At the first rehearsal, Travers was disturbed to see Hawtrey cutting some of his favorite scenes from the script. As the director's pencil slashed through the best line of the play, Travers cried, "Oh, Mr. Hawtrey, must that line go? I always thought it was rather a good line."

"A good line?" repeated Hawtrey. "A good line? It's a very good line indeed, dear boy. You mustn't on account lose it. Put it in another play."

———∞———

HAY, Lord Charles (d. 1760), *British soldier.*

1 At the battle of Fontenoy in 1745, Lord Charles Hay was leading the 1st Footguard Regiment over a low hill when he suddenly and unexpectedly came face to face with the French Guards, who were as little prepared for action as were their English counterparts. Hay immediately stepped forward from the ranks. His French opposite number, M. D'Auteroches, did the same. "Gentlemen of the French Guards, fire," said Hay, bowing low. "Monsieur," said the Frenchman, "we never fire first; do you fire."

———∞———

HAYDN, Franz Joseph (1732–1809), *Austrian composer.*

1 Haydn was composing a passage to give the effect of a storm at sea. He tried various arrangements of discords and harmonies on the piano, but the librettist kept shaking his head. In exasperation, Haydn eventually threw his hands to the far ends of the keyboard and brought them together, exclaiming, "The deuce take the tempest; I can make nothing of it!"

"That is the very thing!" cried his delighted collaborator.

2 The musicians for the Esterházy family spent much of the year at Schloss Esterházy in a remote corner of northwestern Hungary, separated from their wives and families. During one particularly long spell of service, Haydn composed his "Farewell" Symphony (no. 5), in the last movement of which the instruments drop out of the score one by one. At the first performance each player, on completing his part, blew out his candle and tiptoed away from the orchestra. Prince Esterházy took the hint, and granted his musicians leave of absence.

3 Haydn enjoyed traveling because it took him away from his difficult wife, One day a caller remarked on the large pile of unopened letters on Haydn's desk. "They're from my wife," the composer explained. "We write to each other monthly, but I do not open her letters and I am certain she doesn't open mine."

4 Though old and ill, Haydn continued to live in Vienna despite the bombardment of the city by Napoleon's troops. Every day he was carried to his piano, where he would play the Austrian imperial anthem. One day his household was horrified when a French sol-

dier burst through the front door. But the young man had come only to pay his respects to Europe's greatest composer and asked if the maestro would agree to accompany him on the piano as the soldier sang an aria from Haydn's *The Creation*.

HAYES, Helen (1900–93), *US actress.*

1 When Helen Hayes first went to Hollywood, she already had a reputation as a stage star. At first Hollywood did not quite know what to make of her, so different was she from any conventional image of a film star. Louis B. Mayer decided that he must discover whether she had sex appeal. There was, he said, only one way to find out: he would make her a present of a white satin gown exactly like the one Norma Shearer had worn in *A Free Soul*. Miss Hayes firmly turned down the offer: "That wasn't a dress; that was an invitation."

2 As she retired to the kitchen to put the finishing touches to the dinner preparations, Helen Hayes warned her family: "This is the first turkey I've ever cooked. If it isn't right, I don't want anybody to say a word. We'll just get up from the table, without comment, and go down to the hotel for dinner." She returned some ten minutes later to find the family seated expectantly at the dinner table — wearing their hats and coats.

3 Hayes entered the theater world at the age of five and never turned back. Throughout her long life she was a star, winning an Academy Award for her first movie and triumphing in scores of plays. But, she noted, the life of a great actress did not always glow: "Stardom can be a gilded slavery," she commented ruefully.

4 Hayes often spoke to groups of elderly people, exhorting them to stay active. One group asked her how she was able to continue acting for so many decades. "If you rest, you rust," she quipped.

HAYES, Rutherford B. (1822–93), *US politician; 19th President of the United States (1877–81).*

1 Hayes and his wife were fervent advocates of temperance. During Hayes's presidency liquor and tobacco were banned from the White House. William M. Evarts, secretary of state, observed of one official dinner, "It was a brilliant affair; water flowed like champagne."

HAYWARD, Leland (1902–71), *US impresario, agent, and film producer.*

1 Hayward acted as agent for so many different actors, writers, and other clients that some confusion was inevitable. Ginger Rogers was once sent a script she found totally unacceptable. Hayward went straight to the producer's office to complain. "How can you insult Ginger with such trash, such drivel, such rot?" he said indignantly. "Get out of here before I throw you out," roared the producer. "*You* sold us that story!"

HAYWORTH, Rita (1918–87), *US movie star.*

1 At their wedding singer Dick Haymes was asked whether Rita Hayworth had ever cooked anything for him. "Who'd marry Rita for her cooking?" he replied.

2 Comedian Jack Lemmon once found Miss Hayworth working her way through a heap of correspondence, tearing up most of the letters unopened. "Stop!" he cried horrified. "There may be checks in there."

"There are," replied Rita, shrugging her shoulders. "But there are also bills. I find it evens up."

—◦◦—

HAZLITT, William (1778–1830), *British critic and essayist.*

1 Hazlitt's literary friends were confirmed book borrowers. He observed plaintively that he visited them from time to time, "just to look over my library."

2 Editor William Gifford once criticized Hazlitt's work with the terse observation: "What we read from your pen, we remember no more." Hazlitt completed the couplet with the caustic line: "What we read from your pen, we remember before."

—◦◦—

HEAP, Jane (c. 1880–1964), *US editor, publisher, and artist.*

1 Together with Margaret Anderson, Heap was the founder and publisher of *The Little Review,* a literary magazine that flourished in the early part of this century. In 1920 the two women were prosecuted for publishing excerpts from James Joyce's work-in-progress, the great novel-to-be *Ulysses.* Charged by the court that *Ulysses* would endanger the minds of young girls, Heap retorted, "If there is anything I really fear it is the mind of a young girl."

—◦◦—

HEARST, William Randolph (1863–1951), *US newspaper proprietor whose nationwide empire based its commercial success on sensationalism.*

1 Hearst sent the artist Frederic Remington, who made a specialty of depicting soldiers and warfare, to cover events in Cuba after the US battleship *Maine* had been blown up in Havana harbor in February 1898. The expected conflict between the United States and Spain did not immediately materialize and Remington cabled Hearst, asking whether he should return. Hearst cabled back: "Please remain. You furnish the pictures and I'll furnish the war."

2 In the 1890s Hearst's *New York Journal* was locked in a titanic circulation battle with Joseph Pulitzer's *World,* with Hearst pouring his resources into the struggle. Someone observed to his mother that he was losing a million dollars a year. Mrs. Hearst was unmoved. "Is he?" she said. "Then he will only last about thirty years."

3 Hearst offered columnist Arthur Brisbane a six-month vacation on full pay as a reward for his dedicated and successful work. When Brisbane refused, Hearst asked him why. The journalist advanced two reasons: "The first is that if I quit writing for six months it might damage the circulation of your newspapers." He paused for a moment; then: "The second reason is that it might not."

4 Considering the high moral tone expected of people in public life at that time, Hearst's thirty-year relationship with actress Marion Davies evoked surprisingly little scandal, even in newspapers owned by rivals. Hearst himself refused to discuss it. "I'm not saying it's right, I'm saying it *is,*" he declared flatly.

—◦◦—

HECHT, Ben (1894–1964), *US playwright, novelist, and scriptwriter.*

1 Although Ben Hecht was paid $2,500 a week to promote Florida real estate during the Florida property boom of the early 1920s, he himself never believed the boom would last. Soon people began remarking how plump Hecht was becoming; this was because he hid all his earnings in bankrolls about his person and never deposited any of the money in a bank. When the crash came, he was one of the few people to escape with the money he had made during the boom years.

HEGEL, Georg Wilhelm (1770–1831), *German idealist philosopher.*

1 On his deathbed Hegel complained, "Only one man ever understood me." He fell silent for a while and then added, "And he didn't understand me."

HEGGEN, Thomas (1919–49), *US writer.*

1 When Heggen's *Mister Roberts* appeared, the publishers arranged for him to make some public appearances to advertise the book. His first speaking engagement was at a luncheon in a New York hotel. Throughout the meal he sat among the ladies at the head table, paralyzed with apprehension and unable to swallow anything. Called upon to speak, he stood up and, overcome with nerves, failed to utter a single word. A neighbor, seeing his agony, tried to get him started by saying kindly, "Perhaps you can tell us how you wrote your book." Heggen gulped and the words suddenly came: "Well, shit, it was just that I was on this boat . . ."

HEIDEGGER, John James (?1659–1749), *Swiss impresario.*

1 Heidegger was famous for his ugliness, recorded for posterity in a number of William Hogarth's prints. He once bet Lord Chesterfield that he would not be able to produce anyone uglier. The earl eventually came up with an old woman who was said to be marginally more hideous. Heidegger quickly borrowed his rival's bonnet, settled it on his head, and was awarded the victory.

HEIFETZ, Jascha (1901–87), *Russian-born violinist.*

1 Jascha Heifetz once attended a vaudeville show at which a man performed various acrobatic feats while playing a violin: standing on his head, holding the instrument behind his back, turning somersaults. Heifetz watched for some time, frowned, and then said to his companion, "Why doesn't he play it straight?"

2 When he played in trios with pianist Artur Rubinstein and cellist Gregor Piatigorsky, Heifetz complained that Rubinstein always got first billing. "If the Almighty himself played the violin," he once said, "the credits would still read, 'Rubinstein, God, and Piatigorsky,'" in that order."

3 In New York for a Carnegie Hall recital, Heifetz was still practicing in his hotel room at midnight on the eve of the concert. An irate fellow guest phoned to complain about the noise. "But I'm Jascha Heifetz," said the violinist. "I don't care if you're Lawrence Welk," retorted the female voice at the other end of the line. "I want to get some sleep."

4 Shortly after his appointment as professor of music at the University of California, Los Angeles, Heifetz was asked what had prompted this change of direction in his career. "Violin-playing is a perishable art," said Heifetz solemnly. "It must be passed on as a personal skill; otherwise it is lost." Then, with a smile, he continued: "I remember my old violin professor in Russia. He said that someday I would be good enough to teach."

HEINE, Heinrich (1797–1856), *German poet.*

1 In 1841 Heine married Eugénie Mirat, a saleswoman in a Parisian boot shop. She was uneducated, foolish, and vain. Heine's affection for her did not preclude an awareness of

her shortcomings. At his death he left her his whole estate on condition that she marry again, "because then there will be at least one man who will regret my death."

2 In 1845 Heine first showed the symptoms of the crippling spinal disease that condemned him to a "mattress grave" for many years before his end. He viewed the approach of death calmly, refusing to be drawn into a display of religious zeal. "God will pardon me," he said. "It's his profession." It was with less equanimity, however, that he viewed the possibility of leaving things unsaid. His last words were, "Write . . . write . . . pencil . . . paper."

3 Heine died in poverty, deserted by his friends. The sole person to attend his deathbed in his squalid Parisian garret was the composer Berlioz. "I always thought you were an original, Berlioz," observed the dying man.

⌘

HELD, Woodie (1932–), *US baseball player.*

1 An undistinguished major league player, Held served on various teams without ever achieving distinction. But his well-meant advice to fellow players has survived: "Don't forget to swing hard, in case you hit the ball."

⌘

HELLMAN, Lillian (1905–84), *US dramatist*

1 *Harper's Magazine* once sent out a questionnaire to a selected number of prominent men. One question was: "During what activity, situation, moment, or series of moments do you feel most masculine?" Having processed the replies, the editor felt it might be interesting to send the questionnaire to a similar group of celebrated women. Lillian Hellman was among the chosen number. She

replied: "It makes me feel masculine to tell you that I do not answer questions like this without being paid for answering them."

⌘

"Most of the rich have liked partying, and since the less rich like being the admiring guests of their financial betters, there is a never-ending stream of party fodder. Though perhaps not always with the happiest of results — as the slightly down-market guests of the Emperor Heliogabalus discovered when one of them remarked how pleasant it would be to be smothered in the scent of roses that adorned the imperial table, and the rest agreed. Taking them at their word, the next time the same guests came to dinner the emperor had several tons of petals dumped over the dinner table. The guests' reaction on this occasion passed unrecorded. They had suffocated."

— DAVID FROST AND MICHAEL DEAKIN,
*David Frost's Book of Millionaires,
Multimillionaires, and Really Rich People*

⌘

HELMSLEY, Leona (1921–), *US real estate entrepreneur.*

1 After she and her husband and business partner, Harry Helmsley, were convicted of tax evasion, the multimillionaire and real estate baroness snapped at reporters, "Only the little people pay taxes."

⌘

HEMINGWAY, Ernest (1899–1961), *US novelist and short-story writer.*

1 The threat of starvation can bring unusual foods to the table, as Hemingway discovered during the course of a particularly hard Paris winter. In order to feed his family, which he was unable to do by selling stories, he resorted to catching pigeons in the Luxembourg Gardens when the gendarme on duty

went into a café for a glass of wine. Having lured the pigeons with a handful of corn, Hemingway dispatched the luckless creatures with an expert twist of the neck. He then concealed the bodies under the blanket in his son Bumby's carriage in order to take them home to be cooked and eaten.

2 Hemingway left his wife, Hadley, and their small son in 1926 and moved to 2 *bis* rue Feron, Paris, where Pauline Pfeiffer, whom he would later marry, awaited him. He was asked why he had left Hadley. In his best Hemingway prose the novelist answered, "Because I am a bastard."

3 Hemingway's contract with his publishers, Scribner's, contained a clause prohibiting the publishers from changing a single word in his manuscripts. Maxwell Perkins, then an editor with Scribner's, was reading *Death in the Afternoon* when he came across the word "fuck." He decided to apply to the highest authority to get a ruling on whether to delete it. He read the passage to the elderly Charles Scribner, head of the firm, who was just about to leave the office and did not feel capable of reaching an immediate decision. "We will have to discuss this fully when I come back from lunch," said the distinguished publisher, and on his notepad headed "What To Do Today" jotted down the one word: "Fuck."

4 F. Scott Fitzgerald remarked to Hemingway that the rich "are not as we are." "No," replied Hemingway, unimpressed. "They have more money."

5 In 1918, toward the end of World War I, Hemingway was wounded at Fossalta di Piave on the Austro-Italian front. Some thirty years later, passing the same spot on his way to Venice, he got out of his car and buried a 1,000-lira note in the ground. With this gesture, he reasoned, he had now contributed both blood and money to Italian soil.

6 Hemingway won the Nobel Prize for Literature in 1954. Five years earlier it had been awarded to another American novelist, William Faulkner. The two writers did not have a very high opinion of each other. Faulkner said of Hemingway that he had no courage, that "he had never been known to use a word that might send the reader to the dictionary." When Hemingway heard this, he said, "Poor Faulkner. Does he really think big emotions come from big words? He thinks I don't know the ten-dollar words. I know them all right. But there are older and simpler and better words, and those are the ones I use."

7 Hemingway's son Patrick asked his father to edit a story he had written. Hemingway went through the manuscript carefully, then returned it to his son. "But, Papa," cried Patrick in dismay, "you've only changed one word."

"If it's the right word," said Hemingway, "that's a lot."

8 (Yousuf Karsh tells of preparing to photograph Hemingway.)

"I had gone the evening before to La Floridita, Hemingway's favorite bar [in Havana] to do my 'homework' and sample his favorite concoction, the daiquiri. But one can be overprepared! When, at nine the next morning, Hemingway called from the kitchen, 'What will you have to drink?' my reply was, I thought, letter-perfect: 'Daiquiri, sir.' 'Good God, Karsh,' Hemingway remonstrated, 'at *this* hour of the day?'"

9 In a Sun Valley restaurant a stranger asked Hemingway for his autograph. "Thanks, Mr. Hemingway," the pleased visitor said cheerily when he got the signature. He passed the table again and said, "Hello, Mr. Hemingway." Intoxicated by being so near the great man, the stranger permitted himself another walk past, this time calling out, "Hi,

Ernest!" Further giddied by Hemingway's acknowledging nod, the man made one final pass, this time calling, "Hello, Papa!" Hemingway lowered his beard and raised his arms. "Hellooo!" he roared. "And good-byyyyye!"

HENRI IV (1553–1610), *king of France.*

1 One of the turning points in Henri's struggle to assert his claim to the throne of France was at Arques in September 1589, when his force of seven thousand men defeated the twenty-three-thousand-strong army of the Duke of Mayenne. Henri announced his victory to an absent comrade-at-arms with the famous message: *"Pends-toi, brave Crillon; nous avons combattu à Arques, et tu n'y étais pas"* (Hang yourself, brave Crillon; we fought at Arques, and you were not there).

2 Paris was one of the centers that held out most stubbornly against the Protestant forces. Henri, who had made a feigned abjuration of his faith to escape the massacre of the Protestants in 1572, decided once again that a lasting peace between the warring religious groups was more important than his personal religious inclinations. In July 1593 he solemnly converted to Roman Catholicism. All opposition collapsed and Paris opened its gates to him. As he rode into his capital city, he is said to have remarked, "Paris is well worth a mass."

3 Greatly taken by the beauty of one of the young ladies of his court, the king asked her to tell him how to reach her bedchamber. "Through the church, sire," was the reply.

4 As the king passed through a small town, a deputation of burgesses was drawn up at the gates to receive him. Just as the leading dignitary began his speech of welcome, a donkey nearby started to bray. The king turned toward the noisy creature and said with great gravity, "Gentlemen, one at a time, please."

5 On his way to dinner, Henri was accosted by a suppliant who began his address with "Sire, Agesilaus, king of Lacedaemon —" Alert to the danger signs of a bore, Henri interrupted, "I have heard of him — but he has dined, and I have not."

6 Henri IV, who disliked long-windedness, happened to meet an ecclesiastic on the road one day. "Where do you come from? Where are you going? What is your purpose?" demanded the king. "From Bourges — to Paris — a benefice," replied the priest. Delighted at this terse response, the king exclaimed, "You shall have it!"

HENRY, O. (1862–1910), *US short-story master, born William Sidney Porter.*

1 Characteristic of O. Henry are the words he is reputed to have uttered (quoting from a popular song of the day) just before his death: "Don't turn down the light. I'm afraid to go home in the dark."

2 Henry wrote to his publisher, Frank Munsey, requesting an advance of $50. Munsey replied that as Henry was already several stories in arrears, there would be "no advance unless I know what you want it for." He received by return mail a sealed envelope containing a single long blonde hair. Henry got the advance.

HENRY II (1133–89), *king of England (1154–89).*

1 One of Henry's advisers and friends in the early part of his reign was Thomas à Becket. He appointed Becket chancellor in 1154 and archbishop of Canterbury in 1162, hoping to bring the powers of church and state into

harmony under his control. Becket, however, resigned the chancellorship and went into exile in France. After nearly seven years abroad, he and Henry were reconciled. Becket returned, only to defy the king again over his attempts to exert control over the church. Henry was spending Christmas near Bayeux, in France, when a deputation of bishops came to him to tell him of Becket's continuing intransigence. "Will no one rid me of this turbulent priest!" Henry raged. Four knights, members of his household, took him literally. They crossed the Channel, rode posthaste to Canterbury, and murdered Becket at the altar of Canterbury cathedral.

HENRY IV (1367–1413), *king of England (1399–1413)*.

1 Henry's cherished wish was to lead a crusade to the Holy Land and recapture Jerusalem from the infidel, as an expiation for his deposition of Richard. Since the threats to his throne from internal feuding made it seem impossible that he would realize this ambition, he was encouraged when a soothsayer told him he would die only in Jerusalem. Early in 1413 he suffered a stroke while praying in Westminster Abbey, and was carried into the abbot's house. The name of the room in which he died was the Jerusalem Chamber.

HENRY VIII (1491–1547), *king of England (1509–47)*.

1 Henry VIII designated a particular nobleman as his ambassador to King Francis I of France, at a time when relations between the two countries were at a very low ebb. The peer, listening to Henry's aggressive message, begged to be excused because, he said, the hot-tempered French king might well have him executed if he delivered it. Henry reassured him by saying that if Francis killed him, there were a dozen Frenchmen in England whose heads Henry could strike off. "But of all these heads, there may not be one to fit my shoulders," persisted the reluctant ambassador.

2 Henry's powerful minister Thomas Cromwell, wishing to strengthen England's links with Protestant Europe, arranged that Henry should marry the Flemish Anne of Cleves as his fourth wife. Hans Holbein painted a delightful portrait of the princess, which was sent to Henry and encouraged him to look forward to his new bride with joyful anticipation. When she finally arrived, the princess turned out to be much homelier than her portrait. "You have sent me a Flanders mare," exclaimed the disappointed bridegroom in disgust.

Thomas Jefferson Hogg, biographer of Percy Bysshe Shelley, once told the story of a Cambridge mathematician who, having never read Milton's *Paradise Lost*, was finally prevailed upon to do so. "I have read your famous poem," the mathematician is reported to have said. "I have read it attentively: but what does it prove? There is more instruction in half a page of Euclid! A man might read Milton's poem a hundred, aye, a thousand times, and he would never learn that the angles at the base of an isosceles triangle are equal!"

HENSON, Josiah (1789–1883), *US leader in the early abolitionist movement*.

1 Henson was introduced to the archbishop of Canterbury, who was so impressed by his bearing and speech that he inquired the name of the university at which he had studied. "The university of adversity," replied Henson.

HENZE, Hans Werner (1926–), *German composer.*

1 The German composer was premiering his newest work, a pro-Marxist opera that found few fans. Critics disliked it, as did many of its cast members. And Henze himself was not popular. One night the tenor Robert Tear told his fellow musicians that the audience for that night's performance would be let in for free, to boost attendance. After a pause he added, "But they are having to pay to get out."

HEPBURN, Katharine (1907–), *US actress, winner of four Academy Awards.*

1 During the earlier part of her great career, Katharine Hepburn made a series of pictures she herself considered "boring." In the trade she was put down as "Box Office Poison." Reviews were not flattering. Just about this time, however, the writer Cleveland Amory noticed in a Hartford, Connecticut, paper a glowing pro-Hepburn notice. Amory, in conversation with Kate's father, a Hartford urologist, commented on this pleasant shift in journalistic appreciation of Miss Hepburn. Dr. Hepburn fixed his gaze on Mr. Amory. "Do you know what I do?"

"No."

"I specialize in what is known as the 'Old Man's Operation.' I have operated on half of the newspaper publishers of this city and I confidently expect to operate on the other half."

2 A reporter noticed that Miss Hepburn, during the filming of *The Lion in Winter,* was wearing sneakers under her twelfth-century robes. Asked why she had made such an odd choice of footwear, Miss Hepburn replied, "I play Eleanor of Aquitaine, queen of England — and also a practical woman who believed in comfort."

3 Later in her life Hepburn dressed in very comfortable, if not glamorous, clothes. She was said to own twenty identical sets of slacks (beige), shirts (white), and sweaters (black) that she could don every day, thus avoiding having to choose an outfit. "Dressing up is a bore," she said. "At a certain age, you decorate yourself to attract the opposite sex, and at a certain age, I did that. But I'm past that age."

HERFORD, Oliver (1863–1935), *US humorist, illustrator, and writer of light verse.*

1 Herford was short of money in the early days of his career. The manager of his hotel, aware of his guest's precarious financial situation, did not insist on immediate payment, but simply added any money owing at the end of a week to the bill for the following week. One day, as the two men passed in the hotel foyer, the manager asked Herford if he had received his latest bill. Herford simply replied, "Yes."

"Is that all you have to say?"

"At the moment, yes," said the humorist. "But if the bill gets any larger, I'll have to ask you for a larger room."

HERMAN, Floyd (1903–87), *US baseball player.*

1 "Babe" Herman, so-called because he used extra-weighty bats in an effort to out-hit his idol, Babe Ruth, played so well one year that Dodgers' owner Charles Ebbets offered him a trip around the world. "Frankly," said Herman, "I'd prefer someplace else."

HERSCHEL, Sir William (1738–1822), *British astronomer, discoverer of the planet Uranus.*

1 As news of Herschel's discoveries became known in the 1780s, what most caught the popular imagination was that the astronomer's powerful new telescopes revealed stars to be circular objects instead of the rayed or spiky shapes that they appeared to the naked eye. At a dinner Herschel was placed next to the great physicist Henry Cavendish. Conversation between these two scientific giants did not flourish, no doubt mainly on account of Cavendish's notorious awkwardness in public. At length Cavendish leaned forward. "Is it true, Dr. Herschel, that you see the stars round?" he asked, very slowly. "Round as a button," replied Herschel. Cavendish lapsed into a silence that lasted until the end of the meal. Then he leaned forward again. "Round as a button?" he asked. "Round as a button," affirmed Herschel. And that was the end of their conversation.

———— ✧ ————

HESS, Dame Myra (1890–1965), *English pianist and harpsichordist.*

1 Dame Myra approached Sir Thomas Beecham before a concert one evening. "Are you going to conduct by heart again tonight, Sir Thomas?" she asked. "Of course," replied the conductor. "In that case," announced Dame Myra, "*I* am going to use my music."

———— ✧ ————

HEVESY, Georg de (1885–1966), *Hungarian chemist, awarded the 1943 Nobel Prize for Chemistry.*

1 Suspecting the quality of food served at his lodgings, Hevesy decided to conduct a simple experiment at dinner one evening. While his landlady's back was turned he slipped a microscopic amount of a certain radioactive substance into a piece of rather fatty meat that he had left at the side of his plate. The following day, meat hash was served for dinner. Hevesy passed a Geiger counter over his plate: its ominous clicks confirmed his worst suspicions. Within a few days he had changed his lodgings.

———— ✧ ————

HEYERDAHL, Thor (1914–), *Norwegian anthropologist and explorer.*

1 On a visit to London, Heyerdahl had a busy schedule of appointments. Shortly after recording a program for the Independent Television Network, he was due at the BBC studios for an interview. Having been assured by the BBC that a taxi would be sent to pick him up from the ITN studios, Heyerdahl waited expectantly in the lobby. As the minutes ticked by, however, he began to grow anxious. He approached a little man in a flat cap, who looked as if he might be a taxi driver and was obviously searching for someone. "I'm Thor Heyerdahl," said the anthropologist. "Are you looking for me?" "No, mate," replied the taxi driver. "I've been sent to pick up four Airedales for the BBC."

———— ✧ ————

HIDEYOSHI (1536–98), *Japanese warlord.*

1 Hideyoshi commissioned a colossal statue of Buddha for a shrine in Kyoto. It took fifty thousand men five years to build, and Hideyoshi himself sometimes worked incognito alongside the laborers. The work had scarcely been completed when the earthquake of 1596 brought the roof of the shrine crashing down and wrecked the statue. In a rage Hideyoshi loosed an arrow at the fallen colossus. "I put you here at great expense," he shouted, "and you can't even look after your own temple!"

HILBERT, David (1862–1943), *German mathematician.*

1 The Hungarian-American mathematician George Pólya likes to tell stories about Hilbert's absentmindedness. At a party at the great mathematician's house his wife noticed that her husband had neglected to put on a clean shirt. She ordered him to do so. He went upstairs; ten minutes passed; Hilbert did not return. Mrs. Hilbert went up to the bedroom to find Hilbert lying peacefully in bed. As Pólya puts it, "You see, it was the natural sequence of things. He took off his coat, then his tie, then his shirt, and so on, and went to sleep."

2 George Pólya tells another story about the Göttingen of more than half a century ago. Each new member of the faculty, dressed in black coat and top hat, was supposed to make a brief, formal call on the senior professors. One such knocked on Hilbert's door; Mrs. Hilbert decided for her husband that he was at home. The new colleague entered, sat down, put his top hat on the floor, started a conversation. Hilbert, whose mind may well have been on some profound mathematical problem, listened to the flow of talk with growing impatience. Finally he took the top hat from the floor, put it on his head, took his wife's arm, said, "My dear, I think we have delayed our good colleague long enough," and walked out of his own house.

HILL, John (?1716–75), *British botanist, miscellaneous writer, and charlatan.*

1 Failing to secure a nomination to the Royal Society, Hill switched his considerable satirical powers from the theater, hitherto his favorite target, to the sciences. From Portsmouth he sent a bogus communication to the society describing the case of a sailor who had broken a leg in a fall from the rigging and who had had it treated with bandages and tarwater to such good effect that within three days he was able to use the leg as well as ever. This revelation occasioned some solemn discussion, in the midst of which another letter arrived from the joker: he had forgotten to mention in his first communication that the leg in question was wooden.

HILL, Rowland (1744–1833), *British preacher.*

1 During a heavy rainstorm a number of people took shelter in the chapel where Hill was preaching. "People who make religion their cloak are rightly censured," he remarked, "but I consider that those who make it their umbrella are not much better."

2 Hill received an anonymous letter attacking him for driving to chapel in his carriage and reminding him that this was not the example set by Christ. Hill agreed, adding, "If the writer of this letter would come to my house saddled and bridled next Sunday, I will gladly follow our Lord's example."

HILLARY, Sir Edmund (1919–), *New Zealand explorer and mountaineer who, with his Sherpa guide, Tenzing Norgay, first climbed Mount Everest.*

1 The dramatic photograph of Tenzing Norgay on the summit of Everest went around the world. Later people wondered why there was no companion picture of Hillary. The explorer wrote that he had not asked the Sherpa to reciprocate because "as far as I knew, he had never taken a photograph before, and the summit of Everest was hardly the place to show him how."

HINDEMITH, Paul (1895–1963), *German composer.*

1 "The composer Paul Hindemith was once conducting a rehearsal of one of his more dissonant orchestral compositions. At one point, he rapped his baton and said, 'No, no, gentlemen; even though it sounds wrong, it's still not right!'"

HINDENBURG, Paul von (1847–1934), *German general and president of the Weimar Republic (1925–34).*

1 Early on the morning of the presidential election, Hindenburg was woken up by his son, who excitedly told him that he'd just been elected president of Germany. "Why did you wake me?" exclaimed the general. "It still would have been true at eight o'clock."

HITCHCOCK, Sir Alfred (1889–1980), *British film director.*

1 Hitchcock, who enjoyed food, was put out to find totally inadequate quantities served up at a private dinner he attended. Toward the end of the evening the host said, "I do hope you will dine with us again soon."

"By all means," assented Hitchcock. "Let's start now."

2 Working with Hitchcock early in her career, actress Ingrid Bergman was uncomfortable about the way he had asked her to play a certain scene. "I don't think I can do that naturally," she told him, and went on to explain her difficulties and suggest possible alternatives. Hitchcock listened solemnly, nodding from time to time; Miss Bergman felt she had won her case. "All right," he finally said, "if you can't do it naturally, then *fake* it."

3 Hitchcock had a habit of falling asleep at parties. On one occasion, he had been asleep for nearly four hours when his wife woke him up and suggested that they go home. "But it's only one o'clock," protested Hitchcock. "They'll think we aren't enjoying ourselves!"

4 Hitchcock watched with fascination as his wife prepared a cheese soufflé. After she had put the dish into the oven his eyes remained glued to the oven door. "What *is* going on behind that door?" he asked every few minutes, lowering his voice to a whisper in case a sudden noise should prevent the soufflé from rising. By the time the dish was ready, and Mrs. Hitchcock opened the oven door to reveal a perfect soufflé, Hitchcock was in a state of nervous exhaustion. "No more soufflés until we have an oven with a glass door," he said. "I can't *stand* the suspense."

5 Hitchcock never sat among the audience to watch his films. "Don't you miss hearing them scream?" he was once asked. "No," replied Hitchcock. "I can hear them when I'm making the picture."

6 Driving through a Swiss city one day, Hitchcock suddenly pointed out of the car window and said, "That is the most frightening sight I have ever seen." His companion was surprised to see nothing more alarming than a priest in conversation with a little boy, his hand on the child's shoulder. "Run, little boy," cried Hitchcock, leaning out of the car. "Run for your life!"

7 When the shooting of *The 39 Steps* began, Hitchcock amused himself by handcuffing the star, Madeleine Carroll, to her co-star Robert Donat and pretending to lose the key until the end of the day. He was particularly interested in seeing how the unfortunate cou-

ple would cope with the inevitable demands of nature.

HOBSON, Laura Z. (1900–86), *US writer.*

1 Laura Zametkin married Thayer Hobson and thenceforward used the name Hobson both socially and professionally. During the pre–World War II period, when Hitler's Nazis were beginning their murderous attacks on Jews, she was a guest at a fashionable New York dinner party. Some deplored "those awful Germans." Others took their excesses lightly. One remarked, "The chosen people ask for it, wherever they are." Another came up with the conventional cliché: "Some of my best friends are Jews." At which point Mrs. Hobson spoke up quietly: "Some of mine are, too. Including my father and mother."

There was a moment's silence. Then the conversation resumed.

HOBSON, Thomas (?1544–1631), *English carrier.*

1 When customers came to Hobson to hire a horse, he would take them into the stable to make their choice, telling them that they must take the horse standing nearest to the stable door. Thus Hobson ensured that each customer had an equal chance of hiring a good or bad horse and that each horse had an equal chance of receiving good or bad treatment.

HOFFMANN, Ernst Theodor Wilhelm (1776–1822), *German novelist, composer, and theatrical manager.*

1 Hoffmann was once the guest of a Berlin *nouveau riche,* who after dinner showed him around his lavishly decorated house. Speaking of his domestics, the millionaire mentioned casually that he needed three servants for his personal attendance. Hoffmann replied that he had four just to take care of his bath: one to lay out the towels, one to test the temperature of the water, and the third to make sure the faucets were in good order.

"And the fourth?"

"Oh, he's the most important of all — he takes my bath for me."

HOFMANN, Josef Casimir (1876–1957), *Polish-born pianist.*

1 Hofmann was just five feet five inches tall, his hands so small that he had to have a keyboard specially made for him. A musician called Felix Salmond went backstage after a Hofmann concert. Salmond was a very tall man, more than a foot taller than Hofmann. As he bent over to congratulate the pianist, he said solemnly, "You are a giant."

2 During a train ride Hofmann sat gazing straight ahead, motionless, his eyes apparently unfocused. "What are you doing?" inquired his traveling companion. "Practicing," said the pianist.

3 At a concert one evening, members of the orchestra were concerned to see a look of bewilderment pass over Hofmann's face as he settled himself at the piano. Leaning toward a lady in the front row of the audience, the pianist whispered, "May I please see your program, madam? I forget what comes first."

HOGAN, Ben (1912–97), *US golfer.*

1 An amateur player once called Hogan to ask for some advice on his game. Hogan, not known for his sociability, asked what brand of golf clubs the caller used. When told he

used Dunlop clubs, Hogan barked, "Then you can call Mr. Dunlop and ask him!"

HOGARTH, William (1697–1764), *British painter and engraver.*

1 Hogarth was commissioned to paint the portrait of an exceptionally ugly nobleman. As was his custom, he depicted the sitter with the utmost frankness and realism. When the nobleman saw the portrait, he refused to pay for it. An acrimonious discussion ensued. Eventually Hogarth, needing the money, sent a letter to his client, saying that a certain showman who specialized in exhibiting wild beasts and freaks or monstrosities was interested in the portrait. Unless Hogarth received payment within three days, he proposed to embellish the picture with a tail and other appendages and to sell it to the showman for exhibition. The nobleman paid up, took delivery of the portrait, and burned it.

HOKUSAI (1760–1849), *Japanese painter and illustrator.*

1 Looking back toward the end of his long life on his artistic output, Hokusai dismissed as nothing all the work he had done before the age of fifty; it was only after he had reached seventy that he felt he was turning out work of note. At age eighty-nine, on his deathbed, he lamented, "If heaven had granted me five more years, I could have become a real painter."

HOLLES, Denzil Holles, 1st Baron (1599–1680), *British statesman.*

1 The first great constitutional crisis of Charles I's reign occurred in 1629 when the king, finding that Parliament would not do as he wished but instead had produced a document censuring his policies, tried to dissolve the sitting. Uproar ensued in the House, as the Speaker made as if to obey the king's command and leave the chamber. Denzil Holles shouted, "God's wounds! You shall sit here till we please to rise," and, going to the Speaker's chair, he and another man held the Speaker down in it while the paper condemning illegal taxes and Roman Catholicism was read.

HOLLIDAY, Judy [Judith Tuvim] (1922–65), *US comedienne.*

1 At a movie interview, Judy Holliday found herself being chased around the room by a lecherous studio head. Unperturbed, she put her hand inside her dress and pulled out her falsies. "Here," she said, handing them to her dumfounded pursuer, "I think this is what you want."

HOLMES, Fanny Dixwell (1841–1929), *wife of Oliver Wendell Holmes, Jr.*

1 When her husband was appointed Supreme Court justice, Fanny Holmes was rather apprehensive about the social life she would encounter in Washington. Their first White House function was a big formal dinner to welcome the new justice. Fanny was greeted by President Theodore Roosevelt, who chatted with her, asking her whether she had seen much of Washington yet, whether she had been to Congress, whether she had met many people. Fanny replied politely that a number of congressmen's wives had called on her. But there was a certain note in her voice that caused the President to ask, "You found the ladies pleasant?" Fanny replied, "Washington is full of famous men and the women they married when they were young." The

President laughed heartily and, with Fanny on his arm, led everyone in to dinner. Fanny was never again nervous attending functions in Washington.

2 Justice Holmes was very fussy about his books. One day in their Washington home, discovering that a volume that he wanted was either lost or misplaced, he made an uproar, worrying his secretary, the butler, and the servants about it before he went off to the Supreme Court. Fanny did not say a single word, but when her husband returned, he found the book in its place on the shelf. An American flag stuck out above it, and underneath Fanny had hung a neatly printed sign: "I am a very old man. I have had many troubles, most of which never happened."

3 Mr. Larcum, who ran the livery stable at Beverly Farms where the Holmeses spent their summers, used to drive Mrs. Holmes about on various errands. One afternoon when he was driving her to meet Justice Holmes, the horse bolted and could not be stopped until they reached their destination. Mrs. Holmes did not panic, nor even appear to be scared; she just leaned out, waving her parasol, and called, "Larcum! If you kill me, tell him I loved him."

———— cᴎɔ ————

HOLMES, John (1812–99), *US lawyer; brother of Oliver Wendell Holmes, Sr.*

1 A kind, unassuming man, John Holmes learned early on to live with his brother's fame and reputation. At a party attended by numerous celebrities, a boy went around collecting autographs. When offered the piece of paper to sign, John Holmes wrote simply, "John Holmes, *frère de mon frère*" (my brother's brother).

2 John Holmes was most often described as "homely." Contented to be outshone by his elder brother, he claimed that he had been

paid only one compliment in his life. When he was six, the maid brushing his hair turned to his mother and said, "I don't think John's so *awful* cross-eyed, ma'am."

3 When John Holmes lay dying, he had been comatose and motionless for such a long time that the people around his bed began to wonder whether he might not already have died. The nurse, finding no pulse, announced that she would just feel his feet to see if they were warm. "If they are, he's alive," she said. "Nobody ever died with warm feet." "John Rogers did," said Holmes distinctly. He never spoke again.

———— cᴎɔ ————

HOLMES, Oliver Wendell, Sr. (1809–94), *US writer and physician.*

1 Holmes arrived at the house of a poor patient one morning to find the priest about to depart. "Your patient is very ill," said the priest solemnly. "He is going to die." Holmes nodded. "Yes, and he's going to hell," he said. The priest was horrified. "I have just given him extreme unction," he exclaimed. "You must not say such things!" Holmes shrugged his shoulders. "Well, you expressed a medical opinion," he retorted, "and I have just as much right to a theological opinion."

2 Oliver Wendell Holmes proved that money has a universal appeal that can affect the great as well as the lowly. On receiving an invitation to deliver a lecture, he sent back the following reply: "I have at hand your kind invitation. However, I am far from being in good physical health. I am satisfied that if I were offered a fifty-dollar bill after my lecture, I would not have strength enough to refuse it."

3 Henry James, father of the novelist, once said to his friend Holmes, "You are intellectually the most alive man I ever knew." "I am, I

am," cried Holmes. "From the crown of my head to the sole of my foot, I'm alive, I'm alive!"

4 Holmes's love of flattery continued unabated into his old age, and he used his hardness of hearing to indulge it. "I am a trifle deaf, you know," he would say to someone who had just praised his latest work. "Do you mind repeating that a little louder?"

5 In old age, Holmes was often bothered by the attentions of devoted admirers who would follow him home from church and even attempt to follow him into his house. On one occasion he tried to elude some pursuers by taking back alleys, but found them still on his trail as he neared home. He summoned enough energy to run up the steps and open the front door. Then he turned to confront the group who rushed after him. "Don't come in," he said. "It's catching and I've got it."

———— ✺ ————

HOLMES, Oliver Wendell, Jr. (1841–1935), *US lawyer, Supreme Court judge.*

1 Oliver Wendell Holmes, Jr., fought in the Civil War and was wounded three times. While he was recovering at home from his second injury, visitors came to the family home to pay their respects to the wounded hero. Expecting reflections on glory and patriotism, they were offended by what he said: "War? War is an organized bore."

2 When he recovered from his third Civil War wound Oliver Wendell Holmes, Jr., decided to return to law school as the army did not need him for a while. He knocked on the door of his father's study so that he could inform him of this decision. He found his father at work, and said without preamble, "I am going to the law school." Dr. Holmes looked up from his desk. "What's the use of that, Wendell?" he said. "A lawyer can't be a great man."

3 (After his father's death Wendell had to settle into the house that his father had so dominated by his presence.)

"Gradually [Wendell assumed] the privileges of the manor. Things he had not dared to touch he began now to use as his own. Grandfather Jackson's high desk stood in a corner of the library. Wendell had always been proud of Judge Jackson, pleased when in court he had to refer to his opinions. Now he stood at the desk to write his opinions. 'Doesn't it tire you?' Fanny asked, watching him write, one knee propped against the desk. 'Yes,' Wendell replied. 'But it's salutary. Nothing conduces to brevity like a caving in of the knees.'"

4 Charles Hopkinson's impressive portrait of Justice Holmes, which hangs in the library of the Law School at Harvard, is a full-length picture of the judge in judicial robes, with distinguished white hair and mustache. When Justice Holmes saw the finished picture, he said, "That isn't me, but it's a damn good thing for people to think it is."

5 In his eighty-seventh year Justice Holmes was out walking with another elderly friend when a pretty girl passed them. The judge turned to watch her and then sighed, "Oh, to be seventy again!"

6 Throughout his judicial career Holmes had a reputation for independence of judgment that earned him the title of "the Great Dissenter." It is said that when he was in his eighty-eighth year, a newspaperman in search of copy about the old judge asked passersby in Capitol Square whether they had heard of Justice Holmes. "Holmes?" replied an overalled mechanic, looking up from the sports page of his newspaper. "Oh, sure! He's the young judge on the Supreme

Court that's always disagreeing with the old guys."

7 At the age of ninety-one, Justice Holmes resigned from the Supreme Court and spent the following summer at his country house in Massachusetts. Old friends from Boston came to see him, bringing their grandchildren, whose company Holmes greatly enjoyed. Sitting on the porch with Betsy Warder, aged sixteen, and discussing life with her, he said, "I won't refrain from talking about anything because you're too young, if you won't because I'm too old."

8 Holmes often scoffed at death, asserting that he was not afraid of what he called his "old friend." In his nineties he liked to say that his last words would surely be "Have faith and pursue the unknown end." When, at the age of ninety-four, he was sent to the hospital deathly ill, he saw the medical machinery that awaited him and uttered his true last words: "Lot of damn foolery."

———— ✺ ————

HOMER, Winslow (1836–1910), *US painter.*

1 The artist Leon Kroll was having trouble with a seascape. "My boy," said Winslow Homer, "if you want to make a great sea, use only two waves."

———— ✺ ————

HOOK, Theodore Edward (1788–1841), *British journalist and wit.*

1 Hook's most famous practical joke was the Berners Street hoax. A certain Mrs. Tottenham, who lived on this fashionable London thoroughfare, had offended Hook. He took his revenge by sending out hundreds of letters inviting people of all ranks of society on various pretexts to visit her house on the same day. Hook and his friends then watched from a vantage point opposite as the car-

riages of the Duke of Gloucester, the lord mayor of London, and other notables struggled through the bedlam of chimney sweeps, draymen, and tradesmen of all sorts, besieging Mrs. Tottenham's house and bringing the usual business of Berners Stret to a chaotic standstill.

2 Hook was rowing up the Thames on an excursion with the comic actor Charles Mathews when their attention was caught by a notice in a waterside garden forbidding unauthorized landings. Incensed, the two men moored, disembarked, and, using their fishing lines as impromptu surveyor's tape, paced to and fro across the lawn, measuring and working out distances. Out came the owner of the property, an alderman of London, to demand what they were doing. Hook introduced himself as an official of a canal company that he said was planning to cut a new canal. This — as far as he could judge it — would go straight through the alderman's garden, right underneath the windows of his house. The poor alderman, dumbfounded, was unable to decide whether to wheedle or bluster. In an attempt to propitiate these unwelcome emissaries, he invited them to dinner, served them excellent food and wine, and tried to dissuade them from ruining his property. It was only over the last bottle of wine that Hook owned up to the hoax.

3 Hook was the guest of an alderman who entertained him with much ostentation and plied him lavishly with food and drink. When Hook was already surfeited, his overattentive host pressed yet another delicacy upon him. "I thank you," said Hook, "but if it's all the same to you, I'll take the rest in money."

4 Toward the end of a successful dinner party, Hook observed that one of his fellow guests, a bookseller, had had rather too much to

drink. Leaning toward his host, Hook remarked in a whisper: "You appear to have emptied your wine cellar into your bookseller."

———— ∽ ————

HOOKER, Joseph (1814–79), *US federal commander.*

1 At the height of the battle of Williamsburg in 1862, reports on the fighting were circulated to the newspapers every few hours. At one point a dispatch arrived relating to an earlier report on General Hooker, whose troops were heavily engaged. The dispatch was labeled "Fighting — Joe Hooker," indicating that it was the continuation of the previous report. However, the typesetter mistook this for a heading, and the dispatch duly appeared in print under the title "Fighting Joe Hooker." Hooker was subsequently nicknamed "Fighting Joe," and the sobriquet remained with him for the rest of his life.

———— ∽ ————

HOOVER, Herbert (1874–1964), *US statesman; 31st President of the United States (1929–33).*

1 Hoover lamented to former President Calvin Coolidge that his attempts to promote economic recovery seemed to be making little impact and that his critics were becoming increasingly angry. "You can't expect to see calves running in the field the day after you put the bull to the cows," said Coolidge soothingly. "No, but I would at least expect to see contented cows," replied the unhappy President.

2 During the Boxer Rebellion Hoover had been in China. In later years his campaign managers wanted to boost his political image by describing in dramatic terms an incident during which Hoover had rescued a Chinese child trapped by gunfire. Hoover read the draft of the story, then threw it into the wastebasket. "You can't make a Teddy Roosevelt out of me," he said.

3 An autograph collector sent a request to President Hoover asking for three signatures; he explained that he wanted one for himself and two to trade for one of Babe Ruth's since "it takes two of yours to get one of Babe Ruth's." Hoover, amused, obliged with three signatures.

4 After suffering some particularly torrid criticism, Hoover pointed from the South Portico of the White House toward the Washington Monument and said, "This, apparently, is the only stable thing in my administration."

———— ∽ ————

HOPE, Bob [Leslie Townes] (1903–), *US comedian and film actor.*

1 On a show one evening, Hope cracked the classic joke about theatrical accommodation: "The hotel room where I'm staying is so small that the rats are round-shouldered." The hotel proprietor was not amused, however, and threatened to sue for damages. Hope agreed to take back the remark. At the beginning of his next show he announced: "I'm sorry I said that the rats in that hotel were round-shouldered. They're not."

———— ∽ ————

HOPKINSON, Francis, *signer of the Declaration of Independence.*

1 Hopkinson was fond of doodling. As he sat in meetings during the momentous days as the Colonies debated the merits of independence from England, he wrote, over and over, the year: "1776." Idly adding up the numbers 1, 7, 7, and 6, the total, 21, intrigued him. Why not institute a 21-gun salute for dignitaries of the new republic? He submitted his idea to Congress, and it has been in use ever since.

HORNE, Lena (1917–), *US singer and entertainer.*

1 (Al Duckett, a freelance journalist during World War II, recounts the following story about Lena Horne.)

"She had been sent to a camp in the south to entertain the troops. She was scheduled to do a performance for the white troops and a separate performance for the black troops and the German prisoners of war. When I was in the service in Fort Dix, the German prisoners would be in the mess line with black troops and you'd have a separate line for white troops. Lena entertained the blacks and the German prisoners and then she left."

HOROWITZ, Vladimir (1904–89), *Russian-born pianist.*

1 As a young pianist Horowitz was shocked by the advice he was given by Artur Schnabel: "When a piece gets difficult, make faces."

2 Horowitz was to perform at Chicago after a long absence from the public stage. Franz Mohr, the chief concert technician of Steinway and Sons, was given the task of ensuring that the piano was in perfect condition. This he did to the best of his ability, but he was not able to relax until Horowitz had given a brilliant rendering of his first number. As was his custom, the pianist then left the stage — but on this occasion did not return. Mohr was summoned backstage. "Where have you been?" exclaimed Horowitz. "I cannot play again. The piano stool is far too high!" Mohr nervously enquired as to the magnitude of the problem. Horowitz held up his hand, his thumb and forefinger about a quarter of an inch apart.

3 Horowitz occasionally had trouble with the English language. At an audience with Mrs. Hoover, wife of the then President of the United States, Herbert Hoover, he bowed and said courteously, "I am delightful."

HORTHY DE NAGYBÁNYA, Miklós (1868–1957), *Hungarian statesman and admiral.*

1 Admiral Horthy always retained his loyalty to the concept of the Hapsburg empire and the Austro-Hungarian axis that had seemed so immutable in his youth. His reactionary yearnings were the target of many malicious tales. Once on a hunting party Horthy shot a big bird, which someone told him was an eagle. "What? An eagle? I always thought an eagle had two heads!" he is reputed to have said, referring to the symbol of the Hapsburg monarchy.

HOUDINI, Harry [Ehrich Weiss] (1874–1926), *US escape artist and magician.*

1 Houdini had a reputation for not paying his fair share of the bill when he dined out with friends. On one occasion, however, a conjuror called Meyenberg managed to get the better of him. After lunching in a restaurant with Houdini and a number of other vaudeville artists, Meyenberg turned to the escapologist and asked, "Would you like to see a new trick? Lay your hands flat on the table, with your palms down." Houdini did as he was told. The conjuror then filled two glasses with water and carefully balanced one on each of Houdini's hands. "Let's see you get out of *that* without paying the bill!" he cried as he and the other performers beat a hasty retreat.

2 Broadway producers Charles Dillingham and Florenz Ziegfeld were among the pallbearers at Houdini's funeral. As they carried

the coffin out of the church, Dillingham leaned across to Ziegfeld and whispered, "Ziggie, I bet you a hundred bucks he ain't in here."

3 Houdini had undergone many rigorous physical challenges in his career. In 1926, as he was sitting in his dressing room reading his mail, an amateur boxer came with some friends to visit the magician and asked if Houdini could really withstand the heaviest blow to his midriff, as he claimed. Casually, and without looking up, Houdini said that he could, whereupon the boxer landed three brutal blows to Houdini's abdomen without warning. Within a day he was feverish and collapsed during his act. A ruptured appendix and peritonitis killed him within a week.

HOUSMAN, A[lfred] E[dward] (1859–1936), *British poet and classical scholar.*

1 As Housman lay dying in a Cambridge nursing home, his doctor, Dr. Woods, remembering his patient's pleasure in risqué anecdotes, repeated to him a witticism ascribed to an English actor who had been asked what actors did to pass the time when they were not working: "We spend half our time lying on the sands looking at the stars and the other half lying on the stars looking at the sands." Housman gasped out, "Indeed — very good. I shall — have to repeat — that — on the Golden Floor."

HOWARD, Catherine (1520–42), *the fifth queen consort of Henry VIII.*

1 After two happy years with Catherine, Henry discovered that she had previously had an affair with a certain Francis Dereham. Henry tried to laugh this off but flew into a rage when he found out that she was still in love with a favorite courtier, Thomas

Culpeper, who had been her fiancé. Catherine and her two lovers were ordered to be beheaded. Defiant as she stood before the block, Catherine announced, "I die a queen. But I would rather die the wife of Thomas Culpeper."

HOWARD, Leslie (1890–1943), *British actor.*

1 The small repertory company in which Howard obtained his early acting experience put on a different show every night and sometimes two different shows in a day. One afternoon Howard forgot his lines. He froze on the stage, but no help came from the prompt corner. "What's my line?" he hissed desperately to the prompter. "What's the play?" came back the equally desperate whisper.

HOWARTH, Humphrey (fl. 1800), *British surgeon.*

1 Challenged to a duel, Howarth appeared at the appointed venue stark naked. His challenger, understandably nonplussed, asked what he thought he was doing. Howarth solemnly explained that if any bit of cloth is carried into the body by gunshot, festering inevitably follows. His opponent averred it would be ridiculous to fight a naked man and the duel was called off.

HOWE, Elias (1819–67), *US inventor of the sewing machine.*

1 A major problem in the development of Howe's sewing machine was the location of the eye of the needle. The inventor was rapidly running out of money and ideas when one night he had a peculiar dream. He was being led to his execution for failing to

design a sewing machine for the king of a strange country. He was surrounded by guards, all of whom carried spears that were pierced near the head. Realizing instantly that this was the solution to his problem, Howe woke up and rushed straight to his workshop. By nine o'clock that morning, the design of the first sewing machine was well on the way to completion.

HOWE, Irving (1920–93), *US literary critic.*

1 The literary critic Howe won a National Book Award for his evocation of Jewish immigation to the United States in a book he called *World of Our Fathers.* At a lecture one evening a woman suggested he might better have titled his book *World of Our Fathers and Mothers.* "*World of Our Fathers* is a title," he snapped. "*World of Our Fathers and Mothers* is a speech."

HOWE, Julia Ward (1819–1910), *US writer and social reformer, remembered chiefly for "The Battle Hymn of the Republic."*

1 Senator Charles Sumner was one of Mrs. Howe's New England circle. On one occasion she invited him to meet the actor Edwin Booth, who was just beginning to become known. Sumner wrote back declining the invitation, remarking loftily, "The truth is, I have got beyond taking an interest in individuals." Mrs. Howe commented in her diary on this arrogant remark: "God Almighty has not got so far."

2 At the age of ninety Mrs. Howe was still playing an active part in public life. On her birthday that year an admirer sent her a card reading, "Greetings to Boston's greatest trinity: Howe, Higginson, and Hale." The other two also were of very advanced age. Mrs.

Howe smilingly remarked, "Well, they can't say we drop our *H*s in Boston."

HOWELLS, William Dean (1837–1920), *US novelist, critic, and editor.*

1 An author was boring Howells with his efforts to extract a compliment from him. "I don't seem to *write* as well as I used to," said the man fretfully. "Oh, yes, you do," said Howells reassuringly. "You write as well as ever you did. But your *taste* is improving."

2 Mrs. Howells engaged a young girl to do housework for her. For several weeks the newcomer observed the novelist constantly about the house. One day she came to Mrs. Howells, and after some preamble and embarrassment said, "You pay me four dollars a week, madam, and — "

"I'm afraid I really can't afford to pay you more," broke in Mrs. Howells apologetically.

"Well, what I was wanting to say, madam," the girl went on, "was that I would be willing to take three until Mr. Howells lands a job."

HOY, William (1862–1951), *US baseball player.*

1 The Washington Statesman outfielder played in the major leagues for fourteen years, from 1888 to 1902 — and was completely deaf and mute. His teammates, exhibiting the cruelty of another age, called him "Dummy." But he was a champion base stealer and earned the respect of his teammates. The form baseball umpires use for hand signals emphasizing the calls "out," "strike," and "safe" were adopted for his benefit — and continue today.

HRUSKA, Roman Lee (1904–), *US politician.*

1 On January 19, 1970, President Richard Nixon submitted to the senate the nomination of G. Harrold Carswell to the Supreme Court. That Mr. Carswell was hardly qualified was apparent to most, though not to Mr. Nixon. He was rejected, of course, but has attained a certain immortality through his defense by Senator Hruska: "Even if he was mediocre, there are a lot of mediocre judges and people and lawyers. They are entitled to a little representation, aren't they, and a little chance? We can't have all Brandeises and Cardozos and Frankfurters and stuff like that there."

HUDSON, Rock (1925–85), *US movie actor.*

1 At a lunch for reporters during a publicity swing through Texas, Hudson took questions. One of the first was from a young, unseasoned reporter who launched into her prepared question with great embarrassment. "I've heard this rumored for years but there's no way to know for sure unless I ask you." The room was silent as Hudson awaited her point. "Is it true," she continued, "that your teeth are capped?"

HUGHES, Langston (1902–67), *US writer and poet.*

1 Hughes worked as a busboy in a Washington, D.C., hotel where Vachel Lindsay once stayed on a reading tour. Hughes approached the poet at breakfast, laying his own poems next to Lindsay's plate and walking away without saying a word. The next morning Hughes read in the newspaper that Lindsay had discovered a significant new voice in poetry and had read aloud some of Hughes's poems at his reading the night before. When he reached the hotel to go to work, Hughes was mobbed by reporters and photographers, and so began his career as an author.

HUGO, Victor (1802–85), *French poet, novelist, and dramatist.*

1 When Victor Hugo wanted to know what his publishers thought of the manuscript of *Les Misérables,* he sent them a note reading simply: "?" They replied: "!"

2 (Richard Monckton Milnes, the British writer and politician, went to call on Victor Hugo in Paris.)

"I was shown into a large room . . . with women and men seated in chairs against the walls, and Hugo at one end throned. No one spoke. At last Hugo raised his voice solemnly, and uttered the words: '*Quant à moi, je crois en Dieu!*' (As for me, I believe in God!) Silence followed. Then a woman responded as if in deep meditation: '*Chose sublime! un Dieu qui croit en Dieu!*' (How sublime! A God who believes in God!)"

3 Hans Christian Andersen on his travels around Europe met Victor Hugo and asked the great French writer for his autograph. Hugo, suspicious of the strange young Dane, worried that he might later write an acknowledgment of debt above the signature or make some other improper use of the autograph. To prevent this he squeezed the name "Victor Hugo" into one corner at the top of a sheet of paper.

4 Goethe was not among Hugo's favorite writers. "Goethe never wrote anything worth reading except *The Robbers,*" he once declared. One of his listeners immediately pointed out that *The Robbers* was written by Schiller, not Goethe. Undaunted, Hugo continued, "And even that is Schiller's."

HULL, Cordell (1871–1955), *US statesman.*

1 A biographer of Cordell Hull submitted his manuscript to his subject for approval. It was returned with just one correction; in a passage describing an incident during the Spanish-American War in which Cordell Hull had won all his company's money at poker, the word "company" was struck out and in Cordell Hull's own handwriting the word "regiment" had been written in.

———cↄ———

HULL, Isaac (1773–1843), *US naval commander and commodore.*

1 When Hull was informed that he would not survive the night, he called for his lawyer, his biographer, and an undertaker to be assembled by his side. After putting his worldly affairs in order, he then said, "I strike my flag," and died.

———cↄ———

HUME, David (1711–76), *Scottish philosopher and historian.*

1 Hume, who enjoyed an annual income of £1,000 from his pensions and literary productions, was on all sides urged to continue his *History* and bring it up to date. "Gentlemen, you do me too much honor," said Hume, "but I have four reasons for not writing: I am too old, too fat, too lazy, and too rich."

2 Hume regularly attended church services conducted by a sternly orthodox minister. A friend once suggested to the skeptical philosopher that he was being inconsistent in going to listen to such a preacher. Hume answered, "I don't believe all he says, but *he* does, and once a week I like to hear a man who believes what he says."

3 Hume was visited by the poet Thomas Blacklock, who complained at great length about his misfortunes: blind and penniless, he no longer had the means to support his large family and did not know where to turn for help. Hume, in financial difficulties himself at that time, had just managed to secure, through the influence of a friend, a university appointment worth about forty pounds a year. Nevertheless, he was so moved by the poet's tale of woe that he offered him the only means of assistance within his power to give. Taking from his desk the grant for the university post, he handed it to his unfortunate friend and promised to have the name changed from Hume to Blacklock. This generous sacrifice almost certainly saved Blacklock and his family from destitution.

4 While Hume was living in Paris, some of the *philosophes* grew jealous of him and made fun of his stoutness. Once when he entered a room d'Alembert quoted from the beginning of St. John's Gospel: *"Et verbum caro factum est"* (And the word was made flesh). *"Et verbum carum factum est* [And the word was made lovable]," reposted a lady admirer of Hume's.

5 At a supper party at Hume's shortly before his death, a guest complained of the spitefulness of the world. Hume contradicted him: "No, no, here am I who have written on all sorts of subjects calculated to excite hostility, moral, political, and religious, and yet I have no enemies, except, indeed, all the Whigs, all the Tories, and all the Christians."

———cↄ———

HUMPHREY, Hubert Horatio (1911–78), *US politician, vice president (1965–69).*

1 Humphrey was noted for his long-windedness on the stump. Once asked to limit a speech to no more than twelve minutes, Humphrey said, "The last time I spoke for

only twelve minutes was when I said hello to my mother."

2 Of Humphrey's speaking style, Barry Goldwater once commented, "Hubert has been clocked at 275 words a minute with gusts up to 340."

3 Humphrey's job was not enviable. The President under whom he served was a larger-than-life egotist who had little respect for underlings — and who had suffered in the same job himself. "All Hubert needs over there," Johnson once said, "is a gal to answer the phone and a pencil with an eraser on it."

4 Humphrey visited Lyndon Johnson at the LBJ ranch in Texas during the 1964 campaign. As he walked into a field to take the tour, he stepped in a pile of manure. "Mr. President," quipped Humphrey for the benefit of reporters, "I just stepped on the Republican platform."

—— ᴄⱱᴏ ——

HUNTER, John (1728–93), *British physician.*

1 A sufferer from angina, Hunter found that his attacks were often brought on by anger. He declared, "My life is at the mercy of any scoundrel who chooses to put me in a passion." This proved prophetic: at a meeting of the board of St. George's Hospital, London, of which he was a member, he became involved in a heated argument with other board members, walked out of the meeting, and dropped dead in the next room.

—— ᴄⱱᴏ ——

HUSTON, John (1906–87), *US film director.*

1 (David Niven recalled the moment of Huston's call-up for military service during World War II.)

"The word came by phone when he was in the middle of directing Bogie in a scene in which the Japanese enemy had surrounded hero Bogart in a small building. His escape had been carefully rehearsed — who he shot, who he knifed and through which window he would jump, etc.

"Huston never said a word about the receipt of his 'call-up,' he just tripled the number of Japanese around the building, boarded it up with the hero inside and left for Europe. A hastily summoned take-over director found a note on the door. 'I'm in the Army — Bogie will know how to get out.' "

2 Huston had gotten through many tough films, but never one as challenging as *The Bible.* When asked how the work was going, Huston barked, "I don't know how God managed. I'm having a terrible time."

—— ᴄⱱᴏ ——

HUTTON, E. F., *US stockbroker.*

1 Hutton wanted land in the south to hunt on, and he found a plantation, Hickory Hill, for sale. After the deal was concluded, Hutton said to the former owner, "Mr. Ravenel, it's been nice knowing you, but you're about the poorest businessman I know. I would have paid you twice the price for it." Said Ravenel, smiling, "I would have sold it for half as much."

—— ᴄⱱᴏ ——

HUTTON, Lauren (1944–), *US model and actress.*

1 At the age of forty-nine, Hutton still had an active career as a model, with a style that had always been casual and natural — the less makeup, the better. Her ambition, she said as she contemplated turning fifty, was to be "the first model who becomes a woman."

HUXLEY, Aldous Leonard (1894–1963), *British writer, grandson of Thomas Henry Huxley.*

1 As a child Aldous Huxley was precocious and thoughtful. A member of the family once asked him (he was about four) what he was thinking about. "Skin," replied Aldous.

2 (Aldous Huxley seems to have developed an individual approach to visiting the sick, which, from the description Osbert Sitwell gave of Huxley's visit to him in the hospital, can hardly have failed to distract the sufferer from his ailments.)

"Versed in every modern theory of science, politics, painting, literature, and psychology, he was qualified by his disposition to deal in ideas and play with them. Nor would gossip or any matter of the day be beneath his notice: though even these lesser things would be treated as by a philosopher, with detachment and an utter want of prejudice. But he preferred to discourse on more erudite and impersonal scandals, such as the incestuous mating of melons, the elaborate love-making of lepidoptera, or the curious amorous habits of cuttle-fish. He would speak with obvious enjoyment, in a voice of great charm, unhurried, clear, without being loud, and utterly indifferent to any sensation he was making. Thus the most surprising statements would hover languidly in air heavy with hospital disinfectants. 'From his usual conduct,' I remember his announcing on one occasion, 'one must presume that every octopus has read Ovid on Love.'"

3 Aldous Huxley's fame rested largely upon his novels, such as *Brave New World,* in which he examined humanity's choice between a fully human life and the mechanized servitude of the anthill. In his sixties he admitted, "It is a bit embarrassing to have been con-

cerned with the human problem all one's life and find at the end that one has no more to offer by way of advice than 'Try to be a little kinder.'"

HUXLEY, Thomas Henry (1825–95), *British biologist, philosopher, and paleontologist.*

1 The controversy between the supporters of Darwin and the Church came into the open at a famous meeting in Oxford in June 1860. No one took down what was said, so accounts are based on recollections of the participants as pieced together afterward. Samuel Wilberforce, bishop of Oxford and professor of mathematics, was on the platform to support the religious viewpoint; Huxley was the spokesman for the Darwinian side. As Wilberforce was expected to smash the scientific forces, the room was packed to capacity. His speech was a savage invective against Darwin and Huxley; at the end he asked Huxley, "If anyone were to be willing to trace his descent through an ape as his *grandfather,* would he be willing to trace his descent similarly on the side of his *grandmother?*" The audience greeted this with rapturous applause.

Although Huxley had come to the meeting with the idea of averting a head-on clash between religion and science, Wilberforce's arrogance and the inadequacy of his answer to the Darwinian position stung Huxley into fighting back. "A man has no reason to be ashamed of having an ape for his grandfather," he said. "If there were an ancestor whom I should feel shame in recalling, it would rather be a man who, not content with an equivocal success in his own sphere of activity, plunges into scientific questions with which he has no real acquaintance."

At this slur on the clergy bedlam broke out in the lecture room and ladies fainted from shock. From that moment the relationship of science to religion would never again be the same.

2 Huxley was late setting off to give a lecture. He jumped into a cab, crying, "Top Speed!" The cabman whipped up his horse and they set off as fast as the horse could go. A thought then dawned on Huxley; sticking his head out of the window, he called to the cabman, "Hey, do you know where I want to go?"

"No, your honor," shouted back the cabman, "but I'm driving as fast as I can!"

———— ⌘ ————

HYDE, Lady Catherine (1700–77), *British noblewoman who became Duchess of Queensberry by her marriage (1720) to Charles Douglas, the third duke.*

1 She kept her beauty into her seventies, and her friend Horace Walpole drank her health, wishing that she might live long enough even to grow ugly. "I hope then that you will keep your taste for antiquities," the duchess replied.

———— ⌘ ————

HYDE, William (dates unknown), *English painter.*

1 William Hyde often told the tale of an odd literary coincidence that happened to him when he came to live in Westminster. On the evening of his very first day in London, returning to his new lodgings, he found the slumped form of a stranger on his step. Noting that the man was evidently ill, and as-

suming him to be a fellow lodger, Hyde summoned the maid to help him. "Why," exclaimed the woman with some concern on seeing the sick man, "it's Dr. Jekyll. He lives here, poor gentleman."

———— ⌘ ————

HYLAN, John F. (1868–1936), *US lawyer and politician.*

1 "Honest John" Hylan was, if not the worst, surely one of the least bright mayors New York City has ever had. In 1922, during his administration, he solemnly swore to the citizenry that the much-publicized crime wave did not exist. He went on to assert, "The police are full able to meet and compete with the criminals."

———— ⌘ ————

HYRTL, Joseph (1810–94), *Austrian anatomist.*

1 Hyrtl was examining a candidate for the medical degree who seemed more than ordinarily nervous. "What can you tell me about the function of the spleen?" was the first question. The candidate wiped his forehead. "Herr Professor, I did know exactly what it was, I knew it just a minute ago, but now I've forgotten," he stammered.

"Miserable creature," cried Hyrtl. "You're the only man in the whole world who knows anything about the function of the spleen — and now you've forgotten it!"

I

IBN SAUD (?1880–1953), *first king of Saudi Arabia (1932–53).*

1 A woman came to Ibn Saud, asking a death sentence for the man who had killed her husband. The man had been in a palm tree gathering dates when he had slipped and fallen upon her husband, fatally injuring him. Ibn Saud inquired: Was the fall intentional? Were the two men enemies? The widow knew neither the man nor why he fell, but, according to the law, she demanded the blood price due her. "In what form will you have the compensation?" Ibn Saud asked. The widow demanded the head of the guilty party. Ibn Saud tried to dissuade her, pointing out that she needed money and that exaction of a life for a life would profit neither her nor her children. But the widow, set on vengeance, would not listen.

Ibn Saud said, "It is your right to exact compensation, and it is also your right to ask for this man's life. But it is my right to decree how he shall die. You shall take this man with you immediately and he shall be tied to the foot of a palm tree and then you yourself shall climb to the top of the tree and cast yourself down upon him from that height. In that way you will take his life as he took your husband's." There was a pause. "Or perhaps," Ibn Saud added, "you would prefer after all to take the blood money?" The widow took the money.

2 Ibn Saud, advanced in years, visited the town of Hofuf to bathe in its hot springs. During the cure one of the men of Hofuf presented the king with a handsome gray horse. Ibn Saud, delighted with the gift, called for the ledger in which he personally recorded the details of the presents that he bestowed upon visitors and well-wishers. Against the name of the donor of the horse he wrote "300 riyals," a sum greatly in excess of the real worth of the beast. As he was writing, the nib of his pen sputtered and a shower of little ink blobs scattered across the page, turning "300 riyals" into "300,000 riyals" (the Arabic sign for zero is a dot, like a period, rather than an open o). The vizer respectfully drew his lord's attention to the spattered page. "I see my pen has clearly stated 300,000," said Ibn Saud, "so that is what you must pay. My hand wrote it, and I cannot have anyone say that my hand is more generous than my heart."

IBRAHIM PASHA (1789–1848), *Egyptian general.*

1 The sultan at Constantinople commanded his viceroy in Egypt, Muhammad Ali, to punish the Wahhabis, who had defied his authority. Although he had some success,

Muhammad Ali found that he could make no impression upon the heartland of Wahhabi power, the area called Nejd, where the strength of these desert fighters was greatest.

One day Muhammad Ali was sitting in his apartments with his generals, each one contending that if *he* were given command of the armies in Arabia, he would conquer Nejd with no difficulty. Muhammad Ali placed an apple in the center of a large carpet and said, "The task of conquering Nejd is a difficult one. It is like seizing this apple without setting foot on the carpet. The man who is able to perform such a thing is the man capable of capturing Nejd." The generals were puzzled, but Muhammad Ali's son, Ibrahim Pasha, asked permission to attempt it. This was granted. The young man went to one side of the carpet and began to roll it up. When the carpet was half rolled up, he reached out and grasped the apple with ease. His father appointed him commander of the Egyptian forces in Arabia, and after a bloody two-year campaign Ibrahim Pasha captured Nejd and completely crushed Wahhabi power.

IBSEN, Henrik (1828–1906), *Norwegian playwright.*

1 Two middle-class ladies were discussing a revival of *A Doll's House,* which they had recently seen. "I just loved it," said the first. "Ibsen is so timeless, isn't he?"

"I'm not so sure," said the second lady doubtfully. "It's a good deal easier to borrow money these days."

2 In Rome one day, Ibsen noticed a number of people gathered around a large red poster. Intrigued, he reached for his spectacles, only to find that he had left them in his hotel room. "Signore," he said, turning to the man beside him, "could you please tell me what those signs say? I've forgotten my glasses."

"Sorry, Signore," replied the Italian in a confidential whisper, "I don't know how to read either."

3 The great playwright found his inspiration by hanging a picture of fellow dramatist August Strindberg over his desk. "He is my mortal enemy," said Ibsen, " and shall hang there and watch while I write."

4 After suffering a stroke in 1900, Ibsen was forced to abandon his writing and spent the remaining six years of his life as a helpless invalid. One day he heard his nurse suggest that he was feeling a little better. "On the contrary!" he snapped, and promptly died.

IKKU, Jippensha (d. 1831), *Japanese writer.*

1 Shortly before his death Ikku entrusted a number of small packages to his disciples, asking that they be placed unopened upon his funeral pyre. When the prayers had been said, the disciples reverently placed the packets around the body of their deceased master, and the pyre was then set alight. At that point the funeral proceedings broke up in disorder: Ikku's packages contained firecrackers.

"Prince Michael Golitsyn of Russia had taken an Italian Catholic wife, to the intense displeasure of Czarina Anna Ivanovna. Although the prince's bride soon died, the czarina remained bent on punishing him. She had a vendetta against the prince and his family, who opposed her rule; she also had a vicious sense of humor. She ordered an ice palace built in St. Petersburg in the winter of 1739, completely outfitted with ice furnishings — dishes, toilets, tables, even a four-poster ice bed. When all was finished, she selected the ugliest woman she could find to be the prince's second bride and forced the couple to parade about town on an elephant before the wedding. Accompanying them was a procession of freaks.

"The procession made its way to the ice palace, where 'the Bridal Pair of Fools' were stripped and sent to their icy nuptial chamber. Then all exits were sealed. The couple survived the frigid night, and nine months later, the prince's wife gave birth to twins."

— IRVING WALLACE, DAVID WALLECHINSKY, AND AMY WALLACE, *Significa*

INGE, William Ralph (1860–1954), *British clergyman; dean of St. Paul's (1911–35).*

1 One of the gloomy dean's articles provoked the wrath of a lady who wrote to him: "I am praying nightly for your death. It may interest you to know that in two other cases I have had great success." Inge was delighted with this missive.

INGERSOLL, Robert Green (1833–99), *US lawyer and orator.*

1 Ingersoll was famous as a free-thinker and for his attacks on the Bible. His extensive library reflected his views and interests. A reporter once asked him if he would mind telling him how much his library had cost him. Ingersoll looked over the rows of shelves for a moment and then said, "These books cost me the governorship of Illinois, and maybe the presidency of the United States as well."

INGYO (mid-5th century AD), *Japanese emperor.*

1 The administration was much bothered during Ingyo's reign by families who laid claim to nobility to which they were not entitled. In the end Ingyo announced that it had been revealed to him that he could separate those with true claims from the pretenders by hav-

ing all claimants immerse their arms in boiling water; only those with genuine claims would suffer no ill effects. This had the result of drastically reducing the number who turned up on the day appointed for the trial, as only those with legitimate claims saw fit to appear.

IPHICRATES (d. 353 BC), *Athenian general.*

1 Harmodius and Aristogiton were greatly revered in Athens for their attack on the tyrant Hippias in 514 BC. As a result, their descendants were granted certain privileges. A descendant of Harmodius scoffed at Iphicrates for being the son of a shoemaker. The general replied, "The difference between us is that my family begins with me, whereas yours ends with you."

IRVING, Sir Henry (1838–1905), *British actor and theater manager.*

1 In London's Garrick Club, the haunt of actors, a new member, anxious to establish himself on a familiar footing with the great Irving, approached him, greeted him casually, and launched into an anecdote about having been stopped in the street by a total stranger who had said, "God bless me, is that you?" Irving said: "And — er — was it?"

IRVING, Washington (1783–1859), *American satirist and short-story writer.*

1 Irving hated looking at his books once they had been published, as he could only see their weaknesses. Near the end of his life he was asked which of his books he prized the

most. Irving said, "I scarcely look with full satisfaction upon any; for they do not seem what they might have been. I often wish that I could have twenty years more, to take them down from the shelf one by one, and write them over."

2 One evening he was preparing to retire for the evening and said to his niece, Sarah, "Well, I must arrange my pillows for another night. When will this end?" Upon which he promptly fell dead of a stroke.

ISABEY, Jean-Baptiste (1767–1855), *French painter.*

1 Isabey visited Vienna in 1815 to make a pictorial record of the participants in the Congress. The great French diplomat Talleyrand indicated that he expected to have the place of honor at the center of the picture. A similar stipulation was made by the Duke of Wellington. Isabey solved the difficulty with masterly diplomacy. He showed the Duke of Wellington entering the hall, with every eye turned toward him, and Talleyrand sitting in an armchair at the center of the picture.

J

JACKSON, Andrew (1767–1845), *US military commander, 7th President of the United States* (1829–37).

1 In 1791 Jackson married his dearly loved Rachel Donelson Robards in the belief that her first husband had deserted and divorced her. A legitimate divorce was eventually obtained and the Jacksons remarried, but the affair caused much scandal. Jackson was touchy about his wife's reputation, and when a certain Charles Dickinson made an insulting allusion to Rachel, Jackson immediately challenged him to a duel. The knowledge that Dickinson was a crack pistol shot did not deflect him from his defense of his wife's name.

Dickinson took aim quickly and fired, but the impact of his bullet was blunted by the loose coat Jackson was wearing and it merely broke one of his ribs. Jackson then took very slow and deliberate aim and shot Dickinson dead. He later said, "I intended to kill him. I would have stood up long enough to kill him if he had put a bullet in my brain."

2 While Jackson was presiding judge at a small town in Tennessee in 1798, a notorious badman called Russell Bean created a disturbance outside the courthouse. The sheriff was unable to arrest him single-handed. Nor could he assemble a posse, as no one wanted to tackle the heavily armed Bean, who was swearing to shoot the first person to come within ten feet of him. Finally, Jackson took his pistols and sought out Bean himself. Making his way through the crowd, he walked coolly up to the troublemaker, pistols in hand, and commanded, "Surrender this instant, or I'll blow you through!" To everyone's amazement, Bean eyed Jackson for a moment, then meekly allowed himself to be led away. Asked later why he had allowed himself to be cowed by Jackson, Bean answered, "When he came up I looked him in the eye, and I saw shoot, and there wasn't any shoot in nary other eye in the crowd; and so I says to myself, says I, hoss, it's about time to sing small, and so I did."

3 When the British admiral Sir Alexander Cochrane was about to attack New Orleans, he boasted that he would eat his Christmas dinner in the town. The remark was reported to Jackson, who said, "It may be so, but I shall have the honor of presiding at that dinner."

4 Scandal broke out during Jackson's first administration because of his friendship with Peggy Eaton, the attractive wife of Jackson's secretary of war. This lady had a rather dubious background, and John Eaton's marriage to her did not restore her reputation; all the

Washington ladies boycotted receptions at which she was present and clergymen denounced her in public. Jackson called two of the latter into a cabinet meeting to discuss the question. The ministers admitted that there was no evidence of improper behavior on the part of John Eaton. "Nor Mrs. Eaton, either!" said the angry president. "I would prefer not to venture an opinion on that point," replied the clergyman. "She's as chaste as a virgin!" snapped Jackson. When this last remark was repeated to Daniel Webster, he paraphrased the line from Shakespeare's *Antony and Cleopatra:* "Age cannot wither her, nor custom stale her infinite virginity."

5 Thomas Hart Benton became an enthusiastic Jackson supporter, but in 1813 they had had a fight that left one of Benton's bullets lodged in Jackson's left arm. There it remained for many years, until in 1832 a surgeon removed it. It was suggested that the bullet be returned to Benton as it was his property. Benton thanked Jackson, who by now was his friend, but declined the offer, saying that twenty years' possession of the bullet had made it Jackson's property. It was pointed out that it was only nineteen years since the duel. Benton replied, "In consideration of the extra care he has taken of it — kept it about his person and so on — I'll waive the odd year."

———— ⌘ ————

JACKSON, Joe (1887–1951), US baseball player.

1 Some reporters and a group of small boys were waiting in the courthouse corridor when Jackson emerged after giving testimony in the "Black Sox Scandal" case, in which Jackson and other White Sox players were accused of accepting bribes to throw the World Series. One of the boys came forward and asked, "It ain't true, is it, Joe?" to

which the player replied, "Yes, I'm afraid it is."

———— ⌘ ————

JACKSON, Reggie (1946–), US baseball player.

1 Jackson liked to display a baseball he had that was signed, "To Reggie, your friend, The Babe." But Babe Ruth died in 1948. Investigation revealed that Ruth routinely signed baseballs in his free time, choosing names at random on the chance someone with that name would like to have a signed ball. So he would write, "To John . . . ," "To Bill . . . ," "To Pete . . . ," and so on. "To Reggie . . ."

2 Jackson claimed he disliked playing in the World Series. Asked why, he said, "I can't watch myself play."

3 Jackson's popularity was such that a candy bar was created and named for him. But Catfish Hunter noted how similar it was to the real thing: "When you unwrap it, it tells you how good it is."

———— ⌘ ————

JACKSON, Shirley (1919–65), US novelist and short-story writer.

1 After writing her infamous story "The Lottery," Jackson became obsessed with witchcraft. One day, angry with publisher Alfred Knopf, whom she heard was headed to Vermont on a skiing trip, she fashioned a wax doll in his likeness and stuck pins in one of its legs. And indeed, Knopf broke his leg — in three places — while skiing.

———— ⌘ ————

JACKSON, Thomas Jonathan ["Stonewall"] (1824–63), American Confederate general.

1 At the first battle of Bull Run in 1861 the fierceness of the Union onslaught caused

some confusion in the Confederate ranks. General Barnard Bee, commanding a battalion adjacent to Jackson's, rode up to him. "General, they are beating us back," he cried.

"Give them the bayonet," shouted Jackson. Heartened by this, Bee galloped back to his own men and encouraged them: "There is Jackson standing like a stone wall! Rally behind the Virginians!" The Confederates rallied and beat off the enemy, and the nickname "Stonewall" was permanently attached to Jackson.

2 Jackson blamed the failure of an attempt to destroy the canal leading to Washington on the fact that the raid had taken place on a Sunday. In order not to break the Sabbath a second time, he planned the next attempt for early Monday morning, and ordered that the necessary gunpowder be obtained on Saturday. Unfortunately the quartermaster was unable to find a suitable supply of powder that day and was obliged to procure it on Sunday. Jackson learned of this and sent for more powder first thing on Monday morning. He commanded the colonel in charge of the expedition, "I desire that you will see that the powder which is used for this expedition is not the powder that was procured on Sunday."

3 General Ewell was so impressed by the conspicuous gallantry of a certain Federal cavalry officer in rallying his troops on the field of battle that he ordered his soldiers not to shoot at the man. Jackson later reprimanded Ewell for this quixotic action, remarking shrewdly, "Shoot the brave officers and the cowards will run away and take their men with them!"

4 Jackson had strictly forbidden his men to ride into the fields alongside the roads so as not to damage the crops. Returning to his camp near Richmond one day, Jackson became impatient with the slow progress he was making along a road cluttered with wagon trains and led his men through a nearby field of oats. The farmer, witnessing this blatant violation of well-publicized orders, rushed over and blocked Jackson's path. Purple with rage, he threatened to report the miscreant to Stonewall Jackson himself and have all his men arrested. With some embarrassment the general admitted that *he* was Stonewall Jackson. The farmer's manner changed instantly. With tears in his eyes and waving his bandanna around his head, he cried, "Hurrah for Stonewall Jackson! By God, general, please do me the honor to ride all over my damned old oats!"

5 An enemy sergeant had been captured and was taken to Jackson's tent for further questioning. While waiting for the general to arrive, the prisoner began to stroke the rump of Jackson's horse and run his finger through the tail in an absentminded manner. One of Jackson's staff noticed hat he was actually pulling a few hairs out of the tail every time he did this and ordered him to stop. At this point Jackson arrived, and, seeing the prisoner's hand full of horsehair, asked for an explanation. The man replied, respect and admiration in his voice, that every hair from the general's horse would be worth a dollar in New York. Jackson was so moved by this tribute to his renown that he sent the prisoner away without further interrogation, still clutching his handful of horsehair.

6 General J. E. B. Stuart arrived at Jackson's camp late one night. Everyone was asleep, and Stuart lay down beside Jackson's bed to get some rest. It was a cold night. In his sleep Stuart gradually began to pull Jackson's blankets over himself and unconsciously slipped in between the sheets. When he awoke in the early morning, he was astonished to find himself in Jackson's bed, still fully clothed, and got out as quickly as possi-

ble. Emerging from the tent some time later, he was greeted by Jackson with the words: "General Stuart, I'm always glad to see you here. You might select better hours sometimes, but I'm always glad to have you. But, general, you must not get into my bed with your boots and spurs on and ride me around like a cavalry horse all night!"

7 Jackson was much amused by the pompous proclamations issued by General John Pope under the rubric "Headquarters in the Saddle." He noted that Pope seemed unable to distinguish "his hindquarters from his headquarters."

8 After a brilliantly successful maneuver Jackson outflanked a greatly superior number of Union troops at Chancellorsville, Virginia. On May 2, 1863, as dusk was falling, the Federals began to flee and Jackson rode out to organize the pursuit. Some of his own men, not recognizing their general in the twilight, shot and wounded him so badly that he lost his left arm. Pneumonia set in and Jackson died. His last words were: "Let us cross over the river and sit under the shade of the trees."

JACOBI, Karl Gustav Jacob (1804–51), *German mathematician.*

1 Jacobi's brother, M. H. Jacobi, had a prodigious contemporary reputation as the founder of the fashionable "science" of galvanoplasty. The professor of mathematics was constantly being mistaken for M. H. Jacobi or even congratulated on having such a famous sibling. Conscious of the lasting value of his own work, K.G.J. found this tiresome. When a lady complimented him on having such a distinguished brother, he retorted, "Pardon me, madame, but *I* am my brother!"

JAMES, Henry (1843–1916), *US novelist and critic.*

1 (According to David Cecil:)
"Henry James was all that Max [Beerbohm] liked a great man to be: majestic, benignant and slightly comical. . . . Henry James, on his side, took to Max. He liked courteous, elegant, intelligent young men. He treated Max on flatteringly equal terms. Once, at a wedding reception, a woman friend saw the two standing together. 'How terribly distinguished you look,' she said. 'We *are* distinguished,' Henry James replied. 'But you need not look so terribly so,' said the friend. 'We are shameless, shameless!' said Henry James."

2 Though invitations to the literary parties of Sir Edmund Gosse were eagerly sought by aspiring writers, the parties themselves were often somewhat uncomfortable occasions. At one party, crushed against the wall in the overcrowded room, Henry James was among those forced to watch a rather dreary puppet show. After a time he groaned, "An interesting example of economy. Economy of means and . . . economy of effect."

3 Edith Wharton recalled a moment that captured the essence of James. While driving near Windsor they got lost, and, spotting an old man, approached him for directions. "My good man," James began. "To put it to you in two words, this lady and I have just arrived here from Slough; that is to say, to be more strictly accurate, we have recently *passed through* Slough on our way here, having actually motored to Windsor from Rye, which was our point of departure; and the darkness having overtaken us, we should be much obliged if you would tell us where we are in relation, say, to the High Street, which, as you of course know, leads to the Castle,

after leaving on the left hand the turn down to the railway station." The old man looked dazed, at which point Wharton leaned over and asked where King's Road was. "Ye're in it," snapped the man.

4 James had dinner with Guy de Maupassant in a restaurant, where the French writer saw an interesting-looking woman nearby and asked James to "get her for me." James demurred, noting the English custom of needing proper introductions. De Maupassant then saw another woman, and asked to meet her. Again James declined. After several such tries, de Maupassant snapped at James, "Really, you don't seem to know anyone in London!"

5 As they were driving in her new car, Edith Wharton mentioned to James that it had been bought with the proceeds of her last novel. James then replied, "With the proceeds of *my* last novel I purchased a small go-cart, or hand-barrow, on which my guests' luggage is wheeled from the station to my house. It needs a coat of paint. With the proceeds from my next novel I shall have it painted."

6 At dinner with his sister Alice in Florence, he developed a severe pain in his throat. Having recently had a toothache, he arranged to go to the dentist the next day. All through the night he suffered; even the dentist was unable to alleviate the discomfort. So he went to a doctor, who looked into his throat and exclaimed, "Why, you have got something sticking in it and it is green!" He pulled and pulled; out came a very long string bean, which had become wrapped around the root of his tongue.

7 When James suffered his first stroke, he thought he was dying. He told a friend that the thought had come into his mind: "So it has come at last — the Distinguished Thing." He lived for a further three months.

8 After James's stroke the literary establishment rallied around and recommended him for the Order of Merit. When the honor was announced, Sir Edmund Gosse went to his bedside to deliver the news. James paid him no attention, apparently not even taking in the honor that was being paid him, but after Gosse had left, the invalid called out, "Nurse, take away the candle and spare my blushes."

JAMES, Jesse (1847–82), *US train- and bank-robber.*

1 On one occasion Jesse James and his gang sought food and rest at a lonely farmhouse. The woman there gave them what food she could and apologized for the poor hospitality. A widow and deeply in debt, she was even then waiting for the debt collector to visit her to demand $1,400, which she could not possibly afford to pay. Jesse James had the spoils of one of his bank raids with him. He gave the astonished woman enough money to pay off her debt, telling her to be sure to get a receipt from the debt collector. Then he and his gang withdrew to watch the road leading to the farmhouse. Along came the debt collector, looking very grim. A short while later he emerged from the farm, looking altogether more pleased with himself. Jesse James and his men stopped him, recovered their $1,400, and rode off.

2 The St. Louis–Texas express train was robbed by Jesse James's gang on January 31, 1874. As they boarded the train, one of the gang members handed the conductor an envelope. It contained the following press release, which appeared in the newspapers the next day: "THE MOST DARING TRAIN ROBBERY ON RECORD! The southbound train of the Iron Mountain Railroad was stopped here this evening by five heavily armed men and robbed of —— dollars.

The robbers arrived at the station a few minutes after the arrival of the train, arrested the agent, put him under guard and then threw the train on the switch. The robbers were all large men, all being slightly under six feet. After robbing the train they started in a southerly direction. They were all mounted on handsome horses. P.S. There is a hell of an excitement in this part of the country."

---------- ⌘ ----------

In England in the years following World War I, the universal obsession was dancing — as Thomas Beecham once described it, "a funeral assemblage of creatures, tightly packed together in an exiguous space, bumping and banging into one another, hardly moving the while and all looking as if they were practicing some painful penitential exercise." Beecham in turn related a French diplomat's comment on the phenomenon, *"Les visages sont si tristes, mais les derrières sont si gais."*

— THOMAS BEECHAM, *A Mingled Chime*

---------- ⌘ ----------

JAMES, William (1842–1910), *US philosopher and psychologist, brother of Henry James.*

1 Josiah Royce, who succeeded James in the Harvard chair of philosophy, was among a group of philosophers who were close personal friends of James, even though they might disagree on philosophical matters. On one occasion Royce was standing in for James at a lecture, using the latter's copies of texts for reference. He picked up one of his own works, opened it at a page marked by James, was about to read from it, then paused. After a long look at the passage, he glanced up at the class, smiled, and said, "Gentlemen, the marginal note says 'Damn fool!'"

2 At Radcliffe, Gertrude Stein was a favorite pupil of William James. Confronted with an exam paper the day after a session of opera-going and parties, she wrote on her paper,

"Dear Professor James, I am so sorry but I do not feel a bit like writing an examination paper on philosophy today." James wrote back, "Dear Miss Stein, I understand perfectly. I often feel like that myself."

3 James was walking along a Cambridge, Massachusetts, street accompanied by a pair of his students, a boy and a girl. A large, imposing figure, white-bearded, swinging his cane, talking to himself, oblivious to the others, approached them. Remarked the girl: "Whoever he is, he's the epitome of the absent-minded professor." "What you really mean," said James, "is that he is present-minded somewhere else."

4 Professor James was once asked by a young writer what his views were about the use of dictation in writing. "Never dictate any of your creative work," the professor answered. "Now let me tell you, I have a brother [Henry James] who used to be a pretty good novelist. But of late he has taken to dictating his stuff, and it has ruined his style. I can't read him anymore!"

---------- ⌘ ----------

JAMES I (1566–1625), *king of England and Ireland (1603–25) and, as James VI, king of Scotland (1567–1625). The son of the luckless Mary, Queen of Scots.*

1 Shortly after ascending the throne of England, James was attending the hearing of a court case. The counsel for the plaintiff spoke so eloquently that when he had finished, James said, "'Tis a clear case," and made as if to leave the court. His advisers insisted that he stay and hear the other side, which the king with a bad grace agreed to do. The counsel for the defendant also spoke very eloquently. When he had finished, James jumped to his feet, crying out, "They are all rogues alike," and left the courtroom.

2 A preacher as renowned for his fearless attacks on personalities and abuses as James was for his irresolution was invited to preach before the king. He entered the pulpit and gave as his text: "James One, Six. 'But let him ask in faith, nothing wavering. For he that wavereth is like a wave of the sea, driven with the wind and tossed.'" "God's faith!" exclaimed the monarch. "He's at me already."

3 A young girl was presented to James I as a prodigy. Impressed by her proficiency in Latin, Greek, and Hebrew, the king was not without reservation. "These are rare attainments for a damsel," he remarked, "but pray tell me, can she spin?"

———⟨⟩———

JARRY, Alfred (1873–1907), *French surrealist writer.*

1 Jarry demonstrated his eccentricity one day in a Paris restaurant. Wishing to communicate with a woman fellow diner who was engaged in staring contemplatively at her reflection in a mirror on the wall, Jarry drew out a pistol and shot at the mirror. In the stunned silence that followed Jarry repocketed the pistol and smiled engagingly. "Now that the mirror is gone," he said to the lady, "can we talk to each other?"

2 Another time Jarry fired his pistol into a hedge. From behind it appeared a furious woman shouting, "My child is playing here. You might have killed him!"

"Madame, I would have given you another!" responded Jarry gallantly.

3 Jarry was a small man, only five feet tall. In his room on the mantel he displayed an enormous stone phallus. A lady visitor inquired if this were a cast. Jarry at once rapped out, "No, madame, it is a re-duc-tion."

4 One night Jarry was stopped in the street by man who asked for a light. Jarry said politely, "Voilà," pulled out his pistol and shot it in the air.

———⟨⟩———

JEFFERSON, Joseph (1829–1905), *US actor.*

1 (Jefferson once told this story to a friend:)
"'I was coming down the elevator of the Stock Exchange building, and at one of the intermediate floors a man whose face I knew as well as I know yours got in. He greeted me very warmly at once, said it was a number of years since we had met, and was very gracious and friendly, but I couldn't place him for the life of me. I asked him as a sort of feeler how he happened to be in New York, and he answered, with a touch of surprise, that he had lived there for several years. Finally, I told him in an apologetic way that I couldn't recall his name. He looked at me for a moment and then he said very quietly that his name was U. S. Grant.'

"'What did you do, Joe?' his friend asked.

"'Do?' he replied, with a characteristic smile. 'Why, I got out at the next floor for fear I'd ask him if he had ever been in the war.'"

———⟨⟩———

JEFFERSON, Thomas (1743–1826), *US statesman, chief author of the Declaration of Independence (1776), and 3d President of the United States (1801–09).*

1 While Jefferson and his mother were away from home, the house caught fire and was destroyed with all its contents. One of their slaves came to report the bad news. "Not one of my books saved?" cried Jefferson in distress. The slave shook his head: "No, master — but we saved the fiddle."

2 The young widow Martha Skelton, whom Jefferson married in 1772, had many suitors.

Two gentlemen among their number decided to visit her together. Arriving at her house, they heard as they stood in the hall the sound of music — a violin accompanied by a harpsichord, and a lady and a gentleman singing. At once the gentlemen realized who it was: Jefferson was the only violinist in the vicinity. Acknowledging to each other that they were wasting their time, they stole out of the house and returned home.

3 When Jefferson arrived to represent his country in France in 1785, he went to pay his respects to the French minister for foreign affairs. "You replace Monsieur Franklin?" asked the minister.

"I succeed him," was Jefferson's reply. "No one can replace him."

4 While ambassador to France, Jefferson and the naturalist Georges Buffon disagreed on the physical properties of certain animals, including the moose, which was then common in New England. Jefferson wrote to a friend in New Hampshire, who sent him the entire skeleton of a moose he had shot for the purpose. When it arrived Jefferson showed it to Buffon, who acknowledged his error. "I should have consulted you," said Buffon, "before publishing my book on natural history, and then I should have been sure of my facts."

5 Jefferson often told how the Declaration of Independence had been ratified and signed so quickly. The committee overseeing the document had their rooms near a stable, and members were much annoyed by constant swarms of biting flies who were adept at getting into their leggings. So impatient did the members become, waving at the flies and running from their aggressions, that their hurry to be done with the pestilential place insured the Declaration's signing.

6 During his term as vice president, Jefferson once asked for a room in Baltimore's princi-pal hotel. Not recognizing the vice president, who had no servants with him and was dressed in soiled working clothes, the proprietor, a Mr. Boyden, turned him away. Soon after Jefferson's departure, Boyden was informed that he had just sent away the vice president. Horrified, Boyden promptly dispatched a number of his servants to find Jefferson and offer him as many rooms as he required. Jefferson had already taken a room at another hotel and sent the man who found him back with the message: "Tell Boyden that I value his good intentions highly, but if he has no room for a dirty farmer, he shall have none for the vice president."

7 One morning Thomas Jefferson woke up in a modest Washington rooming house, dressed, and then left the house in order to attend his inauguration as the third President. When he got back, duly sworn in, he found no space left for him at the dinner table. Quietly accepting the democratic principle of first come, first served, the President of the United States went up to his room without dinner.

8 In bygone days affairs of state were tackled with a good deal less frenetic haste than they are today, as this remark by Thomas Jefferson, speaking of the US minister to Spain, illustrates: "I haven't heard from him in two years. If I don't hear from him next year, I will write him a letter."

9 Baron Alexander von Humboldt, the German scientist and explorer, was surprised to find in Jefferson's office a newspaper containing the most scurrilous abuse of the President. "Why is this libelous journal not suppressed?" asked the baron. "Or why do you not fine the editor, or imprison him?" Jefferson smiled. "Put that paper in your pocket, baron," he said, "and if you hear the reality of our liberty, the freedom of the press, questioned, show them this paper and tell them where you found it."

10 While riding to Washington one day, Jefferson overtook a traveler on the road. After exchanging greetings, the man, who clearly did not recognize his fellow traveler, began to abuse the President in vile terms. Asked if he knew the President, the man replied, "No, nor do I wish to." Jefferson asked if the man would consent to meeting the President if Jefferson could arrange it, and they parted. The traveler suddenly realized his error, but nevertheless he appeared at Monticello and sent in his card, which read, "Mr. X, Mr. Jefferson's yesterday's companion." Jefferson appeared and warmly greeted him. "I have called," the man said, "to apologize for having said to a stranger —" and Jefferson broke in, saying, "Hard things of an imaginary being who is no relation of mine."

11 Jefferson and his grandson were out riding one day when a slave took off his hat and bowed to them. Jefferson courteously raised his hat and bowed in acknowledgment. His grandson, engrossed in conversation, ignored the man. Jefferson said severely, "Do you permit a slave to be more of a gentleman than you?"

12 The code of discipline at the University of Virginia was at first very lax, as Jefferson trusted that the students would take their studies seriously. This trust proved misplaced and the misbehavior of the students culminated in a riot in which the professors who tried to restore order were attacked with bricks and canes.

The following day a meeting was held between the university's board of visitors, of which Jefferson was of course a member, and the defiant students. Jefferson began by saying, "This is one of the most painful events of my life," was overcome by emotion, and burst into tears. No amount of oratory or scolding could have had such an extraordinary effect. Another member of the board took over the meeting and asked the rioters to come forward and give their names. Nearly every one of them did so. As one of the students said afterward, "It was not Mr. Jefferson's words, but his tears."

13 By a strange coincidence Jefferson and his old rival John Adams both died on the fiftieth anniversary of the Declaration of Independence — July 4, 1826. On the evening of July 3 Jefferson was in bed, his life ebbing rapidly. "This is the Fourth?" he whispered to a young friend watching by his bedside. The man could not bring himself to say that it was not yet, so kept silent. Jefferson repeated the question, and this time the friend nodded. A look of deep satisfaction came over Jefferson's face, he sighed deeply, lay back, sank into a deep sleep, and died shortly after noon on the Fourth.

14 Jefferson's grandson Jefferson Randolph once asked an old man, who remembered the President as a young lawyer, how his grandfather had been as a speaker in the courtroom. "Well," said the man, "it's hard to tell, because he always took the right side."

JEFFREYS, George, 1st Baron Jeffreys of Wem (?1645–89), *English judge, notorious for his brutality.*

1 Pointing with his cane at a man about to be tried, Jeffreys remarked, "There is a rogue at the end of my cane." The accused looked Jeffreys straight in the eye. "At which end, my lord?" he asked.

JÉRÔME (1784–1860), *king of Westphalia (1807–13), brother of Napoleon Bonaparte.*

1 When Napoleon III heard that his uncle was on his deathbed, he sent for Cardinal Moriot,

told him that he wished Jérôme to die with the full benefit of the last rites of the Roman Catholic Church, and dispatched him to attend on the dying man. Arriving at Jérôme's house, the cardinal asked his majordomo, *"Le roi a-t-il sa connaissance?"* (Is the king in possession of his senses?) But the majordomo, interpreting *connaissance* in its more colloquial sense as "mistress," replied, "Yes, your eminence, Mme de Plancy has spent the whole night at his bedside."

JERROLD, Douglas (1803–57), *English writer, humorist, and playwright.*

1 Jerrold had been seriously ill and was recuperating at a seaside resort, with reading prohibited. One day a parcel arrived containing Robert Browning's abstruse philosophical poem *Sordello,* and Jerrold indulged in the illicit pleasure. After reading a few lines he was seized with a mounting panic. He could not understand the poem at all. He sat down on his sofa, murmuring, "Oh, God, I *am* an idiot!" Had the illness softened his brain? When Mrs. Jerrold came in, he thrust the book into her hands, demanding to know what she made of it. She read it carefully under the anxious scrutiny of her husband. "I don't understand what the man means," she declared at last. "It is gibberish." A delighted smile broke out on Jerrold's face. "Thank God, I am *not* an idiot!" he cried.

2 "What's going on, Jerrold?" asked a talkative bore, stopping Jerrold one day in the street. "*I am,*" said Jerrold firmly, and did.

3 A certain member of Jerrold's acquaintance was notorious for his demands upon his friends' purses. Finding himself once again short of money, he sent an intermediary to Jerrold to ask him to subscribe. Jerrold viewed the go-between with disfavor as he made his case. "How much does he want this time?" he asked. "Just a four and two noughts will put him straight," said the man uneasily. "Put me down for one of the noughts," Jerrold replied.

JESSEL, George (1898–1981), *US entertainer.*

1 Jessel arrived at the Stork Club one day with the beautiful and talented Lena Horne. Sherman Billingsley, the owner of the Stork Club, and his headwaiters were not fervent believers in racial equality, but Jessel was a regular customer. The headwaiter stalled, paging through his reservation book, pretending that all the tables were filled. Finally, the headwaiter said to Jessel, "Mr. Jessel, who made the reservation?" And Jessel answered, "Abraham Lincoln." Billingsley signaled the headwaiter from across the room, and Mr. Jessel and Miss Horne were seated.

JOHN, Augustus [Edwin] (1878–1961), *British painter.*

1 Augustus John had a reputation for exaggeration. One of his favorite stories featured a meeting he claimed to have had with Abdul Hamid II, sultan of Turkey, before the latter was deposed in 1909. The sultan was known to be a ruthless man and several of his wives had disappeared in mysterious circumstances. John was asked to paint the beheading of John the Baptist. All went well until the two men began to argue over the appearance of a severed neck after decapitation. Before the artist had time to protest the sultan had sent for one of his wives and had her beheaded on the spot. "See how right I was?" said the sultan calmly.

JOHN XXIII [Angelo Roncalli] (1881–1963), *pope (1958–63).*

1 As papal nuncio to France, the future pope was once invited to a banquet. His dinner partner wore an extremely low-cut dress, which the prelate affected not to notice during the course of the meal. When dessert was served, however, he selected a rosy apple and offered it to the lady. She politely refused. "Please do take it, madam," he urged. "It was only after Eve ate the apple that she became aware of how little she had on."

2 While serving as papal nuncio in Paris, Pope John, then Monsignor Roncalli, was created a cardinal. At a reception given in his honor the new cardinal was asked if he had any family connections with the Marquis of Roncalli. Roncalli, a farmer's son, smiled. "Up to now we did not belong to the same family," he replied, "but I think that starting from this moment we will become more and more related."

3 Photographer Yousuf Karsh had been commissioned to take an official portrait of the pope. He was accompanied to the Vatican by Bishop Fulton Sheen. Pope John watched uneasily as Karsh set up his equipment. Turning to Sheen, he remarked with a sigh, "God knew seventy-seven years ago that someday I would be pope. Why couldn't he have made me a little more photogenic!"

4 Pope John reported that frequently when he was drowsing off some important thought would come into his mind and he would make a mental note, "I must speak to the pope about that." "Then," he went on, "I would be wide awake and remember that I am pope."

5 Pope John had some confidential advice for an ambitious young priest who was trying rather too hard to impress the Vatican dignitaries. "My dear son," he said, "stop worrying so much. You may rest assured that on the day of judgment Jesus is not going to ask you, 'And how did you get along with the Holy Office?'"

6 Pope John once received a courtesy visit from the Anglican bishop of Gibraltar, whose see covers the whole Mediterranean region. Stepping forward to greet his guest, the pope cried heartily, "Ah, good day, Bishop. I believe I'm in your diocese?"

—⟡—

JOHN III SOBIESKI (1624–96), *king of Poland (1674–96).*

1 In 1683 John Sobieski drove the Turks back from the walls of Vienna. He announced his victory to the pope with a paraphrase of Caesar: "I came; I saw; God conquered."

—⟡—

JOHNSON, Andrew (1808–75), *US politician; 17th President of the United States (1865–69).*

1 Johnson fiercely denounced secession and as senator from Tennessee courageously did his best to keep his state in the Union. This made him exceedingly unpopular in the southern states and for a period his life was in danger from mobs. In one incident at Lynchburg, Virginia, the mob actually succeeded in dragging him out of the train in which he was traveling to his home town of Greenville, Tennessee, assaulted him, and was about to hang him, when an old man in the crowd shouted, "His neighbors at Greenville have made arrangements to hang their senator on his arrival. Virginians have no right to deprive them of that privilege." Swayed by this argument, the mob released its victim and he resumed his journey.

——

JOHNSON, Lyndon Baines (1908–73), *US statesman; 36th President of the United States (1963–69).*

1 Appointed director of the National Youth Administration for Texas at the age of twenty-six, LBJ sometimes seemed to his staff to deliver cutting remarks for their own sake. Passing a colleague whose desk was piled high with papers, he commented in a voice intended to be heard by others in the room, "I hope your mind's not as messy as that desk." By tremendous exertion the man managed to deal with the papers and clear the desk before Johnson made his next round of the office. Viewing the vacant surface, the boss remarked, "I hope your mind's not as empty as that desk."

2 (David Halberstam tells this story:)

"Early in 1961, Russell Baker, then covering Capitol Hill for the *New York Times,* was coming out of the Senate when he ran into Vice President Johnson. Johnson grabbed him, cried, '*You,* I've been looking for *you,*' pulled him into his office, and began a long harangue about how important he was to the Kennedy administration and what an insider he really was. While talking, he scribbled something on a piece of paper and rang the buzzer. His secretary came in, took the paper, and left the room; she returned a few minutes later and handed the paper back to him. Still talking, LBJ glanced at the paper, crumpled it up, threw it away, and finally finished his monologue. Later Baker learned that Johnson had written on the paper: 'Who is this I'm talking to?'"

3 The Senate worked hard and late when Johnson was majority leader. One weary senator complained to a colleague, "What's all the hurry? Rome wasn't built in a day." "No, but Lyndon Johnson wasn't foreman on that job," said the other.

4 At one stage Johnson looked for a way to get rid of the head of the FBI, J. Edgar Hoover, but the difficulties appeared insuperable. Philosophically accepting Hoover's continuance in office, he observed, "It's probably better to have him inside the tent pissing out, than outside pissing in."

5 Johnson tried to persuade his secretary of defense, Robert McNamara, to let a certain Pentagon speechwriter move over to the White House. McNamara was anxious not to lose the young man, but he could not give the President a straight refusal. Instead, he implied that the speechwriter's work was not up to the high standards of the White House. Some weeks later, Johnson repeated his request, taking McNamara by surprise. "But I can't spare him," he protested. "Why, you told me yourself he wasn't any good at all," replied Johnson triumphantly. "I just want to take him off your hands." McNamara admitted defeat, and the speechwriter was transferred.

6 One of Johnson's daughters was once asked by an inquisitive journalist to describe her relationship with her famous father. After no more than a moment's hesitation, she replied: "Blood."

7 Bill Moyers, Johnson's press secretary, was saying grace at lunch one day. "Speak up, Bill," shouted Johnson, "I can't hear a damn thing." "I wasn't addressing you, Mr. President," replied Moyers quietly.

8 Johnson often liked to talk about speeches, singling out two kinds for especial notice: "The Mother Hubbard speech, which, like the garment, covers everything but touches nothing; and the French bathing suit speech, which covers only the essential points."

9 Hubert Humphrey liked to tell of his initial meeting with Johnson, after he had been se-

lected to be Johnson's running mate in 1964. The President looked at Humphrey and asked him, "Do you think you can keep your mouth shut for the next four years?" Humphrey immediately assented, "Yes, Mr. President." "There you go interrupting me again," Johnson barked.

10 Johnson was often frustrated by the violent differences within the Democratic party. He once asked a fellow politician, "Do you know what the difference between cannibals and liberals is? Cannibals eat only their enemies."

11 Johnson was well known for his machismo. At one point during a heated discussion of the course of the war in Vietman he began cursing Ho Chi Minh, asking how he had the nerve to push around America. He then unzipped his trousers and asked the staffers present, "Has Ho Chi Minh got anything like that?"

———— cᴺᴏ ————

JOHNSON, Nunnally (1897–1977), *US screenwriter and film producer.*

1 When first asked how he would adjust to writing for the wide screen, Nunnally replied: "Very simple. I'll just put the paper in sideways."

2 Johnson had arranged to have lunch with a lady friend, unaware that she was intending to use the occasion to air certain grievances concerning their relationship. He had ordered shad roe, his favorite dish, and was tucking in with a hearty appetite when the emotional scene was launched. Unable to abandon the roe, which was delicious, he attempted between mouthfuls to make the right noises of contrition and regret. The young lady was fully aware, however, that she was not receiving her lover's undivided attention. "Look at you," she cried, "our very lives are at the crossroads, and you sit there smacking your lips like a pig!" Johnson was genuinely distressed. "I'm so sorry," he replied. "If I'd known it was going to be like this, I'd have ordered something I didn't like."

———— cᴺᴏ ————

JOHNSON, Samuel (1709–84), *English journalist, critic, poet, and lexicographer.*

1 When Johnson was a very young child in petticoats and had just learned to read, his mother gave him the Book of Common Prayer, pointed to the collect for the day, and told him to learn it by heart. Leaving him with that task, she went upstairs, but by the time she reached the second story, she heard him following her. "What's the matter?" she asked. "I can say it," he replied, and repeated the collect from memory although he had not had time to read it more than twice.

2 Johnson was explaining to his former tutor from Oxford how he would complete his dictionary in three years. The other objected, "But the French Academy, which consists of forty members, took forty years to compile their dictionary."

"Sir, thus it is. This is the proportion. Let me see; forty times forty is sixteen hundred. As is three to sixteen hundred, so is the proportion of an Englishman to a Frenchman."

3 Andrew Millar, the bookseller who published Johnson's *Dictionary,* had great difficulty in extracting the copy for this work from the author. At last a messenger was dispatched to Millar with the final page. Upon the messenger's return Johnson asked, "Well, what did he say?"

"Sir," replied the messenger, "he said, 'Thank God I have done with him.'"

"I am glad," said Johnson, "that he thanks God for anything."

4 Two ladies were complimenting Dr. Johnson on his *Dictionary,* then recently published. In

particular they praised his omission of all naughty words. "What! My dears! Then you have been looking for them?" exclaimed Johnson. The ladies, deeply embarrassed, changed the subject.

5 Dr. Johnson was taken to task by a lady who asked why he had defined "pastern" as "the knee of a horse" in his dictionary. She expected an elaborate defense. He replied, "Ignorance, madam, pure ignorance."

6 Johnson once offered a lift in his coach to a poor woman who was trudging along in the rain with her baby, but only on condition that she refrain from indulging in baby talk, to which he had a strong aversion. At first the woman sat quietly in her corner and the baby slept, but after a while the motion of the coach awakened the infant. "The little dearie, is he going to open his eyesy-pysies then," said the woman, forgetting her benefactor's prohibition. "Stop the coach," Johnson ordered, and promptly turned her and the child out onto the road.

7 Johnson started work on a new edition of Shakespeare, and, to pay for the project, took subscriptions. A bookseller's apprentice, calling with yet another subscription for him, was startled to see him pocket the money without making any note of the subscriber's name or address. Diffidently he suggested that Johnson should take a note of this for the printed list of subscribers that should appear in the completed work. "I shall print no list of subscribers," said Johnson emphatically and abruptly, and then, supposing that some explanation was required, he added, "Sir, I have two very cogent reasons for not printing any list of subscribers — one, that I have lost all the names, the other, that I have spent all the money."

8 Johnson had no great feeling for music and tended to be somewhat dismissive of it.

When someone tried to impress upon him the virtuosity of a celebrated violinist's performance, he replied, "Difficult, do you call it, sir? I wish it were impossible."

9 A lady who had just performed to perfection on the harpsichord in Johnson's presence asked the philosopher if he was fond of music. "No, madam," he replied frankly, "but of all the noises I think music is the least disagreeable."

10 Johnson maintained the superiority of England and the English at all times. Visiting North Wales with friends and viewing the local scenery, he inquired, "Has this *brook* e'er a name?" He was assured that it was the *River* Ustrad. "Let us jump over it directly," he said to his companions, "and show them how an Englishman should treat a Welsh river."

11 After several attempts to meet Johnson, Boswell was finally introduced to him and, knowing how much Johnson disliked Scotland, begged the friend who was performing the introductions, "Don't tell where I come from."

"From Scotland," his friend announced immediately, and Boswell, anguished, cried, "Mr. Johnson, I do indeed come from Scotland, but I cannot help it."

"That, sir, I find," retorted Johnson, "is what a very many of your countrymen cannot help."

12 A Scot talking to Johnson unfortunately chose his native land as a topic of conversation. He claimed that Scotland had a great many noble wild prospects. "I believe, sir, you have a great many," said Johnson. "Norway, too, has noble wild prospects; and Lapland is remarkable for prodigious noble wild prospects. But, sir, let me tell you, the noblest prospect which a Scotchman ever sees, is the high-road that leads him to England."

13 On his tour of Scotland with Boswell, Johnson visited the island of Mull, which amply justified his prejudices about the bleakness of Scottish landscapes. While they were there, Johnson mislaid his stout oak staff. Boswell was hopeful that they might recover it, but Johnson immediately gave it up for lost. "It is not to be expected that any man in Mull who had got it will part with it. Consider, sir, the value of such a piece of timber here."

14 Boswell and Johnson on an excursion to Bristol were not at all pleased with the inn in which they stayed. Writing his journal, Boswell wondered out loud how he should describe it. "Describe it, sir?" said Johnson. "Why, it was so bad, that Boswell wished to be in Scotland!"

15 At a party held in his honor during his tour of the Hebrides, Johnson found himself with a pretty little married girl of sixteen sitting on his knee. She had taken a bet to do this and to kiss him because some other girls had said that he was too ugly for any woman to kiss. So the girl put her arms round his neck and kissed his cheek. "Do it again," he said, "and let us see who will tire first."

16 It was mentioned to Johnson that a certain female political writer, whose doctrines he disliked, had become very fond of her appearance and her clothes, and would spend many hours on them. "She is better employed at her toilet, than using her pen," said Johnson. "It is better that she should be reddening her own cheeks, than blackening other people's characters."

17 Johnson and Boswell were discussing Bishop Berkeley's theory of the nonexistence of matter, which held that all things in the universe exist solely in the mind as ideas. Boswell remarked that he found it impossible to refute this theory, although it was clearly untrue. Johnson promptly aimed a hefty kick at a large stone and, as his foot struck it, announced, "I refute it *thus.*"

18 One Sunday morning Boswell went to a Quaker meeting, where he heard a woman preach. He hastened to tell Johnson about this singular experience. "Sir," said Johnson, "a woman's preaching is like a dog's walking on his hind legs. It is not done well, but you are surprised to find it done at all."

19 The volume of poems allegedly written by the Highland bard Ossian and translated by James Macpherson attracted a large number of admirers. Johnson, however, was quick to see through its spurious antiquity, and denied that the poems (which were entirely the work of the "translator") had any literary merit. In this he was in a minority and found himself arguing with one of Ossian's admirers, who asked, "Do you think, sir, that any man of a modern age could have written such poems?"

"Yes, sir," replied Johnson, "many men, many women, and many children."

20 Dr. Johnson was once asked his opinion of Laurence Sterne's *Sermons of Mr. Yorick.* He replied that he knew nothing about them, but was later heard censuring the work. On being reminded of his earlier assertion, he explained, "I did read them, but it was in a stagecoach. I should not have even deigned to have looked at them had I been at large."

21 On being told that a gentleman who had been very unhappy in marriage married again immediately after his wife died, Johnson observed that it was the triumph of hope over experience.

22 Dr. Johnson's attention was one directed to the discrepancy between the epitaph that had been carved upon the tombstone of a certain gentleman and the way in which the deceased had actually conducted his life. With typical wryness, the doctor observed that "in

lapidary inscriptions a man is not upon oath."

23 Johnson's wife in later years insisted that her failing health made it impossible for her to sleep with him, and Johnson's friends accordingly commiserated with him on this "conjugal infelicity." Garrick related a conversation with Johnson in which, when asked what was the greatest pleasure in life, "he answered fucking and the second was drinking. And therefore he wondered why there were not more drunkards, for all could drink tho' all could not fuck."

24 Pestered once too often by Boswell for minute biographical data, Johnson snapped, "Sir, you have but two topics, yourself and me. I am sick of both!"

25 A very disdainful young man was introduced to the elderly Johnson and looking at him closely said, "Tell me, Doctor, what would you give to be as young and sprightly as I am?"

"Why, sir," replied the doctor, "I should almost be content to be as foolish and conceited."

———— ❧ ————

JOHNSON, Sir William (1715–74), *British soldier and administrator of American Indian affairs.*

1 Sir William Johnson had ordered some suits of rich clothing from England. When they were unpacked, the Mohawk chief Hendrick admired them greatly. Shortly afterward he told Sir William that he had had a dream in which Sir William had given him one of the suits. Sir William took the hint and presented Hendrick with one of the handsomest outfits. Not long after that when Sir William and Hendrick were again together, Sir William said that he too had had a dream. Hendrick asked him what it was. Sir William explained that he had dreamed that Hendrick had presented him with a certain tract of land on the Mohawk River, comprising about five thousand acres of the most fertile terrain. Immediately Hendrick presented the land to Sir William, remarking as he did so that he would dream no more with him. "You dream too hard for me, Sir William," he observed.

———— ❧ ————

JOLLEY, Smead (1902–91), *US baseball player, known for his good hitting and bad fielding.*

1 Smead Jolley could hit, but the problem was finding a position for him where he could get by in the field. He was being tried as an outfielder in Boston's Fenway Park, where there was an incline leading to the wall. The coaches worked with him at running back and taking the little hill in stride, when he had to go to the wall to catch a fly ball. In the game Jolley ran back for one, but went too far. Realizing this, he came forward again, down the incline, and fell flat on his face. The ball hit him on the head and bounced away. Afterward Jolley came to the bench, rubbing his head and muttering, "Ten days you guys spend teaching me how to go up the hill and there isn't one of you with the brains to teach me how to come down."

———— ❧ ————

JOLSON, Al [Asa Yoelson] (1886–1950), *US singer and songwriter, born in Russia.*

1 At one point during the making of *The Jazz Singer,* Al Jolson called out to the technicians and extras on the set, "Wait a minute! Wait a minute! You ain't heard nothin' yet." The unscripted words went into the sound track, from which they were due to be cut. By a last-minute decision they were left in, and became part of movie history.

JONES, James (1921–77), *US author.*

1 While fighting in the Pacific in World War II, Jones was hit in the head by fragments of a Japanese shell. He was taken to the hospital, where a doctor looked at him bloody and disoriented and said, "Getting more material for that book of yours you're going to write?" Jones replied, "More than I want, Doc."

2 Shortly after the publication of *From Here to Eternity,* Jones was known to carry around with him a pocketful of envelopes, each containing 67 cents, which he handed to friends who had bought a copy of his book. "That's my royalty on each copy," he explained. "I don't want to make money on my friends."

3 Jones, whose novel *From Here to Eternity* had made him a rich man, lived in Paris while he wrote *The Thin Red Line.* As he worked on an especially emotional scene, which had Jones in tears, a large wrestler employed by the local laundry knocked on his door to collect the laundry bill. When Jones answered the door still crying, the man mistook the reason for Jones's tears. "It's okay," he said. "You no have to pay now."

4 Jones had a love of practical jokes. He and his friends liked a certain café in Paris, where the owner, Jean Castel, was strangely haunted by a filthy old woman who stood outside the front door shouting insults at customers and playing an out-of-tune mandolin. Eventually Castel had to get away, and flew to Tahiti on vacation to escape her torments. But when he arrived at the airport, the old lady was standing at the foot of the ramp, playing her mandolin and singing, "Welcome to Tahiti, M. Castel!" Jones's group had chipped in to get her a ticket there as well.

JONES, John Paul (1747–92), *US sailor of Scots origin.*

1 On September 23, 1779, off Flamborough Head in northeast England, Jones, sailing the rather ramshackle *Le Bonhomme Richard,* encountered a convoy of British merchantmen under the escort of the royal naval ship *Serapis.* The commander of the *Serapis,* Richard Pearson, recognized the *Richard* and attacked. His ship battered by forty-four hostile guns, Jones closed on his enemy and lashed the *Richard*'s bowsprit to the mizzenmast of the *Serapis.* The sides of the *Richard* had been so pounded by the *Serapis*'s guns that Pearson sent a signal inviting Jones to surrender. Back came the immortal reply, "I have not yet begun to fight."

2 When Pearson eventually returned to England, the loss of the *Serapis* was forgotten in the general praise for the heroic fight he had put up. Despite his ill luck, he received a knighthood. When Jones heard that his opponent had been made a knight, he remarked, "Should I have the good fortune to fall in with him again, I'll make a lord of him."

JONSON, Ben (1572–1637), *British dramatist.*

1 When Ben Jonson asked his benefactor, Charles I of England, for a square foot in hallowed Westminster Abbey after he died, that is exactly what he got. He was buried in an upright position in order that he take up no more space than he had bargained for.

2 A certain Sir John Young, who happened to be in Westminster Abbey when Jonson's grave was being covered over, paid the mason 18 pence to inscribe upon the gravestone the words: "O rare Ben Jonson." It was later

thought that the first two words of the inscription should have been joined together as the Latin word *orare* (pray). The epitaph would then translate as "Pray for Ben Jonson."

JORDAN, Michael (1963–), *US basketball player.*

1 At the end of an All-Star game Jordan threw a full-court shot that barely missed the basket. When asked if he actually thought the shot would go in, he replied, "I expect them *all* to go in."

JOWETT, Benjamin (1817–93), *English classical scholar.*

1 Jowett was once approached by a rather conceited young student. "Master," he said, "I have searched everywhere in all philosophies, ancient and modern, and nowhere do I find the evidence of a God." Jowett, who had little time for such pretentious attitudes, issued the following ultimatum: "If you don't find a God by five o'clock this afternoon you must leave the college."

2 Jowett once submitted a matter to a vote of the dons of Balliol College. The result did not please him, he announced. "The vote is twenty-two to two. I see we are deadlocked."

JOYCE, James (1882–1941), *Irish novelist, author of* Ulysses *and* Finnegans Wake.

1 In his impoverished youth, Joyce once applied for a job in a bank. "Do you smoke?" asked the bank manager.

"No," replied his would-be employee.

"Do you drink?"

"No."

"Do you go with girls?"

"No."

The manager was unimpressed by this display of virtue. "Away with you!" he cried. "You'd probably rob the bank."

2 (The story of the first meeting in Dublin between the youthful James Joyce and William Butler Yeats, then at the height of his poetic powers, exists in a number of versions. George Russell wrote from memory a version of this encounter that is published in Richard Ellmann's biography of Joyce.)

"Yeats asked Joyce to read him some of his poems. 'I do so since you ask me,' said Joyce, 'but I attach no more importance to your opinion than to anybody one meets in the street.' Yeats made him some compliments on the verses, which were charming. But Joyce waved aside the praise. 'It is likely both you and I will soon be forgotten.' He then questioned Yeats about some of his later poetry. Yeats began an elaborate and subtle explanation, the essence of which was that in youth he thought everything should be perfectly beautiful but now he thought one might do many things by way of experiment. 'Ah,' said the boy, 'that shows how rapidly you are deteriorating.' He parted with Yeats with a last shaft. 'We have met too late. You are too old for me to have any effect on you.'"

3 A woman was singing one evening at a private gathering, when a moth headed straight for her open mouth. She stopped abruptly, and there was an awkward silence, broken by Joyce's saying, "The desire of the moth for the star."

4 When Joyce was sitting for the painter Patrick Tuohy, the artist "began to philosophize about the importance to an artist of capturing his subject's soul. Joyce replied, 'Never mind my soul. Just be sure you have my tie right.'"

5 Asked about the demands his writing made upon the reader, Joyce replied, "The demand I make of my reader is that he should devote his whole life to reading my works."

6 "Joyce had no patience with monuments. Valery Larbaud said to him as they drove in a taxi in Paris past the Arc de Triomphe with its eternal fire, 'How long do you think that will burn?' Joyce answered, 'Until the Unknown Soldier gets up in disgust and blows it out.' "

7 "When a young man came up to him in Zurich and said, 'May I kiss the hand that wrote *Ulysses?*' Joyce replied, somewhat like King Lear, 'No, it did lots of other things too.' "

8 "One night drinking with Ottocaro Weiss, who had returned from the army in January 1919, he sampled a white Swiss wine called Fendant de Sion. This seemed to be the object of his quest, and after drinking it with satisfaction, he lifted the half-emptied glass, held it against the window like a test tube, and asked Weiss, 'What does this remind you of?' Weiss looked at Joyce and at the pale golden liquid and replied, '*Orina.*' '*Si,*' said Joyce laughing, '*ma di un'arciduchessa*' ('yes, but an archduchess's'). From now on the wine was known as the Archduchess, and is so celebrated in *Finnegans Wake.*"

9 "Once or twice Joyce dictated a bit of *Finnegans Wake* to Samuel Beckett, though dictation did not work very well for him; in the middle of one such session there was a knock at the door that Beckett didn't hear. Joyce said, 'Come in,' and Beckett wrote it down. Afterwards he read back what he had written and Joyce said, 'What's that "Come in"?' 'Yes, you said that,' said Beckett. Joyce thought for a moment, then said 'Let it stand.' "

JOYCE, John (1849–1931), *father of Irish writer James Joyce.*

1 (John Joyce, who worked as a tax collector in Dublin, had a dry native wit.)

"On one occasion someone complained that his name had been spelled with two *ll*'s instead of one. 'Which *l* would you like to have removed?' asked John Joyce gravely."

2 The Rumanian sculptor Brancusi and James Joyce were friends during the twenties. Harry and Caresse Crosby, wealthy American expatriates, proposed to illustrate their Black Sun edition of Joyce's *Tales Told of Shem and Shaun* with a portrait of the author by Brancusi. Brancusi's portrait was a sketch of an abstract spiral intended to suggest the labyrinthine nature of Joyce's thought processes. When the portrait was shown to John Joyce in Dublin, he remarked, "The boy seems to have changed a good deal."

3 John Joyce was renowned as a heavy drinker and was frequently in debt. After his death, when his son was asked what his father had been, James Joyce replied, "He was a bankrupt."

JUANG-ZU (4th century BC), *Chinese philosopher, a major interpreter of Taoism.*

1 Juang-zu's disciples wished to give their master an elaborate burial, but when the dying sage's views were asked he vetoed the idea of interment. "Above ground I shall be food for kites; below I shall be food for mole-crickets and ants. Why rob one to feed the other?"

JULIA (39 BC–AD 14), *daughter of Augustus Caesar, the first Roman emperor.*

1 By Marcus Vipsanius Agrippa, her second husband, Julia had three sons and two daughters. Her infidelities were common

gossip among Roman high society. Someone once observed that it was remarkable in the circumstances how like Agrippa all her children looked. "That," said Julia, "is because passengers are never allowed on board until the hold is full."

2 One day Julia came into her father's presence wearing a rather immodest dress. Though shocked, the emperor did not rebuke her. The following day, to his great pleasure, she appeared in a dress entirely suitable to her age and status. "This dress," he said to her, "is much more becoming to the daughter of Augustus." Julia excused herself: "Today I dressed to meet my father's eyes; yesterday it was for my husband's."

3 At a gladiatorial display, the groups of people attending the two first ladies of Rome — Julia and her stepmother, Livia — appeared in striking contrast. Livia was surrounded by mature men who held important positions in public life, while Julia's suite comprised mainly wild and pleasure-loving youngsters. Augustus sent Julia a note, remarking on this difference. Julia countered: "These friends of mine will be old men too, when I am old."

4 A friend once tried to persuade Julia that she should abandon her extravagant lifestyle and live more in accordance with her father's simple tastes. Julia refused: "He sometimes forgets that he is Caesar, but I always remember that I am Caesar's daughter."

JULIAN (c. 332–363), *Roman emperor at Constantinople (361–363).*

1 A former provincial governor was accused of embezzlement, which he strongly denied. He was put on trial and his evidence could not be faulted under examination. Eventually the judge, irritated by the absence of proof and the accused's protestations of innocence,

turned to Julian and demanded, "Can anyone ever be proved guilty if it is enough just to deny the charge?" Julian replied, "Can anyone be proved innocent if it is enough just to accuse him?"

JULIUS II (1443–1513), *pope (1503–13), born Giuliano della Rovere.*

1 Michelangelo was commissioned to make a statue of Julius II in bronze. He suggested a design showing the pope's right hand raised and a book held in his left hand. The pope did not approve. "Put a sword there," he said, "for I know nothing of letters."

JULLIEN, Louis Antoine (1812–60), *French composer and conductor.*

1 Jullien was born at Sisteron in the Basses Alpes. His father, a violinist, had been invited to play a concerto with the local Philharmonic Society orchestra and thought it only proper that he should ask one of the musicians to be the child's godfather. A problem arose, however, when all thirty-six members of the orchestra claimed the privilege. In the end the society's secretary held the infant at the font and he was duly baptized with all thirty-six names.

2 In his last year Jullien toyed with the scheme of setting the Lord's Prayer to music. He said it was the idea of the wording on the title page that really attracted him: "THE LORD'S PRAYER. Words by Jesus Christ. Music by Jullien."

JUSSERAND, Jean Adrien Antoine Jules (1855–1932), *French diplomat and scholar.*

1 Theodore Roosevelt's enthusiasm for exercise was a challenge to which the Washington

diplomatic corps never became fully accustomed. When Jusserand, garbed in afternoon suit, top hat, and kid gloves, turned up one day for a stroll with the President, he was not a little disconcerted to find Roosevelt in a rough tweed suit and stout boots. The stroll soon became something of a marathon as Roosevelt bounded off cross-country, with his unhappy companions toiling fretfully in his wake. At a stream too wide to jump and too deep to ford, they were sure that there would be a respite. But Roosevelt merely said, "We'd better strip, so as not to wet our things in the creek." With the honor of his country at stake, the urbane Jusserand removed his clothing, except for the kid gloves. As Roosevelt cast a disapproving eye at him, Jusserand forestalled comment by saying, "With your permission, Mr. President, I will keep these on, otherwise it would be embarrassing if we should meet ladies." Thus they crossed the stream.

2 Jusserand eventually found Roosevelt's phenomenal energy too much for him. After two sets of tennis at the White House, Roosevelt invited Jusserand to go jogging. Then they had a workout with the medicine ball. "What would you like to do now?" the President asked his guest when his enthusiasm for the exercise seemed to be flagging. "If it's all the same to you," gasped the exhausted Frenchman, "lie down and die."

3 When Jusserand was once talking with Mrs. Theodore Roosevelt, she said, "Why don't you learn from the United States and Canada? We have a three-thousand-mile unfortified peaceful frontier. You people arm yourselves to the teeth." The ambassador replied: "Ah, madame. Perhaps we could exchange neighbors!"

K

KAHN, Otto H. (1867–1934), *US financier.*

1 The great magnate was incensed one day to notice on the front of a run-down store the sign: "ABRAM CAHN. COUSIN OF OTTO H. KAHN." As soon as he arrived home, he directed his lawyer to get the offending sign removed, under threat of legal proceedings. A few days later Kahn drove past the store again to make sure that the sign had been taken down. It had. In its place was a new one: "ABRAM CAHN. FORMERLY COUSIN OF OTTO H. KAHN."

KALLIO, Kyösti (1873–1940), *Finnish statesman; prime minister (1924–25, 1929–30, 1936–37) and president (1937–40).*

1 In the Winter War of 1939–40 the Finnish army with nine divisions held off forty-five Soviet divisions for 105 days after the unprovoked Soviet onslaught. The Finns, inevitably, were crushed, and terms were imposed upon them in a treaty signed in Moscow in March 1940. As President Kallio picked up the pen to sign, he exclaimed, "Let the hand wither that signs this monstrous treaty!" Within a few months his arm had become paralyzed.

KAMES, Henry Home, Lord (1696–1782), *Scottish lawyer and psychologist.*

1 Meeting his old rival Lord Monboddo in an Edinburgh street shortly after the publication of *Elements of Criticism,* Lord Kames inquired whether Lord Monboddo had read it. "I have not, my lord," was the response. "You write a great deal faster than I am able to read."

KANT, Immanuel (1724–1804), *German transcendentalist philosopher.*

1 In 1802 Kant discharged Lampe, the faithful servant who had been with him for years. But he could not dismiss him from his mind, and this began to trouble him greatly. He therefore made an entry in his memorandum book: "Remember, from now on the name of Lampe must be completely forgotten."

KARL ALEXANDER (1818–1901), *grand duke of Saxe-Weimar (1853–1901).*

1 About Karl Alexander cluster many anecdotes, most of them based on his absentmindedness and the difficulty he found in paying attention to matters that didn't interest him. In the course of his duties he fre-

quently had to receive and welcome the reserve officers of his Eisenach battalion. One such occasion is well remembered:

"Your name?"

"Schulze, Your Highness."

"And what do you do?"

"I am chief forester, Your Highness."

"Where do you come from?"

"Strassburg, Your Highness."

A look of joyful recognition appeared on the archduke's face. He gave the young officer a hearty handshake and exclaimed, "Ah, then you must be Chief Forester Schulze from Strassburg!"

KAUFMAN, George S[imon] (1889–1961), *US dramatist, wit, director, and journalist.*

1 Kaufman looked in at the theater while William Gaxton was starring in *Of Thee I Sing* to make sure that all was running smoothly. He was appalled at the liberties that Gaxton was taking with the script. In the intermission Kaufman hurried out and sent Gaxton a wire: "Am sitting in the last row. Wish you were here."

2 Walking on Fifth Avenue one day, Mrs. Kaufman saw so many acquaintances from her home town of Rochester that she observed, "All Rochester seems to be in New York this week."

"What an excellent time to visit Rochester," suggested George Kaufman.

3 The head of the great Bloomingdale's department store in New York once backed a Kaufman production, which opened out of town. Early the following morning Bloomingdale was in touch with Kaufman for news of how the play had fared. "Close the play and keep the store open nights," advised Kaufman.

4 (Marc Connelly tells this story:)

George C. Tyler [a producer] commissioned George Kaufman to adapt Jacques Deval's French farce *Someone in the House.* George did a good job, but a weak cast plus a city-wide epidemic of influenza shortened its life. Tyler reluctantly turned down George's suggestion for an advertising slogan for the faltering play: 'Avoid crowds, see *Someone in the House* at the Knickerbocker Theater.'"

5 Kaufman went on business to the office of theatrical producer Jed Harris, notorious for doing outrageous things to attract attention to himself. When Kaufman was ushered in, he found Harris seated at his desk completely nude. "Jed, your fly is open," said Kaufman.

6 Though Dorothy Parker was half-Jewish, Kaufman could not always count on her support against Alexander Woollcott, who liked to pretend to be anti-Semitic. At the Round Table one day Woollcott loudly addressed Kaufman as "you Christ-killer." Kaufman stood up and announced, "I will not stay here and listen to any more slurs on my race. I am now leaving this table and the Algonquin." He turned on his heel, then paused and glared at Dorothy Parker, who was sitting silent. "And I hope Mrs. Parker will follow me — halfway."

7 Kaufman, though deploring the liberties taken by the Marx Brothers with the text of *Animal Crackers,* which he and Morrie Ryskind had written specially for them, could do little to control their ad-libbing. At one performance, he and Ryskind were talking quietly together at the back of the theater, when Kaufman suddenly broke into what Ryskind was saying: "Excuse me, Morrie, but I think I just heard one of the original lines."

8 Dropping in on a matinee performance in New York, Kaufman was incensed to discover that the Marx Brothers were up to their usual tricks and went backstage to protest. "Well, they laughed at Edison, didn't

they?" said Groucho defensively. "Not at the Wednesday matinee, they didn't," replied Kaufman.

9 During a game of bridge Kaufman's partner asked to be excused to make a visit to the men's room. "Gladly," said Kaufman. "For the first time today I'll know what you have in your hand."

10 Actress Ruth Gordon was telling Kaufman about her latest play. "In the first scene I'm on the left side of the stage," she explained, "and the audience has to imagine I'm eating dinner in a crowded restaurant. Then in scene two I run over to the right side of the stage and the audience imagines I'm in my own drawing room."

Kaufman was unimpressed. "And the second night," he said, "*you* have to imagine there's an audience out front."

11 The Canadian stage and screen actor Raymond Massey clearly reveled in his tremendous success in the role of Abraham Lincoln. "Massey won't be satisfied until he's assassinated," commented Kaufman.

12 Kaufman became embarrassingly famous when the diary of the film actress Mary Astor was disclosed, revealing the playwright as Public Lover No. 1. Subpoenaed to appear at Miss Astor's divorce trial, he fled Hollywood and remained secluded for some time. When the case was settled, he returned to Hollywood, and thereafter is said to have asked every woman who attracted him, "Do you keep a diary?"

13 Asked to suggest his own epitaph, Kaufman came up with "Over my dead body!"

14 A famed hypochondriac, Kaufman disliked touching doorknobs with his bare hands and seemed to be under a doctor's care continually. Once he tested a new doctor by demanding his right to smoke, even though he was a nonsmoker. Only when the doctor dis-

agreed did Kaufman trust him. The only kind of doctor he would not see was a psychiatrist. He had tried one out, but quickly stopped. "She's asking too damn many personal questions," he told his friends.

KAUNITZ-RIETBURG, Wenzel Anton, Prince von (1711–94), *Austrian statesman and diplomat.*

1 Empress Maria-Theresa relied greatly upon Prince von Kaunitz, but she disapproved of his personal morals. Once she rebuked him for riding openly through the Viennese streets with his mistress seated beside him. To this von Kaunitz replied, "I have come here, madame, to speak about your affairs, not mine."

KAZAN, Elia (1909–), *US film director.*

1 Kazan, who hoped for a career in the movies, was advised by a Hollywood studio executive to change his name to Cezanne. "You make just one good picture," Kazan was told, "and nobody will ever remember the other guy."

KEATS, John (1795–1821), *British Romantic poet.*

1 In the spring of 1819 Keats was staying with his friend Charles Armitage Brown and found great pleasure in listening to the song of a nightingale that had built its nest near Brown's house. One morning he took his chair out into the garden for two or three hours. When he returned, Brown noticed that he had some scraps of paper in his hand that he was quietly tucking behind some books. Knowing Keats's habits of composition, Brown got his friend to show him the almost illegible scraps and together they

arranged the stanzas. The poem was "Ode to a Nightingale," and at once Brown instigated a search for other scraps of paper tucked into books or carelessly abandoned, and in that way rescued a number of poems. After that Keats agreed that Brown should make fair copies of everything he wrote.

2 (Keats's medical training left him in no doubt about the nature of the disease that was to kill him. Charles Armitage Brown was with Keats at the moment that he realized that he had tuberculosis.)

"On entering the cold sheets, before his head was on the pillow, he slightly coughed, and I heard him say, 'That is blood from my mouth.' I went towards him; he was examining a single drop of blood upon the sheet. 'Bring me the candle, Brown, and let me see this blood.' After regarding it steadfastly, he looked up in my face, with a calmness of countenance that I can never forget, and said, 'I know the color of that blood; it is arterial blood; I cannot be deceived in that color; that drop of blood is my death-warrant — I must die.'"

3 Keats's room in Rome was near the Spanish Steps, and he could hear from his sickbed the sound of the water playing in the fountain there. Lines from the play *Philaster* by the seventeenth-century playwrights Beaumont and Fletcher came into his mind: "All your better deeds / Shall be in water writ." He told his friend Joseph Severn, who was nursing him, that he wished for no inscription upon his grave, nor even his name, but simply the words: "Here lies one whose name was writ in water."

KEKULÉ VON STRADONITZ, [Friedrich] August (1829–96), *German chemist.*

1 The structural formula for benzene eluded Kekulé for a long time. He claimed that the initial insight came to him in 1865 while he was dozing before his fireplace in Ghent. He saw atoms dancing before his eyes and then things like snakes, which contorted and took their tails in their mouths, thus creating rings. The ancient alchemical symbol of the snake biting its tail suggested that the two ends of the benzene chain were joined, and the Kekulé formula for benzene was thus established.

KELLER, Helen Adams (1880–1968), *US social worker and writer.*

1 With her teacher, Anne Mansfield Sullivan, Helen Keller lectured all over the country, answering questions from the audience that were communicated to her by Miss Sullivan. A stock question was: "Do you close your eyes when you go to sleep?" Helen Keller's stock response was: "I never stayed awake to see."

KELLY, George (1887–1974), *US playwright, uncle of actress Grace Kelly.*

1 On his deathbed Kelly was visited by his sister Mary's daughter, who had come to see her uncle for the last time. As she learned forward to kiss him the old man whispered softly, "My dear, before you kiss me goodbye, fix your hair. It's a mess."

KELLY, Michael (?1764–1826), *Irish singer, actor, and composer.*

1 In 1802 Kelly embarked on a new venture as wine merchant. He proposed to put up a shop sign reading, "Michael Kelly, Composer of Music, Importer of Wine." His friend and colleague Richard Brinsley Sheridan suggested that this should be amended to

read "Michael Kelly, Importer of Music, Composer of Wine," for "none of his music is original and all his wine is, since he makes it himself."

———— ❧ ————

KELVIN, William Thomson, 1st Baron (1824–1907), *British physicist.*

1 Kelvin worked out an improved method for measuring the depth of the sea, using piano wire and a narrow-bore glass tube, stoppered at the upper end. While experimenting with this invention, he was interrupted one day by his colleague James Prescott Joule. Looking with astonishment at the lengths of piano wire, Joule asked him what he was doing. "Sounding," said Thomson. "What note?" asked Joule. "The deep C," returned Thomson.

2 Lost in a scientific reverie at lunch one day, Kelvin suddenly became aware that his wife was discussing plans for an afternoon excursion. Looking up, he asked abstractedly, "At what time does the dissipation of energy begin?"

———— ❧ ————

KEMBLE, Charles (1775–1845), *English actor, father of Fanny Kemble.*

1 Kemble had received and ignored insistent demands for income-tax payment. Eventually, however, he was forced to give in. As he presented the money to the tax collector he remarked: "Sir, I now pay you this exorbitant charge, but I must ask you to explain to Her Majesty that she must not in future look upon me as a source of income."

———— ❧ ————

Richard Kowalski was one of the greatest black marketeers in the history of modern Poland. He was a total illiterate poor Jew whose wife, mother, and three children had been slaughtered by the Germans. He blamed his fate on poverty. In the 1960s he sold to the state 26 million zlotys' worth of water, a remarkable coup in view of the fact that the contract called for wine. When his increasing wealth could no longer be ignored, the militia called him in for interrogation. The interrogator said, "Mr. Kowalski, do us a favor. Stop making money. Don't you understand our economic system?" Kowalski reflected sadly, then said, "I never learned to read and I never learned to write. What else is there left for me to do but make money?"

— FROM STEWART STEVEN, *The Poles*

———— ❧ ————

KEMBLE, Fanny [Frances Anne] (1809–93), *British actress.*

1 Wishing to explore the countryside of Massachusetts, where she was spending a summer vacation, Miss Kemble hired a local farmer to drive her around. As they set off on their first excursion, the farmer embarked on a detailed description of the area. Fanny brusquely interrupted him: "I hired you to drive me, not talk to me." The farmer said no more until the end of the holiday, when he presented his bill. Miss Kemble studied it for a moment or two. Pointing to one entry, she asked: "What is this item?"

"Sass, five dollar," drawled the farmer. "I don't often take it, but when I do I charge."

———— ❧ ————

KEMBLE, John Philip (1757–1823), *British tragic actor and theatrical manager, brother of Sarah Siddons and uncle of Fanny Kemble.*

1 Playing one of his celebrated roles in a country theater, Kemble was constantly interrupted by the crying of a young child. Finally Kemble came to the front of the stage and announced, "Ladies and gentlemen, unless the play is stopped, the child cannot possibly go on."

2 Kemble was once in conversation with a gentleman who had just returned from a visit to Sydney, Australia, and who spoke of the flourishing condition of the theater there. "Yes," remarked Kemble, "the performers ought to be all good, for they have been selected and sent to that situation by very excellent judges."

———⟳———

KEMBLE, Stephen (1758–1822), *British actor and theatrical manager; brother of John Philip Kemble.*

1 As an actor Stephen Kemble was eclipsed by other members of his illustrious clan. His main claim to fame was his huge bulk, which enabled him to play Falstaff without any padding. One night, Kemble awoke early at the country inn at which he was staying to find a diminutive figure standing at his bedside. Raising his massive body to a sitting position, Kemble asked for an explanation. "I am a dwarf come to exhibit at the fair tomorrow, and I have mistaken the bedchamber," replied the intruder. "I suppose you are a giant come for the same purpose."

———⟳———

KENNEDY, Edward (1936–), *US politician, brother of John and Robert.*

1 In 1964 Kennedy was hospitalized after an airplane crash. When his brother Robert came to visit him, a photographer said to Ted, "Move over, you're in your brother's shadow." "Well," said Ted, "that's the way it will be when we're in the Senate."

2 After his disastrous run for the presidency in 1980, a campaign in which he was soundly rejected by voters even before the Democratic nomination was settled, Kennedy was asked how he felt. "Frankly," he said, "I don't mind not being President. I just mind that someone else is."

3 Kennedy's brief run for the presidency in 1980 has become famous as an utter disaster. Much of the aura of doom can be laid at the door of the interview Roger Mudd conducted with the candidate, a televised showing that underlined Kennedy's unsuitability for the job and his own clouded view of his potential role as President. The night Mudd's interview was shown, a rival television station showed the popular movie *Jaws*. Of Mudd's coup de grâce, Senator Bob Dole of Kansas remarked, "Seventy-five percent of the country watched *Jaws*, twenty-five percent watched Roger Mudd, and half of those couldn't tell the difference."

———⟳———

KENNEDY, John Fitzgerald (1917–63), *US politician; 35th President of the United States (1961–63).*

1 JFK was known as something of a rake during his bachelor days. To further his political career, however, it was clear the junior senator from Massachusetts would have to get married. Asked to describe what he wanted in a wife, he replied, "Intelligent, but not too brainy."

2 During World War II Kennedy held a commission in the US Navy and served in the Pacific. In August 1943 in Blackett Strait in the Solomon Islands, a Japanese destroyer rammed his ship. Kennedy, with some others, reached a nearby island but found it was held by the Japanese. He and another officer then swam to another island, where they persuaded the inhabitants to send a message to other US forces, who rescued them. Kennedy's comment on his reputation as a hero: "It was involuntary. They sank my boat."

3 When John F. Kennedy was first persuaded to enter politics, his father orchestrated the campaigns that took him into Congress.

Joseph Kennedy remarked, "We're going to sell Jack like soap flakes," and did so.

4 After he had lost the vice presidential nomination to Estes Kefauver in 1956, Kennedy flew to Europe to rest. He was basking in the sun at his father's rented Riviera home when Michael Canfield, former husband of Jackie Kennedy's sister, Lee, came by. Canfield asked Jack why he wanted to be President. His eyes still closed, Jack replied, "I guess it's the only thing I can do."

5 During the contest for the 1960 Democratic presidential nomination, Kennedy visited a mine in West Virginia. "Is it true you're the son of one of our wealthiest men?" asked one of the miners there. Kennedy admitted that this was true.

"Is it true that you've never wanted for anything and had everything you wanted?"

"I guess so."

"Is it true you've never done a day's work with your hands all your life?"

Kennedy nodded.

"Well, let me tell you this," said the miner. "You haven't missed a thing."

6 As Democratic candidate for the presidency in 1960, Kennedy was surprised to receive the endorsement of the *New York Times,* which usually supported the Republicans. Once elected, the new President remarked: "In part, at least, I am one person who can truthfully say, 'I got my job through the *New York Times.*'"

7 Kennedy enjoyed telling this story against himself. He said that during an election campaign his father sent him the following telegram: "Don't buy a single vote more than necessary. I'll be damned if I'm going to pay for a landslide."

8 Addressing a group of donors who had paid a great deal to meet the Democratic presidential nominee, Kennedy said, "I am deeply touched. Not as deeply touched as you have been by coming to this dinner; nevertheless, it is a sentimental occasion."

9 When Kennedy got the news that he had won the presidency against Richard Nixon in the closest election ever held, he turned to his wife and her friend Toni Bradlee, both of whom were pregnant, and said, "All right, girls, you can take the pillows out. We won!"

10 Sir Rudolf Bing, manager of the Metropolitan Opera House in New York, invited the whole company to a party to watch the ticker-tape parade for President Kennedy soon after his inauguration. As the cavalcade went by, Bing was standing next to one of the Italian ladies who sang in the chorus. He overheard her say to her little daughter, "Now watch. This is President Kennedy and he's the first Catholic President of the United States."

"All the others were Jews?" asked the child in surprise.

11 When Kennedy made his brother Robert attorney general in 1961, a great cry of nepotism went up across the land. Kennedy retorted, "I can't see that it's wrong to give him a little legal experience before he goes out to practice law."

12 Shortly after Kennedy blocked the hike in steel prices in 1961, he was visited by a businessman who expressed wariness about the national economy. "Things look great," said JFK. "Why, if I wasn't President, I'd be buying stock myself."

"If you weren't President," said the businessman, "so would I."

13 Senator Barry Goldwater, a talented amateur photographer, once took a picture of President Kennedy and sent it to him, requesting an autograph. Back it came with this inscription: "For Barry Goldwater, whom I urge to follow the career for which he has shown so

much talent — photography. From his friend, John Kennedy."

14 Kennedy resigned from the Metropolitan, an exclusive Washington club, as a gesture of disapproval of its refusal to admit blacks. At around the same time he refused Moise Tshombe, the rebel Congolese leader, an entry visa to the United States. Arthur Krock of the *New York Times* remained a member of the Metropolitan and took up Tshombe's cause with the President. "Arthur," said Kennedy, "I'll give Tshombe a visa if you'll take him to lunch at the Metropolitan Club."

15 Pierre Salinger was mystified one day when the President called him and asked him how many Cuban cigars there were available in Washington. Salinger couldn't make a guess, but offered to find out how many cigar stores there were. "Buy every Havana they've got," Kennedy told him. Later that evening the President announced an embargo on Cuban products, including cigars, for every American.

16 After the fiasco of the Bay of Pigs invasion of Cuba, the American people rallied around their President. Kennedy's popularity rating was never higher, with 82 percent expressing their approval of him. Kennedy was dumbfounded. "My God! It's as bad as Eisenhower. The worse I do, the more popular I get."

17 After a speech he gave in the Midwest, Kennedy said, "There is no city in the United States in which I get a warmer welcome and fewer votes than Columbus, Ohio."

18 In October 1962 the world was brought to the brink of nuclear war when the United States confronted the Soviet Union over the Russian decision to install ballistic missiles in Cuba. President Kennedy made plain his determination to have the missiles removed. After days of acute tension, the Soviet premier, Nikita Khrushchev, ordered their withdrawal. At the height of the crisis Kennedy observed, "I guess this is the week I earn my salary."

19 When President Kennedy and his wife visited Paris in 1962, Jacqueline charmed everyone, including President de Gaulle. At departure time, Kennedy held a press conference. He began: "I do not think it is altogether inappropriate to introduce myself to this audience. I am the man who accompanied Jacqueline Kennedy to Paris, and I have enjoyed it."

20 When Kennedy entertained a group of Nobel Prize winners at the White House in December 1962, he welcomed them as the most distinguished gathering of intellects to have dined at the Executive Mansion — "with the possible exception of when Mr. Jefferson dined here alone."

21 Joseph Kennedy once remarked of his granddaughter Caroline, Jack's daughter: "Caroline's very bright, smarter than you were, Jack, at that age."

"Yes, she is," agreed Jack. "But look who *she* has for a father!"

22 William Haddad was an associate of Kennedy's. After JFK was assassinated, his young son, John, asked Mr. Haddad, "Are you a daddy?" Haddad admitted that he was. Said little John, "Then will you throw me up in the air?"

KENNEDY, Joseph Patrick (1888–1969), *US businessman and diplomat, father of President John F. Kennedy and Senators Robert and Edward Kennedy.*

1 Kennedy objected to being referred to as an Irishman in the Boston newspapers. Although he could not claim to be a "Proper Bostonian," he felt he was at least eligible for

American status. "I was born here," he complained. "My children were born here. What the hell do I have to do to be an American?"

2 In 1926 Joseph Kennedy became involved in the film industry, rising to the chairmanship of Pathé, Inc. Many Hollywood people disliked him and his methods. Marcus Loew is said to have inquired, "What's Kennedy doing in the movie business? He's not a furrier."

3 In 1926 Kennedy and his family moved from Boston to New York, which offered wider financial horizons. Shortly before he left, a friend asked him, "What is it you really want?" Kennedy reflected a moment. Then he replied, "Everything."

4 Joseph Kennedy, on reading the latest bills that had been charged to him, often would lecture his family about extravagance as they sat at the dinner table. On one occasion his son Bobby's wife, Ethel, was subjected to one of these tirades and fled from the room, very distressed. Only after much soothing from her indignant husband did she return to the table. Father and son confronted each other in an ominous silence. Then Jack shrugged his shoulders and, breaking the tension, told Bobby: "We've found the solution. Dad's just got to go out and make more money."

5 As ambassador to Britain, Kennedy had abolished the tradition of presenting American debutantes to the Court, reserving, however, the right to present his own daughters and those of selected friends. When George Bernard Shaw was told of this and asked if he approved, he snorted, "Certainly not. We don't want the Court to have only *selected* riff-raff."

KENNEDY, Robert (1925–68), *US lawyer and politician.*

1 Campaigning for New York's Senate seat in 1964, he told an audience, "People say I am ruthless. I am not ruthless. And if I find the man who is calling me ruthless, I shall destroy him."

2 Kennedy was once hugged and kissed vigorously on the cheek by his daughter Kerry, to which he said, "Please, Kerry, I told you — only when there are cameras around!"

3 Once he decided to enter the presidential race in 1968, he revealed his plans to his sister-in-law Jacqueline Kennedy, who said excitedly, "Won't it be wonderful when we get back into the White House again!" Robert's wife, Ethel, turned to her and said, icily, "What do you mean, *we*?"

KEPLER, Johannes (1571–1630), *German astronomer.*

1 Kepler also believed in the Pythagorean music of the spheres, that each celestial body in its course gave out a characteristic note or notes. The notes sounded by Earth, he said, were *mi, fa, mi,* indicating *mi*sery *(miseria)*, *fa*mine *(fames)*, and *mi*sery.

KEPPEL, Augustus Keppel, 1st Viscount (1725–86), *British statesman and admiral.*

1 When Keppel was still in his mid-twenties, he was sent as an emissary to the dey of Algiers to insist that he restrain his corsairs, who were then a major menace on the high seas. The dey scornfully queried the wisdom of the king of England who had sent a beardless boy to negotiate with him. "Had my master supposed that wisdom was measured by the

length of the beard, he would have sent your deyship a he-goat," retorted Keppel.

{This remark so enraged the dey that he threatened Keppel with instant death; Keppel pointed toward the naval squadron riding in the bay and observed that there were enough Englishmen there to make a glorious funeral pyre for him. The dey thought better of it.}

———— ⌘ ————

KER, William Paton (1855–1923), *British scholar.*

1 Visiting a natural history museum, Ker and a young woman acquaintance paused in front of a display of seafowl. "What's that bird?" the girl inquired.

"That's a guillemot."

"That's not my idea of a guillemot."

"It's God's idea of a guillemot," said Ker.

2 An energetic walker and lover of mountain scenery, Ker revisited the Italian Alps in 1923. Walking up the slopes of the Pizzo Bianco at Macugnaga, he paused to remark to his companions, "I thought this was the most beautiful spot in the world, and now I know it." So saying, he dropped dead of a heart attack.

———— ⌘ ————

KERN, Jerome [David] (1885–1945), *US composer best known for his musical comedy* Show Boat.

1 An actress had been irritating Kern all afternoon with her theatrical gestures and affected articulation, particularly the exaggerated rolling of her *r*'s. "Tell me, Mr. Kern," she cried at one point, "you want me to cr-r-ross the stage, but I'm behind a table. How shall I get acr-r-ross?"

"Why, my dear," replied Kern, "just r-r-roll over on your *r*'s."

KEROUAC, Jack (1922–69), *US writer and leading chronicler of the Beat Generation of the 1950s.*

1 (In *The Origins of the Beat Generation* Kerouac recalled how he borrowed the term that labeled an entire decade from a broken-down drug addict named Herbert Huncke and how he then went on to use it himself.)

"John Clellon Holmes . . . and I were sitting around trying to think up the meaning of the Lost Generation and the subsequent existentialism and I said, 'You know, this is really a beat generation': and he leapt up and said, 'that's it, that's right.' "

2 The year after he published his first novel, *The Town and the City,* Kerouac appeared in his editor's office with the now-famous continuous roll of teletype paper on which he had written, in a mad rush, *On the Road,* claiming that it had been divinely inspired. Kerouac's editor looked at the massive roll and, suggesting that some revisions might be in order, said, "Even after you have been inspired by the Holy Ghost, you have to sit down and read your manuscript." Kerouac was so incensed by the idea that he might have to change a single word that he turned and left the office and found a new publisher for what would become his greatest book.

———— ⌘ ————

KERR, Deborah (1921–), *British stage and film actress.*

1 Kerr was often approached by publishers to write her autobiography, as most of her peers had done. But she always demurred. "They're all the same," she complained. "It's always rags-to-riches or I-slept-with-so-and-so. Damned if I'm going to say that."

———— ⌘ ————

KERR, Johnny (1932–), *US basketball player and coach.*

1 As coach of the Chicago Bulls, he had lost seven games in a row, and decided to give his players a pep talk before the next game, which was with the Boston Celtics. He told one to pretend he was the best scorer in basketball; another was told to pretend he was the best defensive guard; another was told to pretend he could run offense better than any other guard; and so on. The Bulls lost by seventeen points. In the locker room afterwards, a player approached Kerr and said, "Don't worry about it, coach. Just pretend we won."

KEYNES, John Maynard, 1st Baron (1883–1946), *British economist.*

1 In his late twenties Keynes was traveling in Africa with a Cambridge friend, Walter John Sprott. At one point they had their shoes polished by the native boys. The economist handed the boys a miserly tip. Sprott suggested a more generous handout, but Keynes firmly declined: "I will not be a party to debasing the currency."

2 During the panic and uncertainty of the first days of the Great Depression, a reporter asked Keynes whether anything like it had ever happened before. "Yes, it was called the Dark Ages, and it lasted four hundred years," was the response.

KHRUSHCHEV, Nikita Sergeyevich (1894–1971), *Soviet politician, premier of the Soviet Union* (1958–64).

1 Khrushchev furiously denounced the United Nations for acting to prevent Russian intervention in the postindependence crisis in the Congo. Shortly afterward he sent Dag Hammarskjöld, then UN secretary general, a protocol invitation to a Soviet reception. Hammarskjöld attended the reception and was greeted with great cordiality by the Russian leader. Someone asked Khrushchev why he behaved so warmly toward a man whom he had recently been attacking so bitterly in public. Khrushchev replied, "Do you know the tradition of the mountain people of the Caucasus in our country? When an enemy is inside your home, sharing your bread and salt, you should always treat him with the greatest hospitality. But as soon as he steps outside the door, it is all right to slit his throat."

2 On a trip to Russia, Stewart Udall, US secretary of the interior, visited the Black Sea in Khrushchev's company. Khrushchev asked Udall if he would like to have his photograph taken with him. Udall said he would, so the photographer lined them up. Just as he was about to take the picture, the Russian premier stopped him. "If it will help you out," he said to Udall, "you can go ahead and shake your finger in my face."

3 During a fiery exchange in a summit meeting between Khrushchev and President Kennedy, Kennedy said to the Russian premier, "Do you ever admit a mistake?"

"Certainly I do," Khrushchev replied. "In a speech before the Twentieth Party Congress, I admitted all of Stalin's mistakes."

4 Censuring Stalin at a public meeting, Khrushchev was interrupted by a voice from the audience. "You were one of Stalin's colleagues," shouted the heckler. "Why didn't you stop him?"

"Who said that?" roared Khrushchev. There was an agonizing silence in the room.

Nobody dared to move a muscle. Then, in a quiet voice, Khrushchev said, "Now you know why."

KIDD, William (1645–1701), *British sea commander and pirate.*

1 The famous Captain Kidd started his career as a simple sea captain. But when he was sent to the coast of Madagascar to quell marauding pirates, he joined them instead, and soon became one of the most ferocious raiders on the open seas. After several years of bloody raids on English ships, he came to an agreement with the British Government that he would surrender in return for a full pardon. Once he was in captivity, the pardon was revoked, and he was sent to the scaffold. As the noose was looped around his neck he said to the assembled crowd, "This is a very fickle and faithless generation."

⁂

KINER, Ralph (1922–), *US baseball player.*

1 "Former Pirate slugger Ralph Kiner was telling his broadcasting buddy Lindsey Nelson about his wife, the former tennis star Nancy Chaffee. 'When I married Nancy, I vowed I'd beat her at tennis someday. After six months, she beat me 6–2. After a year, she beat me 6–4. After we were married a year and a half, I pushed her to 7–5. Then it happened — she had a bad day and I had a good one, and I beat her 17–15.' 'Good for you, Ralph,' exclaimed Lindsey. 'Was she sick?' 'Of course not!' Kiner snapped indignantly. 'Well, she was eight months pregnant.'"

⁂

KINGLAKE, Alexander William (1809–91), *British writer.*

1 A skeptic by nature, Kinglake suggested that all churches should bear the inscription: "IMPORTANT IF TRUE."

⁂

KINGSALE, Michael William de Courcy, 32d Baron [28th by some reckonings] (1822–95).

1 Determined to exercise his rights, the 32d Baron Kingsale appeared before Queen Victoria without removing his hat, explaining to the austere queen that he was asserting the ancient privilege. "Don't be so silly," snapped the queen. "It may be your right to keep your hat on before the monarch, but I am a lady, too. Take it off at once." The privilege has not been tested since.

⁂

KIPLING, [Joseph] Rudyard (1865–1936), *British poet and short-story writer, born in India.*

1 A newspaper to which Kipling subscribed published by mistake an announcement of his death. Kipling wrote at once to the editor: "I've just read that I am dead. Don't forget to delete me from your list of subscribers."

2 At the height of Kipling's success, a journal published a report that his earnings worked out at a dollar a word. An autograph hunter who had vainly tried to extract a signature from the great man wrote again to him: "I see you get $1 a word for your writing. I enclose a check for $1. Please send me a sample." Kipling wrote back a single word on an unsigned postcard: "Thanks."

⁂

KIRCHHOFF, Gustav Robert (1824–87), *German physicist.*

1 One of the important results of Kirchhoff's work on spectrum analysis was that for the first time it became possible to ascertain the chemical elements present in celestial bodies. Kirchhoff's banker, however, was skeptical about his customer's work. "What good is gold in the sun if I can't bring it down to earth?" he asked. When Kirchhoff's work be-

came internationally recognized, he was awarded a medal and a prize paid in gold sovereigns. "Here is the gold from the sun," he observed as he handed the money to his banker.

———

KISSINGER, Henry (1923–), *US diplomat, born in Germany. In 1972 he shared the Nobel Peace Prize.*

1 In Moscow for arms control negotiations in 1972, Kissinger, then secretary of state, joked with some of his hosts about bugging. During one session Kissinger held a document up in the air toward the chandelier and said, "Can I have two copies of this delivered to my suite?" Soviet Foreign Minister Andrei Gromyko, who had a sense of humor, said no, he couldn't. The hidden cameras had been installed in the Kremlin, said he, during the time of Ivan the Terrible, and their lenses were not good enough to pick up the fine print.

2 The day after Kissinger was nominated as secretary of state, he held a news conference. Newsman Richard Valeriani wound up the conference by asking, "Do you prefer being called 'Mr. Secretary' or 'Dr. Secretary'?"

"I don't stand on protocol," Kissinger deadpanned. "If you will just call me 'Excellency,' it will be okay."

3 Kissinger's German accent stayed with him all his life, although his younger brother, Walter, managed to lose his. When asked why this was so, Walter answered, "Because I am the Kissinger who listens."

4 Kissinger's aide Winston Lord had worked on a report for days. After giving it to Kissinger, he got it back with the comment, "Is this the best you can do?" Lord reworked it over several days and resubmitted it. It was returned with the same comment. When yet one more revision was treated the same way,

Lord snapped, "Damn it, yes, it's the best I can do," Kissinger then said, "Fine, then I guess I'll read it this time."

5 At a press conference in Brussels a reporter asked Kissinger what he considered his greatest success and what was his greatest failure. Kissinger replied, "I don't quite understand your second point."

6 Kissinger once asked his Secret Service guard what he would do in the event of a kidnap attempt. "Don't worry, Mr. Secretary," the guard replied. "We'll never let them take you alive."

———

KITCHENER, Horatio Herbert, 1st Earl of Khartoum and Broome (1850–1916), *British general.*

1 On June 5, 1916, the British ship *Hampshire* was sailing to Arkhangelsk when she struck a mine shortly after leaving Scapa Flow and sank. Lord Kitchener, along with most of the crew, drowned. When the news broke the following morning, newspaper magnate Lord Northcliffe announced it to his sister with the words: "Providence is on the side of the British Empire after all."

———

KITTREDGE, George (1860–1941), *US academic and scholar.*

1 Invited to a tea at Harvard, Kittredge — a formidable-looking man — knocked on his hostess's door. "My God!" said the maid, opening it. "Not God, madam," Kittredge intoned, "Kittredge."

———

KLEIN, Charles (1867–1915), *US playwright.*

1 Klein wrote a play called *The Ne'er Do Well*, which flopped. As the final curtain fell, a

young lady sitting behind him tapped him on the shoulder. "Are you Mr. Klein?" The disconsolate playwright admitted that he was, "Before the curtain rose," the girl went on, "I took the liberty of cutting off a lock of your hair. Now I would like to give it back."

———∽———

KLEMPERER, Otto (1885–1973), *German-born conductor.*

1 Expecting nothing but the best from his musicians, Klemperer was very sparing with his praise. On one occasion, however, after a particularly excellent performance, he congratulated the orchestra with an enthusiastic "Good!" The players burst into spontaneous applause, and Klemperer's smile faded into the more familiar frown. "Not *that* good," he growled.

2 Klemperer went into a music shop one day accompanied by a recording company executive called George de Mendelssohn-Bartholdy. "Do you have Klemperer conducting Beethoven's Fifth?" he asked the young man behind the counter.

"No," said the clerk. "We have it conducted by Ormandy and Toscanini. Why do you want it by Klemperer?"

Replied the indignant conductor: "Because I *am* Klemperer!"

The clerk looked at him skeptically, then nodded toward George. "And that, I suppose, is Beethoven," he said.

"No," replied Klemperer with a triumphant smile. "That's Mendelssohn."

3 In the middle of a performance of a modern work that he hated, Klemperer heard a member of the audience leave the hall. "Thank God somebody understands it!" exclaimed the conductor.

———∽———

KLÖPFER, Eugene (1886–1950), *German actor.*

1 Klöpfer once dried up on the stage and paused for the prompter, a certain Frau Wesemeier, to help him out. She had apparently lost her place in the prompt book and the embarrassing silence dragged on. To cover the lapse, Klöpfer addressed the fellow actor with whom he was playing the scene: "I wanted to ask you, how is Frau Wesemeier? Is she ill?" The other actor shrugged noncommittally. With increasing desperation Klöpfer went on, "I haven't heard from her for quite some time.

———∽———

KNELLER, Sir Godfrey (1646–1723), *German-born British portrait painter, known for his paintings of royalty and high-society figures.*

1 Alexander Pope had wagered that there was no flattery so gross that Kneller would not believe it. One day as Kneller was painting, Pope observed, "Sir Godfrey, I believe if God Almighty had had your assistance the world would have been formed more perfect."

"'Fore God, sir," said Kneller, "I believe so."

2 A visitor to Kneller's house remarked on a full-length portrait of Lady Kneller, the bottom of which had been very considerably damaged by scratches. The marks, Kneller explained, had been made by his wife's little lapdog, which used to paw at the painted skirt, asking to be taken up into its mistress's arms. The visitor observed that that reminded him of a story of Zeuxis, who painted grapes on a boy's head so realistically that birds came to peck at them. Kneller disparaged this legend: "If the boy had been painted as well as the grapes, the birds would have been afraid to meddle with them."

3 Kneller was greatly attached to his country house at Whitton. When he lay dying, a friend exhorted him to think of death merely

as the passage to a better place. "Ah, my good friend, I wish God would let me stay at Whitton," the painter sighed.

———⁂———

KNOPF, Alfred A. (1892–1984), *US book publisher.*

1 Traveling by train one day, Knopf entered the smoking car and seated himself next to a gentleman of pleasant appearance and manners. He took out one of his special cigars, lit it, and then on an impulse offered one to his neighbor. The man accepted, lit up, and after a few puffs remarked, "A magnificent cigar."

"It should be," replied Knopf. "These cigars are specially put up for me by Upmann."

"Indeed?" said the stranger. "May I ask your name?"

"Alfred Knopf. May I ask yours?"

"Upmann."

———⁂———

KNOX, Philander Chase (1853–1921), *US lawyer and political leader.*

1 In 1903 Theodore Roosevelt acquired the Panama Canal Zone. Though proud of his achievement, he knew that not all citizens approved of it. Philander Knox, his attorney general, was a corporation lawyer, and it was to him that Roosevelt went for a defense of his action. Knox is said to have replied, "Oh, Mr. President, do not let so great an achievement suffer from any taint of legality."

———⁂———

KNOX, Ronald (1888–1957), *British Roman Catholic priest and author.*

1 Knox was engaged in a theological discussion with scientist John Scott Haldane. "In a universe containing millions of planets," reasoned Haldane, "is it not inevitable that life should appear on at least one of them?"

"Sir," replied Knox, "if Scotland Yard found a body in your cabin trunk, would you tell them: 'There are millions of trunks in the world; surely one of them must contain a body?' I think they would still want to know who put it there."

2 Traveling by train from Oxford to London one morning, Knox opened his copy of *The Times* and turned straight to the crossword puzzle, reputed to be the most difficult in the world. One of his fellow passengers, noticing that the priest had been staring at the puzzle for several minutes without filling in any of the answers, offered to lend him a pencil. "No, thanks," replied Knox, looking up with a smile. "Just finished."

———⁂———

KOESTLER, Arthur (1905–83), *British writer, born in Vienna.*

1 Koestler once quelled a gushing fan by saying, "Liking a writer and then meeting the writer is like liking goose liver and then meeting the goose."

———⁂———

KOO, Wellington [Ku Wei-chün] (1887–1985), *Chinese statesman and ambassador.*

1 When Wellington Koo was representing his country at the 1921 Washington Conference, he found some Americans were ill at ease when talking to a sophisticated foreigner. At a banquet he was placed next to a young woman who, after some minutes of embarrassed silence, attempted to begin a conversation with "Likee soupee?" Koo, feeling that there was not much to be said on this level, just nodded and continued with his soup. At the end of the meal he was called upon to address the guests, which he did for

ten minutes in perfect English. As he sat down, he turned to the young woman and said: "Likee speechee?"

KOPPAY, Joszi Arpád, Baron von Drétoma (1859–?), *Hungarian portrait painter.*

1 On an Atlantic crossing Koppay met the sixteen-year-old Iphigene Ochs, daughter of Adolph Ochs, the owner of the *New York Times.* He offered to paint her portrait free of charge, saying he could never be fulfilled as an artist until he had captured such beauty on canvas. Adolph Ochs, flattered, consented. When the portrait was finished Ochs received a bill for $1,000. Koppay met his objection: "Your daughter has such a beautiful face, it was a joy to paint it. But the body was dull and bored me. It is for this that I charge you one thousand dollars."

KORDA, Sir Alexander (1893–1956), *British film producer and director, born in Hungary.*

1 Having offered a part to the English actress Ann Todd, Korda changed his mind and made the film with another actress. Understandably hurt and angry, Miss Todd raged at Korda for his perfidy. "I wouldn't have done it to anyone else," said Korda. Miss Todd was taken aback by this unexpected response. "What do you mean?" she asked. "You and I are such good friends," Korda continued placatingly, "I knew you would forgive me."

2 In 1942 Korda was given a knighthood for his services to the British film industry. Proud of the honor, he resisted the temptation to take it overseriously, though it made a considerable impression upon his Hollywood colleagues. One evening he won nearly $10,000 from Sam Goldwyn at poker. The next day a check arrived, written in red ink with the note: "Signed in my blood. Sam." Soon afterward Korda lost a similar amount of money to Goldwyn. Korda sent a check in blue ink with the inscription: "This check is signed in my blood, too."

3 When Korda was filming Kipling's *Jungle Book,* a rubber and wire python was operated from a barge moored in midstream. On the barge stood the technicians, the camera crew, and Korda's brother Zoli. Korda, on the bank, remarked that the barge appeared rather unstable with so many people on it. A few minutes later it capsized. Everyone swam to the shore, with the exception of Zoli Korda, who remained in the deep water near the python, splashing and shouting. Korda watched his brother's foolery with an indulgent smile. Suddenly someone asked, "Can he swim?" Alexander Korda pondered: "No, we never learned to swim as children. I don't believe he can. Someone help him." A long pole was fetched and Zoli Korda was fished out. As soon as he could speak, he demanded, "Why didn't you bloody help?" Korda replied coolly, "You should have shouted in Hungarian. Always cry for help in your native language — they're the only people who understand."

4 Gossip said that Alexander Korda had an infallible seduction technique. After inviting a woman to stay for a drink at his apartment, he would look wistful, sigh, and say what a sadness it was for him to be impotent. Some of the most desirable women in the world had tried and failed with him, Korda would continue. Most of his guests accepted the irresistible challenge. After a while a "miracle" would happen.

5 On a visit to Marc Chagall's studio, Korda admired a painting that he said he would like

to buy. The artist, declaring that negotiations about money embarrassed and upset him, promptly left the room, leaving Mme Chagall to discuss the price. Leaning forward to speak to her, Korda suddenly noticed a reflection in a mirror. It was Chagall, standing, as he thought, unseen in the hall, and signaling to his wife. First he sketched a dollar sign in the air, then held up five fingers, then ten, and finally crossed his index fingers to indicate that she should multiply. Before Mme Chagall could saying anything, Korda offered $50,000. "Why, that's the sum I was going to ask you for," exclaimed Mme Chagall in some surprise. "How did you guess?"

"Ah, madame, sometimes a painting simply speaks for itself."

6 One afternoon Korda's nephew Michael, then a small boy, was wandering around a soundstage when he suddenly found himself in the middle of a scene his uncle was shooting with David Niven for the movie *Bonnie Prince Charlie*. With great exasperation Alexander Korda stopped the filming, telling his nephew, "My boy, try to remember, as a Korda you are supposed to be behind the camera, not in front!"

———— ⁂ ————

KOUSSEVITZKY, Sergei (1874–1951), *Russian bass player and conductor.*

1 Boston held him in the highest regard. Not only because of his long stay there but also because of his imposing presence and musical inspiration, he was a genuine idol. At one reception, a Boston matron came up to him and with awe said: "Mr. Koussevitzky, you are a god to me." To which Koussevitzky replied: "Ah, madame, what a responsibility!"

2 Koussevitzky was known for his interesting turns of phrase. Once, during rehearsals of

Ravel's *Bolero*, Koussevitzky, losing patience with a struggling tympanist, blurted out, "If you make me more nervous I send you bill from my doctor."

3 Another time, a clarinetist, goaded to the limit, glared at Koussevitzky in the midst of Shostakovitch's First Symphony. Koussevitzky finally said, "Kill me; it will make me more pleasure than listen to you!"

———— ⁂ ————

KREISLER, Fritz (1875–1962), *US violinist of Austrian birth.*

1 Setting out from Hamburg one day to give a concert in London, Kreisler found that he had an hour to kill before the boat sailed. He wandered into a music shop, where the proprietor asked if he could look at the violin Kreisler was carrying. Having looked, he vanished and then reappeared with two policemen, one of whom said to the violinist, "You are under arrest."

"What for?" asked Kreisler.

"You have Fritz Kreisler's violin."

"I am Fritz Kreisler."

"You can't pull that one on us. Come along to the station."

As Kreisler's boat was sailing soon, there was no time for prolonged inquiries and explanations. Kreisler asked if the music shop had any of his records. The proprietor found one, "The Old Refrain," and put it on the Victrola. When it had finished playing, Kreisler asked for his violin and, mustering all the skill at his command, played the piece through again. "Now are you satisfied?" he asked. They were.

2 A society hostess asked Kreisler how much he would charge to play at a private musical evening. The fee was $5,000. To this the lady reluctantly agreed, adding, "Please remember that I do not expect you to mingle with

my guests." Kreisler smiled: "In that case, madam, my fee will be only two thousand dollars."

3 Jascha Heifetz and Mischa Elman were dining together when the waiter brought over a note with the superscription: "To the greatest violinist in the world." Heifetz glanced at it and handed it to Elman: "For you, Mischa." Elman passed it back. "No, no, for *you,* Jascha," he said. The note went back and forth a few more times before they agreed to open it together. The first words were: "Dear Fritz."

4 Kreisler's devoted wife refused to sit next to him at his seventy-fifth birthday party. "I want him to have a good time with other women fussing over him," she explained. "That's my birthday gift."

L

LABOUCHERE, Henry (1831–1912), *British politician and journalist.*

1 When Labouchere was an attaché at the British legation in St. Petersburg, a pompous nobleman paid a call, stating that he wished to see the ambassador immediately. "Pray take a chair," Labouchere told him, "the ambassador will be here soon." The visitor took exception to this offhand treatment. "Young man, do you know who I am?" he demanded, and recited a list of his titles and appointments. "Pray take two chairs," said Labouchere.

2 Labouchere, away from home when his father died, came back in time to see his body. The butler showed him into the room where it lay in the open coffin. Labouchere gazed at his parent's face for a few moments, then remarked to the butler, "The right man in the right place."

3 On the day before Labouchere's death A. L. Thorold (nephew as well as biographer) was sitting by his bedside. A burning spirit lamp was accidentally overturned. Labouchere opened his eyes, murmured, "Flames? — not yet, I think," laughed, and went to sleep.

LADD, Diane (1932–), *US film actress.*

1 Married to actor Bruce Dern, Ladd had a daughter, Laura, who became interested in following in her parents' footsteps (and who indeed did). When Ladd realized her daughter's ambition, she urged her to choose another profession. "Be a doctor!" she pleaded. "Be a lawyer! Be a leper missionary!"

LAEMMLE, Carl (1908–79), *US film producer.*

1 A new writer came from Australia. Laemmle asked him how long he had been in America and was told two weeks. "It's amazing how well you talk English after only two weeks," said Carl.

LAFAYETTE, Marie Joseph Gilbert du Motier, Marquis de (1757–1834), *French general and politician.*

1 The harvest of 1783 was a poor one, but the bailiffs of Lafayette's estates at Chavaniac had managed to fill the barns with wheat. "The bad harvest has raised the price of wheat," said the bailiff. "This is the time to sell." Lafayette thought about the hungry peasants in the surrounding villages. "No," he replied, "this is the time to give."

2 In the heady days of the French Revolution the followers of Lafayette once went to unusual lengths to indicate their admiration. Stopping his carriage in the street, they unhitched the horses and pulled the vehicle to its destination. Some weeks later it was suggested to Lafayette that he must have been much pleased by the gesture. The great man considered for a moment. "Yes, it was delightful, delightful," he agreed slowly, "but one thing disturbs me a little — I never saw anything more of my horses."

3 Upon Lafayette's last visit to the United States, he called on Jefferson at Monticello. The news of the visit drew a great crowd, who watched as the old and feeble former President and the lame French hero, broken from years in prison, were to meet. Jefferson walked down the steps of his house as Lafayette descended from his carriage. At first they walked toward each other, then broke into a run, falling into each other's arms. "Ah, Jefferson!" "Ah, Lafayette!" they cried, tears running down their faces. Among the four hundred witnesses, there was not a sound or a dry eye as the two men slowly walked in Monticello, their arms around each other.

LA FONTAINE, Jean de (1621–95), *French poet renowned for his* Fables *(1668–94).*

1 La Fontaine, engaged to make a speech before the French Academy, had first to attend a society gathering that soon began to bore him. He excused his departure by explaining the circumstances of his engagement. "But," objected his hostess, "the Academy isn't scheduled to meet for a whole hour. Taking the quickest way, you'll need only twenty minutes to get there." La Fontaine made a courteous bow, replying, "But you see, I prefer the longest way."

LA GUARDIA, Fiorello (1882–1947), *US politician and mayor of New York (1933–45), nicknamed the "Little Flower."*

1 (Bennett Cerf records an occasion on which La Guardia was presiding at the police court.)

"One bitter cold day they brought a trembling old man before him, charged with stealing a loaf of bread. His family, he said, was starving. 'I've got to punish you,' declared La Guardia. 'The law makes no exception. I can do nothing but sentence you to a fine of ten dollars.'

"But the Little Flower was reaching into his pocket as he added, 'Well, here's the ten dollars to pay our fine. And now I remit the fine.' He tossed a ten-dollar bill into his famous sombrero. 'Furthermore,' he declared, 'I'm going to fine everybody in this courtroom fifty cents for living in a town where a man has to steal bread in order to eat. Mr. Bailiff, collect the fines and give them to this defendant!' The hat was passed and an incredulous old man, with a light of heaven in his eyes, left the courtroom with a stake of forty-seven dollars and fifty cents."

2 (Journalist John Gunther, interviewing La Guardia, asked him about the large collection of files in his office.)

"I'll tell you a little story. Files are the curse of modern civilization. I had a young secretary once. Just out of school. I told her, 'If you can keep these files straight, I'll marry you.' She did, and so I married her."

3 An important German diplomat was to pay a visit to New York. It was the mid-1930s, and anti-Nazi feeling ran high in the city. La Guardia, as mayor, was duty-bound to protect his visitor, but he found it hard to swallow his own hatred of the Nazis. As a compromise, he surrounded the diplomat

with a bodyguard of specially selected policemen. They were all Jewish.

4 La Guardia felt that the New York police were being rather too hard on young offenders, and tried to point out to them the difference between a mischievous prank and true juvenile delinquency. "When I was a boy," he said, "I used to wander around the streets with my friends until we found a horse tied up to a post. We'd unhitch him, ride him around town, then tie him up again."

"Are you trying to tell us," asked one of the policemen, "that the mayor of New York was once a horse thief?"

"No," replied La Guardia. "I'm telling you that he was once a boy."

———— ❧ ————

LAIRD, Melvin (1922–), *US politician.*

1 When Richard Nixon visited the Vatican in 1970, it was decided that the presidential party should leave from St. Peter's Square in a US military helicopter. In order not to embarrass the Curia with further reminders of warfare, it was suggested to the secretary of defense that he should not accompany the rest of the party to the papal audience. However, Laird was not so easily spurned. When the group gathered inside the Vatican, there he was, smoking his inevitable cigar and ready with the excuse that he was only looking for the President's helicopter. He was persuaded at least to pocket the cigar as the pope began to speak. Unfortunately, the cigar was still alight and in a few moments Laird's jacket was issuing ominous clouds of smoke. Alarmed, Laird began slapping at his pocket. Many of the guests present, interpreting the sound as applause, joined in enthusiastically. Ingrained Vatican decorum, thus challenged, was maintained only with difficulty.

———— ❧ ————

LAÏS (5th century BC), *famous Corinthian beauty.*

1 When she moved to Athens, Laïs posed for several well-known Athenian sculptors. The elderly Myron, who had created the classic *Discus Thrower,* was high on her list. When she removed her clothes and prepared to pose, the old man was instantly rejuvenated and offered her the entire contents of his studio if she would stay the night with him. Glancing at the old man's tangled gray hair and beard and tattered garments, she put her clothes back on and walked out.

The following day, the eager Myron had his hair cut, his beard shaved, and his new robe perfumed. Then, donning a gold chain, he found Laïs and declared his love for her. "My friend," she said, "you are asking me to do for you what I refused your father yesterday."

———— ❧ ————

LAMAR, Lucius Quintus Cincinnatus (1825–93), *US statesman and judge.*

1 When Lamar was appointed secretary of the interior on a salary of $8,000, he looked for a residence to rent. It happened that the widow of Admiral J. H. Dahlgren had a property to let in the neighborhood that Lamar liked. She informed him that the house was indeed for rent — at $7,500 per annum. Secretary Lamar sat quite motionless, eyes downcast, saying nothing, until Mrs. Dahlgren finally asked if he had been taken ill. "No, madam," he replied, "I was simply wondering what I could do with the remainder of my salary."

———— ❧ ————

LAMB, Lady Caroline (1785–1828), *British novelist.*

1 (The *Boston Globe* told this story:)

"Lady Caroline, renowned for her flamboyant style, once celebrated the birthday of her husband, the English prime minister Lord Melbourne, by having herself served to him as a birthday banquet dish. On that occasion, she emerged naked from a large tureen."

2 Lady Caroline was staying with her cousin Lord Hartington at Lismore Castle in Ireland. One evening, after a dispute with Hartington, Lady Caroline suddenly went to the door, opened it wide, and said, "Pray walk in, sir. I have no doubt that you are the rightful possessor, and my cousin only an interloper, usurping your usual habitation." Nothing happened for some minutes, then in hopped a frog. Caroline walked behind it with two lighted candles, "to treat the master of the castle with proper respect."

LAMB, Charles (1775–1834), *British essayist, poet, and literary critic.*

1 When Charles Lamb was little more than a toddler, his sister, Mary, took him for a walk in the graveyard. The precocious little boy read the laudatory epitaphs on the tombstones, commemorating the deceased as "virtuous," "charitable," "beloved," and so on. As they came away, he asked, "Mary, where are all the naughty people buried?"

2 A superior in the office where Lamb worked reproached him for bad time-keeping. "You arrive late, Mr. Lamb," the senior clerk began. Lamb is reputed to have replied, "But see how early I leave!"

3 Lamb had been advised for medical reasons to take a course of sea-bathing at Hastings. Shivering with cold and trepidation, he stood at the door of his bathing machine and issued instructions to the men who were to "dip" him. Unfortunately, his stammer got the better of him: "Hear me, men! Take notice of this. I am to be d-d-d-dipped . . ." Tired of waiting, the two men assumed their instructions to be complete and plunged the protesting writer into the sea. Emerging from the icy water, Lamb was only able to stutter, "I tell you I am to be d-d-d-dipped . . ." before being plunged for a second time. After his third ducking, Lamb was finally allowed to complete his sentence: "I tell you that I am — no, that I *was* — to be d-d-d-dipped only *once*."

4 Lamb's farce, *Mr. H——* was a complete failure on its first night. Sitting in the pit at Drury Lane Theatre, he joined in the hissing, because, as he later explained, he was "so damnably afraid of being taken for the author."

5 "Don't introduce me to him," said Lamb urgently when a friend offered to present a man whom Lamb had for a long time disliked by hearsay. "I want to go on hating him, and I can't do that to a man I know."

6 Lamb was a generally acquiescent audience for the garrulous Coleridge. One day when Coleridge had been particularly voluble, he suddenly interjected the question, "Charles, have you ever heard me preach?"

"I've never heard you do anything else," replied Lamb resignedly.

7 In the course of a lecture, Lamb was interrupted by a hiss from the audience. "There are only three things that hiss," said Lamb calmly, "a goose, a snake, and a fool. Stand forth, and let us identify you."

LANDERS, Ann (1918–), *US advice columnist.*

1 Landers, born Eppie Lederer, was raised in a comfortable Midwestern home (with her sister, who writes the "Dear Abby" advice column), and had experienced little emotional turmoil or distress as a young woman. When asked how she felt qualified to give advice to

others about their problems, given her own serene upbringing, she answered, "I don't believe that you have to be a cow to know what milk is."

———∞———

LANDIS, Kenesaw Mountain (1866–1944), *US jurist, the first commissioner of baseball (1920–44).*

1 An old offender was severely reprimanded by Landis and sentenced to five years in prison.
  "But I'm a sick man, I'll be dead long before that," he protested. "I can't do five years!"
  Landis fixed the felon with an icy glare. "You can try, can't you?" he thundered.

———∞———

LANDOR, Walter Savage (1775–1864), *British poet, essayist, and critic.*

1 Landor's cook displeased his master one day by serving an indifferent meal. Landor in a passion threw him through an open window. The cook landed awkwardly in the flower bed below and broke a limb. Landor cried out, "Good God, I forgot the violets!"

———∞———

LANDOWSKA, Wanda (1879–1959), *Polish harpsichordist.*

1 Landowska was famous for her interpretation of Bach. Meeting a woman who also was a Bach specialist, she was soon deeply engrossed in discussion. The other lady's views on Bach ornamentation differed from Landowska's. "Well, my dear," said Landowska, "you continue to play Bach your way, and I'll continue to play him his way."

———∞———

LANDRU, Henri Désiré (1869–1922), *French multiple murderer.*

1 Landru's trial was a popular sensation, with fashionable ladies, complete with picnic baskets and pet dogs, contending for seats in the courtroom. Landru's comment: "If any lady would care to have my place, I would willingly surrender it."

2 Landru was sentenced to die for murdering ten women in Paris. As he approached the guillotine he was seen to have been shorn of the long black beard of which he was so proud. He had asked for a shave that morning, saying to the prison barber, "It will please the ladies."

———∞———

LANG, George (b. 1924–), *Hungarian-born US restaurateur.*

1 Lang's first job in New York was as a busboy in a busy and chic restaurant. One night he was rushing through the kitchen when the German chef thrust a huge and beautiful lobster platter at him, barking instructions — of which Lang understood only the words "go" and "fast." Lang disappeared with it. Fifteen minutes later, as he reappeared in the kitchen, the staff fell silent. The chef asked him what he had done with the lobster meant for the table of Claudette Colbert; Lang replied, to everyone's horror, including his own,"Thank you very, very much. It was absolutely delicious." He had thought he was being asked to eat an unusually magnificent staff meal quickly.

2 Lang worked for a time at London's Savoy Hotel, learning the intricacies of the grand hotel business. One afternoon a very casually dressed young woman approached the manager and complained that she had been refused tea. When the manager, observing her dress, noted that the Savoy did not serve

people in jeans, she said, "You certainly don't keep up with the times." "No, madame," replied the man, "we try to keep up with our past."

———— ⚮ ————

LANGTRY, Lillie [Emilie Charlotte le Breton] (1853–1929), *British actress.*

1 Lillie Langtry was the mistress of the Prince of Wales (later King Edward VII). During a quarrel, the prince complained, "I've spent enough on you to buy a battleship." Lillie retorted, "And you've spent enough in me to float one."

———— ⚮ ————

LAPLACE, Pierre-Simon, Marquis de (1749–1827), *French mathematician and astronomer.*

1 Laplace presented a copy of an early volume of his *Mécanique céleste* to Napoleon, who studied it very carefully. Sending for Laplace, he said, "You have written a large book about the universe without once mentioning the author of the universe." "Sire," Laplace replied, "I have no need of that hypothesis."

2 Joseph-Louis Lagrange worked with Laplace on the *Mécanique céleste* and indeed made an original contribution to the thinking behind it. Laplace failed to acknowledge this contribution, an omission that the generous Lagrange appears not to have resented. When Lagrange heard of Laplace's reply to Napoleon, he is said to have shaken his head at his colleague's skepticism, commenting, "But it is a beautiful hypothesis just the same. It explains so many things."

———— ⚮ ————

LARDNER, Ring [Ringgold Wilmer] (1885–1933), *US writer.*

1 Lardner was drinking at a club frequented by actors when an individual came in whose

flamboyance of dress and hairstyle were remarkable even in those theatrical surroundings. Lardner scrutinized the man for some minutes and then said to him, "How do you look when I'm sober?"

2 On an excursion Ring Lardner and Arthur Jacks stocked their hotel room with supplies of liquor, including a good Canadian whiskey and some inferior Midwestern corn. They made a heavy night of it. When Jacks awoke the following morning, he felt rather ill and in need of a drink. He poured himself some of the Canadian whiskey, which promptly made him sick. He tried again, with the ame result. On Jacks's third or fourth unsuccessful attempt to keep the liquor down, Lardner opened one eye and said, "Arthur, if you're just practicing, would you mind using the corn?"

———— ⚮ ————

LASORDA, Tommy (1927–), *US baseball manager.*

1 The Dodgers manager believed that managerial direction was more effective in winning games than any kind of team unity. Once he was overheard from his office loudly arguing with Kirk Gibson, who strongly objected to being traded. As Lasorda left his office, the eavesdropping team members wondered if his bitter words would have a negative effect on team chemistry. "Chemistry?" responded Lasorda. "What's that? I think I took it in high school."

———— ⚮ ————

LATIMER, Hugh (?1485–1555), *English cleric, bishop of Worcester (1535–39).*

1 After a show trial at Oxford, Latimer and the bishop of London, Nicholas Ridley, were condemned to be burned at the stake for heresy. As the fire was lighted, Latimer turned to his co-martyr and said, "Be of

good comfort, Master Ridley, and play the man; we shall this day light such a candle, by God's grace, in England as I trust shall never be put out."

LAUGHTON, Charles (1899–1962), *British character actor and director.*

1 Laughton, married to actress Elsa Lanchester, was once asked the hypothetical question: "Would you ever consider marrying again?" Having answered emphatically in the negative, the actor was asked his reasons. "During courtship," replied Laughton, "a man reveals only his better qualities. After marriage, however, his real self gradually begins to emerge, and there is very little his wife can do about it." After a moment's pause he concluded: "I don't believe I would ever put a woman through that again."

2 Having invited Laughton and a number of other film stars to dinner one evening, pianist Artur Rubinstein entertained his guests before the meal by showing home movies of his children's amateur stage performances. The "audience" was visibly relieved when the last reel came to an end and dinner was served. "I've always regretted that I never had children," remarked Laughton to his host as they passed into the dining room, "and never more so than now. Because, Mr. Rubinstein, if I had children, I would make them play the piano for you."

LAUZUN, Armand Louis de Gontaut, Duc de (1747–93), *French aristocrat and soldier.*

1 When the executioner came to fetch the duke from his cell, he found him eating oysters and drinking wine. "Allow me to finish, citizen," said the condemned man. "And take a glass of this wine. In your profession you must need courage."

LAVOISIER, Antoine Laurent (1743–94), *French chemist, discoverer of the two gases he named oxygen and nitrogen.*

1 "But I'm a scientist," protested Lavoisier to the officer who had been sent to arrest him on the charge of tax-farming. "The Republic has no need of scientists," replied the man.

LAWRENCE, D[avid] H[erbert] (1885–1930), *British novelist and poet.*

1 Lawrence's first novel, *The White Peacock,* was published in 1911. He was able to give it to his mother on her deathbed. His father, after struggling through half a page, asked Lawrence how much he had got for the book. "Fifty pounds, father," he replied. The old miner was incredulous: "Fifty pounds! An' tha's niver done a day's hard work in thy life!"

2 Much of his life Lawrence battled bad health. He had almost died of pneumonia, and tuberculosis ravaged his lungs. Together with his wife, Frieda, he traveled in search of a healthful climate. They finally settled on a lovely house on the French Riviera. As Frieda looked at the beautiful flowers filling his room, she said, "Why, oh why, can't you flourish like these?"

LAWRENCE, James (1781–1813), *US naval hero.*

1 During the War of 1812 the US frigate *Chesapeake* engaged the British frigate *Shannon* off Boston and was badly beaten. In the fighting James Lawrence, the *Chesapeake's* captain, was mortally wounded. His dying words are now part of American legend: "Don't give up the ship."

LAWRENCE, T[homas] E[dward] (1888–1935), *British soldier and writer, known as "Lawrence of Arabia" for leading the Arab revolt against the Turks*

1 (It was Lawrence's greatest source of pride that he was a Fellow of All Souls College, Oxford; it is, with his birth and death dates, the only fact about his career recorded on his tombstone in the quiet country churchyard in Dorset. Robert Graves recalls how, shortly after World War I, Lawrence acquired the two heavy leather chairs that were part of the furnishing in his rooms in All Souls.)

"An American oil-financier had come in suddenly one day when I was there and said, 'I am here from the States, Colonel Lawrence, to ask a single question. You are the only man who will answer it honestly. Do Middle-Eastern conditions justify my putting any money in South Arabian oil?' The always self-assured Lawrence, without rising, quietly answered, 'No.' 'That's all I wanted to know; it was worth coming for. Thank you, and good day!' In his brief glance about the room he missed something and, on his way home through London, chose the chairs and had them sent to Lawrence with his card."

2 (Edward Marsh relates this story:)

"On one of his spells in the ranks [Lawrence] was assigned as batman to an officer of the class who used to be known in the War as 'temporary gentlemen.' Lawrence hated him at sight, and on the first evening, when he was unpacking his kit, looked round and said: 'I beg your pardon, sir, but I can only find one of your razors.' 'I've only got one razor.' 'Indeed, sir? I thought most gentlemen had a razor for every day in the week.' After a moment he looked round again. 'Sir, I can't find your left-handed nail-scissors.' The poor man rushed out of the tent and applied for a less exacting batman."

3 At a cocktail party in Egypt on a day of intense heat, Lawrence was approached by a lady of uncertain age who had the reputation of perseveringly courting the acquaintance of celebrities. Seizing upon the heat wave as a conversational gambit, she remarked, "Ninety-two today, Colonel Lawrence. Just think of it! Ninety-two."

"Many happy returns, madam," responded Lawrence.

LAWSON, Wilfrid [Wilfrid Worsnop] (1900–66), *British character actor.*

1 Lunching in a pub before a matinee performance, Lawson met fellow-actor Richard Burton and invited him to the show that afternoon. As Lawson was not due to appear at the beginning of the play, he sat with Burton to watch the opening scenes. Some twenty minutes into the performance, however, Burton was a little concerned to find Lawson still sitting beside him, having made no move to leave and prepare for his entrance. A few moments later, Lawson tapped Burton on the arm. "You'll like this bit," he whispered excitedly. "This is where I come on."

LEAHY, William Daniel (1875–1959), *US admiral.*

1 When Truman came to office in 1945, Leahy was present at meetings at which the new President was briefed upon the development of an atomic weapon. Leahy's comment: "That is the biggest fool thing we have ever done. . . . The bomb will never go off."

LEAR, Edward (1812–88), *British artist and poet.*

1 In 1846 Lear was asked to give Queen Victoria a course of drawing lessons. These progressed very well and Lear soon felt quite at east in the royal apartments. He liked to stand in front of the fire, warming his coattails, but every time he took up his position on the hearthrug, facing the queen, one of the lords-in-waiting would invite him to look at something on the far side of the room, thus obliging him to move. No one explained, and the episode was repeated several times before it dawned upon Lear that etiquette forbade a subject to adopt such a relaxed and comfortable posture in his sovereign's presence.

2 Queen Victoria took a liking to Lear. Following one of the drawing lessons, she showed him some miniatures and other treasures kept in display cases in her apartments. Lear in his enthusiasm exclaimed, "Oh, where did you get all these beautiful things?" The queen replied, "I inherited them, Mr. Lear."

3 Traveling in southern Italy in 1847, Lear was overtaken by the beginnings of the Italian revolution at Reggio. He returned to his hotel to find the waiter deliriously drunk, and his pleas for the keys to his room fell on oblivious ears. *"Non ci sono più chiavi; non ci sono più passaporti, non ci sono più Ré — più legge — più giudici — più niente! Non è altro che l'amore, la libertà — l'amicizia e la constituzione . . ."* (There are no more keys, there are no more passports, no more kings, no more laws, no more judges, no more nothing! Nothing but love, liberty, friendship, and the constitution.)

4 When a man is in full flight upon some learned topic that tests the intellect and demands the greatest concentration, he does not especially welcome another's irrelevant witticisms. Just such a man was Lear's old friend Lord Westbury, the ex-lord chancellor. One evening, in the midst of a discussion on Tennyson, Lear could not help slipping in a small pun or two. "Lear," said the old man sternly, "I abominate the forcible introduction of ridiculous images calculated to distract the mind from what it is contemplating."

━━━━━━━━ ⌘ ━━━━━━━━

LEDRU-ROLLIN, Alexandre Auguste (1807–74), *French politician.*

1 During the Revolution of February 1848 Ledru-Rollin was caught up in a mob at the barricades. Amid the confusion he was heard to shout, "Let me pass, I have to follow them, I am their leader!"

━━━━━━━━ ⌘ ━━━━━━━━

LEE, Gypsy Rose [Rose Louise Hovick] (1919–70), *US entertainer and professional celebrity.*

1 In his book about his mother, Gypsy's son, Erik Lee Preminger, recalls that one of her favorite (and always financially productive) hobbies was sewing. In the spring of 1955 her friend Mr. John, the famous milliner, showed her his spring collection in advance. Gypsy bought one of the hats, took it apart, made a dozen copies, and distributed them to her friends as Easter gifts. Mr. John noticed one of these friends, complete with hat, walking past his shop and at once phoned Gypsy. She cut him off with, "Oh, John darling, I'm so glad you called. I made a few copies of your marvelous hat, and I need some labels. The hats look so naked without them." The labels arrived shortly. They read: "A Mr. John design stolen by Gypsy Rose Lee." Gypsy put one inside each hat.

━━━━━━━━ ⌘ ━━━━━━━━

Thérèse Lachmann, one of the *grandes horizontales* of the era of Napoleon III, played with francs like a child playing with sand. Once an impecunious admirer pursued her for months, passionately. At length she instructed him to bring her 10,000 francs in small notes. "We'll waste them together," she promised him. He somehow acquired the necessary investment and arrived at Thérèse's boudoir to find her gracefully arranged on a couch beside which a marble table had been placed. On this altar she piled the crumpled notes and set a match to them. "I promise that your flame shall be allowed to burn as long as the notes," she told him. In very short order, money and passion were consumed, and she looked ironically at her lover. To her astonishment his face wore the same expression. "They were counterfeit," he said.

LEE, Nathaniel (?1653–92), *British playwright.*

1 A friend visited Lee in Bedlam and, finding him calm and reasonable, hoped he had recovered. Lee offered to show him around the asylum. As they proceeded, Lee's conversation was so rational that the friend's hopes soared. At length they came out on the lofty roof of the building. Lee suddenly gripped his visitor's arm. "Let us immortalize ourselves; let us leap down this moment!" he burst out excitedly. "Any man could leap *down*," said Lee's friend coolly, "so we should not immortalize ourselves that way. But let us go down and try if we can leap *up*." Delighted with the idea, Lee at once ran down the stairs to see if he could put into practice his friend's novel idea for achieving immortality.

LEE, Robert E[dward] (1807–70), *US Confederate general.*

1 Confederate troops held a low ridge called Marye's Heights at Fredericksburg (1862). The Union divisions sent to assault it had exposed ground to cross before they could reach the Confederate positions. Wave after wave of federal troops charged with bayonets and were cut down by the Confederate fire before any could reach the stone wall marking the enemy front line. More than twelve thousand were killed. Watching the dying federal soldiers, Lee remarked to General James Longstreet, whose men were holding Marye's Heights, "It is well that war is so terrible; else we would grow too fond of it."

2 One day in 1864 Lee visited General Henry Heth at Petersburg to inspect his defenses. As they rode down the line, Lee was displeased to see a large stretch without fortification. Heth was surprised, for he had given orders for the defenses to be completed. He assured the general that the work would be undertaken immediately, but when Lee returned a few days later nothing had been done. He was obviously very annoyed, and Heth waited anxiously for the storm to break. However, much to Heth's relief, Lee began talking instead about the rather boisterous horse being ridden by Heth's wife. To quiet the horse down, Lee recommended plenty of exercise. He concluded, "For the sake of your wife, as well as your own, I beg you to try the experiment; and I know of no better place for you to ride the horse than just up and down in front of the gap I ordered you to have closed, until a good breastwork has been completed."

3 Shortly before the battle of Spotsylvania in 1864, it was reported that General Grant had lost many men and was preparing to retreat. General John Gordon was therefore surprised when Lee ordered him to move his troops to Spotsylvania Courthouse. Lee, however, having great faith in Grant's military genius, had reasoned thus: "General Grant ought to move to Spotsylvania. That is his best maneuver and he will do what is best. I am so sure of it that I have had a short road cut to that point, and you will move by that route." The prediction was fulfilled:

Grant's troops arrived at Spotsylvania at almost exactly the same moment as the Confederate forces under Gordon.

4 Toward the end of the Civil War, when meat was an almost unobtainable luxury for Lee, he lived chiefly on boiled cabbage. One day, when he had several important guests dining with him, the table was set with the usual heap of cabbage and a very small piece of meat. The guests politely refused to eat the meat, and Lee looked forward to having it all to himself the following day. However, on the next day there was nothing but the usual cabbage. Lee inquired as to the whereabouts of the meat. He learned to his dismay that his servant had only borrowed the meat to impress the guests, and had duly returned it, untouched, to its rightful owner.

5 One Sunday morning in 1865, a black man entered a fashionable Episcopalian church in Richmond, Virginia. When Communion was served, he walked down the aisle and knelt at the altar. A rustle of resentment swept the congregation — how dare he! Episcopalians use the common cup. Then a distinguished layman stood up, stepped forward to the altar, and knelt beside the black man. It was Robert E. Lee. Said he to the congregation, "All men are brothers in Christ. Have we not all one Father?" Humbly, the congregation followed his lead.

6 After the Civil War Lee was encouraged to write his memoirs. He refused: "I should be trading on the blood of my men."

———— ❧ ————

LEHMANN, Lilli (1848–1929), *German coloratura soprano who specialized in Wagnerian roles.*

1 At a reception given by Wagner's widow, Cosima, during the 1894 Bayreuth festival, soprano Lillian Nordica, who was singing Elsa in *Lohengrin* at the festival, approached Lilli Lehmann and asked if she might call on her. Glaring frostily at her potential rival, Lehmann replied: "I am not taking any pupils this season."

———— ❧ ————

LEIGHTON, Frederic, Baron Leighton of Stretton (1830–96), *British painter and sculptor.*

1 Leighton, who prided himself on the thoroughness of his draftsmanship, met Whistler one day in Piccadilly, and took it upon himself to remark upon the other artist's technique. "My dear Whistler, you leave your pictures in such a crude, sketchy state. Why don't you ever finish them?"

"My dear Leighton," was the response, "why do you ever begin yours?"

———— ❧ ————

LENCLOS, Ninon de (1620–1705), *French courtesan.*

1 Ninon de Lenclos's sexual expertise was so renowned that daughters of the aristocracy were sent to her to learn the art of love. One such student asked, "How large should a woman's breast be to attract a lover?"

"Large enough to fill the hand of an honest man," replied her instructress.

2 Ninon de Lenclos had no time for the fashionable group of writers known as the *précieuses,* and poked fun at their literary and social affectations. When a man complained to her that his daughter had lost her memory, she answered, "Be thankful, monsieur, for that will prevent her from quoting."

3 A nobleman forced to flee Paris entrusted half his savings of twenty thousand crowns to a clergyman and the other half to Ninon, asking them both to look after the money for him until he returned. When the nobleman eventually came back to Paris, he found that the clergyman had given away his ten thousand crowns to the poor to enhance his own

charitable reputation. If this was how the saint behaved, then what could he expect from the sinner? Ninon, however, had kept her share intact and was delighted to be able to hand back his ten thousand crowns.

4 In her sixties Ninon de Lenclos still received a few young men, the sons of close friends, to educate them in the skills of being a gentleman. One, a certain Monsieur de Gersay, fell in love with her. Knowing him to be her own son, Ninon ridiculed him, pleading that at her age no sexual relationship could even be contemplated. The youth persisted until his mother had no alternative but to say, "This dreadful love cannot continue. Do you realize who you are and who I am?" The boy, stunned, murmured the word "Mother," ran outside into the garden, drew his sword, and fell upon it.

5 In her will Ninon de Lenclos left only 10 écus to provide for her funeral. She wished it to be as simple as possible. However, she did ask her attorney, M. Arouet, if she might leave a thousand francs to his son, a clever lad who was studying with the Jesuits, so that he could buy books. The attorney's son grew up to be Voltaire.

LENNON, John (1940–80), *British singer and composer, founding member of The Beatles.*

1 At a performance in England at which members of the Royal Family were in attendance, John asked fans to clap their hands in time with the music. Nodding to the royal box, he said, "Those upstairs, just rattle your jewelry."

LENYA, Lotte (1900–81), *Austrian-born actress and singer.*

1 Although she had a magnetic stage personality, Lotte Lenya was no beauty. She would of-

ten tell the story of how Kurt Weill proposed to her. They were boating one afternoon on a lake, Weill wearing his thick glasses, since he was very nearsighted. Accidentally, she knocked them into the water. Later that afternoon he asked her to marry him. Sometime afterward she asked him, "Would you have married me with your glasses on?" He peered at her closely and said, "I *think* so."

LEO X (1475–1521), *pope (1513–21). Born Giovanni de' Medici, second son of Lorenzo the Magnificent.*

1 As Leo was a smiling sybarite infected with the popular neopagan culture of his day, his pontificate was a gorgeous carnival that left the Church bankrupt. To his flair for bacchanalian diversions, he added a reckless patronage of the arts, worked Raphael to death, and adorned his court with all the entertainers, scholars, and poets money could buy. When he was enthroned, he remarked: "Since God has given us the papacy, let us enjoy it."

LEONARD, Elmore (1925–), *US writer of crime novels and westerns.*

1 The author of *Glitz* and other popular detective thrillers was once asked how he managed to keep the action in his books moving so quickly. He said, "I leave out the parts that people skip."

LEONIDAS (d. 480 BC), *king of Sparta (487–480).*

1 The Persians sent an envoy to Leonidas urging the futility of resistance to the advance of their huge army. "Our archers are so numerous," said the envoy, "that the flight of their arrows darkens the sun."

"So much the better," replied Leonidas, "for we shall then fight in the shade."

LEOPOLD II (1835–1909), *king of the Belgians (1865–1909).*

1 A zealous republican once observed to King Leopold that although he had no liking for monarchies he did acknowledge Leopold's superior qualities. "I admit you would make an excellent president of a republic," he went on. "Really?" said the king. "I must remember to pass that compliment along to my doctor. 'Thiriar,' I'll say, 'you are an excellent doctor and I think you would make an admirable vet.'"

2 Once while King Leopold was in consultation with his ministers, a breeze blew a pile of documents from his desk onto the floor. "You pick them up," said the king, pointing to his nephew, the heir apparent, Prince Albert. "Leave him alone," he went on, addressing the ministers, who were clearly embarrassed to see their future monarch groveling on the floor. "A constitutional king must learn to stoop."

LESCHETIZKY, Theodor (1830–1915), *Polish pianist.*

1 Leschetizky considered that there were three essentials for pianistic greatness. He used to ask prospective pupils three questions: "Were you a child prodigy? Are you of Slavic descent? Are you a Jew?" If the answer to all three was "Yes," Leschetizky was delighted and would undertake the young player's tuition.

LESSING, Gotthold Ephraim (1729–81), *German dramatist, historian, and theologian.*

1 Many stories are told of Lessing's absentmindedness. One evening, returning home after dark without his key, he knocked on the front door of his house. A servant looked out of a window and, not recognizing his master in the gloom, called out, "The professor is not at home."

"Oh, very well," said Lessing, turning away. "No matter. Tell him I'll call another time."

LEVANT, Oscar (1906–72), *US pianist, writer, and wit.*

1 During World War II Oscar Levant appeared before the draft-board examiner. "Do you think you can kill?" the official asked. "I don't know about strangers," replied Oscar, "but friends, yes."

2 Levant was playing a virtuoso passage at a college concert when a telephone began ringing offstage. The pianist carried on, but the ringing continued and soon the audience became restless. Levant, without pausing in his playing, glanced at the audience and said, "If that's for me, tell them I'm busy."

3 The model for the face on the Liberty Head dime was Mrs. Wallace Stevens, wife of the famous poet. Introduced once to Stevens, Oscar Levant's first words were: "Why shouldn't you be a great poet? I'd be inspired too if my wife had little wings where her ears should be."

4 As a houseguest in the Kaufman household, Levant rather overstayed his welcome. At the end of one of his prolonged visits, Mrs. Kaufman hinted, "The servants always expect a little something, and I know you haven't any money, so I tipped them each three dollars and told them it was from you." Levant was

outraged. "You should have given them five!" he exclaimed. "Now they'll think I'm stingy."

5 (Oscar Levant describes his reprisals against a woman who arrived late for one of his recitals and distracted the audience as she walked down the center aisle.)

"I stopped my performance of a Poulenc piece and began choreographing her walk by playing in time with her steps. She hesitated and slowed down — I slowed down. She stopped — I stopped. She hurried — I hurried. By the time she reached her seat, the audience was in hysterics and the matron in a state of wild confusion."

———— ⌀ ————

LÉVIS, Duc Guston Pierre Marc de (?1764–1830), *French aristocrat.*

1 The de Lévis family considered itself to be the oldest in Christendom. Their château was reputed to contain two paintings to prove it: one of Noah going into the Ark with a box full of the Lévis papers under his arm; the other of the Virgin Mary addressing the founder of the house as *mon cousin* and begging him to put his hat back on.

———— ⌀ ————

LEWIS, C[live] S[taples] (1898–1963), *British writer and scholar of medieval and renaissance history, author of theological works.*

1 An important part of the selection procedure for Oxford fellowships — and one much dreaded by shy candidates — was dinner at the high table with the assembled dons, who would put aspirants through their social paces. When C. S. Lewis was a candidate for a fellowship in English at Magdalen College, Oxford, he was placed next to the elderly and formidable Sir Herbert Warren, president of the college. Throughout the first two

courses the president did not speak a word. Then, as the meat course was served, Warren spoke: "Do you like poetry, Mr. Lewis?" Lewis replied, "Yes, President, I do." As there seemed to be no further reaction from his eminent neighbor, he added, "I also like prose." That was the whole extent of their conversation. Lewis was awarded his fellowship.

2 The medievalist Nevill Coghill once encountered C. S. Lewis walking in the grounds of Magdalen College. Lewis was wearing a happy smile. Coghill greeted him with, "You're looking very pleased with yourself. What is it?"

"I believe," Lewis replied modestly but triumphantly, "I have proved that the Renaissance never happened in England." Coghill was about to interrupt in astonishment, but Lewis checked him and went on: "Alternatively, that if it did it had no importance."

3 Lewis had been on a walking tour. As he boarded the train for his return journey, his unkempt appearance startled an old lady in the first-class compartment. "Have you a first-class ticket?" she asked. "Yes, madam," replied Lewis, "but I'm afraid I'll be needing it for myself."

———— ⌀ ————

LEWIS, Matthew Gregory (1775–1818), *British novelist and poet.*

1 The immensely successful *Monk* brought its author the adulation of high society, an attention he greatly enjoyed. Byron records seeing Lewis with red eyes and air "sentimental" and asking him what was the matter. "I am so deeply affected by kindness," said the author, "and just now the Duchess of York said something so kind to me —" Here he broke off as his tears began to flow again. "Never mind, Lewis," said a colonel

who was standing nearby, "never mind, don't cry. She couldn't mean it."

———— ✃ ————

LEWIS, Sinclair (1885–1951), *US novelist, awarded the 1930 Nobel Prize for Literature, the first American author to receive the award.*

1 Sinclair Lewis met journalist Dorothy Thompson a few days after her divorce had come through and immediately proposed marriage to her. She hesitated, saying that she knew him only as a public figure, not as a private person. He replied that he would continue to ask her in public and private to marry him until she consented. Shortly afterward, called upon at a dinner party to make a speech, he stood up, said, "Dorothy, will you marry me?" and sat down again.

2 In 1927, when he began his courtship of Dorothy Thompson, Sinclair Lewis followed her across Europe, all the way to Moscow. At Moscow airport, says John Jakes in *Great Women Reporters,* the press was waiting to greet him. "What brought you to Russia?" Lewis was asked.

"Dorothy," he said.

"We mean, what's your business here?" the press persisted.

"Dorothy," said Lewis.

"You misunderstand. What do you plan to see in Russia?"

"Dorothy," said Lewis.

3 Booked to give a lecture at Columbia University on the writer's craft, Sinclair Lewis began by asking, "How many of you here are really serious about being writers?" A forest of hands shot up. "Well, why the hell aren't you all home writing?" said Lewis, and sat down.

4 After Lewis's death in Rome from alcoholism, his body was cremated and the urn containing his ashes sent to the US embassy for safekeeping until their final disposal. A caller was surprised to find one of the con-

sular officials on her knees, busy with a broom and pan, an overturned funerary urn beside her. "Whatever are you doing?" he said. "Sweeping up Sinclair Lewis," was the response.

———— ✃ ————

LIBERACE, Wladziu Valentino ["Liberace"] (1919–1987), *US pianist renowned for his sequined suits and flamboyant lifestyle as much as for his piano playing.*

1 Liberace's concert in Madison Square Garden, New York, in June 1954 was vastly successful with his fans, but the critics loathed him. Sometime later Liberace observed to the latter, "What you said hurt me very much. I cried all the way to the bank."

———— ✃ ————

LI BO (701–762), *Chinese poet, considered one of China's greatest men of letters.*

1 A lover of beauty and wine, Li Bo met his death appropriately. According to popular tradition, he was out in a boat one evening. Trying to embrace the reflection of the moon, which shone full on the water, he fell in and drowned.

———— ✃ ————

LICHTENBERG, Georg Christoph (1742–99), *German physicist and satirist.*

1 One day a person not noted for his tact made a slighting remark to Lichtenberg about his notably large ears. Lichtenberg replied: "Well, just think of it — with my ears and your brains we'd make a perfectly splendid ass, wouldn't we?"

———— ✃ ————

LIEBERMANN, Max (1847–1935), *German painter and etcher.*

1 Despite the growing anti-Semitism in Germany in the early 1930s, President Paul von Hindenburg sent emissaries to Liebermann, asking him to make a portrait of Hindenburg, but specifying that it must be done within a very short space of time. Liebermann promptly showed Hindenburg's agents the door. As he flung it open, he pointed to the snow that lay deep outside and said, "If I were to piss on that snow, I could do a very good likeness of Hindenburg."

LIEBLING, Abbott Joseph (1904–63), *US journalist noted for his work in* The New Yorker.

1 (Brendan Gill describes how he and Liebling were trying to cross the street when they got caught up in one of the numerous "ethnic" parades that periodically snarl up the New York streets.)

"We waited in vain on the curb as the band of Our Lady of Sorrows blocked every foot of space in front of us. 'One of the great things about the Jews,' I said to Liebling, 'is that they're the only large group in New York that doesn't insist on a parade. Why should that be?' Liebling thought and thought. 'Their feet hurt,' he said at last."

LIEVEN, Dariya Khristoforovna, Princess de (1784–1857), *Russian aristocrat.*

1 The widowed Princess de Lieven was asked whether she would marry François Guizot, the utterly middle-class politician and historian with whom she had been living for several years, and with whom she continued to live until her death. "Oh! my dear," she replied, "can you see me being announced as Mrs. Guizot?"

Jean Cocteau, in his old age, related the following in conversation with William Fifield:

"I will recount one thing. Then you must let me rest. You perhaps know the work of the painter Domergue? The long girls? Calendar art, I am afraid. He had a domestic in those days — a 'housemaid' — who would make the beds, fill the coal scuttles. We all gathered in those days at the Café Rotonde. And a little man with a bulging forehead and a black goatee would come there sometimes for a glass and to hear us talk. This was the 'housemaid' of Domergue, out of funds. We asked him once (he said nothing and merely listened) what he meant to do with himself. He said he meant to overthrow the government of Russia. We all laughed, because of course we did too. That is the kind of time it was. It was Lenin."

— WILLIAM FIFIELD, *In Search of Genius*

LILIENCRON, Detlev von (1844–1909), *German lyric poet and novelist.*

1 Dining one evening with a group of local noblemen, Liliencron listened while one of them boasted at length about his aristocratic ancestors who had fought in the Crusades, sailed with Columbus, and so forth. "You remind me of a potato," Liliencron said at last.

"How so?"

"The best part is underground."

2 Liliencron was often in dire financial straits. One of his creditors stopped him in the street and demanded payment. "Sorry, but I have no money," said Liliencron. "Please be patient."

"But that's what you said four weeks ago."

"Well," said Liliencron triumphantly, "haven't I kept my word?"

LILLIE, Beatrice (1898–1989), *Canadian-born actress.*

1 Beatrice Lillie was dining at Buckingham Palace, wearing an exquisite model gown, when a waiter spilled a ladleful of soup down her dress. There was a horrified silence as he desperately mopped at the stain. Miss Lillie broke the hush by saying in ringing tones, "Never darken my Dior again."

2 Miss Lillie, in a Chicago beauty salon with several members of her company, overheard a conversation between the receptionist and a client who was annoyed at being kept waiting. "Oh, if I'd known all these theatrical people would be here today, I'd never have come," said the woman in a loud and affected voice. Miss Lillie found out that she was Mrs. Armour, wife of the Chicago meat-packing tycoon. As Miss Lillie was leaving, she saw Mrs. Armour still in the reception area. Without looking at her, she said to the receptionist in her clear English tones, "You may tell the butcher's wife that Lady Peel has finished."

3 (Clifton Daniel tells the following story.)
"One bright day on Piccadilly I saw an unmistakable figure approaching — Bea on the arm of a man. She had been abroad entertaining the 'troooops,' as she called them, and I hadn't seen her for a long time. As she came down the street I maneuvered myself so that she could not avoid running into me. When she did she threw open her arms and embraced me.
" 'Darling,' she cried, 'how *are* you?' Still holding me, she leaned back and examined my face. 'And *who* are you?' "

4 In Hollywood one day, Miss Lillie was absentmindedly driving on the left-hand side of the road when she suddenly noticed another car bearing down on her. She swerved to the left and crashed, wrecking the car but escaping with a few cuts and bruises. She staggered to the nearest house, which happened to be that of film star John Gilbert. "Why, Bea! What's up?" cried Gilbert as he opened the door. "Heard there was a party," gasped Miss Lillie. "Came."

LINCOLN, Abraham (1809–65), *US statesman; 16th President of the United States (1861–65).*

1 As a young man Lincoln was captain of a militia company during the Black Hawk War of 1832. He was not well versed in military procedures. One day, as he was leading a squad of some twenty men across a field, the appropriate word of command for getting them into position for marching through a gate went right out of his mind. In desperation, he shouted, "This company is dismissed for two minutes, and will fall in again on the other side of the gate."

2 When Lincoln was a lawyer, an out-of-town case required him to hire a horse from the local livery stables. Returning the animal, he asked the liveryman whether he kept the horse for funerals. "Certainly not," said its owner indignantly. "I am glad to hear it," said Lincoln, "because if you did, the corpse would not get there in time for the resurrection."

3 Lincoln's friend and fellow-lawyer Ward Lamon was on circuit in Illinois. While waiting outside the courtroom, Lamon was challenged to a wrestling match and in the struggle tore the seat of his trousers. Immediately afterward he was summoned into court for a case. His short coat did not conceal the damaged condition of his trousers. One of the other lawyers facetiously started a subscription paper to buy him a new pair, and it was passed around the various members of the bar. When the paper reached Lincoln, he

wrote his name and under the column for the amount the words: "I can contribute nothing to the end in view."

4 In his legal practice Lincoln was never greedy for fees and discouraged unnecessary litigation. A man came to him in a passion, asking him to bring a suit for $2.50 against an impoverished debtor. Lincoln tried to dissuade him, but the man was determined upon revenge. When he saw that the creditor was not to be put off, Lincoln asked for and got $10 as his legal fee. He gave half of this to the defendant, who thereupon willingly confessed to the debt and paid up the $2.50, thus settling the matter to the entire satisfaction of the irate plaintiff.

5 (A clerk of the court relates the only occasion on which he was fined for contempt of court.)

"David fined me five dollars. Mr. Lincoln had just come in, and leaning over my desk had told me a story so irresistibly funny that I broke out into a loud laugh. The judge called me to order, saying, 'This must be stopped. Mr. Lincoln, you are constantly disturbing this court with your stories.' Then to me: 'You may fine yourself five dollars.' I apologized, but told the judge the story was worth the money. In a few minutes the judge called me over to him. 'What was that story Lincoln told you?' he asked. I told him, and he laughed aloud in spite of himself. 'Remit your fine,' he ordered."

6 A New York firm wrote to Lincoln, then practicing law, requesting information about the financial circumstances of one of his neighbors. The reply was as follows: "I am well acquainted with Mr. ——, and know his circumstances. First of all, he has a wife and baby; together, they ought to be worth $50,000 to any man. Secondly, he has an office in which there is a table worth $1.50, and three chairs, worth $1.00. Last of all, there is in one corner a large rat-hole which will bear looking into. Respectfully yours, A. Lincoln."

7 During his time as a lawyer in Springfield, Lincoln was walking into town one day when he was overtaken by a man driving in the same direction. Lincoln hailed him and asked, "Will you have the goodness to take my overcoat to town for me?"

"With pleasure," responded the stranger, "but how will you get it again?"

"Oh, very easily; I intend to remain in it."

8 On hearing the anguished cries of children in the street, one of Lincoln's neighbors in Springfield rushed out of his house in alarm. There he found Lincoln with two of his sons, both of whom were sobbing uncontrollably. "Whatever is the matter with the boys, Mr. Lincoln?" he asked. "Just what's the matter with the whole world," replied Lincoln resignedly. "I've got three walnuts, and each wants two."

9 In 1858 the Illinois legislature elected Stephen A. Douglas senator instead of Lincoln. A sympathetic friend asked Lincoln how he felt. "Like the boy who stubbed his toe; I am too big to cry and too badly hurt to laugh."

10 Stephen Douglas was attempting to discomfit Lincoln by making allusions to his lowly start in life. He told a gathering that the first time he had met Lincoln it had been across the counter of a general store in which Lincoln was serving. "And an excellent bartender he was too," Douglas concluded. When the laughter had died away, Lincoln got up and said, "What Mr. Douglas says is quite true; I did keep a general store and sold cotton and candles and cigars and sometimes whiskey, and I particularly remember Mr. Douglas, as he was a very good customer. Many a time I have been on one side of the counter and sold whiskey to Mr. Douglas on

the other side. But now there's a difference between us: I've left my side of the counter, but he sticks to his as tenaciously as ever."

11 Lincoln was called in as arbiter in many disputes, serious and frivolous. Two men who had been arguing for hours about the correct proportion of the length of a man's legs to the size of his body called on Lincoln to settle the question. Lincoln listened gravely to the points on both sides, and then gave his summing up in full legal fashion. It seemed to him, he said, that this was a question of the utmost significance and one that had caused much bloodshed in the past and would doubtless do so again in the future, so it was not without much mental anguish and exertion that he reached his opinion. Nonetheless, he concluded, "It is my opinion, all side issues being swept aside, that a man's lower limbs, in order to preserve harmony of proportion, should be at least long enough to reach from his body to the ground."

12 Holding the copy of his speech, his hat, and a cane, Lincoln arrived at the rostrum to be sworn in as President. He laid the cane down, but there was nowhere to put the hat. Senator Stephen A. Douglas quickly came forward and relieved him of it. As he sat down, he observed to one of Mrs. Lincoln's cousins, "If I can't be President, I can at least hold his hat."

13 After his election in 1861 Lincoln spoke to a crowd at Pennsylvania Station in Washington who were anxious to catch a glimpse of his wife, about whom they were very curious. Calling to her to make herself visible, the tall Lincoln said of his five-foot-three-inch Mary Todd, "Well, here's the long and short of it."

14 A delegation of Southerners came to see him just before the outbreak of the war, and told him that the cause of the South would prevail, for God was on their side. Lincoln re-

sponded, "It is more important to know that we are on God's side."

15 As Lincoln was walking down a corridor in the War Department building, an army officer in a hurry barged straight into him. When the man saw who it was, he offered "ten thousand pardons."

"One is quite enough," said Lincoln, adding, "I wish the whole army would charge like that!"

16 A delegation called on Lincoln to ask that the commissionership of the Sandwich Islands be given to a particular man. After setting out his qualifications they concluded by saying that their candidate was in poor health and the climate in the Sandwich Islands would be beneficial to him. "I am sorry to say, gentlemen," said Lincoln, "that there are eight other applicants for the post, and they are all sicker than your man."

17 President Lincoln turned down an applicant for a job and gave as his reason: "I don't like his face." One of the members of his cabinet indicated that he did not think this was a sufficient and satisfactory explanation. Lincoln disagreed: "Every man over forty is responsible for his face."

18 Lincoln particularly enjoyed a story that circulated in Washington during the Civil War concerning him and the president of the Confederate States, Jefferson Davis. Two Quaker ladies were discussing the relative merits and prospects of the opposing leaders. "I think Jefferson will succeed because he is a praying man," said one. "But so is Abraham a praying man," said the other. "Yes," rejoined the first lady, "but the Lord will think that Abraham is joking."

19 A woman once approached Lincoln, demanding a colonel's commission for her son. "My grandfather fought at Lexington, my father fought at New Orleans, my husband

was killed at Monterey. I ask the commission not as a favor, but as a right."

"I guess, madam," answered Lincoln, "your family has done enough for the country. It's time to give somebody else a chance."

20 When the Confederate forces were attacking Fort Stevens, Lincoln made a tour of inspection of the Union defenses. He was shown around by the general's aide, Oliver Wendell Holmes, Jr. As Holmes pointed out the enemy lines, Lincoln, wearing his customary tall hat, stood up to get a better view. At once there was a crackle of musketry fire from the opposing trenches. "Get down, you fool!" shouted Holmes, grabbing the President and hauling him under cover. An instant later he realized what he had said, and wondered what kind of disciplinary action would be taken against him. As Lincoln was leaving, he bade the young officer farewell with the words, "Good-bye, Captain Holmes. I'm glad to see you know how to talk to a civilian."

21 In a discussion on the manpower and resources in the Civil War someone asked Lincoln how many men the Confederates had in the field. "Twelve hundred thousand," was the prompt and astonishing reply. Seeing the amazement and disbelief on the faces of those around him, Lincoln went on, "No doubt of it — twelve hundred thousand. You see, all our generals, every time they get whipped, they tell me that the enemy outnumbered them at least three to one, and I must believe them. We have four hundred thousand men in the field, and three times four equals twelve. Twelve hundred thousand men, no doubt about it."

22 In the later months of 1863 Lincoln was angered by General George B. McClellan's inactivity, despite his superiority in numbers over the Confederate forces. In the end he wrote McClellan a single-sentence letter: "If

you don't want to use the army, I should like to borrow it for a while. Yours respectfully, A. Lincoln."

23 When General Joseph Hooker, nicknamed "Fighting Joe," was appointed commander in chief of the Union army, he was anxious to dispel the impression of incompetence and inaction left by his predecessors in the post, though, as it turned out, he was temperamentally unsuited to supreme command. On one occasion he reported his energetic activities to Lincoln in a dispatch datelined "Headquarters in the saddle." Lincoln received it and sighed: "The trouble with Hooker is that he has got his headquarters where his hindquarters ought to be."

24 In September 1862 Lincoln called a special session of his closest advisers. When they arrived, he was reading a book. At first he paid little attention to their entrance, then started to read aloud to them a piece by the humorist Artemus Ward entitled, "A High-Handed Outrage at Utica," which Lincoln found very funny. At the end he laughed heartily but no one joined in; the cabinet members sat in stony disapproval of the President's frivolity. Lincoln rebuked them: "Why don't you laugh? With the fearful strain that is upon me night and day, if I did not laugh I should die, and you need this medicine as much as I do." Then turning to business, he told them that he had privately prepared "a little paper of much significance." It was the draft of the Emancipation Proclamation.

25 The Emancipation Proclamation was laid before Lincoln for his signature at noon on January 1, 1863. Lincoln twice picked up the pen and twice laid it down. To the secretary of state he said, "I have been shaking hands since nine o'clock this morning, and my right arm is almost paralyzed. If my name ever goes into history, it will be for this act, and my whole soul is in it. If my hand trembles

when I sign the Proclamation, all who examine the document hereafter will say, 'He hesitated.'" He then picked up the pen and slowly and firmly wrote his signature.

26 Lincoln was much plagued by people seeking offices or favors. He was unwell one day and not feeling inclined to listen to such requests. One petitioner, however, managed to get into his office. Just as the man was settling down for a lengthy interview, Lincoln's physician entered. Holding out his hands to him, Lincoln asked what the blotches on them were. The doctor instantly diagnosed varioloid, a mild form of smallpox. "It's contagious, I believe?" asked Lincoln. "Very contagious," was the answer. The visitor got to his feet at this point. "Well, I can't stop now, Mr. Lincoln, I just called to see how you were," he said. "Oh, don't be in a hurry," said Lincoln affably. "Thank you, sir, I'll call again," said the visitor, heading speedily for the door. As it closed behind him, Lincoln observed, "A good thing about this is that I now have something that I can give to everybody."

27 Lincoln's secretary of war, Edwin Stanton, had some trouble with a major general who accused him, in abusive terms, of favoritism. Stanton complained to Lincoln, who suggested that he write the officer a sharp letter. Stanton did so, and showed the strongly worded missive to the President, who applauded its powerful language: "What are you going to do with it?" he asked. Surprised at the question, Stanton said, "Send it." Lincoln shook his head. "You don't want to send that letter," he said. "Put it in the stove. That's what I do when I have written a letter while I am angry. It's a good letter and you had a good time writing it and feel better. Now, burn it, and write another."

28 A Prussian nobleman, who had been involved in revolutionary activities in his own country, came to the United States seeking a commission in the Union army. In an audience with the President, he expatiated on the high and ancient nobility of his family. Lincoln eventually broke in, saying, "That need not trouble you. It will not stand in your way if you behave yourself as a soldier."

29 Lincoln's mail one day contained a letter from a lady requesting not only his autograph but also a "sentiment" with his signature. Irritated by this demand at a time of national crisis, the president responded: "Dear Madam: When you ask from a stranger that which is of interest only to yourself, always enclose a stamp. There's your sentiment, and here's my autograph. A. Lincoln."

30 On the night of December 23, 1863, Lincoln dreamed that he was in a party of undistinguished, unattractive people; when they found out who he was, they commented on his appearance. One of them said, "He's a very common-looking man." Lincoln retorted, "The Lord prefers common-looking people; that's the reason that he makes so many of them."

31 A guest at a reception told Lincoln that in his home state people said that the welfare of the nation depended on God and Abraham Lincoln. "You are half right," said Lincoln.

32 During the Civil War Lincoln had occasion at an official reception to refer to the Southerners rather as erring human beings than as foes to be exterminated. An elderly lady, a fiery patriot, rebuked him for speaking kindly of his enemies when he ought to be thinking of destroying them. "Why, madam," said Lincoln, "do I not destroy my enemies when I make them my friends?"

33 A delegation of businessmen from Wilmington, Delaware, came to see Lincoln to give him their views on winning the war. Their spokesman announced pompously that they

represented the "weighty men" of Delaware. "So you're the weighty men of Delaware," said Lincoln when he had heard them out. "All from New Castle County?"

"Yes, all from the same city."

"Did it ever occur to you gentlemen," asked the President, "that there was danger of your little state tipping up in your absence?"

34 When a gentleman called on the President, asking for a pass to allow him to visit Richmond (the Confederate capital), the President replied, "I would be very happy to oblige you if my passes were respected; but the fact is, sir, I have, within the last two years, given passes to two hundred and fifty thousand men to go to Richmond, and not one has got there yet."

35 Just a week before he was assassinated Lincoln had a dream that he discussed with several people. It seemed that he was walking through the silent White House toward the sound of sobbing. When he entered the East Room he was confronted by the sight of a catafalque covered in black. He asked the guard on duty there who was dead. "The President," said the soldier.

36 On April 13, 1865, the Civil War being over, orders were given to end the draft of soldiers. The following day Lincoln made his fatal visit to the theater to see *Our American Cousin*. At one point in the play the heroine, reclining on a garden seat, calls for a shawl to protect her from the draft. The actor Edward Southern, to whom the request was addressed, replied on this occasion with the impromptu line: "You are mistaken, Miss Mary, the draft has already been stopped by order of the President!" Lincoln joined in the audience's appreciation of this remark with what was to be his last laugh.

LINCOLN, Robert Todd (1843–1926), *US diplomat and businessman, son of Abraham Lincoln.*

1 Robert Todd Lincoln was home from Harvard on a visit at the time that his father was assassinated. After the shooting he sat by his father's bedside until he died. He had no political ambitions, preferring the life of a lawyer. But President James Garfield called him away from his practice to occupy the post of secretary of war in 1881. He reluctantly accepted. Later that same year Robert Lincoln arrived at the Washington railroad station just in time to see Garfield shot. Twenty years later, as president of the Pullman Company, Robert Lincoln was invited to bring his family to meet President William McKinley. As they arrived they heard the news: the President had just been shot. Robert Lincoln observed, "There is a certain fatality about presidential functions when I am present."

LIND, Jenny (1820–87), *Swedish operatic soprano known as "the Swedish Nightingale."*

1 A group of American tourists knocked on Jenny Lind's door. The star asked them what they wanted. The spokesman said that they merely wanted to have a look at her. "This is my face," she said, and then turned around: "This is my back. Now you can go home and say you have seen me." With that she shut the door.

LINDBERGH, Charles Augustus (1902–74), *US aviator.*

1 Lindbergh's solo flight across the Atlantic, in 1925, had made him a hero of gigantic proportions. His reception in England, where he went after landing in Paris, was tumultuous. The crowd was so huge that the planned

welcome had to be cancelled; instead, Lindbergh was driven to Buckingham Palace to meet the king. At the palace Lindbergh was told the king had a very private question for him and was shown into the royal study, where George V awaited. As soon as he entered, the king asked quietly, "Tell me, how do you pee?"

2 On a flight to Mexico in 1927 Lindbergh encountered rainy, foggy weather. It soon became apparent that, once he had crossed over from Texas, he had lost his way. Railroad tracks on the ground provided a landmark of sorts, and he followed them, flying low until he saw a railroad station sign that read "Caballeros." But he could not find Caballeros on his map. Onward he flew until he reached the next station sign: "Caballeros." Only gradually did he realize that the signs he was reading indicated the entrance to the men's bathrooms.

———— ⌀ꞷ ————

LINDEMANN, Frederick Alexander, Viscount Cherwell (1886–1957), *German-born British physicist.*

1 In 1931 Churchill was hit by a taxi on Fifth Avenue in New York and taken to a hospital. From there he sent a cable to Lindemann asking him to calculate the shock, to a stationary body weighing 200 pounds, of a car weighing 2,400 pounds traveling between 30 and 35 miles an hour. He also asked the professor to bear in mind that the brakes did not operate before he was hit by the car and that he had been "carried forward on the cowcatcher" until he dropped off, adding that the information "must be impressive." Lindemann soon sent the following reply, "Collision equivalent falling thirty feet on pavement. Equal six thousand foot pounds energy. Equivalent stopping ten-pound brick dropped six hundred feet or two charges buckshot pointblank range. Rate inversely

proportional thickness cushion surrounding skeleton and give of frame. If assume average one inch your body transferred during impact at rate eight thousand horsepower. Congratulations on preparing suitable cushion and skill in bump."

———— ⌀ꞷ ————

LIPPERT, Barbara, *US advertising critic.*

1 As part of her job, Lippert watched a great deal of television. As a trend started toward shorter ads on TV, Lippert noted, "Watching fifteen seconds of nasal passages unblocking sure beats watching thirty seconds."

———— ⌀ꞷ ————

LISTER, Joseph, 1st Baron Lister (1827–1912), *British surgeon.*

1 Lister was once summoned to attend a rich lord who had a fishbone stuck in his throat. Dextrously the great surgeon removed the bone. Overcome with gratitude, the patient asked Lister what was owned him. Lsiter replied, with a smile, "My lord, suppose we settle for half of what you would be willing to give me if the bone were still lodged in your throat."

———— ⌀ꞷ ————

LISZT, Franz (1811–86), *Hungarian composer, acclaimed as the greatest virtuoso pianist of his time.*

1 (According to Samuel Butler:)

"It is said, with what truth I know not, that Liszt got Verdi to give him a letter of introduction to Rossini and went to call on him. Rossini was exceedingly polite, asked him to play, and when he had done inquired what the piece was. Liszt said, 'It is a march I have written on the death of Meyerbeer; how do you like it, maestro?' Rossini said he liked it very much, but presently added, 'Do you not think it would have been better if it had been you who had died, and Meyerbeer who had written the music?'"

2 It has been said of Liszt that Wagner was indebted to him for much besides money — including sympathy and a wife. The two men were friends, if somewhat tempestuously on Wagner's part, and Wagner came to rely on Liszt as mentor and guide. Musically they influenced each other considerably. Wagner, by far the more popular composer, once wrote to Liszt to say that he had unconsciously used a theme of his. Liszt replied, "Now at least it will be heard."

3 Liszt was invited to take tea with a noblewoman, who then invited a number of her friends to come, hoping Liszt would play for them. To make her hint more evident she arranged her piano right in the middle of the room, where no one could miss it. When Liszt arrived he saw what was in store, and asked his hostess where the piano was. "Oh!" she said, "Would you really? *Here* it is." "Ah, true," said Liszt. "I wanted to put my hat on it."

———— ✺ ————

LIVERMORE, Mary Ashton Rice (1821–1905), *US suffragette and temperance reformer.*

1 (May Saxton tells this story:)

"One of Mary Livermore's favorite stories was about the time she and five other girls had gone to see President Josiah Quincy of Harvard about studying at the university. They demonstrated their learning for him and he said, 'Very smart girls . . . unusually capable, but can you cook?' They assured him they were expert domestics. 'Highly important,' he said. He continually diverted them from asking their questions until finally Mary burst out that they wanted to go to college with their brothers: 'You say we are sufficiently prepared, is there anything to prevent our admission?' He told them that the place for girls was at home. 'Yes, but, Mr. Quincy, if we are prepared, we would not ask to recite but may we not attend the recitations and sit silent in the class?'

" 'No, my dear, you may not.'

" 'Then I wish —'

" 'What do you wish?'

" 'I wish I were God, for the instant, that I might kill every woman from Eve down and let you have the masculine world all to yourselves and see how you would like that!'"

———— ✺ ————

LLOYD GEORGE, David, 1st Earl (1863–1945), *British statesman; prime minister (1916–22).*

1 In the early days of his political career Lloyd George appeared as a speaker at a rally in favor of Home Rule. His speech advocated extension of the principle to other parts of the British Empire. "Home Rule in Ireland, Home Rule in India, Home Rule in South Africa —" At this point he was interrupted by a heckler shouting, " 'Ome Rule for 'Ell." Lloyd George's glance swept round the audience until he had picked out the speaker. "Yes," he thundered back, pointing his finger at the interrupter, "Home Rule for Hell. I like every man to speak for his own country."

2 When popular patriotism was at its zenith at the outbreak of World War I, and the slogan "The war that will end war" was on every tongue, Lloyd George expressed a gloomy skepticism. "This war, like the next war, is a war to end war," he remarked.

3 During his ministry Lloyd George had to contend with World War I, the economic crisis, and the Sinn Fein movement for Irish liberation, among other difficulties. Asked how he retained his good spirits, he replied,

"Well, I find that a change of nuisances is as good as a vacation."

4 The chairman of a meeting introduced Lloyd George with the jocular remark: "I had expected to find Mr. Lloyd George a big man in every sense, but you see for yourselves he is quite small in stature."

"In North Wales," replied Lloyd George, "we measure a man from his chin up. You evidently measure from his chin down."

5 Lloyd George was once approached by explorer Ernest Shackleton, seeking a sponsor for his next expedition. Proud to be considered a friend of the rich and famous, Lloyd George introduced the explorer to a millionaire of his acquaintance. Some time later, Lloyd George inquired of Shackleton how the meeting had gone. "Very well indeed," replied the explorer, "your friend was most charming and considerate. He offered me ten thousand pounds for my expenses, provided I would take you along with me to the Pole. And he promised me one million pounds if I were to leave you there by mistake."

LLOYD WEBER, Andrew (1948–), *British popular composer.*

1 Lloyd Weber was searching for someone to write the lyrics for his latest production, and paid a visit to Alan Jay Lerner, who had written the lyrics for *My Fair Lady*. Lloyd Weber expressed disappointment that he had not been able to find a steady collaborator. "I don't know why," he said, "but some people dislike me as soon as they meet me." Lerner replied, "Perhaps it saves time."

LOBENGULA (c. 1836–94), *king of the Matabele (1870–94).*

1 Lobengula was anxious until the last minute to avoid open conflict with the encroaching Europeans. Unfortunately, a party of *indunas* (chiefs) whom he sent as emissaries to the British were attacked and killed through a misunderstanding. Lobengula, enraged at what he saw as treachery, declared war. He did this in the traditional way, by driving an *assegai* (short stabbing spear) into the ground in sight of the assembled army. The shaft of the *assegai* snapped. Despite this bad omen the Matabele warriors marched out to war — and defeat.

LOCKE, John (1632–1704), *British philosopher.*

1 Locke had been introduced by his patron Lord Shaftesbury to two other noblemen. Rather than take the opportunity to converse with the philosopher, the three men sat down to play cards. Locke said nothing, but began to scribble in his notebook. Some time later, intrigued by the philosopher's behavior, one of the players asked what he was doing. "My lord," replied Locke, "I am endeavoring, as far as possible, to profit by my present situation; for having waited with impatience for the honor of being in company with the greatest geniuses of the age, I thought I could do nothing better than to write down your conversation, and indeed I have set down the substance of what you have said for this hour or two." This remark had the desired effect, and the noblemen, suitably embarrassed, abandoned their game.

LOMBARDI, Vince (1913–70), *US football coach.*

1 Lombardi was a stern disciplinarian but also an inspirational leader who hated to lose. After one noteworthy victory, he was asked how important it was to him to win. He said,

"Winning isn't everything, but wanting to win is."

2 One of the Green Bay Packers remarked on Lombardi's fairness, the fact that he treated every man the same. "He treats us all like dogs."

———cs2———

LONG, Huey Pierce (1893–1935), *US lawyer and politician.*

1 Before beginning his electoral campaign in southern Louisiana, Long was reminded by a colleague that a large number of the voters there were Catholics. In accordance with this advice, he opened his first speech with the words: "When I was a boy, I would get up at six o'clock in the morning on Sunday, and I would hitch our old horse up to the buggy and I would take my Catholic grandparents to mass. I would bring them home, and at ten o'clock I would hitch the old horse up again, and I would take my Baptist grandparents to church."

"Why, Huey," remarked his colleague later, "you've been holding out on us. I didn't know you had any Catholic grandparents."

"Don't be a damn fool," replied Long. "We didn't even have a horse."

2 Although an ardent supporter of the New Deal, Long was wary of wholehearted support for Roosevelt. The only difference between Hoover and Roosevelt, he once said, was that Hoover was a hoot owl while Roosevelt was a scrootch owl. "A hoot owl bangs into the roost and knocks the hen clean off, and catches her while she's falling. But a scrootch owl slips into the roost and talks softly to her. And the hen just falls in love with him, and the first thing you know, *there ain't no hen.*"

———cs2———

LONGWORTH, Alice Roosevelt (1884–1980), *US society hostess, daughter of Theodore Roosevelt.*

1 Alice's antics scandalized the staid society of Washington during her father's tenure at the White House. When a visitor objected to the girl's wandering in and out of the President's office while he was discussing important business with her father, Roosevelt said, "I can be President of the United States or I can control Alice. I cannot possibly do both."

2 Alice's barbed comments on political figures quickly became current Washington gossip. When Thomas E. Dewey was seeking the Republican presidential nomination, she exclaimed, "How can the Republican party nominate a man who looks like the bridegroom on a wedding cake?"

———cs2———

LOUIS, Joe (1914–81), *US boxer, world heavyweight champion.*

1 Joe Louis defended his heavyweight title against Billy Conn, "the Pittsburgh Kid," in June 1941. Although Conn was much smaller and lighter than Louis, his speed and agility made him a serious challenger. As his opponent darted around him and managed to get in some telling punches, Louis grew increasingly confused and his own punches appeared to have no effect. By the end of the twelfth round Conn was a long way ahead on points and the huge crowd of fans were confident they would see a new champion. At the start of the thirteenth round Conn delivered a heavy punch to Louis and went in for the kill, only to meet a tremendous uppercut from Louis that stretched him out cold on the canvas.

Several years later the two boxers were talking about this famous battle, and Conn asked jokingly why Louis had not let him win that one fight. "You could have sort of loaned me the crown for six months," he said. Louis replied seriously, "Billy, you *had* that title for twelve rounds."

2 Joe Louis defended the rights of his race before there really was a civil rights movement. Touring the army bases of the South during World War II, giving boxing exhibitions, he and black fighter Sugar Ray Robinson were once confronted by a military policeman while waiting at an Alabama bus station.

"You soldiers belong in the rear of the station," said the M.P.

When the two men didn't respond, they were arrested and severely reprimanded by an officer at the provost marshal's office.

"I'm sorry, sir," Joe Louis replied. "But I'm in this war like anybody else. I expect to be treated like anybody else."

3 Knocked down by a surprise left from Tony Galento, Louis was back on his feet before the referee could start the count. Joe's trainer later reproached him: "I keep teaching you to take a count when you're knocked down. Now why didn't you stay down for nine like I've always taught you?"

"What," growled Louis, "and let him get all that rest?"

4 In 1946 Joe Louis once again prepared to defend his title against Billy Conn. He was warned to watch out for Conn's great speed and his tactic of darting in to the attack and then moving quickly out of his opponent's range. In a famous display of (justified) confidence, Louis replied, "He can run, but he can't hide."

———— ✧ ————

LOUIS XI (1423–83), *king of France (1461–83).*

1 A devout believer in astrology, Louis was deeply impressed when an astrologer correctly foretold that a lady of the court would die in eight days' time. Deciding that the too-accurate prophet should be disposed of, he summoned the man to his apartments, having first told his servants to throw the visitor out of the window when he gave the signal. "You claim to understand astrology and to know the fate of others," Louis said to the man, "so tell me at once what your fate will be and how long you have to live." "I shall die just three days before Your Majesty," answered the astrologer. Louis decided not to risk defenestration.

———— ✧ ————

LOUIS XIV (1638–1715), *king of France (1643–1715), known as* **Le Roi Soleil** *(the Sun King) because of the brilliance of his court and the prestige that France achieved during his reign.*

1 When Louis's father, Louis XIII, knew himself to be dying, he took much consolation and pleasure in the precocious energy and intelligence of the four-year-old dauphin. "What is your name?" the king asked playfully. "Louis the Fourteenth," replied the child promptly. "Not quite yet, my son," said the king with a smile.

2 The etiquette that attended every portion of the king's day was minutely prescribed. The *grand lever* ceremony, at which the king dressed and made ready, was attended by over a hundred courtiers. Despite living surrounded by grandeur and formality, Louis was capable of showing genuine concern for the feelings of others. A valet who had made a mistake in the details of the royal *lever* was immediately abused and scolded by the assembled courtiers. "Let us not forget," Louis interposed, "that he is far more upset about it than I am."

3 Louis's great general, Maréchal Villars, made enemies among the king's favorites. A pretext was found to send him off to a dangerous posting in Germany. The marshal took his leave of Louis with these words: "I leave

Your Majesty surrounded by my enemies, and I go to be surrounded by yours."

4 Louis XIV was one day expatiating to his courtiers on the absolute power great kings have over their subjects. The Comte de Guiche objected that such power must have its limits, to which Louis replied, "If I commanded you to throw yourself into the sea, you would be the first to obey me." The count, instead of replying, turned his back and walked toward the door. Astonished, Louis asked him where he was going. "To learn to swim, sire," replied de Guiche.

5 The insatiable ambition of one of his courtiers was well known to the king. "Do you know Spanish?" Louis asked.

"No, sire."

"What a pity."

The courtier at once concluded that Louis had an ambassadorship in mind for him. He devoted himself strenuously to learning the language, and then presented himself before the monarch, stating that he was now master of it.

"Do you know it so well that you can actually converse with Spaniards?"

"Yes, sire."

"I congratulate you. Now you can read *Don Quixote* in the original."

6 When hunting, Louis XIV never wore gloves, even in the coldest weather. Two peasants watched him ride by; one voiced his surprise that the king took no precautions against the cold. The other replied, "Why should he? He always has his hands in our pockets."

7 Louis was very fond of billiards. On one occasion a dispute arose over a shot, and Louis asked the Comte de Gramont, who was sitting nearby, to adjudicate. "Sire, you are in the wrong," said Gramont immediately, without budging from his seat. "Why, sir, you didn't even see the shot!" exclaimed the king. "No, sire," replied Gramont, "but if

there had been the slightest doubt about the shot, the gentlemen who did see it would have all cried out that you were in the right."

8 The English ambassador Lord Stair was described to Louis as being one of the best-bred men in Europe. Louis decided to put this to the test. The next time Lord Stair was in attendance as Louis was about to set out in his coach, the king gestured for the ambassador to go ahead of him into the conveyance. Lord Stair bowed and climbed in, as bidden. "It is true what they say of Lord Stair," observed Louis afterward. "Another man would have troubled me with ceremonious objections."

9 News of the French army's crushing defeat at Blenheim was brought to Louis. "How could God do this to me," he exclaimed, "after all I have done for him?"

10 As Louis lay dying in great pain, with his left leg gangrenous, he noticed that the two attendants at the foot of his bed were weeping. "Why are you weeping?" he said. "Did you imagine that I was immortal?"

———⚭———

LOUIS XV (1710–74), *king of France (1715–74).*

1 Mme d'Esparbés, one of Louis's many mistresses, did not confine her favors to the royal couch. "You have slept with all my subjects," protested Louis one day. Mme d'Esparbés denied this.

"You have slept with the Duc de Choiseul?"

"Yes, sire, but he is so powerful."

"The Maréchal de Richelieu?"

"But he is so witty!"

"Mainville?"

"But he has such beautiful legs!"

"Very well, but how about the Duc d'Aumont, who has none of these attractions?"

"Ah, sire, he is so devoted to Your Majesty!"

2 The Comte de Charolais, the king's cousin, was a notorious eccentric. One of his oddities was to order his coachman to run over any monks they might encounter on the road. He went too far, however, when, for the pleasure of seeing him fall, he shot a man who was putting tiles on a roof. Louis pardoned him but said, "Let it be understood: I will similarly pardon anyone who shoots you."

3 Louis was playing cards with members of his entourage when a certain M. de Chauvelin was stricken by a fit of apoplexy, of which he died. "M. de Chauvelin is ill," exclaimed a courtier, seeing him fall. Louis turned and surveyed the fallen body coldly. "Ill?" he said. "He is dead. Take him away. Spades are trumps, gentlemen."

4 Marie Antoinette was on her way from Austria to marry Louis XV's grandson, the future Louis XVI. The elderly roué greatly looked forward to seeing the fifteen-year-old dauphine-to-be. A courtier who had been in the party sent from France to meet Marie Antoinette at the French border galloped back ahead of the bridal party to report to his master. "What do you think of her?" was Louis's first question. "Has she any bosom?"

5 During his last illness Louis's doctor was called in to try to save his patient. During the course of his efforts he used the word "must." The king was shocked at this expression, which was never used around the monarch. With his last breath he murmured, "Must! Must!"

— ∽ —

LOUIS XVI (1754–93), *king of France (1774–93)*.

1 On his wedding day the gluttonous Louis ate a prodigious quantity of food. His grandfather, Louis XV, thinking of the pleasures of the wedding night, warned him against filling his stomach too much, to which the sixteen-year-old Louis replied, "Why not? I sleep so much better that way."

2 The Maréchal de Richelieu suggested that Louis take a certain lady as his mistress. "No," said the king, "she would be too expensive to dismiss."

3 On July 14, 1789, a Paris mob stormed and captured the Bastille, the old royal prison in Paris. That day Louis XVI, who had been out hunting, returned to Versailles and entered a note in his diary: "July 14: Nothing." Then the Duc de la Rochefoucauld-Liancourt hurried in from Paris to tell the king of the successful attack. "Why, this is a revolt!" said the monarch. "No, Sire," replied the duke. "It is a revolution."

4 When the arrangements were being made in December 1792 for the trial of Louis XVI before the Revolutionary Convention, the distinguished lawyer Chrétien de Malesherbes came out of retirement to offer his services to his king. Louis accepted sadly and reluctantly. "Your sacrifice is the greater," he said, "for you are jeopardizing your own life while you cannot possibly save mine."

— ∽ —

LOUIS XVIII (1755–1824), *king of France (1814–24)*.

1 At his restoration "fat Louis" was fully and sympathetically aware of his subjects' need to let bygones be bygones. The elderly M. de Barentin was stumblingly explaining to Louis how it was that he had not — strictly speaking — in actual fact — sworn an oath of allegiance to Napoleon Bonaparte. "I quite understand," Louis broke in. "At our age one only does things by halves. You didn't swear an oath to Bonaparte, you swore an oathlet."

— ∽ —

LOUIS PHILIPPE (1773–1850), *king of France (1830–48), known as the "Citizen King."*

1 Fleeing from Paris in 1848, Louis Philippe climbed into the carriage that would take him into exile; an unknown man closed the door. "Thank you," said the king absently. "Not at all," replied the man. "I've waited eighteen years for this day."

LOWELL, Abbott Lawrence (1856–1943), *US educator and lawyer.*

1 During William Howard Taft's administration President Lowell was summoned from Harvard to the White House on business. In his absence his secretary received a visitor who asked where Lowell was. "The president is in Washington seeing Mr. Taft," was the reply.

LOWELL, Amy (1874–1925), *US poet and critic.*

1 The Cabots, one of Boston's leading families, were held in low esteem by Miss Lowell. She would go to the extent of refusing invitations to parties and dinners if she knew that one or more Cabots had also been invited. One day, as she set off for her annual trip to Europe aboard the *Devonian,* she happened to glance at the passenger list and promptly disembarked. "There are sixteen Cabots aboard the *Devonian* this trip," she told a newspaper reporter, "and God isn't going to miss such an opportunity."

2 At the time of the declaration of war in 1914 Miss Lowell was in London. Late for an appointment, hindered by the crowds in the street, indignant at the police for not helping her, as she returned to her hotel she burst out, "Don't they know I'm Amy Lowell? And it was this month that my book of poems was coming out here! What attention will it get with this going on? What has happened to England? Why doesn't she simply stop the war?"

LOWELL, Robert (1917–77), *US poet.*

1 Due to present the Duff Cooper Memorial Prize before an illustrious gathering that included Duff Cooper's widow, Lady Diana, Lowell suffered a serious nervous breakdown and was taken to a mental home. A substitute was arranged, but at the last moment Lowell discharged himself and set off for the ceremony. Lady Diana's son was informed of this and told that Lowell must on no account touch alcohol. He rushed to pass the news to his mother, and found her talking to Lowell, then on his third glass of champagne. "Darling," she said brightly, "I've just been telling this gentleman how the principal speaker has lost his marbles and been carted off to a loony-bin!"

2 As a punishment for refusing to serve in the army, Lowell was imprisoned for five months by the US courts. While waiting to be transferred to Connecticut to serve the sentence, Lowell spent a few days in New York's West Street Jail. During his stay there he was put in a cell next to Louie Lepke, a convicted member of Murder Incorporated. "I'm in for killing," Lepke told the poet. "What are you in for?" Lowell answered: "Oh, I'm in for refusing to kill."

3 Lowell's first wife, novelist Jean Stafford, recalled that he revised his work so extensively that a poem he once began as "To Jean: On Her Confirmation" ended up as "To a Whore at the Brooklyn Navy Yard."

LUCAS, George (1944–). *US film director.*

1 Lucas was vastly underpaid for his work on *Star Wars.* As a writer he received $50,000;

as director, $100,000. But Lucas had arranged to retain merchandising and licensing rights — called "garbage" provisions — to his characters, a first in the film business. *Star Wars,* which was released in 1977, went on to become the most successful film up to that time in movie history, and Lucas a rich man. When the time came to do the sequel, *The Empire Strikes Back,* Lucas made sure he kept complete control over not just licensing but artistic choices and all other decisions as well. So tough were his terms — which the studio had to accept — that his negotiator, Tom Pollack, presented the contract to the head of Twentieth Century Fox with a flourish on Yom Kippur, saying, "This is your day of atonement."

2 Lucas cast nineteen-year-old Carrie Fisher as Princess Leia. But her character was to be a virginal innocent, so Lucas draped Fisher's body in a long robe and even had her breasts taped to her chest, to accentuate Leia's youthfulness. Fisher noted later, "No jiggling in the Empire."

3 Throughout the making of *Star Wars* novice actor Harrison Ford struggled with his dialogue, finally exploding to writer-director Lucas, "You can type this shit, George, but you sure can't say it."

4 Told his *Star Wars* sequel, *The Empire Strikes Back,* lacked any kind of depth, he said, "If we have enough action, no one will notice."

———— ✛ ————

LUCE, Clare Boothe (1903–87), *US journalist, playwright, and politician, wife of Henry R. Luce.*

1 Lady Jeanne Campbell, the granddaughter of Lord Beaverbrook, worked as a researcher on *Life* and it was well known that Henry Luce was having an affair with her. It is said that he even went so far as to ask Clare for a divorce so that he could marry Jeanne. Clare replied that, curiously enough, Lord Beaverbrook had been showing considerable interest in *her,* and if she married him that would make her the grandmother of Luce's intended bride. Luce decided against the marriage.

2 A certain congressman, intending to flatter Mrs. Luce, said of her in the House of Representatives one day: "She has the best mind of any woman in the House." Mrs. Luce was enraged by the patronizing tone of the compliment. "The mind knows no sex," she retorted. "If the lady believes that," remarked a second congressman, "she doesn't know the mind of man."

3 Asked by a reporter to comment on a certain senator's move from the Republican to the Democratic party, Mrs. Luce replied: "Whenever a Republican leaves one side of the aisle and goes to the other, it raises the intelligence quotient of both parties."

———— ✛ ————

LUCE, Henry R. (1898–1967), *US publisher, founder of the Time-Life publishing concern.*

1 Stanley Karnow, once based in Hong Kong for *Time* magazine, told Sterling Seagrave of a trip made to Taiwan with his boss Henry Luce. (Chiang Kai-shek had fled after losing China to the Communists. He had been, of course, a hero to Luce.) On their way to the Palace Hotel in Taipei, Luce noticed that their luggage seemed to be missing and muttered peevishly, "I think they've lost our bags." Karnow commented, "It won't be the first thing they've lost."

"Within a year," Karnow told Seagrave, "I was no longer working for *Time.*"

———— ✛ ————

LUCULLUS, Lucius Licinius (c. 114–57 BC), *Roman general and statesman.*

1 Lucullus's dinners became proverbial for their sumptuousness. On one of the rare occasions when Lucullus was dining alone, he noticed to his displeasure that the preparations for the meal were not up to their usual standard. He summoned the servant responsible, who explained that as no one had been invited, he had assumed that his master would want a less lavish meal. Lucullus frowned: "Do you not know that this evening Lucullus sups with Lucullus?"

———⌁———

LULLY, Jean-Baptiste (1632–87), *French composer.*

1 The baton used by a seventeenth-century conductor was a much longer and heavier affair than the little wand used today. On January 8, 1687, in the course of conducting a *Te Deum,* Lully struck his foot with his baton, injuring it so seriously that gangrene set in and he died ten weeks later.

———⌁———

LUNT, Alfred (1893–1977), *US actor who with his wife, Lynn Fontanne (1887–1983), constituted a famous husband-and-wife acting team.*

1 The Lunts made one motion picture, *The Guardsman.* On the day of the premier Lunt was ill and Fontanne went alone. She returned distraught. "Alfred, it was a total disaster," she babbled. "I cannot imagine what they were thinking of. You were all right, just occasionally it looked as if you had thin lips, but in the close-ups of me all you could see were my nostrils, or else my eyelashes cast such a shadow that it looked as if I had great bags under my eyes, and my hair was a mess,

a total mess, and there is something wrong with the sound that makes my voice sound like either a squeak or a groan . . ." She paused for breath. Lunt said thoughtfully, "Thin lips, eh?"

2 In one of the plays in which they co-starred Lynn Fontanne had to hit Alfred Lunt across the face. A devoted wife, she tried for some time without bringing herself to do it. Everyone became exasperated as the scene stuck at that point. Finally Lunt burst out, "For God's sake, you're the lousiest actress I've ever played opposite." Miss Fontanne, her hang-up overcome, struck him sharply. Thereafter at every performance, Lunt used to whisper, "Don't be lousy, dear."

———⌁———

LUTHER, Martin (1483–1546), *German Protestant theologian.*

1 Luther's colleague, Philipp Melanchthon, vexed his more ebullient friend by his quiet and virtuous ways. "For goodness' sake, why don't you go and sin a little?" cried Luther in exasperation. "Doesn't God deserve to have something to forgive you for!"

2 Cornered by a persistent young theologian with the question of where God had been before the world was created, Luther snapped, "He was building hell for such presumptuous, fluttering, and inquisitive spirits as you are."

3 And to another overly inquisitive student who wanted to know what God had been doing before He created the world, Luther replied, "He sat under a birch tree cutting rods for those who ask nosy questions."

4 Arraigned for his heresies before the Diet of Worms in 1521, Luther refused to recant. *"Hier stehe ich, ich kann nicht anders* [Here I stand, I can do no other]," he declared.

LYAUTEY, Louis Hubert Gonzalve (1854–1934), *French general.*

1 After the war was over, Lyautey asked his gardener to plant a tree in a particular part of his estate. The gardener objected that the tree the marshal had chosen was particularly slow-growing and would not reach maturity for at least a century. The marshal replied, "In that case, there is no time to lose. Plant it this afternoon."

LYCURGUS (7th century BC), *Spartan statesman.*

1 Lycurgus is credited with having created the Spartan constitution, with its strict military discipline and repressive state control of the peasantry. When someone asked why it was that he had not made the constitution of Sparta a democratic one, Lycurgus retorted, "Try the experiment in your own family."

LYNDHURST, John Singleton Copley, Lord (1772–1863), *British lawyer; lord chancellor (1827–28, 1834–35, 1841–46).*

1 A society lady asked Lord Lyndhurst whether he believed in platonic friendship between men and women. "After, not before," replied his lordship.

LYTTON, Edward George Earle Lytton Bulwer-Lytton, 1st Baron (1803–73), *British novelist and politician.*

1 When Wilkie Collins's detective novel *The Woman in White* appeared in 1860, it created a considerable stir. A feature much remarked upon was the villain, Count Fosco. One lady reader, however, was not so impressed and wrote to tell Collins, "You really do not know a villain. Your Count Fosco is a very poor one." She then offered to supply Collins with a villain next time he wanted one. "Don't think that I am drawing upon my imagination. The man is alive and constantly under my gaze. In fact, he is my husband." The writer was Bulwer-Lytton's wife.

M

MABLY, Gabriel Bonnet, Abbé de (1709–85), *French political writer and philosopher.*

1 It was proposed to Mably that he campaign for election to the French Academy. He replied, "If I were a member, people would ask: 'Why is he there?' I prefer them to ask: 'Why is he not there?'"

McCARTHY, Joseph R[aymond] (1908–57), *US politician.*

1 Senator McCarthy stalked out of a congressional committee room in a rage, to be met by a bevy of reporters who asked him to comment upon a shocking allegation that had just been made. "Why, it's the most unheard-of thing I've ever heard of," McCarthy exploded.

McCORMACK, John (1884–1945), *US operatic tenor, born in Ireland.*

1 McCormack was noted for his performance as the naval officer Pinkerton in *Madame Butterfly.* Having watched a production of the opera by a different company, he sought out the tenor playing Pinkerton and told him, "You sang very well but you must have been a rotten naval officer." The tenor looked puzzled. "You began with a little bit of braid on your sleeve," continued McCormack, "then, years later, when you return to Japan and your little Butterfly, you're still wearing the same bit of braid. Don't you ever get promoted? When I sang Pinkerton I took good care to promote myself to commander in the third act."

McCORMICK, Edith Rockefeller (1872–1932), *daughter of John D. Rockefeller.*

1 Edith McCormick always maintained a large staff in her huge and magnificent house. One rule applied to all of them, from the first butler to the personal maid's assistant: they were not permitted to speak to her. Only once was that rule broken. One evening in 1901, when Edith McCormick's young son was suffering from scarlet fever, a dinner party was in progress at the family's country retreat in Lake Forest. During the meal the news arrived that the unfortunate boy had died. Following a discussion in the servants' quarters, the tragic news was whispered to Mrs. McCormick at the table. Mrs. McCormick merely nodded her head, and the dinner party continued without pause.

—✣—

McCOY, Kid [Norman Selby] (1873–1940), *US welterweight boxer, world champion.*

1 The expression "the real McCoy" originated in a barroom brawl, when a drunk insisted that the boxer was not who he said he was. McCoy flattened his opponent, who struggled back onto his feet and said, "It's the real McCoy."

2 (P. G. Wodehouse, having watched Kid McCoy training at a gymnasium at White Plains, impulsively asked if he could step into the ring with him. The world champion agreed and he and Wodehouse began to make themselves ready for the bout, when McCoy suddenly laughed.)

"He had been reminded, he said, of an entertaining incident in his professional career, when he was fighting a contender who had the misfortune to be stone deaf. It was not immediately that he became aware of the other's affliction, but when he did he acted promptly and shrewdly. As the third round entered its concluding stages he stepped back a pace and pointed to his adversary's corner, to indicate to him that the bell had rung, which of course was not the case but far from it.

" 'Oh, thank you so much,' said the adversary, 'Very civil of you.'

"He dropped his hands and turned away, whereupon Kid McCoy immediately knocked him out."

—✣—

McCULLERS, Carson (1917–67), *US novelist and playwright.*

1 Carson McCullers's mother was on a bus en route to visit her daughter in New York when she fell into conversation with a lady of aristocratic mien who said she was fond of reading. The proud mother immediately began a lengthy monologue on her daughter's extraordinary literary talents. After some time the other woman mentioned that her father had also been a writer. Carson's mother asked her name. "Countess Tolstoy," was the answer.

2 McCullers was a great admirer of Katherine Anne Porter, whom she once pointed out to a friend as "the greatest female writer in America now — but just wait until next year." They found themselves together at the writer's colony Yaddo, where McCullers tried to meet her. Porter, who disliked her, refused to answer repeated knocks on her door, despite McCullers's calling out, "I do love you so much." Dinner was served at 6:30, and residents were expected to attend on time. Thinking she heard McCullers walking away down the hall, she opened her door only to find the young writer prostrate across her doorstep, waiting silently. "I had had enough," Porter later recalled. "I merely stepped over her and continued on my way to dinner. And that was the last time she ever bothered me."

3 McCullers shared a house in Brooklyn Heights with a revolving cast of characters that included, at one time or another, Benjamin Britten, Gypsy Rose Lee, W. H. Auden, Louis MacNeice, and a chimpanzee. One Thanksgiving Day the group was roused from their post-dinner stupor by the screaming sounds of a fire engine. They all ran down the street to find the fire, but suddenly McCullers stopped and grabbed Gypsy Rose Lee's arm, shouting, "Frankie is in love with her brother and the bride, and wants to become a member of the wedding!" Both walked silently home, McCullers trembling and Lee aware that the writer had suddenly broken through to her muse.

—✣—

McGRAW, Frank "Tug" (1944–), *US baseball player.*

1 "Tug" played for the Mets during the 1973 season, when the team was slumping in epic proportion. As he walked onto the field one day, an autograph seeker called out, "What's with the Mets?" McGraw turned and said, "There's nothing wrong with the Mets — you gotta believe!" The retort quickly became the rallying cry for the team and was eagerly embraced by fans and press, continuing today.

2 Pitcher McGraw often became unduly anxious about his pitches, especially in crucial situations. Eventually he developed a philosophy that worked every time: just before a pitch he would think to himself, "In a billion years the sun is going to burn out and the earth will become a frozen iceball hurtling through space. And when that happens, nobody's going to care what [any great hitter] does with the bases loaded."

McKINLEY, William B. (1843–1901), *US politician; 25th President of the United States (1897–1901).*

1 On a visit to Niagara Falls in 1901, McKinley was careful to walk only halfway along the bridge connecting the United States with Canada. He simply didn't want to be the first President to leave the boundaries of the United States during his term of office.

2 On September 6, 1901, while greeting people at an official reception at Buffalo, McKinley was shot at point-blank range by an anarchist named Leon Czolgosz. McKinley slumped in a chair, his first thoughts for the safety of his assailant, who was being tackled by people nearby, and his second thoughts for his wife, Ida, a semi-invalid who suffered from seizures. "My wife," he gasped, "be careful how you tell her." He was taken to a hospital where he lingered for a few days. His wife was at his bedside as his end approached. "I want to go too, I want to go too," she sobbed. "We are all going," said McKinley faintly. He did not speak again.

MacARTHUR, Douglas (1880–1964), *US general.*

1 (Alexander Woollcott tells this story about MacArthur in World War I.)

"As the sun came up . . . he might have been seen by his fellow officers (and he certainly was seen by the Germans) standing erect, adventurous, and oblivious on a painfully exposed parapet. One hand held his field glasses to his eyes, the other was clenched in excitement as the infantry just ahead charged through a wood. His adjutant — call him Smith, for the purpose of this story — stood at his elbow. Machine-gun bullets were hissing and hitting all around. A captain jumped up out of the trench and touched the general on the arm. 'If I might suggest, sir,' he said, 'your position is dangerous. The machine guns are reaching here.'

"'Eh, eh, what's that? Oh, yes, quite right, quite right. Thank you. Smith' — this with a glare at his adjutant — 'get down in that trench at once.'"

2 When it became clear early in 1942 that Bataan, the last American foothold in the Philippines, would fall to the Japanese, President Roosevelt, in order to save MacArthur for tasks elsewhere, commanded him to leave the Philippines. As he left on March 11, MacArthur promised, "I shall return."

3 (Eisenhower, who had been on MacArthur's staff before World War II, called on his former commander in Tokyo. At the time, the names of both generals were being mentioned in connection with the presidency.)

"Eisenhower could not get a word in for three-quarters of an hour, while MacArthur reminisced about old times. Then Eisenhower interrupted to say, with emphasis and much elaboration, that he did not think that any military man should be president of the United States. His sincerity was manifest. But MacArthur cocked a wary eye at him and said, 'That's the way to play it, Ike.'"

MACAULAY, Thomas Babington, 1st Baron (1800–59), *Scottish statesman and historian.*

1 There is a story, of unknown origin, that bears on Macaulay's fabulous memory. It seems that one day an acquaintance of his, calling on him, found the noble lord pacing up and down in his study, reciting, line after line, hundreds of alexandrines from some obscure French medieval epic romance. After listening patiently for some time, the visitor at last interrupted: "Why in God's name, Macaulay, did you ever bother to memorize all that tedious nonsense?" Macaulay at once turned to him, saying, "Sir, do you not see that I am doing my best to *forget* it?"

2 Macaulay was known as a prodigious talker. After his return from India, Sydney Smith professed to notice an improvement. "His enemies might have said before that he talked rather too much; but now he has occasional flashes of silence that make his conversation perfectly delightful."

3 As Macaulay was notoriously clumsy about shaving himself, his rooms were always scattered with fragments of strops and broken razors. On one occasion when he had injured a hand, he had to send for a barber to shave him. "What should I give you?" he asked, uncertain what fee would be expected. "Whatever you usually give the person who shaves you, sir," replied the barber equably.

"In that case I should give you a great gash on each cheek," Macaulay observed.

4 At a political meeting in Macaulay's Edinburgh constituency, he was standing on a balcony beside his opponent when he suffered the unpleasant experience of being hit by a dead cat thrown by a member of the audience. The man at once apologized, explaining that he had intended the cat for Macaulay's opponent. "In that case," said Macaulay, "I wish you had intended it for me and hit him."

5 (In June 1850 huge queues formed to see the first living hippopotamus to be displayed at London Zoo. By this time Macaulay's *History of England* had made him something of a celebrity too. Macaulay wrote to his friend Thomas Flower Ellis to tell him of what he described as "the proudest event of my life.")

"Two damsels were just about to pass that doorway [to the hippopotamus's quarters] when I was pointed out to them. 'Mr. Macaulay!' cried the lovely pair. 'Is that Mr. Macaulay? Never mind the hippopotamus.' And having paid a shilling to see Behemoth, they left him in the very moment at which he was about to display himself — but spare my modesty. I can wish for nothing more on earth."

MACK, Connie (1862–1956), *US baseball player and manager.*

1 The manager of the Philadelphia A's was in church one Sunday morning when an usher, holding the collection plate, leaned over and whispered, "Why did you sell Jimmy Foxx?" Mack whispered back, "For the same reason that you're taking up this collection. I need the money."

MacLAINE, Shirley (1934–), *US actress.*

1 After many years as an actress, MacLaine began to explore the paranormal world, writing several bestselling books about other dimensions and past lives she had led. Much of her public scoffed, including fellow actor Yves Montand, who said, "Shirley MacLaine — who does she think she isn't?"

MACMAHON, Marie Edmé Patrice Maurice, Comte de (1808–93), *French general and statesman; president (1873–79).*

1 Visiting a field hospital one day, the marshal addressed a few words to a soldier who lay ill with a tropical fever. "Yes, that's a nasty disease you've got there. You either die of it, or go crazy. I've been through it myself."

MACMILLAN, [Maurice] Harold, 1st Earl of Stockton (1894–1986), *British statesman and prime minister.*

1 At the United Nations in September 1960, Macmillan was interrupted in the middle of his speech by Nikita Khrushchev, the Soviet premier, who had taken off his shoe and was banging on the table with it. Unperturbed, Macmillan simply remarked, "I'd like that translated, if I may."

MacNEIL, Robert (1931–), *Canadian author and public television journalist.*

1 Upon receiving an award for his work promoting the integrity of the First Amendment, MacNeil commented on the present state and future of public television, saying, "Public television should be more than English people talking and animals mating, occasionally interrupted by English people mating and animals talking."

MACREADY, William Charles (1793–1873), *British actor.*

1 Macready's handwriting was notoriously difficult to decipher. When he wrote a complimentary letter of admission to a theater during one of his American tours, the recipient remarked that it looked every bit as illegible as a doctor's prescription. He and a friend thereupon decided to take it along to the apothecary to see what he made of it. The young assistant took the piece of paper and with scarcely a glance at it began pulling down phials and jars to make a compound. After mixing a number of ingredients with great confidence, he seemed to come to an item that bothered him; he paused and puzzled over it and at last summoned his boss from the back of the shop. The older man studied the paper and then with a contemptuous snort at his assistant's ignorance, pulled down another bottle and completed the mixture. Handing the result to his customers, he remarked with a smile, "A cough mixture, and a very good one. Fifty cents, if you please."

2 Macready once directed a production of *Hamlet* in Norwich, playing the title role himself. His innovative ideas made him a number of enemies among the cast, notably the actor playing Claudius. On the opening night, having received his deathblow from Hamlet, Claudius staggered to center stage to die. Macready was incensed: he had made it quite clear at rehearsals that Claudius was to die upstage, leaving the center free for his own death scene. "Die further up the stage," hissed the irate director. "Get up and die elsewhere." The "dead" Claudius sat up and said, in tones heard by the entire audience, "Look here, Mr. Macready, you've had your

way at rehearsals, but I'm king now, and I shall die just where I please."

MADISON, Dolley (1768–1849), *US wife of President James Madison (1809–17).*

1 In 1812 the British army invaded Washington, burning much of the city. As the White House was ablaze, Dolley Madison fled the building, after having assured the safety of some of the furniture. She first went to the house of an acquaintance, asking for shelter, but was refused. The woman of the house barred the door, saying to her, "Your husband has got mine out fighting and, damn you, you shan't stay in my house."

MADISON, James (1751–1836), *US statesman; 4th President of the United States (1809–17).*

1 At the Constitutional Convention Madison was one of the most active speakers, and many wise provisions owe their origin to his foresight and learning. Apt to get carried away when addressing the Convention, he asked a friend to sit by him and tweak his coattails if he seemed to be getting overexcited. After a particularly impassioned speech he sat down, almost exhausted, and reproached his friend for not pulling at his coat. "I would as soon have laid a finger on the lightning," said his friend.

MADONNA [CICCONE] (1958–), *US singer and actress.*

1 The immensely busy and visible singer was asked, at the height of her career, what was her ambition. "I have the same goal I've had ever since I was a girl," was her response. "I want to rule the world."

MAETERLINCK, Maurice (1862–1949), *Belgian poet and dramatist.*

1 Modern amenities were sometimes sparse in old French country houses at the end of the nineteenth century, but Maeterlinck was nonetheless pleased to accept an invitation for a prolonged stay in a remote château to enable him to relax and write in peace. Arriving while his hostess was out, he asked the maid to direct him to the bathroom. She led him down a corridor at the end of which was a huge, apparently solid, oak throne. From behind the contraption she pulled a large cloak and a face mask. "Here you are, monsieur," she said. "You wear these so no one knows who is sitting here." Maeterlinck thanked her and was well away from the château by the time his hostess returned.

2 Maeterlinck's well-publicized romance with the French actress Georgette Leblanc came to a mysterious end after twenty years. The sixty-year-old writer then married a young girl of nineteen. He refused to speak to the press on the subject, but an enterprising young American reporter managed to secure an interview with him at his Mediterranean villa. She sent him a note bearing the following message: "I am an American writer in great difficulties. If I can do an interview on you for my paper I can pay my passage home, and all will be well. If not, my only alternative will be to commit suicide." Even Maeterlinck could not reject such an appeal. The woman duly arrived for her interview, opened up her notebook, and began: "May I ask why you left Georgette Leblanc?" Maeterlinck glared at the reporter and snapped, "Go and commit suicide, madame."

MAGRUDER, John B. (1810–71), *US Confederate commander.*

1 While Magruder was in command at Yorktown in 1861, he forbade soldiers to bring liquor into the camp. One day he noticed a certain Private Sharpe drinking from his canteen with a relish suggesting the canteen contained something more potent than water. Magruder, known to be fond of alcoholic refreshment, ordered Sharpe to let him have a drink of his "water." Magruder took a draught, returned the canteen, and promptly promoted the terrified private to the rank of corporal. Some time later Magruder called for another drink, and this time returned the canteen with the words: "You are no longer Corporal Sharpe, sir; you are Sergeant Sharpe!" Sharpe realized he would merit his instant promotions as long as the liquor in his canteen lasted. Unfortunately, he had only attained the rank of lieutenant when the canteen was found to be empty. When Magruder next called for a drink, the disappointed Sharpe, having searched the camp in vain for further supplies, could only reply, "General, it is played out, and I am sorry for it; for if it had held out I'll be damned if I would not have been a brigadier general before night!"

MAHAFFY, Sir John Pentland (1839–1919), *Irish scholar.*

1 Dr. Mahaffy was out shooting when another member of the party carelessly put some shot through the crown of his hat. He inspected the damage calmly. "Two inches lower, and you would have shot away ninety percent of the Greek in Ireland."

2 A lady seeking to embroil Dr. Mahaffy in a feminist argument opened her attack with "You are a man. I am a woman. What is the essential difference between us?"

"Madame," said Dr. Mahaffy urbanely, "I can't conceive."

MAHLER, Gustav (1860–1911), *Austrian composer.*

1 Mahler found the inspiration for much of his music in the beautiful scenery of the Austrian countryside. "Don't bother looking at the view," he once told a visitor to his country house. "I have already composed it."

MAINTENON, Françoise d'Aubigné, Madame de (1635–1719), *French noblewoman, second wife of Louis XIV.*

1 Louis built a château at Marly as a country retreat. The central building, called the Sun, was flanked by twelve other buildings, each named for a sign of the zodiac and arranged six on either side of a pool of water. In this exquisite artificial pond swam Louis's favorite carp, which boasted glamorous names like Golden Sun, Beautiful Mirror, the Dauphine, Topaz, and Dawn. To the eyes of a lady walking by the pond with Mme de Maintenon, the fish looked melancholy in the crystal-clear water, and she mentioned the fact to her companion. "The carp are like me," said Mme de Maintenon. "They regret their native mud." {Hence the French phrase *"nostalgie de la boue."*}

2 Mme de Maintenon, an excellent conversationalist, could keep a company of witty and malicious courtiers charmed by her talk. Even the servants recognized her powers in this direction. At a private dinner when some culinary hitch had occurred, one of them whispered to her. "Madame, be pleased to tell another story. There is no roast today."

MALHERBE, François de (1555–1628), *French poet and critic.*

1 Even on his deathbed Malherbe retained his passionate concern with purity of diction and style. As he lay dying, his confessor tried to encourage him with a fulsome description of the joys of paradise. Malherbe begged him to stop: "Your ungrammatical style is giving me a distaste for them."

—◈—

MALLARMÉ, Stéphane (1842–98), *French Symbolist poet.*

1 The picture dealer Ambroise Vollard was walking in the woods near Paris with a friend when they came upon a small gray-haired gentleman spearing pieces of paper and other litter with a nailed stick and putting them into a basket. "That's Mallarmé," said the friend, and going up to the poet asked him what on earth he was doing. "I have invited some Parisians to come to tea tomorrow," Mallarmé explained, "so I am cleaning up the banquet hall."

—◈—

MALLORY, George Leigh (1886–1924), *British mountaineer.*

1 Mallory, a veteran of several Everest expeditions when he went on a lecture tour of the United States in 1923, was frequently asked why he wanted to climb Mount Everest. He always gave the same answer: "Because it is there."

—◈—

MANKIEWICZ, Herman J. (1897–1953), *US journalist and film scriptwriter.*

1 After Mankiewicz had been out of a job for some time, his agent succeeded in getting him a post at the Columbia studio, with a warning to steer clear of Harry Cohn, head of the studio. For some weeks Mankiewicz obeyed, but the sound of laughter and talk from the executive dining room penetrated his office and finally proved too much for him. When the Columbia executives assembled one day, they found Mankiewicz seated at the end of the table. "I won't say a word," he promised. Cohn came in and immediately launched into an attack on a film he had seen the night before in his private projection room. Someone suggested he might feel otherwise if he had seen it with a public audience. Audience reaction made no difference to him, Cohn replied. "When I'm alone in a projection room I have a foolproof device for judging whether a picture is good or bad. If my fanny squirms, it's bad. If my fanny doesn't squirm, it's good. It's as simple as that." The sudden silence was broken by Mankiewicz's voice from the foot of the table: "Imagine — the whole world wired to Harry Cohn's ass!"

2 Mankiewicz's wife, Sara, had a difficult time with her husband's drinking problem and the frequent interruptions to his career caused by his falling out with studio bosses. A friend whom he had not seen for a while asked Mankiewicz, "How's Sara?"

Mankiewicz looked puzzled: "Sara? Who?"

"Sara. Your wife, Sara."

"Ah, you mean Poor Sara."

—◈—

MANN, Thomas (1875–1955), *German novelist, winner of the 1929 Novel Prize for Literature.*

1 Mann was introduced to an American writer of some note who abased himself before the famous novelist, saying that he scarcely considered himself to be a writer in comparison with Mann. Mann answered him civilly, but afterward he remarked, "He has no right to make himself so small. He's not that big."

—⬧—

MANSART, François (1598–1666), *French architect.*

1 Louis XIV was walking with Mansart in the sun. The architect was bareheaded, as court etiquette demanded. Louis told him to put on his hat. To his courtiers, who expressed astonishment at the king's condescension, he said, "I can make twenty dukes in a quarter of an hour, but it takes centuries to make a Mansart."

—⬧—

MANSFIELD, William Murray, 1st Earl of (1705–93), *British judge.*

1 On one occasion an old woman, accused of being a witch, was brought before him. She was also charged with walking through the air. The judge listened attentively to all the evidence and then dismissed the accused woman. "My opinion," he said, "is that this good woman should be suffered to return home, and whether she shall do this, walking on the ground or riding through the air, must be left entirely to her own pleasure, for there is nothing contrary to the laws of England in either."

—⬧—

MANTLE, Mickey [Charles] (1931–98), *US baseball player.*

1 The son of a miner from Oklahoma, Mantle was led to baseball at an early age by his father. But he struggled with the Yankees and was sent down to their farm team in Kansas City, where he went 0 for 22 in a strong slump. He called his father, saying, "I don't think I can play baseball anymore." The next day his father appeared unannounced in Mantle's hotel room and started packing a suitcase, jamming Mantle's clothes into it. Asked what he was doing, Mantle's father told him, "You're going home. You're going to work in the mines, that's what we'll do. You can work back down there." Shocked, Mantle bounced back out of his slump, hitting .360 for Kansas City and returning to the Yankees. Looking back years later, he said, "That was the turning point of my life."

2 Mantle was considered the best switch hitter in baseball's history. Commenting on his ability, he said, "Hitting the ball was easy. Running around the bases was the tough part."

3 Mantle loved the game for its own sake, and never for a moment considered a route gone down by many other players too old to continue as active players: being a manager. As he himself said, "All I have is natural ability."

4 After his retirement in 1968, Mantle was haunted by dreams of returning to the field. They occurred often enough that he spoke of them on several occasions. In his dream he would drive up to Yankee Stadium but would find himself unable to get in. Hearing his name called out over the public address system, he would see his old teammates — Whitey Ford, Casey Stengel, Yogi Berra, Billy Martin — searching for him. At last a hole presented itself in the fence around the stadium, but, as he remembered it, "I try to get through but there I'm stuck."

5 When a major league player hit forty home runs and stole forty bases one season — a feat that was later duplicated — the attendant publicity was enormous. Mantle, reading the press accolades, was not impressed. "Hell," he said, "if I'd known they were going to make such a fuss about it, I'd have done it a few times myself."

—⬧—

MAO ZEDONG (1893–1976), *Chinese statesman, founder of the People's Republic of China and chairman of the Chinese Communist party.*

1 It is reported that Mao was fond of a little set speech he would make to visitors: "Our fathers were indeed wise. They invented printing, but not newspapers, They invented gunpowder, but used it only for fireworks. Finally, they invented the compass, but took care not to use it to discover America."

2 When someone asked him what he thought about the French Revolution, Mao replied, "It is too early to say."

———— ✿ ————

MARGARET [Rose] (1930–), *princess of Great Britain, Countess of Snowdon, and sister of Queen Elizabeth II.*

1 While attending a small dinner given in her honor during a visit to San Francisco in 1966, Princess Margaret was introduced to Barnaby Conrad. "You have a very English name," the princess observed. "Are you English?"

"No, ma'am," Conrad replied, "but my sixth great-grandmother was. Then she married a lieutenant colonel and soon after became an American. His name was George Washington."

"Oh," she said, as only the English can say that word.

———— ✿ ————

MARIA FËDOROVNA (1847–1928), *empress of Russia as the wife of Czar Alexander III (1845–94).*

1 The czarina was known throughout Russia for her philanthropy. She once saved a prisoner from transportation to Siberia by transposing a single comma in a warrant signed by Alexander. The czar had written: "Pardon impossible, to be sent to Siberia." After

Maria's intervention, the note read: "Pardon, impossible to be sent to Siberia." The prisoner was subsequently released.

———— ✿ ————

MARIA THERESA (1717–80), *empress of Austria (1740–80).*

1 Maria Theresa spent the last few days of her life propped up in a chair as she was unable to breathe if she lay down. Her son Joseph was constantly by her side. After one particularly agonizing spasm she struggled from the chair and dropped awkwardly onto the sofa. "Your Majesty cannot be comfortable like that," said Joseph, trying to support her. "No, but comfortable enough to die," said Maria Theresa, and within a few minutes she died without further struggle.

———— ✿ ————

MARIE ANTOINETTE (1755–93), *wife of King Louis XVI of France.*

1 Told that her people had no bread to eat, Marie Antoinette is reported to have said, *"Qu'ils mangent de la brioche"* (Let them eat cake).

2 Marie Antoinette was painted several times by Marie-Louise Vigée-Lebrun. During one sitting the artist, who was far advanced in pregnancy, dropped some of her colors. The queen at once said, "You are too far along," and stooped to pick up the fallen colors herself.

3 At her trial before the revolutionary tribunal, Marie Antoinette defended herself with skill and courage, but the verdict and sentence were a foregone conclusion. She behaved with great composure when brought to the guillotine. As she was standing on the platform, she accidentally stepped on the executioner's foot. "Monsieur," she said, "I ask your pardon. I did not do it on purpose."

MARIE de Médicis (1573–1642), *Italian-born wife of King Henri IV of France.*

1 The queen mother was visited on her deathbed by Fabio Chigi, then papal nuncio in France. To him she vowed to forgive all her enemies, including Cardinal Richelieu. "Madame," asked Chigi, "as a mark of reconciliation, will you send him the bracelet you wear on your arm?"

"No," she replied firmly, "that would be too much."

MARIS, Roger (1934–85), *US baseball player.*

1 Maris arrived from out of town to join the Yankees in 1959. It was not something the country boy looked forward to. Showing up at the clubhouse in white bucks, he was taken aside by an official who said, "Listen, kid, Yankee ballplayers don't dress like you. You got them Pat Boone shoes, they gotta go." So he took Maris to a nearby Thom McCan's store, where Maris bought two pairs of new shoes — both white bucks.

2 During the 1961 season Maris hit sixty-one home runs, more than any other player in the game, breaking Babe Ruth's record set in 1927. When told that people expected the same performance the following year, Maris replied, "As a ballplayer I'd be delighted to do it again. But as an individual, I doubt if I could possibly go through it again."

MARLBOROUGH, John Churchill, 1st Duke of (1650–1722), *British general and statesman.*

1 Marlborough's notorious love of money remained with him through his life. In his last years he was once playing picquet with a certain Dean Jones, with stakes of sixpence a game. When they stopped, Marlborough was one game ahead and he asked the dean for his sixpence. The dean said he had no silver at that moment, but would pay the duke the next time he saw him. Marlborough replied that he needed the sixpence to pay for a sedan chair to take him home, and made such a fuss that the dean eventually went to the trouble of sending a servant out to get change for a guinea. Marlborough took his sixpence and departed. The dean watched him leave the house and walk on down the street, conserving his winnings by going home on foot.

MARLBOROUGH, John Spencer-Churchill, 10th Duke of (1897–1972), *British aristocrat.*

1 The duke lived in some style at Blenheim. Once he had occasion to stay overnight in the much more modest home of one of his three daughters. Before breakfast the daughter was surprised to hear her father bellowing down the stairs that his toothbrush was "not working." Upon investigation it turned out the toothbrush was not foaming as it should and the duke was angrily demanding a new one. The daughter had to explain that toothbrushes foamed only if toothpaste or powder was applied to them — a task habitually performed for the duke by his valet at Blenheim.

MARQUAND, J[ohn] P[hillips] (1893–1960), *US novelist.*

1 (The novelist Louis Auchincloss recalls an incident at a party soon after Marquand was released from the hospital.)

"John was back in his old form, swinging his glass in his hand as he entertained his audience, holding forth on what he called 'the lack of taste and reticence' in younger American writers. A few minutes later, he was talking about his weeks in the Newburyport hospital and how, as part of his therapy, an abdominal massage had been prescribed. His nurse, John confided, had whispered to him during the procedure, 'How lucky I am to be able to manipulate the lower abdominal muscles of a man like you!' One of the guests at the gathering was the New York *grande dame* Mrs. August Belmont. When Marquand had finished this anecdote, Mrs. Belmont inquired, 'And where, Mr. Marquand, was the taste and reticence in that remark?'"

MARQUIS, Don[ald Robert Perry] (1878–1937), *US journalist and poet.*

1 After a month on the wagon, Don Marquis came up to the bar at the Players' Club and ordered a double martini. "I've conquered my goddam willpower," he announced to the assembled company.

MARSHALL, John (1755–1835), *US lawyer; Chief Justice of the Supreme Court (1801–35).*

1 On hearing it said that they were drinking too much, the justices of the Supreme Court decided that they would henceforth drink nothing on their weekly consultation day unless it was raining. The following consultation day Marshall duly asked Joseph Story to go to the window and see if there was any sign of rain. Story reported: "Mr. Chief Justice, I have very carefully examined this case, and I have to give it as my opinion that there is not the slightest sign of rain." Marshall, not content with this assessment of the situation, replied, "Justice Story, I think that is the shallowest and most illogical opinion I have ever heard you deliver; you forget that our jurisdiction is as broad as the Republic, and by the laws of nature it must be raining some

place in our jurisdiction. Waiter, bring on the rum."

MARSHALL, Thomas Riley (1854–1925), *US politician.*

1 During a tedious debate a senator embarked upon a boring enumeration of "what this country needs."

"What this country needs is a good five-cent cigar," chipped in Marshall.

2 Thomas Marshall was never under any illusion about the role and scope of the vice presidency. He once said, "The vice president of the United States is like a man in a cataleptic state: he cannot speak; he cannot move; he suffers no pain; and yet he is perfectly conscious of everything that is going on about him."

MARTIN, Billy (1928–89), *US baseball player and manager.*

1 At one point during the 1972 playoffs between the Tigers and the A's, Martin told his pitcher, Lerrin LaGrow, to throw the ball directly at Bert Campaneris, who had stolen several bases during the game. LaGrow hit the batter in the ankle, upon which Campaneris threw his bat at LaGrow and a general brawl started. Campaneris was asked after the game if he felt regret for his action. "Yeah," he said, "I should have thrown the bat at Martin."

2 Martin was well known for being paranoid that his players were secretly in league against him. He often suspected that people in the locker rooms were spies sent to watch him. As one player described him, "Billy was the only guy who could hear someone giving him the finger."

MARTINELLI, Giovanni (1885–1969), *Italian opera singer*.

1 Martinelli was once questioned by a newspaper reporter about his smoking habits. "Tobacco, cigarettes, bah!" exclaimed the singer in disgust. "I would not think of it." The reporter, a little puzzled, reminded Martinelli of an advertisement in which he had asserted that a particular brand of cigarettes did not irritate his throat. "Yes, yes, of course I gave that endorsement," said Martinelli impatiently. "How could they irritate my throat? I have never smoked."

MARX, Chico [Leonard] (1891–1961), *US comedian, one of the Marx Brothers*.

1 Chico wrote Heywood Broun a check to pay off some gambling debts, warning him not to cash it before twelve o'clock the following day. Broun later complained to Chico that the check had bounced. Chico asked: "What time did you try to cash it?"

"Twelve-o-five."

"Too late."

MARX, Groucho [Julius] (1895–1977), *US comedian, one of the Marx Brothers*.

1 Groucho was working in the garden of his California house, dressed in tattered and ancient clothes. A wealthy matron in a Cadillac caught sight of him, stopped, and wondered whether she might persuade the supposed gardener to come and work for her. "Gardener," she called, "how much does the lady of the house pay you?"

Groucho looked up. "Oh, I don't get paid in dollars," he replied. "The lady of the house just lets me sleep with her."

2 Groucho was descending in the elevator of the Hotel Danieli in Venice. On the third floor the elevator stopped and a group of priests entered. One of them, recognizing Groucho, told him that his mother was a great fan of his. "I didn't know you guys were allowed to have mothers," said Groucho.

3 When Groucho wanted to join a certain beach club in Santa Monica, California, he was told by a friend that as the club was known to be anti-Semitic, he might as well not bother to apply. "But my wife isn't Jewish," replied Groucho, "so will they let my son go into the water up to his knees?"

4 Groucho sent a telegram to the exclusive Friar's Club in Hollywood, to which he belonged: "Please accept my resignation. I don't want to belong to any club that will accept me as a member."

5 The maître d'hôtel stopped Groucho as he was about to enter the dining room of a smart Los Angeles hotel. "I am sorry, sir, but you have no necktie."

"That's all right," said Groucho, "don't be sorry. I remember the time when I had no pants."

"I am sorry, sir," repeated the man, "you cannot enter the dining room without a necktie."

Groucho caught sight of a bald man in the center of the dining room and yelled, "Look! Look at him! You won't let me in without a necktie, but you let him in without his hair!"

6 A tipsy man lumbered up to Groucho Marx, slapped him on the back, and said, "You old son-of-a-gun, you probably don't remember me." Marx glared at him and said, "I never forget a face, but in your case I'll be glad to make an exception."

7 The Marx Brothers, though a closely knit group, also understood their relative values as performers. When they were working on Broadway, Zeppo, the straight man and con-

sequently replaceable, decided to quit the show. Sam Harris, the producer, gave him permission to leave. When Groucho, Harpo, and Chico heard about it, they went to Harris. Groucho said, "Sam, if Zeppo leaves, you'll have to give us more money."

8 Groucho Marx intensely disliked producer Harry Cohn, who worked for Columbia Pictures. Once, with his brother Chico, he viewed Cohn's latest film. When the words "Columbia Pictures Presents" came up, Groucho turned to Chico and remarked, "Drags, doesn't it?"

9 Warner Brothers threatened to sue Groucho Marx when they heard that the next Marx Brothers film was to be called *A Night in Casablanca,* arguing that the title was too close to their own *Casablanca.* Groucho's reply: "I'll sue you for using the word *Brothers.*"

10 During his stint as comedian on a show called *You Bet Your Life,* Groucho interviewed many participants. On one occasion he interviewed a Mrs. Story, who had given birth to twenty-two children. "I love my husband," Mrs. Story said enthusiastically. "I like my cigar, too," said Groucho, "but I take it out once in a while."

11 Invited to a bachelor dinner at a fashionable restaurant before a high-society wedding, Groucho and Harpo noted that the automatic elevator opened directly into the dining rooms on the various floors. As the elevator went up, they gleefully arranged a surprise for the assembled bachelors and emerged — carrying their clothes in valises and wearing nothing but top hats.

To their consternation, they were greeted not by raucous roars of male hilarity but by high-pitched feminine shrieks. The bride was entertaining *her* friends on the floor above the bachelor dinner, and Groucho and Harpo had pressed the wrong button. No ready escape appeared; they took refuge behind a large potted plant until they could drape themselves in tablecloths secured by a kindly waiter, murmur abject apologies to the horrified ladies, and slink ignominiously from the room.

12 Marx despised the empty clichés of business correspondence. A letter from his bank manager ended with the standard phrase, "If I can be of any service to you, do not hesitate to call on me." Marx immediately put pen to paper. "Dear Sir," he wrote, "The best thing you can do to be of service to me is to steal some money from the account of one of your richer clients and credit it to mine."

13 For many years, every time they met, Samuel Goldwyn's first words to Groucho Marx would be "How's Harpo?" Marx grew rather tired of this. Finally, on meeting Goldwyn again and facing the inevitable inquiry, he said, "Listen, Sam, every time we meet — every time for *years* — you always ask, 'How's Harpo?' You never ask me anything else, and to tell you the truth, I'm getting goddamn sick and tired of it. Why don't you ever ask me how *I* am?"

"How are you?" asked Goldwyn obligingly.

"I'm fine," replied Groucho.

"And how's Harpo?"

MARX, Harpo [Arthur] (1893–1964), *US comedian, the member of the Marx Brothers team who often pretended to be mute.*

1 Among the guests at a dinner party were Harpo Marx and his wife, Susan. The English writer Jonathan Miller quizzed one of the other guests afterward, hoping to hear firsthand some of Harpo's witticisms. "What did Harpo say?" he asked.

"He didn't say anything."

"How about his wife?"

"She didn't say anything, either."

"Oh," said Miller in pretended disgust, "stealing Harpo's bit, eh?"

2 Harpo Marx on a visit to New York was plagued by representatives of charities wanting him to appear at benefits. One persistent lady telephoned him no fewer than twelve times in forty-eight hours. Harpo eventually agreed to appear for her charity. To ensure that he would not escape her at the last minute, she called to escort him personally to the benefit. As they were leaving the hotel suite, the telephone began ringing. "Don't you want to go back and answer it?" the lady asked. "Why bother?" responded Harpo with a weary sigh. "It's undoubtedly you again."

MARY I (1516–58), *queen of England (1553–58), known as "Bloody Mary."*

1 Calais, England's last possession in France, was lost to the French in 1558. This disaster further undermined Mary's health, which had been weakened by a phantom pregnancy. A lady-in-waiting suggested to her during her last illness that her distress was caused by the absence of her husband, Philip, from her side. "Not only that," said the unhappy queen, "but when I am dead and opened you shall find 'Calais' lying in my heart."

In his *Encyclopedia of Eccentrics* De Morgan tells the story of the slow-witted royal duke of the previous century who was once out riding with noble members of his retinue. "The rain comes into my mouth," complained the royal rider with a grimace. An equerry politely suggested that His Highness would be wise to shut his mouth in that case. The duke did so. A few minutes later he commented thoughtfully, "It doesn't come in now."

— AUGUSTUS DE MORGAN,
The Encyclopedia of Eccentrics

MARY (1867–1953), *queen consort of George V of Great Britain.*

1 As Prince and Princess of Wales, George and Mary once visited Portsmouth, where they were entertained by the commander in chief of the British fleet, Admiral Sir John Fisher. Sir John offered to take the prince down in a submarine, and the invitation was eagerly accepted. Mary was not altogether happy about this idea, but with true regal self-control managed to suppress her feelings. As the vessel disappeared below the surface, she simply murmured, "I shall be very disappointed if George doesn't come up again."

2 When she was informed of the death of her son, King George VI, all that escaped Queen Mary's lips was the smallest "Oh!" She looked so upset, however, that the members of her household asked her daughter, the Princess Royal, to come to her as quickly as possible. The princess, then in her mid-fifties, hurried to Queen Mary, full of concern for the old lady. To her surprise she was greeted with disapproval. "When you come before the queen," said her mother, "please do your hair properly." The princess retreated to her room.

MARY, Queen of Scots (1542–87). *The daughter of James V of Scotland, she became queen soon after her birth.*

1 Surviving portraits of Mary show her with exquisite auburn hair. After she had been beheaded, the executioner stooped to pick up her head to exhibit it, as the custom was, to the crowd. As he stood and cried, "Long live the queen!" he found he was holding only a kerchief to which was fastened an auburn

wig. At his feet lay the head of the queen of Scots, almost completely bald.

—✦—

MASARYK, Jan (1886–1948), *son of the founding president of Czechoslovakia, politician.*

1 Early in his career Jan Masaryk served as Czech ambassador to the United States. At a party he was prevailed upon by the hostess to play the violin. He graciously accepted the invitation and played a Czech nursery song, to rapturous applause from all present. He left the party with a Czech friend, who wanted to know why on earth he had been asked to play the violin. Masaryk explained, "Oh, it's all very simple — don't you see? They have mixed me up with my father; they mixed him up with Paderewski. And they mixed the piano up with the violin."

—✦—

MASCAGNI, Pietro (1863–1945), *Italian composer.*

1 Mascagni was much irritated by an organ-grinder who stood outside his apartment playing tunes from *Cavalleria Rusticana* at about half the correct speed. Eventually he could stand it no longer, went out into the street, and said to the organ-grinder, "I am Mascagni. Let me show you how to play this music correctly." He gave the handle of the hurdy-gurdy a few vigorous turns.

The following day Mascagni again heard the organ-grinder in the street outside. When he looked out, he noticed a sign over the instrument: "PUPIL OF MASCAGNI."

2 When in 1901 the time came to dedicate his opera *Le Maschere,* Mascagni solved the problem neatly. He dedicated it to himself "with highest esteem and unchanging affection."

—✦—

MASSENET, Jules (1842–1912), *French opera composer.*

1 Massenet was conducting a rehearsal of *Manon* with a particularly lackluster chorus. Finally he rapped on the rostrum and exhorted them, saying, "Brother and sister artists! Sing it like an encore! Sing it as though the audience had applauded!" The appeal was immediately successful.

—✦—

MASTROIANNI, Marcello (1923–97), *Italian actor.*

1 Film producer Joseph Levine once presented Mastroianni with a magnificent gold wristwatch. It could have been an embarrassing moment, for the actor was already wearing a gold watch. On seeing what was inside the package, however, Mastroianni took off his own watch and nonchalantly dropped it into the nearest wastebasket.

—✦—

MATHILDE, Princess (1820–1904), *French noblewoman.*

1 Separated from her husband within five years of their marriage, Princess Mathilde had a long affair with Count Niewekerke. The liaison was public knowledge, but because of Princess Mathilde's position in the imperial family, no one was supposed to know about it. She was entertaining a group of ladies one afternoon when her dog, a miniature greyhound, came running up to her to be caressed. "Go away, you naughty dog," said the princess, pushing it from her. "Don't you know you're in disgrace?" Then turning to her guests she explained: "Last night he kept jumping on the bed all night and I couldn't get any sleep at all." A short while later Count Niewekerke joined the party. The little dog ran to fawn on him as well, but he

pushed it away. "You're a very bad dog and I'm not going to pet you. You kept jumping on the bed all night and I didn't sleep a wink."

2 At the end of a pleasant social evening at Saint Gratien, her summer residence, the princess rose and said to her *chevalier d'honneur,* General Bougenel, "Now let's go to bed." Admiral Duperré was also present. "I wish I were in the general's place," he murmured. "I'm afraid you'd be cheated, *mon cher,*" said the princess, playfully slapping the admiral's wrist with her fan. "In this house we don't provide night service."

MATISSE, Henri (1869–1954), *French painter.*

1 At a museum in Antibes, Matisse sat down in front of a Picasso painting and began copying it. Curious bystanders came over to see what this old man was doing, and one asked the painter, "Can you tell me what this picture represents?" Matisse replied, "You see, I'm trying to find out for myself."

2 Matisse's painting *Le Bateau* hung upside down in the Museum of Modern Art, New York, for forty-seven days before anyone noticed (October 18–December 4, 1961). In that period 116,000 people had visited the gallery.

MATTHEWS, A[lfred] E[dward] (1869–1960), *British actor.*

1 Toward the end of his career Matthews was acting in a West End play. One scene involved a crucial telephone call, which Matthews was to answer. The telephone rang on cue; he crossed the stage, picked up the receiver, and promptly dried up. In despera-

tion, he turned to the only other actor on the stage and said, "It's for you."

2 Matthews's last memorable stage appearance was in *The Manor of Northstead* in 1953. During rehearsals, it was obvious that the eighty-four-year-old actor was having some difficulty learning his part, and his director was rather concerned. "I know you think I'm not going to know my lines," said Matthews when approached on the subject, "but I promise you that even if we had to open next Monday, I would be all right."

"But, Matty," replied his director anxiously, "we *do* open next Monday."

MATURE, Victor (1915–99), *US film actor.*

1 Victor Mature applied for membership in the exclusive Los Angeles Country Club, only to be told "We don't accept actors." "I'm no actor," Mature is supposed to have protested, "and I've got sixty-four pictures to prove it."

2 Groucho Marx was among the audience invited to a private screening of Victor Mature's new film *Samson and Delilah,* in which he co-starred with Hedy Lamarr. "What did you think?" asked the producer buoyantly at the end. "I have one major criticism," said Groucho. "You can't expect the public to get excited about a film where the leading man's bust is bigger than the leading lady's."

3 During a break in the filming of a historical picture, Mature slipped out with one of his fellow actors for a quick drink. As time was short, they did not bother changing out of their Roman gladiator costumes and strode into the local bar in full armor, complete with helmets and swords. The barman, speechless, stood rooted to the spot. "What's the matter?" asked Mature. "Don't you serve members of the armed forces?"

—◆—

MAUCH, Gene (1925–), *US baseball executive.*

1 The manager of many teams, Mauch was known for making bad decisions that adversely affected his team's chances in playoff games and often prevented them from getting into the World Series. Attempting to console him, a friend noted that one learned best from adversity. "If it's true you can learn from adversity," he shot back, "then I must be the luckiest sonofabitch in the whole world."

—◆—

MAUGHAM, W[illiam] Somerset (1874–1965), *British novelist and playwright.*

1 Somerset Maugham's *Liza of Lambeth,* his first novel, was published in 1897. Drawing on his experiences as a medical student when he spent some weeks as an obstetric clerk in the London slums, it achieved sufficient success to encourage Maugham to abandon his medical career for writing. Ten years passed before that success was repeated, and in the meantime his numerous novels and plays made no further mark. Edmund Gosse, then the doyen of the literary and social circles to which Maugham aspired, had been particularly enthusiastic about *Liza of Lambeth,* but for many years after that he rubbed salt into the wounds in Maugham's self-esteem by saying every time they met, "My dear Maugham, I liked your *Liza of Lambeth* so much. How wise of you never to have written anything else!"

2 Somerset Maugham believed that early nights would keep him young, a habit his friend, the society hostess Emerald Cunard, found irritating. As he was preparing as usual to leave soon after dinner one night, Lady Cunard pressed him to stay. Maugham demurred: "I can't stay, Emerald. I have to keep my youth."

"Then why didn't you bring him with you?" Lady Cunard asked. "I should be delighted to meet him."

3 Asked why he always chose to sail in French ships, Maugham replied, "Because there's none of that nonsense about women and children first."

4 Unable to take his Spanish royalties out of the country, Maugham decided to use the money to pay for a luxury holiday there. He chose one of the best hotels and dined extravagantly every evening, until he felt satisfied that he had spent most of the accumulated sum. He informed the manager that he would be leaving the following day, and asked for his bill. The manager beamed at his distinguished guest. "It has been an honor having you here," he replied. "You have brought much good publicity to us. Therefore, there is no bill."

5 His ex-wife, who was about to leave for America, worried that she would never make the crossing alive — a torpedo would surely sink their ship. "I have only one piece of advice to give you," Maugham told her. "Keep your mouth open, and you will drown the sooner."

6 During the course of his eightieth-birthday celebrations, Maugham spoke at a dinner in his honor at the Garrick Club in London. "There are many virtues in growing old," he began, then paused and looked down at the table. The pause grew uncomfortably long. Maugham fumbled with his notes, looked around the room, shifted uneasily from one foot to the other. The guests exchanged embarrassed glances. The writer cleared his throat and continued: ". . . I'm just trying to think what they are."

—◆—

MAUREPAS, Jean-Frédéric Phélippeaux, Comte de (1701–81), *French statesman.*

1 When Louis XVI ascended the throne, he cast about for experienced advisers. Two names were suggested to him: Comte de Machault as prime minister and Comte de Maurepas as master of ceremonies to arrange the court mourning for Louis XV. Both were summoned. Maurepas arrived first and, like the experienced courtier he was, quickly insinuated himself into the young king's favor. When the king was called to a council meeting, Maurepas was still with him, and as Louis did not dismiss him, he followed him into the council chamber and sat down at the table. Seeing that Louis was nonplussed as to how to deal with him, Maurepas said boldly, "Is Your Majesty wishing to appoint me prime minister?"

"No," said Louis, "I did not intend that."

"Ah," said Maurepas, "I understand; Your Majesty wishes me to teach him how to govern without one."

{After this Maurepas became de facto prime minister, Machault returned home empty-handed, and the consequences for Louis's government were disastrous.}

MAURY, Jean Siffrein (1746–1817), *French cardinal.*

1 In 1781 Maury was the Lenten preacher at Louis XVI's court. The king observed of his preaching, "If the abbé had only said a few words about religion, he would have covered every possible subject."

2 During the period 1789–92 Maury's wit stood him in good stead in the Constituent Assembly; it was said that a single *bon mot* might preserve his life for a month. On one occasion he was followed as speaker by Mirabeau, who announced, "I shall enclose the abbé in a vicious circle."

"Ah, Mirabeau," interjected the abbé, "are you proposing to embrace me?"

MAYER, Louis B. (1885–1957), *US film producer.*

1 When Mayer visited Franklin Roosevelt in the White House, he laid his watch down on the President's desk at the start of their meeting and said, "I'm told, Mr. President, that when anyone spends eighteen minutes with you, you have them in your pocket." Their interview lasted seventeen minutes.

2 Driving away from the funeral of Irving Thalberg, his protégé, longtime colleague, and finally rival, Mayer was very quiet. MGM executive Edgar J. Mannix, who was in the limousine with him, wondered what the thoughts were going through his chief's head. Suddenly a smile broke across Mayer's face and he said, "Isn't God good to me?"

3 Trying to persuade Mayer to give money to charity, a colleague reasoned: "You can't take it with you when you go."

"If I can't take it with me," retorted Mayer, "I won't go."

4 Mayer admired "class" and wanted badly to possess it. Told that golf was a classy American sport, he once took it up. But he never seemed to get the hang of it, never quite understood that it was scored in strokes. Instead, he saw it as a kind of race. He employed two caddies. One caddy was posted down the fairway to locate the ball at once. Meanwhile caddy number two would run ahead, Mayer pelting behind him, to station himself for the next shot. The game over, Mayer would consult his watch. "We made it in one hour and seven minutes! Three minutes better than yesterday."

5 When Mayer appointed his daughter's husband to an executive position at MGM over

the heads of more experienced staff, a studio employee noted, "The son-in-law also rises."

6 Mayer's funeral was attended by huge crowds, a fact that could not in his case be attributed to universal popularity. Goldwyn explained: "The reason so many people showed up for his funeral was because they wanted to make sure he was dead."

MAYO, Charles Horace (1865–1939), US surgeon.

1 In Dr. Mayo's mail one morning was a letter from a spiritualist. "Ever since your late great father passed over," it read, "he has been my doctor. What do you say to that?" Mayo picked up his pen and drafted a reply: "Fine! Please estimate what my father's services have amounted to and send the money to me."

MAZARIN, Jules, Cardinal (1602–61), *French statesman.*

1 A court gossip once told Cardinal Mazarin of a dreadful row between two ladies of the court. The ladies had bombarded each other with insults, each trying to blacken the other's reputation with accusations and slander. "Have they called each other ugly?" asked the cardinal. His informant thought for a moment. "No, Monseigneur," he replied. "Well, then," said Mazarin, "it should not be too difficult to reconcile them."

2 As Mazarin lay dying, the night skies of France were lit by a comet, which the superstitious saw as heralding the great statesman's death. When Mazarin was told of the fears aroused by the phenomenon, he remarked drily, "The comet does me too much honor."

MEDICI, Lorenzo de' (1449–92), *Florentine ruler, known as "Lorenzo the Magnificent."*

1 Lorenzo was on one occasion watching a young apprentice carving the face of an old satyr. He remarked that he was surprised such an old face had a full set of teeth. When he next saw the young man at work again, he noted that one of the satyr's teeth had been knocked out and the gums carefully aged and wrinkled. Impressed, Lorenzo invited the young man to live in the Palazzo Medici with his family. The youth was Michelangelo.

MEHMED II (1432–81), *Ottoman sultan (1451–81) known as "the Conqueror."*

1 The son of Sultan Murad II and an obscure slave girl, Mehmed had an unhappy childhood and turbulent adolescence while his status as heir to the throne was being established. These early events probably instilled in him his inordinate deviousness and secretiveness. Once when asked what he intended to do, he replied, "If a hair of my beard knew, I would pluck it out."

MEHTA, Zubin (1936–), *Indian-born conductor.*

1 Asked which orchestra gave him the most pleasure to conduct, Mehta tactfully refused to single out any particular favorite. "What would a devout Muslim answer as to which of his wives he preferred?" he reasoned. "One can have preferences about details only — a dimple here, an oboe there."

MELBA, Dame Nellie [Helen Porter Armstrong, *née* Mitchell] (1861–1931), *Australian opera singer.*

1 According to the traditional account, the invention of Melba toast was an accident. While Dame Nellie Melba was staying at the Savoy Hotel in London, whoever prepared the star's toast left it too long in the oven and it was brought to her in a thin, dried-up, fragile state. When the maître d'hôtel hastened to apologize, Dame Nellie cut him short, saying the toast was delicious.

2 Opera, in the days before World War I, was often a much more emotional experience than it became in later years. Nellie Melba played Desdemona so heartrendingly during tours of America that many women in the audience burst into tears when she was strangled by Otello. If the applause was particularly persistent, Nellie would rise from her deathbed and signal for a piano to be brought on to the stage. She would then accompanying herself for an encore by singing *Home, Sweet Home,* with the audience joining in. When the ovation following the encore died down, she would collapse again upon the bed and the unfortunate Otello was allowed to finish the act.

MELBOURNE, William Lamb, 2d Viscount (1779–1848), *British statesman; prime minister (1834, 1835–41).*

1 In Dublin as secretary for Ireland, Lamb very quickly assessed the way in which the government there worked and was regarded by the Irish. The young son of one of his subordinates came in to be shown the office one day. "Is there anything here you would like?" asked Lamb, gesturing toward the top of his desk. The child selected a stick of official red sealing wax. "Quite right, my boy," said the secretary for Ireland, pressing some pens into

his hand as well, "begin life early. All the things here belong to the public, and it's your business to get as much out of the public as you can."

2 Lord Melbourne had a strong distaste for religious zeal. Having been forced to sit through an evangelical sermon on the consequences of sin, he grumbled, "Things have come to a pretty pass when religion is allowed to invade private life."

3 Melbourne also had little patience with the ecclesiastical squabbles of the day and frequently ran into difficulties over the appointment of bishops, particularly as he favored the more liberal theologians in the church hierarchy. Consequently, he was distressed when the death of a bishop entailed a vacancy in the House of Lords which it was the prime minister's duty to fill. "Damn it! Another bishop dead! I think they die just to vex me."

4 When the death in 1832 of the poet George Crabbe was announced, Lord Melbourne observed, "I am always glad when one of these fellows dies, for then I know I have the whole of him on my shelf."

MELLON, Andrew William (1855–1937), *US financier, secretary of the Treasury, art collector, and philanthropist.*

1 (The writer Lucius Beebe recalls a breakfast at the Mellon establishment.)

"The old man was very fond of thin little hot cakes and sausages, and their service was ritual. One morning in the midst of their presentation, one at a time by the day footman, another lackey brought in the telephone on a cord and announced that the Minister of Finance of France wished to speak with Mr. Mellon on the transocean. 'Not with the hot cakes,' said the old gentleman testily. . . .

'These foreigners have no sense of propriety.'"

———⚭———

MELVILLE, Herman (1819–91), *US novelist.*

1 On a visit one evening to Nathaniel Hawthorne and his wife, Melville told them a story of a fight he had witnessed on an island in the South Seas, in which one of the Polynesian warriors had wreaked havoc among his foes with a heavy club. Striding about the room, Melville demonstrated the feats of valor and the desperate drama of the battle. After he had gone, Mrs. Hawthorne thought she remembered that he had left empty-handed, and wondered, "Where is that club with which Mr. Melville was laying about him so?" Mr. Hawthorne maintained that he must have taken it with him, and indeed a search of the room revealed nothing. The next time they saw him they asked what had happened to the club. It turned out that there was no club; it had simply been a figment of their imagination, conjured up by the vividness of Melville's narrative.

———⚭———

MENCKEN, H[enry] L[ouis] (1880–1945), *US critic and journalist.*

1 Mencken coined his own epitaph: "If after I depart this vale, you ever remember me and have thought to please my ghost, forgive some sinner and wink your eye at some homely girl."

———⚭———

MENELIK II (1844–1913), *emperor of Ethiopia (1889–1913).*

1 In the late nineteenth century, news of the success of the electric chair as a means of dispatching criminals reached Ethiopia. Mene-lik II eagerly ordered one. When it arrived, however, he was disappointed to find that it did not work: no one had warned him that Ethiopia's lack of electricity would be a problem. The criminals of the nation sighed with relief and the emperor, anxious that his new acquisition should not go to waste, had the chair converted into a throne.

2 The emperor had one eccentricity. If he felt unwell, he was convinced that he had only to eat a few pages of the Bible in order to feel better. This odd behavior did him little harm, as long as his testamentary intake was modest. However, in December 1913 he was recovering from a stroke, when he suddenly felt extremely ill. On his instructions the complete Book of Kings was torn from the Bible and fed to him, page by page. He died before he had consumed the entire book.

———⚭———

MENSHIKOV, Alexander Sergeievich, Prince (1787–1869), *Russian general, commander in chief of the Russian forces during the Crimean War.*

1 During a sortie near Sevastopol a young British army officer was captured by the Russians, who searched him and found a number of letters in his possession. The man was particularly reluctant to part with one from his sweetheart, but the Russians insisted on having it and it was sent to Prince Menshikov along with the others. When the prince read it, he was amused to find that the girl had written flippantly that she hoped her young man would have the good fortune to capture Prince Menshikov and that if he did so he was to be sure to send her one of his buttons. Much to the man's surprise the letter was returned to him, along with a note from Menshikov and a button. The note said that although events had not happened quite as the lady had envisaged, nonetheless here was

one of Prince Menshikov's buttons and it was to be sent to her.

———∽———

MERMAN, Ethel (1909–84), *US entertainer.*

1 During Mary Martin's Broadway run in *Leave It to Me!* Ethel Merman was asked her opinion of her rival. "Well," replied Ethel rather tartly, "if you like talent . . ."

———∽———

MESSIER, Charles (1730–1817), *French astronomer.*

1 Nursing his dying wife, Messier was obliged to abandon his search for a certain comet. In the meantime, the comet was discovered by a rival astronomer, Montaigue of Limoges. A friend, hearing of the death of Mme Messier, expressed his sympathy for Messier's loss. The astronomer nodded in acknowledgment, his eyes filling with tears. "To think that when I had discovered twelve," he said, "this Montaigue should have got my thirteenth."

———∽———

METAXAS, Ioannis (1871–1941), *Greek general.*

1 During a visit of inspection to an air base Metaxas was invited to test a new flying boat. He took the aircraft up for a short flight and was coming in to land when the commander of the base intervened: "Excuse me, General; it would be better to come down on the water; this is a flying boat." Metaxas, who had been about to put the aircraft down on a runway, swerved quickly upward, made another circuit, and touched the flying boat down safely on the surface of the water. Metaxas switched off the engine and turned to his host. "Thank you, Commander, for preventing me from making a stupid

blunder" — and so saying, briskly opened the aircraft's door and jumped out into the water.

———∽———

METTERNICH, Klemens, Prince von (1773–1859), *Austrian statesman.*

1 Metternich, who had a contempt for the average Englishman's inability to speak French fluently, observed to Lord John Dudley that he was the only Englishman he knew who could speak French well: "The common people of Vienna speak French better than the educated men of London." Lord Dudley replied, "That may be so, but Your Highness will recall that Bonaparte has not been twice in London to teach them."

———∽———

METTERNICH, Princess Pauline [*née Countess Sándor*] (1859–1921), *autocratic wife of Prince Richard Metternich (1829–95).*

1 The princess was traveling on a train one day toward Compiègne. The other occupant of her compartment asked politely if smoking would bother her. The princess replied: "I have no idea, monsieur. No one has ever dared to smoke in my presence."

———∽———

MEURISSE, Paul (1912–79), *French actor.*

1 Meurisse, renowned for his taciturnity, once caught sight of a sign in a florist's window: SAY IT WITH FLOWERS. He went in and asked for a rose. "Just one," he told the young clerk. "To be delivered to this address with my card." The girl picked out a delicate red rose and asked, "Is there any message?" Meurisse took the flower and plucked out all

the petals except two. "There you are," he said, handing back the mutilated bloom. "And even then, I wonder if I haven't said too much."

———ᴕᴕ———

MEYERBEER, Giacomo (1791–1864), *German pianist and opera composer.*

1 Meyerbeer took care to be on good terms with the Parisian critics, a policy he was able to implement with the help of his great wealth. Heinrich Heine was among those convinced by the lavishness of Meyerbeer's generosity that his forthcoming works were very good indeed. Unfortunately for the impoverished critic, Meyerbeer suddenly cut off the flow of funds just at a moment when Heine's resources were especially depleted. Heine avenged himself by remarking, "Meyerbeer will be immortal while he lives and maybe for a little while after, because he always pays in advance."

2 The rival composers Meyerbeer and Rossini, though polite, cordially disliked each other. One day Rossini was complaining to Meyerbeer that he felt in the lowest possible spirits, bored, melancholy, and so forth. Meyerbeer consoled him: "You listen to too much of your own music."

3 In 1839 a young German composer left his native land for Paris, where he hoped to obtain recognition for his work. One of his compatriots referred him to Meyerbeer, who received the young German amiably enough and gave him a sealed letter of recommendation to Léon Pillet, at that time director of the Opéra. What the letter actually contained were the words: "Take this imbecile off my hands."

The imbecile was Richard Wagner.

———ᴕᴕ———

MICHELANGELO BUONARROTI (1475–1564), *Italian sculptor, architect, painter, and poet.*

1 One day Michelangelo happened to overhear a group of people admiring his *Pietà*. One man attributed the sculpture to Il Gobbo, much to the chagrin of Michelangelo, who took particular pride in the *Pietà*. Returning to the sculpture after dark that evening, he carved his name on it, so that no similar mistake could occur in the future.

2 The figures Michelangelo completed for the Medici tombs ordered by Pope Clement VII represent the members of the family in highly idealized form. Someone remarked on this absence of realism. "Who will care," replied the sculptor, "in a thousand years' time, whether these are their features or not?"

3 The pope's master of ceremonies pestered Michelangelo to allow him a glimpse of the *Last Judgment* fresco before the artist was ready to unveil it. Michelangelo took his revenge by including the official among the damned in hell, being tormented by devils. When the master of ceremonies complained to Pope Paul III, the latter replied: "God has given me authority in heaven and on earth, but my writ does not extend to hell. You will just have to put up with it."

4 Michelangelo was once assisted in his work by a marble-hewer, who, by following Michelangelo's detailed instructions — "Cut this away . . . level that . . . polish here" — was amazed to find that he had created a splendid marble figure. "What do you think of it?" asked Michelangelo. "I think it's fine," replied the man, "and I am much obliged to you. By your means I have discovered a talent that I did not know I possessed."

5 A certain painter had produced a picture that was a pastiche of details stolen from other

artists. Asked by a friend his opinion of the picture, Michelangelo praised the workmanship but added wryly, "I don't know what will become of this scene on the Day of Judgement, when all the bodies shall recover their members, for there will be nothing left of it."

6 A priest once remarked to Michelangelo that it was a pity that he had not married and had many children to whom he could have bequeathed his works. Michelangelo answered, "I have too much of a wife in this art of mine, which has afflicted me throughout my life, and my children shall be the works I leave. What would have become of Lorenzo Ghiberti's reputation if he had not made the gates of San Giovanni? His children and grandchildren sold or squandered all he left, but the gates are still standing."

7 Michelangelo began the Rondanini *Pietà* when he was nearly ninety. The effort of cutting the marble exhausted him and revealed how far his power and genius had withered with age. He himself was tragically aware of his decline. One night Vasari, visiting the old sculptor, found his eyes irresistibly drawn to the unfinished *Pietà* standing in a corner. Michelangelo said, "I am so old that death often plucks at my mantle to bear me away, and one day my body will fall — like this." As he spoke he dropped the lantern he had been holding, cutting off the scene from Vasari's eyes.

———— ⌇ ————

MICHELET, Jules (1798–1874), *French historian.*

1 The July Revolution of 1830, which ousted the autocratic Charles X and ushered in the constitutional monarchy of Louis Philippe, broke out on July 27, when Michelet was delivering a lecture at the École Normale. As the sound of cannon fire became audible, the students grew restless. "Gentlemen," Michelet said, "they are making history. We shall write it."

———— ⌇ ————

MIES VAN DER ROHE, Ludwig (1886–1969), *German architect.*

1 Mies van der Rohe did not believe that an architect should indulge in self-expression. Once a student asked him for his opinion on this subject. He handed her a pencil and paper and told her to write her name. When she had done so, he said, "That's for self-expression. Now we get to work."

———— ⌇ ————

MILL, John Stuart (1806–73), *British political philosopher and social reformer.*

1 As John Stuart Mill, in Parliament, was expounding his famous principle of "the greatest good for the greatest number," Disraeli, from the Tory benches, breathed, "Ah — the nursery governess!"

———— ⌇ ————

MILLAY, Edna St. Vincent (1892–1950), *US poet and dramatist.*

1 The poet's middle name is that of a New York hospital. How did this come about? On a February day in 1892 a young man named Charles Buzzell boarded the ship *El Monte*, then in New Orleans loading cotton for New York, to watch the loading. Suffering from a slight fever, he fell asleep on a bale of hay, cotton stacked all about him. He awoke in the hold, all hatches battened down. Calls for help were unheard. Nine days later the hold was opened and Charles was found at the foot of the hatchway. The captain rushed him to St. Vincent's Hospital, where he was given up for dead. But the doctors plus a strong constitution pulled him through. It

was said then that he had survived "longer than anyone ever had without food or water."

At about that time a little girl was born to Mrs. Henry Tolman Millay, Charles's sister. She gave the little girl a middle name in memory of the hospital in which her brother had recovered. These facts are recorded in a letter to *The New York Times Book Review* from Edna's sister Norma, who concludes, "Had it been Doctor's Hospital or Lenox Hill, she doubtless would have reconsidered — they wouldn't scan."

———— ⚬⁄ₒ ————

MILLER, Arthur (1915–), *US dramatist.*

1 "Arthur Miller, sitting alone in a bar, was approached by a well-tailored, slightly tiddly fellow who addressed him thus:

" 'Aren't you Arthur Miller?'

" 'Why, yes, I am.'

" 'Don't you remember me?'

" 'Well . . . your face seems familiar.'

" 'Why, Art, I'm your old buddy Sam! We went to high school together! We went out on double dates!'

" 'I'm afraid I —'

" 'I guess you can see I've done all right. Department stores. What do *you* do, Art?'

" 'Well, I . . . write.'

" 'Whaddya write?'

" 'Plays, mostly.'

" 'Ever get any produced?'

" 'Yes, some.'

" 'Would I know any?'

" 'Well . . . perhaps you've heard of *Death of a Salesman?*'

"Sam's jaw dropped; his face went white. For a moment he was speechless. Then he cried out, 'Why, you're ARTHUR MILLER!' "

———— ⚬⁄ₒ ————

MILLIKAN, Robert Andrews (1868–1953), *US physicist.*

1 Millikan's wife was passing through the hall of their home when she overheard the maid answering the telephone. "Yes, this is where Dr. Millikan lives," she heard the girl say, "but he's not the kind of doctor that does anybody any good."

———— ⚬⁄ₒ ————

MILNE, A[lan] A[lexander] (1882–1956), *British journalist and writer, best known for his Winnie-the-Pooh.*

1 (Christopher Milne explains how his father tactfully corrected his table manners.)

"Once, when I was quite little, he came up to the nursery while I was having my lunch. And while he was talking I paused between mouthfuls, resting my hands on the table, knife and fork pointing upwards. 'You oughtn't really to sit like that,' he said, gently. 'Why not?' I asked, surprised. 'Well . . . ,' he hunted around for a reason he could give. Because it's considered bad manners? Because you mustn't? Because . . . 'Well,' he said, looking in the direction that my fork was pointing, 'suppose somebody suddenly fell through the ceiling. They might land on your fork and that would be very painful.' 'I see,' I said, though I didn't really."

———— ⚬⁄ₒ ————

MILNES, Richard Monckton, 1st Baron Houghton (1809–85), *British writer and politician.*

1 As he lay on his deathbed the bon vivant Monckton Milnes observed, "My exit is the result of too many entrées."

———— ⚬⁄ₒ ————

MILO (late 6th century BC), *Greek wrestler famed for his feats in the Olympic games.*

1 Milo's strongman antics were his eventual downfall. He came upon a tree trunk in which woodmen, who had been trying to split it, had left a wedge. Milo attempted to split the tree apart with his bare hands, the wedge sprang out, and the trunk closed upon his hands. Trapped, he was found by a pack of wolves who tore him limb from limb.

MILTON, John (1608–74), *British poet.*

1 In April 1667 Milton signed an agreement with Samuel Simmons, a London bookseller (i.e., publisher), by which he sold the copyright of *Paradise Lost* for £5, plus £5 for the sale of each of three subsequent editions, an edition comprising fifteen-hundred copies. Milton received a second £5 in April 1669, making a grand total of £10 to the author of England's greatest epic. After his death, Milton's widow, his third wife, Elizabeth, sold all remaining rights for £8 to Simmons, who became perpetual owner of the copyright.

2 In the course of a visit to Milton, James II, then Duke of York, suggested that the poet's blindness was a divine punishment for his having written a defense of the execution of Charles I. Milton retorted, "If Your Highness thinks that misfortunes are indexes of the wrath of heaven, what must you think of your father's tragical end? I have only lost my eyes — he lost his head."

3 Even after he went blind Milton was able to produce magnificent poetry. He simply organized his life into a secure routine. Rising early, he would have a man read to him from the Bible, after which he would contemplate the ways of God. Then the man would return to take Milton's dictation. Once the man returned very late. Milton complained, "I want to be milked."

MINGUS, Charlie (1922–79), *US jazz musician.*

1 Mingus played at a nightclub on one occasion where patrons at several tables paid no attention to his music but talked throughout his performance. After a considerable time had passed and the chatterers still talked on, Mingus announced that he would play a few bars, then turn the "music" over to the talkers for a few bars, back and forth — and did so for an extended piece. The talkers never noticed, and even joined in the applause at the end.

MIRABEAU, Honoré Gabriel Riqueti, Comte de (1749–91), *French revolutionary statesman.*

1 Mirabeau received numerous challenges, to which he always returned the same answer: "Sir, your favor is received and your name is on my list, but I must warn you that the list is long, and I grant no preferences."

2 Mirabeau, who was badly pockmarked, addressed one of the first sessions of the constitutional convention, describing in his best oratorical style the proper qualifications of the to-be-elected president. Talleyrand remarked, "He has forgotten only one thing: he must also be pockmarked."

3 Although not noted for his own sincerity, Mirabeau was quick to recognize the quality in others. On hearing Robespierre speak for the first time, he leaned toward his neighbor and observed, "That man will go far; he believes all he says."

4 A group of students, observing the proceedings of the French Assembly, listened to the pompous and long-winded debates with expressions of disgust. Mirabeau mocked them gently for their naiveté. "Laws are like

sausages," he said. "You should never watch them being made."

———⌀———

MISES, Ludwig von (1881–1973), *Austrian economist.*

1 At the age of eighty-eight Mises was asked how he felt upon getting up in the morning. "Amazed," he replied.

———⌀———

MITCHELL, MARGARET (1900-49), *US author of one novel,* Gone with the Wind.

1 When New York editor Harold Latham visited Atlanta looking for new writers, he heard a great deal about a woman, Margaret Mitchell, who was writing a vast epic about the Civil War. Latham contacted her, but a very modest Mitchell declined to share her novel, saying she had nothing to show. Latham was preparing to leave Atlanta when he received a phone call from the lobby; when he got there, he was stunned to see Mitchell, a tiny woman, sitting surrounded by two huge towers of her manuscript. What had happened? A young woman whom Mitchell introduced to Latham during the course of his visit had boasted of her own writing genius and her intention to win the Pulitzer Prize, although, as she said, she had already been rejected by "the best" publishers. "You know, you don't take life seriously enough to be a novelist," the catty young lady had said to Mitchell. "I think you are wasting your time trying. You really aren't the type." Mitchell was energized. And her book, *Gone with the Wind*, won the Pulitzer Prize.

2 While crossing Atlanta's Peachtree Street with her husband to see a movie, Mitchell was struck by a speeding car and died a few days later. The car was driven by Hugh Gravitt, an off-duty cab driver who had been cited twenty-eight times the previous decade for speeding. As he was sentenced to jail for involuntary manslaughter, he was asked why he had ignored the twenty-five-mile-per-hour limit. "Everybody does it," he said nonchalantly. The next day, just before he was to report to jail, he and his wife were injured when the car he was driving crashed into a truck.

———⌀———

MITCHUM, Robert (1917–97), *US film actor.*

1 Mitchum, happily married for thirty years, was asked what he thought had made his marriage last, when those of so many of his show-business colleagues had failed. "Mutual forbearance," he replied. "We have each continued to believe that the other will do better tomorrow."

———⌀———

MITFORD, Nancy (1904–73), *British author.*

1 The British police were having one of their periodic drives to stamp out prostitution in London. "But," protested Nancy Mitford, "where will the young men learn?"

———⌀———

MIZNER, Addison (?-1933), *US architect and entrepreneur.*

1 Despite an almost complete lack of formal qualifications, Addison Mizner sprang to wealth and fame as the chief architect employed by those who bought land in Florida during the great property boom. The rich and celebrated scrambled for the cachet of a Mizner-designed residence, despite certain structural drawbacks (engrossed in aesthetic considerations, Mizner once forgot to install a stairway between the first and second stories). When client William Gray Warden asked for a copy of the blueprints of his Palm

Beach house in order to show his friends, Mizner remonstrated, "Why, the house isn't built yet! Construction first, blueprints afterward."

———— ❧ ————

MIZNER, Wilson (1876–1933), *US writer and wit who tried his hand at a score of respectable and disreputable means of earning a living.*

1 In the hospital for an appendectomy, Mizner was not reassured when a nurse came to write his name, illness, and other information on his chest for purposes of identification. He kept quiet about his misgivings and when her back was turned added a postscript to her notes: "Store in a cool place until opened."

2 Mizner's opponent at a game of draw poker took out his wallet and tossed it onto the table, saying, "I call you." Mizner calmly took off his right shoe and put it on the table and announced, "If we're playing for leather, I raise."

3 In 1907 Mizner managed the Hotel Rand on West Forty-ninth Street in New York. He put up two signs for guests: "No opium-smoking in the elevators" and "Carry out your own dead."

4 The friend and associate of boxers, Mizner was himself a talented pugilist. One night in a San Francisco bar to which he had been accompanied by a group that included the middleweight known as "Mysterious" Billy Smith, Mizner started a fight with some longshoremen. At the end only one longshoreman was left standing; although Mizner was raining punches upon him, he remained obstinately upright, causing Mizner to worry that his punch had lost its power. Suddenly Mysterious Billy Smith noticed what was happening. "Leave him alone, Wilson!" he shouted. "I knocked him out five minutes ago." On investigation it turned out that a punch from Smith had indeed knocked the longshoreman out cold, but had also wedged him vertically between two pieces of furniture.

5 When in June 1906 Harry Thaw shot the well-known architect Stanford White in a quarrel over Evelyn Nesbit, the scandal gripped the entire country. Some years later Wilson Mizner, observing with distaste a Palm Beach hotel designed by Joseph Urban, remarked, "Harry Thaw shot the wrong architect."

6 During the 1920s property boom in Florida the Mizner brothers ran an "antiquing" factory at which pieces of furniture, timber, statuary and other items were treated to give the impression of venerable age. Showing friends around the factory, Wilson Mizner handed them air rifles and offered to let them take part in inflicting the ravages of time upon a too-new dining-room suite. "Don't shoot straight at it," he instructed. "Remember a worm always charges at a piece of furniture from an angle."

7 On his deathbed Mizner awoke briefly from a coma to find a priest bending over him offering words of comfort. Mizner waved the man away. "Why should I talk to you? I've just been talking to your boss."

———— ❧ ————

MODIGLIANI, Amedeo (1884–1920), *Italian painter and sculptor.*

1 Modigliani's admiration of Utrillo was reciprocated. On the occasion of their first meeting, they began by paying each other extravagant compliments. "You are the world's greatest painter," said one.

"No, *you* are the world's greatest painter," said the other.

"I forbid you to contradict me."

"I forbid you to forbid me."

The argument became heated. "If you say that again, I'll hit you."

"You are the greatest —" and they fell to blows.

Later, they made up over several bottles of wine at a nearby bistro. As they went out into the street, one said, "You are the world's greatest painter."

"No, you are."

And so the fight broke out again, until both combatants were down in the gutter, where they went to sleep. In the early dawn they woke up to discover that they had been robbed.

MOLIÈRE [Jean-Baptiste Poquelin] (1622–73), *French actor and dramatist.*

1 On February 17, 1673, the desperately ill Molière insisted on going on stage so as not to let the rest of the company down. When the play was over he had to be carried home, where he died shortly afterward.

Religious prejudices against the theater were so powerful that it was customary for a dying actor solemnly to abjure his profession so as to obtain burial in consecrated ground. Molière's sudden death prevented this formality and appeals to the archbishop of Paris were fruitless. Molière's widow sought the aid of the king. Louis sent to the ecclesiastical authorities to ask how deep consecrated ground may run. Back came the answer: "Fourteen feet."

"Very good," said Louis. "Let Molière's grave be dug in the churchyard sixteen feet deep and then it cannot be said that he is buried in consecrated ground, nor need it scandalize the clergy."

MOLNÁR, Ferenc (1878–1952), *Hungarian dramatist and novelist.*

1 Molnár was a late riser, never emerging until 1:00 PM. On one occasion in Budapest, called as a witness in a lawsuit, he had to present himself at court by 9:00 AM. The combined efforts of his servants got him out of bed and dressed, and they propelled him out of the house at 8:30 into the rush-hour crowd. Molnár looked in amazement at the hurrying workers and exclaimed, "Good heavens, are all these people witnesses in this fool case?"

2 During the Béla Kun revolution the streets of Budapest became unsafe, the haunt of thugs who attacked passersby with impunity. People went about in groups or stayed off the streets at night. Molnár remained home during much of this period, but he encouraged friends to visit him. One evening they brought a giant of a man along with them. Molnár eyed him in a worried way all evening. When he came to bid the giant farewell, he shook his hand and said in a concerned voice, "Aren't you afraid to go home by yourself? Aren't you horribly worried that you'll attack somebody?"

3 While Molnár was living in a hotel in Vienna during the 1920s, a large contingent of his relatives came to see him in the hope of sharing some of the fruits of the playwright's fabulous success. They were prepared for a hostile reception, but to their surprise Molnár greeted them kindly, even insisting that they all sit for a group portrait to mark the occasion. The print ready, Molnár presented it to the hotel doorman. "And whenever you see any of the persons in the picture trying to get into the hotel, don't let them in."

4 Expatriate Hungarians, all of them coffeehouse habitués, gathered around Molnár in New York and soon established a semblance of the former café society of Budapest —

gossiping, playing games, writing, and arguing for up to twelve hours a day. Once the talk turned to the topic of learning English. Molnár asked his friends which words of sentences had been the first they had learned. One man replied, "I love you." Others cited the conventional greetings — "Hello," "Goodbye," "Good morning," and so on. "The first sentence I learned," said Molnár, "was 'Separate checks, please!'"

———— ✧ ————

MONET, Claude (1840–1926), *French painter, founder of the Impressionist school.*

1 Unlike a portraitist, Monet worked under tight time limits. His painting, which was done outdoors, had to be completed in short segments and done very quickly, to take advantage of conditions of light, weather, atmosphere, and time of day. Once an art dealer saw him arrive at Varengeville in haste, look at the sun, then look at his watch. Monet said to him, "I'm half an hour late. I'll come back tomorrow."

2 When he first put on a pair of glasses, he exclaimed, "Good lord, I see things like Bouguereau!" [a popular academic painter of the period]

———— ✧ ————

MONROE, Marilyn (1926–62), *US film actress.*

1 Marilyn Monroe was difficult to direct, often unsure of her lines, frequently late — yet what finally emerged on the screen was usually triumphant. Director Billy Wilder once recalled an episode that occurred during the shooting of *Some Like It Hot.* It was simple enough. The script required Miss Monroe to knock on a door, enter the room, and ask for a slug of bourbon from a bottle in a bureau drawer. But, try as she would, the line of dialogue eluded her, and it never quite came out as fitting the action. Wilder recalled: "On the fifty-third take I told her we had put the line on pieces of paper and they were in every drawer she would open. . . . She went to the wrong piece of furniture."

2 She once admitted that as a woman she felt like a failure; she had been turned into something she wasn't. "Men expect bells to ring and whistles to whistle," she said sadly, "but my anatomy is the same as any other woman's and I can't live up to it."

3 Considered one of the goddesses of the screen, Monroe never felt satisfied with her acting abilities. Despite the enormous sums she was paid to star in movies such as *Some Like It Hot* and *Bus Stop,* Monroe continued to take private acting classes, working hard on her craft. She noted, "I don't want to make money. I just want to be wonderful."

4 When asked why she had posed for some nude photographs early in her career, Monroe said, "Why? It paid the rent!"

5 At a press conference shortly after her marriage to baseball great Joe DiMaggio, a reporter boldly asked her what she wore to bed. Looking over at her new husband, she said, very softly, "Chanel No. 5."

6 In 1954 Monroe was paired with Robert Mitchum in the western saga *River of No Return.* Friends warned her about Mitchum, reminding her that he was known to be a scene stealer. "Oh, I'm not scared of Bob stealing scenes," she told them. "It's those darned hammy horses that worry me."

7 Monroe's inability to be on time for a shoot was legendary in the business, but things seemed worse than ever during the filming of *Some Like It Hot.* She would appear terribly late, looking tired and hesitant about her script. Director Billy Wilder was exasperated but showed her great patience. "My Aunt Minnie would always be punctual and never hold up production," he explained to a har-

ried cast member, "but who would pay to see my Aunt Minnie?"

8 On the set of *Something's Got to Give,* her last movie, and one she never completed, Monroe was later than ever to rehearsals and shoots. Director Billy Wilder needed her one morning and was unable to find her. "It used to be you'd call her at nine AM, she'd show up at noon," he groaned. "Now you call her in May, she shows up in October."

———— ∽ ————

MONTAGU, Lady Mary Wortley (1689–1762), *British letter writer and traveler.*

1 In Constantinople Lady Mary lost no opportunity to tell the Turkish ladies of the superior status of women in England. Her propaganda suffered a serious setback, however, when her friends invited her to go with them to a public bath. The Turkish lady who helped her undress was amazed at the sight of Lady Mary's stays, and called all her friends to come and have a look. "See how cruelly the poor English ladies are used by their husbands!" she cried. "How can you boast of your greater liberty when your husbands lock you up in a box like this?"

2 The breadth of Lady Mary's experience is perhaps best summed up in her alleged dying words: "It has all been most interesting."

———— ∽ ————

MONTAGUE, Charles Edward (1867–1928), *British journalist and writer.*

1 At the outbreak of World War I, Montague dyed his gray hair black in order to conceal his age and join the army. H. W. Nevinson remarked that Montague was "the only man on record whose hair turned black in a single night from fearlessness."

———— ∽ ————

MONTCALM [DE SAINT-VÉRAN], Louis Joseph Marquis de (1712-59), *French military commander in Canada.*

1 Montcalm's last breaths were taken within the walls of Quebec, where he was taken after being mortally wounded in battle with the British. When told he would not live to see out the day, he said, "So much the better. I am happy that I shall not live to see the surrender of Quebec."

———— ∽ ————

MONTECUCCOLI, Raimund, Count (1609–80), *Austrian general.*

1 The Roman Catholic (and ordinarily pious) general had dutifully ordered an omelet for his dinner one Friday. Being exceptionally hungry, however, he decided that there would be no harm in having a little ham sliced up in it. Just as the dish was set in front of him, an exceptionally loud clap of thunder announced the start of a storm. Without a word, the general strode to the window, opened it, and threw out the omelet. Looking up toward the source of the thunder, he exclaimed petulantly, *"Voilà bien du bruit pour une omelette au jambon!"* (What a lot of fuss over a mere ham omelet!)

———— ∽ ————

MONTEFIORE, Sir Moses (1784–1885), *Jewish philanthropist.*

1 At a dinner party Montefiore found himself seated next to an anti-Semitic nobleman who opened the conversation by saying, "I have just returned from Japan, and it's a most unusual country. Did you know that it has neither pigs nor Jews?"

"In that case," Montefiore replied, "you and I should go there, so it will have a sample of each."

MONTEUX, Pierre (1875–1964), *French conductor.*

1 After hearing André Previn conduct the final movement of a Haydn symphony, Monteux called the younger man over to him. "Did you think the orchestra was playing well?" he asked. Previn, who had been rather pleased with the rendering, hesitated, then replied, "Yes, I thought they played very well." Monteux nodded. "So did I," he said. "Next time don't interfere with them."

2 A rehearsal of Richard Strauss's *Till Eulenspiegel* with the Philadelphia Orchestra was not going well. Monteux suspected that the trouble lay with the orchestra's overfamiliarity with the piece. Stopping the music suddenly, he said, "Gentlemen, I know that you know this piece backwards, but please do not let us play it that way."

MONTGOMERY, Bernard Law, 1st Viscount Montgomery of Alamein (1887–1976), *British field marshal, nicknamed "Monty."*

1 When Paris was recaptured by the Allies from the Germans in 1944 a jubilant General de Gaulle invested Monty with the Grande Croix of the Légion d'Honneur. The British Embassy was packed with a wildly excited crowd who would take no orders from anyone but Monty himself. Monty mustered his best French and said, *"Merci — et maintenant — allez-vous en."* The crowd dispersed, but some people grumbled that Monty had said the wrong thing, been ungracious, and so on. Monty sought out A. P. Herbert. "'Allez-vous en' means 'go away,' doesn't it?"

"Yes, sir."

"Well," said Monty, "that's what I wanted, and that's what they did."

2 In 1944 Alan Brooke, chief of the imperial general staff and later to become first Viscount Alanbrooke, remarked to George VI that Montgomery was "a very good soldier, but I think he is after my job." Replied the king, "I thought he was after mine."

3 Climbing into a London cab one afternoon, Montgomery gave his destination as Waterloo. "Station?" quipped the driver. Monty glanced at his watch. "Certainly," he replied. "We're a bit late for the battle."

4 Montgomery carried his flair for the dramatic into civilian life. One day during a sitting of the House of Lords, he turned to the man next to him and, with his expression unruffled and voice calm, said, "Excuse me, but I'm having a coronary thrombosis." And away he went to look for medical attention.

{The doctors discovered that he had indeed suffered a heart attack.}

MONTGOMERY, James (1771–1854), *Scottish poet and journalist.*

1 From 1792 Montgomery lived in Sheffield, where he attained a position of prominence as a writer and philanthropist. In 1812, however, his house was burgled. A treasured inkstand, presented to him by the ladies of Sheffield, was among the items stolen. There was a great public outcry, and some time later the inkstand was returned to its rightful owner with the following message: "Honored sir: When we robbed your house we did not know that you wrote such beautiful verses as you do. I remember my mother told some of them to me when I was a boy. I found what house we robbed by the writing on the inkstand. Honored sir, I send it back. It was my share of the booty, and I hope you and God will forgive me."

MONTMORENCY, Anne, Duc de (1493–1567), *French nobleman and general.*

1 Montmorency was fatally wounded leading the Roman Catholic forces against the Huguenots at the battle of St. Denis in 1567, and was taken back to Paris to die. When a priest came to exhort him to make a good end, Montmorency said, "Father, do you believe that a man who knew how to live for nearly eighty years with honor does not know how to die for a quarter of an hour?"

MOORE, George Augustus (1852–1933), *British author.*

1 Moore was at the center of London literary life and gossip for many years. His various love affairs were well publicized — usually by the author. One woman acquaintance complained, "Some men kiss and do not tell; some kiss and tell; but George Moore told and did not kiss."

2 Moore had trouble keeping a cook. Yeats tells how he fired six in three weeks. One of them, in protest, summoned a policeman. Moore took the officer into his dining room and demanded, "Is there a law in this country to compel me to eat that abominable omelet?" The cook left.

3 (In George Moore's *Ulick and Soracha* the old harper Tadgh dies gazing at the beautiful naked back of the young peasant woman Bridgit, whom he had married in his extreme old age. In a chapter suppressed from the published version of her *G. M.: Memories of George Moore,* Nancy Cunard, the daughter of one of George Moore's great lovers, Emerald Cunard, and herself a friend of the aged novelist, records the incident that gave rise to this scene. From time to time in the early 1920s, without any other amorous overtures, Moore had asked Nancy whether he might see her naked. She had always refused.)

"The words were as sudden as ever, said this time with a good deal of wistfulness: 'I *do* wish you would let me see you naked. I am an old man.... Oh, let me at least see your naked back.'

"Now, equally suddenly, something within me said, 'Do this!' and without more ado, facing away from him, I took off all my clothes, standing motionless a few feet from where he sat. How lightly, how easily, it came about. My clothes left me, lying in a graceful summer pool on the floor, as if they had slipped away of themselves. The night was warm and the mood serene. Without hesitation, my long, naked back and legs were at last in front of him and the silence was complete. It would be full-on he was looking at them and I did not turn my head. Of what could he be thinking? At length came a slow, murmuring sigh: 'Oh, what a beautiful back you have, Nancy! It is as long as a weasel's! What a beautiful back!'

"Then, never turning, I put my clothes on again with the same ease."

MOORE, Marianne (1887-1972), *US poet.*

1 A young man arrived at the great elderly poet's apartment in Brooklyn with an armload of books for her to sign. As she was doing so, he looked around the dwelling and saw a trapeze hanging from a doorway. "Miss Moore," he finally asked after thinking about it, "what is that up in the doorway?" "Oh," said Moore without looking up, "that is my trapeze."

MORE, Hannah (1745-1833), *British moralistic writer and philanthropist.*

1 Mrs. More was spending a pleasant evening with a group of friends, when a late arrival to

the party introduced a note of tragedy by relating a harrowing scene he had just witnessed along the road. A young mother had heroically rushed back into her blazing house to rescue her child, but in the dense smoke had mistakenly seized upon the child of another woman, leaving her own to die. The company, distressed by this tale, immediately set up a collection for the poor woman. Mrs. More played a prominent part in organizing the collection, in the course of which she approached a wealthy peer, who was not known for his generosity. "I will give you . . ." he began, as Mrs. More held out her hand expectantly, ". . . I will give you this afflicting incident for the subject of your next tragedy."

MORE, Sir Thomas (1478–1535), *British statesman, author of* Utopia.

1 When young Thomas More was looking for a wife, the three daughters of a certain John Colte seemed to him eligible and attractive girls. More's inclinations led him to fix his choice first upon the second daughter, but then he thought what an affront it would be to the eldest if her younger sister was married before she was. He accordingly asked for the hand of the eldest daughter, Jane.

2 In *Utopia* More recommends that young people should see each other naked before marriage in order to avoid disappointments and recriminations later. When Sir William Roper came early one morning to More's house at Chelsea with a request to marry one of his daughters, More led him upstairs to the room where the two young girls were sleeping. They were lying on their backs, with the sheet lightly over them. The father whipped off the sheet. The startled girls awoke and turned quickly over onto their stomachs. "Now I have seen both sides," said Sir William, and then and there made his choice of the elder daughter, Margaret.

3 "Ascending the scaffold, [More] seemed so weak that he was ready to fall; whereupon he merrily said to the Lieutenant, 'I pray you Mr. Lieutenant see me safe up, and for my coming down let me shift for myself.' Then desired he all the people to pray for him, and to bear witness with him, that he should suffer death, in, and for the Faith of the Holy Catholic Church, a faithful servant both of God and the King. Which done, he kneeled down, and after his prayers ended, he turned to the executioner, and with a cheerful countenance, said, 'Pluck up thy spirits, man, and be not afraid to do thine office. My neck is very short, take heed therefore thou strike not awry for saving thine honesty.' Then laying his head upon the block he had the executioner stay until he had removed aside his beard, saying that that had never committed any treason. So with much cheerfulness he received the fatal blow of the axe, which at once severed his head from his body."

MOREL, Fédéric (1552–1630), *French scholar and printer.*

1 Morel was engrossed in a translation of Libanius when a messenger arrived to tell him that his wife was seriously ill. "I have only two or three passages left to translate," said Morel, without looking up from his work, "then I shall come directly." After some time, a second messenger brought the news that Mme Morel had not long to live. "Just two more words," cried the scholar, "and I shall be there." A third messenger appeared. "Your wife is dead," he announced solemnly. Morel sighed. "I am grieved indeed," he said. "She was a good woman." With that, he settled down to his translation again.

---⟡---

MORGAN, John Pierpont, Sr. (1837–1913), *US banker, financier, and benefactor of the arts.*

1 J. P. Morgan was as sharp an art collector as he was a banker; so the young Joseph Duveen, who in later years became one of the world's foremost art dealers, found out to his cost. Young Joseph was convinced that his uncle, Henry Duveen, was not getting as much as he should from Morgan. Accordingly, Joseph put before the great man a collection of thirty miniatures, of which six were very rare and the rest unremarkable. Morgan cast his eye briefly over the collection and then asked what the thirty pieces cost. Duveen gave him the figure, upon which Morgan pocketed the six good miniatures, divided Duveen's figure by thirty, multiplied by six, and handed over that amount. "You're only a boy, Joe," Uncle Henry told the exasperated Joseph afterward. "It takes a man to deal with Morgan."

2 Morgan once told a jeweler of his acquaintance that he was interested in buying a pearl scarf pin. Just a few weeks later, the jeweler happened upon a magnificent pearl. He had it mounted in an appropriate setting and sent it to Morgan, together with a bill for $5,000. The following day the package was returned. Morgan's accompanying note read: "I like the pin, but I don't like the price. If you will accept the enclosed check for $4,000, please send back the box with the seal unbroken." The enraged jeweler refused the check and dismissed the messenger in disgust. He opened up the box to reclaim the unwanted pin, only to find that it had been removed. In its place was a check for $5,000.

3 The Cathedral of St. John the Divine, near Columbia University in New York City, has attached to it a Gothic château called the Cathedral House. It is an opulent structure, originally intended to be the bishop's house. At the time of its completion there were critics who felt that it was perhaps too elegant to house a humble servant of God. One of the trustees, J. P. Morgan, defended it thus: "Bishops should live like everyone else."

4 Morgan was looking for a new director of the Metropolitan Museum. Sir Caspar Purdon Clarke, director of the Victoria and Albert Museum in South Kensington, London, seemed the ideal choice. To the dismay of his English colleagues, Clarke accepted the new appointment. The secretary of the Victoria and Albert Museum was on vacation at the time; on his return he asked about some Chinese porcelains and tapestries that had come up for auction in his absence, which he had hoped to acquire for the museum. "I'm afraid J. P. Morgan bought them, sir," replied the clerk. "Good God," said the secretary, "I must tell Sir Purdon." The clerk looked a little uneasy. "Sorry, sir," he said. "Mr. Morgan bought him also."

5 Morgan's nose was disfigured by a skin disease that made it swollen and fiery. People, while pretending politely not to notice anything extraordinary, were nonetheless mesmerized by it. There is the story of the nervous hostess at the tea table, who inquired, "Do you take nose in your tea, Mr. Morgan?"

6 Morgan disliked haggling and tended to make offers in his business dealings on a "take-it-or-leave-it" basis. The figure quoted for the purchase of Andrew Carnegie's steel interests was almost a quarter of a billion dollars. When the slip of paper bearing the figure was handed to him, he barely glanced at it before saying, "I accept." Later Carnegie met him by chance and said he regretted not having set the price 100 million dollars higher. "You'd have got it if you had," said Morgan.

7 Morgan was asked to contribute to an Ivy League medical school. Meeting representatives from the school, he said he was in a hurry and asked them quickly to show him the plans of the proposed buildings. The plans were spread out. "I'll give that, and that, and that," said Morgan, pointing to three buildings, and hurried from the room before he could even be thanked.

8 Morgan fell afoul of Theodore Roosevelt over an antitrust action that the president brought in 1902 against one of his companies. When Roosevelt left office and immediately headed for Africa on a big game safari, Morgan is said to have exclaimed, "Health to the lions!"

MORGAN, John Pierpont, Jr. (1867–1943), *US head of the banking house of Morgan.*

1 A man who had been gazing enviously at J. P. Morgan's yacht said to its owner, "I'm thinking of buying a yacht myself. Can you give me an idea of the annual upkeep?" Morgan replied, "Anyone who has to ask about annual upkeep can't afford one."

2 One of J. P. Morgan's servants availed himself of every opportunity to better and enrich himself. Eventually he decided that he had saved enough to retire in style, and so notified Morgan that he would be leaving his service. Morgan asked him to find a suitable replacement. The following day the man presented to his employer two likely candidates. Morgan interviewed them and selected one. "And I'll take the other, Mr. Morgan," said the retiring servant.

MORLEY, Christopher (1890–1957), *US writer and editor.*

1 Christopher Morley and William Rose Benét were gazing at the window of a wig shop in which were displayed two small identical wigs on their stands. "They're alike as toupees in a pod," observed Morley.

MORLEY, Robert (1908–92), *British actor.*

1 Playwright William Douglas-Home boasted to Morley over lunch one day that actor Alfred Marks was to appear in his new play. "I've always admired Mr. Marks tremendously," said Morley enthusiastically. Then, without thinking, he continued, "Unfortunately, he always seems to choose the wrong play."

MORRIS, Clara (1847–1925), *US actress, born in Canada.*

1 (Clara Morris told the following story of her own experience:)

"Somewhere in the wide world there is an actor — and a good one — who never eats celery without thinking of me. It was years ago, when I was playing Camille. In the first scene, you will remember, the unfortunate Armand takes a rose from Camille as a token of love. We had almost reached that point, when, as I glanced down, I saw that the flower was missing from its accustomed place on my breast.

"What could I do? On the flower hung the strength of the scene. However, I continued my lines in an abstracted fashion, and began a still hunt for that rose or a substitute. My gaze wandered around the stage. On the dinner table was some celery. Moving slowly toward it, I grasped the celery and twisted the tops into a rose form. Then I began the fateful lines: 'Take this flower. The life of a camellia is short. If held and caressed it will fade in a morning or an evening.'

"Hardly able to control his laughter, Armand spoke his lines, which ran: 'It is a cold, scentless flower. It is a strange flower.' I agreed with him."

---cⁿᵒ---

MORRIS, William (1834–96), *British poet, designer, artist, and typographer.*

1 During William Morris's last visit to Paris, he spent much of his time in the restaurant of the Eiffel Tower, either eating or writing. When a friend observed that he must be very impressed by the tower to spend so much time there, Morris snorted, "Impressed! I remain here because it's the only place in Paris where I can avoid seeing the damn thing."

---cⁿᵒ---

MORSE, Samuel Finley Breese (1791–1872), *US inventor of the telegraph.*

1 In May 1844 Morse sent the first public telegram over the specially constructed line built between Baltimore and Washington. The text of the telegram was: "WHAT HATH GOD WROUGHT."

2 Morse was a successful artist as well as inventor. He once painted a picture of a man in his death agony and showed it to a friend, who happened to be a doctor. "Well, what's your opinion?" he demanded, after the doctor had studied the painting. "Malaria," said the medical man without hesitation.

---cⁿᵒ---

MOSCARDÓ, José (1876–1956), *Spanish soldier.*

1 As the defenders of the Alcázar were reduced to near-starvation rations, an officer notorious for grumbling came to see Moscardó to demand that he receive more than the usual daily allowance of food. Moscardó heard his demand through, then pulled out a 50-peseta bill and handed it to him. "Take this," he said, "and go outside and buy something if you like. It's the best I can do for you."

---cⁿᵒ---

MOTT, Lucretia Coffin (1793–1880), *US Quaker reformer who campaigned for women's rights and the abolition of slavery.*

1 A meeting of the Anti-Slavery Society in New York was broken up by thugs, who attacked some of the speakers as they left the hall. Lucretia Mott told the gentleman accompanying her to escort some of the other ladies who were alone and frightened in the tumult. "But who will look after you?" he asked. "This gentleman," she said, turning to one of the roughest-looking members of the mob and laying her hand on his arm. "He will see me safely through." The thug was so astonished that he did as she requested and escorted her respectfully through the crowd to safety.

---cⁿᵒ---

MOUNTBATTEN of Burma, Louis, 1st Earl (1900–79), *British naval commander, great-grandson of Queen Victoria.*

1 During the most controversial period of the Vietnam War, Mountbatten, in Los Angeles, was Johnny Carson's guest on the *Tonight* show. He had previously warned Carson that he would answer no questions about Vietnam. On the show, after a few minutes of conversation that went quite smoothly, Carson apparently decided to slip one over on Mountbatten. "Sir," he asked, "if you were President of the United States, what would you do about Vietnam?" Replied Mountbatten, "I'd tell the British to keep their noses out of it."

---cⁿᵒ---

MOZART, Wolfgang Amadeus (1756–91), *Austrian composer.*

1 At the age of two Mozart was taken to visit a farm, where he heard a pig squeal. "G-

sharp!" he exclaimed. Someone ran to the piano. G-sharp was right.

2 On his 1762 visit to Schönbrunn, the Austrian royal palace, Mozart slipped on the polished floor while romping with the young princesses and burst into tears. He was picked up and comforted by the seven-year-old Marie Antoinette. The little boy kissed the future queen of France and told her, "You are good. I will marry you."

3 Mozart was approached by a young man, little older than a boy, who sought his advice on composing a symphony. Mozart pointed out that he was still very young and it might be better if he began by composing ballads. "But you wrote symphonies when you were only ten years old," objected the lad. "But I didn't have to ask how," Mozart retorted.

4 At an evening party, Mozart bet Haydn a case of champagne that the older man could not play at sight a piece he had composed that afternoon. Haydn accepted the bet, the piece was placed on the spinet rack, Haydn briskly played the first few bars, then stopped short. He found it impossible to continue, for the composition prescribed playing with the two hands at the two ends of the keyboard and striking a note in the very center. Haydn confessed himself beaten. Mozart took his place at the piano and, reaching the fatal note, bent forward and hit it with his nose.

5 The Emperor Franz Joseph II commissioned the creation of *The Abduction from the Seraglio,* but when he first heard it, he complained to Mozart, "That is too fine for my ears — there are too many notes." Mozart replied, "There are just as many notes as there should be."

6 During the final rehearsal for the premiere of *Don Giovanni,* Mozart was unhappy with one of the singers, a young girl whose purity of voice had little power. In one scene she had to scream, but the singer was quite unconvincing. Mozart climbed up onstage, and in the gloom of the few candles that lit the scene crept up behind her without being seen. At the crucial moment, as she was about to scream, he pinched her arm violently, eliciting a bloodcurdling yell. "Admirable!" he exclaimed. "Mind you scream like that tonight!"

7 When traveling through beautiful countryside, Mozart would often start humming, then singing, while looking around delightedly. "If only I could put the subject down on paper!" he would exclaim.

8 After his death a fellow composer noted, "It is a pity to lose such a great genius, but a good thing for us that he is dead. For if he had lived much longer, we should not have earned a crust of bread by our compositions."

———— ☙ ————

MUGGERIDGE, Malcolm (1903–90), *British writer, broadcaster, and journalist.*

1 Muggeridge had little time for politicians and admitted that he had voted only once in his life. "On that occasion," he said, "I just had to. There was this one candidate who had been committed to an asylum and upon discharge was issued a Certificate of Sanity. Well, now, how could I resist? What other politician anywhere has an actual medical report that he is sane? I simply had to support him!"

———— ☙ ————

MUGNIER, Abbé Arthur (1853–1944), *French divine.*

1 A rather plump and also rather vain actress confessed to Mugnier that she sometimes admired her naked body in the mirror. "Is it a

sin?" she asked. The abbé, glancing at her ample figure, replied, "No, madame, it's an error."

2 At a social gathering, Mugnier, sitting beside an exceptionally attractive young lady, was asked by a gentleman present if he would dare to kiss her. "Certainly not!" replied the abbé. "She's not yet a relic!"

MUHAMMAD SHAH I (fl. 14th century), *sultan of the Bahmani kingdom in southern India (1358–75).*

1 A ragged messenger arrived one day at the sultan's capital, bearing dreadful news. The Hindus had captured his native town; he was the sole survivor of the ensuing massacre. Muhammad Shah was so outraged at the report that he immediately sentenced the unfortunate messenger to death. "I could never bear in my presence," he said, "a wretch who could survive the sight of the slaughter of so many brave companions."

MUIR, John (1838–1914), *US naturalist, born in Scotland.*

1 Financial consideration played only a small part in the satisfaction John Muir derived from life. On one occasion he declared that he was richer than magnate E. H. Harriman: "I have all the money I want and he hasn't."

MURAVIEV, Count Mikhail (?1796–1866), *Russian statesman.*

1 Although his cousin Sergei Muraviev-Apostol was one of the leaders of the December uprising in 1825 and was subsequently hanged for his part in it, Count Mikhail Muraviev attained prominence in the councils of

Czar Alexander II. When Russian mismanagement in Poland led to a revolt there in 1863, he was one of those entrusted with the task of pacifying the country. The savagery with which he did this caused adverse comment, which the count brushed off by saying, "I am one of the hanging Muravievs, not one of the ones who are hanged."

MURRAY, Sir George (1772–1846), *British soldier.*

1 During the expedition against the French in Egypt in 1801, Murray and his troops found themselves in the vicinity of Alexandria without water. Having had a classical education, Murray recalled that Julius Caesar had suffered the same problem in almost exactly the same spot. He lost no time in consulting the copy of Caesar's writings that he always carried with him, and was delighted to discover that the Romans had found water by digging wells in the sand to a specified depth. Murray set his men to work and before long a plentiful water supply was found.

MURRAY, [George] Gilbert [Aimé] (1866–1957), *British classical scholar.*

1 Gilbert Murray's wife, Lady Mary Howard, was a teetotaler and a vegetarian. She converted her husband to her way of thinking, but when guests were present she allowed a joint of meat to be served. Murray, carving the joint, would ask the guests, "Will you have some of the corpse, or will you try the alternative?"

2 (As a student coming belatedly to Oxford after active service in World War I, poet Robert Graves was discussing Aristotle's *Poetics* with Gilbert Murray in the latter's study. Murray was pacing up and down.)

"I suddenly asked, 'Exactly what is the principle of that walk of yours? Are you trying to avoid the flowers on the rug, or are you trying to keep to the squares?' My own compulsion-neuroses made it easy for me to notice them in others. He wheeled around sharply: 'You're the first person who has caught me out,' he said. 'No, it's not the flowers or the squares; it's a habit that I have got into of doing things in sevens. I take seven steps, you see, then I change direction and go another seven steps, then I turn around. I consulted Browne, the Professor of Psychology, about it the other day, but he assured me it isn't a dangerous habit. He said, "When you find yourself getting into multiples of seven, come to me again."'"

MUSIAL, Stan (1920–), *US baseball player.*

1 In the 1951 All-Star game, Yankees pitcher Ed Lopat told Brooklyn's pitcher Preacher Roe that he had found a perfect way to pitch against Musial. In the fourth inning he had his chance — and Musial hit a home run. Roe stood in the stands and shouted at Lopat, "I see what you mean, but I found that way to pitch to him a long time ago, all by myself."

MUSSET, Alfred de (1810–57), *French poet, novelist, and playwright.*

1 Alfred de Musset's affairs caused considerable scandal. A Théâtre Français actress accosted the famous poet familiarly, but in her ignorance left out the particle in his name: "Monsieur Musset, they tell me you boast of having slept with me." Musset replied, "Pardon me, but I have always boasted of the exact opposite."

MYTTON, John (1796–1834), *British sportsman and eccentric.*

1 The impetuous Mytton once set fire to his nightshirt in order to get rid of the hiccups. He succeeded, but it should be mentioned that he happened to be inside the nightshirt at the time.

N

NABOKOV, Vladimir (1899–1977), *US novelist, born in Russia.*

1 (One summer in the 1940s Nabokov and his family stayed with James Laughlin at Alta, Utah, where Nabokov took the opportunity of enlarging his collection of butterflies and moths.)

"Nabokov's fiction has never been praised for its compassion; he was single-minded if nothing else. One evening at dusk he returned from his day's excursion saying that during hot pursuit over Bear Gulch he had heard someone groaning most piteously down by the stream. 'Did you stop?' Laughlin asked him. 'No, I had to get the butterfly.' The next day the corpse of an aged prospector was discovered in what has been renamed, in Nabokov's honor, Dead Man's Gulch."

2 After the publication of *Lolita* Nabokov (who characterized himself, probably quite accurately, as a "mild old gentleman") was on occasion besieged by aspiring nymphets. In his latter years he retired from teaching and took up residence in Montreux at the Palace Hotel.

Interviewed by Alan Levy (*New York Times Magazine,* October 31, 1971), the great stylist described a post-*Lolita* experience that turned on a delicate question of rhetoric:

"Not long ago there was someone with an American name who kept leaving vague messages for me all over Montreux. I started leaving messages too, that I was unavailable. Then I got one more message — a slip of paper that said, 'F—— you.' Well, this was so much more explicit than the others that I asked the desk what kind of person had left this message, and the desk said, 'That wasn't a person, sir; that was two rather wild-looking American girls.' This intrigued me even more, so I looked at the paper again. And there I found something at the end of the message which I hadn't noticed on my first reading: a question mark!"

3 (Nabokov describes a visit to the distinguished French novelist Alain Robbe-Grillet.)

"Robbe-Grillet's petite pretty wife, a young actress, had dressed herself *à la gamine* in my honor, pretending to be Lolita, and she continued the performance the next day, when we met again at a publisher's luncheon in a restaurant. After pouring wine for everyone but her, the waiter asked, '*Voulez-vous un Coca-Cola, Mademoiselle?*'"

4 Nobokov loved puns, of course, and was given a golden opportunity when one of his students complained to him that a young couple in class was always spooning. Replied

Nabokov, "Be grateful they were not fork-ing."

———— ⚘ ————

NAGURSKI, Bronko (1908–90), *Canadian-born US football player and wrestler.*

1 Carrying the ball, Nagurski ran right over people. In one game against the New York Giants, Benny Friedman hit him on the twelve-yard line but did not bring him down until the one-yard line. "He hits hard enough to knock down a horse," muttered Friedman. On the next play, Nagurski did just that: he crashed through the end zone so hard, head down, that he ran into a mounted policeman and bowled over man and beast. Not quite sure what had happened, Nagurski stood up groggily, complaining, "That last man hit me awful hard."

2 Bruised and battered, the Pittsburgh Steelers were on their way home from a meeting with the Bears and Nagurski, when their train came to a jolting halt, spilling players into the aisles. "Run for your lives, men," counseled a Steeler. "Nagurski has struck again."

3 As a result of some horseplay with a team-mate, Nagurski once fell out of a second-floor window. A crowd gathered. A policeman appeared. He asked, "What happened?" Replied Nagurski, "I don't know. I just got here myself."

———— ⚘ ————

NAMATH, Joe (1943–), *US football player.*

1 (Frank Howard, a former Clemson football coach, told the following story about Namath and Bear Bryan, the winningest college football coach of his period:)

"Bear had a squad meeting one time and he told his players, 'This is a class operation. I want your shoes to be shined. I want you to have a tie on, get your hair cut and keep a crease in your pants. I also want you to go to class. I don't want no dumbbells on this team. If there is a dumbbell in the room, I wish he would stand up.'

"Joe Namath rose to his feet, and Bear said, 'Joe, how come you're standing up? You ain't dumb.' Namath told him, 'Coach, I just hate like the devil for you to be standing up there by yourself.'"

———— ⚘ ————

NAPIER, Sir Charles James (1782–1853), *British soldier and administrator.*

1 In August 1842 Napier annexed the province of Sind, thus giving the British control of the Indus River in what is now southeast Pakistan. Of this action Napier wrote in his journal: "We have no right to seize Sind, but we shall do so, and a very advantageous, useful, humane piece of rascality it will be." He is reputed to have dispatched news of the conquest of Sind in one Latin word: *"Peccavi"* (I have sinned).

———— ⚘ ————

NAPOLEON I (1769–1821), *soldier and emperor of France (1804–15).*

1 (Napoleon always hated being on the losing side: when he played chess he would surreptitiously replace a forfeited piece on the board. His elder brother told a revealing story about Napoleon's school days.)

For an ancient history lesson the teacher brought in two huge flags, one the flag of Rome with the legend SPQR on it, and the other the flag of Carthage. With the flags set up on either side of the classroom, the children were divided into two groups to go and stand under them. Napoleon's elder brother was sent to stand under the Roman flag, Napoleon under the Carthaginian flag. When Napoleon discovered that he was standing under the flag of the defeated, he protested until the teacher allowed him to change places with his brother.

2 During Napoleon's time as first consul it was the fashion for women to wear transparent gauze dresses. Somewhat incensed at this practice, one evening Napoleon ordered the servants to build up the drawing-room fire until the room reached ovenlike temperature. As he sourly explained: "It is extremely cold and these ladies are almost naked." Joséphine understood the situation and inaugurated new fashions in dress of somewhat more seemly nature.

3 As first consul, Napoleon often worked a sixteen-hour day. He expected that the Council of State would have stamina and zeal to match his own. One night when the councillors began to doze off, he reprimanded them, "Do let's keep awake, citizens. It's only two o'clock. We must earn our salaries." These superhuman efforts were much applauded by Napoleon's admirers, but not by royalists. One such admirer, singing the first consul's praises, remarked, "God made Bonaparte and then rested." An emigré count commented, "God should have rested a little earlier."

4 After an overnight journey Napoleon arrived at the palace of the king of Saxony and found himself in the middle of a full-scale reception. But Frederick Augustus discreetly led Napoleon into an anteroom where there was a chamber pot, saying, "I've often found that great men, like everybody else, sometimes require to be alone."

5 Receiving intelligence that seemed to link the Duc d'Enghien with royalist conspiracies against him, Napoleon authorized his agents to seize and execute him. Despite pleas for his life from Joséphine, Napoleon had the duke summarily shot. Although the matter aroused no immediate open opposition, it had the long-term effect of strengthening an-

tagonism toward Napoleon and evoked from Comte Boulay de la Meurthe the observation: *"C'est pire qu'un crime, c'est une faute"* (It's worse than a crime, it's a blunder).

6 In a moment of vanity, Napoleon observed to his secretary, Bourrienne, "You too will be immortal."

"Why?"

"Well, are you not my secretary?"

"Name Alexander the Great's secretary," was the response.

7 Searching for a book one day in his library, Napoleon eventually located it on the topmost shelf, beyond his reach. "Permit me, sire," said the tall Marshal Moncey, stepping forward. "I am higher than Your Majesty."

"No, Marshal, you are longer," Napoleon corrected him, scowling.

8 In the path of Napoleon's advancing army, the Russians abandoned the city of Smolensk and set fire to it. Napoleon, watching the blaze with his aides, compared it to an eruption of Vesuvius, and asked his master of horse whether it was not a fine sight. "Horrible, sir," said the man. Napoleon snorted contemptuously. "Remember, gentlemen," he said, "as one of the Roman emperors remarked, 'The corpse of an enemy always smells sweet!'"

9 A little later, Napoleon may have had a change of heart. When the French defeated the Russians at Borodino, their losses were almost as great as those of the Russians. Napoleon considered Borodino the most terrible battle he had ever fought. On the following day he and his aides rode over the battlefield in silence, reckoning up the dead. They came across a prostrate body and, hearing a cry of pain, Napoleon ordered a stretcher. "It's only a Russian, sire," said one of his aides. Napoleon retorted, "After a victory there are no enemies, only men."

10 Later still all trace of compassion — even for his own — was gone. After the French victory at Eylau over the combined Russian and Prussian forces, Napoleon walked across the battlefield, turning over with his foot the corpses of French soldiers. "Small change, small change," he said. "One Parisian night will soon adjust these losses."

11 After the Russian debacle Napoleon, fearing his position at home was precarious, left the French army in the lurch and hurried back to France almost unaccompanied. Arriving at the banks of the river Neman in his miserable sleigh, he inquired of the ferryman whether many deserters had come through that way. "No," replied the Russian, "you are the first."

12 When Napoleon made his triumphant return from Elba in March 1815, the restored Bourbon king, Louis XVIII, fled, leaving a large sum of money with the banker Jacques Laffitte. An official thinking to curry favor with the emperor, informed Napoleon of the existence of the deposit. Napoleon, however, had it transferred to England, where Louis could have access to it. After Waterloo, when Napoleon himself was about to flee Paris, he made arrangements with Laffitte to leave a similarly large amount of money on deposit. When Laffitte sat down at his desk to write out a receipt for the deposit, Napoleon stopped him: "If I am captured and the receipt is found on me it will compromise you." And he absolutely refused to accept one.

13 Napoleon had a general, one Bisson, whom he called "Gargantua" for his appetite. Bisson once challenged an English admiral to a duel. The weapon he chose was food, and in the course of their "battle," Bisson ate blood sausage, six chickens, and six lambs. After the admiral withdrew, Bisson went on to desserts and cheeses.

14 The death of Napoleon on St. Helena was announced in a crowded Paris salon attended by Wellington and Talleyrand, among others. In the hush that followed the announcement, someone exclaimed, "What an event!"

"It is no longer an event!" broke in the voice of Talleyrand. "It is only a piece of news."

———— ✵ ————

NAPOLEON III (1808–73), *emperor of France (1852–70), nephew of Napoleon I.*

1 The emperor was once implored by a lady to forbid all smoking on the grounds that it was a great vice. Laying aside his cigar, he replied, "This vice brings in one hundred million francs in taxes every year. I will certainly forbid it at once — as soon as you can name a virtue that brings in as much revenue."

2 For years Napoleon suffered agonies from stones in the bladder. The pain undermined his health and prematurely aged him. Before giving a public audience, he was seen once to hold his arm against the flame of a candle in an attempt to find some relief through a change of pain.

3 The battle of Solferino in 1859 was technically a French victory, as the Austrian forces retreated. There was appalling carnage on both sides, and Napoleon, alarmed by unrest at home, made peace three weeks later. "I don't care for war," he remarked at the time. "There's far too much luck in it for my liking."

———— ✵ ————

NAPOLEON, Eugène Louis Jean Joseph (1856–79), *French pretender to the imperial throne, known as the "Prince Imperial."*

1 On a holiday at Biarritz, when the Prince Imperial was little more than a toddler, he seemed afraid to enter the sea, so he was

picked up and hurled in bodily. He struggled out and ran away as fast as he could, howling in terror. He was caught and soothed, and then an attempt was made to rationalize his fears. Why, he was asked, was he afraid of the sea when he had stood by while soldiers fired off their cannon and had not been frightened? The child thought this one over for a moment, then said, "Because I'm in command of the soldiers, but I'm not in command of the sea."

———— ✧ ————

NAPOLEON, Joseph Charles Paul, Prince (1822–91), *Bonapartist heir to the French throne.*

1 The courtesan Anna Deslion at one time shared her favors between Plon-Plon and the playwright Lambert Thiboust. Though the rivals met occasionally on the stairs of Anna's house, neither of them was inclined to make a fuss. "To be dishonored by a prince is something of an honor," said Thiboust. Plon-Plon was likewise philosophical: "To be deceived by a man of brains is no serious misfortune."

———— ✧ ————

NARVÁEZ, Ramón María (1800–68), *Spanish general and statesman, prime minister (1844–47, 1856–57, 1864–65, 1866–68).*

1 A priest asked the dying Narváez, "Does your Excellency forgive all your enemies?" "I do not have to forgive me enemies," retorted Narváez. "I have had them all shot."

———— ✧ ————

NASH, Ogden (1902–71), *US writer of humorous verse.*

1 Radio director Tom Carlson's dog had chewed up an autographed copy of one of Nash's works. Though the book was out of print, Carlson finally managed to acquire a replacement. He sent it to Nash, explaining what had happened and asking for another autograph. The book was returned — with the dedication: "To Tom Carlson or his dog — depending on whose taste it best suits."

———— ✧ ————

NASSER, Gamal Abdel (1918–70), *Egyptian soldier and statesman.*

1 With emotions high on the night before the coup of 1952, one of Nasser's associates was close to tears. "Tonight there is no room for sentiment," said Nasser firmly. "We must be ready for the unexpected." Some minutes later, when the man had regained his composure, he asked Nasser, "Why did you address me in English?" Nasser laughed. "Because Arabic," he replied, "is hardly a suitable language in which to express the need for calm."

———— ✧ ————

In the 1930s Guido Nazzo, an Italian tenor, sang only once in New York. The sole review read: "Guido Nazzo: nazzo guido."

— WILLARD R. ESPY,
Another Almanac of Words at Play

———— ✧ ————

NAST, Thomas (1840–1902), *US cartoonist.*

1 Nast's greatest campaign was his war against corruption in New York politics during the 1870s. He pilloried the Tammany Hall machine in *Harper's* until "Boss" Tweed writhed. "We gotta stop them damned pictures," Tweed told his henchmen. "I don't care so much what the papers write about me — my constituents can't read. But they can see pictures."

{It was one of "them damned pictures" that stopped Tweed. After being sentenced to jail, he escaped in 1875 and made his way to Spain. While staying incognito at Vigo he was recognized from one of Nast's caricatures, arrested, and returned to the United States.}

NAVRATILOVA, Martina (1956–), *US tennis player, born in Czechoslovakia.*

1 Navratilova played singles tennis matches for over twenty years, and was ranked the best woman tennis player in the world. After a time, though, she fell to third place in the ranking. Soon she was playing competitors young enough to be her daughters. But to a comment that she was at last nearing the end of her life in professional sports, she replied, "I've been in the twilight of my career longer than most people have had their career."

2 When asked about the prospect of life in retirement, she said, "It sure beats the heck out of life after death, that's for sure."

NECKER, Suzanne (1739–94), *Swiss society leader; wife of Jacques Necker, finance minister to Louis XVI, and mother of Mme de Staël.*

1 The Marquis de Chastellux was once invited to one of Mme Necker's dinner parties. Having arrived early, he was left alone in the drawing-room where he found a notebook under Mme Necker's chair. Idly leafing through the pages, he discovered that the book contained detailed notes for the dinner-table conversation that evening. He carefully replaced it under the chair and later, during the course of the meal, was amused to hear Mme Necker recite word for word everything she had written down in her notebook.

NELSON, Horatio, Viscount (1758–1805), *British admiral.*

1 Shortly after the loss of his right arm, Nelson was presented to King George III, who congratulated him upon his naval victories, then added prophetically, "But your country has a claim for a bit more of you."

2 When he tried to obtain compensation for his lost eye, Nelson was told that no money could be paid without a surgeon's certificate. Annoyed by this petty bureaucracy, since his wounds were well known, Nelson nevertheless obtained the necessary documentation. As a precaution, he asked the surgeon to make out a second certificate attesting to the obvious loss of his arm. He presented the eye certificate to the clerk, who paid out the appropriate sum, commenting on the smallness of the amount. "Oh, this is only for an eye," said Nelson. "In a few days I'll come back for an arm, and probably, in a little longer, for a leg." Later that week he returned to the office and solemnly handed over the second certificate.

3 After pursuing the French fleet around the Mediterranean for some weeks, Nelson caught up with it at Alexandria. As preparations were made for the battle, Nelson sat down for dinner with his officers. "Before this time tomorrow I shall have gained a peerage, or Westminster Abbey," he said to them as they went out to their various stations.

4 In the middle of the battle of Copenhagen, after the Danish bombardment had continued unabated for three hours, Nelson's commander, Sir Hyde Parker, sent him the signal to "discontinue action." Clapping his telescope to his blind eye, Nelson said that he did not see the signal. When the officers

around him insisted it was there, he merely reiterated, "I have only one eye — I have a right to be blind sometimes — I really do not see the signal!"

5 Sir William Hamilton, husband of Nelson's Emma, behaved with perfect generosity toward his wife's lover. When he died at an advanced age in 1803, he breathed his last in Emma's arms, holding Nelson by the hand. He left Nelson a favorite portrait of Emma, done in enamel, and the codicil containing the bequest ended with the words: "God bless him, and shame fall on those who do not say, Amen."

6 Before the battle of Trafalgar, Nelson on board HMS *Victory* discussed their chances with Thomas Masterman Hardy, his captain. Hardy said that, all things considered, he would think the capture of fourteen ships a glorious outcome. "I shall not be satisfied with anything less than twenty," replied Nelson. He then ordered the sending of his last signal: "ENGLAND EXPECTS EVERY MAN WILL DO HIS DUTY."

7 (Mortally wounded, Nelson lingered for several hours in fearful agony, but knew before he died that the English had gained a magnificent victory. Robert Southey reports his final moments, after he had given his last orders concerning the fleet.)

"Presently, calling Hardy back, he said to him in a low voice, 'Don't throw me overboard'; and he desired that he might be buried by his parents, unless it should please the king to order otherwise. Then reverting to private feelings: 'Take care of my dear Lady Hamilton, Hardy; take care of poor Lady Hamilton. — Kiss me, Hardy.' Hardy knelt down and kissed his cheek; and Nelson said, 'Now I am satisfied. Thank God, I have done my duty.' Hardy stood over him in silence for a moment or two, then knelt again and kissed his forehead. 'Who is that?' said

Nelson; and being informed, he replied, 'God bless you, Hardy.' And Hardy then left him — for ever."

⁂

NERO (AD 37–68), *Roman emperor (AD 54–68).*

1 Agrippina was determined to secure the imperial throne for her son despite Claudius's plans to name Britannicus as his successor. She therefore fed the elderly emperor poisonous mushrooms, and he died in agony without having made plain his wishes concerning the succession. Nero ascended the throne, gave Claudius a splendid funeral, and later deified him. He remarked that mushrooms were indeed the food of the gods, because by eating them Claudius had become divine.

2 "Pretending to be disgusted by the drab old buildings and narrow, winding streets of Rome, he brazenly set fire to the City; and though a group of ex-consuls caught his attendants, armed with oakum and blazing torches, trespassing on their property, they dared not interfere. He also coveted the sites of several granaries, solidly built in stone, near the Golden House [Nero's palace]; having knocked down their walls with siege-engines, he set the interiors ablaze. This terror lasted for six days and seven nights, causing many people to take shelter in the tombs. . . . Nero watched the conflagration from the Tower of Maecenas, enraptured by what he called 'the beauty of the flames'; then put on his tragedian's costume and sang *The Fall of Ilium* from beginning to end."

3 When he signed his first death warrant, he said, "Why did they teach me how to write?"

4 Fleeing from Rome with his enemies hard on his heels, Nero took refuge in a villa a few miles out of the city. The four faithful servants who attended him insisted that he should commit suicide honorably, rather than fall into the hands of those who had

seized power in Rome. Still obsessed with the greatness of his own gifts as an actor, poet, and singer, Nero watched the men preparing his funeral pyre and as he watched muttered through his tears, *"Qualis artifex pereo!"* (How great an artist dies here!)

5 Nero could not bring himself to face death, despite the hopelessness of his situation. Weeping and howling, he first tried to persuade his retinue to commit suicide first, to pave the way for his own death. When they refused, the abandoned despot finally stabbed himself. Only then did a centurion rush in, half-heartedly pretending to staunch Nero's fatal wound with his cloak. "Too late!" gasped Nero. "But, ah, what *loyalty*!"

NERVAL, Gérard de (1808–55), *French poet, translator, and playwright.*

1 Gérard de Nerval walked in the gardens of the Palais-Royal in Paris, leading a lobster on a pale blue ribbon. Asked why he did so, he replied that he preferred lobsters to dogs or cats because they could not bark at one, and besides, they knew the secrets of the sea.

2 For some time Gérard de Nerval had carried around with him an old apron string that, he maintained, was the Queen of Sheba's garter — or a corset-string belonging to Mme de Maintenon or Marguerite de Valois. In the small hours of the morning of January 26, 1855, he knocked on the door of a dosshouse in a poor quarter of Paris. The concierge heard the knock but decided it was too cold to open up. When daylight dawned, the poet was discovered hanged from some iron railings with the Queen of Sheba's garter. As a final macabre touch, a pet raven was hovering nearby, repeating the only words it knew: *"J'ai soif!"* (I'm thirsty!)

NESBIT, Evelyn (1884–1967), *US model and showgirl.*

1 In 1905 Evelyn Nesbit married millionaire Harry K. Thaw. The following year the couple were dining in a smart restaurant when Harry Thaw noticed his wife's former lover, architect Stanford White, at a nearby table. He walked over, pulled out a gun, and shot his rival three times in the face. Evelyn Thaw's reaction was memorable: "My, you are in a fix, Harry!"

NEWMAN, Paul (1925–), *US film actor and director.*

1 Despite an extraordinary range of films, as well as a large and fanatical audience, Newman was passed over for an Academy Award for many years. Finally, in the late 1980s, he was given a special award for his body of work — a reward usually given to actors much older, and certainly much less active. As he thanked the Academy, Newman said, "I'm grateful this award didn't come wrapped in a gift certificate to Forest Lawn."

NEWTON, Sir Isaac (1642–1727), *British physicist and mathematician.*

1 In an eighteen-month period during 1665 to 1666 the plague forced Newton to leave Cambridge and live in his mother's house at Woolsthorpe in Lincolnshire (a house that can still be seen and is preserved as a museum). One day he was sitting in the orchard there, pondering the question of the forces that keep the moon in its orbit, when the fall of an apple led him to wonder whether the force that pulled the apple toward the earth might be the same kind of force that held the moon in orbit round the earth. This train of

thought led him eventually to the law of gravitation and its application to the motion of the heavenly bodies.

2 Newton owned a pet dog called Diamond, which one day knocked over the candle on the scientist's desk and started a blaze that destroyed records of many years' research. Newton, viewing the destruction, said only, "O Diamond, Diamond, thou little knowest the damage thou hast done."

3 An admirer asked Newton how he had come to make discoveries in astronomy that went far beyond anything achieved by anyone before him. "By always thinking about them," replied Newton simply.

4 Newton once lived next door to a rather inquisitive widow, who was unaware of her neighbor's identity and renown. The lady was visited one day by a Fellow of the Royal Society of London, to whom she related the strange behavior of "the poor crazy gentleman" next door. "Every morning," she said, "when the sun shines so brightly that we are obliged to draw the window-blinds, he takes his seat in front of a tub of soap-suds and occupies himself for hours blowing bubbles through a common clay pipe and intently watches them until they burst." Following his hostess to the window, the visitor saw Newton at his work. Turning to the widow, he said, "The person you suppose to be a poor lunatic is none other than the great Sir Isaac Newton, studying the refraction of light upon thin plates — a phenomenon which is beautifully exhibited upon the surface of common soap bubbles."

5 Newton, Cambridge University's representative to Parliament in 1689, was not well adapted to life as a parliamentarian. Only on one occasion did he rise to his feet, and the House of Commons hushed in expectation of hearing the great man's maiden speech. Newton observed that there was a window open, which was causing a draft, asked that it be closed, and sat down.

6 One evening during the Anglo-Dutch wars Newton came into the hall at Trinity College, Cambridge, announcing to the Fellows that there had been a naval battle that day between the Dutch and the English, and that the English had got the worst of it. As Cambridge is a considerable distance from the sea and as it was the first the Fellows had heard of any battle, they were naturally skeptical; they asked him how he knew. Newton explained that he had been in his observatory and heard a great firing of cannon, such as could only be between two great fleets. The noise had become louder and louder, which suggested that the English ships were retreating toward the English coast. The following day a full report of the battle exactly bore out Newton's summary.

7 In 1696 Jean Bernoulli and G. W. Leibniz concocted two teasing problems they sent to the leading mathematicians in Europe. After the problem had been in circulation for about six months, a friend communicated them to Newton, who, when he had finished his day's work at the Mint, came home and solved both. The next day he submitted his solutions to the Royal Society anonymously, as he did not like to be distracted from the business of the Mint by embroilment in scientific discussions. The anonymity did not, however, deceive Bernoulli. "I recognize the lion by his paw!" he exclaimed.

8 Newton invited a friend to dinner but then forgot the engagement. When the friend arrived, he found the scientist deep in meditation, so he sat down quietly and waited. In due course dinner was brought up — for one. Newton continued to be abstracted. The friend drew up a chair and, without disturbing his host, consumed the dinner. After he had finished, Newton came out of his reverie,

looked with some bewilderment at the empty dishes, and said, "If it weren't for the proof before my eyes, I could have sworn that I have not yet dined."

9 By 1720 the South Sea Company, a speculative organization in England, had captured the fortunes of many, many people who dreamt of the millions to be made in shares of an enterprise that exploited fishing and slaving in the South Seas. The values of the company's shares had risen to an extraordinary high, despite the comparative lack of fish and the complete absence of slavery in that part of the world. Newton had invested, too, but just before the company peaked he sold out for a £7000 profit, saying, "I can calculate the motions of heavenly bodies, but not the madness of people."

10 To the very end of his life Newton's scientific curiosity was unquenched. According to one authority his (somewhat improbable) last words were: "I do not know what I may appear to the world. But to myself, I seem to have been only like a boy playing on the seashore, diverting myself in now and then finding a smoother pebble or a prettier shell than ordinary, whilst the great ocean of truth lay all undiscovered before me."

———— ⌀ ————

NICHOLAS I (1796–1855), *czar of Russia (1825–55).*

1 One of the Decembrist conspirators condemned to be hanged was Kondraty Ryleyev. The rope broke. Ryleyev, bruised and battered, fell to the ground, got up, and said, "In Russia they do not know how to do anything properly, not even how to make a rope." Ordinarily an accident of this sort resulted in a pardon, so a messenger was sent to the Winter Palace to know the czar's pleasure. Nicholas asked, "What did he say?"

"Sire, he said that in Russia they do not even know how to make a rope properly."

"Well, let the contrary be proved," said the czar.

———— ⌀ ————

NICHOLSON, Jack (1937–), *US film actor.*

1 While shooting a western, Nicholson, who was not accustomed to horses, fell off his mount, hurting himself. But he climbed back on gamely and redid the shoot. "I wouldn't have gotten back on the horse if I were a real person," he said.

———— ⌀ ————

NICKLAUS, Jack William (1940–), *US golfer.*

1 Nicklaus dethroned Arnold Palmer as the reigning king of golf when he came from five strokes back to tie after 72 holes in the 1962 US Open, and then won the 18-hole playoff next day. Palmer noted, "Now that the big bear's out of the cage, everybody better run for cover." Nicklaus's comment was: "I'm hungry as a bear. But I'm gonna slim down and go for the gold." Slimmed down, he became know as "the Golden Bear."

———— ⌀ ————

NIJINSKY, Vaslav (1890–1950), *Russian ballet dancer and choreographer.*

1 When Nijinsky choreographed *Le Sacre du Printemps* (The Rite of Spring) to Stravinsky's music, most critics loathed the ballet as a disturbing departure from the themes and conventions of the classical dance to which they were accustomed. In fact, one early critic gave it a title that quickly caught on: *Le Massacre du Printemps.*

———— ⌀ ————

NILSSON, Birgit Marta (1918–), *Swedish soprano celebrated for her Wagnerian interpretations.*

1 (Miss Nilsson appeared in *Turandot* with the tenor Franco Corelli on a Metropolitan Opera tour under the management of Rudolf Bing.)

"Mr. Corelli, after having been thoroughly outshouted in 'In questa reggia,' immediately left the stage (he had no more to sing, but he was supposed to be there), sulked in his dressing room, and declared that he would not come out again. At this point, Rudolf Bing is said to have entered the dressing room with an idea wonderfully calculated to appeal to the tenor's *amour propre*. 'In America, a man cannot retreat before a woman,' Mr. Bing is reported to have said. 'Continue! And in the last act, when the time comes to kiss her, *bite* her instead.' Mr. Corelli is said to have followed instructions, and Mr. Bing, according to the story, fled to New York, where Miss Nilsson telephoned him, saying, 'I cannot go on to Cleveland. I have rabies.'"

2 "Once she was negotiating a contract with Herbert von Karajan, at the time director of the Vienna Opera, when a string of pearls she was wearing broke and scattered all over the floor. Von Karajan and several others who were present got down on their knees to search for the pearls. 'We must find every one of them,' von Karajan said. 'These are the expensive pearls that Miss Nilsson buys with her high fees from the Metropolitan.' 'No,' Miss Nilsson replied. 'These are just imitation ones, which I buy with my low fees from the Vienna Opera.'"

3 Sir Rudolf Bing, who had often engaged Miss Nilsson, was asked if the star was difficult. "Not at all," he replied. "You put enough money in and glorious sound comes out."

4 Asked what was needed for a successful Isolde, Miss Nilsson replied, "Comfortable shoes."

NIVEN, David (1909–83), *British movie actor.*

1 At the Academy Awards presentations in April 1974, the proceedings were interrupted by a streaker who dashed across the stage where Niven and other celebrities were sitting. "Just think," said Niven, "probably the only laugh that man will ever get is for stripping and showing his shortcomings."

2 Niven found it hard to come to terms with the aging process and, in later life, still thought of himself as a young man. He recalled a visit to the London boat show with an attractive girl many years his junior. "Suddenly this hideous couple hove into view; a foul old creature with a crone of a wife. To my horror, the man came over and introduced himself. 'Good heavens, Niven,' he said, 'I haven't seen you since you were at school.' When they'd gone, I could sense that the girl was looking at me warily. 'Were you really at school with him?' she asked. 'Absolutely,' I told her. 'He was the music master.'"

NIVERNAIS, Louis Jules Mancini Mazarin, Duc de (1716–98), *French soldier and diplomat.*

1 The widowed Duc de Nivernais was in the habit of calling on the Comtesse de Rochefort, also a widow, every morning without fail. The regularity of these visits did not escape the notice of the duke's friends, who suggested to the widower that it would be far simpler for him to marry the lady. "Oh, yes, certainly," replied the duke, "but where would I then spend my evenings?"

NIXON, Richard Milhous (1913–94), *US politician; 37th President of the United States (1969–74).*

1 The first major attack on Nixon's integrity came in 1952 when there were some unexplained contributions from wealthy California businessmen to a fund upon which Nixon had apparently been drawing for his own use. Eisenhower wanted to drop Nixon as his running mate on the Republican ticket, but Nixon appeared on television to defend himself in what became known as the Checkers speech. Having dwelt at length on his humble origins and his advancement in life through his own efforts, Nixon admitted that he had accepted a gift after the nomination — namely, a spaniel puppy, which his daughter had christened Checkers. He told how his kids loved the dog and how, whatever anyone said, the family was going to keep it. Thousands of telegrams of support poured into Republican headquarters, and Nixon remained on the Republican ticket, though cynical observers described the Checkers speech as "a slick production."

2 As he prepared for an important political appearance in the early 1950s, Nixon commented, "No TV performance takes such special preparation as an off-the-cuff talk."

3 Of Nixon's integrity, his old rival Harry Truman said, "He is one of the few men in the history of this country to run for high office talking out of both sides of his mouth at the same time and lying out of both sides."

4 At a Gridiron Club dinner in Washington Truman and Nixon were guests. That year the theme of the annual event was Love. When Nixon rose to give a short speech, he mentioned that during the predinner cocktail hour, he had been asked to pass a bourbon-and-water to President Truman. This he presumably did. "When Harry Truman," he said, "will accept a drink from the hand of Richard Nixon without having someone else taste it first — that's Love."

5 In one of the televised debates between presidential candidates Nixon and Kennedy in 1960, Nixon demanded that Kennedy disown the earthy language used by ex-President Truman, a vigorous Kennedy supporter, and applauded the way in which Eisenhower had restored "the dignity of the office." Kennedy just laughed. A few minutes after the ending of the debate, Nixon raged to the newsmen waiting for comments, "That fucking bastard, he wasn't supposed to be using notes!"

6 Meeting Kennedy's aide Ted Sorenson shortly after Kennedy's inaugural address, Nixon remarked that there were things in the speech that he would have liked to have said. "Do you mean the part about 'Ask not what your country can do for you . . . ?'" said Sorenson. "No," replied Nixon, "the part beginning 'I do solemnly swear. . . .'"

7 On October 28, 1970, the presidential motorcade through St. Petersburg, Florida, came to an abrupt halt when the policeman at the head of the procession was hit by a truck. Nixon rushed to the scene and offered his sympathies to the injured policeman, Don Leadbeter. By way of reply, Leadbeter apologized for holding up the motorcade. There was an awkward silence as the President searched for something else to say. He finally blurted out, "Do you like the work?"

8 Signing copies of his book *Six Crises* at a local bookstore, Nixon asked each customer to what name he should address the inscription. One gentleman replied with a grin: "You've just met your seventh crisis. My name is Stanislaus Wojechzleschki."

9 "President Nixon was shaking hands and talking with members of a crowd at an airport when a little girl shouted to him, 'How

is Smokey the Bear?' referring to the famous fire-fighting symbol who was then residing at the Washington Zoo. Nixon smiled at the girl and turned away, but she kept waving and asking her question. Unable to make out her words, Nixon sought help from his aide-de-camp, Steve Bull. Bull whispered, "Smokey the Bear, Washington National Zoo.' Nixon walked over to the little girl, shook her hand and said, 'How do you do, Miss Bear?'"

10 Questioned by the British television interviewer David Frost about his approval of a plan of action that entailed such criminal ingredients as burglary and the opening of other people's mail, Nixon replied, "Well, when the President does it, that means it is not illegal."

11 Nixon once returned to his cabin at Camp David and announced, "I scored 126." Henry Kissinger, in a flattering voice, said, "Your golf is improving, Mr. President." "I was bowling," Nixon snapped.

12 After his wife, Pat, died, Nixon remembered the time his youngest granddaughter, Jennie Eisenhower, asked her grandmother what she should call her. "Grandmother" seemed too stiff, and "Grandma" too old, so they settled on "Ma." Jennie then asked Nixon the same question. "Oh, you can call me anything," Nixon told her, "because I've been called everything."

NORBURY, John Toler, 1st Earl of (1745–1831), *Irish lawyer.*

1 Norbury was riding with another Irish lawyer, John Parsons, in Parsons's carriage. Their route took them past a gibbet with a corpse still hanging on it. The melancholy sight prompted Lord Norbury to remark, "Ah, Parsons, if we all had our deserts, where would you be?"

"Alone in my carriage," was the response.

2 A Dublin attorney having died in poverty, his legal colleagues set up a subscription to pay for his funeral. Lord Norbury was asked to contribute. On inquiring what sum would be appropriate, he was told that no one else had subscribed more than a shilling. "A shilling!" exclaimed the judge, reaching into his pocket. "A shilling to bury an attorney? Why, here's a guinea! Bury one and twenty of the scoundrels."

3 Even as he lay dying, Lord Norbury could not resist a jest. Realizing that his end was imminent, he sent his valet around to another aged peer who was also on his deathbed. "James," he said, "present my compliments to Lord Erne and tell him it will be a dead heat between us."

NORTH, Frederick, Lord (1732–92), *British statesman; prime minister (1770–82).*

1 When North was visiting Algiers, he asked the dey if he might see the women of his harem. The dey's reaction was not at all what might have been expected of a jealous oriental potentate: "He is so ugly, let him see them all."

2 Sir Joseph Mawbey rose during a parliamentary sitting and roundly attacked Lord North for his part in the revolt of the American colonists. He asserted that it was entirely due to North's mismanagement that so much blood had been spilled and so many resources wasted in an unnecessary war. Lord North listened to the onslaught with his eyes shut. "Furthermore," continued Sir Joseph, "he is so little affected by consciousness of his misdeeds that he is even now asleep." Lord North stirred in his seat and opened his eyes. "I wish to God, Mr. Speaker, I was asleep," he remarked, and closed his eyes again.

3 After one of his frequent quarrels with his father, the Prince of Wales (later King George IV) asked Lord North to act as mediator and bring about a reconciliation. Having made the prince's peace with George III, Lord North reported his success to the prince, adding a little homily for the occasion: "Now, my dear prince, do in future conduct yourself differently — do so for God's sake, do so for your own sake, do so for your excellent father's sake, do so for the sake of that good-natured man Lord North, and don't oblige him again to tell your good father so many lies as that good-natured man has been obliged to tell him this morning."

4 In his old age Lord North became blind. He was visited by a friend who had likewise lost his sight. "Colonel, no one will suspect us of insincerity if we say we should be overjoyed to see each other," said the old man in greeting his friend.

NORTHCOTE, James (1746–1831), *British artist.*

1 Sitting for Northcote, the Duke of Clarence (afterward William IV) asked if the artist knew his brother, the Prince Regent. Northcote said he did not, and the duke was surprised: "Why, my brother says he knows you."

"That's only his brag," replied Northcote.

NOYES, John Humphrey (1811–86), *US social reformer.*

1 Noyes envisioned a society in which there was no money, no private property, food and shelter for all, and thus no need for competition. A visitor to the community is said to have asked her guide the nature of the fragrance that she smelt in "the Honorable John's" house. "The odor of crushed selfishness, maybe," was the reply.

NURMI, Paavo (1897–1973), *Finnish athlete.*

1 During the 1924 Olympics in Paris, Nurmi ran seven races in six days. Adrian Pavlen, former president of the IAAF and himself an Olympic long-distance runner, recalls the day in which Nurmi won the 1,500-meter event, then seventy-five minutes later won the 5,000. That night Pavlen and some friends were on a bus going from Colombes, the Olympic village, to a party in Paris. The distance was about six miles. "We looked out the window and there was Nurmi *walking* to Paris, even though he had competed in the 1,500 and 5,000 a few hours earlier."

OATES, Lawrence Edward Grace (1880–1912), British explorer and member of Robert Falcon Scott's ill-fated expedition to the South Pole.

1 On their return journey from the Pole, Scott's party was beset by fearful blizzards. Oates suffered badly from frostbitten feet, which were turning gangrenous. He begged to be left behind so as not to slow up the others. His companions would not hear of it, and they struggled on for another day. The following morning the blizzard was still raging. Oates said, "I am just going outside and may be some time." He then walked out of the tent and vanished forever into the storm.

OFFENBACH, Jacques (1819–80), French composer of operettas.

1 Offenbach dismissed his valet, but gave the man such an excellent reference that a friend wondered why he should have let him go. "Oh, he's a good fellow," said Offenbach, "but he won't do for a composer. He beats my clothes outside my door every morning and his tempo is nonexistent."

O'HARA, Frank(1926–66), US writer and poet.

1 On Mother's Day 1958, O'Hara remarked on a *New York Times* book review titled "The Arrow That Flieth by Day," and suggested it would make a fine title for a poem. At the same time his roommate, John LeSueur, was worrying about neglecting his mother on this day and wanted to send a telegram, but neither man could come up with a good message. So LeSueur went out in the rain to hear a performance of Aaron Copland's "Piano Fantasy." Upon his return he found that O'Hara had written a poem called "Ode on the Arrow That Flieth by Day," which managed to incorporate Western Union, the "Fantasy," Mother's Day and the rain.

O'HARA, John [Henry] (1905–70), US novelist, short-story writer, and playwright.

1 Pooling their money during the Spanish Civil War, Ernest Hemingway, James Lardner, and Vincent Sheean found they had some to spare. There followed a discussion as to how the surplus should be spent. Suggested Hemingway: "Let's take the bloody money and start a bloody fund to send John O'Hara to Yale."

2 (Someone once said of O'Hara that he was master of the fancied slight.)

Robert Benchley and his daughter-in-law Marjorie, catching sight of O'Hara at the restaurant 21, called him over to their table. Marjorie said, "John, we've just been seeing *Pal Joey* again, and do you know, I like it even better than I did the first time."

"What was the matter with it the first time?" said O'Hara.

3 Writing to John Steinbeck to congratulate him on winning the Nobel Prize for Literature, O'Hara added, "I can think of only one other author I'd rather see get it."

4 O'Hara told Bennett Cerf he wanted to use as the title of his new book a Richard Rodgers song, "A Small Hotel." O'Hara had known Rodgers from their collaboration on the musical version of *Pal Joey*, but even so, Cerf suggested he get permission. When O'Hara broached the subject, Rodgers agreed, but noted that the song was actually called "There's a Small Hotel." "When I need you to name my books," fumed O'Hara before storming out, "I'll tell you!"

OLDFIELD, Anne (1683–1730), *British actress.*

1 Mrs. Oldfield was a passenger on a ferry that appeared in imminent danger of capsizing. When the other passengers broke into lamentations at what seemed to be their approaching doom, Mrs. Oldfield rebuked them with great dignity. Their deaths would be merely a matter for private grief, but, she reminded them, "I am a public concern."

OLIVIER, Laurence [Kerr], Baron (1907–89), *British stage and film actor.*

1 At the tender age of ten, Olivier gave a highly acclaimed performance as Brutus in a school production of *Julius Caesar.* The actress Ellen Terry saw the play and declared: "The boy who plays Brutus is *already* a great ac-

tor." These words of praise were relayed to the young Olivier. "Who is Ellen Terry?" he asked.

2 On a visit to Jamaica as the guest of Noël Coward, Sir Laurence Olivier accompanied Coward to a mountaintop to see the playwright's favorite view. Looking out at the terraces of jungle sprawled beneath him, Olivier had but one comment: "It looks like rows and rows of empty seats."

3 Olivier and American actor Dustin Hoffman were paired for the filming of *Marathon Man,* a thriller involving an attempt by aging Nazis to recover diamonds hidden in the United States. To prepare for his role, Hoffman, who famously adhered to the school of method acting, didn't wash and stayed up for days to achieve the look and feeling of an exhausted man. Appearing on the set in this condition, he was spotted by Olivier, who said, "My dear boy, you look absolutely awful. Why don't you try acting ?"

'OMAR (d. AD 664), *Muslim caliph.*

1 'Omar's general 'Amr Ibn Al-as conquered Egypt in 640. In 642, when the city of Alexandria surrendered to him, 'Amr sent to 'Omar for instructions about how to deal with its great library, which contained hundreds of thousands of texts from classical antiquity. 'Omar replied, "If the writings of the Greeks agree with the Koran they are superfluous and need not be preserved; if they disagree they are pernicious, and ought not to be preserved." 'Amr therefore ordered the irreplaceable manuscripts to be used to fuel the furnaces for the public baths. It is said that they kept the furnaces going for six months.

ONASSIS, Aristotle [Socrates] (1906–75), *Greek shipping magnate who married the widowed Jacqueline Kennedy in 1968.*

1 On the *Christina* Onassis had installed a luxurious private bathroom adjoining his office. The door was a one-way mirror, which enabled him to observe unsuspecting visitors from the privacy of the bathroom. During a business meeting one afternoon Onassis excused himself and went to the bathroom. Comfortably enthroned, he looked up at the door and was horrified to see his own reflection staring back at him. A workman making minor repairs to the door earlier in the day had replaced the mirror the wrong way around.

———✥———

ONASSIS, Jacqueline Bouvier Kennedy (1929–97), *wife of John F. Kennedy, 35th President of the United States (1961–63); subsequently married to Aristotle Onassis.*

1 Jacqueline Bouvier first met her future husband, John Kennedy, at a dinner party in Washington in 1951. It took time for the courtship to develop between the junior senator from Massachusetts and the young newspaper reporter. After their engagement John Kennedy told her that he had decided upon their initial meeting that, were he ever to marry, she would be his bride. "How *big* of you," she teased.

2 At a dinner party a Democratic party official asked her what would be a sensible place to hold the 1960 National Convention (at which her husband became the presidential nominee). Instantly she replied, "Acapulco."

3 During the campaign her hairstyles generated enormous attention — providing quite a change from the image of Mamie Eisenhower. Eventually she released the following statement to the press: "What does my

hairdo have to do with my husband's ability to be President?"

4 French Culture Minister André Malraux commented to President Charles de Gaulle that Mrs. Kennedy was a most unusual First Lady. "Yes, she's unique," replied de Gaulle. "I can see her in about ten years on the yacht of a Greek petrol millionaire."

5 Jacqueline Kennedy was much occupied with her young children during her husband's presidency but confessed that she was unable to cope alone and felt she needed help. Dr. Spock's book provided her the assistance she needed, she said. "I find it such a relief to know that other people's children are as bad as yours at the same age."

6 When he heard that Fidel Castro's friend and companion-in-arms Che Guevara had expressed a strong desire to meet Jacqueline Kennedy, John Kennedy said, "He'll have to wait in line."

7 As First Lady, Jacqueline Kennedy was inundated with advice and literally tons of mail suggesting she redecorate this, begin that, look into such-and-such. Once she confessed her recipe for happiness to a staffer, with a delicious smile: "People have told me ninety-nine things that I have to do as a First Lady, and I haven't done one of them!"

8 She was once very late arriving at a rally for her husband in Houston, Texas, which caused the assembled crowd to begin chanting her name over and over. Her husband, in explanation, called out to the crowd, "It takes a little longer but, of course, she looks better than the rest of us when she does it."

9 The world was shocked when, in 1968, she decided to marry Greek shipping magnate Aristotle Onassis. Americans especially felt they had lost a national treasure. A friend with whom she shared her news before telling the public said to her, "You're going

to fall off your pedestal." "That's better than freezing there," Jacqueline Kennedy replied.

10 Later in her life, long after the turbulent days of the 1960s, during which she witnessed death and unhappiness in her personal life, she was asked what she considered her greatest achievement. After a pause she replied, "I think it is that after going through a rather difficult time, I consider myself comparatively sane."

———— ✧ ————

O'NEAL, Tatum (1963–), *US film actress, daughter of actor Ryan O'Neal.*

1 When fourteen-year-old Tatum O'Neal was making the film *International Velvet*, a school inspector came to make sure that she was not falling behind in her studies. Noting that her math was not very good, he asked whether that did not bother her. The child star was unconcerned: "Oh, no, I'll have an accountant."

———— ✧ ————

O'NEILL, Eugene (1888–1953), *US dramatist, winner of the 1936 Nobel Prize for Literature.*

1 Working as a news reporter on the *New London Telegraph*, O'Neill sometimes found it difficult to deliver his stories in a form acceptable to his editor. One contribution came back with the following note: "This is a lovely story, but would you mind finding out the name of the gentleman who carved the lady and whether the dame is his wife or daughter or who? And phone the hospital for a hint as to whether she is dead or discharged or what? Then put the facts into a hundred and fifty words and send this literary batik to the picture framers."

2 O'Neill always strongly objected to cutting any of his plays. When director and playwright Russel Crouse asked him to shorten the script of *Ah, Wilderness!* he was very reluctant. The following day he telephoned Crouse to tell him that he had cut fifteen minutes. Surprised and pleased, Crouse said, "I'll be right over to get the changes." "Oh, there aren't any changes to the text," O'Neill explained, "but you know we have been playing this thing in four acts. I've decided to cut out the third intermission."

3 O'Neill greatly disliked any kind of publicity. The one time in his life that he went to a nightclub, the excited owner announced to the audience that America's greatest playwright was in the room and would take a bow. O'Neill obliged, standing in a bright spotlight. As he was leaving, a waiter rushed over with a bill for $60 for his dinner. O'Neill took out a pencil and scrawled across the bottom, "One bow — sixty dollars," and left.

3 O'Neill spent his last days in Suite 401 of Boston's Shelton Hotel, broke and desperately ill. Just before falling into unconsciousness he sat up, looked wildly around his room, and cried out, "I knew it! I knew it! Born in a hotel room — goddamn it — and dying in a hotel room!"

———— ✧ ————

OPPENHEIMER, J. Robert (1904–67), *US physicist in charge of the development of the atomic bomb at the end of World War II.*

1 Physicist James Franck was professor of Göttingen University when the twenty-three-year-old Oppenheimer was being examined for his doctorate. On emerging from the oral examination, Franck remarked, "I got out of there just in time. He was beginning to ask *me* questions."

2 As Oppenheimer watched the first atomic bomb explode in a test at Alamogordo, New Mexico, on July 16, 1945, a passage from the Hindu scripture the *Bhagavad Gita* came

into his mind: "If the radiance of a thousand suns were to burst into the sky, that would be like the splendor of the Mighty One." Then, as the enormous mushroom cloud darkened the sky, another sentence from the same source came to him: "I am become Death, the shatterer of worlds."

———cNa———

ORSAY, Alfred-Guillaume-Gabriel, Count d' (1801–52), *French dandy.*

1 After 1841 Count d'Orsay was beset by fear of arrest for debt. The curious laws of the time, however, put him in no danger of being served with a writ or arrested between sunset and sunrise. During daylight hours, visitors to his house had to establish their identity before they were allowed in, and two mastiffs prowled in the garden. Despite these precautions an enterprising bailiff, disguised as an errand boy, managed to gain admittance late one afternoon. He surprised the count in his dressing room and revealed his true identity. D'Orsay, who was halfway through his toilet, did not lose his head. He asked the officer if he might finish dressing and courteously bade him take a chair. For over an hour the man sat and watched, fascinated, oblivious to the rapidly approaching sunset. The count, however, was carefully monitoring the progress of the sun. As it slipped below the horizon, he gently reminded the officer that now his authority no longer ran and sent for a servant to show him out.

2 Seated at dinner next to the willful Lady Holland, Count d'Orsay found her ladyship determined to monopolize his attention; whenever it seemed to wander, she would reclaim it by dropping something, which, of course, the count had to retrieve for her. First her napkin fell to the floor, then a spoon, then her ladyship's fan. Finally the count lost patience and turning to the footman behind

his chair, told him to place his plates and cutlery on the floor. "I shall finish my dinner there," he announced. "It will be so much more convenient for my Lady Holland."

———cNa———

OSCAR II (1829–1907), *king of Sweden (1872–1907) and Norway (1872–1905).*

1 Visiting a village school one day, the king asked the pupils to name the greatest kings of Sweden. The answers were unanimous: Gustavus Vasa, Gustavus Adolphus, Charles XII. Then the teacher leaned over to one little boy and whispered something in his ear. "And King Oscar," volunteered the child. "Really? And what has King Oscar done that's so remarkable?" asked the king. "I — I — I don't know," stammered the unhappy child. "That's all right, my boy," said the king. "Neither do I."

———cNa———

O'TOOLE, Peter (1932–), *British film actor.*

1 As a young actor Peter O'Toole landed a bit part as a Georgian peasant in a Chekhov play. All he had to do was to come on stage, announce, "Dr. Ostroff, the horses are ready," and exit. Determined to obtain what mileage he could out of this unpromising role, O'Toole conceived of the peasant as a youthful Stalin: he made himself up to look like Stalin, practiced a slight limp like Stalin's, and rehearsed his line to indicate his furious resentment against his social betters. The first-night audience was duly aroused by the entry of this ominous figure. Concentrating intensely, O'Toole made his announcement: "Dr. Horsey, the ostroffs are ready."

2 Besides being an enormously talented actor, O'Toole was known for his enormous ego on

and off the sets of movies. His reputation for this started with his first starring role, in *Lawrence of Arabia*. Not long after casting the unknown O'Toole in the film, Sam Spiegel said of him, "You make a star, you make a monster."

"Walter O'Keefe, an actor in the US in the 1930s, was once invited to address a medical convention. He found on arrival at the banquet that the convention was in fact one of chiropodists.

"O'Keefe had hardly tucked his napkin into his collar when a fanfare rang through the hall and the chiropodists leaped to attention. A spotlight roved across the heads of the multitude and picked up, on a wall bracket, Old Glory rippling in the breeze of an electric fan. After a properly patriotic salute, O'Keefe and the chiropodists again attacked their meal, an interval largely given over to a long, unhappy account by the chairman of his troubles in organizing the luncheon. Just as the ladyfingers and bombe glacée were arriving a second fanfare brought everyone up again.

"The spotlight settled on the swinging doors to the kitchen where stood a chef in a tall hat and apron. He bowed, flourished to his staff inside, and a huge foot sculptured out of ice rolled into view on a tea wagon. Amid thunderous applause, it made a slow, majestic circuit of the tables. As it drew abreast the speaker's table, the already irascible chairman turned a rich mulberry.

"'God damn it,' he snarled into O'Keefe's ear, 'they've gone and dropped the metatarsal arch!'"

— S. J. PERELMAN, "Two Years Down the Drain," in '47, *The Magazine of the Year*

OTTO (1865–1900), *archduke of Austria, father of Emperor Charles I.*

1 The archduke submitted to a medical examination by a renowned Viennese physician. The latter made careful, exhaustive inquiries about his patient's symptoms, pains, and so forth. These insistent questions irritated the archduke and he was frank enough to say so. The doctor replied, "Your Highness, I suggest the next time you ask for a veterinarian. He cures without asking any question."

OUIDA [Marie Louise de la Ramée] (1839–1908), *British novelist.*

1 Ouida, who never suffered from false modesty, enjoyed the chagrin of "serious" writers whose success was a fraction of her own. Once when Oscar Wilde asked her the secret of her popularity, she confided, "I am the only woman who knows how two dukes talk when they are alone."

OWEN, Robert (1771–1858), *Welsh manufacturer and founder of the New Harmony, Indiana, utopian community.*

1 There are many heart-breaking records of nineteenth-century child labor in the coal mines of England. The philanthropist Owen once talked to a twelve-year-old breaker boy, coal-black, weary from digging shale from broken coal. "Do you know God?" asked Owen. Replied the boy, "No. He must work in some other mine."

P

PACHMANN, Vladimir de (1848–1933), *Russian pianist whose eccentric manners on the platform made him highly popular with audiences.*

1 Pachmann's eccentricities were not confined to his own stage appearances. During a concert by Leopold Godowsky, Pachmann once rushed onto the stage saying, "No, no, Leopold, you moost play it like *so*." He then gave a demonstration to the delighted audience as Godowsky sat by, crimson-faced. He explained that he would not have bothered for just any old player. "But Godowsky is *ze zecond* greatest liffing pianist," he announced.

2 During a London recital at which he played Chopin's *Minute* Waltz Pachmann adopted a curious hunched position, crouching over the keyboard so that no one could see his hands. Feeling the audience was owed some explanation, he said, "Vy I do zis? I vill tell. I see in ze owdience *mein alte freund* Moriz Rosenthal, and I do not vish him to copy my fingering."

3 One of de Pachmann's favorite tricks before a recital was to play about with the piano stool, adjusting and readjusting it, until the audience became desperate. Then he would rush into the wings to fetch a large book, place it on the seat, and try that. He would indicate that all was still not satisfactory and would tear one page from the book and try again. Finally, if the audience was lucky, he would begin.

PACKER, Alfred (1842–1907), *US gold prospector.*

1 In 1873, in Utah, Alfred Packer and some friends went on a gold prospecting trip. The weather proved too difficult, and most of the party went home. Packer and six men continued on into the mountains. But it was Packer alone who returned, insisting he had been deserted by his friends, of whom there was no trace. He claimed he had subsisted on roots and small game, but he looked rosy and flush indeed. It was not long before the half-eaten bodies of his companions were found, and Packer confessed that in a dispute he had killed and consumed them all. As he was sentenced to death, the judge said to him, "Alfred Packer, you depraved Republican cannibal — there were only six Democrats in Hinsdale County and, by God, you've et five of them!"

PADEREWSKI, Ignace Jan (1860–1941), *Polish pianist, composer, and statesman.*

1 When Paderewski played before Queen Victoria, he won her enthusiastic approval. "Mr. Paderewski," she exclaimed, "you are a genius." Paderewski, who liked to allude to the number of hours he spent practicing every day, shook his head. "Perhaps, Your Majesty, but before that I was a drudge."

2 Paderewski's enormous reputation was not taken as seriously by fellow pianists as by the adoring public. Moriz Rosenthal went to hear Paderewski play in London and is reported to have said after the concert, "He plays well, I suppose, but he's no Paderewski."

3 A young American student visiting the Beethoven museum in Bonn was fascinated by the piano on which Beethoven had composed some of his greatest works. She asked the museum guard if she could play a few bars on it; she accompanied the request with a lavish tip, and the man agreed. The girl sat down at the piano and tinkled out the opening of the *Moonlight* Sonata. As she was leaving, she said to the guard, "I suppose all the great pianists who come here want to play on that piano." The guard shook his head; "Well, Paderewski was here a few years ago and he said he wasn't worthy to touch it."

4 Paderewski had been asked to play for the dinner guests of a certain English duchess. Somewhat taken aback by the size of the fee demanded by the pianist, the duchess decided not to invite him for the meal itself and wrote: "Dear Maestro, accept my regrets for not inviting you to dinner. As a *professional* artist you will be more at ease in a nice room where you can rest before the concert." Paderewski promptly replied: "Dear Duchess, thank you for your letter. As you so kindly informed me that I am not obliged to be present at your dinner, I shall be satisfied with half of my fee."

5 Paderewski attended the 1919 Paris Peace Conference as the new premier of Poland. The French premier, Georges Clemenceau, was introduced to the great musician. "Are you a cousin of the famous pianist Paderewski?" he asked mischievously. "I *am* the famous pianist," replied Paderewski. "And you have become prime minister?" exclaimed Clemenceau. "What a comedown!"

———

PAIGE, Leroy Robert ["Satchel"] (1904–82), *US baseball player.*

1 "Paige worked briefly as a coach for the now-defunct Tulsa Oilers in 1976 and every night youngsters trooped to him for autographs. He gave them a small, white business card and said, 'Look on the back. That's where my secret is.' The little leaguers turned over the card and read Satchel Paige's 'Six Rules for a Happy Life':

"'1. Avoid fried meats which angry up the blood.

"'2. If your stomach disputes you, lie down and pacify it with cool thoughts.

"'3. Keep the juices flowing by jangling around gently as you move.

"'4. Go very light on vices such as carrying on in society. The social ramble ain't restful.

"'5. Avoid running at all times.

"'6. Don't look back. Something may be gaining on you.'"

2 One night Paige was pitching for the Kansas City Monarchs against the Lynn Frasers. At one point in the game he asked his outfielders to leave the field, upon which he casually struck out all three batters to finish the inning.

"Sir William Perry, 17th-century English political economist, had a boy (that is, a young servant) that whistled incomparably well. He after wayted on a Lady, a widowe, of good fortune. Every night this boy was to whistle his Lady asleepe. At last she could hold out no longer, but bids her chamber-mayd withdraw: bids him come to bed, setts him to worke, and marries him the next day."

— *Aubrey's Brief Lives*

PAINE, Thomas (1737–1809), *British political theorist and writer.*

1 Benjamin Franklin said to Paine, "Where liberty is, there is my country." Paine answered, "Where liberty is not, there is mine."

2 When Paine was traveling through Baltimore, he was accosted by a Swedenborgian minister who had recognized him as the author of *The Age of Reason.* The deistic thesis expounded by that book had led to a large number of answers from divines of various persuasions, and the minister was clearly anxious to present the Swedenborgian viewpoint. Having introduced himself, he began, "I am minister of the New Jerusalem Church here, and we explain the true meaning of the Scripture. The key had been lost above four thousand years, but we have found it." "It must have been very rusty," said Paine coolly.

3 During a serious illness Paine's doctor, a man given to his dinner, noted that Paine's stomach had diminished alarmingly. "And yours augments!" snapped Paine.

4 One day Paine was unexpectedly visited by an old lady, who interrupted his afternoon nap, saying, "I came from Almighty God to tell you that if you do not repent of your sins and believe in the blessed Saviour, you will be damned." "Poh! poh! It is not true," Paine

snapped back. "You were not sent on any such impertinent mission. God would not send such a foolish ugly old woman as you about with his messages!"

PALEY, William (1743–1805), *British clergyman.*

1 Appointed archdeacon of Carlisle, Paley made no secret of his feeling that his position entitled him to lord it over the lesser clergy. Feeling a draft on his back during a diocesan dinner, he summoned a footman and instructed him, "Close the window behind me and open one behind one of the curates."

PALMERSTON, Henry John Temple, 3d Viscount (1784–1865), *British statesman; prime minister (1855–58, 1859–65).*

1 When Palmerston was a young man, the Duke of Wellington made an appointment with him for half past seven in the morning. Someone expressed doubt that Palmerston, who kept late hours, would be able to keep the appointment. "Of course I shall," he retorted. "It's perfectly easy: I shall keep it the last thing before I go to bed."

2 Standing with Palmerston at a military review on a particularly hot day, the queen watched a company of perspiring volunteers doubling past her. Their proximity caused her to put her handkerchief to her nose. She remarked to Palmerston, "Don't you think there is rather a . . . ?"

"Oh, that's what we call *esprit de corps,* ma'am," he replied.

3 A certain Frenchman, eager to flatter the patriotic Lord Palmerston, once remarked, "If I were not a Frenchman, I should wish to be an Englishman." Palmerston was unimpressed. "If I were not an Englishman," he

replied, "I should wish to be an Englishman."

4 Palmerston's physician broke the news to the elderly statesman that he was going to die. "Die, my dear doctor?" Palmerston is said to have exclaimed. "That's the last thing I shall do!"

---⌘---

PAQUIN, Anna (1982–), *New Zealand actress, born in Canada.*

1 The nine-year-old Paquin had never acted professionally before auditioning for a role in Jane Campion's film *The Piano*. And she only tried out because her older sister was trying out as well. Her acting led to an Academy Award for Best Supporting Actress. When she was asked if she was similar to the character she played, Paquin said, "A wee bit. Actually, she tells more lies than I do."

---⌘---

PARK, Mungo (1771–1806), *Scottish explorer of Africa.*

1 While exploring a particularly wild and uncultivated region of Africa, Park unexpectedly came across a gibbet. "The sight of it," he later remarked, "gave me infinite pleasure, as it proved that I was in a civilized society."

---⌘---

PARKER, Dorothy (1893–1967), *US short-story writer, theater critic, doyenne of light verse, and wit.*

1 While a book reviewer for *The New Yorker*, Dorothy Parker went on her honeymoon. Her editor, Harold Ross, began pressuring her for her belated copy. She replied, "Too fucking busy, and vice versa."

2 At one time Dorothy Parker had a small, dingy cubbyhole of an office in the Metropolitan Opera House building in New York. As no one ever came to see her, she became depressed and lonely. When the signwriter came to paint her name on the office door, she got him to write instead the word "GENTLEMEN."

3 William Randolph Hearst lived with his movie-star mistress Marion Davies in his spectacular castle, San Simeon. Hollywood personalities were frequent guests. Hearst always insisted upon the observation of certain rules. Despite his own irregular association with Marion Davies, one of these rules was that there should be no lovemaking between unmarried couples. Dorothy Parker broke the rule and received a note from her host asking her to leave. In the San Simeon visitors' book she left these lines:

> Upon my honor,
> I saw a Madonna
> Standing in a niche,
> Above the door
> Of the famous whore
> Of a prominent son of a bitch.

4 After some years apart Dorothy Parker and her second husband, Alan Campbell, were remarried. At the reception following the ceremony she remarked, "People who haven't talked to each other for years are on speaking terms again today — including the bride and groom."

5 Dorothy Parker wrote a report on a Yale prom at which the number and beauty of the girls present had obviously made a deep impression on her. "If all those sweet young things were laid end to end," she announced, "I wouldn't be at all surprised."

6 She was asked to use the word *horticulture* in a sentence. "You can lead a horticulture, but

you can't make her think," said Dorothy Parker promptly.

7 Looking at a worn-out toothbrush in their hostess's bathroom, a fellow guest said to Dorothy Parker, "Whatever do you think she does with that?"

"I think she rides it on Halloween," was the reply.

8 Attending the dress rehearsal of her play *Close Harmony*, Dorothy Parker was discouraged by the performance. The leading lady was amply endowed. At one point the producer, sitting with Dorothy, whispered, "Don't you think she ought to wear a brassiere in this scene?"

"God, no," said Dorothy. "You've got to have something in the show that moves."

9 Gossiping about an acquaintance, Dorothy Parker murmured in bogus admiration, "You know, she speaks eighteen languages. And she can't say 'No' in any of them."

10 In the hospital Dorothy Parker was visited by her secretary, to whom she wished to dictate some letters. Pressing the button marked NURSE, Dorothy observed, "That should assure us of at least forty-five minutes of undisturbed privacy."

11 Leaving her place at the Round Table one day, Dorothy said, "Excuse me, I have to go to the bathroom." She paused, then went on, "I really have to telephone, but I'm too embarrassed to say so."

12 Coming to pay her last respects to Scott Fitzgerald as he lay in an undertaker's parlor in Los Angeles, Dorothy Parker used the words spoken by the anonymous mourner at the funeral of Jay Gatsby in Fitzgerald's *The Great Gatsby*: "The poor son-of-a-bitch!"

13 Dorothy Parker once attended a party with Somerset Maugham where the guests challenged each other to complete nursery

rhymes. Somerset Maugham presented Mrs. Parker with the lines: "Higgledy piggledy, my white hen / She lays eggs for gentlemen." Dorothy Parker added the following couplet: "You cannot persuade her with gun or lariat / To come across for the proletariat."

14 (Lillian Hellman records an incident that took place as the body of Alan Campbell was being carried from the house where he had died.)

"Among the friends who stood with Dottie on those California steps was Mrs. Jones, a woman who had liked Alan, pretended to like Dottie, and who had always loved all forms of meddling in other people's troubles. Mrs. Jones said, 'Dottie, tell me, dear, what I can do for you.'

"Dottie said, 'Get me a new husband.'

"There was a silence, but before those who would have laughed could laugh, Mrs. Jones said, 'I think that is the most callous and disgusting remark I ever heard in my life.'

"Dottie turned to look at her, sighed, and said gently, 'So sorry. Then run down to the corner and get me a ham and cheese on rye and tell them to hold the mayo.'"

15 Dorothy Parker once collided with Clare Boothe Luce in a narrow doorway. "Age before beauty," said Mrs. Luce, stepping aside. "Pearls before swine," said Dorothy Parker, gliding through.

16 At a Halloween party she saw a group of people standing around a tub of water and asked what they were doing. When she was told they were ducking for apples, she noted sadly, "There, but for a typographical error, is the story of my life."

17 During her later years Dorothy Parker increasingly found refuge in alcohol. Admitted to a sanatorium, she approved the room but told the doctor she would have to go out every hour or so for a drink. He solemnly

warned her that she must stop drinking or she would be dead within a month. "Promises, promises," she said with a sigh.

PARKER, Henry Taylor (1867–1934), *US music critic.*

1 During a symphony concert Parker had the misfortune to be seated near some persistent talkers. At last he rounded on the offenders: "Those people on the stage are making such a noise I can't hear a word you're saying."

PARKER, Quannah (late 18th–early 19th centuries), *North American Comanche Indian chief.*

1 "In his old age, after he quit the warpath, Quannah Parker . . . adopted many of the white man's ways. But in one respect he clung to the custom of his fathers. He continued to be a polygamist. He was a friend and admirer of Theodore Roosevelt and on one occasion when Roosevelt was touring Oklahoma he drove out to Parker's camp to see him. With pride Parker pointed out that he lived in a house like a white man, his children went to a white man's school, and he himself dressed like a white man. Whereupon Roosevelt was moved to preach him a sermon on the subject of morality. 'See here, chief, why don't you set your people a better example? A white man has only one wife — he's allowed only one at a time. Here you are living with five squaws. Why don't you give up four of them and remain faithful to the fifth?' Parker stood still a moment, considering the proposition. Then he answered, 'You are my great white father, and I will do as you wish — on one condition.' 'What is the condition?' asked Roosevelt. 'You pick out the one I am to live with and then you go kill the other four,' answered Parker."

PARR, Samuel (1747–1825), *British author, schoolmaster, and clergyman.*

1 His contemporaries valued highly Parr's talents as a composer of Latin epitaphs. Once he said to a friend, "My lord, should you die first, I mean to write your epitaph." His friend replied, "It is a temptation to commit suicide."

2 On Easter Tuesday in 1800 Parr preached a famous sermon before the lord mayor of London. Asked his opinion, his worship replied that he heard only four things in it that he disliked — the four quarters of the hour struck by the church clock.

3 Parr rated highly his own skill at whist. He was correspondingly intolerant of lack of skill in other players. One evening he was playing with a partner who committed blunder after blunder. A lady asked Parr how the game was going. "Pretty well, madam," was the reply, "considering that I have three adversaries."

PARRISH, Maxfield (1870–1966), *US illustrator, painter, and poster designer.*

1 Parrish specialized in painting beautiful nudes and was thus accustomed to having lovely young models in his studio. One morning, when a model arrived, Parrish suggested that they have a cup of coffee before getting down to work — a habit he had recently acquired to postpone confronting the blank canvas. They had hardly started to drink the coffee when the studio buzzer rang. Panic seized the artist. "Young lady," he cried, "for God's sake, take your clothes off — my wife's coming up to check on me."

---cᴺᴐ---

PARTRIDGE, John (1644–1715), *British cobbler turned almanac maker.*

1 In 1707 Jonathan Swift decided to laugh the fraudulent Partridge out of business. As "Isaac Bickerstaff" he published a spoof, *Predictions for the Year 1708.* "Bickerstaff" professed his concern to rescue the noble art of astrology from the hands of the quacks. In particular he would make precise predictions in place of the vague prophecies put forth by the ordinary almanac makers. Thus his very first prediction: the death of John Partridge "upon 29 March next, about 11 at night, of a raging fever."

On the morning of March 30 the London booksellers did a brisk trade in another pamphlet, hot off the presses, announcing that Bickerstaff's prediction had come true and Partridge had died the previous evening. It gave a detailed account of his deathbed, followed by an "Elegy on the Death of Mr. Partridge." Partridge hurriedly printed and distributed a denial of his death, but by then no one believed him. Other writers joined in the fun with pamphlets urging Partridge to abandon his perverse insistence that he was still alive. The Stationers' Company struck his name off their records. It was four years before Partridge recovered sufficiently from this onslaught to resume publication of his almanac, and by then "Isaac Bickerstaff" had become a household name.

2 One day Partridge, journeying to a country town, paused to rest at an inn. As he was remounting his horse to resume his journey, the ostler said, "If you take my advice you'll stay here, because if you go on you will certainly be overtaken by heavy rain." "Nonsense!" exclaimed Partridge, and away he rode. After he had ridden a short distance, he was drenched by a heavy shower. Interested in the ostler's accuracy of prediction, he returned to the inn, admitted that the man had been quite correct, and offered him a large tip if he would divulge his secret.

Pocketing the tip, that man said, "You see, we have an almanac in the house called Partridge's almanac, and the fellow is such a notorious liar that whenever he promises fine weather we can be sure it will rain. Now today he had put down 'settled weather, fine; no rain,' so when I looked that up before I saddled your horse I was able to put you on your guard."

---cᴺᴐ---

PASCAL, Blaise (1623–62), *French mathematician and writer on religion.*

1 Pascal's father began his son's education with a course of reading in ancient languages. When the nine-year-old Pascal inquired as to the nature of geometry, he was told that it was the study of shapes and forms. The boy immediately proceeded to discover for himself the first thirty-two theorems of Euclid — in the correct order. The elder Pascal saw that it was no use attempting to steer his son away from mathematics and allowed him to pursue his studies as he wished.

---cᴺᴐ---

PATER, Walter (1839–94), *British writer and critic.*

1 Pater's lectures at Oxford were notoriously inaudible, in fact virtually whispered. Max Beerbohm once asked Wilde if he had heard Pater lecture and got the response: "I overheard him."

---cᴺᴐ---

PATTI, Adelina (1843–1919), *Italian operatic soprano.*

1 Patti's successful tour of Europe brought her great acclaim from all operagoers, including

royalty. "Which crowned head do you like best?" she was once asked by a critic. Patti thought for a moment. "The Czar Alexander gives the best jewelry," she replied.

———— ᴄⱴɔ ————

PATTON, George S[mith], Jr. (1885–1945), *US general, nicknamed "Old Blood-and-Guts."*

1 In August 1943, when Patton was commanding American forces in Italy, he visited the hospital at Sant'Agata. While being shown around by the colonel in charge, he spied a man who did not seem to be wounded at all. He snapped at the colonel, "I want you to get that man out of bed right away. Get him back to the front. I won't have these men who really are wounded see that man babied so." When the soldier himself did not immediately respond, Patton struck him. It turned out that he was seriously shell-shocked. When the incident became known three months later, there was an outcry, and Patton was forced to make a public apology.

2 On August 26, 1944, one of Patton's units crossed the Seine at Melun, outflanking Paris. Patton sent Eisenhower a formal military report of the operation with the postscript: "Dear Ike, Today I pissed in the Seine."

3 Psychologists have often noted that in their final moments men often speak not of their mothers but their fathers. Patton's last word was "Papa?"

———— ᴄⱴɔ ————

The classic children's book *Make Way for Ducklings* by Robert McCloskey has a real-life analogue.

One of the events in the 1928 Olympics was single-scull rowing. Henry Pearce, representing Australia, was in the lead when a fam-

ily of ducks passed in front of him single file. Courteously, he pulled in his oars.

Yes, he won.

— Dᴀᴠɪᴅ Wᴀʟʟᴇᴄʜɪɴsᴋʏ, *The Complete Book of the Olympics*

———— ᴄⱴɔ ————

PEALE, Norman Vincent (1898–1993), *US clergyman and inspirational writer.*

1 Peale arrived to speak at a bankers' association annual dinner, and began chatting with one of the attendees in the elevator. The man was dismayed that "some preacher from New York" was the keynote speaker. "I'm telling you," he said, "it won't be any good." Replied Peale, "Brother, I *know* it won't be any good." After the dinner Peale gave his speech, at the conclusion of which the banker from the elevator came up to him and shook his hand. "Buddy," said the man, "we were both right, weren't we?"

———— ᴄⱴɔ ————

PEARD, John Whitehead (1811–80), *British country squire and soldier.*

1 Dumas *fils,* also in Garibaldi's entourage, gave a colorful account of Peard's first meeting with the Italian leader. Peard was introduced to Garibaldi on the field of battle, during a lull. They exchanged brief preliminary greetings. Then a movement in the Austrian lines attracted Peard's attention. "Pardon me, there's a devil of an Austrian over there who's catching my eye." So saying, he raised his gun and fired. The group around Garibaldi trained their field glasses on the obtrusive Austrian, who staggered forward a couple of paces and then pitched face downward and lay still. Peard nodded with satisfaction, and held out his hand to Garibaldi: "Good day, general. I hope I see you well."

———— ᴄⱴɔ ————

PEARY, Robert Edwin (1856–1920), *US Arctic explorer.*

1 A young lady had been questioning Peary for some time on various matters relating to his polar expeditions. "But how does anyone know when he has reached the North Pole?" she asked with a puzzled frown. "Nothing easier," replied Peary. "One step beyond the pole, you see, and the north wind becomes a south one."

———— ✃ ————

PECK, Gregory (1916–), *US film actor.*

1 Entering a crowded restaurant with a companion, Gregory Peck found no table available. "Tell them who you are," murmured the friend. "If you have to tell them who you are, you aren't anybody," said Peck.

———— ✃ ————

PECKINPAH, Sam (1925–84), *US movie director.*

1 Peckinpah was hired to direct a movie that was to star Paul Newman and Robert Redford, but the actual story was still vague. Many conversations with the writer produced no clear direction until Peckinpah said he wanted a western. "Jesus, Sam," exploded the writer, "it's about two cops in New York City." Replied the director, "Every story is a western."

———— ✃ ————

PEMBROKE, Thomas Herbert, 8th Earl of (1656–1733), *British military commander.*

1 Strict with his servants, Lord Pembroke would dismiss on the spot any that were found drunk. He generally turned a blind eye, however, to the misdeeds of a trusty old footman called John. But on one occasion this proved impossible, for John had appeared in full view of his master almost too drunk to stand, and the incident had been witnessed by other members of the household. Unperturbed, Lord Pembroke went straight up to the tottering footman, felt his pulse, and exclaimed, "God bless us, he is in a raging fever! Get him to bed directly and send for the apothecary." The apothecary was ordered to bleed the patient copiously and give him a strong dose of medicine every twenty-four hours, with the result that after a few days John staggered out looking weaker and paler than the most severe illness could have left him. "I am truly glad to see thee alive," cried the earl, "though you have had a wonderful escape, and ought to be thankful. Why, if I had not passed by at that time and spied the condition you were in, you would have been dead before now. But John," he added emphatically, "no more of these fevers!"

———— ✃ ————

PENICK, Harvey (1905–95), *US golfing amateur and author.*

1 Penick's *Little Red Book* remains the best-selling book ever published about the game of golf. It was written with a collaborator, Bud Shrake, whose agent negotiated the sale to a large New York publisher. When told his share of the money would be $85,000, Penick, who had never written a book before, panicked. "Bud," he said worriedly to his co-author, "I don't think I can raise that kind of money."

———— ✃ ————

PERELMAN, S[idney] J[oseph] (1904–79), *US humorist and screenwriter.*

1 On a visit to Taipei, Perelman, accosted by a group of prostitutes, had some difficulty in escaping from their importunities. Having at last shaken them off he headed back to his hotel, remarking, "A case of the tail dogging the wag."

PERICLES (c. 495–429 BC), *Athenian statesman and orator.*

1 During the Peloponnesian War an eclipse occurred when Pericles was about to set out to sea. As the pilot was too terrified to perform his duties, Pericles stepped forward and covered the man's head with his cloak. "Does this frighten you?" he asked. "No," said the pilot. "Then what difference is there between the two events," inquired Pericles, "except that the sun is covered by a larger object than my cloak?"

PERLMAN, Itzhak (1945–), *Israeli violinist.*

1 In 1980 Mike Wallace interviewed the great violinist on the television program *60 Minutes.* Wallace recalled the names of masters of the instrument — Jascha Heifetz, Yehudi Menuhin, Isaac Stern, Perlman himself — and then asked why so many great violinists were Jewish. Holding up his fingers and twiddling them, Perlman replied: "You see, our fingers are circumcised, which gives it a very good dexterity, you know, particularly in the pinky."

PERÓN, Eva Duarte de (1919–52), *Argentinian actress who became the second wife of President Juan Perón.*

1 Eva rose from the obscurity of a poor working-class background through a combination of talent, beauty, and unscrupulousness. She had a series of increasingly influential lovers whom she used to further her career and then discarded. As the wife of President Juan Perón, she was sent on a tour to win friends for Argentina among the European powers. Her reception was somewhat mixed. As she drove through the streets of Milan, accompa-

nied by a retired admiral, the crowd shouted "Whore." Angrily Eva turned to her escort, "They are calling me a whore!"

"That's all right," said the admiral soothingly. "I haven't been to sea for fifteen years, yet they still call me admiral."

PEROT, H. Ross (1930–), *US business executive and Independent candidate for President (1992 and 1996).*

1 "Looking around for a suitable way of serving the community, Mr. Perot decided that he would give a Christmas present to every American prisoner-of-war in Vietnam. Accordingly, thousands of parcels were wrapped and packed, and a fleet of Boeing 707s was chartered to deliver them to Hanoi. Then the message came from the government of Vietnam — no such gesture could be considered during the course of the bloody war, which was then at its height. Perot argued. The Vietnamese replied that any charity was impossible while American B-52s were devastating Vietnamese villages.

"'No problem,' Perot replied. He would hire an expert American construction company in order to rebuild anything the Americans had knocked down.

"The puzzled Vietnamese declined to continue this dialogue. Christmas drew closer, the parcels remained undelivered. Finally in despair Perot took off in his chartered fleet and flew to Moscow where his aides posted the parcels, one at a time, at the Moscow Central post office. They were delivered intact."

PERRY, Oliver Hazard (1785–1819), *US naval commander.*

1 During the battle of Lake Erie in 1813, Perry's flagship, the *Lawrence,* was so badly

damaged that he was obliged to abandon it and row to the *Niagara*. After finally forcing the British fleet to surrender, Perry made no reference to the exigencies of the battle in the dispatch announcing his victory. It read simply, "We have met the enemy, and they are ours."

PERUGINO, Pietro [Pietro di Cristoforo Vannucci] (1446–1523), *Italian painter.*

1 Perugino was commissioned to paint frescoes (now lost) in a convent in Florence. The niggardly prior stood over the artist while he worked, holding the little bag that contained the expensive ultramarine pigment and allowing Perugino only tiny quantities at a time. Every now and then he would wail, "How much blue that wall is eating!" Perugino said nothing, but worked steadily, occasionally cleaning his brush in a bowl of water. When he had completed his day's work, he drained the bowl and handed it back to the prior with its sediment of pure ultramarine at the bottom. "Here you are, Father. And please learn to trust an honest man."

2 On his deathbed, Perugino refused to send for the priest. His last words were: "I am curious to see what happens in the next world to one who dies unshriven."

PÉTAIN, [Henri] Philippe (1856–1951), *French general and statesman.*

1 From February to December 1916, one of the fiercest battles of World War I was fought at Verdun-sur-Meuse in northeast France. Marshal Pétain was in command of the Allied troops; Crown Prince Frederick William

commanded the Germans. At the beginning of the battle a determined Pétain said of the German troops, "They shall not pass." The resolution was upheld and the Allies ultimately triumphed, but only after one million lives had been lost.

2 In June 1940 Charles de Gaulle returned to France from England to bring Marshal Pétain an offer from Winston Churchill of "union" between the two countries to resist German onslaught. Pétain, knowing that France's capitulation was only hours away and believing that England was doomed too, rejected the offer, saying, "What use is fusion with a corpse?"

PETER I [Peter the Great] (1672–1725), *czar (1682–1721) and later emperor (1721–25) of Russia.*

1 In the Russian army there was a secret society whose members gained promotion by their ability to withstand torture and who practiced inuring themselves against greater and greater degrees of pain. One of these officers was involved in a plot against Peter, and although tortured four times refused to confess. Peter, realizing that pain would not break him, went up to him and kissed him. "I know full well that you were party to the plot against me, but you have been punished enough. Now, confess freely to me on account of the love you owe to your czar, and I swear that I will grant you a complete pardon. Not only that, but as a special sign of my mercy I will make you a colonel." The man was so unnerved by Peter's tactics that he embraced him and made a full confession. Peter kept his side of the bargain and made him a colonel.

2 Peter, greatly interested in medicine, often assisted surgeons and dentists in their opera-

tions. One morning one of his valets appealed to the czar to help his wife; she was suffering dreadfully from a toothache, he said, but refused to have the offending tooth pulled and pretended to be in no pain when approached by a dentist. Peter collected his dental instruments and followed the valet to his apartments, where, ignoring the cries and protests of the struggling woman, he extracted the tooth. Some days later the czar discovered that the poor woman had never had a toothache; the painful extraction had been her husband's revenge for a domestic quarrel.

PETERBOROUGH, Charles Mordaunt, 3d Earl of (1658–1735), *British diplomat, soldier, and admiral.*

1 In 1710, when the Duke of Marlborough was out of favor with the London populace, a mob attacked Peterborough in the street, mistaking him for the hated and ungenerous duke. He finally convinced them that he was not Marlborough by saying, "In the first place, I have only five guineas in my pocket; and in the second, they are very much at your service."

PETRONIUS, Gaius ["Petronius Arbiter"] (fl. AD 60), *Roman writer, a favorite at the court of Emperor Nero. He is believed to have been the author of the* Satyricon, *a satirical romance.*

1 Petronius had received an invitation to a special banquet at Nero's palace. The meal was to be followed by a "licentious entertainment" featuring a hundred naked virgins. Petronius refused the invitation. "Tell the emperor," he instructed his messenger, "that one hundred naked virgins are not one hundred times as exciting as one naked virgin."

PHELPS, William Lyon (1865–1943), *US scholar and critic.*

1 Marking an examination paper written shortly before Christmas, Phelps came across the note: "God only knows the answer to this question. Merry Christmas." Phelps returned the paper with the annotation: "God gets an A. You get an F. Happy New Year."

PHILIP, John Woodward (1840–1900), *US naval commander.*

1 During the Spanish-American War of 1898 Captain Philip was in command of the battleship *Texas.* The entire Spanish fleet, blockaded by the Americans in the bay of Santiago de Cuba, was destroyed when it emerged on July 3. As the *Texas* sailed past the burning Spanish cruiser *Vizcaya* in pursuit of another Spanish ship, Philip checked the natural jubilation of his crew with the words: "Don't cheer, boys; the poor devils are dying."

PHILIP, Prince, Duke of Edinburgh (1921–), *husband of Queen Elizabeth II of the United Kingdom.*

1 During a tour of Canada in the early years of their marriage, Prince Philip and Princess Elizabeth had a rather turbulent crossing to Vancouver Island on a Canadian destroyer. Tea was served in the royal suite by a young petty officer. As he entered with a large tray of cakes, the ship lurched violently and the cakes were thrown to the floor. To the officer's amazement, Prince Philip immediately went down on his hands and knees and crawled around the floor, retrieving about half of the cakes. Returning to his seat, he smiled triumphantly at Elizabeth and said, "I've got mine — yours are down there."

2 Visiting an Australian university during a royal tour in 1954, Prince Philip was introduced to a "Mr. and Dr. Robinson."

"My wife is a doctor of philosophy," explained Mr. Robinson. "She is much more important than I."

"Ah, yes," replied Prince Philip sympathetically. "We have that trouble in our family, too."

3 Prince Philip was asked by a hostile questioner what kind of work he would say that he did. "I'm self-employed," he replied.

4 An official greeted Prince Philip as he stepped from an aircraft with the words: "And how was your flight, sir?"

"Have you ever flown?" asked the prince.
"Yes, sir, often."
"Well, it was like that."

5 During a royal visit to a small English town, Prince Philip stopped to talk to two very old ladies. "I'm a hundred and four," boasted one of the women, "and my friend here is a hundred and one."

"I don't believe it," said Philip, his eyes twinkling. "Ladies always take ten years off their age."

6 Prince Philip has developed a reputation for startlingly brusque comments made off the cuff. Sometimes he is answered in kind. Once, on a visit to the capital city of Brasilia, he asked a Brazilian admiral if the colorful array of medals he wore had been won on Brasilia's artificial lake. The admiral suavely nodded. "Yes sir," he said, "not by marriage."

———⌘———

PHILIP II (382–336 BC), *king of Macedon (359–336 BC).*

1 Like Alexander the Great, Philip had the reputation of being a heavy drinker. Once when drunk he gave an unjust verdict in the case of a woman who was being tried before him. "I appeal!" cried the unfortunate litigant. "To whom?" asked the monarch, who was the highest tribunal in the land. "From Philip drunk to Philip sober," was the bold reply. The king, somewhat taken aback, gave the case further consideration.

2 After Philip had subdued or formed alliances with all the major Greek city-states, Sparta still remained aloof. Finding that diplomacy had no effect on its stubborn independence, Philip sent a threat: "You are advised to submit without further delay, for if I bring my army into your land, I will destroy your farms, slay your people, and raze your city." The Spartans replied: "If." Recalling Sparta's glorious military past, Philip thought better of it and left them alone.

3 Philip was always accompanied by two men whose duty it was to say to him each morning, "Philip, remember that you are but a man." Each evening they said, "Philip, have you remembered that you are but a man?"

———⌘———

PHILIP III (1578–1621), *king of Spain (1598–61).*

1 Politically indecisive and incompetent, Philip is said to have died of a fever. This was the consequence of overheating himself by sitting too long near a hot brazier. It did not occur to him to move away from the heat. How could he? The palace functionary whose job it was to remove the brazier could not be found. Philip's death was inevitable.

———⌘———

PHILIP V (1683–1746), *king of Spain (1700–46).*

1 Louis XIV hesitated for nearly a week after receiving news of the death of Charles II and

his bequest to Philip. He wondered whether to accept the legacy. On November 16, 1700, he made the formal announcement, after his *lever,* to the assembled court. "Gentlemen," he said, leading Philip forward, "here is the king of Spain." He then made a brief but touching speech, exhorting his grandson to be a good Spaniard and keep the peace in Europe. Overcome with emotion, the Spanish ambassador fell on his knees before Philip and kissed his hand and said, "The Pyrenees have ceased to exist."

PHILLIPS, Wendell (1811–84), *US reformer and orator.*

1 In the days before he became well known, Phillips spent a night in a hotel at Charleston, South Carolina. His breakfast was brought up by a slave, to whom Phillips began to expound his abolitionist ideals. After a time, realizing that his discourse was making little impression, Phillips gave up and told him he could go. The man stood firm. "You must excuse me," he said. "I am obliged to stay here, 'cause I'm responsible for the silverware."

2 While Wendell Phillips was on a lecture tour in the northern states, he was accosted by a minister from Kentucky who attacked him for his abolitionist views. "You want to free the slaves, don't you?" demanded the minister.

"Indeed I do."

"Then why are you preaching your doctrines up here? Why don't you try going to Kentucky?"

Phillips retorted, "You're a minister, aren't you?"

"Yes, I am."

"And you try to save souls from hell?"

"Yes, I do."

"Well, why don't you go there then?" said Phillips.

PIATIGORSKY, Gregor (1903–76), *Russian cellist.*

1 Piatigorsky was having problems with one of his pupils. No matter how many times the master played a piece to show how it should sound, his student failed to make any significant progress; in fact, his playing seemed to deteriorate. It occurred to Piatigorsky that he was perhaps discouraging the young man by performing the pieces too well himself. He therefore began to introduce a few deliberate mistakes; miraculously, the pupil showed marked signs of improvement. This method of teaching continued for some weeks, with Piatigorsky taking a perverse pleasure in being free to play as badly as he pleased.

The young man went on to perform with brilliant success at his graduation. Fighting through the crowd of well-wishers to congratulate his pupil, Piatigorsky heard someone ask the new graduate what he thought of the great cellist. "As a teacher," replied the young man, "excellent. But as a cellist, lousy."

PICABIA, Francis (1879–1953), *French painter of Spanish descent, one of the first exponents of Dadaism.*

1 In Picabia's château the rooms were designed with different themes; the children's room was furnished with grotesque masks, instruments of torture, witchcraft trappings, and a mechanical ghost that could be animated at night to rattle chains. The painter chose this theme for the children's room because he believed in training them in fearlessness from an early age. "When they get a bit older, I shall replace the ghost with a creditor waving an unpaid bill," he said.

—⚭—

PICASSO, Pablo (1881–1973), *Spanish artist, sculptor, and ceramist.*

1 (Picasso recalls his mother's ambitions for him.)

"When I was a child, my mother said to me, 'If you become a soldier, you'll be a general. If you become a monk, you'll end up as Pope.' Instead I became a painter and wound up as Picasso."

2 In 1906 Gertrude Stein sat to Picasso for her portrait. At the end of many sittings he simply obliterated the picture, saying he could no longer "see" her. Later he completed the picture, in the absence of a sitter, and gave the portrait to Miss Stein. She complained that she did not look like that. Picasso said, "But you will," and this prediction was borne out as Miss Stein aged.

3 When Picasso painted his famous portrait of Gertrude Stein, he was virtually unknown. Some years later the millionaire art collector Dr. Albert Barnes, interested in the picture, asked Miss Stein straight out how much she had paid for it. "Nothing," Miss Stein replied. "Naturally, he gave it to me." Dr. Barnes was incredulous. She subsequently recounted the incident to Picasso, who smiled and said, "He doesn't understand that at that time the difference between a sale and a gift was negligible."

4 Not long after the outbreak of World War I Gertrude Stein and Picasso were standing on a street corner in Paris, watching a procession of camouflaged trucks passing, the sides of the vans disguised by blotches of gray and green paint. Picasso, in his amazement, blurted out, *"C'est nous qui avons fait ça"* (It is we who have created that).

5 During World War II Picasso suffered some harassment from the Gestapo in Nazi-occu-

pied Paris. An inquisitive German officer, coming into his apartment, noticed a photograph of *Guernica* lying on a table. "Did you do that?" he asked Picasso. "No, you did," said Picasso.

6 Picasso fell into conversation with an American GI in Paris, who told him that he did not like modern paintings because they were not realistic. Picasso did not immediately respond, but when the soldier a few minutes later showed him a snapshot of his girlfriend, he exclaimed, "My, is she really as small as that?"

7 As the market value of Picasso's works grew, so too did the cottage industry of faking his paintings. A poor artist who owned a supposed Picasso sent it via a friend for the master to authenticate so that he could sell it. Picasso said, "It's false." From a different source the friend brought another Picasso and then a third. On each occasion Picasso disowned them. Apropos the third painting the man protested, "But I saw you paint this one with my own eyes."

"I can paint false Picassos as well as anyone," retorted Picasso. Then he bought the first painting from the impoverished artist for a sum four times as high as the owner had originally hoped it would fetch.

8 Friends lunching at Picasso's home in the south of France commented on the fact that their host had none of his own pictures on the walls. "Why is that, Pablo?" one of them asked. "Don't you like them?"

"On the contrary," replied the painter, "I like them very much. It's just that I can't afford them."

9 Picasso visited his local cabinetmaker to commission a mahogany wardrobe for his château. To illustrate the shape and dimensions he required, he drew a hasty sketch on a sheet of paper and handed it to the craftsman. "How much will it cost?" he asked.

"Nothing at all," replied the cabinetmaker. "Just sign the sketch."

10 Picasso was relaxing on a beach in the south of France when he was accosted by a small boy clutching a blank sheet of paper. The child had evidently been dispatched by his parents to solicit an autographed drawing. After a moment's hesitation, Picasso tore up the paper and drew a few designs on the boy's back instead. He signed his name with a flourish and sent the child back to his parents. Relating the incident at a later date, Picasso remarked thoughtfully, "I wonder if they'll ever wash him again?"

11 Picasso was asked whether it didn't tire him to stand in front of a canvas for three or four hours while he was painting. "No," he replied. "That is why painters live so long. While I work, I leave my body outside the door, the way Muslims take off their shoes before entering the mosque."

12 A visitor to Picasso's studio found the artist gazing disconsolately at a painting on the easel. "It's a masterpiece," said the visitor, hoping to cheer Picasso up.

"No, the nose is all wrong," Picasso said. "It throws the whole picture out of perspective."

"Then why not alter the nose?"

"Impossible," replied Picasso. "I can't find it."

13 A rich Dutch grocer who prided himself on his art collection managed to obtain an introduction to Picasso. He examined the works in the studio and then said, "Master, I understand every one of your productions except one."

"And that is?"

"Your dove. It seems to me so simple, so primitive that I cannot understand it."

"Sir," Picasso asked, "do you understand Chinese?"

"No."

"Six hundred million people do." And Picasso politely showed him out.

14 "I had lunched at the Catalan for months," Picasso said, "and for months I looked at the sideboard without thinking more than 'it's a sideboard.' One day I decide to make a picture of it. I do so. The next day, when I arrived, the sideboard had gone, its place was empty. . . .I must have taken it away without noticing by painting it."

15 "Do you remember that head of a bull I had in my last show? I'll tell you how it was conceived. One day I noticed in a corner the handle-bar and the seat of a bicycle, lying in such a way as to look like a bull's head. I picked them up and put them together so that nobody could possibly fail to realize that this seat and this handle-bar from a bike were really a bull's head. My metamorphosis was successful, and now I wish there could be another one, this time in reverse. Suppose that one day my head of a bull were to be thrown on a junk heap. Maybe a little boy would come along and notice it and say to himself, 'Now there's something I could use as a handle-bar for my bike.' If that ever happens, we will have brought off a double metamorphosis."

16 (David Douglas Duncan describes a conversation during a meal at Picasso's house.)

"During the meal I mentioned that it seemed really eerie to me to watch his gaze leap from article to article on the table and around the room, knowing perfectly well he was not seeing *anything* as I saw it, and never had. I added that it seemed incredible that one person ever dreamed of such varied images throughout a lifetime and could still be doing it today without apparently even trying. Picasso answered very simply, 'If I tried, they would all look the same.'"

17 (Ronald Penrose, Picasso's biographer, recalls a visit to the artist in his Paris apartment.)

"I happened to notice that a large Renoir hanging over the fireplace was crooked. 'It's better like that,' [Picasso] said, 'if you want to kill a picture all you have to do is to hang it beautifully on a nail and soon you will see nothing of it but the frame. When it's out of place you see it better.'"

18 When Picasso married Olga Koklova, their honeymoon was spent at the luxurious villa of a well-known hostess in the south of France. Picasso happily painted portraits of the other guests, and adorned the white-washed walls of the villa with playful murals. But one guest was not at all pleased with the portrait he did of her holding her son. She told him that, in fact, she would much rather have had the portrait done in the style of a currently fashionable portraitist, Boldini. Without a word Picasso took out a canvas and, within minutes, gave her a portrait done perfectly in Boldini's style and signed with his name.

19 One art patron Picasso disliked was Peggy Guggenheim. She came to see him one day with a list in hand, hoping to go over his collection to see what she might purchase. Picasso ignored her and made a show of talking to other guests in the house. Then he approached her and said, "Lingerie is on the next floor."

20 In later life Picasso visited an exhibition of children's drawings. He observed, "When I was their age, I could draw like Raphael, but it took me a lifetime to learn to draw like them."

———— ✤ ————

PICCARD, Auguste (1884–1962), *Swiss physicist.*

1 Auguste and his twin brother, Jean Felix, had spent the night in a strange town and were both in need of a shave. Entering the local barber's shop alone, Auguste settled down in the chair and said, "Make sure you give me a close shave. My beard grows so rapidly that two hours after I've had a shave, I need another." The barber looked at him in disbelief. "If your beard grows in two hours," he said skeptically, "I'll give you another shave free." Auguste left the shop in due course, clean-shaven and apparently satisfied. Two hours later, the barber was horrified to see his customer return with a dark growth of stubble on his chin. "Now do you believe me?" asked Jean Felix as he sat down for his free shave.

———— ✤ ————

PINTER, Harold (1930–), *British dramatist.*

1 Besides writing plays, Pinter occasionally liked to write poetry. Once he wrote a verse, which follows in its entirety: "I knew Len Hutton in his prime. / Another time, another time." Pinter then sent it off, as was his custom, to numerous friends for their reaction. After two weeks he had heard nothing and so called someone to whom he had sent the poem, claiming to be worried about the mail service. Had he received it? Yes, came the reply, indeed, it arrived ten days ago. And what did he think of it? Said the friend, "Actually, I haven't quite finished it."

———— ✤ ————

PINZA, Ezio (1892–1957), *US opera singer, born in Italy.*

1 Soon after opening in the Broadway production of *South Pacific*, Pinza called at his favorite restaurant for his customary twelve-course dinner. Noticing the look of astonishment on the waiter's face as he took the order, Pinza snapped, "What's the matter with you? I may be singing musical comedy these days — but I still *eat* grand opera!"

———— ✤ ————

PITT, William (1759–1806), *British statesman; prime minister (1783–1801, 1804–06), known as William Pitt the Younger to distinguish him from his father, the Earl of Chatham.*

1 A number of volunteers in London offered Pitt their services as militia. Although they were prepared to organize and equip themselves, the offer was hedged about with a number of provisos that substantially reduced its usefulness. Pitt read through their proposal until he reached a clause stating that they should never be required to leave the kingdom. At this point he picked up a pen and added in the margin, "except in the case of actual invasion."

2 Pitt had been urging Parliament to approve the immediate dispatch of the British fleet against the French. In order to secure the necessary appropriation, he had to persuade Lord Newcastle, the chancellor of the exchequer, who opposed his policy. Pitt called on the chancellor to pursue the question and found him in bed, suffering from gout. It was autumn, the room was unheated, and Pitt remarked how cold it was. Newcastle ironically replied that the weather would hinder any fleet movements and indeed hinder any comfortable discussion of the point at issue. Pitt answered that he did not so lightly relinquish his plans. Then, asking pardon, he removed his boots, climbed into the room's other bed, drew up the cover, and began a unique conference. He won his point.

3 Napoleon's victory at Austerlitz in December 1805 left him master of Europe and spelled the end of Pitt's alliance against him with Sweden, Austria, and Russia. When the news of the battle was brought to Pitt, he pointed to a large map of Europe on the wall and said, "Roll up that map; it will not be wanted these ten years."

4 Pitt died in office, worn out by overwork and crushed by the overthrow of his coalition against Napoleon. Desperately aware of the dangerous ebb of England's fortunes, he murmured as he died, "My country, oh, how I leave my country!

{Alternative last words attributed to Pitt are the far more touching "I think I could eat one of Bellamy's veal pies."}

PLATH, Sylvia (1932–63), *US poet and novelist.*

1 One day Alfred Kazin was interviewing prospective students for his writing class at Smith. The last girl he saw showed him some samples of her work, which Kazin spotted instantly as the product of a great talent. "The writing was so coolly professional that I scented plagiarism, and said with some bitterness, 'These could be published in *X* and *Y*.'" "They've already taken them," said Plath. Then why would she take Kazin's class? "I'm lonesome here, and want to talk to you."

PLATO (c. 428–c. 348 BC), *Greek philosopher who founded the Academy at Athens.*

1 A student, struggling with the abstract concepts of Platonic mathematics, asked Plato, "What practical end do these theorems serve? What is to be gained from them?" Plato turned to his attendant slave and said, "Give this young man an obol [a small coin] that he may feel that he has gained something from my teachings, and then expel him."

2 Plato considered the abstract speculations of pure mathematics to be the highest form of thought of which the human mind was capable. He therefore had written over the entrance to the Academy "Let no one ignorant of mathematics enter here."

3 Diogenes came to Plato's house one day and was disgusted to find rich and exquisite carpets on the floor. To show his contempt he stamped and wiped his feet upon them, saying, "Thus do I trample upon the pride of Plato."

"With greater pride," observed Plato mildly.

———— ✧ ————

PLINY [the Younger] (c. 61–c. 133), *Roman orator, statesman, and lawyer.*

1 At dinner Pliny noticed that his host distributed the food and wine according to the social standing of the diners. Rich and elegant dishes and the best wine were served to himself and his most honored guests, while cheap and paltry food and drink were set before the rest. Another guest, sensing Pliny's disapproval of these parsimonious measures, inquired how he managed in his own home. Pliny answered, "I provide each guest with the same fare, for when I invite a man to my table I have placed him on a footing of equality with me and I will therefore treat him as an equal." The other man was surprised. "Even freedmen?" he asked. "Even freedmen," replied Pliny, "because on these occasions I regard them as companions, not as freedmen." The other remarked that this must run Pliny into a great deal of expense. "Not at all," said Pliny, "for my freedmen don't drink the same wine as I do, but *I* drink what *they* do."

———— ✧ ————

PLOTINUS (205–270), *Greek philosopher.*

1 A friend urged Plotinus to have his portrait painted. The philosopher refused: "It is bad enough to be condemned to drag around this image in which nature has imprisoned me. Why should I consent to the perpetuation of the image of this image?"

———— ✧ ————

POE, Edgar Allan (1809–49), *US poet, short-story writer, and literary critic.*

1 An old literary and military tradition has it that Poe was expelled from West Point in 1831 for "gross neglect of duty" because he appeared naked at a public parade. Parade dress instructions called for "white belts and gloves, under arms." Poe took this literally and appeared with rifle over his bare shoulder, wearing belt and gloves — and nothing else.

———— ✧ ————

POGGIO BRACCIOLINI, Gian Francesco (1380–1459), *Italian humanist scholar and writer.*

1 As holder of a secretarial post in the papal Curia, Poggio wore ecclesiastical dress although he was never formally ordained a priest. A cardinal reprimanded him for having children, which did not become a man wearing ecclesiastical garb, and for having a mistress, which was unbecoming even to a layman. Poggio retorted, "I have children, which is suitable for a layman, and I have a mistress, which is a time-honored custom of the clergy."

———— ✧ ————

POLK, James K. (1795–1849), *US politician; 11th President of the United States (1845–49).*

1 Like another southern President over a hundred years later, Polk disliked alcohol and banned dancing and card playing in the White House. His opponent Sam Houston once said that the only problem with Polk was that he drank too much water.

POMPADOUR, Jeanne-Antoinette Poisson, Marquise d'Étoiles (1721–64), *French lady of the court; mistress of Louis XV.*

1 (Mme de Pompadour enjoyed surrounding herself with intellectuals and supported the *Encyclopédistes* against the church. Despite her efforts, at one time the religious and anti-rationalist factions in the court persuaded Louis to ban the *Encyclopédie*. Soon after this a duke wondered aloud at a royal supper party what gunpowder was made of.) "'It seems so funny that we spend our time killing partridges, and being killed ourselves on the frontier, and really we have no idea how it happens.' Madame de Pompadour, seeing her opportunity, quickly went on: 'Yes, and face powder? What is that made of? Now, if you had not confiscated the *Encyclopédie*, Sire, we could have found out in a moment.' The King sent to his library for a copy, and presently a footman staggered in under the heavy volumes; the party was kept amused for the rest of the evening looking up gunpowder, rouge, and so on. After this subscribers were allowed to have their copies, though it was still not on sale in the bookshops."

2 As she lay dying, Madame de Pompadour summoned her last strength and called to God, "Wait a second," as she dabbed her cheeks with rouge.

3 Mme de Pompadour, whose interest not just in her king but in the welfare of his people resulted in her being called "the mistress of France," was cut down early in life by cancer. After her confessor gave her last rites, he rose to go. "One moment," she said with a smile as she grasped his hand. "We will leave together." Upon which she died.

POPE, Alexander (1688–1744), *British poet, satirist, and translator.*

1 Statesman and financier Charles Montagu, first Earl of Halifax, prided himself upon his literary acumen. When Pope had completed the first few books of his translation of the *Iliad*, Montagu invited him to give a reading at his house. Other eminent literary figures also attended. Pope considered that the reading had gone off very well, even though Lord Halifax had interrupted, most politely, four or five times to say that there was something about that particular passage he did not think quite right and that Pope could improve it with some more thought. On the way home with physician and poet Samuel Garth, Pope confessed that he was much perplexed by Lord Halifax's rather vague objections. He went on to say that although he had been thinking about the offending passages ever since, he could not for the life of him see what should be done to make them more acceptable to his lordship. Dr. Garth reassured him; he knew Lord Halifax very well, he said, and all Pope needed to do was to leave the passages as they were, wait a couple of months, and then go back to Lord Halifax, thank him for his kind criticisms, and read him the "corrected" passages. In due course Pope had another session with Lord Halifax, reading him the passages exactly as they had been. His lordship was delighted, and congratulated Pope on getting them absolutely right.

2 Pope's translation of Homer's *Iliad* and *Odyssey* offended the classical scholar Richard Bentley. Of Pope's *Iliad* he said, "It is a pretty poem, Mr. Pope, but you must not call it Homer."

3 Pope's father was a linen draper, and, although his family was respectable, it was by no means aristocratic. George II, alert to social distinctions, advised Lord Hervey, "You

ought not to write verses, 'tis beneath your rank; leave such work to little Mr. Pope; it is his trade."

4 When Pope was lying on his deathbed, the doctor assured him that his breathing was easier, his pulse steadier, and various other encouraging things. "Here am I," commented Pope to a friend, "dying of a hundred good symptoms."

POPE, Arthur Upham (1881–1969), *US eccentric authority on the art and archaeology of Iran (in his day Persia) and neighboring Arab cultures.*

1 Pope was single-minded in his intellectual interests. In 1943 he agreed to deliver the annual Lincoln's Day address at Cooper Union, New York, where Lincoln had once made an epochal speech. According to a *New Yorker* magazine account he spoke for about an hour and a half on his favorite topic, Middle Eastern cultures. At the very end, recalling his assigned subject, he discharged his obligation by stating: "Lincoln knew no Arabs, but he would have enjoyed meeting them, and they would have recognized him as a great sheik."

PORSON, Richard (1759–1808), *British classical scholar.*

1 Porson had an outstanding memory, first revealed during his schooldays at Eton. A classmate, as a practical joke, had borrowed his copy of Horace's *Odes,* artfully replacing it with a different text. As the Latin lesson began, Porson was asked to read and translate one of the odes. This he did without faltering, but the master, noticing that the boy appeared to be reading from the wrong side of the page, asked which edition he was using. Porson sheepishly handed the book to his master, who was amazed to find that he had just recited the Latin ode from memory while looking at an English version of Ovid.

2 Porson was once traveling in a stagecoach with a young Oxford student who, in an attempt to impress the ladies present, let slip a Greek quotation which he said was from Sophocles. The professor was not taken in by the young man's bluff and, pulling a pocket edition of Sophocles from the folds of his coat, challenged him to find the passage in question. Undeterred, the student said that he had made a mistake and that the quotation was in fact from Euripides. To the great amusement of the young ladies, Porson immediately produced a copy of Euripides from his pocket and issued the same challenge. In a last desperate attempt to save face, the young man announced with conviction that the passage was, of course, from Aeschylus. However, on seeing the inevitable copy of Aeschylus emerge from Porson's pocket, he finally admitted defeat. "Coachman!" he cried. "Let me out! There's a fellow here has the whole Bodleian Library in his pocket."

3 Porson arrived unexpectedly to stay with the portrait painter John Hoppner. Hoppner told him he could not offer much in the way of hospitality as Mrs. Hoppner was away and had taken with her the key to the wine closet. In the course of the evening Porson became increasingly restless, declared that he was sure Mrs. Hoppner would keep some wine for her own private enjoyment hidden somewhere in her bedroom, and asked that he might be allowed to search for it. With some irritation Hoppner agreed, and was greatly chagrined when Porson returned from his search clutching a bottle and pronouncing it to be the best gin he had tasted for a long time.

When Mrs. Hoppner returned, her husband rather angrily told her that Porson had found and consumed her hidden drink.

"Good heavens," she cried, "that was spirit of wine for the lamp!"

4 Porson was once asked for his opinion of the poetical works of his younger contemporary Robert Southey. "Your works will be read," he told him, "after Shakespeare and Milton are forgotten — and not till then."

5 A junior scholar once rashly suggested to Porson that they could collaborate. Porson applauded the notion: "Put in all I know and all you don't know, and it will make a great work."

6 On a walk together, Porson and a Trinitarian friend were discussing the nature of the Trinity. A buggy passed them with three men in it. "There," said the friend, "that's an illustration of the Trinity."

"No," said Porson, "you must show me one man in three buggies — if you can."

———— ∽ ————

POUSSIN, Nicolas (1594–1665), *French classical painter.*

1 Exasperated by his failure to produce a satisfactory depiction of the foam around the mouth of a spirited horse, Poussin dashed his sponge against the canvas. The effect thus created was exactly what he had been striving for so laboriously.

———— ∽ ————

PREVIN, André (1929–), *German-born conductor.*

1 After a rehearsal with the London Symphony Orchestra, Previn was sitting in the bar of the Westbury Hotel, having a drink with the soloist. He saw a young American composer whose work he had admired come into the room, and Previn beckoned him over and ordered him a drink. "I heard your orchestra a few nights ago," the composer said. "It sounded absolutely marvelous. It was the night the Beethoven Sixth was played in the first half."

"Oh, God," Previn replied, "that was the night Pollini was supposed to play the Fourth Piano Concerto in the second half, and he canceled, and we were stuck with one of those last-minute substitutions, that really appalling third-rate lady pianist. I'm sorry you had to suffer through that."

The young composer gave Previn a long and thoughtful look. "That's all right," he said coolly, "I didn't mind. That pianist is my wife."

2 To assess their suitability for adopting a Vietnamese orphan, a Miss Taylor, who had run a Saigon orphanage, stayed with the Previn family for a weekend. At breakfast on the first morning, she asked if she might have a bowl of cereal. Eager to please, Previn reached for the health-food cereal that his two small sons consumed with delight every morning and poured Miss Taylor a generous bowlful. While she ate, he held forth on the nutritional value of the cereal. Miss Taylor made no reply, however, until her bowl was empty. "To be quite honest," she admitted, "I'm not crazy about it." Previn's glance happened to fall on the jar from which he had served Miss Taylor. "I'm not surprised," he said slowly. "I've just made you eat a large dish of hamster food."

———— ∽ ————

PRINGLE, Sir John (1707–82), *Scottish physician.*

1 Ill health is the cause generally given for Pringle's resignation of the presidency of the Royal Society, but there is also another explanation. Benjamin Franklin's invention of the lightning rod had given him unique status as a scientist all over the Western world. George III, however, who found Franklin's revolutionary sentiments uncongenial, was eager to discredit his scientific achievements.

He therefore ordered that blunt ends should be substituted for the pointed ends on the lightning rods used on Kew Palace. Sir John Pringle is reputed to have remonstrated with the king, saying, "The laws of nature are not changeable at royal pleasure." For this undiplomatic remark he was compelled to forfeit his position in the Royal Society.

PROKOFIEV, Sergei (1891–1953), *Russian composer.*

1 One regular concert-goer at the Brussels Philharmonic always arrived at the concert hall armed with a sketchbook and pencil. She would sketch the guest artist during the performance and have the portrait autographed afterward. When Prokofiev's turn came, however, he refused to sign the picture, considering it a poor likeness. "It looks more like Furtwängler," he said. The usher who was acting as intermediary for the lady pleaded with the composer: "Please, Mr. Prokofiev. She is such a good subscriber. Please do this little thing for the Brussels Philharmonic!" Prokofiev looked at the picture again. "All right," he sighed, picking up his pen and writing with a flourish. The usher examined the "autograph" more closely. Prokofiev had signed the picture: "Furtwängler."

PUCCINI, Giacomo (1858–1924), *Italian opera composer.*

1 Puccini worked on *Turandot,* his greatest opera, for more than four years, and kept worrying that he would never finish it. In his anxiety he kept pestering his librettists to get their own part of the opera done. "If they wait much longer," he fretted, "I shall have to get them to put paper, pen, and inkpot in my tomb."

PULITZER, Joseph (1847–1911), *US newspaper baron, born in Hungary.*

1 Like most great newspaper and magazine owners, Pulitzer was mildly megalomaniacal. He felt the *World* "should be more powerful than the President." He even thought it might influence the inhabitants of other planets. He once considered erecting an advertising sign in New Jersey that would be visible on Mars, and was dissuaded only when one of his assistants asked, "What language shall we print it in?"

PUSHKIN, Alexander (1799–1837), *Russian poet, novelist, and playwright.*

1 Pushkin once listened to Gogol reading *Dead Souls.* He laughed heartily. Then suddenly his face grew grave and he exclaimed, "Oh God, how sad our Russia is!"

PUTNAM, Israel (1718–90), *US Revolutionary commander.*

1 During the French and Indian War Putnam was challenged to a duel by a British major whom he had insulted. Realizing that he would stand little chance in a duel with pistols, Putnam invited the major to his tent and suggested an alternative trial of honor. The two men were sitting on small powder kegs, into each of which Putnam had inserted a slow-burning fuse. The first to squirm or move from his seat would be the loser. As the fuses burned, the major showed increasing signs of anxiety, while Putnam continued to smoke his pipe with a casual air. Seeing the spectators gradually disappear from the tent to escape the impending explosion, the major finally leaped from his keg, acknowledging

Putnam as the victor. Only then did Putnam reveal that the kegs contained onions, not gunpowder.

——— ⌀ᴢ ———

PYLE, Ernest Taylor (1900–45), *US war correspondent.*

1 Reporting on the Normandy landings, Ernie Pyle always seemed to be there when the action was toughest, though without any parade of heroics. Entering Cherbourg, the correspondents found everything superficially calm, when suddenly a shell hit a tank only a few yards from them. When the men in the street stopped running and went back, they found Ernie Pyle taking down the names of those who had come out of the tank. By way of explanation he said, "They seemed to know me, so I had to stick around."

——— ⌀ᴢ ———

PYRRHUS (319–272 BC), *king of Epirus, in northwestern Greece (306–272 BC).*

1 In 279 BC the invading Greek forces under Pyrrhus met and defeated the Romans at the battle of Asculum in Apulia. The engagement, however, cost Pyrrhus many men, some of his closest associates, and all his baggage. One of the Greeks congratulated the king on his victory, to which he replied, "Another such victory and we are ruined." Hence the phrase "Pyrrhic victory" for one that costs the victor too high a price.

——— ⌀ᴢ ———

PYTHAGORAS (fl. 530 BC), *Greek philosopher born on Samos.*

1 Seeing a puppy being beaten one day, Pythagoras took pity, saying, "Stop, do not beat it; it is the soul of a friend which I recognized when I heard it crying out."

Q

QUAYLE, Dan (1947–), *US politician; vice president (1989–1993).*

1 President Bush's adviser, the fearless southern political strategist Lee Atwater, once said to Quayle, "You were the best rabbit we ever had. Let them chase you and they'll stay off the important things."

2 At a Thanksgiving festival in Virginia, Quayle said, "I suppose three important things certainly come to my mind that we want to say thank you. The first would be our family. Your family, my family — which is composed of an immediate family of a wife and three children, a larger family with grandparents and aunts and uncles. We all have our family, whichever that may be."

3 Speaking at a college graduation, Quayle managed to mangle the slogan of the United Negro College Fund ("A mind is a terrible thing to waste"), saying, "What a terrible thing it is to lose one's mind."

QUEENSBERRY, William Douglas, 4th Duke of (1724–1810), *British nobleman.*

1 Old Q was entertaining at his villa in Richmond, which had a magnificent view of the Thames River. Guest after guest admired the panorama until the duke burst out, "What is there to make so much of in the Thames? I am quite tired of it. Flow, flow, flow, always the same."

2 With advancing years Old Q became very infirm and spent much of his time at the porch or bow window of his London house, overlooking Piccadilly. In those days great households included a class of retainer called a "running footman," whose job was to run messages and errands and to clear a way through crowds for their employers. Applicants for the post of running footman in Old Q's establishment had to run a kind of trial up Piccadilly, dressed in full ducal livery, while Old Q himself watched from his vantage point.

One particular candidate ran so speedily that Old Q shouted down in delight, "You'll do very well for me."

"And your lordship's livery will do very well for me," replied the man, taking off at top speed, never to be seen again.

QUESNAY, François (1694–1774), *French economist and physician.*

1 Louis XV once asked Quesnay, who was originally the king's physician, what he would do if he were king. "Nothing," replied

Quesnay. "But then, who would govern?" asked Louis. "The laws," was the response.

———◦﹍◦———

QUIN, James (1693–1766), *British actor.*

1 William Warburton, bishop of Gloucester, was holding forth about royal prerogative, of which he was an ardent supporter. Quin tried to shut him up by asking him to spare his feelings, as he was a republican. "Perhaps I even think that the execution of Charles I might have been justified," he added. "Oh? By what law?" demanded Warburton. "By all the laws that he had left to the country," retorted Quin. The bishop replied that Charles would have been spared in a proper court of law, and in any case all the regicides had come to violent ends. "I would not advise your lordship to make use of *that* inference," said Quin, "for, if I am not mistaken, that was the case of the twelve apostles."

———◦﹍◦———

QUISENBERRY, Dan (1953–98), *US baseball player.*

1 The closer for the Royals had only one pitch in his repertory when he first began playing baseball: the sinker. After a game his catcher would say, "Way to mix 'em up." Quisenberry would reply, "Way to call 'em."

2 When his pitching was at the top of its form, Quisenberry was given a contract for a great deal of money. But eventually he began to lose power, and the Royals used him less and less. Once he asked the director of the Players' Association, Donald Fehr, what recourse he had if the Royals chose not to use him again. "Well," said Fehr, "you could always buy them."

R

RABELAIS, François (?1494–1553), *French friar, monk, physician, and writer.*

1 On the way to Paris one day, Rabelais found himself stranded at a small country inn with no money to pay his bill or to continue his journey. So he made up three small packets, labeled them "Poison for the King," "Poison for Monsieur," and "Poison for the Dauphin" and left them where the landlord of the inn was sure to find them. That patriotic citizen informed the police, who promptly arrested Rabelais and hauled him off to Paris. When the packets were examined and found to be empty, Rabelais explained his subterfuge and was set free, having accomplished his journey at no expense to himself.

2 A short time before Rabelais died, he put on a domino (cloak and mask) and was seen sitting by his bed in this unusual garb. Reproached for being so frivolous at this dark and serious hour, he quipped in Latin, *"Beati qui in Domino moriuntur"* (Blessed are they who die in the Lord — or — in a domino).

RACHEL (1820–58), *French actress.*

1 One of Rachel's numerous lovers was François d'Orléans, Prince de Joinville, third son of Louis-Philippe. He sent her his visiting card on which he had written: *"Où? — quand? — combien?"* (Where? — when? — how much?) Rachel, equally businesslike, scrawled: *"Chez toi — ce soir — pour rien"* (Your place — tonight — free of charge) and sent the card back. Their affair lasted for seven or eight years.

2 Because of her itinerant upbringing Rachel was virtually uneducated, and to the end of her life her letters remained full of errors in spelling and grammar. Rachel was quite aware of her failings. When an admirer begged her for *"un bel autographe"* (a nice autograph), she replied, *"Un bel autographe avec ou sans orthographe?"* (A nice autograph — with or without proper spelling?)

3 Despite her lack of education, Rachel excelled at the interpretation of the classical French heroines in the tragedies of Racine and Corneille, restoring their plays to the repertoire of the Comédie-Française. Someone once pompously congratulated her on saving the French language. She answered, "Clever of me, isn't it, seeing that I never learned it."

4 Rachel was notorious for her avarice and for her guile at persuading people to give her presents. Dining at the Comte Duchâtel's, she pointedly admired the great silver centerpiece on the table. The count, completely un-

der her spell, said he would be happy to give it to her. Rachel accepted eagerly, but was a little nervous that the count might change his mind. She mentioned that she had come to the dinner in a cab. The count offered her his carriage to take her home. "Indeed," said Rachel, "that will suit me very well, as there will then be no danger of my being robbed of your gift, which I had better take with me." The count bowed. "With pleasure," he said, "but you *will* send my carriage back, won't you?"

5 Boasted Rachel after a successful opening night: "*Mon dieu!* When I came out on the stage the audience simply sat there open-mouthed."

"Nonsense!" snapped a fellow actress. "They never all yawn at once."

———— ∞ ————

RACHMANINOFF, Sergei (1873–1943), *Russian composer, pianist, and conductor.*

1 Artur Rubinstein gave a dinner party in honor of Rachmaninoff, in the course of which the composer mentioned that he thought the Grieg piano concerto the greatest ever written. Rubinstein said that he had just recorded it. Rachmaninoff insisted on hearing the recording then and there. During coffee, Rubinstein put on the proofs of the record and Rachmaninoff, closing his eyes, settled down to listen. He listened right through without saying a word. At the end of the concerto he opened his eyes and said, "Piano out of tune."

2 Rachmaninoff, taken ill in the middle of a concert tour, was admitted to a hospital in Los Angeles, where cancer was diagnosed. Knowing he was dying, the pianist looked at his hands and murmured, "My dear hands. Farewell, my poor hands."

———— ∞ ————

RACINE, Jean (1639–99), *French dramatist.*

1 The actress Marie Champmêlé once asked Racine from what source he had drawn his religious drama *Athalie*. "From the Old Testament," he replied. "Really?" said the actress. "From the Old Testament? I always thought there was a new one."

———— ∞ ————

RAFT, George (1895–1980), *US film actor.*

1 George Raft acquired and disposed of about $10 million in the course of his career. "Part of the loot went for gambling," he later explained, "part for horses, and part for women. The rest I spent foolishly."

———— ∞ ————

RAGLAN, FitzRoy James Henry Somerset, 1st Baron (1788–1855), *British field marshal.*

1 At the close of the battle of Waterloo Raglan was standing beside Wellington when a bullet shattered his right elbow. The arm had to be amputated, an operation Raglan bore without a murmur, but as the limb was being taken away for disposal he cried out, "Don't carry away that arm till I have taken off my ring." The arm was brought back, and Raglan retrieved a ring that his wife had given him.

———— ∞ ————

RAINIER III [Rainier Louis Henri Maxence Bertrand de Grimaldi] (1923–), *prince of Monaco (1949–).*

1 On a tour of the Astrodome, a huge sports stadium covering some nine acres of land in Houston, Texas, Prince Rainier was asked, "How would you like to have the Astrodome in Monaco?"

"Marvelous," he replied. "Then we could be the world's only indoor country."

———— ∞ ————

RALEIGH, Sir Walter (?1552–1618), *British soldier, explorer, and writer.*

1 Although primarily a man of action, the courtly Raleigh exemplified the ideal of the Renaissance gentleman. There is an old tradition that he first caught the attention of Queen Elizabeth sometime in 1581 when she was walking along a muddy path. As she hesitated in front of a particularly large puddle, Raleigh sprang forward and, taking off his new plush cloak, laid it on the ground for his sovereign to step upon.

2 At the outset of his career as courtier Raleigh scratched with a diamond the following words on a window of the royal palace: "Fain would I climb, yet fear I to fall." The queen, as he had intended, read the line. She completed the couplet: "If thy heart fail thee, climb not at all."

3 Raleigh brought back tobacco from the New World and introduced smoking to Britain. The novelty caused much comment and considerable discussion pro and con. Raleigh was once enjoying a pipe when his servant, seeing his master enveloped in clouds of smoke, thought that he must be on fire, and quickly emptied a bowl of water over Raleigh's head.

4 (John Aubrey recounts an incident that led to Raleigh's temporary loss of favor with Queen Elizabeth.)

"He loved a wench well; and one time getting one of the Maids of Honour up against a tree in a wood ('twas his first lady) who seemed at first boarding to be something fearful of her honour, and modest, she cried, 'Sweet Sir Walter, what do you me ask? Will you undo me? Nay, sweet Sir Walter! Sweet Sir Walter! Sir Walter!' At last, as the danger and the pleasure at the same time grew higher, she cried in the ecstasy, 'Swisser Swatter, Swisser Swatter!' She proved with child, and I doubt not but this hero took care of them both, as also that the product was more than an ordinary mortal."

5 Like his father, Raleigh's eldest son and namesake was quick-tempered and a womanizer. At a dinner in great company young Walter, sitting next to his father, began to tell a discreditable anecdote, about how he had visited a whore and she had refused to lie with him because "your father lay with me but an hour ago."

Incensed and embarrassed, Raleigh hit young Walter across the face. The young man was wild, but not so wicked as to strike his father. So he turned to the man sitting on his other side and hit him, saying as he did so, "Box about; it will come to my father anon."

6 In his role as Elizabeth's favorite Raleigh was quick to seek benefits and rewards. The queen once rebuked him mildly for his rapacity, saying, "When will you cease to be a beggar?"

"When you cease to be a benefactress, ma'am," replied Raleigh.

7 The sentence of death on Raleigh was confirmed on October 28, 1618, with the execution set for the following morning. As Raleigh was led back to prison from the tribunal at Westminster, he spied an old acquaintance, Sir Hugh Beeston, whom he greeted cheerfully. "You will come tomorrow?" he asked Beeston. "But I do not know how you will manage to get a place. For my own part I am sure of one, but you will have to shift for yourself."

8 Raleigh's courage and dignity on the scaffold were part of the legend that grew up around him as a martyr to the unpopular pro-Spanish policy of James I. He tested the ax's edge, saying, "It is a sharp remedy, but a sure one for all ills." As he laid his head on the

block, someone protested that it should be placed so that his head should point toward the east. "What matter how the head lie, so the heart be right?" said Raleigh.

RAMANUJAN, Srinivasa (1887–1920), *Indian mathematician.*

1 (J. E. Littlewood, a mathematician who collaborated with Hardy, recounts a conversation with Ramanujan.)

"I remember once going to see him when he was lying ill at Putney. I had ridden in taxicab number 1729, and remarked that the number seemed to me rather a dull one, and that I hoped it was not an unfavorable omen. 'No,' he replied, 'it is a very interesting number; it is the smallest number expressible as the sum of two cubes in two different ways.'"

RAMSEY, Alice Huyler (1886–1983).

1 Ramsey was the first woman (though not the first person) to drive across the country, from San Francisco to New York. She did this in 1909, when good roads were all but unknown. "Good driving has nothing to do with sex," she said. "It's all above the collar."

RAPHAEL [Raffaello Sanzio] (1483–1520), *Italian artist and architect.*

1 A couple of cardinals, watching Raphael at work on his Vatican frescoes, annoyed the artist by keeping up a stream of ill-informed criticism. "The face of the apostle Paul is far too red," complained one. "He blushes to see into whose hands the church has fallen," said Raphael.

RATHER, Dan (1931–), *US journalist.*

1 When Rather covered a summit meeting between Reagan and Gorbachev, he appeared on television wearing an open-necked shirt that showed his hairy chest. A gossip columnist quipped, "One good thing came out of the summit. We got to see that Dan Rather is definitely a he-man and no wimp."

RAYNAL, Abbé Guillaume Thomas François (1713–96), *French historian.*

1 The Abbé Raynal and the Abbé Galiani were both incessant talkers. A friend decided to amuse himself by inviting them together to a gathering at his house. Abbé Galiani seized the first opening and took over the conversation so completely that no one, not even the Abbé Raynal, could get a word in edgewise. After listening in growing frustration, Raynal turned to his host and muttered, *"S'il crache, il est perdu"* (If he spits, he's lost).

Fanny Ronalds was a nineteenth-century society beauty and singer. Leonard Jerome, a Wall Street magnate, was one of her most ardent admirers, financing her performance as a singer and being frequently seen out driving with her. At a ball she came unexpectedly face to face with Jerome's wife, Clara. As Mrs. Ronalds held out her hand, the spectators held their breath, wondering how Mrs. Jerome would react to meeting the lady with whom her husband's name was so publicly linked. Mrs. Jerome took her rival's hand and said, "I don't blame you. I know how irresistible he is."

— ANITA LESLIE,
The Remarkable Mr. Jerome

REAGAN, Nancy (1921–), *wife of Ronald Reagan, 40th President of the United States (1981–89).*

1 The 1980 presidential elections were thought to be a very close call; no one would predict whether Jimmy Carter or Ronald Reagan would be the winner. On the evening of the election both of the Reagans had taken baths and were standing wrapped in towels when they heard the news that Carter was conceding the election — well in advance of the polls' closing in California. Nancy recalled that moment, as the couple stood staring at each other, dripping wet. "Is this really the way it is supposed to be?" she exclaimed to her husband.

2 As she visited a school, she was asked how she liked being married to the President of the United States. "Fine," was her reply, "as long as the president is Ronald Reagan."

3 Nancy worried a great deal during the time her husband was recuperating in the hospital from John Hinckley's assassination attempt. When unthinking friends asked about her method for losing weight, assuming she was trying a new diet, she said, "Just have your husband go into politics."

4 The great pianist Vladimir Horowitz gave a performance at the White House, after which Ronald Reagan rose to thank him. Somehow Nancy's chair slipped off the dais, and she fell into a row of decorative flowers. When she called out that she was fine and joked that she just wanted to liven up the affair, her husband quipped, "Honey, I told you to do it only if I didn't get any applause."

5 Despite the constant criticism of her style, Nancy had a sense of humor about her reputation as a lover of high style. When she saw a picture of herself that had been circulating showing her as Queen Nancy, she said,

"Now that's silly, I'd never wear a crown — it musses up your hair."

———— ✂ ————

REAGAN, Ronald (1911–), *US film actor and politician; 40th President of the United States (1981–89).*

1 As a young radio announcer in Des Moines, Iowa, Reagan once interviewed the famed evangelist Aimee Semple McPherson, who spoke with passion about her need to find adequate financial support for her revival meetings. The interview ended early, and Reagan had four minutes to fill. He asked that appropriate music be played, expecting a hymn or a stirring choral piece. Instead, and Reagan claimed it was completely by accident, the station played the then-wildly popular song "Minnie the Moocher."

2 During a student demonstration in the 1960s Reagan's limousine was hemmed in by a crowd of chanting demonstrators waving placards. The demonstrators were chanting, "We are the future." Reagan scribbled on a piece of paper and held it up to the window so they could read the words: "I'll sell my bonds."

3 Reagan loved to discuss politics, but when he finally decided to run for governor of California, producer Jack Warner, who had worked with him in many movies, was incredulous. "No, no, no!" he cried. "Jimmy Stewart for governor — Reagan for best friend."

4 In the early 1970s, Reagan was already a fiscal conservative, a theme he would evoke over and over throughout the eight years of his presidency. In one of his speeches he said, "Do you remember back in the days when you thought that nothing could replace the dollar? Today, it practically has."

5 Reagan often joked about his age. At a party honoring the bicentennial of the U.S.S. *Constitution,* he joked, "History is no easy subject. Even in my day it wasn't, and we had so much less to learn then."

6 Just before Reagan gave his speech at the Republican national convention accepting the 1980 presidential nomination, a nomination he had sought with fervor for years, Reagan quipped, "My first thrill tonight was to find myself, for the first time in a long time, in a movie in prime time."

7 Reagan had been casual friends with fellow actor Richard Widmark for many years. Widmark enjoyed his company; but when Reagan ran for President in 1980, Widmark voted for his opponent, Jimmy Carter. Surprised reporters, aware they had an acquaintance, were sure he had voted for his friend, but Widmark denied it: "Of course not. I said, I've known him for a long time."

8 Shortly after his election to the presidency, a group of CEOs was being addressed by journalist Art Buchwald. He asked them how many had voted for Reagan. Almost every hand was raised. "And how many here would let him be CEO of your company?" Not one hand was raised.

9 In March 1981 a would-be assassin fired several shots at the President and his party as they left a Washington hotel. Reagan was taken to the hospital with a serious chest wound that needed emergency surgery. As he was wheeled into the operating theater he smiled, looked around at the team of surgeons, and said, "Please assure me that you are all Republicans!"

10 After leaving the hospital upon recovering from being shot, he thanked the doctors at George Washington University Hospital who had saved his life. "If I'd had this much at-

tention in Hollywood, I'd have stayed there," he said.

11 Even the Democrats were impressed by Reagan's first televised budget speech, in which he used a handful of small change to illustrate the current value of the dollar. "It takes an actor to do that," admitted one of his rivals. "Carter would have emphasized all the wrong words. Ford would have fumbled and dropped the cash. Nixon would have pocketed it."

12 Reagan, who built his career on anti-Communism, once quipped, "The Soviet Union would remain a one-party state even if an opposition party were permitted, because everyone would join that party."

13 On April 6, 1984, Reagan ended a foreign policy address at Georgetown University by recalling his entrance to a recent state dinner for François Mitterrand: "Mrs. Mitterrand and I started through the tables, the butler leading us through the people, and suddenly Mrs. Mitterrand stopped. She calmly turned her head and said something to me in French, which unfortunately I did not understand. And the butler was motioning for us to come on, and I motioned to her that we should go forward, that we were to go to the other side of the room. And again, very calmly, she made her statement to me." An interpreter finally explained to Mr. Reagan that Madame Mitterrand was telling him he was standing on her gown.

14 At a Salute to Congress Dinner in the early 1980s, Reagan was asked to talk about age. "I can define middle-aged," he said. "That's when you're faced with two temptations and you choose the one that'll get you home at nine o'clock."

15 In 1983 Reagan's popularity took a dip, mostly due to a rise in unemployment. One of his advisers came to him with the bad

polling data, announcing that for the first time since he took office, a majority of Americans disapproved of his job performance. Reagan thought for a moment, then said, "I know what we can do. I'll just have to go and get shot again."

16 Reagan disliked wearing his bullet-proof vest because he felt it made him look fat. A few years after Hinckley's assassination attempt he was in full swing delivering his usual stump speech. "We can make America stronger, not just economically and militarily, but also morally and spiritually. We can make our beloved country the source of all the dreams and the opportunities that she was — " at which point a balloon exploded, making a sound like a gunshot. Reagan paused only to say, "Missed me," and resumed in midsentence the remainder of his speech.

17 Reagan's answers to questions posed during his press conferences were convoluted and often factually in error. But he continued to go through the exercise with good humor. When he was asked by the White House correspondents if anything could be done to improve his answers, he responded, "Yes, ask better questions."

18 Reagan was unable to remember the name of the Japanese prime minister, whom he was about to meet for the first time. Undaunted, his staff quickly supplied him with a mnemonic, which Reagan used to flawlessly address the host: "You can knock a Panasonic, but you can't Nakasone."

19 Never known as a dedicated worker, Reagan was often criticized for his lack of focus and his shaky grasp of issues. But he clearly relished the role of President and sometimes made fun of his own perceived indolence, saying, "It's true hard work never killed anybody, but I figure, why take the chance?"

20 To a congressional group that had gathered shortly before the election of 1988, Reagan said, "Just for the record, I'm speaking in jest here. Of course, some of you think I've been doing that for eight years."

21 Many Republicans in Congress began proposing that the Constitution be changed to allow the enormously popular President to run for a third term. Realistically the movement lost steam, but many, including perhaps Reagan, were wistful about the possibility. Not long after he left office Reagan appeared at a journalists' dinner and discussed the most recent crop of presidential candidates. "I heard one say that what this country needed was a President for the nineties," he said. "I was set to run again. I thought he said a President in his nineties."

22 Andrei Voznesensky paid a call to Reagan at the White House, during which he asked the President which Russian author had influenced him the most — Dostoevsky, Tolstoy, or Chekhov. Reagan paused for a very long time, then said, "When I was young, I studied the classics of world literature." When Voznesensky later asked why Reagan hadn't given him a clear answer, he was told, "He probably thought one of them was a Commie."

23 As the oldest President to serve, Reagan had a natural source of inspiration for his genial quips about his longevity. To one group of reporters he once said, "When I go in for a physical, they no longer ask how old I am. They just carbon-date me." And at another gathering he noted, "Of course, when you're my age, everything brings back memories — even other memories."

REDGRAVE, Sir Michael (1908–85), *British stage actor, father of actresses Lynn and Vanessa.*

1 During one play his scene called for him to be left onstage with one attendant as he prepared to commit suicide. His line was to be "Bring me a pint of port and a pistol." With the audience in a high state of tension, Redgrave called, "Bring me a pint of piss and a portal." Trying to help the situation, the young actor who played the attendant asked, "A pint of *piss*, my lord?" "Aye," responded a furious Redgrave, "*and* a portal."

———— ⌘ ————

REED, Thomas Brackett (1839–1902), *US lawyer and politician.*

1 Speaker Reed was chatting with lawyer and diplomat Joseph H. Choate and a senator of the time. Choate said pompously, "I have not drunk whiskey, played cards for money, or attended a horse race in twenty-eight years." The senator said admiringly, "I wish I could say that!" Remarked Reed: "Well, why don't you? Choate said it."

2 In the course of debate when Reed was Speaker, William M. Springer of Illinois quoted Henry Clay's famous "I had rather be right than be president." In an undertone Reed interjected, "The gentleman need not worry, for he will never be either."

———— ⌘ ————

REGER, Max (1873–1916), *German composer and organist.*

1 After playing the piano part in Schubert's "Trout" Quintet, Max Reger received a basket of trout from an admirer. Reger wrote to thank the sender, mentioning casually that his next concert program was to include Haydn's "Minuet of the Ox."

2 After receiving a bad review from Munich critic Rudolf Louis, Reger wrote to him: "I am sitting in the smallest room of my house. I have your review before me. In a moment it will be behind me."

———— ⌘ ————

REHAN, Ada (1860–1916), *US actress, born in Ireland.*

1 Miss Rehan was playing opposite an inexperienced young actor in a romantic comedy. During one scene the young hero asks the heroine a vital question and she pauses to consider her answer. The hero's next line should have been: "You don't reply," but at this point the young actor lost his nerve and dried up. "You don't reply . . . you don't reply," came a hoarse whisper from the wings. "How the hell can I," retorted the young actor impatiently, "when I don't know what to say?"

———— ⌘ ————

REINHARDT, Max (1873–1943), *Austrian theater director.*

1 A clever young man was instructing Reinhardt in the art of producing Shakespeare: "No lavish spectacle, no gorgeous scenery, just simple black curtains; that's how it should be done. So much more artistic." Reinhardt nodded. "Also much easier," he said.

———— ⌘ ————

REISENAUER, Alfred (1863–1907), *German pianist, a pupil of Liszt.*

1 "Reisenauer . . . had given a concert at the palace of some German princeling. The next day, the *Hofmarschall* came to his hotel on behalf of the grand duke and offered him the choice of either 1,000 marks or the Order of the Bear or the Falcon, or something like

that. 'What would they charge for such a medal in shops?' asked the artist. 'Oh, I think twenty marks,' replied the courtier. 'Well,' said Reisenauer, 'I will accept the medal and nine hundred and eighty marks.'"

RENOIR, Pierre-Auguste (1841–1919), *French Impressionist painter.*

1 Renoir was once asked how he managed to produce such natural flesh tints and shapely forms in his nude paintings. "I just keep painting till I feel like pinching," he replied. "Then I know it's right."

2 When both were in their seventies, Renoir and sculptor Aristide Maillol exchanged views on art. Maillol said, "My ambition is to be able to sculpt a young girl between sixteen and seventeen, in accord with my ideal conception of the figure." "And mine," said Renoir, "is to be able to paint a white napkin."

3 Renoir continued painting, magnificently, for years after he was crippled by arthritis; the brush had to be strapped to his arm. "You don't need your hand to paint," he said.

4 When Renoir became so old and crippled that he could not hold a brush, he took to modeling nudes in clay for his own entertainment. Auguste Rodin, the sculptor, asked why he did not stick to painting. Renoir replied gently, "I am too old to paint. I must do something easier."

REUTHER, Walter (1907–70), *US labor leader.*

1 Reuther once visited an auto factory in Cleveland. A young manager talked on and on about a new process they had for automating the line. It would be, he said, highly robotized, and it would work far more efficiently and cheaply than the current line. On and on he went, describing the glory of the robots.

"And tell me," Reuther finally interrupted, "these wonderful new robots — will they go out and buy cars from your company?"

Fanny Ronalds crowned her artistic and social triumphs by giving a grand ball to which only the cream of New York society was invited. The hostess's dress in her role as the spirit of music was one of the highlights of an evening in which no expense was spared. Some twenty years later two of Mrs. Ronalds's most devoted beaux were recalling those days. "Do you remember Fanny's celebrated ball?" Leonard Jerome asked August Belmont. "I most certainly do," Belmont replied. "After all, I paid for it." There was a slight pause. "Why, how very strange," said Jerome. "So did I."

— ANITA LESLIE,
The Remarkable Mr. Jerome

REYNOLDS, Burt (1936–), *US film actor.*

1 After Sean Connery temporarily stopped participating in the James Bond movies, wanting a change, George Lazenby substituted for the great spy in one movie, *On Her Majesty's Secret Service,* which was a dud. One day director Guy Hamilton and producer Albert Broccoli spotted a young actor on television and were immediately sure they had found the next James Bond. It was Reynolds. But a casting director talked them out of contacting him, saying, "He's just a stunt guy — he's going nowhere at all."

2 An early role for Reynolds was in the television show *Riverboat.* One afternoon Reynolds, on a break from the set, wandered across the Universal lot and into the filming of *Inherit the Wind,* where he watched Spencer Tracy acting as Clarence Darrow without seeming to act at all. During a quiet

moment Tracy asked if Reynolds was an actor, and said, "It's a great profession, as long as nobody ever catches you at it."

3 The bane of Reynolds's young acting career was to be mistaken, as he often was, for Marlon Brando. In an airport one day a couple approached him and greeted him as Marlon Brando. When Reynolds denied being Brando, the couple conferred together for a moment, then insisted he was the star of *On the Waterfront*. "Damn it to hell, lady, I am not Brando!" The woman beamed as she said, "Ah, now I know for sure that you *are* Brando."

———— ✑ ————

REYNOLDS, Sir Joshua (1723–92), *English portrait painter.*

1 The Scottish painter Robert Barber was out sketching on Carlton Hill, Edinburgh. He noticed a curious effect caused by the prevailing atmospheric conditions: it was as if the entire view were contained within a cylinder. Inspired with the idea of reproducing this effect artistically, he made a model of a panorama and showed it to Reynolds. The great artist was skeptical. If Barber were able to put his idea into practice, said Sir Joshua, he would get out of his bed in the middle of the night to see the outcome. Barber persevered and set up his first panorama in a house in Leicester Square, London, not far from Sir Joshua's own residence. Reynolds carried out his promise. He arrived to view the panorama wearing his dressing gown and slippers.

———— ✑ ————

RHODES, Cecil John (1853–1902), *South African statesman and financier.*

1 Rhodes was a stickler for correct dress and behavior, but not at the expense of someone else's feelings. A young man invited to dine with him in Kimberley arrived by train and had to go directly to Rhodes's house in his travel-stained clothes. Here he was appalled to find the other guests already assembled, wearing full evening dress. Feeling very uncomfortable, he waited with the rest of the company for their host to appear. After what seemed a long time, Rhodes finally appeared, in a shabby old blue suit. The young man later learned that when he arrived Rhodes had been dressed in evening clothes and was about to welcome his guests. Told of the traveler's dilemma, Rhodes had at once returned to his room and put on an old suit.

2 When asked why he had come to South Africa, Rhodes replied that there was some truth in the reasons his friends usually ascribed to him — love of adventure or on account of his health. But, he confided, "The real fact is that I could no longer stand English eternal cold mutton."

3 Rhodes died from heart disease at a low ebb in his fortunes, beset by personal scandals and discredited by the tragedy of the Boer War, which his own misjudgments and policies had helped to foment. Lewis Michell, who was at his bedside in Rhodes's cottage at Muizenberg, near Cape Town, heard the dying man murmur, "So little done, so much to do."

4 The distribution of Rhodes's vast fortune under the terms of his will, with much of the money directed toward the setting up of the Rhodes scholarships, caused some resentment in the immediate family. "Well, there it is," said his brother Arthur. "It seems to me I shall have to win a scholarship."

———— ✑ ————

RICHARD I (1157–99), *king of England (1189–99), known as Richard Coeur de Lion (the Lionheart).*

1 When Richard was captured by the Austrians, it was some time before anyone in England discovered where he was. A minstrel called Blondel searched for his master throughout Europe in vain. Returning home through Austria, however, he learned that in an ancient stronghold near Linz there was a closely guarded prisoner whose identity no one knew. Blondel, suspecting the mysterious captive was his master, went to the castle but was unable to catch a glimpse of the prisoner. He eventually located a tiny barred window, high up on the castle wall, which he thought was the prisoner's cell. Under this window he sang the first couplet of a troubadour's song, the first part of which had been composed by himself and the second by Richard. From the window a voice responded with the second part, and Blondel knew that he had found his master.

2 Richard I was once warned by an eminent preacher that he would be severely punished by God if he did not soon marry off his three daughters. The king protested that he had no daughters, to which the priest replied, "Your Majesty has three — ambition, avarice, and luxury. Get rid of them as fast as possible, else assuredly some great misfortune will be the consequence."

"If it must be so," replied Richard contemptuously, "then I give my ambition to the templars, my avarice to the monks, and my luxury to the prelates."

———— ❧ ————

RICHARDSON, Sir Ralph (1902–82), *British actor.*

1 Ralph Richardson seemed destined to have bad luck at the home of his friends, Vivien Leigh and Laurence Olivier. At a house-warming for the couple's first home in Chelsea, Richardson brought along some fireworks to set off in the tiny backyard in celebration. He lit the first (and largest) one, but instead of soaring into the London skies, it shot straight through the open patio windows into the dining room, burned up the curtains, and set the cornice ablaze. Vivien Leigh was not amused.

Some years later, Richardson and his wife were invited to the Oliviers' new home, Notley Abbey. Recalling the disaster of the fireworks, they promised each other to be exceedingly careful. All went well at first. After dinner, Olivier mentioned that the medieval monks who had owned the abbey had left some interesting paintings on the roof beams; would anyone like to see them? The ladies declined, but Richardson and Olivier, armed with flashlights, went up to the attics. A few minutes later there came an anguished cry and a fearful crash. The women rushed upstairs to find Richardson on the bed in the main guestroom, dust and plaster everywhere, and a jagged hole in the ceiling. In his enthusiasm over the paintings, Richardson had not noticed that the attic floor was unboarded, had stepped backward from a rafter, and, like the firework through the patio door, shot straight down through the ceiling.

———— ❧ ————

RICHELIEU, Armand-Emmanuel du Plessis, Duc de (1766–1822), *French statesman.*

1 Married at fifteen to a deformed girl three years his junior, Richelieu never had more than a formal relationship with his wife. The duchess inevitably sought her consolation elsewhere. Coming upon her *flagrante delicto*, Richelieu rebuked her: "Madame, you must really be more careful. Suppose it had been someone else who found you like this."

2 Richelieu and his officers were planning a campaign. "We shall cross the river at this point," said one of the officers, placing his finger on the map. "Excellent, sir," remarked Richelieu, "but your finger is not a bridge."

3 When Richelieu learned an old, rich, and stupid widow of his acquaintance had died the previous day, his only comment was, "What a pity! She would have been a fine catch the day before that."

———— ✿ ————

RICHTER, Hans (1843–1916), *Hungarian conductor.*

1 An orchestra player who had yearned to try his hand at conducting finally realized his ambition. As he left the podium, he observed to Richter, "You know, this conducting business is really very straightforward."

"Ssh!" said Richter. "I beg you, don't give us away!"

2 Richter once lost his temper (and, temporarily, his command of the English language) with an incompetent second flutist at Covent Garden. "Your damned nonsense can I stand twice or once," he roared, "but sometimes always, by God, never."

———— ✿ ————

RICKEY, Branch (1881–1965), *US baseball executive.*

1 A former catcher and the inventor of the farm-team system for the Cardinals in the 1920s, Rickey was determined to economize with his new team, the Dodgers. Once he sent a telegram to Bobby Brager, manager of the Dodgers' Fort Worth farm team, asking, "Do you need a shortstop or can you go with your present infield." Brager wired back one word: "Yes." When Rickey sent another message, saying, "Yes, what?" Brager's reply was, "Yes sir!"

2 Near the end of his life Rickey was interviewed by *Sports Illustrated* about his life and career in the sport. He held up a baseball and looked at it for a moment, then said carefully, "This ball — this symbol. Is it worth a man's whole life?"

———— ✿ ————

RIGAUD, Hyacinthe (1659–1743), *French painter.*

1 A heavily made-up lady was having her portrait painted by Rigaud. She complained that his colors were much too bright. "We buy them at the same shop, madame," retorted the artist.

———— ✿ ————

RILEY, James Whitcomb (1849–1916), *US versifier, known as the "Hoosier poet."*

1 Riley's Washington landlady told the poet one day of the sad fate of her neighbor's cook. Having worked for the family for many years, the unfortunate woman had fallen asleep over her stove and burned to death. An appropriate epitaph sprang immediately to Riley's lips: "Well done, good and faithful servant."

2 Standing on a curb directly in front of a saloon, he asked a policeman who was walking by where was the nearest place a man could buy a drink. When the policeman pointed out the saloon not two steps away, Riley asked, "Are you sure it's the nearest?"

———— ✿ ————

RIVAROL, Antoine de (1753–1801), *French writer and wit.*

1 A bitter and merciless critic of others, who had himself produced nothing, was attacking his usual targets. Rivarol said to him, "It is a great advantage to have produced nothing, but you must not abuse it."

———cℵ∂———

RIVERA, Antonio (d. 1936), *Spanish National-ist hero, known as "the Angel of the Alcázar."*

1 Antonio Rivera, son of a former mayor of Toledo, took refuge with other Nationalists in the Alcázar in the summer of 1936 at the start of the famous siege during the Spanish Civil War. As a pacifist, the youth refused at first to help defend the ancient stronghold, and was put on latrine duty. When the situa-tion of the besieged became more desperate, he decided that it would not be inconsistent with his principles to aid in the defense, pro-vided that he did not kill in hatred. He was assigned the position of loader to a heavy machine gun. It was said that he would give the signal to fire with the words: *"Tirad — pero sin odio"* (Fire — without hatred).

———cℵ∂———

RIZZUTO, Phil (1918–), *US sports figure.*

1 "While broadcasting a Yankee game Rizzuto was informed that Pope Paul VI had died. He commented on the air, 'Well, that kind of puts the damper on even a Yankee win.'"

———cℵ∂———

ROBERT I [Robert the Bruce] (1274–1329), *king of Scotland (1306–29).*

1 There are many popular stories and legends about Robert the Bruce and his daring deeds against the English oppressors. One, made famous by Walter Scott, concerns the period when Robert the Bruce was on the run from the troops of Edward I. Hiding in a cave, and suffering from deep despondency and uncer-tainty as to what he ought to do next, he watched a small spider spinning its web, try-ing and failing time and time again to secure it properly. The fugitive king read the spider's persistence and its eventual success as a para-

ble for himself: he must not be discouraged by his failures, but go out and continue the struggle until he achieved the liberation of his country.

———cℵ∂———

ROBERT, Léopold (1794–1835), *Swiss painter and etcher.*

1 Léopold Robert, brought up in a pious household, was himself highly moral. In 1827, however, he painted two pictures, enti-tled *Two Girls Disrobing for Their Bath,* that offended by their "freedom." Robert de-fended himself by saying that, although ordi-narily all his figures were clothed from head to foot, this time he had wanted to choose a different subject. He went on, "But I assure you that I have placed the figures in a com-pletely secluded spot so that they would not possibly encounter any observation from cu-rious onlookers."

———cℵ∂———

ROBINSON, Edwin Arlington (1869–1935), *US poet.*

1 Robinson used to spend his summers at the MacDowell Colony near Peterborough, New Hampshire. Arriving at breakfast one morn-ing, he found the writer Nancy Byrd Turner and a new member of the colony already seated at his table. "This is Mr. Robinson," said Nancy Byrd Turner to her companion. "Robinson! Not E. A. Robinson — not *the* Mr. Robinson?" gushed the other woman. There followed a long, uncomfortable pause, then Robinson said, "*A* Mr. Robinson."

2 In 1905 one of President Theodore Roo-sevelt's sons brought to his father's attention a book of poems by Robinson, *The Children of the Night.* Impressed, Roosevelt created in the New York Custom House a sinecure for the virtually destitute poet. "I expect you to

think poetry first and customs second," he told Robinson when he took up the post.

{Robinson was required only to open his desk, read the morning newspaper, close his desk, and leave the newspaper on his chair as proof that he had turned up at the office. This lasted four years, during which time Robinson established himself as a poet. When Taft became President and intimated that Robinson would have to put in a full day's work, the poet resigned.}

3 At the MacDowell Colony a young poet often threatened to kill himself and liked to mope about, hoping for attention. One day after lunch the poet went outside and lay down, swearing to stay there until he starved to death. A group of writers gathered round, offering help, but the poet lay still on the grass. Robinson came out, looked him over for a long time, then said, "The ants will get him."

4 A very shy man, Robinson found himself tongue-tied around women. One day he walked into the village of Peterborough with a young woman, saying as they left, "I'm afraid I'm not going to be able to say anything." Ten minutes later, he said, "I'm not saying anything." And upon their return to the MacDowell Colony, he said, "Well, I don't seem to have said anything."

ROBINSON, Jackie (1919–72), *US baseball player.*

1 On the day of his first appearance with the Dodgers, Robinson kissed his wife good-bye at their hotel before setting out. "If you come down to Ebbets Field today," he said, "you won't have any trouble recognizing me." He paused for a moment, then added, "My number's forty-two."

ROCHE, Sir Boyle (1743–1807), *Irish politician.*

1 Sir Boyle Roche was well known in Parliament and beyond for his extraordinary "bulls," or Irishisms, some of which are preserved in the records of parliamentary proceedings. He was an ardent advocate of the union of England and Ireland in 1800 and declared that his love for the two countries was so great that he would like to see "the two sisters embrace like one brother."

2 John Philpot Curran took the opposite view to Roche's on the union of England and Ireland, and they often clashed in parliamentary debates on the subject. Replying to some aspersion, Curran proclaimed that he needed no help from anyone but was well able to be "the guardian of my own honor." "Indeed," commented Sir Boyle Roche, "why, I always thought the right honorable member was an enemy to sinecures."

ROCHEFORT, [Victor] Henri, Marquis de Rochefort-Luçay (1830–1913), *French journalist.*

1 On one occasion when Rochefort had been arrested, the authorities confronted him with evidence of his links with international revolutionaries. "In one of your drawers were found two photographs of Garibaldi and Mazzini with their autographs."

"That is true," said Rochefort, "for those two great patriots did send me their photos."

"But that is not all," went on the interrogator, "for there were also seized several pictures of Henri Rochefort."

Somewhat baffled, Rochefort said, "But I am Henri Rochefort."

"I am not denying that," said the interrogator, "but it is nonetheless significant that you should have so many portraits of that notorious socialist in your house."

2 Rochefort found it difficult to make ends meet by his writing. He used to observe, "My scribbling pays me zero francs per line — not including the white spaces."

ROCKEFELLER, John D[avison], Sr. (1839–1937), *US oil magnate and philanthropist.*

1 Rockefeller found out that his family had ordered an electric car as his surprise birthday present, to enable him to get around his vast estate more easily. "If it's all the same to you," said the multimillionaire, "I'd rather have the money."

ROCKEFELLER, John D[avison], Jr. (1874–1960), *US capitalist and philanthropist, son of John D. Rockefeller, Sr.*

1 Rockefeller once made a collect call from a coin box, which failed to refund the money he had put in. He called the operator, who asked for his name and address so that the money could be mailed to him. Rockefeller began: "My name is John D. . . . Oh, forget it; you wouldn't believe me anyway."

ROCKEFELLER, Nelson Aldrich (1908–79), *US politician, son of John D. Rockefeller, Jr.*

1 Rockefeller never became President, an office for which he had a deep ambition. But he did become vice president, when Gerald Ford appointed him to the post once he had replaced Richard Nixon after the latter's resignation in 1974. His experience of the job was not unlike that of other vice presidents; he held high office but in fact had little true responsibility. When asked what his chief responsibilities were, Rockefeller said, "I go to funerals. I go to earthquakes."

RODGERS, Richard Charles (1902–79), *US composer.*

1 Dick Rodgers's collaborators Larry Hart and Oscar Hammerstein II were first-rate lyric writers. He was often asked how they differed. It should be mentioned that Hart was a very short man, about five feet three inches; Rodgers himself a few inches taller; and Hammerstein over six feet. Said Rodgers, "When I worked with Larry and people recognized us walking together, they'd say, 'The little fellow is okay but watch out for the big son-of-a-bitch.' Now, when I'm with Oscar and am recognized, people say, 'The big guy is okay, but watch out for the little son-of-a-bitch.' And that's the difference between working with Larry and working with Oscar."

2 Rodgers composed the score for the musical *Chee-Chee,* the story of which is based upon a novel by Charles Pettit, *The Son of the Grand Eunuch.* The plot hinges upon the efforts of the hero to avoid being emasculated in order to inherit his father's exalted office. At the point in the story at which the youth is taken away for the operation Rodgers inserted into the score a few bars from Tchaikovsky's *Nutcracker Suite.*

{Rodgers commented, "At almost every performance there were two or three individuals with ears musically sharp enough to appreciate the joke."}

RODZINSKI, Artur (1892–1958), *US orchestra conductor.*

1 On a vacation Rodzinski noticed that there was to be a radio broadcast of an open-air concert conducted by Fabien Sevitzky and that the program included one of Rodzinski's own specialties, Shostakovich's Fifth Symphony. Tuning in shortly after the concert had begun, Rodzinski listened to Sevitzky's

rendering with increasing respect. "How well he sustains the line!" he murmured. "Listen to that balance! He must have studied my recording." And he ended by saying that he had done Sevitzky an injustice, that he had always thought that he had no talent but that really he was a great conductor. At the end of the performance, instead of the expected applause there was a moment of silence. Then the announcer came on, saying that the concert had been rained out and in its place the station had played a recording of Shostakovich's Fifth conducted by Artur Rodzinski.

ROETHKE, Theodore (1908–63), *US poet.*

1 Roethke affected, in person and in his poetry, a rough masculine swagger that belied his true sensitivity. Once, as a young teacher, he was asked to identify a bird call. "It's a vireo," he said instantly, and launched into a lengthy and passionate monologue about birds and their habits. Suddenly, remembering his affectation, he stopped. "Aw, shit, who wants to know about birds, anyhow?" he growled, and walked off.

2 At a party given for him by Robert Lowell, Roethke was asked to read a poem. And then other poets at the party read a favorite poem of their own as well. The critic and budding poet I. A. Richards then was asked to read his poem. He looked in one book, then another. Shaking his head, he said, "Well, perhaps I have not yet published it." And then, "No, actually I think that I have not yet *written* it."

ROGERS, Samuel (1763–1855), *British writer.*

1 Discussing the approaching marriage of a lady whom they both knew, Lord Lansdowne observed to Rogers that she had made a good match. "I'm not so sure," replied Rogers. "Why not? All her friends approve it," said Lord Lansdowne. "Then she is able to satisfy everyone," said Rogers. "Her friends are pleased and her enemies are delighted."

2 Rogers had a considerable reputation for his biting and sarcastic wit. Once when accused of being ill-natured, he justified himself by saying, "They tell me I say ill-natured things. I have a weak voice; if I did not say ill-natured things, no one would hear what I said."

3 Rogers had a bare, polished head and a somewhat cadaverous appearance. He and Lord Dudley once spent an hour or two exploring the catacombs in Paris. As they were leaving, the keeper caught sight of Rogers and rushed toward him with a look of horror, shouting, "No, no. You have no right to come out. Go back inside. Go back."

Lord Dudley fled from the scene in paroxysms of laughter, leaving Rogers to extricate himself from the situation as best as he might. When Rogers later taxed him for his desertion, he replied, "My dear Rogers, you looked so much at home I did not like to interfere."

4 A gathering of society leaders was praising one of its absent members, a young duke who had recently come of age; they extolled his looks, his talents, his wealth, his prospects. . . . In a pause in the chorus of admiration the voice of Rogers could be heard saying malevolently, "Thank God he has bad teeth!"

ROGERS, Will (1879–1935), *US comedian.*

1 One of the many legends about William Randolph Hearst's fabulous weekend houseparties at San Simeon concerns Will Rogers. Throughout the weekend Hearst kept him

busy amusing the rest of the company. A few days later Hearst received a large bill from Rogers for services as a professional entertainer. Hearst telephoned Rogers to protest: "I didn't engage you as an entertainer. You were invited as a guest." Rogers retorted, "When someone invites me as a guest, they invite Mrs. Rogers as well. When they ask me to come alone, I come as a professional entertainer."

2 On a visit to Paris, Rogers sent a picture postcard of the Venus de Milo to his young niece. On the back he wrote: "See what will happen to you if you don't stop biting your fingernails."

3 Rogers had been asked by a firm of piano manufacturers to write a short testimonial for their instruments. Unwilling to endorse any product that he could not put to the test, Rogers simply replied, "Dear Sirs, I guess your pianos are the best I ever leaned against. Yours truly, Will Rogers."

4 Rogers, having paid too much income tax one year, tried in vain to claim a rebate. His numerous letters and queries remained unanswered. Eventually the form for the next year's return arrived. In the section marked "DEDUCTIONS," Rogers listed: "Bad debt, US Government — $40,000."

ROLAND, Jeanne Manon (1754–93), *wife of the French statesman Jean Roland* (1734–93).

1 Mme Roland's calm courage in prison and at her execution became famous. As she mounted the steps to the guillotine, she looked toward the clay statue of Liberty set up in the Place de la Révolution and exclaimed, *"O liberté! O liberté! Que de crimes on commet en ton nom!"* (O liberty! O liberty! What crimes are committed in thy name!)

ROOSEVELT, [Anna] Eleanor (1884–1962), *wife of President Franklin D. Roosevelt* (1933–45), *diplomat and writer.*

1 At a lecture Eleanor gave in Akron, Ohio, a hostile member of the audience asked her if she felt her husband's illness had affected his mind. "Yes," she replied. "Anyone who has gone through great suffering is bound to have a greater sympathy and understanding of the problems of mankind."

2 Eleanor Roosevelt had found the wife of China's leader Chiang Kai-shek a "gentle and sweet" character. But when Madame Chiang paid another visit to the White House, a very different personality was on display. Over dinner the company was discussing labor issues when FDR asked Madame Chiang how she would deal with labor leader John Lewis in China. Without a word she drew her hand across her throat. "Well," FDR asked his wife, "how about your gentle and sweet character now?"

3 Giving a group of Russian diplomats a tour of New York, she took them to the Independence Day parade. A group of uniformed youth went by, and she was asked, "Military?" "Boy Scouts," she said. Next, an impressive gang of men marched past. "Military?" "No," she said. "Fire department." When a car drove past holding just a few older men who sat uncomfortably in rather threadbare old uniforms, she turned to her guests and said, "Military."

4 In 1946, a year after the death of her husband, Franklin Delano Roosevelt, Eleanor was approached by an admirer who gushed over her importance to the world. "I'm so glad I never *feel* important," Roosevelt responded kindly. "It does complicate life."

ROOSEVELT, Franklin Delano (1882–1945), *US statesman; 32d President of the United States (1933–45).*

1 As a small boy Roosevelt was introduced to President Cleveland. Cleveland put his hand on the child's head and said, "I'm making a strange wish for you, little man, a wish I suppose no else would make. I wish for you that you may never be President of the United States."

2 In 1885, as a three-year-old, Roosevelt was returning on the ship *Germanic* when a storm broke out, leaking water into the cabins. His mother wrapped a fur coat about him, saying, "Poor little boy, if he must go down, he is going down warm."

3 FDR appointed Frances Perkins as secretary of labor — the first woman to hold a cabinet office — over the heads of several men who had been suggested for the position by labor leaders. The trade unionists, opposed as always to the idea of a woman's holding real power, had a stormy meeting with the President about the appointment. According to a Washington story current at the time, Mrs. Roosevelt sympathized with her husband over the confrontation. "That's all right," he replied. "I'd rather have trouble with them for an hour than trouble with you for the rest of my life."

4 The novelist Fannie Hurst wanted to surprise FDR with the change in her appearance since she had been on a diet. She managed to slip unannounced into his office. The President looked up as she entered, then gestured for her to turn around in front of him. When she completed the turn, he commented, "The Hurst may have changed, but it's the same old fanny."

5 Eleanor Roosevelt was particularly fond of sweetbreads. In one week they appeared on the White House menu no fewer than six times. The President eventually complained in a note to his wife: "I am getting to the point where my stomach rebels, and this does not help my relations with foreign powers. I bit two of them today."

6 The many details which an inaugural committee must cope with in a short time inevitably produce a few mistakes. Thus FDR, in 1937, received an invitation to his own inauguration.

Through the White House social bureau he solemnly sent word that the press of official business would keep him away. Then, relenting, he sent a further note in his own handwriting: "I have rearranged my engagements and think I may be able to go. Will know definitely January 19. F.D.R."

7 Roosevelt found the polite small talk of social functions at the White House somewhat tedious. He maintained that those present on such occasions rarely paid much attention to what was said to them. To illustrate the point, he would sometimes amuse himself by greeting guests with the words, "I murdered my grandmother this morning." The response was invariably one of polite approval. On one occasion, however, the President happened upon an attentive listener. On hearing Roosevelt's outrageous remark, the guest replied diplomatically, "I'm sure she had it coming to her."

8 In 1938 Roosevelt was invited to address the Daughters of the American Revolution. His speech began, "My fellow immigrants . . ."

9 One morning the President asked his secretary to take down a brief message to Congress. As he dictated every word, including punctuation marks, she wrote out, "Yesterday, December 7, 1941, a date which will live in world history, the United States was suddenly and deliberately attacked . . ." After the five-hundred-word message was typed, she returned it to Roosevelt, who, while con-

ducting other business simultaneously, made only one change, crossing out "world history" and replacing it with "infamy."

10 After a long and exhausting Gridiron Club dinner, he was asked how he composed his mind in order to get to sleep. "It's very easy," he said. "I coast down the hills at Hyde Park in the snow, and then I walk slowly up. I know every curve."

11 Roosevelt was visited by a clergyman at Hyde Park. As the two men were discussing a book, Roosevelt descended from his wheelchair, crawled across the floor to get a book, put it between his teeth, and crawled back to his chair. When the clergyman asked why he had not asked for help, Roosevelt said, "I felt I had to do it to show that I could."

12 In 1944 Roosevelt decided to try for an unprecedented fourth term. When criticized by the Republicans for his decision, he joked, "The first twelve years are the hardest."

———— ∽ ————

ROOSEVELT, Theodore (1858–1919), *US statesman; 26th President of the United States (1901–09).*

1 During his time as a rancher, Roosevelt and one of his cowpunchers, riding over the range, lassoed a maverick, a two-year-old steer that had never been branded. They lit a fire then and there and prepared the branding irons. The part of the range they were on was claimed by Gregor Lang, one of Roosevelt's neighbors. According to the rule among cattlemen the steer therefore belonged to Lang, having been found on his land. As the cowboy applied the brand, Roosevelt said, "Wait, it should be Lang's brand, a thistle."

"That's all right, boss," said the cowboy, continuing to apply the brand.

"But you're putting on my brand."

"That's right," said the man, "I always put on the boss's brand."

"Drop that iron," said Roosevelt, "and get back to the ranch and get out. I don't need you anymore."

The cowboy protested, but Roosevelt was adamant. "A man who will steal *for* me will steal *from* me," he declared. So the cowboy went, and the story spread all over the Badlands.

2 When the hotel in which Vice President Roosevelt was staying caught fire, he was ordered down to the lobby with the other guests. After some time, prevented from returning to his room, he protested: "But I'm the vice president!"

"Oh, that's different," said the hotel official. Then, as Teddy started up the stairs, "Wait a minute. What are you vice president *of*?"

"Why, of the United States, of course!"

"Then get the hell back down there. I thought you were vice president of this hotel!"

3 Before retiring to bed, Roosevelt and his friend the naturalist William Beebe would go out and look at the skies, searching for a tiny patch of light near the constellation of Pegasus. "That is the Spiral Galaxy in Andromeda," they would chant. "It is as large as our Milky Way. It is one of a hundred million galaxies. It consists of one hundred billion suns, each larger than our sun." Then Roosevelt would turn to his companion and say, "Now I think we are small enough. Let's go to bed."

4 Some of Roosevelt's critics complained of his tendency to introduce moral issues in matters where none existed. Speaker of the House Thomas B. Reed once told Roosevelt, "If there is one thing more than another for which I admire you, Theodore, it is your

original discovery of the Ten Commandments."

5 Shot in the chest in an assassination attempt in October 1912, Roosevelt was determined to carry on with the speech he had been about to make. "I will deliver this speech or die, one or the other," he declared.

6 Shortly before he left the White House, Roosevelt, planning a big-game hunting trip to Africa, heard that a famous white hunter was visiting Washington. He invited the man to come along and give him some advice. After a two-hour tête-à-tête the hunter came out of the President's office looking dazed. "What did you tell the President?" someone asked idly. "My name," said the bemused visitor. "After that he did all the talking."

———— ✧ ————

ROOSEVELT, Theodore, Jr. (1887–1944), *US soldier, explorer, and politician, the son of President Theodore Roosevelt.*

1 Roosevelt had arranged to meet his wife's train. Arriving at the railroad station at the appointed time, he was dismayed to see the train speed past the platform without stopping. His wife waved anxiously from the rear car, tossing out an envelope as she passed her husband. Roosevelt retrieved the envelope with some difficulty and was amused to read the following message: "Dear Ted: This train doesn't stop here."

———— ✧ ————

ROOT, Elihu (1845–1937), *US lawyer and statesman who won the Nobel Peace Prize in 1912.*

1 When a frail old man in his eighties, Root was frequently visited by Sol M. Linowitz, who used to read to him. One day Root asked the young man what he wanted to do in life. Linowitz replied, "I'm not sure. Maybe be a rabbi or perhaps a lawyer." Root's reply was immediate: "Be a lawyer. A lawyer needs twice as much religion as a rabbi."

———— ✧ ————

ROPS, Félicien (1833–98), *French painter, engraver, and lithographer.*

1 Art dealer Ambroise Vollard had occasion to visit Rops a few years before the painter's death. Rops warned him: "I'm expecting a woman. When the bell rings three times, you must leave by the other end of the studio." After some time the bell rang as predicted and Vollard took his leave. Glancing behind him as he closed the door, he saw an old housemaid enter the room. "Come now, monsieur," she said, "it's time for your *tisane*" (herbal tea).

———— ✧ ————

ROSE, Pete (1941–), *US baseball player.*

1 "Charlie Hustle" was one of the greatest players in the history of baseball. A veteran of the Phillies and the Reds, he was a leader in the World Series and played five different positions in five different All-Star games. Once his young daughter Fawn asked Rose's manager Sparky Anderson why her father didn't get a summer vacation like her friends' fathers. "Because I need him, dear, " Anderson replied.

2 Anderson was awed by Rose's abilities on the field — he seemed sheer muscle and vitality. Said the manager when trying to describe Rose's skills, "Pete Rose is the best thing to happen to the game since, well, the game."

3 A fellow player once said of Rose, "If I had his head, I'd make a butcher-block coffee table out of it." When Rose heard this he responded, "Your face would look old, too, if you'd been sliding on it for twenty-three years."

4 In August 1985, Rose broke Ty Cobb's record of 4,191 hits. In the days before, as he closed in on Cobb's hitherto unbeatable statistic, a reporter asked him if he thought Ty Cobb was looking down on Rose as he chased the record. "From what I hear about the guy," said Rose, "he may not be up there. He may be down there."

5 After his imprisonment for gambling, Rose was invited to appear on the *Tonight* show. After thanking Doc Severinsen's orchestra for not playing "Jailhouse Rock," he mentioned that he had never before been invited to be on the show, despite the many baseball records he had achieved. Said Rose to the audience, "You gotta go to prison to get on this show!"

ROSS, Harold (1892–1951), *US journalist, founder, and for many years editor of* The New Yorker.

1 Shortly after Ross had obtained his discharge from the armed forces at the end of World War I, he met the former war secretary, Newton D. Baker. He and Ross discussed the war at length, and Ross was delighted with the frankness with which Baker covered a wide range of topics. Taking leave of him, Ross remarked, "Well, Mr. Secretary, that cleans up everything except how Joe Higgins was made corporal of my squad."

2 Ross launched *The New Yorker* in 1925 on a shoestring budget. The magazine's finances continued to be very shaky for some time; its equipment and resources were therefore minimal. When Ross asked Dorothy Parker why she had not come in to do a piece she had promised him, she retorted, "Someone else was using the pencil."

3 (Ross's unavailing but persistent attempts to bring order to the *New Yorker* offices made life miserable for a series of assistants, who included James Thurber and M. B. Levick.)

"Levick's final frantic response to the editor's demand for a method of keeping track of everything was an enormous sheet of cardboard, six feet by four, divided into at least eight hundred squares, with fine hand lettering in each of them covering all phases of the scheduling of departments and other office rigmaroles. This complicated caricature of System, this concentration of all known procedural facts, hung on a wall of the Talk meeting room until one day it fell down of its own weight. Ross had stared at it now and then without saying a word. When it crashed, he told his secretary, 'Get rid of that thing.'"

4 A promising young lad, possibly James Thurber, sought a place on the staff of *The New Yorker* and Ross hired him. "Don't be too pleased with yourself," he warned the new employee, "I hire any damn fool who sticks his nose in here. And don't think you'll be starting as a reporter. You'll begin as managing editor, like everyone else."

5 As a practical joke Thurber once rolled a very large water bottle along the corridor past the offices of *The New Yorker*. Hearing the racket, Ross instructed the new managing editor: "Go and find out what the hell is happening. But don't tell me."

6 For years Harold Ross had *The New Yorker*'s cover-design character, Eustace Tilley, listed in the Manhattan telephone book. He was delighted when the city authorities eventually sent this imaginary figure a personal-property tax bill.

7 Ross's turnout was never very smart. After a winter sports holiday in Connecticut with Franklin P. Adams, someone asked Ross's host what Ross had looked like tobogganing. "Well, you know what Ross looks like *not* tobogganing," said Adams.

8 Hemingway's *Death in the Afternoon* was reviewed for *The New Yorker* by critic Robert M. Coates. After he had read the review, Ross telephoned Coates in the country and said, "Woollcott tells me there's a hell of a bad word in the book — bathroom stuff." Coates asked what the word was. "I can't tell you over the phone," said Ross.

9 (Peter De Vries tells the story of Ross at an art meeting during which sketches were selected for possible inclusion in *The New Yorker*.)

"The cover on the board showed a Model T driving along a dusty country road, and Ross turned his sharpshooting eye on it for a full two minutes. 'Take this down, Miss Terry,' he said. 'Better dust.'"

10 Many of Ross's *New Yorker* writers were lured away to Hollywood. When John McNulty headed west, Ross bade him farewell with what Thurber describes as "a memorable tagline": "Well, God bless you, McNulty, goddamn it."

11 A rival cartoonist once grumbled to Ross, "Why do you reject my drawings and print stuff by that fifth-rate artist, Thurber?"

"Third-rate," corrected Ross.

12 On December 11, 1936, King Edward VIII of Great Britain broadcast to the world his historic "the woman I love" abdication speech. At a cocktail party in New York, the polished Noël Coward and the unbuttoned Harold Ross listened to the broadcast. Ross burst into uncontrollable laughter. Coward, an Establishment man to his fingertips, was shocked, and he reproved Ross for this unseemly exhibition. Ross would have none of it. "You mean," he said incredulously, "the king of England runs away with an old American hooker and *that* ain't funny?"

13 When Ross asked writer Ring Lardner how he wrote his short stories, Lardner replied that he wrote a few words or phrases very widely spaced apart on a piece of paper and then went back to fill in the blank spots.

ROSSETTI, Dante Gabriel (1828–82), *British painter and poet.*

1 Rossetti announced that he wanted to buy an elephant, and, when his friends asked what on earth for, he replied, "So I can teach it to wash the windows of my house." When they still seemed puzzled, he added, "Then everyone would stare and say, 'That elephant is washing the windows of the house in which lives Dante Gabriel Rossetti, the famous artist.'"

2 When Rossetti's beautiful wife, Elizabeth Siddal, killed herself with an overdose of laudanum in 1862, just two years after their marriage, Rossetti's grief was overwhelming. Most of his poems had been written for her or to her. At her burial he wrapped the little book containing the unique copies of these poems in her long golden hair and consigned them to the grave with her. As the years passed, Rossetti began to think with regret of the poems that he had lost, concluding that it was pointless to leave some of the finest works he had produced to molder in the grave with the dead. After much business to obtain permission, the grave was opened and the book retrieved. Its contents, with a few additions, were published in 1870 under the title *Poems,* and the book was immediately successful.

3 The negotiations on behalf of the Liverpool art gallery to buy Rossetti's great picture *Dante's Dream* seemed likely to be abortive when Rossetti discovered that one of the intermediaries was a critic who he considered had insulted him. A third party, called in to make peace, succeeded in convincing Rossetti that the man was "quite a good fellow

at bottom." Rossetti observed afterward, "I did not mention that if he came here he had better take care that the place at which he was a good fellow did not get kicked."

———— ✧ ————

ROSSINI, Gioacchino Antonio (1792–1868), *Italian composer.*

1 Jacques François Halévy, another popular composer, was driven nearly to distraction by an organ-grinder who had stationed himself outside his window and was busy grinding out the hit tunes from his rival's *Barber of Seville.* Halévy went out and said to the man, "I will give you one louis d'or if you will go to Rossini's lodgings and play one of my tunes outside his window." The organ-grinder smiled. "But, monsieur, M. Rossini has paid me *two* louis d'or to play his music outside your window."

2 In a Paris music store in 1856 Rossini encountered the celebrated music theorist and scholar François-Joseph Fétis. On the counter was displayed Fétis's *Treatise on Counterpoint and Fugue.* "Must all this be learned?" inquired Rossini, gesturing toward the volume. "Not at all," replied Fétis. "You yourself are the living proof to the contrary."

3 Rossini congratulated the diva Adelina Patti on her singing. "Madame, I have cried only twice in my life," he informed her, "once when I dropped a wing of truffled chicken into Lake Como, and once when for the first time I heard you sing."

4 A singer gave a rendering of Rossini's famous aria *"Una voce,"* embellished with many showy *fioriture.* When she had finished, Rossini courteously congratulated her upon her technique. "And whose is the music?" he asked.

5 Rossini, who usually marked errors in his pupils' compositions with crosses, returned a manuscript to a mediocre student with very few crosses on it. The young man was delighted. "I'm so pleased that there are so few mistakes," he said happily. "If I had marked all the blunders in the music with crosses, your score would have looked like a cemetery," said Rossini.

6 One day a composer unknown to Rossini brought him the score of two oratorios, seeking his opinion. Rossini tried to excuse himself, citing poor health. But the composer insisted, stating that he would return in a week for Rossini's judgment. He did so, finding Rossini in his armchair, serene and smiling, but quick to say that he had been so ill and had slept so little that he had been able to examine only one of the scores. "And what did you think of it?" was the eager question. "There are good things in it . . . but I prefer the other one."

7 When Rossini was old and eminent but still not rich, a group of his admirers raised a subscription of twenty thousand francs for a statue of their hero.

"Give me the twenty thousand," said Rossini, "and I'll stand on the pedestal myself."

8 Baron Rothschild sent Rossini some beautiful grapes from his conservatory. Rossini wrote back, thanking him but adding, "Although your grapes are superb, I don't like my wine in capsules."

{Rothschild then sent him some of his celebrated Chateau-Lafitte, enjoying the hint.}

———— ✧ ————

ROTHSCHILD, Sir Nathan Meyer, 1st Baron (1840–1915), *member of the London branch of the famous family of financiers.*

1 Alighting from a hansom cab one evening, Lord Rothschild gave the driver what he felt to be an adequate tip. "Your lordship's son always gives me a good deal more than this,"

said the driver, eyeing the money disdainfully. "I daresay he does," retorted Lord Rothschild. "But then, you see, he has got a rich father: I haven't."

———⟨∿⟩———

ROUSSEAU, Jean-Jacques (1712–78), *French philosopher and writer.*

1 Rousseau owed a great deal to his patroness, Mme De Vercelles. As she was readying to die, Rousseau waited by her bedside. She could no longer speak, and it was clear death was near. Suddenly, she broke wind loudly. "Good," she said, "a woman who can fart is not dead." Upon which she died.

———⟨∿⟩———

ROUTH, Martin (1755–1854), *British academic.*

1 The ups and downs of college life had little effect on the Venerable Dr. Routh, as he was generally called. A breathless don once stumbled into the president's room, gasping, "A Fellow of this college has killed himself!" Dr. Routh held up a calming hand. "Pray don't tell me who," he is reported to have said. "Allow me to guess."

2 Routh suffered an injury that troubled him for a long time; it was caused when he reached up for a weighty volume on a high shelf and the book fell, striking his left leg. The elderly scholar was incensed. "To be lamed by a book written by a dunce!" he cried. "A worthless volume! A worthless volume!"

———⟨∿⟩———

ROWLAND, Henry Augustus (1848–1901), *US physicist.*

1 Professor Rowland was summoned as an expert witness at a trial. During cross-examination a lawyer demanded, "What are your qualifications as an expert witness in this case?"

"I am the greatest living expert on the subject under discussion," replied the professor quietly.

Later a friend, well acquainted with the professor's modest and retiring disposition, observed that he had been amazed to hear him praise himself in this way; it was completely out of character. Rowland asked, "Well, what did you expect me to do? I was under oath."

———⟨∿⟩———

RUBINSTEIN, Anton (1829–94), *Russian pianist and composer.*

1 The telephone rang at a bad time while the maestro was practicing. His servant, François, answered the phone. It was a feminine voice tenderly asking to speak with Rubinstein. Although the sounds of the piano were clearly audible, François assured the lady that Rubinstein was not in. "But I hear him playing," she said. "You are mistaken, madame," replied François. "I'm dusting the piano keys."

2 Anton Rubinstein liked to sleep late in the mornings, often missing early appointments as a result. Mme Rubinstein worked out a ruse to get him out of bed. She would play an unresolved chord on the piano upstairs, and her husband, who could not bear unresolved dissonances, would run up in his nightshirt to resolve it into a perfect triad. While he did this, Mme Rubinstein would sneak downstairs and remove the bedclothes to prevent him from returning to bed.

———⟨∿⟩———

RUBINSTEIN, Artur (1886–1982), *Polish-born pianist.*

1 (Clifton Fadiman recalls a lunch with Rubinstein.) "We . . . awaited him in the restau-

rant. He entered, his stride thirty-five years his junior, sat down at the table, ordered drinks in Italian (from the eight languages he speaks he selects one as an ordinary man would a tie), and started to apologize: 'So sorry to be late. For two hours I have been at my lawyer's, making my will. What a nuisance, this business of a will. One figures, one schemes, one arranges, and in the end — what? It is practically impossible to leave anything for yourself!'"

2 Rubinstein was standing in the lobby of a concert hall watching the capacity crowd streaming in to hear one of his recitals. The attendant at the box office, thinking that he had not seen the "SOLD OUT" sign, called out to him, "I'm sorry, mister, but we can't seat you."

"May I be seated at the piano?" inquired Rubinstein meekly.

———— ‹›› ————

RUGGLES, Carl (1876–1971), *US composer.*

1 Henry Cowell, visiting Ruggles at his studio, found the composer at his piano playing the same chordal agglomerate over and over again. Eventually Cowell shouted, "What on earth are you doing to that chord? You've been playing it for at least an hour." Ruggles shouted back, "I'm giving it the test of time."

———— ‹›› ————

RUSKIN, John (1819–1900), *British critic, writer, and social reformer.*

1 In accordance with his ideas on the dignity of labor Ruskin encouraged his Oxford students to try their hand at manual work. He hit on the scheme of building a road from the nearby village of North Hinksey to Oxford to enable the villagers to reach the town by a direct route across low-lying and often muddy fields. Among the undergraduates he recruited was — of all people — Oscar

Wilde. They set to work with a will under the direction of Ruskin's gardener, but somehow the charm of manual labor diminished after a while and the road was never completed. Final comment on the episode came from an anonymous resident of North Hinksey: "I don't think the young gentlemen did much harm."

2 In the heyday of his career as art critic, Ruskin used always to maintain that it should in no way affect his friendship with an artist if he panned his work. The artists, of course, saw matters in a rather different light. "Next time I meet you I shall knock you down," one of his victims retorted, "but I trust it will make no difference to our friendship."

3 Ruskin, no lover of technological progress, was asked to comment on the completion of the British-Indian cable. "What have we to say to India?" he asked.

———— ‹›› ————

RUSSELL, Bertrand Arthur William, 3d Earl (1872–1970), *British philosopher who won the 1950 Nobel Prize for Literature.*

1 The American publisher William Jovanovich in his student days at Harvard often ate at a cafeteria that served cheap, rather bad food. Bertrand Russell also used to eat at the same place. One day Jovanovich, unable to restrain his curiosity, said to Russell, "Mr. Russell, I know why I eat here. It is because I am poor; but why do you eat here?" Russell replied, "Because I am never interrupted."

2 Russell's friend G. H. Hardy, who became professor of pure mathematics at Cambridge in 1931, once told him that if he could find a proof that Russell would die in five minutes' time, he would naturally be sorry to lose him, but the sorrow would be quite outweighed by pleasure in the proof. Russell, wise in the ways of mathematics, observed,

"I entirely sympathized with him and was not at all offended."

3 (G. H. Hardy reports a nightmare once experienced by Bertrand Russell. In his dream he found himself on the top floor of a great library in about AD 2100.)

"A library assistant was going around the shelves carrying an enormous bucket, taking down book after book, glancing at them, restoring them to the shelves or dumping them into the bucket. At last he came to three large volumes which Russell could recognize as the last surviving copy of *Principia Mathematica*. He took down one of the volumes, turned over a few pages, seemed puzzled for a moment by the curious symbolism, closed the volume, balanced it in his hands and hesitated . . ."

4 When Bertrand Russell refused to grant interviews after a serious illness in China, in 1920, a resentful Japanese press carried the news he had died. Even when Russell appealed to them, they refused to retract the story. On his way home he stopped in Japan, and the press again sought to interview him. By way of reprisal he had his secretary hand out printed slips to each reporter. The slips read: "Since Mr. Russell is dead he cannot be interviewed."

5 A young friend of Russell's once found the philosopher in a state of profound contemplation. "Why so meditative?" asked the young man. "Because I've made an odd discovery," replied Russell. "Every time I talk to a savant I feel quite sure that happiness is no longer a possibility. Yet when I talk with my gardener, I'm convinced of the opposite."

———— ✧ ————

RUSSELL, John, 1st Earl (1792–1878), *British statesman; prime minister (1846–52, 1865–66).*

1 During a fiery debate, the Tory Sir Francis Burdett objected to some sentiments from the other side that he called "the cant of patriotism." Russell immediately retorted, "There is something worse than the cant of patriotism; that is the recant of patriotism."

2 Asked his opinion as to what would be the proper punishment for bigamy, Russell promptly answered, "Two mothers-in-law."

———— ✧ ————

RUTH, George Herman ["Babe"] (1895–1948), *US baseball player.*

1 During the Depression Babe Ruth, asked to take a cut in salary, held out for his $80,000 contract. A club official protested, "But that's more money than Hoover got for being President last year."

"I know," said the Babe, "but I had a better year."

2 Babe Ruth was enormously popular, a larger-than-life figure in many respects, given to overeating and overdrinking. The most notorious occasion was in the course of preseason training when, on a railroad ride to New York, the Babe got off at a train stop and consumed an estimated twelve hot dogs and eight bottles of lemon-lime soda pop in a few minutes. Soon afterward he was stricken with "the stomachache heard 'round the world." (Less publicized were rumors that he had contributed to his misery with the consumption of large amounts of beer and booze.) For days ominous headlines had his fans across the country fearing for his life. Recovering, Ruth is reported to have said, "That soda pop will get you every time."

3 Babe Ruth loved kids. On one occasion when the family of a fan of the Babe's, a youngster who was seriously ill in the hospital, requested an autographed baseball for the boy, the Babe went along to the hospital himself, gave him the baseball, and promised to hit a home run for him in the game that after-

noon. Sure enough, the Babe came through with the home run. The lad recovered and Babe Ruth observed, "Best medicine in the world, a home run."

4 Another version of the sick-boy-and-home-run story relates as follows: The boy, Johnny Sylvester, was injured in a fall from his horse. His uncle brought him baseballs autographed by Yankee team members and prevailed on Ruth to visit him in the hospital. When Ruth promised to hit a home run for him, and did — hit four, in fact, in the next game — the press picked up on it and the legend grew. The next year Ruth was chatting with reporters when the uncle approached him and thanked him for his kindness to Johnny Sylvester. "Glad to do it," said Ruth, who asked after Johnny. "Send him my regards." When the grateful uncle left Ruth turned to his cronies and asked, "Now who the hell is Johnny Sylvester?"

5 "Grantland Rice, the prince of sportswriters, used to do a weekly radio interview with some sporting figure. Frequently, in the interest of spontaneity, he would type out questions and answers in advance. One night his guest was Babe Ruth.

"'Well, you know, Granny,' the Babe read in response to a question, 'Duke Ellington said the Battle of Waterloo was won on the playing fields of Elkton.'

"'Babe,' Granny said after the show, 'Duke Ellington for the Duke of Wellington I can understand. But how did you ever read Eton as Elkton? That's in Maryland, isn't it?'

"'I married my first wife there,' Babe said, 'and I always hated the goddamn place.'"

6 Ruth once suffered the humiliation of having the great Walter Johnson of the Washington Senators throw three straight fastballs past him. He asked the umpire if he had seen any of the pitches. "No," replied the umpire. "Neither did I," said Ruth, "but that last one sounded kinda high to me."

7 At an exhibition game in Chattanooga, Tennessee, a teenaged girl was allowed as a joke to pitch to the Yankees. In short order she struck out Lou Gehrig and Babe Ruth. Only after she walked Tony Lazzeri was she taken out of the game by the manager.

8 The Babe was once asked if he had any superstitions. "Just one," he said. "Whenever I hit a home run, I make sure I touch all four bases."

9 Near the end of his career with the Red Sox, Ruth was in a bitter negotiation with owner Harry Frazee over his salary. Frazee professed amazement that Ruth would ask for so much money, claiming that not even the great actor John Barrymore made that amount. "I don't give a damn about any actors," Ruth retorted. "What good will John Barrymore do you with the bases loaded and two down in a tight ball game? Either I get the money or I don't play!"

S

SAGE, Russell (1816–1906), *US financier.*

1 Sage's lawyer was delighted by the case his client had just laid before him. "It's an iron-clad case," he exclaimed with confidence. "We can't possibly lose!"

"Then we won't sue," said Sage. "That was my opponent's side of the case I gave you."

SAINTE-BEUVE, Charles Augustin (1804–69), *French critic and literary historian.*

1 Although himself unpugnacious, Sainte-Beuve was once compelled to fight a duel with pistols. At the critical moment, just as the order to fire was about to be given, it started to rain. Sainte-Beuve called for a pause in the proceedings while he went to his carriage and fetched and opened a large umbrella. He then faced his opponent with the umbrella held in his left hand and the pistol in his right. The opponent protested at the derogation of the dignity of the occasion. "I don't mind being killed," Sainte-Beuve responded, "but I do mind getting wet."

SAINT-SAËNS, [Charles] Camille (1835–1921), *French composer.*

1 Sir Thomas Beecham conducted a concert in London given in honor of Saint-Saëns, for which the principal piece was Saint-Saëns's Third Symphony. Beecham found the tempi in the symphony depressingly slow; so did the players, as they made clear by the way they played in rehearsal. Nor was the situation helped by Saint-Saëns's presence.

Beecham finally exaggerated the accentuation on purpose to give a semblance of life to the music without actually speeding it up. Later he asked Saint-Saëns what he thought of the interpretation. The aged composer replied, "My dear young friend, I have lived a long while, and I have known all the *chefs d'orchestre.* There are two kinds; one takes the music too fast, and the other too slow. There is no third."

SALINGER, J. D. (1919–), *US writer.*

1 When *The Catcher in the Rye* was chosen as the main selection of the Book-of-the-Month Club in 1951, the president of the club, who had invited Salinger to lunch, expressed anxiety over the book's somewhat ambiguous title. Asked if he would consider a change, Salinger thought for a moment, then replied

simply, "Holden Caulfield wouldn't like that." The suggestion was not revived.

———— ❧ ————

SALISBURY, Robert Arthur Talbot Gascoyne-Cecil, 3d Marquess of (1830–1903), *British statesman.*

1 In 1896, Salisbury made the undistinguished poet Alfred Austin Poet Laureate. It was widely believed that the decision was based on Austin's political leanings rather than on his talent. Asked why he had chosen a poet of such inferior ability, Salisbury simply replied, "I don't think anyone else applied for the post."

———— ❧ ————

SALK, Jonas E. (1914–95), *US virologist.*

1 Salk worked hard to publicize his discovery, although he received no money from the sale of it. Someone once asked him who owned the patent. He replied, "The people — could you patent the sun?"

———— ❧ ————

SAMUELSON, Paul (1915–), *US economist.*

1 When Samuelson completed his oral examination for a Ph.D. degree, an examiner turned to his colleagues in the room and asked, "Did we pass?"

———— ❧ ————

SANDBURG, Carl (1878–1967), *US poet, novelist, and biographer.*

1 A young dramatist, anxious for Sandburg's opinion of his new serious play, asked the poet to attend the dress rehearsal. Sandburg slept throughout the performance. When the dramatist complained, saying that Sandburg had known how much he wanted his opinion, Sandburg replied, "Sleep *is* an opinion."

2 Carl Sandburg was a guest of honor at a banquet along with a famous general. Suddenly the hostess without prior warning announced, "Mr. Oliver Herford will now improvise a poem in honor of this occasion." Herford, a shy and modest man, protested. "Oh, no," he said, shrinking back in his chair, "have the general fire a cannon."

———— ❧ ————

SANDERS, George (1906–72), *British stage and film actor, born in Russia.*

1 After a lifetime of playing cynical, world-weary characters on stage and in the movies, Sanders committed suicide. His final note read, "I am leaving because I am so bored."

———— ❧ ————

SANDWICH, John Montagu, 4th Earl of (1718–92), *British politician.*

1 Entertaining at a dinner at which his chaplain was present, the earl brought in a large baboon dressed in clerical garb to say grace. The affronted chaplain left the room, pausing on his way out to observe, "I did not know your lordship had so near a relative in holy orders."

2 Lord Sandwich was remarkable for his ungainliness; a contemporary wit said that he could be recognized from afar by the fact that "he walked down both sides of the street at once." He liked to tell the following story: During a stay in Paris he took dancing lessons. Bidding farewell to his dancing master, he offered to recommend him to members of London society who might be visiting Paris. The man bowed and said earnestly, "I would take it as a particular favor if your lordship would never tell anyone of whom you learned to dance."

3 As Sandwich was dining with the actor Samuel Foote, he asked him how Foote

thought he would die: from the pox or on the gallows? Foote replied, "My Lord, that will depend upon one of two contingencies — whether I embrace your Lorship's mistress or your Lorship's principles."

———— ᴏⱴꜱ ————

SANTAYANA, George (1863–1952), *Spanish-born philosopher and poet.*

1 Santayana inherited his simple and unostentatious habits from his father. Once he asked the senior Santayana why he always traveled third class. "Because there's no fourth class."

2 When Santayana came into a sizable legacy, he was able to relinquish his post on the Harvard faculty. The classroom was packed for his final appearance, and Santayana did himself proud. He was about to conclude his remarks when he caught sight of a forsythia beginning to blossom in a patch of muddy snow outside the window. He stopped abruptly, picked up his hat, gloves, and walking stick, and made for the door. There he turned. "Gentlemen," he said softly, "I shall not be able to finish that sentence. I have just discovered that I have an appointment with April."

———— ᴏⱴꜱ ————

SARASATE [y Navascués], Pablo de (1844–1908), *Spanish violinist.*

1 By inviting Sarasate to dinner, his wealthy hostess had hoped to obtain a free violin recital for her guests after the meal. During the course of dinner she broached the subject, asking Sarasate whether he had brought his violin. *"Mais non, madame,"* replied the violinist, *"mon violon ne dine pas"* (No, madame, my violin does not dine).

2 In the latter part of his career, Sarasate received a visit from a famous music critic who acclaimed him as a genius. Sarasate accepted the compliment with little enthusiasm. "A genius!" he said. "For thirty-seven years I've practiced fourteen hours a day, and now they call me a genius!"

———— ᴏⱴꜱ ————

SARGENT, John Singer (1856–1925), *US portrait painter.*

1 The commission to paint the coronation of Edward VII went to an artist named Edwin A. Abbey. This huge canvas contained about 120 portraits, and Abbey worked on it from 1902 to 1904. One important sitter was the Prince of Wales, the future George V. He surprised Abbey by asking him about Sargent's income, which apparently was much discussed among the portraitist's friends, of whom the prince was one. "Do you suppose it's ten thousand pounds?" guessed the prince. "I would say more likely twenty thousand," replied Abbey. The heir apparent was amazed: "My God! I wish I had twenty thousand pounds a year!"

2 Sargent did not take kindly to criticism of his work by his subjects. When a woman objected to his treatment of the mouth in a portrait he had done of her, his rejoinder was: "Perhaps, madam, we'd better leave it out altogether."

{Sargent suggested "A little something wrong with the mouth" should be written on his tombstone.}

3 A woman who was paying $5,000 for her portrait by Sargent said that there was something wrong with the nose. "Oh, you can easily put a little thing like that right when you get it home," said Sargent, handing her the canvas.

4 Sargent had been commissioned to do a portrait of Teddy Roosevelt. Determined to find the right setting, he and the President scoured the White House for a suitable backdrop. By the end of the second afternoon, af-

ter trying a succession of poses against various settings, Roosevelt had had enough. Pausing at the bottom of a staircase, his elbow on the newel post, he turned to the painter and said, "We're after the impossible; we'd better give it up." Sargent took in at a glance the President's pose and exclaimed, *"Don't move, Mr. President! We've got it!"*

5 Sargent once found himself sitting beside an effusive young admirer at a dinner party. "Oh, Mr. Sargent," she gushed, "I saw your latest painting and kissed it because it was so much like you."

"And did it kiss you in return?" asked the artist.

"Why, no."

"Then it was not like me," said Sargent with a smile.

SARGENT, Sir Malcolm (1895–1967), *British conductor and organist.*

1 At the age of seventy, Sargent was asked by an interviewer: "To what do you attribute your advanced age?"

"Well," replied the conductor, "I suppose I must attribute it to the fact that I haven't died yet."

SAROYAN, William (1908–81), *US writer.*

1 Before his death in 1981, Saroyan phoned in to the Associated Press a final Saroyanesque observation: "Everybody has got to die, but I have always believed an exception would be made in my case. Now what?"

SATIE, Erik (1866–1925), *French composer of songs and piano pieces.*

1 Satie wrote the following direction on one of his piano compositions: "To be played with both hands in the pocket."

2 Satie attended the premiere of Debussy's *La Mer,* the first part of which is entitled "From Dawn to Noon on the Sea." Asked by the composer what he thought of the work, Satie replied, "I liked the bit about quarter to eleven."

SCARRON, Paul (1610–60), *French poet, playwright, and novelist.*

1 Scarron dedicated a collection of poems to his sister's dog: *"A Guillemette, chienne de ma soeur."* Shortly before the publication of the poems, however, Scarron quarreled with his sister, and as a result the following notice appeared among the errata of the book: "For *chienne de ma soeur* [my sister's bitch] read *ma chienne de soeur* [my bitch of a sister]."

2 At their marriage the notary drawing up the contract asked Scarron what dowry he intended to bestow upon his beautiful but penniless young bride. "Immortality," he replied.

SCHEFFEL, Josef Victor von (1826–86), *German writer.*

1 While Scheffel was a student and had already achieved some literary fame, he set out on a walking trip along the right bank of the Rhine. As the day was hot, he decided on a swim, threw off all his clothes, and plunged in. The current, however, was far stronger than he expected. After an exhausting struggle he managed to reach shore — but found himself on the *left* bank. Stark naked, he had no option but to walk to the nearest inn and appeal for help. It happened that the district military policeman had also stopped by at the inn. The latter grimly surveyed the naked, dripping Scheffel. "Where did you come from?" he demanded.

"From the opposite bank, Officer."

"And what's your name?"

"I'm the writer Josef Victor von Scheffel."

"Indeed. Show me your papers!"

SCHIFFER, Claudia (1970–), *German fashion model.*

1 Asked about her background and her ambitions, Schiffer told an interviewer, "My education was to become a miss. A *Miss*. Like Miss Venezuela, Miss World . . ."

SCHLEIERMACHER, Friedrich Daniel Ernst (1768–1834), *German philosopher and theologian.*

1 When complimented on the popularity of his sermons, which drew large audiences from many walks of life, Schleiermacher explained, "My audiences comprise mainly students, women, and officers. The students come to hear me preach, the women come to look at the students, and the officers come to look at the women."

SCHLIEMANN, Heinrich (1822–90), *German archaeologist, discoverer of Troy.*

1 "I have looked upon the face of Agamemnon," exulted Schliemann when his excavations in the citadel of Mycenae unearthed a gold death mask of a warrior king. Later, doubts crept in, and his more scientifically inclined colleagues almost persuaded him that he had discovered the remains of a generation far earlier than the presumed date of Homer's Agamemnon. Schliemann resisted these suggestions hotly at first, but later came to accept them philosophically. "What," he said, "this is not Agamemnon's body and these are not his ornaments? All right, let's call him Schulze." (Schulze is the German equivalent of Smith or Jones.) After that, these remains were always referred to as "Schulze."

SCHMIDT, Mike (1949–), *US baseball player.*

1 The Phillies' third baseman who won ten Golden Gloves over his career and led his league in home runs eight times attended a banquet given for his team when they won the World Series in 1980. During his speech Ruly Carpenter, owner of the team, said to the audience, "What can I say about Mike Schmidt after his being named Most Valuable Player for both the National League and the World Series?" Schmidt shouted from his seat, "Renegotiate!"

2 The Philadelphia media were always highly critical of the Phillies, even when the team played well. Schmidt once said about the city's sportswriters, "Philadelphia is the only city in the world where you can experience the thrill of victory and the agony of reading about it the next day."

3 Philadelphia's resident fans were tough, too. After losing the World Series to the Orioles in 1983, Schmidt was driving up to a bus carrying his daughter home from school when the schoolchildren inside spotted him and began chanting "Choke! Choke! Choke!" "Ah," said Schmidt, "that's your Philadelphia fan in the making."

SCHNABEL, Artur (1882–1951), *Austrian pianist.*

1 A piano student came to Schnabel to ask him if he could study with him. Schnabel tested him and agreed to take him on as a pupil. "How much are your lessons?" the student asked.

"Five guineas each."

"I'm afraid I can't afford that."

"I also give lessons at three guineas — but I don't recommend them."

2 In 1940, Schnabel's son Stefan, an actor, was visited by a publicity agent. Toward the end of the interview she asked: "Are your parents in America?"

"Yes," replied Stefan.

"And your father — what does he do?"

"He is Artur Schnabel."

The lady looked bemused. "I see," she said. "But what does he do?"

"He's a pianist," replied Stefan. "He played at Carnegie Hall several times this season."

"That's nice," said the agent. "I'm always so glad to hear of a refugee getting on well."

3 An elderly lady in the front row slept right through one of Schnabel's concerts, waking with a start as the final ovation rang around the auditorium. Schnabel leaned across to apologize. "It was the applause, madame," he whispered. "I played as softly as I could."

SCHÖDL, Max (1834–1921), *Austrian still-life painter.*

1 Schödl was noted for his absentmindedness. "Where to?" asked the driver of a horse-cab that the painter had hailed. Schödl reflected. "Number six," he said. "I'll tell you the street later on."

SCHOLL, Aurélien (1833–1902), *notorious Belle Epoque boulevardier, journalist, and amorist.*

1 "One challenger of Scholl's was a banker of rather shady reputation who, on certain occasions, had carried out a number of deals which had all but landed him in prison. Angered by some insinuating remarks Scholl had written about him in his newspaper, the banker burst into Tortoni's and challenged Scholl to a duel. Scholl, as always adjusting his monocle, stared coolly at the man and asked, 'You really want to fight?'

"'Oui, monsieur!' roared the banker.

"Scholl shrugged. *'Bon,'* he said. 'I daresay that when we arrive on the grounds they'll remove your handcuffs.'"

3 "He eventually married the daughter of a rich London brewer, a far from felicitous marriage which in no way interfered with his successful pursuit of other women. His witty approach had an individuality of its own. When one little married woman, wanting to give way yet struggling with her conscience, pleaded piteously, 'Let me be for a time, my friend! Let me retire into myself,' Scholl replied with gallant ardor: 'Allow me, madame, to accompany you.'"

SCHÖNBEIN, Christian Friedrich (1799–1868), *German-Swiss chemist.*

1 In 1845 Schönbein was carrying out an experiment with a mixture of sulfuric and nitric acid in the kitchen of his home. This was a practice expressly forbidden by his wife, who had banned the professor from her kitchen. In her absence he became so absorbed in his experiment that he spilled a little of the dangerous mixture on her kitchen table. Aware that his disobedience might be disclosed by a permanent stain on the woodwork, he grabbed the first thing at hand, his wife's cotton apron, and mopped up the offending liquid. He then hung it before the fire so that it would be dry before his wife returned. The resulting explosion, caused by the nitration of the cellulose in the cotton, eventually enabled the browbeaten chemist to invent, market, and exploit the smokeless gunpowder that became known as guncotton.

SCHÖNBERG, Arnold (1874–1951), *Austrian composer, pioneer of atonality, the so-called twelve-tone system.*

1 Schönberg was strolling through the streets of his home town with a visiting friend one day, nodding graciously at the respectful greetings from the local people, many of them young boys. His friend was impressed and not a little surprised. "You really are famous," he remarked. "Even the children know you."

"That is quite true," remarked Schönberg with a smile. "You see, my son is a halfback on the high-school football team."

2 (The pianist Artur Schnabel in the course of a lecture told this story about the composers Schönberg and Stravinsky.)

"You may find this hard to believe, but Igor Stravinsky has actually published in the papers the statement, 'Music to be great must be completely cold and unemotional'! And last Sunday, I was having breakfast with Arnold Schönberg, and I said to him, 'Can you imagine that Stravinsky actually made the statement that music to be great must be cold and unemotional'? At this, Schönberg got furious and said, 'I said that first!' "

SCHOPENHAUER, Arthur (1788–1860), *German philosopher.*

1 Visiting a greenhouse in Dresden, Schopenhauer became absorbed in contemplation of one of the plants. His eccentric gestures drew the attention of the attendant. "Who are you?" he asked. Schopenhauer looked at him for some moments, then said slowly, "If you could only answer that question for me, I'd be eternally grateful."

2 Schopenhauer, living in lodgings at Frankfurt for the last years of his life, used to take his meals at an inn frequented by English military personnel. At the start of each meal he would place a gold coin on the table in front of him. At the end of the meal he would drop the coin back in his pocket. A waiter, who had been eyeing the coin with interest, asked him why he did this. Schopenhauer explained that he had a little wager with himself every day: he would drop the coin into the poor box on the first occasion that the English officers talked of anything other than horses, dogs, or women.

SCHUMANN-HEINK, Ernestine (1861–1936), *German contralto.*

1 Schumann-Heink was an unashamed gourmand. Enrico Caruso, another lover of good food in quantity, entered the restaurant at which she was dining. Seeing her about to begin on a vast steak, he said, "Stina, surely you are not going to eat that alone?" "No, no, not alone," replied the lady, "mit potatoes."

2 When Mme Schumann-Heink appeared as the witch in *Hansel and Gretel,* her children, watching from the auditorium, were appalled at her fate at the end of the opera. "Mother! Mother!" her little boy screamed as she was pushed into the oven. A few minutes later she was back on the stage for her curtain calls. "There she is!" he cried out in relief. "There's Mother! They didn't burn her after all!"

3 Conditions were rather cramped in the Detroit concert hall where Schumann-Heink was to perform. As the portly singer struggled through the orchestra pit to make her entrance, music racks crashed to the floor. The conductor looked on in alarm. "Side-

ways, madam," he whispered urgently, "go sideways."

"Mein Gott!" cried the singer in reply. "I haff no sideways."

4 In the Depression of the 1930s financial problems forced Schumann-Heink out of retirement. Despite her age and ill health, she signed a music-hall contract and took to the road. A newspaper reporter interviewing her remarked: "Things must be really bad when a great Wagnerian contralto is forced to do ten-cent shows."

"Young man," said Ernestine reprovingly, "how can times be bad when children can hear Schumann-Heink for a dime?"

SCHWAB, Charles (1862–1939), *US financier.*

1 Schwab's first big job in finance was in 1901, when J. P. Morgan hired him to run U.S. Steel. Before starting, Schwab went to Paris to cut loose, but his party-going and high living were loud enough to reverberate back in America. Upon his return to New York Morgan called him into his office and told him to stop acting like a fool. Schwab, defending himself, said, "Mr. Morgan, you're being unfair. You know perfectly well I'm not doing anything you don't do behind closed doors." Replied Morgan, "That is what doors are for, Mr. Schwab."

SCHWARTZ, Delmore (1913–66), *US poet and writer.*

1 After years of marriage, Schwartz and his first wife, Gertrude, agreed to a divorce. But in New York, divorce was granted only for such grounds as adultery, not simple incompatibility. So Delmore staged a scene in a hotel room: friends would stop by for a visit, only to find him *flagrante delicto* with a stranger. The friends duly arrived to see a woman rushing into the bathroom. It was Gertrude herself — who said later, "This was the one time when he wasn't with another woman."

2 Schwartz's severe alcoholism proved a permanent source of paralysis. He was unable to travel, or often to work at all, due to bouts with the bottle. When asked why he had never even crossed the Atlantic, Schwartz said, "How could I go to Europe when I can't even shave at home?"

SCHWARTZ, Maurice (1890–1964), *Polish-born actor and theater director.*

1 Schwartz was frequently accused of monopolizing all the best roles. A friend of his hotly denied the allegations. "On occasion Mr. Schwartz has been very generous with the leading parts," he said. "Take, for example, his recent production of the *Brothers Ashkenazi.* Did he play both brothers?"

SCHWARZENBERG, Felix, Prince (1800–52), *Austrian statesman and diplomat.*

1 Austria was forced to rely on the help of Czar Nicholas I of Russia to crush the Hungarian uprising against Austrian dominion in 1849. After this had been achieved, Schwarzenberg showed no signs in his policy of favoring Russia in any way. Asked whether he did not feel under an obligation to the czar, Schwarzenberg replied, "Austria will astound the world with the magnitude of her ingratitude."

2 After the quelling of the 1849 uprising, it was suggested to Schwarzenberg that it would be prudent to show mercy toward the captured Hungarian rebels. "Yes, indeed, a good idea," he replied, "but first we will have a little hanging."

3 Schwarzenberg's health failed quite suddenly when he was still comparatively young. A doctor called in to examine him warned him to take more rest or he would die of an apoplectic stroke. "That manner of death has my full approval," snapped back the patient.

———— ∽ ————

SCHWEITZER, Albert (1875–1965), *Alsatian-born medical missionary, theologian, and musician who was awarded the Nobel Peace Prize for his work in Africa in 1952.*

1 The phrase "reverence for life" aptly sums up Schweitzer's philosophy. On a visit to the United States he was importuned by many visitors, a group of whom interrupted his dinner to try to persuade him to explain his ethics. He talked patiently for twenty minutes. One of the visitors wanted him to give a specific example of "reverence for life." Schweitzer said, "Reverence for life means my answering your kind inquiries; it also means your reverence for my dinner hour." Schweitzer was able to return to his meal.

2 His doctrine of "reverence for life" was to be literally obeyed. It accounted for his vegetarianism, as well as for his attitude toward all animals. The American TV star Jack Paar once visited him at his hospital in Lambaréné. A dog appeared, chasing a chicken. In French Dr. Schweitzer shouted, "No! No! Remember we have won the Nobel Peace Prize!"

3 Jack Paar also recalls Schweitzer's standard attire: white pith helmet, white shirt and pants, black tie. He had worn one hat for forty years, the tie for twenty. Told that some men owned dozens of neckties, he remarked, "For one neck?"

4 (African patients leaving Schweitzer's hospital frequently stole his chamber pots to use as cooking utensils in their jungle homes.) Traveling by train in Europe, Schweitzer was asked by an inquisitive fellow passenger, "What do you do for a living?" "I supply Gabon with chamber pots," he replied.

5 On a train journey in the American Midwest, Schweitzer was approached by two ladies. "Have we the honor of speaking to Professor Einstein?" they asked. "No, unfortunately not," replied Schweitzer, "though I can quite understand your mistake, for he has the same kind of hair as I have." He paused to rumple his hair. "But inside, my head is altogether different. However, he is a very old friend of mine — would you like me to give you his autograph?" Taking a slip of paper from his pocket he wrote: "Albert Einstein, by way of his friend, Albert Schweitzer."

———— ∽ ————

SCIPIO NASICA SERAPIO, Publius Cornelius (fl. 138 BC), *Roman politician.*

1 Scipio Nasica called on his friend, poet Quintus Ennius, only to be told by Ennius's slave that his master was not at home. Nasica caught sight of the poet disappearing into a room at the back of the house. He did not attempt to contradict the slave, however, and left without a word. Sometime later, Ennius returned the visit. "Not at home!" cried Nasica as his friend arrived at the door. "You can't expect me to believe that — I recognize your voice," replied Ennius. "Why, you're a nice fellow," retorted Nasica. "I believed your slave, and you won't believe me."

———— ∽ ————

SCOTT, Sir Walter (1771–1832), *Scottish novelist.*

1 As a boy Scott was always the runner-up in his class at school. Try as he might, he could never displace the fluent, quick-witted, and studious boy who stood at the top of the class. One day Scott, watching his rival

speaking in class, noticed that the lad always fumbled with a particular button on his vest while he talked. Stealthily Scott took a pair of scissors and snipped off the button. The next time the master called upon the boy to answer a question, he stood up and began to speak, feeling for the button. Failing to find it, he was so disconcerted that he stuttered and fell silent. Scott seized his opportunity, answered the question, and displaced his rival from the head of the class, a position he maintained thereafter.

2 Walking around the Abbotsford estate in spring, Sir Walter and Lady Scott passed a field full of gamboling lambs. "No wonder," said Scott, "that poets from the earliest times have made lambs the symbols of peace and innocence."

"Delightful creatures indeed," Lady Scott assented, "especially with mint sauce."

3 Scott gleaned many of the anecdotes and traditional stories used in his novels from an old Scottish lady, Mrs. Murray Keith. At the height of the speculation about the authorship of *Waverley,* Mrs. Keith challenged Scott with being "the Great Unknown" and refused to accept his customary denial. "D'ye think I dinna ken my ain groats among other folks' kail [broth]?" she exclaimed.

4 Scott's young son was ignorant of his father's fame as a novelist, but loved and admired him for reasons closer to a boy's heart. Once when he was in his teens he was in the company of some older people who were discussing Scott's genius. "Aye," put in young Scott, "it's commonly him is first to see the hare."

5 When Scott was declared bankrupt in 1826, his friends rallied around with offers of money. Scott declined their assistance, saying, "No, this right hand shall work it all off." This promise he kept, although the incessant writing ruined his health, and he dic-

tated his last works from his deathbed while suffering great pain.

---ᐱ---

SEBASTIANO DEL PIOMBO, Fra (?1485–1547), *Italian painter.*

1 In later life Sebastiano ceased painting and was censured for his idleness by certain busybodies. He rebutted such criticism by pointing out, "There are now men of genius who do in two months what I used to do in two years, and I believe if I live long enough I shall find that everything has been painted. As these stalwarts can do so much, it is as well that there should also be someone who does nothing, so that they may have the more to do."

---ᐱ---

SEDGWICK, Catharine Maria (1789–1867), *US writer.*

1 Like most Sedgwicks, Catharine was very fond of her native town, Stockbridge, Massachusetts, where the burial markers of the clan are arranged in concentric circles known as the Sedgwick Pie. Someone once remarked to Miss Sedgwick that she spoke about Stockbridge as if it were heaven. "I expect no very violent transition," she replied.

---ᐱ---

SEDGWICK, John (1813–64), *US general.*

1 During the battle of the Wilderness in the Civil War, the general was inspecting his troops. At one point he came to a parapet over which he gazed out in the direction of the enemy. His officers suggested that this was unwise and perhaps he ought to duck while passing the parapet. "Nonsense,"

snapped the general. "They couldn't hit an elephant at this dist — "

———⌥———

SEDGWICK, Theodore (1746–1813), *US judge; Speaker of the House of Representatives (1799–1801).*

1 The Sedgwicks had a black servant called Mumbet, who reared the Sedgwick children when their mother became insane. One day Mumbet heard the Declaration of Independence being read out at a town meeting. The following day she went to see Theodore Sedgwick in his office. "Sir," she said, "I heard that we are all born equal, and every one of us has the right to be free." Mr. Sedgwick promptly began a suit on Mumbet's behalf and a decree was obtained in her favor. Mumbet was so grateful she remained with the Sedgwick family for the rest of her life.

———⌥———

SEDLEY, Sir Charles (1639–1701), *British playwright and wit. His writings enjoyed a high reputation among his contemporaries, who also reveled in gossip about the author's scandalous personal life.*

1 Sir Charles had one daughter, Catharine, a shrewd and witty girl whom James, the Duke of York, made his mistress. When the duke ascended the throne as James II, he resolved not to see her again, but within three months their intrigue was revived. In 1686 James created Catharine Countess of Dorchester. Sir Charles, despite his own notoriety as a libertine, was sincerely upset by his daughter's situation. "I hate ingratitude," he said, "and as the king has made my daughter a countess I will endeavor to repay the civility by making his daughter a queen."

This he did by voting James II out of office in the Parliament preceding the Glorious Revolution of 1688, which brought James's daughter Mary and her husband, William of Orange, to the English throne.

———⌥———

SEELEY, Sir John Robert (1834–95), *British historian and essayist.*

1 In 1869 Seeley succeeded Charles Kingsley in the chair of Modern History at Cambridge, which Kingsley had resigned on grounds of ill health. Dr. William Thompson, the Master of Trinity College, observed after Seeley's inaugural lecture, "Well, well, I did not think we could so soon have had occasion to regret poor Kingsley."

———⌥———

SEFERIS, George [George Seferiades] (1900–71), *Greek poet and diplomat who won the Nobel Prize for Literature in 1963.*

1 (The British writer and classical scholar Peter Levi met Seferis in Athens in 1963).

"We talked about mermaids. He said people knew he had a passion for them, and sent him presents of mermaids. There was a mermaid of bread, I think from southern Italy, hanging against the white garden wall. It had been there three years. I said she was young, for a mermaid. 'But it is old,' he said, 'for bread.'"

———⌥———

SEGOVIA, Andrés (1893–1987), *Spanish guitar virtuoso.*

1 During a recital in Berlin, Segovia's guitar was heard to emit a loud cracking sound. Segovia rushed offstage and, cradling his instrument, kept repeating, "My guitar, my guitar." It was soon learned that the man who had built the guitar had died in Madrid

at the exact moment in the concert that Segovia's guitar had split.

———— ⌘ ————

SELLERS, Peter (1925–80), *British comic actor.*

1 Sellers once received the following letter from a *Goon Show* fan: "Dear Mr. Sellers, I have been a keen follower of yours for many years now, and should be most grateful if you would kindly send me a singed photograph of yourself." Encouraged by fellow-comedian Harry Secombe, Sellers took the writer at his word. With the flame of his cigarette lighter, he carefully burned the edges of one of his publicity photographs and sent it off by return mail. A couple of weeks later, another letter arrived from the same address. "Dear Mr. Sellers," it read, "Thank you very much for the photograph, but I wonder if I could trouble you for another as this one is signed all round the edge."

2 Blake Edwards, who directed Sellers in the "Pink Panther" films, did not find him the easiest person to work with. One night, having wasted an entire day on one particular scene, Edwards was awakened by a phone call from Peter. "I just talked to God," he said excitedly, "and He told me how to do it."

The following day, Edwards set the cameras rolling to capture the results of Sellers's divine inspiration. "Peter," sighed the harassed director, "next time you talk to God, tell Him to stay out of show business."

3 In *The Mask Behind the Mask,* Peter Evans, biographer of Peter Sellers, says that Sellers played so many roles he sometimes was not sure of his own identity. Approached once by a fan who asked him, "Are you Peter Sellers?" Evans said Sellers answered briskly, "Not today," and walked on.

———— ⌘ ————

SELWYN, George Augustus (1719–91), *British politician, eccentric, and wit.*

1 When Henry Fox, Lord Holland, was dying, Selwyn called on him and left his card. His lordship, told that his old friend had called, instructed his footman, "If Mr. Selwyn calls again, show him up. If I am alive, I shall be glad to see him, and if I am dead, I am sure he will be delighted to see me."

2 Politician Charles Fox asked Selwyn if he had attended the execution of a highwayman, also called Charles Fox. Replied Selwyn, "I never attend rehearsals."

3 Robert Walpole once remarked in Selwyn's hearing that the British system of politics was the same under George III as it had been under his grandfather, George II, and that there was nothing new under the sun. "Nor under the grandson," put in Selwyn.

4 Staying at the fashionable resort of Bath out of season, Selwyn was compelled for want of better company to cultivate the acquaintance of an elderly bore. Some months later they met again by chance in a smart London thoroughfare at the height of the London season. Selwyn tried to slip past unnoticed, but the older gentleman hailed him, saying, "Don't you recollect me?"

"Perfectly," said Selwyn, "and when I next go to Bath I shall be most happy to become acquainted with you again."

5 A fashionable society beauty was showing off her new gown, which was covered with silver spangles the size of shillings. "How do you like it?" she asked George Selwyn. "You will be change for a guinea, madam," he replied.

6 Selwyn once asserted that no woman could write a letter without adding a postscript. One of the ladies present, determined to prove him wrong, sent him a letter the following day. To Selwyn's glee, however, his

triumphant correspondent had added after her signature: "P.S. Who is right now, you or I?"

———— ✤ ————

SENECA, Lucius Annaeus (?4 BC–65 AD), *Roman statesman, author, and philosopher.*

1 Seneca's influence upon the vicious and mad Nero grew weaker as the years passed. Nonetheless, Seneca tried to curb his charge's cruelty, warning him on one occasion, "However many you put to death, you will never kill your successor."

———— ✤ ————

SERVETUS, Michael (1511–53), *Spanish-born theologian and physician.*

1 Hiding from the Inquisition in Calvin's Geneva, Servetus was caught, tried, and condemned to be burned at the stake for his views. He said to his judges, "I will burn, but this is a mere incident. We shall continue our discussion in eternity."

———— ✤ ————

SEWARD, William Henry (1801–72), *US statesman.*

1 After a debate in which Stephen A. Douglas had delivered a fiery diatribe against "niggerworshipers," Seward walked home with him from the Capitol. Aware that Douglas hoped to secure the Democratic presidential nomination, Seward remarked, "Douglas, no man will ever be President of the United States who spells negro with two *g*'s."

2 Seward was in an assembly of people who were speculating about the probable destination of a secret movement of troops. A lady, noticing his silence, challenged him: "Well, Governor Seward, what do you make of it? Where do you think they are going?" Seward

smiled. "Madam," he replied, "if I did not know I would tell you."

———— ✤ ————

SHAFTESBURY, Anthony Ashley Cooper, 1st Earl of (1621–83), *British statesman.*

1 Shaftesbury's religious beliefs remained a mystery; very likely he was a deist. He once remarked that all wise men are of but one religion. "Which is that?" he was promptly asked. "Wise men never tell," he replied.

2 Charles II, hearing some gossip about Lord Shaftesbury, remarked to him jestingly, "I believe you're the wickedest rogue in England."

"Of a subject, sire, I believe I am," was the prompt reply.

———— ✤ ————

SHAKESPEARE, William (1564–1616), *British dramatist.*

1 At a time when Richard Burbage was playing the title role in *Richard III,* he made an assignation with a lady who lived near the playhouse. "Announce yourself as Richard III," she suggested cautiously — a suggestion Shakespeare overheard. The dramatist slipped out of the theater before the end of the play and hastened to the woman's lodgings. Here he announced himself as Richard III and was admitted to her bedroom. A short while afterward a message was brought up that "Richard III" was at the door. Shakespeare sent the message back to Burbage, saying that William the Conqueror came before Richard III.

2 Once when Shakespeare was acting the role of a king, Queen Elizabeth thought she would see if she could distract him from his part and purposely let her handkerchief flutter to the stage at the actor's feet. Shakespeare did not hesitate. "Take up our sister's handkerchief," he instructed one of the stage courtiers in his train.

---⁕---

SHARP, William (1855–1905), *British writer.*

1 The English scholar W. P. Ker learned from a mutual acquaintance that Sharp always wore women's clothing to write his "Fiona Macleod" romances. "Did he? The bitch!" said Ker.

---⁕---

SHATNER, William (1931–), *US actor.*

1 Shatner's most embarrassing moment occurred when he was still a novice in his profession. He was asked to attend a party at Joshua Logan's house and did, bringing his baby daughter and his eighty-pound dog along. He immediately saw that he had dressed wrong; he was in T-shirt and jeans, while every other guest was in a tuxedo or a long formal gown. And almost as quickly, his dog jumped into the pool, got out, ran over to a beautifully dressed Gloria Vanderbilt, and jumped up on her with its muddy paws, soiling and soaking her dress. Shatner left as quickly as possible. Years later he ran into Henry Fonda on an airplane. "Mr. Fonda," said Shatner, "I don't suppose you remember me . . ." Fonda interrupted him, saying, "Aren't you the young actor who was at Logan's party and whose dog dirtied Gloria Vanderbilt's dress?"

---⁕---

SHAW, George Bernard (1856–1950), *Irish playwright.*

1 Before Shaw became famous, one of his plays was consistently turned down by a certain producer. After Shaw achieved success, the producer suddenly cabled an offer to stage the rejected work. Shaw cabled in reply: "Better never than late."

2 While Shaw was still a music critic, he was dining with a friend in a restaurant that provided for entertainment an orchestra that was at best mediocre. The leader, recognizing Shaw, wrote him a note asking him what he would like the orchestra to play next. "Dominoes," replied Shaw.

3 The first performance of *Arms and the Man* (April 21, 1894) was boisterous. The author took a curtain call and was received with cheers. While they were subsiding, before Shaw could utter a syllable, a solitary hiss was heard from the gallery. It was made by R. Goulding Bright, who later became a very successful literary agent. Bright hissed, it later appeared, under the misapprehension that Shaw's satire on florid Balkan soldiers was, in fact, a reflection on the British army. Shaw did not know this at the time, however, and as he stood on the stage he raised his hand to silence the cheers. Bowing in Bright's direction, he said, "I quite agree with you, sir, but what can two do against so many?"

4 The Theatre Guild had started rehearsals for the American premiere of Shaw's *Saint Joan.* Everything was progressing smoothly, except that the play was found to run for three and a half hours, long past the normal curtain time. Suburban playgoers would miss the last trains home. This information was cabled to Shaw, together with a request that he cut the play. Back came the reply: "Begin at eight or run later trains."

5 The success of Shaw's dramatic writings was an embarrassment to his socialistic ideals. To the play representative who had sent him a draft of money with promise of more to come, he wrote: "Rapacious Elisabeth Marbury: What do you want me to make a fortune for? Don't you know that the draft you sent me will permit me to live and preach Socialism for six months? The next time you have so large an amount to remit, please send

it to me by installments, or you will put me to the inconvenience of having a bank account."

6 "George Bernard Shaw, a staunch vegetarian, refused to attend a gala testimonial because the bill of fare was a vegetarian menu. He said: 'The thought of two thousand people crunching celery at the same time horrified me.'"

7 At a dinner party Shaw sat next to a young man who proved to be a bore of historic proportions. After suffering through a seemingly interminable monologue, Shaw cut in to observe that between the two of them, they knew everything there was to know in the world. "How is that?" asked the young man. "Well," said Shaw, "you seem to know everything except that you're a bore. And I know that!"

8 It is said that the dancer Isadora Duncan wrote to Shaw that good eugenics indicated they should have a child together. "Think of it! With my body and your brains, what a wonder it would be," she said. Shaw replied, "Yes, but what if it had my body and your brains?"

9 "At a performance given by an Italian string quartet, Shaw's companion remarked approvingly, 'These men have been playing together for twelve years.' 'Surely,' said Shaw, 'we have been here longer than that.'"

10 The military theorist and historian B. H. Liddell Hart once observed to Shaw, "Do you know that 'sumac' and 'sugar' are the only two words in the English language that begin with *su* and are pronounced *shu?*"

"Sure," answered Shaw.

11 Shaw was once approached by the advertising executive of a company manufacturing electric razors, in the hope that the great writer would endorse their new product by shaving off his beard. By way of reply, Shaw explained the reason why he, and his father before him, had chosen to grow a beard. "I was about five at the time," said Shaw, "and I was standing at my father's knee whilst he was shaving. I said to him, 'Daddy, why do you shave?' He looked at me in silence for a full minute, before throwing the razor out the window, saying, 'Why the hell do I?' He never did again."

12 An anthologist wrote to Shaw requesting permission to include one of his pieces in an anthology. He explained that he was a very young man and therefore would not be able to pay Shaw's usual fee. GBS responded, "I'll wait for you to grow up."

13 Arnold Bennett visited Shaw in his apartment and, knowing his host's love of flowers, was surprised that there was not a single vase of flowers to be seen. He remarked on their absence to Shaw: "But I thought you were so fond of flowers." "I am," said Shaw, "but I don't chop their heads off and stand them in pots around the house."

14 A lady notorious for courting celebrities sent Shaw an invitation reading: "Lady — will be at home on Tuesday between four and six o'clock." Shaw returned the card annotated, "Mr. Bernard Shaw likewise."

15 "Are you enjoying yourself, Mr. Shaw?" anxiously inquired the hostess, who had noticed that her distinguished guest was standing alone in a corner. "Certainly," he replied. "There is nothing else here to enjoy."

16 Sam Goldwyn, the American movie magnate, attempted to buy from Shaw the film rights to one of his plays. There was a protracted haggle over what the rights should cost, which ended in Shaw's declining to sell. "The trouble is, Mr. Goldwyn," said Shaw, "you are interested only in art and I am interested only in money."

17 A country clergyman, hearing that Shaw was an expert in the brewing of coffee, wrote to him for the recipe. Shaw obliged, adding as an afterthought that he hoped the request was not an underhanded way of obtaining his autograph. The clergyman cut Shaw's signature from the letter, returned it with a note thanking him for the coffee recipe, and concluded, "I wrote in good faith, so allow me to return what is obvious you infinitely prize, but which is of no value to me, your autograph."

18 Shaw once came across a copy of one of his works in a secondhand bookshop. Opening the volume, he found the name of a friend inscribed in his own hand on the flyleaf: "To — with esteem, George Bernard Shaw." He promptly bought the book and returned it to his friend, adding the inscription, "With renewed esteem, George Bernard Shaw."

19 In conversation with Shaw and his wife, writer Patrick Mahony asked Mrs. Shaw how she had coped with her husband's many female admirers. By way of reply, Mrs. Shaw began to recount an anecdote: "After we were married there was an actress who pursued my husband. She threatened suicide if she were not allowed to see him . . ." "And did she die of a broken heart?" "Yes, she did," interrupted Shaw. "Fifty years later."

20 Showing a friend the portrait bust sculpted for him by Renoir, Shaw remarked: "It's a funny thing about that bust. As time goes on, it seems to get younger and younger."

21 Once when sitting for the photographer Yousuf Karsh, Shaw said that Karsh "might make a good picture of him — but none as good as the picture he had seen at a recent dinner party, where he glimpsed, over the shoulder of his hostess, a perfect portrait of himself: "Cruel, you understand, a diabolical caricature, but absolutely true." He had pushed by the lady, approaching the living image, and found he was looking into a mirror!

22 Among his guests George Bernard Shaw received on his ninetieth birthday was Fabian, Scotland Yard's celebrated detective. At Fabian's suggestion Shaw agreed to have his fingerprints recorded for posterity. To the amazement of both, Shaw's fingerprints were so faint no impression could be obtained. "Well," announced Shaw, "had I known this sooner I should certainly have chosen another profession."

23 On a visit to GBS shortly after Shaw's ninetieth birthday, comedian Danny Kaye sought to compliment the playwright by saying, "You're a young-looking ninety." "Nonsense," came the crusty reply, "I look exactly like a man of ninety should look. Everyone else looks older because of the dissolute lives they lead."

24 At the age of ninety-four Shaw refused a crucial kidney operation, telling his doctor, "You won't be famous if I recover. Surgeons only become famous when their patients die."

———— ✳ ————

SHEARING, George [Albert] (1919–), *British-born US jazz pianist.*

1 One afternoon, at rush hour, he was waiting at a busy intersection for someone to take him across the street when another blind man tapped him on the shoulder and asked if Shearing would mind helping him to get across.

"What could I do?" said Shearing afterward. "I took him across and it was the biggest thrill of my life."

———— ✳ ————

Asked why he robbed banks, the notorious American bank robber Willie Sutton is reputed to have remarked, "Because that's where the money is."

— THEODORE WHITE,
America in Search of Itself

SHELBURNE, William Petty, 1st Marquis of Lansdowne (1737–1805), *British politician.*

1 In March 1780 Lord Shelburne fought a duel with a Lieutenant Colonel William Fullerton over some remarks that the former had made in the House of Lords. Shelburne was slightly wounded in the groin. As his anxious seconds bent over him, he reassured them, saying, "I don't think Lady Shelburne will be the worse for it."

SHELLEY, Mary Wollstonecraft Godwin (1797–1851), *British author.*

1 During the summer of 1816 Byron and Shelley were neighbors on the shores of the lake of Geneva. The two poets, together with Byron's friend Dr. John Polidori and Shelley's companions, Mary Godwin and her stepsister Claire Clairmont, spent many an evening conversing. One night Byron initiated a discussion of ghosts and the supernatural. Polidori recalled that Shelley was so distressed at the conversation that he ran from the room, maintaining that he had seen the women's breasts as eyes. Meanwhile Byron suggested that all of them write their own ghost stories. From this evening emerged an effort begun by Byron about the ruins of Ephesus, never completed; a tale by Polidori eventually published as *The Vampyre;* and, by the seventeen-year-old Mary, the tale of *Frankenstein* — a story that probably has frightened more people and led to more spin-offs than any other ghost story in the world.

2 Shelley's utter disregard for convention may have been a trial to his wife. After his death she was urged to send her surviving son, Percy Florence, to an advanced school at which the boy would be taught to think for himself. "To think for himself!" exclaimed his mother. "Oh, my God, teach him to think like other people!"

SHELLEY, Percy Bysshe (1792–1822), *British Romantic poet.*

1 As a young man he went on a short journey in rural Sussex. There was a full complement of passengers on the outside of the coach, but Shelley took an inside seat and for a time had the interior to himself. Then the coach stopped and picked up a large elderly woman carrying two vast panniers, one filled with apples, the other with onions. In the stuffy coach the smell of apples, onions, and sweaty old woman soon became overwhelming. Seating himself on the floor, Shelley fixed his unwanted companion with a wild glare and began to recite Richard II's lament from Shakespeare's play — "For God's sake let us sit upon the ground . . ." When he got to the words, "All murder'd," the old woman's nerve could stand it no longer and she yelled at the coach driver to stop and let her out. She duly exited, and Shelley was able to complete his journey in comfort.

2 Early in 1822 Shelley's household was joined by the young English adventurer Edward J. Trelawny, a sportsman and extrovert who greatly admired the impractical and wayward poet. Trelawny found a deep pool in the river where he liked to bathe. One day, after watching Trelawny performing various aquatic feats, Shelley said wistfully, "Why can't I swim?" Trelawny immediately offered to teach him. Shelley stripped off his clothes and leaped in — plunging straight to the bottom of the pool, where he lay motionless. Trelawny jumped into the water and man-

aged to haul the poet out. Shelley was not at all flustered by the narrowness of his escape. "I always find the bottom of the well and they say truth lies there. In another minute I should have found it, and you would have found an empty shell. It is an easy way to get rid of the body." Only a few months later Shelley was drowned while sailing near Leghorn in squally weather.

SHERIDAN, Philip Henry (1831–88), *US army officer.*

1 In January 1869 Sheridan held a conference with Indian chiefs at Fort Cobb in the then Indian Territory (now part of Oklahoma). When the Comanche chief Toch-a-way was introduced, he said to Sheridan, "Me Toch-a-way, me good Indian." "The only good Indians I ever saw were dead," retorted Sheridan.

2 While commanding the Military Division of the Gulf, Sheridan spent time at San Antonio, Texas. Asked by a local reporter his opinion of Texas as a country to live in, he answered, "If I owned two plantations and one was located in Texas and the other one was in hell, I'd rent out the one in Texas and live on the other one." This comment was printed with a note from the editor that read: "Well, damn a man that won't stand up for his own country."

SHERIDAN, Richard Brinsley (1751–1816), *Anglo-Irish playwright.*

1 Lord Thurlow produced a bottle of particularly good Constantia wine, specially sent from the Cape of Good Hope, at a dinner at which Sheridan was a guest. Sheridan greatly appreciated the wine and tried, by praising and hinting, to persuade Lord Thurlow to bring out another bottle. The host, however, was determined not to be overgenerous with this rare treat, and Sheridan eventually saw that his efforts were in vain. Turning to his next neighbor, he gestured toward the decanter of Madeira and said, "Pass the decanter. I must return to Madeira since I cannot double the Cape."

2 A lady anxious to take a walk with Sheridan observed that the weather had cleared up sufficiently for them to set out. Sheridan, equally anxious to avoid the tête-à-tête, replied, "It may have cleared up enough for one, but not enough for two."

3 Two royal dukes, meeting Sheridan in London's Piccadilly, greeted him familiarly. Said one, "I say, Sherry, we were just discussing whether you are more rogue or fool."

"Why," replied Sheridan, taking each duke by the arm, "I believe I am between both."

4 Once a servant dropped a heap of plates with a tremendous crash. Sheridan rebuked the man, saying, "I suppose you've broken all of them."

"No, sir, not one," said the man.

"Then, you mean to say you have made all that noise for nothing!"

5 Sheridan's financial affairs were constantly in disorder, and debt was a chronic state with him. "Thank God, that's settled," he is reported to have said, handing over an IOU to a creditor.

6 A long-suffering creditor importuned Sheridan to name a date for payment. "The day of judgment," cried the harassed author. "But, no — stay — that will be a busy day. Make it the day after."

7 Sheridan had borrowed £500 from a friend, who took every opportunity to remind him

of the debt. On one such occasion Sheridan added insult to injury by asking for a further £25 to pay for a journey he had to make. On receiving the inevitable refusal Sheridan complained, "My dear fellow, be reasonable; the sum you ask me for is a very considerable one, whereas I only ask you for twenty-five pounds."

8 Sheridan's tailor grew tired of asking the writer to pay off his bill. "At least you could pay me the interest on it," he reasoned. "It is not my interest to pay the principal," replied Sheridan, "nor my principle to pay the interest."

9 Edmund Burke was delivering one of his stupendous orations in the House of Commons. At the climax he underlined his point by brandishing the dagger he had brought into the chamber with him and plunging it into the desk in front of him. In the stunned hush that followed this piece of histrionics the voice of Sheridan was heard saying, "The honorable gentleman has brought his knife with him, but where's his fork?"

10 Sheridan had been asked to apologize for insulting a fellow member of Parliament. "Mr. Speaker," replied Sheridan, "I said the honorable member was a liar it is true and I am sorry for it. The honorable member may place the punctuation where he pleases."

11 Richard Cumberland was a dramatist specializing in a brand of sentimental comedy that was rendered unfashionable by the comedy of Goldsmith and Sheridan. Nonetheless, he agreed to take his children to see Sheridan's *School for Scandal*. The children would have enjoyed themselves hugely, but every time they laughed, Cumberland hissed, "What are you laughing at, my dear little folks? You should not laugh, my angels. There is nothing to laugh at." Finally, in exasperation, he snapped: "Keep still, you little dunces." When this story was retailed to

Sheridan sometime later, he observed, "It was very ungrateful in Cumberland to have been displeased with his poor children for laughing at my comedy; for I went the other night to see his tragedy, and laughed at it from beginning to end."

12 Like his father, Sheridan's son Tom was perpetually short of money. Father and son once had a disagreement. A few days later, Sheridan told Tom that he had made his will and cut him off with a shilling. "I'm sorry to hear that, sir," said Tom. Then, after a moment's thought, he added, "You don't happen to have the shilling about you now, do you?"

13 On the night of February 24, 1809, the House of Commons was suddenly illuminated by a blaze of light. It was learned that the Drury Lane Theatre, of which Sheridan was the manager at that time, was on fire. A motion was made to adjourn the House, but Sheridan, who was in the chamber, said calmly, "Whatsoever might be the extent of the private calamity, I hope it will not interfere with the public business of the country." He then left the House and walked to Drury Lane, where he watched the blazing theater with apparent calm. While he was sitting in the nearby Piazza coffeehouse, a friend approached him and remarked on the philosophic calmness with which he bore his misfortune. Sheridan answered, "A man may surely be allowed to take a glass of wine by his own fireside."

14 Sheridan was sufficiently intimate with the future George IV to make gentle fun of his idiosyncrasies, such as his habit of taking the credit for anything good that happened in England. After an unusually fine summer one year, Sheridan remarked, "What His Royal Highness most particularly prides himself upon is the excellent harvest."

———— ∞ ————

SHERMAN, Roger (1721–93), *US revolutionary patriot, signer of the Declaration of Independence.*

1 As a young politician he was asked to give a speech on the opening of a new bridge in Connecticut. He walked out onto the bridge, walked back, and gave his entire speech: "I don't see but that it stands steady."

———— ᖀᕒ ————

SHERMAN, William Tecumseh (1820–91), *US general.*

1 After the Mexican War, Sherman was sent by President Zachary Taylor to survey the newly acquired lands of New Mexico, Arizona, and California. On his return, Taylor asked Sherman: "Well, Captain, will our new possessions pay for the blood and treasure spent in the war?" Recalling the arid lands he had just explored, Sherman replied, "Between you and me, General, I feel that we'll have to go to war again." Taylor was aghast. "What for?" he asked. "To make 'em take the darn country back!" said Sherman.

2 During one of his many engagements in Georgia in 1864, Sherman was having difficulty breaking through the enemy front. He decided to send General Cox's division to attack the opposing left. Sherman positioned himself on a high hill to watch the operations and gave Cox his final orders for the circuitous march: "See here, Cox, burn a few barns occasionally as you go along. I can't understand those signal flags, but I know what smoke means."

3 Receiving a telegram from the Republican convention asking him to be the presidential candidate in 1884, Sherman wired back: "I will not accepted if nominated, and will not serve if elected."

———— ᖀᕒ ————

SHI HUANGDI (late 3d century BC), *first emperor of China.*

1 Shi Huangdi died while on a journey to seek the elixir of life. Two of his confidants, Zhao Gao and Li Si, feared that the crown prince, who objected to his father's harsh regime, would dismiss and perhaps even execute them if he became emperor. They therefore hatched a plan to place another of Shi Huangdi's sons on the throne. The first part of this plan involved concealing the old emperor's death from the world. Enclosing the body in his traveling carriage, they gave orders to return to the capital. The weather was warm and the corpse soon began to putrefy. Zhao Gao and Li Si therefore arranged for the imperial carriage to be closely followed by a cart laden with rotting fish. The stench of fish was so overpowering that not even the emperor's bodyguard detected the smell of the putrefying body, and the conspirators succeeded in reaching the capital without the emperor's death being discovered. There they used the emperor's seal to sign a decree commanding the crown prince to commit suicide, whereupon they established their own candidate on the throne of China.

———— ᖀᕒ ————

SHUTER, Edward (1728–76), *British comic actor.*

1 Chided for having holes in his stocking, Shuter replied that he would rather have twenty holes than one darn. "A hole is the accident of a day, while a darn is premeditated poverty."

———— ᖀᕒ ————

SIBELIUS, Jean (1865–1957), *Finnish composer.*

1 Sibelius was hosting a party at which many of those invited were businessmen. "Why

businessmen?" asked one of his other guests. "What do you talk about with them?" "About music, of course," replied the composer. "I can't talk about music with musicians. All they talk about is money."

---∾---

SIDDONS, Sarah (1755–1831), *British tragic actress, sister of John and Charles Kemble and aunt of Fanny Kemble.*

1 The daughter of the theatrical manager Roger Kemble, Sarah was brought up in the stage environment. Her father nonetheless strictly forbade his beautiful and talented daughter to marry an actor. Despite this prohibition, she bestowed her affections on William Siddons, a lowly constituent of her father's company. The exasperated Roger Kemble lectured Sarah on her choice, concluding with the statement that not only was William Siddons a member of a dubious profession but also the worst one in the troupe. "Exactly," said Sarah sweetly. "No one can call him an actor."

2 When Sir Joshua Reynolds painted his famous portrait of Sarah Siddons as the Tragic Music, he added his name by working it into the border of her robe. Mrs. Siddons examined the picture minutely and smiled. Reynolds said, "I could not lose this opportunity of sending my name to posterity on the hem of your garment."

3 (In 1783 Sarah Siddons paid a call on Dr. Johnson, then in his seventies.)

"When Mrs. Siddons came into the room, there happened to be no chair ready for her, which he observing, said with a smile, 'Madam, you who so often occasion a want of seats to other people, will the more easily excuse the want of one yourself.'"

4 Sarah Siddons's high dramatic style tended to spill over into her everyday life. (As Sydney Smith observed of her at the dinner table, "It

was never without awe that one saw her stab the potatoes.") In Bath to play some of her favorite tragic roles, she visited a draper's shop to buy some fabric. Picking up a piece of muslin, she looked with great intensity at the shopman and said with the utmost solemnity and dramatic effect, "Did you say, sir, that this would wash?" The draper suspected that he had a lunatic in his shop. Mrs. Siddons recollected herself at the sight of his surprise, apologized, and repeated the question in a more normal tone of voice.

5 During a tour of the north of England, Mrs. Siddons was playing the role of a tragic queen who commits suicide by taking poison. At one performance, as she raised the cup of poison to her lips, the spellbound silence of the audience was shattered by a shout of encouragement from the gallery: "That's reet, Molly. Soop it oop, ma lass, soop it oop."

---∾---

SIDNEY, Sir Philip (1554–86), *British writer, soldier, and courtier, whose talents and charm made him the model of Elizabethan behavior.*

1 At Zutphen Sidney was wounded in the thigh. As he was being carried along to have the wound dressed, he suffered greatly from thirst, owing to loss of blood. A water bottle was found and brought to him. Putting it to his lips, he caught sight of another wounded man, a humble soldier, looking longingly at the water. Sidney at once passed the bottle to him with the words, "Thy need is yet greater than mine."

---∾---

SIEYÈS, Emmanuel-Joseph, Abbé de (1748–1836), *French cleric and statesman.*

1 After the Terror, a friend inquired of the abbé what he had done during those terrible years. "*J'ai vécu* [I survived]," he said.

can see the look in the eyes of the approaching men."

SIGISMUND (1368–1437), *Holy Roman Emperor (1414–37)*.

1 The emperor was once asked his recipe for lasting happiness in this world. "Only do always in health what you have often promised to do when you are sick," he replied.

SILVERMAN, Fred (1937–), *US broadcaster and television executive*.

1 A few days before Yom Kippur Fred Silverman was asked by a friend if he would be going home for the holiday. Silverman asked on what day the event fell. "Wednesday," the friend informed him. "Wednesday?" cried Silverman. "You mean they've scheduled Yom Kippur opposite *Charlie's Angels?*"

SIMENON, Georges (1903–89), *Belgian novelist, creator of the character Inspector Maigret*.

1 One of the reasons for Simenon's prolific output was the speed at which he was able to produce a novel. Director Alfred Hitchcock happened to telephone him from the United States while he was working on his 158th novel. Madame Simenon took the call. "I'm sorry," she said, "Georges is writing and I would rather not disturb him."

"Let him finish his book," replied Hitchcock. "I'll hang on."

2 Strolling down a Parisian boulevard with the playwright Marcel Pagnol one afternoon, Simenon suddenly exclaimed, "Goodness, she must be very pretty!" Looking ahead, Pagnol could see only a couple of young men walking in their direction. "Who? Where?" he asked. "She's behind us," replied Simenon. "Then how can you see her?" asked Pagnol. "I can't," said Simenon. "But I

SIMON, Richard Leo (1889–1960), *US publisher. In 1924, with Max L. Schuster (1897–1971), he founded the publishing company Simon and Schuster*.

1 Launching a new children's book, *Dr. Dan the Bandage Man*, Simon decided to include a free gift of six Band-Aids with each copy. He cabled a friend at the manufacturers, Johnson and Johnson: "Please ship half million Band-Aids immediately." Back came the reply: "Band-Aids on the way. What the hell happened to you?"

SINATRA, Frank (1915–98), *US singer and film actor*.

1 Having suffered a series of fainting fits, Sinatra consulted his doctor. "How much money do you earn, Mr. Sinatra?" asked the doctor. "Somewhere between four hundred thousand and a million dollars a year," replied Sinatra carelessly. "In that case," advised the doctor, "I suggest you go right out and buy yourself some red meat. You're suffering from malnutrition."

2 Sinatra often traveled many miles out of his way to visit hospitalized friends and sing to them. It was said that the more serious the illness, the more punctilious he was in visiting. One friend, who was suffering from a minor complaint but was afraid the doctors were not telling him the truth, awoke suddenly in his hospital room to find Sinatra at his bedside. The singer had been in the neighborhood and had just called in. The patient was appalled. "I knew it!" he yelled. "They've been lying to me!"

SINGER, Isaac Bashevis (1904–91), *US writer, born in Poland, who was awarded the 1978 Nobel Prize for Literature.*

1 An interviewer asked Singer whether he was a vegetarian for religious reasons or because of his health. "It is out of consideration for the chicken," he replied.

2 Singer was asked whether he believed in free will or predestination. "We have to believe in free will," he replied. "We've got no choice."

———— ✑ ————

SITWELL, Dame Edith (1887–1964), *British poet.*

1 (Osbert Sitwell tells about a guest at the Sitwells' home, Renishaw Hall:)

"A man whom we had never seen before was wished on us for luncheon one day. He was placed next to my sister, and took it into his head to enquire of her: 'Do you remember this house being built, Miss Sitwell?' Mrs. [Alice] Keppel overheard this, and said to him quickly: 'My dear man, be careful! Not even the nicest girl in the world likes to be asked if she is four hundred years old.'"

2 Edith Sitwell was accustomed to ferocious attacks on her poetry. At one gathering at which she had been reading some of her poems aloud, a woman came up to her and announced, "I just wanted to tell you, Miss Sitwell, that I *quite* enjoyed your last book of poems." She paused and then seemed about to go on when Edith Sitwell interrupted her.

"Now please don't say any more," she said. "You mustn't spoil me. It isn't good for me to be spoiled."

3 In 1954 Edith Sitwell was given the title Dame of the British Empire. On a visit to the United States an American came up to her and said rather aggressively, "Why do you call yourself 'Dame'?"

"I don't," she replied. "The queen does."

———— ✑ ————

SITWELL, Sir George Reresby (1860–1943), *British antiquarian and eccentric.*

1 Having in a fit of unsociability banished all visitors from his home, Renishaw Hall, Sir George was soon overcome by boredom. He confided to his son Osbert that he felt like taking a holiday and described the sort of hotel that he thought would suit him: a secluded country house with fine grounds, good views, and a few congenial fellow guests to whom he could talk. Osbert immediately recalled a newspaper advertisement he had seen that morning for what was clearly an expensive private institution for the mentally deranged. He described the "hotel" in glowing and inventive terms. Sir George agreed that it sounded exactly what he was looking for. Sir George's secretary was told to book a room for the month of September, and the whole Sitwell family joined in extolling the virtues of the supposed hotel. The eagerly awaited confirmation of the booking arrived. Unfortunately, the asylum director had added a postscript: "Ought a strait-waistcoat to be sent for Sir George to wear during the journey, which will be made by van? Three strong and practised male nurses will, of course, be in attendance, and prepared to quell any disturbance on the way."

2 (Sir Osbert Sitwell recalls a narrowly averted contretemps at a tea party at which one of the guests was a certain Mrs. Brooke. Sir George had begun the conversation with a spirited attack on modern art and from there he moved on to modern poetry.)

"He was just saying: 'Then there was that young man who died in the Dardanelles — I forget his name — they try to make out he was a genius, but no good, no good, I can assure you,' when with a startling suddenness I realized *why* Mrs. Brooke's face was so familiar — from photographs in the Press of Rupert Brooke: the resemblance was very marked; she must be his mother. I gave my father a good kick under the tea-table, but he did not even pause; only the as yet undreamt-of H-bomb could have stopped him. He went on: 'His poems were grossly over-praised in the Press.' . . . I could hardly believe my ears. Could it be true that this was really happening, or was it just a nightmare instalment of an instant in hell? Before, however, his memory could supply the missing name, the crowning horror was skilfully averted. . . . 'Sir George,' our hostess bravely intervened, 'you are sitting next to Mrs. Brooke, the mother of that wonderful young poet, Rupert Brooke. I *must* tell you, because,' she proceeded, drawing on her imagination, 'before tea you were just saying to me — but we were interrupted — how much you admired his work,' and continued, 'how different it is from the work of that other young poet — I, too, forget his name for the moment — of whom you were speaking.'

My father looked puzzled but said no more."

SKELTON, John (?1460–1529), *English poet at the court of Henry VIII.*

1 Enjoying the position of a licensed jester at Henry VIII's court, Skelton could satirize the great and powerful with virtual impunity. At last, however, with *Why Come Ye Not to Courte?* he went too far in his attack on Cardinal Wolsey, and the cardinal threw him into prison. In the *Merie Tales,* which contain a number of (probably fictional) anecdotes about Skelton, he is shown as kneeling before Wolsey to ask for pardon. The cardinal ranted at him for some time. At last Skelton said, "I pray Your Grace to let me lie down and wallow, for I can kneel no longer."

SKINNER, Cornelia Otis (1901–79), *US actress and writer.*

1 Cornelia Otis Skinner was playing the title role in a revival of George Bernard Shaw's *Candida.* Shaw cabled her: "Excellent. Greatest." The actress cabled back: "Undeserving such praise." Shaw sent another cable: "I meant the play." Miss Skinner replied: "So did I."

SKINNER, Otis (1858–1942), *US stage actor, father of Cornelia Otis Skinner.*

1 At the rehearsal for his daughter's wedding, Skinner asked the minister what he was supposed to say in reply to the question: "Who giveth this woman . . ."

"You don't say a thing, Mr. Skinner," replied the minister. "You just hand your daughter over."

"Nonsense," said Skinner, "I've never played a walk-on part in my life."

SLEZAK, Leo (1873–1946), *Czechoslovak tenor.*

1 At the end of Wagner's opera *Lohengrin* a magic swan appears, drawing a boat to take the hero back to rejoin the fellowship of the Knights of the Holy Grail. On one occasion when Slezak was singing Lohengrin, the apparatus failed to function properly and sailed off back into the wings, leaving the tenor stranded on the stage. Amid consternation among performers and stage hands Slezak muttered, "When does the next swan leave?"

2 Slezak had just left his residence in Vienna for a performance in Zurich when his valet discovered that the singer had left behind an important part of his costume — a magnificent crown studded with artificial jewels. He wrapped it up in a sheet of newspaper and

rushed off to the station, where he just had time to thrust the package into his employer's hands as the train moved away. During the long overnight journey, a customs officer boarded the train. "Anything to declare?" he asked as he passed through Slezak's compartment. "No, nothing," replied the singer, who had been trying to catch a few hours' sleep. The customs officer glanced around the compartment. "Open that!" he snapped, pointing at the hastily wrapped package. With ill-disguised irritation, Slezak tore off the newspaper and uncovered the crown. The customs officer gasped. Then, standing to attention, he exclaimed, "Oh! Incognito! Please excuse me, Your Majesty."

SMITH, Adam (1723–90), *Scottish economist and philosopher.*

1 Smith was known for his absentmindedness. One Sunday morning he wandered into his garden wearing only a nightgown and soon became engrossed in philosophical contemplation. Totally absorbed in his train of thought, he went out into the street and began walking in the direction of Dunfermline. He had covered the twelve miles to the town before the ringing of the church bells aroused him from his reverie. Regular churchgoers arriving for the morning service were astonished to find the eminent philosopher in their midst, still clad only in his nightgown.

SMITH, Alfred Emanuel (1873–1944), *US politician.*

1 Smith was in Albany for a political convention, along with James Walker, Herbert Lehman, and many others. One morning, after a night of heavy drinking, Smith and Walker, both Catholic, felt that they ought to go to early mass as it was a Roman Catholic holy day. Tiptoeing through the hotel suite, they looked wistfully at Lehman and their other Jewish colleagues, who were still peacefully sleeping off the effects of the previous night's excesses. Turning to Walker, Smith said, "Gee, I hope we're right!"

2 Irritated by the constant interruptions of a heckler, Smith once paused in the middle of a speech. "Go ahead, Al, don't let me bother you," shouted the heckler. "Tell 'em all you know. It won't take you long." Smith was quick to respond. "If I tell 'em all we both know," he cried, "it won't take me any longer."

3 During one of his terms as governor of New York, Smith was late for a broadcast he was due to make. He hailed a taxi to take him to the radio station, but the driver, who did not recognize the governor, refused to take him. He explained that he was in a hurry himself, anxious to be home in time to hear Governor Smith talk on the radio. Smith, flattered, held out a five-dollar bill and repeated his request. The driver's eyes lit up. "Hop in, mister," he said, "and to hell with the governor."

SMITH, Bessie (1894–1937), *US jazz singer.*

1 In September 1937 Bessie Smith, traveling with her white business manager near Clarksdale, Mississippi, was seriously injured in an auto accident. The doctor who arrived on the scene directed that the manager, who was suffering from concussion, should be sent to the nearby hospital but that the singer should go to a "blacks only" hospital many miles away. She bled to death before she got there.

SMITH, Charlotte (1973–), *US college basketball player.*

1 The University of North Carolina women's basketball team, National College Athletic

Association champions, had less than one second to play, and were facing a 59–57 loss against rival team Louisiana Tech. At the buzzer Smith sank a three-point basket, winning the game 60–59 and taking the team to the next championship. Her secret for the amazing shot? "I knew I had to do it. It was an order from the coach."

———∽———

SMITH, F[rederick] E[dwin], 1st Earl of Birkenhead (1872–1930), *British barrister and Conservative politician.*

1 A distinguished Oxford don had a particular way of snubbing clever young undergraduates. He would invite the student to accompany him on a long walk, leaving it to his companion to start the conversation. After a lengthy silence the embarrassed student would usually make some banal remark, and would immediately be crushed by the don's reply.

The undergraduate F. E. Smith, aware of the don's tactics, set off for the walk with his own plan of action carefully worked out. The two men walked in complete silence for more than an hour, and for once it was the don's turn to feel embarrassed. "They tell me," he was finally compelled to utter, "they tell me you're clever, Smith. Are you?"

"Yes," replied Smith.

No further word was exchanged until the men returned to the college. "Good-bye, sir," said Smith. "I've so much enjoyed our talk."

2 As a young man Smith represented a tramway company in a suit brought by a boy who had been blinded. The judge directed that the boy be lifted onto a chair so that the jury could see him properly. Thinking this made an undue emotional appeal to the jury's sympathy, Smith protested: "Your Honor, why not pass the boy around the jury box?" The judge rebuked him for his improper remark. "Prompted," Smith said, "by

an equally improper suggestion." Preferring not to pursue that one, the judge tried to quash the young lawyer by quoting Francis Bacon at him: "Youth and discretion are ill-wedded companions." Smith was ready with a counter-quotation: "My lord, the same Bacon also said that a much-talking judge was like an ill-tuned cymbal." The judge frowned. "Now you are being offensive, Mr. Smith," he said. "We both are," agreed Smith. "The difference is that I am trying to be, and you can't help it."

3 Smith once cross-examined a young man claiming damages for an arm injury caused by the negligence of a bus driver. "Will you please show us how high you can lift your arm now?" asked Smith. The young man gingerly raised his arm to shoulder level, his face distorted with pain. "Thank you," said Smith. "And now, please will you show us how high you could lift it before the accident?" The young man eagerly shot his arm up above his head. He lost his case.

4 Smith was cross-examining a rather nervous witness. "Have you ever been married?" he asked.

"Yes, sir," replied the witness, "once."

"Whom did you marry?"

"A — er — a woman, sir."

"Of course, of course," snapped Smith impatiently. "Did you ever hear of anyone marrying a man?"

"Er — yes, sir," ventured the witness. "My sister did."

5 Smith was conducting a lengthy and complicated case before a judge whom he regarded as slow and pedantic. As the case drew to its close, the judge intimated that some of the issues involved were no longer clear to him, upon which Smith gave the judge a short but very cogent account of all the issues and their implications. As Smith sat down, the judge thanked him courteously, but added, "I'm

sorry, Mr. Smith, but I regret that I am none the wiser." Smith rose wearily to his feet again. "Possibly, my lord, but you are better informed."

6 Smith annoyed the patrons of London's Athenaeum Club, of which he was not a member, by frequently making use of their toilet facilities on his way to the House of Lords. One day a porter drew his attention to the fact that the club was for members only. "Oh," said Smith, "is it a club as well?"

7 Smith had many contentious moments in the particular courtroom of a Judge Willis. Once Willis, deeply exasperated and tired from the constant tangles with Smith, asked him, "What do you suppose I am on the bench *for?*" Smith replied instantly, "It is not for me, your Honour, to attempt to fathom the inscrutable workings of Providence."

8 Trapped by a club bore who would not stop talking, Smith in desperation called over a waiter, to whom he said, "Would you mind listening to the end of this gentleman's story?"

SMITH, Sydney (1771–1845), *British clergyman and author.*

1 At a gathering Sydney Smith met the lawyer and philosopher Sir James Mackintosh with his young Scottish cousin, an ensign in one of the Scots regiments. The young man asked Sir James in an undertone whether this was "the great Sir Sidney Smith," hero of the defense of Acre against Napoleon in 1799. Before Sir James could put the young man right, Sydney Smith had embarked on an account of the siege of Acre, complete with description of guns and attacks and counterattacks. The young ensign was entranced by this display of friendliness on the part of the famous admiral, while the rest of the

party scarcely knew how to keep a straight face.

A few days later Sir James and his cousin met Sydney Smith and his wife walking in the street. Smith introduced his wife and they talked for a few minutes. As the Smiths moved on, the young Scot said in a low voice, "I didna think the great Sir Sidney was married."

"Why, er, no," said Sir James, floundering for a moment before inspiration struck, "no, not exactly married — only an Egyptian slave he brought over with him. Fatima — you know — you understand."

The nickname "Fatima" stuck to Mrs. Smith for a long time thereafter among her friends.

2 When Francis Jeffrey was lord advocate, the polar explorer John Ross tried to persuade him to get the government to finance an expedition to the North Pole. A man who agreed to act as intermediary called on Jeffrey at an unlucky moment, when he was just about to go out riding and did not want to be detained. Jeffrey became more and more impatient and eventually burst out, "Damn the North Pole!" The aggrieved intermediary complained to Sydney Smith about Jeffrey's language. "Never mind," said Smith, "never mind his damning the North Pole. *I* have heard him speak disrespectfully of the equator."

3 Sydney Smith became embroiled in an argument with a country squire who was being abusive about the Church of England. The squire concluded by saying that if he had a son who was a fool he would make him a parson. "Very probably," retorted Smith, "but I see your father was of a different mind."

4 The lady seated next to him at dinner rejected an offer of gravy. "Madam," said Sydney Smith, "I have been looking for a person

who disliked gravy all my life; let us swear eternal friendship."

5 Sydney Smith was disturbed one morning at his work by a self-important little man who announced that he was compiling a history of the distinguished families of Somerset and was calling to identify the Smith arms. Sydney Smith regretted he was unable to help: "The Smiths have never had any arms, and have invariably sealed their letters with their thumbs."

6 Smith once complained of the prosiness of some sermons, saying, "They are written as if sin were to be taken out of man like Eve out of Adam — by putting him to sleep."

7 On receiving a basket of strawberries from one of his parishioners, Smith wrote in reply, "What is real piety? What is true attachment to the Church? How are these fine feelings best evinced? The answer is plain: by sending strawberries to a clergyman. Many thanks."

8 Sydney Smith never attained the eminence in the church that might have been expected, mainly because the Anglican establishment disapproved of his attitude toward Roman Catholic emancipation, evinced in the *Peter Plymley Letters* (1807–08). Comparing his own career with that of his brother, Robert Percy, Sydney Smith observed, "He rose by gravity; I sank by levity."

SMUTS, Jan Christiaan (1870–1950), *South African philosopher and statesman.*

1 Writer and journalist Wynford Vaughan-Thomas once accompanied Smuts on a "morning stroll" up Table Mountain. The year was 1947; Smuts was seventy-six and Vaughan-Thomas some thirty-eight years younger. As the writer arrived at the summit, a full ten minutes after his companion, Smuts remarked with a smile: "Young man, at my age I haven't as much time as you for loitering."

SMYTH, Dame Ethel (1858–1944), *British composer and author.*

1 (Leonard and Virginia Woolf invited Dame Ethel, then quite elderly, to dinner at their house at Rodmell in Sussex.)

"Dame Ethel bicycled the twenty miles from the village where she lived to Rodmell, dressed in rough tweeds. About two miles from her destination she decided that perhaps she was not suitably dressed for a dinner party. She thought that possibly corsets were required to smarten up her figure. Accordingly, she went into a village shop and asked for some corsets. There were none. Distressed, she looked round the shop and her eye lighted on a bird cage, which she purchased. About twenty minutes later, Virginia went into her garden to discover Dame Ethel in a state of undress in the shrubbery struggling with the bird cage, which she was wrenching into the shape of corsets and forcing under her tweeds."

SNEAD, Sam (1912–), *US golfer.*

1 Passing through Rome in 1961, Snead stopped for an audience with Pope John. The golfer had not been playing well for some time, and he confessed to one of the papal officials: "I brought along my putter, on the chance that the pope might bless it." The monsignor nodded sympathetically. "I know, Mr. Snead," he said. "My putting is absolutely hopeless too." Snead looked at him in amazement. "If you *live* here and can't putt," he exclaimed, "what chance is there for me?"

SOBHUZA II (1899–1982), *king of Swaziland (1921–82).*

1 King Sobhuza called a meeting of his ministers and advisers to discuss recent missions to other African states. Suddenly, for no apparent reason, he asked all his officials, with the exception of Dr. Samuel Hynd, the minister of health, to leave. Turning to the doctor, Sobhuza said, "I am going." Hynd, a little surprised, asked the obvious question, "Where are you going?" By way of reply, the king simply smiled, raised his hand in a farewell gesture, and died.

———cлɔ———

SOCRATES (c. 469–399 BC), *Greek philosopher.*

1 Knowing the frugality of Socrates' way of life, a friend was surprised to discover the philosopher studying with rapt attention some flashy wares on display in the marketplace. He inquired why Socrates came to the market, since he never bought anything. "I am always amazed to see how many things there are that I don't need," replied Socrates.

2 Socrates' wife, Xanthippe, visited him in prison and bewailed the jury's condemnation. "They are by their nature also condemned," Socrates said. "But the condemnation is unjust!" persisted Xanthippe. "Would you prefer it to be just?" asked Socrates.

———cлɔ———

SOLOMON (c. 973–c. 933 BC), *king of Israel.*

1 Two prostitutes living alone in the same house had babies within three days of each other. One baby died, and its mother stole the other while the mother slept, substituting the corpse of her own baby. Although the other woman noticed the deception, the first woman refused to relinquish the baby. So they came before King Solomon, each claiming that the living child was hers. The king commanded his officers to bring a sword and when it was brought ordered that the baby be cut in two; one half would then be given to one woman and the other half to the other. The rightful mother, stirred with love and pity for her child, said, "O my lord, give her the living child, and in no wise slay it." But the other woman said, "Let it be neither mine or thine, but divide it." The king, perceiving that the compassion of the first woman had identified her as the true mother, ordered that the baby should be given to her.

———cлɔ———

SOLON (c. 639–559 BC), *Greek legislator and statesman.*

1 Solon's sweeping changes naturally came in for a good deal of criticism. Solon himself acknowledged that there were imperfections in his legal code. Challenged to say whether he had given the Athenians the best laws, he replied mildly, "No, but the best that they could receive."

2 Asked what measures could be taken to eliminate law breaking and crime within the state, Solon replied, "Wrongdoing can only be avoided if those who are not wronged feel the same indignation at it as those who are."

———cлɔ———

SOMERSET, Charles Seymour, 6th Duke of (1662–1748), *British courtier.*

1 The duke's first wife was Elizabeth, heiress to the great name and fortune of the Percys, dukes of Northumberland. When she died in 1722, he married again; his second wife was Charlotte Finch, third daughter of the Earl of Nottingham. Charlotte once made the mistake of tapping playfully on her husband's arm with her fan to attract his attention. He turned on her and said icily, "Madam, my

first wife was a Percy, and *she* never took such a liberty."

———— ✧ ————

SOPHOCLES (496–406 BC), *Greek dramatist.*

1 At the age of eighty-nine Sophocles was brought before a court of law by his son, who, suspecting that the playwright intended to cut him out of his will, wished to have him certified as suffering from senility. Sophocles said simply, "If I am Sophocles, I am not out of my mind; if I am out of mind, I am not Sophocles." He then proceeded to read to the court passages from the *Oedipus at Colonus,* which he had lately written but not yet staged. The judges dismissed the case.

———— ✧ ————

SOUTHEY, Robert (1774–1843), *British poet and prose writer; poet laureate (1813–43).*

1 Southey enjoyed making a parade of the regularity of his life and the industriousness of his habits. Intending to impress a certain Quaker lady, he told her the full routine of his day; rising at 5:00 AM, reading Spanish from 6:00 to 8:00, reading French from 8:00 to 9:00, writing poetry for two hours, writing prose ditto, and so on through to bedtime. The lady heard his recital out and then asked, "And pray, Friend, when dost thou think?"

———— ✧ ————

SPELLMAN, Francis Joseph (1889–1967), *US Roman Catholic cardinal.*

1 As a boy of eight Frank Spellman used to help out in his father's grocery store. One piece of advice that Spellman Sr. gave his son stuck in the future cardinal's mind: "Always associate with people smarter than yourself, and you'll have no difficulty finding them."

2 In conversation with a local businessman in a busy New York post office, Cardinal Spellman happened to remark that he was feeling rather tired. "Tell me, Your Eminence," asked the businessman, "with all the work you do, do you ever get so tired that you forget to say your prayers at night?"

"No," replied Spellman with a smile. "When I'm so tired I can't keep my eyes open, I simply say: 'Dear God, you *know* I've been working in your vineyard all day. If you don't mind, could we skip the details till morning?'"

———— ✧ ————

SPENCER, Herbert (1820–1903), *British philosopher and economist.*

1 Spencer was playing billiards with a subaltern who was a highly proficient player. In a game of fifty up Spencer gave a miss in balk and his opponent made a run of fifty and out in his first inning. The frustrated philosopher remarked, "A certain dexterity in games of skill argues a well-balanced mind, but such a dexterity as you have shown is evidence, I fear, of a misspent youth."

———— ✧ ————

SPENSER, Edmund (?1552–99), *British poet.*

1 Spenser presented some of his poetry to Queen Elizabeth, who received it graciously and instructed the lord treasurer, Lord Burghley, to pay the poet a hundred pounds. Burghley, a prudent keeper of the royal purse-strings, protested that it was far too generous a recompense. "Then give him what is reason," said the queen. Burghley, however, conveniently forgot to make the payment, and Spenser waited patiently for some months. Eventually he decided that he would have to petition the queen himself, so

he found an opportunity to present to her the following rhyme: "I was promised on a time / To have reason for my rhyme; / From that time unto this season, / I received not rhyme nor reason." Elizabeth scolded Lord Burghley and ordered immediate payment.

2 When Spenser first showed portions of *The Faerie Queen* to the Earl of Southampton, that great connoisseur of literature was enchanted by what he read. "Go bear Master Spenser a gift of twenty pounds," he commanded his attendants. He read on, and again the charms of the poetry encouraged him to further generosity: "Go bear Master Spenser another twenty pounds." Still he went on reading, and then cried out a third time, "Go turn that fellow out of my house, for I shall be ruined if I read further."

SPILLANE, Mickey [Frank Morrison] (1918–98), *US writer of detective stories featuring the character Mike Hammer.*

1 Authors become impatient with eager students of their work who find symbolism where none was intended. When the subject came up at a meeting of the Mystery Writers of America, Spillane dismissed any profound conclusions that might have been drawn from the drinking habits of his most famous character. "Mike Hammer drinks beer, not cognac, because I can't spell cognac," he declared.

SPOONER, William Archibald (1844–1930), *British scholar, Warden of New College, Oxford (1903–24). He gave his name to the verbal trick, accidental or otherwise, known as a spoonerism — the transposition of the initial letters of words, especially to give a comic effect; for in-*

stance, "a half-warmed fish" for "a half-formed wish."

1 Meeting a stranger in the New College quadrangle, Warden Spooner could recall only that the man was a recent addition to the college Fellows. "Come to tea tomorrow," he said hospitably, "I'm giving a little party for the new mathematics Fellow."

"But Warden," said the stranger. "*I am the* new mathematics Fellow."

"Never mind. Come all the same."

2 "Mr. Spooner was one evening found wandering disconsolately about the streets of Greenwich. 'I've been here two hours,' he said. 'I had an important appointment to meet someone at "The Dull Man, Greenwich," and I can't find it anywhere; and the odd thing is no one seems to have heard of it.' Late at night he went back to Oxford. 'You idiot!' exclaimed his wife; 'why, it was the Green Man, Dulwich, you had to go to.'"

3 (Sprinkling salt over wine spilled on a linen tablecloth is said to prevent a stain.)

At dinner one day, Dr. Spooner accidentally upset the salt cellar on the clean white linen tablecloth. Without a moment's hesitation, he reached for his wine glass and poured a few drops of claret over the spilled salt.

4 He once stopped a student in the street, asking him, "Was it you or your dear brother who was killed in the war?"

SPURGEON, Charles Haddon (1834–92), *British Baptist minister.*

1 When Spurgeon was involved in one of the many controversies that marked his career, a friend remarked jocularly, "I hear you are in hot water again."

"I'm not the one in hot water," retorted Spurgeon. "The other fellows are. I'm the man who makes the water boil."

2 "Oh, Mr. Spurgeon, that was wonderful!" cried an admirer after one of Spurgeon's sermons.

"Yes, madam — so the devil whispered into my ear as I came down the steps of the pulpit."

———— ✤ ————

STAËL, Anne Louise Germaine, Baronne de (1766–1817), *French writer.*

1 In 1797 Napoleon still seemed to Mme de Staël the epitome of the hero who would bring peace and sanity back to France. She pursued and flattered him, but he eluded her attentions whenever possible. On one occasion she called at his house, demanding to be admitted at once to Napoleon's presence. The butler explained that that was impossible since the general was in his bathtub. "No matter!" Mme de Staël cried. "Genius has no sex!"

2 In 1803 Mme de Staël published her feminist novel *Delphine,* in which she herself appears, flimsily concealed, as the heroine. The opinions and character of Talleyrand are embodied in the fictional figure of the book's villainess, Mme de Vernon. When Talleyrand next saw Mme de Staël, he greeted her with the words: "They tell me we are both of us in your novel, in the disguise of women."

3 Mme de Staël's officiousness could be a trial even to her friends. Talleyrand remarked that she was such a good friend that she would throw all her acquaintances into the water for the pleasure of fishing them out again.

4 Mme de Staël told the story of how she and the beautiful Mme Récamier were seated at dinner on either side of a young fop, who an-

nounced, "Here I am between wit and beauty."

"Quite so," said Mme de Staël, "and without possessing either."

5 Told by Napoleon that it was not fitting for a woman to take an interest in politics, Madame de Staël retorted, "In a country where women have been decapitated, it is only natural for other women to ask 'Why?'"

———— ✤ ————

STAFFORD, Jean (1915–79), *US writer.*

1 An old cowhand in Colorado, learning that Jean Stafford was a writer, observed, "That's real nice work, Jean. It's something you can do in the shade."

———— ✤ ————

STALIN, Joseph [Iosif Dzhugashvili] (1879–1953), *Russian leader.*

1 Lady Astor was one of a group of eminent English visitors to Russia in 1931. Never one to mince her words, she asked Stalin, "How long are you going to go on killing people?"

"As long as it's necessary," replied Stalin.

2 At the Teheran conference Churchill had argued that opening a second front in France would result in the unnecessary death of tens of thousands of soldiers. Replied Stalin, "When one man dies it is a tragedy. When thousands die it is a statistic."

3 During the 1945 conference at Yalta in the Soviet Union, Winston Churchill and the British delegation were housed in the Alubka palace. On the grounds was a marble statue of a dozing lion, its head resting on its front paws, to which Churchill took a great liking. As he explained to Stalin, "It's so like me." He added that he understood there was a Russian tradition of presenting the best things in the country to important visitors.

"Yes, indeed," responded Stalin. "The best thing we have in Russia now is socialism." The lion stayed where it was.

———— ✺ ————

STANLEY, Sir Henry Morton (1841–1904), *British explorer and journalist.*

1 (Stanley, encouraged by rumors of a white man on the shores of Lake Tanganyika, reached Ujiji on November 10, 1871.)

"As I advanced slowly towards him, I noticed he was pale, looked wearied, had a gray beard, wore a bluish cap with a faded gold band round it, had on a red-sleeved waistcoat and a pair of gray tweed trousers. I would have run to him, only I was a coward in the presence of the mob — would have embraced him, only, he being an Englishman, I did not know how he would receive me. So I did what cowardice and false pride suggested was the best thing — walked deliberately up to him, took off my hat and said, 'Dr. Livingstone, I presume?' 'Yes,' said he with a kind smile, lifting his cap slightly. I replaced my hat on my head, and he puts on his cap, and we both grasp hands, and I then say aloud — 'I thank God, Doctor, I have been permitted to see you.' He answered, 'I feel thankful that I am here to welcome you.'"

———— ✺ ————

STANTON, Charles E. (1859–1933), *US colonel.*

1 On the Fourth of July 1917 the American Expeditionary Forces, newly arrived in Europe to fight in World War I, sent a contingent to visit the grave of Lafayette in Paris. General Pershing asked Colonel Stanton to make a speech on behalf of the A. E. F. Stanton made the memorably simple announcement: "Lafayette, we are here!"

———— ✺ ————

STANTON, Elizabeth Cady (1815–1902), *US reformer and campaigner for women's rights.*

1 At a women's rights convention in Rochester, a married clergyman rebuked Mrs. Stanton for speaking in public. "The apostle Paul enjoined silence upon women," he said. "Why don't you mind him?" "The apostle Paul also enjoined celibacy upon the clergy," retorted Mrs. Stanton. "Why don't *you* mind him?"

———— ✺ ————

STARK, John (1728–1822), *US general.*

1 On August 16, 1777, Stark's men faced two detachments of Burgoyne's troops at Bennington, Vermont. Before the battle Stark made an impassioned appeal to his men's pride and courage. "Yonder are the Hessians. They were bought for seven pounds and tenpence a man. Are you worth more? Prove it. Tonight the American flag floats from yonder hill or Molly Stark sleeps a widow!"

———— ✺ ————

STEELE, Sir Richard (1672–1729), *British dramatist and essay writer.*

1 Steele was frequently in debt. A group of friends invited to dine at his house one day were therefore astonished to see the number of servants who attended them at dinner. After dinner a guest inquired how it was that Steele could afford such a lavish establishment. Steele explained that the attendants were in fact bailiffs, who were in the house on their official business. As he could not get rid of them, he had made the best of the situation by dressing them up in servants' liveries, and stationing them around his dining room. His guests were so amused that they pooled their money to pay Steele's debts and rid him of the bailiffs.

———— ✺ ————

STEFFENS, Lincoln (1866–1936), *US journalist*.

1 When Steffens visited Russia in 1919, he was able to observe the Bolshevik revolution at first hand. On his return he made the famous statement: "I have seen the future, and it works."

———— ⌀ ————

STEIN, Gertrude (1874–1946), *US expatriate writer of experimental prose*.

1 Stein appeared on a nationwide radio show, arranged by her publisher Bennett Cerf to introduce her writing to a wider audience. In welcoming her, Cerf announced that he was proud to be her publisher but, in truth, he had never really understood her work at all. Stein responded instantly, "I've always told you, Bennett, you're a nice boy but you're rather stupid."

2 In 1929 Gertrude Stein was invited to lecture at Oxford. She delivered a well-argued address in her customary style. Her lucidity and platform presence confounded those who had mainly come to jeer, although there was some laughter when she said in the course of her lecture, "Everything is the same and everything is different." At the end two hecklers jumped to their feet in different parts of the lecture hall and fired the same question at her: "Miss Stein, if everything is the same, how can everything be different?" Miss Stein replied, "Consider, the two of you, you jump up one after the other, that is the same thing and surely you admit that the two of you are always different."

3 (Ernest Hemingway describes the probable origin of a famous phrase.)

"She had some ignition trouble with the old Model T Ford she then drove and the young man who worked in the garage and had served in the last year of the war had not been adept, or perhaps had not broken the priority of other vehicles, in repairing Miss Stein's Ford. Anyway, he had not been *sérieux* and had been corrected severely by the *patron* of the garage after Miss Stein's protest. The *patron* had said to him, 'You are all a *génération perdue*.'

"'That's what you are. That's what you all are,' Miss Stein said. 'All of you young people who served in the war. You are a lost generation.'"

4 Stein once remarked to Ernest Hemingway that his soul was 90 percent Rotarian. "Couldn't you make it eighty percent?" asked Hemingway. "No," said Stein, "I can't."

5 A friend asked Gertrude Stein what it was that writers most wanted. "Praise, praise, praise," she replied, laughing.

6 Gertrude Stein had a good opinion of herself, which gave rise to a number of pronouncements recorded by her contemporaries. She told the sculptor Jacques Lipchitz that he knew very little about English literature. "Besides Shakespeare and me, who do you think there is?" she said.

7 One of the few people who refused to be overawed by Miss Stein's astounding flow of rhetoric was Mortimer Adler, the philosopher, educator, and author of *How to Read a Book*. He and Gertrude got into a violent argument one evening. Alice B. Toklas, trembling on the outskirts of the battlefield, was heard to remark, "Dear me! Gertrude is saying some things tonight that she won't understand herself for six months."

8 The poet William Carlos Williams visited her one day, upon which she showed him a huge cabinet full of her unpublished manuscripts. She described each one, reading aloud its title, then asked him what he would do if all of the manuscripts were his. "I should probably select what I thought were the best and

throw the rest into the fire," responded Williams. After a brief and shocked silence, Stein said stiffly, "No doubt. But then writing is not, of course, your métier."

9 Picasso once read a poem he had written aloud at a gathering at Stein's house, saying that if he applied his energies to writing as he did to painting, he could become a great poet. After he had finished reading, he awaited Stein's response. After a pause, she said, "Pablo, go home and paint."

10 When Gertrude Stein was dying of cancer, she turned to Alice B. Toklas and murmured, "What is the answer?" Miss Toklas made no reply. Miss Stein nodded and went on, "In that case, what is the question?"

11 The American composer and writer Ned Rorem made his first visit to Alice B. Toklas's home after Gertrude Stein's death. He noticed on the wall two remarkable Picassos with which he was not familiar. He expressed his admiration. Miss Toklas said thoughtfully, "Yes, Gertrude always used to say: if the house were on fire and I could only take one picture, it would be those two."

STEINBECK, John (1902–68), *US novelist, winner of the Nobel Prize for Literature in 1962.*

1 Steinbeck in his earlier days genuinely disliked personal publicity. After years of penury and unrewarded labor, he finally achieved success with *Tortilla Flat* and so could not entirely escape interviewers. He was enraged when the journalist Ella Winter, in a profile of him, did not abide by his request that he be judged by his work, not his personality. "What did I say that was so personal?" asked Miss Winter. "You mentioned that I had blue eyes," he replied.

2 Five thousand copies of Steinbeck's novel *The Wayward Bus* were destroyed by fire when the truck carrying them from the bindery was involved in a collision. The cause of the accident was a wayward bus, traveling on the wrong side of the road.

3 In 1965 Steinbeck passed through San Francisco on an automobile journey with his poodle, Charlie. He sat at a sidewalk café with advertising executive Howard Gossage and remarked, "Yesterday in Muir Woods Charlie lifted his leg on a tree that was fifty feet across, a hundred feet high, and a thousand years old. What's left in life for that dog after that supreme moment?" Gossage reflected a moment and then said, with his slight stammer, "W-w-well, he could always t-t-teach."

4 During a conversation about women, a conceited young man remarked derisively, "Women? They're a dime a dozen."

"Sure, women are a dime a dozen," agreed Steinbeck. "It's when you cut the number down to one that it gets expensive."

5 During his later years, when he was famous, his wife, Elaine, brought home a paperback book entitled *John Steinbeck,* by Frank William Watt. Steinbeck, who often felt he had been misinterpreted by many of the commentators on his life and work, read it with great interest. Finished, he remarked, "This book doesn't seem to be about me, but it's pretty interesting about somebody."

STEINBERG, William (1899–1978), *US conductor, born in Germany.*

1 With time William Steinberg became totally bald. Relating an episode in his musical career, he once told his audience, "And there I was tearing my hair." Then he paused, gripped his bare skull, and added, "*What* am I saying?"

———⌀———

STEINBRENNER, George (1930–), *US baseball executive.*

1 The owner of the New York Yankees since 1973, when he bought the team from CBS for $10 million, Steinbrenner was the ultimate hands-on boss, firing at will and often causing havoc in the clubhouse. At one point in the early 1980s the Yankees were losing game after game, and Steinbrenner flew from city to city in a panic, watching them play and trying to devise new strategies for victory. One player noted, "The more we lose, the more often Steinbrenner will fly in. And the more he flies, the better chance there is of a plane crashing."

2 One year Steinbrenner released star player Reggie Jackson, "Mr. October," from the team. In 1982 Jackson returned to Yankee Stadium as a member of the Angels. After he hit a huge home run the crowd went wild, hurling abuse at Steinbrenner. After the game Jackson was in the ground-floor lobby of the clubhouse when the elevator doors opened, revealing Steinbrenner standing inside. They looked at each other, and the doors closed. After a moment the doors opened again, and again they looked at each other. As Steinbrenner mumbled something about a malfunctioning elevator, Jackson quietly walked away, not wishing to further embarrass his former boss.

3 At the Fiftieth Anniversary All-Star game in Chicago, which had been the site of the first All-Star game, White Sox president Jerry Reinsdorf was fined $500 for saying of his fellow owner Steinbrenner, "How do you know when he's lying? His lips are moving."

4 Discussing the personalities of Steinbrenner and Reggie Jackson while drinking in a bar with some journalists, Billy Martin — who had been fired three times by the tempestuous Yankees owner — said, "They deserve each other. One's a born liar and the other's convicted."

———⌀———

STEINMETZ, Charles Proteus (1865–1923), *US electrical engineer.*

1 When "the Electrical Wizard" was working at General Electric, he was annoyed to find in his office a sign reading NO SMOKING. Steinmetz left a note reading NO SMOKING — NO STEINMETZ. After that it was decided that the rule should not be applied to him.

2 After retiring, Steinmetz was recalled by General Electric to try to locate a breakdown in a complex system of machines. The cause of the breakdown baffled all GE's experts. Steinmetz spent some time walking around and testing the various parts of the machine complex. Finally, he took out of his pocket a piece of chalk and marked an X on a particular part of one machine. The GE people disassembled the machine, discovering to their amazement that the defect lay precisely where Steinmetz's chalk mark was located.

Some days later GE received a bill from Steinmetz for $10,000. They protested the amount and asked him to itemize it. He sent back an itemized bill:

Making one chalk mark $ 1
Knowing where to place it $9,999

———⌀———

STENGEL, Casey (1890–1975), *US baseball player and manager.*

1 "Stengel was coaching at third one afternoon in a ding-dong contest at the Polo Grounds when a Dodger batter named Cuccinello hammered a hit to the bull pen in right field. [Mel] Ott fielded the ball brilliantly, and threw to third base. 'Slide! Slide!' screamed

Stengel, but Cuccinello came in standing up, and was tagged out. 'I told you to slide,' roared Stengel. 'You'd have been safe a mile! Why didn't you do what I told you?' 'Slide?' repeated Cuccinello with some dignity, 'and bust my cigars?'"

2 The manager of the Yankees from 1949 to 1960, Stengel led the team to seven World Championships. But he was more famous for his verbosity than for his managerial skills. Asked a question by a reporter one day, Stengel talked for forty minutes straight until the reporter cut in, saying his question had not been answered. "Don't rush me," Stengel admonished.

3 Asked about the art of managing, Stengel replied, "Managing is getting paid for home runs someone else hits."

4 "Casey Stengel's eye for talent was often as keen as his wit. Early in his managerial career with the New York Mets, he was asked about the future prospects for two of his twenty-year-old players. 'In ten years, Ed Kranepool has a chance to be a star,' said Casey. 'In ten years the other guy has a chance to be thirty.'"

5 At a baseball game one day Stengel was exasperated by demands from the crowd for a player he had on the bench. He finally called for the player in question. "Am I going in?" asked the player eagerly. "No," replied Stengel, "I don't want you. Go up in the stands with your fans. *They* want you."

6 Told by a pitcher he wanted to remove from the mound, "I'm not tired," Stengel said, "Well, I'm tired of you."

7 During a famous exchange with Senator Kefauver in 1958, when Stengel testified before a committee investigating antitrust issues, Stengel kept talking and talking, while the senator kept repeating his question about Stengel's opinion of some proposed legisla-

tion. Finally Kefauver said, "Mr. Stengel, I am not sure that I made my question clear." Stengel replied, "Well, that is all right. I am not sure I'm going to answer you perfectly, either."

8 As he aged, Stengel slowed considerably. Gone were the days of Joe DiMaggio, Roger Maris, and Yogi Berra, when Stengel was at the top of his form. In 1959, when the Yankees finished third, many blamed his failing health for the loss. But not White Sox owner Bill Veeck, who said, "I know Casey well, and he's no different now than he was when he was winning pennants. He just hasn't got the horses."

9 Explaining a point of strategy to young baseball star Mickey Mantle, seventy-year-old Stengel described an incident from his own days as a player. "You played?" asked Mantle, astonished. "Sure I played," said Stengel. "Did you think I was born at the age of seventy sitting in a dugout trying to manage guys like you?"

10 Finally, in 1960, Stengel was fired. Of his end, he said, "I'll never make the mistake of being seventy again."

11 In his old age, Stengel was asked how he was doing. He sighed and said, "Not bad. Most people my age are dead. You could look it up."

———◦ℕ◦———

STERN, Isaac (1920–), *US violinist, born in Russia.*

1 On Election Night in Copenhagen, Stern was playing when he noticed that the audience was quite inattentive. After intermission he returned to the stage, but before playing he announced the results of the election, saying that the audience could now resume sneezing and snoring. The hall was filled with laugh-

ter, and for the rest of the concert an attentive quiet was kept.

———— ⁊ ————

STERNE, Laurence (1713–68), *British writer and clergyman.*

1 "Soon after *Tristram* appeared, Sterne asked a Yorkshire lady of fortune and condition whether she had read his book. 'I have not, Mr. Sterne,' was the answer; 'and to be plain with you, I am informed it is not proper for female perusal.' 'My dear good lady,' replied the author, 'do not be gulled by such stories; the book is like your young heir there [pointing to a child of three years old, who was rolling on the carpet in his white tunic]: he shows at times a good deal that is usually concealed, but it is all in perfect innocence!'"

———— ⁊ ————

STEVENS, Thaddeus (1792–1868), *US politician and lawyer.*

1 At the beginning of the 1861 congressional session, a woman admirer broke into Stevens's office and begged for a lock of his hair. Stevens removed his chestnut wig and invited her, "Pray, madam, select any curl that strikes your fancy."

2 In a scandal over the awarding of army contracts in the early 1860s, it was widely rumored that Simon Cameron, the secretary of war, had been less than strictly honest. Thaddeus Stevens was on record as saying that Cameron would steal anything except a red-hot stove. Cameron appealed to Lincoln, who asked Stevens to say that he had been misquoted. "Certainly I'll say I've been misquoted," said the unrepentant Stevens. "What I actually said was that Cameron would steal anything, *even* a red-hot stove."

3 A visitor who called on Stevens during his last illness remarked on the patient's appear-

ance. "It's not my appearance that troubles me right now," Stevens replied. "It's my disappearance."

———— ⁊ ————

STEVENSON, Adlai E[wing] (1900–65), *US statesman.*

1 Harry Truman finally persuaded Stevenson to campaign for the Democratic nomination in 1952. Stevenson stayed overnight at the White House and was put in the Lincoln Room. He wandered around the room, gazing with awe at the things in it, unable to bring himself to lie in the bed. So he spent the night on the sofa. He was unaware that in Lincoln's time the bed was not there, but the sofa was.

2 It was probably during his first campaign against Eisenhower that Stevenson was approached by an enthusiastic woman supporter who said to him, "Governor, every thinking person will be voting for you." Stevenson replied, "Madam, that is not enough. I need a majority."

3 At a Labor Day rally during the 1952 presidential campaign a photographer took a famous picture of Stevenson, showing him with a hole in the bottom of one shoe. When the photographer won a Pulitzer Prize for the picture, Stevenson sent him a telegram reading: "Congratulations. I'll bet this is the first time anyone ever won a Pulitzer Prize for a hole in one."

4 Alistair Cooke, talking to Stevenson shortly after his defeat in the 1952 election, was heartened to find him able to view the situation with objective humor. "After all," he said, "who did I think I was, running against George Washington?"

Four years later Eisenhower again defeated Stevenson in the presidential election, and Cooke sent Stevenson a cable reading simply: "How now?" Back came the reply:

"Who did I think I was, running against George Washington twice?"

5 Stevenson was much praised in the European press for his condemnation of the American U-2 reconnaissance flights over Europe. Stevenson read the favorable comments and said wryly, "The trouble is, I always run in the wrong continent."

6 Stevenson arrived late to address the American Society of Newspaper Editors. Apologizing, he said he had been delayed at the airport by the arrival of President de Gaulle from France. "It seems to be my fate always to be getting in the way of national heroes," he added.

7 During his 1956 election campaign Stevenson asked some children, "How many children in this audience would like to be a candidate for President of the United States?" A number of hands went up. Stevenson continued: "How many candidates for President of the United States would like to be children again?" He raised his own hand.

8 The *New York Times* reported that when Stevenson was the US delegate to the United Nations, the question was put to him: "Here's Soviet Russia pushing for votes for her satellites, even one as improbable as Outer Mongolia; how can that be counterbalanced?" Stevenson replied: "It's easy. We give Texas her independence and change her name to Outer Arkansas."

9 Stevenson once reflected, "In America, any boy may become President, and I suppose that's just the risk he takes."

———— ⁂ ————

STEVENSON, Robert Louis (1850–94), *Scottish writer.*

1 A young friend of Stevenson's had complained to him about being born on Christmas Day. She received presents only once a year and felt cheated. When Stevenson drew up his will as death approached, he remembered the girl and bequeathed his own birthday to her. He subsequently added the following clause: "If, however, she fails to use this bequest properly, all rights shall pass to the President of the United States."

———— ⁂ ————

STILLMAN, James A. (1850–1918), *US banker.*

1 After visiting the famous 1913 Armory Show, the first exhibition of the work of avant-garde European painters for the American public, Stillman remarked, "Something is wrong with the world. These men know."

———— ⁂ ————

STIMSON, Henry Lewis (1867–1950), *US attorney and statesman.*

1 Secretary of State Stimson once tried to close down the American counterintelligence and decipherment sources (known as "the Black Chamber"). Said Stimson: "Gentlemen do not read each other's mail."

———— ⁂ ————

STOKOWSKI, Leopold (1882–1977), *British conductor.*

1 During a performance of Beethoven's *Leonora* Overture No. 3, the offstage trumpet call twice failed to sound on cue. The overture finished, Stokowski dashed from the rostrum in a fury to seek out the errant trumpeter. He found the player in the wings wrestling with a burly janitor. "You can't blow that damn thing here, I tell you," the janitor was insisting. "There's a concert going on."

2 Stokowski was intensely irritated by members of the audience who coughed during a performance. At the end of a series of concerts with the Philadelphia orchestra, shortly

before his departure on a six-month tour of the Far East, he turned to the audience and said, "Good-bye for a long time. I hope when I come back your colds will all be better."

STOPPARD, Tom (1937–), *British playwright, born in Czechoslovakia.*

1 *Rosencrantz and Guildenstern Are Dead* became a sensational success in England, the United States, and even Tokyo and Buenos Aires. On its first production a friend, puzzled by its enigmatic character, asked, "Tom, what's it about?" Replied Stoppard, "It's about to make me a rich man."

STOUT, Rex (1886–1973), *US novelist, creator of the fictional detective Nero Wolfe.*

1 Stout was surrounded by books from an early age. His father had a personal library of over a thousand volumes, and his mother, Lucetta, was constantly engrossed in one book or another. Although she had nine children, her reading was rarely interrupted — thanks to a simple expedient. She kept a bowl of cold water and a washcloth beside her chair: any child who dared to disturb her would have his or her face thoroughly washed.

2 As a young man Rex Stout decided to join the navy. Examined by a medical board, he was told that he would have to have his tonsils out before he could be accepted. This was a blow; $2 was all the money he possessed. He managed, however, to find a young doctor who agreed to perform the operation at a bargain rate. No operating theater was available, of course, but a local barber offered surgeon and patient the use of one of his chairs during a slack period. The doctor duly removed the tonsils. Stout bled profusely, and the barber, alarmed at the sight of the gore and thinking that it might deter other clients, begged Stout to leave. Stout, feeling rather groggy, remained in the chair. "I'll give you two bits to go away," said the barber in desperation. The mention of cash roused Stout; he accepted the money, crawled out of the shop, and, after lying down for a time in a vacant lot, went back to the recruiting board, which forthwith accepted him.

STOWE, Harriet Beecher (1811–96), *US novelist.*

1 *Uncle Tom's Cabin* quickly achieved fame. A woman came up to Mrs. Stowe and asked if she could clasp the hand of the woman who had written the great work. "I did not write it," said Mrs. Stowe. "God wrote it. I merely did his dictation."

{William D. Howells saw it differently: "As for the author of *Uncle Tom's Cabin,* her syntax was such a snare to her that it sometimes needed the combined skill of the proofreaders and the assistant editor to extricate her. Of course nothing was ever written into her work, but in changes of diction, in correction of solecisms, in transposition of phrases, the text was largely rewritten in the margin of her proofs. The soul of her art was present, but the form was so often absent, that when it was clothed on anew, it would have been hard to say whose cut the garment was of in many places." The practical inspiration for *Uncle Tom's Cabin* came from a reading of a pamphlet written by a runaway Maryland slave, Josiah Henson, describing the degradation of a slave's life.}

2 The feelings engendered by *Uncle Tom's Cabin* did much to polarize opinion between North and South, contributing to the outbreak of the Civil War. In 1862, when Mrs. Stowe visited President Lincoln at the White House, he greeted her (as recollected by Harriet's son, who was present) with: "So this is

the little lady who wrote the book that made the big war."

—⚬—

STRACHEY, [Giles] Lytton (1880–1932), *British writer and a leading member of the Bloomsbury group.*

1 (Osbert Sitwell tells the following story:)

"We might recall what [Lytton Strachey] said to a clever, charming, rather noisy young man who had once been taken to stay with him. I do not know whether the visit could be considered a success, but when the guest next saw his former host, a whole lustrum had passed. 'Mr. Strachey, do you realize it's five years since we met?' the young man asked. He received the reply: 'Rather a nice interval, don't you think?' "

2 When military conscription became compulsory during World War I, Strachey applied for exemption as a conscientious objector. This meant that he had to appear before a tribunal that would assess the genuineness of his objections and rule accordingly. The military representative on the board boomed out questions that he usually found disconcerted the applicants. "I understand, Mr. Strachey, that you have a conscientious objection to all wars?" he began. "Oh, no, not at all," replied Strachey. "Only to this one." The military man tried again: "Tell me, Mr. Strachey, what would you do if you saw a German soldier attempting to rape your sister?" Strachey looked around at his sisters, who were sitting in the public gallery of the courtroom, and said in his piping voice, "I should try and come between them."

3 The basis of Dora Carrington's devotion to the homosexual, egocentric Strachey puzzled all their friends. When Arthur Waley asked her what it was about Strachey that could possibly appeal to her, she replied ecstatically, "Oh, it's his knees!"

4 Asked what he considered the greatest thing in life, Strachey inclined his reedlike body, complete with owl eyes and spectral beard, and, in his elegant, high-pitched voice, languidly piped: "Why, passion, of course."

5 As he lay dying at his house, Ham Spray, in Berkshire, Strachey looked about and said, "If this is death, then I don't think much of it."

—⚬—

STRAUSS, Richard (1864–1949), *German composer and conductor.*

1 When *Salome* was produced, Kaiser Wilhelm II, no lover of modern music, remarked, "It will do Strauss a great deal of harm." The royal remark came to Strauss's ears; he commented, "I was able to build my villa in Garmisch, thanks to the harm."

—⚬—

STRAVINSKY, Igor (1882–1971), *Russian-born composer.*

1 Although the more discriminating members of the audience at the historic Paris premiere of *Le Sacre du printemps* recognized the work as a masterpiece, the fashionable and ignorant were outraged at its novelty. Sporadic interruptions swelled to a full-scale tumult. Over the noise could be heard the voice of the impresario Gabriel Astruc yelling at the hecklers, "First listen! *Then* boo."

2 (The young music critic Carl Van Vechten attended the premiere of *Le Sacre du printemps*.)

"I was sitting in a box in which I had rented one seat. . . .Three ladies sat in front of me and a young man occupied the place behind me. The intense excitement under which he was laboring, thanks to the potent force of the music, betrayed itself presently when he began to beat rhythmically on the top of my head with his fists. My emotion was so great that I did not feel the blows for some time. They were perfectly synchronized with the beat of the music. When I did, I turned around. His apology was sincere. We had both been carried beyond ourselves."

3 When Stravinsky was fifty-seven, he settled in the United States and a year later decided to apply for American citizenship. He made an appointment to see the appropriate official. At his first interview the official asked the famous composer his name. "Stra-vin-sky," he replied, speaking each syllable distinctly. "You could change it, you know," suggested the official.

4 Stravinsky wrote a ballet for Billy Rose's Broadway shoe *The Seven Lively Arts*. After the opening one of the dancers sent a wire to the composer: "Ballet great success but if you would allow violin to play *pas de deux* instead of trumpet it would be a triumph." Stravinsky cabled back: "Satisfied with great success."

5 Stravinsky once had an argument with an airport official who insisted that he pay a charge for excess weight. The official, quite used to dealing with such situations, began to explain the reason for the extra charge. "I quite understand the *logic* of it," Stravinsky said impatiently. "What I am objecting to is the money."

6 In the 1950s the Venice Festival commissioned Stravinsky to write an original composition. When the piece was submitted, its length — only fifteen minutes — was found unsatisfactory. Stravinsky was unruffled. "Well, then," he said, "play it again."

7 In 1952, thirty-nine years after its tumultuous premiere, *Le Sacre du printemps* was again performed in Paris and received ecstatic applause. Pierre Monteux, the conductor

on both occasions, commented, "There was just as much noise the last time, but the tonality was different."

8 A lady approached Stravinsky and told him that, of all his works, she liked *Scheherazade* best. "But, madame, I did not compose *Scheherazade*," he protested. "Oh," said his admirer, "don't be modest."

9 Stravinsky was inveighing against some critics who had treated his work rather harshly. A friend tried to reassure him: "No one can please everyone. Even God does not please everyone." Stravinsky jumped up, shouting, "Especially God!"

10 Choreographer George Balanchine tells the following story: "Stravinsky's *Circus Polka* was composed precisely for the circus — for the Ringling Brothers, Barnum and Bailey Circus in 1942. The circus impresarios wanted to do a ballet for elephants. They asked me to arrange the dance and told me I could choose the composer. Who else but Stravinsky? I telephoned him, not giving away the whole story.

" 'What kind of music?' he asked.
" 'A polka,' I said.
" 'For whom?' he wanted to know.
" 'Elephants.'
" 'How old?'
" 'Young!'
" 'Okay, if they are very young, I'll do it.'
"What he did served its purpose very well, and our ballet . . . was done no less than 425 times."

11 Stravinsky, greatly concerned with his health, would sometimes put himself on a diet of raw vegetables. During one such period he dined on raw tomatoes and potatoes at a restaurant with composer Nicholas Nabokov. Nabokov left some of his cutlet at the side of his plate, and Stravinsky asked if he might finish it. Swallowing the morsel with a generous helping of sour cream, he declared:

"I want to astonish the raw potato in my stomach."

12 Stravinsky's publisher, impatient to publish his latest composition, urged him to hurry its completion. "Hurry!" exclaimed the enraged composer. "I never hurry. I have no time to hurry."

13 A librettist commiserated with Stravinsky over the very bad reviews he had received for *The Rake's Progress.* Stravinsky seemed unconcerned, and taking out the check he had received for conducting the performance, said, "This is the only review I read."

STRUG, Kerri (1977–), *US Olympic gymnast.*

1 The famously retiring young gymnast completed her final vault in the 1996 Olympics despite great pain caused by a sprained ankle, and thus led her team to the first American gold medal in the women's team event. Her coach, Bela Karolyi, said of her, "Always a little shy, always standing behind someone else. But sometimes this is the person with the biggest ggrrrrr."

STUART, James Ewell Brown (1833–64), *US Confederate commander.*

1 In the summer of 1862 Stuart was visiting a house that was raided by Union cavalrymen, and in the confusion of his hasty departure left behind his hat and plume. A week or two later, Stuart and his men attacked the forces of General Pope and plundered the Federal camp. In the morning Stuart displayed his booty — the blue uniform coat of General Pope himself. He lost no time in sending the following proposition to Pope: "General: You have my hat and plume. I have your best coat. I have the honor to propose a cartel for a fair exchange of the prisoners."

STUBBS, John (1543–91), *British pamphleteer.*

1 In 1579 it seemed that Queen Elizabeth was likely to marry the Duke of Anjou, much to the consternation of her Protestant subjects. Stubbs wrote an intemperate pamphlet against the marriage entitled *The Discovery of a Gaping Gulf to Swallow England.* The queen was furious; author, printer, and bookseller were apprehended and condemned to have their right hands cut off. The printer was pardoned, but the historian William Camden was an eyewitness to the execution of sentence on Stubbs and the bookseller. He records that as soon as his right hand had been struck off, Stubbs raised his hat with his left hand, waved it, and shouted, "God save the Queen!"

SUDERMANN, Hermann (1857–1928), *German playwright and novelist.*

1 Sudermann and fellow-dramatist Richard Voss disliked each other. When a dramatists' guild was founded, their colleagues brought them together to effect a reconciliation, as their names were of importance to the guild. After much hesitation they were persuaded to shake hands. Voss added, "Herr Sudermann, I wish for your next play the same success as you wish me." Sudermann turned to the onlookers: "Do you hear that? There he goes again!"

SULLIVAN, Sir Arthur Seymour (1842–1900), *British composer and conductor. His greatest successes were the comic Savoy operas on which he collaborated with W. S. Gilbert.*

1 Returning home one night after a convivial party, Sullivan found he could not identify

his own house in the terraced row of identical dwellings on his street. Fortunately his acute tonal sense did not desert him. He walked along the row, pausing to kick the metal shoe scrapers that stood by the sides of the front entrances. One rang a familiar note. Sullivan kicked it again. "That's it: E-flat," he muttered and walked confidently into the house.

SULLIVAN, John Lawrence (1858–1918), *US heavyweight boxer.*

1 Sullivan was once accosted in a bar by a puny little drunk, who challenged the burly champion to a fight. "Listen, you," growled Sullivan. "If you hit me just once — and I find out about it . . ."

SUMMERALL, Charles Pelot (1867–1955), *US general.*

1 Summerall's division had suffered heavy casualties at the Argonne in World War I. Asked how much longer he could continue, he replied, "As long as there are enough men for my division to be organized in depth."
"How many men will that take?"
"Two," replied Summerall. "One behind the other."

SUMNER, Charles (1811–74), *US statesman.*

1 A possibly apocryphal story tells how Sumner in his younger days was suddenly taken dangerously ill, so ill that he could not be conveyed home. He was laid upon a couch in his office in great pain. The friend who was with him, expecting his imminent death, asked if there was anything that he would wish to do by way of spiritual preparation. "I am prepared to die," whispered Sumner,

"I have read Calvin's *Institutes* through in the original."

SUSANN, Jacqueline (1918–74), *US author of highly popular novels, of which* Valley of the Dolls *and* The Love Machine *were perhaps the most successful.*

1 *The Love Machine* was competing in the bestseller lists with Philip Roth's *Portnoy's Complaint,* which dealt in part with masturbation. Asked her opinion of Roth, Jackie replied, "He's a fine writer, but I wouldn't want to shake hands with him."

2 Jackie and her husband were dining at Maurice Chevalier's country home. The dinner was elegantly served, but the portions were extremely small. After this insubstantial meal, the party retired to Chevalier's study. "What would you like to drink, Jacqueline, *ma chère?"* asked her host. "Maurice," she replied, "I never drink on an empty stomach."

3 She once called her editor at three o'clock in the morning, complaining that her current book was underrepresented in bookstores. When he mentioned the hour to her, she snapped, "You son of a bitch, I can't sleep, so why should you?"

4 Susann left her publisher for another just as her new book, *Once Is Not Enough,* was being published. On publication day he sent her a single rose with a note that read, "For us, once *was* enough."

5 A certain young lady, eager to appear on the television show *Talent Scouts,* produced by Susann's husband, Irving Mansfield, sent Mansfield a provocative photograph of herself. "I'll do anything to get on your show," she wrote, "and when I say anything, I mean anything." Unfortunately, it was Jackie who opened the letter. "I am Mrs. Mansfield," she

replied, "and I do everything for my husband — and when I say everything, I mean everything."

---cлo---

SUTTON, Don (1945–), *US baseball player.*

1 As a nineteen-year-old pitcher from Alabama, Sutton hoped to be drafted into the major leagues. He got a call from A's owner Charles Finley, who, after some conversation, asked him his nickname. Sutton told him that everyone just called him Don. Finley, a great lover of and bestower of nicknames, professed astonishment. "Why, we've just signed three kids called Catfish, Blue Moon, and Jumbo Jim. If you don't have a nickname, we can't give you the money." And he didn't.

2 The Dodgers pitcher was occasionally accused of altering baseballs to heighten the power of his pitches. When asked if it was true that he used a "foreign substance" on baseballs, Sutton replied, "Not true at all. Vaseline is manufactured right here in the United States of America."

3 An umpire once searched Sutton for evidence of ball doctoring but found only a note in his glove that read, "You're getting warm but it is not there."

---cлo---

SUVOROV, Alexander Vasilievich (1729–1800), *Russian general.*

1 On his campaign Suvorov lived as an ordinary soldier. Asked if he ever took off his clothes at night, he replied, "No; when I get lazy and want to have a comfortable sleep I generally take off one spur."

---cлo---

SVYATOPOLK (11th century AD), *grand prince of Kiev and son of Saint Vladimir.*

1 The city-state of Novgorod liked to consider itself a free republic. Although it was under the nominal charge of an elected prince, control was really exercised by the merchant-aristocrats of the area. Thus, the suggestion forcibly put forward by Grand Prince Svyatopolk that the city accept his son as its prince was coolly received. The Novgorodvans discussed the idea and sent back their message: "Send him here if he has a spare head."

---cлo---

SWEDENBORG, Emanuel (1688–1772), *Swedish mystic, scientist, and philosopher.*

1 Swedenborg was a very practical man. In a little inn in London one day, he was eating his dinner very rapidly when he thought he saw in the corner of the room a vision of Jesus Christ. The vision uttered two words: "Eat slower." This sensible advice was the beginning of all his visionary experiences.

---cлo---

SWIFT, Jonathan (1667–1745), *Anglo-Irish clergyman, satirist, and journalist.*

1 When Swift first started to visit a fashionable London coffeehouse, the regular clientele, comprising some of the foremost literary men in England, were so amazed by the eccentric behavior of the unknown parson that they concluded he must be mad. Dr. John Arbuthnot, the queen's physician, was writing a letter and needed some sand, as the custom then was, to blot it. Spying the strange parson nearby and thinking to have some fun with him, he said, "Pray, sir, have you any sand about you?"

"No, sir," said Swift, "but I have the gravel, and if you will give the letter to me, I'll piss upon it." From this unlikely start, a warm friendship grew up between the doctor and the divine.

2 On his travels Swift stopped at a house where the hostess, anxious to please her eminent visitor, asked him what he would like for dinner. "Will you have an apple pie, sir? Will you have a gooseberry pie, sir? A plum pie? A currant pie? A cherry pie? A pigeon pie — "

"Any pie but a magpie, madam," interrupted Swift.

3 On a journey by foot one day Swift was caught in a heavy thunderstorm and took shelter under a large tree. Presently he was joined by a rough-looking man and a pregnant woman. Falling into conversation with them, Swift learned that they were en route to the nearby town to be married. As the woman seemed likely to give birth at any moment, Swift's offer to marry them was happily accepted and Swift performed the marriage ceremony. The pair were about to go on their way when the husband remembered that a certificate was necessary to validate the marriage. Swift obliged by writing: "Under an oak, in stormy weather, / I joined this rogue and whore together; / And none but he who rules the thunder / Can put this rogue and whore asunder."

4 Dean Swift was reprimanded for preaching a charity sermon at such inordinate length that by the end the audience was very little inclined to contribute to the cause concerned. On the next occasion the dean determined to make it terse. He announced his text from Prov. 19: " 'He that hath pity upon the poor lendeth unto the Lord; and that which he hath given will he pay him again.' You have heard the terms of the loan," Swift continued, "and if you like the security, put down

your money." Then he sat down. The resulting donations were generous.

5 Lady Carteret, wife of the English viceroy in Ireland, was on friendly terms with Swift. One day when she happened to remark on how good the air was in Ireland, Swift fell on his knees and besought her, "For God's sake, madam, don't say that in England, for if you do, they will surely tax it."

6 At the age of fifty Swift gazed at the withered crown of a tree and remarked to the poet Edward Young, "I shall be like that tree; I shall die from the top."

{This prediction, sadly, was fulfilled by Swift's mental decay in his last years.}

---❦---

SWINBURNE, Algernon Charles (1837–1909), *British poet.*

1 (Swinburne had a hard time at school; Sir Osbert Sitwell records the reminiscences of an eighty-six-year-old former schoolmate.)

"He told me how much he had enjoyed his long life. 'If a man — or a schoolboy for that matter — ' he continued, 'does not get on well, it's his own fault. I well remember, when I first went to Eton, the head-boy called us together, and pointing to a little fellow with a mass of curly red hair, said, "If ever you see that boy, kick him — and if you are too far off to kick him, throw a stone."... He was a fellow named Swinburne,' he added. 'He used to write poetry for a time, I believe, but I don't know what became of him.' "

---❦---

SZILARD, Leo (1898–1964), *Hungarian-born US physicist.*

1 On one occasion Szilard was discussing with his colleague Enrico Fermi the possibility of

the existence of other life in the cosmos. Fermi held forth on the vastness of the universe, the likelihood that stars other than the sun would have planetary systems, the aeons of time that would enable life to emerge on some of these planets, and the probability that intelligent beings not only would exist elsewhere in the universe but would be capable of traveling to our own Earth. "If all this has been happening," concluded Fermi, "how is it that they have not arrived? Where are they?"

"They are already among us," replied Szilard, "but they call themselves Hungarians."

T

TAFT, Horace Dutton (1890–1936), *US educator, brother of William Howard Taft and founder of the Taft School in Connecticut.*

1 When the son of a pompous businessman was expelled from Taft's school, his enraged father was determined to have him readmitted. He stormed into Taft's office without knocking and roared, "Mr. Taft, you think you can run this school any damned way you please, don't you?" Taft looked at him calmly. "Your manner is crude and your language vulgar," he replied, "but you have somehow got the point."

TAFT, Lorado (1860–1936), *US sculptor.*

1 Taft was working on a classical sculpture that required the effect of windblown robes. Leaving the Art Institute of Chicago one windy day, the sculptor found himself walking on the opposite side of the street from two nuns, whose swirling robes offered a perfect model of the effect he hoped to create. Taft then realized that a man was closely following the nuns. Somewhat concerned, he crossed the street and accosted the man — only to find himself face to face with a fellow sculptor.

TAFT, William Howard (1857–1930), *27th President of the United States (1909–13) and Chief Justice of the Supreme Court (1921–30).*

1 When a blizzard hit Washington in the spring of 1909, Taft's inauguration ceremony had to be moved inside. "I've always said it would be a cold day when I got to be President of the United States," noted Taft.

2 On one occasion Taft, stranded at a small country railroad station, was informed that the express train would stop only if a number of people wanted to board it. Taft wired the conductor: "Stop at Hicksville. Large party waiting to catch train." When the train stopped, Taft boarded and reassured the confused conductor: "You can go ahead. I am the large party."

3 At Beverly Bay, Massachusetts, clad in a vast bathing suit, Taft plunged into the waves and was disporting himself in the water when one of his neighbors suggested to a friend that they also should go for a swim. "Better wait," the friend replied. "The President is using the ocean."

4 During a political speech a listener threw a cabbage at Taft, who then paused, examined the cabbage and said, "I see that one of my opponents has lost its head."

5 Taft was asked to comment on his spectacular defeat in the 1912 presidential election, when he ran for reelection against Woodrow Wilson and Theodore Roosevelt. "Well, I have one consolation," remarked Taft. "No candidate was ever elected ex-President by such a large majority."

6 Upon leaving the White House Taft was offered a Chair of Law by his alma mater, Yale. Taft noted that, given his size of over 350 pounds, a Sofa of Law would be more appropriate.

7 Taft spent many years in public service. When asked by a reporter how he had managed to occupy so many posts, he answered, "Like every well-trained Ohio man, I always had my plate the right side up when offices were falling."

———— ✺ ————

TALLEYRAND-PÉRIGORD, Charles Maurice de (1754–1838), *French statesman.*

1 Talleyrand had a faithful but inquisitive servant. One day, after entrusting a letter to him for delivery, he glanced out of the window and observed the man reading the letter. The following day Talleyrand sent another letter, this time with a postscript: "You may send a verbal answer by the bearer; he is perfectly acquainted with the whole business, having taken the precaution of reading this prior to its delivery."

2 Examining a draft budget prepared by Louis XVIII, Talleyrand pointed out that no provision had been made for payment of the deputies. "I think they should perform their duties without any payment," said the king. "It should be an honorary position."

"Without any payment?" exclaimed Talleyrand. "Your Majesty, that would cost us too much!"

3 During the French Revolution, Talleyrand spent some time in exile in America. On his return to France he said of the United States, "I found there a country with thirty-two religions and only one sauce."

4 Talleyrand was sitting between Mme de Staël and the famous beauty Mme Récamier, his attention very much engaged with the latter. Mme de Staël made a bid to get into the conversation. "Monsieur Talleyrand, if you and I and Madame Récamier were shipwrecked together and you could save only one of us, which would you save?" Talleyrand replied with his deepest bow, "Madame, you know everything, so clearly you know how to swim."

5 Claude Rulhières, author of a celebrated work on the Polish Revolution, *Histoire de l'anarchie de Pologne* (1807), complained in Talleyrand's hearing that people said that he was mischievous, "although I have done only one mischievous thing in my whole life."

"And when will that end?" inquired Talleyrand.

6 During Napoleon's reign the military were at their most arrogant, referring contemptuously to civilians as *pequins* (weaklings). Talleyrand asked a certain general for an explanation of the derogatory term. *"Nous appelons pequin tout ce qui n'est pas militaire* [We call weakling anybody who is not military]," he replied. *"Ah, oui,"* said Talleyrand, *"comme nous autres appelons militaires tous ceux qui ne sont pas civiles"* (Ah, yes, we call military all those who are not civil).

7 Talleyrand made no secret of his opposition to Napoleon's invasion of Spain and Portugal. This led to the notorious scene of January 28, 1809, when Napoleon abused Talleyrand in the grossest language in front of his other ministers, ending by shouting, *"Tenez, vous êtes de la merde dans un bas de*

soie" (You're shit in a silk stocking). Talleyrand said nothing under this attack, only remarking as he left the council chamber, "What a pity such a great man should be so ill bred!"

8 At the Congress of Vienna Alexander I of Russia inveighed against those who, like King Frederick Augustus of Saxony, had "betrayed the cause of Europe" in not joining the alliance against Napoleon. Talleyrand, mindful of the czar's own former conciliatory attitude toward the erstwhile French emperor, observed, "But that, sire, is merely a question of dates."

9 A rationalist colleague complained to Talleyrand about the difficulty of converting the French peasants. "What can one do to impress these people?" he asked. "Well," replied Talleyrand, "you might try getting crucified and rising again on the third day."

10 Talleyrand once reprimanded a visitor for swallowing a glass of expensive brandy in a single gulp. "The first thing you should do," explained Talleyrand, "is take your glass in the palms of your hands and warm it. Then shake it gently, with a circular movement, so that the liquid's perfume is released. Then, raise the glass to the nose and breathe deeply." His visitor was fascinated. "And then, my lord?" he asked. "And then, sir," continued Talleyrand, "you replace the glass on the table and talk about it."

11 The role played by Talleyrand behind the scenes in the July Revolution of 1830, which brought Louis Philippe to the throne, remains as obscure now as it was to his contemporaries. A widely told story relates how the elderly statesman, sitting in his house in Paris during the three days of riots, heard the pealing of the bells and remarked, "Ah, the tocsin! We're winning."

"Who's we, *mon prince?*"

Talleyrand gestured for silence: "Not a word. I'll tell you who we are tomorrow."

12 The veteran statesman was unimpressed by Louis Philippe's handling of the many crises that beset his reign. "How do you think this government will end?" someone once asked. "Accidentally," said Talleyrand.

TALMADGE, Norma (1895–1957), *US silent movie actress.*

1 Some years into her retirement, after making over fifty movies and reigning as a queen of Hollywood for years, she was besieged by a crowd of admirers when she was spotted leaving a restaurant in Los Angeles. As she drove away, she called out to her fans, "Go away! I don't need you anymore."

TAMAGNO, Francesco (1851–1905), *Italian tenor.*

1 The leading tenor of an American opera company, rehearsing Tamagno's famous role in *Otello,* was puzzled by a request from the stage director. During a brief rest in the tenor part he was to walk upstage, pause, then return downstage and continue singing. The action seemed pointless and difficult to execute in the time allowed. "But it is the tradition of the role," insisted the director. "Tamagno did it." The tenor submitted with reluctance. In Italy the following year, he visited Tamagno and asked him to explain this strange "tradition." The old man's face lit up. "It is very simple," he said. "Note that in the final passage Otello must sing a high B-flat. So while the chorus was singing I went upstage to spit."

TARANTINO, Quentin (1963–), *US film director.*

1 The graphic violence of Tarantino's movies had caused both widespread criticism and acclaim by the time he was awarded the Cannes Film Festival grand prize for *Pulp Fiction*. Onstage to accept his award, he was booed by some members of the audience, to whom he responded with an obscene gesture. "I don't make movies that bring people together," he barked. "I make movies that split people apart."

———— ✿ ————

TAYLOR, Elizabeth (1932–), *US film actress.*

1 Miss Taylor's fabulous diamond ring drew the notice of Princess Margaret, who remarked, "That's a bit vulgar." Miss Taylor persuaded the princess to try on the ring. "There, it's not so vulgar now, is it?" she said.

———— ✿ ————

TAYLOR, John (1703–72), *British oculist.*

1 At dinner in Edinburgh, Taylor was holding forth with much impudence, boasting among other things that he could read anybody's thoughts by looking at their eyes. His hostess, the Countess of Dumfries, angered by his behavior, contemptuously inquired whether he knew what she was thinking. Taylor confidently asserted that he did. "Then," said the countess, "it's very safe, for I am sure you will not repeat it."

———— ✿ ————

TAYLOR, Laurette (1884–1946), *US actress.*

1 At a party after a poorly attended performance one evening, Miss Taylor was engaged in amiable conversation with one of her fellow guests, a complete stranger. After some time, he politely took his leave and walked over to a group of people at the opposite side of the room. Miss Taylor's smile suddenly disappeared and she turned angrily to her hostess. "That man walked out on me tonight at the theater!" she cried. "Are you sure?" asked the hostess. "Of course I'm sure. I sometimes forget a face, but I *never* forget a back!"

———— ✿ ————

TAYLOR, Paul (1930–), *US dancer and choreographer.*

1 During a modern-dance program, Paul Taylor contributed a solo in which he simply stood motionless onstage for four minutes. The reviewer for *Dance Observer* magazine responded in kind: his review consisted of just four inches of white space.

———— ✿ ————

TECUMSEH (c. 1768–1813), *chief of the American Shawnee Indians, who organized an Indian confederacy to resist white encroachments.*

1 In 1810 Harrison, then governor of Indiana Territory, was negotiating with Tecumseh in order to try to prevent open hostilities. He ordered a chair to be brought for the Indian chief. The man who brought it said, "Your father, General Harrison, offers you a seat."

"My father!" Tecumseh exclaimed. "The sun is my father and the earth is my mother, and on her breast will I lie." Ignoring the chair, he stretched himself out on the ground.

———— ✿ ————

TELFORD, Thomas (1757–1834), *British engineer.*

1 In his later years Telford was something of a celebrity, as well as being delightful company. In London he stayed at the Ship Inn in

Charing Cross, which was always crowded with his friends. A new landlord purchased the inn without knowing that Telford was about to move into a house of his own in Abingdon Street. When he found out, he was utterly dismayed. "Not *leaving!*" he exclaimed. "I have just paid seven hundred and fifty pounds for you."

TEMPLE, Frederick (1821–1902), *British clergyman.*

1 Archbishop Temple had a reputation for intimidating his clergy, and ordinands particularly dreaded their pre-ordination interview with him. To one man he said, "I will lie down on that couch and pretend to be ill. You leave the room, come in again, and 'sick-visit' me." The ordinand did as he was told. Coming up to the archiepiscopal couch, he gazed intently at the recumbent figure and then said reprovingly, "Why, Freddie, you're on the drink again!"

TENG SHIH (6th century BC), *Chinese philosopher and administrator.*

1 A wealthy man from Teng's state had drowned in the Wei River. The corpse was recovered by a man who refused to return it to the mourning family until he had received a large payment. The relatives of the drowned man sought Teng's advice. He told them, "Wait, no other family will pay for the body." Fortified by this counsel, they waited, and in due course the finder of the corpse grew worried and also consulted Teng. "Wait," Teng advised, "for nowhere else can they obtain the body."

TENNYSON, Alfred, 1st Baron Tennyson (1809–92), *British poet; poet laureate (1850–92).*

1 The Duke of Argyll and his family, on holiday near the Tennysons, were invited for dinner. When the Argylls arrived, Tennyson apologized for not having changed: "I can't dress for you, for I never dress for anyone. If I made an exception and dressed for a duke, my butler would set me down as a snob."

2 The great Shakespearean actor Henry Irving was staying with the Tennysons. One evening after dinner when they were having port, the butler filled Irving's glass, then set the decanter down by Tennyson. Tennyson was talking and continued absentmindedly to fill his own glass, failing to notice when Irving's was empty. The decanter emptied, he called for another bottle. Again the butler filled Irving's glass and left Tennyson the decanter, which he finished as before. Next morning Irving found Tennyson standing solicitously at his bedside, inquiring how he felt. "Ah, but pray, Mr. Irving, do you always drink two bottles of port after dinner?"

3 The critics' reception of Tennyson's *Maud* was predictably hostile, for the poem dealt with love, madness, murder, suicide, hysteria. One reviewer suggested that *Maud* had one vowel too many in the title, and that it would make sense no matter which was deleted.

4 One of Tennyson's admirers, a little girl called Elspeth Thompson, used to accompany the poet on his long walks around London. As he tramped through the streets, the child trotting beside him, the poet made a striking figure in his swirling Spanish cloak and great sombrero. Passersby would often turn to look at him. Tennyson grumbled to Elspeth, "Child, your mother should dress you less conspicuously; people are staring at us."

5 Tennyson was offered a baronetcy four times, as a mark of honor from the nation, and each time he declined. He came around to thinking that he had made a mistake in declining and wished to accept. Accordingly, a friend, acting as intermediary between him and Gladstone, the prime minister, conveyed Tennyson's willingness. It was further suggested that Tennyson might be offered a peerage rather than a baronetcy, but Gladstone mused, "Ah! Could I be an accessory to introducing *that hat* into the House of Lords?"

6 Tennyson was entertaining a Russian nobleman at his house on the Isle of Wight. One morning the Russian set off on a shooting expedition, returning later that day with the proud news that he had shot two peasants. Tennyson politely corrected his guest's pronunciation: "You mean 'two pheasants,'" he said. "No," replied the Russian, "two peasants. They were insolent, so I shot them."

7 As a young man Tennyson was afflicted with a painful attack of piles. Accepting advice, he visited a young but well-known proctologist and was so successfully treated that for many years he had no further trouble. However, after he had become a famous poet and had been raised to the peerage, he suffered a further attack. Revisiting the proctologist, he expected to be recognized as the former patient who had become the great poet. The proctologist, however, gave no signs of recognition. It was only when the noble lord had bent over for examination that the proctologist exclaimed, "Ah, Tennyson!"

8 On his first meeting with Lady Duff Gordon, who later became a very good friend, Tennyson lay full length on the carpet, then rolled over to her and said, "Will you please to put your foot on me for a stool."

9 Ambassador to the Court of Saint James's and distinguished poet James Lowell was invited to dine at Tennyson's with a group of writers. The meal began in silence and lasted in silence until Tennyson turned to Lowell and said, "Do you know anything about Lowell?" Mrs. Tennyson rescued the meal: "Why, my dear, this *is* Mr. Lowell."

10 When the great poet had but days left before his death, he was asked if he felt any better. "The doctor says I do," he replied.

TERESA of Ávila, Saint (1515–82), *Spanish Carmelite nun.*

1 A young nun came to Saint Teresa with exaggerated tales of her spiritual trials and the fearful sins into which she had lapsed. After listening to her recitation, Saint Teresa said briskly, "We know, sister, that none of us is perfect. You must just be sure that your sins don't turn into bad habits."

TERRY, Dame Ellen (1847–1928), *British actress.*

1 Ellen Terry was at the height of her career when the director of a production in which she was starring turned out to be a rather opinionated and fussy young man. He told her exactly how she should play a particular scene, down to the most minute details of action and delivery. The star listened patiently and did precisely as she was told. When she had finally gone through the scene to his satisfaction, she turned to him and said, "Now, if you don't mind, I'll just do that little extra something for which I am paid my enormous fee."

2 At the turn of the century Ellen Terry was in her early fifties and, though still at the height of her powers as an actress, complained:

"Now I am a grandmother, nobody will ever write a play for me." When Bernard Shaw heard this remark, he immediately wrote *Captain Brassbound's Conversion* for her. Consequently, in 1901 she enjoyed a great success in the role of Lady Cicely Waynflete. "He only did it," Ellen Terry observed of Shaw, "out of a natural desire to contradict."

TETRAZZINI, Luisa (1871–1940), *Italian soprano.*

1 Tetrazzini was concerned neither about her size nor about the amount she needed to eat. She shared her predilection for Neapolitan dishes with her friend Enrico Caruso. On one occasion after a late spaghetti lunch with Caruso she had to sing Violetta in *La Traviata*. When her co-star John McCormack attempted to raise the dying Violetta in his arms, it felt, as he said later, as if he were fondling a pair of Michelin tires. He did not know that she had consumed so much spaghetti that she had had to remove her corsets. The amazement that he could not conceal started her giggling, and to the audience's astonishment both performers in this tragic death scene were soon convulsed with laughter.

THACKERAY, William Makepeace (1811–63), *British writer.*

1 On a lecturing tour of the United States Thackeray was invited to a feast of Massachusetts oysters by his publisher James T. Fields, who knew the author's great desire to taste these delicacies. Thackeray, overcome at the sight of the six huge oysters set before him, asked in a tremulous voice how he should begin on them. Fields promptly gave a demonstration and swallowed his first oyster. Plucking up courage, Thackeray did likewise. Fields asked him how he felt. "As if I had swallowed a baby," replied Thackeray.

2 Thackeray blackballed a man named Hill, proposed for membership in London's Garrick Club. This Mr. Hill was a self-made man with a strong cockney accent. "I blackballed him because he is a liar," Thackeray explained. "He calls himself 'ill' when he isn't."

3 At his club one day Thackeray was accosted by a pompous Guards officer who exclaimed, "Ha, Thackeray, old boy, I hear you're having your portrait painted." Disliking the man's patronizing tone, Thackeray briefly assented. "Full length?" inquired the officer superciliously. "No, full-length portraits are for soldiers, so we can see their spurs," replied Thackeray. "With authors, the other end of the man is the principal thing."

THALBERG, Irving J. (1899–1936), *US movie producer.*

1 Thalberg usually had his working hours double- or triple-booked with conferences on the many films currently in production. Important and self-important people might have to wait weeks for appointments, and when they arrived often found they had to cool their heels for hours in Thalberg's anteroom. When the Marx brothers came to talk to Thalberg about *A Night at the Opera*, they were displeased to be told they would have to wait. Lighting up two cigars apiece, they stationed themselves around the door of his sanctum and busily puffed smoke through the crack. Eventually Thalberg emerged. "Is there a fire?" he asked. "No, there's the Marx brothers," Groucho, Chico, and Harpo told him.

2 In 1936, shortly before Thalberg's early death from pneumonia, his literary scout Al Lewin brought him the synopsis of a book about to be published. He was greatly excited about its potential as a film and as a vehicle for Clark Gable. The book's title was *Gone with the Wind*. Thalberg agreed to read the synopsis, but kept putting it off. Lewin went on reminding him and asking him about it until at last Thalberg said that he had read it and he agreed with everything Lewin had said about it. "But," he continued, "I have just made *Mutiny on the Bounty* and *The Good Earth*. And now you're asking me to burn Atlanta. No, absolutely not! No more epics for me now. Just give me a little drawing-room drama. I'm just too tired."

———— ✿ ————

THALES (?640–?546 BC), *Greek philosopher.*

1 According to Herodotus (writing a century after Thales' death), Thales used his knowledge of Babylonian astronomy to predict an eclipse of the sun. The eclipse occurred just as the Medes and the Lydians were on the point of advancing into battle. It so terrified their armies that they packed their tents and returned home. Modern astronomical investigations have pinpointed the only eclipse in Thales' time as that occurring on May 28, 585 BC, a rare instance of establishing a precise date for an early historical event.

2 Aristotle (writing about two centuries after Thales' death) shows the philosopher as entrepreneur. People often taunted Thales, saying that all his wisdom had failed to make him rich. Thales responded by buying up all the olive presses in Miletus in a year when his knowledge of meteorology enabled him to predict a bumper crop of olives. By charging monopolistic prices for the use of his newly acquired presses, he became extremely wealthy in one season. Having proved his point, Thales then sold all the presses again and returned to philosophy.

3 Plato (writing about a century and a half after Thales' death) tells a more typical story of philosophical unworldliness. Thales was walking along a road with his head thrown back, studying the stars, when he stumbled into a well. In response to his cries for help a servant girl came and pulled him out, observing that while he was eager to know about things in the sky, he failed to see what lay at his own feet.

4 When Thales entertained the great Athenian lawgiver Solon at Miletus, Solon teased the philosopher about why he did not marry and have children. Thales made no reply. Shortly afterward a stranger came to his house and Thales took him aside for a few words before introducing him to Solon. The man informed Solon that he came from Athens. Solon eagerly asked for news.

"No news," said the stranger, "apart from the funeral of a great man's son."

"Whose son was this?" inquired Solon.

"I cannot recollect the name," replied the stranger, "but the father is a man of great honor, who is currently traveling abroad."

Solon, whose forebodings had been growing throughout the conversation, burst out with, "Was it the son of Solon?"

"Yes, that was the name," said the stranger.

When Solon began to weep and express extreme grief, Thales took him by the hand and said gently, "These things that can strike down even a man as resolute as Solon with uncontrollable grief are the things that prevent me from marrying and raising a family. But take courage, not a word of the man's story is true."

5 Thales used to say that there was no essential difference between being alive and being dead. Someone asked why, if that was the

case, he chose life instead of death. "Because there is no difference," Thales replied.

---cᴧɔ---

THEMISTOCLES (?527–460 BC), *Athenian statesman.*

1 Themistocles alienated the allies of Athens by extorting money from them. Anchoring his fleet off a small island, he sent a message saying that he had two powerful deities on his side who would compel them to pay up — Persuasion and Force. The islanders sent back a message saying they had two equally potent gods on their side — Poverty and Despair.

2 Themistocles was overheard to remark that his young son ruled all Greece. Asked to explain, he said, "Athens holds sway over all Greece; I dominate Athens; my wife dominates me; our newborn son dominates her."

---cᴧɔ---

THEODORIC [Theodoric the Great] (c. 454–526), *king of the Ostrogoths and of Italy (493–526).*

1 Although an Arian, Theodoric had a Catholic minister whom he trusted. This minister, thinking to ingratiate himself with the king, announced that he was renouncing his tenets to embrace Arianism. Theodoric had him beheaded, saying, "If this man is not faithful to his God, how can he be faithful to me, a mere man?"

---cᴧɔ---

THIERS, Louis Adolphe (1797–1877), *French statesman and historian; first president (1870–73) of the Third Republic.*

1 Someone remarked in Thiers's hearing that the great statesman's mother had been a cook. Thiers, intending to imply that she had been worthy of a higher estate in life, rushed to her defense: "She was — but I assure you that she was a very bad cook."

---cᴧɔ---

THOMAS, Dylan (1914–53), *Welsh poet.*

1 On one occasion when Dylan Thomas had been drinking and talking freely for some time, he suddenly stopped. "Somebody's boring me," he said. "I think it's me."

2 (Donald Hall, who later wrote about his friendship with Thomas, once had an exchange with the poet that became particularly poignant after Thomas's death.)

"I was complaining about some Sunday paper critic who used phrases like 'death-wish.' Out of brutal innocence I asked, 'What a dumb idea anyway. Who wants to die?' Dylan looked up at me. 'Oh, I do,' he said. 'Why?' I demanded. 'Just for the change,' he said."

3 "There is a story of [Thomas's] wife in the funeral parlour, who looked down at the poet's painted face, loud suit, and carnation in his buttonhole, only to declare, 'He would never have been seen dead in it.'"

---cᴧɔ---

After a successful career on stage, Julius Tannen came upon hard times in Hollywood. Unable to get an acting job, he finally at least obtained an audition for an editor's role in a newspaper drama.

He dressed carefully and, worried about his baldness, wore a toupee. After the audition the producer shook his head and said, "I'm sorry. I don't think you will do for the part. I've always visualized a bald-headed man for the part."

Julius pulled the toupee from his head. "I think I can satisfy you on that score," he beamed.

The producer studied Tannen's polished skull but shook his head again. "I'm sorry, Mr. Tannen, I simply can't visualize you as a bald-headed man."

— BEN HECHT, *A Child of the Century*

THOMAS, M. Carey (1857–1935), *US educator.*

1 Thomas, who had earned her doctorate summa cum laude in Switzerland and who later became the president of Bryn Mawr College, was denied admittance to higher studies in the United States because she was a woman. "One thing I am determined on," she vowed, "is that by the time I die *my brain* shall weigh as much as a man's if study and learning can make it so."

THOMAS, Norman (1884–1968), *US socialist politician and reformer.*

1 Norman Thomas campaigned regularly and unsuccessfully for the presidency from 1928 to 1948. When Franklin D. Roosevelt was President, Thomas visited him in the White House. In the course of the interview Roosevelt said, "Norman, I'm a damned sight better politician than you." Thomas replied, "Certainly, Mr. President; you're on that side of the desk, and I'm on this."

2 Thomas had many distinguished supporters, but lacked mass popular backing. Complimented on the lofty character of his campaigns, he replied, "I appreciate the flowers; only I wish the funeral weren't so complete."

3 Looking back at his record of failure in his campaigns for the presidency, Thomas commented, "While I'd rather be right than president, at any time I'm ready to be both."

THOMPSON, Emma (1959–), *British actress.*

1 Moviegoers commented on Thompson's radiance in the film *Howards End*. Her natural beauty was of course striking, but somehow a glow seemed to suffuse her presence on screen. After she won the Academy Award for Best Actress for her role, she revealed her secret, claiming she was in debt to the corset she was forced to wear throughout the film. "Every day they laced me up in these whalebone contraptions," she said. "And the blood rushes to your face when you wear those things. So that explains 'radiant.'"

THOMSON, Sir George Paget (1892–1975), *British physicist.*

1 The Maud Committee was given its name as a result of a telegram that Niels Bohr, the famous Danish physicist, managed to send to his friends in England shortly after the German occupation of Denmark. The telegram ended: "Please inform Cockcroft and Maud Ray, Kent," after having assured his friends that he was well. The message was mistakenly thought to be in code and skillfully decoded to mean "make uranium day and night." It was later found that Maud Ray had been Bohr's English governess.

THOMSON, Joseph (1858–94), *British explorer.*

1 In 1878 Thomson made his first journey to Africa as geologist and natural historian in an expedition led by Alexander Keith Johnston. Barely six weeks after departing Zanzibar for the interior, Johnston died, leaving the twenty-one-year-old Thomson leader of the expedition. He carried on to the great lakes and brought the expedition to an al-

most entirely successful conclusion. On his return to London he wrote the book *To African Lakes and Back,* and became a celebrity. J. M. Barrie asked Thomson what was the most dangerous part of his travels. "Crossing Piccadilly Circus," said Thomson.

———— ❧ ————

THOMSON, Robert (b. 1923), *US baseball player, born in Scotland.*

1 No team in the history of American baseball has come from as far behind to win a league pennant as did the National League's New York Giants in 1951. In mid-August they trailed the Brooklyn Dodgers by 13½ games, but in the last seven weeks of the season moved up to tie for the top spot, forcing a best-of-three play-off. After each team had won one game, the Giants, in the final game, with the score 4 to 1 against them, went into the last half of the last inning, scored a run, picked up one out, and had two men on base. Dodgers pitcher Ralph Branca entered the fray to try to get the other two outs his team needed. Then Bobby Thomson came to bat and hit a three-run home run to win the game 5 to 4 and the league pennant for the Giants. Pandemonium broke out in New York's Polo Ground, and this became one of the best-remembered moments in American baseball history.

Looking back on his career, Thomson said, "I played fourteen or fifteen years in the majors. I got more than 11,700 hits and more than 100 home runs. But I'd be forgotten except for that one."

{Curiously, Ralph Branca expressed a similar sentiment about the same moment: "I pitched nine or ten years in the big leagues. I threw thousands of pitches. And no one has ever let me forget that one."}

———— ❧ ————

THOREAU, Henry David (1817–62), *US writer and transcendentalist philosopher.*

1 A friend asked Thoreau what he thought of the world to come. "One world at a time," said Thoreau.

2 Thoreau's *A Week on the Concord and Merrimack Rivers* did not sell. Eventually his publisher, who needed the space, wrote to ask Thoreau how he should dispose of the remaining copies. Thoreau asked that they be sent to him — 706 copies out of the edition of 1,000. When they arrived and were safely stowed away, Thoreau noted in his journal, "I now have a library of nearly nine hundred volumes, over seven hundred of which I wrote myself."

3 (Thoreau made the following entry in his journal on September 8, 1859:)

"I went to the store the other day to buy a bolt for our front door, for as I told the storekeeper, the Governor was coming here. 'Aye,' said he, 'and the Legislature too.' 'Then I will take two bolts,' said I. He said that there had been a steady demand for bolts and locks of late, for our protectors were coming."

4 Thoreau was languishing in jail after he had refused to pay the Massachusetts poll tax in 1843. Ralph Waldo Emerson came to visit him and asked him why he was there. "Waldo, why are you *not* here?" said Thoreau.

5 Thoreau, whose father had been a manufacturer of lead pencils, was confident that he could improve on the type of pencil in use at that time. His early experiments were a great success and presented him with the opportunity to make his fortune. Thoreau, however, surprised his friends by announcing that he had no intention of making any further pencils. "Why should I?" he said. "I would not do again what I have done once."

6 Asked whether he had traveled much, Thoreau replied, "Yes — around Concord."

7 Toward the end of his life Thoreau was urged to make his peace with God. "I did not know that we had ever quarreled," he replied.

THORNDIKE, Dame Sybil (1882–1976), *British actress.*

1 Dame Sybil was the daughter of the canon of Rochester. At evensong one Sunday, she noticed that her father seemed a little distracted as he gave the blessing. She later asked him what he had been thinking about at the time. "My dear!" he exclaimed. "I was thinking how wonderful it would have been if I had been on a trapeze swinging across the aisle."

2 Sybil Thorndike was married to Sir Lewis Casson, himself a distinguished actor, and they frequently toured together, giving dramatic recitals. After his death she was asked about their long and happy marriage. "Did you ever think of divorce?" was one of the questions. "Divorce?" she said. "Never. But murder often!"

3 Dame Sybil Thorndike appeared in a play with Dame Edith Evans. The theater manager was faced with a dilemma — to which of the two distinguished actresses should the Number One dressing room be allocated? In desperation, he consulted Dame Sybil herself. "The Number Two dressing room is equally luxurious," he explained, "but it has the disadvantage of being at the top of a flight of stairs."

"There's no problem at all, my dear," replied Dame Sybil. "Let Edith have Number One. *I* can climb stairs."

THORPE, Jim (1888–1953), *US athlete of American Indian descent.*

1 Questioned about his running ability in football, Thorpe smiled and said, "I give 'em the hip, then I take it away."

Stories involving amnesia are not rare. One of the most endearing is told about the father of the poet Alfred Tennyson. Once, visiting a new parishioner, he was politely asked by the servant admitting him to identify himself. He found he could not remember his own name, turned away, walked, lost in thought, through the village, and encountered a rustic who respectfully greeted him: "Good day to 'ee, Dr. Tennyson."

"By God, my man, you're right!" exclaimed Dr. Tennyson.

— MICHAEL INNES, *The Gay Phoenix*

THRONBERRY, Marv (1933–), *US professional baseball player.*

1 "During their worst early years no one symbolized the hapless condition of the New York Mets better than first baseman Marv Thronberry. He was the good-natured butt of many of the better (and somewhat exaggerated) Mets stories. Like the time manager Casey Stengel got a cake for his birthday and someone in the clubhouse asked why Marvelous Marv hadn't got one on *his* birthday. 'We were afraid he might drop it,' Stengel explained."

THURBER, James (1894–1961), *US cartoonist, short-story writer, and humorist who contributed to* The New Yorker *for many years.*

1 The offices of *The New Yorker* were constantly being altered on editor Harold Ross's orders and the sound of hammering and drilling filled the air as partitions were moved around by squads of workmen.

Thurber once hung up a sign outside the elevator that read: "ALTERATIONS GOING ON AS USUAL DURING BUSINESS."

2 When *The Secret Life of Walter Mitty,* with Danny Kaye in the title role, became a hit movie, Sam Goldwyn decided that he would like to have Thurber as a permanent part of his team of writers. He tried to lure Thurber to Hollywood with an offer of $500 a week. Thurber, quite content to go on working for Harold Ross at *The New Yorker,* wrote back after a decent interval, declining Goldwyn's offer with "Mr. Ross has met the increase." Goldwyn wrote again, raising the offer to $1,000 a week, then $1,500, and finally $2,500. On each occasion the response was the same. Goldwyn decided to drop the matter for a while. Then one day he wrote again, but this time the offer had dropped to $1,500. Back came Thurber's reply: "I am sorry, but Mr. Ross has met the decrease."

3 Having overdrawn his bank account, Thurber was summoned to a meeting with the bank manager. The humorist freely admitted that he kept no record of the checks he wrote. "Then how do you know how much money is in your account?" asked the manager. "I thought that was *your* business," retorted Thurber.

4 One of Thurber's favorite stories concerned a conversation he had with a nurse while he was in the hospital. "What seven-letter word has three *u*'s in it?" he asked. The nurse pondered and then said, "I don't know, but it must be unusual."

5 At a party a woman lurched drunkenly up to Thurber and told him she would like to have a baby by him. "Surely you don't mean by unartificial insemination?" protested Thurber.

6 At another cocktail party a woman waxed enthusiastic over Thurber's work, saying that she found it even funnier in French than in English. "Yes, I always seem to lose something in the original," agreed Thurber.

7 Thurber and a friend attended the premiere of a Hollywood spectacular. As they were leaving the theater, Thurber inquired what his companion had thought of the movie. "Well, not to mince words, I thought it stank," was the response. "I can't say I liked it that well," murmured Thurber thoughtfully.

8 After he lost his sight Thurber was in a restaurant with Harold Ross when Ross picked up a bottle of Worcestershire sauce and exasperatedly said, "Goddammit, that's the ten thousandth time I've read the label on this bottle." Thurber said to him, "Goddammit, Harold, that's because you're handicapped by vision."

9 Thurber attended a friend's party after he had lost his sight. As a certain couple departed, he remarked to his host, "They're going to break up."

"That's not possible!" exclaimed his friend. "I've never seen such friendliness and smiling."

"Yes," said Thurber, "you *saw* them. I *heard* them."

Six months later, the couple separated.

10 In the fall of 1961 Thurber underwent surgery for a blood clot on the brain. He made a partial recovery but then contracted pneumonia and died on the afternoon of November 2. According to legend, his last words were: "God bless . . . God damn."

THURLOW, Edward, 1st Baron (1731–1806), *British statesman.*

1 As an undergraduate at Gonville and Caius College, Cambridge, Thurlow was principally distinguished for his idleness and unruliness. His tutor summoned him and began

to rebuke him: "Sir, I never come to the window but I see you idling in the court." Adopting the tutor's tone, Thurlow replied, "Sir, I never come into the court but I see you idling at the window."

2 As lord chancellor, Thurlow held the disposal of a number of church benefices and so was constantly being approached by various eminent people who wished him to confer such wealthy benefices, or livings, on their protégés. One day a poor country curate came to his office. Thurlow addressed him in his usual brusque manner: who was he? what did he want? in which lord's name did he come? and so on. The curate stammered out his name and the name of the parish for which he had come to apply. "I have no interest, my lord," he said, "and I come to you in no lord's name, but in the name of the Lord of Hosts."

"The Lord of Hosts!" said Thurlow. "The Lord of Hosts! You are the first person to apply to me in that lord's name, and I'll be damned if you don't have the living."

3 The lord chancellor and a certain bishop had the right to take turns in presenting a particular living. Thurlow got into an argument with the bishop as to whose turn it was to make the presentation. Eventually the bishop sent his secretary along to see Thurlow. The secretary said, transmitting his superior's compliments, that he believed the next turn belonged to the bishop. Thurlow replied, "Give your lord my compliments and tell him that I will see him damned before he shall present." The secretary turned pale. "My lord, this is a very unpleasant message to have to give to a bishop." Thurlow considered. Then he said, "You are right. It is indeed. Tell my lord bishop that *I* will be damned before he shall present."

4 At the adjournment of the court for the long vacation, Lord Thurlow, failing to take the customary leave of the bar, was about to depart the room in silence. "He might at least have said, 'Damn you,'" said a young barrister in a stage whisper. Thurlow heard, returned, and obliged.

TINTORETTO [Jacopo Robusti] (1518–94), *Italian painter.*

1 The satirist Aretino was a highly partisan supporter of the other great Venetian painter of the High Renaissance, Titian. He lost no opportunity to jeer at the dyer's young son. When Tintoretto began to obtain commissions that Aretino considered should have been Titian's, the satirist doubled his venom, Tintoretto's poverty and pride making him an easy target. Tintoretto let it be known that he was willing to paint Aretino's portrait gratis, an offer Aretino could not resist. He went to his victim's studio, took a chair, and struck a pose. "Stand up," ordered Tintoretto. "First I must measure you." Aretino stood, and Tintoretto came toward him, drawing out a long horse-pistol, which he ran slowly over his sitter. "I find you are two and a half pistols tall," the painter concluded. "Now — go!" From that time on, Tintoretto had no further trouble with Aretino.

TITIAN (c. 1488–1576), *Italian painter who worked mainly in Venice.*

1 The Duchess of Urbino, although ugly and advanced in years, persuaded her husband to commission Titian to paint her in the nude. As Titian was reluctant, his friend the satirist and poet Pietro Aretino suggested a way around the problem. They hired a prostitute, a girl with an exquisitely beautiful figure, to pose for the body, and Titian produced an idealized portrait of the duchess for the head.

She was delighted, particularly as the picture was christened *The Venus of Urbino*. When it was shown to the duke, he sighed and said, "If I could have had that girl's body, even with my wife's head, I would have been a happier man." Aretino, to whom this remark was addressed, laughed so much that he suffered a stroke and died.

TOLSTOY, Leo [Nikolaevich], Count (1828–1910), *Russian writer.*

1 Tolstoy once gave a lecture about the need for pure passive nonresistance and nonviolence to all living creatures. A member of the audience asked what he should do if a tiger were to attack him in the woods. "Do the best you can," replied Tolstoy. "It doesn't happen very often."

2 In his last hours Tolstoy firmly resisted the efforts of those who tried to persuade him to reconcile himself with the Russian Orthodox church. "Even in the valley of the shadow of death, two and two do not make six," he said.

TOOKE, John Horne (1736–1812), *British radical politician and philologist. His support of the French Revolution occasioned his trial (1794) for high treason; he was acquitted.*

1 When Tooke was at school, a master asked him in a grammar lesson why a certain verb governed a particular case. "I don't know," answered Tooke. "That is impossible," said the master. "I know you're not ignorant, but obstinate." Tooke, however, persisted in saying that he didn't know, so the master beat him. The beating over, the master quoted the rule that covered the verb in question. "Oh, I know that," said Tooke at once, "but you asked me the *reason,* not the *rule.*"

2 Horne Tooke was advised to take a wife. "With all my heart," said he. "Whose wife shall it be?"

TOSCANINI, Arturo (1867–1957), *Italian conductor.*

1 During a rehearsal Toscanini flew into a tantrum with a player and ended by ordering him from the stage. As the man reached the exit he turned around and shouted, "Nuts to you!"

"It's too late to apologize," yelled back Toscanini.

2 A trumpet player had attracted Toscanini's wrath during a rehearsal. "God tells me how the music should sound," shouted the exasperated conductor, "but *you* stand in the way!"

3 Every Christmas, composer Giacomo Puccini would have a cake baked for each of his friends. One year, having quarreled with Toscanini just before Christmas, he tried to cancel the order for the conductor's cake. But it was too late — the cake had already been dispatched. The following day, Toscanini received a telegram from Puccini: "Cake sent by mistake." He replied by return: "Cake eaten by mistake."

4 Puccini having died shortly before finishing his opera *Turandot,* the work was completed for performance by Franco Alfano. When Toscanini, who had a profound reverence for Puccini's music, used to conduct *Turandot,* he always laid down his baton at the point in the last act at which Puccini broke off. "Here died the maestro," he would announce to the audience, and two minutes' silence would then be kept before Toscanini launched into Alfano's finale.

5 Exasperated by the shortcomings of an orchestra, Toscanini suddenly burst out, "When

I retire, I open a bordello. You know what that is? Or are you all *castrati*? I will attract the most beautiful women in the world for my bordello — it will be the La Scala of passion. But I will lock the door against *every one of you!*"

6 Toscanini used to sing with the orchestra during rehearsals. Engrossed in the music, he sometimes forgot about this habit. At Salzburg once during a dress rehearsal, his voice could be heard above the instruments. Suddenly he stopped the orchestra and exclaimed, "For the love of God, who's singing here?"

7 The orchestra's librarian was vexed by Toscanini's habit of hurling valuable scores at the orchestra if things went badly during a rehearsal. Observing him closely, he noticed that the conductor's first action when enraged was to take his baton in both hands and attempt to snap it. If the baton snapped, Toscanini usually calmed down and the rehearsal went on; if it did not, he began throwing scores. The librarian therefore arranged for a supply of relatively flimsy batons to be available during rehearsals. If things went badly, Toscanini might break as many as six batons and the librarian would have to send for spares. "Lumber, lumber," he would shout to his assistant.

8 Arriving at a town on July 3 during a South American tour with the NBC Symphony Orchestra, Toscanini told the disgruntled players that he wished them to assemble at the theater the following morning. The players, who had been traveling for some time, were looking forward to a couple of days' rest from rehearsals. They obeyed with an ill grace. When they were assembled, Toscanini asked them to rise and led them through "The Star-Spangled Banner." "Today is the Fourth of July," he announced at the end, and dismissed them.

9 During a rehearsal of Debussy's *La Mer*, Toscanini found himself unable to describe the effect he hoped to achieve from a particular passage. After a moment's thought, he took a silk handkerchief from his pocket and tossed it high into the air. The orchestra, mesmerized, watched the slow, graceful descent of the silken scarf. Toscanini smiled with satisfaction as it finally settled on the floor. "There," he said, "play it like that."

TOULOUSE-LAUTREC, Henri de (1864–1901), *French nobleman and painter.*

1 The famed portrayer of Montmartre nightlife eventually succumbed to the ravages of alcohol and syphilis. To the priest, who had come to ease his soul and asked how he was, the painter said, "I'm happier now than I shall be in a few days when you come with your little bell [signifying Last Rites]."

TOWNSHEND, Charles (1725–67), *British politician.*

1 A certain James Harris, author of some moralistic treatises and a once-celebrated book on a universal grammar, was elected to Parliament. After he had made his maiden speech, Townshend demanded to know who he was. "Mr. Harris of Salisbury, who has written a very ingenious book of grammar and another on virtue," someone informed him. "What the devil brings him here?" Townshend demanded. "I am sure he will find neither one nor the other in the House of Commons."

TRACY, Spencer (1900–67), *US film actor.*

1 When asked what he looked for in a script, Tracy's immediate reply was, "Days off."

2 Tracy was asked by director Garson Kanin why he always insisted on first billing when he co-starred in films with Katharine Hepburn. "Why not?" asked Tracy. "Well, after all," reasoned Kanin, "she's the lady and you're the man. Ladies first?" Retorted Tracy: "This is a movie, not a lifeboat."

3 When a young actor asked Spencer Tracy for help with his acting, Tracy gave some of the most valuable advice to date: "Just learn your lines and don't bump into the furniture."

TRAVERS, William R. (1819–87), *US lawyer and wit.*

1 A bore who had been discoursing tediously throughout dinner turned to William Travers and inquired, "Do you think oysters have brains?"

"Y-y-yes," Travers replied in his celebrated stutter. "J-j-just enough b-b-brains to k-k-keep their mouths s-s-shut."

TRAVOLTA, John (1954–), *US film actor and dancer.*

1 Audiences loved seeing Travolta dance with Uma Thurman in the movie *Pulp Fiction.* Dancing had brought fame and fortune to Travolta years earlier, when he played Tony Manero in *Saturday Night Fever,* an iconic film for its generation in the 1970s. Thurman described the filming of her dance scene by saying, "To dance with Travolta was like being able to do a western with John Wayne — you'd happily play some barroom slut just for the opportunity."

2 Travolta was nominated for Best Actor for *Pulp Fiction,* and that same year Paul Newman was nominated for the same award for his work in *Nobody's Fool.* One day a partisan Travolta fan approached him and said, "Watch out for Newman!" asserting that Newman, stiff competition, was campaigning for the Academy Award harder than any other actor. When Travolta demurred, the fan said, "Oh really? I went into a supermarket and saw his face on the front of a bottle of salad dressing!"

TREE, Sir Herbert Beerbohm (1853–1917), *British actor and theater manager.*

1 Tree was directing a rehearsal of a play in which he felt that the actresses, with their rather sophisticated appearance, had not captured the essential spirit of their roles. Stopping them, he said, "Ladies, just a little more virginity, if you don't mind."

2 Tree showed Max Beerbohm a letter that he had received from an admirer who had seen him act the night before. Max read it and commented, "That's very nice." "Very," said Tree happily. "I can stand any amount of flattery so long as it's fulsome enough."

3 One of the more bizarre productions of the silent-film era was a version of *Macbeth* produced in 1916 by D. W. Griffith, who was ambitious to raise the cultural standing of the film industry. Cast in the title role, Tree did not take easily to the medium; it is said that on the first day of shooting he pointed to the camera and said, "Take that black box away. I can't act in front of it."

4 During the rehearsal of a scene that was not working out too well, Tree directed a young actor to step back a little. The man did so. After a while Tree stopped the rehearsal again: "A little further back, please." Again the actor did as he was bidden and the rehearsal carried on. Tree stopped it a third time: "Further back still," he requested. "But if I go any further back, I'll be right off the

stage," protested the actor. "Yes, that's right," said Tree.

5 The writer Hesketh Pearson was once waiting to speak to Tree at His Majesty's Theatre in London. Another man, a stranger to Pearson, was also present on the same mission. When Tree finally arrived, he looked at the two men for a moment, then sat down between them. "Consider yourselves introduced," he said, "because I only remember one of your names, and that wouldn't be fair to the other."

6 Tree had little money sense, and his financial manager at the Haymarket Theatre was constantly warning him against being overgenerous. As an example of unnecessary expenditure, he once cited Tree's habit of taking him to lunch at the Carlton every day and paying the bill out of petty cash. Tree thanked him for his advice and promised immediate reform. At lunchtime that day, he dutifully took his manager to a nearby teashop and said to the waitress, "Madam, will you please give this gentleman a nice glass of milk and a large bun." Then, turning to his colleague, Tree said amicably, "Pick me up at the Carlton when you have had enough — but do have enough."

7 Tree once had cause to criticize a young actor for his overbearing conceit. "I assure you, sir," retorted the actor indignantly, "that I am not suffering from a swelled head."

"It isn't the swelling that causes suffering," remarked Tree. "It's the subsequent shrinkage that hurts."

———— ⚭ ————

TRENCH, Richard Chenevix (1807–86), *British divine and biblical scholar.*

1 In 1875 a fall fractured both of Trench's knees, after which he never fully recovered his health, living in fear of paralysis. A lady sitting next to him at dinner noticed that the elderly cleric was agitated and muttering to himself. "It's come at last; I can't feel a thing; I'm paralyzed." She asked Trench what was wrong. "I've been pinching my leg for the last five minutes and I can't feel a thing," he replied. "I must be paralyzed." The lady colored. "It's all right, Your Grace," she said, "it's my leg you've been pinching."

2 In 1884 Trench resigned his archbishopric on grounds of ill health. Some time later his successor invited him and Mrs. Trench back for a short stay at the bishop's palace in Dublin. Feeling comfortable and at home in the house where he had lived for so long, Trench forgot that he was not the host. At a meal at which the food was rather poor he suddenly boomed out across the table to his wife, "My dear, you must count this cook as one of your failures."

———— ⚭ ————

TRILLING, Lionel (1905–76), *US educator and author.*

1 "The erudite Lionel Trilling and the erudite Jacques Barzun [also a Columbia professor] got into a punning match when a student, discussing Malthus's *Essay on Population,* cited the motto of the Order of the Garter, *Honi soit qui mal y pense* — 'Shame on him who imputes ill to it.' Barzun remarked, 'Honi soit que Malthus pense.' Trilling rejoined, 'Honi soit qui mal thus puns.'"

———— ⚭ ————

TROLLOPE, Anthony (1815–82), *British novelist.*

1 Michael Sadleir describes Trollope as one "scarcely giving himself time to think, but spluttering and roaring out an instantly-formed opinion couched in the very strongest of terms." At a meeting of surveyors, Trollope suddenly fired at the speaker who pre-

ceded him, "I disagree with you entirely. What was it you said?"

2 A lady sitting next to Trollope at dinner observed that he helped himself liberally from every dish that was offered to him. "You seem to have a very good appetite, Mr. Trollope," she remarked, rather impertinently. "None at all, madam," he replied, "but, thank God, I am very greedy."

3 The character of Mrs. Proudie, the insufferable wife of the bishop of Barchester, in the Barsetshire novels is one of Trollope's greatest successes. In his *Autobiography* he owns to taking great delight in his creation of her. One morning he was sitting writing in the drawing room of his London club, the Athenaeum, when he overheard two clergymen talking about his work. They were complaining that in different books Trollope kept on introducing the same characters again and again. "If I could not invent new characters, I would not write novels at all," said one. Then the other began to complain about Mrs. Proudie. This was too much for Trollope, who approached them, confessing that he was the author of the novels they were criticizing. "As to Mrs. Proudie, I will go home and kill her before the week is over," he promised. The two clergymen, much embarrassed, begged Trollope to overlook their comments, but Trollope kept his word. The novel he was working on was *The Last Chronicle of Barset,* and in it he describes the sudden and shocking death of his old favorite, Mrs. Proudie.

4 (In 1858 the Post Office dispatched Trollope to the West Indies with the title of "missioner" to investigate and make suggestions for reorganizing the postal system in Britain's Caribbean and Central American colonies.)

"Trollope was determined to prove that a certain distance could be covered on mule-back in two days. The local postal authorities declared that the journey would take three, and to support their claim purposely provided the troublesome visitor with an uncomfortable saddle. In consequence the first day's ride reduced the missioner to the extremes of raw discomfort. The morrow (if he were to carry his point) must be another, equally fatiguing day. Only one remedy was possible, and that a drastic one. He ordered two bottles of brandy, poured them into a washbasin, and sat in it."

TROLLOPE, Frances (1780–1863), *British novelist, traveler, and mother of Anthony Trollope.*

1 (The novelist Sabine Baring-Gould remembers meeting Mrs. Trollope at Pau one winter when she was a child and Mrs. Trollope an old lady.)

"The English residents were not a little shy of her, fearing lest she should take stock of them and use them up in one of her novels; for she had the character of delineating members of her acquaintance, and that not to their advantage. Someone asked her whether this was not her practice. 'Of course,' answered Mrs. Trollope, 'I draw from life — but I always pulp my acquaintances before serving them up. You would never recognize a pig in a sausage.'"

TROTSKY, Leon [Lev Davidovich Bronstein] (1879–1940), *Russian revolutionary.*

1 A Russian émigré in Vienna during World War I, Trotsky spent much of his time playing chess in the Café Central and was regarded by those who knew him as a harmless, almost pathetic figure. In March 1917, the Austrian foreign minister was informed by an excited official that revolution had broken out in Russia. "Russia is not a land where revolutions break out," said the

minister skeptically, dismissing the credulous young man. "Besides, who on earth would make a revolution in Russia? Perhaps Herr Trotsky from the Café Central?"

TROY, Hugh (1906–64), *US artist and practical joker.*

1 In 1935 the Museum of Modern Art sponsored the first American exhibition of van Gogh's art. Troy suspected that many of the vast crowds of people who thronged to the show were more attracted by the sensational details of van Gogh's life than sincerely interested in his art. He made a replica of an ear out of chipped beef and had it mounted in a little blue velvet display case. Under it was a card reading: "This was the ear that Vincent van Gogh cut off and sent to his mistress, a French prostitute, 24 December 1888." The ear was placed on a table in the gallery and was immediately a prime draw for the crowd.

TRUMAN, Harry S. (1884–1972), *US politician; 33d President of the United States (1945–53).*

1 When Harry Truman first took his seat in the Senate, majority whip "Ham" Lewis sat down beside him and gave him his first look at the workings of the august body. "For the first six months you'll wonder how the hell you got here, and after that you'll wonder how the hell the rest of us got here."

2 Every·presidential couple who lived in the White House had their own china pattern. It was tradition. And the choosing of the right china was often a lengthy affair. Not so for Truman, who walked his decorator into the dining room and said, "Just match the wallpaper!"

3 Truman had accepted the vice presidency with extreme reluctance. On April 12, 1945, he was summoned to the White House. There he was shown into Eleanor Roosevelt's sitting room and she told him gently that President Roosevelt was dead. After a moment's stunned silence, Truman asked her, "Is there anything I can do for you?" She shook her head. "Is there anything *we* can do for *you?*" she said. "For you're the one in trouble now."

4 In December 1950 President Truman's daughter, Margaret, gave a public singing recital in Washington, which was unenthusiastically received by Paul Hume, the *Washington Post*'s music critic. He characterized her voice as having "little size and fair quality," said she sang flat much of the time, and complained that there were "few moments . . . when one can relax and feel confident that she will make her goal, which is the end of the song."

Truman penned the following letter: "I have just read your lousy review buried in the back pages. You sound like a frustrated old man who never made a success, an eight-ulcer man on a four-ulcer job, and all four ulcers working. I have never met you, but if I do you'll need a new nose and plenty of beefsteak and perhaps a supporter below. Westbrook Pegler, a guttersnipe, is a gentleman compared to you. You can take that as more of an insult than as a reflection on your ancestry."

5 After Truman had referred to a certain politician's speech as "a bunch of horse manure," it was suggested to Bess Truman that she persuade her husband to tone down his language. Mrs. Truman replied, "You don't know how many years it took me to tone it down to that!"

6 It may have been Truman who started the joke about one-handed economists. "All my economists say, 'on the one hand . . . on the other.' Give me a one-handed economist!"

7 As President, Truman kept two signs on his desk. One quoted Mark Twain: "Always do right. This will gratify some people and astonish the rest." The other read, "The buck stops here."

8 During an informal discussion with Truman, an eager young student asked, "How do I get started in politics, sir?"

"You've already started," replied the former President. "You're spending somebody else's money, aren't you?"

9 Truman liked to take walks around Washington. One evening he decided to go see a bridge that had been put up over the Potomac. Walking down some steps by the river's edge, he came upon a man who seemed completely unsurprised to see the President of the United States in front of him. "You know, Mr. President,' the man said, "I was just thinking about you."

10 It is said that Truman read more books than any President of this century. One day a friend visited him at New York's Waldorf-Astoria Hotel after he had left the presidency. Beside Truman's chair were two enormous stacks of new books. His friend commented that he supposed Truman read them to fall asleep at night. "No," replied Truman, "I read myself awake."

11 In her book *Souvenir* Margaret Truman recalls the Christmas of 1955. The President found his wife at the fireplace disposing of letters he had written to her over the years. "But think of history," he protested. "I *have,*" replied Bess.

12 Of the ego of politicians, Truman liked to say that a statesman was a politician who had been dead for fifteen years.

TRUTH, Sojourner [Isabella Van Wagener] (c. 1797–1838), *US evangelist, abolitionist, feminist, and orator.*

1 Sojourner Truth was one of the first blacks to test the streetcar antidiscrimination law in Washington, D.C. Having failed to get a trolley to stop for her when she signaled, she shouted at the top of her voice, "I want to ride! I want to ride! *I want to ride!*" A large crowd gathered, and the streetcar was unable to continue on its way. Sojourner Truth jumped aboard and was told by the angry conductor to go forward to where the horses were or he would put her out. Truth sat down quietly and informed the conductor that she was a passenger and would not be bullied: "As a citizen of the Empire State of New York, I know the law as well as you do." So saying, she rode the car to the end of the line and left it with the words, "Bless God! I have had a ride."

TURNER, Joseph Mallord William (1775–1851), *British landscape painter.*

1 A naval officer complained to Turner that the ships in his view of Plymouth had no portholes. The painter retorted, "My business is to paint not what I know, but what I see."

2 Handed a salad at the table, Turner remarked to his neighbor, "Nice cool green, that lettuce, isn't it? and the beetroot pretty red — not quite strong enough; and the mixture, delicate tint of yellow that. Add some mustard, and then you have one of my pictures."

3 Other artists loathed being hung next to Turner at exhibitions, as the brilliance of his colors had a disastrous effect on the pictures

on either side. When *Cologne* was hung between two paintings by Sir Thomas Lawrence, the great portraitist complained so bitterly that Turner good-naturedly toned down the golden sky in his painting to an overall dullness. "What have you done to your picture?" asked a friend in horror when he saw the change. "Well, poor Lawrence was so unhappy," explained Turner. "It's only lampblack. It'll all wash off after the exhibition."

4 Turner always regretted selling his paintings and would wear an expression of woe for days after a sale. "I've lost one of my children this week," he would explain.

5 The watercolorist Thomas Girtin was the exact contemporary of Turner, and their talents for evoking atmosphere by use of color were astonishingly similar. When Girtin died young in 1802, Turner observed in his characteristically generous way, "If Girtin had lived, I would have starved."

6 One of Turner's most famous and popular pictures was his painting of the fire that destroyed the old Houses of Parliament in 1834. It is remarkable for its evocation of an immensely complex scene caught at a moment of high drama. First exhibited at the British Institution, it was hung in a far from complete state. For three hours before the public were admitted, Turner worked busily on it. When he had finished, he just walked away, never turning his head to have a look at the completed picture. The historical painter Daniel Maclise, who witnessed this extraordinary scene, observed, "There, that's masterly; he does not stop to look at his work; he *knows* it is done and he is off."

7 Turner found the color green difficult to use, as the greens available were unsatisfactory and costly as well. His habit was to paint palm trees yellow. One gentleman who disliked his use of yellow rebuked him, telling him that palm trees are never yellow, but always green. "Umph!" said Turner. "I can't afford it! Can't afford it!"

———— ojo ————

TWAIN, Mark [Samuel Langhorne Clemens] (1835–1910), *US humorist, writer, and lecturer.*

1 In order to apply for the post of reporter-at-large on the *Territorial Enterprise,* Samuel Clemens walked 130 miles to Virginia City in Nevada Territory. He arrived at the newspaper's offices one hot afternoon in August, a dust-covered, weary stranger in a slouch hat, with a revolver slung on his belt, and a roll of blankets on his back. He wore a blue woolen shirt and dusty trousers tucked into his boots. Dropping into a chair, he announced, "My starboard leg seems to be unshipped. I'd like about one hundred yards of line; I think I am falling to pieces." He added, "My name is Clemens, and I've come to write for the paper."

2 As a cub reporter, Mark Twain was told never to state as fact anything that he could not personally verify. Following this instruction to the letter, he wrote the following account of a gala social event: "A woman giving the name of Mrs. James Jones, who is reported to be one of the society leaders of the city, is said to have given what purported to be a party yesterday to a number of alleged ladies. The hostess claims to be the wife of a reputed attorney."

3 On board ship on an expedition to the Holy Land, Clemens made the acquaintance of Charles J. Langdon, a young man from Elmira, New York, who was a great admirer of his. At some point Langdon showed him a miniature of his sister, Olivia. Clemens could not forget her face and resolved to meet her. He later maneuvered an invitation to visit the Langdon home for a week, and in that week

he fell thoroughly for Livy, as the family called her. On the last day of his visit he said to Langdon, "Charley, my week is up, and I must go home." Langdon did not press him to stay longer, but said, "We'll have to stand it, I guess, but you mustn't leave before tonight."

"I ought to go by the first train," said Clemens gloomily. "I am in love."

"In what?"

"In love — with your sister, and I ought to get away from here."

Langdon was now genuinely alarmed: no one was good enough for his sister, the family's darling. "Look here, Clemens," he said, "there's a train in half an hour. I'll help you catch it. Don't wait till tonight. Go now."

4 Mark Twain's wife did her best to censor the more picturesque flights of her husband's language. One morning he cut himself shaving and cursed long and loud. When he stopped, his wife tried to shame him by repeating to him verbatim all the profanities that he had just uttered. Twain heard her out and then remarked, "You have the words, my dear, but I'm afraid you'll never master the tune."

5 A businessman notorious for his ruthlessness announced to Mark Twain, "Before I die I mean to make a pilgrimage to the Holy Land. I will climb Mount Sinai and read the Ten Commandments aloud at the top."

"I have a better idea," said Twain. "You could stay home in Boston and keep them."

6 Arriving at a small town in the course of a lecture tour, Mark Twain went to the local barbershop for a shave, and told the barber that it was his first visit to the town.

"You've chosen a good time to come," said the barber. "Mark Twain is going to lecture here tonight. You'll want to go, I suppose?"

"I guess so," responded Twain.

"Have you bought your ticket yet?"

"No, not yet."

"Well, it's sold out, so you'll have to stand."

"Just my luck," said Twain with a sigh. "I always have to stand when that fellow lectures."

7 There were always cats at Mark Twain's farm, and favorite cats had their own names — Blatherskite, Sour Mash, Stray Kit, Sin, Satan. His children inherited his love of them. His daughter Susy once said, "The difference between Papa and Mamma is that Mamma loves morals and Papa loves cats."

8 As Twain and his good friend the writer William Dean Howells were leaving church one Sunday, it started to rain heavily. Howells looked up at the clouds and said, "Do you think it will stop?"

"It always has," replied Twain.

9 When the printing plates were being prepared for the illustrations to *Huckleberry Finn,* a mischievous engraver (whose identity was never discovered despite the posting of a reward) made an addition to the picture of old Silas Phelps. He drew in a male sex organ, thus altering entirely the implications of the pictured Aunt Sally's question, "Who do you think it is?" The alteration was discovered only after thousands of the books had been printed and bound, and the offending illustration had to be cut out by hand and replaced.

10 After several attempts, Mark Twain at last obtained an appointment to see General Ulysses S. Grant at home. He was elated at this prospect, but when he actually confronted Grant and looked at the square, imperturbable, unsmiling face, he found himself, for the first time, unable to think of what to say. Grant, noted for his taciturnity, nodded slightly and waited. Mark Twain hesitated, and then inspiration came. "General," he said, "I seem to be a little embarrassed, are you?" This broke the ice, and there were no further difficulties.

Twelve years later the two men met again in Chicago, at a reception for General Grant after his world tour. Twain arrived in time for the large welcoming procession. On the way to the reviewing stand, the mayor of Chicago said, "General, let me present Mr. Clemens, a man almost as great as yourself." The two men shook hands, and there was a pause. Then the general looked at Twain gravely. "Mr. Clemens," he said, "*I am not embarrassed, are you?*" They both laughed.

11 Mark Twain often did his writing in bed, regardless of the time of day. On one occasion his wife came in to tell him that a reporter had arrived to interview him. When Twain showed no sign of being ready to get up, she said, "Don't you think it will be a little embarrassing for him to find you in bed?"

"Why, if you think so, Livy," Twain responded, "we could have the other bed made up for him."

12 Henry Irving was telling Mark Twain a story. "You haven't heard this, have you?" he inquired after the preamble. Mark Twain assured him he had not. A little later Irving again paused and asked the same question. Mark Twain made the same answer. Irving then got almost to the climax of the tale before breaking off again — "Are you quite sure you haven't heard this?" The third time was too much for his listener. "I can lie once," said Twain, "I can lie twice for courtesy's sake, but I draw the line there. I can't lie the third time at any price. I not only heard the story, I invented it."

13 When Mark Twain was in London, a rumor of his death or imminent death reached the editor of the *New York Journal,* who sent its London correspondent the following cablegrams: "IF MARK TWAIN DYING IN POVERTY IN LONDON SEND 500 WORDS" and "IF MARK TWAIN HAS DIED IN POVERTY SEND 1000 WORDS." The *Journal*'s man showed the cables to Mark Twain, who suggested the substance of

a reply to the effect that a cousin, James Ross Clemens, had been seriously ill in London, but had recovered. The reply ended with "REPORT OF MY DEATH GREATLY EXAGGERATED."

14 One night a group of Twain's friends and admirers in New York, remembering it was the writer's birthday, resolved to send him birthday greetings. The globe-trotting Twain was away on his travels and none of them knew his address. So they mailed a letter superscribed "Mark Twain, God Knows Where." Some weeks later they received an acknowledgment reading simply: "He did."

15 After attending a service conducted by Dr. Doane, later bishop of Albany, Mark Twain congratulated him on an enjoyable service. "I welcomed it as an old friend," he went on. "I have a book at home containing every word of it." Dr. Doane bristled. "I am sure you have not," he replied huffily. "Indeed I have," Twain persisted. "Well, I'd like to have a look at it then. Could you send it over to me?" The following day Twain sent him an unabridged dictionary.

16 A devotee of cigars, Mark Twain was contemptuous of those who made a great to-do about giving up smoking. He always claimed that it was easy to quit: "I've done it a hundred times!"

17 Mark Twain, careless about his dress, one day called on Harriet Beecher Stowe without his necktie. On his return Mrs. Clemens noticed the omission and scolded him. A little later a messenger turned up on Mrs. Stowe's doorstep and handed her a small package. Inside was a black necktie, and a note: "Here is a necktie. Take it out and look at it. I think I stayed half an hour this morning without this necktie. At the end of that time, will you kindly return it, as it is the only one I have. Mark Twain."

18 Mark Twain loved to brag about his hunting and fishing exploits. He once spent three weeks fishing in the Maine woods, regardless of the fact that it was the state's closed season for fishing. Relaxing in the lounge car of the train on his return journey to New York, his catch iced down in the baggage car, he looked for someone to whom he could relate the story of his successful holiday. The stranger to whom he began to boast of his sizable catch appeared at first unresponsive, then positively grim. "By the way, who are you, sir?" inquired Twain airily. "I'm the state game warden," was the unwelcome response. "Who are you?" Twain nearly swallowed his cigar. "Well, to be perfectly truthful, warden," he said hastily, "I'm the biggest damn liar in the whole United States."

19 Twain was tired of receiving photographs from men claiming to be his double. To cope with the heavy correspondence this entailed he composed the following form letter and had his printer run off a few hundred copies: "My dear Sir, I thank you very much for your letter and your photograph. In my opinion you are more like me than any other of my numerous doubles. I may even say that you resemble me more closely than I do myself. In fact, I intend to use your picture to shave by. Yours thankfully, S. Clemens."

20 "In a world without women," Twain was once asked, "what would men become?" "Scarce, sir," replied Twain. "Mighty scarce."

21 In later life Mark Twain suffered periodically from bronchitis and arthritis. Whenever the newspapers reported that he had had another attack, well-wishers would send him prescriptions, remedies, nostrums, and elixirs of life in the hope of bringing about his recovery. He had a standard reply for acknowledging these unsolicited items: "Dear Sir (or Madam), I try every remedy sent to me. I am now on No. 87. Yours is 2,653. I am looking forward to its beneficial results."

22 Twain remembered his childhood as one of constant illness. Besides having to live on medicine until he was seven, he recalled that his family thought of him as a "precarious and tiresome and uncertain child." When his mother was in her eighties, he asked her whether she had worried about him. "Yes, the whole time," she told him. "Afraid that I wouldn't live?" he asked. After a pause, she replied, "No, afraid you would."

23 When Mark Twain was born in November 1835, Halley's comet blazed in the night sky. Twain often referred to this, and came to think of himself and the comet as "unaccountable freaks" which, having come in together, must go out together. He was right: when he died in April 1910, Halley's comet was again in the sky.

———⚭———

TYLER, Anne (1941–), *US novelist.*

1 Tyler was standing in a schoolyard waiting for one of her children when another mother approached her. "Have you found work yet?" she asked. "Or are you still just writing?

———⚭———

TYSON, Mike (1966–), *US boxer, world heavyweight champion.*

1 Tyson was known for his savage, sudden knockouts — and for the pain he inflicted on his opponents. "This is about hurt," Tyson said. "It doesn't matter whether you be a Kennedy, a Rockefeller, a Donald Trump — you come to see someone get hurt." Only a few of his opponents survived on their feet. Many did not make it to the second round. When Pinklon Thomas entered the ring to fight Tyson, Thomas's trainer looked at Tyson and said to the other assistant, "You take the head and I'll take the feet."

U

UCCELLO, Paolo (1397–1475), *Italian painter and craftsman.*

1 Uccello's fascination with perspective kept him up all night drawing elaborate polygons and other figures. When his wife tried to get him to come to bed, he responded, "What a delightful thing this perspective is!"

ULBRICHT, Walther (1893–1973), *East German statesman.*

1 Extolling the glories of the East German state, Ulbricht declared: "The millennium is on the horizon."

"That was a wonderful speech," an aide said to him afterward. "But is the millennium truly on the horizon?"

"Of course," said Ulbricht. "Don't you know the dictionary defines 'horizon' as 'an imaginary line which recedes as you approach it'?"

UNTERMEYER, Louis (1885–1977), *US poet and writer.*

1 Untermeyer once returned his speaker's fee to a small and impoverished group, enjoining them to put the money to good use. A little while later, happening to inquire what good use they had found for the money, he was told that they had put it into "a fund to get better speakers next year."

2 At a New Year's Eve costume party Louis Untermeyer entered fully into the spirit of the thing, donning a funny paper hat and making an uproarious racket upon a horn. A student walked up, looked closely at him, then turned on her heel, snorting contemptuously, "And *he's* Required Reading!"

UNZELMANN, Karl Wilhelm Ferdinand (1753–1832), *German actor and singer.*

1 When Unzelmann was playing at the Berlin theater, the other actors found his ad libs so distracting that the management told him to stop. The following night, as he made his entrance on horseback, the horse committed an indiscretion. Laughter spread through the audience. "Don't you remember," said Unzelmann sternly to his steed, "that we are forbidden to improvise?"

URBAN VIII (1568–1644), *Italian pope (1632-44).*

1 A member of the aristocratic Barberini family of Florence, Urban loved architecture and

was a patron of Bernini. In 1632 he had inscribed on the Pantheon, "Pantheon, the most celebrated edifice in the whole world," after which he stripped the Pantheon of the bronze from its roof beams to use in one of his own projects. Said a Roman wit, "*Quod non fecerunt barbari fecerunt Barberini*" (What was not done by the barbarians was done by the Barberinis).

———⌘———

USTINOV, *Peter (1921–), British actor, director, playwright, and raconteur.*

1 As a father taking his very well brought-up young daughter to the opera for the first time, Ustinov was unwise enough to choose the Baths of Caracalla in Rome. The opera was *Aida:* during one particular scene the whole stage seemed to be covered with animals — camels, elephants, horses, unwanted cats, and so on. At a climactic point, almost all the animals relieved themselves simultaneously. As he stared aghast at this incredible sight, Ustinov felt a light tapping on his shoulder, and his daughter's earnest voice — "Daddy, is it all right if I laugh?"

2 Ustinov once received an irate letter from the headmaster of his son's school. The boy persistently played the fool in lessons, making his classmates laugh, and it was felt that Ustinov should use his influence to control the child. Ustinov reminded the headmaster that the only reason he was able to afford the school's high fees was that he was paid for doing precisely the same thing.

V

VAN BUREN, Martin (1782–1862), *US politician, 8th President of the United States (1837–41)*.

1 Van Buren was so obnoxious to the southern states that he received only nine popular votes there in his 1848 campaign, all from Virginia. His supporters raised a cry of fraud. "Yes, fraud," said a Virginian, "and we are still looking for the son-of-a-bitch who voted nine times."

VANDERBILT, Alice (c. 1845–c. 1930), *wife of Cornelius Vanderbilt II, the financier*.

1 While having luncheon one day at the old Ambassador Hotel with her son Reggie and his new second wife, Gloria, Alice Vanderbilt enquired whether Gloria had received her pearls. When Reggie answered that he had not yet bought any because the only pearls worthy of his bride were far beyond his price, his mother calmly ordered that a pair of scissors be brought to her. When the scissors arrived, she proceeded to cut off about one-third of her own pearls, worth some $70,000, and handed them to her daughter-in-law. "There you are, Gloria," she said. "All Vanderbilt women have pearls."

VANDERBILT, Cornelius (1794–1875), *US businessman, nicknamed "Commodore."*

1 After a prolonged absence from his office the commodore returned to find that Charles Morgan and C. K. Garrison, his associates in the Accessory Transit Company, had taken advantage of the power of attorney he had vested in them and had done considerable damage to his interests. Recovering from his initial rage, Vanderbilt dictated the following letter to them: "Gentlemen: You have undertaken to cheat me. I won't sue you, for the law is too slow. I'll ruin you."

2 One of Vanderbilt's sons-in-law, needing $50,000 to set up a business, approached the commodore for the loan. The old man inquired how much he expected to make from the investment. "About five thousand a year," was the reply. "I can do better than that with fifty thousand dollars," said Vanderbilt. "Tell you what I'll do. I'll pay you five thousand a year hereafter, and you may consider yourself in my employ at that salary."

3 Cornelius Vanderbilt was an admirer of the famous and unconventional Woodhull sisters, one of whose interests was spiritualism. In his seventies he expressed a wish to get financial advice from his dear friend, Jim Fiske. Victoria Woodhull offered to contact

his spirit. In the ensuing séance she managed to materialize the spirit of Vanderbilt's dead wife, Sophia. The old man was not interested. "Business before pleasure," he declared. "Let me speak to Jim."

———— ✂ ————

VANDERBILT, William Henry (1821–85), *US railroad magnate, son of Cornelius Vanderbilt.*

1 William asked if could buy the manure from his father's horse-car stables to enrich his land at New Drop on Staten Island. The elder Vanderbilt agreed, and the price was settled at $4 per load — a generous figure. A few weeks later, the commodore was surprised to learn from his son that only one load had been ferried across to the island; he had seen at least twenty wagonloads put on the scow. The younger Vanderbilt replied, "No, Father, I never let them put more than one load on at a time — one *scow* load, I mean." Cornelius was quick to realize that his son's talent could be put to better use and persuaded him to enter the world of finance.

2 A reporter cornered William Vanderbilt, head of the New York Central Railroad, declaring that the public had a right to know his mind on a particular issue. Vanderbilt pushed past him snapping, "The public be damned. I am working for my stockholders."

3 After William Vanderbilt's death his fortune was estimated at $200,000,000. Shortly before he died he said of this wealth, "I have had no real gratification or enjoyment of any sort more than my neighbor on the next block who is worth only half a million."

———— ✂ ————

VAN DOREN, Mark (1894–1972), *US poet and literary critic.*

1 A bore once blundered in uninvited to a literary gathering hosted by Mark Van Doren, and immediately spread a pall of dullness over the whole party. After his departure the interloper became the topic of discussion. Someone observed that it must be heartbreaking for someone like that to see the face of everyone to whom he spoke freeze with distaste and boredom. "You forget that a person like that has never encountered any other kind of expression," said Van Doren.

2 A group of young men asked Van Doren what they should do with their lives. The professor was quite clear in his answer. "Whatever you want," he told them, "just so long as you don't miss the main thing!" When the young men asked what that was, he said simply, "Your own lives."

———— ✂ ————

VAN SLYKE, Andy (1960–), *US baseball player.*

1 During one bad year — 1989 — Van Slyke was unable to hit a ball. Nothing was hittable, not easy lobs, not straight-on pitches. Van Slyke even tried *not* hitting, to defeat his demon, but to no effect. Asked about his slump, he said, "Right now, I couldn't drive home Miss Daisy."

———— ✂ ————

VARAH, Chad (1911–), *British clergyman.*

1 When Chad Varah decided to start his telephone service for the despairing, he wanted to find a simple, easily remembered number that had something of an emergency feel about it. His center, in the crypt of the church of St. Stephen Walbrook, was in the Mansion House telephone area of London, so its telephone number would have the prefix MAN. Varah decided on MAN 9000. His next step was to find out from the Post Office whether the number was available for his use. Standing in the crypt, he noticed for the first time that there was a dusty old telephone in the corner. To his surprise, he found it was still

working. He rang the Post Office telephone sales department and made his request. The Post Office clerk asked him from what number he was calling. Rubbing the center of the dial with his handkerchief, Varah was astounded to read the number — MAN 9000.

———— ◁▷ ————

VATEL (?1622–71), *French chef.*

1 Louis XIV was to be the guest of honor at a dinner at Chantilly prepared by Vatel. The chef, having ordered a large quantity of fish from the nearest ports, rose early to inspect the quality of the fish as it was delivered. He found to his horror that only two hampers had been brought, not nearly enough for the royal party. "Is that all there is?" he asked. "Yes," said the fishmonger, meaning that no more would be coming from his particular fishing fleet. Vatel misunderstood; he thought that there would be no more fish coming at all. "I cannot endure this disgrace," he cried. Going to his room, he fixed his sword into the door and ran upon the point.

———— ◁▷ ————

VEECK, Bill (1914–86), *US baseball player and executive.*

1 Veeck was asked for his take on the game of baseball; had it declined, or was it still the national pastime? "Baseball is the only game left for people," he said. "To play basketball now, you have to be seven feet six inches. To play football, you have to be the same width."

———— ◁▷ ————

VEGA CARPIO, Lope Félix de (1562–1635), *Spanish playwright and poet.*

1 On his deathbed in 1635, Vega asked how much time he had left. Assured that his death

was at hand, he murmured, "All right, then, I'll say it: Dante makes me sick."

———— ◁▷ ————

VERDI, Giuseppe (1813–1901), *Italian operatic composer.*

1 Though patriotic Italians cheered Verdi at every performance, the enthusiasm was not solely ascribable to their devotion to grand opera. By a fortunate chance the composer's surname was the acronym of a phrase dear to all Italian nationalists after 1861: "Vittorio Emmanuele, Re d'Italia."

2 One summer Verdi rented a large cottage in a fashionable Italian resort. A visitor was somewhat surprised to find the composer apparently occupying only one room, which served as bedroom, sitting room, and study. "Why don't you use the rest of the house?" he asked. Verdi took him into the other rooms; every one of them was packed to the ceiling with barrel organs — ninety-five in all. "They were all churning out operas of mine," Verdi explained, "*Rigoletto — Il Trovatore* — and all the others. It was clearly impossible for me to work under such conditions, so I have hired the organs from their owners. It will cost me about fifteen hundred lire for the summer, but that is not too large a price to pay for peace."

———— ◁▷ ————

VERLAINE, Paul (1844–96), *French poet, a precursor of the Symbolist movement.*

1 Poet and painter F. A. Cazals, a friend of Verlaine, arranged to meet the poet at a café, but was unavoidably late. When he finally did arrive, he was a trifle nervous, for Verlaine drunk was unpredictable. A mutual friend met Cazals at the door and warned him that Verlaine, hopelessly drunk, was "furious

with you." Cazals entered to find Verlaine surrounded by his acolytes, but a little less drunk than he had been described. Cazals took courage: "I hear that you were abusing me just a few minutes ago."

"Who told you that?" cried the furious Verlaine.

"Somebody you don't know," replied Cazals prudently.

"Somebody I don't know!" exclaimed Verlaine. He began to weave his way through the crowded café. "I'm going outside, and the first passerby I don't know, I'll — I'll — *I'll smash his jaw!*"

VERRALL, Arthur Woollgar (1851–1912), *British classical scholar.*

1 A pupil of Verrall's told him that mutual friends of theirs had moved to 58 Oakley Street and remarked that he was afraid that 58 would be a difficult number to remember. "Not at all," Verrall contradicted him. "The Septuagint minus the Apostles."

VESEY, Elizabeth (?1715–91), *British society hostess.*

1 In the late 1740s, Mrs. Vesey invited the naturalist Benjamin Stillingfleet to her salon at Bath. She countered his protest that he had no clothes suitable for such a fashionable gathering by assuring him he need not mind about dress. His arrival at the salon in blue worsted stockings caused some comment among the society leaders. Stillingfleet soon became a *habitué,* however, and so the salon gained the nickname of the "Blue Stocking Society."

VESPASIAN [Titus Flavius Sabinus Vespasianus] (AD 9–79), *Roman emperor (70–79).*

1 Vespasian's avarice was one of the few faults held against him. On one occasion a favorite servant of Vespasian's asked for a stewardship for a man he claimed was his brother. Vespasian told him to wait and asked the candidate for the stewardship to come to him for a private interview. "How much commission would you have paid my servant?" he inquired. The applicant mentioned a sum. "You may pay that directly to me," said the emperor and granted him the desired post. Later the servant alluded to the matter, and Vespasian told him, "You'd better go and find yourself another brother. The one you mistook for yours turned out to be mine."

2 Vespasian imposed taxes on many commodities to restore the Roman state to solvency; he even taxed Rome's public urinals. When Vespasian's son Titus objected to this tax as beneath the dignity of the state, Vespasian took a handful of coins obtained from this source and held them to his son's nose, saying, "See, my boy, if they smell."

3 The emperor once happened to meet, while traveling, the retinue of Demetrius the Cynic, who had been banished from Rome. Despite the visible power of the royal presence, Demetrius made no effort to acknowledge him, and instead barked out a rude comment. "Good dog!" said Vespasian, smiling, and rode on.

VICTOR AMADEUS II (1666–1732), *Duke of Savoy (1675–1732).*

1 In the eighteenth century the little kingdom of Sardinia suffered severely under the burden of taxation imposed by its ambitious rulers. Once Victor Amadeus on a journey stopped to ask a laboring peasant how he

was faring. "Well, master, about as well as things can go in a holy land like ours."

"Holy land?"

"Yes, surely we must be a holy land because here the Passion of the Savior repeats itself — except in reverse."

"I don't understand."

"What's to understand? In those days One died for us all. Here all of us die for one."

———∽———

VICTORIA (1819–1901), *queen of the United Kingdom (1837–1901)*.

1 Victoria was eleven years old when she learned that she stood next in line to the throne. Her governess showed her a list of the kings and queens of England with her own name added after those of George IV and William IV. The child burst into tears as the implications sank in. Then she controlled herself and said solemnly, "I will be good."

2 As a young woman Victoria was a keen theatergoer. At a performance of *King Lear,* however, the tragedy failed to engage her attention, and for most of the early part of the play she chatted to the lord chamberlain, who was in her box. At last she began to pay more attention to the stage. After a while the lord chamberlain ventured to ask her what she thought of the play. "A strange, horrible business," she replied, "but I suppose good enough for Shakespeare's day."

3 Victoria's mother, the Duchess of Kent, totally dominated her daughter's upbringing and clearly had ambitions to be the power behind the throne once Victoria became queen. The princess slept in her mother's room and was never allowed to talk to anyone except in the presence of her German governess or the duchess. The very day that William IV died and Victoria ascended the throne, the Duchess of Kent came to Victoria after the state dignitaries had departed and

inquired if there was anything she could do for her. "I wish to be left alone," replied Victoria, and the same day she gave orders for her bed to be moved from the duchess's room.

4 Stafford House, the London house of the Duke and Duchess of Sutherland, was the center of high society in the early years of Queen Victoria's reign. The duchess was a close friend of the queen. The magnificence of Stafford House led Victoria to remark to her hostess on one of her frequent visits, "I have come from my house to your palace."

5 Before she made the announcement to her councilors of her decision to marry Prince Albert, Queen Victoria was seen to be trembling. Someone asked her if she was nervous. "Yes, but I have just done a far more nervous thing," replied the queen. "I proposed to Prince Albert."

6 When Victoria was about to marry Prince Albert, she wished to have the title "King Consort" bestowed upon him by act of Parliament. Lord Melbourne, knowing the depth of opposition to such a move on behalf of an unknown German princeling, strongly advised against it. "For God's sake, ma'am, let's have no more of that. If you get the English people into the way of making kings, you'll get them into the way of *un*making them."

7 Victoria and Albert had a quarrel shortly after their marriage. Albert stalked out of the room and locked himself in his private apartments. Victoria hammered furiously upon the door. "Who's there?" called Albert. "The queen of England, and she demands to be admitted." There was no response and the door remained locked. Victoria hammered at the door again. "Who's there?" The reply was still "The queen of England," and still the door remained shut. More fruitless and furious knocking was followed by a pause. Then

there was a gentle tap. "Who's there?" The queen replied, "Your wife, Albert." The prince at once opened the door.

8 In the early years of their marriage, Victoria and Albert visited Florence several times, greatly impressed by the city's architectural treasures. Of these, the Brunelleschi dome surmounting the cathedral was their personal favorite. Victoria returned to Florence some years after Albert's death to find that the dome had been magnificently restored. She ordered the carriage to stop in the piazza outside the cathedral and rolled down the window. Opening up the locket that hung around her neck, she turned the miniature of her beloved husband to face the building, so that he could share with her the splendor of the newly restored dome. Then, after a few moments' silent contemplation, she closed the locket and drove away.

9 It was well known that the queen disapproved of tobacco and had banned smoking in the royal residences. Her sons, however, smoked a great deal, and, according to a popular story, had appropriated a room in Windsor to use as a smoking room. Panic ensued when they learned that their mother intended to make an inspection of every room in the castle, until the Prince of Wales thought up a solution. The letters WC were without delay put up over the door.

10 The queen and her daughter, the Empress Frederick of Prussia, who had distinctly different literary tastes, were arguing about the merits of the popular romantic novelist Marie Corelli. The queen claimed that Marie Corelli would rank as one of the greatest writers of the time; the Empress Frederick thought her writings were trash. The empress summoned a gentleman-in-waiting, who had not heard the beginning of the discussion, and asked his opinion of Marie Corelli. He replied that he thought the secret of her pop-

ularity was that her writings appealed to the semi-educated. The subject was dropped very quickly.

11 On a crossing to Ireland the ship in which Queen Victoria was traveling encountered rough weather. A gigantic wave caused such a violent lurch that the queen was almost knocked off her feet. Recovering her balance she said to an attendant, "Go up to the bridge, give the admiral my compliments, and tell him he's not to let that happen again."

12 "In order to hear how HMS *Eurydice,* a frigate sunk off Portsmouth, had been salvaged, Queen Victoria invited Admiral Foley to lunch. Having exhausted this melancholy subject, Queen Victoria inquired after her close friend, the Admiral's sister. Hard of hearing, Admiral Foley replied in his stentorian voice, 'Well, Ma'am, I am going to have her turned over, take a good look at her bottom and have it well scraped.' The queen put down her knife and fork, hid her face in her handkerchief, and laughed until the tears ran down her cheeks."

13 On visits to the London home of Baroness Burdett-Coutts, Victoria could often be found sitting beside the window on the top floor. From there she would watch, with a childlike fascination, the traffic stream pass below her in Piccadilly. She once explained to the baroness: "Yours is the only place where I can go to see the traffic without stopping it."

14 During a visit by some of her grandchildren, the queen heard them roaring with laughter and proceeded to investigate. It appeared that one of them had made a joke of a somewhat "advanced" nature, and they were reluctant to repeat it. Eventually the queen prevailed upon one of the boys to comply with her royal command, and, hearing the joke, realized that it was not to her taste. She

drew herself up and, with the dignified rebuke, "We are not amused!" left the room.

15 Victoria asked after the health of one of her ladies-in-waiting, who had been quite ill. Told that the lady in question was recovering nicely, and that her ailment had been centered in her legs, the famously prudish Victoria coughed and replied that in her day, "Young ladies did not used to have legs."

16 After the defeat of a British army unit in South Africa, Victoria wished to send them a telegraph. When told by her private secretary that the custom was to send a message only in the event of a victory, Victoria said, "And since when have I not been proud of my troops whether in success or defeat? Clear the line."

17 On her deathbed the queen noted that she would be soon reunited with her beloved, and long-dead, husband Albert. "Ah yes," said a lady-in-waiting, "you'll soon meet Albert in Abraham's bosom." "I will *not* meet Abraham," snapped Victoria.

18 On the anniversary of Queen Victoria's death, her children would visit the mausoleum at Frogmore. One year, as they knelt piously in prayer, a dove entered the mausoleum and flew about. "It is dear Mama's spirit," they murmured. "No, I am sure it's not," contradicted Princess Louise. "It must be dear Mama's spirit," they persisted. "No, it isn't," said Princess Louise. "Dear Mama's spirit would never have ruined Beatrice's hat."

———— ⌘ ————

VIDAL, Gore (1925–), *US writer.*

1 The English novelist Anthony Powell, attending an international writers' conference in Sofia, Bulgaria, found himself alongside Vidal, inspecting some pictures taken of the session. Several of these showed Vidal beside an Indian delegate. "I always sit next to a man in a turban," explained Vidal. "You get photographed more."

———— ⌘ ————

VILLA, Pancho (?1877–1923), *Mexican revolutionary.*

1 As Pancho Villa lay dying, his last words were, "Don't let it end like this. Tell them I said something."

———— ⌘ ————

VILLIERS de L'Isle-Adam, Auguste, Comte de (1839–89), *French writer of the Symbolist school.*

1 "Villiers de L'Isle-Adam, who was leaving the following day for London to be married, an expectation which was never realized, came to see Mallarmé and . . . asked to be taught English at once. 'Willingly,' replied Mallarmé, 'but I cannot begin the lessons for two days.' 'Oh,' replied Villiers, 'we can simplify matters. As it is a question of a coming marriage, you might teach me only the future tenses of the verbs.'"

———— ⌘ ————

VIRCHOW, Rudolf (1821–1902), *German pathologist and politician.*

1 Bismarck, enraged at Virchow's constant criticisms, had his seconds call upon the scientist to challenge him to a duel. "As the challenged party, I have the choice of weapons," said Virchow, "and I choose these." He held aloft two large and apparently identical sausages. "One of these," he went on, "is infected with deadly germs; the other is perfectly sound. Let His Excellency decide which one he wishes to eat, and I will eat the other." Almost immediately the mes-

sage came back that the chancellor had decided to laugh off the duel.

2 The French ethnologist Armand de Quatrefages was incensed by the damage done to Paris's natural history museum by German shells during the Franco-Prussian War of 1870. He declared that the Prussians were by race not Nordic or Teutonic but descendants of the barbarian hordes of Huns who ravished eastern Europe during the Middle Ages. Virchow was outraged by this racial slur. As a member of the Prussian Parliament, he introduced a bill by which the physical characteristics of every schoolchild in Prussia — six million in number — could be examined and assessed. The survey was carried out, head measurements, bones, hair, and teeth were all analyzed, and Virchow proved scientifically that the Prussians were in origin Franks — cousins, in fact, of the French themselves. But the epithet "Hun" was applied derogatorily to the Germans thereafter, especially by Germany's enemies in the two world wars.

VOLTAIRE [François-Marie Arouet] (1694–1778), *French philosopher, writer, and wit.*

1 In 1717 Voltaire, in consequence of a satire directed against the regent, Philippe d'Orléans, was imprisoned in the Bastille for eleven months. Liberated, Voltaire, a highly adaptable man, thanked the regent for the gracious pardon. The latter, aware of Voltaire's power, was equally anxious to effect a reconciliation and made all the appropriate apologies. Voltaire replied: "Your Highness, I am most grateful for your generosity with respect to my board but in the future you need not worry yourself about my lodging."

2 Voltaire and a select group of friends were running through Voltaire's latest play before its production. During the reading of a lengthy speech, Montesquieu fell asleep. "Wake him up," said Voltaire. "He seems to imagine that he's in the audience."

3 In 1725 Voltaire became involved in a stupid quarrel with the Chevalier de Rohan-Chabot, a short-tempered aristocrat, possibly over Voltaire's mistress, the famous actress Adrienne Lecouvreur. There was an exchange of insults at the Opéra, in which the chevalier came out badly and left the theater threatening revenge. A few days later Voltaire was dining with a patron when he was told that someone wished to speak to him. In the street a number of ruffians hired by the chevalier fell on him and beat him up. The chevalier, who watched the whole episode from his own coach, cried out, "Be careful not to hit him on the head. Something might come out of that one day."

4 Voltaire was in exile in London at a time when popular feelings ran high against the French. One day on the street he was surrounded by an angry mob shouting, "Hang him. Hang the Frenchman!" Turning to face the mob, Voltaire said, "Men of England! You wish to kill because I am a Frenchman. Am I not punished enough in not being born an Englishman?" This tactful speech so pleased the crowd that they cheered and escorted him safely back to his lodgings.

5 Rousseau sent a copy of his "Ode to Posterity" hot off the press to Voltaire for his opinion. Voltaire read it through and commented, "I do not think this poem will reach its destination."

6 A notoriously dissolute group of Parisians invited Voltaire to participate in an orgy. He accepted, giving such a satisfactory account of himself that the very next night he was asked to come again. "Ah, no, my friends," said Voltaire with a slight smile. "Once: a philosopher; twice: a pervert!"

7 Though it enjoyed an unprecedented success, Voltaire's *Oedipe* drew the criticism of the aged Fontenelle, who told the author that he considered some of the verses "too strong and full of fire."

"To correct myself I shall read your *Pastorales,*" Voltaire replied.

8 After a long absence a royal favorite returned to the court of Frederick the Great. Many rumors circulated as to the reason for her absence. She complained to Voltaire, "The things they say about me are incredible! They even say I retired to the country in order to give birth to twins!" Voltaire replied, "Don't let that disturb you. I believe only half of what I hear at the court."

9 At the funeral of a certain nobleman, Voltaire declared, "He was a great patriot, a humanitarian, a loyal friend — provided, of course, that he really is dead."

10 In 1759 Casanova, the author of the famous *Mémoires,* set out from Paris on a two-year journey around Europe, in the course of which he visited Voltaire in Switzerland. Voltaire had been reading some of the works of the Swiss physiologist and polymath Albrecht von Haller. He praised them to his guest. "That praise is ill returned," said Casanova, "for he has been saying that your work is nonsense." Voltaire smiled. "Perhaps we are both mistaken," he said.

11 Voltaire drank prodigious quantities of coffee throughout his life. Some killjoy warned him that he should give up the beverage because it was a slow poison. "I think it must be slow," the elderly philosopher replied, "for I have been drinking it for sixty-five years and I am not dead yet."

12 Visitors to Voltaire's model village at Ferney near Geneva remarked on the church that the old skeptic had built there for the villagers.

Over the door was the dedication: "DEO EREXIT VOLTAIRE." Voltaire liked to observe that it was the only church in Europe that was erected to God.

13 At Ferney, Voltaire once had as guests a certain Huber and also the noted mathematician Jean d'Alembert. It was proposed that each ad-lib a story involving thieves. Huber's invention was received with acclamation, as was d'Alembert's. It was now Voltaire's turn. "Gentlemen," he said, "there was once a tax collector . . . good Lord, I've forgotten the rest of the story."

14 Voltaire was approached by a man who thanked him for having destroyed credibility in religion, and asked for his advice since he wanted to found a new religion without the flaws that Voltaire had found so easily in Christianity. "Simple enough," said Voltaire. "Go get yourself crucified and rise from the dead."

15 In the last year of his life the famous invalid, domiciled at the Marquis de Villette's mansion, was visited by hordes of admirers, anxious to pay their last respects. Among them were two mediocre dramatists, Antoine Lemierre and Dormont de Belloy. Voltaire remarked to them, "Gentlemen, as I take farewell of life, I am consoled by the knowledge that I leave behind me Lemierre and de Belloy." After Voltaire's death Lemierre was fond of recalling these words, never failing to add, "And poor de Belloy never suspected that Voltaire was making fun of him."

16 When Voltaire lay on his deathbed a priest arrived to shrive him. The philosopher asked: "Who sent you here, Monsieur l'Abbé?"

"God himself, Monsieur Voltaire."

"Ah, my dear sir, and where are your credentials?"

W

WADDELL, Rube (1876–1914), *US baseball player, pitcher for the Philadelphia Athletics.*

1 "He wielded a pretty hefty bat for a pitcher, and was allowed to swing for himself one day in the eighth inning with the score 2-1 against the Athletics, two out, and tying run on second. The catcher of the opposing nine saw a chance to pick off the runner at second and heaved the ball in that general direction. It ended in center field, and the runner hot-footed for the plate. He'd have made it, too, with plenty to spare, but as the throw came into the plate, Waddell, to the amazement of everybody in the park, swung at the ball, bashed it out over the right field fence, and was promptly declared out for interference. 'Why did you do it?' wailed Manager Connie Mack. 'They'd been feeding me curves all afternoon,' explained the Rube sheepishly, 'and this was the first straight ball I'd looked at!'"

WALKER, James John (1881–1946), *US politician, mayor of New York (1926–32).*

1 Henry ("Light-Horse Harry") Lee's famous toast to George Washington, "To the memory of the man, first in war, first in peace, and first in the hearts of his countrymen," was repeated at a Washington's Birthday celebration banquet by Jimmy Walker. After a brief pause the mayor went on, "No one's ever understood how he happened to marry a widow."

WALLER, Edmund (1606–87), *British lyric poet.*

1 One of Waller's most successful poems with a political theme is his panegyric on Oliver Cromwell. His later laudatory verses on Charles II were generally considered inferior in poetic merit. The king having commented upon this difference, Waller replied, "Poets, sire, succeed better in fiction than in truth."

WALN, Nicholas (1742–1813), *US lawyer.*

1 A Quaker meeting having detected some fault in Waln, a deputation of elders was sent to remonstrate with him. They knocked and knocked at his front door but without result. At last an upstairs window was thrown open and Waln's head poked out. "My Friends," he called down, "you need not come in; the Master has been here before you."

WALPOLE, Horace, 4th Earl of Orford (1717–97), *British writer.*

1 Walpole had a stormy interview with an elderly uncle concerning a proposed marriage in the family. Departing unplacated, he wrote his relative a furious letter ending: "I am, sir, for the last time in my life, Your Humble Servant Horace Walpole."

WALPOLE, Sir Robert, 1st Earl of Orford (1676–1745), *British statesman.*

1 Walpole's father encouraged him to drink deep. For every time he filled his own glass he filled his son's twice. "Come, Robert," said the senior Walpole, "you shall drink twice while I drink once, for I cannot permit the son in his sober senses to witness the intoxication of his father."

2 After his arduous years in office, Walpole looked forward to retirement in his splendid mansion, Houghton Castle. Entering the library, he took down a book, perused it for a few minutes, and then returned it to the shelf. He took down another, but held that only half as long before replacing it and taking a third. This he immediately put back, and, bursting into tears, exclaimed, "I have led a life of business so long that I have lost my taste for reading, and now — what shall I do?"

WALTER, Bruno (1876–1962), *German conductor.*

1 When Bruno Walter first conducted the New York Philharmonic, Alfred Wallenstein was the first cellist. Walter noticed that Wallenstein ostentatiously ignored him during both rehearsals and concerts. Rather than make a scene in public, Walter asked Wallenstein to come and speak to him privately. "What is your ambition, Mr. Wallenstein?" Walter inquired mildly. "Someday I'd like to be a conductor," replied the cellist. "Well, when you are, I hope you never have Wallenstein in front of you," said Walter.

WALTON, Sir William [Turner] (1902–83), *British composer.*

1 At the rehearsals for the first performance of *Façade*, the players were at first irritated, then interested, and finally delighted by the strange and difficult new sounds that the young Walton, as composer-conductor, asked them to make. During one of the pauses in the rehearsal the clarinetist looked up from his score and asked, "Excuse me, Mr. Walton, has a clarinet player ever done you an injury?"

2 Until the success of his film score for Laurence Olivier's *Henry V* in 1942 Walton was poor, and as he himself admitted in later life, lived by scrounging off the Sitwell family. Lady Aberconway, a close friend of the Sitwells and a well-known London hostess of the 1930s, recalled that Walton was known to them by the nickname "Lincrusta." It was the tradename for a particular kind of embossed wallpaper that was extremely difficult to detach.

WARBURTON, William (1698–1779), *British clergyman and literary scholar; bishop of Gloucester (1759–79).*

1 During a debate in the House of Lords upon the Test Laws, under which those who wished to stand for public office were obliged to profess the Anglican faith, the witty and profligate Earl of Sandwich complained, "I have heard frequent use of the words 'orthodoxy' and 'heterodoxy' but I confess myself at a loss to know precisely what they mean." Bishop Warburton enlight-

ened him in a whisper, "Orthodoxy is my doxy; heterodoxy is another man's doxy."

WARD, Artemus [Charles Farrar Browne] (1834–67), *US humorist.*

1 After a successful and lucrative lecture tour of the eastern states, Ward headed west in October 1863. The manager of the San Francisco opera house sent him a telegram asking what he would take for forty nights in California. Ward wired back: "Brandy and water. A. Ward."

2 Artemus Ward spent Christmas Eve 1863 with Mark Twain and some other cronies at Barnum's Restaurant in Virginia City. A great deal of liquor was consumed, and toward the end of the evening Ward proposed "a standing toast." He made several ineffectual attempts to get to his feet, while his companions remained slumped at the table. "Well," he said, abandoning his efforts, "*consider* it standing."

WARNER, Jack (1892–1978), *US movie producer, co-founder of Warner Brothers.*

1 The actor Pat O'Brien recalls that Jack Warner bought Sinclair Lewis's worldwide bestseller *Main Street* and changed the title to *I Married a Doctor* on the grounds that nobody "would want to see a picture about a street." The movie died.

2 In 1946, when British Field Marshal Bernard Montgomery visited California, Mr. and Mrs. Samuel Goldwyn gave a dinner for him. Goldwyn began: "It gives me great pleasure to welcome to Hollywood a very distinguished soldier. Ladies and gentlemen, I propose a toast to Marshall Field Montgomery." The silence was broken by Jack Warner's voice saying, "Montgomery Ward, you mean."

3 Warner was in the habit of taking an afternoon nap in his office at Warner Brothers, and it was an unwritten rule of the studios that he should not be disturbed. On one occasion, however, Bette Davis burst into the office while Warner was asleep and began ranting about a script that did not meet with her approval. Without opening his eyes, Warner reached for the phone and called his secretary. "Come in and wake me up," he said. "I'm having a nightmare." Miss Davis could not help laughing, and the crisis over the script was resolved in a few minutes.

WASHINGTON, George (1732–99), *US general and statesman, 1st President of the United States (1789–97).*

1 Parson Weems's *Life of Washington* (1800) contains many apocryphal stories about his hero and ranks more as hagiography than factual biography. His best-known fabrication (introduced into the 1806 edition) is the story of George Washington and the cherry tree. According to Weems, when he was about six, George Washington was given a hatchet. He went around his father's farm, testing it on all manner of things, including a fine young cherry tree. His father, discovering the damage, summoned the boy and said sternly, "Do you know who killed this beautiful little cherry tree?" The child was silent for a moment but then cried out, "I cannot tell a lie; you know I cannot tell a lie. I cut it with my hatchet." His father at once forgot his anger in his delight at the child's truthfulness.

2 After a skirmish in the course of the Seven Years' War, Washington was reported to have said, "I heard the bullets whistle, and believe me, there is something charming in the sound." When King George II of England heard of this remark, he said, "He would not say so had he been used to hear many."

3 During the American Revolution an officer in civilian clothes rode past a group of soldiers busy repairing a small redoubt. Their commander was shouting instructions but making no attempt to help them. Asked why, he retorted with great dignity, "Sir, I am a corporal!" The stranger apologized, dismounted, and proceeded to help the exhausted soldiers himself. When the job was completed he turned to the corporal and said, "Mr. Corporal, next time you have a job like this and not enough men to do it, go to your commander in chief, and I will come and help you again." Too late, the corporal recognized General Washington.

4 During the bitterly cold winter at Valley Forge, Washington constantly went the rounds of his men, encouraging and comforting them. One day he came across Private John Brantley drinking some stolen wine with his companions. Already a little drunk, Brantley cheerily invited his commander to "drink some wine with a soldier." Replied Washington, "My boy, you have no time for drinking wine." And he turned away. "Damn your proud soul," exclaimed Brantley. "You're above drinking with soldiers." Washington turned back. "Come, I will drink with you," he said and took a pull at the jug and handed it back. "Give it to your servants," said Brantley, gesturing toward Washington's aides. The jug was duly passed around. "Now," said Brantley, when he once more had his jug, "I'll be damned if I don't spend the last drop of my heart's blood for you."

5 Early in the Revolutionary War, Washington sent one of his officers to requisition horses from the local landowners. Calling at an old country mansion, the officer was received by the elderly mistress of the house. "Madam, I have come to claim your horses in the name of the government," he began. "On whose orders?" demanded the woman sternly. "On the orders of General George Washington, commander in chief of the American army," replied the officer. The old lady smiled. "You go back and tell General George Washington that his mother says he cannot have her horses," she said.

6 As Washington was sitting at dinner one evening, the heat from the fire behind him became so intense that he said he had better move farther from the hearth. Someone in the company said jokingly that it was only right and proper for a general to be able to stand fire. "But it doesn't look good if he receives it from behind," replied Washington.

7 During the Constitutional Convention someone suggested that the size of the army be restricted to five thousand men at any one time. Washington saw the impracticality of this, but as chairman he was prevented from making a counterproposal. Instead he whispered to a delegate sitting near him that they ought to amend the proposal to provide that "no foreign army should invade the United States at any time with more than three thousand troops."

8 Walking in Philadelphia with an American acquaintance, an English visitor expressed a wish to see President Washington. A few moments later, the President happened to pass the two men on the opposite side of the street. Pointing at the solitary figure, the American said, "There he goes." The Englishman was surprised. "Is that President Washington?" he exclaimed. "Where's his guard?" The American struck his breast proudly. "Here," he declared.

9 Gilbert Stuart, who painted a famous portrait of Washington in 1795, remarked afterward to General Henry ("Light-Horse Harry") Lee on the strong passions that he could perceive beneath the President's dignified exterior. A few days later General Lee mentioned to the Washingtons that he had

seen the portrait, adding, "Stuart says you have a tremendous temper." Mrs. Washington's color rose and she said sharply, "Mr. Stuart takes a great deal on himself to make such a remark." General Lee checked her: "But he added that the President has wonderful control." Washington said, almost smiling, "He's right."

10 In 1797 the French revolutionist and freethinker Constantin Volney visited the United States and asked Washington for a letter of recommendation. Not wishing to offend the Frenchman, but also anxious to avoid controversy over the man's opinions, Washington simply wrote: "C. Volney needs no recommendation from Geo. Washington."

WATERTON, Charles (1782–1865), *British eccentric and naturalist.*

1 While in the United States, as Edith Sitwell describes it, Waterton sprained his ankle, and "being extremely annoyed by inquiries of other less-adventurous gentlemen, staying in the hotel, as to the progress of his 'gout,' he remembered that in the past, when his ankle had been badly sprained, a doctor had ordered him to hold it under the pump two or three times a day. It struck him therefore that it might be a kind of super-cure if he held his ankle under the Niagara Falls." Which he did.

WATSON, Richard (1737–1816), *British clergyman, bishop of Llandaff (1782–1816).*

1 The landlord of the well-known Cock Inn at Windermere in northwest England wished to compliment Dr. Watson, who had a house nearby. He changed the name of the inn to "The Bishop" and hung out a sign bearing a portrait of the eminent cleric. A rival landlord of a less popular establishment across the street thereupon changed his inn sign to "The Cock," and thus attracted a lot of the customers of the former Cock Inn. The landlord of the latter decided that he must make the identity of his inn clear to visitors to the town. When Dr. Watson next passed through Windermere, he was not at all flattered to see painted underneath his portrait on the inn sign the words: "This is the old Cock."

WATT, James (1736–1819), *British engineer.*

1 According to tradition, the solution to the problem of preventing the loss of energy in the Newcomen engine occurred to Watt as he observed a kettle boiling on the fire at his home. His aunt came in and rebuked him for idly fiddling about with the kettle, holding a spoon over the spout, pressing it down, and so on. She suggested that he go out and do something useful.

WAUGH, Evelyn (1903–66), *British novelist.*

1 Evelyn Waugh and Harold Acton toured southern Italy together. It turned out to be one of those vacations when everything conspires to go wrong. When they got to Naples, the British consul came to pay them a courtesy call. They were both feeling rather out of sorts, and the conversation flagged. In a desperate attempt to enliven it, the consul said to Waugh, "I have a map of Mount Ararat, which I think might interest you."

"Why should it?" said Waugh. "Has the Ark been found?"

2 In 1935, Waugh was sent to cover the Italian invasion of Ethiopia. While he was there, his editor heard a rumor that an English nurse had been killed in an Italian air raid and cabled: "Send two hundred words upblown nurse." Waugh made exhaustive inquiries,

but was unable to substantiate the story. He finally cabled back: "Nurse unupblown."

3 Waugh's commanding officer was impressed by his courage during the battle of Crete in 1941. On the return journey, the writer was asked for his impression of the battle, his first experience of military actions. "Like German opera," he replied, "too long and too loud."

4 (Joseph Epstein tells this story about Evelyn Waugh:)

"Once, when he had behaved with particular rudeness to a young French intellectual at a dinner party in Paris at the home of Nancy Mitford, Miss Mitford, angry at his social brutality, asked him how he could behave so meanly and yet consider himself a believing and practicing Catholic. 'You have no idea,' Waugh returned, 'how much nastier I would be if I was not a Catholic. Without supernatural aid I would hardly be a human being.'"

5 As a captain in the British Army during World War II, he once came out of a foxhole during a bombardment by the German air force. Looking up at the sky, he said, "Like all things German, this is vastly overdone."

6 Waugh once declined to be interviewed by the critic Edmund Wilson. "I don't think that Americans have much to say that is much of interest, do you?"

———— ↔ ————

WAVELL, Archibald Percival, 1st Earl (1883–1950), *British field marshal; viceroy of India (1943–47).*

1 (One of the greatest disappointments of Wavell's life came at the end of June 1941, when he was replaced by Claude Auchinleck as commander in the Middle Eastern battle zone.)

"A signal from the prime minister [Churchill] telling him that Auchinleck and

he were to change places had arrived in the small hours of the morning, and been taken to General Arthur Smith, who had at once dressed and gone round to Wavell's house on Gezira. He found him shaving, with his face covered with lather and his razor poised. He read out the signal. Wavell showed no emotion. He merely said: 'The prime minister's quite right. This job wants a new eye and a new hand'; and went on shaving."

———— ↔ ————

WAYNE, John [Marion Michael Morrison] (1907–79), *US movie actor.*

1 While playing a cameo role in the biblical epic *The Greatest Story Ever Told,* Wayne had a line he spoke too laconically: "Truly, this was the Son of God." The director, George Stevens, reminded him he was talking about Jesus and said, "You've got to deliver the line with a little more awe." On his next take Wayne said, "Aw, truly this was the Son of God."

2 Wayne went to Harvard College to receive the famous, and famously satirical, Hasty Pudding Award. At the ensuing press conference he was asked, "Do you look at yourself as an American legend?" Replied Wayne, "Well, not being a Harvard man, I don't look at myself any more than necessary."

———— ↔ ————

WEAVER, Earl (1930–), *US baseball player and executive.*

1 Outfielder and born-again Christian Pat Kelly once called out to Weaver, "You got to walk with the Lord, Skip!" "Hell," replied Weaver, "I'd rather you walk with the bases loaded."

2 After a series of bad pitches Jim Palmer headed to the dugout followed by Weaver, who was jumping up and down, visibly an-

gry and yelling. Finally Palmer turned around and faced Weaver, saying, "Why Earl, I've never seen you so tall."

WEBB, Sidney [James], Baron Passfield (1859–1947), *British socialist politician and economist.*

1 Asked to account for the harmonious front the Webbs presented on the important issues of the time, Beatrice explained that they had agreed early in their married life always to vote alike on great issues. "Sidney was to decide which way we voted. I was to decide which were the great issues."

WEBSTER, Daniel (1782–1852), *US lawyer and statesman.*

1 Temporarily absent from home, Captain Webster left Daniel and his brother Ezekiel with specific instructions as to the work they were to do that day. On his return he found the task still unperformed, and questioned his sons severely about their idleness. "What have you been doing, Ezekiel?" he asked.

"Nothing, sir."

"Well, Daniel, what have you been doing?"

"Helping Zeke, sir."

2 As a boy, Daniel Webster worked in his father's fields. One day, told to do the mowing, he made a thoroughly bad job of it; sometimes his scythe struck the ground and sometimes it swung too high and missed the grass entirely. He complained to his father that the scythe was not hung right. Various attempts were made to hang it better, but with no success. At last his father told him that he might hang it to suit himself, whereupon he hung it on a tree and said, "There, that's just right."

3 As a lad at school Webster committed some peccadillo for which he was called up to the teacher's desk to have the palm of his right hand caned. Aware that his hands were very dirty, he made an effort to rub off some of the dirt as he walked up to the desk. Nevertheless, the hand he held out was exceedingly grimy. The teacher looked at it sternly. "Daniel, if you can find another hand as dirty as that in this schoolroom, I'll let you off." Out from behind the boy's back came the left hand. "Here it is, sir," said young Webster. The teacher had to abide by his offer.

4 Webster was not chosen to be valedictorian of his Dartmouth class, an honor he felt he deserved. When he received his diploma, he led a group of friends behind the college, where he ripped up the document, saying, "My industry can make me a great man, but this miserable parchment cannot!"

5 A friend advised young Webster not to attempt to enter the legal profession, which was already overcrowded and posed formidable obstacles to a man without either money or family connections to help him. "There's always room at the top," said Webster calmly.

6 Daniel Webster met Grace Fletcher, who was to become his first wife, when he was a young lawyer at Portsmouth. He was allowed to call on her, and on one of his visits was making himself useful by holding skeins of silk thread for her. Suddenly he stopped and said, "Grace, we have been engaged in untying knots; let us see if we can tie a knot which will not untie for a lifetime." Then Webster took a piece of tape and began to tie a complicated knot in it, which he gave to her to complete — this they regarded as the ceremony of their engagement.

7 At the beginning of his legal career, Daniel Webster was engaged as associate counsel by

a lawyer acting for a gentleman from Grafton County. The lawyer made known his choice to the client, who asked if this was Daniel Webster, son of old Ebenezer of Salisbury. Receiving an affirmative reply, he cried, "What! That little black stable-boy who once brought me some horses! Then I think we might as well give up the case." It was too late to engage another associate counsel, and the case went ahead. The dejected client sat in court, not listening to the proceedings. Then he found that his attention was gradually arrested by the associate counsel's voice. He was held spellbound until the end of the speech. The lawyer turned to his client and asked, "What do you think of him now?"

"Think! Why, I think he is an angel sent down from Heaven to save me from ruin, and my wife and children from misery!"

8 (Webster had an immensely impressive presence, especially in court, where his magnificent voice and his dark, beetle-browed eyes were of great advantage. Van Wyck Brooks recounts the story of how Daniel Webster looked a witness out of court.)

"He had set his great eyes on the man and searched him through and through; then, as the cause went on, and this fellow's perjury was not yet called for, Webster looked round again to see if he was ready for the inquisition. The witness felt for his hat and edged toward the door. A third time Webster looked on him, and the witness could sit no longer. He seized his chance and fled from the court and was nowhere to be found."

9 A Nantucket gentleman stopped a friend in the street and told him, "I am in trouble and wish your advice."

"What's the matter?"

"Oh, I'm in a lawsuit, and Webster is against me. What shall I do?"

"My advice is that your only chance of escape is to send to Smyrna and import a young earthquake."

10 The lawyer Jeremiah Mason was Webster's colleague and friend in Portsmouth. The two were often opposed in important cases, and performed impressively against each other in court. One day when a new case was called, the clerk of the court asked who was counsel on each side. "Which side are you on in this case?" Mason asked Webster. "I don't know," said Webster. "Take your choice."

11 Daniel Webster attended a particularly illustrious dinner party. After the ladies had retired, the host produced a bottle of Madeira for the gentlemen. The wine, he said, had been bottled by his grandfather more than seventy years before. One of the guests did some calculations on the back of a letter and remarked that if the wine was worth 25 cents when bottled, its present value at current interest would reach $100. At that moment a servant announced that the carriage had arrived to take Mr. Webster to a ball given in his honor. Some of the guests escorted Webster to his carriage. As one of them was folding up the carriage step after he had climbed in, he found Webster's foot in the way, and asked whether he wished to alight. "Yes," said Webster quickly, "I want to go back and help our mathematical friend stop the interest on that damned expensive bottle of wine."

WEBSTER, Noah (1758–1843), *US lexicographer. His* American Dictionary of the English Language *(1828) was the forerunner of a great procession of American dictionaries bearing the name Webster in their titles.*

1 Going unexpectedly into the parlor of their house one day, Mrs. Webster discovered her husband embracing their maid. "Noah, I am surprised!" she exclaimed. Webster released the maid and reassumed his professional dignity. "No, my dear," he corrected his wife,

"it is *I* who am surprised; you are merely astonished."

2 When Webster arrived in Philadelphia on a visit, he was met by Benjamin Rush, who greeted him by saying, "My dear friend, I congratulate you on your arrival in Philadelphia." "Sir," replied Webster, "you may congratulate Philadelphia on the occasion."

———— ✂ ————

WEIZMANN, Chaim (1874–1952), *Jewish statesman; first president of Israel (1949–52)*.

1 As a chemist at Manchester University, Weizmann came into the constituency of the Conservative politician Arthur Balfour. There was a proposal at that time to establish a Jewish "homeland" in Uganda, a suggestion hotly countered by the Zionists. A mediator arranged for Weizmann to meet Balfour to put him straight on the unacceptability of Uganda and to explain the emotional and spiritual attraction of Palestine. Trying to get this idea across to Balfour, Weizmann said, "Just suppose, Mr. Balfour, I were to offer you Paris instead of London; would you accept it?" Balfour, off guard, said somewhat crassly, "But, Dr. Weizmann, we already *have* London." Replied Weizmann: "But we had Jerusalem when London was a marsh."

———— ✂ ————

WELLES, Orson (1915–85), *US film actor and director*.

1 When Welles was given a tour of the Hollywood studio where he would be able to make his first film, *Citizen Kane,* he clapped his hands in delight, saying, "It's the biggest train set a boy ever had."

2 One Saturday during the production of his film *The Lady from Shanghai,* Welles decided that a certain set needed repainting for the following Monday's filming. Having been told by production manager Jack Fier that this was quite impossible, Welles gathered together a group of friends. They broke into the paint department late on Saturday evening, repainted the set themselves, and left a huge sign over the entrance to the studio: "THE ONLY THING WE HAVE TO FEAR IS FIER HIMSELF." When the official set painters arrived for work on Monday, they immediately called a strike. Fier was obliged to pay a hefty sum to each member of the crew as compensation for the work done by nonunion labor. He deducted the money from Welles's fee and had a new banner painted "ALL'S WELL THAT ENDS WELLES." Whereupon the two men, bitter enemies up to that point, called a truce and ultimately became great friends.

3 Film director Vincent Korda and his son Michael once had to chase Orson Welles, who was running from contract obligations, across Europe. Landing in Venice, Naples, Capri, and Nice, they finally caught up with him in Cagnes-sur-Mer and hoisted him off to a private airplane. Michael and Welles shared the back seats with a giant basket of fruit, which Vincent had carefully selected in Nice, wedged between them. Michael eventually fell asleep. When he awoke, he eyed the basket — and realized that Welles had systematically taken a single bite out of each piece of fruit. Having thus effectively destroyed Vincent's fruit, Welles now slept soundly, his immaculate appearance marred only by a few spots of juice on his shirt front.

———— ✂ ————

WELLINGTON, Arthur Wellesley, 1st Duke of (1769–1852), *British general and statesman, nicknamed "the Iron Duke."*

1 On a sea voyage the vessel in which Wellington was traveling encountered a violent

storm and seemed in imminent danger of sinking. The captain came to Wellington's cabin at dusk and said, "It will soon be all over with us." Wellington, about to go to bed, replied, "Very well, then I shall not take off my boots."

2 When the young Arthur Wellesley was in India, he was in charge of negotiations after the battle of Assaye with an emissary of an Indian ruler who was anxious to know what territories would be ceded to his master as a result of the treaty. Having tried various approaches and found that the general was not to be drawn on the subject, the Indian offered him five lacs of rupees (about £50,000) for the information. "Can you keep a secret?" asked Wellesley. "Yes, indeed," said the Indian eagerly. "So can I," said Wellesley.

3 Wellington's soldiers nicknamed him "Old Nosey" on account of his prominent nose. Riding up one day during his Spanish campaigns to inspect an exposed position, Wellington, about to be challenged, forgot the countersign. The sentry, an Irishman, nonetheless brought his musket to the salute and said, "God bless your crooked nose; I would rather see it than ten thousand men!"

4 During the Peninsular War a detachment of energetic but inexperienced young officers arrived to strengthen Wellington's forces. Wellington observed, "I don't know what effect they will have upon the enemy, but by God, they frighten me."

5 Although the cavalry regiments tended to get more of the limelight, Wellington was fully aware of the crucial importance of the infantry. A few weeks before the battle of Waterloo an Englishman encountered the duke in a square in Brussels and asked if he thought he could defeat Napoleon. Wellington pointed to a soldier from one of the infantry regiments, who was doing some off-duty sightseeing in the town. "It all de-

pends upon that article there," he said. "Give me enough of it, and I am sure."

6 At one point during the battle of Waterloo an officer commanding a gun battery sent a message to Wellington saying that he could clearly discern Napoleon among the enemy troops, his guns were in position, and he requested permission to fire. Wellington forbade him. "It is not the business of generals to shoot one another."

7 At Waterloo, the Marquess of Anglesey, who was in command of the British, Hanoverian, and Belgian horse, was standing by the Duke of Wellington when a shot hit his right knee. "By God, sir," he remarked to Wellington, "I have lost my leg." "By God, I believe you have," replied Wellington laconically.

8 Traveling to Belgium from his great victory at Waterloo, he was mobbed by a crowd of ecstatic citizens. Asked if he was pleased by the turnout, Wellington replied in the negative. "Not in the least; if I had failed they would have shot me."

9 The hero of Waterloo was sitting in his office one day when the door flew open and a man rushed in, crying, "I must kill you!" Wellington did not raise his head from his papers. He merely said, "Does it have to be today?" The intruder looked confused. "Well, they didn't tell me . . . but soon, surely," he replied. "Good," said Wellington briskly. "A little later on then, I'm busy at the moment." The man withdrew and was promptly seized by the police, who had been informed that there was an escaped lunatic on the rampage.

10 At Vienna Wellington was compelled to sit through a performance of Beethoven's *Battle of Victoria* (or, *Wellington's Victory*). Afterward a Russian envoy asked him if the music had been anything like the real thing. "By God, no," said the duke. "If it had been like that I'd have run away myself."

11 When some French officers, cut to the heart at France's defeat, turned their backs on Wellington at Vienna, an onlooker spoke sympathetically to the snubbed duke. Wellington smiled. "I have seen their backs before, madam," he said.

12 When Sir John Steell was executing the colossal equestrian statue of Wellington to be placed in Edinburgh, he was troubled by the fact that his sitter did not look particularly warlike. All his efforts to get a more animated expression, by urging the duke to recall the glorious victories of the Peninsular campaigns and Waterloo, failed to produce their effect. At last in desperation, he suggested that he should model the duke as he was on the morning of the Battle of Salamanca, "as you galloped about the field inspiring your troops to deeds of valor." The duke snorted. "If you really want to model me as I was on the morning of Salamanca, you must show me crawling along a ditch on my stomach, holding a telescope."

13 Lord Douro, the duke's eldest son, was extraordinarily like him in appearance. A lady once asked the duke if the numerous caricatures of him that had been published had ever annoyed him. "Not a bit, not a bit," said Wellington, then added after a pause, "There is only one caricature that has ever caused me annoyance — Douro."

14 Sparrows invaded the newly built Crystal Palace and became trapped under the glass roof, with predictably messy results for the exhibits and visitors. Queen Victoria sought the views of her eldest statesman on how to deal with the problem.

"Sparrowhawks, ma'am," was Wellington's laconic advice.

15 The French actress Mlle George boasted that she had slept with both Napoleon and Wellington. Asked in later life who was the better lover, she replied, *"Ah, monsieur, le duc était de beaucoup le plus fort"* (Ah, sir, the duke was by far the more vigorous).

16 Wellington once came upon a little boy sitting at the side of the road, crying as if his heart would break. "Come now, that's no way for a young gentleman to behave. What's the matter?" he asked. "I have to go away to school tomorrow," sobbed the child, "and I'm worried about my pet toad. There's no one else to care for it and I shan't know how it is." The duke reassured him, promising to attend to the matter personally. After the boy had been at school for little more than a week, he received the following letter: "Field Marshal the Duke of Wellington presents his compliments to Master ——— and has the pleasure to inform him that his toad is well."

17 In his later years Wellington resented any kind of attention that implied he was decrepit. One evening, as Wellington was waiting to cross Piccadilly to reach his house, a gentleman nearly as old forcibly took the Duke's arm and made a considerable parade of escorting him across the busy thoroughfare. "I thank you, sir," said Wellington when he reached his door. The other clasped his hand and broke into effusive speech, concluding with, "I never dared to hope that I might see the day when I might render the slightest assistance to the greatest man that ever lived." Wellington surveyed him serenely. "Don't be a damn fool, sir," he said, and walked into his house.

———ⲝⲟ———

WELLS, H[erbert] G[eorge] (1866–1946), *British novelist.*

1 On leaving a Cambridge party, Wells accidentally picked up a hat that did not belong to him. Discovering his mistake, he decided not to return the headgear to its rightful owner, whose label was inside the brim. The

hat fit Wells comfortably; furthermore, he had grown to like it. So he wrote to the erstwhile owner: "I stole your hat; I like your hat; I shall keep your hat. Whenever I look inside it I shall think of you and your excellent sherry and of the town of Cambridge. I take off your hat to you."

2 At a dinner one evening H. G. Wells expounded his theory that mankind had failed. The dinosaur had failed because he had concentrated upon size. *Homo sapiens* had failed because he had not developed the right type of brain. So, Wells claimed, we will first destroy ourselves, then die out as a species, and revert to mud and slime. "And we shall deserve it," he added. One of the guests objected that surely it wouldn't be as bad as that. "One thousand years more," said Wells. "That's all *Homo sapiens* has before him."

3 Wells refused to leave his London home during the Blitz, but the writer Elizabeth Bowen found him one evening after an air raid alert shaking with fright. "It's not the bombs," Wells told her. "It's the dark; I've been afraid of darkness all my life."

4 (C. P. Snow recounts a sobering conservation with H. G. Wells that took place well after midnight in a hotel lounge, where they were sitting under the potted palms, glasses of whiskey by their chairs. Snow comments that Wells's bursts of intimacy tended to be lugubrious.)

"Untypically for [Wells] the conversation tailed off. The silences got longer and longer. Without any introduction, he broke into the quiet. It was a simple question. He said, 'Ever thought of suicide, Snow?' I reflected. I said, 'Yes, H. G., I have.' He replied, 'So have I. But not till I was past seventy.' He was then seventy-two. We drank some more whisky and looked sombrely at the palms."

WERFEL, Alma Mahler (1879–1964), *wife of composer Gustav Mahler, then architect Walter Gropius, and finally writer Franz Werfel.*

1 The German playwright Gerhart Hauptmann was a great admirer of Alma's, although he had never been her lover. He said to her, "Alma, in another life we two must be lovers. May I make my reservation now?" Frau Hauptmann was standing close enough to overhear her husband's remark. "Oh, darling," she said, "I am sure Alma will be booked up there, too."

WESLEY, John (1703–91), *British religious leader.*

1 At a stormy meeting a ruffian raised his hand to strike John Wesley on the head, but as he brought it down he checked his blow and murmured, "What soft hair he has!"

2 Preaching one day, Wesley noticed that some of his congregation were fast asleep. "Fire! Fire!" he suddenly cried. The sleepers awoke with a start and leaped to their feet. "Where?" they asked, looking anxiously around them. "In hell," replied Wesley, "for those who sleep under the preaching of the word."

WEST, Mae (1892–1980), *US movie star and actress; the sex symbol of the 1930s.*

1 "Goodness, Mae," said a friend, on greeting her, "where did you get those beautiful pearls?"

"Never mind," said Mae West, "but you can take it from me that goodness had nothing to do with it."

2 Asked how she knew so much about men, West said, "Baby, I went to night school."

3 When she heard that, in the blaze of her fame, even a life jacket had been named after her, she said, "I've been in *Who's Who* and I know what's what, but this is the first time I've ever been in the dictionary."

4 Gerald Ford once invited her to the White House, but she declined. "It's an awful long way to go for just one meal."

———— ✧ ————

WESTINGHOUSE, George (1846–1914), *US inventor and manufacturer.*

1 In 1872 Westinghouse took out his first patent for an automatic air brake that would function far more quickly and safely than the clumsy hand brakes then in use. The railroad companies, however, were deeply suspicious of the invention. When he wrote to Cornelius Vanderbilt, president of the New York Central Railroad, pointing out the advantages of the air brake, Vanderbilt returned the letter with the words "I have no time to waste on fools," scrawled on the bottom.

　　Alexander J. Cassatt of the Pennsylvania Railroad, next approached, saw possibilities in the new brake, and gave Westinghouse money to continue developing his invention. The tests were successful. News of them reached Vanderbilt. He wrote Westinghouse a letter inviting him to come and see him. Back came the letter, endorsed "I have no time to waste on fools. George Westinghouse."

———— ✧ ————

WHARTON, Edith Newbold (1862–1937), *US writer.*

1 At the age of eleven, Edith Wharton attempted her first novel. It began: "'Oh, how do you do, Mrs. Brown?' said Mrs. Tompkins. 'If only I had known you were going to call, I should have tidied up the drawing room.'" Her mother's sole comment, on perusing this promising effort, was a gelid "Drawing rooms are always tidy."

2 Appalled by the rude behavior of a French visitor to her house, she was bidding him good-bye when he remarked that he generally liked her house and its furnishings, except for the ugly bas-relief in the front hall. "I assure you," she said icily, "that you will never see it again."

———— ✧ ————

WHEELER, Joseph (1836–1906), *US army officer and politician.*

1 Wheeler had been a Confederate general in the Civil War. In the Spanish-American War he commanded six regiments in the attack on Santiago. On the road to the city his men suffered serious casualties from the superior fire power of the enemy. Nevertheless, at a certain point the Spanish abandoned their entrenchments. General Wheeler, directly behind his men, inspired them with his imperishable and unreconstructed cry, "We've got the damn Yankees on the run!"

———— ✧ ————

WHEWELL, William (1794–1866), *British scientist.*

1 During the Victorian era the River Cam in Cambridge was still used as the town sewer. On a visit to Cambridge Queen Victoria paused on one of the bridges, surrounded by college dignitaries. She remarked on the quantity of paper she could see in the stream. "All that paper, ma'am," said Whewell, "carries notices to inform visitors that the river is unfit for bathing."

2 Whewell, well read in many subjects, could speak with authority on any topic of conversation that arose in the Trinity Senior Common Room, to the infuriation of some of his colleagues. Gathering up a number of reference books, including an old encyclopedia, they selected the obscure subject of Chinese musical instruments and studied it assiduously for several days. During the after-dinner conversation the next Sunday, they introduced the topic. Those who knew nothing of the conspiracy were astounded at the unexpected erudition of their colleagues; even Whewell remained silent for a while. Then, turning to one of the conspirators, he remarked, "I gather you have been reading the encyclopedia article on Chinese musical instruments I wrote some years back."

WHISTLER, James Abbott McNeill (1834–1903), *US painter who lived most of his life in London after 1860.*

1 During a West Point examination Whistler scandalized his examiners by not knowing the date of the battle of Buena Vista. "What!" said one of them, "Suppose you went out to dinner and the company got talking about the Mexican War, and you, a West Point man, did not know the date of this battle. What would you do?" Politely but decisively Whistler replied, "I should refuse to associate with people who talked of such things at dinner."

2 Whistler's failure in his West Point chemistry examination once provoked him to remark later in life, "If silicon had been a gas, I should have been a major general."

3 A snobbish Bostonian approached Whistler at a party one evening. "And where were you born, Mr. Whistler?" she asked. "Lowell, Massachusetts," replied the painter. "Whatever possessed you to be born in a place like that?" exclaimed the lady. "The explanation is quite simple," said Whistler. "I wished to be near my mother."

4 An American self-made millionaire visited Whistler's Paris studio, intending to buy some pictures for his palatial house. He glanced around the studio with its clutter of canvases and said, "How much for the lot?"
"Four million," said Whistler.
"What!"
"My posthumous prices."

5 Whistler, priding himself on his fluency in French, insisted on doing the ordering in a fashionable Paris restaurant. His companion tried to intervene and was told, "I am quite capable of ordering a meal in France without your assistance." "Of course you are," said his friend placatingly, "but I just distinctly heard you order a flight of steps."
{Did he use *escalier* for *escalope*?}

6 Whistler had been commissioned to paint a life-size nude portrait of French actress Cléo de Mérode. With her mother sitting nearby as chaperone, Mlle de Mérode draped herself on the couch, wearing nothing but a bandeau around her head. Whistler was not totally satisfied with the effect. He stepped forward to readjust the bandeau, which completely covered the actress's ears. Her mother instantly rose to her feet. "Oh, no, no, no, monsieur!" she cried. "My daughter's ears are for her husband."

7 Whistler had dined and wined extremely well at a friend's house. He left the party and a few seconds later a loud crash announced that he had fallen down the stairs. As he was picked up, he indignantly demanded the name of his host's architect. "Norman Shaw," was the reply. "I might have known it," said Whistler. "The damned teetotaler."

8 A female admirer asked Whistler whether he thought genius hereditary. "I cannot tell you

that, madam," he replied. "Heaven has granted me no offspring."

9 A notorious bore approached Whistler at a gathering and launched into conversation with "You know, Mr. Whistler, I passed your house last night — "

"Thank you," said Whistler.

10 Someone annoyed by Whistler's constant self-applause said pointedly, "It's a good thing we can't see ourselves as others see us."

"Isn't it?" responded Whistler. "I know in my case I would grow intolerably conceited."

11 Some blank canvases that Whistler had ordered had been lost in the mail. Asked whether the canvases were of any great value, Whistler replied, "Not yet, not yet."

12 "A woman said to Whistler, 'I just came up from the country this morning along the Thames, and there was an exquisite haze in the atmosphere which reminded me so much of some of your little things. It was really a perfect series of Whistlers.'

"'Yes, madam,' responded Whistler gravely, 'Nature is creeping up.'"

13 A friend of Whistler's came up to him in a London street as the artist was talking to a particularly grimy urchin selling newspapers. Whistler asked the lad how long he had been doing the work.

"Three years, sir."

"How old are you?"

"Seven, sir."

"Oh, come, you must be older than that."

"No, I ain't, sir."

Whistler turned to his friend. "I don't think he could get that dirty in seven years. Do you?"

14 A supposed conversation between Whistler and Oscar Wilde having been published in *Punch*, Wilde sent Whistler the following telegram: "*Punch* too ridiculous. When you

and I are together we never talk about anything except ourselves." Back came the reply from Whistler: "No, no, Oscar, you forget. When you and I are together we never talk about anything except me."

15 Whistler was once printing etchings with the painter Walter Sickert. During the course of their work, Sickert clumsily dropped one of the copper plates. "How like you!" said Whistler derisively.

A few minutes later, however, the same accident befell Whistler himself. "How unlike me!" he exclaimed.

16 Whistler disliked Joseph Turner's work and made no secret of his opinion. Someone once asked him if he would give advice as to whether a certain picture was a genuine Turner or an imitation. "That is a fine distinction," said Whistler.

17 Whistler's presidency of the Royal Society of British Artists was short-lived. In 1888 he resigned after his autocratic ways had caused him to quarrel with most of the members. To his followers he said of this debacle, "It is very simple. The artists retired. The British remained."

18 When an Englishman remarked to Whistler that he found the courtesy of the French false, being only on the surface, Whistler replied, "That is a very good place for it."

———— ❧ ————

WHITMAN, Walt (1819–92), *US poet*.

1 The stir caused by Whitman's poetry was such that some people hailed him as a prophet and others abused him as a monster of depravity. One day, as Whitman was walking past the White House, he was pointed out to President Lincoln. "Well, he looks like a man" was the President's comment.

———— ❧ ————

WHITNEY, Stephen (c. 1850–c. 1920), *US businessman*.

1 On hearing the news of Stephen Whitney's death, the diarist George Templeton Strong commented that he had never used any of his money for the benefit of either himself or anyone else. "His last act was characteristic and fitting," Strong observed. "He locked up his checkbook and died."

—◇—

WIENIAWSKI, Henri (1835–80), *Polish violinist and composer*.

1 Wieniawski once played to a half-empty auditorium in Boston. Despite the poor attendance, he was urged to return and perform there again. "Oh, no," replied the violinist. "I'll get out of the habit of playing in public."

—◇—

WILD, Jonathan (?1682–1725), *British criminal*.

1 Wild remained a criminal literally to his death. As he stepped up to the gallows at Tyburn, the unrepentant rogue deftly picked the pocket of the priest administering the last rites. He died waving his trophy, a corkscrew, triumphantly at the crowd below.

—◇—

WILDE, Oscar (1854–1900), *British aesthete, writer, and wit*.

1 In the nineteenth-century Oxford examinations there was a compulsory divinity section, and candidates were required to translate aloud from the Greek version of the New Testament. Wilde, assigned a passage dealing with the Passion, began to translate fluently and accurately. The examiners, satisfied, told him he could stop. Ignoring them, he continued to translate. Eventually they succeeded in halting him. "Oh, do let me go on," Wilde said. "I want to see how it ends."

2 In 1882 Wilde went on a lecture tour of the United States. A New York customs official asked if he had anything to declare. "No. I have nothing to declare" — Wilde paused — "except my genius."

3 "Wonderful man, Columbus!" exclaimed an American eager to strike up a conversation with Wilde. "Why?" asked Wilde. "He discovered America," replied the other. Wilde shook his head: "Oh no, it had often been discovered before, but it had always been hushed up."

4 The great French actor Coquelin asked Wilde about the progress of his new play, *The Duchess of Padua*. "The ending is quite tragic," said Wilde. "My hero, at his moment of triumph, makes an epigram which falls flat."

5 Frank Harris, then editor of the *Saturday Review*, gave a dinner at the Café Royal to which some of London's most brilliant wits were invited. Harris dominated the conversation, ignoring all hints to quiet down. Oscar Wilde grew more and more restless as Harris told the company about all the great houses at which he had been a guest. Eventually he broke in with "Dear Frank, we believe you; you have dined in every house in London — *once*."

6 Wilde was asked his opinion of a play that had been generally accounted a fiasco. "The play was a great success," he replied, "but the audience was a disaster."

7 Wilde and Whistler frequently exchanged insults in a feud that owed more to both parties' addiction to the limelight than to any genuine rancor. "I wish I had said that!" exclaimed Wilde after a particular scintillating remark from Whistler. "You will, Oscar, you will," said Whistler.

8 In the course of their well-publicized feud, Whistler accused Wilde of plagiarizing his ideas on art. Wilde replied: "As for borrowing Mr. Whistler's ideas about art, the only thoroughly original ideas I have ever heard him express have had reference to his own superiority as a painter over painters greater than himself."

9 When the poet laureateship fell vacant on the death of Tennyson, the names of several likely candidates came up frequently. Not included was that of the prolific poetaster Sir Lewis Morris. "It's a complete conspiracy of silence against me," Morris complained to Oscar Wilde. "What ought I to do, Oscar?"
"Join it," said Wilde.

10 Talking to an admirer of Dickens, Wilde moved his hearer almost to tears by the eloquence of his enthusiasm for the master's powers. And then Wilde concluded, "One would have to have a heart of stone to read the death of Little Nell without laughing."

11 After playing for some time the role of Lord Illingworth in Wilde's play *A Woman of No Importance,* Beerbohm Tree showed signs of unconsciously adopting the character's mannerisms in real life. Wilde was delighted with this phenomenon. "Ah, every day dear Herbert becomes *de plus en plus Oscarisé,*" he declared. "It is a wonderful case of nature imitating art."

12 When asked to make certain changes in one of his plays, Wilde protested: "Who am I to tamper with a masterpiece?"

13 Wilde was staying with friends at a country house, where his eccentric behavior and manner of dress startled his fellow guests. One morning he came down to breakfast looking very pale and drawn. "I'm afraid you are ill, Mr. Wilde," remarked another member of the party. "No, not ill," replied Wilde, "only tired. The fact is, I picked a primrose in the wood yesterday, and it was so ill I have been sitting up with it all night."

14 Wilde's legal battle with the Marquis of Queensberry, father of Lord Alfred Douglas, began when Wilde brought a case of criminal libel against the marquis for publicly accusing him of sodomy. Shortly after the trial began, Wilde met an actor friend, Charles Goodhart, in Piccadilly Circus, where every newspaper placard displayed his name and the newsboys were shouting it on every corner. Goodhart, feeling embarrassed, talked about the weather. Wilde, however, put him at his ease: "You've heard of my case? Don't distress yourself. All is well. The working classes are with me . . . to a boy."

15 Sentenced to two years' hard labor, Wilde stood handcuffed in driving rain waiting for transport to prison. "If this is the way Queen Victoria treats her prisoners," he remarked, "she doesn't deserve to have any."

16 Ada Leverson was a devoted friend of Oscar Wilde, who always called her "Sphinx." It was she who gave him refuge when he had nowhere to go to escape the public scandal after his first trial in 1895. When Wilde was released from prison two years later, she, her husband, and a very few others went early in the morning to the house of a mutual friend to greet him before he departed for France. It was a difficult ordeal for all concerned, but Wilde immediately put his friends at their ease. "Sphinx," he said as soon as he entered the room, "how marvelous of you to know exactly the right hat to wear at seven o'clock in the morning to meet a friend who has been away."

17 (Yeats recounts a story he was told of Wilde's visit to a brothel in Dieppe after he had been released from prison. "Dowson" is the poet Ernest Dowson.)
"Dowson pressed upon him the necessity of acquiring a 'more wholesome taste.' They

emptied their pockets onto the café table, and though there was not much, there was enough, if both heaps were put into one. Meanwhile the news had spread, and they set out accompanied by a cheering crowd. Arrived at their destination, Dowson and the crowd remained outside, and presently Wilde returned. He said in a low voice to Dowson, 'The first these ten years, and it will be the last. It was like cold mutton' . . . and then aloud, so that the crowd might hear him, 'But tell it in England, for it will entirely restore my character.' "

18 Wilde died of cerebral meningitis in a hotel in Paris. He was offered and accepted a drink of champagne, remarking as he did so, "I am dying beyond my means."

19 Still another version of Wilde's last words has him staring at his shabby Paris bedroom. He is reputed to have said, "Either that wallpaper goes, or I do."

———— ✂ ————

WILDER, Billy [Samuel] (1906–), *US film director and screenwriter, born in Austria.*

1 Wilder wanted Gloria Swanson's attempted suicide in *Sunset Boulevard* to look authentic, and instructed his cameraman John Seitz to angle the camera just so. "Johnny, it's the usual slashed-wrist shot," he said. Later in the film, filming the funeral of Swanson's pet monkey, he said, "Johnny, it's the usual dead-chimpanzee setup."

2 While shooting *Sunset Boulevard* Wilder instructed the cameraman to keep the film a little out of focus. When the cameraman objected, Wilder said, "I want to win the foreign picture award."

3 Wilder was asked by a journalist to name his personal favorite among his many films. "*Some Like It Hot,*" he replied instantly. The journalist was surprised that Wilder had not

named one of his classics, such as *Sunset Boulevard.* "A nice little picture," agreed Billy, "but in those days I wasn't getting a percentage of the gross."

———— ✂ ————

WILDING, Michael (1912–79), *British actor.*

1 Wilding was once asked whether actors had any distinguishing features that set them apart from other human beings. "Without a doubt," he replied. "You can pick out actors by the glazed look that comes into their eyes when the conversation wanders away from themselves."

———— ✂ ————

WILHELMINA HELENA PAULINE MARIA (1880–1962), *queen of the Netherlands (1890–1948).*

1 At a meeting with Wilhelm II during World War I, Queen Wilhelmina was not intimidated by the kaiser's exaggerated boasts. "Our guardsmen," he declared, "are seven feet tall."

   "And when we open our dikes," replied the queen, "the waters are ten feet deep."

———— ✂ ————

WILKES, John (1725–97), *British politician and journalist.*

1 After James Boswell had dined with the sheriffs and judges at a formal dinner at London's Old Bailey law courts, he complained that his pocket had been picked and his handkerchief stolen. "Pooh," said Wilkes, "this is nothing but the ostentation of a Scotsman to let the world know that he had possessed a pocket handkerchief."

2 After 1786, when Wilkes became a supporter of Pitt, and hence of the government, the Whigs liked to taunt him for his fickleness. The Prince of Wales, Wilkes's *bête noire*, one

evening recited to him Sheridan's mocking verses beginning, "Johnny Wilkes, Johnny Wilkes, You greatest of bilks." Wilkes waited for revenge until a gathering at Carlton House, when the prince called for toasts. Knowing the prince's loathing for his father and his glee at the king's illness, Wilkes gave the toast: "The king; long life to him."

"Since when," sneered the prince, "have you been so anxious about my parent's health?"

"Since I had the pleasure of Your Royal Highness's acquaintance," replied Wilkes with a most courteous bow.

3 Wilkes dined one night with the Earl of Sandwich in London's Covent Garden, at the famous Beef Steak Club. After a fair amount to drink Lord Sandwich said to Wilkes, "I have often wondered what catastrophe would bring you to your end; I think you must die of the pox or the halter." "My lord," replied Wilkes instantaneously, "that will depend on whether I embrace your lordship's mistress or your lordship's principles."

WILLES, Sir John (1685–1761), *British lawyer, lord chief justice (1737–61).*

1 Rumors of irregular conduct in the lord chief justice's household became so rife that a dissenting clergyman decided to talk with him and perhaps bring him to repentance. After approaching the matter in a roundabout way, which Willes affected not to understand, the clergyman came to the point: "They say that one of your maidservants is now with child."

"What's that to me?" said Willes.

"But they say she is with child by your lordship."

"What's that to you?"

WILLIAM I [William the Conqueror] (1027–87), *king of England (1066–87).*

1 Leading his army of invasion ashore at Pevensey in southeast England, William stumbled and fell. The superstitious men around him exclaimed at the bad omen, but William quickly stood up and, holding out his muddied hands, cried, "By the splendor of God I have taken possession of my realm; the earth of England is in my two hands."

WILLIAM I (1797–1888), *king of Prussia (1861–88) and emperor of Germany (1871–88).*

1 At a Berlin subscription ball, open to those of lesser rank as well as to high society, the emperor noticed his court tailor and greeted him amiably: "A lovely ball, isn't it?" The tailor bowed deeply, observing in a tone of servility, "These balls, Your Majesty, seem to draw a somewhat more mixed group of guests than formerly." The emperor smiled, then said, "True, but what can we do about it? We can't invite tailors only."

2 Daily at noon the emperor would station himself at the corner of his Berlin palace and show himself to the thousands of subjects and visitors who came to pay homage to this embodiment of imperial power. During his later years as his health declined, his doctors were emphatic in beseeching him not to weaken himself with this daily activity. It was in fact difficult for the old emperor, but he refused to obey his doctors. "No, there's no help for it. My daily appearance is listed in Baedeker."

WILLIAM II (1859–1941), *emperor of Germany (1888–1918).*

1 As part of his program to build up the German navy, the kaiser himself designed a war-

ship. When the plans were complete, he sent them to the Italian minister of the marine, Admiral Brin, who was then considered the world's leading naval architect. In due course the admiral's report was transmitted to the kaiser. The ship would easily outgun any existing battleship; its range and speed were likewise far in excess of any other vessel. Moreover, its internal arrangements were so well thought out that everyone sailing in it, from the commander to the humblest cabin boy, would find it a miracle of convenience and efficiency. The only problem, the report concluded, was that if the ship were actually put in the water it would sink like a lump of lead.

WILLIAM III (1650–1702), *king of England (1689–1702) and Stadholder of the United Provinces (1672–1702).*

1 During a journey by carriage through a village not far from Windsor, a woman who was determined to see the king pressed up close to the window to peer at the occupant. Having satisfied her curiosity, she stepped back and remarked, "Is that the king? My husband is a handsomer man than he." King William overheard her, leaned out, and said, "Good woman, do not speak so loud. Pray consider that I am a widower."

WILLIAMS, Ted (1918–), *US baseball player.*

1 The great outfielder for the Red Sox had a reputation for being personally unpleasant. One evening Williams signed into a hotel under the name "G. C. Luther." The clerk looked at his name, and then at him, and asked if he was in fact Ted Williams. Williams denied it, and the two began a conversation about fishing. Finally the clerk said, "I thought you really were Ted. But I can see you're not. You've got a much nicer disposition."

2 Williams never wore ties, a fact that was anticipated to cause problems with new manager Joe McCarthy, who was known as a stickler for a dress code. But at the first formal team meal he attended, McCarthy wore a brightly colored sports shirt to everyone's surprise. "If I don't get along with a .400 hitter," McCarthy later said, "it'll be my fault."

3 When he turned forty-one in 1959, Williams was not playing up to his standard; his batting average had dipped below .316 for the first time ever. The owner of the Red Sox approached him and suggested it might be time to consider retirement, but Williams declined. "I may not have been the greatest hitter who ever lived, but I knew I was the greatest old hitter."

4 Williams was known to be a fishing fanatic. Once he mentioned to a Boston sportswriter that no one knew more about fishing than he did. "Sure there is," said the writer. "God, who made the fish."

"Yeah, all right," said Williams. "But you had to go pretty far back."

WILLIAMS, Tennessee [Thomas Lanier Williams] (1911–83), *US dramatist.*

1 Newspaper reports in 1961 announced that Williams had decided not to attend any further sessions with his psychoanalyst. Asked the reason for this decision, the playwright replied, "He was meddling too much in my private life."

2 (When Williams received the gold medal for drama from the National Institute of Arts and Letters, his brief acceptance speech consisted almost entirely of an anecdote:)

"One time, Maureen Stapleton received a phone call from a friend who said that so-

and-so was getting married, and the caller said, 'Why is she marrying that man, you know he is a homosexual,' and Maureen said, 'Well, what about the bride?' And the caller said, 'Well, of course we know she's a lesbian. And you know they're not even being married by a real minister, but by one who's been defrocked!' And Maureen said, 'Will you do me a favor? Will you please invite Tennessee Williams? Because he'll say, "Oh, they're just plain folks!"'"

WILLS, Maury (1932–), *US baseball player.*

1 A former shortstop, Wills became the manager of the Seattle Mariners in the early 1980s, but it didn't take long for him to reveal his basic ignorance of his new team. At the press conference announcing his hire, he was asked who he would name as center fielder. "I wouldn't be a bit surprised if it was Leon Roberts," he said, not realizing that Roberts had been traded to another team five weeks earlier.

2 Wills quickly earned a reputation as an incompetent manager. He changed pitchers before allowing his replacements to warm up, and he often demoted players to the minor leagues for no apparent reason. His players were in despair, but soon they hit on the strategy of losing as a means of getting rid of Wills. After one victory over the Tigers, a player said ruefully, "Hell, we screwed up. We won."

WILSON, Charles Erwin (1890–1961), *US industrialist.*

1 Wilson, president of General Motors, was nominated by President Eisenhower to be secretary of defense. At his Senate confirmation hearing, Wilson uttered perhaps the only words for which he will be remembered:

"What is good for the country is good for General Motors, and what's good for General Motors is good for the country."

WILSON, Edmund (1895–1972), *US literary critic and essayist.*

1 Like all successful writers, Wilson was beset by people wanting his advice or help in all manner of literary and other matters. To deal with the flood of letters he had the following postcard printed: "Edmund Wilson regrets that it is impossible for him to: Read manuscripts, write articles or books to order, write forewords or introductions, make statements for publicity purposes, do any kind of editorial work, judge literary contests, give interviews, take part in writers' conferences, answer questionnaires, contribute to or take part in symposiums or 'panels' of any kind, contribute manuscripts for sales, donate copies of his books to libraries, autograph works for strangers, allow his name to be used on letterheads, supply personal information about himself, supply opinions on literary or other subjects." He was then pestered by people who wrote to him simply in order to obtain a copy of the postcard.

WILSON, Sir Harold (1916–95), *British statesman; Labour prime minister (1964–70, 1974–76).*

1 At a rally in the mid-1960s, Wilson was interrupted by a cry of "Rubbish!" from a heckler at the back of the crowd. Without missing a beat, Wilson replied: "We'll take up your special interest in a moment, sir."

2 On one occasion during Harold Wilson's administration, Willie Hamilton, the vociferous member for Fife Central, harangued the prime minister for his indecisiveness on the issue of Britain's entry into the European Common Market. "First we're in, then we're

out," cried the irate Labour member. "It's exactly like coitus interruptus." The House, stunned into silence, erupted with laughter when a Tory member shouted, "Withdraw."

———∞———

WILSON, Harriette (1786–1846), *British courtesan.*

1 Around 1820 Harriette, finding herself short of money, decided to write her memoirs. The enterprise was widely publicized, Harriette making no secret of the fact that she was naming names. Some former "friends" were able to buy themselves out of the narrative by substantial cash payments. The Duke of Wellington, on being offered such a deal, is said to have responded with "Publish and be damned!" Harriette did publish; the publisher sold thirty editions of the book within a year.

———∞———

WILSON, Richard (1714–82), *Welsh painter.*

1 The Italian tradition of landscape painting and the beauties of the Italian landscape were the factors that caused Wilson's change of allegiance in mid-career. On a visit to the famous waterfall at Terni, he is said to have exclaimed, "Well-done water — by God!"

———∞———

WILSON, [Thomas] Woodrow (1856–1924), *US politician; president of Princeton University (1902–10); 28th President of the United States (1913–21).*

1 As president of Princeton University, Wilson was once interrogated at length by an anxious mother who wanted to be sure that Princeton was the best place to send her son. "Madam," said Wilson, his patience exhausted, "we guarantee satisfaction or you will get your son back."

2 One afternoon during his time as governor of New Jersey, Wilson received news of the sudden death of a personal friend, a New Jersey senator. He was still recovering from the shock when the telephone rang again. It was a prominent New Jersey politician. "Governor," he said, "I would like to take the senator's place." Wilson replied, "It's perfectly agreeable to me if it's agreeable to the undertaker."

3 Shortly after the 1912 presidential election, Wilson visited an aged aunt whom he had not seen for some time. "What are you doing these days, Woodrow?" she asked. "I've just been elected President," replied Wilson. "Oh, yes? President of what?" inquired the aunt. "Of the United States." The old lady snorted impatiently. "Don't be silly!" she said.

4 President Wilson had refused to receive a deputation of Irish-American leaders headed by the agitator Daniel F. Cohalan. Wilson's private secretary, Joseph P. Tumulty, aware of Cohalan's great influence, tried to persuade the President to change his mind. "Think what a terrible impression it will make on his followers if you don't," he said. "That's just what I wanted it to do," replied Wilson, "but I think it will make a good impression on decent people."

5 During the Versailles peace negotiations, Wilson opposed the ceding of the Adriatic port of Fiume to Italy. The head of the Italian delegation, V. E. Orlando, argued eloquently that Italy's right to the city was undeniable, since its language, population, and cultural affinities were all predominantly Italian. "I hope you won't press the point in respect to New York City," countered Wilson, "or you might feel like claiming a sizable piece of Manhattan Island."

———∞———

WINTERS, Shelley [Shirley Schrift] (1922–), *US actress of stage, screen, and television.*

1 Al Horwits worked at one time for Universal Pictures in the publicity department. One of his clients was the young Shelley Winters. Scheduled to meet a certain Italian producer, she called Horwits to get some background information. Said Horwits, "He's a terrible wolf. He'll tear the clothes off your back."

"So I'll wear an old dress," said Shelley.

———⚬ঌ———

WITTGENSTEIN, Ludwig (1889–1951), *British philosopher and writer, born in Austria.*

1 A neighbor heard the sound of animated conversation as he approached Wittgenstein's cottage in Connemara, Ireland, but was quite surprised when he entered to find the great philosopher alone. "I thought you had company," he said. "I did," replied Wittgenstein. "I was talking to a very dear friend of mine — myself."

———⚬ঌ———

WODEHOUSE, Sir P[elham] G[renville] (1881–1975), *British humorist, called Plum by his friends.*

1 Ethel Wodehouse was a natural party giver, and on occasion her inclinations were allowed to override Plum's. Once when Ethel gave a party, some guests arrived rather late. When they rang the bell, the front door was opened not by the butler but by Plum. He surveyed them carefully and, recognizing them as friends, put out both hands in a gesture to push them away. "Don't come in," he said, "don't come in. You'll hate it!"

2 Wodehouse's terror of casual human contacts assumed almost pathological proportions. The Wodehouses were looking for an apartment in New York, and as Mrs. Wodehouse was about to go out to continue the search her husband called her back. "Get one on the ground floor," he said. "Why?" she asked. "I never know what to say to the lift boy," was the answer.

3 On a visit to the zoo Wodehouse wandered into the monkey house and was confronted by ferocious-looking monkey. For a while the two stared at one another. Finally the monkey turned and stalked off, revealing for the first time its scarlet, purple, and orange behind. Plum shook his head sadly. "That monkey," he declared, "is wearing its club colors in the wrong place."

———⚬ঌ———

WOLF, Hugo (1860–1903), *Austrian composer.*

1 In 1897, Wolf went mad and was committed to an asylum. He was still sane enough, however, to be aware of his condition. "Is that clock right?" he once asked, pointing to a large clock that hung in the dining room of the asylum. "As far as I know," replied one of the attendants. "Then what's it doing here?" inquired Wolf.

———⚬ঌ———

WOLFE, James (1727–59), *British soldier who died leading the attack on Quebec in which the British seized the city from the French during the Seven Years' War.*

1 Wolfe's energy and self-confidence did not endear him to his fellow commanders. One of them complained to King George II that Wolfe was mad. "Mad, is he?" said the monarch. "Then I wish he'd bite some of my other generals."

———⚬ঌ———

WOLFE, Thomas (1900–38), *US novelist.*

1 In *Look Homeward, Angel,* Wolfe based the stonecutter Gant on his own father ("It's the God's truth! It's the God's truth!" exclaimed

his mother, when she read the finished book). At his meeting with Max Perkins to go over the manuscript, though, Wolfe worried about the nature of Gant's portrayal. When Perkins began focusing on a scene involving the girls in a brothel, Wolfe cut in, "I know you can't print that. I'll take it out immediately." "Take it out?" cried Perkins. "Why, it's one of the greatest short stories I've ever read!"

2 Descending from his apartment to the street, Wolfe found himself sharing the elevator with a woman whose large German Shepherd was straining on its leash. The dog leaped up onto Wolfe, causing the woman to cry out, "Wolfe! You great, obnoxious beast!" Wolfe, whose literary celebrity had caused him embarrassment all over New York, spent the day walking in the rain, depressed that even a total stranger would address him so brutally. Later, he learned that the dog's name was Wolf.

WOOLLCOTT, Alexander (1887–1943), *US writer, drama critic, and New York wit.*

1 In his early years of service in World War I, as a sergeant in the Medical Corps, Woollcott and his outfit camped at Le Mans in appalling conditions. The tents leaked, and the men were obliged to put up their rickety beds in muddy pools of rainwater. Shortly afterward, Woollcott was transferred to the Paris office of *The Stars and Stripes,* the US army newspaper. He spent the remaining war years in luxury, frequenting the boulevard cafés and dining at the Ritz each evening. After the Armistice he happened to meet one of his former colleagues from the Medical Corps. "You made an awful mistake leaving our unit when you did," said the soldier. "The week after you went, they put wooden floors in our tents."

2 Opening an account at a New York department store, Dorothy Parker and her new husband, Alan Campbell, cited Woollcott as a reference for their financial reliability. They were soon to regret their choice. Woollcott's endorsement read: "Mr. Alan Campbell, the present husband of Dorothy Parker, has given my name as a reference in his attempt to open an account at your store. We all hope you will extend this credit to him. Surely Dorothy Parker's position in American letters is such as to make shameful the petty refusals which she and Alan have encountered at many hotels, restaurants, and department stores. What if you never get paid? Why shouldn't you stand your share of the expense?"

3 Woollcott was constantly referred to in the Broadway and literary columns. At one stage, the popular columnist Walter Winchell quoted a whole series of jokes and wisecracks he attributed to Woollcott. In fact, they had been made up by Irving Mansfield, whom Woollcott had hired for the purpose. Mansfield, who later became a well-known television producer, soon ran out of funny things to say, and Winchell's column no longer contained *bons mots* attributed to Woollcott. After a couple of weeks Woollcott sent Mansfield a telegram: "Dear Irving, whatever happened to my sense of humor?"

4 On seeing playwright Moss Hart's sumptuous country mansion and landscaped grounds, Woollcott remarked, "Just what God would have done if he had the money."

5 The writer Ludwig Lewisohn complained to Woollcott about getting a bad review. Woollcott remarked, "Ludwig thinks he gets bad reviews because the critics are anti-Semitic. Actually it's because Ludwig has halitosis."

6 While Woollcott was a regular contributor to *The New Yorker,* he attended a dinner party in London at which the guest of honor was

the Prince of Wales, the future Edward VIII. The ladies had left the room and the gentlemen had started on their port and cigars, when the prince intimated that he would like a few words in private with Mr. Woollcott. The gentlemen withdrew after the ladies, leaving Woollcott tête-à-tête with royalty, his head filled with visions of splendid commissions from the prince. "I understand, Mr. Woollcott, that you have something to do with that magazine from the States, *The New Yorker*," began the prince. Woollcott admitted that he had. "Then why the devil don't I get it more regularly?" demanded His Highness. "Do look into it, will you?" Then they joined the rest of the party.

7 After Woollcott gave a lecture in a midwestern town, an elderly lady approached him and told him that his lecture had given her much pleasure. "And," she went on, "I was encouraged to speak to you because you said that you loved old ladies."

"Yes, I do," replied Woollcott, "but I also like them your age."

8 Childless himself, the redoubtable Alexander Woollcott was, on nineteen occasions, godparent to the children of friends. At the baptism of Mary MacArthur, daughter of Charles MacArthur and Helen Hayes, Woollcott was heard to exclaim with characteristic gusto: "Always a godfather, never a god!"

9 Woollcott once participated in a radio panel for CBS. The question under discussion was, "Is Germany Incurable?" Just as he was making a comment, Woollcott pushed the microphone away. "I AM SICK," he wrote on a piece of paper. Mystery writer Rex Stout, who was also on the panel, knew something was wrong. Said he, "A healthier Woollcott would have written, 'I AM ILL.'"

10 Visiting the playwright Moss Hart at his house in rural Pennsylvania, Woollcott im-

mediately began insulting Hart, Hart's taste, his friends, his house and its furnishings, and the other house guests. He then demanded to be given the master bedroom and that the heat be turned off in the house. And finally he insisted on having someone bring him a milkshake and chocolate cake in bed. Just before retiring for the night, Woollcott remembered to sign Hart's guest book, in which he wrote, "I wish to say that on my first visit to Moss Hart's house, I had one of the most unpleasant evenings I can ever remember having." Later, Hart said to his collaborator George Kaufman that it could have been worse — what if Woollcott had broken his leg and had had to stay for an extended period? Kaufman thought for a minute, then put a sheet of paper in his typewriter and wrote, "Act One, Scene One."

WORDSWORTH, William (1770–1850), *British Romantic poet.*

1 As Wordsworth's poetic arteries hardened, he became an ardent patriot and an establishment figure. At a gathering at which the youthful John Keats was present, Keats attempted to break into Wordsworth's monologue with an enthusiastic agreement with what the older poet was saying. Mrs. Wordsworth leaned over and checked him. "Mr. Wordsworth is never interrupted," she whispered.

2 Wordsworth boasted in Charles Lamb's hearing, "I could write like Shakespeare if I had a mind to."

"So it's only the mind that's lacking," murmured Lamb.

3 At the time when Wordsworth and Tom Moore were the heroes of London literary society, both were invited to a reception at which Moore promptly became the center of attraction, monopolizing the guests' atten-

tion with his wit and gaiety. The hostess noticed Wordsworth standing on the fringes of the group, looking a little sour. "Oh, Mr. Wordsworth," she said, thinking to draw him into the fun, "isn't Mr. Moore amusing? He says such entertaining things."

"Very amusing; very entertaining," said Wordsworth glumly. "You know I have only once in my life ever said anything very amusing." The hostess clapped her hands for silence and asked Wordsworth to repeat that *mot* for the guests, who all fell silent and waited expectantly. "I was walking along near Grasmere," Wordsworth began, "when I met a dalesman who appeared to be looking for something, and when he saw me the man hurried over and asked me if I had seen his wife anywhere along the road. And you know what I said? I said, 'My good man, I didn't even know that you had a wife.' That was the one time in my life that I have ever said anything very amusing."

WREN, Sir Christopher (1632–1723), *British architect, mathematician, and astronomer.*

1 When Wren designed the inside of Windsor Town Hall, his ceiling was supported by pillars. The building inspectors felt he had not put up enough. Wren felt differently. He put in four more pillars that did not actually touch the ceiling; they only looked as if they did. The inspectors were fooled, and the four fake pillars still stand.

WRIGHT, Frank Lloyd (1869–1956), *US architect.*

1 In 1937, Wright built a house in Wisconsin for industrialist Hibbard Johnson and his family. One rainy evening Johnson was entertaining some distinguished guests for dinner when the roof began to leak. The water

seeped through the ceiling directly above Johnson himself, dripping steadily onto the top of his bald head. Irate, he put a call through to Wright in Phoenix, Arizona. "Frank," he said, "you built this beautiful house for me and we enjoy it very much. But I have told you the roof leaks, and right now I am with some friends and distinguished guests and it is leaking right on top of my head." Wright's reply was heard by all. "Well, Hib," he said, "why don't you move your chair?"

2 In 1930 novelist Rex Stout built a fourteen-room house, with his own hands, on a hilltop in Danbury, Connecticut. Later he invited Frank Lloyd Wright out to see it and waited patiently for his evaluation. Wright examined it carefully and then said, "A superb spot. Someone should build a house here."

WRIGHT, Orville (1871–1948) and Wilbur (1867–1912), *US pioneer aviators. In December 1903 they made the first powered flight at Kitty Hawk, North Carolina.*

1 Weary of explaining the principles of their Flyer's performance to the inquisitive, the Wright brothers said simply, "The airplane stays up because it doesn't have the time to fall."

WRIGHT, Richard (1908–60), *US writer.*

1 Traveling from Mexico back to the United States with John Steinbeck, Wright had included in his luggage several books bound to make trouble at the border; including Lenin's *What Is to Be Done?* and Karl Marx's *Das Kapital*. Wright decided to risk it despite Steinbeck's worry. The customs inspector found the books and, holding them up, asked, "Boy, these books ain't Communistic,

are they?" "Oh, no, sir," Wright replied. "They are books dealing with writing." They were waved through.

———— ❧ ————

WYCHERLEY, William (1640–1716), *British playwright.*

1 One day when Wycherley and a friend were in a bookstore they overheard a fashionable young lady asking the bookseller if he had *The Plain Dealer.* Wycherley's friend at once pushed him across to the lady and said, "Here, madam, is the Plain Dealer himself." The lady turned out to be the widowed Countess of Drogheda. She and Wycherley exchanged compliments, and as they parted she said, "I love plain dealing best of all." Acting on this hint, Wycherley wooed her in the manner approved by the heroes of his comedies and they married in 1680.

———— ❧ ————

WYLIE, Elinor (1885–1928), *US poet and novelist.*

1 The novelist and short-story writer Katherine Anne Porter was roused from sleep by the doorbell at 4:00 AM. On the step was Elinor Wylie, who announced, "I have stood the crassness of the world as long as I can and I am going to kill myself. You are the only person in the world to whom I wish to say good-bye." Since at the time Elinor Wylie was richly endowed with all the material advantages her friend lacked, Katherine Anne Porter was not disposed to be sympathetic. "Elinor," she said, "it was good of you to think of me. Good-bye."

X

XERXES (d. 465 BC), *King of Persia (485–465 BC), who led the great Persian expedition against Greece in 480 BC.*

1 Xerxes, surveying the great army he had assembled for the invasion of Greece, seemed at first very happy, but presently began to weep. "I am moved to pity," he said, "when I think of the brevity of human life, seeing that of all this host of men not one will still be alive in a hundred years' time."

2 On his retreat from Greece Xerxes boarded a Phoenician ship to transport him back to Asia Minor. On the way a fearful storm blew up and the ship seemed likely to founder, especially as it was overloaded with Persians who had accompanied Xerxes. The king asked the pilot if there was any hope of safety. The man replied that there was none, unless the ship's load was substantially lightened. Xerxes then turned to the Persians on deck and said, "It is on you that my safety depends. Now let some of you show your regard for your king." A number of those who heard him made obeisance to him and then threw themselves overboard. Thus lightened, the ship came safely to harbor.

After he landed Xerxes immediately ordered that a golden crown be presented to the pilot for preserving the king's life; however, he also commanded that the man's head should be cut off, as he had caused the loss of so many Persian lives.

Y

YEATS, William Butler (1865–1939), *Irish poet and playwright.*

1 (Yeats had a lifelong interest in the occult. That conversation centered on this topic when Louis MacNeice and E. R. Dodds, professor of Greek at Oxford, went to tea with him in 1934.)

"He talked a great deal about the spirits to whom his wife, being a medium, had introduced him. 'Have you ever seen them?' Dodds asked (Dodds could never keep back such questions). Yeats was a little piqued. No, he said grudgingly, he had never actually seen them . . . but — with a flash of triumph — he had often *smelt* them."

2 In the 1930s a certain Dr. Steinach claimed to be able to rejuvenate aging men by implanting new sex glands. Yeats read a pamphlet about this treatment and was impressed enough to ask his physician as to the advisability of the operation. When the physician refused to commit himself, Yeats went ahead and had the operation in London in May 1934. Back in Dublin he was fully convinced of the success of the treatment. His friend Oliver St. John Gogarty, also a doctor by training, was appalled and questioned Yeats closely about it. "What was wrong with you?" Gogarty inquired. "I used to fall asleep after lunch," replied Yeats.

YUSUPOV, Prince Feliks *(dates unknown), Russian nobleman. He was one of the chief conspirators in the murder of Rasputin in 1916.*

1 In the Metro-Goldwyn-Mayer film *Rasputin and the Empress* the studio sought to avoid trouble with Prince Yusupov by changing to Prince Chegodieff the name of the character who played his role in the story. They had reckoned without the prince's proprietary attitude to the murder. He sued the studio in a London court for depriving him of the credit for his actions. He won his case and the studio had to pay a considerable sum in damages. Then a real Prince Chegodieff came forward and sued for the libelous use of his name. He also won his case and MGM paid off once more.

Z

ZAHARIAS, Babe Didrikson (1911–56), *US athelete.*

1 In the 1930s Didrikson, who was one of the first professional women athletes, was asked what her advice would be for women who wanted to emulate her and get involved in sports. "Loosen your girdle and let 'er fly!" was her response.

ZANGWILL, Israel (1864–1926), *British novelist and playwright.*

1 Andrew Lang wrote to inquire of his friend Israel Zangwill whether he planned to attend a certain event. The reply came back: "If you, Lang, will, I. Zangwill."

2 A *nouveau-riche* peer, whose accent did not match his social position, was feeling the effects of a heavy drinking session of the night before. "Oh, my 'ead! My 'ead!" he moaned. "What you need is two aspirates," recommended Zangwill.

ZENO (c. 335–c. 263 BC), *Greek philosopher, founder of the Stoic school of philosophy.*

1 Zeno caught his slave stealing, and gave him a good beating. The slave, something of a philosopher himself, pleaded, "But it was fated that I should steal."

"And that I should beat you," retorted Zeno.

ZEUXIS (c. 424–380 BC), *Greek painter.*

1 Zeuxis's painting of a boy holding a dish of grapes (*see* SIR GODFREY KNELLER 2) was executed by Zeuxis to prove that he could outdo his rival Parrhasius in trompe-l'oeil effects. When the birds attacked the grapes, it seemed certain that victory would go to Zeuxis, who then called upon Parrhasius to draw back the curtain concealing his own painting. But this supposed curtain was itself painted, and Zeuxis had to concede that while he had been able to deceive the birds, Parrhasius had been able to deceive him.

ZHOU ENLAI (1898–1976), *Chinese revolutionary, prime minister of the Peoples' Republic of China (1949–76).*

1 Khrushchev and Zhou got into a terrible argument, at the end of which the Russian premier said angrily to Zhou that the two statesmen had nothing in common and could therefore not communicate. One was the son of an aristocratic landlord while Khrushchev

himself was the son of a poor peasant. Zhou agreed, but noted that, in fact, the two men did have one thing in common. "Oh, what's that?" asked Khrushchev. Said Zhou, "We're both traitors to our class."

———— ⠑⠺ ————

ZOELLER, "Fuzzy" (1951–), *US golfer.*

1 Zoeller had lived life to the full on the golf circuit, thoroughly enjoying his time on and off the green. In discussion about the next generation of golfers, he dismissed their seemingly ascetic habits. "They eat their ba-

nanas and drink their fruit drinks, then go to bed. It's a miserable way to live."

———— ⠑⠺ ————

ZOG I (1895–1961), *king of Albania (1928–39), forced into exile by Mussolini.*

1 In 1940 Zog, accompanied by his royal retinue, arrived at the Ritz Hotel in London. Some of the luggage seemed remarkably heavy, exciting the curiosity of George, the hall porter. George asked the king whether they contained anything very valuable. "Yes," replied Zog, "gold."

Nicholas Murray Butler and Professor Brander Matthews of Columbia University were having a conversation and Professor Matthews was giving his ideas as to plagiarism, from an article of his own on that subject. "In the case of the first man to use an anecdote," he said, "there is originality; in the case of the second, there is plagiarism; with the third, it is lack of originality; and with the fourth it is drawing from a common stock."

"Yes," broke in President Butler, "and in the case of the fifth, it is research."

— B. A. BOTKIN, *A Treasury of American Anecdotes*

SOURCE LIST

———⌇———

Sources for the anecdotes are given wherever possible. Only names and titles are cited; full bibliographical information is given in the bibliography, which follows this list. Abbreviations used in the list:

DBQ   Richard Kenin and Justin Wintle, *Dictionary of Biographical Quotation*

DNB   *Dictionary of National Biography*

EB   *Encyclopaedia Britannica*

OBALA   *Oxford Book of American Literary Anecdotes*, ed. Donald Hall

OBLA   *Oxford Book of Literary Anecdotes*, ed. John Sutherland

Aaron 1: B. Uecker and M. Herskowitz, *Catcher in the Wry;* 2: D. Okrent and S. Wolf, eds., *Baseball Anecdotes;* 3: P. Dickson, *Baseball's Greatest Quotations;* 4: J. McBride, *High and Inside: The A–Z Guide to the Language of Baseball*

Abernethy 1: T. Pettigrew, *Medical Portrait Gallery,* in Kenin and Wintle, *DBQ;* 2: S. Smiles, *Self-Help,* in Kenin and Wintle, *DBQ;* 3: F. Winslow, *Physic and Physicians,* in D. George, *A Book of Anecdotes;* 4: G. Macilwain, *Memoirs of John Abernethy F.R.S.,* in Kenin and Wintle, *DBQ;* 5: E. Fuller, *2500 Anecdotes;* 6: W. Keddie, *Literary and Scientific Anecdote*

Acheson 1: *Time,* Dec. 22, 1952; 2: A. Schlesinger, Jr., in K. Halle, *Randolph Churchill*

Acton 1: P. Quennell, *The Sign of the Fish*

Adams, Alexander, 1: Oxfam, *Pass the Port*

Adams, Ansel, 1: *Ansel Adams: An Autobiography*

Adams, F. P., 1–2: R. Drennan, *The Algonquin Wits;* 3: O. Levant, *The Unimportance of Being Oscar;* 4–5: R. Drennan, *Wit's End*

Adams, H., 1: M. T. Chanler, *Roman Spring: Memoirs,* in D. Hall, ed., *OBALA*

Adams, J., 2: P. Smith, *John Adams,* in P. Boller, ed., *Presidential Anecdotes;* 4: *Columbian Sentinel,* July 12, 1826, in Boller, *Presidential Anecdotes*

Adams, J. Q., 1: E. Colman, *Seventy-Five Years of White House Gossip,* in P. Boller, ed., *Presidential Anecdotes;* 2: E. Fuller, *2500 Anecdotes;* 3: N. and B. Donaldson, *How Did They Die?*

Addams 1: E. Wagenknecht, *American Profile, 1900–1909*

Addison 1: R. Hendrickson, *The Literary Life*; 2: A. Bespaloff, *The Fireside Book of Wine*; 3: E. Fuller, *2500 Anecdotes*

Ade 1: J. Braude, *Speaker's and Toastmaster's Handbook*

Adee 1: '47, *The Magazine of the Year*, I

Adenauer 1: J. Gunther, *Procession*; 3: K. Edwards, *More Things I Wish I'd Said*

Adler 1: J. Braude, *Braude's Second Encyclopedia*

Aeschylus 1: *EB*

Agassiz 1: E. Fuller, *2500 Anecdotes*

Agrippina 1: 1–2: Tacitus, *Annals*

Aidan 1: Bede, *History of the English Church and People*

Albemarle 1: E. Guérard, *Dictionnaire Encyclopédique*

Albert 1: Sir S. Lee, *Queen Victoria*, in A. Hardy, *Queen Victoria Was Amused*; 2: B. Disraeli, *Reminiscences*, in Kenin and Wintle, *DBQ*

Albert, D', 1: H. Hoffmeister, *Anekdotenschatz*

Alcibiades 1: L. Harris, *The Fine Art of Political Wit*

Alcott, A., 1: C. Meigs, *Invincible Louisa*

Alcott, L., 1: M. Worthington, *Miss Alcott of Concord*

Alembert 1: I. Asimov, *Biographical Encyclopedia*

Alençon 1: C. Skinner, *Elegant Wits and Grand Horizontals*

Alexander, G., 1: J. Aye, *Humour in the Theatre*

Alexander, S., 1: Oxfam, *Pass the Port*

Alexander I 1: M. Paléologue, *The Enigmatic Czar*; 2: *Harper's Magazine*, April 1883, in C. Shriner, *Wit, Wisdom, and Foibles of the Great*; 3: L. Wechsler, "The Boy Wonder," *The New Yorker*, Nov. 17, 1986

Alexander III 1: 1–7: Plutarch, *Lives*; 8: F. Paley, *Greek Wit*

Alexander VI 1: O. Prescott, *Princes of the Renaissance*

Alexandra 1: R. Collier, *The Rainbow People*

Alfonso X 1: I. Asimov, *Biographical Encyclopedia*

Alfonso XIII 1: W. Churchill, *Great Contemporaries*

Alfred 2: *Asser's Life of King Alfred*

Ali 2–3: R. Crouser, *It's Unlucky to Be Behind at the End of the Game*; 5: P. O'Brian, *Talkin' Sports*

Allais 1: M. Pedrazzini and J. Gris, *Autant en apportent les mots*; 2: C. Skinner, *Elegant Wits and Grand Horizontals*

Allen, D. 1: D. Okrent and S. Wolf, eds., *Baseball Anecdotes*

Allen, E., 1: *Harper's Magazine*, July 1875, in C. Shriner, *Wit, Wisdom, and Foibles of the Great*; 2: C. Fadiman and C. Van Doren, *The American Treasury*; 3: D. Fisher, *Vermont Tradition*, in B. Botkin, *A Treasury of American Anecdotes*; 4: D. Wallechinsky and I. Wallace, *The People's Almanac*

Allen, F., 1: J. Bryan III, "Funny Man," *Saturday Evening Post*, Sept. 23, 1965; 2: C. Fadiman and C. Van Doren, *The American Treasury*; 3: J. Paar, *P.S. Jack Paar*

Allen, W., 1: P. Boller, ed., *Hollywood Anecdotes*; 2: P. Hay, ed., *Movie Anecdotes*

Allingham 1: J. Thorogood, *Margery Allingham: A Biography*

Alma-Tadema 1: W. Scholz, *Das Buch des Lachens*

Altenberg 1: S. Radecki, *Das ABC des Lachens*

Altman 1: M. Wiley and D. Bona, *Inside Oscar*

Alvanley 1–2: W. Adams, *Treasury of Modern Anecdote*

Ambrose 1: W. Durant, *The Story of Civilization*, IV

Ammonius 1: J. C. Roy, *Islands of Storm*

Anaxagoras 1: W. Durant, *The Story of Civilization*, II

Anaximenes 1: H. Hoffmeister, *Anekdotenschatz*

Anders 2: T. Ferris, *Coming of Age in the Milky Way*

Andersen 1–2: E. Bredsdorff, *Hans Christian Andersen*; 3: R. Godden, *Hans Christian An-*

dersen; 4: N. and B. Donaldson, *How Did They Die?*

Anderson 1: R. Nelson, *The Almanac of American Letters*

Andre 1: N. and B. Donaldson, *How Did They Die?*

Andrew 1: P. Bussard, *The New Catholic Treasury of Wit and Humor*

Anne, Princess, 2–3: E. Longford, *The Oxford Book of Royal Anecdotes*

Antheil 1: S. Beach, *Musicdotes*

Anthony, M., 1: Plutarch, *Lives*

Anthony, S., 1: W. Abbot, *Notable Women in History;* 2–3: M. Biggs, ed., *Women's Words: The Columbia Book of Quotations by Women*

Antisthenes 1: W. Durant, *The Story of Civilization,* II; 2: H. Hoffmeister, *Anekdotenschatz*

Apelles 1: W. Durant, *The Story of Civilization,* II; 2: E. Fuller, *2500 Anecdotes*

Aquinas 1: H. and D. L. Thomas, *Living Biographies of the Great Philosophers*

Archelaus 1: W. Durant, *The Story of Civilization,* II

Archer, G., 1: R. T. Sommers, *Golf Anecdotes*

Archer, W., 1: S. Behrman, *Portrait of Max*

Archimedes 1: *New Columbia Encyclopedia;* 2: W. Durant, *The Story of Civilization,* II; 3: E. Bell, *Men of Mathematics;* 4: I. Asimov, *Biographical Encyclopedia*

Arditi 1: F. Berger, *Reminiscences, Impressions, and Anecdotes*

Aristides 1: Plutarch, *Lives*

Aristippus 1–2: F. Callières, *Des Bons mots et des bons contes;* 3: E. Guérard, *Dictionnaire Encyclopédique*

Arlen 1: M. Arlen, *Exiles;* 2: *Book-of-the-Month Club News,* Mar. 1944

Armour 1: E. Fuller, *2500 Anecdotes*

Armstrong, L., 1: J. Collier, *Louis Armstrong;* 2: C. Fadiman and C. Van Doren, *The American Treasury;* 4–6: B. Crow, *Jazz Anecdotes*

Armstrong, N., 1: D. Wallechinsky and I. Wallace, *The People's Almanac;* 3: T. Friedman, *From Beirut to Jerusalem*

Arne 1: W. Cummings, *Dr. Arne and Rule, Britannia*

Arnim 1: W. Scholz, *Das Buch des Lachens*

Arno 1: B. Gill, *Here at The New Yorker*

Arnold 1: L. Trilling, *Matthew Arnold,* in J. Sutherland, ed., *OBLA;* 2: C. Sifakis, *Dictionary of Historic Nicknames*

Arnould 1, 3–4: L. Russell, *English Wits;* 2: E. Guérard, *Dictionnaire Encyclopédique*

Arria 1: *Oxford Classical Dictionary*

Asche 1: D. Knox, *More Quotable Anecdotes*

Asoka 1: W. Durant, *The Story of Civilization,* I

Asquith, H., 1: D. Frost and M. Deakin, *David Frost's Book of Millionaires*

Asquith, M., 1: W. Espy, *Another Almanac of Words at Play;* 2: C. Bowra, *Memories 1898–1939;* 3: J. Abdy and C. Grere, *The Souls;* 4: E. Longford, *The Queen*

Astaire 1–3: D. Niven, *Bring On the Empty Horses*

Astor, J. J., 1: C. Fadiman and C. Van Doren, *The American Treasury;* 2: E. Rachlis and J. Marquese, *The Landlords*

Astor, M. D., 1: J. Smith, *Elsie de Wolfe*

Astor, N.W., 1: *Observer,* Feb. 7, 1982; 2–3: *DNB;* 5: M. Ringo, *Nobody Said It Better;* 6: W. Manchester, *The Last Lion*

Atkinson 1: L. Missen, *Quotable Anecdotes*

Atlas 1: D. Wallechinsky and I. Wallace, *The People's Almanac 2*

Auber 1: L. Russell, *English Wits;* 2: E. Guérard, *Dictionnaire Encyclopédique;* 4: W. Scholz, *Das Buch des Lachens*

Aubernon 1–3: C. Skinner, *Elegant Wits and Grand Horizontals*

Aubigné 1: L. Missen, *After-Dinner Stories and Anecdotes*

Auden 1: H. Carpenter, *W. H. Auden;* 2, 4: W. Espy, *An Almanac of Words at Play;* 3: *Book-of-the-Month Club News,* Dec. 1946; 5, 8: C. Osborne, *W. H. Auden: The Life of a Poet,* in D. Hall, ed., *OBALA;* 6–7: S. Spender, ed., *W. H. Auden: A Tribute,* in D. Hall, ed., *OBALA;* 9: W. S. Johnson, *W. H. Auden*

Auerbach 1: *Los Angeles Times*, Nov. 11, 1982; 2: A. Barra, *That's Not the Way It Was*

Augustine 1: *Oxford Dictionary of Quotations*

Augustus 1: Plutarch, *Lives;* 2–5: Macrobius, *Saturnalia;* 6: W. Durant, *The Story of Civilization*, III

Aumale 1: A., Castelot, *Paris: The Turbulent City;* 2–5: C. Skinner, *Elegant Wits and Grand Horizontals*

Austin, A., 1: E. Marsh, *A Number of People*

Austin, W., 1: C. Fadiman and C. Van Doren, *The American Treasury*

Avempace 1: W. Durant, *The Story of Civilization*, IV

Avery 1: L. Thomas, *Late Night Thoughts*

Aymé 1: M. and A. Guillois, *Liberté, Egalité, Hilarité*

Azeglio 1: H. Morton, *A Traveller in Italy*

Babbage 1: R. Hendrickson, *The Literary Life;* 2: C. Darwin, *Autobiography,* in Kenin and Wintle, *DBQ*

Bacall 1: O. Levant, *The Unimportance of Being Oscar;* 2: D. Wallechinsky and I. Wallace, *The People's Almanac 2;* 3: P. Hay, ed., *Movie Anecdotes*

Bach, C., 1: H. Schonberg, *The Great Pianists*

Bach, J. S., 1: S. Sadie, *New Grove Dictionary of Music and Musicians*

Bacon 1: J. Aubrey, *Brief Lives;* 2: E. Fuller, *2500 Anecdotes;* 3: L. Missen, *After-Dinner Stories and Anecdotes;* 4–5: H. Hoffmeister, *Anekdotenschatz*

Bader 1: *Los Angeles Times*, Sept. 7, 1982

Baeyer 1: J. Read, *Humour and Humanism in Chemistry*

Bahr 1: W. Scholz, *Das Buch des Lachens*

Bailly 1: H. Hoffmeister, *Anekdotenschatz*

Baker 1–2: I. Wallace et al., *Intimate Sex Lives of Famous People*

Bakst 1: A. Dolin, *Friends and Memories*

Balanchine 1: B. Taper, *Balanchine: A Biography*

Baldwin 1: *DNB;* 2: *The Times* (London), Mar. 17, 1982

Balfour 1: J. Abdy and C. Grere, *The Souls*

Balmain 1: R. Buckle, ed., *Self-Portrait with Friends*

Balsan 1: C. Canfield, *Up and Down and Around*

Balzac 1: I. Wallace et al., *Intimate Sex Lives of Famous People;* 2, 5: E. Fuller, *2500 Anecdotes;* 3: J. Timbs, *Century of Anecdote;* 4: D. George, *A Book of Anecdotes;* 6: E. de Goncourt, *Journal des Goncourts;* 7: D. Wallechinsky and I. Wallace, *The People's Almanac;* 8: J. Train, *True Remarkable Occurrences;* 9: D. Boorstin, *The Creators*

Bancroft 1: S. Behrman, *Portrait of Max*

Bankhead 1: L. Hellman, *Pentimento;* 2: R. Drennan, *Wit's End;* 3: H. Teichmann, *Smart Aleck;* 4: M. Ringo, *Nobody Said It Better;* 5–6: D. Herrmann, *With Malice Toward All;* 7: J. Paar, *P.S. Jack Paar;* 8: A. Faulkner and T. Hartman, *All the Best People;* 11: Celebrity Research Group, *The Bedside Book of Celebrity Gossip*

Banks 1: C. Fadiman, *Any Number Can Play*

Barbirolli 1: A. Previn, ed., *Orchestra*

Barham 1: W. Adams, *Treasury of Modern Anecdote;* 2: *DNB*

Barnes 1: *New York Times Book Review,* June 26, 1983; 2: G. Davenport, *The Geography of the Imagination;* 3: N. D. Murray, *Darlinghissima: Letters to a Friend*

Barnum 1: H. Rawson, *Dictionary of Euphemisms;* 2: I. Wallace, *The Fabulous Showman;* 3: L. Lucaire, *Celebrity Trivia;* 4: N. and B. Donaldson, *How Did They Die?*

Barr 1: *Los Angeles Times,* Feb. 8, 1981

Barrie 1–2, 4–5: C. Asquith, *Portrait of Barrie;* 3: I. Wallace, "Significa," July 24, 1983; 6: J. Dunbar, *J. M. Barrie;* 7: R. Marquard, *Jokes and Anecdotes;* 8: E. Fuller, *2500 Anecdotes;* 9: E. Adams, ed., *Mrs. J. Comyns Carr's Reminiscences,* in J. Sutherland, ed., *OBLA;* 10: J. Aye, *Humour in the Theatre*

Barrow 1: J. Larwood, *Anecdotes of the Clergy*

Barrows 1: M. Biggs, ed., *Women's Words: The Columbia Book of Quotations by Women*

Barrymore, E. 1: J. Braude, *Speaker's and Toastmaster's Handbook;* 2: J. McAleer, "Globe

Man's Daily Story," *Boston Globe,* 1967; 3: N. and B. Donaldson, *How Did They Die?*

Barrymore, J., 1, 9: I. Wallace et al., *Intimate Sex Lives of Famous People;* 2: G. Lieberman, *The Greatest Laughs of All Time;* 3: B. Cerf, *Try and Stop Me;* 4: D. Niven, *Bring On the Empty Horses;* 5: E. Fuller, *2500 Anecdotes;* 6: R. Marquard, *Jokes and Anecdotes;* 7: M. Griffin, *From Where I Sit;* 8: J. Train, *Wit: The Best Things Ever Said*

Barrymore, M., 1: G. Fowler, *Good Night, Sweet Prince*

Bartók 1: V. Thomson, *A Virgil Thomson Reader*

Barton 1: J. C. Humes, *Speaker's Treasury;* 2: M. Biggs, ed., *Women's Words: The Columbia Book of Quotations by Women*

Baruch 1: *The New Yorker,* Jan. 10, 1948; 2: B. Cerf, *Bumper Crop of Anecdotes*

Basie 1: S. Dance, *The World of Count Basie*

Baum 2: D. P. Mannix, "The Father of Oz," in *A Sense of History*

Baylis 1: B. Forbes, *Ned's Girl;* 2: *The New Yorker,* Sept. 16, 1950

Bean 1: B. Botkin, *Treasury of American Anecdotes*

Beaton 1–2: R. Buckle, ed., *Self-Portrait with Friends*

Beatty 1: *DNB*

Beaumont 1: J. Boswell, *Life of Johnson*

Beckett 1: W. Lowenfels, *The Paris Years;* 2: D. Bair, *Samuel Beckett*

Beckford 1: W. P. Frith, *My Autobiography and Reminiscences,* in J. Sutherland, ed., *OBLA;* 2: J. Gere and J. Sparrow, *Geoffrey Madan's Notebooks*

Beecham, T., 1: Kenin and Wintle, *DBQ*

Beecham, Sir T., 1–2, 5–10: H. Atkins and A. Newman, eds., *Beecham Stories;* 4: L. Humphrey, *The Humor of Music;* 11: S. Beach, *Musicdotes*

Beecher 1: L. and F. Copeland, *10,000 Jokes, Toasts, and Stories;* 2: T. Masson, *The Best Stories in the World;* 3: T. Masson, ed., *Little*

Masterpieces of American Wit and Humor, in R. Shenkman and K. Reiger, *One-Night Stands with American History;* 4: E. Fuller, *2500 Anecdotes*

Beerbohm 2–4: D. Cecil, *Max: A Biography*

Beethoven 2: E. Forbes, ed., *Thayer's Life of Beethoven;* 3: A. Hopkins, *Music All Around Me;* 4, 6: S. Sadie, *New Grove Dictionary of Music and Musicians;* 5: F. Bonavia, ed., *Musicians on Music;* 7–8: N. Lebrecht, *The Book of Musical Anecdotes;* 9: N. and B. Donaldson, *How Did They Die?*

Begin 1: I. Wallace et al., *Book of Lists 2*

Behan 1: R. Jeffs, *Brendan Behan, Man and Showman;* 2: B. Behan, *My Life with Brendan;* 3: G. Brandreth, *Great Theatrical Disasters*

Bell, A., 1: J. J. Carty, *The Smithsonian Report for 1922,* in Kenin and Wintle, *DBQ;* 2: I. Wallace et al., *Intimate Sex Lives of Famous People*

Bell, J., 1–2: I. Wallace, *The Fabulous Originals*

Belloc 1: R. Hendrickson, *The Literary Life;* 2: *New York Times Book Review,* Aug. 2, 1982; 3: A. Wilson, *Hilaire Belloc*

Bellows 1: E. Speicher, *A Personal Reminiscence,* in Kenin and Wintle, *DBQ*

Bembo 1: S. Radecki, *Das ABC des Lachens*

Benchley 1: N. Rees, *Quote . . . Unquote;* 2: E. Fuller, *2500 Anecdotes;* 3: *Saturday Evening Post,* Sept. 23, 1965; 4: H. Teichmann, *Smart Aleck;* 5: B. Cerf, *Try and Stop Me;* 6: K. Tynan, *Show People;* 7: H. Thurber and E. Weeks, eds., *Selected Letters of James Thurber;* 8: D. Herrmann, *With Malice Toward All;* 9–10: R. Drennan, *The Algonquin Wits;* 11: N. Benchley, *Robert Benchley,* in D. Hall, ed., *OBALA;* 12: N. and B. Donaldson, *How Did They Die?*

Bennett, A., 1: B. Cerf, *Shake Well Before Using;* 2: R. Hendrickson, *The Literary Life;* 3: J. McAleer, "Globe Man's Daily Story," Aug. 31, 1966; 4: E. Goossens, *Overture and Beginners*

Bennett, J., 1: B. Morton, *Americans in Paris;* 2: P. Brendon, *The Life and Death of the Press*

Barons; 3–4: D. Frost and M. Deakin, *David Frost's Book of Millionaires*

Benton 1: E. Fuller, *2500 Anecdotes;* 2: *Harper's Magazine,* in R. Shenkman and K. Reiger, *One-Night Stands with American History*

Berg 1: J. McBride, *High and Inside: The A–Z Guide to the Language of Baseball*

Beria 1: J. Gunther, *Inside Russia Today*

Bernadotte 1: S. Radecki, *Das ABC des Lachens*

Bernard 1, 5–7: C. Skinner, *Elegant Wits and Grand Horizontals;* 4: E. Kelen, *Peace in Their Time*

Berners 1–3: E. Sitwell, *Taken Care Of;* 4: E. Salter, *Helpmann;* 5: J. Bryan, III, ed., *Hodge-podge: A Commonplace Book*

Bernhardt 1–2, 4, 6: A. May, *Different Drummers;* 3: *Oxford Dictionary of Quotations;* 5: L. and M. Cowan, *The Wit of Women;* 7, 10–11: C. Skinner, *Elegant Wits and Grand Horizontals;* 8: E. Fuller, *2500 Anecdotes;* 9: L. Missen, *Quotable Anecdotes;* 12: J. Braude, *Speaker's and Toastmaster's Handbook*

Bernoulli 1: J. E. Bell, *Men of Mathematics*

Bernstein, H., 1: B. Cerf, *The Life of the Party*

Bernstein, L., 1: H. Temianka, *Facing the Music;* 3–4: N. Lebrecht, *The Book of Musical Anecdotes*

Bernstein, R., 1: P. Schwed, *Turning the Pages*

Berra 4: L. Rosten, *People I Have Loved, Known, or Admired;* 5: W. Espy, *An Almanac of Words at Play;* 6: R. Crouser, *It's Unlucky to Be Behind at the End of the Game;* 7–8, 10–13: D. Okrent and S. Wolf, eds., *Baseball Anecdotes;* 9: Y. Berra, *The Yogi Book;* 14–15: J. McBride, *High and Inside: The A–Z Guide to the Language of Baseball;* 16: A. Stevens, "Shell Shocked; More Baseball Memories with Jim Bouton," *The Sanibel/Captiva Islander,* Dec. 1, 1992; 18: A. Barra, *That's Not the Way It Was*

Betty 1: A. Matthews, *Anecdotes of Action,* in F. Muir, *Irreverent Social History*

Beuno 1: '48, *The Magazine of the Year,* vol. 2, no. 4

Bialik 1: W. Novak and M. Waldoks, *The Big Book of Jewish Humor*

Bing 1–6, 8: Sir R. Bing, *5000 Nights at the Opera;* 7: Sir. R. Bing, *A Knight at the Opera*

Bion 1: E. Fuller, *2500 Anecdotes*

Bismarck 1, 7: E. Crankshaw, *Bismarck;* 2: C. Shriner, *Wit, Wisdom, and Foibles of the Great;* 3: W. Scholz, *Das Buch des Laches;* 4: H. Ziegler, *Heitere Muse;* 5–6: H. Hoffmeister, *Anekdotenschatz;* 8: R. K. Massie, *Dreadnought: Britain, Germany and the Coming of the Great War*

Blackwell 1: A. Powell, *London Walks*

Blake, E., 1–2: *The Times* (London), Feb. 15, 1983

Blake, W., 1: R. Hendrickson, *The Literary Life;* 2–3: J. Timbs, *English Eccentrics*

Blech 1: H. Hoffmeister, *Anekdotenschatz*

Blessington 1: D. Duff, *Eugénie and Napoleon III*

Blomberg 1: C. Jones, *What Makes Winners Win*

Blume 1: J. Wintle and E. Fisher, *The Pied Pipers*

Blumenthal 1: H. Hoffmeister, *Anekdotenschatz*

Bogart 1: V. Thompson, *Bogie and Me*

Bogdanovich 1: P. Hay, ed., *Movie Anecdotes*

Boileau 1: R. Hendrickson, *The Literary Life;* 2: V. Cronin, *Louis XIV*

Boleyn 1: I. Wallace et al., *Intimate Sex Lives of Famous People;* 2: W. Abbot, *Notable Women in History*

Bolingbroke 1: *DNB*

Bolt 1–2: *Los Angeles Times,* Mar. 13, 1982

Bonner 1: G. Taylor, *The Great Evolution Mystery*

Boone 1: *Book-of-the-Month Club News,* Oct. 1972

Booth, J. B., 1, 4: W. Winter, *Other Days;* 2: E. Fuller, *2500 Anecdotes;* 3: G. Vidal, *Lincoln*

Borges 1: R. Alifano, *Twenty-Four Conversations with Borges*

Borghese 1: M. Marmont, *Memoirs,* in C. Shriner, *Wit, Wisdom, and Foibles of the Great*

Borromeo 1: P. Bussard, *The New Catholic Treasury of Wit and Humor*

Bosquet 1: C. Woodham-Smith, *The Reason Why*

Bossuet 1: W. Keddie, *Literary and Scientific Anecdote;* 2: J. Larwood, *Anecdotes of the Clergy*

Boswell 1: *EB;* 2: H. Pearson, *Johnson and Boswell*

Botticelli 1: G. Vasari, *Lives of the Painters*

Bottomley 1: A. Sylvester, *Life with Lloyd George;* 2: A. J. P. Taylor, *English History 1914–1945,* in Kenin and Wintle, *DBQ*

Bouhours 1: B. Conrad, *Famous Last Words*

Boulanger, G., 1: I. Wallace, *The Nympho & Other Maniacs*

Boulanger, N., 1: A. Kendall, *The Tender Tyrant*

Boult 1: A. Boyle, *Only the Wind Will Listen*

Bowen, E., 1: H. Moss, *Whatever Is Moving*

Bowen, L., 1: M. Cable, *Top Drawer*

Bowles, P., 1: M. Dillon, review of P. Bowles's *Two Years Beside the Strait: Tangier Journal 1967–1987, Times Literary Supplement,* Sept. 7–14, 1990

Bowles, W., 1–2: S. C. Hall, *A Book of Memories,* in D. George, *A Book of Anecdotes*

Bowra 1: Oxfam, *Pass the Port*

Bradford 1: J. Bartlett, *Bartlett's Familiar Quotations*

Bradley 1: R. Bridges, *Three Friends,* in J. Sutherland, ed., *OBLA*

Brady 1: B. Cerf, *Bumper Crop of Anecdotes*

Brahe 1: N. and B. Donaldson, *How Did They Die?*

Brahms 1, 3–4: P. Latham, *Brahms;* 5: A. Rubinstein, *My Younger Years;* 6, 8: N. Slominsky, *A Thing or Two About Music;* 7: P. Méras, *The Mermaids of Chenonceaux;* 10: J. Braude, *Braude's Second Encyclopedia*

Braithwaite 1: G. Brandreth, *Great Theatrical Disasters;* 2: A. Faulkner and T. Hartman, *All the Best People*

Brancusi 1: *Compton's Encyclopedia*

Braque 1: R. Penrose, *Ronald Penrose Scrapbook*

Brendel 1: Letter from Emily Misser, *London Review of Books,* May 25, 1992

Briand 1–2: E. Kelen, *Peace in Their Time*

Bridger 1–2: *American Scholar,* VIII (1938–39)

Brillat-Savarin 1: D. Wallechinsky and I. Wallace, *The People's Almanac*

Britten 1–2: N. Lebrecht, *The Book of Musical Anecdotes*

Brodie, Sir B., 1: L. Cliffe, *Anecdotal Reminiscences*

Brodie, W., 1: *"Daily Mirror" Old Codger's Little Black Book 4*

Brontë, C., 1: A. Harrison and D. Stanford, *Anne Brontë;* 2: D. Frost, *Book of the World's Worst Decisions*

Brookfield 1: J. Aye, *Humour in the Theatre*

Brooks, P., 1: J. Braude, *Speaker's and Toastmaster's Handbook*

Brougham 1: N. McPhee, *The Book of Insults;* 2: S. Smith, *Memoir of the Rev. Sydney Smith by His Daughter;* 3: K. Arvine, *Cyclopaedia of Anecdotes*

Broun 1: G. Brandreth, *Great Theatrical Disasters;* 2: H. Broun, *Whose Little Boy Are You?*

Brown, C. B., 1: D. L. Clark, *Charles Brockden Brown: Pioneer Voice of America,* in D. Hall, ed., *OBALA*

Brown, G., 1–2: D. Okrent and S. Wolf, eds., *Baseball Anecdotes*

Brown, J., 1: *The New Yorker,* Oct. 18, 1952; 2: C. Canfield, *Up and Down and Around*

Browning, E., 1: F. Winwar, *The Immortal Lovers;* 2: A. Bernard, *Now All We Need Is a Title*

Browning, R., 1: B. Cerf, *Laughing Stock;* 2: G. W. E. Russell, *Collections,* in J. Sutherland, ed., *OBLA;* 3: F. Winwar, *The Immortal Lovers*

Bruce 1: J. Pinkerton, *Walpoliana,* in Kenin and Wintle, *DBQ*

Brummell 1–5: J. Timbs, *Century of Anecdote;* 6: D. George, *A Book of Anecdotes;* 8: E. Sitwell, *English Eccentrics*

Brunet 1: D. Okrent and S. Wolf, eds., *Baseball Anecdotes*

Bruno 1: *EB*

Bryan 1: E. Fuller, *2500 Anecdotes;* 2: I. Stone,

They Also Ran; 3: C. Fadiman and C. Van Doren, *The American Treasury*

Buchanan 1: A. C. Buell, *History of Andrew Jackson,* in P. Boller, ed., *Presidential Anecdotes;* 2: C. Fadiman and C. Van Doren, *The American Treasury*

Buckingham 1: C. Roberts, *And So to Bath*

Buckland 1: J. Morris, *The Oxford Book of Oxford;* 2: W. Keddie, *Literary and Scientific Anecdote*

Buckley 1: *Los Angeles Times,* Apr. 11, 1982

Buddha 1: R. Tung, *A Portrait of Lost Tibet;* 2: W. Durant, *The Story of Civilization,* I

Budé 1: C. Fadiman, *Any Number Can Play*

Buffalmacco 1: G. Vasari, *Lives of the Painters*

Bull 1: P. Phillips, *A Brief Chronicale;* 2: Anthony à Wood, *Fasti Oxonienses,* in Kenin and Wintle, *DBQ*

Buller 1: S. Weintraub, *The London Yankees*

Bülow 1: H. Schonberg, *The Great Pianists;* 2–3: N. Slominsky, *A Thing or Two About Music;* 4: H. Schonberg, *The Great Conductors*

Bunsen 1: J. Read, *Humour and Humanism in Chemistry*

Burke 1: K. C. Balderston, ed., *Thraliana,* in J. Sutherland, ed., *OBLA;* 2–3: J. Timbs, *Century of Anecdote;* 4: W. Keddie, *Literary and Scientific Anecdote;* 5: W. Adams, *Treasury of Modern Anecdote*

Burns 1: S. Allen, *Funny People;* 2: G. Burns, *Third Time Around*

Burr 2: N. and B. Donaldson, *How Did They Die?*

Burton, R., 2: Interview with Dick Cavett, PBS, 1986

Burton, Sir R., 1: M. Hastings, *Richard Burton;* 2: L. Blanch, *The Wilder Shores of Love*

Busby 1–2: E. Fuller, *2500 Anecdotes*

Busch 1: Sir R. Bing, *5000 Nights at the Opera*

Bush, B., 1–3: B. Dole, *Great Political Wit*

Bush, G., 1–3: B. Dole, *Great Political Wit;* 4: C. Jones, *What Makes Winners Win*

Butler, B. F., 1: D. Wallechinsky and I. Wallace, *The People's Almanac;* 2: Herbert W. Beecher, *History of the First Light Battery Connecticut*

Volunteers 1861–1865, in B. Botkin, *A Civil War Treasury*

Butler, H. M., 1: A. Milne, *It's Too Late Now*

Butler, S., 1: H. Festing Jones, *Samuel Butler: A Memoir,* in J. Sutherland, ed., *OBLA;* 2: M. MacCarthy, *A Nineteenth-Century Childhood,* in Sutherland, *OBLA;* 3–5: G. Keynes and B. Hill, eds., *Samuel Butler's Notebooks*

Byng 1: H. Walpole, *Memoirs,* in Kenin and Wintle, *DBQ*

Byrd 1: A. Hatch, *The Byrds of Virginia*

Byron 1: W. Keddie, *Literary and Scientific Anecdote;* 2: S. Rogers, *Table Talk;* 3–4: K. Arvine, *Cyclopaedia of Anecdotes*

Cabell 1: B. Cerf, *The Life of the Party*

Cadbury 1: I. and R. Poley, *Friendly Anecdotes*

Caen 1: B. Conrad, *Fun While It Lasted*

Caesar, Julius, 1–4, 8–9: Suetonius, *The Twelve Caesars;* 5–7: Plutarch, *Lives*

Cagliostro 1: W. Scholz, *Das Buch des Lachens*

Cagney 1: *Parade,* Aug. 5, 1984; 2–3: Charles Champlin, *Los Angeles Times*

Caine 1: *Book-of-the-Month Club News,* 1947

Calhern 1: *New York Times Book Review,* July 12, 1981

Caligula 1, 3–5: Suetonius, *The Twelve Caesars;* 2: W. Durant, *The Story of Civilization,* III

Callas 1: Sir R. Bing, *5000 Nights at the Opera;* 3: N. Lebrecht, *The Book of Musical Anecdotes*

Cambridge 1: H. and D. L. Thomas, *Living Biographies of Famous Women*

Cambronne 1: D. Wallechinsky and I. Wallace, *The People's Almanac*

Cambyses II 1: W. Durant, *The Story of Civilization,* I

Cameron, J. 1: R. Martin, *Tennyson: The Unquiet Heart*

Cameron of Lochiel 1: T. Mason, *The Best Stories in the World*

Campbell, Mrs. P., 1: G. Fallon, *Sean O'Casey, The Man I Knew,* in J. Sutherland, ed., *OBLA;* 2: G. Kanin, *Hollywood;* 3: L. Missen, *Quotable Anecdotes;* 5, 8: M. Peters, *Mrs. Pat;* 6: C. Tomkins, *Living Well Is the*

Best Revenge; 7: J. Braude, *Speaker's and Toastmaster's Handbook*

Campbell, T., 1: Sir G. Trevelyan, *The Life and Letters of Lord Macauley;* 2: W. Keddie, *Literary and Scientific Anecdote*

Cane 1: C. Speroni, *Wit and Wisdom of the Italian Renaissance*

Canning 1: J. Timbs, *Century of Anecdote;* 2: C. Sifakis, *Dictionary of Historic Nicknames*

Cannon 1: M. Schlesinger, *Snatched from Oblivion*

Canute 1: Henry of Huntingdon, *Historia Anglorum*

Capa 1: *'47, The Magazine of the Year*

Capone 1: J. Kobler, *Capone*

Capus 1: C. Skinner, *Elegant Wits and Grand Horizontals*

Caray 1–2: D. Okrent and S. Wolf, eds., *Baseball Anecdotes*

Cardano 1: I. Asimov, *Biographical Encyclopedia*

Cardozo 1: R. Marquard, *Jokes and Anecdotes*

Carême 1: W. H. Auden, *A Certain World: A Commonplace Book*

Carillo 1: M. Biggs, ed., *Women's Words: The Columbia Book of Quotations by Women*

Carleton 1: E. Fuller, *2500 Anecdotes*

Carlos I 1: H. Prochnow, *The Public Speaker's Treasure Chest*

Carlton 1: D. Okrent and S. Wolf, eds., *Baseball Anecdotes;* 2: M. Shannon, *Tales from the Dugout: The Greatest True Baseball Stories Ever*

Carlyle 2: Sir Mountstuart Elphinstone Grant Duff, *Notes from a Diary,* in Sutherland, *OBLA;* 3: N. Rees, *Quote . . . Unquote;* 4: A. J. C. Hare, *The Story of My Life*

Carnegie 1: G. Fowler, *Beau James;* 2: E. Wagenknecht, *American Profile;* 3: E. Fuller, *2500 Anecdotes;* 4: *Book-of-the-Month Club News,* Dec. 1952; 5: R. L. Heilbroner, "Carnegie & Rockefeller" in *A Sense of History*

Carol II 1: J. Braude, *Speaker's and Toastmaster's Handbook*

Caroline, Duchesse De Berri, 1: A. Castelot, *Paris: The Turbulent City*

Caroline of Ansbach 1: J. Timbs, *Century of Anecdote;* 2: Hervey, *Memoirs of George the Second,* in *Oxford Dictionary of Quotations*

Caroline of Brunswick 1: E. Fuller, *2500 Anecdotes;* 2: M. Ringo, *Nobody Said It Better;* 3: A. Bryant, *The Age of Elegance;* 4: The Journal of Hon. Henry Edward Fox, 25 Aug. 1821, in Kenin and Wintle, *DBQ*

Caroto 1–2: G. Vasari, *Lives of the Painters*

Carroll, L. 1: L. Missen, *Quotable Anecdotes;* 2: R. Green, *Diaries of Lewis Carroll;* 3: N. and B. Donaldson, *How Did They Die?*

Carson 1: K. Tynan, *Show People;* 2–3: S. Cox, *Here's Johnny;* 4: E. Drew, *Portrait of an Election,* in P. F. Boller, ed., *Presidential Campaigns*

Carter 2, 4, 9–10: B. Dole, *Great Political Wit;* 3: Kandy Stroud, *How Jimmy Won,* in P. Boller, ed., *Presidential Campaigns;* 5: Bill Adler, ed., *Wit and Wisdom of Jimmy Carter,* in Boller, *Presidential Anecdotes;* 6: J. Carter, *Keeping Faith;* 7: "He Can Catch Fire," *Time,* Jan. 5, 1981, in Boller, *Presidential Anecdotes;* 8: R. Byrne, *The 637 Best Things Anybody Ever Said*

Cartland 1: J. Cooper, *Class*

Caruso 1: D. Wallechinsky and I. Wallace, *The People's Almanac;* 2: H. Greenfield, *Caruso;* 3: E. Van de Velde, *Anecdotes Musicales*

Casals 1: A. Whitman, *Come to Judgment;* 2–3: M. Eastman, *Great Companions;* 4: Y. Karsh, *Karsh*

Cassatt 1: A. Vollard, *Recollections of a Picture Dealer*

Castiglione 1: I. Wallace et al., *Intimate Sex Lives of Famous People*

Castlerosse 1: P. Ziegler, *Diana Cooper*

Castracani 1: Ludovico Domenichi in C. Speroni, *Wit and Wisdom of the Italian Renaissance*

Castro 1–2: C. Franqui, *Family Portrait with Fidel*

Cather 1: W. Bynner, *Prose Pieces,* in D. Hall, ed., *OBALA*

Catherine of Aragon 1: W. Abbot, *Notable Women in History*

Catherine II 1: W. Abbot, *Notable Women in History*

Cato 1: *Oxford Companion to Classical History;* 2: J. Braude, *Speaker's and Toastmaster's Handbook;* 3: F. Callières, *Des Bons mots et des bons contes*

Cavell 1: *The Times* (London), Oct. 23, 1915, in *Oxford Dictionary of Quotations*

Cecil 1: J. Train, *True Remarkable Occurrences*

Cervantes 1: *Compton's Encyclopedia*

Cetewayo 1: J. Smail, *With Shield and Assegai*

Cézanne 1: *Compton's Encyclopedia*

Chaliapin 1–2: S. Beach, *Musicdotes;* 3: R. Merrill, *Between Acts*

Chaloner 1: *The New Yorker,* Nov. 26, 1955

Chamberlain, J., 1: T. Masson, *The Best Stories in the World*

Chamberlain, Sir J. A., 1: Frances Stevenson diary, Mar. 5, 1919, in Kenin and Wintle, *DBQ*

Chandler 1: F. MacShane, *The Life of Raymond Chandler,* in D. Hall, ed., *OBALA*

Chanel 1: F. Steegmuller, *Cocteau;* 3: M. Biggs, ed., *Women's Words: The Columbia Book of Quotations by Women*

Channing 1: B. Adler, *My Favorite Funny Story*

Chaplin 1: C. Seelig, *Albert Einstein;* 2: L. Lucaire, *Celebrity Trivia;* 3: D. Niven, *Bring On the Empty Horses;* 4: E. Fuller, *2500 Anecdotes*

Chapman, John, 1: Robert Price, *Johnny Appleseed, Man and Myth,* in B. Botkin, *Treasury of American Anecdotes;* 2: P. Smith, *The Nation Comes of Age*

Chapman, John Jay, 1: C. Canfield, *Up and Down and Around*

Charlemagne 1: Draper and Esquin sales brochure

Charles II 1: T. Blount, *Boscobel;* 2: J. Aubrey, *Miscellanies;* 3: Gilbert Burnet, *History of My Own Time,* in Kenin and Wintle, *DBQ;* 4: James Granger, *Biographical History of England,* in Kenin and Wintle, *DBQ;* 5: I. and R. Poley, *Friendly Anecdotes;* 6: William King,

Anecdotes, in D. George, *A Book of Anecdotes;* 7: Jonathan Richardson, *Richardsoniana,* in J. Sutherland, ed., *OBLA;* 8: J. Bartlett, *Bartlett's Familiar Quotations;* 9: Gilbert Burnet, *History of My Own Time,* in B. Conrad, *Famous Last Words*

Charles V 1: W. Durant, *The Story of Civilization,* V; 2: H. Prochnow, *The Public Speaker's Treasure Chest*

Charles X 1–2: W. Adams, *Treasury of Modern Anecdote*

Charles Francis Joseph 1: H. Hoffmeister, *Anekdotenschatz*

Charlotte of Mecklenburg-Strelitz 1: J. Timbs, *Century of Anecdote*

Charondas 1: W. Durant, *The Story of Civilization,* II

Chase, I., 1: E. Fuller, *2500 Anecdotes*

Chase, S., 1: B. Cerf, *Bumper Crop of Anecdotes*

Chateaubriand 1: M. Ringo, *Nobody Said It Better;* 2: C. Brinton, *The Lives of Talleyrand*

Chekhov 1: A. Chekhov, *The Image of Chekhov;* 2: J. Epstein, "Chekhov's Last Souls," *The New Criterion,* May 1986; 3: H. Troyat, *Chekhov*

Cherubini 1: W. Gates, *Anecdotes of Great Musicians;* 2: H. Hoffmeister, *Anekdotenshatz;* 3: J. Papesch, *Europa Lächelt Noch Immer;* 4: H. Sievers, *Musica Curiosa*

Chesterfield 1, 4: E. Fuller, *2500 Anecdotes;* 2: J. Timbs, *Century of Anecdote;* 3: *DNB*

Chesterton 1, 7–8: A. Dale, *The Outline of Sanity;* 2–3, 12: G. Chesterton, *Charles Dickens* (foreword); 4: H. Hoffmeister, *Anekdotenschatz;* 6: W. Scholz, *Das Buch des Lachens;* 9: H. Pearson, *Lives of the Wits;* 10: J. Braude, *Speaker's and Toastmaster's Handbook;* 11: C. Asquith, *Portrait of Barrie;* 14: B. Cerf, *Try and Stop Me;* 15: J. Train, *Wit: The Best Things Ever Said*

Chigi 1: P. Méras, *The Mermaids of Chenonceaux*

Choate 1–2, 4: T. Strong, *Joseph Choate;* 3: M. Ringo, *Nobody Said It Better;* 5: E. Fuller, *2500 Anecdotes*

Chopin 1: H. Finck, *Musical Laughs;* 2: N. Slonimsky, *A Thing or Two About Music*

Christian X 1: K. Edwards, *More Things I Wish I'd Said*

Christie, A. 1: B. Cerf, *The Life of the Party;* 2: I. Wallace, "Significa," Nov. 13, 1983

Christina 1: W. Abbot, *Notable Women in History*

Churchill, R., 1: K. Halle, *Randolph Churchill;* 2: W. Manchester, *The Last Lion,* vol. II: *Alone: Winston Churchill 1932–1940*

Churchill, Lord R., 1: A. Leslie, *The Remarkable Mr. Jerome*

Churchill, Sir W. 1: *Book-of-the-Month Club News,* Apr. 1954; 2, 25, 35: L. Rosten, *People I Have Loved, Known, or Admired;* 3–4: E. Marsh, *A Number of People;* 5: V. Bonham Carter, *Winston Churchill, An Intimate Portrait,* in W. Manchester, *The Last Lion;* 6: A. Sylvester, *Life with Lloyd George;* 7: E. Langhorne, *Nancy Astor and Her Friends,* in Kenin and Wintle, *DBQ;* 8: K. Halle, *Randolph Churchill;* 9: W. Churchill, *Thoughts and Adventures;* 11: M. MacDonald, *Titans and Others;* 12: L. Missen, *Quotable Anecdotes;* 14: *DNB;* 15, 20: R. Collier, *The Road to Pearl Harbor;* 16, 28–30: W. Manchester, *The Last Lion;* 18, 21, 36: O. Levant, *The Unimportance of Being Oscar;* 19: J. Green, *Morrow's Dictionary of Quotations;* 23: N. Rees, *Quote . . . Unquote;* 24: *Penguin Dictionary of Quotations;* 26: M. and A. Guillois, *Liberté, Egalité, Hilarité;* 27: *Los Angeles Times,* Mar. 25, 1982; 32: S. Shadegg, *Clare Boothe Luce*

Chwolson 1: L. Rosten, *Joys of Yiddish*

Cibber 1: T. Davies, *Dramatic Miscellanies,* in Kenin and Wintle, *DBQ*

Cicero 1–2: Macrobius, *Saturnalia*

Cimon 1: Plutarch, *Lives*

Cinque 1: D. Wallechinsky and I. Wallace, *The People's Almanac*

Claire 1: R. Lamparski, *Whatever Became Of . . . ?*

Clark, G. R., 1: P. Smith, *The Shaping of America*

Clark, M. W., 1: J. Braude, *Speaker's and Toastmaster's Handbook*

Clay, C., 1: S. Sifakis, *Dictionary of Historic Nicknames*

Clay, H., 1: R. Marquard, *Jokes and Anecdotes;* 2: E. Fuller, *2500 Anecdotes;* 3: H. Wright and S. Rapport, *The Great Explorers;* 4: T. H. Clay, *Henry Clay,* in C. Shriner, *Wit, Wisdom, and Foibles of the Great;* 5: C. Fadiman and C. Van Doren, *The American Treasury;* 6: D. Knox, *More Quotable Anecdotes;* 7: L. Harris, *The Fine Art of Political Wit*

Clemenceau 1: E. Fuller, *2500 Anecdotes;* 2: M. and A. Guillois, *Liberté, Egalité, Hilarité;* 3: J. Braude, *Speaker's and Toastmaster's Handbook;* 4: A. Sylvester, *Life with Lloyd George;* 5: H. Acton, *More Memoirs of an Aesthete;* 6: B. Cerf, *Try and Stop Me;* 7: L. Missen, *After-Dinner Stories and Anecdotes;* 8: P. Smith, *America Enters the World;* 9: I. Hamilton, *Koestler*

Cleopatra 1: N. and B. Donaldson, *How Did They Die?*

Cleveland, 1: J. Schermerhorn, *Schermerhorn Stories,* in P. Boller, ed., *Presidential Anecdotes;* 2: *American Scholar* III (1934)

Clinton 1–5: B. Dole, *Great Political Wit*

Clive 1: Sir G. Trevelyan, *Life and Letters of Lord Macauley,* in D. George, *A Book of Anecdotes;* 2: D. George, *A Book of Anecdotes*

Clurman 1–2: R. Lewis, *Slings and Arrows*

Cobb 1: R. Marquard, *Jokes and Anecdotes;* 2: J. C. Humes, *Speaker's Treasury*

Cocteau 1: H. Acton, *More Memoirs of an Aesthete;* 2: H. Hoffmeister, *Anekdotenschatz;* 3: J. Braude, *Speaker's and Toastmaster's Handbook*

Cohan 1: O. Levant, *The Unimportance of Being Oscar;* 2: S. Marx and J. Clayton, *Rodgers and Hart;* 3: *Book-of-the-Month Club News,* Mar. 1944; 4: S. Alexander, *Talking Woman*

Cohn 1: M. Ringo, *Nobody Said It Better;* 2: *Los*

Angeles Times, June 25, 1982; 3: G. Kanin, *Hollywood*

Coke 1: J. Aubrey, *Brief Lives*

Colavito 1: J. C. Humes, *Speaker's Treasury*

Cole 1: *DNB*

Coleridge 1: W. Keddie, *Literary and Scientific Anecdote;* 2: S. T. Coleridge, *Kubla Khan;* 3: L. Russell, *English Wits;* 4: J. Braude, *Speaker's and Toastmaster's Handbook;* 5: C. R. Leslie, *Autobiographical Recollections,* in J. Sutherland, ed., *OBLA;* 6: T. Moore, *Memoirs, Journal, and Correspondence*

Colette 1: J. McAleer, "Globe Man's Daily Story," *Boston Globe,* Aug. 4, 1969

Collins, J., 1: *New York Times Book Review,* May 6, 1984

Collins, M., 1: W. Churchill, *Great Contemporaries*

Columbus 1: S. E. Morison, ed., *Journals and Other Documents of Columbus,* in L. B. Young, *The Blue Planet;* 2: Benzoni, *Historia del Mondo Nuevo,* in D. George, *A Book of Anecdotes;* 3: I. Wallace et al., *The Book of Lists 2*

Comte 1: B. Conrad, *Famous Last Words*

Condorcet 1: E. Bell, *Men of Mathematics*

Confucius 1: W. Durant, *The Story of Civilization,* I; 2: H. Margolius, *Der Lächelnde Philosoph*

Congreve 1: Voltaire, *Letters Concerning the English Nation,* in J. Sutherland, ed., *OBLA*

Connelly 1: H. Teichmann, *Smart Aleck;* 2: C. Stinnett, "Travels with Marc," *Signature,* Dec. 1981

Connolly 1: *Times Literary Supplement,* Dec. 6, 1974

Constable 1: W. Adams, *Treasury of Modern Anecdote;* 2: D. Piper, *Painting in England;* 3: P. Johnson, *The Birth of the Modern: World Society 1815–1830*

Constantine the Great 1: W. Durant, *The Story of Civilization,* III

Cook 1: F. Muir, *Irreverent Social History*

Coolidge 1: BBC Radio 4, Oct. 11, 1981; 2: I. Ross, *Grace Coolidge and Her Era,* in Kenin and Wintle, *DBQ;* 3, 6–7, 18, 24: E. Fuller,

2500 Anecdotes; 4: J. Braude, *Braude's Second Encyclopedia;* 5: *Los Angeles Times,* Aug. 6, 1982; 8: L. Missen, *After-Dinner Stories and Anecdotes;* 10: B. Cerf, *Try and Stop Me;* 11: B. Cerf, *Shake Well Before Using;* 12: E. C. Lathem, *Meet Calvin Coolidge;* 13: B. House, *Laugh Parade of States,* in P. Boller, ed., *Presidential Anecdotes;* 14: Edmund W. Starling, *Starling of the White House,* in Boller, *Presidential Anecdotes;* 15–16: Cameron Rodgers, *The Legend of Calvin Coolidge,* in B. Botkin, *Treasury of American Anecdotes;* 17: A. Krock, *Memoirs;* 19: R. Shenkman and K. Reiger, *One-Night Stands with American History;* 22: J. Braude, *Speaker's and Toastmaster's Handbook;* 23: "The Well-Known Human Race," *Reader's Digest,* June 1933, in Boller, *Presidential Anecdotes;* 25: M. Ringo, *Nobody Said It Better*

Cooper, Lady D., 1: P. Ziegler, *Diana Cooper;* 2: W. Amos, *The Originals: An A–Z of Fiction's Real-Life Characters*

Cooper, G., 1: P. Hay, ed., *Movie Anecdotes;* 2: H. Smith, *The Life and Legend of Gene Fowler;* 3: G. Herman, *The Book of Hollywood Quotes*

Cooper, Dame G., 1: R. Morley, *A Musing Morley*

Cooper, J. F., 1: D. Hall, ed., *OBALA*

Cooper, Sir W., 1: A. Lawson, *Discover Unexpected London*

Coote 1: S. Morley, *Tales from the Hollywood Raj*

Cope 1: I. Asimov, *Biographical Encyclopedia*

Corday 1: M. Pedrazzini and J. Gris, *Autant en apportent les mots*

Cornett 1: M. Biggs, ed., *Women's Words: The Columbia Book of Quotations by Women*

Corot 1: T. Craven, *Men of Art;* 2: E. Chubb, *Sketches of Great Painters;* 3: N. Rorem, *Later Diaries*

Corrigan 1: R. Lamparski, *Whatever Became Of . . . ?*

Cotten, E., 1: M. Biggs, ed., *Women's Words: The Columbia Book of Quotations by Women*

Courteline 1: C. Skinner, *Elegant Wits and Grand Horizontals*

Coward 2: R. Drennan, *Wit's End;* 3: R. Marquard, *Jokes and Anecdotes;* 4: R. Massey, *A Hundred Different Lives;* 5: G. Brandreth, *Great Theatrical Disasters;* 6: S. Morley, *A Talent to Amuse;* 7: R. Buckle, *In the Wake of Diaghilev;* 8: G. Payn and S. Morley, *The Noel Coward Diaries;* 9: B. Conrad, *Fun While It Lasted*

Cowl 1: E. Fuller, *2500 Anecdotes*

Crane 1: R. W. Stallman, *Stephen Crane,* in D. Hall, ed., *OBALA*

Cranmer 1: J. Foxe, *Acts and Monuments*

Crawford, J., 3: P. Boller, ed., *Hollywood Anecdotes*

Crenshaw 1: D. Wade, *And Then Fuzzy Told Seve;* 2: R. T. Sommers, *Golf Anecdotes*

Crockett 1: D. C. Roper and F. Lovette, *Fifty Years of Public Life,* in B. Botkin, *Treasury of American Anecdotes;* 2: H. Greeley, ed., *The Tribune Almanac for the Years 1838–1868,* in R. Shenkman and K. Reiger, *One-Night Stands with American History*

Crockford 1: W. Walsh, *Handy Book of Curious Information*

Croesus 1: Herodotus, *Histories,* I

Croll 1: W. Espy, *An Almanac of Words at Play*

Cromwell 1: H. Walpole, *Anecdotes of Painting;* 2: C. Hill, *God's Englishman;* 3: C. Shriner, *Wit, Wisdom, and Foibles of the Great;* 4: J. Spence, *Anecdotes;* 5: H. Hoffmeister, *Anekdotenschatz*

Crosby 1: C. Thompson, *Bing*

Cukor 1: *Los Angeles Times,* July 31, 1984

Cummings 1: S. Cheever, *Home Before Dark*

Cunard 1: H. Acton, *Nancy Mitford: A Memoir;* 2: E. Marsh, *A Number of People*

Cunninghame Graham 1: *Book-of-the-Month Club News,* Apr. 1950

Curie 1: H. and D. L. Thomas, *Living Adventures in Science*

Curley 1: W. Manchester, *One Brief Shining Moment*

Curran 1–2: W. Adams, *Treasury of Modern Anecdote;* 3: D. George, *A Book of Anecdotes*

Curtiz 1: D. Niven, *Bring On the Empty Horses;*

2: O. Levant, *The Unimportance of Being Oscar*

Cushman 1: W. Winter, *Other Days*

Cuvier 1: I. Asimov, *Biographical Encyclopedia*

Cyrus II 1: K. Edwards, *I Wish I'd Said That*

Dahn 1: H. Hoffmeister, *Anekdotenschatz*

Dale 1: W. Keddie, *Literary and Scientific Anecdote*

Dali 1: L. Buñuel, *My Last Breath;* 2: P. Horgan, *Encounters with Stravinsky;* 3: J. Gruen, *The Party's Over Now;* 7: J. Bryan III, ed., *Hodgepodge: A Commonplace Book*

Dalton 1: I. Asimov, *Biographical Encyclopedia*

Dana 1: C. Fadiman, *Any Number Can Play*

D'Annunzio 1: E. Fuller, *2500 Anecdotes*

Dante Alighieri 1–2: C. Speroni, *Wit and Wisdom of the Italian Renaissance*

Danton 1: B. Conrad, *Famous Last Words*

Darius I 1: Herodotus, *Histories,* IV; 2: F. Paley, *Greek Wit*

Darrow 1–2: E. Fuller, *2500 Anecdotes;* 3: M. Ringo, *Nobody Said It Better;* 4: H. Prochnow, *The Public Speaker's Treasure Chest;* 5: T. Arnold, *Fair Fights and Foul*

Darwin, C., 1: J. Chancellor, *Charles Darwin;* 2: A. Moorhead, *Darwin and the Beagle;* 3: G. Keynes and B. Hill, eds., *Samuel Butler's Notebooks*

Darwin, E., 1: E. Kraus, *Erasmus Darwin,* in Kenin and Wintle, *DBQ*

Daudet 1: E. Van de Velde, *Anecdotes Musicales*

Davenant 1: *DNB;* 2: B. Conrad, *Famous Last Words*

Davies, Lady E., 1: W. Keddie, *Literary and Scientific Anecdote*

Davies, M., 1: S. Marx, *Mayer and Thalberg*

Davis, A., 1: N. and B. Donaldson, *How Did They Die?*

Davis, B., 1: I. Wallace et al., *Book of Lists 2*

Davis, M., 1–2: B. Crow, *Jazz Anecdotes*

Davy 1–2: C. R. Weld, *A History of the Royal Society,* in Kenin and Wintle, *DBQ;* 3: E. Fuller, *2500 Anecdotes*

Dean 1: C. Fadiman and C. Van Doren, *The American Treasury;* 2: J. Nash, *Zanies;*

3: C. Sifakis, *Dictionary of Historic Nicknames*

Debs 1: D. Wallechinsky and I. Wallace, *The People's Almanac*

Degas 1: R. McMullen, *Degas: His Life, Times, and Work*; 3: E. Lucie-Smith, ed., *The Faber Book of Art Anecdotes*; 4: J. Krantz, *Mistral's Daughter*

De Gaulle 1: R. Buckle, ed., *Self-Portrait with Friends*; 2: M. Ringo, *Nobody Said It Better*; 3: J. Bartlett, *Bartlett's Familiar Quotations*; 4, 10: P. Frederick, *Ten First Ladies of the World*; 5: *The Times* (London), Aug. 30, 1983; 7: L. Lucaire, *Celebrity Trivia*; 8: B. Walters, *How to Talk with Practically Anybody*; 9: R. Morley, *Book of Bricks*

De la Mare 1: *John Bailey 1864–1931: Letters, Edited by his Wife*, in J. Sutherland, ed., *OBLA*

De Mille 1: Barry Paris, "The Godless Girl," *The New Yorker*, 1989

De Moivre 1: C. Fadiman, *The Mathematical Magpie*

Demosthenes 1: N. McPhee, *Second Book of Insults*; 2: Plutarch, *Lives*

Dempsey 1: M. Ringo, *Nobody Said It Better*; 2: G. Perrett, *America in the Twenties*

Denham 1: C. Sifakis, *Dictionary of Historic Nicknames*

Denis 1: Dugas de Bois St. Just, *Paris, Versailles et les provinces*

Dennis 1–2: R. Hendrickson, *The Literary Life*

Depew 1: E. Fuller, *2500 Anecdotes*; 2: I. Asimov, *Treasury of Humor*

Descartes 1: D. Wallechinsky and I. Wallace, *The People's Almanac 2*; 2: I. Asimov, *Biographical Encyclopedia*; 3: W. Keddie, *Literary and Scientific Anecdote*

De Seversky 1: B. Cerf, *Shake Well Before Using*

Detourbey 1: C. Skinner, *Elegant Wits and Grand Horizontals*

De Valera 1: I. Asimov, *Treasury of Humor*; 2: E. Fuller, *2500 Anecdotes*; 3: J. Gunther, *Procession*

De Valois 1: *The New Yorker*, Sept. 16, 1950

Devonshire, Duke of 1: Duchess of Devonshire, *The House*; 2: J. Pearson, *The Serpent and the Stag*

De Wolfe 1: J. Smith, *Elsie de Wolfe*

Diaghilev 1: D. Boorstin, *The Creators*; 2: B. Taper, *Balanchine: A Biography*; 3: M. Georges-Michel, *From Renoir to Picasso*

Diana, Princess of Wales 1: *The Times* (London), Apr. 13, 1983

Dicaprio 1: M. Wiley and D. Bona, *Inside Oscar*

Dickens 1: G. Chesterton, *Charles Dickens*; 2: R. Hendrickson, *The Literary Life*; 3: J. Forster, *The Life of Charles Dickens (1872–74)*, in J. Sutherland, ed., *OBLA*; 4: F. Locker-Lampson, *My Confidences*, in Sutherland, *OBLA*; 5: E. Johnson, *Charles Dickens*

Diderot 1: E. Bell, *Men of Mathematics*

Dietz 1: *Los Angeles Times*, Mar. 30, 1983

Diogenes 1: Plutarch, *Lives*; 2–3: Diogenes Laertius, *Eminent Philosophers*; 4: E. Fuller, *2500 Anecdotes*; 5: H. Hoffmeister, *Anekdotenschatz*; 6: J. Braude, *Speaker's and Toastmaster's Handbook*; 7: H. Margolius, *Der Lächelnde Philosoph*

Dionysius II 1: W. Keddie, *Literary and Scientific Anecdote*

Dirichlet 1: H. Hoffmeister, *Anekdotenschatz*

Disney 1: C. Finch, *The Art of Walt Disney*

Disraeli 1: *DNB*; 2: B. Cerf, *Try and Stop Me*; 3: R. Marquard, *Jokes and Anecdotes*; 4: F. Muir, *Irreverent Social History*; 5: M. MacDonagh, *Fortnightly Review*, Aug. 1902, in Shriner, *Wit*; 6: Shriner, *Wit*; 7: H. Hoffmeister, *Anekdotenschatz*; 8: L. Harris, *The Fine Art of Political Wit*; 9: N. McPhee, *Second Book of Insults*; 10: I. Wallace et al., *Intimate Sex Lives of Famous People*; 11: E. Longford, *The Oxford Book of Royal Anecdotes*; 12: H. H. Marie Louise, *My Memories of Six Reigns*, in A. Hardy, *Queen Victoria Was Amused*

Divine 1: D. Wallechinsky and I. Wallace, *The People's Almanac*; 2: L. Rosten, *People I Have Loved, Known, or Admired*

Dix 1: P. Smith, *Trial by Fire*

Doherty 1: W. Adams, *Treasury of Modern Anecdote*

Dole, R. 1: J. Simpson, *Simpson's Contemporary Quotations*; 2–5: B. Dole, *Great Political Wit*

Donatello 1: A. Poliziano, *Diario*

Donne 1: Sir J. Prior, *Life of Edmond Malone . . .* , in J. Sutherland, ed., *OBLA;* 2: I. Walton, *The Lives of John Donne, . . . Robert Sanderson,* in Sutherland, *OBLA*

Douglass 1: B. Botkin, *Treasury of American Anecdotes*

Doyle 2: P. Mahony, *Barbed Wit and Malicious Humor;* 3: J. Nash, *Zanies*

Drake 1: J. Williamson, *The English Channel;* 2: *DNB*

Dreiser 1: S. Mayfield, *The Constant Circle;* 2: Bennett Cerf, *At Random,* in D. Hall, ed., *OBALA*

Drew 1: E. Fuller, *2500 Anecdotes*

Dreyschock 1: H. Schonberg, *The Great Pianists*

Dryden 1: W. Keddie, *Literary and Scientific Anecdote;* 2: J. Prior, *Life of E. Malone;* 3: G. Colman, *Circle of Anecdote*

Du Barry 1: L. and M. Cowan, *The Wit of Women*

Duclos 1: Dugas de Bois St. Just, *Paris, Versailles et les provinces*

Du Deffand 1–2: C. Pedrazzini and J. Gris, *Autant en apportent les mots*

Dudley 1: W. Adams, *Treasury of Modern Anecdote*

Dulles 1: H. Temianka, *Facing the Music*

Dumas, A. (Père), 1: B. Cerf, *Shake Well Before Using;* 2: E. Fuller, *2500 Anecdotes;* 3–6: H. Hoffmeister, *Anekdotenschatz;* 7: L. and F. Copeland, *10,000 Jokes, Toasts, and Stories*

Dumas, A. (Fils), 1–2: C. Skinner, *Elegant Wits and Grand Horizontals;* 3: A. Castelot, *Paris: The Turbulent City*

Dunsany 1: S. Winchester, *Their Noble Lordships*

Du Pont 1: *The New Yorker,* Dec. 13, 1952

Durocher 1: C. Fadiman and C. Van Doren, *The American Treasury*

Duse 1: S. Radecki, *Das ABC des Lachens;* 2: E. Fuller, *2500 Anecdotes*

Duval 1: C. Roberts, *And So to Bath*

Duveen 1: S. Holbrook, *The Age of the Moguls*

Dyson 1: Oxfam, *Pass the Port*

Eastwood 1–2: P. Hay, ed., *Movie Anecdotes;* 3: P. Boller, ed., *Hollywood Anecdotes*

Eddy 1: H. and D. L. Thomas, *Living Biographies of Religious Leaders*

Eden, A., 1: A. Cooke, *Six Men*

Eden, Sir W., 1: C. Fadiman, *Any Number Can Play*

Edison, C., 1: J. Braude, *Speaker's and Toastmaster's Handbook*

Edison, T., 1: Henry Ford, *My Friend, Mr. Edison,* in Kenin and Wintle, *DBQ;* 2–5: E. Fuller, *2500 Anecdotes;* 6: D. Wallechinsky and I. Wallace, *The People's Almanac;* 7: J. Braude, *Speaker's and Toastmaster's Handbook;* 8: N. and B. Donaldson, *How Did They Die?*

Edman 1: *Book-of-the-Month Club News,* 1947; 2: B. Cerf, *Try and Stop Me*

Edward I 1: E. C. Brewer, *Dictionary of Phrase and Fable*

Edward III 1: B. Vincent, ed., *Haydn's Dictionary of Dates;* 2: *Oxford Dictionary of Quotations*

Edward VII 1: *Private Life of Edward VII, by a Member of the Royal Household,* in C. Shriner, *Wit, Wisdom, and Foibles of the Great;* 2: C. Skinner, *Elegant Wits and Grand Horizontals;* 3–4, 6: R. Collier, *The Rainbow People;* 5: G. Lieberman, *The Greatest Laughs of All Time;* 7: H. Atkins and A. Newman, eds., *Beecham Stories;* 8: P. Mahony, *Barbed Wit and Malicious Humor;* 9: C. Aslet, *The Last Country Houses*

Edward VIII 1: D. Herrmann, *With Malice Toward All;* 3: A. Chambers, *Dream Resorts*

Einstein 1: P. David and R. Hersh, *The Mathematical Experience;* 2: I. Rosenthal-Schneider, *Reality and Scientific Truth;* 3: T. Ferris, *Coming of Age in the Milky Way;* 4: P. Frank, *Einstein;* 5: C. Seelig, *Albert Einstein;* 6: J.

Bernstein, *Einstein;* 7: G. Whitrow, *Einstein;* 8: M. and A. Guillois, *Liberté, Egalité, Hilarité;* 9: E. Fuller, *2500 Anecdotes;* 10: A. Toynbee, *Acquaintances;* 12: W. Novak and M. Waldoks, *The Big Book of Jewish Humor;* 13, 18: S. Harris, *Pieces of Eight;* 15: *New York Times Book Review,* Sept. 26, 1982; 16: O. Levant, *The Unimportance of Being Oscar;* 20: D. Halberstam, *The Fifties;* 21: E. Longford, "Continuity and Change," in *Testament,* ed. C. Fadiman; 22: *British Medical Journal,* 1985; 23: L. LeShain, *From Newton to ESP*

Eisenhower 1: Merlo J. Pusey, *Eisenhower the President,* in P. Boller, ed., *Presidential Anecdotes;* 2: M. Dietrich, *Marlene;* 3: D. Eisenhower, *Eisenhower at War;* 4: D. Halberstam, *The Fifties;* 6: R. Crouser, *It's Unlucky to Be Behind at the End of the Game;* 5: R. Sommers, *Golf Anecdotes*

Eleanor of Aquitaine 1: W. Durant, *The Story of Civilization,* IV

Eliot, C., 1: J. McAleer, "Globe Man's Daily Story," *Boston Globe,* June 27, 1963

Eliot, J., 1: W. Keddie, *Literary and Scientific Anecdote*

Eliot, T. S., 1: I. A. Richards, "On T.S.E.," in *T. S. Eliot: The Man and His Work,* in J. Sutherland, ed., *OBLA;* 2: D. Wallechinsky and I. Wallace, *The People's Almanac 2;* 3: A. Tate, ed., *T. S. Eliot, The Man and His Work;* 4: S. Weintraub, *The London Yankees;* 5: P. Ackroyd, *T. S. Eliot;* 6: *Publishers Weekly,* Jan. 8, 1982; 7: P. Horgan, *Approaches to Writing*

Elizabeth I 1: E. Longford, *The Oxford Book of Royal Anecdotes;* 2: D'Israeli, *Curiosities of Literature;* 3: J. Aubrey, *Brief Lives;* 4: W. Keddie, *Literary and Scientific Anecdote;* 5–7: M. Biggs, ed., *Women's Words: The Columbia Book of Quotations by Women*

Elizabeth II 1–3, 8–12: E. Longford, *The Oxford Book of Royal Anecdotes;* 5: V. Wade, *Courting Triumph;* 7: R. Lacey, *Majesty*

Elizabeth, the Queen Mother, 3: J. Bartlett, *Bartlett's Familiar Quotations;* 4: D. Duff, *Elizabeth of Glamis;* 5: B. Cerf, *Good for a Laugh;* 6: K. Edwards, *I Wish I'd Said That*

Ellenborough 1: L. Russell, *English Wits;* 2: W. Adams, *Treasury of Modern Anecdote*

Elliott 1: W. Adams, *Treasury of Modern Anecdote*

Elliston 1: T. Moore, *Memoirs, Journal, and Correspondence,* in Kenin and Wintle, *DBQ*

Elman 1: E. Fuller, *2500 Anecdotes*

Emerson 1, 3, 9: O. Holmes, *Ralph Waldo Emerson;* 2: H. and D. L. Thomas, *Living Biographies of the Great Philosophers;* 4: I. Wallace et al., *Book of Lists 2;* 5: Mary B. Claflin, *Personal Recollections of John Greenleaf Whittier,* in *OBALA;* 6: C. Fadiman and C. Van Doren, *The American Treasury;* 8: Edward Wilson, *The Shock of Recognition,* in D. Hall, ed., *OBALA*

Empedocles 1: *Oxford Classical Dictionary*

Enesco 1: W. Espy, *Another Almanac of Words at Play*

Engels 1: G. Pijet, *Duell mit der Vergangenheit*

Epstein 1: J. Braude, *Speaker's and Toastmaster's Handbook*

Erasmus 1: E. Guérard, *Dictionnaire Encyclopédique*

Eric the Red 1: H. Rawson, *Dictionary of Euphemisms*

Erskine 1: J. Timbs, *Century of Anecdote;* 2: W. Keddie, *Literary and Scientific Anecdote*

Erving 1: P. O'Brian, *Talkin' Sports*

Este 1: C. Speroni, *Wit and Wisdom of the Italian Renaissance*

Euclid 1: I. Asimov, *Treasury of Humor*

Eugénie 1: D. Duff, *Eugénie and Napoleon III;* 2: F. Loliée, *Gilded Beauties of the Second Empire*

Euler 1: E. Bell, *Men of Mathematics*

Euripides 1: W. Keddie, *Literary and Scientific Anecdote*

Evans, Sir A., 1: C. Bowra, *Memories 1898–1939*

Evans, Dame E., 1–2: B. Forbes, *Ned's Girl*

Everett 1: D. Wallechinsky and I. Wallace, *The People's Almanac*

Fagiuoli 1: J. Papesch, *Europa Lächelt Noch Immer*

Fairbanks 1: V. Castlerosse, *Valentine's Days*

Fallières 1: M. and A. Guillois, *Liberté, Egalité, Hilarité*

Faraday 1: S. Bolton, *Famous Men of Science*

Farouk I 1: R. Byrne, *The 637 Best Things Anybody Ever Said*

Farquhar 1: W. Adams, *Treasury of Modern Anecdote*

Farr 1: M. Biggs, ed., *Women's Words: The Columbia Book of Quotations by Women*

Farragut 1: D. Wallechinsky and I. Wallace, *The People's Almanac*

Faulkner 1: C. Fadiman and C. Van Doren, *The American Treasury*; 2: G. Herman, *The Book of Hollywood Quotes*; 3: S. Mayfield, *The Constant Circle*; 4: S. Graham, *The Garden of Allah*; 5: Robert Coughlin, *The Private World of William Faulkner*, in D. Hall, ed., *OBALA*; 6: B. Cerf, *At Random*, in D. Hall, ed., *OBALA*; 7: J. Bryan III, ed., *Hodgepodge Two*

Fauré 1: N. Rorem, *Later Diaries*

Favras 1: M. Pedrazzini and J. Gris, *Autant en apportent les mots*

Fawkes 1: J. Kenyon, *Dictionary of British History*

Feller 1: C. Jones, *What Makes Winners Win*

Ferdinand I (Austria) 1: E. Crankshaw, *The Fall of the House of Hapsburg*

Ferdinand I (Bulgaria) 1: C. Skinner, *Elegant Wits and Grand Horizontals*

Ferdinand IV 1: E. C. Brewer, *Dictionary of Phrase and Fable*

Ferguson 1: M. Biggs, ed., *Women's Words: The Columbia Book of Quotations by Women*

Fergusson 1: *DNB*

Fermat 1: I. Asimov, *Biographical Encyclopedia*

Fermi 1: P. Dunaway and G. De Kay, eds., *Turning Point*

Feydeau 1–4: C. Skinner, *Elegant Wits and Grand Horizontals*

Feynmann 1: M. Biggs, ed., *Women's Words: The Columbia Book of Quotations by Women*; 2: J. Gleick, *Chaos: The Life and Science of Richard Feynmann*

Field, J., 1: E. Van de Velde, *Anecdotes Musicales*

Field, M., 1: J. Braude, *Speaker's and Toastmaster's Handbook*

Fielding 1: J. Timbs, *Century of Anecdote*; 2: J. Nichols, *Literary Anecdotes of the Eighteenth Century*, in J. Sutherland, ed., *OBLA*

Fields 1: G. Fowler, *Minutes of the Last Meeting*; 2: R. Lewis, *W. C. Fields*; 3: C. Fadiman and C. Van Doren, *The American Treasury*; 4: E. Fuller, *2500 Anecdotes*; 5: "Daily Mirror" *Old Codger's Little Black Book 1*

Fiennes 1: M. Wiley and D. Bona, *Inside Oscar*

Fillmore 1: J. Morgan, *Our Presidents*, in P. Boller, ed., *Presidential Anecdotes*

Finley 1: M. Shannon, *Tales from the Dugout: The Greatest True Baseball Stories Ever*

Fisher, M. F. K. 1: M. Biggs, ed., *Women's Words: The Columbia Book of Quotations by Women*

Fiske 1: H. Prochnow, *Public Speaker's Treasure Chest*; 2: M. Biggs, ed., *Women's Words: The Columbia Book of Quotations by Women*

Fitzgerald, E., 1: *Los Angeles Times*, Jan. 30, 1983

Fitzgerald, F. S., 1: A. Latham, *Crazy Sundays*; 3: A. Turnbull, *F. Scott Fitzgerald, A Biography*, in D. Hall, ed., *OBALA*

Fitzsimmons 1: C. Fadiman and C. Van Doren, *The American Treasury*

Flaherty 1: *The New Yorker*, June 11, 1949

Flanner 1: J. Krementz, *The Writer's Image*

Flaubert 1: *Book-of-the-Month Club News*, 1955; 2: P. Stitt, *The World's Hieroglyphic Beauty: Five American Poets*

Fleetwood 1: J. Aubrey, *Brief Lives*

Fleming 1: *New York Times*, Apr. 9, 1983

Foch 1–2, 4–5: E. Fuller, *2500 Anecdotes*; 3: J. Braude, *Speaker's and Toastmaster's Handbook*

Fonda, H., 1: B. Adler, *My Favorite Funny Story*; 2: P. Boller, ed., *Hollywood Anecdotes*

Fonda, J., 1: M. Wiley and D. Bona, *Inside Oscar*; 2: P. Boller, ed., *Hollywood Anecdotes*

Fontanne 1: S. Marx, *Mayer and Thalberg*

Fontenelle 1: H. Hoffmeister, *Anekdotenschatz*; 2, 4: M. Pedrazzini and J. Gris, *Autant en apportent les mots*; 3: E. Fuller, *2500 Anecdotes*; 5: B. Conrad, *Famous Last Words*

Foote 1: R. Hendrickson, *The Literary Life*; 2–3: E. Fuller, *2500 Anecdotes*; 4, 7: W. Adams, *Treasury of Modern Anecdote*; 6: G. Lieberman, *The Greatest Laughs of All Time*

Ford, B., 1: B. Dole, *Great Political Wit*; 2: B. Ford, *The Times of My Life*, in P. Boller, ed., *Presidential Wives: An Anecdotal History*; 3: Myra MacPherson, "Betty Ford at 60: My Life Is Just Beginning," *McCall's*, Mar. 1979, in Boller, *Presidential Wives*

Ford, G., 1–2, 4: B. Dole, *Great Political Wit*; 3: Gerald Ford, *A Time to Heal*, in P. Boller, ed., *Presidential Campaigns*

Ford, H., 1: C. Bowen, *Yankee from Olympus*; 3: E. Fuller, *2500 Anecdotes*; 6: D. Halberstam, *The Reckoning*

Ford, J., 1: *Tonight* show, July 28, 1981; 2–4: M. Corey and G. Ochoa, *The Man in Lincoln's Nose*

Fordyce 1: S. Rogers, *Table Talk*

Forgy 1: *Los Angeles Times,* June 3, 1982

Forrest 1: B. W. Duke, *Reminiscences of Gen. Basil W. Duke, C.S.*, in B. Botkin, *A Civil War Treasury*

Fosdick 1: S. Harris, *Pieces of Eight*

Foster 1: L. Humphrey, *The Humor of Music*

Fouché 1: W. and A. Durant, *The Story of Civilization,* XI; 2: A. Duff Cooper, *Talleyrand*

Fowler 1: H. Smith, *The Life and Legend of Gene Fowler*

Fox, C., 1, 5: E. Fuller, *2500 Anecdotes*; 2–3: J. Timbs, *Century of Anecdote*; 4: Lord Broughton, *Recollections of a Long Life*, in Kenin and Wintle, *DBQ*

Fox, G., 1: H. and D. L. Thomas, *Living Biographies of Religious Leaders*

Fraguier 1: J. Papesch, *Europa Lächelt Noch Immer*

Francis I 1: W. Walsh, *Handy Book of Curious Information*

Francis II 1: A. Bryant, *The Age of Elegance*; 2: E. Crankshaw, *The Fall of the House of Hapsburg*

Francis Ferdinand 1: E. Crankshaw, *The Fall of the House of Hapsburg*

Francis Joseph 1: S. Radecki, *Das ABC des Lachens*; 2: P. Méras, *The Mermaids of Chenonceaux*

Francis of Assisi 1: H. Morton, *A Traveller in Italy*

Franco 1: S. Bellow, *Him with His Foot in His Mouth*

Franklin 1: C. Fadiman and C. Van Doren, *The American Treasury*; 2: H. S. Randall, *The Life of Thomas Jefferson*, in P. Boller, ed., *Presidential Anecdotes*; 3: D. George, *A Book of Anecdotes*; 4–5, 12–13: P. Zall, *Ben Franklin Laughing*; 6: Arthur D. Graeff, "Anecdotes Related in Pennsylvania-German Almanacs," *The American-German Review,* VI (June 1940), in Boller, *Presidential Anecdotes*; 7: C. Shriner, *Wit, Wisdom, and Foibles of the Great*; 8: C. Van Doren, *Benjamin Franklin*, in D. Hall, ed., *OBALA*; 9: Sarah Randolph, *The Domestic Life of Thomas Jefferson*, in D. Hall, *OBALA*; 10: P. Smith, *A New Age Now Begins*; 14: M. Strauss, *Familiar Medical Quotations*; 15: J. Train, *Wit: The Best Things Ever Said*

Franks 1: G. Moorhouse, *The Diplomats*

Frederick II 1: Sholto and Reuben Percy, *The Percy Anecdotes*, in D. George, *A Book of Anecdotes*; 2: I. Asimov, *Treasury of Humor*; 3–4: W. and A. Durant, *The Story of Civilization,* X; 5–7, 11: H. Hoffmeister, *Anekdotenschatz*; 8: G. Colman, *Circle of Anecdote*; 9: H. Prochnow, *The Public Speaker's Treasure Chest*; 10: V. Nikolaev and A. Parry, *The Loves of Catherine the Great*

Frederick Augustus I 1: W. Scholz, *Das Buch des Lachens*

Frederick William I 1: *EB*; 2: Sylvester Douglas, *Lord Glenbervie, Journals,* in D. George, *A Book of Anecdotes*; 3: B. Conrad, *Famous Last Words*

Frederick William IV 1: G. Craig, *The Germans;* 2: H. Hoffmeister, *Anekdotenschatz*

Freud 1: D. Wallechinsky and I. Wallace, *The People's Almanac;* 2: *Los Angeles Times,* July 4, 1982; 3: P. Méras, *The Mermaids of Chenonceaux*

Frith 1: W. Walsh, *Handy Book of Curious Information*

Frohman 1: B. Conrad, *Famous Last Words*

Fugger 1: T. Robards, *The New York Times Book of Wine*

Fuller, Margaret, 1: F. Muir, *Irreverent Social History;* 2: E. Fuller, *2500 Anecdotes*

Fuller, Melville, 1: E. Fuller, *2500 Anecdotes*

Fuller, R. B., 1: B. Taper, *The Arts in Boston*

Fulton 1: M. Bishop, *The Exotics*

Furtwängler 1: H. Schonberg, *The Great Conductors*

Fuseli 1–2: P. Wescher, *Schweitzer Künstler-Anekdoten*

Gabin 1: E. Fuller, *2500 Anecdotes*

Gainsborough 1: W. and A. Durant, *The Story of Civilization,* X; 2: A. Cunningham, *Lives of the Most Eminent British Painters,* in D. George, *A Book of Anecdotes*

Gaisford 1: J. Morris, *The Oxford Book of Oxford*

Galbraith 1: J. Galbraith, *A Life in Our Times*

Galen 1: R. Calder, *Medicine and Man*

Galiani 1: H. Sievers, *Musica Curiosa*

Galileo 1: J. Bartlett, *Bartlett's Familiar Quotations*

Galois 1: E. Bell, *Men of Mathematics*

Galvani 1: W. Penfield, *The Second Career,* in M. Strauss, *Familiar Medical Quotations*

Gandhi 2: H. and D. L. Thomas, *Living Biographies of Religious Leaders;* 3: M. Ringo, *Nobody Said It Better;* 5: G. Brandreth, *Joy of Lex*

Garbo 1: N. Zierold, *The Moguls;* 2: D. Niven, *Bring On the Empty Horses;* 3–4: M. Biggs, ed., *Women's Words: The Columbia Book of Quotations by Women*

Gardner 1: J. McAleer, "Globe Man's Daily Story," *Boston Globe,* Jan. 8, 1960; 2: L.

Tharp, *Mrs. Jack;* 4: A. Saarinen, *The Proud Possessors*

Garland 1: A. King and M. Sheraton, *Is Salami and Eggs Better Than Sex?*

Garrick 1: J. Boswell, *Life of Johnson;* 2: E. Fuller, *2500 Anecdotes*

Garrison 1: E. Fuller, *2500 Anecdotes*

Garrod 1: D. Balsdon, *Oxford Now and Then*

Garth 1: F. Winslow, *Physic and Physicians,* in D. George, *A Book of Anecdotes*

Garvey 1: D. Okrent and S. Wolf, eds., *Baseball Anecdotes*

Gates 1: C. Sifakis, *Dictionary of Historic Nicknames*

Gauss 1: E. Bell, *Men of Mathematics;* 2: I. Asimov, *Biographical Encyclopedia*

Gelon 1: W. Durant, *The Story of Civilization,* II

Geoffrin 1: Dugas de Bois St. Just, *Paris, Versailles et les provinces*

George I 1: J. Spence, *Anecdotes*

George II 1: A. Isaacs and E. Martin, *Dictionary of Music;* 2: E. Guérard, *Dictionnaire Encyclopédique*

George III 2: B. Wilson, *George III,* in Kenin and Wintle, *DBQ;* 3: J. Timbs, *Century of Anecdote;* 4: W. Gates, *Anecdotes of Great Musicians;* 5: R. Hendrickson, *The Literary Life;* 6: A. Bennett, "The King and I," *London Review of Books,* Jan. 30, 1992; 7: E. Longford, *The Oxford Book of Royal Anecdotes*

George IV 1: B. Disraeli, *Lothair,* in Kenin and Wintle, *DBQ;* 2: H. L. Bulwer, *Historical Characters,* in D. George, *A Book of Anecdotes;* 3: E. Longford, *The Oxford Book of Royal Anecdotes*

George V 1: B. Cerf, *The Life of the Party;* 3: K. Rose, *King George V;* 4: R. Collier, *The Rainbow People;* 5: M. Pye, *The King over the Water;* 6: W. Manchester, *The Last Lion;* 8: J. Bryan, III, ed., *Hodgepodge: A Commonplace Book;* 9: N. Rees, *Quote . . . Unquote*

George VI 1: P. Berton, *The Royal Family;* 2: P. Vandyke Price, *The Penguin Book of Spirits and Liqueurs*

Gerard 1: P. Smith, *America Enters the World*

Gershwin, George, 1: E. Fuller, *2500 Anecdotes;* 2–3: O. Levant, *Memoirs of an Amnesiac,* in Kenin and Wintle, *DBQ;* 4: M. Ringo, *Nobody Said It Better;* 5: A. Rubinstein, *My Many Years*

Gesvres 1: L. Norton, *Saint-Simon at Versailles*

Ghiberti 1: T. Craven, *Men of Art*

Giamatti 1: J. McBride, *High and Inside: The A–Z Guide to the Language of Baseball*

Giampetro 1: H. Hoffmeister, *Anekdotenshatz*

Gibbon 1: D. George, *A Book of Anecdotes;* 2: Thomas Moore's Journal, Dec. 12, 1844, in D. George, *A Book of Anecdotes;* 3: H. Beste, *Personal and Literary Memorials*

Gibbons 1: N. and B. Donaldson, *How Did They Die?*

Gibson 1: D. Okrent and S. Wolf, eds., *Baseball Anecdotes*

Gide 1: N. Jones, *A Book of Days for the Literary Year*

Gielgud 1: B. Forbes, *Ned's Girl;* 2: R. Morley, *Book of Bricks;* 4: *Time,* Aug. 15, 1983

Gilbert, Sir H., 1: T. Fuller, *The Worthies of England,* in D. George, *A Book of Anecdotes*

Gilbert, J., 1: G. Brandreth, *Great Theatrical Disasters*

Gilbert, Sir W., 1: H. Evans, *Personal Recollections;* 2: E. Fuller, *2500 Anecdotes;* 3: M. Ringo, *Nobody Said It Better;* 4–5: N. McPhee, *Second Book of Insults;* 6–7: J. Aye, *Humour in the Theatre;* 8: G. Brandreth, *Great Theatrical Disasters;* 9: N. and B. Donaldson, *How Did They Die?*

Gillespie 1: B. Crow, *Jazz Anecdotes*

Giolotti 1: P. Hoffmann, *Rome — The Sweet, Tempestuous Life*

Giorgione 1: G. Vasari, *Lives of the Painters*

Giotto 1–2: G. Vasari, *Lives of the Painters;* 3: P. Méras, *The Mermaids of Chenonceaux*

Gipp 1: D. Wallechinsky and I. Wallace, *The People's Almanac*

Gladstone 1: E. Fuller, *2500 Anecdotes;* 2: J. Papesch, *Europa Lächelt Noch Immer*

Gluck 1: E. Guérard, *Dictionnaire Encyclopédique*

Glyn 1: P. Mahony, *Barbed Wit and Malicious Humor*

Godard 1: *Time,* Sept. 14, 1981

Godiva 1: *EB*

Godowsky 1: H. Taubman, *Music on My Beat*

Goering 1: E. Fuller, *2500 Anecdotes*

Goethe 1: D. Enright, *The Oxford Book of Death;* 2: W. and A. Durant, *The Story of Civilization,* X; 3: *Oxford Dictionary of Quotations;* 4: S. Behrman, *Portrait of Max*

Gogarty 1: P. Bussard, *The New Catholic Treasury of Wit and Humor;* 2: W. Yeats, *The Oxford Book of Modern Verse*

Goldsmith 1: C. Hibbert, *The Personal History of Samuel Johnson*

Goldwater 1–2: B. Dole, *Great Political Wit*

Goldwyn 1: M. Ringo, *Nobody Said It Better;* 2–3: D. Niven, *Bring On the Empty Horses;* 4–5: E. Fuller, *2500 Anecdotes;* 6: R. Marquard, *Jokes and Anecdotes;* 7–8: B. Cerf, *Try and Stop Me;* 9: H. Dietz, *Dancing in the Dark;* 10–11: J. Nash, *Zanies;* 12: G. Lieberman, *The Greatest Laughs of All Time;* 13: S. Graham, *The Garden of Allah;* 14, 18: S. Birmingham, *"The Rest of Us";* 15–16: N. Zierold, *The Moguls;* 17: *Life,* Feb. 1984; 19: G. Herman, *The Book of Hollywood Quotes*

Gordon, Lord George 1: J. Timbs, *Century of Anecdote*

Gorki 1: E. Fuller, *2500 Anecdotes*

Gossage 1: B. Shlain, *Baseball Inside Out*

Gosse 1: A. Noyes, *Two Worlds for Memory*

Gould 1: D. Wallechinsky and I. Wallace, *The People's Almanac;* 2: J. Wheeler, *"The Old Second Guesser," Omaha World-Herald,* Feb. 20, 1955, in B. Botkin, *Treasury of American Anecdotes*

Grable 1: B. Cerf, *Laughing Stock*

Grafton 1: M. Biggs, ed., *Women's Words: The Columbia Book of Quotations by Women*

Grant, C. 1: R. Webb and T. Carle, *The Laughs on Hollywood*

Grant, U. S. 1: H. Garland, *McClure's Magazine,* Feb. 1897, in C. Shriner, *Wit, Wisdom, and Foibles of the Great;* 2: *The New York Sun,*

July 26, 1885, in B. Botkin, *A Civil War Treasury*; 3: E. B. Long, ed., *U. S. Grant: Personal Memoirs*, in P. Boller, ed., *Presidential Anecdotes*; 4: "Anecdotes of General Grant," *New York Daily Tribune*, Aug. 5, 1885, in B. Botkin, *A Civil War Treasury*; 5: M. Ringo, *Nobody Said It Better*; 6: B. Cerf, *The Life of the Party*; 7: H. Greene, *General Grant's Last Stand*, in Boller, *Presidential Anecdotes*; 8, 13: D. Wecter, *The Hero in America*, in Boller, *Presidential Anecdotes*; 9: C. Tuckerman, "Personal Recollections of Notable People," *Magazine of American History*, in Shriner, *Wit*; 10: L. Untermeyer, *A Treasury of Laughter*, in Boller, *Presidential Anecdotes*; 11: S. Frank, *The Presidents*, in R. Shenkman and K. Reiger, *One-Night Stands with American History*; 12: *New York Review of Books*, Mar. 1981

Grassini 1: J. Papesch, *Europa Lächelt Noch Immer*

Graves 1: M. Seymour-Smith, *Robert Graves: His Life and Work*

Gray 1: W. Keddie, *Literary and Scientific Anecdote*

Graziano 1: R. Crouser, *It's Unlucky to Be Behind at the End of the Game*

Greeley 1: G. Fowler, *Timber Line*; 2, 4: R. Marquard, *Jokes and Anecdotes*; 3: E. Fuller, *2500 Anecdotes*; 5: J. H. Browne, "Horace Greeley," *Harper's New Monthly Magazine*, Apr. 1873, in B. Botkin, *Treasury of American Anecdotes*; 6: P. Mahony, *Barbed Wit and Malicious Humor*; 7: G. Lieberman, *The Greatest Laughs of All Time*; 8: J. H. Trietsch, *The Printer and the Prince*, in D. Hall, ed., *OBALA*

Green, H., 1: I. Ross, *Charmers and Cranks*; 2: *Parade*, Oct. 17, 1982

Green, J., 1: B. Conrad, *Famous Last Words*

Greene 1: *Book-of-the-Month Club News*, Oct. 1949; 2: M. Korda, *Another Life*; 3: C. Fadiman

Greenwood 1: J. W. Robertson Scott, *The Story of the Pall Mall Gazette*, in J. Sutherland, ed., *OBLA*

Gregory I 1: Bede, *History of the English Church and People*; 2: W. Durant, *The Story of Civilization*, IV

Grey 1: B. Tuchman, *The Guns of August*; 2: W. Churchill, *Great Contemporaries*

Grimm 1: J. Braude, *Braude's Second Encyclopedia*

Grote 1: J. Gere and J. Sparrow, *Geoffrey Madan's Notebooks*

Guggenheim 1: P. Méras, *The Mermaids of Chenonceaux*

Guimond 1: F. Loliée, *Gilded Beauties of the Second Empire*

Guines 1: S. Alsop, *Yankees at the Court*

Guitry 1: J. Braude, *Speaker's and Toastmaster's Handbook*

Gunther 1: *Book-of-the-Month Club News*, Aug. 1947

Guthrie 1: A. Guinness, *Blessings in Disguise*

Gwyn 1: *DNB*; 2: L. and M. Cowan, *The Wit of Women*

Hadrian 1: W. Durant, *The Story of Civilization*, III

Haeseler 1: H. Hoffmeister, *Anekdotenschatz*

Hagen 2: A. Cooke, *The Patient Has the Floor*

Halbe 1: H. Hoffmeister, *Anekdotenschatz*

Haldane 1: V. Castlerosse, *Valentine's Days*

Hale 1: I. Wallace et al., *The Book of Lists 2*

Halifax, C., 1: W. and A. Durant, *The Story of Civilization*, VIII

Halifax, E., 1: *Book-of-the-Month Club News*, Jan. 1954

Hall 1: W. Walsh, *Handy Book of Curious Information*

Hamilton 1: C. Fadiman and C. Van Doren, *The American Treasury*

Hammerstein II 1: H. Fordin, *Getting to Know Him*; 3: N. and B. Donaldson, *How Did They Die?*

Hammett 1: D. Johnson, *Dashiell Hammett*; 3: L. Hellman, *An Unfinished Woman*

Hamsun 1: H. Hoffmeister, *Anekdotenschatz*

Handel 1: E. Jones, *A Food Lover's Companion*; 2–4: H. C. Robbins Landon, *Handel and His World*

Hannibal 1: Livy, *Annals*

Hardy 1: *New York Review of Books,* Oct. 7, 1982

Harlow 1: C. Bowen, *The Curse of the Misbegotten: A Tale of the House of O'Neill,* in D. Hall, ed., *OBALA*

Harriman 1: *The New Yorker,* May 10, 1952; 2: *The New Yorker,* May 3, 1952

Harris 1: E. Fuller, *2500 Anecdotes;* 2: S. Beach, *Shakespeare and Co.,* in D. Hall, ed., *OBALA;* 3: D. Cecil, *Max: A Biography*

Harrison, Benjamin, 1: D. Wallechinsky and I. Wallace, *The People's Almanac*

Harrison, President Benjamin, 1: H. L. Stoddard, *As I Knew Them: Presidents and Politics from Grant to Coolidge,* in P. Boller, ed., *Presidential Anecdotes*

Hart 1: O. Levant, *The Unimportance of Being Oscar*

Harte 1: W. Scholz, *Das Buch des Lachens*

Hartleben 1: H. Hoffmeister, *Anekdotenschatz*

Hatto 1: W. Walsh, *Handy Book of Curious Information*

Havemeyer 1: J. Braude, *Speaker's and Toastmaster's Handbook*

Hawthorne, Nathaniel, 2: N. and B. Donaldson, *How Did They Die?;* 3: R. Stewart, *Nathaniel Hawthorne,* in D. Hall, ed., *OBALA*

Hawthorne, Nigel, 1: M. Wiley and D. Bona, *Inside Oscar*

Hawtrey 1: G. Brandreth, *Great Theatrical Disasters*

Hay 1: *Quarterly Review,* no. 218, 1861, in D. George, *A Book of Anecdotes*

Haydn 1: *Quarterly Review,* no. 218, 1861, in D. George, *A Book of Anecdotes;* 2: W. and A. Durant, *The Story of Civilization,* X; 3: N. Slonimsky, *A Thing or Two About Music;* 4: N. and B. Donaldson, *How Did They Die?*

Hayes, H., 1: B. Thomas, *Thalberg: Life and Legend;* 3–4: M. Biggs, ed., *Women's Words: The Columbia Book of Quotations by Women*

Hayes, R., 1: G. F. Hoar, *Autobiography of Seventy Years,* in P. Boller, ed., *Presidential Anecdotes*

Hayworth 1: C. Fadiman and C. Van Doren, *The American Treasury*

Hazlitt 1: E. Fuller, *2500 Anecdotes;* 2: W. Keddie, *Literary and Scientific Anecdote*

Heap 1: M. Biggs, ed., *Women's Words: The Columbia Book of Quotations by Women*

Hearst 1: Kenin and Wintle, *DBQ;* 2: P. Kael, *The Citizen Kane Book;* 3: R. Marquard, *Jokes and Anecdotes;* 4: J. Tebbel, *The Inheritors*

Hecht 1: *The New Yorker,* Dec. 13, 1952

Hegel 1: B. Conrad, *Famous Last Words*

Heggen 1: R. Nelson, *The Almanac of American Letters*

Heidegger 1: F. Muir, *Irreverent Social History*

Heifetz 1: O. Levant, *The Unimportance of Being Oscar;* 2: *Los Angeles Times,* Aug. 29, 1982; 3: H. Temianka, *Facing the Music*

Heine 1: D. Wallechinsky and I. Wallace, *The People's Almanac;* 2: B. Conrad, *Famous Last Words;* 3: E. Fuller, *2500 Anecdotes*

Held 1: J. McBride, *High and Inside: The A–Z Guide to the Language of Baseball*

Helmsley 1: M. Biggs, ed., *Women's Words: The Columbia Book of Quotations by Women*

Hemingway 1: P. Méras, *The Mermaids of Chenonceaux;* 2: B. Morton, *Americans in Paris;* 3: B. Cerf, *Try and Stop Me;* 4, 9: C. Fadiman and C. Van Doren, *The American Treasury;* 5: *Signature,* Sept. 1983; 7: A. Hotchner, *Choice People;* 8: Y. Karsh, *Karsh*

Henri IV 1, 5: W. and A. Durant, *The Story of Civilization,* VII; 2: *EB;* 3: E. Guérard, *Dictionnaire Encyclopédique;* 4: K. Arvine, *Cyclopaedia of Anecdotes;* 6: W. Keddie, *Literary and Scientific Anecdote*

Henry 1: O. Henry, *The Voice of the City*

Henry II 1: *DNB*

Henry IV 1: *DNB*

Henry VIII 1: L. and F. Copeland, *10,000 Jokes, Toasts, and Stories;* 2: *"Daily Mirror" Old Codger's Little Black Book 1*

Henson 1: R. Hendrickson, *The Literary Life*

Henze 1: N. Lebrecht, *The Book of Musical Anecdotes*

Hepburn 1: *Parade*, Nov. 27, 1983; 3: M. Biggs, ed., *Women's Words: The Columbia Book of Quotations by Women*

Herman 1: J. McBride, *High and Inside: The A–Z Guide to the Language of Baseball*

Herschel 1: *DNB*

Hess 1: H. Temianka, *Facing the Music*

Hideyoshi 1: W. Durant, *The Story of Civilization*, I

Hilbert 1–2: G. Polya, "Some Mathematicians I Have Known," in D. Campbell and J. Higgins, eds., *Mathematics: People, Problems, Results*

Hill, J., 1: A. de Morgan, *Encyclopedia of Eccentrics*

Hill, R., 1–2: W. Adams, *Treasury of Modern Anecdote*

Hillary 1: E. Hillary, *High Adventure*

Hindemith 1: R. Smullyan, *5000 B.C. and Other Philosophical Fantasies*

Hitchcock 1: E. Fuller, *2500 Anecdotes*; 5–6: C. Madigan and A. Elwood, *Brainstorms and Thunderbolts*; 7: D. Spoto, *The Dark Side of Genius*

Hobson, L., 1: L. Hobson, *Laura Z.*

Hobson, T., 1: *DNB*

Hoffman 1: H. Hoffmeister, *Anekdotenschatz*

Hofman 1: O. Levant, *The Unimportance of Being Oscar*; 2: H. Taubman, *Music on My Beat*; 3: H. Temianka, *Facing the Music*

Hogan 1: S. Snead, *The Game I Love*

Hogarth 1: G. Colman, *Circle of Anecdote*

Hokusai 1: B. Conrad, *Famous Last Words*

Holles 1: A. Fraser, *Cromwell*

Holliday 1: G. Steinem, *Outrageous Acts and Everyday Rebellions*

Holmes, F., 1–3: C. Bowen, *Yankee from Olympus*

Holmes, J., 1–3: C. Bowen, *Yankee from Olympus*

Holmes, O. Sr., 1: M. Howe, *Holmes of the Breakfast Table*; 2: R. Shenkman and K. Reiger, *One-Night Stands with American History*; 3: W. D. Howells, *Literary Friends and Acquaintances*, in D. Hall, ed., *OBALA*; 4: C. Bowen, *Yankee from Olympus*; 5: C. Ticknor, *Dr. Holmes's Boston*

Holmes, O. Jr., 1–4, 6–7: C. Bowen, *Yankee from Olympus*; 5: C. Fadiman and C. Van Doren, *The American Treasury*; 8: B. Conrad, *Famous Last Words*

Homer 1: '47, *The Magazine of the Year*

Hook 1: *DNB*; 2: L. Russell, *English Wits*; 3: K. Arvine, *Cyclopaedia of Anecdotes*; 4: D. Knox, *More Quotable Anecdotes*

Hooker 1: J. Bigelow, Jr., *Sidney V. Lowell in the Campaign at Chancellorsville*, in B. Botkin, *A Civil War Treasury*

Hoover 1: A. Krock, *Memoirs*, in P. Boller, ed., *Presidential Memoirs*; 2: E. Lyons, *Herbert Hoover: A Biography*, in Boller, *Presidential Anecdotes*; 3: I. Wallace et al., *Book of Lists 2*; 4: C. Fadiman and C. Van Doren, *The American Treasury*

Horne 1: S. Terkel, *"The Good War"*

Horowitz 1, 3: O. Levant, *The Unimportance of Being Oscar*; 2: J. Gaines, *Lives of the Piano*

Horthy De Nagybánya 1: E. Kelen, *Peace in Their Time*

Houdini 1: F. Oursler, *Behold This Dreamer*; 2: H. Prochnow, *The Public Speaker's Treasure Chest*; 3: N. and B. Donaldson, *How Did They Die?*

Housman 1: R. Graves, *A. E. Housman*

Howard, C., 1: I. Wallace et al., *Intimate Sex Lives of Famous People*

Howard, L., 1: L. and F. Copeland, *10,000 Jokes, Toasts, and Stories*

Howarth 1: S. Rogers, *Table Talk*

Howe, E., 1: J. Braude, *Speaker's and Toastmaster's Handbook*

Howe, I., 1: A Bernard, *Now All We Need Is a Title*

Howe, J., 1–2: W. Abbot, *Notable Women in History*

Howells 1: M. Howe, *John Jay Chapman*; 2–3: E. Fuller, *2500 Anecdotes*

Hoy 1: C. Jones, *What Makes Winners Win*

Hruska 1: *Congressional Quarterly*, vol. 3

Hudson 1: P. Boller, ed., *Hollywood Anecdotes*

Hughes 1: J. S. Haskins, *Always Movin' On: The Life of Langston Hughes,* in D. Hall, ed., *OBALA*

Hugo 1: R. Hendrickson, *The Literary Life; 2:* E. Samuels, *The Education of Henry Adams; 3:* R. Godden, *Hans Christian Andersen; 4:* G. Lieberman, *The Greatest Laughs of All Time*

Hull, C., 1: J. Braude, *Braude's Second Encyclopedia*

Hull, I., 1: B. Conrad, *Famous Last Words*

Hume 1: E. Guérard, *Dictionnaire Encyclopédique; 2:* E. Fuller, *2500 Anecdotes; 3:* W. Keddie, *Literary and Scientific Anecdote; 4:* W. and A. Durant, *The Story of Civilization,* IX; *5:* H. Brougham, *Men of Letters*

Humphrey 1–4: B. Dole, *Great Political Wit*

Hunter 1: *New Scientist,* Nov. 9, 1981

Huston 1: D. Niven, *Bring On the Empty Horses; 2:* P. Hay, ed., *Movie Anecdotes*

Hutton, E. F., 1: B. Fussell, *I Hear America Cooking*

Hutton, L., 1: M. Biggs, ed., *Women's Words: The Columbia Book of Quotations by Women*

Huxley, A., 1, 3: D. Wallechinsky and I. Wallace, *The People's Almanac 2; 2:* R. Clark, *The Huxleys*

Huxley, T., 1: R. Moore, *Charles Darwin; 2:* E. Fuller, *2500 Anecdotes*

Hyde, Lady C., 1: L. and M. Cowan, *The Wit of Women*

Hyde, W., 1: E. Lucas, *A Fronded Isle*

Hylan 1: C. Sifakis, *Dictionary of Historic Nicknames*

Hyrtl 1: M. Jelusisch, *Geschichten aus dem Wienerwald*

Ibn Saud 1–2: R. Lacey, *The Kingdom*

Ibrahim Pasha 1: R. Lacey, *The Kingdom*

Ibsen 1: C. Fadiman, Introduction to E. Wharton, *Ethan Frome; 4:* J. Train, *True Remarkable Occurrences*

Ikku 1: R. Hendrickson, *The Literary Life*

Inge 1: A. Noyes, *Two Worlds for Memory*

Ingersoll 1: L. and F. Copeland, *10,000 Jokes, Toasts, and Stories*

Ingyo 1: J. Kidder, *Ancient Japan*

Iphicrates 1: L. Missen, *Quotable Anecdotes*

Irving, Sir Henry, 1: E. Heron-Allen, *We Saw Him Act,* in Kenin and Wintle, *DBQ; 2:* B. Conrad, *Famous Last Words*

Irving, W., 1: E. Wagenknecht, *Washington Irving: Moderation Displayed,* in D. Hall, ed., *OBALA; 2:* B. Conrad, *Famous Last Words*

Isabey 1: J. Timbs, *Century of Anecdote*

Jackson, A., 1–2, 5: J. Parton, *Life of Andrew Jackson,* in P. Boller, ed., *Presidential Anecdotes; 4:* B. Poore, *Perley's Reminiscences of Sixty Years,* in Boller, *Presidential Anecdotes*

Jackson, J., 1: D. Wallechinsky and I. Wallace, *The People's Almanac 2*

Jackson, R., 1: P. O'Brian, *Talkin' Sports; 2–3:* B. Adler, *Baseball Wit*

Jackson, S., 1: B. Gill, *Here at The New Yorker,* in D. Hall, ed., *OBALA*

Jackson, T., 1: M. Ringo, *Nobody Said It Better; 2:* M. J. Preston, "Personal Reminiscences of Stonewall Jackson," *Century Magazine,* XXXII (Oct. 1886), in B. Botkin, *A Civil War Treasury; 3:* R. Stiles, *Four Years Under Marse Robert,* in Botkin, *A Civil War Treasury; 4–5:* C. M. Blackford, ed., *Letters from Lee's Army,* in Botkin, *A Civil War Treasury; 6:* Maj. H. K. Douglas, *I Rode with Stonewall,* in Botkin, *A Civil War Treasury; 7:* J. Train, *Wit: The Best Things Ever Said; 8:* B. Conrad, *Famous Last Words*

Jacobi 1: E. Bell, *Men of Mathematics*

James, H., 1–2: D. Cecil, *Max: A Biography; 3:* E. Wharton, *A Backward Glance,* in D. Hall, ed., *OBALA; 4:* L. Edel, *Henry James: The Middle Years 1882–1895,* in D. Hall, ed., *OBALA; 6:* L. Edel, ed., *The Diary of Alice James,* in D. Hall, ed., *OBALA; 7:* D. Hall, ed., *OBALA; 8:* C. Fadiman and C. Van Doren, *The American Treasury*

James, J., 1: R. Love, *The Rise and Fall of Jesse James*

James, W., 1: *American Scholar* I: 4 (1931); *2:* L. Lucaire, *Celebrity Trivia; 3:* J. Barzun, *A*

Stroll with William James; 4: *Book-of-the-Month Club News,* Apr. 1948

James I 1: G. Colman, *Circle of Anecdote;* 2: *"Daily Mirror" Old Codger's Little Black Book 1;* 3: W. Keddie, *Literary and Scientific Anecdote*

Jarry 1: P. Méras, *The Mermaids of Chenonceaux;* 2: A. Vollard, *Recollections of a Picture Dealer;* 3: N. Lennon, *Alfred Jarry: The Man with the Axe;* 4: A. S. Huffington, *Picasso: Creator and Destroyer*

Jefferson, J., 1: T. Masson, *The Best Stories in the World*

Jefferson, T., 1, 3, 11: H. S. Randall, *The Life of Thomas Jefferson,* in P. Boller, ed., *Presidential Anecdotes;* 2, Edward Ellis, *Thomas Jefferson, A Character Sketch,* in Boller, *Presidential Anecdotes;* 4–5, 10, 14: Sarah Randolph, *The Domestic Life of Thomas Jefferson,* in D. Hall, ed., *OBALA;* 6: Arthur D. Graeff, "Anecdotes Related in Pennsylvania-German Almanacs," *The American-German Review* VI (Apr. 1940), in B. Botkin, *Treasury of American Anecdotes;* 8: J. Train, *True Remarkable Occurrences;* 9, 12: M. B. Smith, *The First Forty Years in Washington Society,* in Boller, *Presidential Anecdotes;* 13: C. Wiltse and H. Moser, eds., *The Papers of Daniel Webster — Correspondence,* vol. II

Jeffreys 1: J. Braude, *Speaker's and Toastmaster's Handbook*

Jérôme 1: F. Loliée, *Gilded Beauties of the Second Empire*

Jerrold 1: T. Powell, *The Living Authors of England,* in J. Sutherland, ed., *OBLA;* 2: E. Fuller, *2500 Anecdotes;* 3: W. Adams, *Treasury of Modern Anecdote*

Jessel 1: A. Burrows, *Honest, Abe*

John XXIII 4: P. Bussard, *The New Catholic Treasury of Wit and Humor;* 5: H. Arendt, *Men in Dark Times*

John III Sobieski 1: D. George, *A Book of Anecdotes*

Johnson, A., 1: M. D. Conway, "The President's Defense," *Fortnightly Review,* V (1866), in P. Boller, ed., *Presidential Anecdotes*

Johnson, L., 1: R. Caro, *The Years of Lyndon Johnson,* I; 2: D. Halberstam, *The Best and the Brightest,* in P. Boller, ed., *Presidential Anecdotes;* 3: "Washington Wags," *Reader's Digest,* Oct. 1959, in Boller, *Presidential Anecdotes;* 5, 9–10: B. Dole: *Great Political Wit;* 7: B. Adler, ed., *The Washington Wits,* in Boller, *Presidential Anecdotes;* 11: Larry L. King, "LBJ and Vietnam," in *A Sense of History*

Johnson, N., 1–2: N. Johnson, *Flashback*

Johnson, S., 1, 3, 5, 11–12, 16–19, 21–22: J. Boswell, *Life of Johnson;* 2, 7, 10, 15, 23: C. Hibbert, *The Personal History of Samuel Johnson;* 4: H. Beste, *Personal and Literary Memorials;* 6: J. Timbs, *Century of Anecdote;* 8: W. Seward, *Anecdotes;* 9: J. Braude, *Speaker's and Toastmaster's Handbook;* 13: L. Russell, *English Wits;* 20: W. Keddie, *Literary and Scientific Anecdote;* 24–25: G. Brandreth, *871 Famous Last Words*

Johnson, W., 1: E. Fuller, *2500 Anecdotes*

Jolson 1: C., Fadiman and C. Van Doren, *The American Treasury*

Jones, James, 1, 3–4: W. Morris, *James Jones: A Friendship,* in D. Hall, ed., *OBALA;* 2: *Book-of-the-Month Club News,* Sept. 1951

Jones, John Paul, 1: M. Ringo, *Nobody Said It Better;* 2: *DNB*

Jonson 1: L. Lucaire, *Celebrity Trivia;* 2: J. Aubrey, *Brief Lives*

Jordan 1: C. Jones, *What Makes Winners Win*

Jowett 1: T. Masson, *The Best Stories in the World;* 2: G. F. Will, "Commencement at Duke," *The American Scholar,* Autumn 1991

Joyce, James, 1: P. Mahony, *Barbed Wit and Malicious Humor;* 2: unpublished ms. by G. Russell, in R. Ellmann, *James Joyce;* 3: S. Huddleston, *Paris Salons, Cafés, Studios;* 4: R. Ellmann, interview with F. Budgen, in Ellmann, *James Joyce;* 6: H. Gorman Papers, in Ellmann, *James Joyce;* 7: R. Ellmann, interview with C. Giedion-Welcker, in Ellmann,

James Joyce; 8: R. Ellmann, *James Joyce;* 9: R. Ellmann, interview with S. Beckett, in Ellmann, *James Joyce*

Joyce, John, 1: R. Ellmann, interview with S. Joyce, in Ellmann, *James Joyce;* 2: W. Wiser, *The Crazy Years;* 3: unpublished notes of L. Gillet in Ellmann, *James Joyce*

Juang-Zu 1: B. Conrad, *Famous Last Words*

Julia 1–4: Macrobius, *Saturnalia*

Julian 1: W. Durant, *The Story of Civilization,* IV

Julius II 1: G. Vasari, *Lives of the Painters*

Jullien 1: *Oxford Companion to Music;* 2: H. Schonberg, *The Great Conductors*

Jusserand 1: W. R. Thayer, *Theodore Roosevelt: An Intimate Portrait,* in P. Boller, ed., *Presidential Anecdotes;* 2: Lewis Henry, *Humorous Anecdotes About Famous People,* in Boller, *Presidential Anecdotes;* 3: *Los Angeles Times Book Review,* Sept. 9, 1984

Kahn 1: R. Marquard, *Jokes and Anecdotes*

Kallio 1: A. Ranjanen, *Of Finnish Ways*

Kames 1: John Ramsay of Ochtertyre, *Scotland and Scotsmen in the Eighteenth Century,* in J. Sutherland, ed., *OBLA*

Kant 1: H. Margolius, *Der Lächelnde Philosoph*

Karl Alexander 1: W. Scholz, *Das Buch des Lachens*

Kaufman 1: O. Levant, *The Unimportance of Being Oscar;* 2: B. Cerf, *Try and Stop Me;* 4: M. Connelly, *Voices Offstage;* 5: D. Herrmann, *With Malice Toward All;* 7: J. Nash, *Zanies;* 8: J. Adamson, *Groucho, Harpo, Chico;* 9: D. Hall, ed., *OBALA;* 10, 13: R. Drennan, *The Algonquin Wits;* 11: C. Fadiman and C. Van Doren, *The American Treasury;* 12: C. Sifakis, *Dictionary of Historic Nicknames;* 14: N. and B. Donaldson, *How Did They Die?*

Kaunitz-Rietburg 1: W. and A. Durant, *The Story of Civilization,* X

Kazan 1: G. Herman, *The Book of Hollywood Quotes*

Keats 1–3: C. A. Brown, "Life of John Keats," in

H. E. Rollins, ed., *The Keats Circle: Letters and Papers 1816–78*

Kekulé Von Stradonitz 1: J. Daintith et al., *Biographical Encyclopedia of Scientists*

Keller 1: A. Whitman, *Come to Judgment*

Kelly, G., 1: A. Lewis, *Those Philadelphia Kellys*

Kelly, M., 1: A. Bespaloff, *The Fireside Book of Wine*

Kelvin 1: S. Bolton, *Famous Men of Science;* 2: A. Fleming, *Memories of a Scientific Life*

Kemble, C., 1: J. Aye, *Humour in the Theatre*

Kemble, F., 1: Thomas B. Reed, ed., *Modern Eloquence,* X, in B. Botkin, *Treasury of American Anecdotes*

Kemble, J., 1: Thomas Moore's Diary, in D. George, *A Book of Anecdotes;* 2: J. Aye, *Humour in the Theatre*

Kemble, S., 1: W. Keddie, *Literary and Scientific Anecdote*

Kennedy, E., 1–2: B. Dole, *Great Political Wit;* 3: J. Germond, *Blue Smoke and Mirrors*

Kennedy, J. F., 1: G. Stebben and J. Morris, *White House Confidential;* 2, 11, 18: M. Ringo, *Nobody Said It Better;* 3: A. Whitman, *Come to Judgment;* 4–5: P. Collier and D. Horowitz, *The Kennedys;* 6: R. Shenkman and K. Reiger, *One-Night Stands with American History;* 7: I. Wallace et al., *Intimate Sex Lives of Famous People;* 8, 13, 17: B. Dole, *Great Political Wit;* 9: T. Wicker, *One of Us: The Age of Richard Nixon 1946–1975;* 10: Sir R. Bing, *A Knight at the Opera;* 12: J. McAleer, "Globe Man's Daily Story," *Boston Globe,* Jan. 22, 1965; 13, 16: D. Wallechinsky and I. Wallace, *The People's Almanac;* 14: W. Manchester, *One Brief Shining Moment;* 15: C. Hitchens, "Booze and Fags," review of V. G. Kiernan's *Tobacco: A History, London Review of Books,* Mar. 12, 1922; 19: H. Sidey, *John F. Kennedy, President;* 20: E. Jones, *A Food Lover's Companion;* 21: R. Martin, *A Hero for Our Times;* 22: H. Rainie and J. Quinn, *Growing Up a Kennedy*

Kennedy, Joseph 1: C. Amory, *The Proper*

Bostonians, in B. Botkin, *Treasury of American Anecdotes*; 2: M. Gordon, *Max Gordon Presents*; 3: P. Collier and D. Horowitz, *The Kennedys*; 4: W. Manchester, *One Brief Shining Moment*; 5: N. Hamilton, *JFK: Reckless Youth*

Kennedy, R., 1–2: B. Dole, *Great Political Wit*; 3: F. Saunders, *Torn Lace Curtain*, in P. Boller, ed., *Presidential Wives: An Anecdotal History*

Kepler 1: I. Asimov, *Biographical Encyclopedia*

Keppel 1: G. Colman, *Circle of Anecdote*

Ker 1: J. Gere and J. Sparrow, *Geoffrey Madan's Notebooks*; 2: J. MacCunn, *Recollections of W. P. Ker by Two Friends*

Kerouac 1: R. Nelson, *The Almanac of American Letters*; 2: D. Hall, "A Visit with Robert Giroux," *The New York Times Book Review*, Jan. 1980, in D. Hall, ed., *OBALA*

Kerr, D., 1: M. Biggs, ed., *Women's Words: The Columbia Book of Quotations by Women*

Kerr, J., 1: *Los Angeles Times*, Dec. 8, 1985

Keynes 1: C. Hession, *John Maynard Keynes*; 2: A. Cave Brown, *The Last Hero*

Khrushchev 1: M. Ringo, *Nobody Said It Better*; 2: B. Adler, *My Favorite Funny Story*; 3: K. P. O'Donnell and D. E. Powers, *"Johnny, We Hardly Knew Ye"*; 4: K. Edwards, *I Wish I'd Said That*

Kidd 1: B. Conrad, *Famous Last Words*

Kiner 1: J. C. Humes, *Speaker's Treasury*

Kinglake 1: J. Gere and J. Sparrow, *Geoffrey Madan's Notebooks*

Kingsale 1: S. Winchester, *Their Noble Lordships*

Kipling 1: H. Hoffmeister, *Anekdotenschatz*; 2: E. Fuller, *2500 Anecdotes*

Kissinger 1–2: R. Valeriani, *Travels with Henry*; 3–5: W. Isaacson, *Kissinger in America: A Biography*; 6: *Los Angeles Times*, Sept. 27, 1986

Kitchener 1: A. J. P. Taylor, *English History*

Kittredge 1: D. Hall, ed., *OBALA*

Klein 1: H. Prochnow, *The Public Speaker's Treasure Chest*

Klemperer 3: H. Temianka, *Facing the Music*

Klöpfer 1: H. Hoffmeister, *Anekdotenschatz*

Kneller 1: H. Walpole, *Anecdotes of Painting*; 2: *A Dictionary of Anecdotes* (1809), in D. George, *A Book of Anecdotes*; 3: L. Russell, *English Wits*

Knopf 1: C. Fadiman, *Fifty Years*

Knox, P. 1: T. Buckley, *Violent Neighbors*

Koestler 1: *International Herald Tribune*, Apr. 24–25, 1982

Koo 1: R. Marquard, *Jokes and Anecdotes*

Koppay 1: S. Dryfoos, *Iphigene*

Korda 1–5: M. Korda, *Charmed Lives*; 6: R. Morley, *Pardon Me, But You're Eating My Doily*

Koussevitzky 1: O. Levant, *The Unimportance of Being Oscar*; 2–3: H. Earle Johnson, *Symphony Hall*

Kreisler 1: E. Fuller, *2500 Anecdotes*; 2: B. Cerf, *Try and Stop Me*; 3: S. Beach, *Musicdotes*

Labouchere 2: H. Pearson, *Lives of the Wits*; 3: L. Russell, *English Wits*

Ladd 1: M. Biggs, ed., *Women's Words: The Columbia Book of Quotations by Women*

Laemmle 1: N. Zierold, *The Moguls*

Lafayette 1: P. Buckman, *Lafayette*; 2: H. Prochnow, *The Public Speaker's Treasure Chest*; 3: D. Hall, ed., *OBALA*

La Fontaine 1: W. Sholz, *Das Buch des Lachens*

La Guardia 1: B. Cerf, *Try and Stop Me*; 2: J. Gunther, *Procession*; 3: J. C. Humes, *Speaker's Treasury*

Laird 1: H. Kissinger, *White House Years*

Laïs 1: I. Wallace, *The Nympho & Other Maniacs*

Lamar 1: E. Mayes, *Life of Lucius Q. C. Lamar*, in C. Shriner, *Wit, Wisdom, and Foibles of the Great*

Lamb, Lady C., 1: *Boston Globe*, Feb. 20, 1985; 2: D. Cecil, *Melbourne*

Lamb, Charles, 1–2, 4: L. Russell, *English Wits*; 3: W. Keddie, *Literary and Scientific Anecdote*; 5, 7: E. Fuller, *2500 Anecdotes*; 6: *American Scholar*, VI: 2 (1937)

Landers 1: M. Biggs, ed., *Women's Words: The Columbia Book of Quotations by Women*

Landis 1: J. Braude, *Speaker's and Toastmaster's Handbook*

Landor 1: R. M. Milnes, *Lord Houghton Monographs,* in F. Muir, *Irreverent Social History*

Landowska 1: H. Schonberg, *The Great Pianists*

Landru 1: D. Wallechinsky and I. Wallace, *The People's Almanac*; 2: J. Carey, ed., *The Faber Book of Reportage*

Lang 1–2: G. Lang, *Nobody Knows the Truffles I've Seen*

Langtry 1: I. Wallace et al., *Intimate Sex Lives of Famous People*

Laplace 1–2: E. Bell, *Men of Mathematics*

Lardner 1: J. Yardley, *Ring*; 2: D. Elder, *Ring Lardner*

Lasorda 1: B. Shlain, *Baseball Inside Out*

Latimer 1: B. Conrad, *Famous Last Words*

Lauzun 1: P. Smith, *A New Age Now Begins*

Lavoisier 1: I. Asimov, *Biographical Encyclopedia*

Lawrence, D. H., 1: E. D. McDonald, ed., *D. H. Lawrence, Phoenix: The Posthumous Papers,* in J. Sutherland, ed., *OBLA*; 2: N. and B. Donaldson, *How Did They Die?*

Lawrence, J. 1: D. Wallechinsky and I. Wallace, *The People's Almanac*

Lawrence, T. E., 1: R. Graves, *Goodbye to All That*; 2: E. Marsh, *A Number of People*

Lawson 1: G. Brandreth, *Great Theatrical Disasters*

Leahy 1: A. Hatch, *The Byrds of Virginia*

Lear 1, 3: V. Noakes, *Edward Lear*; 2, 4: A. Davidson, *Edward Lear*

Ledru-Rollin 1: L. Harris, *The Fine Art of Political Wit*

Lee, G., 1: E. Preminger, *Gypsy and Me*

Lee, N., 1: "Liber Facetiarum," in D. George, *A Book of Anecdotes*

Lee, R. E., 1: C. Fadiman and C. Van Doren, *The American Treasury*; 2: J. M. Morgan, *Century Magazine,* LX (May 1900), in B. Botkin, *A Civil War Treasury*; 3: Gen. J. B. Gordon, "Last Days of the Confederacy," *Modern Eloquence,* V, in B. Botkin, *A Civil War Treasury*; 4: G. W. Bagby, *The Old Virginia Gentleman and Other Sketches,* in B. Botkin, *Treasury of American Anecdotes*; 6: M. Ringo, *Nobody Said It Better*

Lehmann 1: C. Gattey, *The Elephant That Swallowed a Nightingale*

Leighton 1: S. Radecki, *Das ABC des Lachens*

Lenclos 1: J. Nash, *Zanies*; 2: G. Boissier, *Mme de Sévigné*; 3: I. Wallace, *The Nympho & Other Maniacs*; 4: I. Wallace et al., *Intimate Sex Lives of Famous People*; 5: W. and A. Durant, *The Story of Civilization,* VIII

Lenya 1: *The Times* (London), Nov. 30, 1981

Leo X 1: T. Craven, *Men of Art*

Leonard 1: W. Zinsser, *A Family of Readers*

Leonidas 1: I. Asimov, *Biographical Encyclopedia*

Leschetizky 1: H. Schonberg, *The Great Pianists*

Lessing 1: J. Timbs, *Century of Anecdote*

Levant 2: B. Adler, *My Favorite Funny Story*; 3: J. McAleer, "Globe Man's Daily Story," *Boston Globe,* July 10, 1964; 4–5: D. Herrmann, *With Malice Toward All*

Lévis 1: D. George, *A Book of Anecdotes*

Lewis, C., 1: D. Balsdon, *Oxford Now and Then*; 2: R. Green, *C. S. Lewis*

Lewis, M., 1: J. Timbs, *Century of Anecdote*

Lewis, S., 1: L. Untermeyer, *Bygones*; 2: J. McAleer, "Globe Man's Daily Story," *Boston Globe,* July 20, 1970; 3–4: B. Conrad, *Fun While It Lasted*

Liberace 1: C. Fadiman and C. Van Doren, *The American Treasury*

Li Bo 1: A. Davis, ed., *Penguin Book of Chinese Verse*

Lichtenberg 1: W. Scholz, *Das Buch des Lachens*

Liebermann 1: C. Bowra, *Memories 1898–1939*

Liebling 1: B. Gill, *Here at The New Yorker*

Lieven 1: J. Griffin, ed., *Snobs*

Liliencron 1–2: H. Hoffmeister, *Anekdotenschatz*

Lillie 2: L. and M. Cowan, *The Wit of Women*; 3: C. Daniel, *Lords, Ladies and Gentlemen*; 4: *Book-of-the-Month Club News,* July 1948

Lincoln, A., 1–2, 11, 15: A. K. McClure, ed., *Lincoln's Own Yarns and Stories;* 3, 27: W. Whipple, *The Story-Life of Abraham Lincoln,* in P. Boller, ed., *Presidential Anecdotes;* 4, 10, 19, 21–23: E. Fuller, *2500 Anecdotes;* 5: I. Tarbell, *The Life of Abraham Lincoln;* 6: B. Cerf, *Shake Well Before Using;* 7: J. M. Scovel, quoting O. H. Browning, in *Lippincott's Magazine,* Mar. 1903, in C. Shriner, *Wit, Wisdom, and Foibles of the Great;* 8: P. Zall, *Abe Lincoln Laughing;* 9, 18: G. S. Hilton, *The Funny Side of Politics,* in Boller, *Presidential Anecdotes;* 12, 26: B. Poore, *Perley's Reminiscences of Sixty Years,* in Boller, *Presidential Anecdotes;* 13: Boller, *Presidential Wives: An Anecdotal History;* 14: A. Barra, *That's Not the Way It Was;* 16, 24–25: P. Selby, ed., *Stories and Speeches of Abraham Lincoln,* in Boller, *Presidential Anecdotes;* 17, 31: C. Fadiman and C. Van Doren, *The American Treasury;* 20: T. Dennett, ed., *Lincoln and the Civil War in the Diaries of John Hay,* in Boller, *Presidential Anecdotes;* 28: P. Smith, *Trial by Fire;* 29: R. Marquard, *Jokes and Anecdotes;* 30: W. R. Thayer, *The Life of John Hay,* in Shriner, *Wit;* 32: C. Sandburg, in D. George, *A Book of Anecdotes;* 33: A. Gross, *Lincoln's Own Stories,* in Boller, *Presidential Anecdotes;* 34: F. Moore, *Anecdotes, Poetry, and Incidents of the War;* 35: D. Wallechinsky and I. Wallace, *The People's Almanac;* 36: W. H. Lamon, *Recollections of Abraham Lincoln 1847–1865,* in B. Botkin, *A Civil War Treasury*

Lincoln, R., 1: I. Wallace, "Significa," Aug. 2, 1981

Lind 1: I. Wallace, *The Fabulous Showman*

Lindbergh 1–2: J. Milton, *Loss of Eden: A Biography of Charles and Anne Morrow Lindbergh*

Lindemann 1: W. Manchester, *The Last Lion*

Lippert 1: M. Biggs, ed., *Women's Words: The Columbia Book of Quotations by Women*

Lister 1: H. Steinbert, *Artz und Patient*

Liszt 1: G. Keynes and B. Hill, *Samuel Butler's Notebooks;* 2: N. Cardus, *Talking of Music;* 3: L. de Heggerman-Lindencrone, "The Sunny Side of Diplomatic Life," in J. Bryan, III, ed., *Hodgepodge: A Commonplace Book*

Livermore 1: M. Saxton, *Louisa May*

Lloyd George 1: S. Spender, *World Within World;* 2: C. Fadiman and C. Van Doren, *The American Treasury;* 3: M. and A. Guillois, *Liberté, Egalité, Hilarité;* 4: E. Fuller, *2500 Anecdotes;* 5: P. Mahony, *Barbed Wit and Malicious Humor*

Lloyd Weber 1: P. Holland, "Whistling in the Dark," review of M. Walsh, *Andrew Lloyd Weber, Times Literary Supplement,* Dec. 8–14, 1989

Lobengula 1: J. Lockhart, *Cecil Rhodes*

Locke 1: W. Keddie, *Literary and Scientific Anecdote*

Lombardi 2: M. Ringo, *Nobody Said It Better*

Long 1: T. H. Williams, *Huey Long,* in R. Shenkman and K. Reiger, *One-Night Stands with American History;* 2: A. Brinkley, *Voices of Protest*

Longworth 1: D. Herrmann, *With Malice Toward All*

Louis, J. 1: R. Lamparski, *Whatever Became Of . . . ?;* 2: B. Conn, "Unforgettable Joe Louis," *Reader's Digest,* July 1983; 4: M. Ringo, *Nobody Said It Better*

Louis XI 1: F. Winslow, *Physic and Physicians,* in D. George, *A Book of Anecdotes*

Louis XIV 1: W. and A. Durant, *The Story of Civilization,* VII; 2, 7, 10: V. Cronin, *Louis XIV;* 3: E. Fuller, *2500 Anecdotes;* 4: M. Pedrazzini and J. Gris, *Autant en apportent les mots;* 5–6: E. Guérard, *Dictionnaire Encyclopédique;* 8: G. Colman, *Circle of Anecdote;* 9: L. Norton, *Saint-Simon at Versailles*

Louis XV 1: M. Pedrazzini and J. Gris, *Autant en apportent les mots;* 2: E. Fuller, *2500 Anecdotes;* 3: T. F. Thiselton-Dyer, *Royalty in All Ages,* in C. Shriner, *Wit, Wisdom, and Foibles of the Great;* 4: A. Castelot, *Marie Antoinette*

Louis XVI 1: R. Chelmiaski, *The French at Table;* 2: W. Merwin, *Products of the Per-*

fected Civilization; 3: W. and A. Durant, The Story of Civilization, X; 4: W. and A. Durant, The Story of Civilization, XI

Louis XVIII 1: A. Castelot, Paris: The Turbulent City

Louis Philippe 1: A. Castelot, Paris: The Turbulent City

Lowell, Abbott, 1: C. Amory, The Proper Bostonians, in P. Boller, ed., Presidential Anecdotes

Lowell, Amy, 1: R. McAlmon, Being Geniuses Together; 2: S. Weintraub, The London Yankees, in D. Hall, ed., OBALA

Lowell, R. 1: P. Ziegler, Diana Cooper; 2: I. Hamilton, Robert Lowell: A Biography; 3: G. Plimpton, The Paris Review Interviews, in A. Bernard, Now All We Need Is a Title

Lucas 1–3: P. Hay, ed., Movie Anecdotes; 4: M. Corey and G. Ochoa, The Man in Lincoln's Nose

Luce, C., 1: W. Sheed, Clare Boothe Luce; 3: J. C. Humes, Speaker's Treasury

Luce, H., 1: S. Seagrave, The Soong Dynasty

Lucullus 1: Plutarch, Lives

Lully 1: EB

Lunt 1: I. Asimov, Treasury of Humor; 2: E. Fuller, 2500 Anecdotes

Luther 1: P. Bussard, The New Catholic Treasury of Wit and Humor; 2: W. Durant, The Story of Civilization, VI; 3: D. Boorstin, The Creators

Lyautey 1: L. Harris, The Fine Art of Political Wit

Lycurgus 1: W. Seward, Biographiana, vol. 5

Lyndhurst 1: B. Disraeli, Reminiscences, in Kenin and Wintle, DBQ

Lytton 1: Sir T. H. H. Caine, My Story, in J. Sutherland, ed., OBLA

Mably 1: E. Guérard, Dictionnaire Encyclopédique

McCarthy 1: S. Allen, Funny People

McCormack 1: C. Gattey, The Elephant That Swallowed a Nightingale

McCormick 1: S. Birmingham, The Grandes Dames

McCoy 1: H. Smith, The Life and Legend of Gene Fowler; 2: B. Green, P. G. Wodehouse

McCullers 1: R. Nelson, The Almanac of American Letters; 2–3: V. S. Carr, The Lonely Hunter: A Biography of Carson McCullers, in D. Hall, ed., OBALA

McGraw 1: J. McBride, High and Inside; 2: B. Shlain, Baseball Inside Out

McKinley 1: R. Shenkman and K. Reiger, One-Night Stands with American History; 2: J. F. Rhodes, The McKinley and Roosevelt Administrations 1897–1909, in P. Boller, ed., Presidential Anecdotes

MacArthur, D., 2: C. Fadiman and C. Van Doren, The American Treasury; 3: J. Gunther, Procession

Macaulay 2: L. Russell, English Wits; 3: W. Adams, Treasury of Modern Anecdote; 4: E. Fuller, 2500 Anecdotes; 5: Sir G. Trevelyan, The Life and Letters of Lord Macauley

Mack 1: A. Barra, That's Not the Way It Was

MacLaine 1: P. Boller, ed., Hollywood Anecdotes

Macmahon 1: H. Hoffmeister, Anekdotenshatz

Macmillan 1: L. Harris, The Fine Art of Political Wit

MacNeil 1: M. Wiley and D. Bona, Inside Oscar

Macready 1: L. and F. Copeland, 10,000 Jokes, Toasts, and Stories; 3: G. Brandreth, Great Theatrical Disasters

Madison, D., P. Boller, ed., Presidential Wives: An Anecdotal History

Madison, J., 1: Virginia Moore, The Madisons, in P. Boller, ed., Presidential Anecdotes

Madonna 1: M. Biggs, ed., Women's Words: The Columbia Book of Quotations by Women

Maeterlinck 1: A. de Stoeckl and W. Edwards, When Men Had Time to Love; 2: P. Mahony, Barbed Wit and Malicious Humor

Magruder 1: North Carolina Branch, Southern Historical Society, "Our Living and Our Dead, Devoted to North Carolina — Her Past, Her Present, and Her Future," in B. Botkin, A Civil War Treasury

Mahaffey 1: L. Missen, Quotable Anecdotes; 2:

F. Delaney and J. Lewinski, *James Joyce's Odyssey*

Mahler 1: K. Bernstein, *Music Lover's Europe*

Maintenon 1: S. R. N. Chamfort, *Characters and Anecdotes*, in C. Shriner, *Wit, Wisdom, and Foibles of the Great*; 2: *The Ladies Companion*, 1853, in Shriner, *Wit*

Malherbe 1: J. Timbs, *Century of Anecdote*

Mallarmé 1: A. Vollard, *Recollections of a Picture Dealer*

Mallory 1: D. Robertson, *George Mallory*

Mankiewicz 1: B. Thomas, *King Cohn*; 2: P. Kael, *The Citizen Kane Book*

Mann 1: E. Fuller, *2500 Anecdotes*

Mansart 1: L. Norton, *Saint-Simon at Versailles*

Mansfield 1: D. George, *A Book of Anecdotes*

Mantle 1: D. Okrent and S. Wolf, eds., *Baseball Anecdotes*; 2–4: P. Dickson, *Baseball's Greatest Quotations*; 5: A. Barra, *That's Not the Way It Was*

Mao 1: M. and A. Guillois, *Liberté, Egalité, Hilarité*; 2: P. Theroux, *Riding the Iron Rooster*

Margaret, Princess, 1: B. Conrad, *Fun While It Lasted*

Maria Fëderovna I 1: I. Wallace et al., *The Book of Lists 3*

Maria Theresa 1: E. Crankshaw, *Maria Theresa*

Marie Antoinette 1: *Oxford Dictionary of Quotations*; 2: W. and A. Durant, *The Story of Civilization*, X; 3: B. Conrad, *Famous Last Words*

Marie De Médicis 1: W. Keddie, *Literary and Scientific Anecdote*

Maris 1: D. Okrent and S. Wolf, eds., *Baseball Anecdotes*; 2: P. Dickson, *Baseball's Greatest Quotations*

Marlborough, 1ˢᵗ Duke of, 1: J. Spence, *Anecdotes*

Marlborough, 10ᵗʰ Duke of, 1: S. Winchester, *Their Noble Lordships*

Marquand 1: S. Birmingham, *The Late John Marquand*

Marquis 1: C. Ford, *The Time of Laughter*

Marshall, J., 1: B. Botkin, *Treasury of American Anecdotes*

Marshall, T., 1: C. Fadiman and C. Van Doren, *The American Treasury*; 2: R. Shenkman and K. Reiger, *One-Night Stands with American History*

Martin 1: A. Barra, *That's Not the Way It Was*; 2: B. Shlain, *Baseball Inside Out*

Martinelli 1: J. Braude, *Speaker's and Toastmaster's Handbook*

Marx, C., 2: J. Adamson, *Groucho, Harpo, Chico*

Marx, G. 1: A. Marx, *Son of Groucho*, in Kenin and Wintle, *DBQ*; 2, 4: K. Edwards, *More Things I Wish I'd Said*; 3: L. Rosten, *Joys of Yiddish*; 5: J. Adamson, *Groucho, Harpo, Chico*; 6: L. Rosten, *People I Have Loved, Known, or Admired*; 7: O. Levant, *The Unimportance of Being Oscar*; 8: E. Wilson, *I Am Gazing into My 8-Ball*; 9: G. Brandreth, *Joy of Lex*; 10–11: D. Herrmann, *With Malice Toward All*; 13: G. Kanin, *Hollywood*

Marx, H., 1: O. Levant, *The Unimportance of Being Oscar*; 2: B. Cerf, *Bumper Crop of Anecdotes*

Mary I 1: *DNB*

Mary, Queen Consort, 2: *Book-of-the-Month Club News*, Apr. 1952

Mary, Queen of Scots, 1: G. Mattingly, *The Defeat of the Spanish Armada*, in Kenin and Wintle, *DBQ*

Masaryk 1: G. Mikes, *Laughing Matter*

Mascagni 1: E. Fuller, *2500 Anecdotes*; 2: H. Sievers, *Musica Curiosa*

Massenet 1: C. Skinner, *Elegant Wits and Grand Horizontals*

Mathilde 1: A. de Stoeckl and W. Edwards, *When Men Had Time to Love*; 2: C. Skinner, *Elegant Wits and Grand Horizontals*

Matisse 1: D. Wallechinsky and I. Wallace, *The People's Almanac*; 2: J. Cocteau, *Past Tense: Diaries*, vol. I

Matthews 1–2: G. Brandreth, *Great Theatrical Disasters*

Mature 2: D. Herrmann, *With Malice Toward All*

Mauch 1: B. Shlain, *Baseball Inside Out*

Maugham 1: W. Maugham, *A Writer's Notebook;* 2: D. Fielding, *Those Remarkable Cunards;* 3: K. Edwards, *I Wish I'd Said That;* 5: Geoffrey Gorer to Edith Sitwell, Oct. 28, 1940, in M. Richler, ed., *Writers and World War II*

Maurepas 1: A. Castelot, *Marie Antoinette*

Maury 1: *EB*, 1971; 2: M. Pedrazzini and J. Gris, *Autant en apportent les mots*

Mayer 1–2: S. Marx, *Mayer and Thalberg;* 3: N. Zierold, *The Moguls;* 4: S. Birmingham, *"The Rest of Us";* 5: G. Herman, *The Book of Hollywood Quotes;* 6: B. Crowther, *Hollywood Rajah,* in Kenin and Wintle, *DBQ*

Mazarin 1: G. Lieberman, *The Greatest Laughs of All Time;* 2: G. Boissier, *Mme de Sévigné*

Medici 1: H. Morton, *A Traveller in Italy*

Mehmed II 1: W. Durant, *The Story of Civilization,* V

Melba 1: E. Fuller, *2500 Anecdotes;* 2: R. Merrill, *Between Acts*

Melbourne 1–3: D. Cecil, *Melbourne;* 4: J. Gere and J. Sparrow, *Geoffrey Madan's Notebooks*

Mellon 1: S. Holbrook, *The Age of the Moguls*

Melville 1: J. Hawthorne, *Nathaniel Hawthorne and His Wife*

Mencken 1: M. Ringo, *Nobody Said It Better*

Menelik II 1: J. Train, *True Remarkable Occurrences*

Menshikov 1: D. George, *A Book of Anecdotes*

Merman 1: H. Pleasants, *The Great American Popular Singers*

Messier 1: G. Murchie, *Music of the Spheres*

Metaxas 1: E. Fuller, *2500 Anecdotes*

Metternich, K. Von, 1: L. Missen, *Quotable Anecdotes*

Metternich, Princess, 1: C. Fadiman

Meyerbeer 1: M. Ringo, *Nobody Said It Better;* 2: H. Sievers, *Musica Curiosa;* 3: E. Van de Velde, *Anecdotes Musicales*

Michelangelo 1, 4–6: G. Vasari, *Lives of the Painters;* 2: W. Durant, *The Story of Civilization,* V; 3: C. Speroni, *Wit and Wisdom of the Italian Renaissance;* 7: H. Morton, *A Traveller in Italy*

Michelet 1: C. Skinner, *Elegant Wits and Grand Horizontals*

Mies van der Rohe 1: A. Whitman, *Come to Judgment*

Mill 1: C. Bowen, *Yankee from Olympus*

Millay 1: *New York Times Book Review,* July 24, 1983

Miller 1: W. Espy, *Another Almanac of Words at Play*

Millikan 1: J. Braude, *Braude's Second Encyclopedia*

Milne 1: C. Milne, *The Enchanted Places*

Milnes 1: B. Conrad, *Famous Last Words*

Milo 1: E. Hauser, *Italy, A Cultural Guide*

Milton 1: *DNB;* 2: W. Keddie, *Literary and Scientific Anecdote;* 3: J. Boorstin, *The Creators*

Mingus 1: B. Crow, *Jazz Anecdotes*

Mirabeau 1: J. S. Smith, *Mirabeau,* in C. Shriner, *Wit, Wisdom, and Foibles of the Great;* 2: W. Sholz, *Das Buch des Lachens;* 3: E. Fuller, *2500 Anecdotes;* 4: J. C. Humes, *Speaker's Treasury*

Mitchell 1: Richard Harwell, ed., *Margaret Mitchell's "Gone with the Wind" Letters,* in D. Hall, ed., *OBALA;* 2: N. and B. Donaldson, *How Did They Die?*

Mitford, N. 1: O. Levant, *The Unimportance of Being Oscar*

Mizner, A., 1: *The New Yorker,* Nov. 22, 1952

Mizner, W., 1: D. Herrmann, *With Malice Toward All;* 2–3, 7: D. Wallechinsky and I. Wallace, *The People's Almanac;* 4: *The New Yorker,* July 29, 1950; 5: C. Fadiman and C. Van Doren, *The American Treasury;* 6: *The New Yorker,* Nov. 22, 1952

Modigliani 1: M. Georges-Michel, *From Renoir to Picasso*

Molière 1: W. Walsh, *Handy Book of Curious Information*

Molnár 1: B. Cerf, *Try and Stop Me;* 2: *The New Yorker,* May 25, 1946; 3: L. Farago, *Strictly from Hungary*

Monet 1: D. Boorstin, *The Creators*

Monroe 1: *Los Angeles Times,* May 3, 1984; 2–4: M. Biggs, ed., *Women's Words: The Columbia Book of Quotations by Women;* 5: G. Brandreth, *871 Famous Last Words;* 7: P. Boller, ed., *Hollywood Anecdotes*

Montagu 1: J. Spence, *Anecdotes;* 2: F. Muir, *Irreverent Social History*

Montague 1: J. Gere and J. Sparrow, *Geoffrey Madan's Notebooks*

Montcalm 1: F. Parkman, *Montcalm and Wolfe,* in D. Boorstin, *The Creators*

Montecuccoli 1: S. and R. Percy, *The Percy Anecdotes*

Montefiore 1: W. Novak and M. Waldoks, *The Big Book of Jewish Humor*

Monteux 1: A. Previn, ed., *Orchestra;* 2: C. O'-Connell, *The Other Side of the Record*

Montgomery, B., 1: A. Herbert, *A.P.H.;* 2: R. Collier, *The Freedom Road;* 4: J. Gunther, *Procession*

Montgomery, J. 1: W. Keddie, *Literary and Scientific Anecdote*

Montmorency 1: M. Strauss, *Familiar Medical Quotations*

Moore, George, 1: O. St. John Gogarty, *As I Was Walking Down Sackville Street,* in Kenin and Wintle, *DBQ;* 2: letter from W. B. Yeats to Lady Gregory, May 1901, in *DBQ;* 3: D. Fielding, *Those Remarkable Cunards*

Moore, M., 1: D. Hall, ed., *OBALA*

More, H., 1: W. Keddie, *Literary and Scientific Anecdote*

More, Sir T., 1: W. Roper, *Life of Sir Thomas More;* 2: J. Aubrey, *Brief Lives;* 3: W. Winstanley, *England's Worthies*

Morel 1: M. Bishop, *A Gallery of Eccentrics*

Morgan, J. P. Sr., 1, 4: C. Tomkins, *Merchants and Masterpieces;* 3: J. Carroll, *Prince of Peace;* 5–7: E. Wagenknecht, *American Profile;* 8: J. L. Gardner, *Departing Glory: Theodore Roosevelt as Ex-President,* in P. Boller, ed., *Presidential Anecdotes*

Morgan, J. P. Jr., 1: B. Cerf, *Laughing Stock;* 2: H. Hoffmeister, *Anekdotenshatz*

Morley, C., 1: C. Fadiman, *Any Number Can Play*

Morley, R., 1: R. Morley, *Book of Bricks*

Morris, C., 1: E. Fuller, *2500 Anecdotes*

Morris, W., 1: L. and F. Copeland, *10,000 Jokes, Toasts, and Stories*

Morse 1: P. Smith, *The Nation Comes of Age;* 2: H. Prochnow, *The Public Speaker's Treasure Chest*

Moscardó 1: C. Eby, *The Siege of the Alcazar*

Mott 1: I. and R. Poley, *Friendly Anecdotes*

Mountbatten 1: P. Ziegler, *Mountbatten*

Mozart 1: O. Sacks, *New York Review of Books,* Feb. 28, 1985; 2: W. and A. Durant, *The Story of Civilization,* X; 3: N. McPhee, *Second Book of Insults;* 4: E. Van de Velde, *Anecdotes Musicales;* 5–8: N. Lebrecht, *The Book of Musical Anecdotes*

Muggeridge 1: J. Paar, *P.S. Jack Paar*

Mugnier 1–2: C. Skinner, *Elegant Wits and Grand Horizontals*

Muhammad Shah I 1: E. Canetti, *Crowds and Power*

Muir 1: C. Fadiman and C. Van Doren, *The American Treasury*

Muraviev 1: E. Crankshaw, *The Shadow of the Winter Palace*

Murray, Sir George, 1: W. Keddie, *Literary and Scientific Anecdote*

Murray, Gilbert, 1: C. Bowra, *Memories 1898–1939;* 2: R. Graves, *Goodbye to All That*

Musial 1: D. Okrent and S. Wolf, eds., *Baseball Anecdotes*

Musset 1: M. Pedrazzini and J. Gris, *Autant en apportent les mots*

Mytton 1: C. Fadiman, *Any Number Can Play*

Nabokov 1: *New York Times Book Review,* Aug. 23, 1981; 2: J. Orgel, *Undying Passion;* 3: V. Nabokov, *Strong Opinions;* 4: Joseph Epstein, "Toys in My Attic," *The American Scholar,* winter, 1992

Nagurski 3: *Los Angeles Times,* Jan. 7, 1985

Namath 1: *Los Angeles Times,* Jan. 20, 1983

Napier 1: I. Asimov, *Treasury of Humor*

Napoleon I 1, 8: C. Barnett, *Bonaparte*; 2–4, 9: V. Cronin, *Napoleon Bonaparte*; 5–6: W. and A. Durant, *The Story of Civilization*, XI; 7: L. and F. Copeland, *10,000 Jokes, Toasts, and Stories*; 10: D. Duff, *Eugénie and Napoleon III*; 11: H. Hoffmeister, *Anekdotenshatz*; 12: A. Castelot, *Paris: The Turbulent City*; 13: R. Chelmiaski, *The French at Table*; 14: A. Duff Cooper, *Talleyrand*

Napoleon III 1: H. Hoffmeister, *Anekdotenschatz*; 2: D. Duff, *Eugénie and Napoleon III*; 3: E. Crankshaw, *The Fall of the House of Hapsburg*

Napoleon, E., 1: D. Duff, *Eugénie and Napoleon III*

Napoleon, J., 1: F. Loliée, *Gilded Beauties of the Second Empire*

Narváez 1: B. Conrad, *Famous Last Words*

Nast 1: *American Scholar* X (1941)

Navratilova 1–2: M. Biggs, ed., *Women's Words: The Columbia Book of Quotations by Women*

Necker 1: W. Keddie, *Literary and Scientific Anecdote*

Nelson 1: A. Lincoln and R. McEwan, eds., *Lord Eldon's Anecdote Book*; 2–3, 5–7: R. Southey, *Life of Nelson*; 4: *DNB*

Nero 1: W. Durant, *The Story of Civilization*, III; 2, 4–5: Suetonius, *The Twelve Caesars*; 4: D. Boorstin, *The Creators*

Nerval 1–2: G. Wagner, *Selected Writing of Gérard de Nerval*

Newman, P. 1: P. Hay, ed., *Movie Anecdotes*

Newton 1, 10: *DNB*; 2: R. Hendrickson, *The Literary Life*; 3, 7: E. Bell, *Men of Mathematics*; 4: W. Keddie, *Literary and Scientific Anecdote*; 5: I. Asimov, *Biographical Encyclopedia*; 6: S. Waterlow, *In Praise of Cambridge*; 8: T. Moore, *Memoirs, Journal, and Correspondence*; 9: L. C. Thurow, *The Zero-Sum Society*

Nicholas I 1: E. Guérard, *Dictionnaire Encyclopédique*

Nicholson 1: P. Hay, ed., *Movie Anecdotes*

Nijinsky 1: R. Buckle, *Nijinsky*

Nilsson 1–2: W. Sargeant, *Divas*; 3: Sir R. Bing, *A Knight at the Opera*

Niven 1: F. Worth, *Complete Unabridged Super Trivia Encyclopedia*; 2: *Los Angeles Times*, Aug. 8, 1983

Nivernais 1: J. Braude, *Speaker's and Toastmaster's Handbook*

Nixon, R. 1: E. Mayo and S. Hess, *President Nixon: A Political Portrait*, in P. Boller, ed., *Presidential Anecdotes*; 4: C. Daniel, *Lords, Ladies and Gentlemen*; 5: D. Wallechinsky and I. Wallace, *The People's Almanac*; 6: Bill Adler, *The Washington Wits*, in Boller, *Presidential Anecdotes*; 7, 9: A. Wallace et al., *The Book of Lists 3*; 10: D. Frost, *"I Gave Them a Sword"*; 11: W. Isaacson, *Kissinger in America: A Biography*

Norbury 1: W. Adams, *Treasury of Modern Anecdote*; 2: A. Lincoln and R. McEwan, eds., *Lord Eldon's Anecdote Book*; 3: *DNB*

North 1: Lord Broughton, *Recollections of a Long Life*; 2–3: A. Lincoln and R. McEwan, eds., *Lord Eldon's Anecdote Book*; 4: W. Adams, *Treasury of Modern Anecdote*

Northcote 1: K. Arvine, *Cyclopaedia of Anecdotes*

Noyes 1: M. Bishop, *The Exotics*

Nurmi 1: *Los Angeles Times*, Aug. 12, 1983

Oates 1: *DNB*

Offenbach 1: S. Beach, *Musicdotes*

O'Hara, F., 1: M. Perloff, *Frank O'Hara: A Critical Introduction*, in D. Hall, ed., *OBALA*

O'Hara, J., 1: M. J. Bruccoli, *The O'Hara Concern*, in J. Sutherland, ed., *OBLA*; 2: B. Gill, *Here at The New Yorker*; 3: J. Simpson, *Simpson's Contemporary Quotations*; 4: B. Cerf, *At Random*, in D. Hall, ed., *OBALA*

Oldfield 1: T. Davies, *Dramatic Miscellanies*

Olivier 1: J. Lasky, *Love Scene*; 2: J. McAleer, *"Globe Man's Daily Story," Boston Globe*, Jan. 1, 1963; 3: P. Boller, ed., *Hollywood Anecdotes*

'Omar 1: W. Walsh, *Handy Book of Curious Information*

Onassis, A., 1: F. Brady, *Onassis*

Onassis, J., 1: W. R. Thayer, *Jacqueline Kennedy*, in P. Boller, ed., *Presidential Wives: An Anecdotal History*; 2: L. David, *The Lonely Lady of San Clemente: The Story of Pat Nixon*, in Boller, *Presidential Wives*; 3: M. B. Gallagher, *My Life*, in Boller, *Presidential Wives*; 4: R. G. Martin, *A Hero for Our Time*, in Boller, *Presidential Wives*; 5: R. Harding and A. L. Holmes, *Jacqueline Kennedy*, in Boller, *Presidential Wives*; 6: G. Hall and A. Pinchot, *Jacqueline Kennedy: A Biography*, in Boller, *Presidential Wives*; 7: Gallagher, *My Life*, in Boller, *Presidential Wives*; 8: K. P. O'Donnell and D. F. Powers, *"Johnny, We Hardley Knew Ye,"* in Boller, *Presidential Wives*; 9: Martin, *A Hero for Our Times*, in Boller, *Presidential Wives*; 10: "Confessions of a Public Son," *Time*, Jan. 20, 1986, in Boller, *Presidential Wives*

O'Neill 1: *The New Yorker*, Feb. 28, 1948; 2: R. Hendrickson, *The Literary Life*; 3: C. Bowen, *The Curse of the Misbegotten: A Tale of the House of O'Neill*, in D. Hall, ed., *OBALA*; 4: N. and B. Donaldson, *How Did They Die?*

Oppenheimer 2: A. Whitman, *Come to Judgment*

Orsay 1: C. Roberts, *And So to Bath*; 2: W. Adams, *Treasury of Modern Anecdote*

Oscar II 1: H. Hoffmeister, *Anekdotenshatz*

O'Toole 1: G. Talese, *Fame and Obscurity*; 2: P. Boller, ed., *Hollywood Anecdotes*

Otto 1: H. Hoffmeister, *Anekdotenshatz*

Ouida 1: W. Abbot, *Notable Women in History*

Owen 1: J. Sanford, *Winters of That Country*

Pachmann 1–3: H. Schonberg, *The Great Pianists*

Packer 1: B. A. Botkin, *A Treasury of American Anecdotes*

Paderewski 1, 3: E. Fuller, *2500 Anecdotes*; 2: H. Schonberg, *The Great Pianists*; 4–5: A. Zamoyski, *Paderewski*

Paige 1: *Los Angeles Times*, June 12, 1982; 2: A. and B. Silverman, eds., *The Twentieth-Century Treasury of Sports*

Paine 1: A. O. Sherman, address before the Huguenot Society of America, New Rochelle, N.Y., July 1910, in C. Shriner, *Wit, Wisdom, and Foibles of the Great*; 2, 4: H. Pearson, *Tom Paine: Friend of Mankind*, in J. Sutherland, ed., *OBLA*, and D. Hall, ed., *OBALA*; 3: N. and B. Donaldson, *How Did They Die?*

Paley 1: W. Adams, *Treasury of Modern Anecdote*

Palmerston 1: R. B. Brett, *The Yoke of Empire*, in C. Shriner, *Wit, Wisdom, and Foibles of the Great*; 2: Arthur Ponsonby, *Henry Ponsonby: His Life and Letters*, in A. Hardy, *Queen Victoria Was Amused*; 4: B. Conrad, *Famous Last Words*

Paquin 1: M. Wiley and D. Bona, *Inside Oscar*

Park 1: E. Fuller, *2500 Anecdotes*

Parker, D., 1, 16: O. Levant, *The Unimportance of Being Oscar*; 2: E. Fuller, *2500 Anecdotes*; 4, 15: R. Drennan, *Wit's End*; 5: B. Cerf, *Try and Stop Me*; 6: D. Wallechinsky and I. Wallace, *The People's Almanac*; 7–8: D. Herrmann, *With Malice Toward All*; 9, 16: John Keats, *You Might As Well Live: The Life and Times of Dorothy Parker*, in D. Hall, ed., *OBALA*; 10–11, 13: R. Drennan, *The Algonquin Wits*; 12: B. Thomas, *Thalberg: Life and Legend*; 14: L. Hellman, *An Unfinished Woman*

Parker, H., 1: L. Humphrey, *The Humor of Music*

Parker, Q., 1: J. C. Humes, *Speaker's Treasury*

Parr 1: R. Hendrickson, *The Literary Life*; 2: *DNB*; 3: J. Timbs, *English Eccentrics*

Parrish 1: J. C. Humes, *Speaker's Treasury*

Partridge 1: *DNB*; 2: W. Walsh, *Handy Book of Curious Information*

Pascal 1: I. Asimov, *Biographical Encyclopedia*

Pater 1: S. Behrman, *Portrait of Max*

Patti 1: C. Gattey, *The Elephant That Swallowed a Nightingale*

Patton 1–2: C. Fadiman and C. Van Doren, *The American Treasury*; 3: Ed Hinton, *The Last Ride of A. J. Foyt*

Peale 1: R. Morley, *Pardon Me, But You're Eating My Doily*

Peard 1: *Country Life*, May 20, 1982

Peck 1: S. Harris, *Pieces of Eight*

Peckinpah 1: P. Hay, ed., *Movie Anecdotes*

Pembroke 1: W. Keddie, *Literary and Scientific Anecdote*

Penick 1: R. T. Sommers, *Golf Anecdotes*

Perelman 1: W. Espy, *Another Almanac of Words at Play*

Pericles 1: Plutarch, *Lives*

Perlman 1: M. Wallace and G. Gates, *Close Encounters*

Perón 1: I. Wallace et al., *Intimate Sex Lives of Famous People*

Perot 1: D. Frost, *Book of Millionaires*

Perry 1: J. Bartlett, *Battlett's Familiar Quotations*

Perugino 1: G. Vasari, *Lives of the Painters*

Pétain 1: P. Méras, *The Mermaids of Chenonceaux*; 2: P. Frederick, *Ten First Ladies of the World*

Peter I 1: R. Massie, *Peter the Great*; 2: W. Keddie, *Literary and Scientific Anecdote*

Peterborough 1: *DNB*

Petronius 1: F. Seymour Smith, *A Treasury of Wit and Wisdom*

Phelps 1: E. Fuller, *2500 Anecdotes*

Philip, J., 1: C. Fadiman and C. Van Doren, *The American Treasury*

Philip, Prince, 3: L. Lucaire, *Celebrity Trivia*; 4: N. McPhee, *Second Book of Insults*; 6: E. Longford, *The Oxford Book of Royal Anecdotes*

Philip II 1: Valerius Maximus, *Facta et Dicta Memorabilia*; 2: I. Asimov, *Treasury of Humor*; 3: E. Guérard, *Dictionnaire Encyclopédique*

Philip III 1: B. Tuchman, *The March of Folly*

Philip V 1: V. Cronin, *Louis XIV*

Phillips 1–2: B. Botkin, *Treasury of Modern Anecdotes*

Piatigorsky 1: H. Temianka, *Facing the Music*

Picabia 1: M. Georges-Michel, *From Renoir to Picasso*

Picasso 1: F. Gilot and C. Lake, *Life with Picasso*; 2, 7: A. Whitman, *Come to Judgment*; 3: E. Burns, ed., *Gertrude Stein on Picasso*, in J. Mellow, *Charmed Circle*; 4: J. Mellow, *Charmed Circle*; 5, 14, 17–18: R. Penrose, *Picasso*; 6: B. Adler, *My Favorite Funny Story*; 12: B. Cerf, *Bumper Crop of Anecdotes*; 13: F. Weiskopf, *Gesammelte Werke*; 15: A. Lanoux, *Paris in the Twenties*; 16: D. Duncan, *Picasso's Picasso*; 18: A. S. Huffington, *Picasso: Creator and Destroyer*; 19: J. Weld, *Peggy: The Wayward Guggenheim*

Pinter 1: J. Epstein, "Merely Anecdotal," *The American Scholar*, spring 1992

Pitt 1: Lord Stanhope, *Conversations with Lord Wellington*, in C. Shriner, *Wit, Wisdom, and Foibles of the Great*; 2: H. Hoffmeister, *Anekdotenshatz*; 3: W. and A. Durant, *The Story of Civilization*, XI; 4: *Stanhope's Life of the Rt. Hon. William Pitt*, in *Oxford Dictionary of Quotations*

Plath 1: D. Hall, ed., *OBALA*

Plato 1–2: I. Asimov, *Treasury of Humor*; 3: E. Fuller, *2500 Anecdotes*

Pliny 1: Pliny, *Letters*

Plotinus 1: E. Monegal and A. Reid, *Borges: A Reader*

Poe 1: R. Hendrickson, *The Literary Life*

Poggio 1: W. Durant, *The Story of Civilization*, V

Polk 1: B. Dole, *Great Political Wit*

Pompadour 1: N. Mitford, *Madame de Pompadour*; 3: N. and B. Donaldson, *How Did They Die?*

Pope, Alexander, 1, 4: J. Spence, *Anecdotes*; 2–3: S. Johnson, *Lives of the English Poets*

Pope, Arthur, 1: J. Howard, *Margaret Mead*

Porson 1–2: W. Keddie, *Literary and Scientific Anecdote*; 3: J. Timbs, *Century of Anecdote*; 4–5: L. Missen, *Quotable Anecdotes*; 6: E. Barker, *Literary Recollections*

Poussin 1: *Quarterly Review*, no. 218, 1861, in D. George, *A Book of Anecdotes*

Previn 1: R. Morley, *Book of Bricks*; 2: R. Morley, *Second Book of Bricks*

Pringle 1: W. Walsh, *Handy Book of Curious Information*

Prokofiev 1: *Book-of-the-Month Club News*, Feb. 1940

Puccini 1: N. and B. Donaldson, *How Did They Die?*

Pulitzer 1: P. Brendon, *The Life and Death of the Press Barons*

Pushkin 1: C. Fadiman, foreword to N. Gogol, *Chichikov's Journeys*

Putnam 1: B. Botkin, *Treasury of American Anecdote*

Pyle 1: '47, *The Magazine of the Year*

Pyrrhus 1: Plutarch, *Lives*

Pythagoras 1: Diogenes Laertius, *Eminent Philosophers*, vol. 8

Quayle 1: J. Simpson, *Simpson's Contemporary Quotations*; 2: B. Bryson, *The Mother Tongue*

Queensberry 1: J. Timbs, *Century of Anecdote*; 2: W. Walsh, *Handy Book of Curious Information*

Quesnay 1: W. and A. Durant, *The Story of Civilization*, X

Quin 1: *DNB*

Quisenberry 1–2: D. Okrent and S. Wolf, eds., *Baseball Anecdotes*

Rabelais 1: R. Hendrickson, *The Literary Life*; 2: F. Winslow, *Physic and Physicians*, in D. George, *A Book of Anecdotes*

Rabi 1: P. Wyden, *Day One*

Rachel 1–3: J. Agate, *Rachel*; 4–5: E. Fuller, *2500 Anecdotes*

Rachmaninoff 1: A. Rubinstein, *My Many Years*; 2: H. Schonberg, *The Great Pianists*

Racine 1: E. Guérard, *Dictionnaire Encyclopédique*

Raft 1: *Santa Barbara News Press*, Nov. 25, 1980

Raglan 1: *DNB*

Raleigh 1–2: T. Fuller, ed., *Worthies of England*; 3: W. Walsh, *Handy Book of Curious Information*; 4–5: J. Aubrey, *Brief Lives*; 6: J. A. St. John, *Life of Sir Walter Raleigh*, in D. Wallechinsky and I. Wallace, *The People's Almanac 2*; 7: I. A. Taylor, *Sir Walter Raleigh*, in C. Shriner, *Wit, Wisdom, and Foibles of the Great*; 8: *DNB*

Ramanujan 1: C. Fadiman, *Any Number Can Play*

Ramsey 1: M. Biggs, ed., *Women's Words: The Columbia Book of Quotations by Women*

Raphael 1: E. Fuller, *2500 Anecdotes*

Rather 1: M. Biggs, ed., *Women's Words: The Columbia Book of Quotations by Women*

Raynal 1: J. Larwood, *Anecdotes of the Clergy*

Reagan, N., 1: "The World of Nancy Reagan," *Newsweek*, Dec. 21, 1981, in P. Boller, ed., *Presidential Wives: An Anecdotal History*; 2–3: Bill Adler, *Ronnie and Nancy: A Very Special Relationship*, in Boller, *Presidential Wives*; 4: "People," *Time*, Oct. 20, 1986, in Boller, *Presidential Wives*; 5: Laurence Leamer, *Make-Believe: The Story of Nancy and Ronald Reagan*, in Boller, *Presidential Wives*

Reagan, R., 1: R. Morley, *Pardon Me, But You're Eating My Doily*; 2: B. Adler and B. Adler, Jr., *The Reagan Wit*; 3, 7: P. Hay, ed., *Movie Anecdotes*; 4–5, 10, 14–17, 19–21, 23: B. Dole, *Great Political Wit*; 6: L. Cannon, *President Reagan: The Role of a Lifetime*; 8: D. Halberstam, *The Next Century*; 9: "Reagan out of Surgery," *Fort Worth Star Telegram*, Mar. 31, 1981; 11: D. McClellan, *Ear on Washington*; 12: J. Train, *Wit: The Best Things Ever Said*; 13: *Los Angeles Times*, Apr. 7, 1984; 22: J. Trelown, "Moscow Notes," *Times Literary Supplement*, Mar. 2–8, 1990

Redgrave 1: M. Bragg, *Richard Burton*

Reed 1: E. Fuller, *2500 Anecdotes*; 2: *McClure's Magazine*, June 1911, in C. Shriner, *Wit, Wisdom, and Foibles of the Great*

Reger 1: N. Slonimsky, *A Thing or Two About Music*; 2: N. Slonimsky, *Lexicon of Musical Invective*

Rehan 1: G. Brandreth, *Great Theatrical Disasters*

Reinhardt 1: A. Milne, *It's Too Late Now*

Reisenhauer 1: A. Rubinstein, *My Young Years*

Renoir 2: H. Hoffmeister, *Anekdotenshatz*; 3: M. Cowley, *The View From 80*; 4: T. Craven, *Men of Art*

Reuther 1: *Parade*, Apr. 10, 1983

Reynolds, B., 1–3: P. Hay, ed., *Movie Anecdotes*

Reynolds, J., 1: E. Lucas, *A Fronded Isle*

Rhodes 1, 3: J. Lockhart, *Rhodes*; 2: G. le Sueur, *Cecil Rhodes*; 4: V. Castlerosse, *Valentine's Days*

Richard I 1: 13th-century chronicle, *Recits d'un menestral de Reims,* in D. George, *A Book of Anecdotes*; 2: W. Keddie, *Literary and Scientific Anecdote*

Richardson 1: K. Tynan, *Show People*

Richelieu 1: D. Wallechinsky et al., *The Book of Lists*; 2: H. Hoffmeister, *Anekdotenschatz*

Richter 1: S. Beach, *Musicdotes*; 2: L. Harris, *The Fine Art of Political Wit*

Rickey 1: D. Okrent and S. Wolf, eds., *Baseball Anecdotes*; 2: J. McBride, *High and Inside: The A–Z Guide to the Language of Baseball*

Rigaud 1: W. Seward, *Biographiana*, vol. 1

Riley 1: B. Cerf, *Treasury of Atrocious Puns*; 2: F. C. Kelly, "The Life and Times of Kim Hubbard," in J. Bryan, III, ed., *Hodgepodge: A Commonplace Book*

Rivarol 1: E. Guérard, *Dictionnaire Encyclopédique*

Rivera 1: C. Eby, *The Siege of the Alcázar*

Rizzuto 1: L. Lucaire, *Celebrity Trivia*

Robert I 1: W. Scott, *Tales of a Grandfather*

Robert 1: P. Wescher, *Schweitzer Künstler-Anekdoten*

Robinson, E., 1, 3–4: C. P. Smith, *Where the Light Falls,* in D. Hall, ed., *OBALA*; 2: I. Wallace et al., *Book of Lists 2*

Robinson, J., 1: B. Adler, *My Favorite Funny Story*

Roche 1: *DNB*; 2: W. Adams, *Treasury of Modern Anecdote*

Rochefort 1: H. Rochefort, *The Adventures of My Life,* in C. Shriner, *Wit, Wisdom, and Foibles of the Great*; 2: M. Pedrazzini and J. Gris, *Autant en apportent les mots*

Rockefeller, N. 1: A. Schlesinger, in *Cycles of American History*

Rodgers 1: H. Fordin, *Getting to Know Him*; 2: S. Beach, *Musicdotes*

Rodzinski 1: H. Rodzinski, *Our Two Lives*

Roethke 1–2: A. Seager, *The Glass House,* in D. Hall, ed., *OBALA*

Rogers, S. 1: E. Fuller, *2500 Anecdotes*; 2: Henry Taylor, *The Autobiography of Henry Taylor,* in D. Sutherland, ed., *OBLA*; 3–4: W. Adams, *Treasury of Modern Anecdote*

Rogers, W. 1: E. Fuller, *2500 Anecdotes*; 2: B. Cerf, *Shake Well Before Using*

Roland 1: *EB*

Roosevelt, E. 1–3: P. Boller, ed., *Presidential Wives: An Anecdotal History*; 4: M. Biggs, ed., *Women's Words: The Columbia Book of Quotations by Women*

Roosevelt, F. D., 1: "Next Week," *Colliers*, June 18, 1932, in P. Boller, ed., *Presidential Anecdotes*; 2, 10, 11: T. Morgan, *FDR: A Biography*; 3: J. Lash, *Eleanor and Franklin*; 4: "Fanny Hurst," *New York Times*, Feb. 24, 1968, in Boller, *Presidential Anecdotes*; 5: D. Wallechinsky and I. Wallace, *The People's Almanac*; 6: J. McAleer, "Globe Man's Daily Story," *Boston Globe*, Mar. 29, 1961; 7: D. McClellan, *Ear on Washington*; 8: P. Boller, ed., *Presidential Anecdotes*; 9: S. Weintraub, *Long Day's Journey into War: December 7, 1941*; 10, 11: T. Morgan, *FDR: A Biography*

Roosevelt, T., 1: H. Hagedorn, *Roosevelt in the Bad Lands*; 2: *Publishers Weekly*, Aug. 5, 1983; 3: William Beebe, *The Book of Naturalists,* in P. Boller, ed., *Presidential Anecdotes*; 4: E. Wagenknecht, *American Profile, 1900–1909*; 5: L. Lucaire, *Celebrity Trivia*; 6: Emily Bax, *Miss Bax of the Embassy,* in Boller, *Presidential Anecdotes*

Roosevelt, T. Jr., 1: E. Fuller, *2500 Anecdotes*

Root 1: J. Baer, *The Self-Chosen*

Rops 1: A. Vollard, *Recollections of a Picture Dealer*

Rose 1–4: D. Okrent and S. Wolf, eds., *Baseball Anecdotes;* 5: S. Cox, *Here's Johnny*

Ross 1, 6: '*48, The Magazine of the Year;* 2, 5, 11: C. Holmes, *The Clocks of Columbus;* 3, 8–10: J. Thurber, *The Years with Ross;* 4: B. Cerf, *Good for a Laugh;* 7: B. Gill, *Here at The New Yorker;* 12: R. Collier, *The Rainbow People;* 13: J. Thurber, *The Years with Ross,* in D. Hall, ed., *OBALA*

Rossetti 1: C. Roberts, *And So to Bath;* 2: Sir T. H. H. Caine, *My Story,* in J. Sutherland, ed., *OBLA;* 3: Sir T. H. H. Caine, *Recollections of Dante Gabriel Rossetti*

Rossini 1, 7: S. Beach, *Musicdotes;* 2, 5: N. Slonimsky, *A Thing or Two About Music;* 3: T. FitzGibbon, comp., *The Pleasures of the Table;* 4: W. Adams, *Treasury of Modern Anecdote;* 6: E. Van de Velde, *Anecdotes Musicales*

Rothschild 1: A. Faulkner and T. Hartman, *All the Best People*

Rousseau 1: D. Boorstin, *The Creators*

Routh 1: J. Morris, *Oxford;* 2: J. Burgon, *Twelve Good Men*

Rowland 1: I. Asimov, *Treasury of Humor*

Rubinstein, Anton 1: H. Hoffmeister, *Anekdotenschatz;* 2: N. Slonimsky, *A Thing or Two About Music*

Rubinstein, Artur 1: C. Fadiman, *Enter, Conversing;* 2: B. Adler, *My Favorite Funny Story*

Ruggles 1: V. Thomson, *A Virgil Thomson Reader*

Ruskin 1: J. Morris, *Oxford;* 2: *DNB*

Russell, B., 1: A. Whitman, *Come to Judgment;* 2: C. Fadiman, *Any Number Can Play;* 3: G. Hardy, *A Mathematician's Apology*

Russell, J., 1: *DNB;* 2: H. Hoffmeister, *Anekdotenschatz*

Ruth 1: B. Cerf, *Good for a Laugh;* 4: A. Barra, *That's Not the Way It Was;* 5: D. Anderson, *The Red Smith Reader;* 6: L. Green, *Sportswit;* 7: P. O'Brian, *Talkin' Sports;*

8–9: P. Dickson, *Baseball's Greatest Quotations*

Sage 1: J. Braude, *Speaker's and Toastmaster's Handbook*

Saint-Saëns 1: T. Beecham, *A Mingled Chime*

Salinger 1: A. Silverman, "The Fragile Pleasure"

Salisbury 1: M. Seymour-Smith, *Robert Graves: His Life and Work*

Salk 1: S. Bolton, *Famous Men of Science*

Sandburg 1: B. Cerf, *Good for a Laugh*

Sanders 1: J. Simpson, *Simpson's Contemporary Quotations*

Sandwich 1: W. Walsh, *Handy Book of Curious Information;* 2: J. Timbs, *Century of Anecdote;* 3: J. Train, *Wit: The Best Things Ever Said*

Santayana 1: H. and D. L. Thomas, *Living Biographies of the Great Philosophers*

Sarasate 1: J. Wechsberg, *Red Plush and Black Velvet;* 2: E. Fuller, *2500 Anecdotes*

Sargent, J., 1: S. Weintraub, *The London Yankees;* 2–3: B. Conrad, *Fun While It Lasted;* 4: P. Boller, ed., *Presidential Anecdotes;* 5: D. Knox, *Quotable Anecdotes*

Sargent, M., 1: K. Edwards, *I Wish I'd Said That*

Saroyan 1: *Time,* Jan. 16, 1984

Satie 1: O. Levant, *The Unimportance of Being Oscar;* 2: J. Williams, *The Magpie's Bagpipe*

Scarron 1: W. Keddie, *Literary and Scientific Anecdote;* 2: H. and D. L. Thomas, *Living Biographies of Famous Women*

Scheffel 1: H. Ziegler, *Heitere Muse*

Schiffer 1: M. Biggs, ed., *Women's Words: The Columbia Book of Quotations by Women*

Schleiermacher 1: H. Hoffmeister, *Anekdotenschatz*

Schliemann 1: W. Durant, *The Story of Civilization,* II

Schmidt 1–3: D. Okrent and S. Wolf, eds., *Baseball Anecdotes*

Schnabel 1: *Sunday Telegraph,* Apr. 11, 1982; 2: A. Faulkner and T. Hartman, *All the Best People*

Schödl 1: M. Jelusisch, *Geschichten aus dem Wienerwald*

Scholl 1–2: C. Skinner, *Elegant Wits and Grand Horizontals*

Schönbein 1: J. Daintith et al., *Biographical Encyclopedia of Scientists*

Schönberg 2: R. Smullyan, *5000 B.C. and Other Philosophical Fantasies*

Schopenhauer 1: W. Scholz, *Das Buch des Lachens*; 2: W. Durant, *The Story of Philosophy*

Schumann-Heink 1: L. Humphrey, *The Humor of Music*; 2: A. May, *Different Drummers*; 3: G. Lieberman, *The Greatest Laughs of All Time*

Schwab 1: T. J. Watson, Jr., with P. Petre, *Thomas J. Watson, Jr.: An Autobiography*

Schwartz, D. 1–2: D. Hall, ed., *OBALA*

Schwartz, M., 1: B. Botkin, *Treasury of American Anecdote*

Schwartzenberg 1–3: E. Crankshaw, *The Fall of the House of Hapsburg*

Schweitzer 1: A. Whitman, *Come to Judgment*; 2–3: J. Paar, *P.S. Jack Paar*

Scipio Nasica 1: E. C. Brewer, *Dictionary of Phrase and Fable*

Scott 1, 5: J. Timbs, *Century of Anecdote*; 2: D. George, *Book of Anecdotes*; 3: W. Keddie, *Literary and Scientific Anecdote*; 4: G. Davenport, *The Geography of the Imagination*

Sebastiano 1: G. Vasari, *Lives of the Painters*

Sedgwick, C., 1: J. Stein, *Edie*

Sedgwick, J., 1: D. Frost, *Book of the World's Worst Decisions*

Sedgwick, T., 1: J. Stein, *Edie*

Sedley 1: Kenin and Wintle, *DBQ*

Seeley 1: J. Sutherland, ed., *OBLA*

Seferis 1: P. Levi, *The Hill of Kronos*

Segovia 1: N. Lebrecht, *The Book of Musical Anecdotes*

Sellers 2: *Life*, Aug. 1983; 3: J. McAleer, "Globe Man's Daily Story," *Boston Globe*, June 17, 1961

Selwyn 1, 3: *DNB*; 2: R. Hendrickson, *The Literary Life*; 4: J. Timbs, *Century of Anecdote*; 5: J. Jesse, *George Selwyn and His Contemporaries*; 6: W. Keddie, *Literary and Scientific Anecdote*

Seneca 1: V. Cronin, *The View from Planet Earth*

Servetus 1: E. Monegal and A. Reid, *Borges: A Reader*

Seward 1: J. Bigelow, *Retrospections of an Active Life*, in C. Shriner, *Wit, Wisdom, and Foibles of the Great*; 2: F. Bancroft, *Life of William H. Seward*, in Shriner, *Wit*

Shaftesbury 1: W. and A. Durant, *The Story of Civilization*, VIII; 2: *DNB*

Shakespeare 1: J. Manningham, *Diary*; 2: K. Arvine, *Cyclopaedia of Anecdotes*

Sharp 1: E. V. Lucas, *Reading, Writing, and Remembering*, in J. Sutherland, ed., *OBLA*

Shatner 1: R. Morley, *Pardon Me, But You're Eating My Doily*

Shaw 1: O. Levant, *The Unimportance of Being Oscar*; 2, 20: K. Edwards, *More Things I Wish I'd Said*; 3: St. John Ervine, *Bernard Shaw: His Life, Work, and Friends*; 4: H. Teichmann, *Smart Aleck*; 5: J. Smith, *Elsie de Wolfe*; 6: G. Lieberman, *The Greatest Laughs of All Time*; 7, 11, 17: J. Braude, *Speaker's and Toastmaster's Handbook*; 9: L. Russell, *English Wits*; 10: B. Cerf, *Try and Stop Me*; 12: B. Cerf, *Shake Well Before Using*; 13: B. Cerf, *The Life of the Party*; 14: N. McPhee, *Second Book of Insults*; 15: Oxfam, *Pass the Port*; 16: N. Rees, *Quote . . . Unquote*; 17: I. Wallace et al., *The Book of Lists 2*; 19: P. Mahony, *Barbed Wit and Malicious Humor*; 21: Y. Karsh, *Karsh*; 23: J. McAleer, "Globe Man's Daily Story," *Boston Globe*, Aug. 3, 1963; 24: N. and B. Donaldson, *How Did They Die?*

Shearing 1: J. McAleer, "Globe Man's Daily Story," *Boston Globe*, Aug. 23, 1962

Shelburne 1: W. and A. Durant, *The Story of Civilization*, X

Shelley, M., 2: I. Wallace, *The Square Pegs*

Shelley, P. 1: T. J. Hogg, *The Life of Percy Bysshe Shelley*, in D. George, *A Book of Ancedotes*; 2: E. Trelawny, *Recollections of the Last Days of Shelley and Byron*

Sheridan, P., 1: D. Wallechinsky and I. Wallace, *The People's Almanac 2*; 2: Adapted from Maj. A. B. Ostrander, *An Army Boy of the Sixties*, in B. Botkin, *Treasury of American Anecedotes*

Sheridan, R., 1: J. Timbs, *Century of Anecdote*; 2–3: L. Russell, *English Wits*; 4. H. Pearson, *Lives of the Wits*; 5–6: W. Sichel, *Sheridan*, in C. Shriner, *Wit, Wisdom, and Foibles of the Great*; 7, 13: T. Moore, *Memoirs of the Life of the Rt. Hon. Richard Sheridan*; 8: E. Fuller, *2500 Anecdotes*; 9: R. Hendrickson, *The Literary Life*; 11: *Sheridaniana*, in J. Sutherland, ed., *OBLA*; 12, 14: L. Harris, *The Fine Art of Political Wit*

Sherman, R., 1: C. D. Bowen, *Miracle at Philadelphia*

Sherman, W., 1: M. D. Landon, *Eli Perkins: Thirty Years of Wit*, in R. Shenkman and K. Reiger, *One-Night Stands with American History*; 2: W. Davis, *Campfire Chats of the Civil War*, in B. Botkin, *A Civil War Treasury*; 3: M. Ringo, *Nobody Said It Better*

Shi Huangdi 1: P. Fitzgerland, *Ancient China*

Shuter 1: *DNB*

Siddons 1: J. Timbs, *Century of Anecdote*; 2: A. Cunningham, *Lives of the Most Eminent British Painters*; 3: J. Boswell, *Life of Johnson*; 4: K. Arvine, *Cyclopaedia of Anecdotes*; 5: J. Aye, *Humour in the Theatre*

Sidney 1: Fulke Greville (Lord Brooke) in D. George, *A Book of Anecdotes*

Sieyès 1: E. Guérard, *Dictionnaire Encyclopédique*

Sigismund 1: W. Seward, *Biographiana*, vol. 1

Silverman 1: *Los Angeles Times*, Aug. 25, 1981

Silvers 1: W. Espy, *Another Almanac of Words at Play*

Simon, 1: B. Cerf, *Good for a Laugh*

Singer 1: D. Straus, *Under the Canopy*; 2: *The Times* (London), June 21, 1982

Sitwell, E., 1: O. Sitwell, *Tales My Father Taught Me*; 2: S. Spender, *World Within World*; 3: L. and M. Cowan, *The Wit of Women*

Sitwell, Sir G., 1–2: O. Sitwell, *Tales My Father Taught Me*

Skelton, J. 1: J. Skelton, *Poems*

Skinner, C., 1: R. Hendrickson, *The Literary Life*

Slezak 1: L. Humphrey, *The Humor of Music*

Smith, Adam, 1: W. Keddie, *Literary and Scientific Anecdote*

Smith, Al, 1: B. Botkin, *Treasury of American Anecdotes*; 2: L. Harris, *The Fine Art of Political Wit*; 3: J. Braude, *Speaker's and Toastmaster's Handbook*

Smith, B., 1: D. Frost, *Book of the World's Worst Decisions*

Smith, C., 1: M. Biggs, ed., *Women's Words: The Columbia Book of Quotations by Women*

Smith, F. E., 1: J. Morris, *The Oxford Book of Oxford*; 2: *The Times* (London), Jan. 8, 1982; 4: S. McCann, *The Wit of the Irish*; 5: K. Edwards, *I Wish I'd Said That*; 7–8: J. Train, *Wit: The Best Things Ever Said*

Smith, S., 1: J. Timbs, *Century of Anecdote*; 2: H. Martineau, *Autobiography*, in J. Sutherland, ed., *OBLA*; 3: H. Pearson, *Lives of the Wits*; 4: *Oxford Dictionary of Quotations*; 5: *A Memoir of the Rev. Sydney Smith by his Daughter, Lady Holland*, in Sutherland, *OBLA*; 6: J. Larwood, *Anecdotes of the Clergy*; 7: N. McPhee, *Second Book of Insults*; 8. M. Ringo, *Nobody Said It Better*

Smuts 1: W. Vaughan-Thomas, *Madly in All Directions*

Smyth 1: S. Spender, *World Within World*

Snead 1: S. Snead and A. Stump, *The Education of a Golfer*

Sobhuza II 1: *The Times* (London), Aug. 25, 1982

Socrates 2: E. Guérard, *Dictionnaire Encyclopédique*

Solomon 1: The Bible

Solon 1: W. Durant, *The Story of Civilization*, II; 2: F. Paley, *Greek Wit*

Somerset 1: C. Roberts, *And So to Bath*

Sophocles 1: *EB*

Southey 1: T. J. Hogg, *The Life of Percy Bysshe Shelley*, in J. Sutherland, ed., *OBLA*

Spellman 1: A. Whitman, *Come to Judgment*

Spencer 1: W. Walsh, *Handy Book of Curious Information*

Spenser 1: T. Fuller, ed., *Worthies of England*; 2: G. Colman, *Circle of Anecdote*

Spillane 1: *New York Times Book Review*, Dec. 27, 1981

Spooner 2: A. Hare, *The Story of My Life*; 4: J. Train, *Wit: The Best Things Ever Said*

Spurgeon 1: J. Ellis, *Spurgeon Anecdotes*; 2: J. Gere and J. Sparrow, *Geoffrey Madan's Notebooks*

Staël 1: J. Herold, *Mistress to an Age*; 2: J. Timbs, *Century of Anecdote*; 3: C. Fadiman, *Party of One*; 4: E. Guérard, *Dictionnaire Encyclopédique*

Stafford 1: *Publishers Weekly*, Jan. 8, 1982

Stalin 1: *Harper's Magazine*, Dec. 1935, in J. Gunther, *Procession*; 2: D. McCullough, *Truman*

Stanley 1: H. Stanley, *How I Found Livingston*

Stanton, C., 1: J. Bartlett, *Bartlett's Familiar Quotations*

Stanton, E., 1: H. and D. L. Thomas, *Living Biographies of Famous Women*

Stark 1: C. Fadiman and C. Van Doren, *The American Treasury*

Steele 1: G. Birkbeck Hill, ed., *Samuel Johnson — Lives of the English Poets*, in J. Sutherland, *OBLA*

Steffens 1: J. Kaplan, *Lincoln Steffens*, in J. Sutherland, ed., *OBLA*

Stein 1: B. Cerf, *At Random*, in D. Hall, ed., *OBALA*; 2, 4: J. Mellow, *Charmed Circle*, in D. Hall, ed., *OBALA*; 3: E. Hemingway, *A Moveable Feast*; 5: '47, *The Magazine of the Year*; Oct.; 6: J. Lipchitz and H. H. Arnason, *My Life in Sculpture*, in Mellow, *Charmed Circle*; 7: B. Cerf, *Try and Stop Me*; 8: *The Autobiography of William Carlos Williams*, in D. Hall, ed., *OBALA*; 9: G. Diliberto, *Hadley*; 10. I. Wallace et al., *Intimate Sex Lives of Famous People*; 11: N. Rorem, *Later Diaries*

Steinbeck 1, 5: J. Benson, *True Adventures of John Steinbeck, Writer*; 2: *Book-of-the-*

Month Club News, May 1947; 3: B. Conrad, *Fun While It Lasted*

Steinberg 1: L. Humphrey, *The Humor of Music*

Steinbrenner 1–2: D. Okrent and S. Wolf, eds., *Baseball Anecdotes*; 3: C. Jones, *What Makes Winners Win*; 4: B. Shlain, *Baseball Inside Out*

Steinmetz 1: C. Fadiman, *Party of One*

Stengel 1: B. Cerf, *Shake Well Before Using*; 2, 6–10: D. Okrent and S. Wolf, eds., *Baseball Anecdotes*; 4: R. Crouser, *It's Unlucky to Be Behind at the End of the Game*

Stern 1: N. Lebrecht, *The Book of Musical Anecdotes*

Sterne 1: W. Scott, *Laurence Sterne*

Stevens 1: G. Vidal, *Lincoln*; 2: R. Marquard, *Jokes and Anecdotes*; 3: T. W. Lloyd, *The Green Bag*, July 1904, in C. Shriner, *Wit, Wisdom, and Foibles of the Great*

Stevenson, A., 1: *Los Angeles Times*, Nov. 25, 1983; 2, 5–6: B. Adler, *The Stevenson Wit*; 3–4: A. Cooke, *Six Men*; 7: M. and A. Guillois, *Liberté, Egalité, Hilarité*; 9: B. Dole, *Great Political Wit*

Stevenson, R., 1: J. Braude, *Speaker's and Toastmaster's Handbook*

Stillman 1: C. Fadiman and C. Van Doren, *The American Treasury*

Stokowski 1: B. Cerf, *Try and Stop Me*; 2: H. Kupferberg, *Those Fabulous Philadelphians*

Stout 2: *The New Yorker*, July 16, 1949

Stowe 1: D. Wallechinsky and I. Wallace, *The People's Almanac*; 2: C. Madigan and A. Elwood, *Brainstorms and Thunderbolts*

Strachey 1: O. Sitwell, *Noble Essences*; 2–3: M. Holroyd, *Lytton Strachey*; 4: C. Fadiman, *Any Number Can Play*; 5: N. and B. Donaldson, *How Did They Die?*

Strauss 1: B. Grun, *Gold and Silver*

Stravinsky 1: G. Astruc, *Le Pavillon des Fantômes*, in F. Steegmuller, *Cocteau*; 2, 8–9: P. Horgan, *Encounters with Stravinsky*; 3: BBC Radio 4, July 5, 1982; 4, 6: O. Levant, *The Unimportance of Being Oscar*; 7: N. Slonimsky, *Lexicon of Musical Invective*; 10: G. Balanchine and F. Mason, *Balanchine's Complete Stories of the Great Ballets;* 11: W. Wiser, *The Crazy Years;* 12: J. Braude, *Speaker's and Toastmaster's Handbook;* 13: E. Mordden, *Opera Anecdotes*

Strug 1: M. Biggs, ed., *Women's Words: The Columbia Book of Quotations by Women*

Stuart 1: Maj. H. K. Douglas, *I Rode with Stonewall,* in B. Botkin, *A Civil War Treasury*

Stubbs 1: W. Camden, *Annales,* in J. Sutherland, ed., *OBLA*

Suderman 1: H. Hoffmeister, *Anekdotenschatz*

Sullivan, 1: E. Fuller, *2500 Anecdotes*

Sumner 1: G. F. Hoar, *The North American Review,* Jan. 1878, in C. Shriner, *Wit, Wisdom, and Foibles of the Great*

Susann 1–2, 5: I. Mansfield, *Life with Jackie;* 3–4: M. Korda, *Another Life*

Sutton; 1: J. McBride, *High and Inside: The A–Z Guide to the Language of Baseball;* 2–3: D. Okrent and S. Wolf, eds., *Baseball Anecdotes*

Suvorov 1: *Harper's Magazine,* Feb. 1852, in C. Shriner, *Wit, Wisdom, and Foibles of the Great*

Svyatopolk 1: W. Durant, *The Story of Civilization,* IV

Swedenborg 1: C. Fox, *Journal,* June 6, 1842, in D. George, *A Book of Anecdotes*

Swift 1: T. Sheridan, *The Life of the Rev. Jonathan Swift,* in J. Sutherland, ed., *OBLA;* 2: E. Fuller, *2500 Anecdotes;* 3–4: G. Colman, *Circle of Anecdote;* 5–6: H. Pearson, *Lives of the Wits*

Swinburne 1: O. Sitwell, *Noble Essences*

Szilard 1: F. Crick, *Life Itself*

Taft, L., 1: J. Braude, *Speaker's and Toastmaster's Handbook*

Taft, W., 3: Lewis Henry, *Humorous Anecdotes About Famous People,* in P. Boller, ed., *Presidential Anecdotes;* 4–7: B. Dole, *Great Political Wit*

Talleyrand-Périgord 1, 5: J. Timbs, *Century of Anecdote;* 2: J. C. Humes, *Speaker's Treasury;* 3: M. Pedrazzini and J. Gris, *Autant en apportent les mots;* 4: Oxfam, *Pass the Port;* 6:

W. Keddie, *Literary and Scientific Anecdote;* 7, 11: C. Brinton, *The Lives of Talleyrand;* 8: A. Duff Cooper, *Talleyrand;* 9: K. Edwards, *I Wish I'd Said That;* 12: F. Mitterand, *The Wheat and the Chaff*

Talmadge 1: R. Webb and T. Carle, *The Laughs on Hollywood*

Tamagno 1: E. Fuller, *2500 Anecdotes*

Tarantino 1: M. Wiley and D. Bona, *Inside Oscar*

Taylor, E., 1: K. Kelley, *Elizabeth Taylor: The Last Star*

Taylor, J., 1: *Boswelliana,* in D. George, *A Book of Anecdotes*

Tecumseh 1: A. W. Dunn, *From Harrison to McKinley,* in P. Boller, ed., *Presidential Anecdotes*

Telford 1: E. Lucas, *A Fronded Isle*

Temple 1: Oxfam, *Pass the Port*

Teng Shih 1: W. Durant, *The Story of Civilization,* I

Tennyson 1, 3: W. R. Nicoll and T. J. Wise, eds., *Literary Anecdotes of the Nineteenth Century,* in R. Martin, *Tennyson: The Unquiet Heart;* 2: G. W. Smalley, *Studies of Man,* in Martin, *Tennyson;* 4: Sir C. Tennyson, *Alfred Tennyson,* in J. Sutherland, ed., *OBLA;* 5: *The Gladstone Papers,* in Martin, *Tennyson;* 6: J. Train, *True Remarkable Occurrences;* 8: Martin, *Tennyson;* 9: Leon Edel, *Henry James: The Conquest of London 1870–1881,* in D. Hall, ed., *OBALA;* 10: N. and B. Donaldson, *How Did They Die?*

Teresa of Ávila 1: P. Bussard, *The New Catholic Treasury of Wit and Humor*

Terry 1: D. Gill, *The Book of the Piano;* 2: *The Times* (London), June 12, 1982

Tetrazzini 1: C. Gattey, *The Elephant That Swallowed a Nightingale*

Thackeray 1: E. Fuller, *2500 Anecdotes;* 2: P. Porzelt, *The Metropolitan Club of New York;* 3: H. Prochnow, *The Public Speaker's Treasury*

Thalberg 1: J. Adamson, *Groucho, Harpo, Chico;* 2: B. Thomas, *Thalberg: Life and Legend*

Thales 1–2: *EB;* 3: Plato, *Theaetetus;* 4: Plutarch, *Lives;* 5: W. Durant, *The Story of Civilization,* II

Themistocles 1: Plutarch, *Lives;* 2: R. Marquard, *Jokes and Anecdotes*

Theodoric 1: E. Guérard, *Dictionnaire Encyclopédique*

Thiers 1: J. Timbs, *Century of Anecdote*

Thomas, D., 1: A. Bespaloff, *The Fireside Book of Wine;* 2: D. Hall, *Remembering Poets;* 3: A. Sinclair, *Dylan Thomas*

Thomas, M. C., 1: M. Biggs, ed., *Women's Words: The Columbia Book of Quotations by Women*

Thomas, N., 1–3: A. Whitman, *Come to Judgment*

Thompson 1: M. Wiley and D. Bona, *Inside Oscar*

Thomson, Sir G., 1: J. Daintith et al., *Biographical Encyclopedia of Scientists*

Thomson, J., 1: J. Dunbar, *J. M. Barrie*

Thoreau 1, 7: M. Saxton, *Louisa May;* 2: H. Thoreau, *Journal,* Oct. 27, 1853; 3: Thoreau, *Journal,* Sept. 8, 1859; 4: C. Fadiman and C. Van Doren, *The American Treasury;* 5: article by Ralph Waldo Emerson in *The Atlantic Monthly,* 1862, in D. Hall, ed., *OBALA;* 6: E. Chubb, *Sketches of Great Painters*

Thurber 1,10: C. Holmes, *The Clocks of Columbus;* 2: B. Cerf, *Good for a Laugh;* 4: B. Bernstein, *Thurber, A Biography;* 5: N. Johnson, letter to Groucho Marx; 7: E. Fuller, *2500 Anecdotes;* 8: M. Rosen, ed., *Collecting Himself*

Thurlow 1, 4: W. Adams, *Treasury of Modern Anecdote;* 2–3: L. Missen, *After-Dinner Stories and Anecdotes*

Tintoretto 1: H. Morton, *A Traveller in Italy*

Titian 1: D. Wallechinsky and I. Wallace, *The People's Almanac*

Tolstoy 1: John Hersey, *Antonietta;* 2: *"Daily Mirror" Old Codger's Little Black Book 4*

Tooke 1: K. Arvine, *Cyclopaedia of Anecdotes;* 2: Lord Broughton, *Recollections of a Long Life,* in Kenin and Wintle, *DBQ*

Toscanini 1: L. Humphrey, *The Humor of Music;* 2: C. Fadiman and C. Van Doren, *The American Treasury;* 4: BBC Radio (Desert Island Discs, Mar. 5, 1982); 5: H. Taubman, *The Maestro;* 6–8: H. Taubman, *Music on My Beat;* 9: J. Braude, *Speaker's and Toastmaster's Handbook*

Toulouse-Lautrec 1: N. and B. Donaldson, *How Did They Die?*

Townshend 1: Sir J. Prior, *Life of Edmond Malone . . .* in J. Sutherland, ed., *OBLA*

Tracy 1: R. Byrne, *The 637 Best Things Anybody Ever Said;* 3: *People,* July 1978

Travers 1: A. Leslie, *The Remarkable Mr. Jerome*

Travolta 1–2: M. Wiley and D. Bona, *Inside Oscar*

Tree 1: H. Teichmann, *Smart Aleck;* 3: K. Brownlow, *Hollywood: The Pioneers;* 4: E. Fuller, *2500 Anecdotes;* 5, 7: J. Braude, *Speaker's and Toastmaster's Handbook;* 6: J. Aye, *Humour in the Theatre*

Trench 1–2: L. Missen, *Quotable Anecdotes*

Trilling 1: W. Espy, *Another Almanac of Words at Play*

Trollope, A., 1–2, 4: M. Sadleir, *Trollope: A Commentary;* 3: A. Trollope, *Autobiography*

Trollope, F., 1: *Outlook,* July 21, 1923

Trotsky 1: G. Mikes, *Coffee Houses of Europe*

Troy 1: D. Wallechinsky and I. Wallace, *The People's Almanac*

Truman 1, 9: D. McCullough, *Truman;* 3: J. Lash, *Eleanor and Franklin;* 4: F. Muir, *Irreverent Social History;* 5: J. B. West, *Upstairs at the White House,* in P. Boller, ed., *Presidential Anecdotes;* 6: "Free to Choose," *The New Republic,* Mar. 22, 1980, in Boller, *Presidential Anecdotes;* 7: M. Miller, *Plain Speaking,* in Boller, *Presidential Anecdotes;* 10: W. Zinsser, ed., *Extraordinary Lives: The Art and Craft of American Biography;* 11: *Los Angeles Times,* Aug. 14, 1983

Truth 1: P. Smith, *Trial by Fire*

Turner 1: G. Painter, *Proust: The Early Years;* 2: W. P. Frith, *My Autobiography and Reminiscences;* 3–4: E. Chubb, *Sketches of*

Great Painters; 5–6: D. Piper, *Painting in England;* 7: P. Johnson, *The Birth of the Modern*

Twain 1, 3, 7, 10, 21: A. Paine, *Mark Twain;* 2: R. Hendrickson, *The Literary Life;* 4: B. Cerf, *Try and Stop Me;* 5: B. Cerf, *Shake Well Before Using;* 6: L. and F. Copeland, *10,000 Jokes, Toasts, and Stories;* 8, 12, 14–15, 19: E. Fuller, *2500 Anecdotes;* 9, 23: J. Kaplan, *Mr. Clemens and Mark Twain;* 11: C. Clemens, *My Father Mark Twain;* 13: S. Weintraub, *The London Yankees,* in D. Hall, ed., *OBALA;* 16: D. Wallechinsky and I. and A. Wallace, *The Book of Lists;* 17: H. Prochnow, *Public Speaker's Treasure Chest;* 18: J. Nash, *Zanies;* 22: D. W. McCullough, ed., *American Childhoods*

Tyler 1: J. Sternberg, ed., *The Writer on Her Work*

Tyson 1: *Los Angeles Times,* June 26, 1988

Uccello 1: T. Craven, *Men of Art*

Untermeyer 1: R. Hendrickson, *The Literary Life;* 2: S. Harris, *Pieces of Eight*

Unzelmann 1: W. Durant, *The Story of Philosophy*

Urban VII 1: D. Boorstin, *The Creators*

Ustinov 1: H. Vickers, *Great Operatic Disasters*

Van Buren 1: H. Alexander, *The American Talleyrand: The Career and Contemporaries of Martin Van Buren,* in P. Boller, ed., *Presidential Anecdotes*

Vanderbilt, A., 1: D. Wallechinsky and I. Wallace, *The People's Almanac*

Vanderbilt, C., 1, 3: S. Holbrook, *The Age of the Moguls;* 2: A. May, *Different Drummers*

Vanderbilt, W., 1: F. Crowninshield, "The House of Vanderbilt," in *Vogue's First Reader,* in B. Botkin, *Treasury of American Anecdotes;* 2: M. Ringo, *Nobody Said It Better;* 3: B. Conrad, *Famous Last Words*

Van Doren 1: B. Cerf, *Shake Well Before Using;* 2: J. C. Humes, *Speaker's Treasury*

Van Slyke 1: B. Shlain, *Baseball Inside Out*

Varah 1: C. Varah, *Samaritans in the 70s*

Vatel 1: D. Wallechinsky and I. Wallace, *The People's Almanac*

Veeck 1: J. McBride, *High and Inside: The A–Z Guide to the Language of Baseball*

Vega Carpio 1: R. Byrne, *The 637 Best Things Anybody Ever Said*

Verdi 1: V. Seligman, *Puccini Among Friends;* 2: N. Slonimsky, *A Thing or Two About Music*

Verlaine 1: J. Bayard, *The Latin Quarter Past and Present*

Verrall 1: E. Marsh, *A Number of People*

Vesey 1: *DNB*

Vespasian 1, 3: Suetonius, *The Twelve Caesars;* 2: W. Durant, *The Story of Civilization,* III

Victor Amadeus II 1: J. Papesch, *Europa Lächelt Noch Immer*

Victoria 1, 5: J. Adair, *The Royal Palaces of Great Britain;* 2, 7: H. and D. L. Thomas, *Living Biographies of Famous Rulers;* 3, 6: D. Cecil, *Melbourne;* 4: Lord Gower, *Records and Reminiscences,* in C. Shriner, *Wit, Wisdom, and Foibles of the Great;* 8: J. Paar, *P.S. Jack Paar;* 9: A. R. Mills, *Two Victorian Ladies,* in A. Hardy, *Queen Victoria Was Amused;* 10: Frederick Ponsonby, *Recollections of Three Reigns,* in Hardy, *Queen Victoria;* 11: B. Cerf, *The Life of the Party;* 12: V. Cowles, *The Kaiser;* 13: J. Bone, *The London Perambulator;* 14: A. H. Bevan, *Popular Royalty,* in Hardy, *Queen Victoria;* 15–16: E. Longford, *The Oxford Book of Royal Anecdotes;* 17: S. Weintraub, *Victoria;* 18: P. Ziegler, *Diana Cooper*

Vidal 1: A. Powell, *The Strangers Are All Gone*

Villa 1: R. Byrne, *The 637 Best Things Anybody Ever Said*

Villiers De L'Isle Adam 1: J. Bayard, *The Latin Quarter Past and Present*

Virchow 1: E. Fuller, *2500 Anecdotes;* 2: R. Calder, *Medicine and Man*

Voltaire 1: J. Papesch, *Europa Lächelt Noch Immer;* 2: L. Russell, *English Wits;* 3: N. Mitford, *Voltaire in Love;* 4, 10: E. Fuller, *2500 Anecdotes;* 5–6: B. Cerf, *Try and Stop Me;* 7: W. and A. Durant, *The Story of Civilization,* IX; 8: W. Scholz, *Das Buch des Lachens;* 9: E.

Kelen, *Peace in Their Time;* 11: W. Ukers, *All About Coffee;* 12: W. Durant, *The Story of Philosophy;* 13, 15: Dugas de Bois St. Just, *Paris, Versailles et les provinces;* 14: W. O'Flaherty, *Other People's Myths;* 16: H. and D. L. Thomas, *Living Biographies of the Great Philosophers*

Waddell 1: B. Cerf, *Bumper Crop of Anecdotes*

Walker 1: C. Fadiman and C. Van Doren, *The American Treasury*

Waller 1: L. Missen, *Quotable Anecdotes*

Waln 1: I. and R. Poley, *Friendly Anecdotes*

Walpole, H., 1: R. Ketton-Cremer, *Horace Walpole*

Walpole, Sir R., 1: *Blackwood's Edinburgh Magazine,* Apr. 1868, in C. Shriner, *Wit, Wisdom, and Foibles of the Great;* 2: K. C. Balderston, ed., *Thraliana*

Walter 1: E. Fuller, *2500 Anecdotes*

Walton 1: O. Sitwell, *Laughter in the Next Room;* 2: *The Observer,* Feb. 7, 1982

Warburton 1: J. Bartlett, *Bartlett's Familiar Quotations*

Ward 1: *The Complete Works of Artemus Ward,* in B. Botkin, *Treasury of American Anecdotes;* 2: J. Kaplan, *Mark Twain and His World*

Warner 1: L. Cannon, *Reagan;* 2: D. Niven, *Bring On the Empty Horses*

Washington 1: M. Weems, *Life of Washington;* 2: W. Gordon, *History of the Independence of the United States,* in P. Boller, ed., *Presidential Anecdotes;* 3: P. Hood, *World of Anecdote;* 4: P. Smith, *A New Age Now Begins;* 5: E. Fuller, *2500 Anecdotes;* 6: Paul Wilstach, *Patriots off Their Pedestals,* in Boller, *Presidential Anecdotes;* 7: F. Hunt, *American Anecdotes,* in Boller, *Presidential Anecdotes;* 8: B. Botkin, *Treasury of American Anecdotes;* 9: F. R. Bellamy, *The Private Life of George Washington,* in Boller, *Presidential Anecdotes;* 10: P. L. Ford, *The True George Washington,* in Boller, *Presidential Anecdotes*

Waterton 1: E. Sitwell, *English Eccentrics*

Watson 1: L. Missen, *After-Dinner Stories and Anecdotes*

Watt 1: W. and A. Durant, *The Story of Civilization,* X

Waugh 1: H. Acton, *More Memoirs of an Aesthete;* 2: R. Claiborne, *Our Marvelous Native Tongue;* 4: J. Epstein, "Evelyn Waugh," *New Criterion,* 3, Apr. 1985; 5: J. Epstein, "Merely Anecdotal," in *The American Scholar,* spring 1992; 6: J. Bryan, III, ed., *Hodgpodge: A Commonplace Book*

Wavell 1: B. Fergusson, *Wavell*

Wayne, J. 1–2: P. Hay, ed., *Movie Anecdotes*

Weaver 1–3: D. Okrent and S. Wolf, eds., *Baseball Anecdotes*

Webb 1: L. Missen, *Quotable Anecdotes*

Webster, D. 1–2: C. Lanman, *The Private Life of Daniel Webster;* 3: B. Botkin, *Treasury of American Anecdotes;* 4: Charles Lanman, *The Private Life of Daniel Webster,* in D. Hall, ed., *OBALA;* 5: *Oxford Dictionary of Quotations;* 6, 10: P. Harvey, *Reminiscences of Daniel Webster;* 7, 9: C. Fuess, *Daniel Webster;* 8: V. Brooks, *Life of Emerson;* 10: Richard Lathers, *Reminiscences,* in C. Shriner, *Wit, Wisdom, and Foibles of the Great*

Webster, N., 1: R. Marquard, *Jokes and Anecdotes;* 2: J. S. Morgan, *Noah Webster,* in D. Hall, ed., *OBALA*

Weizmann 1: R. St. John, *They Came from Everywhere*

Welles 1–2: P. Boller, ed., *Hollywood Anecdotes;* 3: M. Korda, *Charmed Lives*

Wellington 1: J. Timbs, *Century of Anecdote;* 2: *Records of the Conference Between Wellington and Scindiak after the Battle of Assaye,* in D. George, *A Book of Anecdotes;* 3, 5: A. Bryant, *The Age of Elegance;* 4, 10–11: N. McPhee, *Second Book of Insults;* 6: George, *Anecdotes;* 7: D. Duff, *Albert and Victoria;* 8: J. Keegan, *The Masks of Command;* 9: H. Hoffmeister, *Anekdotenschatz;* 12: E. Fuller, *2500 Anecdotes;* 13, 17: W. Fraser, *Words of Wellington,* in C. Shriner, *Wit, Wisdom, and*

Foibles of the Great; 14: *The New Yorker,* Mar. 10, 1951; 16: M. Garland, *The Changing Face of Childhood*

Wells 1: E. Fuller, *2500 Anecdotes;* 2: H. Nicolson, *Diaries;* 3: N. and B. Donaldson, *How Did They Die?;* 4: C. Snow, *Variety of Men*

Werfel 1: I. Wallace et al., *Intimate Sex Lives of Famous People*

Wesley 1: H. and D. L. Thomas, *Living Biographies of Religious Leaders;* 2: E. Fuller, *2500 Anecdotes*

West 1: K. Edwards, *I Wish I'd Said That Too;* 2–3: G. Herman, *The Book of Hollywood Quotes;* 4: G. Vlastos, *Socrates: Ironist and Moral Philosopher*

Westinghouse 1: W. Walsh, *Handy Book of Curious Information*

Wharton 1: E. Wharton, *A Backward Glance;* 2: P. Lubbock, *Portrait of Edith Wharton,* in D. Hall, ed., *OBALA*

Wheeler 1: P. Smith, *The Rise of Industrial America*

Whewell 1: L. Missen, *Quotable Anecdotes;* 2: W. Keddie, *Literary and Scientific Anecdote*

Whistler 1–2: L. Russell, *English Wits;* 3: K. Edwards, *I Wish I'd Said That Too;* 4, 7–8, 12–13, 17: D. Seitz, *Whistler Stories;* 5: B. Cerf, *The Life of the Party;* 6: P. Mahony, *Barbed Wit and Malicious Humor;* 9: L. and F. Copeland, *10,000 Jokes, Toasts, and Stories;* 10: H. Pearson, *The Man Whistler;* 11: H. Gerwig, *Fifty Famous Painters;* 14: J. Whistler, *On the Gentle Art of Making Enemies;* 15: J. Braude, *Speaker's and Toastmaster's Handbook;* 16: E. Fuller, *2500 Anecdotes*

Whitman 1: C. Fadiman and C. Van Doren, *The American Treasury*

Whitney 1: P. Smith, *The Nation Comes of Age*

Wieniawski 1: N. Slonimsky, *A Thing or Two About Music*

Wild 1: H. Bagust, *London Through the Ages*

Wilde 1: Miss J. Hawkins, in J. Sutherland, ed., *OBLA;* 2: H. Pearson, *The Life of Oscar Wilde,* in Sutherland, *OBLA;* 3, 10, 14: H.

Pearson, *Lives of the Wits;* 4: R. Ellmann, *Oscar Wilde;* 5: Sir W. Rothenstein, *Men and Memories,* in Sutherland, *OBLA;* 6: R. Marquard, *Jokes and Anecdotes;* 7: B. Cerf, *Shake Well Before Using;* 8: J. Bartlett, *Bartlett's Familiar Quotations;* 9: Walter Jerrold, *A Book of Famous Wits,* in Sutherland, *OBLA;* 11: G. Brandreth, *Great Theatrical Disasters;* 12: G. Mikes, *Laughing Matter;* 13: A. Hare, *The Story of My Life;* 15: N. McPhee, *Book of Insults;* 17: W. Yeats, *Autobiographies;* 18: D. Wallechinsky and I. Wallace, *The People's Almanac;* 19: *Time,* Jan. 16, 1984

Wilder 3: T. Wood, *The Bright Side of Billy Wilder, Primarily*

Wilkes 1: J. Timbs, *Century of Anecdote;* 2: R. Postgate, *That Devil Wilkes;* 3: P. Stockdale, *Memoirs of the Life and Writings of P. Stockdale*

Willes 1: Lord Campbell, *Lives of the Chief Justices,* in D. George, *A Book of Anecdotes*

William I (England) 1: *DNB*

William I (Prussia) 1: W. Scholz, *Das Buch des Lachens;* 2: F. Syben, *Preussiche Anekdoten*

William II (Germany) 1: E. Benson, *The Kaiser and English Relations*

William III (England) 1: J. H. Jesse, *England Under the House of Hanover,* in C. Shriner, *Wit, Wisdom, and Foibles of the Great*

Williams, Ted, 1–3: D. Okrent and S. Wolf, eds., *Baseball Anecdotes;* 4: R. B. Cramer, "What Do You Think of Ted Williams Now?" *Esquire,* June 1986

Williams, Tennessee, 1: J. Rosner, *A Hater's Handbook;* 2: D. Spoto, *The Kindness of Strangers*

Wills, M. 1–2: D. Okrent and S. Wolf, eds., *Baseball Anecdotes*

Wilson, C., 1: P. Smith, *The Rise of Industrial America*

Wilson, E., 1: A. Whitman, *Come to Judgment*

Wilson, Sir H., 2: BBC Radio 4, Oct. 23, 1984

Wilson, H., 1: *Harriette Wilson's Memoirs of Herself and Others,* in J. Sutherland, ed., *OBLA*

Wilson, R., 1: D. Piper, *Painting in England*

Wilson, W., 1: J. C. Humes, *Speaker's Treasury;* 2: B. Adler, ed., *Presidential Wit from Washington to Johnson*, in P. Boller, ed., *Presidential Anecdotes;* 4–5: E. Fuller, *2500 Anecdotes*

Winters 1: *Los Angeles Times*, Mar. 24, 1984

Wittgenstein 1: F. McLynn, "An Unintegrated Ego," review of R. Monk, *Ludwig Wittgenstein: The Duty of Genius, Literary Review*, Nov. 1990

Wodehouse 1: F. Donaldson, *Freddy Lonsdale;* 2: F. Donaldson, *P. G. Wodehouse;* 3: B. Nichols, *The Sweet Twenties*

Wolf 1: P. Mahony, *Barbed Wit and Malicious Humor*

Wolfe, J., 1: M. Ringo, *Nobody Said It Better*

Wolfe, T., 1–2: A. Turnbull, *Thomas Wolfe: A Biography*, in D. Hall, ed., *OBALA*

Woollcott 2: J. Nash, *The Innovators;* 3: I. Mansfield, *Life with Jackie;* 4: M. Hart, *Act One;* 5: O. Levant, *The Unimportance of Being Oscar;* 6: H. Teichmann, *Smart Aleck;* 7: J. Braude, *Braude's Second Encyclopedia;* 8: J. McAleer, "Globe Man's Daily Story," *Boston Globe*, Dec. 16, 1962; 9: N. and B. Donaldson, *How Did They Die?;* 10: H. Teichmann, *Smart Aleck*, in D. Hall, ed., *OBALA*

Wordsworth 1: F. Muir, *Irreverent Social History;* 2: L. Missen, *Quotable Anecdotes;* 3: E. Marsh, *A Number of People*

Wren 1: N. Lo Bello, *European Detours*

Wright, F., 1: The Johnson Foundation

Wright, O., 1: H. and D. L. Thomas, *Living Adventures in Science*

Wright, R., 1: C. Webb, *Richard Wright: A Biography*, in D. Hall, ed., *OBALA*

Wycherley 1: J. Spence, *Anecdotes*

Wylie 1: V. S. Carr, *The Lonely Hunter: A Biography of Carson McCullers*, in D. Hall, ed., *OBALA*

Xerxes 1: E. Fuller, *2500 Anecdotes;* 2: D. George, *A Book of Anecdotes*

Yeats 1: L. MacNeice, *The Strings Are False;* 2: M. Cowley, *The View from 80*

Yusupov 1: S. Marx, *Mayer and Thalberg*

Zaharias 1: M. Biggs, ed., *Women's Words: The Columbia Book of Quotations by Women*

Zangwill 2: P. Mahony, *Barbed Wit and Malicious Humor*

Zeno 1: W. Durant, *The Story of Civilization*, II

Zeuxis 1: T. Fuller, *The Holy State*

Zhou Enlai 1: D. Edgar, "Apparatchat," review of F. Burlatsky's *Khrushchev and the First Russian Spring, Literary Review*, Aug. 1991

Zoeller 1: R. T. Sommers, *Golf Anecdotes*

BIBLIOGRAPHY

———— ❧ ————

The bibliography is divided into two sections: Books and Periodicals. In many instances, old or classical references do not have specific publication data.

BOOKS

Abbott, Willis J. *Notable Women in History.* Philadelphia: Winston, 1913.

Abdy, Jane, and Charlotte Grere. *The Souls.* London: Sidgwick & Jackson, 1984.

Ace, Goodman. *The Book of Little Knowledge: More Than You Want to Know About Television.* New York: Simon & Schuster, 1955.

Ackroyd, Peter. *T. S. Eliot.* New York: Simon & Schuster, 1984.

Acton, Harold. *Memoirs of an Aesthete.* London: Methuen, 1948.

Acton, Harold. *More Memoirs of an Aesthete.* London: Methuen, 1970.

Acton, Harold. *Nancy Mitford: A Memoir.* New York: Harper & Row, 1975.

Adair, John. *The Royal Palaces of Britain.* London: Thames & Hudson, 1981.

Adams, Ansel. *Ansel Adams: An Autobiography.* Boston: NYGS/Little, Brown, 1985.

Adams, W. Davenport. *Treasury of Modern Anecdote.* London: Thomas D. Morison, 1886.

Adamson, Joe. *Groucho, Harpo, Chico and Sometimes Zeppo: A History of the Marx Brothers and a Satire on the Rest of the World.* New York: Simon & Schuster, 1984.

Adler, Bill. *Baseball Wit.* New York: Crown, 1986.

Adler, Bill. *My Favorite Funny Story, by Billy Graham . . . and Others.* New York: Four Winds Press, 1967.

Adler, Bill, and Bill Adler, Jr. *The Reagan Wit.* Aurora, Ill.: Caroline House, 1981.

Adler, Mortimer. *Philosopher at Large: An Intellectual Biography.* New York: Macmillan, 1977.

Agate, James. *Rachel.* New York: Viking, 1928.

Alexander, Shana. *Talking Woman.* New York: Delcorte, 1976.

Alifano, Roberto. *Twenty-Four Conversations with Borges.* New York: Grove Press, 1984.

Allen, Steve. *Funny People.* New York: Stein & Day, 1981.

Allen, Walter E. *As I Walked Down New Grub Street: Memories of a Writing Life.* Chicago: University of Chicago Press, 1981.

Alsop, Em Bowles, ed. *The Greatness of Woodrow Wilson, 1856–1956.* New York: Rinehart, 1956.

Alsop, Susan Mary. *Yankees at the Court: The*

First Americans in Paris. New York: Doubleday, 1982.

American Jest Book, 1789.

Amos, William. *The Originals: An A–Z of Fiction's Real-Life Characters.* New York: Little, Brown, 1986.

Anderson, Dave. *The Red Smith Reader.* New York: Random House, 1982.

Anson, Robert Sam. *Exile: The Unquiet Oblivion of Richard M. Nixon.* New York: Simon & Schuster, 1984.

Ardoin, John Louis, and Gerald Fitzgerald. *Callas.* New York: Holt, Rinehart & Winston, 1974.

Arendt, Hannah. *Men in Dark Times.* New York: Harcourt, Brace & World, 1971.

Arlen, Michael J. *Exiles.* New York: Farrar, Straus & Giroux, 1970.

Arlott, John. *Cricket: The Great Ones.* London: Pelham Books, 1967.

Arlott, John. *John Arlott's Book of Cricketers.* London: Sphere, 1982.

Arnold, Thurman. *Fair Fights and Foul: A Dissenting Lawyer's Life.* New York: Harcourt, Brace & World, 1965.

Arvine, Kazlitt. *Cyclopaedia of Anecdotes of Literature and the Fine Arts.* Boston: Gould and Lincoln, 1851. Rpt. Detroit: Gale Research Co., 1967.

A Sense of History. New York: American Heritage Publishing Co., Inc., 1985.

Asimov, Isaac. *Asimov's Biographical Encyclopedia of Science and Technology.* New York: Doubleday, 1964.

Asimov, Isaac. *Isaac Asimov's Treasury of Humor.* Boston: Houghton Mifflin, 1971.

Aslet, Clive. *The Last Country Houses.* New Haven: Yale University Press, 1982.

Asquith, Cynthia. *Portrait of Barrie.* New York: Dutton, 1955.

Asser's Life of King Alfred, ed. W. H. Stevenson. London: Oxford University Press, 1959.

Atherton, Gertrude Franklin. *Adventures of a Novelist.* New York: Liveright, 1932.

Atkins, Harold, and Archie Newman, eds. *Beecham Stories: Anecdotes, Sayings and Impressions of Sir Thomas Beecham.* New York: St. Martin's Press. 1979.

Aubrey, John. *Brief Lives and Other Selected Writings.* Rpt. New York: Scribner, 1949.

Aubrey, John. *Miscellanies,* ed. John Buchanan-Brown. Rpt. Arundel, England: Centaur Press, 1972.

Auden, W. H. *A Certain World: A Commonplace Book.* New York: Viking, 1970.

Aye, John. *Humour in the Theatre.* London: Universal Publications Ltd., 1932.

Baer, Jean, *The Self-Chosen: "Our Crowd" Is Dead — Long Live "Our Crowd!"* New York: Priam/Arbor House, 1984.

Bagust, Harold. *London Through the Ages.* Cheltenham, England: Thornhill Press, 1982.

Baillén, Claude. *Chanel Solitaire.* New York: Quadrangle/New York Times Books, 1974.

Bair, Deirdre. *Samuel Beckett: A Biography.* London: Jonathan Cape, 1978.

Baker, Richard. *Richard Baker's Music Guide.* North Pomfret, Vt.: David & Charles, 1979.

Balanchine, George, and Francis Mason. *Balanchine's Complete Stories of the Great Ballets.* Rev. and enl. ed. New York: Doubleday, 1977.

Balderston, Katherine C., ed. *Thraliana: The Diary of Mrs. Hester Lynch Thrale (Later Mrs. Piozzi) 1776–1809.* Oxford: Clarendon Press, 1942.

Balsdon, Dacre. *Oxford Now and Then.* New York: St. Martin's Press, 1970.

Barker, Edmund Hillary. *Literary Recollections and Contemporary Reminiscences of Professor Porson and Others.* London: J. R. Smith, 1852.

Barmash, Isadore. *"Always Live Better Than Your Clients": The Fabulous Life and Times of Benjamin Sonnenberg, America's Greatest Publicist.* New York: Dodd, Mead, 1983.

Barnett, Correlli. *Bonaparte.* London: Allen & Unwin, 1978.

Barra, Allen. *That's Not the Way It Was.* New York: Hyperion, 1995.

Barrow, Andrew. *Gossip.* London: Hamish Hamilton, 1978.

Barson, Michael. *The Illustrated Who's Who of Hollywood Directors.* Vol. I: *The Sound Era.* New York: Farrar, Straus & Giroux, 1995.

Bartlett, John. *Familiar Quotations.* 14th, 15th eds. Boston: Little, Brown, 1968, 1980.

Barzun, Jacques. *A Stroll with William James.* New York: Harper & Row, 1983.

Bayard, Jean Emile. *The Latin Quarter, Past and Present,* trans. Percy Mitchell. New York: Brentano's, 1927.

Beach, Scott, *Musicdotes.* Berkeley, Calif.: Ten Speed Press, 1977.

Bede. *History of the English Church and People.* Rpt. Harmondsworth, England: Penguin, 1968.

Beebe, William. *The Book of Naturalists.* New York: Knopf, 1944.

Beecham, Sir Thomas. *A Mingled Chime.* New York: Putnam, 1943.

Behan, Beatrice, with Des Hickey and Gus Smith. *My Life with Brendan.* Los Angeles: Nash, 1974.

Behrman, Samuel Nathaniel. *Portrait of Max: An Intimate Memoir of Sir Max Beerbohm.* New York: Random House, 1960.

Bell, Eric Temple. *Men of Mathematics.* New York: Simon & Schuster, 1937.

Bellow, Saul. *Him with His Foot in His Mouth and Other Stories.* New York: Harper & Row, 1984.

Benchley, Nathaniel, *Robert Benchley.* New York: McGraw-Hill, 1955.

Benny, Mary Livingstone, and Hilliard Marks, with Marcia Borie. *Jack Benny.* New York: Doubleday, 1978.

Benson, E. F. *The Kaiser and English Relations.* London and New York: Longmans, Green, 1936.

Benson, Ivan. *Mark Twain's Western Years.* Palo Alto, Calif.: Stanford University Press, 1938.

Benson, Jackson J. *The True Adventures of John Steinbeck, Writer.* New York: Viking, 1984.

Berger, Francesco. *Reminiscences, Impressions, and Anecdotes.* London: S. Low, Marston, 1913.

Bernard, André. *Now All We Need Is a Title: Famous Book Titles and How They Got That Way.* New York: Norton, 1994.

Bernard, André, ed. *Rotten Rejections: A Literary Companion.* Wainscott, N.Y.: Pushcart Press, 1990.

Bernard, Robert. *Tennyson: The Unquiet Heart.* Oxford: Clarendon Press, 1983.

Bernstein, Burton. *Thurber: A Biography.* New York: Dodd, Mead, 1975.

Bernstein, Jeremy. *Einstein.* New York: Penguin, 1973.

Bernstein, Kenneth. *Music Lover's Europe: A Guidebook and Companion.* New York: Scribner, 1983.

Berra, Yogi. *The Yogi Book.* New York: Workman Publishing, 1998.

Berton, Pierre. *The Royal Family: The Story of British Monarchy from Victoria to Elizabeth.* New York: Knopf, 1953.

Bespaloff, Alexis. *The Fireside Book of Wine.* New York: World, 1971.

Beste, Henry Digby. *Personal and Literary Memorials.* London: H. Colburn, 1829.

Biggs, Mary, ed. *Women's Words: The Columbia Book of Quotations by Women.* New York: Columbia University Press, 1996.

Bing, Sir Rudolf. *5000 Nights at the Opera.* New York: Doubleday, 1972.

Bing, Sir Rudolf. *A Knight at the Opera.* New York: Putnam, 1981.

Bingham, J. *Courage to Change: An Introduction to the Life and Thought of Reinhold Niebuhr.* New York: Scribner, 1972.

Birmingham, Stephen. *The Grandes Dames.* New York: Simon & Schuster, 1982.

Birmingham, Stephen. *The Late John Marquand: A Biography.* Philadelphia: Lippincott, 1972.

Birmingham, Stephen. *"The Rest of Us": The Rise of America's Eastern European Jews.* Boston: Little, Brown, 1984.

Bishop, Morris. *The Exotics; Being a Collection of Unique Personalities and Remarkable Characters.* New York: American Heritage, 1969.

Bishop, Morris. *A Gallery of Eccentrics.* New York: Minton, Balch, 1928.

Black, David. *King of Fifth Avenue: The Fortunes of August Belmont.* New York: Dial, 1981.

Bland-Sutton, Sir John. *The Story of a Surgeon.* Boston: Houghton Mifflin, 1930.

Blount, Thomas. *Boscobel.* London: for H. Seile, 1662.

Bogarde, Dirk. *An Orderly Man.* New York: Knopf, 1983.

Bogarde, Dirk. *Snakes and Ladders.* New York: Holt, Rinehart & Winston, 1979.

Boissier, Gaston. *Mme de Sévigné,* trans. Arthur Stanley. Paris, 1887–1919.

Boller, Paul. *Hollywood Anecdotes.* New York: Morrow, 1987.

Boller, Paul, ed. *Presidential Anecdotes.* New York: Oxford University Press, 1981.

Boller, Paul. *Presidential Wives: An Anecdotal History.* New York: Oxford University Press, 1988.

Boller, Paul. *Presidential Campaigns.* New York: Oxford University Press. 1984.

Bolton, Sarah K. *Famous Men of Science.* New York: T. Y. Crowell, 1989.

Bonavia, Ferruccio, ed. *Musicians on Music.* New York: McBride, 1956.

Bone, James. *The London Perambulator.* New York: Knopf, 1925.

Bonington, Christian. *Quest for Adventure.* New York: C. N. Potter, 1982.

Boorstin, Daniel. *The Creators.* New York: Random House, 1992.

Boorstin, Daniel J. *The Discoverers.* New York: Random House, 1983.

Boswell, J. *Life of Johnson.* London: Oxford University Press, 1934 (first published in 1791).

Botkin, B. A. *A Civil War Treasury.* New York: Random House, 1960.

Botkin, B. A., ed. *A Treasury of American Anecdotes.* New York: Random House, 1957.

Bouhier, Jean. *Souvenirs de Jean Bouhier.* Paris: Émile Voitelain, 1866.

Bourrienne, Louis. *Memoris of Napoleon Bonaparte.* New York: P. F. Collier, 1891.

Bowen, Catherine Drinker. *Miracle at Philadelphia.* Boston: Atlantic–Little, Brown, 1966.

Bowen, Catherine Drinker. *Yankee from Olympus.* Boston: Atlantic–Little, Brown, 1944.

Bowles, Paul. *Two Years Beside the Straight: Tangier Journal 1987–1989.* London: Owen, 1990.

Bowra, Cecil Maurice. *Memories 1898–1939.* London: Weidenfeld and Nicolson, 1966.

Boyd-Carpenter, John. *Way of Life: The Memoirs of John Boyd-Carpenter.* London: Sidgwick & Jackson, 1980.

Boydell, Thomas. *My Luck Was In: With Spotlights on General Smuts.* Capetown: Stewart, 1947.

Boyle, Andrew. *Only the Wind Will Listen: Reith of the BBC.* London: Hutchinson, 1972.

Bradley, Omar Nelson, and Clay Blair. *A General's Life: An Autobiography.* New York: Simon & Schuster, 1983.

Brady, Frank. *Onassis: An Extravagant Life.* Englewood Cliffs, N.J.: Prentice-Hall, 1977.

Brandreth, Gyles. *Great Theatrical Disasters.* New York: St. Martin's, 1982.

Brandreth, Gyles. *The Joy of Lex: How to Have Fun with 860,341,500 Words.* New York: Morrow, 1980.

Brandreth, Gyles. *871 Famous Last Words.* New York: Bell Publishing, 1979.

Braude, Jacob M. *Braude's Second Encyclopedia of Stories, Quotations and Anecdotes.* Englewood Cliffs, N.J.: Prentice-Hall, 1957.

Braude, Jacob M. *Speaker's and Toastmaster's Handbook of Anecdotes by and About Famous Personalities.* Englewood Cliffs, N.J.: Prentice-Hall, 1971.

Bredsdorff, Elias. *Hans Christian Andersen: The*

Story of His Life and Work 1805–75. New York: Scribner, 1975.

Brendon, Piers. *The Life and Death of the Press Barons*. New York: Atheneum, 1983.

Brewer, Ebenezer Corham. *Brewer's Dictionary of Phrase and Fable* (1870). London: Cassell, 1923; Centenary Ed., ed. Ivor H Evans. New York: Harper & Row, 1981.

Bridges, Robert Seymour. *Three Friends: Memoirs of Digby Mackworth Dolben, Richard Watson Dixon, Henry Bradley*. London: Oxford University Press, 1932.

Brinkley, Alan. *Voices of Protest: Huey Long, Father Coughlin, and the Great Depression*. New York: Knopf, 1982.

Brinton, Crane. *The Lives of Talleyrand*. New York: Norton, 1936.

Brooks, Van Wyck. *The Life of Emerson*. New York: Dutton, 1932.

Brougham, Henry, Lord. *Men of Letters and Science Who Flourished in the Time of George III*. Paris: Baudry's European Library, 1845.

Broughton, Lord. *Recollections of a Long Life*. London: J. Murray, 1909.

Broun, Heywood Hale. *Whose Little Boy Are You?: A Memoir of the Broun Family*. New York: St. Martin's, 1983.

Brown, Anthony Cave. *The Last Hero: Wild Bill Donovan*. New York: Times Books, 1982.

Brown, Ivor. *A Charm of Names*. London: The Bodley Head, 1972.

Brownlow, Kevin. *Hollywood: The Pioneers*. New York: Knopf, 1979.

Bryan III, J. *Hodgepodge: A Commonplace Book*. New York: Atheneum, 1986.

Bryan III, J. *Hodgepodge Two*. New York: Atheneum, 1989.

Bryant, Arthur. *The Age of Elegance, 1812–22*. New York: Harper, 1951.

Bryson, Bill. *The Mother Tongue*. New York: Morrow, 1990.

Buckle, Richard. *In the Wake of Diaghilev*. New York: Holt, Rinehart & Winston, 1983.

Buckle, Richard. *Nijinsky*. New York: Simon & Schuster, 1971.

Buckle, Richard, ed. *Self-Portrait with Friends: The Selected Diaries of Cecil Beaton, 1926–1974*. New York: Times Books, 1979.

Buckley, Tom. *Violent Neighbors*. New York: Times Books, 1983.

Buckman, Peter. *Lafayette*. New York: Paddington Press, 1977.

Buñuel, Luis. *My Last Breath*. New York: Knopf, 1983.

Burgon, John. *Lives of Twelve Good Men*. New York: Scribner & Welford, 1888.

Burney, Charles. *A General History of Music from the Earliest Ages to the Present Period (1789), with Critical and Historical Notes by Frank Mercer*. Rpt. New York: Dover, 1937.

Burns, George. *The Third Time Around*. New York: Putnam, 1980.

Burrows, Abe. *Honest, Abe*. Boston: Little, Brown, 1980.

Bussard, Paul. *The New Catholic Treasury of Wit and Humor*. New York: Meredith, 1968.

Butler, Peter, ed. *The Wit of Prince Philip*. New York: Hawthorne, 1966.

Byrne, Robert. *The 637 Best Things Anybody Ever Said*. New York: Atheneum, 1982.

Byron, George Gordon, Lord. *Byron's Letters and Journals,* ed. Leslie A. Marchand. Cambridge, Mass.: Harvard University Press, 1973–1982.

Cable, Mary. *Top Drawer,* New York: Atheneum, 1984.

Caine, T. Hall. *Recollections of Dante Gabriel Rossetti*. Boston: Roberts Bros., 1883.

Calder, Ritchie. *Medicine and Man: The Story of the Art of Science and Healing*. New York: American Library, 1958.

Callières, Françoise de. *Des Bons mots et des bons contes*. Geneva: Slatkine Reprints, 1971.

Cameron, Kenneth Neill. *Shelley: The Golden Years*. Cambridge, Mass.: Harvard University Press, 1974.

Campbell, Douglas, and John Higgins. *Mathematics: People, Problems, Results*. Vol. I. Belmont, Calif.: Wadsworth, 1984.

Canetti, Elias. *Crowds and Power.* New York: Viking, 1962.

Canfield, Cass. *Up and Down and Around: A Publisher Recollects the Times of His Life.* New York: Harper's Magazine Press, 1971.

Cannon, Lou. *President Reagan: The Role of a Lifetime.* New York: Simon & Schuster, 1991.

Cannon, Lou. *Reagan.* New York: Putnam, 1982.

Cantor, N. F., and M. S. Werthman, eds. *The History of Popular Culture.* New York: Macmillan, 1968.

Cardus, Neville. *Sir Thomas Beecham: A Memoir.* London: Collins, 1961.

Cardus, Neville. *Talking of Music.* New York: Macmillan, 1957.

Carey, John, ed. *The Faber Book of Reportage.* London: Faber & Faber, 1988.

Caro, Robert A. *The Years of Lyndon Johnson.* Vol I: *The Path to Power.* New York: Knopf, 1982.

Carpenter, Humphrey. *W. H. Auden: A Biography.* Boston: Houghton Mifflin, 1981.

Carroll, James. *Prince of Peace.* Boston: Little, Brown, 1984.

Carter, Harry. *A History of the Oxford University Press.* Vol. I. London: Oxford University Press, 1975.

Carter, Jimmy. *Keeping Faith: Memoirs of a President.* New York: Bantam, 1982.

Carter, Rosalynn. *First Lady from Plains.* Boston: Houghton Mifflin, 1984.

Cary, M., et al., eds. *Oxford Classical Dictionary.* Oxford: Clarendon Press, 1940.

Castelot, André. *Marie Antoinette d'après des documents inédits.* Paris: Amiot-Dumont, 1953.

Castelot, André. *Paris: The Turbulent City 1783–1871,* trans. Denise Foliot. New York: Harper & Row, 1962.

Castelot, André. *Philippe Egalité: Le Prince rouge.* Paris: SFELT, 1950.

Castlerosse, Valentine, Viscount. *Valentine's Days.*

Cavett, Dick, and Christopher Porterfield. *Eye on Cavett.* New York: Arbor House, 1983.

Cecil, Lord David. *Max: A Biography.* Boston: Houghton Mifflin, 1965.

Cecil, Lord David. *Melbourne.* New York: Grosset & Dunlap. 1954.

Celebrity Research Group. *The Bedside Book of Celebrity Gossip.* New York: Crown Publishers, 1984.

Cerf, Bennett A. *Bumper Crop of Anecdotes and Stories.* New York: Garden City Books, 1959.

Cerf, Bennett A. *Good for a Laugh.* New York: Hanover House, 1952.

Cerf, Bennett A. *Laughing Stock.* New York: Grosset & Dunlap, 1945.

Cerf, Bennett A. *The Life of the Party.* New York: Hanover House, 1956.

Cerf, Bennett A. *Shake Well Before Using.* New York: Simon & Schuster, 1948.

Cerf, Bennett A. *Treasury of Atrocious Puns.* New York: Harper and Row, 1968.

Cerf, Bennett A. *Try and Stop Me.* New York: Simon & Schuster, 1944.

Chambers, Andrea. *Dream Resorts.* New York: C. N. Potter, 1983.

Chancellor, John. *Charles Darwin.* New York: Taplinger, 1976.

Charteris, E. *Life and Letters of Sir Edmund Gosse.* New York: Haskell House, 1982.

Cheever, Susan. *Home Before Dark.* Boston: Houghton Mifflin, 1984.

Chekhov, Anton. *The Image of Chekhov: Forty Stories in the Order in Which They Were Written,* trans. Robert Payn. New York: Vintage, 1963.

Chelminski, Rudolph. *The French at Table.*

Chesterton, G. K. *Charles Dickens: The Last of the Great Men.* New York: The Press of the Reader's Club, 1942.

Chubb, Edwin W. *Sketches of Great Painters.* Cincinnati: Stewart & Kidd, 1915.

Churchill, Winston S. *Great Contemporaries.* New York: Putnam, 1937.

Churchill, Winston S. *Thoughts and Adventures.* London: T. Butterworth, 1932.

Claiborne, Robert. *Our Marvelous Native Tongue: The Life and Times of the English Language*. New York: New York Times Books, 1983.

Clark, Eric. *Diplomat: The World of International Diplomacy*. New York: Taplinger, 1974.

Clark, Ronald W. *The Huxleys*. New York: McGraw-Hill, 1968.

Clark, Ronald W. *The Life of Bertrand Russell*. New York: Knopf, 1976.

Clemens, Clara. *My Father Mark Twain*. New York: Harper & Bros., 1931.

Cliffe, Leigh. *Anecdotal Reminiscences*.

Cocteau, Jean. *Past tense*. Vol I: *Diaries,* trans. Richard Howard.

Cohen, J. M., and M. J. Cohen. *Penguin Dictionary of Quotations*. New York: Penguin, 1982.

Coleridge, Samuel T. *Kubla Khan*. Boston: Wells and Lilly, 1816.

Coleridge, Samuel T. *Table Talk*. 3rd ed. London: J. Murray, 1851.

Collier, James L. *Louis Armstrong: An American Genius*. New York: Oxford University Press, 1983.

Collier, Peter, and David Horowitz. *The Kennedys: An American Drama*. New York: Summit Books, 1984.

Collier, Richard. *The Freedom Road: 1944–1945*. New York: Atheneum, 1984.

Collier, Richard. *The Rainbow People*. New York: Dodd, Mead, 1984.

Collier, Richard. *The Road to Pearl Harbor 1941*. New York: Atheneum, 1981.

Colman, George. *Circle of Anecdote and Wit*. London: J. Williams, 1826.

Compton's Picture Encyclopedia. Chicago: F. E. Compton, 1968 ed.

Connelly, Marcus. *Voices Offstage: A Book of Memoirs*. New York: Holt, Rinehart & Winston, 1968.

Conrad, Barnaby. *Famous Last Words*. New York: Doubleday, 1961.

Conrad, Barnaby. *Fun While It Lasted*. New York: Random House, 1969.

Considine, Bob. *It's All News to Me: A Reporter's Deposition*. New York: Meredith, 1967.

Cooke, Alistair. *The Patient Has the Floor*. New York: Knopf, 1986.

Cooke, Alistair. *Six Men*. New York: Knopf, 1977.

Cooper, A. Duff. *Tallyrand*. London: Jonathan Cape, 1932.

Cooper, Jilly. *Class*. New York: Knopf, 1981.

Copeland, Lewis, and Faye Copeland. *10,000 Jokes, Toasts and Stories*. New York: Halcyon House, 1939.

Corey, Melinda, and George Ochoa. *The Man in Lincoln's Nose*. New York: Fireside Books, 1990.

Corn, Wanda. *The Art of Andrew Wyeth*. San Francisco: The Fine Arts Museum, 1973.

Cornell, Tim, and John Matthews. *Atlas of the Roman World*. New York: Facts on File, 1982.

Coughlin, Robert. *The Private World of William Faulkner*. New York: Harper, 1954.

Cowan, Lore, and Maurice Cowan. *The Wit of Women*. London: Leslie Frewin, 1969.

Cowles, Virginia. *The Kaiser*. New York: Harper & Row, 1963.

Cowley, Malcolm. *The View from 80*. New York: Viking, 1980.

Cox, Stephen. *Here's Johnny: Thirty Years of America's Favorite Late Night Entertainment*. New York: Harmony Books, 1992.

Craig, Gordon. *The Germans*. New York: Putnam, 1982.

Crankshaw, Edward. *Bismarck*. New York: Viking, 1981.

Crankshaw, Edward. *The Fall of the House of Hapsburg*. New York: Viking, 1963.

Crankshaw, Edward. *Maria Theresa*. New York: Viking, 1970.

Crankshaw, Edward. *The Shadow of the Winter Palace: Russia's Drift to Revolution*. New York: Viking, 1976.

Crankshaw, Edward. *Tolstoy: The Making of a Novelist*. New York: Viking, 1974.

Crankshaw, Edward. *Vienna: The Image of a Culture in Decline.* New York: Macmillan, 1938.

Craven, Thomas. *Men of Art.* Garden City, N.Y.: Halcyon House, 1931.

Creamer, Robert W. *The Babe — The Legend Comes to Life.* New York: Simon & Schuster, 1974.

Crick, Francis. *Life Itself: Its Origins and Nature.* New York: Simon & Schuster, 1981.

Cronin, Vincent. *Louis XIV.* Boston: Houghton Mifflin, 1965.

Cronin, Vincent. *Napoleon Bonaparte: An Intimate Biography.* New York: Morrow, 1972.

Cronin, Vincent. *The View from Planet Earth: Man Looks at the Cosmos.* New York: Morrow, 1981.

Crouser, Richard L. *It's Unlucky to Be Behind at the End of the Game and Other Sports Retorts.* New York: Morrow, 1983.

Crow, Bill. *Jazz Anecdotes.* New York: Oxford University Press, 1990.

Culbertson, Judi, and Tom Randall. *Permanent New Yorkers.* Royalton, Vt.: Chelsea Green, 1987.

Cummings, W. H. *Dr. Arne and Rule, Britannia.*

Cunningham, Allan. *Lives of the Most Eminent British Painters and Sculptors.* New York: J. Harper, 1831.

Curtis, George Ticknor. *Life of Daniel Webster.* New York: D. Appleton and Co., 1870.

Daiches, David. *James Boswell and His World.* New York: Scribner, 1976.

"Daily Mirror" Old Codger's Little Black Book, The. London: Mirror Books, 1977.

Daintith, John, Sarah Mitchell, and Elizabeth Tootill. *Biographical Encyclopedia of Scientists.* New York: Facts on File, 1981.

Dale, Alzina Stone. *The Outline of Sanity: A Biography of G. K. Chesterton.* Grand Rapids, Mich.: Eerdman's, 1982.

Dance, Stanley. *The World of Count Basie.* New York: Scribner, 1980.

Daniel, Clifton. *Lords, Ladies and Gentlemen: A Memoir.* New York: Arbor House, 1984.

Darwin, Charles. *Autobiography.* Rpt., New York: Norton, 1969.

Davenport, Guy. *The Geography of the Imagination: Forty Essays.* San Francisco: North Point Press, 1981.

David, Philip, and Reuben Hersh. *The Mathematical Experience.* Boston: Houghton Mifflin, 1981.

Davidson, Angus. *Edward Lear: Landscape Painter and Nonsense Poet (1812–1888).* New York: Dutton, 1939.

Davin, Dan. *Closing Times.* New York: Oxford University Press, 1975.

Davies, Thomas. *Dramatic Miscellanies.* London, 1783–84.

Davis, A. R., ed. *The Penguin Book of Chinese Verse,* trans. Robert Kotewall and Norman L. Smith. Baltimore: Penguin, 1962.

Deighton, Len. *Action Cook Book: Len Deighton's Guide to Eating.* London: Jonathan Cape, 1965.

Delaney, Frank, and Jorge Lewinski. *James Joyce's Odyssey: A Guide to the Dublin of Ulysses.* New York: Holt, Rinehart & Winston, 1983.

De Morgan, Augustus. *The Encyclopedia of Eccentrics.* La Salle, Ill.: Open Court, 1974.

De Stoeckl, Agnes, and Wilfred S. Edwards. *When Men Had Times to Love.* London: J. Murray, 1953.

Devonshire, Deborah Vivien Freeman-Mitford Cavendish, Duchess of. *The House: A Portrait of Chatsworth.* London: Macmillan, 1982.

Dickson, Paul. *Baseball's Greatest Quotations.* New York: HarperCollins, 1991.

Dictionary of National Bioigraphy. Sir Leslie Stephen and Sir Sidney Lee, eds. 63 vols., supplements. London: Oxford University Press, 1885–1900, 1921–1927, 1960.

Diehl, Digby. *Supertalk.* New York: Doubleday, 1974.

Dietrich, Marlene. *Marlene.* New York: Grove Press, 1989.

Dietz, Howard. *Dancing in the Dark.* New York: Quadrangle, 1974.

Diliberto, Gioia. *Hadley*. New York: Ticknor & Fields, 1992.

Diogenes Laertius. *Lives of Eminent Philosophers*. Cambridge, Mass.: Harvard University Press, 1928.

D'Israeli, Isaac. *Curiosities of Literature*. Boston: Lilly, Wait, Colman & Holden, 1833.

D'Israeli, Isaac. *Miscellanies of Literature*. New York: J. and H. G. Langley, 1841.

Dole, Robert, ed. *Great Political Wit: Laughing (Almost) All the Way to the White House*. New York: Doubleday, 1998.

Dolin, Anton. *Friends and Memories*, ed. Andrew Wheatcroft. London: Routledge & Kegan Paul, 1982.

Donaldson, Frances. *Freddy Lonsdale*. Philadelphia: Lippincott, 1957.

Donaldson, Frances. *P. G. Wodehouse: A Biography*. New York: Knopf, 1982.

Donaldson, Norman, and Betty Donaldson. *How Did They Die?* New York: Greenwich House, 1980.

Donovan, Hedley. *From Roosevelt to Reagan*. New York: Harper & Row, 1983.

Draper & Esquin (San Francisco Wine Merchants). Sales brochure.

Drennan, Robert E. *The Algonquin Wits*. New York: Citadel Press, 1968.

Drennan, Robert E. *Wit's End*. London: Leslie Frewin, 1973.

Dryfoos, Susan W. *Iphigene: Memoirs of Iphigene Ochs Sulzberger of the New York Times Family as Told to Her Granddaughter*. New York: Dodd, Mead, 1981.

Duff, David. *Albert and Victoria*. London: Muller, 1972.

Duff, David. *Elizabeth of Glamis*. London: Muller, 1973.

Duff, David. *Eugénie and Napoleon III*. New York: Morrow, 1978.

Dugas de Bois St. Just, Jean Louis Marie. *Paris, Versailles et les provinces au dix-huitième siècle*. Paris: H. Nicole, 1811.

Dunaway, Philip, and George De Kay, eds. *Turning Points: Fateful Moments That Revealed Men and Made History*. New York: Random House, 1958.

Dunbar, Janet. *J. M. Barrie, The Man Behind the Image*. Boston: Houghton Mifflin, 1970.

Duncan, David Douglas. *Picasso's Picasso*. New York: Harper, 1961.

Durant, Will. *The Story of Philosophy: The Lives and Opinions of the Greater Philosophers*. New York: Simon & Schuster, 1926.

Durant, Will, and Ariel Durant. *The Story of Civilization*. 11 vols. New York: Simon & Schuster, 1935–65.

Eastman, Max. *Great Companions*. New York: Farrar, Straus & Cudahy, 1959.

Eby, Cecil. *The Siege of the Alcazar*. New York: Random House, 1965.

Edwards, Kenneth. *I Wish I'd Said That: An Anthology of Witty Replies*. London: Abelard-Schuman, 1976.

Edwards, Kenneth. *I Wish I'd Said That Too*. London: Abelard-Schuman, 1977.

Edwards, Kenneth. *More Things I Wish I'd Said, and Some I Wish I Hadn't*. London: Abelard-Schuman, 1978.

Eisenhower, David. *Eisenhower at War*. New York: Random House, 1986.

Eisenhower, Dwight D. *At Ease: Stories I Tell to Friends*. New York: Doubleday, 1957.

Elder, Donald. *Ring Lardner: A Biography*. New York: Doubleday, 1956.

Elliot, John Harold. *Berlioz*. London: Dent, 1938; reissued 1967.

Ellis, James J. *Spurgeon Anecdotes: Being Authentic Anecdotes*. London: J. E. Hawkins, 1892.

Ellmann, Richard. *James Joyce*. Oxford: Oxford University Press, 1959; new and rev. edition, 1982.

Ellmann, Richard. *Oscar Wilde*. New York: Knopf, 1988.

Encyclopaedia Britannica. Chicago: Encyclopaedia Britannica, 1960, 1961, 1967, 1969, 1971.

Enright. D. J. *The Oxford Book of Death*. New York: Oxford University Press, 1983.

Erskine, David, ed. *Augustus Hervey's Journal.* London: Kimber, 1953.

Ervine, St. John Greer. *Bernard Shaw: His Life, Work and Friends.* New York: Morrow, 1956.

Espy, Willard. *An Almanac of Words at Play.* New York: C. N. Potter, 1980.

Evans, Christopher. *The Micro Millennium.* New York: Washington Square Press, 1979.

Evans, H. Sutherland. *Personal Recollections.*

Evans, Richard. *Nasty: Ilie Nastase vs. Tennis.* New York: Stein & Day, 1979.

Fadiman, Clifton. *Any Number Can Play.* Cleveland: World Publishing, 1957.

Fadiman, Clifton. *Enter, Conversing.* Cleveland: World Publishing, 1962.

Fadiman, Clifton. *Fifty Years.* New York: Knopf, 1965.

Fadiman, Clifton, ed. *Testament.* New York: Doubleday, 1991.

Fadiman, Clifton. *The Mathematical Magpie.* New York: Simon & Schuster, 1962.

Fadiman, Clifton. *Party of One: The Selected Writings of Clifton Fadiman.* Cleveland: World Publishing, 1955.

Fadiman, Clifton, and Charles Van Doren. *The American Treasury 1455–1955.* New York: Harper & Row, 1955.

Farago, Ladislas. *Strictly from Hungary.* New York: Walker, 1962.

Faulkner, Alex, and Tom Hartman. *All the Best People . . . The Pick of Peterborough, 1929–1945.* Boston: Allen & Unwin, 1981.

Ferris, Timothy. *Coming of Age in the Milky Way.* New York: Morrow, 1988.

Fien, Irving A. *Jack Benny: An Intimate Biography.* Boston: G. K. Hall, 1976.

Fergusson, Bernard. *Wavell: Portrait of a Soldier.* London: Collins, 1961.

Fielding, Daphne. *Those Remarkable Cunards: Emerald and Nancy.* New York: Atheneum, 1968.

Fifield, William. *In Search of Genius.* New York: Morrow, 1982.

Finch, Christopher. *The Art of Walt Disney: From Mickey Mouse to the Magic Kingdoms.* New York: H. N. Abrams, 1973.

Finck, Henry. *Musical Laughs.* New York: Funk & Wagnalls, 1924.

Fitzgerald, Patrick. *Ancient China.* Oxford: Elsevier-Phaidon, 1978.

Fitzgibbon, Theodora, comp. *The Pleasures of the Table.* New York: Oxford University Press, 1981.

Flanner, Janet. *Darlinghissima: Letters to a Friend,* edited and with commentary by Natalia Danesi Murray. New York: Random House, 1985.

Fleming, Sir Ambrose. *Memories of a Scientific Life.* London: Marshall, Morgan & Scott, 1934.

Fonteyn, Margot. *Margot Fonteyn: An Autobiography.* New York: Knopf, 1976.

Foot, Michael. *Aneurin Bevan: A Biography.* New York: Atheneum, 1963.

Forbes, Bryan. *Ned's Girl.* Boston: Little, Brown, 1977.

Forbes, Elliot, ed. *Thayer's Life of Beethoven.* Princeton, N.J.: Princeton University Press, 1964.

Ford, Corey. *The Time of Laughter.* Boston: Little, Brown, 1967.

Ford, Ford Madox. *Ancient Lights* (1911).

Fordin, Hugh. *Getting to Know Him: A Biography of Oscar Hammerstein II.* New York: Random House, 1967.

Forkner, Ben. *Modern Irish Short Stories.* Preface by Anthony Burgess. New York: Penguin, 1980.

Fowler, Gene. *Beau James: The Life and Times of Jimmy Walker.* New York: Viking, 1949.

Fowler, Gene. *Good Night, Sweet Prince.* New York: Viking, 1944.

Fowler, Gene. *Minutes of the Last Meeting.* New York: Viking, 1954.

Fowler, Gene. *Schnozzola: The Story of Jimmy Durante.* New York: Viking, 1951.

Fowler, Gene. *Timber Line: A Story of Bonfils and Fammen.* Garden City, N.Y.: Halcyon House, 1933.

Foxe, John. *Acts and Monuments,* ed. H. M. Seymour. New York: 1855.

François, Jacob. *The Possible and the Actual.* New York: Pantheon, 1982.

Frank, Philipp. *Einstein: His Life and Times.* New York: Knopf, 1947.

Franqui, Carlos. *Family Portrait with Fidel,* trans. Alfred MacAdam. New York: Random House, 1983.

Fraser, Antonia. *Cromwell, The Lord Protector.* New York: Knopf, 1973.

Fraser, Sir William. *Disraeli and His Day.* London: K. Paul, Trench, Trubner, 1891.

Frederick, Pauline. *Ten First Ladies of the World.* New York: Meredith, 1967.

Freud, Sigmund. *Wit and Its Relation to the Unconscious* (1916).

Friedman, Thomas. *From Beirut to Jerusalem.* New York: Farrar, Straus & Giroux, 1989.

Frith, William Powell. *My Autobiography and Reminiscences.* New York: Harper, 1888.

Frommer, Myrna Katz, and Harvey Frommer. *It Happened on Broadway: An Oral History of the Great White Way.* New York: Harcourt Brace & Company, 1998.

Frost, David. *Best of the World's Worst Decisions.* New York: Crown, 1983.

Frost, David. *"I Gave Them a Sword": Behind the Scenes of the Nixon Interviews.* New York: Morrow, 1978.

Frost, David, and Michael Deakin. *David Frost's Book of Millionaires, Multimillionaires, and Really Rich People.* New York: Crown, 1984.

Fuess, Claude Moore. *Daniel Webster.* Boston: Little, Brown, 1930.

Fuller, Edmund. *2500 Anecdotes for All Occasions.* New York: Crown, 1943.

Fuller, Thomas. *Fuller's The Holy State and the Profane State,* ed. Maximilian Graff Walten. New York: Columbia University Press, 1938.

Fuller, Thomas, ed. *The Worthies of England,* intro. and notes by John Freeman. New York: Barnes & Noble, 1952.

Furnas, J. C. *Fanny Kemble: Leading Lady of the Nineteenth-Century Stage.* New York: Dial, 1982.

Fussell, Betty. *I Hear America Cooking.* New York: Viking, 1986.

Gaines, James R., ed. *The Lives of the Piano.* New York: Holt, Rinehart & Winston, 1981.

Galbraith, John Kenneth. *A Life in Our Times.* Boston: Houghton Mifflin, 1981.

Garland, H. *Ulysses S. Grant: His Life and Character.* New York: Doubleday & McClure, 1898.

Garland, Joseph. *Boston's Gold Coast.* Boston: Little, Brown, 1981.

Garland, Madge. *The Changing Face of Childhood.* New York: October House, 1965.

Gates, W. Francis. *Anecdotes of Great Musicians: Three Hundred Anecdotes and Biographical Sketches of Famous Composers and Performers.* Philadelphia: T. Presser, 1898.

Gattey, Charles Neilson. *The Elephant That Swallowed a Nightingale and Other Operatic Wonders.* London: Hutchinson, 1981.

Gay, Peter. *Freud: A Life for Our Time.* New York: Norton, 1988.

George, Daniel, ed. *A Book of Anecdotes: Illustrating Varieties of Experience in the Lives of the Eminent and the Lives of the Obscure.* Secaucus, N.J.: Citadel, 1958.

Georges-Michel, Michel. *From Renoir to Picasso: Artists in Action,* trans. Dorothy and Randolph Weaver. Boston: Houghton Mifflin, 1957.

Gere, J. A., and John Sparrow. *Geoffrey Madan's Notebooks: A Selection.* New York: Oxford University Press, 1984.

Gerin, W. *Anne Thackeray Ritchie: A Biography.* New York: Oxford University Press, 1981.

Germond, J. *Blue Smoke and Mirrors: How Reagan Won and Why Carter Lost the Election of 1980.* New York: Viking, 1991.

Gerwig, Henrietta. *Fifty Famous Painters.* New York: T. Y. Crowell, 1926.

Gibbon, Edward. *The History of the Decline and Fall of the Roman Empire.* 3rd ed. London:

W. S. Strahan & T. Cadell, 1777. Rpt., New York: Modern Library, 1983.

Gilbert, Michael. *The Oxford Book of Legal Anecdotes.* Oxford: Oxford University Press, 1986.

Gilchrist, Alexander. *The Life of William Blake.* New York: Dodd, Mead, [1906?].

Gill, Brendan. *Here at the New Yorker.* New York: Random House, 1975.

Gill, Dominic, ed. *The Book of the Piano.* Ithaca, N.Y.: Cornell University Press, 1981.

Gilot, Françoise, and Carlton Lake. *Life with Picasso.* New York: McGraw-Hill, 1964.

Gipe, George. *The Last Time When.* New York: Newspaper Enterprise Assn., 1980.

Gleick, James. *Genius: The Life and Science of Richard Feynman.* New York: Pantheon Books, 1992.

Godden, Rumer. *Hans Christian Andersen: A Great Life in Brief.* New York: Knopf, 1954.

Gogarty, Oliver St. John. *It Isn't This Time of Year at All! An Unpremeditated Autobiography.* New York: Doubleday, 1954.

Gogol, Nikolai V. *Chichikov's Journeys: Home Life in Old Russia,* trans. Bernard Guilbert Guerney. New York: The Reader's Club, 1942.

Goncourt, Edmond de. *Journal des Goncourt: Mémoires de la vie littéraire.* Paris: E. Fasguelle, 1891–1907.

Goossens, Eugene. *Overture and Beginners: A Musical Autobiography.* Westport, Conn.: Greenwood Press, 1972.

Gordon, Max, with Lewis Funke. *Max Gordon Presents.* New York: Geis, 1963.

Gottfried, Martin, *Jed Harris: The Curse of Genius.* Boston: Little, Brown, 1984.

Graham, Sheila. *The Garden of Allah.* New York: Crown, 1970.

Grant, Michael. *Readings in the Classical Historians.* New York: Scribner, 1992.

Graves, Robert. *Goodbye to All That.* New ed., rev. New York: Doubleday, 1957.

Graves, R. P. *A. E. Housman: The Scholar Poet.* New York: Scribner, 1980.

Green, Benny, comp. *London.* New York: Oxford University Press, 1984.

Green, Horace. *General Grant's Last Stand.* New York: Scribner, 1936.

Green, Jonathan. *Morrow's International Dictionary of Contemporary Quotations.* New York: Morrow, 1982.

Green, Lee. *Sportswit.* New York: Harper & Row, 1982.

Green, Robert Lancelyn. *C. S. Lewis: A Biography.* New York: H. Z. Walck, 1963.

Green, Robert Lancelyn, ed. *The Diaries of Lewis Carroll.* New York: Oxford University Press, 1954.

Greenfield, Howard. *Caruso.* New York: Putnam, 1983.

Griffin, Jasper, ed. *Snobs.* New York: Oxford University Press, 1982.

Griffin, Merv, with Peter Barsocchini. *From Where I Sit: Merv Griffin's Book of People.* New York: Arbor, 1982.

Gruen, John. *Menotti: a Biography.* New York: Macmillan, 1978.

Gruen, John. *The Party's Over Now: Reminiscences of the Fifties — New York's Artists, Writers, Musicians, and Their Friends.* New York: Viking, 1972.

Grun, Bernard. *Gold and Silver: The Life and Times of Franz Lehár.* New York: D. McKay Co., 1970.

Guedalla, Philip. *Supers and Supermen: Studies in Politics, History and Letters.* New York: Knopf, 1921.

Guérard, E. *Dictionnaire Encyclopédique d'anecdotes modernes, anciennes, françaises et étrangères par Edmond Guérard.* Paris: Firmin-Didot, 1879.

Guillois, Mina, and André Guillois. *Liberté, Egailité, Hilarité.* Paris: Fayard, 1972.

Guinness, Alec. *Blessings in Disguise.* Knopf, 1986.

Guinness, Jonathan, with Catherine Guinness. *House of Mitford.* New York: Viking, 1985.

Gunther, John. *Inside Russia Today.* New York: Harper, 1958.

Gunther, John. *Inside South America*. New York: Harper & Row, 1967.

Gunther, John, *Procession*. New York: Harper & Row, 1965.

Hadleigh, Boze. *Hollywood Babble On: Stars Gossip About Other Stars*. New York: Birch Lane Press, 1994.

Hagedorn, Herman. *Roosevelt in the Bad Lands*. Boston: Houghton Mifflin, 1921.

Halberstam, David. *The Fifties*. New York: Villard, 1993.

Halberstam, David. *The Next Century*. New York: Morrow, 1990.

Halberstam, David. *The Reckoning*. New York: Morrow, 1986.

Hall, Donald, ed. *The Oxford Book of American Literary Anecdotes*. New York: Oxford University Press, 1981.

Hall, Donald. *Remembering Poets*. New York: Harper & Row, 1978.

Halle, Kay. *Randolph Churchill, The Young Unpretender: Essays by His Friends*. London: Heinemann, 1971.

Hamburger, Michael, ed. *Beethoven: Letters, Journals and Conversations*. New York: Pantheon, 1952.

Hamilton, Ian. *Koestler: A Biography*. New York: Macmillan, 1982.

Hamilton, Ian. *Robert Lowell: A Biography*. New York: Random House, 1982.

Hamilton, Nigel. *JFK: Reckless Youth*. New York: Random House, 1992.

Hammond, John Winthrop. *Men and Volts: The Story of General Electric*. Philadelphia: Lippincott, 1941.

Hancock, W. K. *Smuts*. London: Cambridge University Press, 1962–1968.

Hardy, Alan. *Queen Victoria Was Amused*. New York: Taplinger, 1977.

Hardy, G. H. *A Mathematician's Apology*. London: Cambridge University Press. 1940.

Hare, Augustus John Cuthbert. *The Story of My Life*. New York: Dodd, Mead, 1896.

Harris, Leon A. *The Fine Art of Political Wit*. New York: Dutton, 1966.

Harris, Sydney J. *Pieces of Eight*. Boston: Houghton Mifflin, 1982.

Harrison, Ada, and Derek Stanford. *Anne Brontë: Her Life and Work*. New York: John Day, 1959.

Hart, Moss. *Act One: An Autobiography*. New York: Random House, 1959.

Harvey, Paul. ed. *Oxford Companion to Classical Literature*. Oxford: Clarendon Press, 1966.

Harvey, Peter. *Reminiscences and Anecdotes of Daniel Webster*. Boston: Little, Brown, 1887.

Hassall, Christopher Vernon. *Biography of Edward Marsh*. New York: Harcourt, Brace, 1959.

Hastings, Michael. *Sir Richard Burton: A Biography*. New York: Coward, McCann & Geoghegan, 1978.

Hatch, Alden. *The Byrds of Virginia*. New York: Holt, Rinehart & Winston, 1969.

Hatch, Alden. *The Mountbattens: The Last Royal Success Story*. New York: Random House, 1965.

Hauser, Ernest O. *Italy, A Cultural Guide*. Atheneum, 1981.

Hauser, Thomas. *Muhammad Ali: His Life and Times*. New York: Touchstone, 1991.

Hawthorne, Julian. *Nathaniel Hawthorne and His Wife*. Boston: James R. Osgood, 1884.

Hay, Peter. *Movie Anecdotes*. New York: Oxford University Press, 1990.

Heath, Sir Thomas. *A History of Greek Mathematics*. New York: Dover Books, 1981.

Hecht, Ben. *A Child of the Century*. New York: Simon & Schuster, 1954.

Heine, Heinrich. *Confessions*, trans. Peter Heinegg. Malibu, Calif.: J. Simon, 1981.

Hellman, Lillian. *Pentimento*. Boston: Little, Brown, 1969.

Hemingway, Ernest. *A Moveable Feast*. New York: Scribner, 1964.

Hendrickson, Robert. *The Literary Life and Other Curiosities*. New York: Viking, 1981.

Henry, O. *The Voice of the City and Other Stories*. New York: Limited Editions Club, 1935.

Henry of Huntingdon. *Historia Anglorum*.

Herbert, Alan Patrick. *A.P.H.: His Life and Times*. London: Heinemann, 1978.

Herman, Gary. *The Book of Hollywood Quotes*. New York: Omnibus, 1979.

Herodotus. *History*, trans. H. Carter. Oxford: Oxford University Press, 1962.

Herold, J. Christopher. *Mistress to an Age: A Life of Madame de Staël*. Indianapolis, Ind.: Bobbs-Merrill, 1958.

Herrmann, Dorothy. *With Malice Toward All*. New York: Putnam, 1982.

Hersey, John. *Antonietta*. New York: Knopf, 1991.

Hession, Charles H. *John Maynard Keynes*. New York: Macmillan, 1984.

Hibbert, Christopher. *The Personal History of Samuel Johnson*. London: Longman Group, Ltd., 1971.

Hill, Christopher. *God's Englishman: Oliver Cromwell and the English Revolution*. New York: Dial, 1970.

Hillary, Edmund. *High Adventure*. New York: Dutton, 1955.

Hobson, Laura Z. *Laura Z: A Life*. New York: Arbor House, 1983.

Hoffmeister, Herbert. *Anekdotenschatz, von der antike bis auf unsere Tage*. Berlin: Verlag Praktisches Wissen, 1957.

Hofman, P. *Rome — The Sweet, Tempestuous Life*. New York: Congdon & Lattès, 1982.

Holbrook, Stewart H. *The Age of the Moguls*. New York: Doubleday, 1953.

Holland, Vyvyan.*Time Remembered After Père Lachaise*. London: Gollancz, 1966.

Holmes, Charles S. *The Clocks of Columbus: The Literary Career of James Thurber*. New York: Atheneum, 1972.

Holmes, Oliver Wendell. *Ralph Waldo Emerson*. Boston: Houghton Mifflin, 1884.

Holroyd, Michael. *Lytton Strachey: A Biography*. New York: Holt, Rinehart & Winston, 1967.

Hood, Paxton. *World of Anecdote*. Philadelphia: Lippincott, 1874.

Hopkins, Anthony. *Music All Around Me: A Personal Choice from the Literature of Music*. London: Frewin, 1967.

Horgan, Paul. *Approaches to Writing*. 2nd ed. Middletown, Conn.: Wesleyan University Press, 1988.

Horgan, Paul. *Encounters with Stravinsky*. New York: Farrar, Straus & Giroux, 1972.

Hotchner, A. E. *Choice People: The Greats, Near-Greats, and Ingrates I Have Known*. New York: Morrow, 1984.

Hough, Richard. *Edward and Alexandra: Their Private and Public Lives*.

Howard, Jane. *Margaret Mead: A Life*. New York: Simon & Schuster, 1984.

Howard, Margo. *Eppie: The Story of Ann Landers*. New York: Putnam, 1982.

Howe, Mark A. DeWolfe. *Holmes of the Breakfast Table*. New York: Oxford University Press, 1939.

Howe, Mark A. DeWolfe. *John Jay Chapman and His Letters*. Boston: Houghton Mifflin, 1937.

Howells, William Dean. *My Mark Twain: Reminiscences and Criticisms*. New York: Harper & Brothers, 1910.

Huddleston, Sisley. *Paris Salons, Cafés, Studios*. Philadelphia: Lippincott, 1928.

Huffington, Arianna Stassinopoulos. *Picasso: Creator and Destroyer*. New York: Simon & Schuster, 1988.

Humes, James C. *Speakers' Treasury of Anecdotes About the Famous*. New York: Harper & Row, 1978.

Humphrey, Laning. *The Humor of Music and Other Oddities in the Art*. Boston: Crescendo, 1971.

Innes, Michael. *The Gay Phoenix*. New York: Penguin, 1981.

Isaacs, Alan, and Elizabeth Martin. *Dictionary of Music*. New York: Hamlyn, 1982.

Isaacson, Walter. *Kissinger in America: A Biography*. New York: Simon & Schuster, 1992.

Jacob, François. *The Possible and the Actual.* New York: Pantheon, 1982.

James, Robert Rhodes, ed. *Chips: The Diaries of Sir Henry Channon.* New York: Penguin, 1970.

Jasen, David A. *P. G. Wodehouse: A Portrait of a Master.* New York: Mason & Lipscomb, 1974.

Jeffs, Rae. *Brendan Behan, Man and Showman.* Cleveland: World Publishing, 1968.

Jelusisch, Mirko. *Geschichten aus dem Wienerwald.* Vienna: Tieck Verlag, 1937.

Jennison, Keith W. *The Humorous Mr. Lincoln.* New York: Crowell, 1965.

Jerome, Jerome A. *My Life and Times.* London: J. Murray, 1983.

Jesse, John Heneage. *George Selwyn and His Contemporaries.* Boston: C. F. Rice, 1843.

Johnson, Diane. *Dashiell Hammett.* New York: Random House, 1983.

Johnson, Doris, and Ellen Leventhal, eds. *The Letters of Nunnally Johnson.* New York: Knopf, 1981.

Johnson, Edgar. *Charles Dickens: His Tragedy and Triumph.* Boston: Little, Brown, 1952.

Johnson, H. Earle. *Symphony Hall.* Boston: Little, Brown, 1950.

Johnson, Nora. *Flashback: Nora Johnson on Nunnally Johnson.* New York: Doubleday, 1979.

Johnson, Paul. *The Birth of the Modern: World Society 1815–1830.* New York: Harper-Collins, 1991.

Johnson, Samuel. *Lives of the English Poets,* ed. John Wain. New York: Dutton, 1975.

Johnson, Wendell Stacy. *W. H. Auden.* New York: Continuum, 1990.

Johnston, Brian. *Rain Stops Play.* London: W. H. Allen, 1979.

Jones, Charlie. *What Makes Winners Win.* New York: Broadway Books, 1999.

Jones, Evan. *A Food Lover's Companion.* New York: Harper & Row, 1979.

Jones, Neal T. *A Book of Days for the Literary Year.* London: Thames & Hudson, 1984.

Jonson, Ben. *Timber; or Discoveries,* ed. G. B. Harrison. New York: Dutton, 1966.

Kac, Mark. *Enigmas of Chance.* New York: Harper & Row, 1985.

Kael, Pauline. *The Citizen Kane Book.* Boston: Little, Brown, 1971.

Kanin, Garson. *Hollywood.* New York: Viking, 1974.

Kaplan, Justin. *Mark Twain and His World.* New York: Simon & Schuster, 1974.

Kaplan, Justin. *Mr. Clemens and Mark Twain.* New York: Simon & Schuster, 1966.

Karsh, Yousuf. *Karsh: A Fifty-Year Retrospective.* Boston: NYGS/Little, Brown, 1983.

Keddie, William. *Cyclopedia of Literary and Scientific Anecdote: Illustrative of the Characters, Habits, and Conversation of Men of Letters and Science.* London: Columbus, Follett, Foster, 1859. Rpt., Ann Arbor, Mich: Gryphon Books, 1971.

Keegan, John. *The Masks of Command.* New York: Viking, 1987.

Keegan, John. *Six Armies in Normandy: From D-Day to the Liberation of Paris, June 6th–August 25th, 1944.* New York: Viking, 1982.

Kelen, Betty. *The Mistresses.* New York: Random House, 1966.

Kelen, Emery. *Peace in Their Time: Men Who Led Us In and Out of War, 1914–1945.* New York: Knopf, 1963.

Kelley, Kitty. *Elizabeth Taylor: The Last Star.* New York: Simon & Schuster, 1981.

Kendall, Alan. *The Tender Tyrant, Nadia Boulanger: A Life Devoted to Music: A Biography.* London: MacDonald & Janes, 1976.

Kenin, Richard, and Justin Winkle. *Dictionary of Biographical Quotation of British and American Subjects.* New York: Knopf, 1978.

Kenyon, John Phillips. *A Dictionary of British History.* New York: Stein & Day, 1983.

Ketton-Cremer, Robert Wyndham. *Horace Walpole.* New York: Longman's, 1864.

Keynes, Geoffrey, and Brian Hill, eds. *Samuel*

Butler's Notebooks — Selections. New York: Dutton, 1951.

Kidder, Jonathan Edward. *Ancient Japan*. New York: John Day, 1965.

Kiernan, V. G. *Tobacco: A History*.

King, Alan, and Mimi Sheraton. *Is Salami and Eggs Better Than Sex?* Boston: Little, Brown, 1985.

Kissinger, Henry. *White House Years*. Boston: Little, Brown, 1979.

Knox, D. B. *More Quotable Anecdotes*. London: T. F. Unwin, 1926.

Knox, D. B. *Quotable Anecdotes for Various Occasions*. New York: Dutton, 1924.

Knox, Ronald Arbuthnott. *Literary Distractions*. New York: Sheed & Ward, 1958.

Kobler, John. *Capone*. New York: Putnam, 1971.

Koestler, Arthur. *Bricks to Babel*. New York: Random House, 1980.

Korda, Michael. *Another Life*. New York: Random House, 1999.

Korda, Michael. *Charmed Lives: A Family Romance*. New York: Random House, 1979.

Krantz, Judith. *Mistral's Daughter*. New York: Crown, 1983.

Krementz, Jill. *The Writer's Image*. Boston: David R. Godine, 1980.

Krock, Arthur. *Memoirs*. New York: Popular Library, 1968.

Kupferberg, Herbert. *Those Fabulous Philadelphians: The Life and Times of a Great Orchestra*. New York: Scribner, 1969.

Lacey, Robert. *The Aristocrats*. London: Hutchinson, 1983.

Lacey, Robert. *The Kingdom: Arabia and the House of Sa'ud*. New York: Harcourt Brace Jovanovich, 1982.

Lacey, Robert. *Majesty: Elizabeth II and the House of Windsor*. New York: Harcourt Brace Jovanovich, 1977.

Lamparksi, Richard. *Whatever Became of . . . ?* New York: Crown, 1966.

Landon, H. C. Robbins. *Handel and His World: A Documentary Biography*. Boston: Little, Brown, 1984.

Lane, Margaret. *Purely for Pleasure*. New York: Knopf, 1967.

Lang, George. *The Cuisine of Hungary*. New York: Atheneum, 1971.

Lang, George. *Nobody Know the Truffles I've Seen*. New York: Knopf, 1998.

Lanman, Charles. *The Private Life of Daniel Webster*. New York: Harper and Brothers, 1852.

Lanoux, Armand. *Paris in the Twenties*. New York: Arts, Inc., 1960.

Larousse, Pierre. *Grand dictionnaire universel du 19ième siècle*. Paris: Union Générale d'Editions, 1975.

Larwood, J. *Anecdotes of the Clergy*. London: Chatto & Windus, 1881.

Lash, Joseph P. *Eleanor: An Appreciation*. New York: Norton, 1984.

Lash, Joseph P. *Eleanor and Franklin: The Story of Their Relationship*. New York: Norton, 1971.

Lasky, Jesse L., and Pat Silver. *Love Scene*. New York: Berkley, 1981.

Latham, Aaron. *Crazy Sundays: F. Scott Fitzgerald in Hollywood*. New York: Viking, 1971.

Latham, Peter. *Brahms*. New York: Pellegrini & Cudahy, 1949.

Lawson, Andrew. *Discover Unexpected London*. Oxford: Elsevier-Phaidon, 1977.

Lebrecht, Norman. *The Book of Musical Anecdotes*. New York: The Free Press, 1985.

Le Gallienne, Richard. *The Romantic '90s*. New York: Doubleday, Page, 1925.

Legouis, Pierre, ed. *André Marvell, Poète, Puritain, Patriote, 1621–1678*. New York: Russell & Russell, 1965.

Leider, Emily Wortis. *Becoming Mae West*. New York: Farrar, Straus & Giroux, 1997.

Lender, Mark Edward, and James Kirby Martin. *Drinking in America: A History*. New York: The Free Press, 1982.

Lennon, Nigey. *Alfred Jarry: The Man with the Axe*. Los Angeles: Panjandrum, 1984.

Leshan, Lawrence. *From Newton to ESP.* Turnstone Press, Ltd.

Leslie, Anita. *The Remarkable Mr. Jerome.* New York: Holt, Rinehart & Winston, 1954.

Le Sueur, Gordon. *Cecil Rhodes: The Man and His Work; By One of His Private and Confidential Secretaries, Gordon le Sueur.* New York: McBride, Nast, 1914.

Levant, Oscar. *A Smattering of Ignorance.* New York: Doubleday, Doran, 1940.

Levant, Oscar. *The Unimportance of Being Oscar.* New York: Putnam, 1968.

Levi, Peter. *The Hill of Kronos.* New York: Dutton, 1981.

Lewis, Arthur H. *Those Philadelphia Kellys, with a Touch of Grace.* New York: Morrow, 1977.

Lewis, Robert. *Slings and Arrows: Theatre in My Life.* New York: Stein & Day, 1984.

Lewis, Robert. *W. C. Fields: His Follies and Fortunes.* New York: New American Library, 1967.

Liddell Hart, B. A. *Reputations, Ten Years After.* Boston: Little, Brown, 1928.

Lieberman, Gerald F. *The Greatest Laughs of All Time.* New York: Doubleday, 1961.

Lincoln, Anthony L. J., and Robert Lindley McEwan, eds. *Lord Eldon's Anecdote Book.* London: Stevens & Sons, 1960.

Linkletter, Art. *I Wish I'd Said That! My Favorite Ad-libs of All Time.* New York: Doubleday, 1968.

Livy (Titus Livius). *Annals of the Roman People.*

Lloyd, Chris Evert. *Chrissie: My Own Story.* New York: Simon & Schuster, 1982.

Lo Bello, Nino. *European Detours: A Travel Guide to Unusual Sites.* Maplewood, N.J.: Hammond, 1981.

Lockhart, John Gibson. *Life of Sir Walter Scott.* New York: Dutton, 1906.

Lockhart, John Gilbert. *Cecil Rhodes.* New York: Macmillan, 1933.

Loliée, Frédéric Auguste. *Gilded Beauties of the Second Empire,* adapted by Bryan O'Donnell. New York: Brentano's, 1910.

Longford, Elizabeth, ed. *The Oxford Book of Royal Anecdotes.* Oxford: Oxford University Press, 1984.

Longford, Elizabeth. *The Queen: The Life of Elizabeth II.* New York: Knopf, 1983.

Love, Robertus. *The Rise and Fall of Jesse James.* New York: Putnam, 1926.

Lowenfels, Walter. *The Paris Years.*

Lucas, Edward Verall. *A Fronded Isle, and Other Essays.* New York: Doubleday, Doran, 1928.

Lucas, Edward Verall. *Reading, Writing and Remembering: A Literary Record.* New York: Harper & Bros., 1932.

Lucie-Smith, Edward, ed. *The Faber Book of Art Anecdotes.* London: Faber & Faber.

Lysons, Daniel. *Environs of London.* London: Cadell, 1795–1811.

Maas, Henry, ed. *The Letters of A. E. Housman.* Cambridge, Mass.: Harvard University Press, 1971.

McAleer, John. *Ralph Waldo Emerson: Days of Encounter.* Boston: Little, Brown, 1984.

McAlmon, Robert. *Being Geniuses Together, 1920–1930.* New York: Doubleday, 1968.

McBride, Joseph. *High and Inside: An A–Z Guide to the Language of Baseball.* Chicago: Contemporary Books, 1997.

McCann, Sean. *The Wit of the Irish.* London: Frewin, 1968.

McCarthy, Joe. *Days and Nights at Costello's.* Boston: Little, Brown, 1980.

McClure, Alexander Kelly. *Lincoln's Own Yarns and Stories.* Philadelphia: Winston, 1900.

McCullough, David. *Truman.* New York: Simon & Schuster, 1992.

McCullough, David Willis, ed. *American Childhoods.* Boston: Little, Brown, 1987.

MacCunn, J. *Recollections of W. P. Ker by Two Friends.*

MacDonald, Malcolm. *Titans and Others.* London: Collins, 1972.

McMullen, Roy. *Degas: His Life, Times, and Work.* Boston: Houghton Mifflin, 1984.

MacNeice, Louis. *The Strings Are False: An Un-*

finished Biography, ed. E. R. Dodds. New York: Oxford University Press, 1966.

McPhee, Nancy. *The Book of Insults.* New York: St. Martin's Press, 1978.

McPhee, Nancy. *The Second Book of Insults.* New York: Penguin, 1983.

Macrobius Ambrosius Theodosius. *Saturnalia.*

Madigan, Carol Orsag, and Ann Elwood. *Brainstorms and Thunderbolts: How Creative Genius Worked.* New York: Macmillan, 1984.

Mahony, Patrick. *Barbed Wit and Malicious Humor.* New York: Citadel Press, 1956.

Maltby, William. *Recollections of the Table Talk of Samuel Rogers. To Which Is Added Porsoniana.* New York: Appleton, 1856.

Manchester, William. *The Last Lion: Winston Spencer Churchill: Alone: 1932–1940.* Boston: Little, Brown, 1988.

Manchester, William. *The Last Lion: Winston Spencer Churchill: Visions of Glory: 1874–1932.* Boston: Little, Brown, 1983.

Manchester, William. *One Brief Shining Moment: Remembering Kennedy.* Boston: Little, Brown, 1983.

Manningham, John. *Diary*

Mansfield, Irving. *Life with Jackie.* New York: Bantam Books, 1983.

Margolius, Hans. *Der lächelnde Philosoph.* Munich: Bechtle Verlag, 1963.

Markham, Felix. *The Bonapartes.* New York: Taplinger, 1975.

Marquand, Ralph L. *Jokes and Anecdotes for All Occasions.* New York: Hart Publishing, 1977.

Marsh, Edward. *A Number of People.* New York: Harper & Bros., 1939.

Martin, Ralph. *A Hero for Our Time: An Intimate Story of the Kennedy Years.* New York: Macmillan, 1983.

Martin, Robert Bernard. *Tennyson: The Unquiet Heart.* London: Oxford University Press, 1980.

Marx, Harpo. *Harpo Speaks!* New York: Geis Associates, 1961.

Marx, Samuel. *Mayer and Thalberg: The Make-Believe Saints.* New York: Random House, 1975.

Marx, Samuel, and Jan Clayton. *Rodgers and Hart, Bewitched, Bothered, and Bedeviled: An Anecdotal Account.* New York: Putnam, 1976.

Massey, Raymond. *A Hundred Different Lives: An Autobiography.* Boston: Little, Brown, 1979.

Massie, Robert K. *Dreadnought: Britain, Germany and the Coming of the Great War.* New York: Random House, 1991.

Massie Robert K. *Peter the Great: His Life and World.* New York: Knopf, 1980.

Masson, Thomas L. *The Best Stories in the World.* New York: Doubleday, 1913.

Maugham, W. Somerset. *A Writer's Notebook.* New York: Doubleday, Doran, 1949.

May, Antoinette. *Different Drummers: They Did What They Wanted.* Millbrae, Calif.: Les Femmes, 1976.

Mayfield, Sara. *The Constant Circle: H. L. Mencken and His Friends.* New York: Dell, 1969.

Meigs, Cornelia Lynde. *Invincible Louisa.* Boston: Little, Brown, 1933.

Mellow, James R. *Charmed Circle: Gertrude Stein & Company.* New York: Praeger, 1974.

Méras, Phyllis. *The Mermaids of Chenonceaux.* New York: Congdon & Weed, 1983.

Merrill, Robert. *Between Acts: An Irreverent Look at Opera and Other Madness.* New York: McGraw-Hill, 1976.

Merwin, W. S., trans. *Products of the Perfected Civilization: Selected Writings of Chamfort,* New York: Macmillan, 1969.

Mignet, François. *Notices historiques* 2nd ed. Paris: Paulin, L'Hereux et cie, 1853.

Mikes, George. *Coffee Houses of Europe.* New York: Thames & Hudson, 1983.

Mikes, George. *Laughing Matter: Towards a Personal Philosophy of Wit and Humor.* New York: Library Press, 1971.

Mills, John. *Up in the Clouds, Gentlemen Please.* New Haven: Ticknor & Fields. 1981.

Milne, Alan Alexander, *It's Too Late Now: The Autobiography of a Writer.* London: Methuen, 1939.

Milne, Christopher. *The Enchanted Places.* New York: Dutton, 1975.

Milton, Joyce. *Loss of Eden: A Biography of Charles and Anne Morrow Lindbergh.* New York: HarperCollins, 1992.

Missen, Leslie Robert. *Quotable Anecdotes.* London: Allen & Unwin, 1966.

Mitford, Nancy. *Voltaire in Love.* New York: Harper & Row, 1957.

Mitterand, François. *The Wheat and the Chaff.* New York: Seaver Books/Lattès, 1982.

Monegal, Emir R., and Alastair Reid. *Borges, a Reader: A Selection from the Writings of Jorge Luis Borges.* New York: Dutton, 1981.

Monk, Ray. *Ludwig Wittgenstein: The Duty of Genius.* London: Jonathan Cape, 1990.

Montgomery-Massingberd, Hugh. *Royal Palaces of Europe.* New York: Vendome, 1983.

Moore, Frank. *Anecdotes, Poetry and Incidents of the War: North and South, 1860–1865.* New York: Arundel, 1882.

Moore, Ruth. *Charles Darwin: A Great Life in Brief.* New York: Knopf, 1973.

Moore, Thomas. *Memoir of the Life of the Right Honourable Richard Brinsley Sheridan.* London: Longman, Rees, Orme, Brown and Green, 1925.

Moore, Thomas. *Memoirs, Journal, and Correspondence of Thomas Moore, ed. By the Right Honorable Lord John Russell, MP.* Boston: Little, Brown, 1853.

Moorehead, Alan. *Darwin and The Beagle.* New York: Harper & Row, 1969.

Moorhouse, Geoffrey. *The Diplomats.* Atlantic Highlands, N.J.: Humanities, 1977.

Mordden, Ethan. *Opera Anecdotes.* New York: Oxford University Press, 1988.

Morgan, Ted. *FDR: A Biography.* New York: Simon & Schuster, 1985.

Morley, Robert. *A Musing Morley: The Selected Writings of Robert Morley,* ed. Sheridan Morley. London: Robson Books, 1974.

Morley, Robert. *Pardon Me, But You're Eating My Doily.* New York: Saint Martin's, 1983.

Morley, Robert. *Robert Morley's Book of Bricks.* New York: Putnam, 1978.

Morley Robert. *A Second Book of Bricks.* London: Weidenfeld & Nicolson, 1981.

Morley, Robert, and Sewell Stokes. *Robert Morley: A Reluctant Autobiography.* New York: Simon & Schuster, 1967.

Morley, Sheridan. *A Talent to Amuse: A Biography of Noel Coward.* New York: Doubleday, 1969.

Morley, Sheridan. *Tales from the Hollywood Raj: The British, the Movies, and Tinseltown.* New York: Viking, 1984.

Morton, Brian N. *Americans in Paris.* Ann Arbor, Mich.: Olivia & Hill, 1984.

Morton, H. V. *A Traveller in Italy.*

Morris, James. *Oxford.* New York: Harcourt, Brace & World, 1965.

Morris, Jan. *Destinations.* Oxford: Oxford University Press, 1980.

Morris, Jan. *The Oxford Book of Oxford.* Oxford: Oxford University Press, 1979.

Moss, Howard. *Whatever Is Moving.* Boston: Little, Brown, 1981.

Muir, Frank. *An Irreverent and Thoroughly Incomplete Social History of Almost Everything.* New York: Stein & Day, 1976.

Murchie, Guy. *Music of the Spheres.* Boston: Houghton Mifflin, 1961.

Murray, William. *Italy: The Fatal Gift.* New York: Dodd, Mead, 1982.

Nabokov, Vladimir. *Strong Opinions.* New York: McGraw-Hill, 1973.

Nash, Jay Robert. *The Innovators: 16 Portraits of the Famous and Infamous.* Chicago: Regnery/Gateway, 1982.

Nash, Jay Robert. *Zanies: The World's Greatest*

Eccentrics. Piscataway, N.J.: New Century, 1982.

Nelson, Randy, F. *The Almanac of American Letters.* Los Altos, Calif.: William Kaufmann, 1981.

New Columbia Encyclopedia, The. William H. Harris and Judith S. Levey, eds. New York: Columbia University Press, 1975.

Nichols, Beverley. *The Sweet Twenties.* New York: British Book Centre, 1958.

Nicolson, Harold. *Harold Nicolson: Diaries and Letters.* New York: Atheneum, 1967.

Nikolaev, Vsevold A., and Albert Parry. *The Loves of Catherine the Great.* New York: Coward, McCann & Geoghegan, 1982.

Niven, David. *Bring On the Empty Horses.* New York: Putnam, 1975.

Nixon, Richard. *Leaders.* New York: Warner Books, 1981.

Noakes, Vivien. *Edward Lear: The Life of a Wanderer.* Boston: Houghton Mifflin, 1969.

Norton, Lucy, ed., trans. *Saint-Simon at Versailles.* New York: Harmony Books, 1980.

Novak, William, and Moshe Waldoks. *Big Book of Jewish Humor.* New York: Harper & Row, 1981.

Noyes, Alfred. *Two Worlds for Memory.* New York: Sheed & Ward, 1953.

O'Brien, Pat. *Talkin' Sports: A.B.S.-er's Guide.* New York: Villard, 1998.

O'Connell, Charles. *The Other Side of the Record.* New York: Knopf, 1947.

O'Donnell, Kenneth, and David F. Powers. *"Johnny We Hardly Knew Ye."* Boston: Little, Brown, 1972.

O'Flaherty, Wendy Doniger. *Other People's Myths.* New York: Macmillan, 1988.

Okrent, Dan, with Steve Wulf. *Baseball Anecdotes.* New York: Harper & Row, 1989.

Orgel, Joseph R. *Undying Passion.* New York: Morrow, 1985.

Oursler, Fulton. *Behold This Dreamer.* New York: Macaulay, 1924.

Oxfam. *Pass the Port.* Cirencester, England: Christian Brann, 1976.

Oxford Dictionary of Quotations. 2nd ed. London and New York: Oxford University Press, 1953.

Paar, Jack. *P.S. Jack Paar: An Entertainment.* New York: Doubleday, 1982.

Paine, Albert Bigelow. *The Adventures of Mark Twain.* New York: Harper & Bros., 1916.

Paine, Albert Bigelow. *Mark Twain: A Biography.* New York: Harper & Bros., 1912.

Painter, George D. *Proust: The Early Years.* Boston: Little, Brown, 1959.

Painter, George D. *Proust: The Later Years.* Boston: Little, Brown, 1959.

Pais, Abraham. *"Subtle Is the Lord . . .": The Science and Life of Albert Einstein.* Oxford and New York: Oxford University Press, 1982.

Paléologue, Maurice. *The Enigmatic Czar: The Life of Alexander I of Russia,* trans. Edwin and Willa Muir. New York: Harper & Bros., 1938.

Paley, F. A. *Greek Wit: A Collection of Smart Sayings and Anecdotes.* London: George Bell & Sons, 1881.

Palmer, George Herbert. *The Life of Alice Freeman Palmer.* Boston: Houghton Mifflin, 1908.

Papesch, Joseph Friedrich. *Europa Lächelt Noch Immer.* Graz: Laykam-Verlag, 1952.

Parkinson, Norman. *Fifty Years of Style and Fashion.* New York: Vendome, 1983.

Parmelin, Hélène. *Picasso Says,* trans. C. Trollope. South Brunswick, N.J.: A. S. Barnes, 1969.

Payn, Graham, and Sheridan Morley. *Noël Coward Diaries.* Boston: Little, Brown, 1982.

Pearson, Hesketh. *Johnson and Boswell.* New York: Harper & Row, 1958.

Pearson, Hesketh. *The Life of Oscar Wilde* (1947). Rpt., Westport, Conn.: Greenwood, 1978.

Pearson, Hesketh. *Lives of the Wits.* New York: Harper & Row, 1962.

Pearson, Hesketh. *The Man Whistler.* New York: Harper & Row, 1952.

Pearson, Hesketh. *The Smith of Smiths: Being the Life, Wit and Humor of Sydney Smith.* New York: Harper & Row, 1934.

Pearson, John. *The Serpent and the Stag.* New York: Holt, Rinehart & Winston, 1984.

Pedrazzini, Marie-Charlotte, and Jeannette Gris. *Autant en apportent les mots.* Paris: Robert Laffont, 1969.

Penrose, Roland. *Picasso: His Life and Work.* New York: Harper & Row, 1959.

Penrose, Roland, *Roland Penrose Scrapbook.* London: Thames & Hudson, 1981.

Pepys, Samuel. *The Diary of Samuel Pepys,* ed. R. Latham and W. Matthews. London: Bell & Hyman, 1983.

Percy, Sholto, and Reuben Percy. *The Percy Anecdotes: Original and Selected.* New York: W. B. Gilley, 1821.

Perrett, Geoffrey. *America in the Twenties: A History.* New York: Simon & Schuster, 1982.

Peters, Margot. *Mrs. Pat: The Life of Mrs. Patrick Campbell.* New York: Knopf, 1984.

Phillips, Peter. *A Brief Chronicle.*

Pijet, Georg W. *Duell mit der Vergangenheit.* Halle (Saale): Mittel Deutscher Verlag, 1976.

Piper, David. *Painting in England 1500–1870.* Harmondsworth: Penguin, 1965.

Plato. *Phaedo,* ed. David Gallop, London: Oxford University Press, 1975.

Plato. *Theaetetus and Sophist,* trans. Harold North Fowler. New York: Putnam, 1928.

Pleasants, Henry. *The Great American Popular Singers.* New York: Simon & Schuster, 1985.

Pliny (Gaius Plinius Caecilius Secundus). *Letters,* trans. William Melmoth. Cambridge, Mass.: Harvard University Press, 1940.

Plutarch. *Plutarch's Lives,* trans. B. Perrin. London: Heinemann, 1914–1926.

Poley, Irvin, and Ruth Poley. *Friendly Anecdotes.* New York: Harper & Bros. 1950.

Poliziano, Angelo. *Diario odeporico-bibliografico inedito del Poliziano: c memoria del Giovanni Pesenti.* Milan: U Hoepli, 1916.

Porzelt, Paul. *The Metropolitan Club of New York.* New York: Rizzoli, 1982.

Postgate, Raymond. *That Devil Wilkes.* New York: Vanguard, 1929.

Powell, Anthony. *The Memoirs of Anthony Powell,* Vol. 3: *Faces in My Time.* New York: Holt, Rinehart & Winston, 1976.

Powell, Anthony. *The Memoirs of Anthony Powell* Vol. 4: *The Strangers Are All Gone.* New York: Holt, Rinehart & Winston, 1982.

Preminger, Erik Lee. *Gypsy and Me: At Home and on the Road with Gypsy Rose Lee.* Boston: Little, Brown, 1984.

Prescott, Orville. *Princess of the Renaissance.* New York: Random House, 1969.

Previn, André, ed. *Orchestra.* New York: Doubleday, 1979.

Price, R. G. G. *A History of Punch.* London: Oxford University Press, 1984.

Priestly, Joseph. *Memoirs of Dr. Joseph Priestly to the Year 1795.* Rpt., Bath: Adams & Dart, 1978.

Prior, Sir James. *Life of Edmond Malone, Editor of Shakespeare.* London: Smith, Elder, 1860.

Pritchett, V. S. *Balzac.* New York: Knopf, 1973.

Pritchett, V. S. *The Myth Makers: Literary Essays.* New York: Random House, 1979.

Prochnow, Herbert V. *The Public Speaker's Treasure Chest.* New York: Harper & Bros., 1942.

Prochnow, Herbert V. *Speaker's and Toastmaster's Handbook.* New York: Prima Publishing, 1993.

Procopius. *Secret History.* Rpt., Ann Arbor, Mich.: University of Michigan Press, 1961.

Pye, M. *The King over the Water.* New York: Holt, Rinehart & Winston, 1981.

Quennell, Peter, *Samuel Johnson: His Friends and Enemies.* New York: American Heritage Press, 1972.

Quennell, Peter. *The Sign of the Fish.* New York: Viking, 1960.

Rachlis, Eugene, and John E. Marquese. *The Landlords*. New York: Random House, 1963.

Radecki, Sigismund von. *Das ABC des Lachens: Ein Anekdotenbuch zur Unterhaltung und Belehrung*. Hamburg: Rowolt, 1953.

Rainie, Harrison, and John Quinn. *Growing Up a Kennedy: The Third Wave Comes of Age*. New York: Putnam, 1983.

Rajanen, Aini. *Of Finnish Ways*. Minneapolis: Dillon, 1981.

Rawson, Hugh. *A Dictionary of Euphemisms and Other Doubletalk*. New York: Crown Publishers, 1981.

Raymond, G. *Memoirs of Robert William Elliston*. New York: B. Blom, 1969.

Read, John. *Humour and Humanism in Chemistry*. London: G. Bell, 1947.

Reagan, R. *The Uncommon Wisdom of Ronald Reagan: A Portrait in His Own Words*, ed. Bill Adler. New York: Little, Brown, 1996.

Rees, Nigel. *Quote . . . Unquote*. Boston: Allen & Unwin, 1978.

Reiman, Donald H., ed. *Shelley and His Circle*, vols. VII, VIII. Cambridge, Mass.: Harvard University Press, 1985.

Rémusat, Claire Elizabeth Jeanne Gravier de Vergennes, Comtesse de. *Mémoires de Madam de Rémusat*. Paris: C. Levy, 1880.

Richard, Ivor. *We, the British*. New York: Doubleday, 1983.

Richler, Mordecai, ed. *Writers and World War II: An Anthology*. New York: Knopf, 1991.

Ridley, Jasper. *Lord Palmerston*. New York: Dutton, 1971.

Ringo, Miriam. *Nobody Said It Better*. Chicago: Rand McNally, 1980.

Riordan, William L. *Plunkitt of Tammany Hall*. New York: Dutton, 1969.

Robards, Terry. *The New York Times Book of Wine*. New York: Quadrangle, 1976.

Roberts, Cecil. *And So to Bath*. New York: Macmillan, 1940.

Robertson, David. *George Mallory*. London: Faber & Faber, 1969.

Rodzinski, Halina. *Our Two Lives*. New York: Scribner, 1976.

Rogers, Samuel. *Table Talk*.

Rollins, Hyder E., ed. *The Keats Circle: Letters and Papers 1816–78*. 2nd ed. Cambridge, Mass.: Harvard University Press, 1965.

Roosevelt, Theodore. *An Autobiography*. New York: Macmillan, 1914.

Roper, William. *The Life of Sir Thomas More*. Rpt., New Haven: Yale University Press, 1962.

Rorem, Ned. *The Later Diaries of Ned Rorem*. San Francisco: North Point Press, 1983.

Rosenthal-Schneider, Ilse. *Reality and Scientific Truth: Discussions with Einstein, von Laue and Others*, ed. Thomas Braun. Detroit: Wayne State University Press, 1980.

Rose, Kenneth. *King George V*. New York: Knopf, 1984.

Rosen, Michael, ed. *Collecting Himself: James Thurber on Writing and Writers, Humor and Himself*. New York: Harper & Row, 1989.

Rosner, Joseph. *A Hater's Handbook*. New York: Delacorte, 1965.

Ross, Ishbel. *Charmers and Cranks*. New York: Harper & Row, 1965.

Rosten, Leo. *The Joys of Yiddish*. New York: McGraw-Hill, 1968.

Rosten, Leo. *People I Have Loved, Known or Admired*. New York: McGraw-Hill, 1970.

Roy, James Charles. *Islands of Storm*. Chester Springs, Pa.: Dufour Editions, Inc., 1991.

Rubinstein, Arthur. *My Many Years*. New York: Knopf, 1980.

Runciman, S. *The Fall of Constantinople*. Cambridge: Cambridge University Press, 1969.

Ruskin, John. *Deucalion: King of the Golden River and The Eagle's Nest*. Boston: Dana Estes, 1865.

Russell, Bertrand. *The Autobiography of Bertrand Russell*. Boston: Little, Brown, 1967.

Russell, John. *Paris*. New York: Viking, 1960.

Russell, Leonard. *English Wits*. Port Washington: Kennikat Press (first pub. 1940).

Saarinen, Aline B. *The Proud Possessors.* New York: Random House, 1958.

Sadie, Stanley. *The New Grove Dictionary of Music and Musicians, in 20 Volumes.* Washington, D.C.: Grove's Dictionaries of Music, 1980.

Sadleir, Michael, *Trollope: A Commentary.* New York: Farrar, Straus, 1947.

Saint-Fois [Germain François Poullain]. *Essais sur Paris de Monsieur de Saint-Fois.* Paris: Veuve Duchesne, 1776–1777.

St. John, Robert. *They Came from Everywhere: Twelve Who Helped Mold Modern Israel.* New York: Coward-McCann, 1962.

Salter, Elizabeth. *Helpmann: The Authorised Biography of Sir Robert Helpmann.* New York: Universe, 1978.

Samuels, Ernest. *The Education of Henry Adams.* Boston: Houghton Mifflin, 1918.

Sandburg, Carl. *Abraham Lincoln: The War Years.* New York: Harcourt, Brace, 1939.

Sanford, John. *Winters of That Country.* Santa Barbara, Calif.: Black Sparrow Press, 1984.

Sargeant, Winthrop. *Divas.* New York: Coward, McCann & Geoghegan, 1973.

Saxton, Martha. *Louisa May: A Modern Biography of Louisa May Alcott.* Boston: Houghton Mifflin, 1977.

Scammel, Michael. *Alexander Solzhenitsyn: A Biography.* New York: Norton, 1984.

Schlesinger, Arthur M., Jr. *Cycles of American History.* Boston: Houghton Mifflin, 1986.

Schlesinger, Marion Cannon. *Snatched from Oblivion: A Cambridge Memoir.* Boston: Little, Brown, 1979.

Scholes, Percy Alfred. ed. *Oxford Companion to Music.* London and New York: Oxford University Press, 1970.

Scholz, Wilhelm von. *Das Buch des Lachens: Schnurren, Schwanke und Anekdoten.* Stuttgart: Verlag Deutsche Volksbücher, 1953.

Schonberg, Harold C. *The Great Conductors.* New York: Simon & Schuster, 1967.

Schonberg, Harold C. *The Great Pianists.* New York: Simon & Schuster, 1963.

Schwartzkopf, Elisabeth. *On and Off the Record: A Memoir of Walter Legge.* New York: Scribner, 1982.

Schwed, Peter. *Turning the Pages: An Insider's Story of Simon & Schuster 1924–1984.* New York: Macmillan, 1984.

Scott, Walter. *Lawrence Sterne.*

Scott, Sir Walter. *The Tales of a Grandfather.*

Seagrave, Sterling. *The Soong Dynasty.* New York: Harper & Row, 1984.

Seaman, Barbara. *Lovely Me: The Life of Jacqueline Susann.* New York: Morrow, 1987.

Secrest, Meryle. *Kenneth Clark: A Biography.* London: Weidenfeld & Nicolson, 1983.

Seelig, Carl. *Albert Einstein: A Documentary Biography.* London: Staples, 1956.

Seitz, Don C. *Whistler Stories.* New York: Harper & Brothers, 1913.

Seligman, Vincent. *Puccini Among Friends.* New York: Macmillan, 1938.

Seward, William. *Anecdotes of Distinguished Persons, Chiefly of the Last and Two Preceding Centuries.* 5th ed. London: T. Cadell and W. Davies, 1804.

Seward, William. *Biographiana.* New York: Garland, 1970.

Seymour Smith, Frank. *A Treasury of Wit & Wisdom.* London: J. Baker, 1966.

Seymour-Smith, Martin. *Robert Graves: His Life and Work.* New York: Holt, Rinehart & Winston, 1983.

Shadegg, Stephen. *Clare Boothe Luce: A Biography.* New York: Simon & Schuster, 1970.

Shaw, George Bernard. *Collected Letters.* New York: Dodd, Mead, 1965.

Sheed, Wilfrid. *Clare Boothe Luce.* New York: Dutton, 1982.

Shenkman, Richard, and Kurt Reiger. *One-Night Stands with American History.* New York: Morrow, 1980.

Shlain, Bruce. *Baseball Inside Out.* New York: Viking, 1992.

Shriner, Charles A. *Wit, Wisdom, and Foibles of the Great.* New York: Funk & Wagnalls, 1918.

Sidey, Hugh. *John F. Kennedy, President.* New York: Atheneum, 1963.

Sievers, H. *Musica Curiosa.* 2nd ed. Tutzing, Germany: Hans Schneider, 1971.

Sifakis, Carl. *Dictionary of Historic Nicknames.* New York: Facts on File, 1984.

Silitch, Clarissa M., ed. *Mad and Magnificent Yankees.* Dublin, N.H.: Yankee, Inc., 1973.

Silverman, Al. "The Fragile Pleasure." *Daedalus.*

Silverman, Al, and Brian Silverman, eds. *The Twentieth-Century Treasury of Sports.* New York: Viking, 1993.

Simpson, Eileen. *Poets in Their Youth: A Memoir.* New York: Random House, 1982.

Simpson, James B. *Simpson's Contemporary Quotations.* New York: HarperCollins, 1997.

Sinclair, Andrew. *Dylan Thomas: No Man More Magical.* New York: Holt, Rinehart & Winston, 1975.

Sitwell, Dame Edith. *English Eccentrics.* New York: Vanguard Press, 1957.

Sitwell, Osbert. *Laughter in the Next Room.* Boston: Little, Brown, 1948.

Sitwell, Osbert. *Noble Essences.* Boston: Little, Brown, 1950.

Sitwell, Osbert. *Tales My Father Taught Me.* Boston: Little, Brown, 1962.

Sitwell, Sacheverell, *Liszt.* Boston: Houghton Mifflin, 1934.

Skelton, John. *John Skelton: The Complete English Poems,* ed. John Scattergood. New Haven: Yale University Press, 1983.

Skelton, John. *Poems of John Skelton.* Oxford: Clarendon Press, 1969.

Skinner, Cornelia Otis. *Elegant Wits and Grand Horizontals.* Boston: Houghton Mifflin, 1962.

Slonimsky, Nicholas. *Lexicon of Musical Invective.* New York: Coleman-Ross, 1953.

Slonimsky, Nicholas. *A Thing or Two About Music.* New York: Allen, Towne & Heath, 1948.

Smail, J. L. *With Shield and Assegai.* Cape Town: H. Timmins, 1969.

Smith, Chard Powers. *Where the Light Falls.* New York: Macmillan, 1965.

Smith, H. Allen. *The Life and Legend of Gene Fowler.* New York: Morrow, 1977.

Smith, Jane S. *Elsie de Wolfe: A Life in the High Style.* New York: Atheneum, 1982.

Smith, Logan Pearsall. *Unforgotten Years.* Boston: Little, Brown, 1939.

Smith, Page. *America Enters the World.* New York: McGraw-Hill, 1984.

Smith, Page. *The Nation Comes of Age: A People's History of the Ante-Bellum Years.* New York: McGraw-Hill, 1981.

Smith, Page. *A New Age Now Begins: A People's History of the American Revolution.* New York: McGraw-Hill, 1976.

Smith, Page. *The Rise of Industrial America: A People's History of the Post-Reconstruction Era.* New York: McGraw-Hill, 1984.

Smith, Page. *The Shaping of America: A People's History of the Young Republic.* New York: McGraw-Hill, 1980.

Smith, Page. *Trial by Fire: A People's History of the Civil War and Reconstruction.* New York: McGraw-Hill, 1982.

Smith, Red. *To Absent Friends from Red Smith.* New York: Atheneum, 1982.

Smith, Richard Norton. *Thomas E. Dewey and His Times.* New York: Simon & Schuster, 1982.

Smith, Sydney. *A Memoir of the Rev. Sydney Smith by His Daughter, Lady Holland.* New York: Harper, 1855.

Smith, Sir William. *Everyman's Smaller Classical Dictionary,* rev. E. H. Blakeney and J. Warrington. New York: Dutton, 1952.

Smullyan, Raymond. *5000 B.C. and Other Philosophical Fantasies.* New York: St. Martin's Press, 1983.

Snead, Sam, and Al Stump. *The Education of a Golfer.* New York: Simon & Schuster, 1962.

Snead, Sam, with Fran Pirozzolo. *The Game I Love.* New York: Ballantine, 1997.

Snow, Charles Percy. *Variety of Men.* New York: Scribner, 1967.

Solberg, Carl. *Hubert Humphrey: A Biography.* New York: Norton, 1984.

Sommers, Robert T. *Golf Anecdotes.* New York: Oxford University Press, 1995.

Southey, Robert. *Life of Nelson.* New York: Eastburn, Kirk; Boston: William Wells, 1813. Rpt., New York: Dutton, 1962.

Spence, Joseph. *Anecdotes, Observations and Characters of Books and Men.* London: W. H. Carpenter, 1820. Rpt., Carbondale, Ill.: Southern Illinois University Press, 1964.

Spender, Stephen. *World Within World: The Autobiography of Stephen Spender,* Berkeley, Calif.: University of California Press, 1966.

Speroni, Charles. *Wit and Wisdom of the Italian Renaissance.* Berkeley, Calif.: University of California Press, 1964.

Spoto, Donald. *The Dark Side of Genius: The Life of Alfred Hitchcock.* Boston: Little, Brown, 1983.

Spoto, Donald. *The Kindness of Strangers: The Biography of Tennessee Williams.* Boston: Little, Brown, 1985.

Spoto, Donald. *Notorious: The Life of Ingrid Bergman.* New York: HarperCollins, 1997.

Stanley, Henry Morton. *How I Found Livingstone.* New York: Scribner, 1872.

Stebben, Gregg, and Jim Morris. *White House Confidential: The Little Book of Weird Presidential History.* Nashville: Cumberland House, 1993.

Steegmuller, Francis. *Cocteau.* Boston: Atlantic–Little, Brown, 1970.

Stein, Jean, with George Plimpton. *Edie: An American Biography.* New York: Knopf, 1982.

Steinberg, Alfred. *The Man from Missouri.* New York: Putnam, 1962.

Steinbert, Hiltrud. *Artz und Patient.*

Steinem, Gloria. *Outrageous Acts and Everyday Rebellions.* New York: Holt, Rinehart & Winston, 1983.

Sternburg, Janet, ed. *The Writer on Her Work.* New York: Norton, 1992.

Stevens, Stewart. *The Poles.* New York: Macmillan, 1982.

Stinnett, Caskie. "Travels with Marc," *Signature.*

Stitt, Peter. *The World's Hieroglyphic Beauty: Five American Poets.* Athens, Ga.: University of Georgia Press.

Stock, Noel. *The Life of Ezra Pound.* New York: Pantheon Books, 1970.

Stockdale, Percival. *Memoirs of the Life and Writings of Percival Stockdale.* London: Longman, Hurst, Rees & Orme, 1809.

Stone, Irving. *They Also Ran.* New York: Doubleday, 1966.

Straus, Dorothea. *Under the Canopy.* New York: G. Braziller, 1982.

Strauss, David, and Fred Worth. *Hollywood Trivia.* New York: Warner, 1981.

Strauss, Maurice B. *Familiar Medical Quotations.* Boston: Little, Brown, 1968.

Strong, Theron G. *Joseph H. Choate.* New York: Dodd, Mead, 1917.

Suetonius (Gaius Suetonius Tranquillus). *The Twelve Caesars,* trans. Robert Graves. Baltimore: Penguin, 1957.

Sutherland, John, ed. *Oxford Book of Literary Anecdotes.* Oxford: Clarendon Press, 1975.

Syben, Friedrich, *Preussische Anekdoten: nach Memoiren und Biographien erzählt.* Berlin: Bernard & Graefe, 1939.

Sylvester, Albert J. *Life with Lloyd George: The Diary of A. J. Sylvester,* ed. Colin Cross. London: Macmillan, 1975.

Sylvester, Robert. *Notes of a Guilty Bystander.* Englewood Cliffs, N.J.: Prentice Hall, 1970.

Tacitus, Gaius Cornelius. *Annals,* ed. C. D. Fisher. London: Oxford University Press, 1906.

Talese, Gay. *Fame and Obscurity.* New York: World Publishing, 1970.

Taper, Bernard. *Balanchine: A Biography.* New York: Times Books, 1984.

Tarbell, Ida M. *The Life of Abraham Lincoln.* New York: Doubleday & McClure, 1900.

Tate, Allen, ed. *T. S. Eliot, The Man and His Work: A Critical Evaluation by Twenty-Six Distinguished Writers.* New York: Delacorte Press, 1966.

Taubman, Howard. *The Maestro: The Life of Arturo Toscanini.* New York: Simon & Schuster, 1951.

Taubman, Howard. *Music on My Beat.* New York: Simon & Schuster, 1943.

Taylor, Alan John Percivale. *Bismarck: The Man and the Statesman.* New York: Vintage Books, 1967.

Taylor, Alan John Percivale. *English History 1914–1945, Oxford History of England,* Vol. 15. New York: Oxford University Press, 1965.

Taylor, Bayard. *Critical Essays and Literary Notes.* New York: Putnam, 1880.

Taylor, Gordon Rattray. *The Great Evolution Mystery.* New York: Harper & Row, 1983.

Tebbel, John. *The Inheritors: A Study of America's Great Fortunes and What Happened to Them.* New York: Putnam, 1962.

Teichmann, Howard. *Smart Aleck: The Wit, World and Life of Alexander Woollcott.* New York: Morrow, 1976.

Temianka, Henri. *Facing the Music: An Irreverent Close-Up of the Real Concert World.* New York: D. McKay, 1973.

Terkel, Studs. *"The Good War": An Oral History of World War Two.* New York: Pantheon, 1984.

Tharp, Louise Hall. *Mrs. Jack.* Boston: Little, Brown, 1965.

Tharp, Louise Hall. *The Peabody Sisters of Salem.* Boston: Little, Brown, 1950.

Theroux, Paul. *Riding the Iron Rooster.* New York: Putnam, 1988.

Thomas, Bob. *King Cohn: The Life and Times of Harry Cohn.* New York: Putnam, 1967.

Thomas, Bob. *Thalberg: Life and Legend.* New York: Doubleday, 1969.

Thomas, Henry, and Dana Lee Thomas. *Living Adventures in Science.* Garden City, N.Y.: Hanover House, 1954.

Thomas, Henry, and Dana Lee Thomas. *Living Biographies of Famous Rulers.* Garden City, N.Y.: Garden City Publishing, 1940.

Thomas, Henry, and Dana Lee Thomas. *Living Biographies of Famous Women.* Garden City, N.Y.: Garden City Publishing, 1942.

Thomas, Henry, and Dana Lee Thomas. *Living Biographies of Religious Leaders.* Garden City, N.Y.: Garden City Publishing, 1942.

Thomas, Henry, and Dana Lee Thomas. *Living Biographies of the Great Philosophers.* Garden City, N.Y.: Garden City Publishing, 1941.

Thomas, Lewis. *Late Night Thoughts on Listening to Mahler's Ninth Symphony.* New York: Bantam, 1983.

Thompson, Charles. *Bing: The Authorized Biography.* New York: McKay, 1975, 1976.

Thompson, Verita, and Donald Shepherd. *Bogie and Me.* Los Angeles: Pinnacle, 1984.

Thompson, Sir Basil. *The Scene Changes.* New York: Doubleday, Doran, 1937.

Thomson, Virgil. *A Virgil Thomson Reader.* Boston: Houghton Mifflin, 1981.

Thoreau, Henry David. *The Journal of Henry D. Thoreau,* ed. Bradford Torrey and Francis H. Allen. Boston: Houghton Mifflin, 1906.

Thorogood, Julia. *Margery Allingham: A Biography.* London: Heinemann, 1991.

Thurber, Helen, and Edward Weeks, eds. *Selected Letters of James Thurber.* Boston: Atlantic–Little, Brown, 1981.

Thurber, James. *The Years with Ross.* Boston: Atlantic–Little, Brown, 1959.

Thurow, Lester. *The Zero-Sum Solution.* New York: Simon & Schuster, 1985.

Thwaite, Ann. *Waiting for the Party: The Life of Frances Hodgson Burnett, 1849–1924.* New York: Scribner, 1974.

Ticknor, C. *Dr. Holmes's Boston.* Boston: Houghton Mifflin, 1915.

Timbs, J. *Century of Anecdote from 1760 to 1860.* London: R. Bentley, 1864.

Timbs, J. *English Eccentrics and Eccentricities.* London: Chatto & Windus, 1890. Rpt. Detroit: Singing Trees Press, 1969.

Tomkins, Calvin. *Living Well Is the Best Revenge.* New York: Dutton, 1982.

Tomkins, Calvin. *Merchants and Masterpieces:*

The Story of the Metropolitan Museum of Art. New York: Dutton, 1970.

Toynbee, Arnold. *Acquaintances*. London: Oxford University Press, 1967.

Train, John. *True Remarkable Occurrences*. New York: C. N. Potter, 1978.

Train, John. *Wit: The Best Things Ever Said*. New York: HarperCollins, 1991.

Trelawny, E. J. *Recollections of the Last Days of Shelley and Byron*. Boston: Ticknor & Fields, 1858.

Trevelyan, G. M. *Trinity College*. London: Cambridge University Press, 1943.

Trilling, Lionel. *Matthew Arnold*. New York: Norton, 1939.

Trollope, Anthony. *Autobiography,* ed. Michael Sadleir and Frederick Page. London: Oxford University Press, 1980.

Troyat, Henri. *Chekhov,* trans. Michael Henry Heim. New York: E. P. Dutton, 1986.

Tuchman, Barbara. *The Guns of August*. New York: Macmillan, 1962.

Tuchman, Barbara. *The March of Folly*. New York: Knopf, 1984.

Tuggle, Robert. *The Golden Age of Opera*. New York: Holt, Rinehart & Winston, 1983.

Tully, Grace. *F.D.R., My Boss*. New York: Scribner, 1949.

Tung, Rosemary J. *A Portrait of Lost Tibet*. New York: Holt, Rinehart & Winston, 1980.

Tynan, Kenneth. *Tynan on Theatre*. Harmondsworth, England: Penguin, 1964.

Tyndall, John. *New Fragments*. New York: Appleton, 1892.

Uecker, Bob, and Mickey Herskowitz. *Catcher in the Wry*. New York: Putnam, 1982.

Ukers, William Harrison. *All About Coffee*. New York: The Tea and Coffee Trade Journal Co., 1922.

Untermeyer, Louis. *Bygones: The Recollections of Louis Untermeyer*. New York: Harcourt, Brace & World, 1965

Untermeyer, Louis. *A Treasury of Laughter*. New York: Simon & Schuster, 1946.

Valerani, Richard. *Travels with Henry*. Boston: Houghton Mifflin, 1979.

Valerius Maximus. *Facta et dicta memorabilia*.

Van de Velde, Ernest. *Anecdotes Musicales*. Tours, France: Editions van de Velde, 1926.

Vandyke Price, Pamela. *The Penguin Book of Spirits and Liqueurs*. New York: Penguin, 1980.

Varah, Chad. *Samaritans in the 70s: To Befriend the Suicidal and Despairing*. London: Constable, 1980.

Vasari, G. *Lives of the Painters,* trans. A. B. Hinds. London: J. H. Dart, 1983.

Vaughan-Thomas, Wynford. *Madly in All Directions*. London: Longmans, 1967.

Vickers, Hugh, *Great Operatic Disasters*. St. Martin's, 1979.

Vidal, Gore. *Lincoln*. New York: Random House, 1984.

Vincent, Benjamin, ed. *Haydn's Dictionary of Fates*. New York: Harper, 1870.

Vlastos, Gregory. *Socrates: Ironist and Moral Philosopher*. Ithaca, N.Y.: Cornell University Press, 1992.

Vollard, Ambroise. *Recollections of a Picture Dealer,* trans. Violet MacDonald. Boston: Little, Brown, 1936.

Wade, Don. *And Then Fuzzy Told Steve: A Collection of the Best True Golf Stories Ever Told*. Chicago: Contemporary Books, 1996.

Wade, Virginia. *Courting Triumph*. New York: Mayflower, 1978.

Wagenknecht, Edward. *American Profile, 1900–1909*. Amherst, Mass.: University of Massachusetts Press, 1982.

Wagner, G., trans. *Selected Writings of Gérard de Nerval*. London: Panther, 1968.

Walker, Stella A. *Horses of Renown*. London: Country Life, 1954.

Wallace, Amy, David Wallenchinsky, and Irving Wallace. *The People's Almanac Presents the Book of Lists 3*. New York: Morrow, 1983.

Wallace, Irving. *The Fabulous Originals: Lives of Extraordinary People Who Inspired Mem-

orable Characters in Fiction. New York: Knopf, 1955.

Wallace, Irving. *The Fabulous Showman: The Life and Times of P. T. Barnum*. New York: Knopf, 1959.

Wallace, Irving. *The Nympho & Other Maniacs*. New York: Simon & Schuster, 1971.

Wallace, Irving. *The Square Pegs: Some Americans Who Dared to Be Different*. New York: Knopf, 1957.

Wallace, Irving, David Wallechinsky, and Amy Wallace. *Significa*. New York: Dutton, 1983.

Wallace, Irving, David Wallechinsky, Amy Wallace, and Sylvia Wallace. *Intimate Sex Lives of Famous People*. New York: Delacorte, 1981.

Wallace, Irving, David Wallechinsky, Amy Wallace, and Sylvia Wallace. *The People's Almanac Presents the Book of Lists 2*. New York: Morrow, 1980.

Wallace, Mike, and Gary Gates. *Close Encounters*. New York: Morrow, 1984.

Wallechinsky, David. *The Complete Book of the Olympics*. Harmondsworth, England: Penguin, 1984.

Wallechinsky, David, and Irving Wallace. *The People's Almanac*. New York: Doubleday, 1975.

Wallechinsky, David, and Irving Wallace. *The People's Almanac 2*. New York: Morrow, 1978.

Wallechinsky, David, and Irving Wallace. *The People's Almanac 3*. New York: Morrow, 1981.

Wallechinsky, David, Irving Wallace, and Amy Wallace. *The People's Almanac Presents the Book of Lists*. New York: Morrow, 1977.

Walpole, Horace. *Anecdotes of Painting*. Rpt., New York: Arno Press, 1969.

Walsh, William S. *Handy Book of Curious Information*. Philadelphia: Lippincott, 1913.

Walters, Barbara. *How to Talk with Practically Anybody About Practically Anything*. New York: Doubleday, 1970.

Waterlow, Sydney. *In Praise of Cambridge: An Anthology in Prose and Verse*. London: Constable, 1912.

Watson, Thomas J., and Peter Petre. *Thomas J. Watson, Jr.: An Autobiography*. New York: Bantam Books, 1990.

Waugh, Evelyn. *The Life of the Right Reverend Ronald Knox*. London: Collins, 1962.

Webb, Richard, and Teet Carle. *The Laughs on Hollywood*. Santa Monica, Calif.: Roundtable Publishing, Inc., 1985.

Wechsberg, Joseph. *Red Plush and Black Velvet: The Story of Melba and Her Times*. Boston: Little, Brown, 1961.

Wecter, Dixon. *The Hero in America: A Chronicle of Hero Worship*. New York: Scribner, 1941.

Weems, M. L. *Life of Washington*. Marcus Cunliffe, ed. Cambridge, Mass.: Harvard University Press, 1962.

Weintraub, Stanley. *The London Yankees: Portrait of American Writers and Artists in England, 1894–1919*. New York: Harcourt Brace Jovanovich, 1979.

Weintraub, Stanley. *Long Day's Journey into War: December 7, 1941*. New York: Penguin Books, 1991.

Weintraub, Stanley. *Victoria*. New York: E. P. Dutton, 1986.

Weiskopf, Franz Carl. *Gesammelte Werke*. Berlin: Dietz, 1960.

Weld, C. R. *A History of the Royal Society*. London: J. W. Parker, 1848.

Weld, Jacqueline. *Peggy: The Wayward Guggenheim*. New York: Dutton, 1986.

Wells, G. P. *H. G. Wells in Love: Postscripts to an Experiment in Autobiography*. Boston: Little, Brown, 1984.

Wells, H. G. *Experiment in Autobiography: Discoveries and Conclusions of a Very Ordinary Brain*. New York: Macmillan, 1934.

Wescher, Paul. *Schweitzer Künstler-Anekdoten aus zwei Jahrhunderten*. Berlin: Holbein, 1942.

West, Geoffrey. *H. G. Wells: A Sketch for a Portrait*. Folcroft, Pa.: Folcroft Library Editions, 1972.

Wharton, Edith. *A Backward Glance*. New York: Appleton-Century, 1934.

Wharton, Edith. *Ethan Frome*. New York: Limited Editions Club, 1939.

Whistler, James McNeill. *On the Gentle Art of Making Enemies*. New York: Putnam, 1890.

White, Theodore. *America in Search of Itself: The Making of a President 1956–1980*. New York: Harper & Row, 1982.

Whitman, Alden. *Come to Judgment*. New York: Viking, 1980.

Whitrow, G. J. *Einstein: The Man and His Achievement*. New York: Dover, 1973.

Wicker, Tom. *One of Us: The Age of Richard Nixon 1946–1975*. New York: Random House, 1990.

Wiley, Mason, and Damien Bova. *Inside Oscar*. New York: Ballantine, 1996.

Williams, Jonathan. *The Magpie's Bagpipe: Selected Essays of Jonathan Williams*. San Francisco: North Point Press, 1982.

Williamson, James Alexander. *The English Channel*. London: Collins, 1959.

Wilson, A. N. *Hilaire Belloc*. New York: Atheneum, 1984.

Wilson, Earl. *Hot Times: True Tales of Hollywood and Broadway*. Chicago: Contemporary Books, 1984.

Wilson, Earl. *I Am Gazing into My 8-Ball*. New York: Doubleday, Doran, 1945.

Wilson, Edith Bolling Galt. *My Memoir*. Rpt., New York: Arno Press, 1980.

Wiltse, Charles, and Harold D. Moser, eds. *The Papers of Daniel Webster: Correspondence*, vol. 2. Hanover, N.H.: University Press of New England, 1976.

Winchester, Simon. *Their Noble Lordships: The Hereditary Peerage Today*. Boston: Faber & Faber, 1978.

Winstanley, William. *England's Worthies*. London: University Microfilms International, 1983.

Winter, William. *Other Days: Being Chronicles and Memories of the Stage*. New York: Moffat, Yard, 1908.

Wintle, Justin, and Emma Fisher. *The Pied Pipers: Interviews with the Influential Creators of Children's Literature*. New York: Paddington Press, 1975.

Winwar, Frances. *The Immortal Lovers: Elizabeth Barrett and Robert Browning*. New York: Harper, 1950.

Wiser, William. *The Crazy Years: Paris in the Twenties*. New York: Atheneum, 1983.

Wolf, I. J. *Aphorisms and Facetiae of Bela Schick*. Baltimore: Waverly Press, 1965.

Wood, Anthony À. *Athenae Oxonienses, with Fasti Oxonienses*. Rpt., London: Lackington, Allen, 1976.

Wood, Tom. *The Bright Side of Billy Wilder, Primarily*. New York: Doubleday, 1969.

Woodham-Smith, Cecil. *The Reason Why*. New York: McGraw-Hill, 1954.

Woodward, Llewellyn. *The Age of Reform*. 2nd ed. Oxford: Clarendon Press, 1962.

Worth, F. L. *Complete Unabridged Super Trivia Encyclopedia*. Los Angeles: Brook House, 1979.

Worthington, Marjorie. *Miss Alcott of Concord: A Biography*. New York: Doubleday, 1958.

Wright, Helen, and Samuel Rapport. *The Great Explorers*. New York: Harper's, 1957.

Wydan, Peter. *Day One: Before Hiroshima & After*. New York: Simon & Schuster, 1984.

Yardley, Jonathan. *Ring: A Biography of Ring Lardner*. New York: Random House, 1977.

Yeats, W. B. *Autobiographies*. London: Macmillan, 1955.

Yeats, W. B. *Letters*, ed. Allan Wade. New York: Macmillan, 1955.

Yeats, W. B., ed. *The Oxford Book of Modern Verse*. Oxford: Clarendon Press, 1936.

Young, Gavin, *Halfway Around the World: An Improbable Journey*. New York: Random House, 1981.

Young, G. M. *Victorian England*. New York: Oxford University Press, 1953.

Young, Louise B. *The Blue Planet*. Boston: Little, Brown, 1983.

Zall, P. M., ed. *Abe Lincoln Laughing: Humorous Anecdotes from Original Sources by and About Abraham Lincoln.* Berkeley, Calif.: University of California Press, 1982.

Zall, P. M. *Ben Franklin Laughing.* Los Angeles: University of California Press, 1980.

Zamoyski, Adam. *Paderewski.* New York: Atheneum, 1982.

Ziegler, Hans Severus. *Heitere Muse: Anekdoten aus Kultur und Geschichte.* Munich: Türmer-Verlag, 1974.

Ziegler, Philip. *Diana Cooper: A Biography.* New York: Knopf, 1981.

Ziegler, Philip. *Mountbatten: A Biography.* New York: Knopf, 1985.

Zierold, Norman. *Moguls.* New York: Coward, McCann, 1969.

Zinsser, William, ed. *Extraordinary Lives: The Art and Craft of American Biography.* Boston: American Heritage/Houghton Mifflin, 1986.

PERIODICALS

The American Scholar
The Atlantic Monthly
Bookman
Book-of-the-Month Club News
The Boston Globe
The Boston Globe Magazine
The Century Magazine
The Chicago Sun-Times
Colliers
Connoisseur
Columbian Centinel
Congressional Quarterly
Country Life
Daedalus
Daily Telegraph
Edinburgh Journal
Esquire
Fortnightly Review
Fort Worth Star Telegram
Harper's Magazine
Holiday
International Herald Tribune
Ladies Literary Cabinet
Life
Lippincott's Magazine
London Review of Books
The Los Angeles Times
The Los Angeles Times Book Review
McClure's Magazine
New Criterion
The New Republic
New Scientist
New York Daily News
New York Daily Tribune
New York Post
The New Yorker
The New York Review of Books
The New York Times
The New York Times Book Review
Newsweek
North American Review
The Observer
Outlook
Parade
People
Publishers Weekly
Quarterly Review
Reader's Digest
Santa Barbara News Press
The Saturday Evening Post
Signature
Sports Illustrated
The Sunday Telegraph
The Sunday Times (London)
Time
The Times (London)
The Times Literary Supplement
Truth
Vanity Fair
Verbatim

INDEX OF NAMES

———— ⌀ ————

This index lists the names of every person appearing in the book (except for those mentioned in the anecdotes set in small type). Boldface type indicates those persons who have anecdotes of their own. These persons may also be mentioned in other persons' anecdotes, and this is indicated by an indented name. Those persons whose names are set in lightface type appear only in other persons' anecdotes. Numbers refer to anecdotes, not pages. Thus:

Lamb, Charles

Coleridge, Samuel Taylor, 3, 7

Elliston, Robert W., 1

Wordsworth, William, 2

means that Charles Lamb has anecdotes under his own name, and he is mentioned in anecdotes 3 and 7 for Samuel Taylor Coleridge, anecdote 1 for Robert W. Elliston, and anecdote 2 for William Wordsworth.

Aaron, Henry "Hank"
Abbey, Edwin A.
  Sargent, John Singer, 1
Abdul Hamid III
  John, Augustus, 1
Aberconway, Lady
  Walton, Sir William, 2
Abernethy, John
Acheson, Dean
Acton, Harold
  Waugh, Evelyn, 1
Adam, William
  Fox, Charles James, 2

Adams, Abigail
  John Adams, 3
Adams, Alexander
Adams, Ansel
Adams, Franklin P.
  Ross, Harold, 7
Adams, Henry
Adams, John
  Jefferson, Thomas, 13
Adams, John Quincy
Addams, Jane
Addison, Joseph
Ade, George

Adee, Alvey A.
Adenauer, Konrad
Adler, Hermann
Adler, Mortimer
  Stein, Gertrude, 7
Adler, Stella
  Clurman, Harold, 1, 2
Adolf of Sweden
  Baker, Josephine, 1
Aeschylus
Agassiz, Jean Louis
Agate, James
  Braithwaite, Dame Lilian, 2

INDEX OF SUBJECTS

Khrushchev, 4
Lamb, Charles, 7
Lloyd George, 1
Macaulay, 4
Shaw, 3
Smith, A. E., 2
Stein, 2
Stravinsky, 1
Wilson, Harold, 1
hedonism
  Leo X, 1
  Zoeller, 1
height
  Barrie, 2
  Benchley, 10
  Busby, 2
  Hofmann, 1
  Jarry, 3
  Lincoln, A., 11, 13
  Lloyd George, 4
  Napoleon I, 7
  Rodgers, 1
  Weaver, 2
hell
  Andrew, 1
  Cocteau, 5
  Greeley, 7
  Labouchere, 3
  Lloyd George, 1
  Luther, 2
  Rose, 4
hemorrhoids
  Tennyson, 7
heredity
  Whistler, 8
heresy
  Servetus, 1
heroes/heroism
  Alençon, 1
  Chaplin, 5
  Churchill, W., 15
  Clark, G. R., 1
  Oates, 1
hiccups
  Mytton, 1
hints
  Haydn, 2

Rossini, 8
hippopotamus
  Darwin, C. R., 3
history
  Churchill, W., 11
  Michelet, 1
  Reagan, R., 5
  Truman, 3
hoaxes
  Hill, J., 1
  Hook, 2
hobbies
  George V, 1
holidays
  Charles, Prince, 2
Hollywood
  Algren, 1
  Bacall, 3
  Carter, 10
  Coote, 1
  Garbo, 4
  Reagan, R., 10
home runs
  Musial, 1
  Ruth, 4, 8
homes. *See also* housing
  Berra, 12
hometowns
  Coolidge, 21
  Cooper, Gary, 1
  Sedgwick, C. M., 1
homosexuality
  Auden, 1
  Goldwyn, 4
  Strachey, 2
  Wilde, 14
  Williams, Tennessee, 2
honesty
  Churchill, W., 18
  Frederick II, 2
  Lenclos, 3
honeymoons
  Parker, D., 1
honor
  Aquinas, 1
  Liliencron, 2
  Napoleon I, 12

honors
  Avempace, 1
  Bialik, 1
  Cato, 3
  Clemenceau, 2
  Disraeli, 9
  James, H., 8
  Mably, 3
  Nelson, 3
hope
  Alexander III, 3
  Johnson, S., 22
horse racing
  Campbell, T., 2
  Crockford, 1
horses
  Alexander III, 2
  Anne, Princess, 3
  Bernard, 6
  Charles II, 1
  Fleetwood, 1
  Fonda, J., 2
  Hobson, T., 1
  Monroe, 6
  Nagurski, 2
  Nicholson, 1
horticulture
  Parker, D., 6
hospitality
  Khrushchev, 1
  Napoleon I, 4
  Spooner, 1
  Stalin, 3
hospitals
  Millay, 1
  Mizner, W., 1
  Parker, D., 10
hosts and hostesses
  Aubernon, 1–2
  Beckford, 1
  Berners, 4
  Bowen, E., 1
  Brahms, 5
  Brummell, 4
  Buckland, 2
  Chamberlain, A., 2
  Chopin, 1

THE PUBLISHER IS GRATEFUL TO THE FOLLOWING PUBLISHERS AND INDIVIDUALS FOR PERMISSION TO QUOTE FROM MATERIAL AS NOTED.

Richard Boehm Literary Agency for excerpts from *5000 Nights at the Opera* by Sir Rudolf Bing.

Christian Brann Limited for excerpts from *Pass the Port* compiled by Oxfam (distributed in the United States by Sterling Publishers under the title *After-Dinner Laughter*). Reprinted by permission.

Cass Canfield, Sr., for excerpts from his book *Up and Down and Around: A Publisher Recollects the Times of His Life.*

Don Congdon Associates, Inc., for excerpts from *Fun While It Lasted* by Barnaby Conrad. Copyright © 1967 by Barnaby Conrad. Reprinted by permission.

Dodd, Mead & Company, Inc., for excerpts from *Joseph H. Choate* by Theron Strong.

Doubleday & Company, Inc., for excerpts from *P.S. Jack Parr: An Entertainment* by Jack Parr. Copyright © 1983 by Jack Parr. Reprinted by permission.

Doubleday & Company, Inc., for excerpts from *The Bright Side of Billy Wilder, Primarily* by Tom Wood. Copyright © 1969 by Tom Wood. Reprinted by permission.

Farrar, Straus and Giroux, Inc., for excerpts adapted by permission of the publisher from *Encounters with Stravinsky* by Paul Horgan. Copyright © 1972 by Paul Horgan.

Hamish Hamilton Ltd. for excerpts from *A Number of People* by Sir Edward Marsh. Reprinted by permission.

Holt, Rinehart and Winston for excerpts from *The Remarkable Mr. Jerome* by Anita Leslie. Copyright 1954 by Henry Holt and Company, Inc. Reprinted by permission.

David Higham Associates Limited for excerpts from *Noble Essences* by Osbert Sitwell, copyright 1950 by Sir Osbert Sitwell; and for excerpts from *Tales My Father Taught Me* by Osbert Sitwell, copyright © 1962 by Osbert Sitwell. Reprinted by permission.

Alfred A. Knopf, Inc., for excerpts from *Peace in Their Time: Men Who Led Us In and Out of War, 1914–1945* by Emery Kelen, copyright © 1963 by Emery Kelen. Also for excerpts from *Diana Cooper: A Biography* by Philip Ziegler, copyright © 1981 by Philip Ziegler. Both excerpts are reprinted by permission.

Robert Merrill for excerpts from his book *Between Acts: An Irreverent Look at Opera and Other Madness.*

William Morrow & Company, Inc., and Howard Miles Teichmann for excerpts from *Smart Aleck: The Wit, World, and Life of Alexander Woollcott* by Howard Teichmann, copyright © 1976 by Howard Teichmann and Evelyn Teichmann. Reprinted by permission.

Oxford University Press for excerpts from *James Joyce, New and Revised Edition* by Richard Ellmann, copyright © 1959, 1982 by Richard Ellmann. Reprinted by permission.

Putnam Publishing Group and International Creative Management for excerpts from *Eppie: The Story of Ann Landers* by Margo Howard, copyright © 1982 by Margo Howard. Reprinted by permission.

Putnam Publishing Group and the Estate of Oscar Levant for excerpts from *The Unimportance of Being Oscar* by Oscar Levant, copyright © 1968 by Oscar Levant. Reprinted by permission.

Putnam Publishing Group and Weidenfeld & Nicolson Limited for excerpts from *Robert Morley's Book of Bricks* by Robert Morley, copyright © 1978 by Robert Morley and Weidenfeld & Nicolson. Reprinted by permission.

Putnam Publishing Group and John Farquharson Ltd. for excerpts from *Bring On the Empty Horses* by David Niven, copyright © 1975 by David Niven. Reprinted by permission.

Random House, Inc., and Weidenfeld & Nicolson Limited for excerpts from *Self-Portrait with Friends: The Selected Diaries of Cecil Beaton, 1926–1974,* edited by Richard Buckle, copyright © 1979 by Richard Buckle. Reprinted by permission of Times Books, a division of Random House, Inc., and Weidenfeld & Nicolson Limited.

Random House, Inc., for excerpts from *Charmed Lives: A Family Romance* by Michael Korda, copyright © 1979 by Success Research Corporation. Reprinted by permission.

Robson Books Ltd. for excerpts from *Beecham Stories: Anecdotes, Sayings and Impressions of Sir Thomas Beecham*, edited by Harold Atkins and Archie Newman.

Patrick Searle for excerpts from *Life with Lloyd George: The Diary of A. J. Sylvester*, edited by Colin Cross.

Simon & Schuster, Inc., for excerpts from *Music on My Beat* by Howard Taubman, copyright 1943 by Howard Taubman, renewed © 1970 by Howard Taubman. Reprinted by permission.

Mrs. Helen Thurber for excerpts from *The Years with Ross* by James Thurber.

Viking Penguin, Inc., and Penguin Books Ltd. for excerpts from *Come to Judgment* by Alden Whitman, copyright © 1980 by Alden Whitman. Reprinted by permission.

Weidenfeld & Nicolson Limited for excerpts from *Memories 1898–1939* by C. M. Bowra. Reprinted by permission.